PhET SIMULATIONS

Available in the Pearson eText and in the Study Area of MasteringPhysics

Extended Edition includes Chapters 1–44. Standard Edition includes Chapters 1–37.
Three-volume edition: *Volume 1 includes Chapters 1–20, Volume 2 includes Chapters 21–37, and Volume 3 includes Chapters 37–44.*

*Indicates an associated tutorial available in the MasteringPhysics Item Library.

ActivPhysics OnLine™ Activities

www.masteringphysics.com

1.1 Analyzing Motion Using Diagrams
1.2 Analyzing Motion Using Graphs
1.3 Predicting Motion from Graphs
1.4 Predicting Motion from Equations
1.5 Problem-Solving Strategies for Kinematics
1.6 Skier Races Downhill
1.7 Balloonist Drops Lemonade
1.8 Seat Belts Save Lives
1.9 Screeching to a Halt
1.10 Pole-Vaulter Lands
1.11 Car Starts, Then Stops
1.12 Solving Two-Vehicle Problems
1.13 Car Catches Truck
1.14 Avoiding a Rear-End Collision
2.1.1 Force Magnitudes
2.1.2 Skydiver
2.1.3 Tension Change
2.1.4 Sliding on an Incline
2.1.5 Car Race
2.2 Lifting a Crate
2.3 Lowering a Crate
2.4 Rocket Blasts Off
2.5 Truck Pulls Crate
2.6 Pushing a Crate Up a Wall
2.7 Skier Goes Down a Slope
2.8 Skier and Rope Tow
2.9 Pole-Vaulter Vaults
2.10 Truck Pulls Two Crates
2.11 Modified Atwood Machine
3.1 Solving Projectile Motion Problems
3.2 Two Balls Falling
3.3 Changing the *x*-Velocity
3.4 Projectile *x*- and *y*-Accelerations
3.5 Initial Velocity Components
3.6 Target Practice I
3.7 Target Practice II
4.1 Magnitude of Centripetal Acceleration
4.2 Circular Motion Problem Solving
4.3 Cart Goes Over Circular Path
4.4 Ball Swings on a String
4.5 Car Circles a Track
4.6 Satellites Orbit
5.1 Work Calculations
5.2 Upward-Moving Elevator Stops
5.3 Stopping a Downward-Moving Elevator
5.4 Inverse Bungee Jumper
5.5 Spring-Launched Bowler
5.6 Skier Speed
5.7 Modified Atwood Machine
6.1 Momentum and Energy Change
6.2 Collisions and Elasticity
6.3 Momentum Conservation and Collisions
6.4 Collision Problems
6.5 Car Collision: Two Dimensions
6.6 Saving an Astronaut
6.7 Explosion Problems
6.8 Skier and Cart
6.9 Pendulum Bashes Box
6.10 Pendulum Person-Projectile Bowling
7.1 Calculating Torques
7.2 A Tilted Beam: Torques and Equilibrium
7.3 Arm Levers
7.4 Two Painters on a Beam
7.5 Lecturing from a Beam
7.6 Rotational Inertia
7.7 Rotational Kinematics
7.8 Rotoride–Dynamics Approach
7.9 Falling Ladder
7.10 Woman and Flywheel Elevator–Dynamics Approach
7.11 Race Between a Block and a Disk
7.12 Woman and Flywheel Elevator–Energy Approach
7.13 Rotoride–Energy Approach
7.14 Ball Hits Bat
8.1 Characteristics of a Gas
8.2 Maxwell-Boltzmann Distribution–Conceptual Analysis
8.3 Maxwell-Boltzmann Distribution–Quantitative Analysis
8.4 State Variables and Ideal Gas Law
8.5 Work Done By a Gas
8.6 Heat, Internal Energy, and First Law of Thermodynamics
8.7 Heat Capacity
8.8 Isochoric Process
8.9 Isobaric Process
8.10 Isothermal Process
8.11 Adiabatic Process
8.12 Cyclic Process–Strategies
8.13 Cyclic Process–Problems
8.14 Carnot Cycle
9.1 Position Graphs and Equations
9.2 Describing Vibrational Motion
9.3 Vibrational Energy
9.4 Two Ways to Weigh Young Tarzan
9.5 Ape Drops Tarzan
9.6 Releasing a Vibrating Skier I
9.7 Releasing a Vibrating Skier II
9.8 One-and Two-Spring Vibrating Systems
9.9 Vibro-Ride
9.10 Pendulum Frequency
9.11 Risky Pendulum Walk
9.12 Physical Pendulum
10.1 Properties of Mechanical Waves
10.2 Speed of Waves on a String
10.3 Speed of Sound in a Gas
10.4 Standing Waves on Strings
10.5 Tuning a Stringed Instrument: Standing Waves
10.6 String Mass and Standing Waves
10.7 Beats and Beat Frequency
10.8 Doppler Effect: Conceptual Introduction
10.9 Doppler Effect: Problems
10.10 Complex Waves: Fourier Analysis
11.1 Electric Force: Coulomb's Law
11.2 Electric Force: Superposition Principle
11.3 Electric Force: Superposition Principle (Quantitative)
11.4 Electric Field: Point Charge
11.5 Electric Field Due to a Dipole
11.6 Electric Field: Problems
11.7 Electric Flux
11.8 Gauss's Law
11.9 Motion of a Charge in an Electric Field: Introduction
11.10 Motion in an Electric Field: Problems
11.11 Electric Potential: Qualitative Introduction
11.12 Electric Potential, Field, and Force
11.13 Electrical Potential Energy and Potential
12.1 DC Series Circuits (Qualitative)
12.2 DC Parallel Circuits
12.3 DC Circuit Puzzles
12.4 Using Ammeters and Voltmeters
12.5 Using Kirchhoff's Laws
12.6 Capacitance
12.7 Series and Parallel Capacitors
12.8 *RC* Circuit Time Constants
13.1 Magnetic Field of a Wire
13.2 Magnetic Field of a Loop
13.3 Magnetic Field of a Solenoid
13.4 Magnetic Force on a Particle
13.5 Magnetic Force on a Wire
13.6 Magnetic Torque on a Loop
13.7 Mass Spectrometer
13.8 Velocity Selector
13.9 Electromagnetic Induction
13.10 Motional emf
14.1 The *RL* Circuit
14.2 The *RLC* Oscillator
14.3 The Driven Oscillator
15.1 Reflection and Refraction
15.2 Total Internal Reflection
15.3 Refraction Applications
15.4 Plane Mirrors
15.5 Spherical Mirrors: Ray Diagrams
15.6 Spherical Mirror: The Mirror Equation
15.7 Spherical Mirror: Linear Magnification
15.8 Spherical Mirror: Problems
15.9 Thin-Lens Ray Diagrams
15.10 Converging Lens Problems
15.11 Diverging Lens Problems
15.12 Two-Lens Optical Systems
16.1 Two-Source Interference: Introduction
16.2 Two-Source Interference: Qualitative Questions
16.3 Two-Source Interference: Problems
16.4 The Grating: Introduction and Qualitative Questions
16.5 The Grating: Problems
16.6 Single-Slit Diffraction
16.7 Circular Hole Diffraction
16.8 Resolving Power
16.9 Polarization
17.1 Relativity of Time
17.2 Relativity of Length
17.3 Photoelectric Effect
17.4 Compton Scattering
17.5 Electron Interference
17.6 Uncertainty Principle
17.7 Wave Packets
18.1 The Bohr Model
18.2 Spectroscopy
18.3 The Laser
19.1 Particle Scattering
19.2 Nuclear Binding Energy
19.3 Fusion
19.4 Radioactivity
19.5 Particle Physics
20.1 Potential Energy Diagrams
20.2 Particle in a Box
20.3 Potential Wells
20.4 Potential Barriers

PEARSON ALWAYS LEARNING

Hugh D. Young • Roger A. Freedman
With contributions from A. Lewis Ford

Sears and Zemansky's University Physics

Custom Edition for University of California, Irvine
Physics 7E

Taken from:
Sears and Zemansky's University Physics, Thirteenth Edition
by Hugh D. Young and Roger A. Freedman
With contributions from A. Lewis Ford

Cover Art: Courtesy of PhotoDisc/Getty Images.

Taken from:

Sears and Zemansky's University Physics, Thirteenth Edition
by Hugh D. Young and Roger A. Freedman
With contributions from A. Lewis Ford

Published by Addison-Wesley
Boston, Massachusetts 02116

Pearson Learning Solutions, 501 Boylston Street, Suite 900, Boston, MA 02116
A Pearson Education Company
www.pearsoned.com

Printed in the United States of America

7 16

000200010270758330

BE

PEARSON

ISBN 10: 1-256-38012-1
ISBN 13: 978-1-256-38012-2

MasteringPHYSICS®

MasteringPhysics® Instructions for Physics 2, Physics 3 and Physics 7 students.

MasteringPhysics® will be used for online homework and tutorial for Physics 2, Physics 3 and Physics 7.

- All Physics 2, Physics 3 and Physics 7 students are **required to have a student access code** for MasteringPhysics®.
- Once you **purchase** a MasteringPhysics® student access code, it is **valid for 2 years** and may be used every quarter (including summer) during that time.
- Each student access code may only be used **for one course per quarter**.

<u>What You Need</u>:

- **A valid email address:** <u>it is recommended that you use your uci.edu email address</u>. Your MasteringPhysics® access code is linked to the email address you enter.
- **Student access code**: included in the Student Access Kit that is packaged with your new textbook.
- **The ZIP code for UCI: 92697**
- **Your 8-digit UCI student ID number**
- **A Course ID:** ______________________ (Instructor provides this)

<u>Register</u>

- Go to http://www.masteringphysics.com
- Under "Students" Click **Register.**
- To register using the Student Access Code inside the MasteringPhysics® Student Access Kit, select **Yes, I have an access code**. Click **Continue**.
- **License Agreement and Privacy Policy:** Click **I Accept** to indicate that you have read and agree to the license agreement and privacy policy.
- Select the appropriate option under "Do you have a Pearson Education account?" and supply the requested information. Upon completion, the **Confirmation & Summary** page confirms your registration. This information will also be emailed to you for your records. You can either click **Log In Now** or return to www.masteringphysics.com later.

<u>Log In</u>

- Go to http://www.masteringphysics.com
- Click **Login to MasteringPhysics.**
- Enter your Login Name and Password and click **Log In**.

Enroll in Your Instructor's Course and/or Access the Self-Study Area

Upon first login, you'll be prompted to do one or more of the following:

- **Join your MasteringPhysics course** by entering the **MasteringPhysics Course ID** provided by your instructor**.**
- **Enter your 8-digit UCI student ID number when prompted**. If you don't use your correct student ID to enroll, you won't get credit for the homework you do. So check this carefully.

Click **Save** and **OK**.

Note: When assignments are created, you may access them in the Assignments Due Soon area, or by clicking the "Assignments" tab. Otherwise, click on Study Area to access self-study material.

MasteringPHYSICS™

Keyboard shortcuts for entering mathematical expressions

When you finish adding values in any of the math templates:
Press the right or left arrow keys to move outside of the specially formatted area and to exit template insertion mode.

To move between the top and bottom parts of a fraction: Use the up and down arrow keys.

For this Math Format Template	Type this...
2.56	. (Period)
y_1	_ (Underscore)
x^2	^
$\sin(\theta)$	(and)
$[2\pi r]$	[and]
$K+U$	+
$x_f - x_i$	– (Hyphen)
$7 \cdot 10^{-8}$	*
$\frac{1}{2}mv^2$	/
$\sqrt{2gh}$	\sqrt
$\sqrt[n]{x}$	\nrt
$\lvert\vec{a}\rvert$	|
$\vec{V}$	\vec
$\hat{j}$	\hat

For this Greek Letter/ Symbol	Type this...	For this Greek Letter/ Symbol	Type this...
α	\alpha	τ	\tau
β	\beta	ϕ	\phi
γ	\gamma	χ	\chi
δ	\delta	ψ	\psi
ϵ	\epsilon	ω	\omega
η	\eta	$\hbar$	\hbar
θ	\theta	Δ	\Delta
κ	\kappa	Σ	\Sigma
λ	\lambda	Φ	\Phi
μ	\mu	Ψ	\Psi
ν	\nu	Ω	\Omega
π	\pi	$\mathcal{E}$	\EMF
ρ	\rho		
σ	\sigma		

For Special Functions, type...
acos
acot
acsc
asec
asin
atan
cos
cot
csc
e
ln
log
sec
sin
tan

BRIEF CONTENTS

Build **Skills**

Learn basic and advanced skills that help solve a broad range of physics problems.

Problem-Solving Strategies coach students in how to approach specific types of problems.

This text's **uniquely extensive set** of **Examples** enables students to explore problem-solving challenges in exceptional detail.

Consistent

The **Identify / Set Up / Execute / Evaluate** format, used in all Examples, encourages students to tackle problems thoughtfully rather than skipping to the math.

Focused

All Examples and Problem-Solving Strategies are revised to be more concise and focused.

Visual

Most Examples employ a diagram—often a **pencil sketch** that shows what a student should draw.

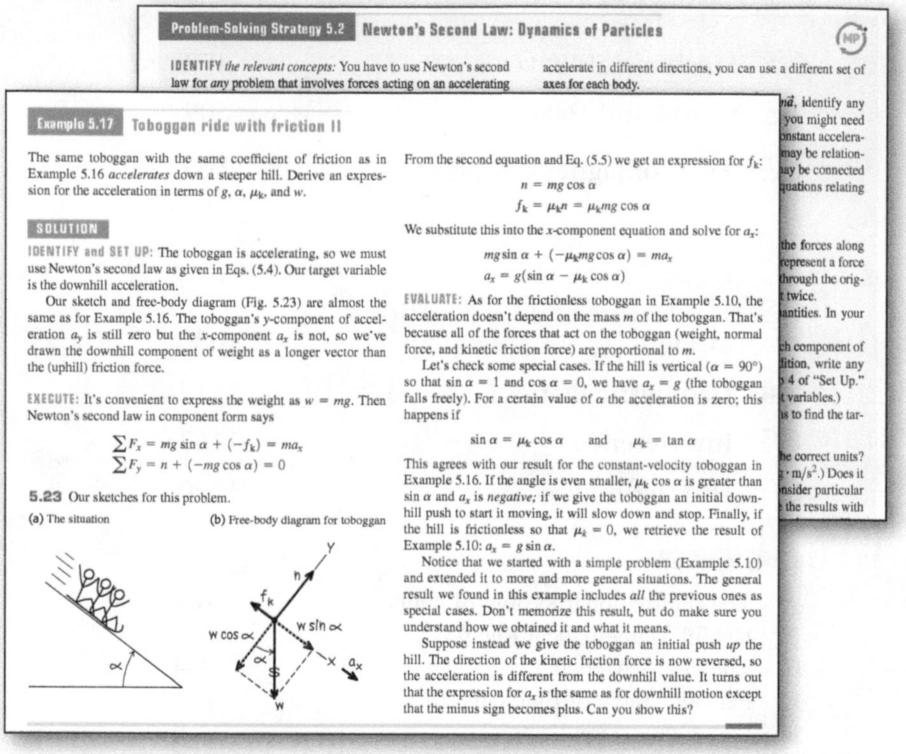

Problem-Solving Strategy 5.2 Newton's Second Law: Dynamics of Particles

IDENTIFY *the relevant concepts:* You have to use Newton's second law for *any* problem that involves forces acting on an accelerating ... accelerate in different directions, you can use a different set of axes for each body.

Example 5.17 Toboggan ride with friction II

The same toboggan with the same coefficient of friction as in Example 5.16 *accelerates* down a steeper hill. Derive an expression for the acceleration in terms of g, α, μ_k, and w.

SOLUTION

IDENTIFY and SET UP: The toboggan is accelerating, so we must use Newton's second law as given in Eqs. (5.4). Our target variable is the downhill acceleration.

Our sketch and free-body diagram (Fig. 5.23) are almost the same as for Example 5.16. The toboggan's y-component of acceleration a_y is still zero but the x-component a_x is not, so we've drawn the downhill component of weight as a longer vector than the (uphill) friction force.

EXECUTE: It's convenient to express the weight as $w = mg$. Then Newton's second law in component form says

$$\sum F_x = mg\sin\alpha + (-f_k) = ma_x$$
$$\sum F_y = n + (-mg\cos\alpha) = 0$$

5.23 Our sketches for this problem.

(a) The situation (b) Free-body diagram for toboggan

From the second equation and Eq. (5.5) we get an expression for f_k:

$$n = mg\cos\alpha$$
$$f_k = \mu_k n = \mu_k mg\cos\alpha$$

We substitute this into the x-component equation and solve for a_x:

$$mg\sin\alpha + (-\mu_k mg\cos\alpha) = ma_x$$
$$a_x = g(\sin\alpha - \mu_k\cos\alpha)$$

EVALUATE: As for the frictionless toboggan in Example 5.10, the acceleration doesn't depend on the mass m of the toboggan. That's because all of the forces that act on the toboggan (weight, normal force, and kinetic friction force) are proportional to m.

Let's check some special cases. If the hill is vertical ($\alpha = 90°$) so that $\sin\alpha = 1$ and $\cos\alpha = 0$, we have $a_x = g$ (the toboggan falls freely). For a certain value of α the acceleration is zero; this happens if

$$\sin\alpha = \mu_k\cos\alpha \quad \text{and} \quad \mu_k = \tan\alpha$$

This agrees with our result for the constant-velocity toboggan in Example 5.16. If the angle is even smaller, $\mu_k\cos\alpha$ is greater than $\sin\alpha$ and a_x is *negative;* if we give the toboggan an initial downhill push to start it moving, it will slow down and stop. Finally, if the hill is frictionless so that $\mu_k = 0$, we retrieve the result of Example 5.10: $a_x = g\sin\alpha$.

Notice that we started with a simple problem (Example 5.10) and extended it to more and more general situations. The general result we found in this example includes *all* the previous ones as special cases. Don't memorize this result, but do make sure you understand how we obtained it and what it means.

Suppose instead we give the toboggan an initial push *up* the hill. The direction of the kinetic friction force is now reversed, so the acceleration is different from the downhill value. It turns out that the expression for a_x is the same as for downhill motion except that the minus sign becomes plus. Can you show this?

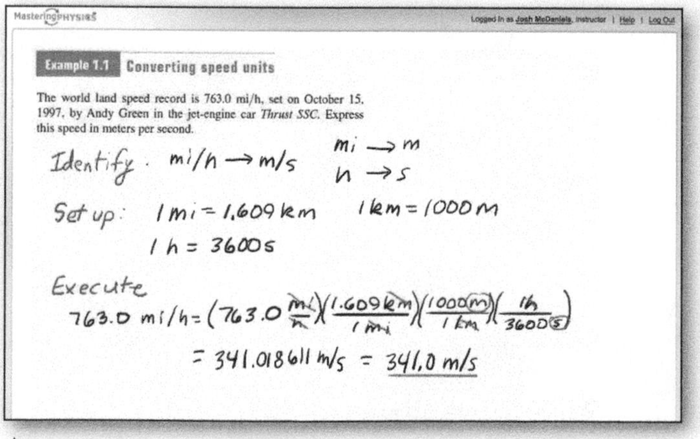

NEW! **Video Tutor Solution for Every Example**

Each Example is explained and solved by an instructor in a Video Tutor solution provided in the Study Area of MasteringPhysics® and in the Pearson eText.

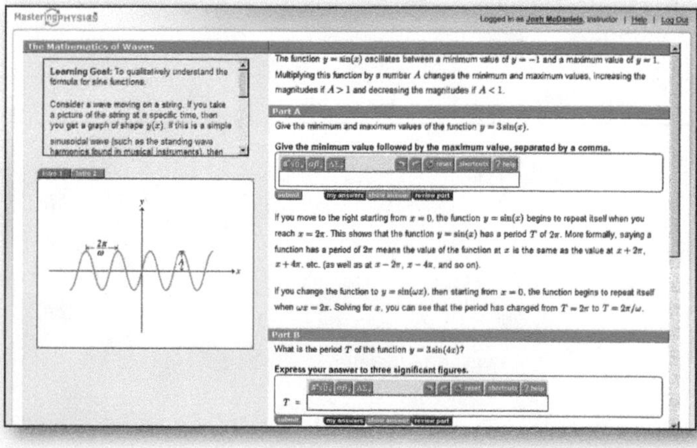

NEW! **Mathematics Review Tutorials**

MasteringPhysics offers an extensive set of assignable mathematics review tutorials—covering differential and integral calculus as well as algebra and trigonometry.

Build **Confidence**

Develop problem-solving confidence through a range of practice options—from guided to unguided.

NEW! **Bridging Problems**
At the start of each problem set, a Bridging Problem helps students make the leap from routine exercises to challenging problems with confidence and ease.

Each Bridging Problem poses a moderately difficult, multi-concept problem, which often draws on earlier chapters. In place of a full solution, it provides a skeleton solution guide consisting of questions and hints.

A full solution is explained in a **Video Tutor**, provided in the Study Area of MasteringPhysics® and in the Pearson eText.

BRIDGING PROBLEM **Billiard Physics**

A cue ball (a uniform solid sphere of mass m and radius R) is at rest on a level pool table. Using a pool cue, you give the ball a sharp, horizontal hit of magnitude F at a height h above the center of the ball (Fig. 10.37). The force of the hit is much greater than the friction force f that the table surface exerts on the ball. The hit lasts for a short time Δt. (a) For what value of h will the ball roll without slipping? (b) If you hit the ball dead center ($h = 0$), the ball will slide across the table for a while, but eventually it will roll without slipping. What will the speed of its center of mass be then?

SOLUTION GUIDE

See MasteringPhysics® study area for a Video Tutor solution.

IDENTIFY and SET UP

1. Draw a free-body diagram for the ball for the situation in part (a), including your choice of coordinate axes. Note that the cue exerts both an impulsive force on the ball and an impulsive torque around the center of mass.
2. The cue force applied for a time Δt gives the ball's center of mass a speed v_{cm}, and the cue torque applied for that same time gives the ball an angular speed ω. What must be the relationship between v_{cm} and ω for the ball to roll without slipping?
3. Draw two free-body diagrams for the ball in part (b): one showing the forces during the hit and the other showing the forces after the hit but before the ball is rolling without slipping.
4. What is the angular speed of the ball in part (b) just after the hit? While the ball is sliding, does v_{cm} increase or decrease? Does ω increase or decrease? What is the relationship between v_{cm} and ω when the ball is finally rolling without slipping?

EXECUTE

5. In part (a), use the impulse–momentum theorem to find the speed of the ball's center of mass immediately after the hit. Then use the rotational version of the impulse–momentum theorem to find the angular speed immediately after the hit. (*Hint:* To write down the rotational version of the impulse–momentum theorem, remember that the relationship between torque and angular momentum is the same as that between force and linear momentum.)
6. Use your results from step 5 to find the value of h that will cause the ball to roll without slipping immediately after the hit.
7. In part (b), again find the ball's center-of-mass speed and angular speed immediately after the hit. Then write Newton's second law for the translational motion and rotational motion of the ball as it is sliding. Use these equations to write expressions for v_{cm} and ω as functions of the elapsed time t since the hit.
8. Using your results from step 7, find the time t when v_{cm} and ω have the correct relationship for rolling without slipping. Then find the value of v_{cm} at this time.

EVALUATE

9. If you have access to a pool table, test out the results of parts (a) and (b) for yourself!
10. Can you show that if you used a hollow cylinder rather than a solid ball, you would have to hit the top of the cylinder to cause rolling without slipping as in part (a)?

10.37

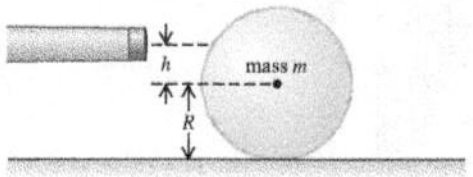

14.95 • CP In Fig. P14.95 the upper ball is released from rest, collides with the stationary lower ball, and sticks to it. The strings are both 50.0 cm long. The upper ball has mass 2.00 kg, and it is initially 10.0 cm higher than the lower ball, which has mass 3.00 kg. Find the frequency and maximum angular displacement of the motion after the collision.

Figure **P14.95**

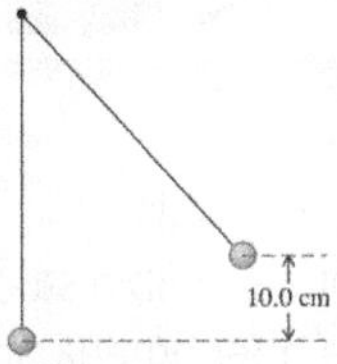

14.96 •• CP BIO *T. rex.* Model the leg of the *T. rex* in Example 14.10 (Section 14.6) as two uniform rods, each 1.55 m long, joined rigidly end to end. Let the lower rod have mass M and the upper rod mass $2M$. The composite object is pivoted about the top of the upper rod. Compute the oscillation period of this object for small-amplitude oscillations. Compare your result to that of Example 14.10.

14.97 •• CALC A slender, uniform, metal rod with mass M is pivoted without friction about an axis through its midpoint and perpendicular to the rod. A horizontal spring with force constant k is attached to the lower end of the rod, with the other end of the spring attached to a rigid support. If the rod is displaced by a small angle Θ from the vertical (Fig. P14.97) and released, show that it moves in angular SHM and calculate the period. (*Hint:* Assume that the angle Θ is small enough for the approximations $\sin \Theta \approx \Theta$ and $\cos \Theta \approx 1$ to be valid. The motion is simple harmonic if $d^2\theta/dt^2 = -\omega^2\theta$, and the period is then $T = 2\pi/\omega$.)

Figure **P14.97**

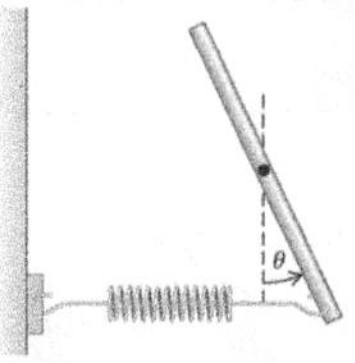

In response to professors, the **Problem Sets** now include more biomedically oriented problems (BIO), more difficult problems requiring calculus (CALC), and more cumulative problems that draw on earlier chapters (CP).

About 20% of problems are new or revised. These revisions are driven by detailed student-performance data gathered nationally through MasteringPhysics.

Problem difficulty is now indicated by a three-dot ranking system based on data from MasteringPhysics.

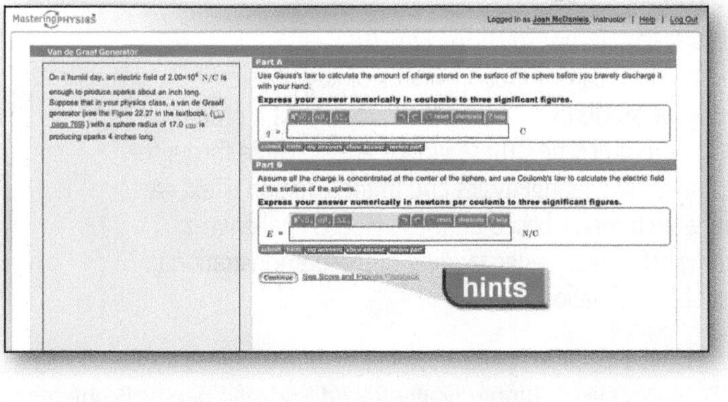

NEW! **Enhanced End-of-Chapter Problems in MasteringPhysics**
Select end-of-chapter problems will now offer additional support such as problem-solving strategy hints, relevant math review and practice, and links to the eText. These new enhanced problems bridge the gap between guided tutorials and traditional homework problems.

Bring Physics **to Life**

Deepen knowledge of physics by building connections to the real world.

NEW! Applications of Physics ▶
Throughout the text, free-standing captioned photos apply physics to real situations, with particular emphasis on applications of biomedical and general interest.

Application Moment of Inertia of a Bird's Wing
When a bird flaps its wings, it rotates the wings up and down around the shoulder. A hummingbird has small wings with a small moment of inertia, so the bird can make its wings move rapidly (up to 70 beats per second). By contrast, the Andean condor (*Vultur gryphus*) has immense wings that are hard to move due to their large moment of inertia. Condors flap their wings at about one beat per second on takeoff, but at most times prefer to soar while holding their wings steady.

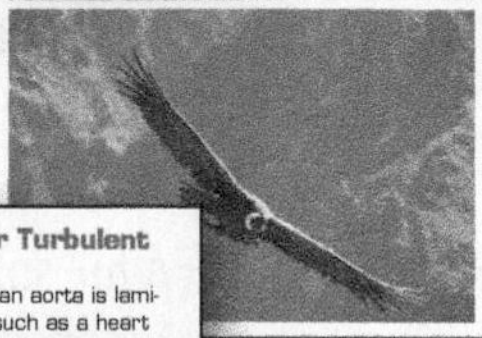

Application Tendons Are Nonideal Springs
Muscles exert forces via the tendons that attach them to bones. A tendon consists of long, stiffly elastic collagen fibers. The graph shows how the tendon from the hind leg of a wallaby (a small kangaroo) stretches in response to an applied force. The tendon does not exhibit the simple, straight-line behavior of an ideal spring, so the work it does has to be found by integration [Eq. (6.7)]. Note that the tendon exerts less force while relaxing than while stretching. As a result, the relaxing tendon does only about 93% of the work that was done to stretch it.

Application Listening for Turbulent Flow
Normal blood flow in the human aorta is laminar, but a small disturbance such as a heart pathology can cause the flow to become turbulent. Turbulence makes noise, which is why listening to blood flow with a stethoscope is a useful diagnostic technique.

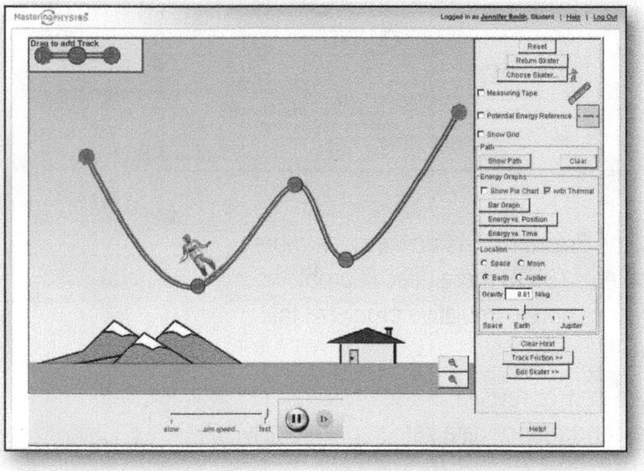

◀ **NEW! PhET Simulations and Tutorials**
Sixteen assignable PhET Tutorials enable students to make connections between real-life phenomena and the underlying physics. 76 PhET simulations are provided in the Study Area of MasteringPhysics® and in the Pearson eText.

The comprehensive library of ActivPhysics applets and applet-based tutorials is also available.

NEW! Video Tutor Demonstrations and Tutorials
"Pause and predict" demonstration videos of key physics concepts engage students by asking them to submit a prediction before seeing the outcome. These videos are available through the Study Area of MasteringPhysics and in the Pearson eText. A set of assignable tutorials based on these videos challenge students to transfer their understanding of the demonstration to a related problem situation.

Figure **E21.23**

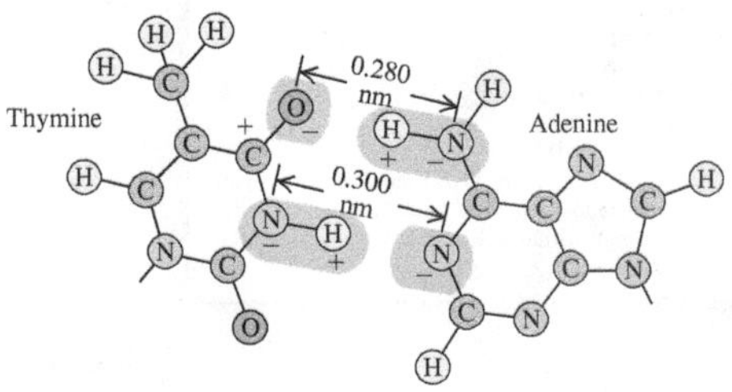

Biomedically Based End-of-Chapter Problems ▶
To serve biosciences students, the text adds a substantial number of problems based on biological and biomedical situations.

21.24 •• BIO **Base Pairing in DNA, II.** Refer to Exercise 21.23. Figure E21.24 shows the bonding of the cytosine and guanine molecules. The O—H and H—N distances are each 0.110 nm. In this case, assume that the bonding is due only to the forces along the O—H—O, N—H—N, and O—H—N combinations, and assume also that these three combinations are parallel to each other. Calculate the *net* force that cytosine exerts on guanine due to the preceding three combinations. Is this force attractive or repulsive?

Make a Difference with **MasteringPhysics®**

Mastering PHYSICS®

www.masteringphysics.com

MasteringPhysics is the most effective and widely used online science tutorial, homework, and assessment system available.

NEW! Pre-Built Assignments ▶

For every chapter in the book, MasteringPhysics now provides pre-built assignments that cover the material with a tested mix of tutorials and end-of-chapter problems of graded difficulty. Professors may use these assignments as-is or take them as a starting point for modification.

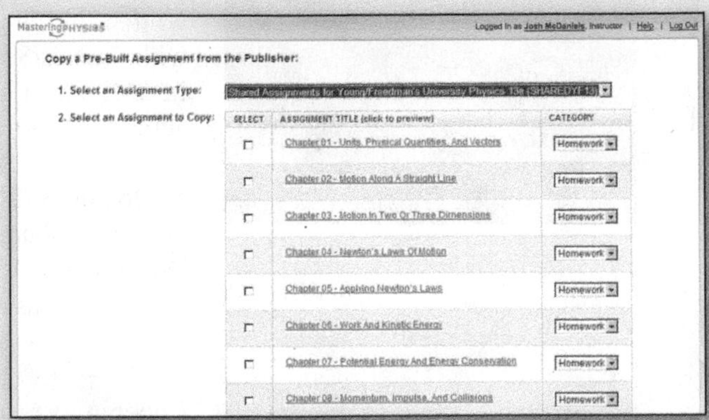

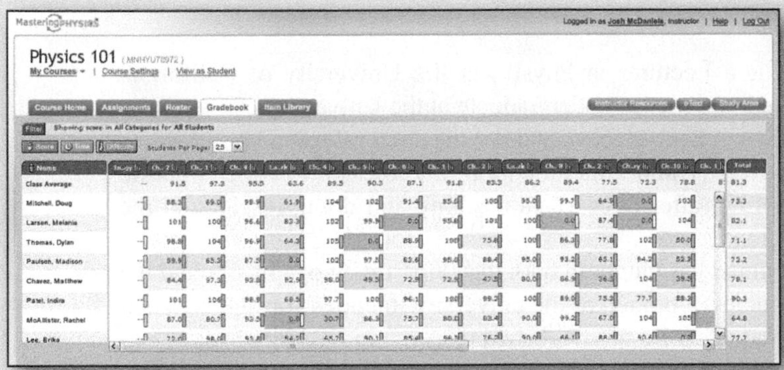

◀ Gradebook

- Every assignment is graded automatically.
- Shades of red highlight vulnerable students and challenging assignments.

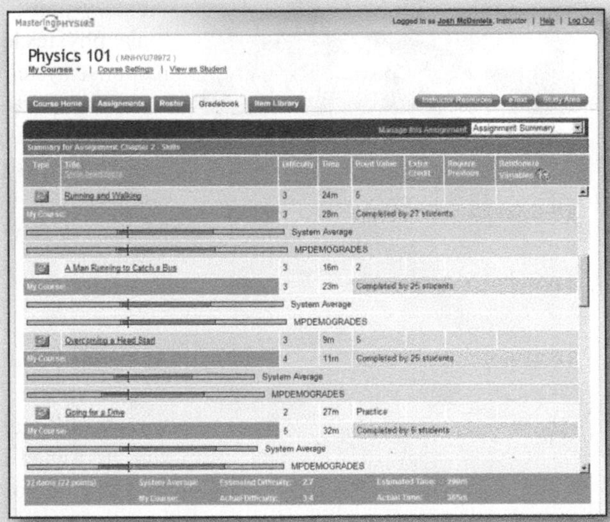

Class Performance on Assignment ▶

Click on a problem to see which step your students struggled with most, and even their most common wrong answers. Compare results at every stage with the national average or with your previous class.

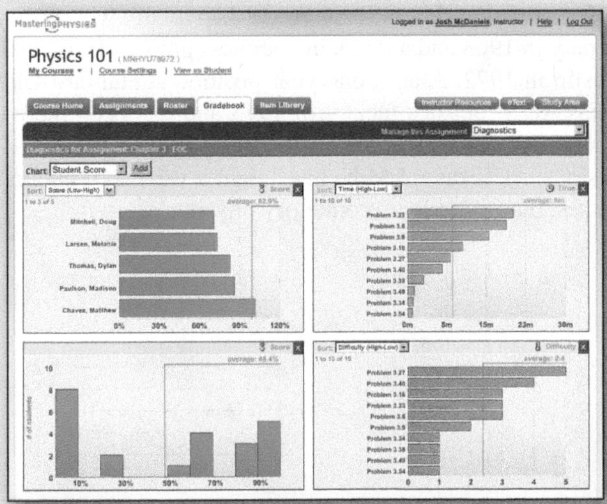

◀ Gradebook Diagnostics

This screen provides your favorite weekly diagnostics. With a single click, charts summarize the most difficult problems, vulnerable students, grade distribution, and even improvement in scores over the course.

ABOUT THE AUTHORS

Hugh D. Young is Emeritus Professor of Physics at Carnegie Mellon University. He earned both his undergraduate and graduate degrees from that university. He earned his Ph.D. in fundamental particle theory under the direction of the late Richard Cutkosky. He joined the faculty of Carnegie Mellon in 1956 and retired in 2004. He also had two visiting professorships at the University of California, Berkeley.

Dr. Young's career has centered entirely on undergraduate education. He has written several undergraduate-level textbooks, and in 1973 he became a coauthor with Francis Sears and Mark Zemansky for their well-known introductory texts. In addition to his role on Sears and Zemansky's *University Physics,* he is also author of Sears and Zemansky's *College Physics*.

Dr. Young earned a bachelor's degree in organ performance from Carnegie Mellon in 1972 and spent several years as Associate Organist at St. Paul's Cathedral in Pittsburgh. He has played numerous organ recitals in the Pittsburgh area. Dr. Young and his wife, Alice, usually travel extensively in the summer, especially overseas and in the desert canyon country of southern Utah.

Roger A. Freedman is a Lecturer in Physics at the University of California, Santa Barbara. Dr. Freedman was an undergraduate at the University of California campuses in San Diego and Los Angeles, and did his doctoral research in nuclear theory at Stanford University under the direction of Professor J. Dirk Walecka. He came to UCSB in 1981 after three years teaching and doing research at the University of Washington.

At UCSB, Dr. Freedman has taught in both the Department of Physics and the College of Creative Studies, a branch of the university intended for highly gifted and motivated undergraduates. He has published research in nuclear physics, elementary particle physics, and laser physics. In recent years, he has worked to make physics lectures a more interactive experience through the use of classroom response systems.

In the 1970s Dr. Freedman worked as a comic book letterer and helped organize the San Diego Comic-Con (now the world's largest popular culture convention) during its first few years. Today, when not in the classroom or slaving over a computer, Dr. Freedman can be found either flying (he holds a commercial pilot's license) or driving with his wife, Caroline, in their 1960 Nash Metropolitan convertible.

A. Lewis Ford is Professor of Physics at Texas A&M University. He received a B.A. from Rice University in 1968 and a Ph.D. in chemical physics from the University of Texas at Austin in 1972. After a one-year postdoc at Harvard University, he joined the Texas A&M physics faculty in 1973 and has been there ever since. Professor Ford's research area is theoretical atomic physics, with a specialization in atomic collisions. At Texas A&M he has taught a variety of undergraduate and graduate courses, but primarily introductory physics.

TO THE STUDENT

HOW TO SUCCEED IN PHYSICS BY REALLY TRYING

Mark Hollabaugh *Normandale Community College*

Physics encompasses the large and the small, the old and the new. From the atom to galaxies, from electrical circuitry to aerodynamics, physics is very much a part of the world around us. You probably are taking this introductory course in calculus-based physics because it is required for subsequent courses you plan to take in preparation for a career in science or engineering. Your professor wants you to learn physics and to enjoy the experience. He or she is very interested in helping you learn this fascinating subject. That is part of the reason your professor chose this textbook for your course. That is also the reason Drs. Young and Freedman asked me to write this introductory section. We want you to succeed!

The purpose of this section of *University Physics* is to give you some ideas that will assist your learning. Specific suggestions on how to use the textbook will follow a brief discussion of general study habits and strategies.

Preparation for This Course

If you had high school physics, you will probably learn concepts faster than those who have not because you will be familiar with the language of physics. If English is a second language for you, keep a glossary of new terms that you encounter and make sure you understand how they are used in physics. Likewise, if you are farther along in your mathematics courses, you will pick up the mathematical aspects of physics faster. Even if your mathematics is adequate, you may find a book such as Arnold D. Pickar's *Preparing for General Physics: Math Skill Drills and Other Useful Help (Calculus Version)* to be useful. Your professor may actually assign sections of this math review to assist your learning.

Learning to Learn

Each of us has a different learning style and a preferred means of learning. Understanding your own learning style will help you to focus on aspects of physics that may give you difficulty and to use those components of your course that will help you overcome the difficulty. Obviously you will want to spend more time on those aspects that give you the most trouble. If you learn by hearing, lectures will be very important. If you learn by explaining, then working with other students will be useful to you. If solving problems is difficult for you, spend more time learning how to solve problems. Also, it is important to understand and develop good study habits. Perhaps the most important thing you can do for yourself is to set aside adequate, regularly scheduled study time in a distraction-free environment.

Answer the following questions for yourself:

- Am I able to use fundamental mathematical concepts from algebra, geometry and trigonometry? (If not, plan a program of review with help from your professor.)
- In similar courses, what activity has given me the most trouble? (Spend more time on this.) What has been the easiest for me? (Do this first; it will help to build your confidence.)

- Do I understand the material better if I read the book before or after the lecture? (You may learn best by skimming the material, going to lecture, and then undertaking an in-depth reading.)
- Do I spend adequate time in studying physics? (A rule of thumb for a class like this is to devote, on the average, 2.5 hours out of class for each hour in class. For a course meeting 5 hours each week, that means you should spend about 10 to 15 hours per week studying physics.)
- Do I study physics every day? (Spread that 10 to 15 hours out over an entire week!) At what time of the day am I at my best for studying physics? (Pick a specific time of the day and stick to it.)
- Do I work in a quiet place where I can maintain my focus? (Distractions will break your routine and cause you to miss important points.)

Working with Others

Scientists or engineers seldom work in isolation from one another but rather work cooperatively. You will learn more physics and have more fun doing it if you work with other students. Some professors may formalize the use of cooperative learning or facilitate the formation of study groups. You may wish to form your own informal study group with members of your class who live in your neighborhood or dorm. If you have access to e-mail, use it to keep in touch with one another. Your study group is an excellent resource when reviewing for exams.

Lectures and Taking Notes

An important component of any college course is the lecture. In physics this is especially important because your professor will frequently do demonstrations of physical principles, run computer simulations, or show video clips. All of these are learning activities that will help you to understand the basic principles of physics. Don't miss lectures, and if for some reason you do, ask a friend or member of your study group to provide you with notes and let you know what happened.

Take your class notes in outline form, and fill in the details later. It can be very difficult to take word for word notes, so just write down key ideas. Your professor may use a diagram from the textbook. Leave a space in your notes and just add the diagram later. After class, edit your notes, filling in any gaps or omissions and noting things you need to study further. Make references to the textbook by page, equation number, or section number.

Make sure you ask questions in class, or see your professor during office hours. Remember the only "dumb" question is the one that is not asked. Your college may also have teaching assistants or peer tutors who are available to help you with difficulties you may have.

Examinations

Taking an examination is stressful. But if you feel adequately prepared and are well-rested, your stress will be lessened. Preparing for an exam is a continual process; it begins the moment the last exam is over. You should immediately go over the exam and understand any mistakes you made. If you worked a problem and made substantial errors, try this: Take a piece of paper and divide it down the middle with a line from top to bottom. In one column, write the proper solution to the problem. In the other column, write what you did and why, if you know, and why your solution was incorrect. If you are uncertain why you made your mistake, or how to avoid making it again, talk with your professor. Physics continually builds on fundamental ideas and it is important to correct any misunderstandings immediately. *Warning:* While cramming at the last minute may get you through the present exam, you will not adequately retain the concepts for use on the next exam.

TO THE INSTRUCTOR

PREFACE

This book is the product of more than six decades of leadership and innovation in physics education. When the first edition of *University Physics* by Francis W. Sears and Mark W. Zemansky was published in 1949, it was revolutionary among calculus-based physics textbooks in its emphasis on the fundamental principles of physics and how to apply them. The success of *University Physics* with generations of several million students and educators around the world is a testament to the merits of this approach, and to the many innovations it has introduced subsequently.

In preparing this new Thirteenth Edition, we have further enhanced and developed *University Physics* to assimilate the best ideas from education research with enhanced problem-solving instruction, pioneering visual and conceptual pedagogy, the first systematically enhanced problems, and the most pedagogically proven and widely used online homework and tutorial system in the world.

New to This Edition

- Included in each chapter, **Bridging Problems** provide a transition between the single-concept Examples and the more challenging end-of-chapter problems. Each Bridging Problem poses a difficult, multiconcept problem, which often incorporates physics from earlier chapters. In place of a full solution, it provides a skeleton **Solution Guide** consisting of questions and hints, which helps train students to approach and solve challenging problems with confidence.
- **All Examples, Conceptual Examples, and Problem-Solving Strategies are revised** to enhance conciseness and clarity for today's students.
- The **core modern physics chapters** (Chapters 38–41) are revised extensively to provide a more idea-centered, less historical approach to the material. Chapters 42–44 are also revised significantly.
- **The fluid mechanics chapter now precedes the chapters on gravitation and periodic motion,** so that the latter immediately precedes the chapter on mechanical waves.
- **Additional bioscience applications** appear throughout the text, mostly in the form of marginal photos with explanatory captions, to help students see how physics is connected to many breakthroughs and discoveries in the biosciences.
- The **text has been streamlined** for tighter and more focused language.
- **Using data from MasteringPhysics, changes to the end-of-chapter content** include the following:
  - **15%–20% of problems are new.**
  - The number and level of **calculus-requiring problems** has been increased.
  - Most chapters include **five to seven biosciences-related problems.**
  - The number of **cumulative problems** (those incorporating physics from earlier chapters) has been increased.
- **Over 70 PhET simulations** are linked to the Pearson eText and provided in the Study Area of the MasteringPhysics website (with icons in the print text). These powerful simulations allow students to interact productively with the physics concepts they are learning. PhET clicker questions are also included on the Instructor Resource DVD.
- **Video Tutors bring key content to life throughout the text:**
  - **Dozens of Video Tutors feature "pause-and-predict" demonstrations of key physics concepts** and incorporate assessment as the student progresses to actively engage the student in understanding the key conceptual ideas underlying the physics principles.

Standard, Extended, and Three-Volume Editions

With MasteringPhysics:

- **Standard Edition:** Chapters 1–37 (ISBN 978-0-321-69688-5)
- **Extended Edition:** Chapters 1–44 (ISBN 978-0-321-67546-0)

Without MasteringPhysics:

- **Standard Edition:** Chapters 1–37 (ISBN 978-0-321-69689-2)
- **Extended Edition:** Chapters 1–44 (ISBN 978-0-321-69686-1)
- **Volume 1:** Chapters 1–20 (ISBN 978-0-321-73338-2)
- **Volume 2:** Chapters 21–37 (ISBN 978-0-321-75121-8)
- **Volume 3:** Chapters 37–44 (ISBN 978-0-321-75120-1)

- **Every Worked Example in the book is accompanied by a Video Tutor Solution** that walks students through the problem-solving process, providing a virtual teaching assistant on a round-the-clock basis.
- **All of these Video Tutors play directly through links within the Pearson eText.** Many also appear in the Study Area within MasteringPhysics.

Key Features of *University Physics*

- Deep and extensive **problem sets** cover a wide range of difficulty and exercise both physical understanding and problem-solving expertise. Many problems are based on complex real-life situations.
- This text offers a larger number of **Examples** and **Conceptual Examples** than any other leading calculus-based text, allowing it to explore problem-solving challenges not addressed in other texts.
- A research-based **problem-solving approach (Identify, Set Up, Execute, Evaluate)** is used not just in every Example but also in the Problem-Solving Strategies and throughout the Student and Instructor Solutions Manuals and the Study Guide. This consistent approach teaches students to tackle problems thoughtfully rather than cutting straight to the math.
- **Problem-Solving Strategies** coach students in how to approach specific types of problems.
- The **Figures** use a simplified graphical style to focus on the physics of a situation, and they incorporate **explanatory annotation.** Both techniques have been demonstrated to have a strong positive effect on learning.
- Figures that illustrate Example solutions often take the form of black-and-white **pencil sketches,** which directly represent what a student should draw in solving such a problem.
- The popular **Caution paragraphs** focus on typical misconceptions and student problem areas.
- End-of-section **Test Your Understanding** questions let students check their grasp of the material and use a multiple-choice or ranking-task format to probe for common misconceptions.
- **Visual Summaries** at the end of each chapter present the key ideas in words, equations, and thumbnail pictures, helping students to review more effectively.

Instructor Supplements

Note: *For convenience, all of the following instructor supplements (except for the Instructor Resource DVD) can be downloaded from the Instructor Area, accessed via the left-hand navigation bar of MasteringPhysics (www.masteringphysics.com).*

Instructor Solutions, prepared by A. Lewis Ford (Texas A&M University) and Wayne Anderson, contain complete and detailed solutions to all end-of-chapter problems. All solutions follow consistently the same Identify/Set Up/Execute/Evaluate problem-solving framework used in the textbook. Download only from the MasteringPhysics Instructor Area or from the Instructor Resource Center (www.pearsonhighered.com/irc).

The cross-platform **Instructor Resource DVD** (ISBN 978-0-321-69661-8) provides a comprehensive library of more than 420 applets from ActivPhysics OnLine as well as all line figures from the textbook in JPEG format. In addition, all the key equations, problem-solving strategies, tables, and chapter summaries are provided in editable Word format. In-class weekly multiple-choice questions for use with various Classroom Response Systems (CRS) are also provided, based on the Test Your Understanding questions in the text. Lecture outlines in PowerPoint are also included along with over 70 PhET simulations.

MasteringPhysics® (www.masteringphysics.com) is the most advanced, educationally effective, and widely used physics homework and tutorial system in the world. Eight years in development, it provides instructors with a library of extensively pre-tested end-of-chapter problems and rich, multipart, multistep tutorials that incorporate a wide variety of answer types, wrong answer feedback, individualized help (comprising hints or simpler sub-problems upon request), all driven by the largest metadatabase of student problem-solving in the world. NSF-sponsored published research (and subsequent studies) show that MasteringPhysics has dramatic educational results. MasteringPhysics allows instructors to build wide-ranging homework assignments of just the right difficulty and length and provides them with efficient tools to analyze both class trends, and the work of any student in unprecedented detail.

MasteringPhysics routinely provides instant and individualized feedback and guidance to more than 100,000 students every day. A wide range of tools and support make MasteringPhysics fast and easy for instructors and students to learn to use. Extensive class tests show that by the end of their course, an unprecedented eight of nine students recommend MasteringPhysics as their preferred way to study physics and do homework.

MasteringPhysics enables instructors to:

- Quickly build homework assignments that combine regular end-of-chapter problems and tutoring (through additional multi-step tutorial problems that offer wrong-answer feedback and simpler problems upon request).
- Expand homework to include the widest range of automatically graded activities available—from numerical problems with randomized values, through algebraic answers, to free-hand drawing.
- Choose from a wide range of nationally pre-tested problems that provide accurate estimates of time to complete and difficulty.
- After an assignment is completed, quickly identify not only the problems that were the trickiest for students but the individual problem types where students had trouble.
- Compare class results against the system's worldwide average for each problem assigned, to identify issues to be addressed with just-in-time teaching.
- Check the work of an individual student in detail, including time spent on each problem, what wrong answers they submitted at each step, how much help they asked for, and how many practice problems they worked.

ActivPhysics OnLine™ (which is accessed through the Study Area within www.masteringphysics.com) provides a comprehensive library of more than 420 tried and tested ActivPhysics applets updated for web delivery using the latest online technologies. In addition, it provides a suite of highly regarded applet-based tutorials developed by education pioneers Alan Van Heuvelen and Paul D'Alessandris. Margin icons throughout the text direct students to specific exercises that complement the textbook discussion.

The online exercises are designed to encourage students to confront misconceptions, reason qualitatively about physical processes, experiment quantitatively, and learn to think critically. The highly acclaimed ActivPhysics OnLine companion workbooks help students work through complex concepts and understand them more clearly. More than 420 applets from the ActivPhysics OnLine library are also available on the Instructor Resource DVD for this text.

The **Test Bank** contains more than 2,000 high-quality problems, with a range of multiple-choice, true/false, short-answer, and regular homework-type questions. Test files are provided both in TestGen (an easy-to-use, fully networkable program for creating and editing quizzes and exams) and Word format. Download only from the MasteringPhysics Instructor Area or from the Instructor Resource Center (www.pearsonhighered.com/irc).

Five Easy Lessons: Strategies for Successful Physics Teaching (ISBN 978-0-805-38702-5) by Randall D. Knight (California Polytechnic State University, San Luis Obispo) is packed with creative ideas on how to enhance any physics course. It is an invaluable companion for both novice and veteran physics instructors.

Student Supplements

The **Study Guide** by Laird Kramer reinforces the text's emphasis on problem-solving strategies and student misconceptions. The *Study Guide for Volume 1* (ISBN 978-0-321-69665-6) covers Chapters 1–20, and the *Study Guide for Volumes 2 and 3* (ISBN 978-0-321-69669-4) covers Chapters 21–44.

The **Student Solutions Manual** by Lewis Ford (Texas A&M University) and Wayne Anderson contains detailed, step-by-step solutions to more than half of the odd-numbered end-of-chapter problems from the textbook. All solutions follow consistently the same Identify/Set Up/Execute/Evaluate problem-solving framework used in the textbook. The *Student Solutions Manual for Volume 1* (ISBN 978-0-321-69668-7) covers Chapters 1–20, and the *Student Solutions Manual for Volumes 2 and 3* (ISBN 978-0-321-69667-0) covers Chapters 21–44.

MasteringPhysics® (www.masteringphysics.com) is a homework, tutorial, and assessment system based on years of research into how students work physics problems and precisely where they need help. Studies show that students who use MasteringPhysics significantly increase their scores compared to hand-written homework. MasteringPhysics achieves this improvement by providing students with instantaneous feedback specific to their wrong answers, simpler sub-problems upon request when they get stuck, and partial credit for their method(s). This individualized, 24/7 Socratic tutoring is recommended by nine out of ten students to their peers as the most effective and time-efficient way to study.

Pearson eText is available through MasteringPhysics, either automatically when MasteringPhysics is packaged with new books, or available as a purchased upgrade online. Allowing students access to the text wherever they have access to the Internet, Pearson eText comprises the full text, including figures that can be enlarged for better viewing. With eText, students are also able to pop up definitions and terms to help with vocabulary and the reading of the material. Students can also take notes in eText using the annotation feature at the top of each page.

Pearson Tutor Services (www.pearsontutorservices.com). Each student's subscription to MasteringPhysics also contains complimentary access to Pearson Tutor Services, powered by Smarthinking, Inc. By logging in with their MasteringPhysics ID and password, students will be connected to highly qualified e-instructors who provide additional interactive online tutoring on the major concepts of physics. Some restrictions apply; offer subject to change.

ActivPhysics OnLine™ (which is accessed through the Study Area within www.masteringphysics.com) provides students with a suite of highly regarded applet-based tutorials (see above). The following workbooks help students work through complex concepts and understand them more clearly.

ActivPhysics OnLine Workbook, Volume 1: Mechanics * Thermal Physics * Oscillations & Waves (978-0-805-39060-5)

ActivPhysics OnLine Workbook, Volume 2: Electricity & Magnetism * Optics * Modern Physics (978-0-805-39061-2)

Acknowledgments

We would like to thank the hundreds of reviewers and colleagues who have offered valuable comments and suggestions over the life of this textbook. The continuing success of *University Physics* is due in large measure to their contributions.

Edward Adelson (Ohio State University), Ralph Alexander (University of Missouri at Rolla), J. G. Anderson, R. S. Anderson, Wayne Anderson (Sacramento City College), Alex Azima (Lansing Community College), Dilip Balamore (Nassau Community College), Harold Bale (University of North Dakota), Arun Bansil (Northeastern University), John Barach (Vanderbilt University), J. D. Barnett, H. H. Barschall, Albert Bartlett (University of Colorado), Marshall Bartlett (Hollins University), Paul Baum (CUNY, Queens College), Frederick Becchetti (University of Michigan), B. Bederson, David Bennum (University of Nevada, Reno), Lev I. Berger (San Diego State University), Robert Boeke (William Rainey Harper College), S. Borowitz, A. C. Braden, James Brooks (Boston University), Nicholas E. Brown (California Polytechnic State University, San Luis Obispo), Tony Buffa (California Polytechnic State University, San Luis Obispo), A. Capecelatro, Michael Cardamone (Pennsylvania State University), Duane Carmony (Purdue University), Troy Carter (UCLA), P. Catranides, John Cerne (SUNY at Buffalo), Tim Chupp (University of Michigan), Shinil Cho (La Roche College), Roger Clapp (University of South Florida), William M. Cloud (Eastern Illinois University), Leonard Cohen (Drexel University), W. R. Coker (University of Texas, Austin), Malcolm D. Cole (University of Missouri at Rolla), H. Conrad, David Cook (Lawrence University), Gayl Cook (University of Colorado), Hans Courant (University of Minnesota), Bruce A. Craver (University of Dayton), Larry Curtis (University of Toledo), Jai Dahiya (Southeast Missouri State University), Steve Detweiler (University of Florida), George Dixon (Oklahoma State University), Donald S. Duncan, Boyd Edwards (West Virginia University), Robert Eisenstein (Carnegie Mellon University), Amy Emerson Missourn (Virginia Institute of Technology), William Faissler (Northeastern University), William Fasnacht (U.S. Naval Academy), Paul Feldker (St. Louis Community College), Carlos Figueroa (Cabrillo College), L. H. Fisher, Neil Fletcher (Florida State University), Robert Folk, Peter Fong (Emory University), A. Lewis Ford (Texas A&M University), D. Frantszog, James R. Gaines (Ohio State University), Solomon Gartenhaus (Purdue University), Ron Gautreau (New Jersey Institute of Technology), J. David Gavenda (University of Texas, Austin), Dennis Gay (University of North Florida), James Gerhart (University of Washington), N. S. Gingrich, J. L. Glathart, S. Goodwin, Rich Gottfried (Frederick Community College), Walter S. Gray (University of Michigan), Paul Gresser (University of Maryland), Benjamin Grinstein (UC San Diego), Howard Grotch (Pennsylvania State University), John Gruber (San Jose State University), Graham D. Gutsche (U.S. Naval Academy), Michael J. Harrison (Michigan State University), Harold Hart (Western Illinois University), Howard Hayden (University of Connecticut), Carl Helrich (Goshen College), Laurent Hodges (Iowa State University), C. D. Hodgman, Michael Hones (Villanova University), Keith Honey (West Virginia Institute of Technology), Gregory Hood (Tidewater Community College), John Hubisz (North Carolina State University), M. Iona, John Jaszczak (Michigan Technical University), Alvin Jenkins (North Carolina State University), Robert P. Johnson (UC Santa Cruz), Lorella Jones (University of Illinois), John Karchek (GMI Engineering & Management Institute), Thomas Keil (Worcester Polytechnic Institute), Robert Kraemer (Carnegie Mellon University), Jean P. Krisch (University of Michigan), Robert A. Kromhout, Andrew Kunz (Marquette University), Charles Lane (Berry College), Thomas N. Lawrence (Texas State University), Robert J. Lee, Alfred Leitner (Rensselaer Polytechnic University), Gerald P. Lietz (De Paul University), Gordon Lind (Utah State University), S. Livingston, Elihu Lubkin (University of Wisconsin, Milwaukee), Robert Luke (Boise State University), David Lynch (Iowa State University), Michael Lysak (San Bernardino Valley College), Jeffrey Mallow (Loyola University), Robert Mania (Kentucky State University), Robert Marchina (University of Memphis), David Markowitz (University of Connecticut), R. J. Maurer, Oren Maxwell (Florida International University), Joseph L. McCauley (University of Houston), T. K. McCubbin, Jr. (Pennsylvania State University), Charles McFarland (University of Missouri at Rolla), James Mcguire (Tulane University), Lawrence McIntyre (University of Arizona), Fredric Messing (Carnegie-Mellon University), Thomas Meyer (Texas A&M University), Andre Mirabelli (St. Peter's College, New Jersey), Herbert Muether (S.U.N.Y., Stony Brook), Jack Munsee (California State University, Long Beach), Lorenzo Narducci (Drexel University), Van E. Neie (Purdue University), David A. Nordling (U. S. Naval Academy), Benedict Oh (Pennsylvania State University), L. O. Olsen, Jim Pannell (DeVry Institute of Technology), W. F. Parks (University of Missouri), Robert Paulson (California State University, Chico), Jerry Peacher (University of Missouri at Rolla), Arnold Perlmutter (University of Miami), Lennart Peterson (University of Florida), R. J. Peterson (University of Colorado, Boulder), R. Pinkston, Ronald Poling (University of Minnesota), J. G. Potter, C. W. Price (Millersville University), Francis Prosser (University of Kansas), Shelden H. Radin, Roberto Ramos (Drexel University), Michael Rapport (Anne Arundel Community College), R. Resnick, James A. Richards, Jr., John S. Risley (North Carolina State University), Francesc Roig (University of California, Santa Barbara), T. L. Rokoske, Richard Roth (Eastern Michigan University), Carl Rotter (University of West Virginia), S. Clark Rowland (Andrews University), Rajarshi Roy (Georgia Institute of Technology), Russell A. Roy (Santa Fe Community College), Dhiraj Sardar (University of Texas, San Antonio), Bruce Schumm (UC Santa Cruz), Melvin Schwartz (St. John's University), F. A. Scott, L. W. Seagondollar, Paul Shand (University of Northern Iowa), Stan Shepherd (Pennsylvania State University), Douglas Sherman (San Jose State), Bruce Sherwood (Carnegie Mellon University), Hugh Siefkin (Greenville College), Tomasz Skwarnicki (Syracuse University), C. P. Slichter, Charles W. Smith (University of Maine, Orono), Malcolm Smith (University of Lowell), Ross Spencer (Brigham Young University), Julien Sprott (University of Wisconsin), Victor Stanionis (Iona College), James Stith (American Institute of Physics), Chuck Stone (North Carolina A&T State

University), Edward Strother (Florida Institute of Technology), Conley Stutz (Bradley University), Albert Stwertka (U.S. Merchant Marine Academy), Kenneth Szpara-DeNisco (Harrisburg Area Community College), Martin Tiersten (CUNY, City College), David Toot (Alfred University), Somdev Tyagi (Drexel University), F. Verbrugge, Helmut Vogel (Carnegie Mellon University), Robert Webb (Texas A & M), Thomas Weber (Iowa State University), M. Russell Wehr, (Pennsylvania State University), Robert Weidman (Michigan Technical University), Dan Whalen (UC San Diego), Lester V. Whitney, Thomas Wiggins (Pennsylvania State University), David Willey (University of Pittsburgh, Johnstown), George Williams (University of Utah), John Williams (Auburn University), Stanley Williams (Iowa State University), Jack Willis, Suzanne Willis (Northern Illinois University), Robert Wilson (San Bernardino Valley College), L. Wolfenstein, James Wood (Palm Beach Junior College), Lowell Wood (University of Houston), R. E. Worley, D. H. Ziebell (Manatee Community College), George O. Zimmerman (Boston University)

In addition, we both have individual acknowledgments we would like to make.

I want to extend my heartfelt thanks to my colleagues at Carnegie Mellon, especially Professors Robert Kraemer, Bruce Sherwood, Ruth Chabay, Helmut Vogel, and Brian Quinn, for many stimulating discussions about physics pedagogy and for their support and encouragement during the writing of several successive editions of this book. I am equally indebted to the many generations of Carnegie Mellon students who have helped me learn what good teaching and good writing are, by showing me what works and what doesn't. It is always a joy and a privilege to express my gratitude to my wife Alice and our children Gretchen and Rebecca for their love, support, and emotional sustenance during the writing of several successive editions of this book. May all men and women be blessed with love such as theirs. — H. D. Y.

I would like to thank my past and present colleagues at UCSB, including Rob Geller, Carl Gwinn, Al Nash, Elisabeth Nicol, and Francesc Roig, for their wholehearted support and for many helpful discussions. I owe a special debt of gratitude to my early teachers Willa Ramsay, Peter Zimmerman, William Little, Alan Schwettman, and Dirk Walecka for showing me what clear and engaging physics teaching is all about, and to Stuart Johnson for inviting me to become a co-author of *University Physics* beginning with the 9th edition. I want to express special thanks to the editorial staff at Addison-Wesley and their partners: to Nancy Whilton for her editorial vision; to Margot Otway for her superb graphic sense and careful development of this edition; to Peter Murphy for his contributions to the worked examples; to Jason J. B. Harlow for his careful reading of the page proofs; and to Chandrika Madhavan, Steven Le, and Cindy Johnson for keeping the editorial and production pipeline flowing. Most of all, I want to express my gratitude and love to my wife Caroline, to whom I dedicate my contribution to this book. Hey, Caroline, the new edition's done at last — let's go flying! — R. A. F.

Please Tell Us What You Think!

We welcome communications from students and professors, especially concerning errors or deficiencies that you find in this edition. We have devoted a lot of time and effort to writing the best book we know how to write, and we hope it will help you to teach and learn physics. In turn, you can help us by letting us know what still needs to be improved! Please feel free to contact us either electronically or by ordinary mail. Your comments will be greatly appreciated.

December 2010

Hugh D. Young
Department of Physics
Carnegie Mellon University
Pittsburgh, PA 15213
hdy@andrew.cmu.edu

Roger A. Freedman
Department of Physics
University of California, Santa Barbara
Santa Barbara, CA 93106-9530
airboy@physics.ucsb.edu
http://www.physics.ucsb.edu/~airboy/

DETAILED CONTENTS

APPENDICES

12
FLUID MECHANICS

? This shark must swim constantly to keep from sinking to the bottom of the ocean, yet the orange tropical fish can remain at the same level in the water with little effort. Why is there a difference?

LEARNING GOALS

By studying this chapter, you will learn:

- The meaning of the density of a material and the average density of a body.
- What is meant by the pressure in a fluid, and how it is measured.
- How to calculate the buoyant force that a fluid exerts on a body immersed in it.
- The significance of laminar versus turbulent fluid flow, and how the speed of flow in a tube depends on the tube size.
- How to use Bernoulli's equation to relate pressure and flow speed at different points in certain types of flow.

Fluids play a vital role in many aspects of everyday life. We drink them, breathe them, swim in them. They circulate through our bodies and control our weather. Airplanes fly through them; ships float in them. A fluid is any substance that can flow; we use the term for both liquids and gases. We usually think of a gas as easily compressed and a liquid as nearly incompressible, although there are exceptional cases.

We begin our study with **fluid statics,** the study of fluids at rest in equilibrium situations. Like other equilibrium situations, it is based on Newton's first and third laws. We will explore the key concepts of density, pressure, and buoyancy. **Fluid dynamics,** the study of fluids in motion, is much more complex; indeed, it is one of the most complex branches of mechanics. Fortunately, we can analyze many important situations using simple idealized models and familiar principles such as Newton's laws and conservation of energy. Even so, we will barely scratch the surface of this broad and interesting topic.

12.1 Density

An important property of any material is its **density,** defined as its mass per unit volume. A homogeneous material such as ice or iron has the same density throughout. We use ρ (the Greek letter rho) for density. If a mass m of homogeneous material has volume V, the density ρ is

$$\rho = \frac{m}{V} \qquad \text{(definition of density)} \tag{12.1}$$

Two objects made of the same material have the same density even though they may have different masses and different volumes. That's because the *ratio* of mass to volume is the same for both objects (Fig. 12.1).

12.1 Two objects with different masses and different volumes but the same density.

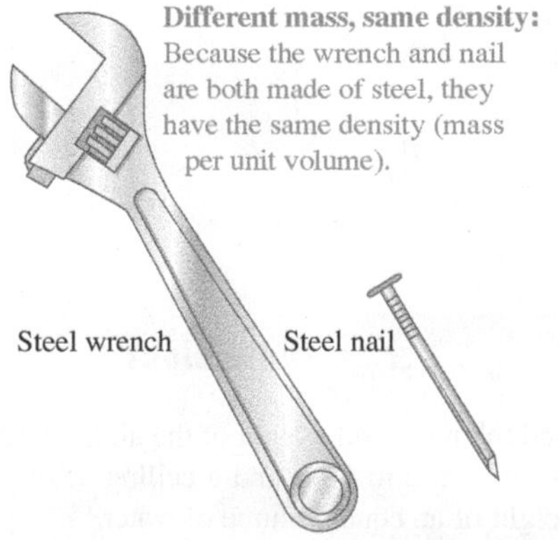

Table 12.1 Densities of Some Common Substances

Material	Density (kg/m^3)*	Material	Density (kg/m^3)*
Air (1 atm, 20°C)	1.20	Iron, steel	7.8×10^3
Ethanol	0.81×10^3	Brass	8.6×10^3
Benzene	0.90×10^3	Copper	8.9×10^3
Ice	0.92×10^3	Silver	10.5×10^3
Water	1.00×10^3	Lead	11.3×10^3
Seawater	1.03×10^3	Mercury	13.6×10^3
Blood	1.06×10^3	Gold	19.3×10^3
Glycerine	1.26×10^3	Platinum	21.4×10^3
Concrete	2×10^3	White dwarf star	10^{10}
Aluminum	2.7×10^3	Neutron star	10^{18}

*To obtain the densities in grams per cubic centimeter, simply divide by 10^3.

The SI unit of density is the kilogram per cubic meter ($1\ kg/m^3$). The cgs unit, the gram per cubic centimeter ($1\ g/cm^3$), is also widely used:

$$1\ g/cm^3 = 1000\ kg/m^3$$

The densities of some common substances at ordinary temperatures are given in Table 12.1. Note the wide range of magnitudes. The densest material found on earth is the metal osmium ($\rho = 22{,}500\ kg/m^3$), but its density pales by comparison to the densities of exotic astronomical objects such as white dwarf stars and neutron stars.

The **specific gravity** of a material is the ratio of its density to the density of water at 4.0°C, $1000\ kg/m^3$; it is a pure number without units. For example, the specific gravity of aluminum is 2.7. "Specific gravity" is a poor term, since it has nothing to do with gravity; "relative density" would have been better.

The density of some materials varies from point to point within the material. One example is the material of the human body, which includes low-density fat (about $940\ kg/m^3$) and high-density bone (from 1700 to $2500\ kg/m^3$). Two others are the earth's atmosphere (which is less dense at high altitudes) and oceans (which are denser at greater depths). For these materials, Eq. (12.1) describes the **average density.** In general, the density of a material depends on environmental factors such as temperature and pressure.

Measuring density is an important analytical technique. For example, we can determine the charge condition of a storage battery by measuring the density of its electrolyte, a sulfuric acid solution. As the battery discharges, the sulfuric acid (H_2SO_4) combines with lead in the battery plates to form insoluble lead sulfate ($PbSO_4$), decreasing the concentration of the solution. The density decreases from about $1.30 \times 10^3\ kg/m^3$ for a fully charged battery to $1.15 \times 10^3\ kg/m^3$ for a discharged battery.

Another automotive example is permanent-type antifreeze, which is usually a solution of ethylene glycol ($\rho = 1.12 \times 10^3\ kg/m^3$) and water. The freezing point of the solution depends on the glycol concentration, which can be determined by measuring the specific gravity. Such measurements can be performed by using a device called a hydrometer, which we'll discuss in Section 12.3.

Example 12.1 The weight of a roomful of air

Find the mass and weight of the air at 20°C in a living room with a 4.0 m × 5.0 m floor and a ceiling 3.0 m high, and the mass and weight of an equal volume of water.

SOLUTION

IDENTIFY and SET UP: We assume that the air density is the same throughout the room. (Air is less dense at high elevations than near sea level, but the density varies negligibly over the room's 3.0-m height; see Section 12.2.) We use Eq. (12.1) to relate the mass m_{air} to the room's volume V (which we'll calculate) and the air density ρ_{air} (given in Table 12.1).

EXECUTE: We have $V = (4.0\text{ m})(5.0\text{ m})(3.0\text{ m}) = 60\text{ m}^3$, so from Eq. (12.1),

$$m_{air} = \rho_{air}V = (1.20\text{ kg/m}^3)(60\text{ m}^3) = 72\text{ kg}$$

$$w_{air} = m_{air}g = (72\text{ kg})(9.8\text{ m/s}^2) = 700\text{ N} = 160\text{ lb}$$

The mass and weight of an equal volume of water are

$$m_{water} = \rho_{water}V = (1000\text{ kg/m}^3)(60\text{ m}^3) = 6.0 \times 10^4\text{ kg}$$

$$w_{water} = m_{water}g = (6.0 \times 10^4\text{ kg})(9.8\text{ m/s}^2)$$

$$= 5.9 \times 10^5\text{ N} = 1.3 \times 10^5\text{ lb} = 66\text{ tons}$$

EVALUATE: A roomful of air weighs about the same as an average adult. Water is nearly a thousand times denser than air, so its mass and weight are larger by the same factor. The weight of a roomful of water would collapse the floor of an ordinary house.

Test Your Understanding of Section 12.1 Rank the following objects in order from highest to lowest average density: (i) mass 4.00 kg, volume $1.60 \times 10^{-3}\text{ m}^3$; (ii) mass 8.00 kg, volume $1.60 \times 10^{-3}\text{ m}^3$; (iii) mass 8.00 kg, volume $3.20 \times 10^{-3}\text{ m}^3$; (iv) mass 2560 kg, volume 0.640 m^3; (v) mass 2560 kg, volume 1.28 m^3.

12.2 Pressure in a Fluid

When a fluid (either liquid or gas) is at rest, it exerts a force perpendicular to any surface in contact with it, such as a container wall or a body immersed in the fluid. This is the force that you feel pressing on your legs when you dangle them in a swimming pool. While the fluid as a whole is at rest, the molecules that make up the fluid are in motion; the force exerted by the fluid is due to molecules colliding with their surroundings.

If we think of an imaginary surface *within* the fluid, the fluid on the two sides of the surface exerts equal and opposite forces on the surface. (Otherwise, the surface would accelerate and the fluid would not remain at rest.) Consider a small surface of area dA centered on a point in the fluid; the normal force exerted by the fluid on each side is $dF_\perp$ (Fig. 12.2). We define the **pressure** p at that point as the normal force per unit area—that is, the ratio of $dF_\perp$ to dA (Fig. 12.3):

12.2 Forces acting on a small surface within a fluid at rest.

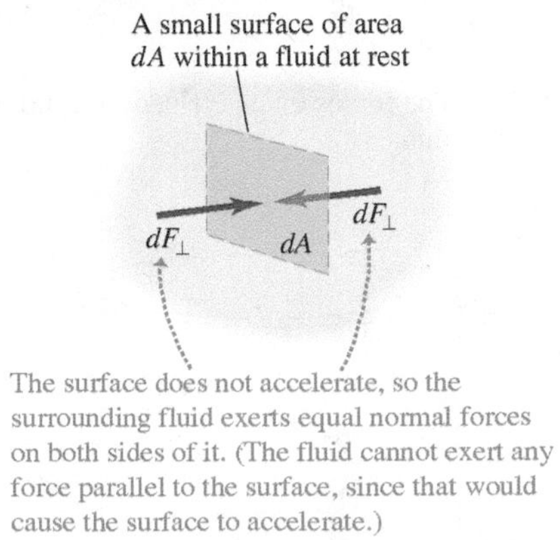

$$p = \frac{dF_\perp}{dA} \quad \text{(definition of pressure)} \tag{12.2}$$

If the pressure is the same at all points of a finite plane surface with area A, then

$$p = \frac{F_\perp}{A} \tag{12.3}$$

where $F_\perp$ is the net normal force on one side of the surface. The SI unit of pressure is the **pascal,** where

$$1\text{ pascal} = 1\text{ Pa} = 1\text{ N/m}^2$$

We introduced the pascal in Chapter 11. Two related units, used principally in meteorology, are the *bar,* equal to 10^5 Pa, and the *millibar,* equal to 100 Pa.

Atmospheric pressure p_a is the pressure of the earth's atmosphere, the pressure at the bottom of this sea of air in which we live. This pressure varies with weather changes and with elevation. Normal atmospheric pressure at sea level (an average value) is 1 *atmosphere* (atm), defined to be exactly 101,325 Pa. To four significant figures,

$$(p_a)_{av} = 1\text{ atm} = 1.013 \times 10^5\text{ Pa}$$
$$= 1.013\text{ bar} = 1013\text{ millibar} = 14.70\text{ lb/in.}^2$$

12.3 The pressure on either side of a surface is force divided by area. Pressure is a scalar with units of newtons per square meter. By contrast, force is a vector with units of newtons.

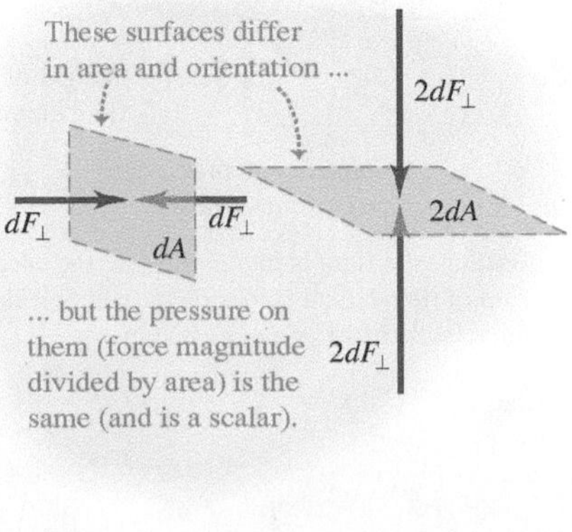

CAUTION **Don't confuse pressure and force** In everyday language the words "pressure" and "force" mean pretty much the same thing. In fluid mechanics, however, these words describe distinct quantities with different characteristics. Fluid pressure acts perpendicular to any surface in the fluid, no matter how that surface is oriented (Fig. 12.3). Hence pressure has no intrinsic direction of its own; it's a scalar. By contrast, force is a vector with a definite direction. Remember, too, that pressure is force per unit area. As Fig. 12.3 shows, a surface with twice the area has twice as much force exerted on it by the fluid, so the pressure is the same.

Example 12.2 The force of air

In the room described in Example 12.1, what is the total downward force on the floor due to an air pressure of 1.00 atm?

SOLUTION

IDENTIFY and SET UP: This example uses the relationship among the pressure p of a fluid (air), the area A subjected to that pressure, and the resulting normal force $F_\perp$ the fluid exerts. The pressure is uniform, so we use Eq. (12.3), $F_\perp = pA$, to determine $F_\perp$. The floor is horizontal, so $F_\perp$ is vertical (downward).

EXECUTE: We have $A = (4.0\text{ m})(5.0\text{ m}) = 20\text{ m}^2$, so from Eq. (12.3),

$$F_\perp = pA = (1.013 \times 10^5\text{ N/m}^2)(20\text{ m}^2)$$
$$= 2.0 \times 10^6\text{ N} = 4.6 \times 10^5\text{ lb} = 230\text{ tons}$$

EVALUATE: Unlike the water in Example 12.1, $F_\perp$ will not collapse the floor here, because there is an *upward* force of equal magnitude on the floor's underside. If the house has a basement, this upward force is exerted by the air underneath the floor. In this case, if we neglect the thickness of the floor, the *net* force due to air pressure is zero.

Pressure, Depth, and Pascal's Law

If the weight of the fluid can be neglected, the pressure in a fluid is the same throughout its volume. We used that approximation in our discussion of bulk stress and strain in Section 11.4. But often the fluid's weight is *not* negligible. Atmospheric pressure is less at high altitude than at sea level, which is why an airplane cabin has to be pressurized when flying at 35,000 feet. When you dive into deep water, your ears tell you that the pressure increases rapidly with increasing depth below the surface.

We can derive a general relationship between the pressure p at any point in a fluid at rest and the elevation y of the point. We'll assume that the density ρ has the same value throughout the fluid (that is, the density is *uniform*), as does the acceleration due to gravity g. If the fluid is in equilibrium, every volume element is in equilibrium. Consider a thin element of fluid with thickness dy (Fig. 12.4a). The bottom and top surfaces each have area A, and they are at elevations y and $y + dy$ above some reference level where $y = 0$. The volume of the fluid element is $dV = A\,dy$, its mass is $dm = \rho\,dV = \rho A\,dy$, and its weight is $dw = dm\,g = \rho g A\,dy$.

12.4 The forces on an element of fluid in equilibrium.

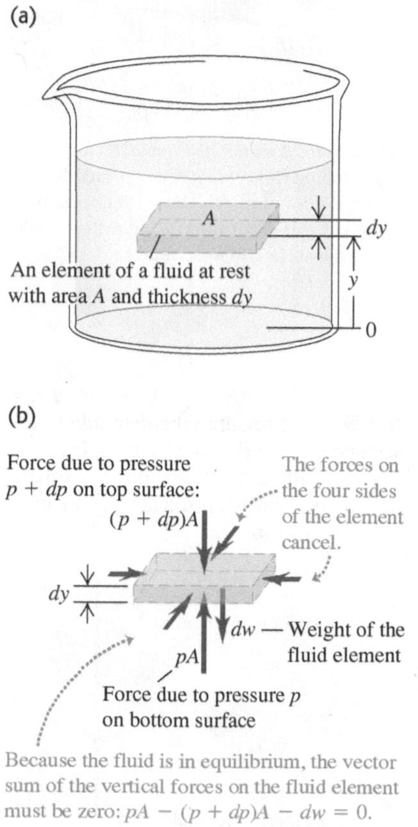

What are the other forces on this fluid element (Fig 12.4b)? Let's call the pressure at the bottom surface p; then the total y-component of upward force on this surface is pA. The pressure at the top surface is $p + dp$, and the total y-component of (downward) force on the top surface is $-(p + dp)A$. The fluid element is in equilibrium, so the total y-component of force, including the weight and the forces at the bottom and top surfaces, must be zero:

$$\sum F_y = 0 \quad \text{so} \quad pA - (p + dp)A - \rho g A\,dy = 0$$

When we divide out the area A and rearrange, we get

$$\frac{dp}{dy} = -\rho g \tag{12.4}$$

This equation shows that when y increases, p decreases; that is, as we move upward in the fluid, pressure decreases, as we expect. If p_1 and p_2 are the pressures at elevations y_1 and y_2, respectively, and if ρ and g are constant, then

$$p_2 - p_1 = -\rho g(y_2 - y_1) \quad \text{(pressure in a fluid of uniform density)} \tag{12.5}$$

It's often convenient to express Eq. (12.5) in terms of the *depth* below the surface of a fluid (Fig. 12.5). Take point 1 at any level in the fluid and let p represent the pressure at this point. Take point 2 at the *surface* of the fluid, where the pressure is p_0 (subscript zero for zero depth). The depth of point 1 below the surface is $h = y_2 - y_1$, and Eq. (12.5) becomes

$$p_0 - p = -\rho g(y_2 - y_1) = -\rho g h \qquad \text{or}$$

$$p = p_0 + \rho g h \quad \text{(pressure in a fluid of uniform density)} \tag{12.6}$$

The pressure p at a depth h is greater than the pressure p_0 at the surface by an amount ρgh. Note that the pressure is the same at any two points at the same level in the fluid. The *shape* of the container does not matter (Fig. 12.6).

Equation (12.6) shows that if we increase the pressure p_0 at the top surface, possibly by using a piston that fits tightly inside the container to push down on the fluid surface, the pressure p at any depth increases by exactly the same amount. This fact was recognized in 1653 by the French scientist Blaise Pascal (1623–1662) and is called *Pascal's law.*

Pascal's law: Pressure applied to an enclosed fluid is transmitted undiminished to every portion of the fluid and the walls of the containing vessel.

The hydraulic lift shown schematically in Fig. 12.7 illustrates Pascal's law. A piston with small cross-sectional area A_1 exerts a force F_1 on the surface of a liquid such as oil. The applied pressure $p = F_1/A_1$ is transmitted through the connecting pipe to a larger piston of area A_2. The applied pressure is the same in both cylinders, so

$$p = \frac{F_1}{A_1} = \frac{F_2}{A_2} \qquad \text{and} \qquad F_2 = \frac{A_2}{A_1}F_1 \tag{12.7}$$

The hydraulic lift is a force-multiplying device with a multiplication factor equal to the ratio of the areas of the two pistons. Dentist's chairs, car lifts and jacks, many elevators, and hydraulic brakes all use this principle.

For gases the assumption that the density ρ is uniform is realistic only over short vertical distances. In a room with a ceiling height of 3.0 m filled with air of uniform density 1.2 kg/m^3, the difference in pressure between floor and ceiling, given by Eq. (12.6), is

$$\rho g h = (1.2\ \text{kg/m}^3)(9.8\ \text{m/s}^2)(3.0\ \text{m}) = 35\ \text{Pa}$$

or about 0.00035 atm, a very small difference. But between sea level and the summit of Mount Everest (8882 m) the density of air changes by nearly a factor of 3, and in this case we cannot use Eq. (12.6). Liquids, by contrast, are nearly incompressible, and it is usually a very good approximation to regard their density as independent of pressure. A pressure of several hundred atmospheres will cause only a few percent increase in the density of most liquids.

Absolute Pressure and Gauge Pressure

If the pressure inside a car tire is equal to atmospheric pressure, the tire is flat. The pressure has to be *greater* than atmospheric to support the car, so the significant quantity is the *difference* between the inside and outside pressures. When we say that the pressure in a car tire is "32 pounds" (actually 32 lb/in.^2, equal to 220 kPa or 2.2×10^5 Pa), we mean that it is *greater* than atmospheric pressure

12.5 How pressure varies with depth in a fluid with uniform density.

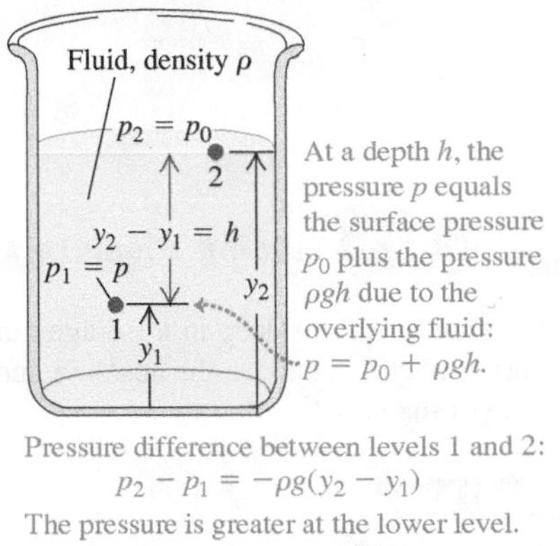

12.6 Each fluid column has the same height, no matter what its shape.

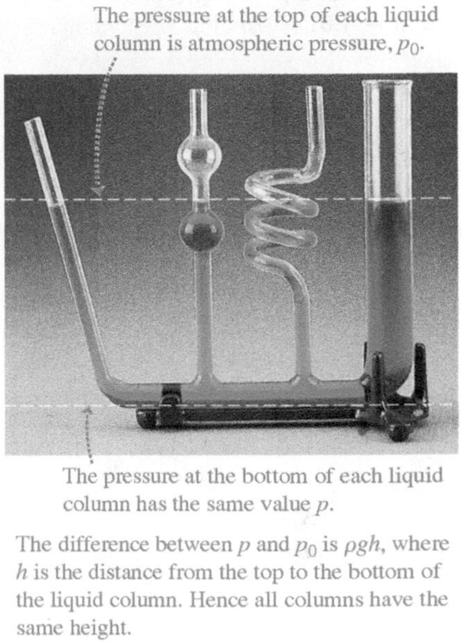

12.7 The hydraulic lift is an application of Pascal's law. The size of the fluid-filled container is exaggerated for clarity.

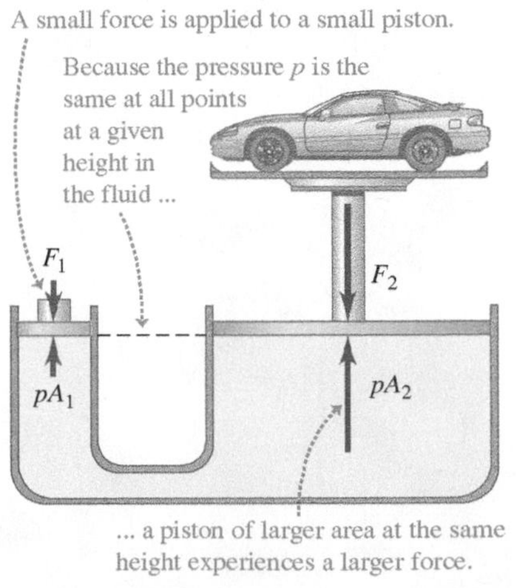

(14.7 lb/in.^{2} or 1.01×10^5 Pa) by this amount. The *total* pressure in the tire is then 47 lb/in.^{2} or 320 kPa. The excess pressure above atmospheric pressure is usually called **gauge pressure,** and the total pressure is called **absolute pressure.** Engineers use the abbreviations psig and psia for "pounds per square inch gauge" and "pounds per square inch absolute," respectively. If the pressure is *less* than atmospheric, as in a partial vacuum, the gauge pressure is negative.

Example 12.3 Finding absolute and gauge pressures

Water stands 12.0 m deep in a storage tank whose top is open to the atmosphere. What are the absolute and gauge pressures at the bottom of the tank?

SOLUTION

IDENTIFY and SET UP: Table 11.2 indicates that water is nearly incompressible, so we can treat it as having uniform density. The level of the top of the tank corresponds to point 2 in Fig. 12.5, and the level of the bottom of the tank corresponds to point 1. Our target variable is p in Eq. (12.6). We have $h = 12.0$ m and $p_0 = 1$ atm $= 1.01 \times 10^5$ Pa.

EXECUTE: From Eq. (12.6), the pressures are

absolute:

$$\begin{aligned} p &= p_0 + \rho g h \\ &= (1.01 \times 10^5 \text{ Pa}) + (1000 \text{ kg/m}^3)(9.80 \text{ m/s}^2)(12.0 \text{ m}) \\ &= 2.19 \times 10^5 \text{ Pa} = 2.16 \text{ atm} = 31.8 \text{ lb/in.}^2 \end{aligned}$$

gauge:

$$\begin{aligned} p - p_0 &= (2.19 - 1.01) \times 10^5 \text{ Pa} \\ &= 1.18 \times 10^5 \text{ Pa} = 1.16 \text{ atm} = 17.1 \text{ lb/in.}^2 \end{aligned}$$

EVALUATE: A pressure gauge at the bottom of such a tank would probably be calibrated to read gauge pressure rather than absolute pressure.

Pressure Gauges

The simplest pressure gauge is the open-tube *manometer* (Fig. 12.8a). The U-shaped tube contains a liquid of density ρ, often mercury or water. The left end of the tube is connected to the container where the pressure p is to be measured, and the right end is open to the atmosphere at pressure $p_0 = p_{atm}$. The pressure at the bottom of the tube due to the fluid in the left column is $p + \rho g y_1$, and the pressure at the bottom due to the fluid in the right column is $p_{atm} + \rho g y_2$. These pressures are measured at the same level, so they must be equal:

$$\begin{aligned} p + \rho g y_1 &= p_{atm} + \rho g y_2 \\ p - p_{atm} &= \rho g (y_2 - y_1) = \rho g h \end{aligned} \tag{12.8}$$

In Eq. (12.8), p is the *absolute pressure,* and the difference $p - p_{atm}$ between absolute and atmospheric pressure is the gauge pressure. Thus the gauge pressure is proportional to the difference in height $h = y_2 - y_1$ of the liquid columns.

12.8 Two types of pressure gauge.

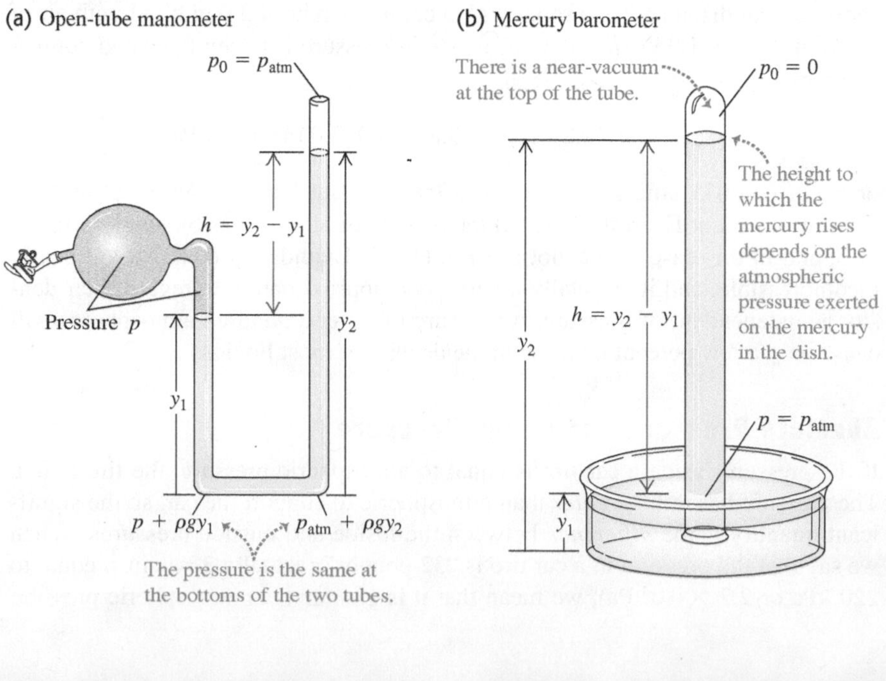

Another common pressure gauge is the **mercury barometer.** It consists of a long glass tube, closed at one end, that has been filled with mercury and then inverted in a dish of mercury (Fig. 12.8b). The space above the mercury column contains only mercury vapor; its pressure is negligibly small, so the pressure p_0 at the top of the mercury column is practically zero. From Eq. (12.6),

$$p_{atm} = p = 0 + \rho g(y_2 - y_1) = \rho g h \quad (12.9)$$

Thus the mercury barometer reads the atmospheric pressure p_{atm} directly from the height of the mercury column.

Pressures are often described in terms of the height of the corresponding mercury column, as so many "inches of mercury" or "millimeters of mercury" (abbreviated mm Hg). A pressure of 1 mm Hg is called *1 torr,* after Evangelista Torricelli, inventor of the mercury barometer. But these units depend on the density of mercury, which varies with temperature, and on the value of g, which varies with location, so the pascal is the preferred unit of pressure.

Many types of pressure gauges use a flexible sealed tube (Fig. 12.9). A change in the pressure either inside or outside the tube causes a change in its dimensions. This change is detected optically, electrically, or mechanically.

Application Gauge Pressure of Blood

Blood-pressure readings, such as 130/80, give the maximum and minimum gauge pressures in the arteries, measured in mm Hg or torr. Blood pressure varies with vertical position within the body; the standard reference point is the upper arm, level with the heart.

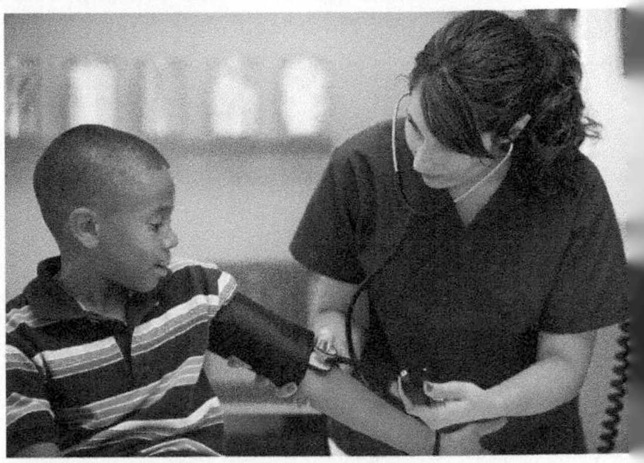

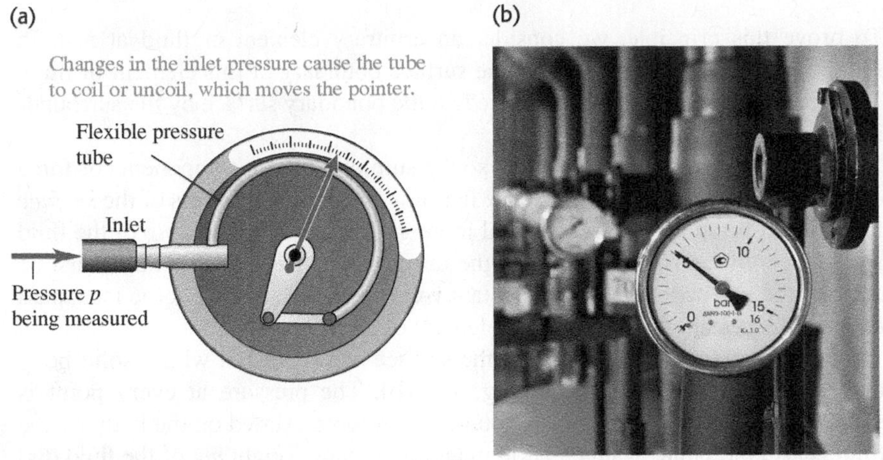

12.9 (a) A Bourdon pressure gauge. When the pressure inside the flexible tube increases, the tube straightens out a little, deflecting the attached pointer. (b) This Bourdon-type pressure gauge is connected to a high-pressure gas line. The gauge pressure shown is just over 5 bars (1 bar $= 10^5$ Pa).

Example 12.4 A tale of two fluids

A manometer tube is partially filled with water. Oil (which does not mix with water) is poured into the left arm of the tube until the oil–water interface is at the midpoint of the tube as shown. Both arms of the tube are open to the air. Find a relationship between the heights h_{oil} and h_{water}.

12.10 Our sketch for this problem.

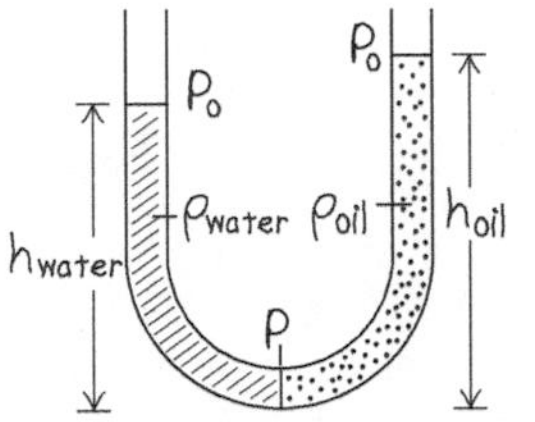

SOLUTION

IDENTIFY and SET UP: Figure 12.10 shows our sketch. The relationship between pressure and depth given by Eq. (12.6) applies only to fluids of uniform density; we have two fluids of different densities, so we must write a separate pressure–depth relationship for each. Both fluid columns have pressure p at the bottom (where they are in contact and in equilibrium) and are both at atmospheric pressure p_0 at the top (where both are in contact with and in equilibrium with the air).

EXECUTE: Writing Eq. (12.6) for each fluid gives

$$p = p_0 + \rho_{water} g h_{water}$$
$$p = p_0 + \rho_{oil} g h_{oil}$$

Since the pressure p at the bottom of the tube is the same for both fluids, we set these two expressions equal to each other and solve for h_{oil} in terms of h_{water}. You can show that the result is

$$h_{oil} = \frac{\rho_{water}}{\rho_{oil}} h_{water}$$

EVALUATE: Water ($\rho_{water} = 1000\ \text{kg/m}^3$) is denser than oil ($\rho_{oil} \approx 850\ \text{kg/m}^3$), so h_{oil} is greater than h_{water} as Fig. 12.10 shows. It takes a greater height of low-density oil to produce the same pressure p at the bottom of the tube.

Test Your Understanding of Section 12.2 Mercury is less dense at high temperatures than at low temperatures. Suppose you move a mercury barometer from the cold interior of a tightly sealed refrigerator to outdoors on a hot summer day. You find that the column of mercury remains at the same height in the tube. Compared to the air pressure inside the refrigerator, is the air pressure outdoors (i) higher, (ii) lower, or (iii) the same? (Ignore the very small change in the dimensions of the glass tube due to the temperature change.)

MasteringPHYSICS

PhET: Balloons & Buoyancy

12.3 Buoyancy

Buoyancy is a familiar phenomenon: A body immersed in water seems to weigh less than when it is in air. When the body is less dense than the fluid, it floats. The human body usually floats in water, and a helium-filled balloon floats in air.

Archimedes's principle: When a body is completely or partially immersed in a fluid, the fluid exerts an upward force on the body equal to the weight of the fluid displaced by the body.

To prove this principle, we consider an arbitrary element of fluid at rest. In Fig. 12.11a the irregular outline is the surface boundary of this element of fluid. The arrows represent the forces exerted on the boundary surface by the surrounding fluid.

The entire fluid is in equilibrium, so the sum of all the y-components of force on this element of fluid is zero. Hence the sum of the y-components of the *surface* forces must be an upward force equal in magnitude to the weight mg of the fluid inside the surface. Also, the sum of the torques on the element of fluid must be zero, so the line of action of the resultant y-component of surface force must pass through the center of gravity of this element of fluid.

Now we remove the fluid inside the surface and replace it with a solid body having exactly the same shape (Fig. 12.11b). The pressure at every point is exactly the same as before. So the total upward force exerted on the body by the fluid is also the same, again equal in magnitude to the weight mg of the fluid displaced to make way for the body. We call this upward force the **buoyant force** on the solid body. The line of action of the buoyant force again passes through the center of gravity of the displaced fluid (which doesn't necessarily coincide with the center of gravity of the body).

When a balloon floats in equilibrium in air, its weight (including the gas inside it) must be the same as the weight of the air displaced by the balloon. A fish's flesh is denser than water, yet a fish can float while

12.11 Archimedes's principle.

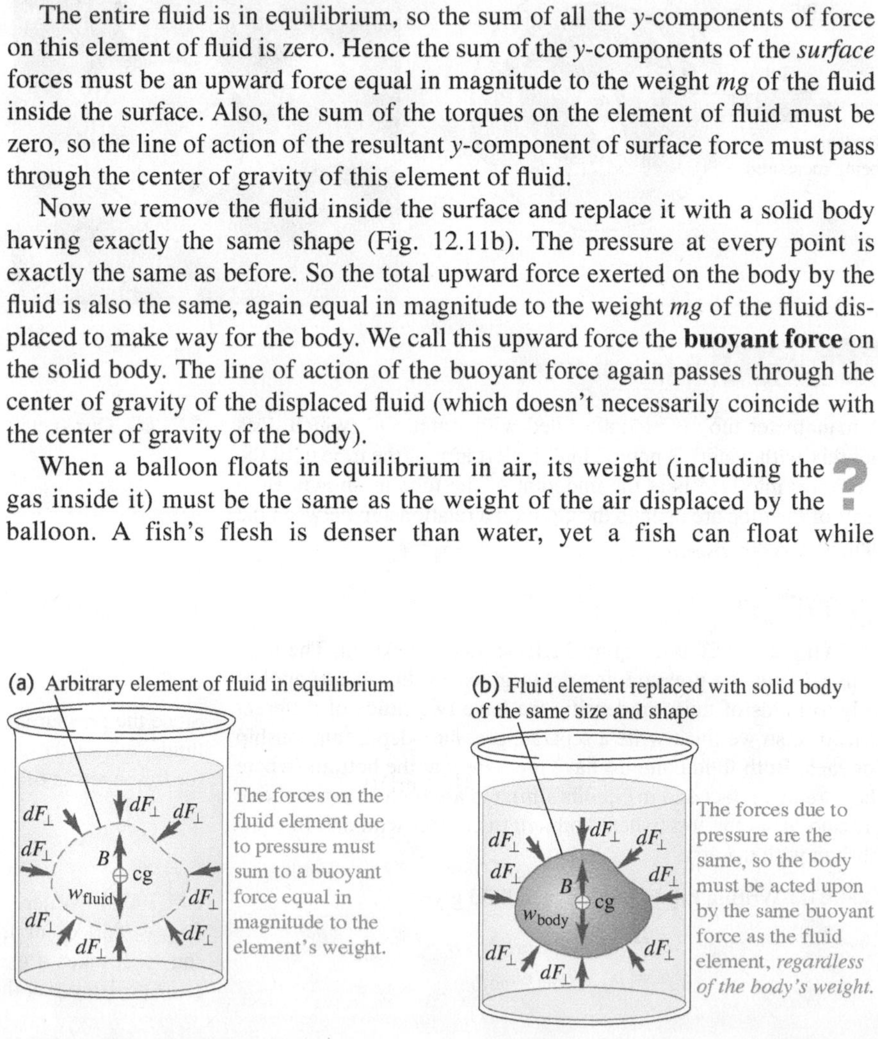

submerged because it has a gas-filled cavity within its body. This makes the fish's *average* density the same as water's, so its net weight is the same as the weight of the water it displaces. A body whose average density is *less* than that of a liquid can float partially submerged at the free upper surface of the liquid. The greater the density of the liquid, the less of the body is submerged. When you swim in seawater (density 1030 kg/m^3), your body floats higher than in fresh water (1000 kg/m^3).

A practical example of buoyancy is the hydrometer, used to measure the density of liquids (Fig. 12.12a). The calibrated float sinks into the fluid until the weight of the fluid it displaces is exactly equal to its own weight. The hydrometer floats *higher* in denser liquids than in less dense liquids, and a scale in the top stem permits direct density readings. Figure 12.12b shows a type of hydrometer that is commonly used to measure the density of battery acid or antifreeze. The bottom of the large tube is immersed in the liquid; the bulb is squeezed to expel air and is then released, like a giant medicine dropper. The liquid rises into the outer tube, and the hydrometer floats in this sample of the liquid.

12.12 Measuring the density of a fluid.

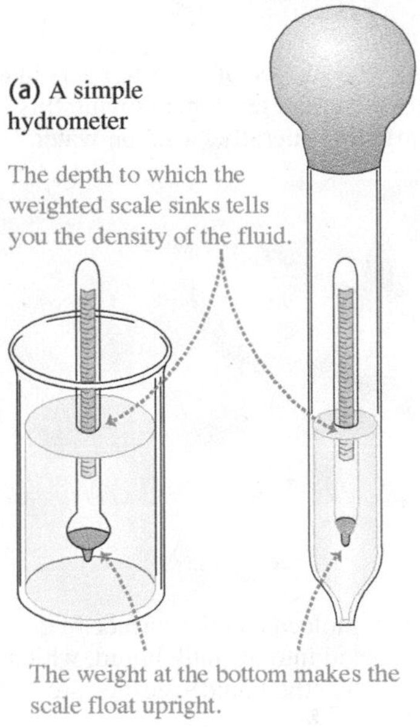

Example 12.5 Buoyancy

A 15.0-kg solid gold statue is raised from the sea bottom (Fig. 12.13a). What is the tension in the hoisting cable (assumed massless) when the statue is (a) at rest and completely underwater and (b) at rest and completely out of the water?

SOLUTION

IDENTIFY and SET UP: In both cases the statue is in equilibrium and experiences three forces: its weight, the cable tension, and a buoyant force equal in magnitude to the weight of the fluid displaced by the statue (seawater in part (a), air in part (b)). Figure 12.13b shows the free-body diagram for the statue. Our target variables are the values of the tension in seawater (T_{sw}) and in air (T_{air}). We are given the mass m_{statue}, and we can calculate the buoyant force in seawater (B_{sw}) and in air (B_{air}) using Archimedes's principle.

EXECUTE: (a) To find B_{sw}, we first find the statue's volume V using the density of gold from Table 12.1:

$$V = \frac{m_{statue}}{\rho_{gold}} = \frac{15.0 \text{ kg}}{19.3 \times 10^3 \text{ kg/m}^3} = 7.77 \times 10^{-4} \text{ m}^3$$

The buoyant force B_{sw} equals the weight of this same volume of seawater. Using Table 12.1 again:

$$\begin{aligned} B_{sw} &= w_{sw} = m_{sw}g = \rho_{sw}Vg \\ &= (1.03 \times 10^3 \text{ kg/m}^3)(7.77 \times 10^{-4} \text{ m}^3)(9.80 \text{ m/s}^2) \\ &= 7.84 \text{ N} \end{aligned}$$

The statue is at rest, so the net external force acting on it is zero. From Fig. 12.13b,

$$\sum F_y = B_{sw} + T_{sw} + (-m_{statue}g) = 0$$

$$\begin{aligned} T_{sw} &= m_{statue}g - B_{sw} = (15.0 \text{ kg})(9.80 \text{ m/s}^2) - 7.84 \text{ N} \\ &= 147 \text{ N} - 7.84 \text{ N} = 139 \text{ N} \end{aligned}$$

12.13 What is the tension in the cable hoisting the statue?

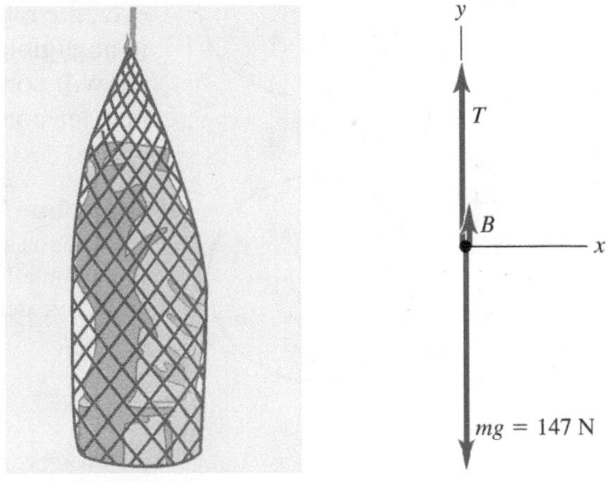

A spring scale attached to the upper end of the cable will indicate a tension 7.84 N less than the statue's actual weight $m_{statue}g$ = 147 N.

(b) The density of air is about 1.2 kg/m^3, so the buoyant force of air on the statue is

$$\begin{aligned} B_{air} &= \rho_{air}Vg = (1.2 \text{ kg/m}^3)(7.77 \times 10^{-4} \text{ m}^3)(9.80 \text{ m/s}^2) \\ &= 9.1 \times 10^{-3} \text{ N} \end{aligned}$$

This is negligible compared to the statue's actual weight $m_{statue}g$ = 147 N. So within the precision of our data, the tension in the cable with the statue in air is $T_{air} = m_{statue}g = 147$ N.

EVALUATE: Note that the buoyant force is proportional to the density of the *fluid* in which the statue is immersed, *not* the density of

Continued

the statue. The denser the fluid, the greater the buoyant force and the smaller the cable tension. If the fluid had the same density as the statue, the buoyant force would be equal to the statue's weight and the tension would be zero (the cable would go slack). If the fluid were denser than the statue, the tension would be *negative:* The buoyant force would be greater than the statue's weight, and a downward force would be required to keep the statue from rising upward.

12.14 The surface of the water acts like a membrane under tension, allowing this water strider to literally "walk on water."

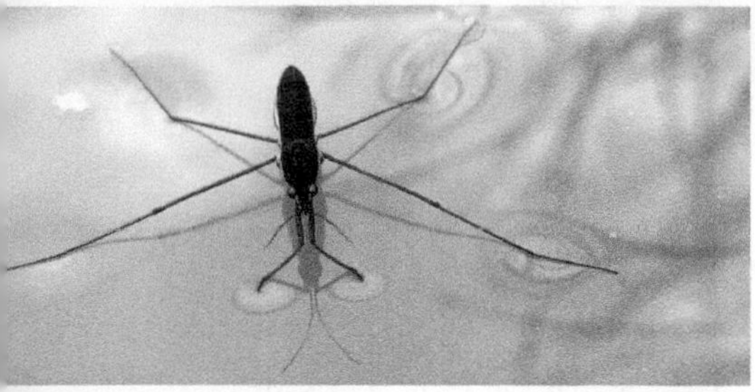

12.15 A molecule at the surface of a liquid is attracted into the bulk liquid, which tends to reduce the liquid's surface area.

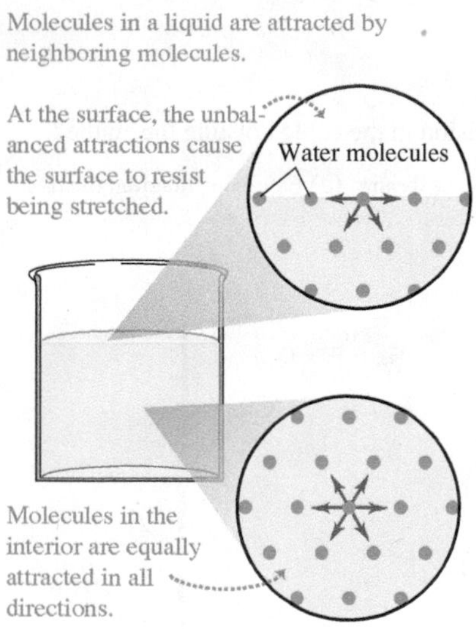

12.16 Surface tension makes it difficult to force water through small crevices. The required water pressure p can be reduced by using hot, soapy water, which has less surface tension.

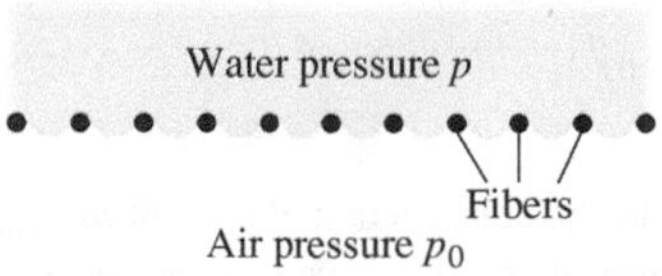

Surface Tension

An object less dense than water, such as an air-filled beach ball, floats with part of its volume below the surface. Conversely, a paper clip can rest *atop* a water surface even though its density is several times that of water. This is an example of **surface tension:** The surface of the liquid behaves like a membrane under tension (Fig. 12.14). Surface tension arises because the molecules of the liquid exert attractive forces on each other. There is zero net force on a molecule inside the volume of the liquid, but a surface molecule is drawn into the volume (Fig. 12.15). Thus the liquid tends to minimize its surface area, just as a stretched membrane does.

Surface tension explains why freely falling raindrops are spherical (*not* teardrop-shaped): A sphere has a smaller surface area for its volume than any other shape. It also explains why hot, soapy water is used for washing. To wash clothing thoroughly, water must be forced through the tiny spaces between the fibers (Fig. 12.16). To do so requires increasing the surface area of the water, which is difficult to achieve because of surface tension. The job is made easier by increasing the temperature of the water and adding soap, both of which decrease the surface tension.

Surface tension is important for a millimeter-sized water drop, which has a relatively large surface area for its volume. (A sphere of radius r has surface area $4\pi r^2$ and volume $(4\pi/3)r^3$. The ratio of surface area to volume is $3/r$, which increases with decreasing radius.) For large quantities of liquid, however, the ratio of surface area to volume is relatively small, and surface tension is negligible compared to pressure forces. For the remainder of this chapter, we will consider only fluids in bulk and hence will ignore the effects of surface tension.

Test Your Understanding of Section 12.3 You place a container of seawater on a scale and note the reading on the scale. You now suspend the statue of Example 12.5 in the water (Fig. 12.17). How does the scale reading change? (i) It increases by 7.84 N; (ii) it decreases by 7.84 N; (iii) it remains the same; (iv) none of these. MP

12.4 Fluid Flow

We are now ready to consider *motion* of a fluid. Fluid flow can be extremely complex, as shown by the currents in river rapids or the swirling flames of a campfire. But some situations can be represented by relatively simple idealized models. An **ideal fluid** is a fluid that is *incompressible* (that is, its density cannot change) and has no internal friction (called **viscosity**). Liquids are approximately incompressible in most situations, and we may also treat a gas as incompressible if the pressure differences from one region to another are not too great. Internal friction in a fluid causes shear stresses when two adjacent layers of fluid move relative to each other, as when fluid flows inside a tube or around an obstacle. In some cases we can neglect these shear forces in comparison with forces arising from gravitation and pressure differences.

The path of an individual particle in a moving fluid is called a **flow line.** If the overall flow pattern does not change with time, the flow is called **steady flow.** In steady flow, every element passing through a given point follows the same flow line. In this case the "map" of the fluid velocities at various points in space remains constant, although the velocity of a particular particle may change in both magnitude and direction during its motion. A **streamline** is a curve whose tangent at any point is in the direction of the fluid velocity at that point. When the flow pattern changes with time, the streamlines do not coincide with the flow lines. We will consider only steady-flow situations, for which flow lines and streamlines are identical.

The flow lines passing through the edge of an imaginary element of area, such as the area A in Fig. 12.18, form a tube called a **flow tube.** From the definition of a flow line, in steady flow no fluid can cross the side walls of a flow tube; the fluids in different flow tubes cannot mix.

Figure 12.19 shows patterns of fluid flow from left to right around three different obstacles. The photographs were made by injecting dye into water flowing between two closely spaced glass plates. These patterns are typical of **laminar flow,** in which adjacent layers of fluid slide smoothly past each other and the flow is steady. (A *lamina* is a thin sheet.) At sufficiently high flow rates, or when boundary surfaces cause abrupt changes in velocity, the flow can become irregular and chaotic. This is called **turbulent flow** (Fig. 12.20). In turbulent flow there is no steady-state pattern; the flow pattern changes continuously.

The Continuity Equation

The mass of a moving fluid doesn't change as it flows. This leads to an important quantitative relationship called the **continuity equation.** Consider a portion of a flow tube between two stationary cross sections with areas A_1 and A_2 (Fig. 12.21). The fluid speeds at these sections are v_1 and v_2, respectively. No fluid flows in or out across the sides of the tube because the fluid velocity is tangent to the wall at every point on the wall. During a small time interval dt, the fluid at A_1 moves a distance $v_1\,dt$, so a cylinder of fluid with height $v_1\,dt$ and volume $dV_1 = A_1 v_1\,dt$ flows into the tube across A_1. During this same interval, a cylinder of volume $dV_2 = A_2 v_2\,dt$ flows out of the tube across A_2.

Let's first consider the case of an incompressible fluid so that the density ρ has the same value at all points. The mass dm_1 flowing into the tube across A_1 in time dt is $dm_1 = \rho A_1 v_1\,dt$. Similarly, the mass dm_2 that flows out across A_2 in the same time is $dm_2 = \rho A_2 v_2\,dt$. In steady flow the total mass in the tube is constant, so $dm_1 = dm_2$ and

$$\rho A_1 v_1\,dt = \rho A_2 v_2\,dt \qquad \text{or}$$

$$A_1 v_1 = A_2 v_2 \qquad \text{(continuity equation, incompressible fluid)} \qquad (12.10)$$

12.17 How does the scale reading change when the statue is immersed in water?

12.18 A flow tube bounded by flow lines. In steady flow, fluid cannot cross the walls of a flow tube.

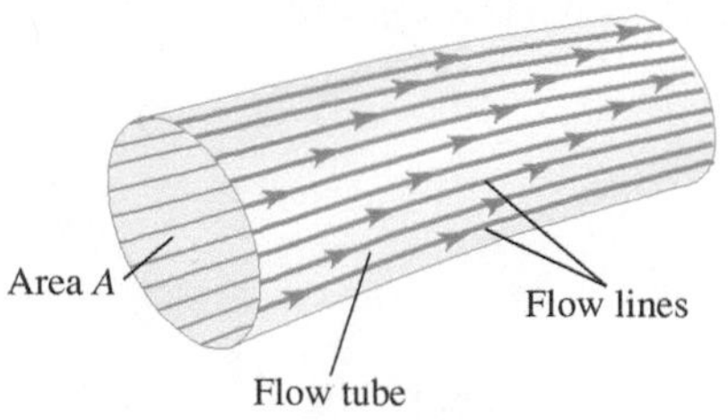

12.19 Laminar flow around obstacles of different shapes.

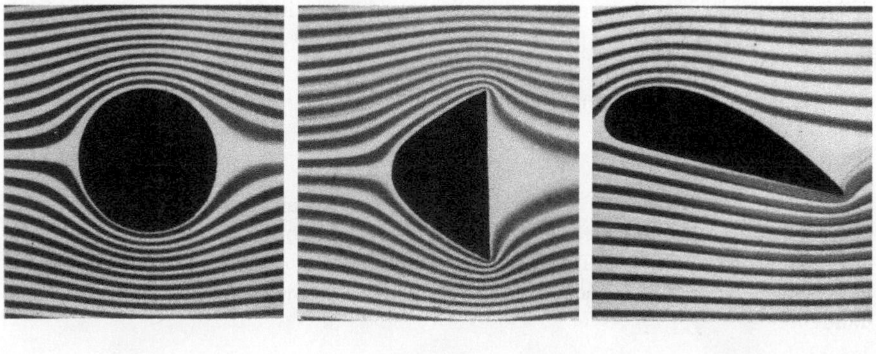

12.20 The flow of smoke rising from these incense sticks is laminar up to a certain point, and then becomes turbulent.

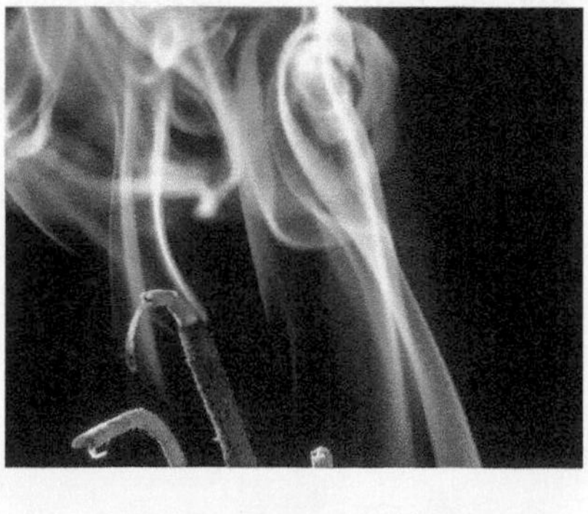

12.21 A flow tube with changing cross-sectional area. If the fluid is incompressible, the product Av has the same value at all points along the tube.

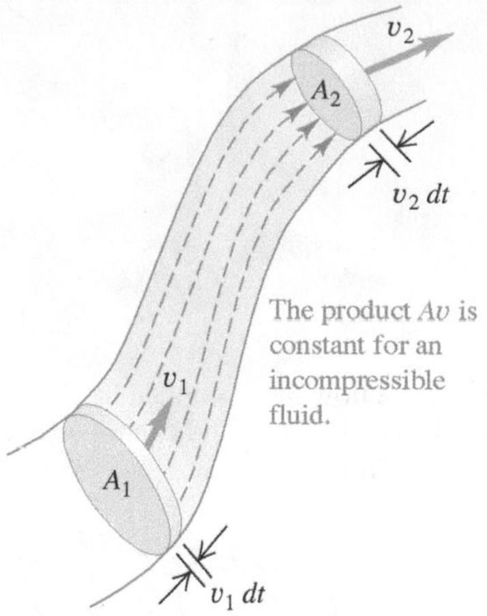

The product Av is the *volume flow rate* dV/dt, the rate at which volume crosses a section of the tube:

$$\frac{dV}{dt} = Av \qquad \text{(volume flow rate)} \qquad (12.11)$$

The *mass* flow rate is the mass flow per unit time through a cross section. This is equal to the density ρ times the volume flow rate dV/dt.

Equation (12.10) shows that the volume flow rate has the same value at all points along any flow tube. When the cross section of a flow tube decreases, the speed increases, and vice versa. A broad, deep part of a river has larger cross section and slower current than a narrow, shallow part, but the volume flow rates are the same in both. This is the essence of the familiar maxim, "Still waters run deep." The stream of water from a faucet narrows as it gains speed during its fall, but dV/dt is the same everywhere along the stream. If a water pipe with 2-cm diameter is connected to a pipe with 1-cm diameter, the flow speed is four times as great in the 1-cm part as in the 2-cm part.

We can generalize Eq. (12.10) for the case in which the fluid is *not* incompressible. If ρ_1 and ρ_2 are the densities at sections 1 and 2, then

$$\rho_1 A_1 v_1 = \rho_2 A_2 v_2 \qquad \text{(continuity equation, compressible fluid)} \qquad (12.12)$$

If the fluid is denser at point 2 than at point 1 ($\rho_2 > \rho_1$), the volume flow rate at point 2 will be less than at point 1 ($A_2 v_2 < A_1 v_1$). We leave the details to you. If the fluid is incompressible so that ρ_1 and ρ_2 are always equal, Eq. (12.12) reduces to Eq. (12.10).

Example 12.6 Flow of an incompressible fluid

Incompressible oil of density 850 kg/m^3 is pumped through a cylindrical pipe at a rate of 9.5 liters per second. (a) The first section of the pipe has a diameter of 8.0 cm. What is the flow speed of the oil? What is the mass flow rate? (b) The second section of the pipe has a diameter of 4.0 cm. What are the flow speed and mass flow rate in that section?

SOLUTION

IDENTIFY and SET UP: Since the oil is incompressible, the volume flow rate has the *same* value (9.5 L/s) in both sections of pipe. The mass flow rate (the density times the volume flow rate) also has the same value in both sections. (This is just the statement that no fluid is lost or added anywhere along the pipe.) We use the volume flow rate equation, Eq. (12.11), to determine the speed v_1 in the 8.0-cm-diameter section and the continuity equation for incompressible flow, Eq. (12.10), to find the speed v_2 in the 4.0-cm-diameter section.

EXECUTE: (a) From Eq. (12.11) the volume flow rate in the first section is $dV/dt = A_1 v_1$, where A_1 is the cross-sectional area of the pipe of diameter 8.0 cm and radius 4.0 cm. Hence

$$v_1 = \frac{dV/dt}{A_1} = \frac{(9.5\ \text{L/s})(10^{-3}\ \text{m}^3/\text{L})}{\pi(4.0 \times 10^{-2}\ \text{m})^2} = 1.9\ \text{m/s}$$

The mass flow rate is $\rho\, dV/dt = (850\ \text{kg/m}^3)(9.5 \times 10^{-3}\ \text{m}^3/\text{s}) = 8.1\ \text{kg/s}$.

(b) From the continuity equation, Eq. (12.10),

$$v_2 = \frac{A_1}{A_2} v_1 = \frac{\pi(4.0 \times 10^{-2}\ \text{m})^2}{\pi(2.0 \times 10^{-2}\ \text{m})^2}(1.9\ \text{m/s}) = 7.6\ \text{m/s} = 4v_1$$

The volume and mass flow rates are the same as in part (a).

EVALUATE: The second section of pipe has one-half the diameter and one-fourth the cross-sectional area of the first section. Hence the speed must be four times greater in the second section, which is just what our result shows.

Test Your Understanding of Section 12.4 A maintenance crew is working on a section of a three-lane highway, leaving only one lane open to traffic. The result is much slower traffic flow (a traffic jam). Do cars on a highway behave like (i) the molecules of an incompressible fluid or (ii) the molecules of a compressible fluid?

12.5 Bernoulli's Equation

According to the continuity equation, the speed of fluid flow can vary along the paths of the fluid. The pressure can also vary; it depends on height as in the static situation (see Section 12.2), and it also depends on the speed of flow. We can derive an important relationship called *Bernoulli's equation* that relates the pressure, flow speed, and height for flow of an ideal, incompressible fluid. Bernoulli's equation is an essential tool in analyzing plumbing systems, hydroelectric generating stations, and the flight of airplanes.

The dependence of pressure on speed follows from the continuity equation, Eq. (12.10). When an incompressible fluid flows along a flow tube with varying cross section, its speed *must* change, and so an element of fluid must have an acceleration. If the tube is horizontal, the force that causes this acceleration has to be applied by the surrounding fluid. This means that the pressure *must* be different in regions of different cross section; if it were the same everywhere, the net force on every fluid element would be zero. When a horizontal flow tube narrows and a fluid element speeds up, it must be moving toward a region of lower pressure in order to have a net forward force to accelerate it. If the elevation also changes, this causes an additional pressure difference.

Deriving Bernoulli's Equation

To derive Bernoulli's equation, we apply the work–energy theorem to the fluid in a section of a flow tube. In Fig. 12.22 we consider the element of fluid that at some initial time lies between the two cross sections a and c. The speeds at the lower and upper ends are v_1 and v_2. In a small time interval dt, the fluid that is initially at a moves to b, a distance $ds_1 = v_1\,dt$, and the fluid that is initially at c moves to d, a distance $ds_2 = v_2\,dt$. The cross-sectional areas at the two ends are A_1 and A_2, as shown. The fluid is incompressible; hence by the continuity equation, Eq. (12.10), the volume of fluid dV passing *any* cross section during time dt is the same. That is, $dV = A_1\,ds_1 = A_2\,ds_2$.

Let's compute the *work* done on this fluid element during dt. We assume that there is negligible internal friction in the fluid (i.e., no viscosity), so the only nongravitational forces that do work on the fluid element are due to the pressure of the surrounding fluid. The pressures at the two ends are p_1 and p_2; the force on the cross section at a is p_1A_1, and the force at c is p_2A_2. The net work dW done on the element by the surrounding fluid during this displacement is therefore

$$dW = p_1A_1\,ds_1 - p_2A_2\,ds_2 = (p_1 - p_2)dV \tag{12.13}$$

The second term has a negative sign because the force at c opposes the displacement of the fluid.

The work dW is due to forces other than the conservative force of gravity, so it equals the change in the total mechanical energy (kinetic energy plus gravitational potential energy) associated with the fluid element. The mechanical energy for the fluid between sections b and c does not change. At the beginning of dt the fluid between a and b has volume $A_1\,ds_1$, mass $\rho A_1\,ds_1$, and kinetic energy $\frac{1}{2}\rho(A_1\,ds_1)v_1^2$. At the end of dt the fluid between c and d has kinetic energy $\frac{1}{2}\rho(A_2\,ds_2)v_2^2$. The net change in kinetic energy dK during time dt is

$$dK = \tfrac{1}{2}\rho\,dV(v_2^2 - v_1^2) \tag{12.14}$$

What about the change in gravitational potential energy? At the beginning of dt, the potential energy for the mass between a and b is $dm\,gy_1 = \rho\,dV\,gy_1$. At

12.22 Deriving Bernoulli's equation. The net work done on a fluid element by the pressure of the surrounding fluid equals the change in the kinetic energy plus the change in the gravitational potential energy.

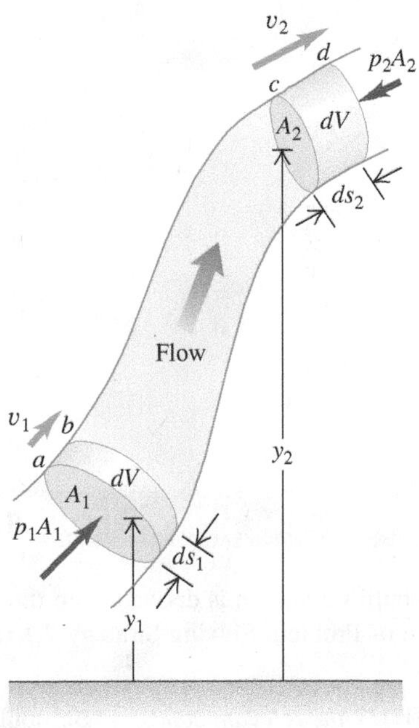

the end of dt, the potential energy for the mass between c and d is $dm\, gy_2 = \rho\, dV\, gy_2$. The net change in potential energy dU during dt is

$$dU = \rho\, dV\, g(y_2 - y_1) \tag{12.15}$$

Combining Eqs. (12.13), (12.14), and (12.15) in the energy equation $dW = dK + dU$, we obtain

$$\begin{aligned}(p_1 - p_2)dV &= \tfrac{1}{2}\rho\, dV(v_2^2 - v_1^2) + \rho\, dV\, g(y_2 - y_1)\\ p_1 - p_2 &= \tfrac{1}{2}\rho(v_2^2 - v_1^2) + \rho g(y_2 - y_1)\end{aligned} \tag{12.16}$$

This is **Bernoulli's equation.** It states that the work done on a unit volume of fluid by the surrounding fluid is equal to the sum of the changes in kinetic and potential energies per unit volume that occur during the flow. We may also interpret Eq. (12.16) in terms of pressures. The first term on the right is the pressure difference associated with the change of speed of the fluid. The second term on the right is the additional pressure difference caused by the weight of the fluid and the difference in elevation of the two ends.

We can also express Eq. (12.16) in a more convenient form as

$$p_1 + \rho g y_1 + \tfrac{1}{2}\rho v_1^2 = p_2 + \rho g y_2 + \tfrac{1}{2}\rho v_2^2 \quad \text{(Bernoulli's equation)} \tag{12.17}$$

The subscripts 1 and 2 refer to *any* two points along the flow tube, so we can also write

$$p + \rho g y + \tfrac{1}{2}\rho v^2 = \text{constant} \tag{12.18}$$

Note that when the fluid is *not* moving (so $v_1 = v_2 = 0$), Eq. (12.17) reduces to the pressure relationship we derived for a fluid at rest, Eq. (12.5).

CAUTION **Bernoulli's principle applies only in certain situations** We stress again that Bernoulli's equation is valid for only incompressible, steady flow of a fluid with no internal friction (no viscosity). It's a simple equation that's easy to use; don't let this tempt you to use it in situations in which it doesn't apply!

Problem-Solving Strategy 12.1 Bernoulli's Equation

MP

Bernoulli's equation is derived from the work–energy theorem, so much of Problem-Solving Strategy 7.1 (Section 7.1) is applicable here.

IDENTIFY *the relevant concepts:* Bernoulli's equation is applicable to steady flow of an incompressible fluid that has no internal friction (see Section 12.6). It is generally applicable to flows through large pipes and to flows within bulk fluids (e.g., air flowing around an airplane or water flowing around a fish).

SET UP *the problem* using the following steps:

1. Identify the points 1 and 2 referred to in Bernoulli's equation, Eq. (12.17).
2. Define your coordinate system, particularly the level at which $y = 0$. Take the positive y-direction to be upward.
3. Make lists of the unknown and known quantities in Eq. (12.17). Decide which unknowns are the target variables.

EXECUTE *the solution* as follows: Write Bernoulli's equation and solve for the unknowns. You may need the continuity equation, Eq. (12.10), to get a relationship between the two speeds in terms of cross-sectional areas of pipes or containers. You may also need Eq. (12.11) to find the volume flow rate.

EVALUATE *your answer:* Verify that the results make physical sense. Check that you have used consistent units: In SI units, pressure is in pascals, density in kilograms per cubic meter, and speed in meters per second. Also note that the pressures must be either *all* absolute pressures or *all* gauge pressures.

Example 12.7 Water pressure in the home

Water enters a house (Fig. 12.23) through a pipe with an inside diameter of 2.0 cm at an absolute pressure of 4.0×10^5 Pa (about 4 atm). A 1.0-cm-diameter pipe leads to the second-floor bathroom 5.0 m above. When the flow speed at the inlet pipe is 1.5 m/s, find the flow speed, pressure, and volume flow rate in the bathroom.

SOLUTION

IDENTIFY and SET UP: We assume that the water flows at a steady rate. Water is effectively incompressible, so we can use the continuity equation. It's reasonable to ignore internal friction because the pipe has a relatively large diameter, so we can also use Bernoulli's equation. Let points 1 and 2 be at the inlet pipe and at the bathroom, respectively. We are given the pipe diameters at points 1 and 2, from which we calculate the areas A_1 and A_2, as well as the speed $v_1 = 1.5$ m/s and pressure $p_1 = 4.0 \times 10^5$ Pa at the inlet pipe. We take $y_1 = 0$ and $y_2 = 5.0$ m. We find the speed v_2 using the continuity equation and the pressure p_2 using Bernoulli's equation. Knowing v_2, we calculate the volume flow rate $v_2 A_2$.

EXECUTE: From the continuity equation, Eq. (12.10),

$$v_2 = \frac{A_1}{A_2}v_1 = \frac{\pi(1.0\text{ cm})^2}{\pi(0.50\text{ cm})^2}(1.5\text{ m/s}) = 6.0\text{ m/s}$$

From Bernoulli's equation, Eq. (12.16),

$$\begin{aligned} p_2 &= p_1 - \tfrac{1}{2}\rho(v_2^2 - v_1^2) - \rho g(y_2 - y_1) \\ &= 4.0 \times 10^5\text{ Pa} \\ &\quad - \tfrac{1}{2}(1.0 \times 10^3\text{ kg/m}^3)(36\text{ m}^2/\text{s}^2 - 2.25\text{ m}^2/\text{s}^2) \\ &\quad - (1.0 \times 10^3\text{ kg/m}^3)(9.8\text{ m/s}^2)(5.0\text{ m}) \\ &= 4.0 \times 10^5\text{ Pa} - 0.17 \times 10^5\text{ Pa} - 0.49 \times 10^5\text{ Pa} \\ &= 3.3 \times 10^5\text{ Pa} = 3.3\text{ atm} = 48\text{ lb/in.}^2 \end{aligned}$$

12.23 What is the water pressure in the second-story bathroom of this house?

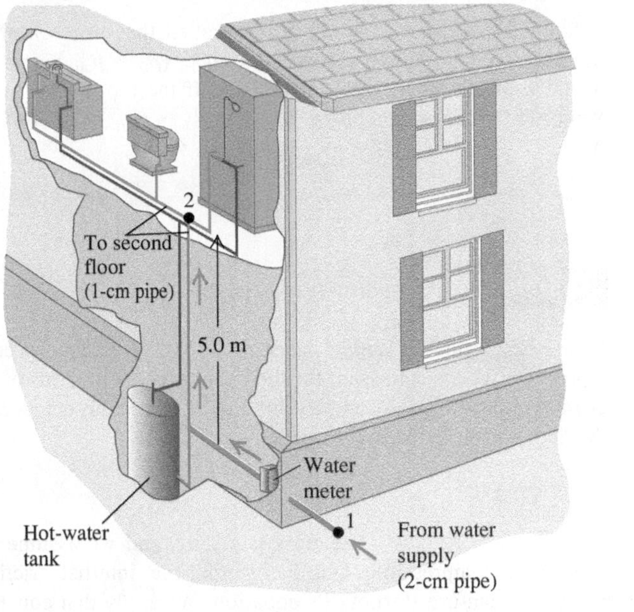

The volume flow rate is

$$\begin{aligned} \frac{dV}{dt} &= A_2 v_2 = \pi(0.50 \times 10^{-2}\text{ m})^2(6.0\text{ m/s}) \\ &= 4.7 \times 10^{-4}\text{ m}^3/\text{s} = 0.47\text{ L/s} \end{aligned}$$

EVALUATE: This is a reasonable flow rate for a bathroom faucet or shower. Note that if the water is turned off, v_1 and v_2 are both zero, the term $\frac{1}{2}\rho(v_2^2 - v_1^2)$ in Bernoulli's equation vanishes, and p_2 rises from 3.3×10^5 Pa to 3.5×10^5 Pa.

Example 12.8 Speed of efflux

Figure 12.24 shows a gasoline storage tank with cross-sectional area A_1, filled to a depth h. The space above the gasoline contains air at pressure p_0, and the gasoline flows out the bottom of the tank through a short pipe with cross-sectional area A_2. Derive expressions for the flow speed in the pipe and the volume flow rate.

12.24 Calculating the speed of efflux for gasoline flowing out the bottom of a storage tank.

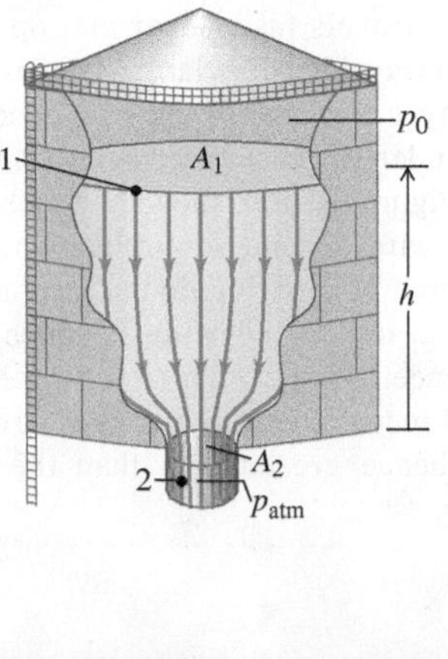

SOLUTION

IDENTIFY and SET UP: We consider the entire volume of moving liquid as a single flow tube of an incompressible fluid with negligible internal friction. Hence, we can use Bernoulli's equation. Points 1 and 2 are at the surface of the gasoline and at the exit pipe, respectively. At point 1 the pressure is p_0, which we assume to be fixed; at point 2 it is atmospheric pressure p_{atm}. We take $y = 0$ at the exit pipe, so $y_1 = h$ and $y_2 = 0$. Because A_1 is very much larger than A_2, the upper surface of the gasoline will drop very slowly and we can regard v_1 as essentially equal to zero. We find v_2 from Eq. (12.17) and the volume flow rate from Eq. (12.11).

EXECUTE: We apply Bernoulli's equation to points 1 and 2:

$$p_0 + \tfrac{1}{2}\rho v_1^2 + \rho g h = p_{atm} + \tfrac{1}{2}\rho v_2^2 + \rho g(0)$$

$$v_2^2 = v_1^2 + 2\left(\frac{p_0 - p_{atm}}{\rho}\right) + 2gh$$

Continued

Using $v_1 = 0$, we find

$$v_2 = \sqrt{2\left(\frac{p_0 - p_{atm}}{\rho}\right) + 2gh}$$

From Eq. (12.11), the volume flow rate is $dV/dt = v_2A_2$.

EVALUATE: The speed v_2, sometimes called the *speed of efflux,* depends on both the pressure difference $(p_0 - p_{atm})$ and the height h of the liquid level in the tank. If the top of the tank is vented to the atmosphere, $p_0 = p_{atm}$ and $p_0 - p_{atm} = 0$. Then

$$v_2 = \sqrt{2gh}$$

That is, the speed of efflux from an opening at a distance h below the top surface of the liquid is the *same* as the speed a body would acquire in falling freely through a height h. This result is called *Torricelli's theorem.* It is valid not only for an opening in the bottom of a container, but also for a hole in a side wall at a depth h below the surface. In this case the volume flow rate is

$$\frac{dV}{dt} = A_2\sqrt{2gh}$$

Example 12.9 The Venturi meter

Figure 12.25 shows a *Venturi meter,* used to measure flow speed in a pipe. Derive an expression for the flow speed v_1 in terms of the cross-sectional areas A_1 and A_2 and the difference in height h of the liquid levels in the two vertical tubes.

12.25 The Venturi meter.

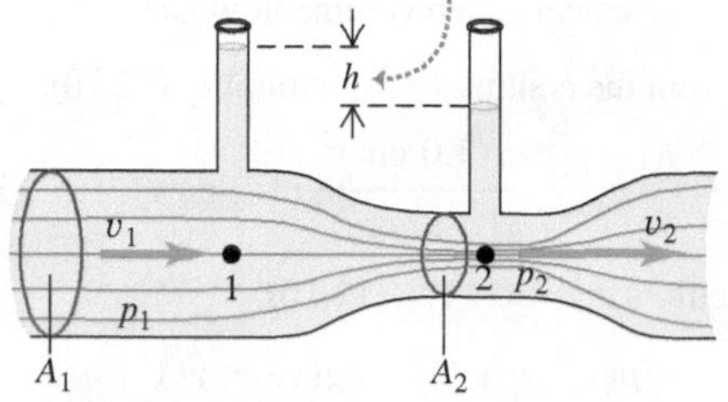

SOLUTION

IDENTIFY and SET UP: The flow is steady, and we assume the fluid is incompressible and has negligible internal friction. Hence we can use Bernoulli's equation. We apply that equation to the wide part (point 1) and narrow part (point 2, the *throat*) of the pipe. Equation (12.6) relates h to the pressure difference $p_1 - p_2$.

EXECUTE: Points 1 and 2 have the same vertical coordinate $y_1 = y_2$, so Eq. (12.17) says

$$p_1 + \tfrac{1}{2}\rho v_1^2 = p_2 + \tfrac{1}{2}\rho v_2^2$$

From the continuity equation, $v_2 = (A_1/A_2)v_1$. Substituting this and rearranging, we get

$$p_1 - p_2 = \tfrac{1}{2}\rho v_1^2\left[\left(\frac{A_1}{A_2}\right)^2 - 1\right]$$

From Eq. (12.6), the pressure difference $p_1 - p_2$ is also equal to ρgh. Substituting this and solving for v_1, we get

$$v_1 = \sqrt{\frac{2gh}{(A_1/A_2)^2 - 1}}$$

EVALUATE: Because A_1 is greater than A_2, v_2 is greater than v_1 and the pressure p_2 in the throat is *less* than p_1. Those pressure differences produce a net force to the right that makes the fluid speed up as it enters the throat, and a net force to the left that slows it as it leaves.

Conceptual Example 12.10 Lift on an airplane wing

Figure 12.26a shows flow lines around a cross section of an airplane wing. The flow lines crowd together above the wing, corresponding to increased flow speed and reduced pressure, just as in the Venturi throat in Example 12.9. Hence the downward force of the air on the top side of the wing is less than the upward force of the air on the underside of the wing, and there is a net upward force or *lift.* Lift is not simply due to the impulse of air striking the underside of the wing; in fact, the reduced pressure on the upper wing surface makes the greatest contribution to the lift. (This simplified discussion ignores the formation of vortices.)

We can also understand the lift force on the basis of momentum changes. The vector diagram in Fig. 12.26a shows that there is a net *downward* change in the vertical component of momentum of the air flowing past the wing, corresponding to the downward force the wing exerts on the air. The reaction force *on* the wing is *upward,* as we concluded above.

Similar flow patterns and lift forces are found in the vicinity of any humped object in a wind. A moderate wind makes an umbrella "float"; a strong wind can turn it inside out. At high speed, lift can reduce traction on a car's tires; a "spoiler" at the car's tail, shaped like an upside-down wing, provides a compensating downward force.

CAUTION **A misconception about wings** Some discussions of lift claim that air travels faster over the top of a wing because "it has farther to travel." This claim assumes that air molecules that part company at the front of the wing, one traveling over the wing and one under it, must meet again at the wing's trailing edge. Not so! Figure 12.26b shows a computer simulation of parcels of air flowing around an airplane wing. Parcels that are adjacent at the front of the wing do *not* meet at the trailing edge; the flow over the top of the wing is much faster than if the parcels had to meet. In accordance with Bernoulli's equation, this faster speed means that there is even lower pressure above the wing (and hence greater lift) than the "farther-to-travel" claim would suggest.

12.26 Flow around an airplane wing.

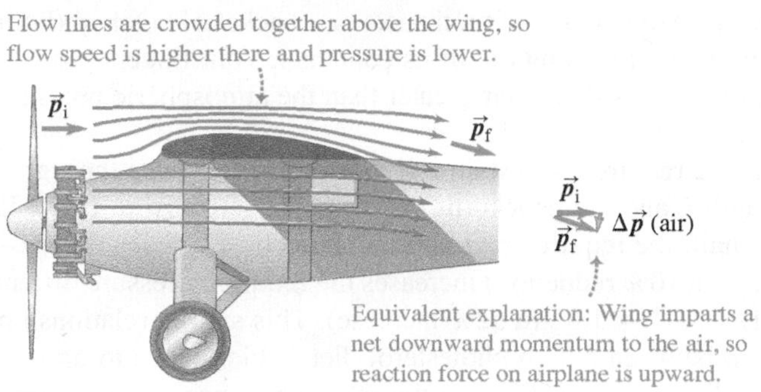

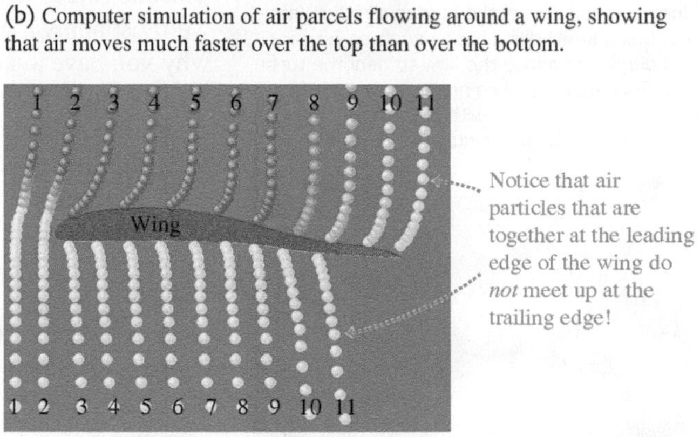

Test Your Understanding of Section 12.5 Which is the most accurate statement of Bernoulli's principle? (i) Fast-moving air causes lower pressure; (ii) lower pressure causes fast-moving air; (iii) both (i) and (ii) are equally accurate. ❙

12.6 Viscosity and Turbulence

In our discussion of fluid flow we assumed that the fluid had no internal friction and that the flow was laminar. While these assumptions are often quite valid, in many important physical situations the effects of viscosity (internal friction) and turbulence (nonlaminar flow) are extremely important. Let's take a brief look at some of these situations.

Viscosity

Viscosity is internal friction in a fluid. Viscous forces oppose the motion of one portion of a fluid relative to another. Viscosity is the reason it takes effort to paddle a canoe through calm water, but it is also the reason the paddle works. Viscous effects are important in the flow of fluids in pipes, the flow of blood, the lubrication of engine parts, and many other situations.

Fluids that flow readily, such as water or gasoline, have smaller viscosities than do "thick" liquids such as honey or motor oil. Viscosities of all fluids are strongly temperature dependent, increasing for gases and decreasing for liquids as the temperature increases (Fig. 12.27). Oils for engine lubrication must flow equally well in cold and warm conditions, and so are designed to have as *little* temperature variation of viscosity as possible.

12.27 Lava is an example of a viscous fluid. The viscosity decreases with increasing temperature: The hotter the lava, the more easily it can flow.

A viscous fluid always tends to cling to a solid surface in contact with it. There is always a thin *boundary layer* of fluid near the surface, in which the fluid is nearly at rest with respect to the surface. That's why dust particles can cling to a fan blade even when it is rotating rapidly, and why you can't get all the dirt off your car by just squirting a hose at it.

Viscosity has important effects on the flow of liquids through pipes, including the flow of blood in the circulatory system. First think about a fluid with zero viscosity so that we can apply Bernoulli's equation, Eq. (12.17). If the two ends of a long cylindrical pipe are at the same height ($y_1 = y_2$) and the flow speed is the same at both ends (so $v_1 = v_2$), Bernoulli's equation tells us that the pressure is the same at both ends of the pipe. But this result simply isn't true if we take viscosity into account. To see why, consider Fig. 12.28, which shows the flow-speed profile for laminar flow of a viscous fluid in a long cylindrical pipe. Due to viscosity, the speed is *zero* at the pipe walls (to which the fluid clings) and is greatest at the center of the pipe. The motion is like a lot of concentric tubes sliding relative to

12.28 Velocity profile for a viscous fluid in a cylindrical pipe.

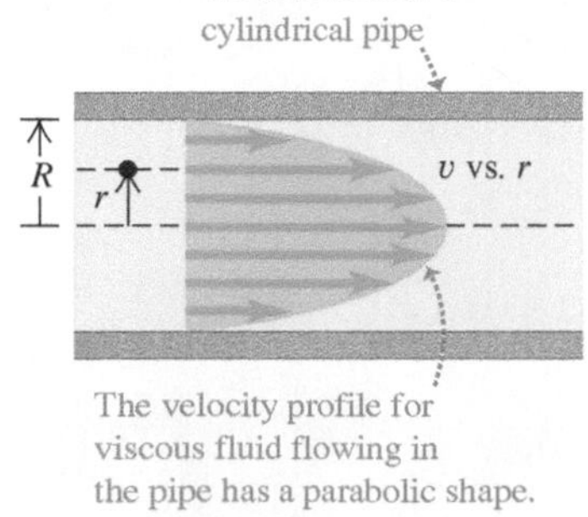

Application Listening for Turbulent Flow
Normal blood flow in the human aorta is laminar, but a small disturbance such as a heart pathology can cause the flow to become turbulent. Turbulence makes noise, which is why listening to blood flow with a stethoscope is a useful diagnostic technique.

one another, with the central tube moving fastest and the outermost tube at rest. Viscous forces between the tubes oppose this sliding, so to keep the flow going we must apply a greater pressure at the back of the flow than at the front. That's why you have to keep squeezing a tube of toothpaste or a packet of ketchup (both viscous fluids) to keep the fluid coming out of its container. Your fingers provide a pressure at the back of the flow that is far greater than the atmospheric pressure at the front of the flow.

The pressure difference required to sustain a given volume flow rate through a cylindrical pipe of length L and radius R turns out to be proportional to L/R^4. If we decrease R by one-half, the required pressure increases by $2^4 = 16$; decreasing R by a factor of 0.90 (a 10% reduction) increases the required pressure difference by a factor of $(1/0.90)^4 = 1.52$ (a 52% increase). This simple relationship explains the connection between a high-cholesterol diet (which tends to narrow the arteries) and high blood pressure. Due to the R^4 dependence, even a small narrowing of the arteries can result in substantially elevated blood pressure and added strain on the heart muscle.

Turbulence

When the speed of a flowing fluid exceeds a certain critical value, the flow is no longer laminar. Instead, the flow pattern becomes extremely irregular and complex, and it changes continuously with time; there is no steady-state pattern. This irregular, chaotic flow is called **turbulence.** Figure 12.20 shows the contrast between laminar and turbulent flow for smoke rising in air. Bernoulli's equation is *not* applicable to regions where there is turbulence because the flow is not steady.

Whether a flow is laminar or turbulent depends in part on the fluid's viscosity. The greater the viscosity, the greater the tendency for the fluid to flow in sheets or lamina and the more likely the flow is to be laminar. (When we discussed Bernoulli's equation in Section 12.5, we assumed that the flow was laminar and that the fluid had zero viscosity. In fact, a *little* viscosity is needed to ensure that the flow is laminar.)

For a fluid of a given viscosity, flow speed is a determining factor for the onset of turbulence. A flow pattern that is stable at low speeds suddenly becomes unstable when a critical speed is reached. Irregularities in the flow pattern can be caused by roughness in the pipe wall, variations in the density of the fluid, and many other factors. At low flow speeds, these disturbances damp out; the flow pattern is *stable* and tends to maintain its laminar nature (Fig. 12.29a). When the critical speed is reached, however, the flow pattern becomes unstable. The disturbances no longer damp out but grow until they destroy the entire laminar-flow pattern (Fig. 12.29b).

12.29 The flow of water from a faucet is (a) laminar at low speeds but (b) turbulent at sufficiently high speeds.

Conceptual Example 12.11 The curve ball

Does a curve ball *really* curve? Yes, it certainly does, and the reason is turbulence. Figure 12.30a shows a nonspinning ball moving through the air from left to right. The flow lines show that to an observer moving with the ball, the air stream appears to move from right to left. Because of the high speeds that are ordinarily involved (near 35 m/s, or 75 mi/h), there is a region of *turbulent* flow behind the ball.

Figure 12.30b shows a *spinning* ball with "top spin." Layers of air near the ball's surface are pulled around in the direction of the spin by friction between the ball and air and by the air's internal friction (viscosity). Hence air moves relative to the ball's surface more slowly at the top of the ball than at the bottom, and turbulence occurs farther forward on the top side than on the bottom. This asymmetry causes a pressure difference; the average pressure at the top of the ball is now greater than that at the bottom. As Fig. 12.30c shows, the resulting net force deflects the ball downward. "Top spin" is used in tennis to keep a fast serve in the court (Fig. 12.30d).

In baseball, a curve ball spins about a nearly *vertical* axis and the resulting deflection is sideways. In that case, Fig. 12.30c is a *top* view of the situation. A curve ball thrown by a left-handed pitcher spins as shown in Fig. 12.30e and will curve *toward* a right-handed batter, making it harder to hit.

A similar effect occurs with golf balls, which acquire "back spin" from impact with the grooved, slanted club face. Figure 12.30f shows the backspin of a golf ball just after impact. The resulting pressure difference between the top and bottom of the ball causes a *lift* force that keeps the ball in the air longer than would be possible without spin. A well-hit drive appears, from the tee, to "float" or even curve *upward* during the initial portion of its flight. This is a real effect, not an illusion. The dimples on the golf ball play an essential role; the viscosity of air gives a dimpled ball a much longer trajectory than an undimpled one with the same initial velocity and spin.

12.30 (a)–(e) Analyzing the motion of a spinning ball through the air. (f) Stroboscopic photograph of a golf ball being struck by a club. The picture was taken at 1000 flashes per second. The ball rotates about once in eight pictures, corresponding to an angular speed of 125 rev/s, or 7500 rpm.

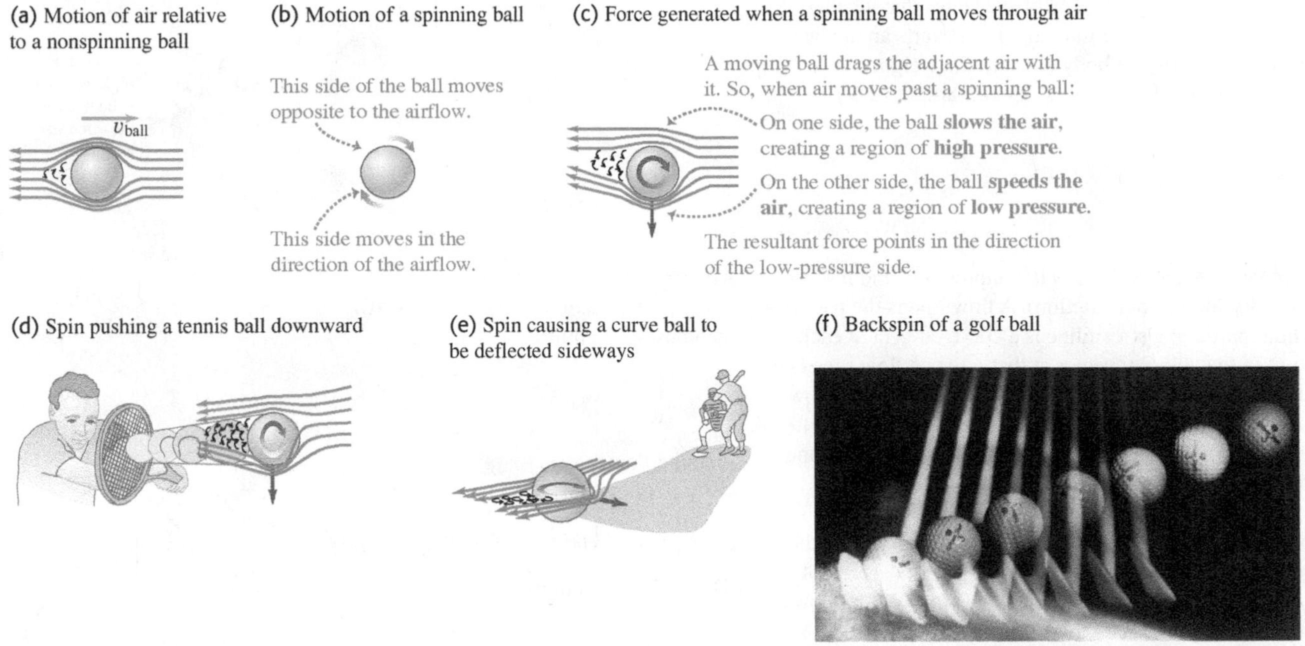

Test Your Understanding of Section 12.6 How much more thumb pressure must a nurse use to administer an injection with a hypodermic needle of inside diameter 0.30 mm compared to one with inside diameter 0.60 mm? Assume that the two needles have the same length and that the volume flow rate is the same in both cases. (i) twice as much; (ii) 4 times as much; (iii) 8 times as much; (iv) 16 times as much; (v) 32 times as much.

CHAPTER 12 SUMMARY

Density and pressure: Density is mass per unit volume. If a mass m of homogeneous material has volume V, its density ρ is the ratio m/V. Specific gravity is the ratio of the density of a material to the density of water. (See Example 12.1.)

Pressure is normal force per unit area. Pascal's law states that pressure applied to an enclosed fluid is transmitted undiminished to every portion of the fluid. Absolute pressure is the total pressure in a fluid; gauge pressure is the difference between absolute pressure and atmospheric pressure. The SI unit of pressure is the pascal (Pa): 1 Pa = 1 N/m^2. (See Example 12.2.)

$$\rho = \frac{m}{V} \quad (12.1)$$

$$p = \frac{dF_\perp}{dA} \quad (12.2)$$

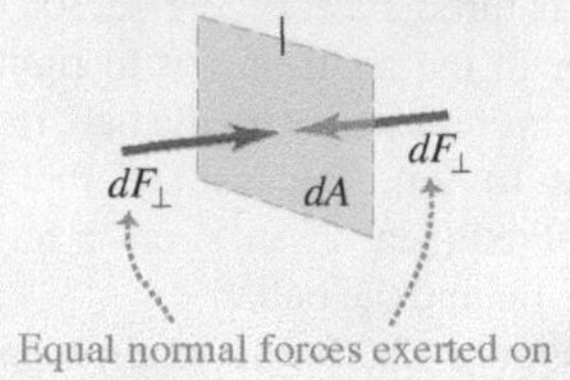

Pressures in a fluid at rest: The pressure difference between points 1 and 2 in a static fluid of uniform density ρ (an incompressible fluid) is proportional to the difference between the elevations y_1 and y_2. If the pressure at the surface of an incompressible liquid at rest is p_0, then the pressure at a depth h is greater by an amount ρgh. (See Examples 12.3 and 12.4.)

$$p_2 - p_1 = -\rho g(y_2 - y_1) \quad (12.5)$$
(pressure in a fluid of uniform density)

$$p = p_0 + \rho gh \quad (12.6)$$
(pressure in a fluid of uniform density)

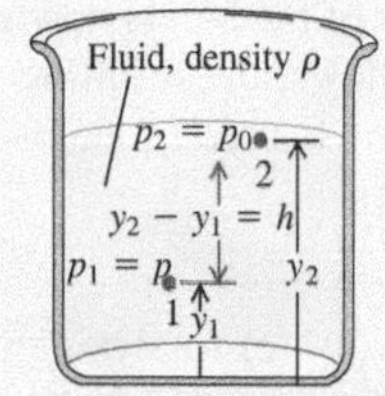

Buoyancy: Archimedes's principle states that when a body is immersed in a fluid, the fluid exerts an upward buoyant force on the body equal to the weight of the fluid that the body displaces. (See Example 12.5.)

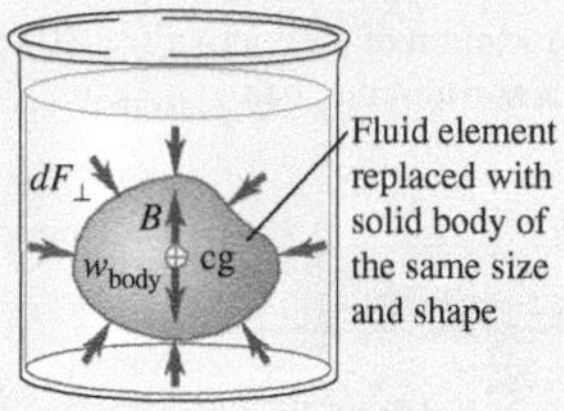

Fluid flow: An ideal fluid is incompressible and has no viscosity (no internal friction). A flow line is the path of a fluid particle; a streamline is a curve tangent at each point to the velocity vector at that point. A flow tube is a tube bounded at its sides by flow lines. In laminar flow, layers of fluid slide smoothly past each other. In turbulent flow, there is great disorder and a constantly changing flow pattern.

Conservation of mass in an incompressible fluid is expressed by the continuity equation, which relates the flow speeds v_1 and v_2 for two cross sections A_1 and A_2 in a flow tube. The product Av equals the volume flow rate, dV/dt, the rate at which volume crosses a section of the tube. (See Example 12.6.)

Bernoulli's equation relates the pressure p, flow speed v, and elevation y for any two points, assuming steady flow in an ideal fluid. (See Examples 12.7–12.10.)

$$A_1v_1 = A_2v_2 \quad (12.10)$$
(continuity equation, incompressible fluid)

$$\frac{dV}{dt} = Av \quad (12.11)$$
(volume flow rate)

$$p_1 + \rho gy_1 + \tfrac{1}{2}\rho v_1^2 = p_2 + \rho gy_2 + \tfrac{1}{2}\rho v_2^2 \quad (12.17)$$
(Bernoulli's equation)

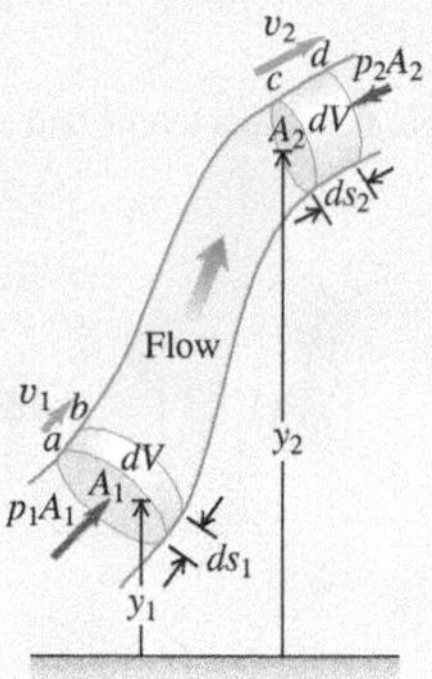

BRIDGING PROBLEM **How Long to Drain?**

A large cylindrical tank with diameter D is open to the air at the top. The tank contains water to a height H. A small circular hole with diameter d, where d is very much less than D, is then opened at the bottom of the tank. Ignore any effects of viscosity. (a) Find y, the height of water in the tank a time t after the hole is opened, as a function of t. (b) How long does it take to drain the tank completely? (c) If you double the initial height of water in the tank, by what factor does the time to drain the tank increase?

SOLUTION GUIDE

See MasteringPhysics® study area for a Video Tutor solution.

IDENTIFY and SET UP

1. Draw a sketch of the situation that shows all of the relevant dimensions.
2. Make a list of the unknown quantities, and decide which of these are the target variables.
3. What is the speed at which water flows out of the bottom of the tank? How is this related to the volume flow rate of water out of the tank? How is the volume flow rate related to the rate of change of y?

EXECUTE

4. Use your results from step 3 to write an equation for dy/dt.
5. Your result from step 4 is a relatively simple differential equation. With your knowledge of calculus, you can integrate it to find y as a function of t. (*Hint:* Once you've done the integration, you'll still have to do a little algebra.)
6. Use your result from step 5 to find the time when the tank is empty. How does your result depend on the initial height H?

EVALUATE

7. Check whether your answers are reasonable. A good check is to draw a graph of y versus t. According to your graph, what is the algebraic sign of dy/dt at different times? Does this make sense?

Problems

For instructor-assigned homework, go to www.masteringphysics.com

•, ••, •••: Problems of increasing difficulty. **CP**: Cumulative problems incorporating material from earlier chapters. **CALC**: Problems requiring calculus. **BIO**: Biosciences problems.

DISCUSSION QUESTIONS

Q12.1 A cube of oak wood with very smooth faces normally floats in water. Suppose you submerge it completely and press one face flat against the bottom of a tank so that no water is under that face. Will the block float to the surface? Is there a buoyant force on it? Explain.

Q12.2 A rubber hose is attached to a funnel, and the free end is bent around to point upward. When water is poured into the funnel, it rises in the hose to the same level as in the funnel, even though the funnel has a lot more water in it than the hose does. Why? What supports the extra weight of the water in the funnel?

Q12.3 Comparing Example 12.1 (Section 12.1) and Example 12.2 (Section 12.2), it seems that 700 N of air is exerting a downward force of 2.0×10^6 N on the floor. How is this possible?

Q12.4 Equation (12.7) shows that an area ratio of 100 to 1 can give 100 times more output force than input force. Doesn't this violate conservation of energy? Explain.

Q12.5 You have probably noticed that the lower the tire pressure, the larger the contact area between the tire and the road. Why?

Q12.6 In hot-air ballooning, a large balloon is filled with air heated by a gas burner at the bottom. Why must the air be heated? How does the balloonist control ascent and descent?

Q12.7 In describing the size of a large ship, one uses such expressions as "it displaces 20,000 tons." What does this mean? Can the weight of the ship be obtained from this information?

Q12.8 You drop a solid sphere of aluminum in a bucket of water that sits on the ground. The buoyant force equals the weight of water displaced; this is less than the weight of the sphere, so the sphere sinks to the bottom. If you take the bucket with you on an elevator that accelerates upward, the apparent weight of the water increases and the buoyant force on the sphere increases. Could the acceleration of the elevator be great enough to make the sphere pop up out of the water? Explain.

Q12.9 A rigid, lighter-than-air dirigible filled with helium cannot continue to rise indefinitely. Why? What determines the maximum height it can attain?

Q12.10 Air pressure decreases with increasing altitude. So why is air near the surface not continuously drawn upward toward the lower-pressure regions above?

Q12.11 The purity of gold can be tested by weighing it in air and in water. How? Do you think you could get away with making a fake gold brick by gold-plating some cheaper material?

Q12.12 During the Great Mississippi Flood of 1993, the levees in St. Louis tended to rupture first at the bottom. Why?

Q12.13 A cargo ship travels from the Atlantic Ocean (salt water) to Lake Ontario (freshwater) via the St. Lawrence River. The ship rides several centimeters lower in the water in Lake Ontario than it did in the ocean. Explain why.

Q12.14 You push a piece of wood under the surface of a swimming pool. After it is completely submerged, you keep pushing it deeper and deeper. As you do this, what will happen to the buoyant force on it? Will the force keep increasing, stay the same, or decrease? Why?

Q12.15 An old question is "Which weighs more, a pound of feathers or a pound of lead?" If the weight in pounds is the gravitational force, will a pound of feathers balance a pound of lead on opposite pans of an equal-arm balance? Explain, taking into account buoyant forces.

Q12.16 Suppose the door of a room makes an airtight but frictionless fit in its frame. Do you think you could open the door if the air pressure on one side were standard atmospheric pressure and the air pressure on the other side differed from standard by 1%? Explain.

Q12.17 At a certain depth in an incompressible liquid, the absolute pressure is p. At twice this depth, will the absolute pressure be equal to $2p$, greater than $2p$, or less than $2p$? Justify your answer.

Q12.18 A piece of iron is glued to the top of a block of wood. When the block is placed in a bucket of water with the iron on top, the block floats. The block is now turned over so that the iron is submerged beneath the wood. Does the block float or sink? Does the water level in the bucket rise, drop, or stay the same? Explain your answers.

Q12.19 You take an empty glass jar and push it into a tank of water with the open mouth of the jar downward, so that the air inside the jar is trapped and cannot get out. If you push the jar deeper into the water, does the buoyant force on the jar stay the same? If not, does it increase or decrease? Explain your answer.

Q12.20 You are floating in a canoe in the middle of a swimming pool. Your friend is at the edge of the pool, carefully noting the level of the water on the side of the pool. You have a bowling ball with you in the canoe. If you carefully drop the bowling ball over the side of the canoe and it sinks to the bottom of the pool, does the water level in the pool rise or fall?

Q12.21 You are floating in a canoe in the middle of a swimming pool. A large bird flies up and lights on your shoulder. Does the water level in the pool rise or fall?

Q12.22 At a certain depth in the incompressible ocean the gauge pressure is p_g. At three times this depth, will the gauge pressure be greater than $3p_g$, equal to $3p_g$, or less than $3p_g$? Justify your answer.

Q12.23 An ice cube floats in a glass of water. When the ice melts, will the water level in the glass rise, fall, or remain unchanged? Explain.

Q12.24 You are told, "Bernoulli's equation tells us that where there is higher fluid speed, there is lower fluid pressure, and vice versa." Is this statement always true, even for an idealized fluid? Explain.

Q12.25 If the velocity at each point in space in steady-state fluid flow is constant, how can a fluid particle accelerate?

Q12.26 In a store-window vacuum cleaner display, a table-tennis ball is suspended in midair in a jet of air blown from the outlet hose of a tank-type vacuum cleaner. The ball bounces around a little but always moves back toward the center of the jet, even if the jet is tilted from the vertical. How does this behavior illustrate Bernoulli's equation?

Q12.27 A tornado consists of a rapidly whirling air vortex. Why is the pressure always much lower in the center than at the outside? How does this condition account for the destructive power of a tornado?

Q12.28 Airports at high elevations have longer runways for takeoffs and landings than do airports at sea level. One reason is that aircraft engines develop less power in the thin air well above sea level. What is another reason?

Q12.29 When a smooth-flowing stream of water comes out of a faucet, it narrows as it falls. Explain why this happens.

Q12.30 Identical-size lead and aluminum cubes are suspended at different depths by two wires in a large vat of water (Fig. Q12.30). (a) Which cube experiences a greater buoyant force? (b) For which cube is the tension in the wire greater? (c) Which cube experiences a greater force on its lower face? (d) For which cube is the difference in pressure between the upper and lower faces greater?

Figure **Q12.30**

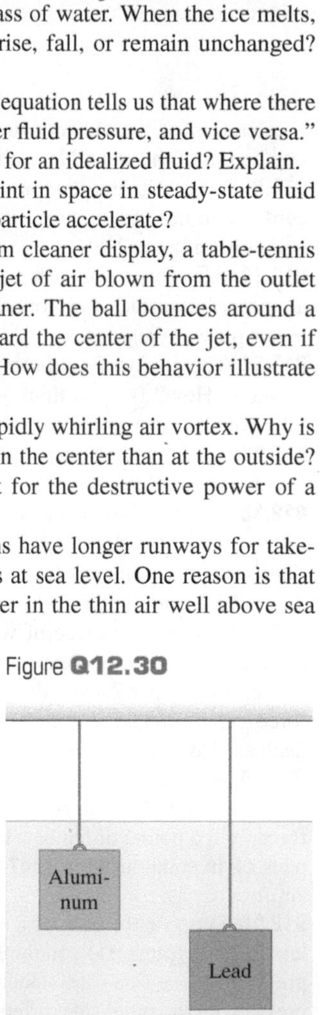

EXERCISES

Section 12.1 Density

12.1 •• On a part-time job, you are asked to bring a cylindrical iron rod of length 85.8 cm and diameter 2.85 cm from a storage room to a machinist. Will you need a cart? (To answer, calculate the weight of the rod.)

12.2 •• A cube 5.0 cm on each side is made of a metal alloy. After you drill a cylindrical hole 2.0 cm in diameter all the way through and perpendicular to one face, you find that the cube weighs 7.50 N. (a) What is the density of this metal? (b) What did the cube weigh before you drilled the hole in it?

12.3 • You purchase a rectangular piece of metal that has dimensions $5.0 \times 15.0 \times 30.0$ mm and mass 0.0158 kg. The seller tells you that the metal is gold. To check this, you compute the average density of the piece. What value do you get? Were you cheated?

12.4 •• **Gold Brick.** You win the lottery and decide to impress your friends by exhibiting a million-dollar cube of gold. At the time, gold is selling for \$426.60 per troy ounce, and 1.0000 troy ounce equals 31.1035 g. How tall would your million-dollar cube be?

12.5 •• A uniform lead sphere and a uniform aluminum sphere have the same mass. What is the ratio of the radius of the aluminum sphere to the radius of the lead sphere?

12.6 • (a) What is the average density of the sun? (b) What is the average density of a neutron star that has the same mass as the sun but a radius of only 20.0 km?

12.7 •• A hollow cylindrical copper pipe is 1.50 m long and has an outside diameter of 3.50 cm and an inside diameter of 2.50 cm. How much does it weigh?

Section 12.2 Pressure in a Fluid

12.8 •• **Black Smokers.** Black smokers are hot volcanic vents that emit smoke deep in the ocean floor. Many of them teem with exotic creatures, and some biologists think that life on earth may have begun around such vents. The vents range in depth from about 1500 m to 3200 m below the surface. What is the gauge pressure at a 3200-m deep vent, assuming that the density of water does not vary? Express your answer in pascals and atmospheres.

12.9 •• **Oceans on Mars.** Scientists have found evidence that Mars may once have had an ocean 0.500 km deep. The acceleration due to gravity on Mars is 3.71 m/s^2. (a) What would be the gauge pressure at the bottom of such an ocean, assuming it was freshwater? (b) To what depth would you need to go in the earth's ocean to experience the same gauge pressure?

12.10 •• BIO (a) Calculate the difference in blood pressure between the feet and top of the head for a person who is 1.65 m tall. (b) Consider a cylindrical segment of a blood vessel 2.00 cm long and 1.50 mm in diameter. What *additional* outward force would such a vessel need to withstand in the person's feet compared to a similar vessel in her head?

12.11 • BIO In intravenous feeding, a needle is inserted in a vein in the patient's arm and a tube leads from the needle to a reservoir of fluid (density 1050 kg/m^3) located at height h above the arm. The top of the reservoir is open to the air. If the gauge pressure inside the vein is 5980 Pa, what is the minimum value of h that allows fluid to enter the vein? Assume the needle diameter is large enough that you can ignore the viscosity (see Section 12.6) of the fluid.

12.12 • A barrel contains a 0.120-m layer of oil floating on water that is 0.250 m deep. The density of the oil is 600 kg/m^3. (a) What is the gauge pressure at the oil–water interface? (b) What is the gauge pressure at the bottom of the barrel?

12.13 • BIO **Standing on Your Head.** (a) What is the *difference* between the pressure of the blood in your brain when you stand on your head and the pressure when you stand on your feet? Assume that you are 1.85 m tall. The density of blood is 1060 kg/m^3. (b) What effect does the increased pressure have on the blood vessels in your brain?

12.14 •• You are designing a diving bell to withstand the pressure of seawater at a depth of 250 m. (a) What is the gauge pressure at this depth? (You can ignore changes in the density of the water with depth.) (b) At this depth, what is the net force due to the water outside and the air inside the bell on a circular glass window 30.0 cm in diameter if the pressure inside the diving bell equals the pressure at the surface of the water? (You can ignore the small variation of pressure over the surface of the window.)

12.15 •• BIO **Ear Damage from Diving.** If the force on the tympanic membrane (eardrum) increases by about 1.5 N above the force from atmospheric pressure, the membrane can be damaged. When you go scuba diving in the ocean, below what depth could damage to your eardrum start to occur? The eardrum is typically 8.2 mm in diameter. (Consult Table 12.1.)

12.16 •• The liquid in the open-tube manometer in Fig. 12.8a is mercury, $y_1 = 3.00$ cm, and $y_2 = 7.00$ cm. Atmospheric pressure is 980 millibars. (a) What is the absolute pressure at the bottom of the U-shaped tube? (b) What is the absolute pressure in the open tube at a depth of 4.00 cm below the free surface? (c) What is the absolute pressure of the gas in the container? (d) What is the gauge pressure of the gas in pascals?

12.17 • BIO There is a maximum depth at which a diver can breathe through a snorkel tube (Fig. E12.17) because as the depth increases, so does the pressure difference, which tends to collapse the diver's lungs. Since the snorkel connects the air in the lungs to the atmosphere at the surface, the pressure inside the lungs is atmospheric pressure. What is the external–internal pressure difference when the diver's lungs are at a depth of 6.1 m (about 20 ft)? Assume that the diver is in freshwater. (A scuba diver breathing from compressed air tanks can operate at greater depths than can a snorkeler, since the pressure of the air inside the scuba diver's lungs increases to match the external pressure of the water.)

Figure **E12.17**

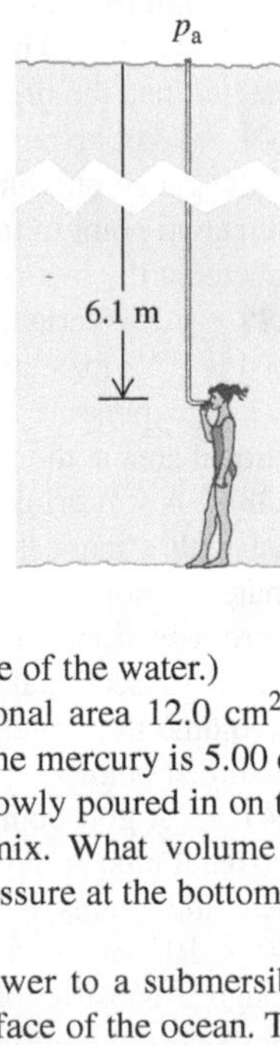

12.18 •• A tall cylinder with a cross-sectional area 12.0 cm^2 is partially filled with mercury; the surface of the mercury is 5.00 cm above the bottom of the cylinder. Water is slowly poured in on top of the mercury, and the two fluids don't mix. What volume of water must be added to double the gauge pressure at the bottom of the cylinder?

12.19 •• An electrical short cuts off all power to a submersible diving vehicle when it is 30 m below the surface of the ocean. The crew must push out a hatch of area 0.75 m^2 and weight 300 N on the bottom to escape. If the pressure inside is 1.0 atm, what downward force must the crew exert on the hatch to open it?

12.20 •• A closed container is partially filled with water. Initially, the air above the water is at atmospheric pressure (1.01×10^5 Pa) and the gauge pressure at the bottom of the water is 2500 Pa. Then additional air is pumped in, increasing the pressure of the air above the water by 1500 Pa. (a) What is the gauge pressure at the bottom of the water? (b) By how much must the water level in the container be reduced, by drawing some water out through a valve at the bottom of the container, to return the gauge pressure at the bottom of the water to its original value of 2500 Pa? The pressure of the air above the water is maintained at 1500 Pa above atmospheric pressure.

12.21 •• A cylindrical disk of wood weighing 45.0 N and having a diameter of 30.0 cm floats on a cylinder of oil of density 0.850 g/cm^3 (Fig. E12.21). The cylinder of oil is 75.0 cm deep and has a diameter the same as that of the wood. (a) What is the gauge pressure at the top of the oil column? (b) Suppose now that someone puts a weight of 83.0 N on top of the wood, but no oil seeps around the edge of the wood. What is the *change* in pressure at (i) the bottom of the oil and (ii) halfway down in the oil?

Figure **E12.21**

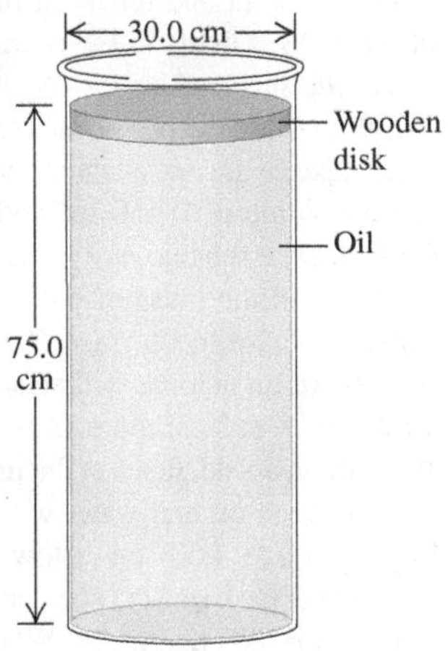

12.22 •• **Exploring Venus.** The surface pressure on Venus is 92 atm, and the acceleration due to gravity there is 0.894*g*. In a future exploratory mission, an upright cylindrical tank of benzene is sealed at the top but still pressurized at 92 atm just above the benzene. The tank has a diameter of 1.72 m, and the benzene column is 11.50 m tall. Ignore any effects due to the very high temperature on Venus. (a) What total force is exerted on the inside surface of the bottom of the tank? (b) What force does the Venusian atmosphere exert on the outside surface of the bottom of the tank? (c) What total inward force does the atmosphere exert on the vertical walls of the tank?

12.23 •• **Hydraulic Lift I.** For the hydraulic lift shown in Fig. 12.7, what must be the ratio of the diameter of the vessel at the car to the diameter of the vessel where the force F_1 is applied so that a 1520-kg car can be lifted with a force F_1 of just 125 N?

12.24 • **Hydraulic Lift II.** The piston of a hydraulic automobile lift is 0.30 m in diameter. What gauge pressure, in pascals, is required to lift a car with a mass of 1200 kg? Also express this pressure in atmospheres.

Section 12.3 Buoyancy

12.25 • A 950-kg cylindrical can buoy floats vertically in salt water. The diameter of the buoy is 0.900 m. Calculate the additional distance the buoy will sink when a 70.0-kg man stands on top of it.

12.26 •• A slab of ice floats on a freshwater lake. What minimum volume must the slab have for a 45.0-kg woman to be able to stand on it without getting her feet wet?

12.27 •• An ore sample weighs 17.50 N in air. When the sample is suspended by a light cord and totally immersed in water, the tension in the cord is 11.20 N. Find the total volume and the density of the sample.

12.28 •• You are preparing some apparatus for a visit to a newly discovered planet Caasi having oceans of glycerine and a surface acceleration due to gravity of 4.15 m/s^2. If your apparatus floats in the oceans on earth with 25.0% of its volume submerged, what percentage will be submerged in the glycerine oceans of Caasi?

12.29 •• An object of average density ρ floats at the surface of a fluid of density ρ_{fluid}. (a) How must the two densities be related? (b) In view of the answer to part (a), how can steel ships float in water? (c) In terms of ρ and ρ_{fluid}, what fraction of the object is submerged and what fraction is above the fluid? Check that your answers give the correct limiting behavior as $\rho \rightarrow \rho_{fluid}$ and as $\rho \rightarrow 0$. (d) While on board your yacht, your cousin Throckmorton cuts a rectangular piece (dimensions $5.0 \times 4.0 \times 3.0$ cm) out of a life preserver and throws it into the ocean. The piece has a mass of 42 g. As it floats in the ocean, what percentage of its volume is above the surface?

12.30 • A hollow plastic sphere is held below the surface of a freshwater lake by a cord anchored to the bottom of the lake. The sphere has a volume of 0.650 m^3 and the tension in the cord is 900 N. (a) Calculate the buoyant force exerted by the water on the sphere. (b) What is the mass of the sphere? (c) The cord breaks and the sphere rises to the surface. When the sphere comes to rest, what fraction of its volume will be submerged?

12.31 •• A cubical block of wood, 10.0 cm on a side, floats at the interface between oil and water with its lower surface 1.50 cm below the interface (Fig. E12.31). The density of the oil is 790 kg/m^3. (a) What is the gauge pressure at the upper face of the block? (b) What is the gauge pressure at the lower face of the block? (c) What are the mass and density of the block?

Figure **E12.31**

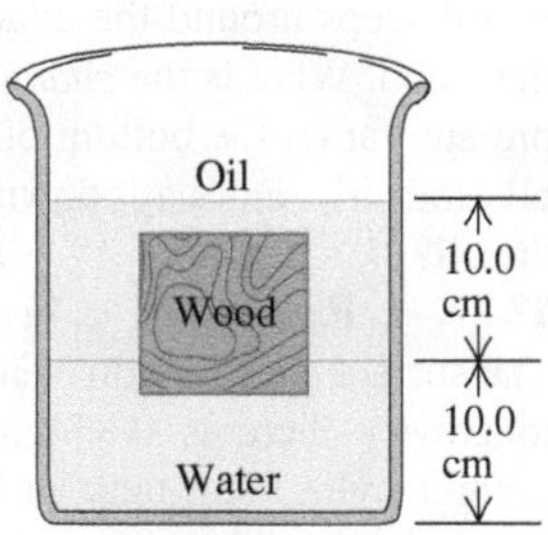

12.32 • A solid aluminum ingot weighs 89 N in air. (a) What is its volume? (b) The ingot is suspended from a rope and totally immersed in water. What is the tension in the rope (the *apparent* weight of the ingot in water)?

12.33 •• A rock is suspended by a light string. When the rock is in air, the tension in the string is 39.2 N. When the rock is totally immersed in water, the tension is 28.4 N. When the rock is totally immersed in an unknown liquid, the tension is 18.6 N. What is the density of the unknown liquid?

Section 12.4 Fluid Flow

12.34 •• Water runs into a fountain, filling all the pipes, at a steady rate of 0.750 m^3/s. (a) How fast will it shoot out of a hole 4.50 cm in diameter? (b) At what speed will it shoot out if the diameter of the hole is three times as large?

12.35 •• A shower head has 20 circular openings, each with radius 1.0 mm. The shower head is connected to a pipe with radius 0.80 cm. If the speed of water in the pipe is 3.0 m/s, what is its speed as it exits the shower-head openings?

12.36 • Water is flowing in a pipe with a varying cross-sectional area, and at all points the water completely fills the pipe. At point 1 the cross-sectional area of the pipe is 0.070 m^2, and the magnitude of the fluid velocity is 3.50 m/s. (a) What is the fluid speed at points in the pipe where the cross-sectional area is (a) 0.105 m^2 and (b) 0.047 m^2? (c) Calculate the volume of water discharged from the open end of the pipe in 1.00 hour.

12.37 • Water is flowing in a pipe with a circular cross section but with varying cross-sectional area, and at all points the water completely fills the pipe. (a) At one point in the pipe the radius is 0.150 m. What is the speed of the water at this point if water is flowing into this pipe at a steady rate of 1.20 m^3/s? (b) At a second point in the pipe the water speed is 3.80 m/s. What is the radius of the pipe at this point?

12.38 • **Home Repair.** You need to extend a 2.50-inch-diameter pipe, but you have only a 1.00-inch-diameter pipe on hand. You make a fitting to connect these pipes end to end. If the water is flowing at 6.00 cm/s in the wide pipe, how fast will it be flowing through the narrow one?

12.39 • At a point where an irrigation canal having a rectangular cross section is 18.5 m wide and 3.75 m deep, the water flows at 2.50 cm/s. At a point downstream, but on the same level, the canal is 16.5 m wide, but the water flows at 11.0 cm/s. How deep is the canal at this point?

12.40 •• BIO **Artery Blockage.** A medical technician is trying to determine what percentage of a patient's artery is blocked by plaque. To do this, she measures the blood pressure just before the region of blockage and finds that it is 1.20×10^4 Pa, while in the region of blockage it is 1.15×10^4 Pa. Furthermore, she knows that blood flowing through the normal artery just before the point of blockage is traveling at 30.0 cm/s, and the specific gravity of this patient's blood is 1.06. What percentage of the cross-sectional area of the patient's artery is blocked by the plaque?

Section 12.5 Bernoulli's Equation

12.41 •• A sealed tank containing seawater to a height of 11.0 m also contains air above the water at a gauge pressure of 3.00 atm. Water flows out from the bottom through a small hole. How fast is this water moving?

12.42 • A small circular hole 6.00 mm in diameter is cut in the side of a large water tank, 14.0 m below the water level in the tank. The top of the tank is open to the air. Find (a) the speed of efflux of the water and (b) the volume discharged per second.

12.43 • What gauge pressure is required in the city water mains for a stream from a fire hose connected to the mains to reach a vertical height of 15.0 m? (Assume that the mains have a much larger diameter than the fire hose.)

12.44 •• At one point in a pipeline the water's speed is 3.00 m/s and the gauge pressure is 5.00×10^4 Pa. Find the gauge pressure at a second point in the line, 11.0 m lower than the first, if the pipe diameter at the second point is twice that at the first.

12.45 • At a certain point in a horizontal pipeline, the water's speed is 2.50 m/s and the gauge pressure is 1.80×10^4 Pa. Find the gauge pressure at a second point in the line if the cross-sectional area at the second point is twice that at the first.

12.46 • A soft drink (mostly water) flows in a pipe at a beverage plant with a mass flow rate that would fill 220 0.355-L cans per minute. At point 2 in the pipe, the gauge pressure is 152 kPa and the cross-sectional area is 8.00 cm^2. At point 1, 1.35 m above point 2, the cross-sectional area is 2.00 cm^2. Find the (a) mass flow rate; (b) volume flow rate; (c) flow speeds at points 1 and 2; (d) gauge pressure at point 1.

12.47 •• A golf course sprinkler system discharges water from a horizontal pipe at the rate of 7200 cm^3/s. At one point in the pipe, where the radius is 4.00 cm, the water's absolute pressure is 2.40×10^5 Pa. At a second point in the pipe, the water passes through a constriction where the radius is 2.00 cm. What is the water's absolute pressure as it flows through this constriction?

Section 12.6 Viscosity and Turbulence

12.48 • A pressure difference of 6.00×10^4 Pa is required to maintain a volume flow rate of 0.800 m^3/s for a viscous fluid flowing through a section of cylindrical pipe that has radius 0.210 m.

What pressure difference is required to maintain the same volume flow rate if the radius of the pipe is decreased to 0.0700 m?

12.49 •• BIO **Clogged Artery.** Viscous blood is flowing through an artery partially clogged by cholesterol. A surgeon wants to remove enough of the cholesterol to double the flow rate of blood through this artery. If the original diameter of the artery is D, what should be the new diameter (in terms of D) to accomplish this for the same pressure gradient?

PROBLEMS

12.50 •• CP The deepest point known in any of the earth's oceans is in the Marianas Trench, 10.92 km deep. (a) Assuming water is incompressible, what is the pressure at this depth? Use the density of seawater. (b) The actual pressure is 1.16×10^8 Pa; your calculated value will be less because the density actually varies with depth. Using the compressibility of water and the actual pressure, find the density of the water at the bottom of the Marianas Trench. What is the percent change in the density of the water?

12.51 ••• In a lecture demonstration, a professor pulls apart two hemispherical steel shells (diameter D) with ease using their attached handles. She then places them together, pumps out the air to an absolute pressure of p, and hands them to a bodybuilder in the back row to pull apart. (a) If atmospheric pressure is p_0, how much force must the bodybuilder exert on each shell? (b) Evaluate your answer for the case $p = 0.025$ atm, $D = 10.0$ cm.

12.52 •• BIO **Fish Navigation.** (a) As you can tell by watching them in an aquarium, fish are able to remain at any depth in water with no effort. What does this ability tell you about their density? (b) Fish are able to inflate themselves using a sac (called the *swim bladder*) located under their spinal column. These sacs can be filled with an oxygen–nitrogen mixture that comes from the blood. If a 2.75-kg fish in freshwater inflates itself and increases its volume by 10%, find the *net* force that the *water* exerts on it. (c) What is the net *external* force on it? Does the fish go up or down when it inflates itself?

12.53 ••• CALC A swimming pool is 5.0 m long, 4.0 m wide, and 3.0 m deep. Compute the force exerted by the water against (a) the bottom and (b) either end. (*Hint:* Calculate the force on a thin, horizontal strip at a depth h, and integrate this over the end of the pool.) Do not include the force due to air pressure.

12.54 ••• CP CALC The upper edge of a gate in a dam runs along the water surface. The gate is 2.00 m high and 4.00 m wide and is hinged along a horizontal line through its center (Fig. P12.54). Calculate the torque about the hinge arising from the force due to the water. (*Hint:* Use a procedure similar to that used in Problem 12.53; calculate the torque on a thin, horizontal strip at a depth h and integrate this over the gate.)

Figure **P12.54**

12.55 ••• CP CALC **Force and Torque on a Dam.** A dam has the shape of a rectangular solid. The side facing the lake has area A and height H. The surface of the freshwater lake behind the dam is at the top of the dam. (a) Show that the net horizontal force exerted by the water on the dam equals $\frac{1}{2}\rho gHA$—that is, the average gauge pressure across the face of the dam times the area (see Problem 12.53). (b) Show that the torque exerted by the water about an axis along the bottom of the dam is $\rho gH^2A/6$. (c) How do the force and torque depend on the size of the lake?

12.56 •• **Ballooning on Mars.** It has been proposed that we could explore Mars using inflated balloons to hover just above the surface. The buoyancy of the atmosphere would keep the balloon aloft. The density of the Martian atmosphere is 0.0154 kg/m^3 (although this varies with temperature). Suppose we construct these balloons of a thin but tough plastic having a density such that each square meter has a mass of 5.00 g. We inflate them with a very light gas whose mass we can neglect. (a) What should be the radius and mass of these balloons so they just hover above the surface of Mars? (b) If we released one of the balloons from part (a) on earth, where the atmospheric density is 1.20 kg/m^3, what would be its initial acceleration assuming it was the same size as on Mars? Would it go up or down? (c) If on Mars these balloons have five times the radius found in part (a), how heavy an instrument package could they carry?

12.57 •• A 0.180-kg cube of ice (frozen water) is floating in glycerine. The gylcerine is in a tall cylinder that has inside radius 3.50 cm. The level of the glycerine is well below the top of the cylinder. If the ice completely melts, by what distance does the height of liquid in the cylinder change? Does the level of liquid rise or fall? That is, is the surface of the water above or below the original level of the gylcerine before the ice melted?

12.58 •• A narrow, U-shaped glass tube with open ends is filled with 25.0 cm of oil (of specific gravity 0.80) and 25.0 cm of water on opposite sides, with a barrier separating the liquids (Fig. P12.58). (a) Assume that the two liquids do not mix, and find the final heights of the columns of liquid in each side of the tube after the barrier is removed. (b) For the following cases, arrive at your answer by simple physical reasoning, not by calculations: (i) What would be the height on each side if the oil and water had equal densities? (ii) What would the heights be if the oil's density were much less than that of water?

Figure **P12.58**

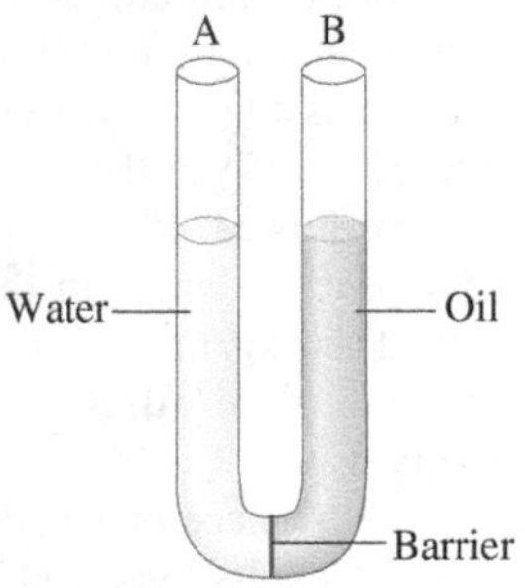

12.59 • A U-shaped tube open to the air at both ends contains some mercury. A quantity of water is carefully poured into the left arm of the U-shaped tube until the vertical height of the water column is 15.0 cm (Fig. P12.59). (a) What is the gauge pressure at the water–mercury interface? (b) Calculate the vertical distance h from the top of the mercury in the right-hand arm of the tube to the top of the water in the left-hand arm.

Figure **P12.59**

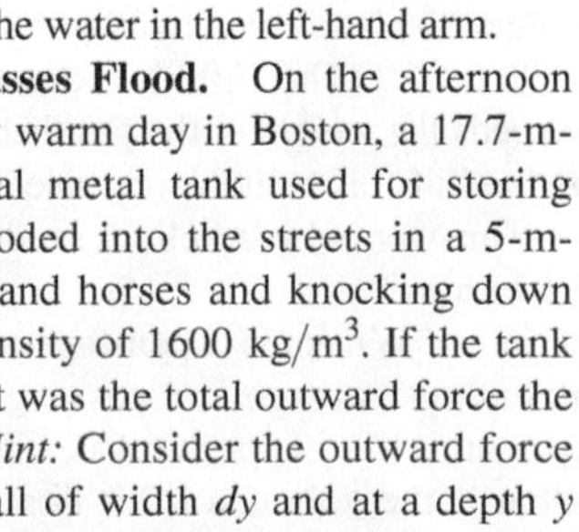

12.60 •• CALC **The Great Molasses Flood.** On the afternoon of January 15, 1919, an unusually warm day in Boston, a 17.7-m-high, 27.4-m-diameter cylindrical metal tank used for storing molasses ruptured. Molasses flooded into the streets in a 5-m-deep stream, killing pedestrians and horses and knocking down buildings. The molasses had a density of 1600 kg/m^3. If the tank was full before the accident, what was the total outward force the molasses exerted on its sides? (*Hint:* Consider the outward force on a circular ring of the tank wall of width dy and at a depth y below the surface. Integrate to find the total outward force. Assume that before the tank ruptured, the pressure at the surface of the molasses was equal to the air pressure outside the tank.)

12.61 • An open barge has the dimensions shown in Fig. P12.61. If the barge is made out of 4.0-cm-thick steel plate on each of its four sides and its bottom, what mass of coal can the barge carry in freshwater without sinking? Is there enough room in the barge to hold this amount of coal? (The density of coal is about 1500 kg/m^3.)

Figure **P12.61**

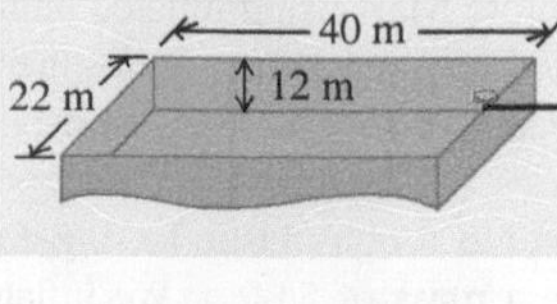

12.62 ••• A hot-air balloon has a volume of 2200 m^3. The balloon fabric (the envelope) weighs 900 N. The basket with gear and full propane tanks weighs 1700 N. If the balloon can barely lift an additional 3200 N of passengers, breakfast, and champagne when the outside air density is 1.23 kg/m^3, what is the average density of the heated gases in the envelope?

12.63 •• Advertisements for a certain small car claim that it floats in water. (a) If the car's mass is 900 kg and its interior volume is 3.0 m^3, what fraction of the car is immersed when it floats? You can ignore the volume of steel and other materials. (b) Water gradually leaks in and displaces the air in the car. What fraction of the interior volume is filled with water when the car sinks?

12.64 • A single ice cube with mass 9.70 g floats in a glass completely full of 420 cm^3 of water. You can ignore the water's surface tension and its variation in density with temperature (as long as it remains a liquid). (a) What volume of water does the ice cube displace? (b) When the ice cube has completely melted, has any water overflowed? If so, how much? If not, explain why this is so. (c) Suppose the water in the glass had been very salty water of density 1050 kg/m^3. What volume of salt water would the 9.70-g ice cube displace? (d) Redo part (b) for the freshwater ice cube in the salty water.

12.65 ••• A piece of wood is 0.600 m long, 0.250 m wide, and 0.080 m thick. Its density is 700 kg/m^3. What volume of lead must be fastened underneath it to sink the wood in calm water so that its top is just even with the water level? What is the mass of this volume of lead?

12.66 •• A hydrometer consists of a spherical bulb and a cylindrical stem with a cross-sectional area of 0.400 cm^2 (see Fig. 12.12a). The total volume of bulb and stem is 13.2 cm^3. When immersed in water, the hydrometer floats with 8.00 cm of the stem above the water surface. When the hydrometer is immersed in an organic fluid, 3.20 cm of the stem is above the surface. Find the density of the organic fluid. (*Note:* This illustrates the precision of such a hydrometer. Relatively small density differences give rise to relatively large differences in hydrometer readings.)

12.67 •• The densities of air, helium, and hydrogen (at p = 1.0 atm and T = 20°C) are 1.20 kg/m^3, 0.166 kg/m^3, and 0.0899 kg/m^3, respectively. (a) What is the volume in cubic meters displaced by a hydrogen-filled airship that has a total "lift" of 90.0 kN? (The "lift" is the amount by which the buoyant force exceeds the weight of the gas that fills the airship.) (b) What would be the "lift" if helium were used instead of hydrogen? In view of your answer, why is helium used in modern airships like advertising blimps?

12.68 •• When an open-faced boat has a mass of 5750 kg, including its cargo and passengers, it floats with the water just up to the top of its gunwales (sides) on a freshwater lake. (a) What is the volume of this boat? (b) The captain decides that it is too dangerous to float with his boat on the verge of sinking, so he decides to throw some cargo overboard so that 20% of the boat's volume will be above water. How much mass should he throw out?

12.69 •• **CP** An open cylindrical tank of acid rests at the edge of a table 1.4 m above the floor of the chemistry lab. If this tank springs a small hole in the side at its base, how far from the foot of the table will the acid hit the floor if the acid in the tank is 75 cm deep?

12.70 •• **CP** A firehose must be able to shoot water to the top of a building 28.0 m tall when aimed straight up. Water enters this hose at a steady rate of 0.500 m^3/s and shoots out of a round nozzle. (a) What is the maximum diameter this nozzle can have? (b) If the only nozzle available has a diameter twice as great, what is the highest point the water can reach?

12.71 •• **CP** You drill a small hole in the side of a vertical cylindrical water tank that is standing on the ground with its top open to the air. (a) If the water level has a height H, at what height above the base should you drill the hole for the water to reach its greatest distance from the base of the cylinder when it hits the ground? (b) What is the greatest distance the water will reach?

12.72 ••• **CALC** A closed and elevated vertical cylindrical tank with diameter 2.00 m contains water to a depth of 0.800 m. A worker accidently pokes a circular hole with diameter 0.0200 m in the bottom of the tank. As the water drains from the tank, compressed air above the water in the tank maintains a gauge pressure of 5.00×10^3 Pa at the surface of the water. Ignore any effects of viscosity. (a) Just after the hole is made, what is the speed of the water as it emerges from the hole? What is the ratio of this speed to the efflux speed if the top of the tank is open to the air? (b) How much time does it take for all the water to drain from the tank? What is the ratio of this time to the time it takes for the tank to drain if the top of the tank is open to the air?

12.73 •• A block of balsa wood placed in one scale pan of an equal-arm balance is exactly balanced by a 0.115-kg brass mass in the other scale pan. Find the true mass of the balsa wood if its density is 150 kg/m^3. Explain why it is accurate to ignore the buoyancy in air of the brass but *not* the buoyancy in air of the balsa wood.

12.74 •• Block A in Fig. P12.74 hangs by a cord from spring balance D and is submerged in a liquid C contained in beaker B. The mass of the beaker is 1.00 kg; the mass of the liquid is 1.80 kg. Balance D reads 3.50 kg, and balance E reads 7.50 kg. The volume of block A is 3.80×10^{-3} m^3. (a) What is the density of the liquid? (b) What will each balance read if block A is pulled up out of the liquid?

Figure **P12.74**

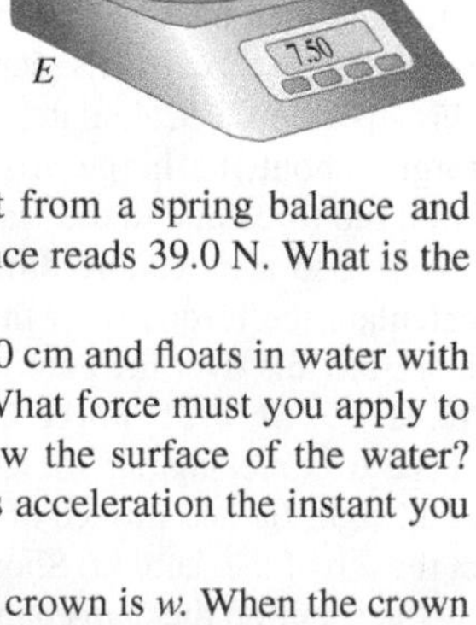

12.75 •• A hunk of aluminum is completely covered with a gold shell to form an ingot of weight 45.0 N. When you suspend the ingot from a spring balance and submerge the ingot in water, the balance reads 39.0 N. What is the weight of the gold in the shell?

12.76 •• A plastic ball has radius 12.0 cm and floats in water with 24.0% of its volume submerged. (a) What force must you apply to the ball to hold it at rest totally below the surface of the water? (b) If you let go of the ball, what is its acceleration the instant you release it?

12.77 •• The weight of a king's solid crown is w. When the crown is suspended by a light rope and completely immersed in water, the tension in the rope (the crown's apparent weight) is fw. (a) Prove that the crown's relative density (specific gravity) is $1/(1 - f)$. Discuss the meaning of the limits as f approaches 0 and 1. (b) If the crown is solid gold and weighs 12.9 N in air, what is its apparent weight when completely immersed in water? (c) Repeat part (b) if the crown is solid lead with a very thin gold plating, but still has a weight in air of 12.9 N.

12.78 •• A piece of steel has a weight w, an apparent weight (see Problem 12.77) w_{water} when completely immersed in water, and an apparent weight w_{fluid} when completely immersed in an unknown fluid. (a) Prove that the fluid's density relative to water (specific gravity) is $(w - w_{fluid})/(w - w_{water})$. (b) Is this result reasonable for the three cases of w_{fluid} greater than, equal to, or less than w_{water}? (c) The apparent weight of the piece of steel in water of density $1000\ kg/m^3$ is 87.2% of its weight. What percentage of its weight will its apparent weight be in formic acid (density $1220\ kg/m^3$)?

12.79 ••• You cast some metal of density ρ_m in a mold, but you are worried that there might be cavities within the casting. You measure the weight of the casting to be w, and the buoyant force when it is completely surrounded by water to be B. (a) Show that $V_0 = B/(\rho_{water}g) - w/(\rho_m g)$ is the total volume of any enclosed cavities. (b) If your metal is copper, the casting's weight is 156 N, and the buoyant force is 20 N, what is the total volume of any enclosed cavities in your casting? What fraction is this of the total volume of the casting?

12.80 • A cubical block of wood 0.100 m on a side and with a density of $550\ kg/m^3$ floats in a jar of water. Oil with a density of $750\ kg/m^3$ is poured on the water until the top of the oil layer is 0.035 m below the top of the block. (a) How deep is the oil layer? (b) What is the gauge pressure at the block's lower face?

12.81 •• **Dropping Anchor.** An iron anchor with mass 35.0 kg and density $7860\ kg/m^3$ lies on the deck of a small barge that has vertical sides and floats in a freshwater river. The area of the bottom of the barge is $8.00\ m^2$. The anchor is thrown overboard but is suspended above the bottom of the river by a rope; the mass and volume of the rope are small enough to ignore. After the anchor is overboard and the barge has finally stopped bobbing up and down, has the barge risen or sunk down in the water? By what vertical distance?

12.82 •• Assume that crude oil from a supertanker has density $750\ kg/m^3$. The tanker runs aground on a sandbar. To refloat the tanker, its oil cargo is pumped out into steel barrels, each of which has a mass of 15.0 kg when empty and holds $0.120\ m^3$ of oil. You can ignore the volume occupied by the steel from which the barrel is made. (a) If a salvage worker accidentally drops a filled, sealed barrel overboard, will it float or sink in the seawater? (b) If the barrel floats, what fraction of its volume will be above the water surface? If it sinks, what minimum tension would have to be exerted by a rope to haul the barrel up from the ocean floor? (c) Repeat parts (a) and (b) if the density of the oil is $910\ kg/m^3$ and the mass of each empty barrel is 32.0 kg.

12.83 ••• A cubical block of density ρ_B and with sides of length L floats in a liquid of greater density ρ_L. (a) What fraction of the block's volume is above the surface of the liquid? (b) The liquid is denser than water (density ρ_W) and does not mix with it. If water is poured on the surface of the liquid, how deep must the water layer be so that the water surface just rises to the top of the block? Express your answer in terms of L, ρ_B, ρ_L, and ρ_W. (c) Find the depth of the water layer in part (b) if the liquid is mercury, the block is made of iron, and the side length is 10.0 cm.

12.84 •• A barge is in a rectangular lock on a freshwater river. The lock is 60.0 m long and 20.0 m wide, and the steel doors on each end are closed. With the barge floating in the lock, a 2.50×10^6 N load of scrap metal is put onto the barge. The metal has density $9000\ kg/m^3$. (a) When the load of scrap metal, initially on the bank, is placed onto the barge, what vertical distance does the water in the lock rise? (b) The scrap metal is now pushed overboard into the water. Does the water level in the lock rise, fall, or remain the same? If it rises or falls, by what vertical distance does it change?

12.85 • **CP CALC** A U-shaped tube with a horizontal portion of length l (Fig. P12.85) contains a liquid. What is the difference in height between the liquid columns in the vertical arms (a) if the tube has an acceleration a toward the right and (b) if the tube is mounted on a horizontal turntable rotating with an angular speed ω with one of the vertical arms on the axis of rotation? (c) Explain why the difference in height does not depend on the density of the liquid or on the cross-sectional area of the tube. Would it be the same if the vertical tubes did not have equal cross-sectional areas? Would it be the same if the horizontal portion were tapered from one end to the other? Explain.

Figure **P12.85**

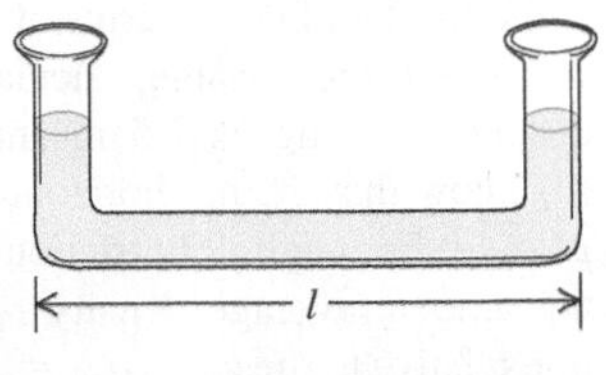

12.86 • **CP CALC** A cylindrical container of an incompressible liquid with density ρ rotates with constant angular speed ω about its axis of symmetry, which we take to be the y-axis (Fig. P12.86). (a) Show that the pressure at a given height within the fluid increases in the radial direction (outward from the axis of rotation) according to $\partial p/\partial r = \rho\omega^2 r$. (b) Integrate this partial differential equation to find the pressure as a function of distance from the axis of rotation along a horizontal line at $y = 0$. (c) Combine the result of part (b) with Eq. (12.5) to show that the surface of the rotating liquid has a *parabolic* shape; that is, the height of the liquid is given by $h(r) = \omega^2 r^2/2g$. (This technique is used for making parabolic telescope mirrors; liquid glass is rotated and allowed to solidify while rotating.)

Figure **P12.86**

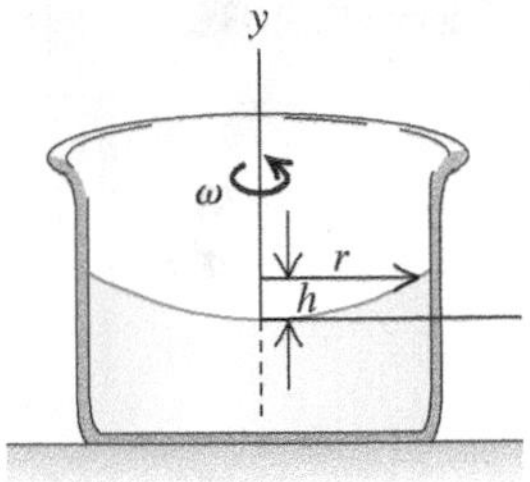

12.87 •• **CP CALC** An incompressible fluid with density ρ is in a horizontal test tube of inner cross-sectional area A. The test tube spins in a horizontal circle in an ultracentrifuge at an angular speed ω. Gravitational forces are negligible. Consider a volume element of the fluid of area A and thickness dr' a distance r' from the rotation axis. The pressure on its inner surface is p and on its outer surface is $p + dp$. (a) Apply Newton's second law to the volume element to show that $dp = \rho\omega^2 r' dr'$. (b) If the surface of the fluid is at a radius r_0 where the pressure is p_0, show that the pressure p at a distance $r \geq r_0$ is $p = p_0 + \rho\omega^2(r^2 - r_0^2)/2$. (c) An object of volume V and density ρ_{ob} has its center of mass at a distance R_{cmob} from the axis. Show that the net horizontal force on the object is $\rho V\omega^2 R_{cm}$, where R_{cm} is the distance from the axis to the center of mass of the displaced fluid. (d) Explain why the object will move inward if $\rho R_{cm} > \rho_{ob}R_{cmob}$ and outward if $\rho R_{cm} < \rho_{ob}R_{cmob}$. (e) For small objects of uniform density, $R_{cm} = R_{cmob}$. What happens to a mixture of small objects of this kind with different densities in an ultracentrifuge?

12.88 ••• **CALC** Untethered helium balloons, floating in a car that has all the windows rolled up and outside air vents closed, move in the direction of the car's acceleration, but loose balloons filled with air move in the opposite direction. To show why, consider only the horizontal forces acting on the balloons. Let a be the magnitude of the car's forward acceleration. Consider a horizontal tube of air with a cross-sectional area A that extends from the windshield, where $x = 0$ and $p = p_0$, back along the x-axis. Now consider a volume element of thickness dx in this tube. The pressure on its front surface is p and the pressure on its rear surface is $p + dp$. Assume the air has a constant density ρ. (a) Apply Newton's second law to the volume element to show that $dp = \rho a\, dx$. (b) Integrate the result of part (a) to find the pressure at the front surface in terms of a and x. (c) To show that considering ρ constant is reasonable, calculate the pressure difference in atm for a distance as long as 2.5 m and a large acceleration of 5.0 m/s^2. (d) Show that the net horizontal force on a balloon of volume V is ρVa. (e) For negligible friction forces, show that the acceleration of the balloon (average density ρ_{bal}) is $(\rho/\rho_{bal})a$, so that the acceleration relative to the car is $a_{rel} = [(\rho/\rho_{bal}) - 1]a$. (f) Use the expression for a_{rel} in part (e) to explain the movement of the balloons.

12.89 • **CP** Water stands at a depth H in a large, open tank whose side walls are vertical (Fig. P12.89). A hole is made in one of the walls at a depth h below the water surface. (a) At what distance R from the foot of the wall does the emerging stream strike the floor? (b) How far above the bottom of the tank could a second hole be cut so that the stream emerging from it could have the same range as for the first hole?

Figure **P12.89**

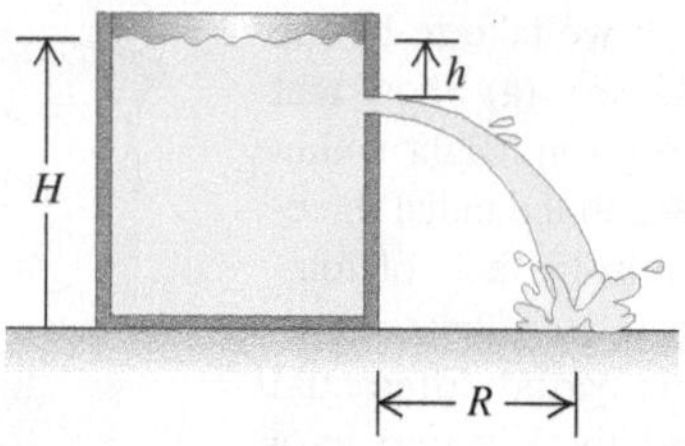

12.90 ••• A cylindrical bucket, open at the top, is 25.0 cm high and 10.0 cm in diameter. A circular hole with a cross-sectional area 1.50 cm^2 is cut in the center of the bottom of the bucket. Water flows into the bucket from a tube above it at the rate of 2.40×10^{-4} m^3/s. How high will the water in the bucket rise?

12.91 • Water flows steadily from an open tank as in Fig. P12.91. The elevation of point 1 is 10.0 m, and the elevation of points 2 and 3 is 2.00 m. The cross-sectional area at point 2 is 0.0480 m^2; at point 3 it is 0.0160 m^2. The area of the tank is very large compared with the cross-sectional area of the pipe. Assuming that Bernoulli's equation applies, compute (a) the discharge rate in cubic meters per second and (b) the gauge pressure at point 2.

Figure **P12.91**

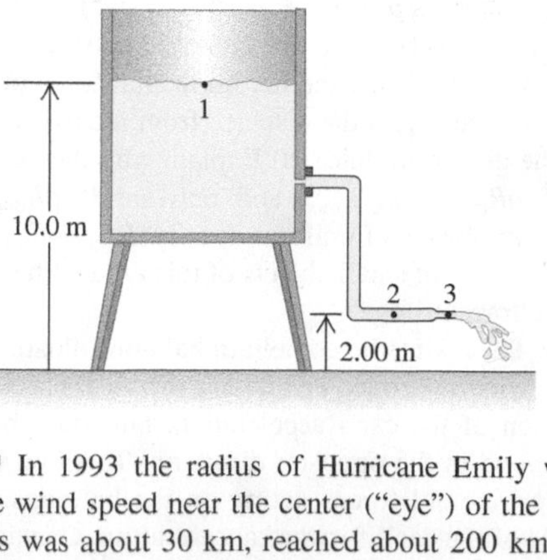

12.92 •• **CP** In 1993 the radius of Hurricane Emily was about 350 km. The wind speed near the center ("eye") of the hurricane, whose radius was about 30 km, reached about 200 km/h. As air swirled in from the rim of the hurricane toward the eye, its angular momentum remained roughly constant. (a) Estimate the wind speed at the rim of the hurricane. (b) Estimate the pressure difference at the earth's surface between the eye and the rim. (*Hint:* See Table 12.1.) Where is the pressure greater? (c) If the kinetic energy of the swirling air in the eye could be converted completely to gravitational potential energy, how high would the air go? (d) In fact, the air in the eye is lifted to heights of several kilometers. How can you reconcile this with your answer to part (c)?

12.93 •• Two very large open tanks A and F (Fig. P12.93) contain the same liquid. A horizontal pipe BCD, having a constriction at C and open to the air at D, leads out of the bottom of tank A, and a vertical pipe E opens into the constriction at C and dips into the liquid in tank F. Assume streamline flow and no viscosity. If the cross-sectional area at C is one-half the area at D and if D is a distance h_1 below the level of the liquid in A, to what height h_2 will liquid rise in pipe E? Express your answer in terms of h_1.

Figure **P12.93**

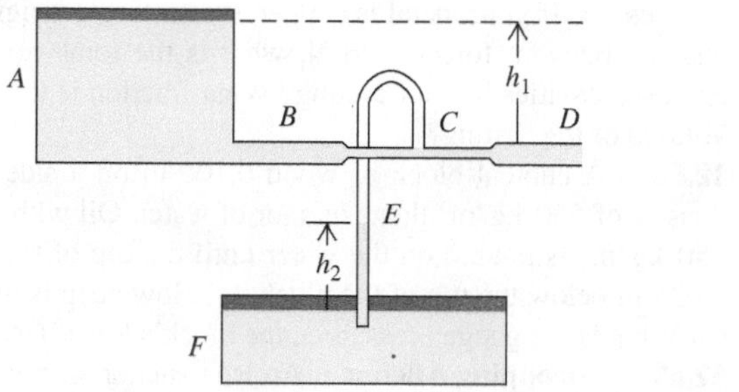

12.94 •• The horizontal pipe shown in Fig. P12.94 has a cross-sectional area of 40.0 cm^2 at the wider portions and 10.0 cm^2 at the constriction. Water is flowing in the pipe, and the discharge from the pipe is 6.00×10^{-3} m^3/s (6.00 L/s). Find (a) the flow speeds at the wide and the narrow portions; (b) the pressure difference between these portions; (c) the difference in height between the mercury columns in the U-shaped tube.

Figure **P12.94**

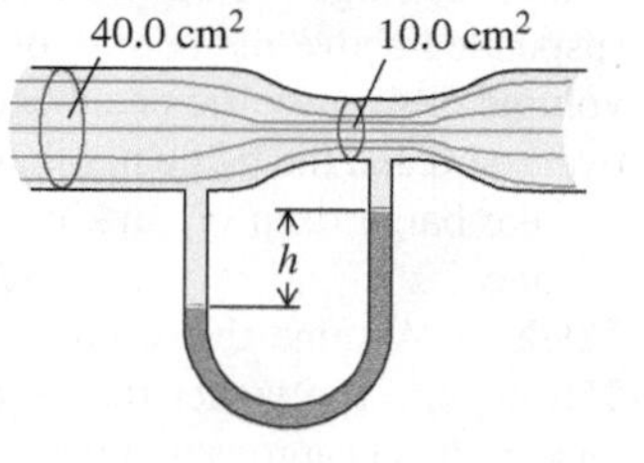

12.95 • A liquid flowing from a vertical pipe has a definite shape as it flows from the pipe. To get the equation for this shape, assume that the liquid is in free fall once it leaves the pipe. Just as it leaves the pipe, the liquid has speed v_0 and the radius of the stream of liquid is r_0. (a) Find an equation for the speed of the liquid as a function of the distance y it has fallen. Combining this with the equation of continuity, find an expression for the radius of the stream as a function of y. (b) If water flows out of a vertical pipe at a speed of 1.20 m/s, how far below the outlet will the radius be one-half the original radius of the stream?

Challenge Problems

12.96 ••• A rock with mass $m = 3.00$ kg is suspended from the roof of an elevator by a light cord. The rock is totally immersed in a bucket of water that sits on the floor of the elevator, but the rock doesn't touch the bottom or sides of the bucket. (a) When the elevator is at rest, the tension in the cord is 21.0 N. Calculate the volume of the rock. (b) Derive an expression for the tension in the cord when the elevator is accelerating *upward* with an acceleration of magnitude a. Calculate the tension when $a = 2.50$ m/s^2

upward. (c) Derive an expression for the tension in the cord when the elevator is accelerating *downward* with an acceleration of magnitude a. Calculate the tension when $a = 2.50\ m/s^2$ downward. (d) What is the tension when the elevator is in free fall with a downward acceleration equal to g?

12.97 ••• **CALC** Suppose a piece of styrofoam, $\rho = 180\ kg/m^3$, is held completely submerged in water (Fig. P12.97). (a) What is the tension in the cord? Find this using Archimedes's principle. (b) Use $p = p_0 + \rho gh$ to calculate directly the force exerted by the water on the two sloped sides and the bottom of the styrofoam; then show that the vector sum of these forces is the buoyant force.

Figure **P12.97**

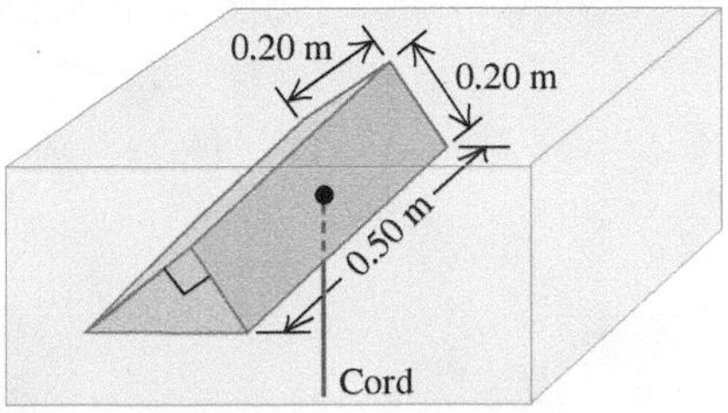

12.98 ••• A *siphon,* as shown in Fig. P12.98, is a convenient device for removing liquids from containers. To establish the flow, the tube must be initially filled with fluid. Let the fluid have density ρ, and let the atmospheric pressure be p_{atm}. Assume that the cross-sectional area of the tube is the same at all points along it. (a) If the lower end of the siphon is at a distance h below the surface of the liquid in the container, what is the speed of the fluid as it flows out the lower end of the siphon? (Assume that the container has a very large diameter, and ignore any effects of viscosity.) (b) A curious feature of a siphon is that the fluid initially flows "uphill." What is the greatest height H that the high point of the tube can have if flow is still to occur?

Figure **P12.98**

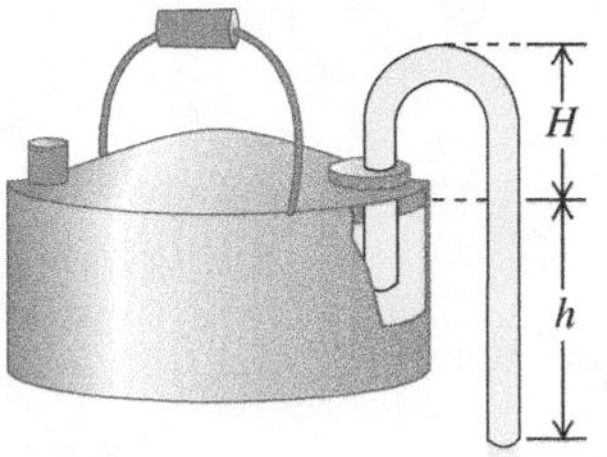

Answers

Chapter Opening Question ?

The flesh of both the shark and the tropical fish is denser than seawater, so left to themselves they would sink. However, a tropical fish has a gas-filled body cavity called a swimbladder, so that the *average* density of the fish's body is the same as that of seawater and the fish neither sinks nor rises. Sharks have no such cavity. Hence they must swim constantly to keep from sinking, using their pectoral fins to provide lift much like the wings of an airplane (see Section 12.5).

Test Your Understanding Questions

12.1 Answer: (ii), (iv), (i) and (iii) (tie), (v) In each case the average density equals the mass divided by the volume. Hence we have (i) $\rho = (4.00\ kg)/(1.60 \times 10^{-3}\ m^3) = 2.50 \times 10^3\ kg/m^3$; (ii) $\rho = (8.00\ kg)/(1.60 \times 10^{-3}\ m^3) = 5.00 \times 10^3\ kg/m^3$; (iii) $\rho = (8.00\ kg)/(3.20 \times 10^{-3}\ m^3) = 2.50 \times 10^3\ kg/m^3$; (iv) $\rho = (2560\ kg)/(0.640\ m^3) = 4.00 \times 10^3\ kg/m^3$; (v) $\rho = (2560\ kg)/(1.28\ m^3) = 2.00 \times 10^3\ kg/m^3$. Note that compared to object (i), object (ii) has double the mass but the same volume and so has double the average density. Object (iii) has double the mass and double the volume of object (i), so (i) and (iii) have the same average density. Finally, object (v) has the same mass as object (iv) but double the volume, so (v) has half the average density of (iv).

12.2 Answer: (ii) From Eq. (12.9), the pressure outside the barometer is equal to the product ρgh. When the barometer is taken out of the refrigerator, the density ρ decreases while the height h of the mercury column remains the same. Hence the air pressure must be lower outdoors than inside the refrigerator.

12.3 Answer: (i) Consider the water, the statue, and the container together as a system; the total weight of the system does not depend on whether the statue is immersed. The total supporting force, including the tension T and the upward force F of the scale on the container (equal to the scale reading), is the same in both cases. But we saw in Example 12.5 that T decreases by 7.84 N when the statue is immersed, so the scale reading F must *increase* by 7.84 N. An alternative viewpoint is that the water exerts an upward buoyant force of 7.84 N on the statue, so the statue must exert an equal downward force on the water, making the scale reading 7.84 N greater than the weight of water and container.

12.4 Answer: (ii) A highway that narrows from three lanes to one is like a pipe whose cross-sectional area narrows to one-third of its value. If cars behaved like the molecules of an incompressible fluid, then as the cars encountered the one-lane section, the spacing between cars (the "density") would stay the same but the cars would triple their speed. This would keep the "volume flow rate" (number of cars per second passing a point on the highway) the same. In real life cars behave like the molecules of a *compressible* fluid: They end up packed closer (the "density" increases) and fewer cars per second pass a point on the highway (the "volume flow rate" decreases).

12.5 Answer: (ii) Newton's second law tells us that a body accelerates (its velocity changes) in response to a net force. In fluid flow, a pressure difference between two points means that fluid particles moving between those two points experience a force, and this force causes the fluid particles to accelerate and change speed.

12.6 Answer: (iv) The required pressure is proportional to $1/R^4$, where R is the inside radius of the needle (half the inside diameter). With the smaller-diameter needle, the pressure is greater by a factor of $[(0.60\ mm)/(0.30\ mm)]^4 = 2^4 = 16$.

Bridging Problem

Answers: (a) $y = H - \left(\frac{d}{D}\right)^2 \sqrt{2gH}\, t + \left(\frac{d}{D}\right)^4 \frac{gt^2}{2}$

(b) $T = \sqrt{\frac{2H}{g}}\left(\frac{D}{d}\right)^2$ **(c)** $\sqrt{2}$

14 PERIODIC MOTION

? Dogs walk with much quicker strides than do humans. Is this primarily because dogs' legs are shorter than human legs, less massive than human legs, or both?

LEARNING GOALS

By studying this chapter, you will learn:

- How to describe oscillations in terms of amplitude, period, frequency, and angular frequency.
- How to do calculations with simple harmonic motion, an important type of oscillation.
- How to use energy concepts to analyze simple harmonic motion.
- How to apply the ideas of simple harmonic motion to different physical situations.
- How to analyze the motions of a simple pendulum.
- What a physical pendulum is, and how to calculate the properties of its motion.
- What determines how rapidly an oscillation dies out.
- How a driving force applied to an oscillator at the right frequency can cause a very large response, or resonance.

Many kinds of motion repeat themselves over and over: the vibration of a quartz crystal in a watch, the swinging pendulum of a grandfather clock, the sound vibrations produced by a clarinet or an organ pipe, and the back-and-forth motion of the pistons in a car engine. This kind of motion, called **periodic motion** or **oscillation,** is the subject of this chapter. Understanding periodic motion will be essential for our later study of waves, sound, alternating electric currents, and light.

A body that undergoes periodic motion always has a stable equilibrium position. When it is moved away from this position and released, a force or torque comes into play to pull it back toward equilibrium. But by the time it gets there, it has picked up some kinetic energy, so it overshoots, stopping somewhere on the other side, and is again pulled back toward equilibrium. Picture a ball rolling back and forth in a round bowl or a pendulum that swings back and forth past its straight-down position.

In this chapter we will concentrate on two simple examples of systems that can undergo periodic motions: spring-mass systems and pendulums. We will also study why oscillations often tend to die out with time and why some oscillations can build up to greater and greater displacements from equilibrium when periodically varying forces act.

14.1 Describing Oscillation

Figure 14.1 shows one of the simplest systems that can have periodic motion. A body with mass m rests on a frictionless horizontal guide system, such as a linear air track, so it can move only along the x-axis. The body is attached to a spring of negligible mass that can be either stretched or compressed. The left end of the spring is held fixed and the right end is attached to the body. The spring force is the only horizontal force acting on the body; the vertical normal and gravitational forces always add to zero.

14.1 A system that can have periodic motion.

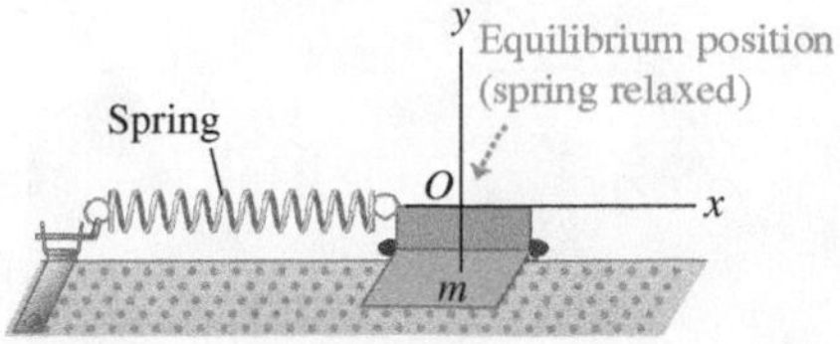

14.2 Model for periodic motion. When the body is displaced from its equilibrium position at $x = 0$, the spring exerts a restoring force back toward the equilibrium position.

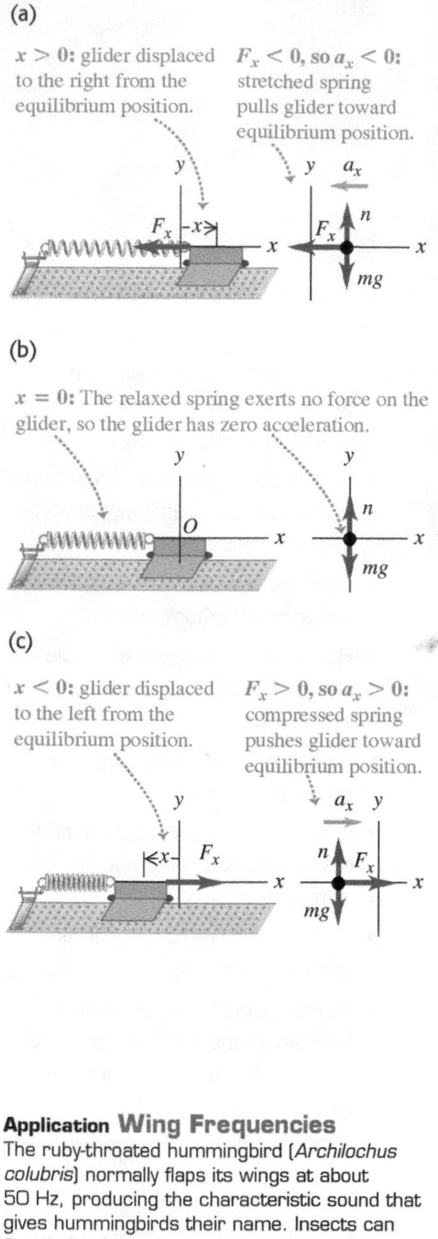

Application Wing Frequencies
The ruby-throated hummingbird (*Archilochus colubris*) normally flaps its wings at about 50 Hz, producing the characteristic sound that gives hummingbirds their name. Insects can flap their wings at even faster rates, from 330 Hz for a house fly and 600 Hz for a mosquito to an amazing 1040 Hz for the tiny biting midge.

It's simplest to define our coordinate system so that the origin O is at the equilibrium position, where the spring is neither stretched nor compressed. Then x is the x-component of the **displacement** of the body from equilibrium and is also the change in the length of the spring. The x-component of the force that the spring exerts on the body is F_x, and the x-component of acceleration a_x is given by $a_x = F_x/m$.

Figure 14.2 shows the body for three different displacements of the spring. Whenever the body is displaced from its equilibrium position, the spring force tends to restore it to the equilibrium position. We call a force with this character a **restoring force.** Oscillation can occur only when there is a restoring force tending to return the system to equilibrium.

Let's analyze how oscillation occurs in this system. If we displace the body to the right to $x = A$ and then let go, the net force and the acceleration are to the left (Fig. 14.2a). The speed increases as the body approaches the equilibrium position O. When the body is at O, the net force acting on it is zero (Fig. 14.2b), but because of its motion it *overshoots* the equilibrium position. On the other side of the equilibrium position the body is still moving to the left, but the net force and the acceleration are to the right (Fig. 14.2c); hence the speed decreases until the body comes to a stop. We will show later that with an ideal spring, the stopping point is at $x = -A$. The body then accelerates to the right, overshoots equilibrium again, and stops at the starting point $x = A$, ready to repeat the whole process. The body is oscillating! If there is no friction or other force to remove mechanical energy from the system, this motion repeats forever; the restoring force perpetually draws the body back toward the equilibrium position, only to have the body overshoot time after time.

In different situations the force may depend on the displacement x from equilibrium in different ways. But oscillation *always* occurs if the force is a *restoring* force that tends to return the system to equilibrium.

Amplitude, Period, Frequency, and Angular Frequency

Here are some terms that we'll use in discussing periodic motions of all kinds:

The **amplitude** of the motion, denoted by A, is the maximum magnitude of displacement from equilibrium—that is, the maximum value of $|x|$. It is always positive. If the spring in Fig. 14.2 is an ideal one, the total overall range of the motion is $2A$. The SI unit of A is the meter. A complete vibration, or **cycle,** is one complete round trip—say, from A to $-A$ and back to A, or from O to A, back through O to $-A$, and back to O. Note that motion from one side to the other (say, $-A$ to A) is a half-cycle, not a whole cycle.

The **period,** T, is the time for one cycle. It is always positive. The SI unit is the second, but it is sometimes expressed as "seconds per cycle."

The **frequency,** f, is the number of cycles in a unit of time. It is always positive. The SI unit of frequency is the hertz:

$$1 \text{ hertz} = 1 \text{ Hz} = 1 \text{ cycle/s} = 1 \text{ s}^{-1}$$

This unit is named in honor of the German physicist Heinrich Hertz (1857–1894), a pioneer in investigating electromagnetic waves.

The **angular frequency,** ω, is 2π times the frequency:

$$\omega = 2\pi f$$

We'll learn shortly why ω is a useful quantity. It represents the rate of change of an angular quantity (not necessarily related to a rotational motion) that is always measured in radians, so its units are rad/s. Since f is in cycle/s, we may regard the number 2π as having units rad/cycle.

From the definitions of period T and frequency f we see that each is the reciprocal of the other:

$$f = \frac{1}{T} \qquad T = \frac{1}{f} \qquad \text{(relationships between frequency and period)} \qquad (14.1)$$

Also, from the definition of ω,

$$\omega = 2\pi f = \frac{2\pi}{T} \quad \text{(angular frequency)} \qquad (14.2)$$

Example 14.1 Period, frequency, and angular frequency

An ultrasonic transducer used for medical diagnosis oscillates at 6.7 MHz = 6.7×10^6 Hz. How long does each oscillation take, and what is the angular frequency?

SOLUTION

IDENTIFY and SET UP: The target variables are the period T and the angular frequency ω. We can find these using the given frequency f in Eqs. (14.1) and (14.2).

EXECUTE: From Eqs. (14.1) and (14.2),

$$T = \frac{1}{f} = \frac{1}{6.7 \times 10^6\ \text{Hz}} = 1.5 \times 10^{-7}\ \text{s} = 0.15\ \mu\text{s}$$

$$\begin{aligned}\omega &= 2\pi f = 2\pi(6.7 \times 10^6\ \text{Hz}) \\ &= (2\pi\ \text{rad/cycle})(6.7 \times 10^6\ \text{cycle/s}) \\ &= 4.2 \times 10^7\ \text{rad/s}\end{aligned}$$

EVALUATE: This is a very rapid vibration, with large f and ω and small T. A slow vibration has small f and ω and large T.

Test Your Understanding of Section 14.1 A body like that shown in Fig. 14.2 oscillates back and forth. For each of the following values of the body's x-velocity v_x and x-acceleration a_x, state whether its displacement x is positive, negative, or zero. (a) $v_x > 0$ and $a_x > 0$; (b) $v_x > 0$ and $a_x < 0$; (c) $v_x < 0$ and $a_x > 0$; (d) $v_x < 0$ and $a_x < 0$; (e) $v_x = 0$ and $a_x < 0$; (f) $v_x > 0$ and $a_x = 0$.

14.2 Simple Harmonic Motion

The simplest kind of oscillation occurs when the restoring force F_x is *directly proportional* to the displacement from equilibrium x. This happens if the spring in Figs. 14.1 and 14.2 is an ideal one that obeys Hooke's law. The constant of proportionality between F_x and x is the force constant k. (You may want to review Hooke's law and the definition of the force constant in Section 6.3.) On either side of the equilibrium position, F_x and x always have opposite signs. In Section 6.3 we represented the force acting *on* a stretched ideal spring as $F_x = kx$. The x-component of force the spring exerts *on the body* is the negative of this, so the x-component of force F_x on the body is

$$F_x = -kx \quad \text{(restoring force exerted by an ideal spring)} \qquad (14.3)$$

This equation gives the correct magnitude and sign of the force, whether x is positive, negative, or zero (Fig. 14.3). The force constant k is always positive and has units of N/m (a useful alternative set of units is kg/s^2). We are assuming that there is no friction, so Eq. (14.3) gives the *net* force on the body.

When the restoring force is directly proportional to the displacement from equilibrium, as given by Eq. (14.3), the oscillation is called **simple harmonic motion,** *abbreviated* **SHM.** The acceleration $a_x = d^2x/dt^2 = F_x/m$ of a body in SHM is given by

$$a_x = \frac{d^2x}{dt^2} = -\frac{k}{m}x \quad \text{(simple harmonic motion)} \qquad (14.4)$$

The minus sign means the acceleration and displacement always have opposite signs. This acceleration is *not* constant, so don't even think of using the constant-acceleration equations from Chapter 2. We'll see shortly how to solve this equation to find the displacement x as a function of time. A body that undergoes simple harmonic motion is called a **harmonic oscillator.**

14.3 An idealized spring exerts a restoring force that obeys Hooke's law, $F_x = -kx$. Oscillation with such a restoring force is called simple harmonic motion.

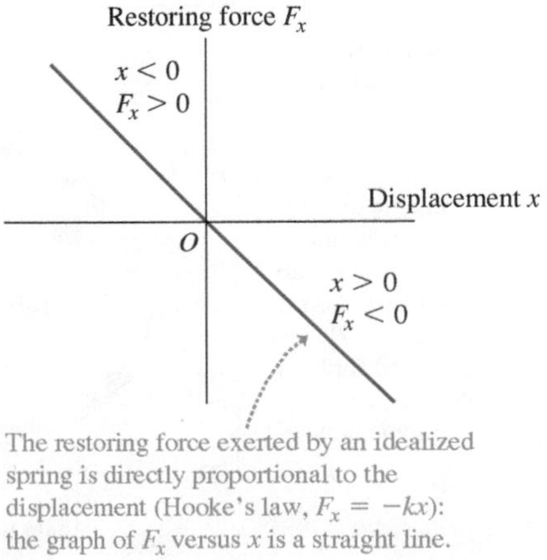

14.4 In most real oscillations Hooke's law applies provided the body doesn't move too far from equilibrium. In such a case small-amplitude oscillations are approximately simple harmonic.

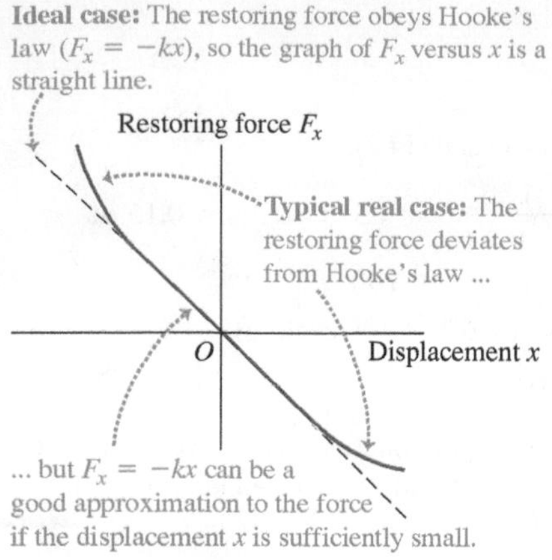

Why is simple harmonic motion important? Keep in mind that not all periodic motions are simple harmonic; in periodic motion in general, the restoring force depends on displacement in a more complicated way than in Eq. (14.3). But in many systems the restoring force is *approximately* proportional to displacement if the displacement is sufficiently small (Fig. 14.4). That is, if the amplitude is small enough, the oscillations of such systems are approximately simple harmonic and therefore approximately described by Eq. (14.4). Thus we can use SHM as an approximate model for many different periodic motions, such as the vibration of the quartz crystal in a watch, the motion of a tuning fork, the electric current in an alternating-current circuit, and the oscillations of atoms in molecules and solids.

Circular Motion and the Equations of SHM

To explore the properties of simple harmonic motion, we must express the displacement x of the oscillating body as a function of time, $x(t)$. The second derivative of this function, d^2x/dt^2, must be equal to $(-k/m)$ times the function itself, as required by Eq. (14.4). As we mentioned, the formulas for constant acceleration from Section 2.4 are no help because the acceleration changes constantly as the displacement x changes. Instead, we'll find $x(t)$ by noticing a striking similarity between SHM and another form of motion that we've already studied.

Figure 14.5a shows a top view of a horizontal disk of radius A with a ball attached to its rim at point Q. The disk rotates with constant angular speed ω (measured in rad/s), so the ball moves in uniform circular motion. A horizontal light beam shines on the rotating disk and casts a shadow of the ball on a screen. The shadow at point P oscillates back and forth as the ball moves in a circle. We then arrange a body attached to an ideal spring, like the combination shown in Figs. 14.1 and 14.2, so that the body oscillates parallel to the shadow. We will prove that the motion of the body and the motion of the ball's shadow are *identical* if the amplitude of the body's oscillation is equal to the disk radius A, and if the angular frequency $2\pi f$ of the oscillating body is equal to the angular speed ω of the rotating disk. That is, *simple harmonic motion is the projection of uniform circular motion onto a diameter.*

We can verify this remarkable statement by finding the acceleration of the shadow at P and comparing it to the acceleration of a body undergoing SHM, given by Eq. (14.4). The circle in which the ball moves so that its projection matches the motion of the oscillating body is called the **reference circle;** we will call the point Q the *reference point.* We take the reference circle to lie in the

14.5 (a) Relating uniform circular motion and simple harmonic motion. (b) The ball's shadow moves exactly like a body oscillating on an ideal spring.

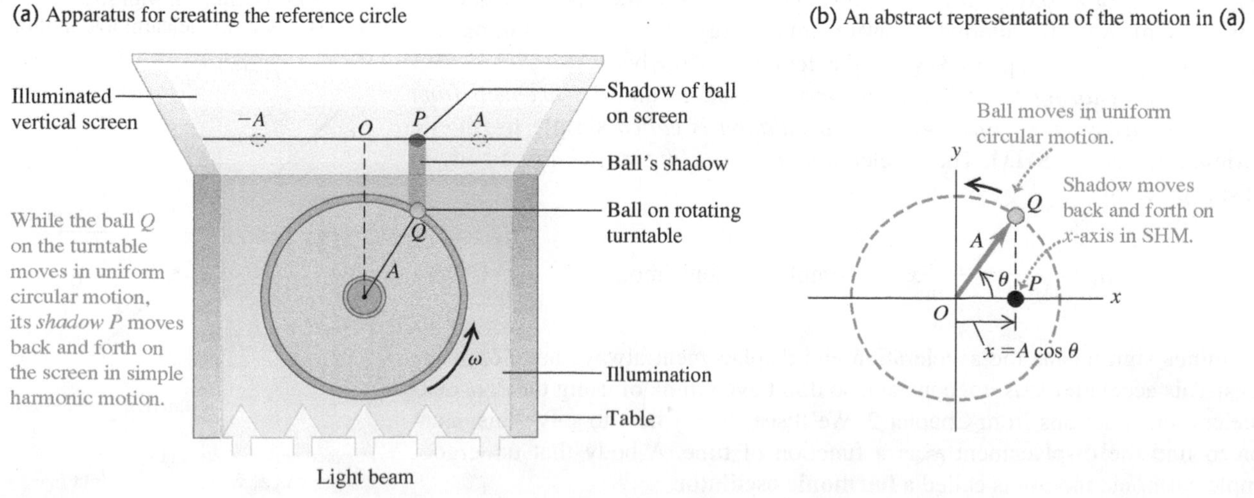

xy-plane, with the origin O at the center of the circle (Fig. 14.5b). At time t the vector OQ from the origin to the reference point Q makes an angle θ with the positive x-axis. As the point Q moves around the reference circle with constant angular speed ω, the vector OQ rotates with the same angular speed. Such a rotating vector is called a **phasor.** (This term was in use long before the invention of the Star Trek stun gun with a similar name. The phasor method for analyzing oscillations is useful in many areas of physics. We'll use phasors when we study alternating-current circuits in Chapter 31 and the interference of light in Chapters 35 and 36.)

The x-component of the phasor at time t is just the x-coordinate of the point Q:

$$x = A\cos\theta \tag{14.5}$$

This is also the x-coordinate of the shadow P, which is the *projection* of Q onto the x-axis. Hence the x-velocity of the shadow P along the x-axis is equal to the x-component of the velocity vector of point Q (Fig. 14.6a), and the x-acceleration of P is equal to the x-component of the acceleration vector of Q (Fig. 14.6b). Since point Q is in uniform circular motion, its acceleration vector $\vec{a}_Q$ is always directed toward O. Furthermore, the magnitude of $\vec{a}_Q$ is constant and given by the angular speed squared times the radius of the circle (see Section 9.3):

$$a_Q = \omega^2 A \tag{14.6}$$

Figure 14.6b shows that the x-component of $\vec{a}_Q$ is $a_x = -a_Q\cos\theta$. Combining this with Eqs. (14.5) and (14.6), we get that the acceleration of point P is

$$a_x = -a_Q\cos\theta = -\omega^2 A\cos\theta \quad \text{or} \tag{14.7}$$

$$a_x = -\omega^2 x \tag{14.8}$$

The acceleration of point P is directly proportional to the displacement x and always has the opposite sign. These are precisely the hallmarks of simple harmonic motion.

Equation (14.8) is *exactly* the same as Eq. (14.4) for the acceleration of a harmonic oscillator, provided that the angular speed ω of the reference point Q is related to the force constant k and mass m of the oscillating body by

$$\omega^2 = \frac{k}{m} \quad \text{or} \quad \omega = \sqrt{\frac{k}{m}} \tag{14.9}$$

We have been using the same symbol ω for the angular *speed* of the reference point Q and the angular *frequency* of the oscillating point P. The reason is that these quantities are equal! If point Q makes one complete revolution in time T, then point P goes through one complete cycle of oscillation in the same time; hence T is the period of the oscillation. During time T the point Q moves through 2π radians, so its angular speed is $\omega = 2\pi/T$. But this is just the same as Eq. (14.2) for the angular frequency of the point P, which verifies our statement about the two interpretations of ω. This is why we introduced angular frequency in Section 14.1; this quantity makes the connection between oscillation and circular motion. So we reinterpret Eq. (14.9) as an expression for the angular frequency of simple harmonic motion for a body of mass m, acted on by a restoring force with force constant k:

$$\omega = \sqrt{\frac{k}{m}} \quad \text{(simple harmonic motion)} \tag{14.10}$$

When you start a body oscillating in SHM, the value of ω is not yours to choose; it is predetermined by the values of k and m. The units of k are N/m or kg/s^2, so k/m is in (kg/s^2)/kg $= \text{s}^{-2}$. When we take the square root in Eq. (14.10), we get s^{-1}, or more properly rad/s because this is an *angular* frequency (recall that a radian is not a true unit).

14.6 The (a) x-velocity and (b) x-acceleration of the ball's shadow P (see Fig. 14.5) are the x-components of the velocity and acceleration vectors, respectively, of the ball Q.

(a) Using the reference circle to determine the x-velocity of point P

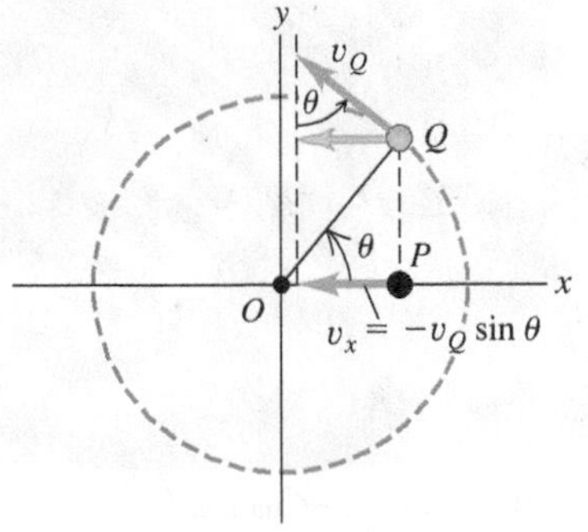

(b) Using the reference circle to determine the x-acceleration of point P

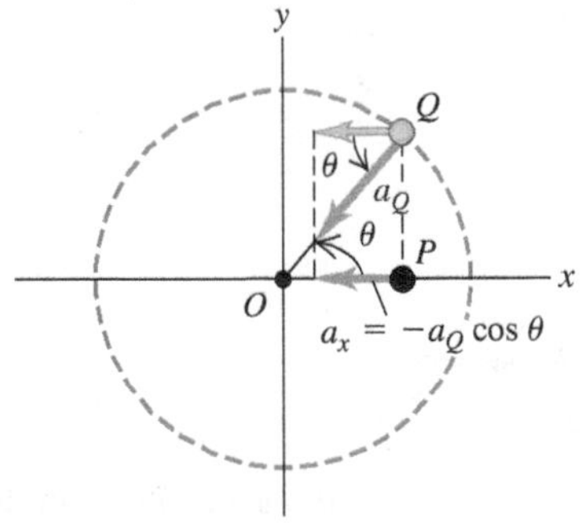

According to Eqs. (14.1) and (14.2), the frequency f and period T are

$$f = \frac{\omega}{2\pi} = \frac{1}{2\pi}\sqrt{\frac{k}{m}} \quad \text{(simple harmonic motion)} \tag{14.11}$$

$$T = \frac{1}{f} = \frac{2\pi}{\omega} = 2\pi\sqrt{\frac{m}{k}} \quad \text{(simple harmonic motion)} \tag{14.12}$$

14.7 The greater the mass m in a tuning fork's tines, the lower the frequency of oscillation $f = (1/2\pi)\sqrt{k/m}$ and the lower the pitch of the sound that the tuning fork produces.

Tines with large mass m: low frequency f = 128 Hz

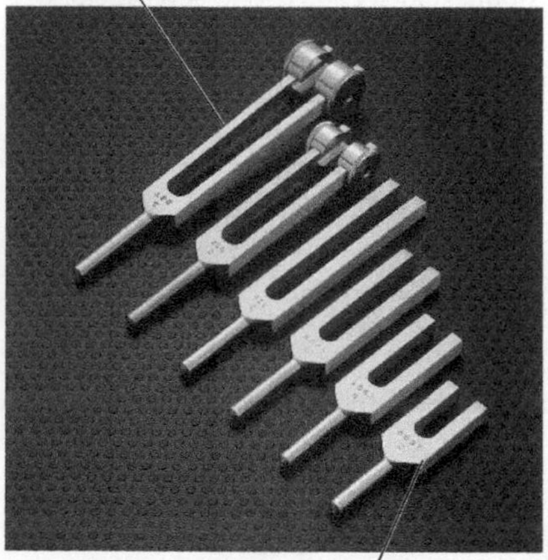

Tines with small mass m: high frequency f = 4096 Hz

We see from Eq. (14.12) that a larger mass m, with its greater inertia, will have less acceleration, move more slowly, and take a longer time for a complete cycle (Fig. 14.7). In contrast, a stiffer spring (one with a larger force constant k) exerts a greater force at a given deformation x, causing greater acceleration, higher speeds, and a shorter time T per cycle.

CAUTION **Don't confuse frequency and angular frequency** You can run into trouble if you don't make the distinction between frequency f and angular frequency $\omega = 2\pi f$. Frequency tells you how many cycles of oscillation occur per second, while angular frequency tells you how many radians per second this corresponds to on the reference circle. In solving problems, pay careful attention to whether the goal is to find f or ω.

Period and Amplitude in SHM

Equations (14.11) and (14.12) show that the period and frequency of simple harmonic motion are completely determined by the mass m and the force constant k. *In simple harmonic motion the period and frequency do not depend on the amplitude A.* For given values of m and k, the time of one complete oscillation is the same whether the amplitude is large or small. Equation (14.3) shows why we should expect this. Larger A means that the body reaches larger values of $|x|$ and is subjected to larger restoring forces. This increases the average speed of the body over a complete cycle; this exactly compensates for having to travel a larger distance, so the same total time is involved.

The oscillations of a tuning fork are essentially simple harmonic motion, which means that it always vibrates with the same frequency, independent of amplitude. This is why a tuning fork can be used as a standard for musical pitch. If it were not for this characteristic of simple harmonic motion, it would be impossible to make familiar types of mechanical and electronic clocks run accurately or to play most musical instruments in tune. If you encounter an oscillating body with a period that *does* depend on the amplitude, the oscillation is *not* simple harmonic motion.

Example 14.2 Angular frequency, frequency, and period in SHM

A spring is mounted horizontally, with its left end fixed. A spring balance attached to the free end and pulled toward the right (Fig. 14.8a) indicates that the stretching force is proportional to the displacement, and a force of 6.0 N causes a displacement of 0.030 m. We replace the spring balance with a 0.50-kg glider, pull it 0.020 m to the right along a frictionless air track, and release it from rest (Fig. 14.8b). (a) Find the force constant k of the spring. (b) Find the angular frequency ω, frequency f, and period T of the resulting oscillation.

14.8 (a) The force exerted *on* the spring (shown by the vector $\vec{F}$) has x-component $F_x = +6.0$ N. The force exerted *by* the spring has x-component $F_x = -6.0$ N. (b) A glider is attached to the same spring and allowed to oscillate.

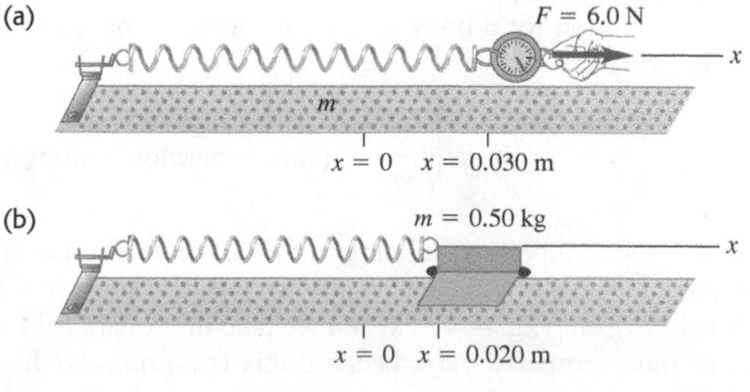

SOLUTION

IDENTIFY and SET UP: Because the spring force (equal in magnitude to the stretching force) is proportional to the displacement, the motion is simple harmonic. We find k using Hooke's law, Eq. (14.3), and ω, f, and T using Eqs. (14.10), (14.11), and (14.12), respectively.

EXECUTE: (a) When $x = 0.030$ m, the force the spring exerts on the spring balance is $F_x = -6.0$ N. From Eq. (14.3),

$$k = -\frac{F_x}{x} = -\frac{-6.0\ \text{N}}{0.030\ \text{m}} = 200\ \text{N/m} = 200\ \text{kg/s}^2$$

(b) From Eq. (14.10), with $m = 0.50$ kg,

$$\omega = \sqrt{\frac{k}{m}} = \sqrt{\frac{200\ \text{kg/s}^2}{0.50\ \text{kg}}} = 20\ \text{rad/s}$$

$$f = \frac{\omega}{2\pi} = \frac{20\ \text{rad/s}}{2\pi\ \text{rad/cycle}} = 3.2\ \text{cycle/s} = 3.2\ \text{Hz}$$

$$T = \frac{1}{f} = \frac{1}{3.2\ \text{cycle/s}} = 0.31\ \text{s}$$

EVALUATE: The amplitude of the oscillation is 0.020 m, the distance that we pulled the glider before releasing it. In SHM the angular frequency, frequency, and period are all independent of the amplitude. Note that a period is usually stated in "seconds" rather than "seconds per cycle."

Displacement, Velocity, and Acceleration in SHM

We still need to find the displacement x as a function of time for a harmonic oscillator. Equation (14.4) for a body in simple harmonic motion along the x-axis is identical to Eq. (14.8) for the x-coordinate of the reference point in uniform circular motion with constant angular speed $\omega = \sqrt{k/m}$. Hence Eq. (14.5), $x = A\cos\theta$, describes the x-coordinate for both of these situations. If at $t = 0$ the phasor OQ makes an angle ϕ (the Greek letter phi) with the positive x-axis, then at any later time t this angle is $\theta = \omega t + \phi$. We substitute this into Eq. (14.5) to obtain

$$x = A\cos(\omega t + \phi) \qquad \text{(displacement in SHM)} \qquad (14.13)$$

where $\omega = \sqrt{k/m}$. Figure 14.9 shows a graph of Eq. (14.13) for the particular case $\phi = 0$. The displacement x is a periodic function of time, as expected for SHM. We could also have written Eq. (14.13) in terms of a sine function rather than a cosine by using the identity $\cos\alpha = \sin(\alpha + \pi/2)$. *In simple harmonic motion the position is a periodic, sinusoidal function of time.* There are many other periodic functions, but none so simple as a sine or cosine function.

The value of the cosine function is always between -1 and 1, so in Eq. (14.13), x is always between $-A$ and A. This confirms that A is the amplitude of the motion.

The period T is the time for one complete cycle of oscillation, as Fig. 14.9 shows. The cosine function repeats itself whenever the quantity in parentheses in Eq. (14.13) increases by 2π radians. Thus, if we start at time $t = 0$, the time T to complete one cycle is given by

$$\omega T = \sqrt{\frac{k}{m}}T = 2\pi \qquad \text{or} \qquad T = 2\pi\sqrt{\frac{m}{k}}$$

which is just Eq. (14.12). Changing either m or k changes the period of oscillation, as shown in Figs. 14.10a and 14.10b. The period does not depend on the amplitude A (Fig. 14.10c).

MasteringPHYSICS

PhET: Motion in 2D
ActivPhysics 9.1: Position Graphs and Equations
ActivPhysics 9.2: Describing Vibrational Motion
ActivPhysics 9.5: Age Drops Tarzan

14.9 Graph of x versus t [see Eq. (14.13)] for simple harmonic motion. The case shown has $\phi = 0$.

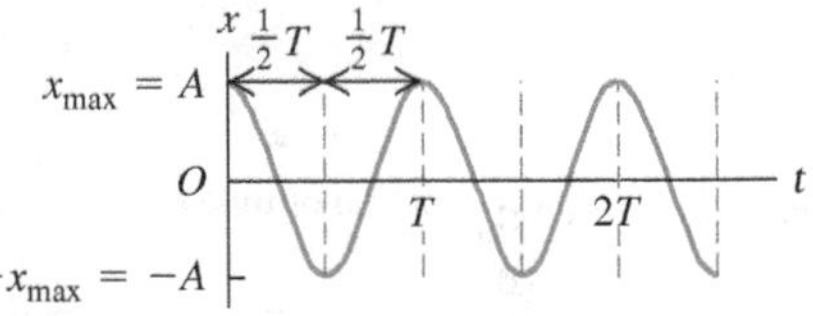

14.10 Variations of simple harmonic motion. All cases shown have $\phi = 0$ [see Eq. (14.13)].

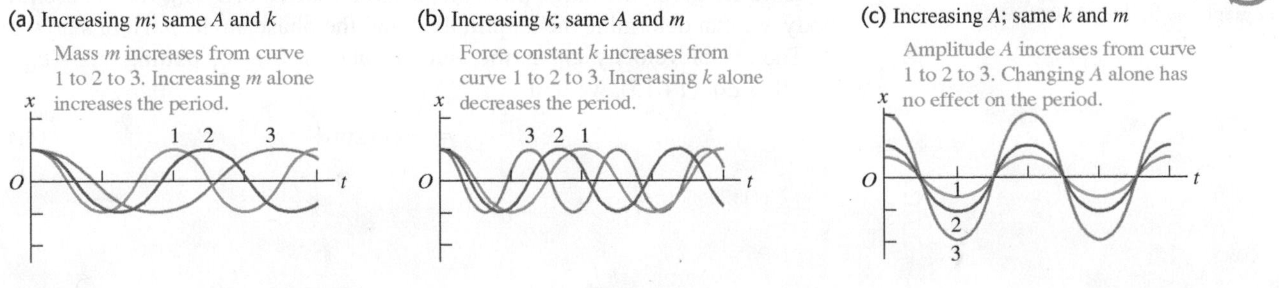

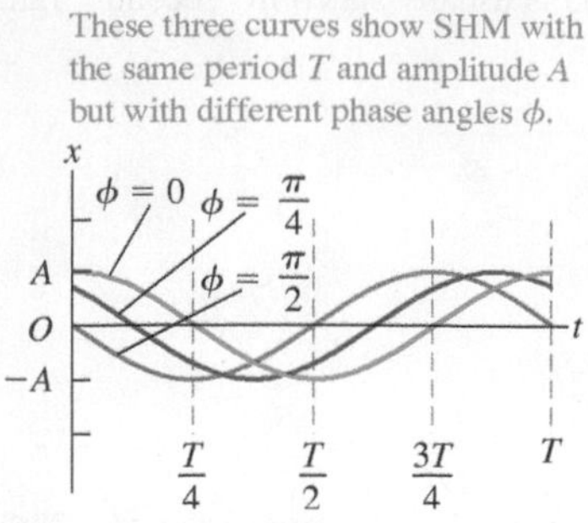

14.11 Variations of SHM: displacement versus time for the same harmonic oscillator with different phase angles ϕ.

The constant ϕ in Eq. (14.13) is called the **phase angle.** It tells us at what point in the cycle the motion was at $t = 0$ (equivalent to where around the circle the point Q was at $t = 0$). We denote the position at $t = 0$ by x_0. Putting $t = 0$ and $x = x_0$ in Eq. (14.13), we get

$$x_0 = A\cos\phi \tag{14.14}$$

If $\phi = 0$, then $x_0 = A\cos 0 = A$, and the body starts at its maximum positive displacement. If $\phi = \pi$, then $x_0 = A\cos\pi = -A$, and the particle starts at its maximum *negative* displacement. If $\phi = \pi/2$, then $x_0 = A\cos(\pi/2) = 0$, and the particle is initially at the origin. Figure 14.11 shows the displacement x versus time for three different phase angles.

We find the velocity v_x and acceleration a_x as functions of time for a harmonic oscillator by taking derivatives of Eq. (14.13) with respect to time:

$$v_x = \frac{dx}{dt} = -\omega A\sin(\omega t + \phi) \qquad \text{(velocity in SHM)} \tag{14.15}$$

$$a_x = \frac{dv_x}{dt} = \frac{d^2x}{dt^2} = -\omega^2 A\cos(\omega t + \phi) \qquad \text{(acceleration in SHM)} \tag{14.16}$$

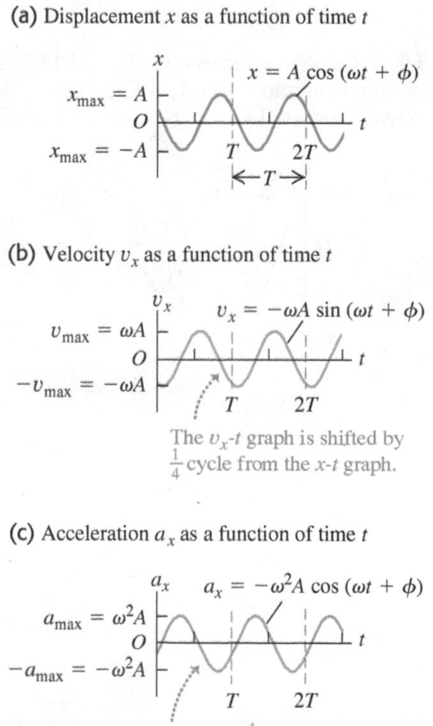

14.12 Graphs of (a) x versus t, (b) v_x versus t, and (c) a_x versus t for a body in SHM. For the motion depicted in these graphs, $\phi = \pi/3$.

The velocity v_x oscillates between $v_{max} = +\omega A$ and $-v_{max} = -\omega A$, and the acceleration a_x oscillates between $a_{max} = +\omega^2 A$ and $-a_{max} = -\omega^2 A$ (Fig. 14.12). Comparing Eq. (14.16) with Eq. (14.13) and recalling that $\omega^2 = k/m$ from Eq. (14.9), we see that

$$a_x = -\omega^2 x = -\frac{k}{m}x$$

which is just Eq. (14.4) for simple harmonic motion. This confirms that Eq. (14.13) for x as a function of time is correct.

We actually derived Eq. (14.16) earlier in a geometrical way by taking the x-component of the acceleration vector of the reference point Q. This was done in Fig. 14.6b and Eq. (14.7) (recall that $\theta = \omega t + \phi$). In the same way, we could have derived Eq. (14.15) by taking the x-component of the velocity vector of Q, as shown in Fig. 14.6b. We'll leave the details for you to work out.

Note that the sinusoidal graph of displacement versus time (Fig. 14.12a) is shifted by one-quarter period from the graph of velocity versus time (Fig. 14.12b) and by one-half period from the graph of acceleration versus time (Fig. 14.12c). Figure 14.13 shows why this is so. When the body is passing through the equilibrium position so that the displacement is zero, the velocity equals either v_{max} or $-v_{max}$ (depending on which way the body is moving) and the acceleration is zero. When the body is at either its maximum positive displacement, $x = +A$, or its maximum negative displacement, $x = -A$, the velocity is zero and the body is instantaneously at rest. At these points, the restoring force $F_x = -kx$ and the acceleration of the body have their maximum magnitudes. At $x = +A$ the acceleration is negative and equal to $-a_{max}$. At $x = -A$ the acceleration is positive: $a_x = +a_{max}$.

If we are given the initial position x_0 and initial velocity v_{0x} for the oscillating body, we can determine the amplitude A and the phase angle ϕ. Here's how to do it. The initial velocity v_{0x} is the velocity at time $t = 0$; putting $v_x = v_{0x}$ and $t = 0$ in Eq. (14.15), we find

$$v_{0x} = -\omega A\sin\phi \tag{14.17}$$

To find ϕ, we divide Eq. (14.17) by Eq. (14.14). This eliminates A and gives an equation that we can solve for ϕ:

$$\frac{v_{0x}}{x_0} = \frac{-\omega A \sin\phi}{A\cos\phi} = -\omega \tan\phi$$

$$\phi = \arctan\left(-\frac{v_{0x}}{\omega x_0}\right) \quad \text{(phase angle in SHM)} \qquad (14.18)$$

It is also easy to find the amplitude A if we are given x_0 and v_{0x}. We'll sketch the derivation, and you can fill in the details. Square Eq. (14.14); then divide Eq. (14.17) by ω, square it, and add to the square of Eq. (14.14). The right side will be $A^2(\sin^2\phi + \cos^2\phi)$, which is equal to A^2. The final result is

$$A = \sqrt{x_0^2 + \frac{v_{0x}^2}{\omega^2}} \quad \text{(amplitude in SHM)} \qquad (14.19)$$

Note that when the body has both an initial displacement x_0 and a nonzero initial velocity v_{0x}, the amplitude A is *not* equal to the initial displacement. That's reasonable; if you start the body at a positive x_0 but give it a positive velocity v_{0x}, it will go *farther* than x_0 before it turns and comes back.

14.13 How x-velocity v_x and x-acceleration a_x vary during one cycle of SHM.

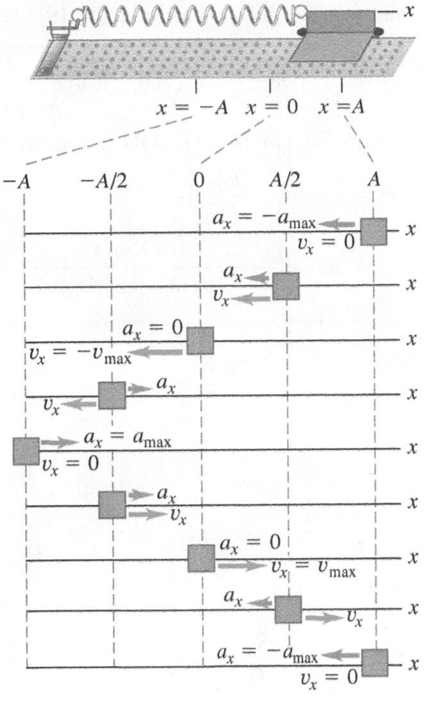

Problem-Solving Strategy 14.1 Simple Harmonic Motion I: Describing Motion

IDENTIFY *the relevant concepts:* An oscillating system undergoes simple harmonic motion (SHM) *only* if the restoring force is directly proportional to the displacement.

SET UP *the problem* using the following steps:

1. Identify the known and unknown quantities, and determine which are the target variables.
2. Distinguish between two kinds of quantities. *Properties of the system* include the mass m, the force constant k, and quantities derived from m and k, such as the period T, frequency f, and angular frequency ω. These are independent of *properties of the motion,* which describe how the system behaves when it is set into motion in a particular way; they include the amplitude A, maximum velocity v_{max}, and phase angle ϕ, and values of x, v_x, and a_x at particular times.
3. If necessary, define an x-axis as in Fig. 14.13, with the equilibrium position at $x = 0$.

EXECUTE *the solution* as follows:

1. Use the equations given in Sections 14.1 and 14.2 to solve for the target variables.
2. To find the values of x, v_x, and a_x at particular times, use Eqs. (14.13), (14.15), and (14.16), respectively. If the initial position x_0 and initial velocity v_{0x} are both given, determine ϕ and A from Eqs. (14.18) and (14.19). If the body has an initial positive displacement x_0 but zero initial velocity ($v_{0x} = 0$), then the amplitude is $A = x_0$ and the phase angle is $\phi = 0$. If it has an initial positive velocity v_{0x} but no initial displacement ($x_0 = 0$), the amplitude is $A = v_{0x}/\omega$ and the phase angle is $\phi = -\pi/2$. Express all phase angles in *radians.*

EVALUATE *your answer:* Make sure that your results are consistent. For example, suppose you used x_0 and v_{0x} to find general expressions for x and v_x at time t. If you substitute $t = 0$ into these expressions, you should get back the given values of x_0 and v_{0x}.

Example 14.3 Describing SHM

We give the glider of Example 14.2 an initial displacement $x_0 = +0.015$ m and an initial velocity $v_{0x} = +0.40$ m/s. (a) Find the period, amplitude, and phase angle of the resulting motion. (b) Write equations for the displacement, velocity, and acceleration as functions of time.

SOLUTION

IDENTIFY and SET UP: As in Example 14.2, the oscillations are SHM. We use equations from this section and the given values $k = 200$ N/m, $m = 0.50$ kg, x_0, and v_{0x} to calculate the target variables A and ϕ and to obtain expressions for x, v_x, and a_x.

Continued

EXECUTE: (a) In SHM the period and angular frequency are *properties of the system* that depend only on k and m, not on the amplitude, and so are the same as in Example 14.2 ($T = 0.31$ s and $\omega = 20$ rad/s). From Eq. (14.19), the amplitude is

$$A = \sqrt{x_0^2 + \frac{v_{0x}^2}{\omega^2}} = \sqrt{(0.015\text{ m})^2 + \frac{(0.40\text{ m/s})^2}{(20\text{ rad/s})^2}} = 0.025\text{ m}$$

We use Eq. (14.18) to find the phase angle:

$$\phi = \arctan\left(-\frac{v_{0x}}{\omega x_0}\right)$$
$$= \arctan\left(-\frac{0.40\text{ m/s}}{(20\text{ rad/s})(0.015\text{ m})}\right) = -53° = -0.93\text{ rad}$$

(b) The displacement, velocity, and acceleration at any time are given by Eqs. (14.13), (14.15), and (14.16), respectively. We substitute the values of A, ω, and ϕ into these equations:

$$x = (0.025\text{ m})\cos[(20\text{ rad/s})t - 0.93\text{ rad}]$$
$$v_x = -(0.50\text{ m/s})\sin[(20\text{ rad/s})t - 0.93\text{ rad}]$$
$$a_x = -(10\text{ m/s}^2)\cos[(20\text{ rad/s})t - 0.93\text{ rad}]$$

EVALUATE: You can check the expressions for x and v_x by confirming that if you substitute $t = 0$, they yield $x = x_0 = 0.015$ m and $v_x = v_{0x} = 0.40$ m/s.

Test Your Understanding of Section 14.2 A glider is attached to a spring as shown in Fig. 14.13. If the glider is moved to $x = 0.10$ m and released from rest at time $t = 0$, it will oscillate with amplitude $A = 0.10$ m and phase angle $\phi = 0$. (a) Suppose instead that at $t = 0$ the glider is at $x = 0.10$ m and is moving to the right in Fig. 14.13. In this situation is the amplitude greater than, less than, or equal to 0.10 m? Is the phase angle greater than, less than, or equal to zero? (b) Suppose instead that at $t = 0$ the glider is at $x = 0.10$ m and is moving to the left in Fig. 14.13. In this situation is the amplitude greater than, less than, or equal to 0.10 m? Is the phase angle greater than, less than, or equal to zero?

MasteringPHYSICS

PhET: Masses & Springs
ActivPhysics 9.3: Vibrational Energy
ActivPhysics 9.4: Two Ways to Weigh Young Tarzan
ActivPhysics 9.6: Releasing a Vibrating Skier I
ActivPhysics 9.7: Releasing a Vibrating Skier II
ActivPhysics 9.8: One- and Two-Spring Vibrating Systems
ActivPhysics 9.9: Vibro-Ride

14.3 Energy in Simple Harmonic Motion

We can learn even more about simple harmonic motion by using energy considerations. Take another look at the body oscillating on the end of a spring in Figs. 14.2 and 14.13. We've already noted that the spring force is the only horizontal force on the body. The force exerted by an ideal spring is a conservative force, and the vertical forces do no work, so the total mechanical energy of the system is *conserved.* We also assume that the mass of the spring itself is negligible.

The kinetic energy of the body is $K = \frac{1}{2}mv^2$ and the potential energy of the spring is $U = \frac{1}{2}kx^2$, just as in Section 7.2. (You'll find it helpful to review that section.) There are no nonconservative forces that do work, so the total mechanical energy $E = K + U$ is conserved:

$$E = \tfrac{1}{2}mv_x^2 + \tfrac{1}{2}kx^2 = \text{constant} \qquad (14.20)$$

(Since the motion is one-dimensional, $v^2 = v_x^2$.)

The total mechanical energy E is also directly related to the amplitude A of the motion. When the body reaches the point $x = A$, its maximum displacement from equilibrium, it momentarily stops as it turns back toward the equilibrium position. That is, when $x = A$ (or $-A$), $v_x = 0$. At this point the energy is entirely potential, and $E = \frac{1}{2}kA^2$. Because E is constant, it is equal to $\frac{1}{2}kA^2$ at any other point. Combining this expression with Eq. (14.20), we get

$$E = \tfrac{1}{2}mv_x^2 + \tfrac{1}{2}kx^2 = \tfrac{1}{2}kA^2 = \text{constant} \quad \text{(total mechanical energy in SHM)} \qquad (14.21)$$

We can verify this equation by substituting x and v_x from Eqs. (14.13) and (14.15) and using $\omega^2 = k/m$ from Eq. (14.9):

$$E = \tfrac{1}{2}mv_x^2 + \tfrac{1}{2}kx^2 = \tfrac{1}{2}m[-\omega A\sin(\omega t + \phi)]^2 + \tfrac{1}{2}k[A\cos(\omega t + \phi)]^2$$
$$= \tfrac{1}{2}kA^2\sin^2(\omega t + \phi) + \tfrac{1}{2}kA^2\cos^2(\omega t + \phi)$$
$$= \tfrac{1}{2}kA^2$$

14.14 Graphs of E, K, and U versus displacement in SHM. The velocity of the body is *not* constant, so these images of the body at equally spaced positions are *not* equally spaced in time.

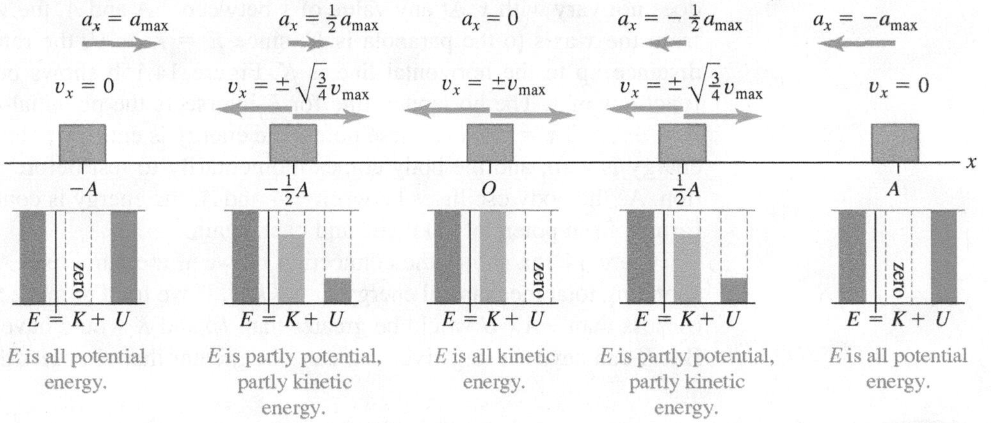

(Recall that $\sin^2\alpha + \cos^2\alpha = 1$.) Hence our expressions for displacement and velocity in SHM are consistent with energy conservation, as they must be.

We can use Eq. (14.21) to solve for the velocity v_x of the body at a given displacement x:

$$v_x = \pm\sqrt{\frac{k}{m}}\sqrt{A^2 - x^2} \tag{14.22}$$

The $\pm$ sign means that at a given value of x the body can be moving in either direction. For example, when $x = \pm A/2$,

$$v_x = \pm\sqrt{\frac{k}{m}}\sqrt{A^2 - \left(\pm\frac{A}{2}\right)^2} = \pm\sqrt{\frac{3}{4}}\sqrt{\frac{k}{m}}A$$

Equation (14.22) also shows that the *maximum* speed v_{max} occurs at $x = 0$. Using Eq. (14.10), $\omega = \sqrt{k/m}$, we find that

$$v_{max} = \sqrt{\frac{k}{m}}A = \omega A \tag{14.23}$$

This agrees with Eq. (14.15): v_x oscillates between $-\omega A$ and $+\omega A$.

Interpreting E, K, and U in SHM

Figure 14.14 shows the energy quantities E, K, and U at $x = 0$, $x = \pm A/2$, and $x = \pm A$. Figure 14.15 is a graphical display of Eq. (14.21); energy (kinetic, potential, and total) is plotted vertically and the coordinate x is plotted horizontally.

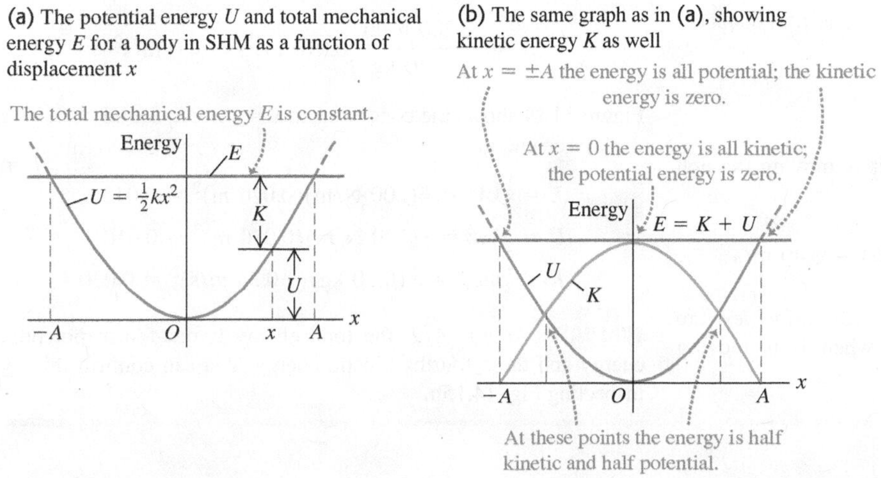

14.15 Kinetic energy K, potential energy U, and total mechanical energy E as functions of position for SHM. At each value of x the sum of the values of K and U equals the constant value of E. Can you show that the energy is half kinetic and half potential at $x = \pm\sqrt{\frac{1}{2}}A$?

The parabolic curve in Fig. 14.15a represents the potential energy $U = \frac{1}{2}kx^2$. The horizontal line represents the total mechanical energy E, which is constant and does not vary with x. At any value of x between $-A$ and A, the vertical distance from the x-axis to the parabola is U; since $E = K + U$, the remaining vertical distance up to the horizontal line is K. Figure 14.15b shows both K and U as functions of x. The horizontal line for E intersects the potential-energy curve at $x = -A$ and $x = A$, so at these points the energy is entirely potential, the kinetic energy is zero, and the body comes momentarily to rest before reversing direction. As the body oscillates between $-A$ and A, the energy is continuously transformed from potential to kinetic and back again.

Figure 14.15a shows the connection between the amplitude A and the corresponding total mechanical energy $E = \frac{1}{2}kA^2$. If we tried to make x greater than A (or less than $-A$), U would be greater than E, and K would have to be negative. But K can never be negative, so x can't be greater than A or less than $-A$.

Problem-Solving Strategy 14.2 Simple Harmonic Motion II: Energy

The SHM energy equation, Eq. (14.21), is a useful relationship among velocity, position, and total mechanical energy. If the problem requires you to relate position, velocity, and acceleration without reference to time, consider using Eq. (14.4) (from Newton's second law) or Eq. (14.21) (from energy conservation). Because Eq. (14.21) involves x^2 and v_x^2, you must infer the *signs* of x and v_x from the situation. For instance, if the body is moving from the equilibrium position toward the point of greatest positive displacement, then x is positive and v_x is positive.

Example 14.4 Velocity, acceleration, and energy in SHM

(a) Find the maximum and minimum velocities attained by the oscillating glider of Example 14.2. (b) Find the maximum and minimum accelerations. (c) Find the velocity v_x and acceleration a_x when the glider is halfway from its initial position to the equilibrium position $x = 0$. (d) Find the total energy, potential energy, and kinetic energy at this position.

SOLUTION

IDENTIFY and SET UP: The problem concerns properties of the motion at specified *positions,* not at specified *times,* so we can use the energy relationships of this section. Figure 14.13 shows our choice of x-axis. The maximum displacement from equilibrium is $A = 0.020$ m. We use Eqs. (14.22) and (14.4) to find v_x and a_x for a given x. We then use Eq. (14.21) for given x and v_x to find the total, potential, and kinetic energies E, U, and K.

EXECUTE: (a) From Eq. (14.22), the velocity v_x at any displacement x is

$$v_x = \pm\sqrt{\frac{k}{m}}\sqrt{A^2 - x^2}$$

The glider's maximum *speed* occurs when it is moving through $x = 0$:

$$v_{max} = \sqrt{\frac{k}{m}}A = \sqrt{\frac{200\ \text{N/m}}{0.50\ \text{kg}}}(0.020\ \text{m}) = 0.40\ \text{m/s}$$

Its maximum and minimum (most negative) *velocities* are $+0.40$ m/s and -0.40 m/s, which occur when it is moving through $x = 0$ to the right and left, respectively.

(b) From Eq. (14.4), $a_x = -(k/m)x$. The glider's maximum (most positive) acceleration occurs at the most negative value of x, $x = -A$:

$$a_{max} = -\frac{k}{m}(-A) = -\frac{200\ \text{N/m}}{0.50\ \text{kg}}(-0.020\ \text{m}) = 8.0\ \text{m/s}^2$$

The minimum (most negative) acceleration is $a_{min} = -8.0\ \text{m/s}^2$, which occurs at $x = +A = +0.020$ m.

(c) The point halfway from $x = x_0 = A$ to $x = 0$ is $x = A/2 = 0.010$ m. From Eq. (14.22), at this point

$$v_x = -\sqrt{\frac{200\ \text{N/m}}{0.50\ \text{kg}}}\sqrt{(0.020\ \text{m})^2 - (0.010\ \text{m})^2} = -0.35\ \text{m/s}$$

We choose the negative square root because the glider is moving from $x = A$ toward $x = 0$. From Eq. (14.4),

$$a_x = -\frac{200\ \text{N/m}}{0.50\ \text{kg}}(0.010\ \text{m}) = -4.0\ \text{m/s}^2$$

Figure 14.14 shows the conditions at $x = 0$, $\pm A/2$, and $\pm A$.

(d) The energies are

$$E = \tfrac{1}{2}kA^2 = \tfrac{1}{2}(200\ \text{N/m})(0.020\ \text{m})^2 = 0.040\ \text{J}$$
$$U = \tfrac{1}{2}kx^2 = \tfrac{1}{2}(200\ \text{N/m})(0.010\ \text{m})^2 = 0.010\ \text{J}$$
$$K = \tfrac{1}{2}mv_x^2 = \tfrac{1}{2}(0.50\ \text{kg})(-0.35\ \text{m/s})^2 = 0.030\ \text{J}$$

EVALUATE: At $x = A/2$, the total energy is one-fourth potential energy and three-fourths kinetic energy. You can confirm this by inspecting Fig. 14.15b.

Example 14.5 Energy and momentum in SHM

A block of mass M attached to a horizontal spring with force constant k is moving in SHM with amplitude A_1. As the block passes through its equilibrium position, a lump of putty of mass m is dropped from a small height and sticks to it. (a) Find the new amplitude and period of the motion. (b) Repeat part (a) if the putty is dropped onto the block when it is at one end of its path.

SOLUTION

IDENTIFY and SET UP: The problem involves the motion at a given position, not a given time, so we can use energy methods. Figure 14.16 shows our sketches. Before the putty falls, the mechanical energy of the block–spring system is constant. In part (a), the putty–block collision is completely inelastic: The horizontal component of momentum is conserved, kinetic energy decreases, and the amount of mass that's oscillating increases. After the collision, the mechanical energy remains constant at its new value. In part (b) the oscillating mass also increases, but the block isn't moving when the putty is added; there is effectively no collision at all, and no mechanical energy is lost. We find the amplitude A_2 after each collision from the final energy of the system using Eq. (14.21) and conservation of momentum. The period T_2 after the collision is a *property of the system*, so it is the same in both parts (a) and (b); we find it using Eq. (14.12).

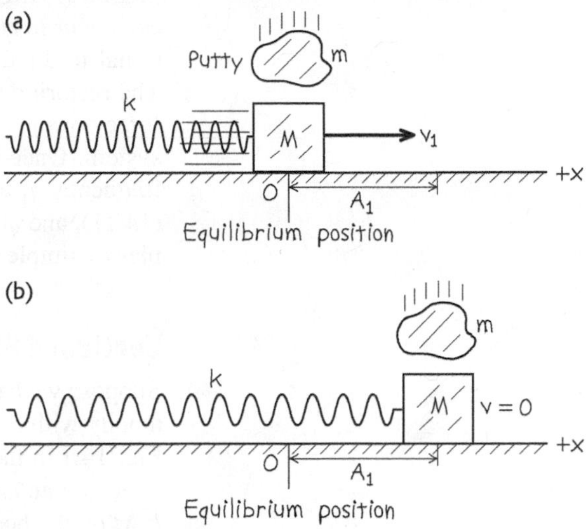

14.16 Our sketches for this problem.

EXECUTE: (a) Before the collision the total mechanical energy of the block and spring is $E_1 = \frac{1}{2}kA_1^2$. The block is at $x = 0$, so $U = 0$ and the energy is purely kinetic (Fig. 14.16a). If we let v_1 be the speed of the block at this point, then $E_1 = \frac{1}{2}kA_1^2 = \frac{1}{2}Mv_1^2$ and

$$v_1 = \sqrt{\frac{k}{M}}A_1$$

During the collision the x-component of momentum of the block–putty system is conserved. (Why?) Just before the collision this component is the sum of Mv_1 (for the block) and zero (for the putty). Just after the collision the block and putty move together with speed v_2, so their combined x-component of momentum is $(M + m)v_2$. From conservation of momentum,

$$Mv_1 + 0 = (M + m)v_2 \qquad \text{so} \qquad v_2 = \frac{M}{M + m}v_1$$

We assume that the collision lasts a very short time, so that the block and putty are still at the equilibrium position just after the collision. The energy is still purely kinetic but is *less* than before the collision:

$$E_2 = \tfrac{1}{2}(M + m)v_2^2 = \tfrac{1}{2}\frac{M^2}{M + m}v_1^2$$
$$= \frac{M}{M + m}\left(\tfrac{1}{2}Mv_1^2\right) = \left(\frac{M}{M + m}\right)E_1$$

Since $E_2 = \frac{1}{2}kA_2^2$, where A_2 is the amplitude after the collision, we have

$$\tfrac{1}{2}kA_2^2 = \left(\frac{M}{M + m}\right)\tfrac{1}{2}kA_1^2$$
$$A_2 = A_1\sqrt{\frac{M}{M + m}}$$

From Eq. (14.12), the period of oscillation after the collision is

$$T_2 = 2\pi\sqrt{\frac{M + m}{k}}$$

(b) When the putty falls, the block is instantaneously at rest (Fig. 14.16b). The x-component of momentum is zero both before and after the collision. The block and putty have zero kinetic energy just before and just after the collision. The energy is all potential energy stored in the spring, so adding the putty has *no effect* on the mechanical energy. That is, $E_2 = E_1 = \frac{1}{2}kA_1^2$, and the amplitude is unchanged: $A_2 = A_1$. The period is again $T_2 = 2\pi\sqrt{(M + m)/k}$.

EVALUATE: Energy is lost in part (a) because the putty slides against the moving block during the collision, and energy is dissipated by kinetic friction. No energy is lost in part (b), because there is no sliding during the collision.

Test Your Understanding of Section 14.3 (a) To double the total energy for a mass-spring system oscillating in SHM, by what factor must the amplitude increase? (i) 4; (ii) 2; (iii) $\sqrt{2} = 1.414$; (iv) $\sqrt[4]{2} = 1.189$. (b) By what factor will the frequency change due to this amplitude increase? (i) 4; (ii) 2; (iii) $\sqrt{2} = 1.414$; (iv) $\sqrt[4]{2} = 1.189$; (v) it does not change.

MP

14.4 Applications of Simple Harmonic Motion

So far, we've looked at a grand total of *one* situation in which simple harmonic motion (SHM) occurs: a body attached to an ideal horizontal spring. But SHM can occur in any system in which there is a restoring force that is directly proportional to the displacement from equilibrium, as given by Eq. (14.3), $F_x = -kx$. The restoring force will originate in different ways in different situations, so the force constant k has to be found for each case by examining the net force on the system. Once this is done, it's straightforward to find the angular frequency ω, frequency f, and period T; we just substitute the value of k into Eqs. (14.10), (14.11), and (14.12), respectively. Let's use these ideas to examine several examples of simple harmonic motion.

Vertical SHM

Suppose we hang a spring with force constant k (Fig. 14.17a) and suspend from it a body with mass m. Oscillations will now be vertical; will they still be SHM? In Fig. 14.17b the body hangs at rest, in equilibrium. In this position the spring is stretched an amount Δl just great enough that the spring's upward vertical force $k\,\Delta l$ on the body balances its weight mg:

$$k\,\Delta l = mg$$

Take $x = 0$ to be this equilibrium position and take the positive x-direction to be upward. When the body is a distance x *above* its equilibrium position (Fig. 14.17c), the extension of the spring is $\Delta l - x$. The upward force it exerts on the body is then $k(\Delta l - x)$, and the net x-component of force on the body is

$$F_{\text{net}} = k(\Delta l - x) + (-mg) = -kx$$

that is, a net downward force of magnitude kx. Similarly, when the body is *below* the equilibrium position, there is a net upward force with magnitude kx. In either case there is a restoring force with magnitude kx. If the body is set in vertical motion, it oscillates in SHM with the same angular frequency as though it were horizontal, $\omega = \sqrt{k/m}$. So vertical SHM doesn't differ in any essential way from horizontal SHM. The only real change is that the equilibrium position $x = 0$ no longer corresponds to the point at which the spring is unstretched. The same ideas hold if a body with weight mg is placed atop a compressible spring (Fig. 14.18) and compresses it a distance Δl.

14.17 A body attached to a hanging spring.

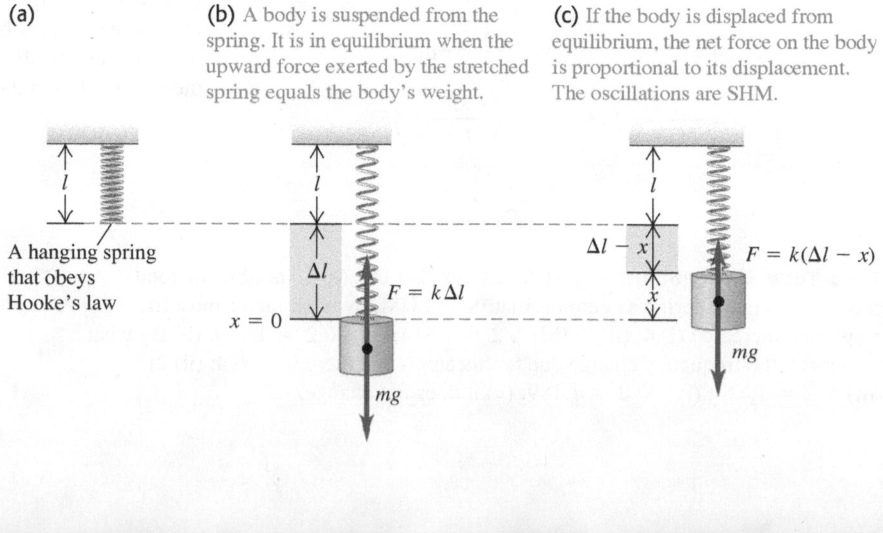

Example 14.6 Vertical SHM in an old car

The shock absorbers in an old car with mass 1000 kg are completely worn out. When a 980-N person climbs slowly into the car at its center of gravity, the car sinks 2.8 cm. The car (with the person aboard) hits a bump, and the car starts oscillating up and down in SHM. Model the car and person as a single body on a single spring, and find the period and frequency of the oscillation.

SOLUTION

IDENTIFY and SET UP: The situation is like that shown in Fig. 14.18. The compression of the spring when the person's weight is added tells us the force constant, which we can use to find the period and frequency (the target variables).

EXECUTE: When the force increases by 980 N, the spring compresses an additional 0.028 m, and the x-coordinate of the car changes by -0.028 m. Hence the effective force constant (including the effect of the entire suspension) is

$$k = -\frac{F_x}{x} = -\frac{980\ \text{N}}{-0.028\ \text{m}} = 3.5 \times 10^4\ \text{kg/s}^2$$

The person's mass is $w/g = (980\ \text{N})/(9.8\ \text{m/s}^2) = 100$ kg. The *total* oscillating mass is $m = 1000\ \text{kg} + 100\ \text{kg} = 1100$ kg. The period T is

$$T = 2\pi\sqrt{\frac{m}{k}} = 2\pi\sqrt{\frac{1100\ \text{kg}}{3.5 \times 10^4\ \text{kg/s}^2}} = 1.11\ \text{s}$$

The frequency is $f = 1/T = 1/(1.11\ \text{s}) = 0.90$ Hz.

EVALUATE: A persistent oscillation with a period of about 1 second makes for a very unpleasant ride. The purpose of shock absorbers is to make such oscillations die out (see Section 14.7).

Angular SHM

A mechanical watch keeps time based on the oscillations of a balance wheel (Fig. 14.19). The wheel has a moment of inertia I about its axis. A coil spring exerts a restoring torque τ_z that is proportional to the angular displacement θ from the equilibrium position. We write $\tau_z = -\kappa\theta$, where κ (the Greek letter kappa) is a constant called the *torsion constant.* Using the rotational analog of Newton's second law for a rigid body, $\Sigma\tau_z = I\alpha_z = I\,d^2\theta/dt^2$, we can find the equation of motion:

$$-\kappa\theta = I\alpha \quad \text{or} \quad \frac{d^2\theta}{dt^2} = -\frac{\kappa}{I}\theta$$

The form of this equation is exactly the same as Eq. (14.4) for the acceleration in simple harmonic motion, with x replaced by θ and k/m replaced by κ/I. So we are dealing with a form of *angular* simple harmonic motion. The angular frequency ω and frequency f are given by Eqs. (14.10) and (14.11), respectively, with the same replacement:

$$\omega = \sqrt{\frac{\kappa}{I}} \quad \text{and} \quad f = \frac{1}{2\pi}\sqrt{\frac{\kappa}{I}} \quad \text{(angular SHM)} \qquad (14.24)$$

The motion is described by the function

$$\theta = \Theta\cos(\omega t + \phi)$$

where Θ (the Greek letter theta) plays the role of an angular amplitude.

It's a good thing that the motion of a balance wheel *is* simple harmonic. If it weren't, the frequency might depend on the amplitude, and the watch would run too fast or too slow as the spring ran down.

Vibrations of Molecules

The following discussion of the vibrations of molecules uses the binomial theorem. If you aren't familiar with this theorem, you should read about it in the appropriate section of a math textbook.

When two atoms are separated from each other by a few atomic diameters, they can exert attractive forces on each other. But if the atoms are so close to each other that their electron shells overlap, the forces between the atoms are repulsive. Between these limits, there can be an equilibrium separation distance at which two atoms form a *molecule.* If these atoms are displaced slightly from equilibrium, they will oscillate.

14.18 If the weight mg compresses the spring a distance Δl, the force constant is $k = mg/\Delta l$ and the angular frequency for vertical SHM is $\omega = \sqrt{k/m}$—the same as if the body were suspended from the spring (see Fig. 14.17).

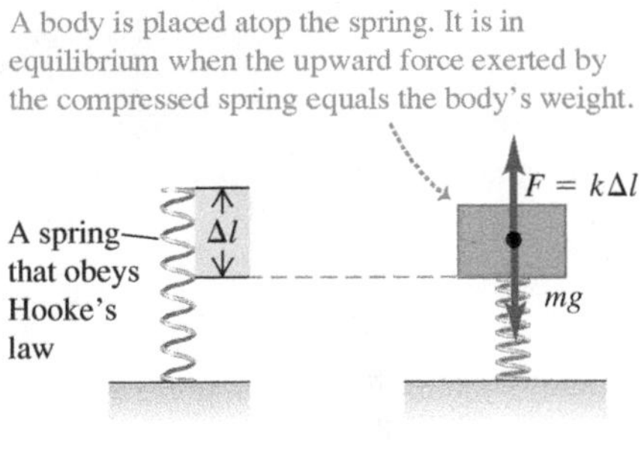

14.19 The balance wheel of a mechanical watch. The spring exerts a restoring torque that is proportional to the angular displacement θ, so the motion is angular SHM.

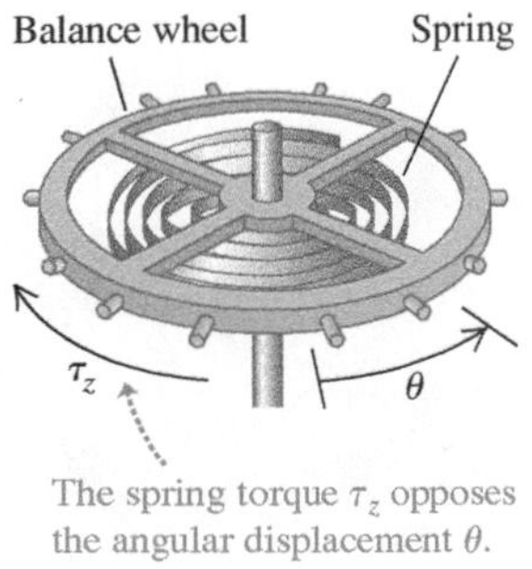

14.20 (a) Two atoms with centers separated by r. (b) Potential energy U in the van der Waals interaction as a function of r. (c) Force F_r on the right-hand atom as a function of r.

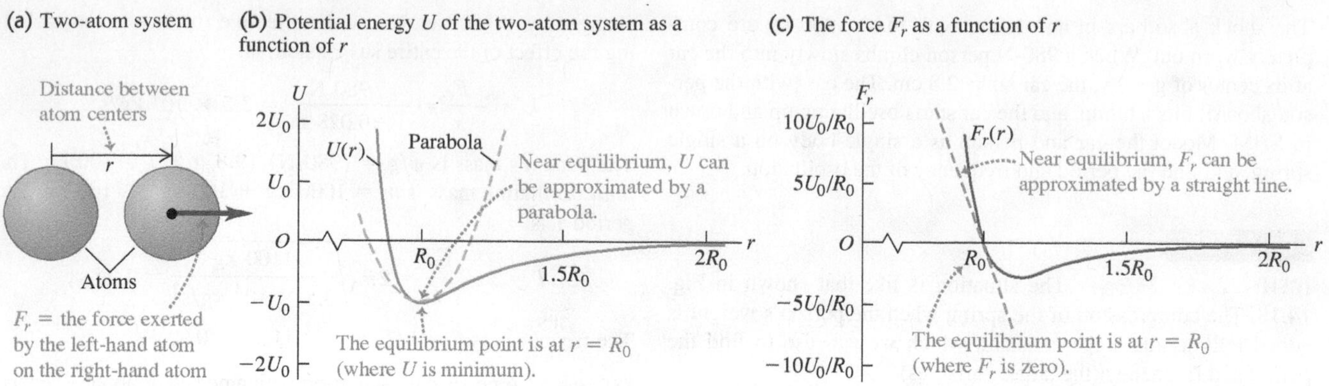

As an example, we'll consider one type of interaction between atoms called the *van der Waals interaction.* Our immediate task here is to study oscillations, so we won't go into the details of how this interaction arises. Let the center of one atom be at the origin and let the center of the other atom be a distance r away (Fig. 14.20a); the equilibrium distance between centers is $r = R_0$. Experiment shows that the van der Waals interaction can be described by the potential-energy function

$$U = U_0\left[\left(\frac{R_0}{r}\right)^{12} - 2\left(\frac{R_0}{r}\right)^{6}\right] \tag{14.25}$$

where U_0 is a positive constant with units of joules. When the two atoms are very far apart, $U = 0$; when they are separated by the equilibrium distance $r = R_0$, $U = -U_0$. The force on the second atom is the negative derivative of Eq. (14.25):

$$F_r = -\frac{dU}{dr} = U_0\left[\frac{12{R_0}^{12}}{r^{13}} - 2\frac{6{R_0}^{6}}{r^{7}}\right] = 12\frac{U_0}{R_0}\left[\left(\frac{R_0}{r}\right)^{13} - \left(\frac{R_0}{r}\right)^{7}\right] \tag{14.26}$$

Figures 14.20b and 14.20c plot the potential energy and force, respectively. The force is positive for $r < R_0$ and negative for $r > R_0$, so it is a *restoring* force.

Let's examine the restoring force F_r in Eq. (14.26). We let x represent the displacement from equilibrium:

$$x = r - R_0 \qquad \text{so} \qquad r = R_0 + x$$

In terms of x, the force F_r in Eq. (14.26) becomes

$$\begin{aligned} F_r &= 12\frac{U_0}{R_0}\left[\left(\frac{R_0}{R_0+x}\right)^{13} - \left(\frac{R_0}{R_0+x}\right)^{7}\right] \\ &= 12\frac{U_0}{R_0}\left[\frac{1}{(1+x/R_0)^{13}} - \frac{1}{(1+x/R_0)^{7}}\right] \end{aligned} \tag{14.27}$$

This looks nothing like Hooke's law, $F_x = -kx$, so we might be tempted to conclude that molecular oscillations cannot be SHM. But let us restrict ourselves to *small-amplitude* oscillations so that the absolute value of the displacement x is small in comparison to R_0 and the absolute value of the ratio x/R_0 is much less than 1. We can then simplify Eq. (14.27) by using the *binomial theorem:*

$$(1 + u)^n = 1 + nu + \frac{n(n-1)}{2!}u^2 + \frac{n(n-1)(n-2)}{3!}u^3 + \cdots \tag{14.28}$$

If $|u|$ is much less than 1, each successive term in Eq. (14.28) is much smaller than the one it follows, and we can safely approximate $(1 + u)^n$ by just the first two terms. In Eq. (14.27), u is replaced by x/R_0 and n equals -13 or -7, so

$$\frac{1}{(1 + x/R_0)^{13}} = (1 + x/R_0)^{-13} \approx 1 + (-13)\frac{x}{R_0}$$

$$\frac{1}{(1 + x/R_0)^{7}} = (1 + x/R_0)^{-7} \approx 1 + (-7)\frac{x}{R_0}$$

$$F_r \approx 12\frac{U_0}{R_0}\left[\left(1 + (-13)\frac{x}{R_0}\right) - \left(1 + (-7)\frac{x}{R_0}\right)\right] = -\left(\frac{72U_0}{R_0^2}\right)x \quad (14.29)$$

This is just Hooke's law, with force constant $k = 72U_0/R_0^2$. (Note that k has the correct units, J/m^2 or N/m.) So oscillations of molecules bound by the van der Waals interaction can be simple harmonic motion, provided that the amplitude is small in comparison to R_0 so that the approximation $|x/R_0| \ll 1$ used in the derivation of Eq. (14.29) is valid.

You can also use the binomial theorem to show that the potential energy U in Eq. (14.25) can be written as $U \approx \frac{1}{2}kx^2 + C$, where $C = -U_0$ and k is again equal to $72U_0/R_0^2$. Adding a constant to the potential energy has no effect on the physics, so the system of two atoms is fundamentally no different from a mass attached to a horizontal spring for which $U = \frac{1}{2}kx^2$.

Example 14.7 Molecular vibration

Two argon atoms form the molecule Ar_2 as a result of a van der Waals interaction with $U_0 = 1.68 \times 10^{-21}$ J and $R_0 = 3.82 \times 10^{-10}$ m. Find the frequency of small oscillations of one Ar atom about its equilibrium position.

SOLUTION

IDENTIFY and SET UP This is just the situation shown in Fig. 14.20. Because the oscillations are small, we can use Eq. (14.29) to find the force constant k and Eq. (14.11) to find the frequency f of SHM.

EXECUTE: From Eq. (14.29),

$$k = \frac{72U_0}{R_0^2} = \frac{72(1.68 \times 10^{-21}\ \text{J})}{(3.82 \times 10^{-10}\ \text{m})^2} = 0.829\ \text{J/m}^2 = 0.829\ \text{N/m}$$

(This force constant is comparable to that of a loose toy spring like a Slinky™.) From Appendix D, the average atomic mass of argon is $(39.948\ \text{u})(1.66 \times 10^{-27}\ \text{kg/1 u}) = 6.63 \times 10^{-26}$ kg.

From Eq. (14.11), if one atom is fixed and the other oscillates,

$$f = \frac{1}{2\pi}\sqrt{\frac{k}{m}} = \frac{1}{2\pi}\sqrt{\frac{0.829\ \text{N/m}}{6.63 \times 10^{-26}\ \text{kg}}} = 5.63 \times 10^{11}\ \text{Hz}$$

EVALUATE: Our answer for f isn't quite right. If no net external force acts on the molecule, its center of mass (halfway between the atoms) doesn't accelerate, so *both* atoms must oscillate with the same amplitude in opposite directions. It turns out that we can account for this by replacing m with $m/2$ in our expression for f. This makes f larger by a factor of $\sqrt{2}$, so the correct frequency is $f = \sqrt{2}(5.63 \times 10^{11}\ \text{Hz}) = 7.96 \times 10^{11}$ Hz. What's more, on the atomic scale we must use *quantum mechanics* rather than Newtonian mechanics to describe motion; happily, quantum mechanics also yields $f = 7.96 \times 10^{11}$ Hz.

Test Your Understanding of Section 14.4 A block attached to a hanging ideal spring oscillates up and down with a period of 10 s on earth. If you take the block and spring to Mars, where the acceleration due to gravity is only about 40% as large as on earth, what will be the new period of oscillation? (i) 10 s; (ii) more than 10 s; (iii) less than 10 s. ❙

14.5 The Simple Pendulum

MasteringPHYSICS

PhET: Pendulum Lab
ActivPhysics 9.10: Pendulum Frequency
ActivPhysics 9.11: Risky Pendulum Walk
ActivPhysics 9.12: Physical Pendulum

A **simple pendulum** is an idealized model consisting of a point mass suspended by a massless, unstretchable string. When the point mass is pulled to one side of its straight-down equilibrium position and released, it oscillates about the equilibrium position. Familiar situations such as a wrecking ball on a crane's cable or a person on a swing (Fig. 14.21a) can be modeled as simple pendulums.

14.21 The dynamics of a simple pendulum.

(a) A real pendulum

(b) An idealized simple pendulum

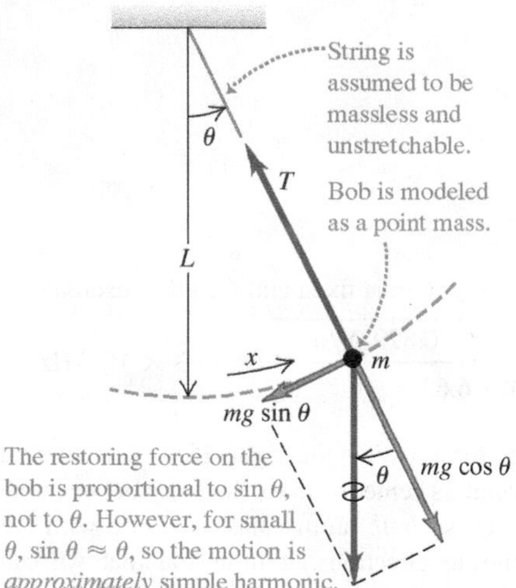

14.22 For small angular displacements θ, the restoring force $F_\theta = -mg\sin\theta$ on a simple pendulum is approximately equal to $-mg\theta$; that is, it is approximately proportional to the displacement θ. Hence for small angles the oscillations are simple harmonic.

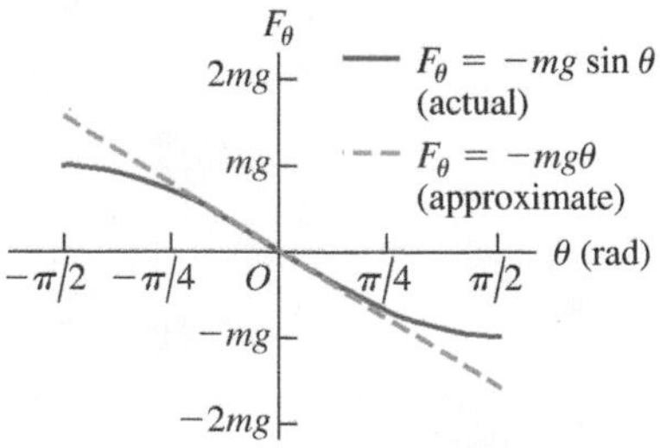

The path of the point mass (sometimes called a pendulum bob) is not a straight line but the arc of a circle with radius L equal to the length of the string (Fig. 14.21b). We use as our coordinate the distance x measured along the arc. If the motion is simple harmonic, the restoring force must be directly proportional to x or (because $x = L\theta$) to θ. Is it?

In Fig. 14.21b we represent the forces on the mass in terms of tangential and radial components. The restoring force F_θ is the tangential component of the net force:

$$F_\theta = -mg\sin\theta \tag{14.30}$$

The restoring force is provided by gravity; the tension T merely acts to make the point mass move in an arc. The restoring force is proportional *not* to θ but to $\sin\theta$, so the motion is *not* simple harmonic. However, if the angle θ is *small*, $\sin\theta$ is very nearly equal to θ in radians (Fig. 14.22). For example, when $\theta = 0.1$ rad (about 6°), $\sin\theta = 0.0998$, a difference of only 0.2%. With this approximation, Eq. (14.30) becomes

$$F_\theta = -mg\theta = -mg\frac{x}{L} \quad \text{or}$$

$$F_\theta = -\frac{mg}{L}x \tag{14.31}$$

The restoring force is then proportional to the coordinate for small displacements, and the force constant is $k = mg/L$. From Eq. (14.10) the angular frequency ω of a simple pendulum with small amplitude is

$$\omega = \sqrt{\frac{k}{m}} = \sqrt{\frac{mg/L}{m}} = \sqrt{\frac{g}{L}} \quad \text{(simple pendulum, small amplitude)} \tag{14.32}$$

The corresponding frequency and period relationships are

$$f = \frac{\omega}{2\pi} = \frac{1}{2\pi}\sqrt{\frac{g}{L}} \quad \text{(simple pendulum, small amplitude)} \tag{14.33}$$

$$T = \frac{2\pi}{\omega} = \frac{1}{f} = 2\pi\sqrt{\frac{L}{g}} \quad \text{(simple pendulum, small amplitude)} \tag{14.34}$$

Note that these expressions do not involve the *mass* of the particle. This is because the restoring force, a component of the particle's weight, is proportional to m. Thus the mass appears on *both* sides of $\Sigma\vec{F} = m\vec{a}$ and cancels out. (This is the same physics that explains why bodies of different masses fall with the same acceleration in a vacuum.) For small oscillations, the period of a pendulum for a given value of g is determined entirely by its length.

The dependence on L and g in Eqs. (14.32) through (14.34) is just what we should expect. A long pendulum has a longer period than a shorter one. Increasing g increases the restoring force, causing the frequency to increase and the period to decrease.

We emphasize again that the motion of a pendulum is only *approximately* simple harmonic. When the amplitude is not small, the departures from simple harmonic motion can be substantial. But how small is "small"? The period can be expressed by an infinite series; when the maximum angular displacement is Θ, the period T is given by

$$T = 2\pi\sqrt{\frac{L}{g}}\left(1 + \frac{1^2}{2^2}\sin^2\frac{\Theta}{2} + \frac{1^2\cdot 3^2}{2^2\cdot 4^2}\sin^4\frac{\Theta}{2} + \cdots\right) \tag{14.35}$$

We can compute the period to any desired degree of precision by taking enough terms in the series. We invite you to check that when $\Theta = 15°$ (on either side of the central position), the true period is longer than that given by the approximate Eq. (14.34) by less than 0.5%.

The usefulness of the pendulum as a timekeeper depends on the period being *very nearly* independent of amplitude, provided that the amplitude is small. Thus, as a pendulum clock runs down and the amplitude of the swings decreases a little, the clock still keeps very nearly correct time.

Example 14.8 A simple pendulum

Find the period and frequency of a simple pendulum 1.000 m long at a location where $g = 9.800\ \text{m/s}^2$.

SOLUTION

IDENTIFY and SET UP: This is a simple pendulum, so we can use the ideas of this section. We use Eq. (14.34) to determine the pendulum's period T from its length, and Eq. (14.1) to find the frequency f from T.

EXECUTE: From Eqs. (14.34) and (14.1),

$$T = 2\pi\sqrt{\frac{L}{g}} = 2\pi\sqrt{\frac{1.000\ \text{m}}{9.800\ \text{m/s}^2}} = 2.007\ \text{s}$$

$$f = \frac{1}{T} = \frac{1}{2.007\ \text{s}} = 0.4983\ \text{Hz}$$

EVALUATE: The period is almost exactly 2 s. When the metric system was established, the second was *defined* as half the period of a 1-m simple pendulum. This was a poor standard, however, because the value of g varies from place to place. We discussed more modern time standards in Section 1.3.

Test Your Understanding of Section 14.5 When a body oscillating on a horizontal spring passes through its equilibrium position, its acceleration is zero (see Fig. 14.2b). When the bob of an oscillating simple pendulum passes through its equilibrium position, is its acceleration zero?

14.6 The Physical Pendulum

A **physical pendulum** is any *real* pendulum that uses an extended body, as contrasted to the idealized model of the *simple* pendulum with all the mass concentrated at a single point. For small oscillations, analyzing the motion of a real, physical pendulum is almost as easy as for a simple pendulum. Figure 14.23 shows a body of irregular shape pivoted so that it can turn without friction about an axis through point O. In the equilibrium position the center of gravity is directly below the pivot; in the position shown in the figure, the body is displaced from equilibrium by an angle θ, which we use as a coordinate for the system. The distance from O to the center of gravity is d, the moment of inertia of the body about the axis of rotation through O is I, and the total mass is m. When the body is displaced as shown, the weight mg causes a restoring torque

$$\tau_z = -(mg)(d\sin\theta) \tag{14.36}$$

The negative sign shows that the restoring torque is clockwise when the displacement is counterclockwise, and vice versa.

When the body is released, it oscillates about its equilibrium position. The motion is not simple harmonic because the torque τ_z is proportional to $\sin\theta$ rather than to θ itself. However, if θ is small, we can approximate $\sin\theta$ by θ in radians, just as we did in analyzing the simple pendulum. Then the motion is *approximately* simple harmonic. With this approximation,

$$\tau_z = -(mgd)\theta$$

The equation of motion is $\sum\tau_z = I\alpha_z$, so

$$-(mgd)\theta = I\alpha_z = I\frac{d^2\theta}{dt^2}$$

$$\frac{d^2\theta}{dt^2} = -\frac{mgd}{I}\theta \tag{14.37}$$

14.23 Dynamics of a physical pendulum.

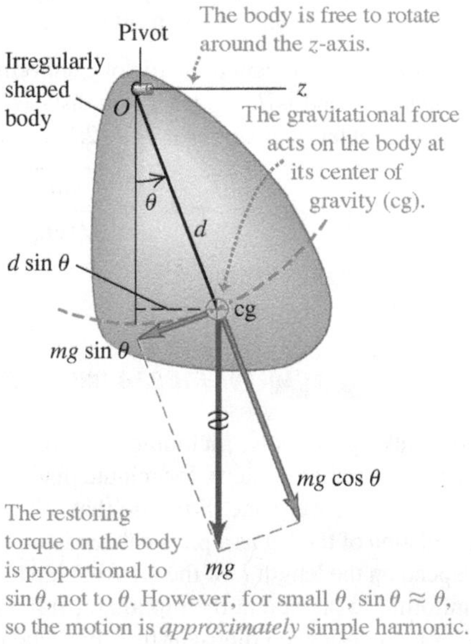

Comparing this with Eq. (14.4), we see that the role of (k/m) for the spring-mass system is played here by the quantity (mgd/I). Thus the angular frequency is

$$\omega = \sqrt{\frac{mgd}{I}} \quad \text{(physical pendulum, small amplitude)} \tag{14.38}$$

The frequency f is $1/2\pi$ times this, and the period T is

$$T = 2\pi\sqrt{\frac{I}{mgd}} \quad \text{(physical pendulum, small amplitude)} \tag{14.39}$$

Equation (14.39) is the basis of a common method for experimentally determining the moment of inertia of a body with a complicated shape. First locate the center of gravity of the body by balancing. Then suspend the body so that it is free to oscillate about an axis, and measure the period T of small-amplitude oscillations. Finally, use Eq. (14.39) to calculate the moment of inertia I of the body about this axis from T, the body's mass m, and the distance d from the axis to the center of gravity (see Exercise 14.53). Biomechanics researchers use this method to find the moments of inertia of an animal's limbs. This information is important for analyzing how an animal walks, as we'll see in the second of the two following examples.

Example 14.9 Physical pendulum versus simple pendulum

If the body in Fig. 14.23 is a uniform rod with length L, pivoted at one end, what is the period of its motion as a pendulum?

SOLUTION

IDENTIFY and SET UP: Our target variable is the oscillation period T of a rod that acts as a physical pendulum. We find the rod's moment of inertia in Table 9.2, and then determine T using Eq. (14.39).

EXECUTE: The moment of inertia of a uniform rod about an axis through one end is $I = \frac{1}{3}ML^2$. The distance from the pivot to the rod's center of gravity is $d = L/2$. Then from Eq. (14.39),

$$T = 2\pi\sqrt{\frac{I}{mgd}} = 2\pi\sqrt{\frac{\frac{1}{3}ML^2}{MgL/2}} = 2\pi\sqrt{\frac{2L}{3g}}$$

EVALUATE: If the rod is a meter stick ($L = 1.00$ m) and $g = 9.80\ \text{m/s}^2$, then

$$T = 2\pi\sqrt{\frac{2(1.00\ \text{m})}{3(9.80\ \text{m/s}^2)}} = 1.64\ \text{s}$$

The period is smaller by a factor of $\sqrt{\frac{2}{3}} = 0.816$ than that of a simple pendulum of the same length (see Example 14.8). The rod's moment of inertia around one end, $I = \frac{1}{3}ML^2$, is one-third that of the simple pendulum, and the rod's cg is half as far from the pivot as that of the simple pendulum. You can show that, taken together in Eq. (14.39), these two differences account for the factor $\sqrt{\frac{2}{3}}$ by which the periods differ.

Example 14.10 *Tyrannosaurus rex* and the physical pendulum

All walking animals, including humans, have a natural walking pace—a number of steps per minute that is more comfortable than a faster or slower pace. Suppose that this pace corresponds to the oscillation of the leg as a physical pendulum. (a) How does this pace depend on the length L of the leg from hip to foot? Treat the leg as a uniform rod pivoted at the hip joint. (b) Fossil evidence shows that *T. rex,* a two-legged dinosaur that lived about 65 million years ago, had a leg length $L = 3.1$ m and a stride length $S = 4.0$ m (the distance from one footprint to the next print of the same foot; see Fig. 14.24). Estimate the walking speed of *T. rex.*

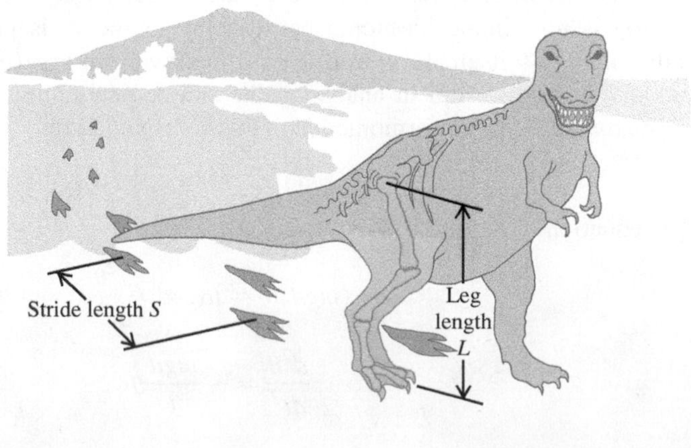

14.24 The walking speed of *Tyrannosaurus rex* can be estimated from leg length L and stride length S.

SOLUTION

IDENTIFY and SET UP: Our target variables are (a) the relationship between walking pace and leg length L and (b) the walking speed of *T. rex.* We treat the leg as a physical pendulum, with a period of oscillation as found in Example 14.9. We can find the walking speed from the period and the stride length.

EXECUTE: (a) From Example 14.9 the period of oscillation of the leg is $T = 2\pi\sqrt{2L/3g}$, which is proportional to $\sqrt{L}$. Each step takes one-half a period, so the walking pace (in steps per second) is twice the oscillation frequency $f = 1/T$, which is proportional to $1/\sqrt{L}$. The greater the leg length L, the slower the walking pace.

(b) According to our model, *T. rex* traveled one stride length S in a time

$$T = 2\pi\sqrt{\frac{2L}{3g}} = 2\pi\sqrt{\frac{2(3.1\text{ m})}{3(9.8\text{ m/s}^2)}} = 2.9\text{ s}$$

so its walking speed was

$$v = \frac{S}{T} = \frac{4.0\text{ m}}{2.9\text{ s}} = 1.4\text{ m/s} = 5.0\text{ km/h} = 3.1\text{ mi/h}$$

This is roughly the walking speed of an adult human.

EVALUATE: A uniform rod isn't a very good model for a leg. The legs of many animals, including both *T. rex* and humans, are tapered; there is more mass between hip and knee than between knee and foot. The center of mass is therefore less than $L/2$ from the hip; a reasonable guess would be about $L/4$. The moment of inertia is therefore *considerably* less than $ML^2/3$—say, $ML^2/15$. Use the analysis of Example 14.9 with these corrections; you'll get a shorter oscillation period and an even greater walking speed for *T. rex*.

Test Your Understanding of Section 14.6 The center of gravity of a simple pendulum of mass m and length L is located at the position of the pendulum bob, a distance L from the pivot point. The center of gravity of a uniform rod of the same mass m and length $2L$ pivoted at one end is also a distance L from the pivot point. How does the period of this uniform rod compare to the period of the simple pendulum? (i) The rod has a longer period; (ii) the rod has a shorter period; (iii) the rod has the same period.

14.7 Damped Oscillations

The idealized oscillating systems we have discussed so far are frictionless. There are no nonconservative forces, the total mechanical energy is constant, and a system set into motion continues oscillating forever with no decrease in amplitude.

Real-world systems always have some dissipative forces, however, and oscillations die out with time unless we replace the dissipated mechanical energy (Fig. 14.25). A mechanical pendulum clock continues to run because potential energy stored in the spring or a hanging weight system replaces the mechanical energy lost due to friction in the pivot and the gears. But eventually the spring runs down or the weights reach the bottom of their travel. Then no more energy is available, and the pendulum swings decrease in amplitude and stop.

14.25 A swinging bell left to itself will eventually stop oscillating due to damping forces (air resistance and friction at the point of suspension).

The decrease in amplitude caused by dissipative forces is called **damping,** and the corresponding motion is called **damped oscillation.** The simplest case to analyze in detail is a simple harmonic oscillator with a frictional damping force that is directly proportional to the *velocity* of the oscillating body. This behavior occurs in friction involving viscous fluid flow, such as in shock absorbers or sliding between oil-lubricated surfaces. We then have an additional force on the body due to friction, $F_x = -bv_x$, where $v_x = dx/dt$ is the velocity and b is a constant that describes the strength of the damping force. The negative sign shows that the force is always opposite in direction to the velocity. The *net* force on the body is then

$$\sum F_x = -kx - bv_x \tag{14.40}$$

and Newton's second law for the system is

$$-kx - bv_x = ma_x \quad \text{or} \quad -kx - b\frac{dx}{dt} = m\frac{d^2x}{dt^2} \tag{14.41}$$

Equation (14.41) is a differential equation for x; it would be the same as Eq. (14.4), the equation for the acceleration in SHM, except for the added term $-bdx/dt$. Solving this equation is a straightforward problem in differential equations, but we won't go into the details here. If the damping force is relatively small, the motion is described by

$$x = Ae^{-(b/2m)t}\cos(\omega' t + \phi) \quad \text{(oscillator with little damping)} \tag{14.42}$$

14.26 Graph of displacement versus time for an oscillator with little damping [see Eq. (14.42)] and with phase angle $\phi = 0$. The curves are for two values of the damping constant b.

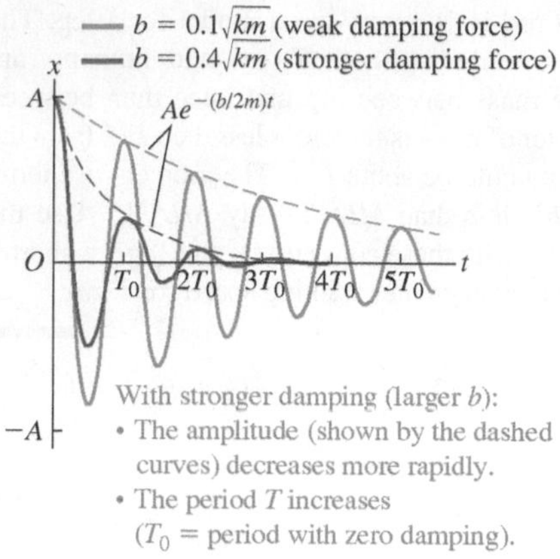

The angular frequency of oscillation ω' is given by

$$\omega' = \sqrt{\frac{k}{m} - \frac{b^2}{4m^2}} \quad \text{(oscillator with little damping)} \tag{14.43}$$

You can verify that Eq. (14.42) is a solution of Eq. (14.41) by calculating the first and second derivatives of x, substituting them into Eq. (14.41), and checking whether the left and right sides are equal. This is a straightforward but slightly tedious procedure.

The motion described by Eq. (14.42) differs from the undamped case in two ways. First, the amplitude $Ae^{-(b/2m)t}$ is not constant but decreases with time because of the decreasing exponential factor $e^{-(b/2m)t}$. Figure 14.26 is a graph of Eq. (14.42) for the case $\phi = 0$; it shows that the larger the value of b, the more quickly the amplitude decreases.

Second, the angular frequency ω', given by Eq. (14.43), is no longer equal to $\omega = \sqrt{k/m}$ but is somewhat smaller. It becomes zero when b becomes so large that

$$\frac{k}{m} - \frac{b^2}{4m^2} = 0 \quad \text{or} \quad b = 2\sqrt{km} \tag{14.44}$$

When Eq. (14.44) is satisfied, the condition is called **critical damping.** The system no longer oscillates but returns to its equilibrium position without oscillation when it is displaced and released.

If b is greater than $2\sqrt{km}$, the condition is called **overdamping.** Again there is no oscillation, but the system returns to equilibrium more slowly than with critical damping. For the overdamped case the solutions of Eq. (14.41) have the form

$$x = C_1 e^{-a_1 t} + C_2 e^{-a_2 t}$$

where C_1 and C_2 are constants that depend on the initial conditions and a_1 and a_2 are constants determined by m, k, and b.

When b is less than the critical value, as in Eq. (14.42), the condition is called **underdamping.** The system oscillates with steadily decreasing amplitude.

In a vibrating tuning fork or guitar string, it is usually desirable to have as little damping as possible. By contrast, damping plays a beneficial role in the oscillations of an automobile's suspension system. The shock absorbers provide a velocity-dependent damping force so that when the car goes over a bump, it doesn't continue bouncing forever (Fig. 14.27). For optimal passenger comfort, the system should be critically damped or slightly underdamped. Too much damping would be counterproductive; if the suspension is overdamped and the car hits a second bump just after the first one, the springs in the suspension will still be compressed somewhat from the first bump and will not be able to fully absorb the impact.

14.27 An automobile shock absorber. The viscous fluid causes a damping force that depends on the relative velocity of the two ends of the unit.

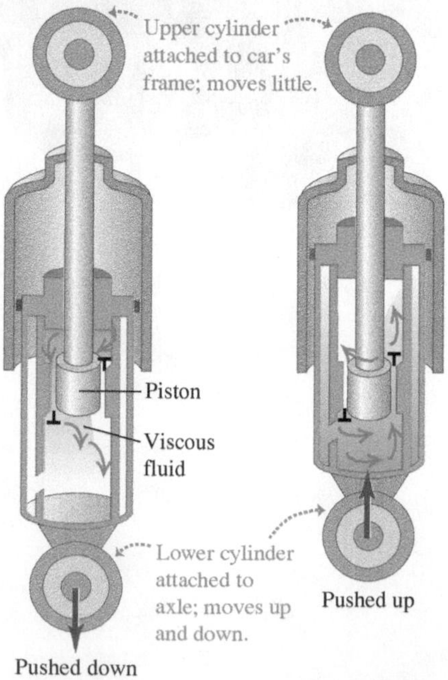

Energy in Damped Oscillations

In damped oscillations the damping force is nonconservative; the mechanical energy of the system is not constant but decreases continuously, approaching zero after a long time. To derive an expression for the rate of change of energy, we first write an expression for the total mechanical energy E at any instant:

$$E = \tfrac{1}{2}mv_x^2 + \tfrac{1}{2}kx^2$$

To find the rate of change of this quantity, we take its time derivative:

$$\frac{dE}{dt} = mv_x\frac{dv_x}{dt} + kx\frac{dx}{dt}$$

But $dv_x/dt = a_x$ and $dx/dt = v_x$, so

$$\frac{dE}{dt} = v_x(ma_x + kx)$$

From Eq. (14.41), $ma_x + kx = -bdx/dt = -bv_x$, so

$$\frac{dE}{dt} = v_x(-bv_x) = -bv_x^2 \quad \text{(damped oscillations)} \tag{14.45}$$

The right side of Eq. (14.45) is **negative** whenever the oscillating body is in motion, whether the x-velocity v_x is positive or negative. This shows that as the body moves, the energy decreases, though not at a uniform rate. The term $-bv_x^2 = (-bv_x)v_x$ (force times velocity) is the rate at which the damping force does (negative) work on the system (that is, the damping *power*). This equals the rate of change of the total mechanical energy of the system.

Similar behavior occurs in electric circuits containing inductance, capacitance, and resistance. There is a natural frequency of oscillation, and the resistance plays the role of the damping constant b. We will study these circuits in detail in Chapters 30 and 31.

Test Your Understanding of Section 14.7 An airplane is flying in a straight line at a constant altitude. If a wind gust strikes and raises the nose of the airplane, the nose will bob up and down until the airplane eventually returns to its original attitude. Are these oscillations (i) undamped, (ii) underdamped, (iii) critically damped, or (iv) overdamped?

14.8 Forced Oscillations and Resonance

A damped oscillator left to itself will eventually stop moving altogether. But we can maintain a constant-amplitude oscillation by applying a force that varies with time in a periodic or cyclic way, with a definite period and frequency. As an example, consider your cousin Throckmorton on a playground swing. You can keep him swinging with constant amplitude by giving him a little push once each cycle. We call this additional force a **driving force.**

Damped Oscillation with a Periodic Driving Force

If we apply a periodically varying driving force with angular frequency ω_d to a damped harmonic oscillator, the motion that results is called a **forced oscillation** or a *driven oscillation.* It is different from the motion that occurs when the system is simply displaced from equilibrium and then left alone, in which case the system oscillates with a **natural angular frequency** ω' determined by m, k, and b, as in Eq. (14.43). In a forced oscillation, however, the angular frequency with which the mass oscillates is equal to the driving angular frequency ω_d. This does *not* have to be equal to the angular frequency ω' with which the system would oscillate without a driving force. If you grab the ropes of Throckmorton's swing, you can force the swing to oscillate with any frequency you like.

Suppose we force the oscillator to vibrate with an angular frequency ω_d that is nearly *equal* to the angular frequency ω' it would have with no driving force. What happens? The oscillator is naturally disposed to oscillate at $\omega = \omega'$, so we expect the amplitude of the resulting oscillation to be larger than when the two frequencies are very different. Detailed analysis and experiment show that this is just what happens. The easiest case to analyze is a *sinusoidally* varying force—say, $F(t) = F_{max} \cos \omega_d t$. If we vary the frequency ω_d of the driving force, the amplitude of the resulting forced oscillation varies in an interesting way (Fig. 14.28). When there is very little damping (small b), the amplitude goes through a sharp peak as the driving angular frequency ω_d nears the natural oscillation angular frequency ω'. When the damping is increased (larger b), the peak becomes broader and smaller in height and shifts toward lower frequencies.

We could work out an expression that shows how the amplitude A of the forced oscillation depends on the frequency of a sinusoidal driving force, with

14.28 Graph of the amplitude A of forced oscillation as a function of the angular frequency ω_d of the driving force. The horizontal axis shows the ratio of ω_d to the angular frequency $\omega = \sqrt{k/m}$ of an undamped oscillator. Each curve has a different value of the damping constant b.

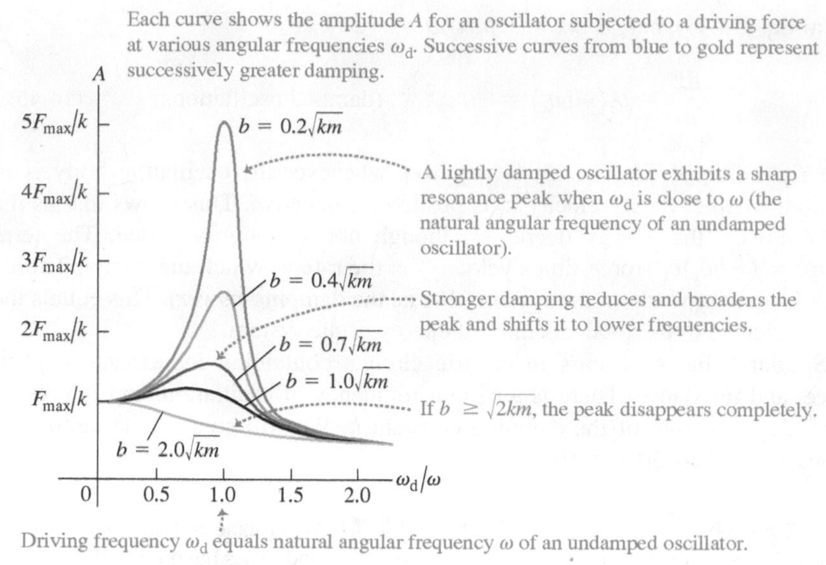

maximum value F_{max}. That would involve more differential equations than we're ready for, but here is the result:

$$A = \frac{F_{max}}{\sqrt{(k - m\omega_d^2)^2 + b^2\omega_d^2}} \quad \text{(amplitude of a driven oscillator)} \qquad (14.46)$$

When $k - m\omega_d^2 = 0$, the first term under the radical is zero, so A has a maximum near $\omega_d = \sqrt{k/m}$. The height of the curve at this point is proportional to $1/b$; the less damping, the higher the peak. At the low-frequency extreme, when $\omega_d = 0$, we get $A = F_{max}/k$. This corresponds to a *constant* force F_{max} and a constant displacement $A = F_{max}/k$ from equilibrium, as we might expect.

Resonance and Its Consequences

The fact that there is an amplitude peak at driving frequencies close to the natural frequency of the system is called **resonance.** Physics is full of examples of resonance; building up the oscillations of a child on a swing by pushing with a frequency equal to the swing's natural frequency is one. A vibrating rattle in a car that occurs only at a certain engine speed or wheel-rotation speed is an all-too-familiar example. Inexpensive loudspeakers often have an annoying boom or buzz when a musical note happens to coincide with the resonant frequency of the speaker cone or the speaker housing. In Chapter 16 we will study other examples of resonance that involve sound. Resonance also occurs in electric circuits, as we will see in Chapter 31; a tuned circuit in a radio or television receiver responds strongly to waves having frequencies near its resonant frequency, and this fact is used to select a particular station and reject the others.

Application Canine Resonance
Unlike humans, dogs have no sweat glands and so must pant in order to cool down. The frequency at which a dog pants is very close to the resonant frequency of its respiratory system. This causes the maximum amount of air to move in and out of the dog and so minimizes the effort that the dog must exert to cool itself.

Resonance in mechanical systems can be destructive. A company of soldiers once destroyed a bridge by marching across it in step; the frequency of their steps was close to a natural vibration frequency of the bridge, and the resulting oscillation had large enough amplitude to tear the bridge apart. Ever since, marching soldiers have been ordered to break step before crossing a bridge. Some years ago, vibrations of the engines of a particular airplane had just the right frequency to resonate with the natural frequencies of its wings. Large oscillations built up, and occasionally the wings fell off.

Test Your Understanding of Section 14.8 When driven at a frequency near its natural frequency, an oscillator with very little damping has a much greater response than the same oscillator with more damping. When driven at a frequency that is much higher or lower than the natural frequency, which oscillator will have the greater response: (i) the one with very little damping or (ii) the one with more damping? ❙

CHAPTER 14 SUMMARY

Periodic motion: Periodic motion is motion that repeats itself in a definite cycle. It occurs whenever a body has a stable equilibrium position and a restoring force that acts when it is displaced from equilibrium. Period T is the time for one cycle. Frequency f is the number of cycles per unit time. Angular frequency ω is 2π times the frequency. (See Example 14.1.)

$$f = \frac{1}{T} \qquad T = \frac{1}{f} \tag{14.1}$$

$$\omega = 2\pi f = \frac{2\pi}{T} \tag{14.2}$$

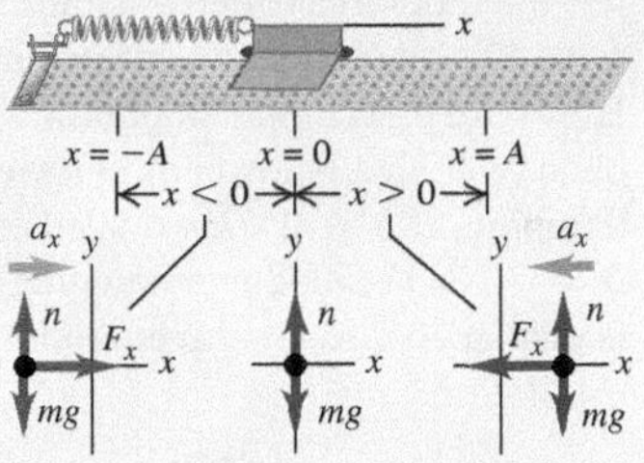

Simple harmonic motion: If the restoring force F_x in periodic motion is directly proportional to the displacement x, the motion is called simple harmonic motion (SHM). In many cases this condition is satisfied if the displacement from equilibrium is small. The angular frequency, frequency, and period in SHM do not depend on the amplitude, but only on the mass m and force constant k. The displacement, velocity, and acceleration in SHM are sinusoidal functions of time; the amplitude A and phase angle ϕ of the oscillation are determined by the initial position and velocity of the body. (See Examples 14.2, 14.3, 14.6, and 14.7.)

$$F_x = -kx \tag{14.3}$$

$$a_x = \frac{F_x}{m} = -\frac{k}{m}x \tag{14.4}$$

$$\omega = \sqrt{\frac{k}{m}} \tag{14.10}$$

$$f = \frac{\omega}{2\pi} = \frac{1}{2\pi}\sqrt{\frac{k}{m}} \tag{14.11}$$

$$T = \frac{1}{f} = 2\pi\sqrt{\frac{m}{k}} \tag{14.12}$$

$$x = A\cos(\omega t + \phi) \tag{14.13}$$

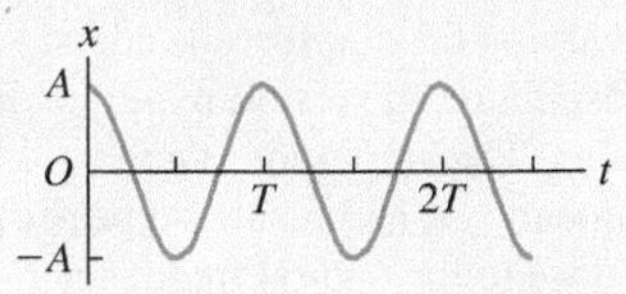

Energy in simple harmonic motion: Energy is conserved in SHM. The total energy can be expressed in terms of the force constant k and amplitude A. (See Examples 14.4 and 14.5.)

$$E = \tfrac{1}{2}mv_x^2 + \tfrac{1}{2}kx^2 = \tfrac{1}{2}kA^2 = \text{constant} \tag{14.21}$$

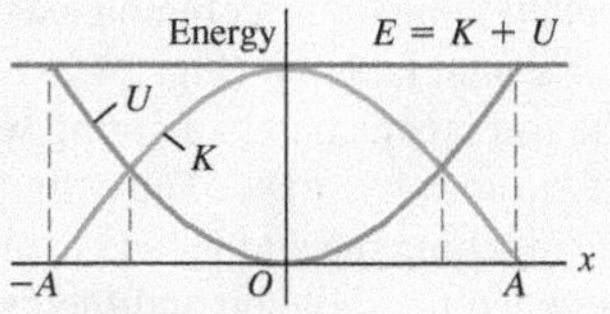

Angular simple harmonic motion: In angular SHM, the frequency and angular frequency are related to the moment of inertia I and the torsion constant κ.

$$\omega = \sqrt{\frac{\kappa}{I}} \quad \text{and} \quad f = \frac{1}{2\pi}\sqrt{\frac{\kappa}{I}} \tag{14.24}$$

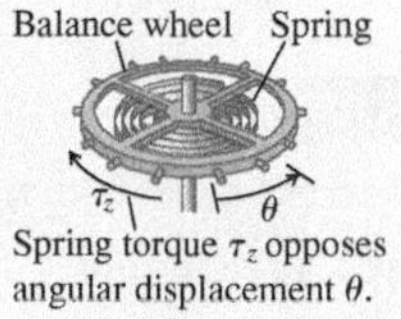

Simple pendulum: A simple pendulum consists of a point mass m at the end of a massless string of length L. Its motion is approximately simple harmonic for sufficiently small amplitude; the angular frequency, frequency, and period then depend only on g and L, not on the mass or amplitude. (See Example 14.8.)

$$\omega = \sqrt{\frac{g}{L}} \tag{14.32}$$

$$f = \frac{\omega}{2\pi} = \frac{1}{2\pi}\sqrt{\frac{g}{L}} \tag{14.33}$$

$$T = \frac{2\pi}{\omega} = \frac{1}{f} = 2\pi\sqrt{\frac{L}{g}} \tag{14.34}$$

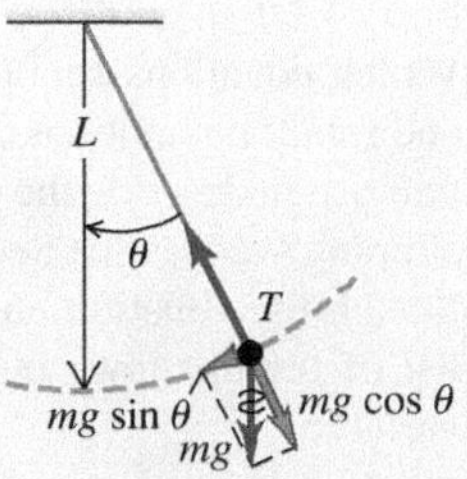

Physical pendulum: A physical pendulum is any body suspended from an axis of rotation. The angular frequency and period for small-amplitude oscillations are independent of amplitude, but depend on the mass m, distance d from the axis of rotation to the center of gravity, and moment of inertia I about the axis. (See Examples 14.9 and 14.10.)

$$\omega = \sqrt{\frac{mgd}{I}} \tag{14.38}$$

$$T = 2\pi\sqrt{\frac{I}{mgd}} \tag{14.39}$$

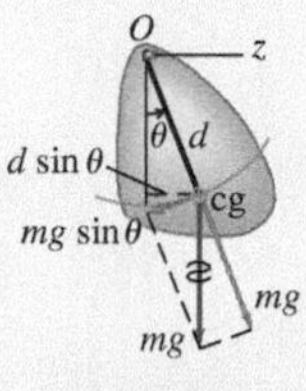

Damped oscillations: When a force $F_x = -bv_x$ proportional to velocity is added to a simple harmonic oscillator, the motion is called a damped oscillation. If $b < 2\sqrt{km}$ (called underdamping), the system oscillates with a decaying amplitude and an angular frequency ω' that is lower than it would be without damping. If $b = 2\sqrt{km}$ (called critical damping) or $b > 2\sqrt{km}$ (called overdamping), when the system is displaced it returns to equilibrium without oscillating.

$$x = Ae^{-(b/2m)t}\cos(\omega' t + \phi) \quad (14.42)$$

$$\omega' = \sqrt{\frac{k}{m} - \frac{b^2}{4m^2}} \quad (14.43)$$

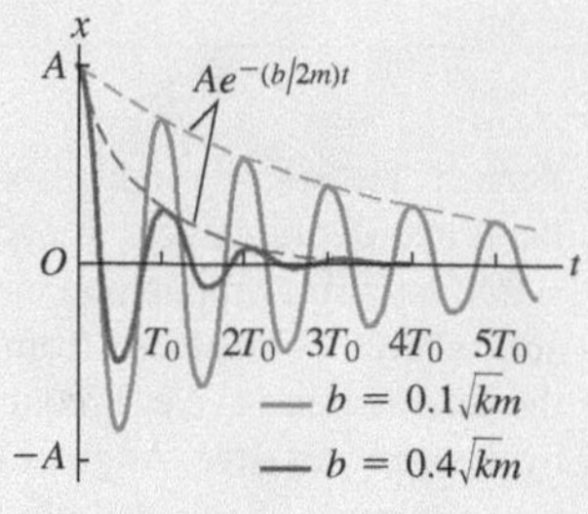

Driven oscillations and resonance: When a sinusoidally varying driving force is added to a damped harmonic oscillator, the resulting motion is called a forced oscillation. The amplitude is a function of the driving frequency ω_d and reaches a peak at a driving frequency close to the natural frequency of the system. This behavior is called resonance.

$$A = \frac{F_{max}}{\sqrt{(k - m\omega_d^2)^2 + b^2\omega_d^2}} \quad (14.46)$$

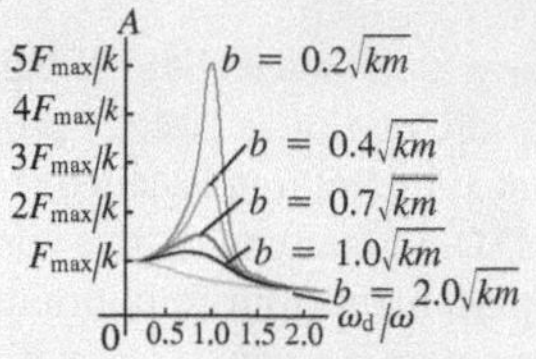

BRIDGING PROBLEM Oscillating and Rolling

Two uniform, solid cylinders of radius R and total mass M are connected along their common axis by a short, light rod and rest on a horizontal tabletop (Fig. 14.29). A frictionless ring at the center of the rod is attached to a spring with force constant k; the other end of the spring is fixed. The cylinders are pulled to the left a distance x, stretching the spring, and then released from rest. Due to friction between the tabletop and the cylinders, the cylinders roll without slipping as they oscillate. Show that the motion of the center of mass of the cylinders is simple harmonic, and find its period.

14.29

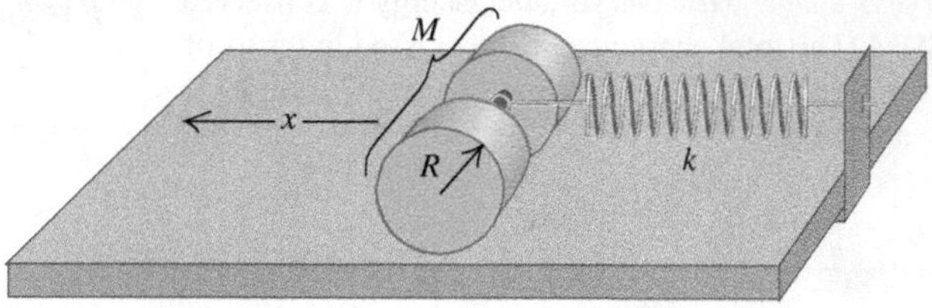

SOLUTION GUIDE

See MasteringPhysics® study area for a Video Tutor solution. MP

IDENTIFY and SET UP

1. What condition must be satisfied for the motion of the center of mass of the cylinders to be simple harmonic? (*Hint:* See Section 14.2.)
2. Which equations should you use to describe the translational and rotational motions of the cylinders? Which equation should you use to describe the condition that the cylinders roll without slipping? (*Hint:* See Section 10.3.)
3. Sketch the situation and choose a coordinate system. Make a list of the unknown quantities and decide which is the target variable.

EXECUTE

4. Draw a free-body diagram for the cylinders when they are displaced a distance x from equilibrium.
5. Solve the equations to find an expression for the acceleration of the center of mass of the cylinders. What does this expression tell you?
6. Use your result from step 5 to find the period of oscillation of the center of mass of the cylinders.

EVALUATE

7. What would be the period of oscillation if there were no friction and the cylinders didn't roll? Is this period larger or smaller than your result from step 6? Is this reasonable?

Problems

For instructor-assigned homework, go to www.masteringphysics.com

•, ••, •••: Problems of increasing difficulty. **CP**: Cumulative problems incorporating material from earlier chapters. **CALC**: Problems requiring calculus. **BIO**: Biosciences problems.

DISCUSSION QUESTIONS

Q14.1 An object is moving with SHM of amplitude A on the end of a spring. If the amplitude is doubled, what happens to the total distance the object travels in one period? What happens to the period? What happens to the maximum speed of the object? Discuss how these answers are related.

Q14.2 Think of several examples in everyday life of motions that are, at least approximately, simple harmonic. In what respects does each differ from SHM?

Q14.3 Does a tuning fork or similar tuning instrument undergo SHM? Why is this a crucial question for musicians?

Q14.4 A box containing a pebble is attached to an ideal horizontal spring and is oscillating on a friction-free air table. When the box has reached its maximum distance from the equilibrium point, the pebble is suddenly lifted out vertically without disturbing the box. Will the following characteristics of the motion increase, decrease, or remain the same in the subsequent motion of the box? Justify each answer. (a) frequency; (b) period; (c) amplitude; (d) the maximum kinetic energy of the box; (e) the maximum speed of the box.

Q14.5 If a uniform spring is cut in half, what is the force constant of each half? Justify your answer. How would the frequency of SHM using a half-spring differ from the frequency using the same mass and the entire spring?

Q14.6 The analysis of SHM in this chapter ignored the mass of the spring. How does the spring's mass change the characteristics of the motion?

Q14.7 Two identical gliders on an air track are connected by an ideal spring. Could such a system undergo SHM? Explain. How would the period compare with that of a single glider attached to a spring whose other end is rigidly attached to a stationary object? Explain.

Q14.8 You are captured by Martians, taken into their ship, and put to sleep. You awake some time later and find yourself locked in a small room with no windows. All the Martians have left you with is your digital watch, your school ring, and your long silver-chain necklace. Explain how you can determine whether you are still on earth or have been transported to Mars.

Q14.9 The system shown in Fig. 14.17 is mounted in an elevator. What happens to the period of the motion (does it increase, decrease, or remain the same) if the elevator (a) accelerates upward at 5.0 m/s^2; (b) moves upward at a steady 5.0 m/s; (c) accelerates downward at 5.0 m/s^2? Justify your answers.

Q14.10 If a pendulum has a period of 2.5 s on earth, what would be its period in a space station orbiting the earth? If a mass hung from a vertical spring has a period of 5.0 s on earth, what would its period be in the space station? Justify each of your answers.

Q14.11 A simple pendulum is mounted in an elevator. What happens to the period of the pendulum (does it increase, decrease, or remain the same) if the elevator (a) accelerates upward at 5.0 m/s^2; (b) moves upward at a steady 5.0 m/s; (c) accelerates downward at 5.0 m/s^2; (d) accelerates downward at 9.8 m/s^2? Justify your answers.

Q14.12 What should you do to the length of the string of a simple pendulum to (a) double its frequency; (b) double its period; (c) double its angular frequency?

Q14.13 If a pendulum clock is taken to a mountaintop, does it gain or lose time, assuming it is correct at a lower elevation? Explain your answer.

Q14.14 When the amplitude of a simple pendulum increases, should its period increase or decrease? Give a qualitative argument; do not rely on Eq. (14.35). Is your argument also valid for a physical pendulum?

Q14.15 Why do short dogs (like Chihuahuas) walk with quicker strides than do tall dogs (like Great Danes)?

Q14.16 At what point in the motion of a simple pendulum is the string tension greatest? Least? In each case give the reasoning behind your answer.

Q14.17 Could a standard of time be based on the period of a certain standard pendulum? What advantages and disadvantages would such a standard have compared to the actual present-day standard discussed in Section 1.3?

Q14.18 For a simple pendulum, clearly distinguish between ω (the angular velocity) and ω (the angular frequency). Which is constant and which is variable?

Q14.19 A glider is attached to a fixed ideal spring and oscillates on a horizontal, friction-free air track. A coin is atop the glider and oscillating with it. At what points in the motion is the friction force on the coin greatest? At what points is it least? Justify your answers.

Q14.20 In designing structures in an earthquake-prone region, how should the natural frequencies of oscillation of a structure relate to typical earthquake frequencies? Why? Should the structure have a large or small amount of damping?

EXERCISES

Section 14.1 Describing Oscillation

14.1 • **BIO** (a) **Music.** When a person sings, his or her vocal cords vibrate in a repetitive pattern that has the same frequency as the note that is sung. If someone sings the note B flat, which has a frequency of 466 Hz, how much time does it take the person's vocal cords to vibrate through one complete cycle, and what is the angular frequency of the cords? (b) **Hearing.** When sound waves strike the eardrum, this membrane vibrates with the same frequency as the sound. The highest pitch that typical humans can hear has a period of 50.0 μs. What are the frequency and angular frequency of the vibrating eardrum for this sound? (c) **Vision.** When light having vibrations with angular frequency ranging from 2.7×10^{15} rad/s to 4.7×10^{15} rad/s strikes the retina of the eye, it stimulates the receptor cells there and is perceived as visible light. What are the limits of the period and frequency of this light? (d) **Ultrasound.** High-frequency sound waves (ultrasound) are used to probe the interior of the body, much as x rays do. To detect small objects such as tumors, a frequency of around 5.0 MHz is used. What are the period and angular frequency of the molecular vibrations caused by this pulse of sound?

14.2 • If an object on a horizontal, frictionless surface is attached to a spring, displaced, and then released, it will oscillate. If it is displaced 0.120 m from its equilibrium position and released with zero initial speed, then after 0.800 s its displacement is found to be

0.120 m on the opposite side, and it has passed the equilibrium position once during this interval. Find (a) the amplitude; (b) the period; (c) the frequency.

14.3 • The tip of a tuning fork goes through 440 complete vibrations in 0.500 s. Find the angular frequency and the period of the motion.

14.4 • The displacement of an oscillating object as a function of time is shown in Fig. E14.4. What are (a) the frequency; (b) the amplitude; (c) the period; (d) the angular frequency of this motion?

Figure **E14.4**

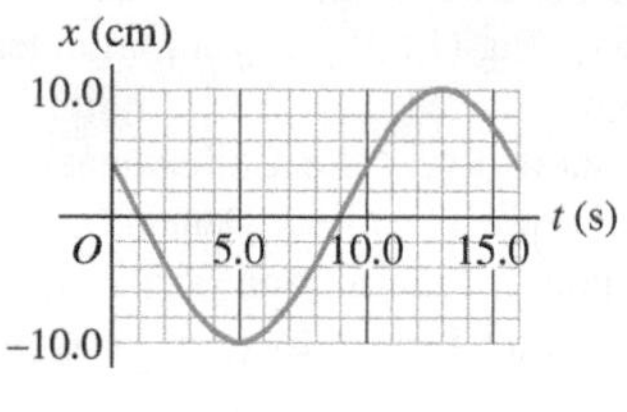

14.5 •• A machine part is undergoing SHM with a frequency of 5.00 Hz and amplitude 1.80 cm. How long does it take the part to go from $x = 0$ to $x = -1.80$ cm?

Section 14.2 Simple Harmonic Motion

14.6 •• In a physics lab, you attach a 0.200-kg air-track glider to the end of an ideal spring of negligible mass and start it oscillating. The elapsed time from when the glider first moves through the equilibrium point to the second time it moves through that point is 2.60 s. Find the spring's force constant.

14.7 • When a body of unknown mass is attached to an ideal spring with force constant 120 N/m, it is found to vibrate with a frequency of 6.00 Hz. Find (a) the period of the motion; (b) the angular frequency; (c) the mass of the body.

14.8 • When a 0.750-kg mass oscillates on an ideal spring, the frequency is 1.33 Hz. What will the frequency be if 0.220 kg are (a) added to the original mass and (b) subtracted from the original mass? Try to solve this problem *without* finding the force constant of the spring.

14.9 •• An object is undergoing SHM with period 0.900 s and amplitude 0.320 m. At $t = 0$ the object is at $x = 0.320$ m and is instantaneously at rest. Calculate the time it takes the object to go (a) from $x = 0.320$ m to $x = 0.160$ m and (b) from $x = 0.160$ m to $x = 0$.

14.10 • A small block is attached to an ideal spring and is moving in SHM on a horizontal, frictionless surface. When the block is at $x = 0.280$ m, the acceleration of the block is $-5.30\ \text{m/s}^2$. What is the frequency of the motion?

14.11 • A 2.00-kg, frictionless block is attached to an ideal spring with force constant 300 N/m. At $t = 0$ the spring is neither stretched nor compressed and the block is moving in the negative direction at 12.0 m/s. Find (a) the amplitude and (b) the phase angle. (c) Write an equation for the position as a function of time.

14.12 •• Repeat Exercise 14.11, but assume that at $t = 0$ the block has velocity −4.00 m/s and displacement +0.200 m.

14.13 • The point of the needle of a sewing machine moves in SHM along the x-axis with a frequency of 2.5 Hz. At $t = 0$ its position and velocity components are +1.1 cm and −15 cm/s, respectively. (a) Find the acceleration component of the needle at $t = 0$. (b) Write equations giving the position, velocity, and acceleration components of the point as a function of time.

14.14 •• A small block is attached to an ideal spring and is moving in SHM on a horizontal, frictionless surface. When the amplitude of the motion is 0.090 m, it takes the block 2.70 s to travel from $x = 0.090$ m to $x = -0.090$ m. If the amplitude is doubled, to 0.180 m, how long does it take the block to travel (a) from $x = 0.180$ m to $x = -0.180$ m and (b) from $x = 0.090$ m to $x = -0.090$ m?

14.15 • BIO **Weighing Astronauts.** This procedure has actually been used to "weigh" astronauts in space. A 42.5-kg chair is attached to a spring and allowed to oscillate. When it is empty, the chair takes 1.30 s to make one complete vibration. But with an astronaut sitting in it, with her feet off the floor, the chair takes 2.54 s for one cycle. What is the mass of the astronaut?

14.16 • A 0.400-kg object undergoing SHM has $a_x = -2.70\ \text{m/s}^2$ when $x = 0.300$ m. What is the time for one oscillation?

14.17 • On a frictionless, horizontal air track, a glider oscillates at the end of an ideal spring of force constant 2.50 N/cm. The graph in Fig. E14.17 shows the acceleration of the glider as a function of time. Find (a) the mass of the glider; (b) the maximum displacement of the glider from the equilibrium point; (c) the maximum force the spring exerts on the glider.

Figure **E14.17**

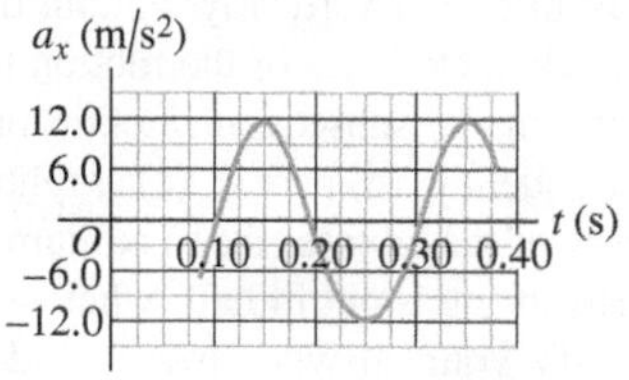

14.18 • A 0.500-kg mass on a spring has velocity as a function of time given by $v_x(t) = -(3.60\ \text{cm/s})\sin[(4.71\ \text{s}^{-1})t - \pi/2]$. What are (a) the period; (b) the amplitude; (c) the maximum acceleration of the mass; (d) the force constant of the spring?

14.19 • A 1.50-kg mass on a spring has displacement as a function of time given by the equation

$$x(t) = (7.40\ \text{cm})\cos[(4.16\ \text{s}^{-1})t - 2.42]$$

Find (a) the time for one complete vibration; (b) the force constant of the spring; (c) the maximum speed of the mass; (d) the maximum force on the mass; (e) the position, speed, and acceleration of the mass at $t = 1.00$ s; (f) the force on the mass at that time.

14.20 • BIO **Weighing a Virus.** In February 2004, scientists at Purdue University used a highly sensitive technique to measure the mass of a vaccinia virus (the kind used in smallpox vaccine). The procedure involved measuring the frequency of oscillation of a tiny sliver of silicon (just 30 nm long) with a laser, first without the virus and then after the virus had attached itself to the silicon. The difference in mass caused a change in the frequency. We can model such a process as a mass on a spring. (a) Show that the ratio of the frequency with the virus attached (f_{S+V}) to the frequency without the virus (f_S) is given by the formula $\dfrac{f_{S+V}}{f_S} = \dfrac{1}{\sqrt{1 + (m_V/m_S)}}$, where m_V is the mass of the virus and m_S is the mass of the silicon sliver. Notice that it is *not* necessary to know or measure the force constant of the spring. (b) In some data, the silicon sliver has a mass of 2.10×10^{-16} g and a frequency of 2.00×10^{15} Hz without the virus and 2.87×10^{14} Hz with the virus. What is the mass of the virus, in grams and in femtograms?

14.21 •• CALC **Jerk.** A guitar string vibrates at a frequency of 440 Hz. A point at its center moves in SHM with an amplitude of

3.0 mm and a phase angle of zero. (a) Write an equation for the position of the center of the string as a function of time. (b) What are the maximum values of the magnitudes of the velocity and acceleration of the center of the string? (c) The derivative of the acceleration with respect to time is a quantity called the *jerk*. Write an equation for the jerk of the center of the string as a function of time, and find the maximum value of the magnitude of the jerk.

Section 14.3 Energy in Simple Harmonic Motion

14.22 •• For the oscillating object in Fig. E14.4, what are (a) its maximum speed and (b) its maximum acceleration?

14.23 • A small block is attached to an ideal spring and is moving in SHM on a horizontal, frictionless surface. The amplitude of the motion is 0.120 m. The maximum speed of the block is 3.90 m/s. What is the maximum magnitude of the acceleration of the block?

14.24 • A small block is attached to an ideal spring and is moving in SHM on a horizontal, frictionless surface. The amplitude of the motion is 0.250 m and the period is 3.20 s. What are the speed and acceleration of the block when $x = 0.160$ m?

14.25 •• A tuning fork labeled 392 Hz has the tip of each of its two prongs vibrating with an amplitude of 0.600 mm. (a) What is the maximum speed of the tip of a prong? (b) A housefly (*Musca domestica*) with mass 0.0270 g is holding onto the tip of one of the prongs. As the prong vibrates, what is the fly's maximum kinetic energy? Assume that the fly's mass has a negligible effect on the frequency of oscillation.

14.26 •• A harmonic oscillator has angular frequency ω and amplitude A. (a) What are the magnitudes of the displacement and velocity when the elastic potential energy is equal to the kinetic energy? (Assume that $U = 0$ at equilibrium.) (b) How often does this occur in each cycle? What is the time between occurrences? (c) At an instant when the displacement is equal to $A/2$, what fraction of the total energy of the system is kinetic and what fraction is potential?

14.27 • A 0.500-kg glider, attached to the end of an ideal spring with force constant $k = 450$ N/m, undergoes SHM with an amplitude of 0.040 m. Compute (a) the maximum speed of the glider; (b) the speed of the glider when it is at $x = -0.015$ m; (c) the magnitude of the maximum acceleration of the glider; (d) the acceleration of the glider at $x = -0.015$ m; (e) the total mechanical energy of the glider at any point in its motion.

14.28 •• A cheerleader waves her pom-pom in SHM with an amplitude of 18.0 cm and a frequency of 0.850 Hz. Find (a) the maximum magnitude of the acceleration and of the velocity; (b) the acceleration and speed when the pom-pom's coordinate is $x = +9.0$ cm; (c) the time required to move from the equilibrium position directly to a point 12.0 cm away. (d) Which of the quantities asked for in parts (a), (b), and (c) can be found using the energy approach used in Section 14.3, and which cannot? Explain.

14.29 • **CP** For the situation described in part (a) of Example 14.5, what should be the value of the putty mass m so that the amplitude after the collision is one-half the original amplitude? For this value of m, what fraction of the original mechanical energy is converted into heat?

14.30 • A 0.150-kg toy is undergoing SHM on the end of a horizontal spring with force constant $k = 300$ N/m. When the object is 0.0120 m from its equilibrium position, it is observed to have a speed of 0.300 m/s. What are (a) the total energy of the object at any point of its motion; (b) the amplitude of the motion; (c) the maximum speed attained by the object during its motion?

14.31 •• You are watching an object that is moving in SHM. When the object is displaced 0.600 m to the right of its equilibrium position, it has a velocity of 2.20 m/s to the right and an acceleration of 8.40 m/s^2 to the left. How much farther from this point will the object move before it stops momentarily and then starts to move back to the left?

14.32 •• On a horizontal, frictionless table, an open-topped 5.20-kg box is attached to an ideal horizontal spring having force constant 375 N/m. Inside the box is a 3.44-kg stone. The system is oscillating with an amplitude of 7.50 cm. When the box has reached its maximum speed, the stone is suddenly plucked vertically out of the box without touching the box. Find (a) the period and (b) the amplitude of the resulting motion of the box. (c) Without doing any calculations, is the new period greater or smaller than the original period? How do you know?

14.33 •• A mass is oscillating with amplitude A at the end of a spring. How far (in terms of A) is this mass from the equilibrium position of the spring when the elastic potential energy equals the kinetic energy?

14.34 •• A mass m is attached to a spring of force constant 75 N/m and allowed to oscillate. Figure E14.34 shows a graph of its velocity v_x as a function of time t. Find (a) the period, (b) the frequency, and (c) the angular frequency of this motion. (d) What is the amplitude (in cm), and at what times does the mass reach this position? (e) Find the maximum acceleration of the mass and the times at which it occurs. (f) What is the mass m?

Figure **E14.34**

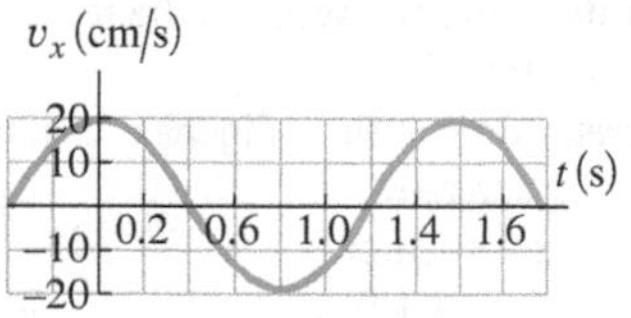

14.35 • Inside a NASA test vehicle, a 3.50-kg ball is pulled along by a horizontal ideal spring fixed to a friction-free table. The force constant of the spring is 225 N/m. The vehicle has a steady acceleration of 5.00 m/s^2, and the ball is not oscillating. Suddenly, when the vehicle's speed has reached 45.0 m/s, its engines turn off, thus eliminating its acceleration but not its velocity. Find (a) the amplitude and (b) the frequency of the resulting oscillations of the ball. (c) What will be the ball's maximum speed relative to the vehicle?

Section 14.4 Applications of Simple Harmonic Motion

14.36 • A proud deep-sea fisherman hangs a 65.0-kg fish from an ideal spring having negligible mass. The fish stretches the spring 0.120 m. (a) Find the force constant of the spring. The fish is now pulled down 5.00 cm and released. (b) What is the period of oscillation of the fish? (c) What is the maximum speed it will reach?

14.37 • A 175-g glider on a horizontal, frictionless air track is attached to a fixed ideal spring with force constant 155 N/m. At the instant you make measurements on the glider, it is moving at 0.815 m/s and is 3.00 cm from its equilibrium point. Use *energy conservation* to find (a) the amplitude of the motion and (b) the maximum speed of the glider. (c) What is the angular frequency of the oscillations?

14.38 • A thrill-seeking cat with mass 4.00 kg is attached by a harness to an ideal spring of negligible mass and oscillates vertically in SHM. The amplitude is 0.050 m, and at the highest point of the motion the spring has its natural unstretched length. Calculate the elastic potential energy of the spring (take it to be zero for the unstretched spring), the kinetic energy of the cat, the gravitational potential energy of the system relative to the lowest point of the motion, and the sum of these three energies when the cat is (a) at its highest point; (b) at its lowest point; (c) at its equilibrium position.

14.39 •• A 1.50-kg ball and a 2.00-kg ball are glued together with the lighter one below the heavier one. The upper ball is attached to a vertical ideal spring of force constant 165 N/m, and the system is vibrating vertically with amplitude 15.0 cm. The glue connecting the balls is old and weak, and it suddenly comes loose when the balls are at the lowest position in their motion. (a) Why is the glue more likely to fail at the *lowest* point than at any other point in the motion? (b) Find the amplitude and frequency of the vibrations after the lower ball has come loose.

14.40 •• A uniform, solid metal disk of mass 6.50 kg and diameter 24.0 cm hangs in a horizontal plane, supported at its center by a vertical metal wire. You find that it requires a horizontal force of 4.23 N tangent to the rim of the disk to turn it by 3.34°, thus twisting the wire. You now remove this force and release the disk from rest. (a) What is the torsion constant for the metal wire? (b) What are the frequency and period of the torsional oscillations of the disk? (c) Write the equation of motion for $\theta(t)$ for the disk.

14.41 •• A certain alarm clock ticks four times each second, with each tick representing half a period. The balance wheel consists of a thin rim with radius 0.55 cm, connected to the balance staff by thin spokes of negligible mass. The total mass of the balance wheel is 0.90 g. (a) What is the moment of inertia of the balance wheel about its shaft? (b) What is the torsion constant of the coil spring (Fig. 14.19)?

14.42 • A thin metal disk with mass 2.00×10^{-3} kg and radius 2.20 cm is attached at its center to a long fiber (Fig. E14.42). The disk, when twisted and released, oscillates with a period of 1.00 s. Find the torsion constant of the fiber.

Figure **E14.42**

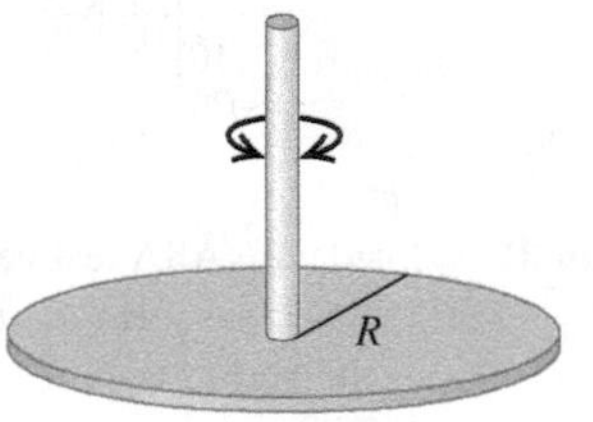

14.43 •• You want to find the moment of inertia of a complicated machine part about an axis through its center of mass. You suspend it from a wire along this axis. The wire has a torsion constant of 0.450 N · m/rad. You twist the part a small amount about this axis and let it go, timing 125 oscillations in 265 s. What is the moment of inertia you want to find?

14.44 •• **CALC** The balance wheel of a watch vibrates with an angular amplitude Θ, angular frequency ω, and phase angle $\phi = 0$. (a) Find expressions for the angular velocity $d\theta/dt$ and angular acceleration $d^2\theta/dt^2$ as functions of time. (b) Find the balance wheel's angular velocity and angular acceleration when its angular displacement is Θ, and when its angular displacement is $\Theta/2$ and θ is decreasing. (*Hint:* Sketch a graph of θ versus t.)

Section 14.5 The Simple Pendulum

14.45 •• You pull a simple pendulum 0.240 m long to the side through an angle of 3.50° and release it. (a) How much time does it take the pendulum bob to reach its highest speed? (b) How much time does it take if the pendulum is released at an angle of 1.75° instead of 3.50°?

14.46 • An 85.0-kg mountain climber plans to swing down, starting from rest, from a ledge using a light rope 6.50 m long. He holds one end of the rope, and the other end is tied higher up on a rock face. Since the ledge is not very far from the rock face, the rope makes a small angle with the vertical. At the lowest point of his swing, he plans to let go and drop a short distance to the ground. (a) How long after he begins his swing will the climber first reach his lowest point? (b) If he missed the first chance to drop off, how long after first beginning his swing will the climber reach his lowest point for the second time?

14.47 • A building in San Francisco has light fixtures consisting of small 2.35-kg bulbs with shades hanging from the ceiling at the end of light, thin cords 1.50 m long. If a minor earthquake occurs, how many swings per second will these fixtures make?

14.48 • **A Pendulum on Mars.** A certain simple pendulum has a period on the earth of 1.60 s. What is its period on the surface of Mars, where $g = 3.71\ \text{m/s}^2$?

14.49 • After landing on an unfamiliar planet, a space explorer constructs a simple pendulum of length 50.0 cm. She finds that the pendulum makes 100 complete swings in 136 s. What is the value of g on this planet?

14.50 •• A small sphere with mass m is attached to a massless rod of length L that is pivoted at the top, forming a simple pendulum. The pendulum is pulled to one side so that the rod is at an angle Θ from the vertical, and released from rest. (a) In a diagram, show the pendulum just after it is released. Draw vectors representing the *forces* acting on the small sphere and the *acceleration* of the sphere. Accuracy counts! At this point, what is the linear acceleration of the sphere? (b) Repeat part (a) for the instant when the pendulum rod is at an angle $\Theta/2$ from the vertical. (c) Repeat part (a) for the instant when the pendulum rod is vertical. At this point, what is the linear speed of the sphere?

14.51 • A simple pendulum 2.00 m long swings through a maximum angle of 30.0° with the vertical. Calculate its period (a) assuming a small amplitude, and (b) using the first three terms of Eq. (14.35). (c) Which of the answers in parts (a) and (b) is more accurate? For the one that is less accurate, by what percent is it in error from the more accurate answer?

Section 14.6 The Physical Pendulum

14.52 •• We want to hang a thin hoop on a horizontal nail and have the hoop make one complete small-angle oscillation each 2.0 s. What must the hoop's radius be?

14.53 • A 1.80-kg connecting rod from a car engine is pivoted about a horizontal knife edge as shown in Fig. E14.53. The center of gravity of the rod was located by balancing and is 0.200 m from the pivot. When the rod is set into small-amplitude oscillation, it makes 100 complete swings in 120 s. Calculate the moment of inertia of the rod about the rotation axis through the pivot.

Figure **E14.53**

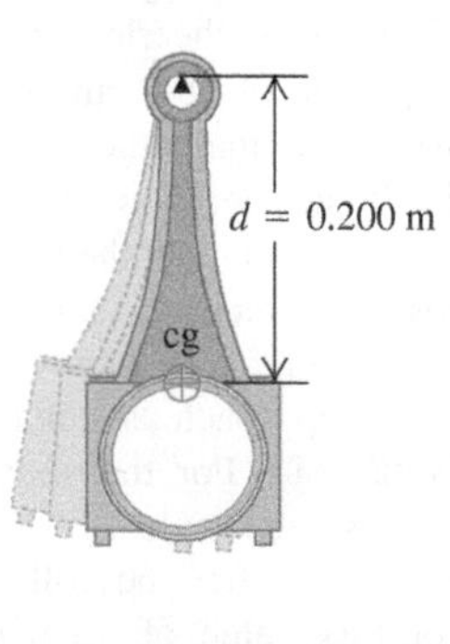

14.54 •• A 1.80-kg monkey wrench is pivoted 0.250 m from its center of mass and allowed to swing as a physical pendulum. The period for small-angle oscillations is 0.940 s. (a) What is the moment of inertia of the wrench about an axis through the pivot? (b) If the wrench is initially displaced 0.400 rad from its equilibrium position, what is the angular speed of the wrench as it passes through the equilibrium position?

14.55 • Two pendulums have the same dimensions (length L) and total mass (m). Pendulum A is a very small ball swinging at the end of a uniform massless bar. In pendulum B, half the mass is in the ball and half is in the uniform bar. Find the period of each pendulum for small oscillations. Which one takes longer for a swing?

14.56 •• **CP** A holiday ornament in the shape of a hollow sphere with mass $M = 0.015$ kg and radius $R = 0.050$ m is hung from a tree limb by a small loop of wire attached to the surface of the sphere. If the ornament is displaced a small distance and released, it swings back and forth as a physical pendulum with negligible friction. Calculate its period. (*Hint:* Use the parallel-axis theorem to find the moment of inertia of the sphere about the pivot at the tree limb.)

14.57 •• The two pendulums shown in Fig. E14.57 each consist of a uniform solid ball of mass M supported by a rigid massless rod, but the ball for pendulum A is very tiny while the ball for pendulum B is much larger. Find the period of each pendulum for small displacements. Which ball takes longer to complete a swing?

Figure **E14.57**

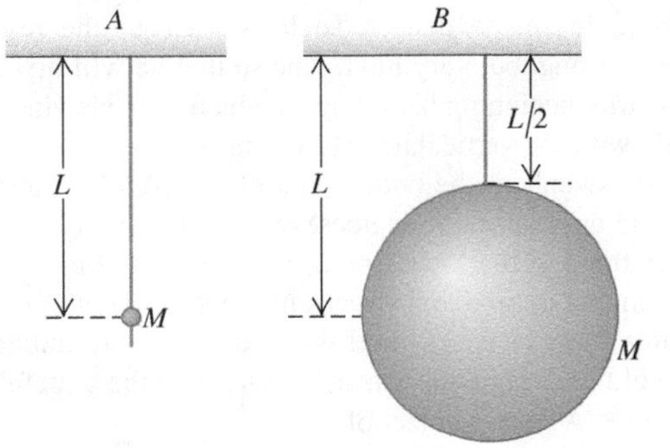

Section 14.7 Damped Oscillations

14.58 • A 2.50-kg rock is attached at the end of a thin, very light rope 1.45 m long. You start it swinging by releasing it when the rope makes an 11° angle with the vertical. You record the observation that it rises only to an angle of 4.5° with the vertical after $10\frac{1}{2}$ swings. (a) How much energy has this system lost during that time? (b) What happened to the "lost" energy? Explain *how* it could have been "lost."

14.59 • An unhappy 0.300-kg rodent, moving on the end of a spring with force constant $k = 2.50$ N/m, is acted on by a damping force $F_x = -bv_x$. (a) If the constant b has the value 0.900 kg/s, what is the frequency of oscillation of the rodent? (b) For what value of the constant b will the motion be critically damped?

14.60 •• A 50.0-g hard-boiled egg moves on the end of a spring with force constant $k = 25.0$ N/m. Its initial displacement is 0.300 m. A damping force $F_x = -bv_x$ acts on the egg, and the amplitude of the motion decreases to 0.100 m in 5.00 s. Calculate the magnitude of the damping constant b.

14.61 •• **CALC** The motion of an underdamped oscillator is described by Eq. (14.42). Let the phase angle ϕ be zero. (a) According to this equation, what is the value of x at $t = 0$? (b) What are the magnitude and direction of the velocity at $t = 0$? What does the result tell you about the slope of the graph of x versus t near $t = 0$? (c) Obtain an expression for the acceleration a_x at $t = 0$. For what value or range of values of the damping constant b (in terms of k and m) is the acceleration at $t = 0$ negative, zero, and positive? Discuss each case in terms of the shape of the graph of x versus t near $t = 0$.

14.62 •• A mass is vibrating at the end of a spring of force constant 225 N/m. Figure E14.62 shows a graph of its position x as a function of time t. (a) At what times is the mass not moving? (b) How much energy did this system originally contain? (c) How much energy did the system lose between $t = 1.0$ s and $t = 4.0$ s? Where did this energy go?

Figure **E14.62**

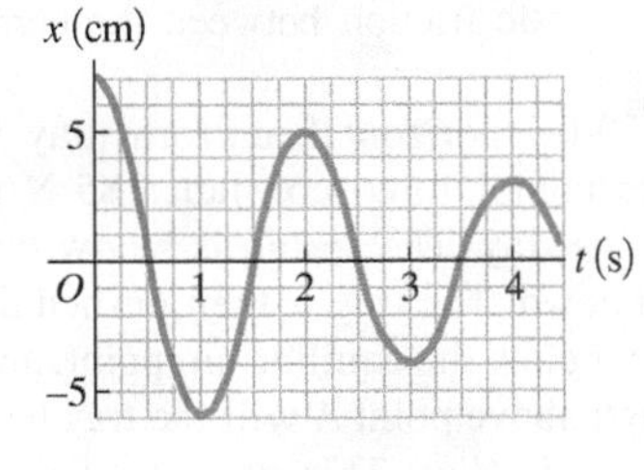

Section 14.8 Forced Oscillations and Resonance

14.63 • A sinusoidally varying driving force is applied to a damped harmonic oscillator. (a) What are the units of the damping constant b? (b) Show that the quantity $\sqrt{km}$ has the same units as b. (c) In terms of F_{max} and k, what is the amplitude for $\omega_d = \sqrt{k/m}$ when (i) $b = 0.2\sqrt{km}$ and (ii) $b = 0.4\sqrt{km}$? Compare your results to Fig. 14.28.

14.64 • A sinusoidally varying driving force is applied to a damped harmonic oscillator of force constant k and mass m. If the damping constant has a value b_1, the amplitude is A_1 when the driving angular frequency equals $\sqrt{k/m}$. In terms of A_1, what is the amplitude for the same driving frequency and the same driving force amplitude F_{max}, if the damping constant is (a) $3b_1$ and (b) $b_1/2$?

PROBLEMS

14.65 •• An object is undergoing SHM with period 1.200 s and amplitude 0.600 m. At $t = 0$ the object is at $x = 0$ and is moving in the negative x-direction. How far is the object from the equilibrium position when $t = 0.480$ s?

14.66 ••• An object is undergoing SHM with period 0.300 s and amplitude 6.00 cm. At $t = 0$ the object is instantaneously at rest at $x = 6.00$ cm. Calculate the time it takes the object to go from $x = 6.00$ cm to $x = -1.50$ cm.

14.67 • **CP SHM in a Car Engine.** The motion of the piston of an automobile engine is approximately simple harmonic. (a) If the stroke of an engine (twice the amplitude) is 0.100 m and the engine runs at 4500 rev/min, compute the acceleration of the piston at the endpoint of its stroke. (b) If the piston has mass 0.450 kg, what net force must be exerted on it at this point? (c) What are the speed and kinetic energy of the piston at the midpoint of its stroke? (d) What average power is required to accelerate the piston from rest to the speed found in part (c)? (e) If the engine runs at 7000 rev/min, what are the answers to parts (b), (c), and (d)?

14.68 • Four passengers with combined mass 250 kg compress the springs of a car with worn-out shock absorbers by 4.00 cm when they get in. Model the car and passengers as a single body on a single ideal spring. If the loaded car has a period of vibration of 1.92 s, what is the period of vibration of the empty car?

14.69 • A glider is oscillating in SHM on an air track with an amplitude A_1. You slow it so that its amplitude is halved. What happens to its (a) period, frequency, and angular frequency;

(b) total mechanical energy; (c) maximum speed; (d) speed at $x = \pm A_1/4$; (e) potential and kinetic energies at $x = \pm A_1/4$?

14.70 ••• **CP** A child with poor table manners is sliding his 250-g dinner plate back and forth in SHM with an amplitude of 0.100 m on a horizontal surface. At a point 0.060 m away from equilibrium, the speed of the plate is 0.400 m/s. (a) What is the period? (b) What is the displacement when the speed is 0.160 m/s? (c) In the center of the dinner plate is a 10.0-g carrot slice. If the carrot slice is just on the verge of slipping at the endpoint of the path, what is the coefficient of static friction between the carrot slice and the plate?

14.71 ••• A 1.50-kg, horizontal, uniform tray is attached to a vertical ideal spring of force constant 185 N/m and a 275-g metal ball is in the tray. The spring is below the tray, so it can oscillate up and down. The tray is then pushed down to point A, which is 15.0 cm below the equilibrium point, and released from rest. (a) How high above point A will the tray be when the metal ball leaves the tray? (*Hint:* This does *not* occur when the ball and tray reach their maximum speeds.) (b) How much time elapses between releasing the system at point A and the ball leaving the tray? (c) How fast is the ball moving just as it leaves the tray?

14.72 •• **CP** A block with mass M rests on a frictionless surface and is connected to a horizontal spring of force constant k. The other end of the spring is attached to a wall (Fig. P14.72). A second block with mass m rests on top of the first block. The coefficient of static friction between the blocks is μ_s. Find the *maximum* amplitude of oscillation such that the top block will not slip on the bottom block.

Figure **P14.72**

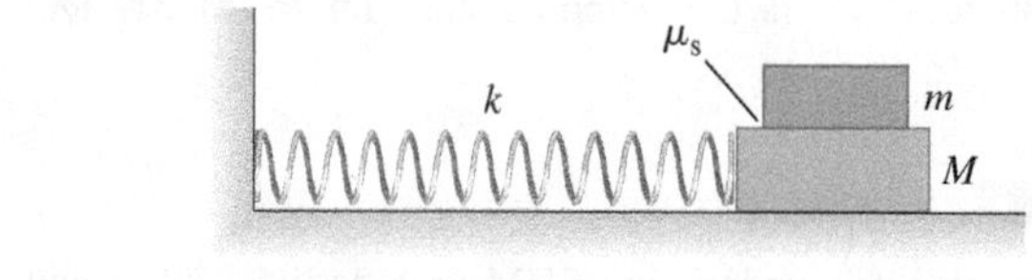

14.73 • **CP** A 10.0-kg mass is traveling to the right with a speed of 2.00 m/s on a smooth horizontal surface when it collides with and sticks to a second 10.0-kg mass that is initially at rest but is attached to a light spring with force constant 110.0 N/m. (a) Find the frequency, amplitude, and period of the subsequent oscillations. (b) How long does it take the system to return the first time to the position it had immediately after the collision?

14.74 • **CP** A rocket is accelerating upward at 4.00 m/s^2 from the launchpad on the earth. Inside a small, 1.50-kg ball hangs from the ceiling by a light, 1.10-m wire. If the ball is displaced 8.50° from the vertical and released, find the amplitude and period of the resulting swings of this pendulum.

14.75 ••• An apple weighs 1.00 N. When you hang it from the end of a long spring of force constant 1.50 N/m and negligible mass, it bounces up and down in SHM. If you stop the bouncing and let the apple swing from side to side through a small angle, the frequency of this simple pendulum is half the bounce frequency. (Because the angle is small, the back-and-forth swings do not cause any appreciable change in the length of the spring.) What is the unstretched length of the spring (with the apple removed)?

14.76 ••• **CP SHM of a Floating Object.** An object with height h, mass M, and a uniform cross-sectional area A floats upright in a liquid with density ρ. (a) Calculate the vertical distance from the surface of the liquid to the bottom of the floating object at equilibrium. (b) A downward force with magnitude F is applied to the top of the object. At the new equilibrium position, how much farther below the surface of the liquid is the bottom of the object than it was in part (a)? (Assume that some of the object remains above the surface of the liquid.) (c) Your result in part (b) shows that if the force is suddenly removed, the object will oscillate up and down in SHM. Calculate the period of this motion in terms of the density ρ of the liquid, the mass M, and the cross-sectional area A of the object. You can ignore the damping due to fluid friction (see Section 14.7).

14.77 •• **CP** A 950-kg, cylindrical can buoy floats vertically in salt water. The diameter of the buoy is 0.900 m. (a) Calculate the additional distance the buoy will sink when a 70.0-kg man stands on top of it. (Use the expression derived in part (b) of Problem 14.76.) (b) Calculate the period of the resulting vertical SHM when the man dives off. (Use the expression derived in part (c) of Problem 14.76, and as in that problem, you can ignore the damping due to fluid friction.)

14.78 ••• **CP Tarzan to the Rescue!** Tarzan spies a 35-kg chimpanzee in severe danger, so he swings to the rescue. He adjusts his strong, but very light, vine so that he will first come to rest 4.0 s after beginning his swing, at which time his vine makes a 12° angle with the vertical. (a) How long is Tarzan's vine, assuming that he swings at the bottom end of it? (b) What are the frequency and amplitude (in degrees) of Tarzan's swing? (c) Just as he passes through the lowest point in his swing, Tarzan nabs the chimp from the ground and sweeps him out of the jaws of danger. If Tarzan's mass is 65 kg, find the frequency and amplitude (in degrees) of the swing with Tarzan holding onto the grateful chimp.

14.79 •• **CP** A square object of mass m is constructed of four identical uniform thin sticks, each of length L, attached together. This object is hung on a hook at its upper corner (Fig. P14.79). If it is rotated slightly to the left and then released, at what frequency will it swing back and forth?

Figure **P14.79**

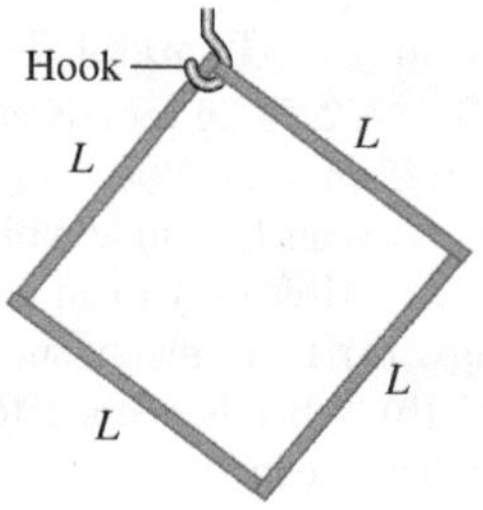

14.80 ••• An object with mass 0.200 kg is acted on by an elastic restoring force with force constant 10.0 N/m. (a) Graph elastic potential energy U as a function of displacement x over a range of x from -0.300 m to $+0.300$ m. On your graph, let 1 cm = 0.05 J vertically and 1 cm = 0.05 m horizontally. The object is set into oscillation with an initial potential energy of 0.140 J and an initial kinetic energy of 0.060 J. Answer the following questions by referring to the graph. (b) What is the amplitude of oscillation? (c) What is the potential energy when the displacement is one-half the amplitude? (d) At what displacement are the kinetic and potential energies equal? (e) What is the value of the phase angle ϕ if the initial velocity is positive and the initial displacement is negative?

14.81 • **CALC** A 2.00-kg bucket containing 10.0 kg of water is hanging from a vertical ideal spring of force constant 125 N/m and oscillating up and down with an amplitude of 3.00 cm. Suddenly the bucket springs a leak in the bottom such that water drops out at a steady rate of 2.00 g/s. When the bucket is half full, find

(a) the period of oscillation and (b) the rate at which the period is changing with respect to time. Is the period getting longer or shorter? (c) What is the shortest period this system can have?

14.82 •• CP A hanging wire is 1.80 m long. When a 60.0-kg steel ball is suspended from the wire, the wire stretches by 2.00 mm. If the ball is pulled down a small additional distance and released, at what frequency will it vibrate? Assume that the stress on the wire is less than the proportional limit (see Section 11.5).

14.83 •• A 5.00-kg partridge is suspended from a pear tree by an ideal spring of negligible mass. When the partridge is pulled down 0.100 m below its equilibrium position and released, it vibrates with a period of 4.20 s. (a) What is its speed as it passes through the equilibrium position? (b) What is its acceleration when it is 0.050 m above the equilibrium position? (c) When it is moving upward, how much time is required for it to move from a point 0.050 m below its equilibrium position to a point 0.050 m above it? (d) The motion of the partridge is stopped, and then it is removed from the spring. How much does the spring shorten?

14.84 •• A 0.0200-kg bolt moves with SHM that has an amplitude of 0.240 m and a period of 1.500 s. The displacement of the bolt is +0.240 m when $t = 0$. Compute (a) the displacement of the bolt when $t = 0.500$ s; (b) the magnitude and direction of the force acting on the bolt when $t = 0.500$ s; (c) the minimum time required for the bolt to move from its initial position to the point where $x = -0.180$ m; (d) the speed of the bolt when $x = -0.180$ m.

14.85 •• CP **SHM of a Butcher's Scale.** A spring of negligible mass and force constant $k = 400$ N/m is hung vertically, and a 0.200-kg pan is suspended from its lower end. A butcher drops a 2.2-kg steak onto the pan from a height of 0.40 m. The steak makes a totally inelastic collision with the pan and sets the system into vertical SHM. What are (a) the speed of the pan and steak immediately after the collision; (b) the amplitude of the subsequent motion; (c) the period of that motion?

14.86 •• A uniform beam is suspended horizontally by two identical vertical springs that are attached between the ceiling and each end of the beam. The beam has mass 225 kg, and a 175-kg sack of gravel sits on the middle of it. The beam is oscillating in SHM, with an amplitude of 40.0 cm and a frequency of 0.600 cycle/s. (a) The sack of gravel falls off the beam when the beam has its maximum upward displacement. What are the frequency and amplitude of the subsequent SHM of the beam? (b) If the gravel instead falls off when the beam has its maximum speed, what are the frequency and amplitude of the subsequent SHM of the beam?

14.87 ••• CP On the planet Newtonia, a simple pendulum having a bob with mass 1.25 kg and a length of 185.0 cm takes 1.42 s, when released from rest, to swing through an angle of 12.5°, where it again has zero speed. The circumference of Newtonia is measured to be 51,400 km. What is the mass of the planet Newtonia?

14.88 •• A 40.0-N force stretches a vertical spring 0.250 m. (a) What mass must be suspended from the spring so that the system will oscillate with a period of 1.00 s? (b) If the amplitude of the motion is 0.050 m and the period is that specified in part (a), where is the object and in what direction is it moving 0.35 s after it has passed the equilibrium position, moving downward? (c) What force (magnitude and direction) does the spring exert on the object when it is 0.030 m below the equilibrium position, moving upward?

14.89 •• **Don't Miss the Boat.** While on a visit to Minnesota ("Land of 10,000 Lakes"), you sign up to take an excursion around one of the larger lakes. When you go to the dock where the 1500-kg boat is tied, you find that the boat is bobbing up and down in the waves, executing simple harmonic motion with amplitude 20 cm. The boat takes 3.5 s to make one complete up-and-down cycle. When the boat is at its highest point, its deck is at the same height as the stationary dock. As you watch the boat bob up and down, you (mass 60 kg) begin to feel a bit woozy, due in part to the previous night's dinner of lutefisk. As a result, you refuse to board the boat unless the level of the boat's deck is within 10 cm of the dock level. How much time do you have to board the boat comfortably during each cycle of up-and-down motion?

14.90 • CP An interesting, though highly impractical example of oscillation is the motion of an object dropped down a hole that extends from one side of the earth, through its center, to the other side. With the assumption (not realistic) that the earth is a sphere of uniform density, prove that the motion is simple harmonic and find the period. [*Note:* The gravitational force on the object as a function of the object's distance r from the center of the earth was derived in Example 13.10 (Section 13.6). The motion is simple harmonic if the acceleration a_x and the displacement from equilibrium x are related by Eq. (14.8), and the period is then $T = 2\pi/\omega$.]

14.91 ••• CP A rifle bullet with mass 8.00 g and initial horizontal velocity 280 m/s strikes and embeds itself in a block with mass 0.992 kg that rests on a frictionless surface and is attached to one end of an ideal spring. The other end of the spring is attached to the wall. The impact compresses the spring a maximum distance of 18.0 cm. After the impact, the block moves in SHM. Calculate the period of this motion.

14.92 •• CP CALC For a certain oscillator the net force on the body with mass m is given by $F_x = -cx^3$. (a) What is the potential energy function for this oscillator if we take $U = 0$ at $x = 0$? (b) One-quarter of a period is the time for the body to move from $x = 0$ to $x = A$. Calculate this time and hence the period. [*Hint:* Begin with Eq. (14.20), modified to include the potential-energy function you found in part (a), and solve for the velocity v_x as a function of x. Then replace v_x with dx/dt. Separate the variable by writing all factors containing x on one side and all factors containing t on the other side so that each side can be integrated. In the x-integral make the change of variable $u = x/A$. The resulting integral can be evaluated by numerical methods on a computer and has the value $\int_0^1 du/\sqrt{1-u^4} = 1.31$.] (c) According to the result you obtained in part (b), does the period depend on the amplitude A of the motion? Are the oscillations simple harmonic?

14.93 • CP CALC An approximation for the potential energy of a KCl molecule is $U = A[(R_0^7/8r^8) - 1/r]$, where $R_0 = 2.67 \times 10^{-10}$ m, $A = 2.31 \times 10^{-28}$ J·m, and r is the distance between the two atoms. Using this approximation: (a) Show that the radial component of the force on each atom is $F_r = A[(R_0^7/r^9) - 1/r^2]$. (b) Show that R_0 is the equilibrium separation. (c) Find the minimum potential energy. (d) Use $r = R_0 + x$ and the first two terms of the binomial theorem (Eq. 14.28) to show that $F_r \approx -(7A/R_0^3)x$, so that the molecule's force constant is $k = 7A/R_0^3$. (e) With both the K and Cl atoms vibrating in opposite directions on opposite sides of the molecule's center of mass, $m_1m_2/(m_1 + m_2) = 3.06 \times 10^{-26}$ kg is the mass to use in calculating the frequency. Calculate the frequency of small-amplitude vibrations.

14.94 ••• CP Two uniform solid spheres, each with mass $M = 0.800$ kg and radius $R = 0.0800$ m, are connected by a short, light rod that is along a diameter of each sphere and are at rest on a horizontal tabletop. A spring with force constant $k = 160$ N/m has one end attached to the wall and the other end attached to a frictionless ring that passes over the rod at the center of mass of the spheres, which is midway between the centers of the two spheres. The spheres are each pulled the same distance from the wall, stretching the spring, and released. There is sufficient friction between the tabletop and the spheres for the spheres to roll without slipping as they move back and forth on the end of the spring. Show that the motion of the center of mass of the spheres is simple harmonic and calculate the period.

14.95 • **CP** In Fig. P14.95 the upper ball is released from rest, collides with the stationary lower ball, and sticks to it. The strings are both 50.0 cm long. The upper ball has mass 2.00 kg, and it is initially 10.0 cm higher than the lower ball, which has mass 3.00 kg. Find the frequency and maximum angular displacement of the motion after the collision.

Figure **P14.95**

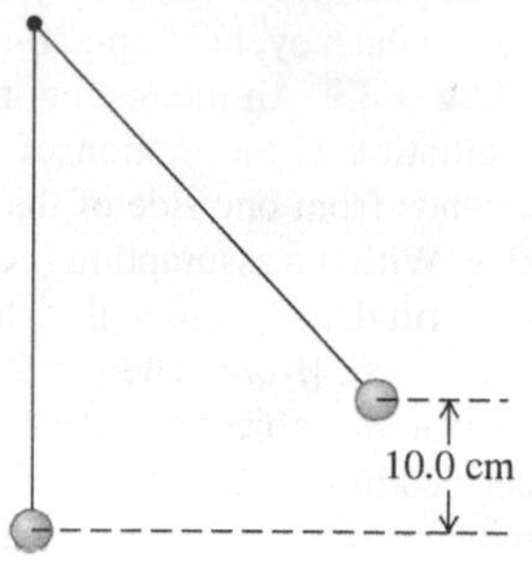

14.96 •• **CP BIO** ***T. rex.*** Model the leg of the *T. rex* in Example 14.10 (Section 14.6) as two uniform rods, each 1.55 m long, joined rigidly end to end. Let the lower rod have mass M and the upper rod mass $2M$. The composite object is pivoted about the top of the upper rod. Compute the oscillation period of this object for small-amplitude oscillations. Compare your result to that of Example 14.10.

14.97 •• **CALC** A slender, uniform, metal rod with mass M is pivoted without friction about an axis through its midpoint and perpendicular to the rod. A horizontal spring with force constant k is attached to the lower end of the rod, with the other end of the spring attached to a rigid support. If the rod is displaced by a small angle Θ from the vertical (Fig. P14.97) and released, show that it moves in angular SHM and calculate the period. (*Hint:* Assume that the angle Θ is small enough for the approximations $\sin\Theta \approx \Theta$ and $\cos\Theta \approx 1$ to be valid. The motion is simple harmonic if $d^2\theta/dt^2 = -\omega^2\theta$, and the period is then $T = 2\pi/\omega$.)

Figure **P14.97**

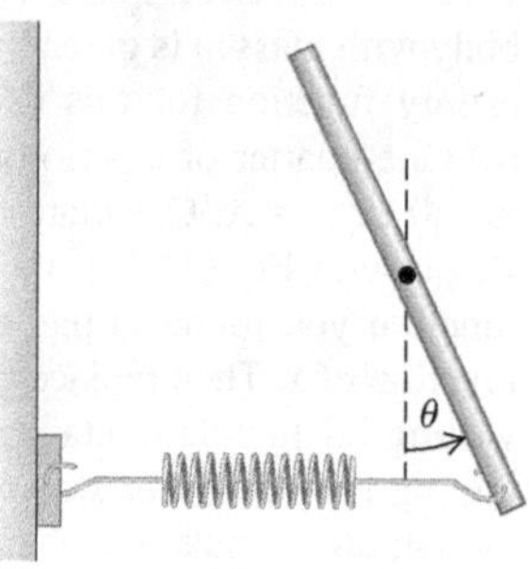

14.98 •• **The Silently Ringing Bell Problem.** A large bell is hung from a wooden beam so it can swing back and forth with negligible friction. The center of mass of the bell is 0.60 m below the pivot, the bell has mass 34.0 kg, and the moment of inertia of the bell about an axis at the pivot is 18.0 kg · m². The clapper is a small, 1.8-kg mass attached to one end of a slender rod that has length L and negligible mass. The other end of the rod is attached to the inside of the bell so it can swing freely about the same axis as the bell. What should be the length L of the clapper rod for the bell to ring silently—that is, for the period of oscillation for the bell to equal that for the clapper?

14.99 ••• Two identical thin rods, each with mass m and length L, are joined at right angles to form an L-shaped object. This object is balanced on top of a sharp edge (Fig. P14.99). If the L-shaped object is deflected slightly, it oscillates. Find the frequency of oscillation.

Figure **P14.99**

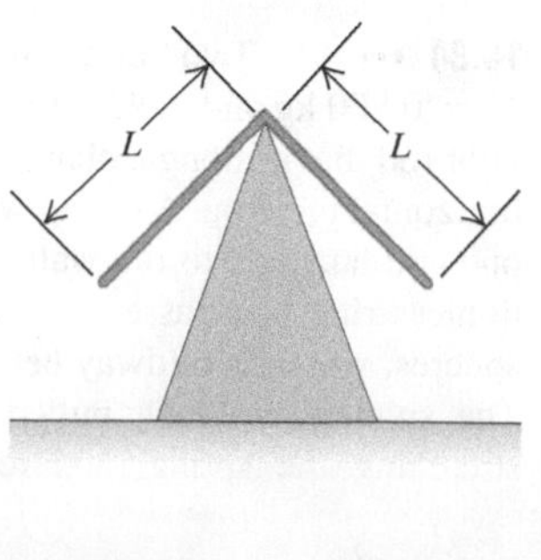

14.100 • **CP CALC** A uniform rod of length L oscillates through small angles about a point a distance x from its center. (a) Prove that its angular frequency is $\sqrt{gx/[(L^2/12) + x^2]}$. (b) Show that its maximum angular frequency occurs when $x = L/\sqrt{12}$. (c) What is the length of the rod if the maximum angular frequency is 2π rad/s?

CHALLENGE PROBLEMS

14.101 ••• **The Effective Force Constant of Two Springs.** Two springs with the same unstretched length but different force constants k_1 and k_2 are attached to a block with mass m on a level, frictionless surface. Calculate the effective force constant k_{eff} in each of the three cases (a), (b), and (c) depicted in Fig. P14.101. (The effective force constant is defined by $\sum F_x = -k_{eff}x$.) (d) An object with mass m, suspended from a uniform spring with a force constant k, vibrates with a frequency f_1. When the spring is cut in half and the same object is suspended from one of the halves, the frequency is f_2. What is the ratio f_2/f_1?

Figure **P14.101**

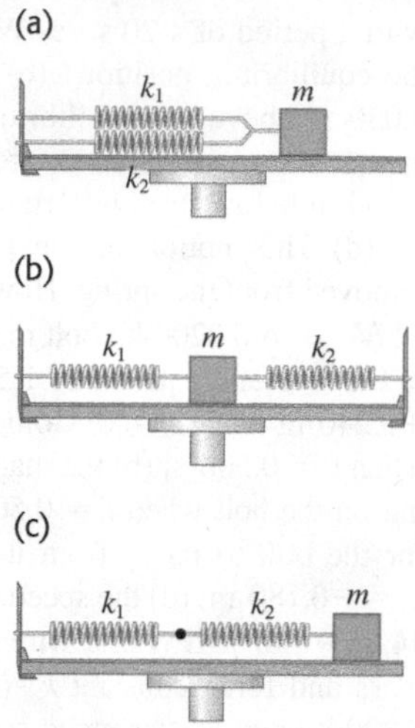

14.102 ••• Two springs, each with unstretched length 0.200 m but with different force constants k_1 and k_2, are attached to opposite ends of a block with mass m on a level, frictionless surface. The outer ends of the springs are now attached to two pins P_1 and P_2, 0.100 m from the original positions of the ends of the springs (Fig. P14.102). Let $k_1 = 2.00$ N/m, $k_2 = 6.00$ N/m, and $m = 0.100$ kg. (a) Find the length of each spring when the block is in its new equilibrium position after the springs have been attached to the pins. (b) Find the period of vibration of the block if it is slightly displaced from its new equilibrium position and released.

Figure **P14.102**

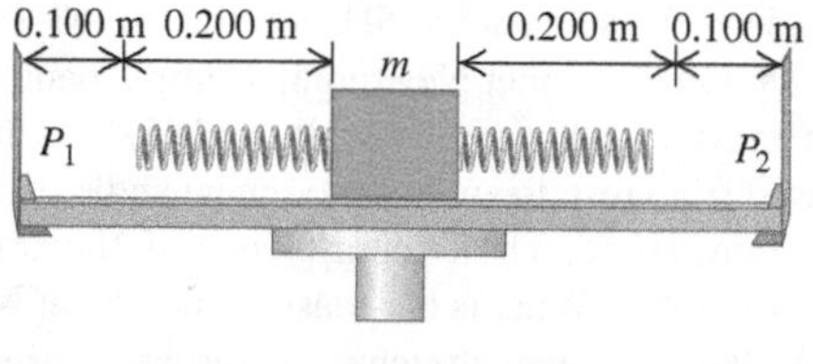

14.103 ••• **CALC A Spring with Mass.** The preceding problems in this chapter have assumed that the springs had negligible mass. But of course no spring is completely massless. To find the effect of the spring's mass, consider a spring with mass M, equilibrium length L_0, and spring constant k. When stretched or compressed to a length L, the potential energy is $\frac{1}{2}kx^2$, where $x = L - L_0$. (a) Consider a spring, as described above, that has one end fixed and the other end moving with speed v. Assume that the speed of points along the length of the spring varies linearly with distance l from the fixed end. Assume also that the mass M of the spring is distributed uniformly along the length of the spring. Calculate the kinetic energy of the spring in terms of M and v. (*Hint:* Divide the spring into pieces of length dl; find the speed of each piece in terms of l, v, and L; find the mass of each piece in terms of dl, M, and L; and integrate from 0 to L. The result is *not* $\frac{1}{2}Mv^2$, since not all of the spring moves with the same speed.) (b) Take the time derivative of the conservation of energy equation, Eq. (14.21), for a mass m moving on the end of a *massless* spring. By comparing your results to Eq. (14.8), which defines ω, show that the angular frequency of oscillation is $\omega = \sqrt{k/m}$. (c) Apply the procedure of part (b) to obtain the angular frequency of oscillation ω of the spring considered in part (a). If the *effective mass* M' of the spring is defined by $\omega = \sqrt{k/M'}$, what is M' in terms of M?

Answers

Chapter Opening Question ?

The length of the leg is more important. The back-and-forth motion of a leg during walking is like a physical pendulum, for which the oscillation period is $T = 2\pi\sqrt{I/mgd}$ [see Eq. (14.39)]. In this expression I is the moment of inertia of the pendulum, m is its mass, and d is the distance from the rotation axis to the pendulum center of mass. The moment of inertia I is proportional to the mass m, so the mass cancels out of this expression for the period T. Hence only the dimensions of the leg matter. (See Examples 14.9 and 14.10.)

Test Your Understanding Questions

14.1 Answers: (a) $x < 0$, (b) $x > 0$, (c) $x < 0$, (d) $x > 0$, (e) $x > 0$, (f) $x = 0$ Figure 14.2 shows that the net x-component of force F_x and the x-acceleration a_x are both positive when $x < 0$ (so the body is displaced to the left and the spring is compressed), while F_x and a_x are both negative when $x > 0$ (so the body is displaced to the right and the spring is stretched). Hence x and a_x always have *opposite* signs. This is true whether the object is moving to the right ($v_x > 0$), to the left ($v_x < 0$), or not at all ($v_x = 0$), since the force exerted by the spring depends only on whether it is compressed or stretched and by what distance. This explains the answers to (a) through (e). If the acceleration is zero as in (f), the net force must also be zero and so the spring must be relaxed; hence $x = 0$.

14.2 Answers: (a) $A > 0.10$ m, $\phi < 0$; (b) $A > 0.10$ m, $\phi > 0$ In both situations the initial ($t = 0$) x-velocity v_{0x} is nonzero, so from Eq. (14.19) the amplitude $A = \sqrt{x_0^2 + (v_{0x}^2/\omega^2)}$ is greater than the initial x-coordinate $x_0 = 0.10$ m. From Eq. (14.18) the phase angle is $\phi = \arctan(-v_{0x}/\omega x_0)$, which is positive if the quantity $-v_{0x}/\omega x_0$ (the argument of the arctangent function) is positive and negative if $-v_{0x}/\omega x_0$ is negative. In part (a) x_0 and v_{0x} are both positive, so $-v_{0x}/\omega x_0 < 0$ and $\phi < 0$. In part (b) x_0 is positive and v_{0x} is negative, so $-v_{0x}/\omega x_0 > 0$ and $\phi > 0$.

14.3 Answers: (a) (iii), (b) (v) To increase the total energy $E = \frac{1}{2}kA^2$ by a factor of 2, the amplitude A must increase by a factor of $\sqrt{2}$. Because the motion is SHM, changing the amplitude has no effect on the frequency.

14.4 Answer: (i) The oscillation period of a body of mass m attached to a hanging spring of force constant k is given by $T = 2\pi\sqrt{m/k}$, the same expression as for a body attached to a horizontal spring. Neither m nor k changes when the apparatus is taken to Mars, so the period is unchanged. The only difference is that in equilibrium, the spring will stretch a shorter distance on Mars than on earth due to the weaker gravity.

14.5 Answer: no Just as for an object oscillating on a spring, at the equilibrium position the *speed* of the pendulum bob is instantaneously not changing (this is where the speed is maximum, so its derivative at this time is zero). But the *direction* of motion is changing because the pendulum bob follows a circular path. Hence the bob must have a component of acceleration perpendicular to the path and toward the center of the circle (see Section 3.4). To cause this acceleration at the equilibrium position when the string is vertical, the upward tension force at this position must be greater than the weight of the bob. This causes a net upward force on the bob and an upward acceleration toward the center of the circular path.

14.6 Answer: (i) The period of a physical pendulum is given by Eq. (14.39), $T = 2\pi\sqrt{I/mgd}$. The distance $d = L$ from the pivot to the center of gravity is the same for both the rod and the simple pendulum, as is the mass m. This means that for any displacement angle θ the same restoring torque acts on both the rod and the simple pendulum. However, the rod has a greater moment of inertia: $I_{\text{rod}} = \frac{1}{3}m(2L)^2 = \frac{4}{3}mL^2$ and $I_{\text{simple}} = mL^2$ (all the mass of the pendulum is a distance L from the pivot). Hence the rod has a longer period.

14.7 Answer: (ii) The oscillations are underdamped with a decreasing amplitude on each cycle of oscillation, like those graphed in Fig. 14.26. If the oscillations were undamped, they would continue indefinitely with the same amplitude. If they were critically damped or overdamped, the nose would not bob up and down but would return smoothly to the original equilibrium attitude without overshooting.

14.8 Answer: (i) Figure 14.28 shows that the curve of amplitude versus driving frequency moves upward at *all* frequencies as the value of the damping constant b is decreased. Hence for fixed values of k and m, the oscillator with the least damping (smallest value of b) will have the greatest response at any driving frequency.

Bridging Problem

Answer: $T = 2\pi\sqrt{3M/2k}$

15 MECHANICAL WAVES

? When an earthquake strikes, the news of the event travels through the body of the earth in the form of seismic waves. Which aspects of a seismic wave determine how much power is carried by the wave?

LEARNING GOALS

By studying this chapter, you will learn:

- What is meant by a mechanical wave, and the different varieties of mechanical waves.
- How to use the relationship among speed, frequency, and wavelength for a periodic wave.
- How to interpret and use the mathematical expression for a sinusoidal periodic wave.
- How to calculate the speed of waves on a rope or string.
- How to calculate the rate at which a mechanical wave transports energy.
- What happens when mechanical waves overlap and interfere.
- The properties of standing waves on a string, and how to analyze these waves.
- How stringed instruments produce sounds of specific frequencies.

Ripples on a pond, musical sounds, seismic tremors triggered by an earthquake—all these are *wave* phenomena. Waves can occur whenever a system is disturbed from equilibrium and when the disturbance can travel, or *propagate,* from one region of the system to another. As a wave propagates, it carries energy. The energy in light waves from the sun warms the surface of our planet; the energy in seismic waves can crack our planet's crust.

This chapter and the next are about mechanical waves—waves that travel within some material called a *medium.* (Chapter 16 is concerned with sound, an important type of mechanical wave.) We'll begin this chapter by deriving the basic equations for describing waves, including the important special case of *sinusoidal* waves in which the wave pattern is a repeating sine or cosine function. To help us understand waves in general, we'll look at the simple case of waves that travel on a stretched string or rope.

Waves on a string play an important role in music. When a musician strums a guitar or bows a violin, she makes waves that travel in opposite directions along the instrument's strings. What happens when these oppositely directed waves overlap is called *interference.* We'll discover that sinusoidal waves can occur on a guitar or violin string only for certain special frequencies, called *normal-mode frequencies,* determined by the properties of the string. The normal-mode frequencies of a stringed instrument determine the pitch of the musical sounds that the instrument produces. (In the next chapter we'll find that interference also helps explain the pitches of *wind* instruments such as flutes and pipe organs.)

Not all waves are mechanical in nature. *Electromagnetic* waves—including light, radio waves, infrared and ultraviolet radiation, and x rays—can propagate even in empty space, where there is *no* medium. We'll explore these and other nonmechanical waves in later chapters.

15.1 Types of Mechanical Waves

A **mechanical wave** is a disturbance that travels through some material or substance called the **medium** for the wave. As the wave travels through the medium, the particles that make up the medium undergo displacements of various kinds, depending on the nature of the wave.

Figure 15.1 shows three varieties of mechanical waves. In Fig. 15.1a the medium is a string or rope under tension. If we give the left end a small upward shake or wiggle, the wiggle travels along the length of the string. Successive sections of string go through the same motion that we gave to the end, but at successively later times. Because the displacements of the medium are perpendicular or *transverse* to the direction of travel of the wave along the medium, this is called a **transverse wave.**

In Fig. 15.1b the medium is a liquid or gas in a tube with a rigid wall at the right end and a movable piston at the left end. If we give the piston a single back-and-forth motion, displacement and pressure fluctuations travel down the length of the medium. This time the motions of the particles of the medium are back and forth along the *same* direction that the wave travels. We call this a **longitudinal wave.**

In Fig. 15.1c the medium is a liquid in a channel, such as water in an irrigation ditch or canal. When we move the flat board at the left end forward and back once, a wave disturbance travels down the length of the channel. In this case the displacements of the water have *both* longitudinal and transverse components.

Each of these systems has an equilibrium state. For the stretched string it is the state in which the system is at rest, stretched out along a straight line. For the fluid in a tube it is a state in which the fluid is at rest with uniform pressure. And for the liquid in a trough it is a smooth, level water surface. In each case the wave motion is a disturbance from the equilibrium state that travels from one region of the medium to another. And in each case there are forces that tend to restore the system to its equilibrium position when it is displaced, just as the force of gravity tends to pull a pendulum toward its straight-down equilibrium position when it is displaced.

Application Waves on a Snake's Body
A snake moves itself along the ground by producing waves that travel backward along its body from its head to its tail. The waves remain stationary with respect to the ground as they push against the ground, so the snake moves forward.

MasteringPHYSICS
ActivPhysics 10.1: Properties of Mechanical Waves

15.1 Three ways to make a wave that moves to the right. (a) The hand moves the string up and then returns, producing a transverse wave. (b) The piston moves to the right, compressing the gas or liquid, and then returns, producing a longitudinal wave. (c) The board moves to the right and then returns, producing a combination of longitudinal and transverse waves.

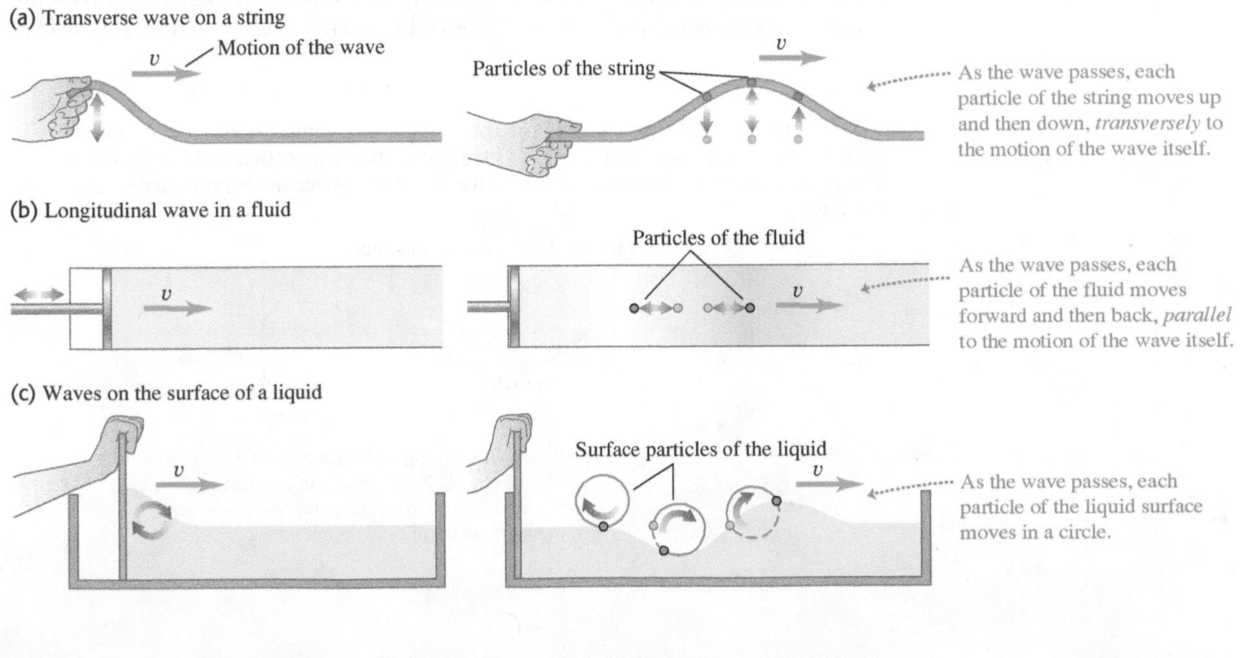

15.2 "Doing the wave" at a sports stadium is an example of a mechanical wave: The disturbance propagates through the crowd, but there is no transport of matter (none of the spectators moves from one seat to another).

These examples have three things in common. First, in each case the disturbance travels or *propagates* with a definite speed through the medium. This speed is called the speed of propagation, or simply the **wave speed.** Its value is determined in each case by the mechanical properties of the medium. We will use the symbol v for wave speed. (The wave speed is *not* the same as the speed with which particles move when they are disturbed by the wave. We'll return to this point in Section 15.3.) Second, the medium itself does not travel through space; its individual particles undergo back-and-forth or up-and-down motions around their equilibrium positions. The overall pattern of the wave disturbance is what travels. Third, to set any of these systems into motion, we have to put in energy by doing mechanical work on the system. The wave motion transports this energy from one region of the medium to another. *Waves transport energy, but not matter, from one region to another* (Fig. 15.2).

Test Your Understanding of Section 15.1 What type of wave is "the wave" shown in Fig. 15.2? (i) transverse; (ii) longitudinal; (iii) a combination of transverse and longitudinal.

15.2 Periodic Waves

The transverse wave on a stretched string in Fig. 15.1a is an example of a *wave pulse.* The hand shakes the string up and down just once, exerting a transverse force on it as it does so. The result is a single "wiggle," or pulse, that travels along the length of the string. The tension in the string restores its straight-line shape once the pulse has passed.

A more interesting situation develops when we give the free end of the string a repetitive, or *periodic,* motion. (You may want to review the discussion of periodic motion in Chapter 14 before going ahead.) Then each particle in the string also undergoes periodic motion as the wave propagates, and we have a **periodic wave.**

Periodic Transverse Waves

In particular, suppose we move the string up and down with *simple harmonic motion* (SHM) with amplitude A, frequency f, angular frequency $\omega = 2\pi f$, and period $T = 1/f = 2\pi/\omega$. Figure 15.3 shows one way to do this. The wave that results is a symmetrical sequence of *crests* and *troughs.* As we will see, periodic

15.3 A block of mass m attached to a spring undergoes simple harmonic motion, producing a sinusoidal wave that travels to the right on the string. (In a real-life system a driving force would have to be applied to the block to replace the energy carried away by the wave.)

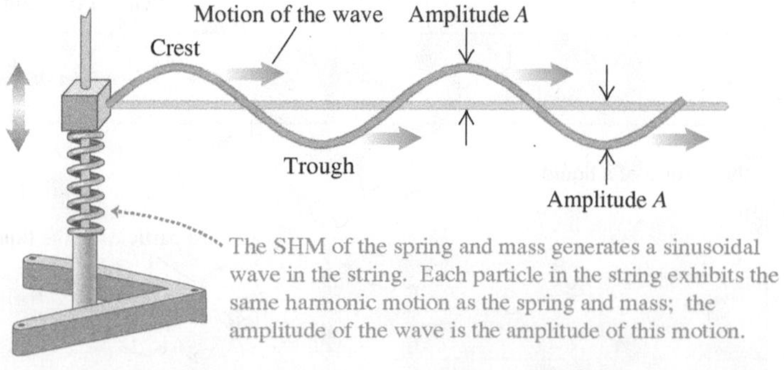

waves with simple harmonic motion are particularly easy to analyze; we call them **sinusoidal waves.** It also turns out that *any* periodic wave can be represented as a combination of sinusoidal waves. So this particular kind of wave motion is worth special attention.

In Fig. 15.3 the wave that advances along the string is a *continuous succession* of transverse sinusoidal disturbances. Figure 15.4 shows the shape of a part of the string near the left end at time intervals of $\frac{1}{8}$ of a period, for a total time of one period. The wave shape advances steadily toward the right, as indicated by the highlighted area. As the wave moves, any point on the string (any of the red dots, for example) oscillates up and down about its equilibrium position with simple harmonic motion. *When a sinusoidal wave passes through a medium, every particle in the medium undergoes simple harmonic motion with the same frequency.*

CAUTION **Wave motion vs. particle motion** Be very careful to distinguish between the motion of the *transverse wave* along the string and the motion of a *particle* of the string. The wave moves with constant speed v *along* the length of the string, while the motion of the particle is simple harmonic and *transverse* (perpendicular) to the length of the string.

For a periodic wave, the shape of the string at any instant is a repeating pattern. The length of one complete wave pattern is the distance from one crest to the next, or from one trough to the next, or from any point to the corresponding point on the next repetition of the wave shape. We call this distance the **wavelength** of the wave, denoted by λ (the Greek letter lambda). The wave pattern travels with constant speed v and advances a distance of one wavelength λ in a time interval of one period T. So the wave speed v is given by $v = \lambda/T$ or, because $f = 1/T$,

$$v = \lambda f \qquad \text{(periodic wave)} \tag{15.1}$$

The speed of propagation equals the product of wavelength and frequency. The frequency is a property of the *entire* periodic wave because all points on the string oscillate with the same frequency f.

Waves on a string propagate in just one dimension (in Fig. 15.4, along the x-axis). But the ideas of frequency, wavelength, and amplitude apply equally well to waves that propagate in two or three dimensions. Figure 15.5 shows a wave propagating in two dimensions on the surface of a tank of water. As with waves on a string, the wavelength is the distance from one crest to the next, and the amplitude is the height of a crest above the equilibrium level.

In many important situations including waves on a string, the wave speed v is determined entirely by the mechanical properties of the medium. In this case, increasing f causes λ to decrease so that the product $v = \lambda f$ remains the same, and waves of *all* frequencies propagate with the same wave speed. In this chapter we will consider *only* waves of this kind. (In later chapters we will study the propagation of light waves in matter for which the wave speed depends on frequency; this turns out to be the reason prisms break white light into a spectrum and raindrops create a rainbow.)

Periodic Longitudinal Waves

To understand the mechanics of a periodic *longitudinal* wave, we consider a long tube filled with a fluid, with a piston at the left end as in Fig. 15.1b. If we push the piston in, we compress the fluid near the piston, increasing the pressure in this

15.4 A sinusoidal transverse wave traveling to the right along a string. The vertical scale is exaggerated.

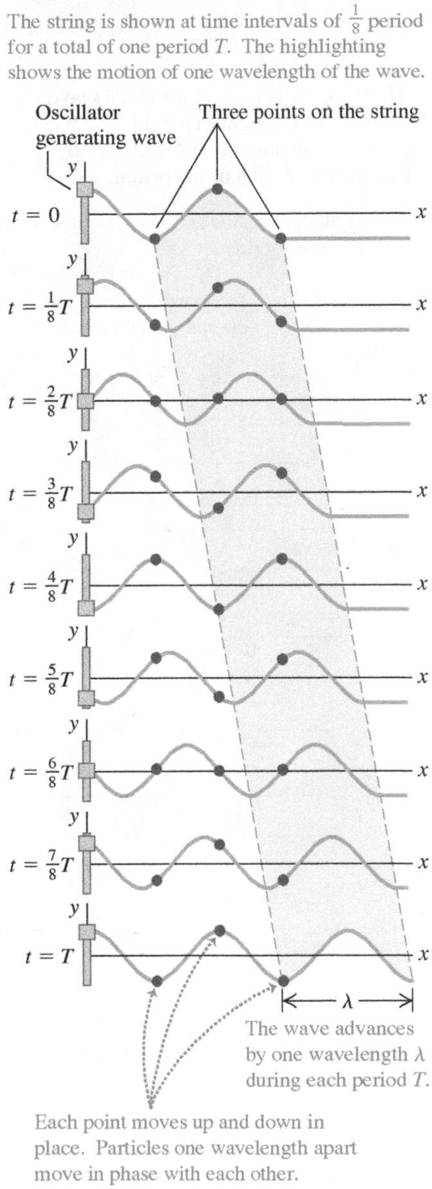

15.5 A series of drops falling into water produces a periodic wave that spreads radially outward. The wave crests and troughs are concentric circles. The wavelength λ is the radial distance between adjacent crests or adjacent troughs.

15.6 Using an oscillating piston to make a sinusoidal longitudinal wave in a fluid.

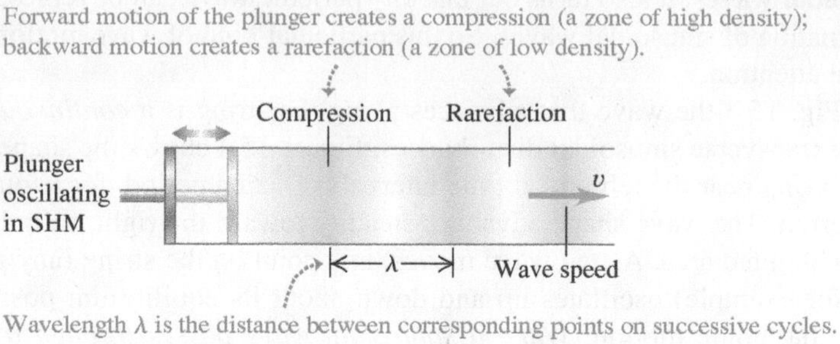

15.7 A sinusoidal longitudinal wave traveling to the right in a fluid. The wave has the same amplitude A and period T as the oscillation of the piston.

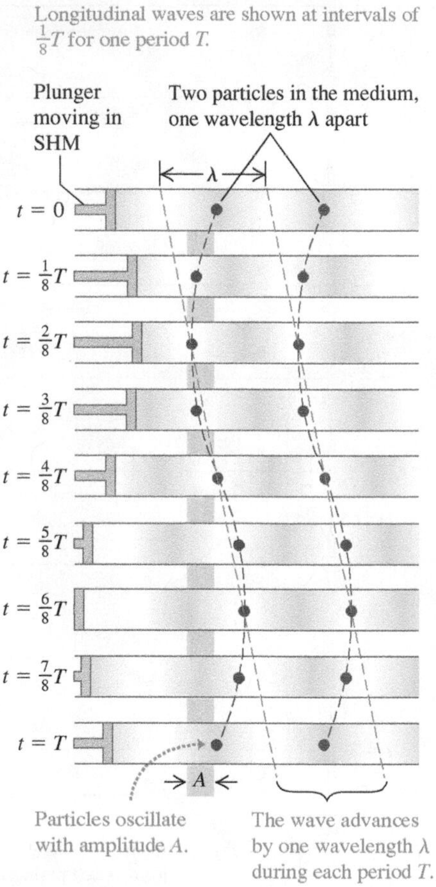

region. This region then pushes against the neighboring region of fluid, and so on, and a wave pulse moves along the tube.

Now suppose we move the piston back and forth with simple harmonic motion, along a line parallel to the axis of the tube (Fig. 15.6). This motion forms regions in the fluid where the pressure and density are greater or less than the equilibrium values. We call a region of increased density a *compression;* a region of reduced density is a *rarefaction.* Figure 15.6 shows compressions as darkly shaded areas and rarefactions as lightly shaded areas. The wavelength is the distance from one compression to the next or from one rarefaction to the next.

Figure 15.7 shows the wave propagating in the fluid-filled tube at time intervals of $\frac{1}{8}$ of a period, for a total time of one period. The pattern of compressions and rarefactions moves steadily to the right, just like the pattern of crests and troughs in a sinusoidal transverse wave (compare Fig. 15.4). Each particle in the fluid oscillates in SHM parallel to the direction of wave propagation (that is, left and right) with the same amplitude A and period T as the piston. The particles shown by the two red dots in Fig. 15.7 are one wavelength apart, and so oscillate in phase with each other.

Just like the sinusoidal transverse wave shown in Fig. 15.4, in one period T the longitudinal wave in Fig. 15.7 travels one wavelength λ to the right. Hence the fundamental equation $v = \lambda f$ holds for longitudinal waves as well as for transverse waves, and indeed for *all* types of periodic waves. Just as for transverse waves, in this chapter and the next we will consider only situations in which the speed of longitudinal waves does not depend on the frequency.

Example 15.1 Wavelength of a musical sound

Sound waves are longitudinal waves in air. The speed of sound depends on temperature; at 20°C it is 344 m/s (1130 ft/s). What is the wavelength of a sound wave in air at 20°C if the frequency is 262 Hz (the approximate frequency of middle C on a piano)?

SOLUTION

IDENTIFY and SET UP: This problem involves Eq. (15.1), $v = \lambda f$, which relates wave speed v, wavelength λ, and frequency f for a periodic wave. The target variable is the wavelength λ. We are given $v = 344$ m/s and $f = 262\ \text{Hz} = 262\ \text{s}^{-1}$.

EXECUTE: We solve Eq. (15.1) for λ:

$$\lambda = \frac{v}{f} = \frac{344\ \text{m/s}}{262\ \text{Hz}} = \frac{344\ \text{m/s}}{262\ \text{s}^{-1}} = 1.31\ \text{m}$$

EVALUATE: The speed v of sound waves does *not* depend on the frequency. Hence $\lambda = v/f$ says that wavelength changes in inverse proportion to frequency. As an example, high (soprano) C is two octaves above middle C. Each octave corresponds to a factor of 2 in frequency, so the frequency of high C is four times that of middle C: $f = 4(262\ \text{Hz}) = 1048$ Hz. Hence the *wavelength* of high C is *one-fourth* as large: $\lambda = (1.31\ \text{m})/4 = 0.328$ m.

Test Your Understanding of Section 15.2 If you double the wavelength of a wave on a particular string, what happens to the wave speed v and the frequency f? (i) v doubles and f is unchanged; (ii) v is unchanged and f doubles; (iii) v becomes one-half as great and f is unchanged; (iv) v is unchanged and f becomes one-half as great; (v) none of these.

15.3 Mathematical Description of a Wave

Many characteristics of periodic waves can be described by using the concepts of wave speed, amplitude, period, frequency, and wavelength. Often, though, we need a more detailed description of the positions and motions of individual particles of the medium at particular times during wave propagation.

As a specific example, let's look at waves on a stretched string. If we ignore the sag of the string due to gravity, the equilibrium position of the string is along a straight line. We take this to be the x-axis of a coordinate system. Waves on a string are *transverse;* during wave motion a particle with equilibrium position x is displaced some distance y in the direction perpendicular to the x-axis. The value of y depends on which particle we are talking about (that is, y depends on x) and also on the time t when we look at it. Thus y is a *function* of both x and t; $y = y(x, t)$. We call $y(x, t)$ the **wave function** that describes the wave. If we know this function for a particular wave motion, we can use it to find the displacement (from equilibrium) of any particle at any time. From this we can find the velocity and acceleration of any particle, the shape of the string, and anything else we want to know about the behavior of the string at any time.

Wave Function for a Sinusoidal Wave

Let's see how to determine the form of the wave function for a sinusoidal wave. Suppose a sinusoidal wave travels from left to right (the direction of increasing x) along the string, as in Fig. 15.8. Every particle of the string oscillates with simple harmonic motion with the same amplitude and frequency. But the oscillations of particles at different points on the string are *not* all in step with each other. The particle at point B in Fig. 15.8 is at its maximum positive value of y at $t = 0$ and returns to $y = 0$ at $t = \frac{2}{8}T$; these same events occur for a particle at point A or point C at $t = \frac{4}{8}T$ and $t = \frac{6}{8}T$, exactly one half-period later. For any two particles of the string, the motion of the particle on the right (in terms of the wave, the "downstream" particle) lags behind the motion of the particle on the left by an amount proportional to the distance between the particles.

Hence the cyclic motions of various points on the string are out of step with each other by various fractions of a cycle. We call these differences *phase differences,* and we say that the *phase* of the motion is different for different points. For example, if one point has its maximum positive displacement at the same time that another has its maximum negative displacement, the two are a half-cycle out of phase. (This is the case for points A and B, or points B and C.)

Suppose that the displacement of a particle at the left end of the string ($x = 0$), where the wave originates, is given by

$$y(x = 0, t) = A\cos\omega t = A\cos 2\pi ft \qquad (15.2)$$

That is, the particle oscillates in simple harmonic motion with amplitude A, frequency f, and angular frequency $\omega = 2\pi f$. The notation $y(x = 0, t)$ reminds us that the motion of this particle is a special case of the wave function $y(x, t)$ that describes the entire wave. At $t = 0$ the particle at $x = 0$ is at its maximum positive displacement ($y = A$) and is instantaneously at rest (because the value of y is a maximum).

The wave disturbance travels from $x = 0$ to some point x to the right of the origin in an amount of time given by x/v, where v is the wave speed. So the motion of point x at time t is the same as the motion of point $x = 0$ at the earlier time $t - x/v$. Hence we can find the displacement of point x at time t by simply

15.8 Tracking the oscillations of three points on a string as a sinusoidal wave propagates along it.

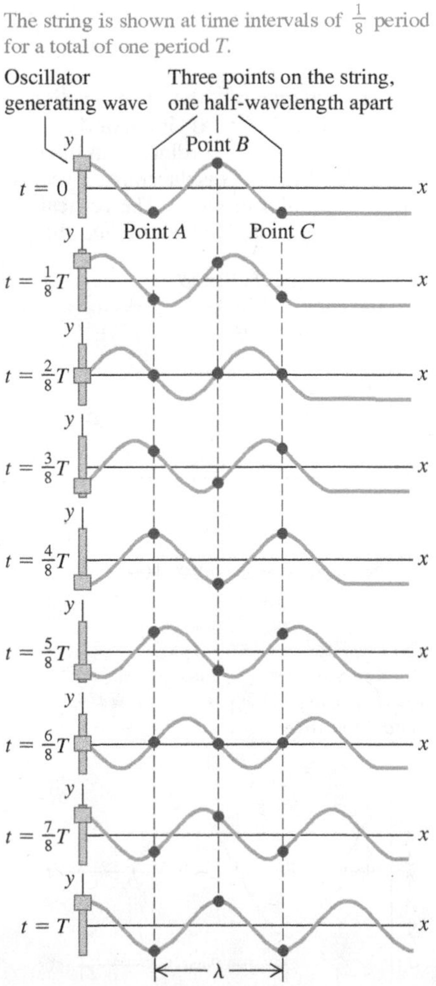

replacing t in Eq. (15.2) by $(t - x/v)$. When we do that, we find the following expression for the wave function:

$$y(x, t) = A\cos\left[\omega\left(t - \frac{x}{v}\right)\right]$$

Because $\cos(-\theta) = \cos\theta$, we can rewrite the wave function as

$$y(x, t) = A\cos\left[\omega\left(\frac{x}{v} - t\right)\right] = A\cos\left[2\pi f\left(\frac{x}{v} - t\right)\right] \quad \text{(sinusoidal wave moving in } +x\text{-direction)} \qquad (15.3)$$

The displacement $y(x, t)$ is a function of both the location x of the point and the time t. We could make Eq. (15.3) more general by allowing for different values of the phase angle, as we did for simple harmonic motion in Section 14.2, but for now we omit this.

We can rewrite the wave function given by Eq. (15.3) in several different but useful forms. We can express it in terms of the period $T = 1/f$ and the wavelength $\lambda = v/f$:

$$y(x, t) = A\cos\left[2\pi\left(\frac{x}{\lambda} - \frac{t}{T}\right)\right] \quad \text{(sinusoidal wave moving in } +x\text{-direction)} \qquad (15.4)$$

It's convenient to define a quantity k, called the **wave number:**

$$k = \frac{2\pi}{\lambda} \quad \text{(wave number)} \qquad (15.5)$$

Substituting $\lambda = 2\pi/k$ and $f = \omega/2\pi$ into the wavelength–frequency relationship $v = \lambda f$ gives

$$\omega = vk \quad \text{(periodic wave)} \qquad (15.6)$$

We can then rewrite Eq. (15.4) as

$$y(x, t) = A\cos(kx - \omega t) \quad \text{(sinusoidal wave moving in } +x\text{-direction)} \qquad (15.7)$$

Which of these various forms for the wave function $y(x, t)$ we use in any specific problem is a matter of convenience. Note that ω has units rad/s, so for unit consistency in Eqs. (15.6) and (15.7) the wave number k must have the units rad/m. (Some physicists define the wave number as $1/\lambda$ rather than $2\pi/\lambda$. When reading other texts, be sure to determine how this term is defined.)

15.9 Two graphs of the wave function $y(x, t)$ in Eq. (15.7). **(a)** Graph of displacement y versus coordinate x at time $t = 0$. **(b)** Graph of displacement y versus time t at coordinate $x = 0$. The vertical scale is exaggerated in both (a) and (b).

(a) If we use Eq. (15.7) to plot y as a function of x for time $t = 0$, the curve shows the *shape* of the string at $t = 0$.

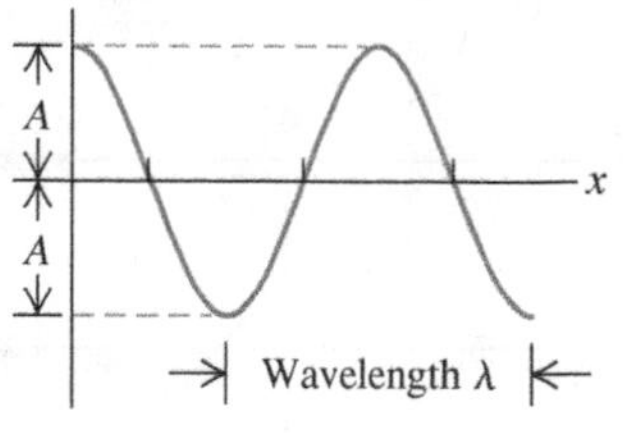

(b) If we use Eq. (15.7) to plot y as a function of t for position $x = 0$, the curve shows the *displacement* y of the particle at $x = 0$ as a function of time.

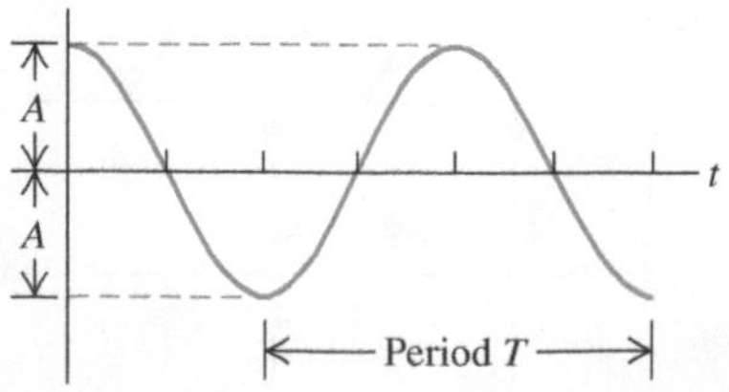

Graphing the Wave Function

Figure 15.9a graphs the wave function $y(x, t)$ as a function of x for a specific time t. This graph gives the displacement y of a particle from its equilibrium position as a function of the coordinate x of the particle. If the wave is a transverse wave on a string, the graph in Fig. 15.9a represents the shape of the string at that instant, like a flash photograph of the string. In particular, at time $t = 0$,

$$y(x, t = 0) = A\cos kx = A\cos 2\pi\frac{x}{\lambda}$$

Figure 15.9b is a graph of the wave function versus time t for a specific coordinate x. This graph gives the displacement y of the particle at that coordinate as a function of time; that is, it describes the motion of that particle. In particular, at the position $x = 0$,

$$y(x = 0, t) = A\cos(-\omega t) = A\cos\omega t = A\cos 2\pi\frac{t}{T}$$

This is consistent with our original statement about the motion at $x = 0$, Eq. (15.2).

CAUTION **Wave graphs** Although they may look the same at first glance, Figs. 15.9a and 15.9b are *not* identical. Figure 15.9a is a picture of the shape of the string at $t = 0$, while Fig. 15.9b is a graph of the displacement y of a particle at $x = 0$ as a function of time.

More on the Wave Function

We can modify Eqs. (15.3) through (15.7) to represent a wave traveling in the *negative* x-direction. In this case the displacement of point x at time t is the same as the motion of point $x = 0$ at the *later* time $(t + x/v)$, so in Eq. (15.2) we replace t by $(t + x/v)$. For a wave traveling in the negative x-direction,

$$y(x, t) = A\cos\left[2\pi f\left(\frac{x}{v} + t\right)\right] = A\cos\left[2\pi\left(\frac{x}{\lambda} + \frac{t}{T}\right)\right] = A\cos(kx + \omega t) \quad (15.8)$$

(sinusoidal wave moving in $-x$-direction)

In the expression $y(x, t) = A\cos(kx \pm \omega t)$ for a wave traveling in the $-x$- or $+x$-direction, the quantity $(kx \pm \omega t)$ is called the **phase.** It plays the role of an angular quantity (always measured in radians) in Eq. (15.7) or (15.8), and its value for any values of x and t determines what part of the sinusoidal cycle is occurring at a particular point and time. For a crest (where $y = A$ and the cosine function has the value 1), the phase could be 0, 2π, 4π, and so on; for a trough (where $y = -A$ and the cosine has the value -1), it could be π, 3π, 5π, and so on.

The wave speed is the speed with which we have to move along with the wave to keep alongside a point of a given phase, such as a particular crest of a wave on a string. For a wave traveling in the $+x$-direction, that means $kx - \omega t =$ constant. Taking the derivative with respect to t, we find $k\,dx/dt = \omega$, or

$$\frac{dx}{dt} = \frac{\omega}{k}$$

Comparing this with Eq. (15.6), we see that dx/dt is equal to the speed v of the wave. Because of this relationship, v is sometimes called the *phase velocity* of the wave. (*Phase speed* would be a better term.)

Problem-Solving Strategy 15.1 Mechanical Waves

MP

IDENTIFY *the relevant concepts:* As always, identify the target variables; these may include mathematical *expressions* (for example, the wave function for a given situation). Note that wave problems fall into two categories. *Kinematics* problems, concerned with describing wave motion, involve wave speed v, wavelength λ (or wave number k), frequency f (or angular frequency ω), and amplitude A. They may also involve the position, velocity, and acceleration of individual particles in the medium. *Dynamics* problems also use concepts from Newton's laws. Later in this chapter we'll encounter problems that involve the relationship of wave speed to the mechanical properties of the medium.

SET UP *the problem* using the following steps:

1. List the given quantities. Sketch graphs of y versus x (like Fig. 15.9a) and of y versus t (like Fig. 15.9b), and label them with known values.
2. Identify useful equations. These may include Eq. (15.1) ($v = \lambda f$), Eq. (15.6) ($\omega = vk$), and Eqs. (15.3), (15.4), and (15.7), which express the wave function in various forms. From the wave function, you can find the value of y at any point (value of x) and at any time t.
3. If you need to determine the wave speed v and don't know both λ and f, you may be able to use a relationship between v and the mechanical properties of the system. (In the next section we'll develop this relationship for waves on a string.)

EXECUTE *the solution:* Solve for the unknown quantities using the equations you've identified. To determine the wave function from Eq. (15.3), (15.4), or (15.7), you must know A and any two of v, λ, and f (or v, k, and ω).

EVALUATE *your answer:* Confirm that the values of v, f, and λ (or v, ω, and k) agree with the relationships given in Eq. (15.1) or (15.6). If you've calculated the wave function, check one or more special cases for which you can predict the results.

Example 15.2 Wave on a clothesline

Cousin Throckmorton holds one end of the clothesline taut and wiggles it up and down sinusoidally with frequency 2.00 Hz and amplitude 0.075 m. The wave speed on the clothesline is $v = 12.0$ m/s. At $t = 0$ Throcky's end has maximum positive displacement and is instantaneously at rest. Assume that no wave bounces back from the far end. (a) Find the wave amplitude A, angular frequency ω, period T, wavelength λ, and wave number k. (b) Write a wave function describing the wave. (c) Write equations for the displacement, as a function of time, of Throcky's end of the clothesline and of a point 3.00 m from that end.

SOLUTION

IDENTIFY and SET UP: This is a kinematics problem about the clothesline's wave motion. Throcky produces a sinusoidal wave that propagates along the clothesline, so we can use all of the expressions of this section. In part (a) our target variables are A, ω, T, λ, and k. We use the relationships $\omega = 2\pi f$, $f = 1/T$, $v = \lambda f$, and $k = 2\pi/\lambda$. In parts (b) and (c) our target "variables" are expressions for displacement, which we'll obtain from an appropriate equation for the wave function. We take the positive x-direction to be the direction in which the wave propagates, so either Eq. (15.4) or (15.7) will yield the desired expression. A photograph of the clothesline at time $t = 0$ would look like Fig. 15.9a, with the maximum displacement at $x = 0$ (the end that Throcky holds).

EXECUTE: (a) The wave amplitude and frequency are the same as for the oscillations of Throcky's end of the clothesline, $A = 0.075$ m and $f = 2.00$ Hz. Hence

$$\omega = 2\pi f = \left(2\pi \frac{\text{rad}}{\text{cycle}}\right)\left(2.00 \frac{\text{cycles}}{\text{s}}\right)$$
$$= 4.00\pi \text{ rad/s} = 12.6 \text{ rad/s}$$

The period is $T = 1/f = 0.500$ s, and from Eq. (15.1),

$$\lambda = \frac{v}{f} = \frac{12.0 \text{ m/s}}{2.00 \text{ s}^{-1}} = 6.00 \text{ m}$$

We find the wave number from Eq. (15.5) or (15.6):

$$k = \frac{2\pi}{\lambda} = \frac{2\pi \text{ rad}}{6.00 \text{ m}} = 1.05 \text{ rad/m}$$

or

$$k = \frac{\omega}{v} = \frac{4.00\pi \text{ rad/s}}{12.0 \text{ m/s}} = 1.05 \text{ rad/m}$$

(b) We write the wave function using Eq. (15.4) and the values of A, T, and λ from part (a):

$$y(x,t) = A\cos 2\pi\left(\frac{x}{\lambda} - \frac{t}{T}\right)$$
$$= (0.075 \text{ m})\cos 2\pi\left(\frac{x}{6.00 \text{ m}} - \frac{t}{0.500 \text{ s}}\right)$$
$$= (0.075 \text{ m})\cos[(1.05 \text{ rad/m})x - (12.6 \text{ rad/s})t]$$

We can also get this same expression from Eq. (15.7) by using the values of ω and k from part (a).

(c) We can find the displacement as a function of time at $x = 0$ and $x = +3.00$ m by substituting these values into the wave function from part (b):

$$y(x = 0, t) = (0.075 \text{ m})\cos 2\pi\left(\frac{0}{6.00 \text{ m}} - \frac{t}{0.500 \text{ s}}\right)$$
$$= (0.075 \text{ m})\cos(12.6 \text{ rad/s})t$$
$$y(x = +3.00 \text{ m}, t) = (0.075 \text{ m})\cos 2\pi\left(\frac{3.00 \text{ m}}{6.00 \text{ m}} - \frac{t}{0.500 \text{ s}}\right)$$
$$= (0.075 \text{ m})\cos[\pi - (12.6 \text{ rad/s})t]$$
$$= -(0.075 \text{ m})\cos(12.6 \text{ rad/s})t$$

EVALUATE: In part (b), the quantity $(1.05 \text{ rad/m})x - (12.6 \text{ rad/s})t$ is the *phase* of a point x on the string at time t. The two points in part (c) oscillate in SHM with the same frequency and amplitude, but their oscillations differ in phase by $(1.05 \text{ rad/m})(3.00 \text{ m}) = 3.15$ rad $= \pi$ radians—that is, one-half cycle—because the points are separated by one half-wavelength: $\lambda/2 = (6.00 \text{ m})/2 = 3.00$ m. Thus, while a graph of y versus t for the point at $x = 0$ is a cosine curve (like Fig. 15.9b), a graph of y versus t for the point $x = 3.00$ m is a *negative* cosine curve (the same as a cosine curve shifted by one half-cycle).

Using the expression for $y(x = 0, t)$ in part (c), can you show that the end of the string at $x = 0$ is instantaneously at rest at $t = 0$, as stated at the beginning of this example? (*Hint:* Calculate the y-velocity at this point by taking the derivative of y with respect to t.)

Particle Velocity and Acceleration in a Sinusoidal Wave

From the wave function we can get an expression for the transverse velocity of any *particle* in a transverse wave. We call this v_y to distinguish it from the wave propagation speed v. To find the transverse velocity v_y at a particular point x, we take the derivative of the wave function $y(x, t)$ with respect to t, keeping x constant. If the wave function is

$$y(x, t) = A\cos(kx - \omega t)$$

then

$$v_y(x, t) = \frac{\partial y(x, t)}{\partial t} = \omega A \sin(kx - \omega t) \qquad (15.9)$$

The ∂ in this expression is a modified d, used to remind us that $y(x, t)$ is a function of *two* variables and that we are allowing only one (t) to vary. The other (x) is constant because we are looking at a particular point on the string. This derivative is called a *partial derivative.* If you haven't reached this point yet in your study of calculus, don't fret; it's a simple idea.

Equation (15.9) shows that the transverse velocity of a particle varies with time, as we expect for simple harmonic motion. The maximum particle speed is ωA; this can be greater than, less than, or equal to the wave speed v, depending on the amplitude and frequency of the wave.

The *acceleration* of any particle is the *second* partial derivative of $y(x, t)$ with respect to t:

$$a_y(x, t) = \frac{\partial^2 y(x, t)}{\partial t^2} = -\omega^2 A \cos(kx - \omega t) = -\omega^2 y(x, t) \quad (15.10)$$

The acceleration of a particle equals $-\omega^2$ times its displacement, which is the result we obtained in Section 14.2 for simple harmonic motion.

We can also compute partial derivatives of $y(x, t)$ with respect to x, holding t constant. The first derivative $\partial y(x, t)/\partial x$ is the *slope* of the string at point x and at time t. The second partial derivative with respect to x is the *curvature* of the string:

$$\frac{\partial^2 y(x, t)}{\partial x^2} = -k^2 A \cos(kx - \omega t) = -k^2 y(x, t) \quad (15.11)$$

From Eqs. (15.10) and (15.11) and the relationship $\omega = vk$ we see that

$$\frac{\partial^2 y(x, t)/\partial t^2}{\partial^2 y(x, t)/\partial x^2} = \frac{\omega^2}{k^2} = v^2 \quad \text{and}$$

$$\frac{\partial^2 y(x, t)}{\partial x^2} = \frac{1}{v^2}\frac{\partial^2 y(x, t)}{\partial t^2} \quad \text{(wave equation)} \quad (15.12)$$

We've derived Eq. (15.12) for a wave traveling in the positive x-direction. You can use the same steps to show that the wave function for a sinusoidal wave propagating in the *negative* x-direction, $y(x, t) = A\cos(kx + \omega t)$, also satisfies this equation.

Equation (15.12), called the **wave equation,** is one of the most important equations in all of physics. Whenever it occurs, we know that a disturbance can propagate as a wave along the x-axis with wave speed v. The disturbance need not be a sinusoidal wave; we'll see in the next section that *any* wave on a string obeys Eq. (15.12), whether the wave is periodic or not (see also Problem 15.65). In Chapter 32 we will find that electric and magnetic fields satisfy the wave equation; the wave speed will turn out to be the speed of light, which will lead us to the conclusion that light is an electromagnetic wave.

Figure 15.10a shows the transverse velocity v_y and transverse acceleration a_y, given by Eqs. (15.9) and (15.10), for several points on a string as a sinusoidal wave passes along it. Note that at points where the string has an upward curvature ($\partial^2 y/\partial x^2 > 0$), the acceleration of that point is positive ($a_y = \partial^2 y/\partial t^2 > 0$); this follows from the wave equation, Eq. (15.12). For the same reason the acceleration is negative ($a_y = \partial^2 y/\partial t^2 < 0$) at points where the string has a downward curvature ($\partial^2 y/\partial x^2 < 0$), and the acceleration is zero ($a_y = \partial^2 y/\partial t^2 = 0$) at points of inflection where the curvature is zero ($\partial^2 y/\partial x^2 = 0$). We emphasize again that v_y and a_y are the *transverse* velocity and acceleration of points on the string; these points move along the y-direction, not along the propagation direction of the

15.10 (a) Another view of the wave at $t = 0$ in Fig. 15.9a. The vectors show the transverse velocity v_y and transverse acceleration a_y at several points on the string. (b) From $t = 0$ to $t = 0.05T$, a particle at point 1 is displaced to point 1′, a particle at point 2 is displaced to point 2′, and so on.

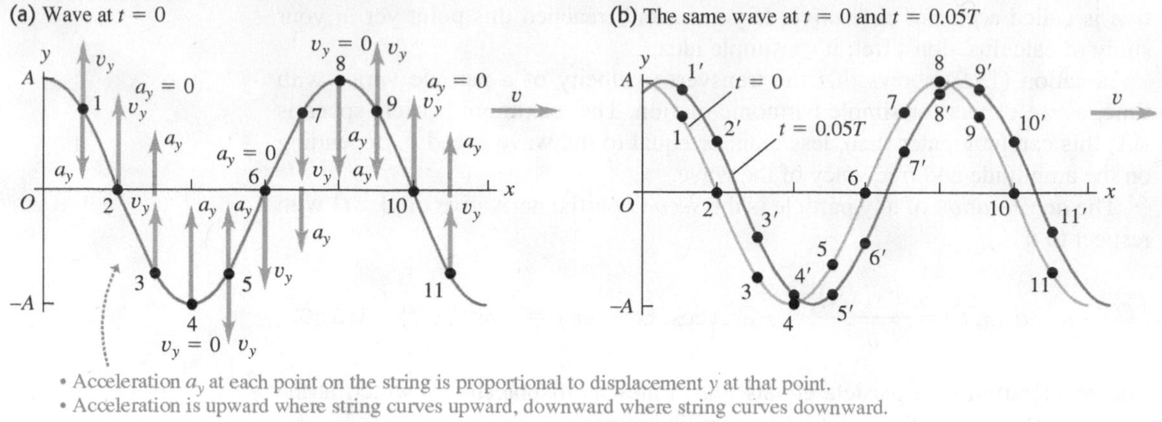

wave. Figure 15.10b shows the transverse motions of several points on the string.

The concept of wave function is equally useful with *longitudinal* waves. The quantity y still measures the displacement of a particle of the medium from its equilibrium position; the difference is that for a longitudinal wave, this displacement is *parallel* to the x-axis instead of perpendicular to it. We'll discuss longitudinal waves in detail in Chapter 16.

Test Your Understanding of Section 15.3 Figure 15.8 shows a sinusoidal wave of period T on a string at times 0, $\frac{1}{8}T$, $\frac{2}{8}T$, $\frac{3}{8}T$, $\frac{4}{8}T$, $\frac{5}{8}T$, $\frac{6}{8}T$, $\frac{7}{8}T$, and T. (a) At which time is point A on the string moving upward with maximum speed? (b) At which time does point B on the string have the greatest upward acceleration? (c) At which time does point C on the string have a downward acceleration but an upward velocity? ❙

MasteringPHYSICS

ActivPhysics 10.2: Speed of Waves on a String

15.4 Speed of a Transverse Wave

One of the key properties of any wave is the wave *speed.* Light waves in air have a much greater speed of propagation than do sound waves in air (3.00×10^8 m/s versus 344 m/s); that's why you see the flash from a bolt of lightning before you hear the clap of thunder. In this section we'll see what determines the speed of propagation of one particular kind of wave: transverse waves on a string. The speed of these waves is important to understand because it is an essential part of analyzing stringed musical instruments, as we'll discuss later in this chapter. Furthermore, the speeds of many kinds of mechanical waves turn out to have the same basic mathematical expression as does the speed of waves on a string.

The physical quantities that determine the speed of transverse waves on a string are the *tension* in the string and its *mass per unit length* (also called *linear mass density*). We might guess that increasing the tension should increase the restoring forces that tend to straighten the string when it is disturbed, thus increasing the wave speed. We might also guess that increasing the mass should make the motion more sluggish and decrease the speed. Both these guesses turn out to be right. We'll develop the exact relationship among wave speed, tension, and mass per unit length by two different methods. The first is simple in concept and considers a specific wave shape; the second is more general but also more formal. Choose whichever you like better.

15.11 Propagation of a transverse wave on a string.

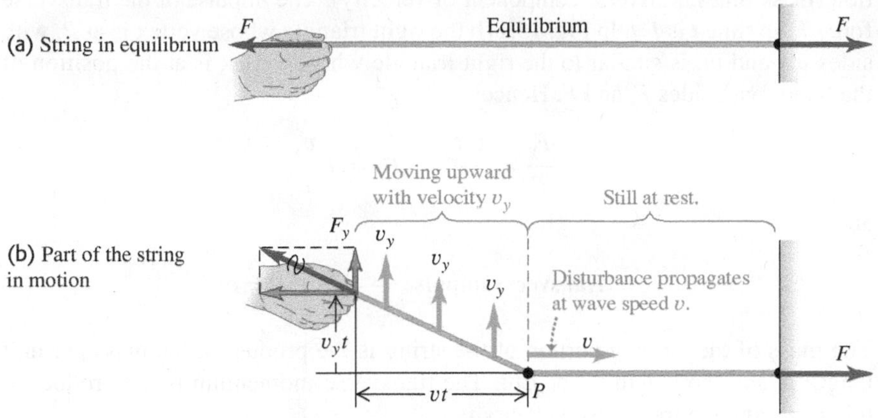

Wave Speed on a String: First Method

We consider a perfectly flexible string (Fig. 15.11). In the equilibrium position the tension is F and the linear mass density (mass per unit length) is μ. (When portions of the string are displaced from equilibrium, the mass per unit length decreases a little, and the tension increases a little.) We ignore the weight of the string so that when the string is at rest in the equilibrium position, the string forms a perfectly straight line as in Fig. 15.11a.

Starting at time $t = 0$, we apply a constant upward force F_y at the left end of the string. We might expect that the end would move with constant acceleration; that would happen if the force were applied to a *point* mass. But here the effect of the force F_y is to set successively more and more mass in motion. The wave travels with constant speed v, so the division point P between moving and nonmoving portions moves with the same constant speed v (Fig. 15.11b).

Figure 15.11b shows that all particles in the moving portion of the string move upward with constant *velocity* v_y, not constant acceleration. To see why this is so, we note that the *impulse* of the force F_y up to time t is $F_y t$. According to the impulse–momentum theorem (see Section 8.1), the impulse is equal to the change in the total transverse component of momentum $(mv_y - 0)$ of the moving part of the string. Because the system started with *no* transverse momentum, this is equal to the total momentum at time t:

$$F_y t = mv_y$$

The total momentum thus must increase proportionately with time. But since the division point P moves with constant speed, the length of string that is in motion and hence the total mass m in motion are also proportional to the time t that the force has been acting. So the *change* of momentum must be associated entirely with the increasing amount of mass in motion, not with an increasing velocity of an individual mass element. That is, mv_y changes because m, not v_y, changes.

At time t, the left end of the string has moved up a distance $v_y t$, and the boundary point P has advanced a distance vt. The total force at the left end of the string has components F and F_y. Why F? There is no motion in the direction along the length of the string, so there is no unbalanced horizontal force. Therefore F, the magnitude of the horizontal component, does not change when the string is displaced. In the displaced position the tension is $(F^2 + F_y^2)^{1/2}$ (greater than F), and the string stretches somewhat.

To derive an expression for the wave speed v, we again apply the impulse–momentum theorem to the portion of the string in motion at time t—that is, the portion to the left of P in Fig. 15.11b. The transverse *impulse* (transverse force times time) is equal to the change of transverse *momentum* of the moving portion (mass times transverse component of velocity). The impulse of the transverse force F_y in time t is $F_y t$. In Fig. 15.11b the right triangle whose vertex is at P, with sides $v_y t$ and vt, is similar to the right triangle whose vertex is at the position of the hand, with sides F_y and F. Hence

$$\frac{F_y}{F} = \frac{v_y t}{vt} \qquad F_y = F\frac{v_y}{v}$$

and

$$\text{Transverse impulse} = F_y t = F\frac{v_y}{v}t$$

15.12 These cables have a relatively large amount of mass per unit length (μ) and a low tension (F). If the cables are disturbed—say, by a bird landing on them—transverse waves will travel along them at a slow speed $v = \sqrt{F/\mu}$.

The mass of the moving portion of the string is the product of the mass per unit length μ and the length vt, or μvt. The transverse momentum is the product of this mass and the transverse velocity v_y:

$$\text{Transverse momentum} = (\mu vt)v_y$$

We note again that the momentum increases with time *not* because mass is moving faster, as was usually the case in Chapter 8, but because *more mass* is brought into motion. But the impulse of the force F_y is still equal to the total change in momentum of the system. Applying this relationship, we obtain

$$F\frac{v_y}{v}t = \mu vtv_y$$

Solving this for v, we find

$$v = \sqrt{\frac{F}{\mu}} \quad \text{(speed of a transverse wave on a string)} \tag{15.13}$$

Equation (15.13) confirms our prediction that the wave speed v should increase when the tension F increases but decrease when the mass per unit length μ increases (Fig. 15.12).

Note that v_y does not appear in Eq. (15.13); thus the wave speed doesn't depend on v_y. Our calculation considered only a very special kind of pulse, but we can consider *any* shape of wave disturbance as a series of pulses with different values of v_y. So even though we derived Eq. (15.13) for a special case, it is valid for *any* transverse wave motion on a string, including the sinusoidal and other periodic waves we discussed in Section 15.3. Note also that the wave speed doesn't depend on the amplitude or frequency of the wave, in accordance with our assumptions in Section 15.3.

15.13 Free-body diagram for a segment of string. The force at each end of the string is tangent to the string at the point of application.

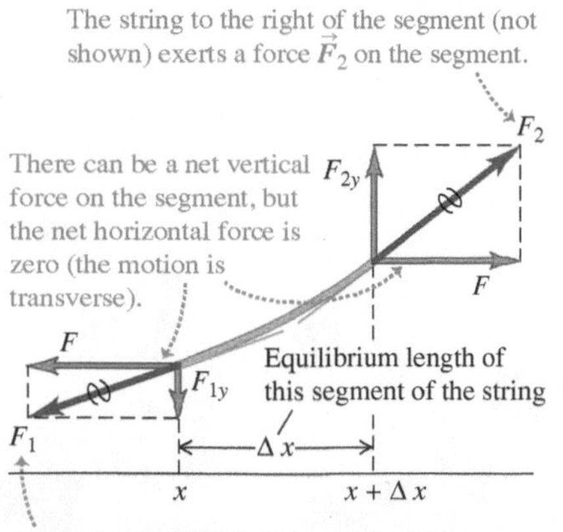

Wave Speed on a String: Second Method

Here is an alternative derivation of Eq. (15.13). If you aren't comfortable with partial derivatives, it can be omitted. We apply Newton's second law, $\sum\vec{F} = m\vec{a}$, to a small segment of string whose length in the equilibrium position is Δx (Fig. 15.13). The mass of the segment is $m = \mu\,\Delta x$; the forces at the ends are represented in terms of their x- and y-components. The x-components have equal magnitude F and add to zero because the motion is transverse and there is no component of acceleration in the x-direction. To obtain F_{1y} and F_{2y}, we note that the ratio F_{1y}/F is equal in magnitude to the *slope* of the string at point x and that F_{2y}/F is equal to the slope at point $x + \Delta x$. Taking proper account of signs, we find

$$\frac{F_{1y}}{F} = -\left(\frac{\partial y}{\partial x}\right)_x \qquad \frac{F_{2y}}{F} = \left(\frac{\partial y}{\partial x}\right)_{x+\Delta x} \tag{15.14}$$

The notation reminds us that the derivatives are evaluated at points x and $x + \Delta x$, respectively. From Eq. (15.14) we find that the net y-component of force is

$$F_y = F_{1y} + F_{2y} = F\left[\left(\frac{\partial y}{\partial x}\right)_{x+\Delta x} - \left(\frac{\partial y}{\partial x}\right)_x\right] \tag{15.15}$$

We now equate F_y from Eq. (15.15) to the mass $\mu\ \Delta x$ times the y-component of acceleration $\partial^2 y/\partial t^2$. We obtain

$$F\left[\left(\frac{\partial y}{\partial x}\right)_{x+\Delta x} - \left(\frac{\partial y}{\partial x}\right)_x\right] = \mu\ \Delta x \frac{\partial^2 y}{\partial t^2} \tag{15.16}$$

or, dividing by $F\Delta x$,

$$\frac{\left(\frac{\partial y}{\partial x}\right)_{x+\Delta x} - \left(\frac{\partial y}{\partial x}\right)_x}{\Delta x} = \frac{\mu}{F}\frac{\partial^2 y}{\partial t^2} \tag{15.17}$$

We now take the limit as $\Delta x \rightarrow 0$. In this limit, the left side of Eq. (15.17) becomes the derivative of $\partial y/\partial x$ with respect to x (at constant t)—that is, the *second* (partial) derivative of y with respect to x:

$$\frac{\partial^2 y}{\partial x^2} = \frac{\mu}{F}\frac{\partial^2 y}{\partial t^2} \tag{15.18}$$

Now, finally, comes the punch line of our story. Equation (15.18) has exactly the same form as the *wave equation,* Eq. (15.12), that we derived at the end of Section 15.3. That equation and Eq. (15.18) describe the very same wave motion, so they must be identical. Comparing the two equations, we see that for this to be so, we must have

$$v = \sqrt{\frac{F}{\mu}} \tag{15.19}$$

which is the same expression as Eq. (15.13).

In going through this derivation, we didn't make any special assumptions about the shape of the wave. Since our derivation led us to rediscover Eq. (15.12), the wave equation, we conclude that the wave equation is valid for waves on a string that have *any* shape.

The Speed of Mechanical Waves

Equation (15.13) or (15.19) gives the wave speed for only the special case of mechanical waves on a stretched string or rope. Remarkably, it turns out that for many types of mechanical waves, including waves on a string, the expression for wave speed has the same general form:

$$v = \sqrt{\frac{\text{Restoring force returning the system to equilibrium}}{\text{Inertia resisting the return to equilibrium}}}$$

To interpret this expression, let's look at the now-familiar case of waves on a string. The tension F in the string plays the role of the restoring force; it tends to bring the string back to its undisturbed, equilibrium configuration. The mass of the string—or, more properly, the linear mass density μ—provides the inertia that prevents the string from returning instantaneously to equilibrium. Hence we have $v = \sqrt{F/\mu}$ for the speed of waves on a string.

In Chapter 16 we'll see a similar expression for the speed of sound waves in a gas. Roughly speaking, the gas pressure provides the force that tends to return the gas to its undisturbed state when a sound wave passes through. The inertia is provided by the density, or mass per unit volume, of the gas.

Example 15.3 Calculating wave speed

One end of a 2.00-kg rope is tied to a support at the top of a mine shaft 80.0 m deep (Fig. 15.14). The rope is stretched taut by a 20.0-kg box of rocks attached at the bottom. (a) The geologist at the bottom of the shaft signals to a colleague at the top by jerking the rope sideways. What is the speed of a transverse wave on the rope? (b) If a point on the rope is in transverse SHM with $f = 2.00$ Hz, how many cycles of the wave are there in the rope's length?

SOLUTION

IDENTIFY and SET UP: In part (a) we can find the wave speed (our target variable) using the *dynamic* relationship $v = \sqrt{F/\mu}$ [Eq. (15.13)]. In part (b) we find the wavelength from the *kinematic* relationship $v = f\lambda$; from that we can find the target variable, the number of wavelengths that fit into the rope's 80.0-m length. We'll assume that the rope is massless (even though its weight is 10% that of the box), so that the box alone provides the tension in the rope.

15.14 Sending signals along a vertical rope using transverse waves.

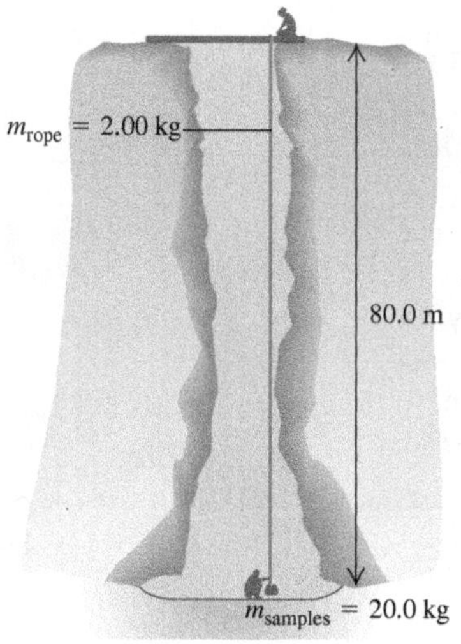

EXECUTE: (a) The tension in the rope due to the box is

$$F = m_{box}g = (20.0\text{ kg})(9.80\text{ m/s}^2) = 196\text{ N}$$

and the rope's linear mass density is

$$\mu = \frac{m_{rope}}{L} = \frac{2.00\text{ kg}}{80.0\text{ m}} = 0.0250\text{ kg/m}$$

Hence, from Eq. (15.13), the wave speed is

$$v = \sqrt{\frac{F}{\mu}} = \sqrt{\frac{196\text{ N}}{0.0250\text{ kg/m}}} = 88.5\text{ m/s}$$

(b) From Eq. (15.1), the wavelength is

$$\lambda = \frac{v}{f} = \frac{88.5\text{ m/s}}{2.00\text{ s}^{-1}} = 44.3\text{ m}$$

There are $(80.0\text{ m})/(44.3\text{ m}) = 1.81$ wavelengths (that is, cycles of the wave) in the rope.

EVALUATE: Because of the rope's weight, its tension is greater at the top than at the bottom. Hence both the wave speed and the wavelength increase as a wave travels up the rope. If you take account of this, can you verify that the wave speed at the top of the rope is 92.9 m/s?

Test Your Understanding of Section 15.4 The six strings of a guitar are the same length and under nearly the same tension, but they have different thicknesses. On which string do waves travel the fastest? (i) the thickest string; (ii) the thinnest string; (iii) the wave speed is the same on all strings. ❙

Application Surface Waves and the Swimming Speed of Ducks
When a duck swims, it necessarily produces waves on the surface of the water. The faster the duck swims, the larger the wave amplitude and the more power the duck must supply to produce these waves. The maximum power available from their leg muscles limits the maximum swimming speed of ducks to only about 0.7 m/s (2.5 km/h = 1.6 mi/h).

15.5 Energy in Wave Motion

Every wave motion has *energy* associated with it. The energy we receive from sunlight and the destructive effects of ocean surf and earthquakes bear this out. To produce any of the wave motions we have discussed in this chapter, we have to apply a force to a portion of the wave medium; the point where the force is applied moves, so we do *work* on the system. As the wave propagates, each portion of the medium exerts a force and does work on the adjoining portion. In this way a wave can transport energy from one region of space to another.

As an example of energy considerations in wave motion, let's look again at transverse waves on a string. How is energy transferred from one portion of string to another? Picture a wave traveling from left to right (the positive x-direction) on the string, and consider a particular point a on the string (Fig. 15.15a). The string to the left of point a exerts a force on the string to the right of it, and vice versa. In Fig. 15.15b the string to the left of a has been removed, and the force it exerts at a is represented by the components F and F_y, as we did in Figs. 15.11 and

15.13. We note again that F_y/F is equal to the negative of the *slope* of the string at a, which is also given by $\partial y/\partial x$. Putting these together, we have

$$F_y(x, t) = -F\frac{\partial y(x, t)}{\partial x} \tag{15.20}$$

We need the negative sign because F_y is negative when the slope is positive. We write the vertical force as $F_y(x, t)$ as a reminder that its value may be different at different points along the string and at different times.

When point a moves in the y-direction, the force F_y does *work* on this point and therefore transfers energy into the part of the string to the right of a. The corresponding power P (rate of doing work) at the point a is the transverse force $F_y(x, t)$ at a times the transverse velocity $v_y(x, t) = \partial y(x, t)/\partial t$ of that point:

$$P(x, t) = F_y(x, t)v_y(x, t) = -F\frac{\partial y(x, t)}{\partial x}\frac{\partial y(x, t)}{\partial t} \tag{15.21}$$

This power is the *instantaneous* rate at which energy is transferred along the string. Its value depends on the position x on the string and on the time t. Note that energy is being transferred only at points where the string has a nonzero slope ($\partial y/\partial x$ is nonzero), so that there is a transverse component of the tension force, and where the string has a nonzero transverse velocity ($\partial y/\partial t$ is nonzero) so that the transverse force can do work.

Equation (15.21) is valid for *any* wave on a string, sinusoidal or not. For a sinusoidal wave with wave function given by Eq. (15.7), we have

$$y(x, t) = A\cos(kx - \omega t)$$

$$\frac{\partial y(x, t)}{\partial x} = -kA\sin(kx - \omega t)$$

$$\frac{\partial y(x, t)}{\partial t} = \omega A\sin(kx - \omega t)$$

$$P(x, t) = Fk\omega A^2\sin^2(kx - \omega t) \tag{15.22}$$

By using the relationships $\omega = vk$ and $v^2 = F/\mu$, we can also express Eq. (15.22) in the alternative form

$$P(x, t) = \sqrt{\mu F}\,\omega^2 A^2\sin^2(kx - \omega t) \tag{15.23}$$

The $\sin^2$ function is never negative, so the instantaneous power in a sinusoidal wave is either positive (so that energy flows in the positive x-direction) or zero (at points where there is no energy transfer). Energy is never transferred in the direction opposite to the direction of wave propagation (Fig. 15.16).

The maximum value of the instantaneous power $P(x, t)$ occurs when the $\sin^2$ function has the value unity:

$$P_{max} = \sqrt{\mu F}\,\omega^2 A^2 \tag{15.24}$$

To obtain the *average* power from Eq. (15.23), we note that the *average* value of the $\sin^2$ function, averaged over any whole number of cycles, is $\frac{1}{2}$. Hence the average power is

$$P_{av} = \tfrac{1}{2}\sqrt{\mu F}\,\omega^2 A^2 \quad \text{(average power, sinusoidal wave on a string)} \tag{15.25}$$

The average power is just one-half of the maximum instantaneous power (see Fig. 15.16).

The average rate of energy transfer is proportional to the square of the amplitude and to the square of the frequency. This proportionality is a general result for mechanical waves of all types, including seismic waves (see the photo that opens this chapter). For a mechanical wave, the rate of energy transfer

15.15 (a) Point a on a string carrying a wave from left to right. (b) The components of the force exerted on the part of the string to the right of point a by the part of the string to the left of point a.

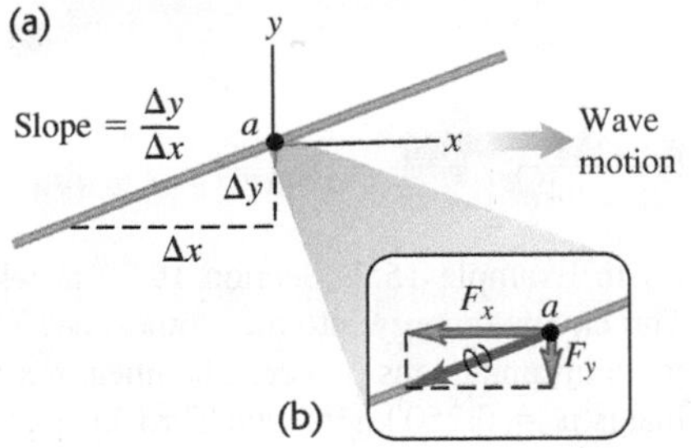

15.16 The instantaneous power $P(x, t)$ in a sinusoidal wave as given by Eq. (15.23), shown as a function of time at coordinate $x = 0$. The power is never negative, which means that energy never flows opposite to the direction of wave propagation.

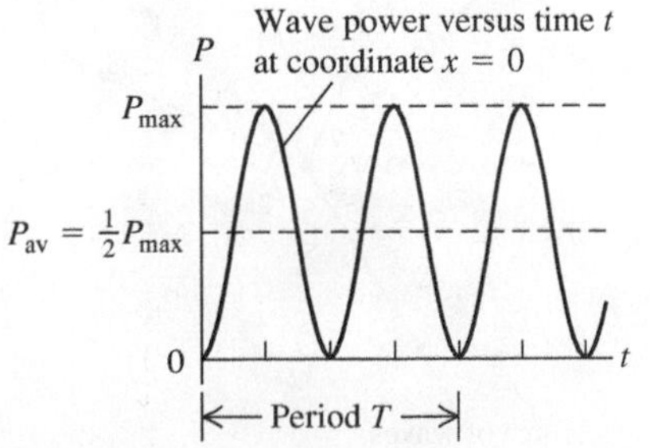

quadruples if the frequency is doubled (for the same amplitude) or if the amplitude is doubled (for the same frequency).

Electromagnetic waves turn out to be a bit different. While the average rate of energy transfer in an electromagnetic wave is proportional to the square of the amplitude, just as for mechanical waves, it is independent of the value of ω.

Example 15.4 Power in a wave

(a) In Example 15.2 (Section 15.3), at what maximum rate does Throcky put energy into the clothesline? That is, what is his maximum instantaneous power? The linear mass density of the clothesline is $\mu = 0.250$ kg/m, and Throcky applies tension $F = 36.0$ N. (b) What is his average power? (c) As Throcky tires, the amplitude decreases. What is the average power when the amplitude is 7.50 mm?

SOLUTION

IDENTIFY and SET UP: In part (a) our target variable is the *maximum instantaneous* power P_{max}, while in parts (b) and (c) it is the *average* power. For part (a) we'll use Eq. (15.24), and for parts (b) and (c) we'll use Eq. (15.25); Example 15.2 gives us all the needed quantities.

EXECUTE: (a) From Eq. (15.24),

$$\begin{aligned} P_{max} &= \sqrt{\mu F}\omega^2 A^2 \\ &= \sqrt{(0.250 \text{ kg/m})(36.0 \text{ N})}(4.00\pi \text{ rad/s})^2(0.075 \text{ m})^2 \\ &= 2.66 \text{ W} \end{aligned}$$

(b) From Eqs. (15.24) and (15.25), the average power is one-half of the maximum instantaneous power, so

$$P_{av} = \tfrac{1}{2}P_{max} = \tfrac{1}{2}(2.66 \text{ W}) = 1.33 \text{ W}$$

(c) The new amplitude is $\frac{1}{10}$ of the value we used in parts (a) and (b). From Eq. (15.25), the average power is proportional to A^2, so the new average power is

$$P_{av} = \left(\tfrac{1}{10}\right)^2(1.33 \text{ W}) = 0.0133 \text{ W} = 13.3 \text{ mW}$$

EVALUATE: Equation (15.23) shows that P_{max} occurs when $\sin^2(kx - \omega t) = 1$. At any given position x, this happens twice per period of the wave—once when the sine function is equal to $+1$, and once when it's equal to -1. The *minimum* instantaneous power is zero; this occurs when $\sin^2(kx - \omega t) = 0$, which also happens twice per period.

Can you confirm that the given values of μ and F give the wave speed mentioned in Example 15.2?

Wave Intensity

Waves on a string carry energy in just one dimension of space (along the direction of the string). But other types of waves, including sound waves in air and seismic waves in the body of the earth, carry energy across all three dimensions of space. For waves that travel in three dimensions, we define the **intensity** (denoted by I) to be *the time average rate at which energy is transported by the wave, per unit area,* across a surface perpendicular to the direction of propagation. That is, intensity I is average power per unit area. It is usually measured in watts per square meter (W/m^2).

If waves spread out equally in all directions from a source, the intensity at a distance r from the source is inversely proportional to r^2 (Fig. 15.17). This follows directly from energy conservation. If the power output of the source is P, then the average intensity I_1 through a sphere with radius r_1 and surface area $4\pi r_1^2$ is

$$I_1 = \frac{P}{4\pi r_1^2}$$

The average intensity I_2 through a sphere with a different radius r_2 is given by a similar expression. If no energy is absorbed between the two spheres, the power P must be the same for both, and

$$4\pi r_1^2 I_1 = 4\pi r_2^2 I_2$$

$$\frac{I_1}{I_2} = \frac{r_2^2}{r_1^2} \quad \text{(inverse-square law for intensity)} \qquad (15.26)$$

15.17 The greater the distance from a wave source, the greater the area over which the wave power is distributed and the smaller the wave intensity.

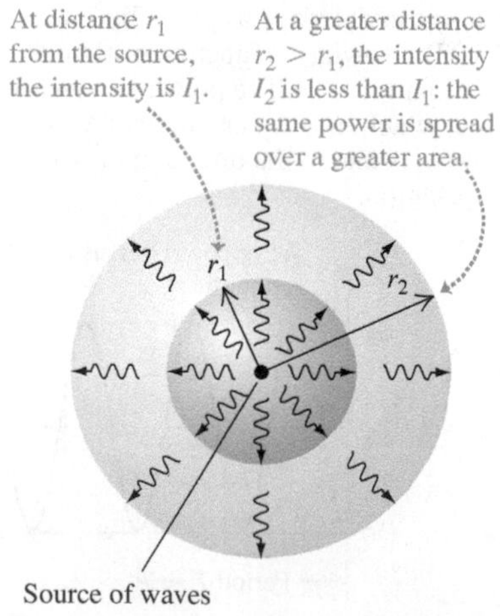

The intensity I at any distance r is therefore inversely proportional to r^2. This relationship is called the *inverse-square law* for intensity.

Example 15.5 The inverse-square law

A siren on a tall pole radiates sound waves uniformly in all directions. At a distance of 15.0 m from the siren, the sound intensity is $0.250\ \text{W/m}^2$. At what distance is the intensity $0.010\ \text{W/m}^2$?

SOLUTION

IDENTIFY and SET UP: Because sound is radiated uniformly in all directions, we can use the inverse-square law, Eq. (15.26). At $r_1 = 15.0$ m the intensity is $I_1 = 0.250\ \text{W/m}^2$, and the target variable is the distance r_2 at which the intensity is $I_2 = 0.010\ \text{W/m}^2$.

EXECUTE: We solve Eq. (15.26) for r_2:

$$r_2 = r_1\sqrt{\frac{I_1}{I_2}} = (15.0\ \text{m})\sqrt{\frac{0.250\ \text{W/m}^2}{0.010\ \text{W/m}^2}} = 75.0\ \text{m}$$

EVALUATE: As a check on our answer, note that r_2 is five times greater than r_1. By the inverse-square law, the intensity I_2 should be $1/5^2 = 1/25$ as great as I_1, and indeed it is.

By using the inverse-square law, we've assumed that the sound waves travel in straight lines away from the siren. A more realistic solution, which is beyond our scope, would account for the reflection of sound waves from the ground.

Test Your Understanding of Section 15.5 Four identical strings each carry a sinusoidal wave of frequency 10 Hz. The string tension and wave amplitude are different for different strings. Rank the following strings in order from highest to lowest value of the average wave power: (i) tension 10 N, amplitude 1.0 mm; (ii) tension 40 N, amplitude 1.0 mm; (iii) tension 10 N, amplitude 4.0 mm; (iv) tension 20 N, amplitude 2.0 mm. ❙

15.6 Wave Interference, Boundary Conditions, and Superposition

Up to this point we've been discussing waves that propagate continuously in the same direction. But when a wave strikes the boundaries of its medium, all or part of the wave is *reflected.* When you yell at a building wall or a cliff face some distance away, the sound wave is reflected from the rigid surface and you hear an echo. When you flip the end of a rope whose far end is tied to a rigid support, a pulse travels the length of the rope and is reflected back to you. In both cases, the initial and reflected waves overlap in the same region of the medium. This overlapping of waves is called **interference.** (In general, the term "interference" refers to what happens when two or more waves pass through the same region at the same time.)

As a simple example of wave reflections and the role of the boundary of a wave medium, let's look again at transverse waves on a stretched string. What happens when a wave pulse or a sinusoidal wave arrives at the *end* of the string?

If the end is fastened to a rigid support, it is a *fixed* end that cannot move. The arriving wave exerts a force on the support; the reaction to this force, exerted *by* the support *on* the string, "kicks back" on the string and sets up a *reflected* pulse or wave traveling in the reverse direction. Figure 15.18 is a series of photographs showing the reflection of a pulse at the fixed end of a long coiled spring. The reflected pulse moves in the opposite direction from the initial, or *incident,* pulse, and its displacement is also opposite. Figure 15.19a illustrates this situation for a wave pulse on a string.

15.18 A series of images of a wave pulse, equally spaced in time from top to bottom. The pulse starts at the left in the top image, travels to the right, and is reflected from the fixed end at the right.

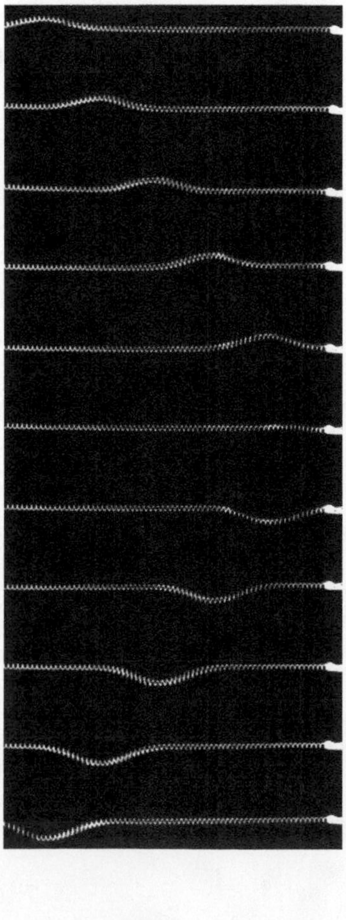

The opposite situation from an end that is held stationary is a *free* end, one that is perfectly free to move in the direction perpendicular to the length of the string. For example, the string might be tied to a light ring that slides on a frictionless rod perpendicular to the string, as in Fig. 15.19b. The ring and rod maintain the tension but exert no transverse force. When a wave arrives at this free end, the ring slides along the rod. The ring reaches a maximum displacement, and both it and the string come momentarily to rest, as in drawing 4 in Fig. 15.19b. But the string is now stretched, giving increased tension, so the free end of the string is

15.19 Reflection of a wave pulse (a) at a fixed end of a string and (b) at a free end. Time increases from top to bottom in each figure.

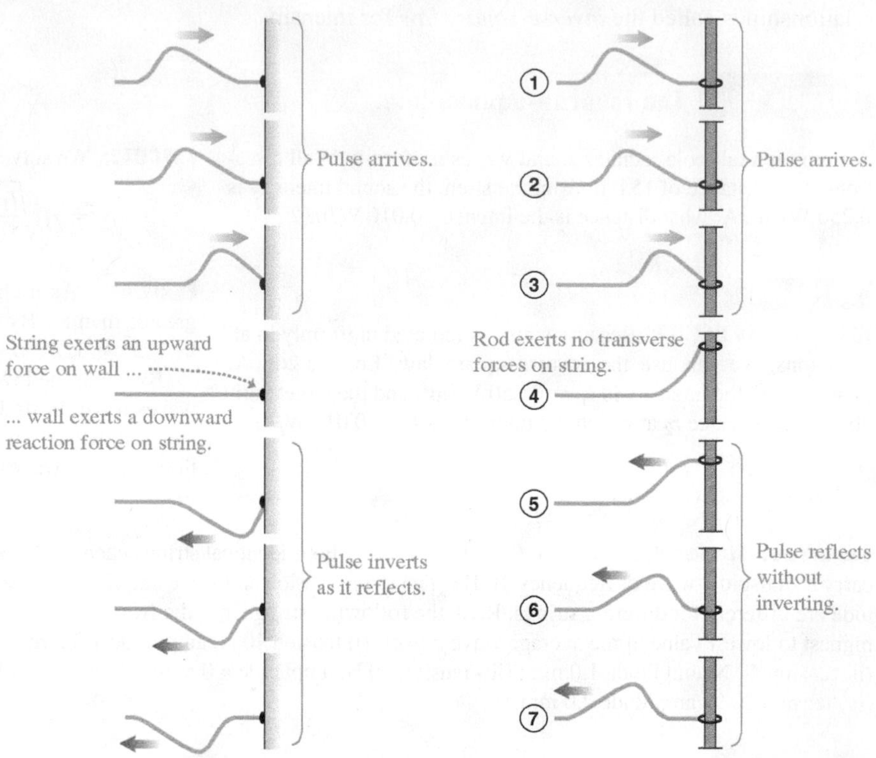

15.20 Overlap of two wave pulses—one right side up, one inverted—traveling in opposite directions. Time increases from top to bottom.

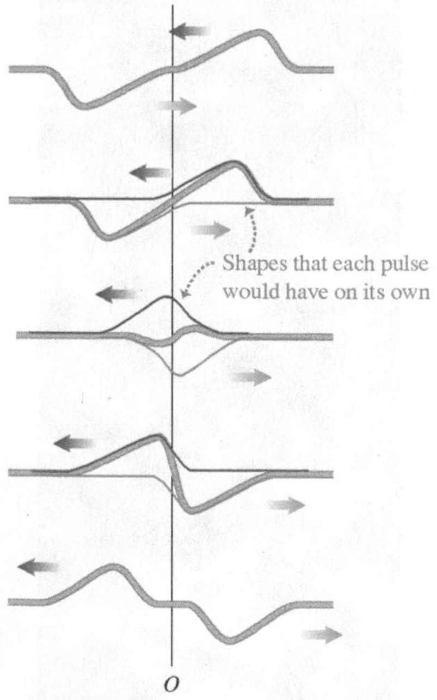

pulled back down, and again a reflected pulse is produced (drawing 7). As for a fixed end, the reflected pulse moves in the opposite direction from the initial pulse, but now the direction of the displacement is the same as for the initial pulse. The conditions at the end of the string, such as a rigid support or the complete absence of transverse force, are called **boundary conditions.**

The formation of the reflected pulse is similar to the overlap of two pulses traveling in opposite directions. Figure 15.20 shows two pulses with the same shape, one inverted with respect to the other, traveling in opposite directions. As the pulses overlap and pass each other, the total displacement of the string is the *algebraic sum* of the displacements at that point in the individual pulses. Because these two pulses have the same shape, the total displacement at point O in the middle of the figure is zero at all times. Thus the motion of the left half of the string would be the same if we cut the string at point O, threw away the right side, and held the end at O fixed. The two pulses on the left side then correspond to the incident and reflected pulses, combining so that the total displacement at O is *always* zero. For this to occur, the reflected pulse must be inverted relative to the incident pulse.

Figure 15.21 shows two pulses with the same shape, traveling in opposite directions but *not* inverted relative to each other. The displacement at point O in the middle of the figure is not zero, but the slope of the string at this point is always zero. According to Eq. (15.20), this corresponds to the absence of any transverse force at this point. In this case the motion of the left half of the string would be the same as if we cut the string at point O and attached the end to a frictionless sliding ring (Fig. 15.19b) that maintains tension without exerting any transverse force. In other words, this situation corresponds to reflection of a pulse at a free end of a string at point O. In this case the reflected pulse is *not* inverted.

The Principle of Superposition

Combining the displacements of the separate pulses at each point to obtain the actual displacement is an example of the **principle of superposition:** When two waves overlap, the actual displacement of any point on the string at any time is obtained by adding the displacement the point would have if only the first wave were present and the displacement it would have if only the second wave were present. In other words, the wave function $y(x, t)$ that describes the resulting motion in this situation is obtained by *adding* the two wave functions for the two separate waves:

$$y(x, t) = y_1(x, t) + y_2(x, t) \qquad \text{(principle of superposition)} \quad (15.27)$$

Mathematically, this additive property of wave functions follows from the form of the wave equation, Eq. (15.12) or (15.18), which every physically possible wave function must satisfy. Specifically, the wave equation is *linear;* that is, it contains the function $y(x, t)$ only to the first power (there are no terms involving $y(x, t)^2$, $y(x, t)^{1/2}$, etc.). As a result, if any two functions $y_1(x, t)$ and $y_2(x, t)$ satisfy the wave equation separately, their sum $y_1(x, t) + y_2(x, t)$ also satisfies it and is therefore a physically possible motion. Because this principle depends on the linearity of the wave equation and the corresponding linear-combination property of its solutions, it is also called the *principle of linear superposition.* For some physical systems, such as a medium that does not obey Hooke's law, the wave equation is *not* linear; this principle does not hold for such systems.

The principle of superposition is of central importance in all types of waves. When a friend talks to you while you are listening to music, you can distinguish the sound of speech and the sound of music from each other. This is precisely because the total sound wave reaching your ears is the algebraic sum of the wave produced by your friend's voice and the wave produced by the speakers of your stereo. If two sound waves did *not* combine in this simple linear way, the sound you would hear in this situation would be a hopeless jumble. Superposition also applies to electromagnetic waves (such as light) and many other types of waves.

15.21 Overlap of two wave pulses—both right side up—traveling in opposite directions. Time increases from top to bottom. Compare to Fig. 15.20.

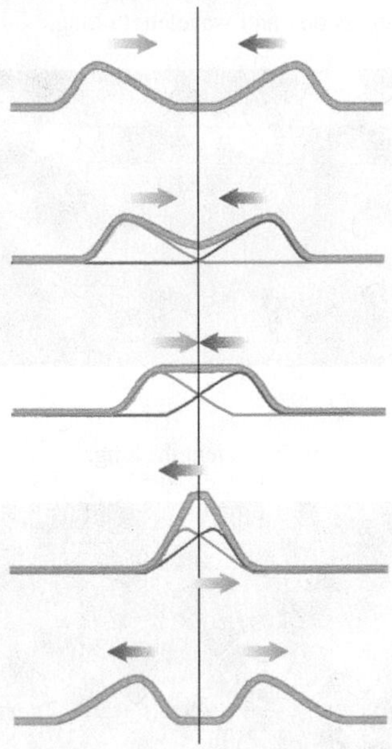

Test Your Understanding of Section 15.6 Figure 15.22 shows two wave pulses with different shapes traveling in different directions along a string. Make a series of sketches like Fig. 15.21 showing the shape of the string as the two pulses approach, overlap, and then pass each other. ❙

15.22 Two wave pulses with different shapes.

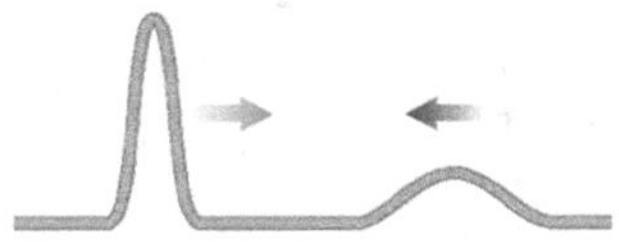

15.7 Standing Waves on a String

We have talked about the reflection of a wave *pulse* on a string when it arrives at a boundary point (either a fixed end or a free end). Now let's look at what happens when a *sinusoidal* wave is reflected by a fixed end of a string. We'll again approach the problem by considering the superposition of two waves propagating through the string, one representing the original or incident wave and the other representing the wave reflected at the fixed end.

Figure 15.23 shows a string that is fixed at its left end. Its right end is moved up and down in simple harmonic motion to produce a wave that travels to the left; the wave reflected from the fixed end travels to the right. The resulting motion when the two waves combine no longer looks like two waves traveling in opposite directions. The string appears to be subdivided into a number of segments, as in the time-exposure photographs of Figs. 15.23a, 15.23b, 15.23c, and 15.23d. Figure 15.23e shows two instantaneous shapes of the string in Fig. 15.23b. Let's compare this behavior with the waves we studied in Sections 15.1 through 15.5. In a wave that travels along the string, the amplitude is constant and the wave pattern moves with a speed equal to the wave speed. Here, instead, the wave pattern remains in the same position along the string and its amplitude

15.23 (a)–(d) Time exposures of standing waves in a stretched string. From (a) to (d), the frequency of oscillation of the right-hand end increases and the wavelength of the standing wave decreases. (e) The extremes of the motion of the standing wave in part (b), with nodes at the center and at the ends. The right-hand end of the string moves very little compared to the antinodes and so is essentially a node.

(a) String is one-half wavelength long.

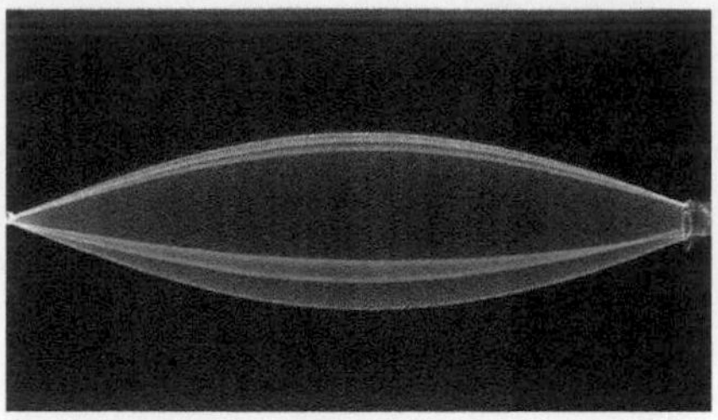

(b) String is one wavelength long.

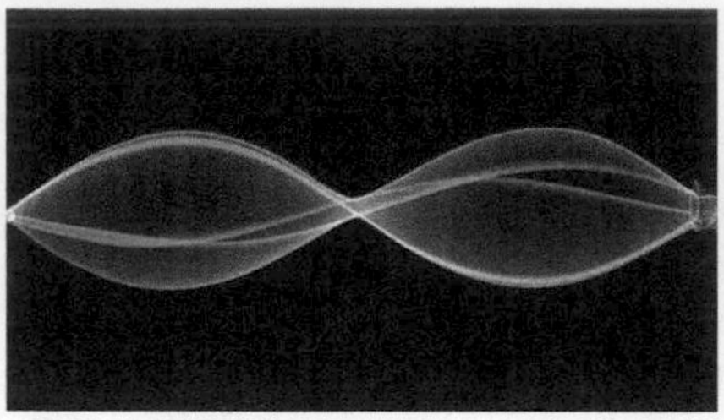

(c) String is one and a half wavelengths long.

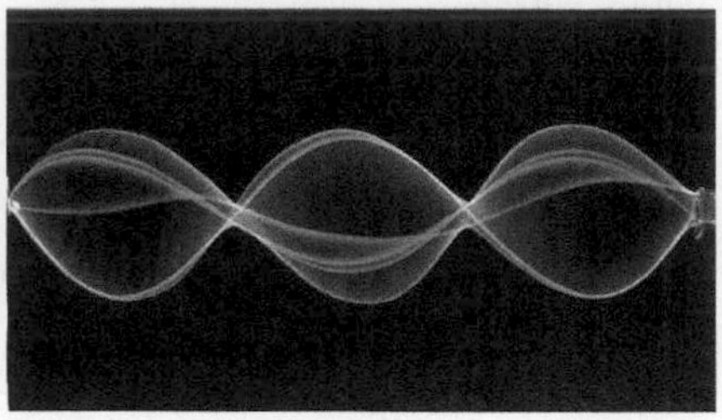

(d) String is two wavelengths long.

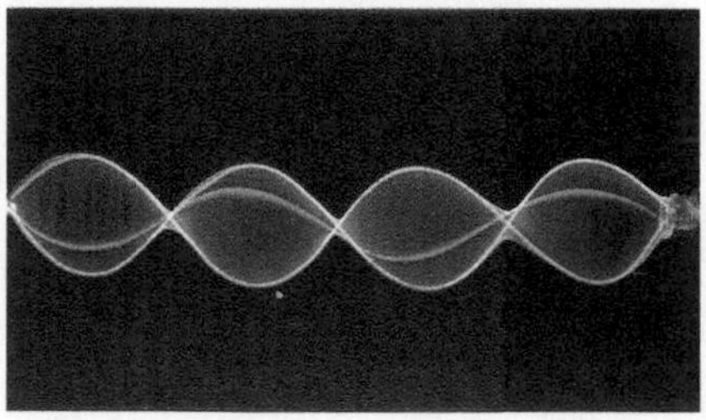

(e) The shape of the string in (b) at two different instants

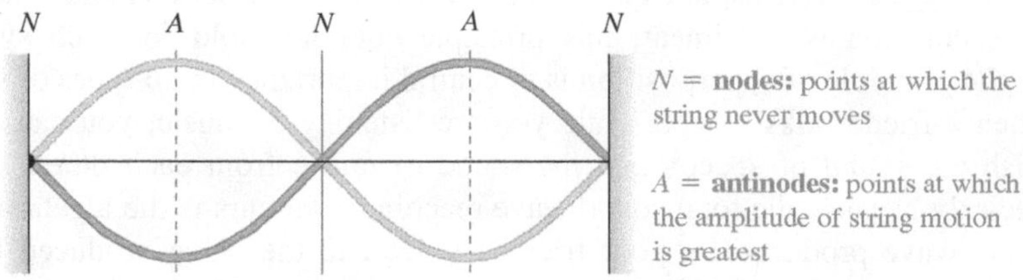

fluctuates. There are particular points called **nodes** (labeled N in Fig. 15.23e) that never move at all. Midway between the nodes are points called **antinodes** (labeled A in Fig. 15.23e) where the amplitude of motion is greatest. Because the wave pattern doesn't appear to be moving in either direction along the string, it is called a **standing wave.** (To emphasize the difference, a wave that *does* move along the string is called a **traveling wave.**)

The principle of superposition explains how the incident and reflected waves combine to form a standing wave. In Fig. 15.24 the red curves show a wave traveling to the left. The blue curves show a wave traveling to the right with the same propagation speed, wavelength, and amplitude. The waves are shown at nine instants, $\frac{1}{16}$ of a period apart. At each point along the string, we add the displacements (the values of y) for the two separate waves; the result is the total wave on the string, shown in brown.

At certain instants, such as $t = \frac{1}{4}T$, the two wave patterns are exactly in phase with each other, and the shape of the string is a sine curve with twice the amplitude of either individual wave. At other instants, such as $t = \frac{1}{2}T$, the two waves are exactly out of phase with each other, and the total wave at that instant is zero. The resultant displacement is *always* zero at those places marked N at the bottom of Fig. 15.24. These are the *nodes.* At a node the displacements of the two waves in red and blue are always equal and opposite and cancel each other out. This cancellation is called **destructive interference.** Midway between the nodes are the points of *greatest* amplitude, or the *antinodes,* marked A. At the antinodes the displacements of the two waves in red and blue are always identical, giving a large resultant displacement; this phenomenon is called **constructive interference.** We can see from the figure that the distance between successive nodes or between successive antinodes is one half-wavelength, or $\lambda/2$.

We can derive a wave function for the standing wave of Fig. 15.24 by adding the wave functions $y_1(x, t)$ and $y_2(x, t)$ for two waves with equal amplitude, period, and wavelength traveling in opposite directions. Here $y_1(x, t)$ (the red curves in Fig. 15.24) represents an incoming, or *incident,* wave traveling to the

15.24 Formation of a standing wave. A wave traveling to the left (red curves) combines with a wave traveling to the right (blue curves) to form a standing wave (brown curves).

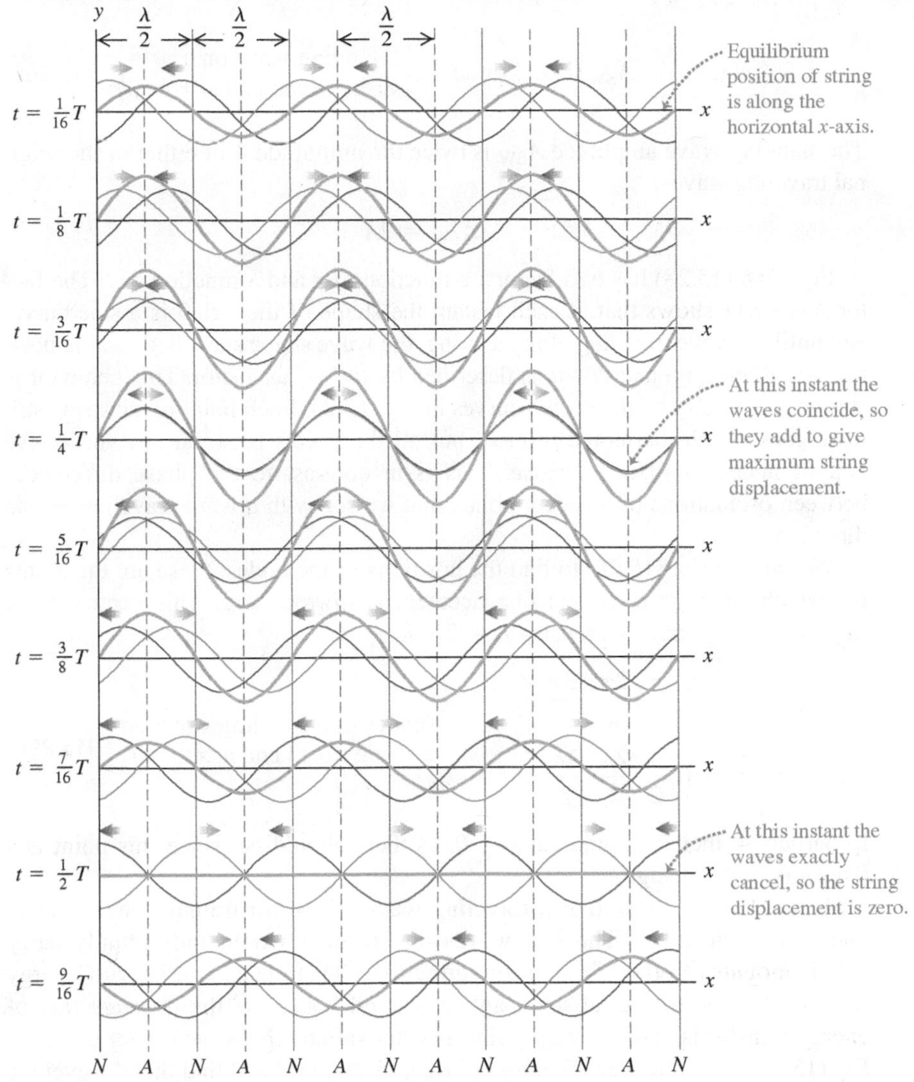

left along the $+x$-axis, arriving at the point $x = 0$ and being reflected; $y_2(x, t)$ (the blue curves in Fig. 15.24) represents the *reflected* wave traveling to the right from $x = 0$. We noted in Section 15.6 that the wave reflected from a fixed end of a string is inverted, so we give a negative sign to one of the waves:

$$y_1(x, t) = -A\cos(kx + \omega t) \quad \text{(incident wave traveling to the left)}$$
$$y_2(x, t) = A\cos(kx - \omega t) \quad \text{(reflected wave traveling to the right)}$$

Note also that the change in sign corresponds to a shift in *phase* of 180° or π radians. At $x = 0$ the motion from the reflected wave is $A\cos\omega t$ and the motion from the incident wave is $-A\cos\omega t$, which we can also write as $A\cos(\omega t + \pi)$. From Eq. (15.27), the wave function for the standing wave is the sum of the individual wave functions:

$$y(x, t) = y_1(x, t) + y_2(x, t) = A[-\cos(kx + \omega t) + \cos(kx - \omega t)]$$

We can rewrite each of the cosine terms by using the identities for the cosine of the sum and difference of two angles: $\cos(a \mp b) = \cos a\cos b \mp \sin a\sin b$.

Applying these and combining terms, we obtain the wave function for the standing wave:

$$y(x, t) = y_1(x, t) + y_2(x, t) = (2A \sin kx) \sin \omega t \qquad \text{or}$$

$$y(x, t) = (A_{SW} \sin kx) \sin \omega t \qquad \begin{array}{l}\text{(standing wave on a}\\ \text{string, fixed end at } x = 0)\end{array} \qquad (15.28)$$

The standing-wave amplitude A_{SW} is twice the amplitude A of either of the original traveling waves:

$$A_{SW} = 2A$$

Equation (15.28) has two factors: a function of x and a function of t. The factor $A_{SW} \sin kx$ shows that at each instant the shape of the string is a sine curve. But unlike a wave traveling along a string, the wave shape stays in the same position, oscillating up and down as described by the $\sin \omega t$ factor. This behavior is shown graphically by the brown curves in Fig. 15.24. Each point in the string still undergoes simple harmonic motion, but all the points between any successive pair of nodes oscillate *in phase.* This is in contrast to the phase differences between oscillations of adjacent points that we see with a wave traveling in one direction.

We can use Eq. (15.28) to find the positions of the nodes; these are the points for which $\sin kx = 0$, so the displacement is *always* zero. This occurs when $kx = 0, \pi, 2\pi, 3\pi, \ldots$, or, using $k = 2\pi/\lambda$,

$$\begin{aligned} x &= 0, \frac{\pi}{k}, \frac{2\pi}{k}, \frac{3\pi}{k}, \ldots \\ &= 0, \frac{\lambda}{2}, \frac{2\lambda}{2}, \frac{3\lambda}{2}, \ldots \end{aligned} \qquad \begin{array}{l}\text{(nodes of a standing wave on}\\ \text{a string, fixed end at } x = 0)\end{array} \qquad (15.29)$$

In particular, there is a node at $x = 0$, as there should be, since this point is a fixed end of the string.

A standing wave, unlike a traveling wave, *does not* transfer energy from one end to the other. The two waves that form it would individually carry equal amounts of power in opposite directions. There is a local flow of energy from each node to the adjacent antinodes and back, but the *average* rate of energy transfer is zero at every point. If you evaluate the wave power given by Eq. (15.21) using the wave function of Eq. (15.28), you will find that the average power is zero.

Problem-Solving Strategy 15.2 Standing Waves

MP

IDENTIFY *the relevant concepts:* Identify the target variables. Then determine whether the problem is purely *kinematic* (involving only such quantities as wave speed v, wavelength λ, and frequency f) or whether *dynamic* properties of the medium (such as F and μ for transverse waves on a string) are also involved.

SET UP *the problem* using the following steps:

1. Sketch the shape of the standing wave at a particular instant. This will help you visualize the nodes (label them N) and antinodes (A). The distance between adjacent nodes (or antinodes) is $\lambda/2$; the distance between a node and the adjacent antinode is $\lambda/4$.
2. Choose the equations you'll use. The wave function for the standing wave, like Eq. (15.28), is often useful.
3. You can determine the wave speed if you know λ and f (or, equivalently, $k = 2\pi/\lambda$ and $\omega = 2\pi f$) or if you know the relevant properties of the medium (for a string, F and μ).

EXECUTE *the solution:* Solve for the target variables. Once you've found the wave function, you can find the displacement y at any point x and at any time t. You can find the velocity and acceleration of a particle in the medium by taking the first and second partial derivatives of y with respect to time.

EVALUATE *your answer:* Compare your numerical answers with your sketch. Check that the wave function satisfies the boundary conditions (for example, the displacement should be zero at a fixed end).

Example 15.6 Standing waves on a guitar string

A guitar string lies along the x-axis when in equilibrium. The end of the string at $x = 0$ (the bridge of the guitar) is fixed. A sinusoidal wave with amplitude $A = 0.750\text{ mm} = 7.50 \times 10^{-4}\text{ m}$ and frequency $f = 440\text{ Hz}$, corresponding to the red curves in Fig. 15.24, travels along the string in the $-x$-direction at 143 m/s. It is reflected from the fixed end, and the superposition of the incident and reflected waves forms a standing wave. (a) Find the equation giving the displacement of a point on the string as a function of position and time. (b) Locate the nodes. (c) Find the amplitude of the standing wave and the maximum transverse velocity and acceleration.

SOLUTION

IDENTIFY and SET UP: This is a *kinematics* problem (see Problem-Solving Strategy 15.1 in Section 15.3). The target variables are: in part (a), the wave function of the standing wave; in part (b), the locations of the nodes; and in part (c), the maximum displacement y, transverse velocity v_y, and transverse acceleration a_y. Since there is a fixed end at $x = 0$, we can use Eqs. (15.28) and (15.29) to describe this standing wave. We will need the relationships $\omega = 2\pi f$, $v = \omega/k$, and $v = \lambda f$.

EXECUTE: (a) The standing-wave amplitude is $A_{SW} = 2A = 1.50 \times 10^{-3}\text{ m}$ (twice the amplitude of either the incident or reflected wave). The angular frequency and wave number are

$$\omega = 2\pi f = (2\pi\text{ rad})(440\text{ s}^{-1}) = 2760\text{ rad/s}$$

$$k = \frac{\omega}{v} = \frac{2760\text{ rad/s}}{143\text{ m/s}} = 19.3\text{ rad/m}$$

Equation (15.28) then gives

$$\begin{aligned} y(x,t) &= (A_{SW}\sin kx)\sin\omega t \\ &= [(1.50\times10^{-3}\text{ m})\sin(19.3\text{ rad/m})x]\sin(2760\text{ rad/s})t \end{aligned}$$

(b) From Eq. (15.29), the positions of the nodes are $x = 0, \lambda/2, \lambda, 3\lambda/2, \ldots$. The wavelength is $\lambda = v/f = (143\text{ m/s})/(440\text{ Hz}) = 0.325\text{ m}$, so the nodes are at $x = 0$, 0.163 m, 0.325 m, 0.488 m, ...

(c) From the expression for $y(x, t)$ in part (a), the maximum displacement from equilibrium is $A_{SW} = 1.50 \times 10^{-3}\text{ m} = 1.50\text{ mm}$. This occurs at the *antinodes,* which are midway between adjacent nodes (that is, at $x = 0.081$ m, 0.244 m, 0.406 m, . . .).

For a particle on the string at any point x, the transverse (y-) velocity is

$$\begin{aligned} v_y(x,t) &= \frac{\partial y(x,t)}{\partial t} \\ &= [(1.50\times10^{-3}\text{ m})\sin(19.3\text{ rad/m})x] \\ &\quad\times[(2760\text{ rad/s})\cos(2760\text{ rad/s})t] \\ &= [(4.15\text{ m/s})\sin(19.3\text{ rad/m})x]\cos(2760\text{ rad/s})t \end{aligned}$$

At an antinode, $\sin(19.3\text{ rad/m})x = \pm1$ and the transverse velocity varies between $+4.15$ m/s and -4.15 m/s. As is always the case in SHM, the maximum velocity occurs when the particle is passing through the equilibrium position ($y = 0$).

The transverse acceleration $a_y(x, t)$ is the *second* partial derivative of $y(x, t)$ with respect to time. You can show that

$$\begin{aligned} a_y(x,t) &= \frac{\partial v_y(x,t)}{\partial t} = \frac{\partial^2 y(x,t)}{\partial t^2} \\ &= [(-1.15\times10^{4}\text{ m/s}^2)\sin(19.3\text{ rad/m})x] \\ &\quad\times\sin(2760\text{ rad/s})t \end{aligned}$$

At the antinodes, the transverse acceleration varies between $+1.15 \times 10^4\text{ m/s}^2$ and $-1.15 \times 10^4\text{ m/s}^2$.

EVALUATE: The maximum transverse velocity at an antinode is quite respectable (about 15 km/h, or 9.3 mi/h). But the maximum transverse acceleration is tremendous, 1170 times the acceleration due to gravity! Guitar strings are actually fixed at *both* ends; we'll see the consequences of this in the next section.

Test Your Understanding of Section 15.7 Suppose the frequency of the standing wave in Example 15.6 were doubled from 440 Hz to 880 Hz. Would all of the nodes for $f = 440$ Hz also be nodes for $f = 880$ Hz? If so, would there be additional nodes for $f = 880$ Hz? If not, which nodes are absent for $f = 880$ Hz? ❙

15.8 Normal Modes of a String

MasteringPHYSICS

PhET: Fourier: Making Waves
PhET: Waves on a String
ActivPhysics 10.4: Standing Waves on Strings
ActivPhysics 10.5: Tuning a Stringed Instrument: Standing Waves
ActivPhysics 10.6: String Mass and Standing Waves

When we described standing waves on a string rigidly held at one end, as in Fig. 15.23, we made no assumptions about the length of the string or about what was happening at the other end. Let's now consider a string of a definite length L, rigidly held at *both* ends. Such strings are found in many musical instruments, including pianos, violins, and guitars. When a guitar string is plucked, a wave is produced in the string; this wave is reflected and re-reflected from the ends of the string, making a standing wave. This standing wave on the string in turn produces a sound wave in the air, with a frequency determined by the properties of the string. This is what makes stringed instruments so useful in making music.

To understand these properties of standing waves on a string fixed at both ends, let's first examine what happens when we set up a sinusoidal wave on such a string. The standing wave that results must have a node at *both* ends of the string. We saw in the preceding section that adjacent nodes are one half-wavelength

$(\lambda/2)$ apart, so the length of the string must be $\lambda/2$, or $2(\lambda/2)$, or $3(\lambda/2)$, or in general some integer number of half-wavelengths:

$$L = n\frac{\lambda}{2} \quad (n = 1, 2, 3, \ldots) \qquad \text{(string fixed at both ends)} \tag{15.30}$$

That is, if a string with length L is fixed at both ends, a standing wave can exist only if its wavelength satisfies Eq. (15.30).

Solving this equation for λ and labeling the possible values of λ as λ_n, we find

$$\lambda_n = \frac{2L}{n} \quad (n = 1, 2, 3, \ldots) \qquad \text{(string fixed at both ends)} \tag{15.31}$$

Waves can exist on the string if the wavelength is *not* equal to one of these values, but there cannot be a steady wave pattern with nodes and antinodes, and the total wave cannot be a standing wave. Equation (15.31) is illustrated by the standing waves shown in Figs. 15.23a, 15.23b, 15.23c, and 15.23d; these represent $n = 1, 2, 3$, and 4, respectively.

Corresponding to the series of possible standing-wave wavelengths λ_n is a series of possible standing-wave frequencies f_n, each related to its corresponding wavelength by $f_n = v/\lambda_n$. The smallest frequency f_1 corresponds to the largest wavelength (the $n = 1$ case), $\lambda_1 = 2L$:

$$f_1 = \frac{v}{2L} \qquad \text{(string fixed at both ends)} \tag{15.32}$$

This is called the **fundamental frequency.** The other standing-wave frequencies are $f_2 = 2v/2L$, $f_3 = 3v/2L$, and so on. These are all integer multiples of the fundamental frequency f_1, such as $2f_1$, $3f_1$, $4f_1$, and so on, and we can express *all* the frequencies as

$$f_n = n\frac{v}{2L} = nf_1 \quad (n = 1, 2, 3, \ldots) \qquad \text{(string fixed at both ends)} \tag{15.33}$$

These frequencies are called **harmonics,** and the series is called a **harmonic series.** Musicians sometimes call f_2, f_3, and so on **overtones;** f_2 is the second harmonic or the first overtone, f_3 is the third harmonic or the second overtone, and so on. The first harmonic is the same as the fundamental frequency (Fig. 15.25).

15.25 Each string of a violin naturally oscillates at one or more of its harmonic frequencies, producing sound waves in the air with the same frequencies.

For a string with fixed ends at $x = 0$ and $x = L$, the wave function $y(x, t)$ of the nth standing wave is given by Eq. (15.28) (which satisfies the condition that there is a node at $x = 0$), with $\omega = \omega_n = 2\pi f_n$ and $k = k_n = 2\pi/\lambda_n$:

$$y_n(x, t) = A_{SW} \sin k_n x \sin \omega_n t \tag{15.34}$$

You can easily show that this wave function has nodes at both $x = 0$ and $x = L$, as it must.

15.26 The first four normal modes of a string fixed at both ends. (Compare these to the photographs in Fig. 15.23.)

(a) $n = 1$: fundamental frequency, f_1

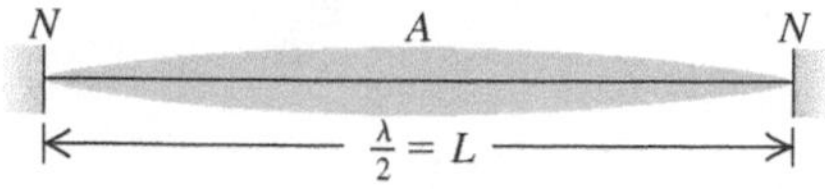

(b) $n = 2$: second harmonic, f_2 (first overtone)

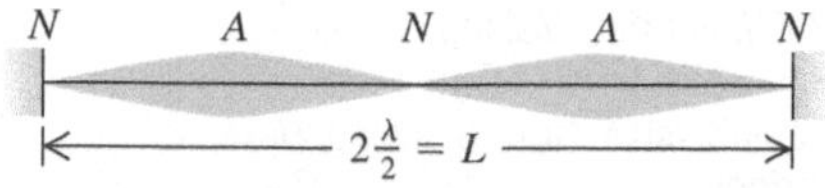

(c) $n = 3$: third harmonic, f_3 (second overtone)

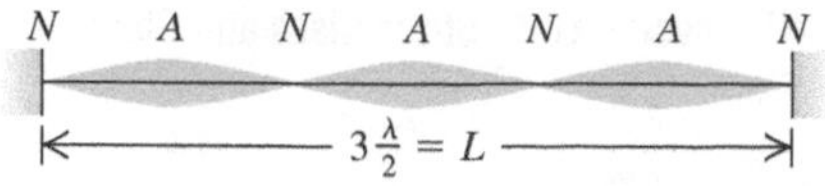

(d) $n = 4$: fourth harmonic, f_4 (third overtone)

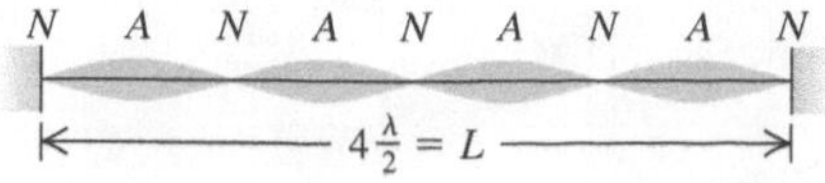

A **normal mode** of an oscillating system is a motion in which all particles of the system move sinusoidally with the same frequency. For a system made up of a string of length L fixed at both ends, each of the wavelengths given by Eq. (15.31) corresponds to a possible normal-mode pattern and frequency. There are infinitely many normal modes, each with its characteristic frequency and vibration pattern. Figure 15.26 shows the first four normal-mode patterns and their associated frequencies and wavelengths; these correspond to Eq. (15.34) with $n = 1, 2, 3$, and 4. By contrast, a harmonic oscillator, which has only one oscillating particle, has only one normal mode and one characteristic frequency. The string fixed at both ends has infinitely many normal modes because it is made up of a very large (effectively infinite) number of particles. More complicated oscillating systems also have infinite numbers of normal modes, though with more complex normal-mode patterns than a string (Fig. 15.27).

Complex Standing Waves

If we could displace a string so that its shape is the same as one of the normal-mode patterns and then release it, it would vibrate with the frequency of that mode. Such a vibrating string would displace the surrounding air with the same frequency, producing a traveling sinusoidal sound wave that your ears would perceive as a pure tone. But when a string is struck (as in a piano) or plucked (as is done to guitar strings), the shape of the displaced string is *not* as simple as one of the patterns in Fig. 15.26. The fundamental as well as many overtones are present in the resulting vibration. This motion is therefore a combination or *superposition* of many normal modes. Several simple harmonic motions of different frequencies are present simultaneously, and the displacement of any point on the string is the sum (or superposition) of the displacements associated with the individual modes. The sound produced by the vibrating string is likewise a superposition of traveling sinusoidal sound waves, which you perceive as a rich, complex tone with the fundamental frequency f_1. The standing wave on the string and the traveling sound wave in the air have similar **harmonic content** (the extent to which frequencies higher than the fundamental are present). The harmonic content depends on how the string is initially set into motion. If you pluck the strings of an acoustic guitar in the normal location over the sound hole, the sound that you hear has a different harmonic content than if you pluck the strings next to the fixed end on the guitar body.

It is possible to represent every possible motion of the string as some superposition of normal-mode motions. Finding this representation for a given vibration pattern is called *harmonic analysis.* The sum of sinusoidal functions that represents a complex wave is called a *Fourier series.* Figure 15.28 shows how a standing wave that is produced by plucking a guitar string of length L at a point $L/4$ from one end can be represented as a combination of sinusoidal functions.

Standing Waves and String Instruments

As we have seen, the fundamental frequency of a vibrating string is $f_1 = v/2L$. The speed v of waves on the string is determined by Eq. (15.13), $v = \sqrt{F/\mu}$. Combining these equations, we find

$$f_1 = \frac{1}{2L}\sqrt{\frac{F}{\mu}} \quad \text{(string fixed at both ends)} \qquad (15.35)$$

This is also the fundamental frequency of the sound wave created in the surrounding air by the vibrating string. Familiar musical instruments show how f_1 depends on the properties of the string. The inverse dependence of frequency on length L is illustrated by the long strings of the bass (low-frequency) section of the piano or the bass viol compared with the shorter strings of the treble section of the piano or the violin (Fig. 15.29). The pitch of a violin or guitar is usually

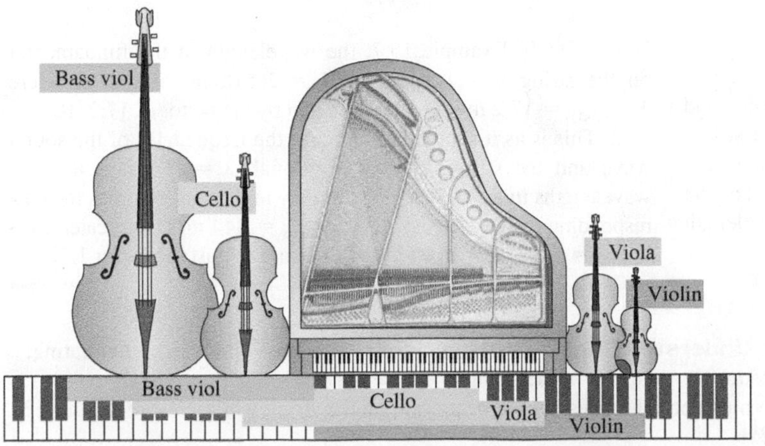

15.29 Comparing the range of a concert grand piano to the ranges of a bass viol, a cello, a viola, and a violin. In all cases, longer strings produce bass notes and shorter strings produce treble notes.

15.27 Astronomers have discovered that the sun oscillates in several different normal modes. This computer simulation shows one such mode.

MasteringPHYSICS

ActivPhysics 10.10: Complex Waves: Fourier Analysis

15.28 When a guitar string is plucked (pulled into a triangular shape) and released, a standing wave results. The standing wave is well represented (except at the sharp maximum point) by the sum of just three sinusoidal functions. Including additional sinusoidal functions further improves the representation.

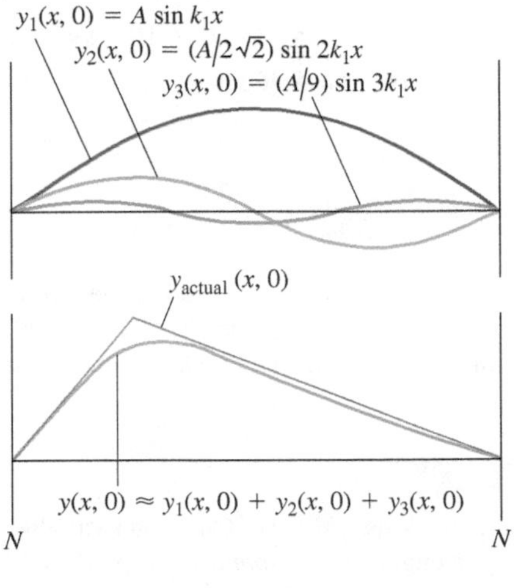

varied by pressing a string against the fingerboard with the fingers to change the length L of the vibrating portion of the string. Increasing the tension F increases the wave speed v and thus increases the frequency (and the pitch). All string instruments are "tuned" to the correct frequencies by varying the tension; you tighten the string to raise the pitch. Finally, increasing the mass per unit length μ decreases the wave speed and thus the frequency. The lower notes on a steel guitar are produced by thicker strings, and one reason for winding the bass strings of a piano with wire is to obtain the desired low frequency from a relatively short string.

Wind instruments such as saxophones and trombones also have normal modes. As for stringed instruments, the frequencies of these normal modes determine the pitch of the musical tones that these instruments produce. We'll discuss these instruments and many other aspects of sound in Chapter 16.

Example 15.7 A giant bass viol

In an attempt to get your name in *Guinness World Records,* you build a bass viol with strings of length 5.00 m between fixed points. One string, with linear mass density 40.0 g/m, is tuned to a 20.0-Hz fundamental frequency (the lowest frequency that the human ear can hear). Calculate (a) the tension of this string, (b) the frequency and wavelength on the string of the second harmonic, and (c) the frequency and wavelength on the string of the second overtone.

SOLUTION

IDENTIFY and SET UP: In part (a) the target variable is the string tension F; we'll use Eq. (15.35), which relates F to the known values $f_1 = 20.0$ Hz, $L = 5.00$ m, and $\mu = 40.0$ g/m. In parts (b) and (c) the target variables are the frequency and wavelength of a given harmonic and a given overtone. We determine these from the given length of the string and the fundamental frequency, using Eqs. (15.31) and (15.33).

EXECUTE: (a) We solve Eq. (15.35) for F:

$$F = 4\mu L^2 f_1{}^2 = 4(40.0 \times 10^{-3}\ \text{kg/m})(5.00\ \text{m})^2(20.0\ \text{s}^{-1})^2$$
$$= 1600\ \text{N} = 360\ \text{lb}$$

(b) From Eqs. (15.33) and (15.31), the frequency and wavelength of the second harmonic ($n = 2$) are

$$f_2 = 2f_1 = 2(20.0\ \text{Hz}) = 40.0\ \text{Hz}$$

$$\lambda_2 = \frac{2L}{2} = \frac{2(5.00\ \text{m})}{2} = 5.00\ \text{m}$$

(c) The second overtone is the "second tone over" (above) the fundamental—that is, $n = 3$. Its frequency and wavelength are

$$f_3 = 3f_1 = 3(20.0\ \text{Hz}) = 60.0\ \text{Hz}$$

$$\lambda_3 = \frac{2L}{3} = \frac{2(5.00\ \text{m})}{3} = 3.33\ \text{m}$$

EVALUATE: The string tension in a real bass viol is typically a few hundred newtons; the tension in part (a) is a bit higher than that. The wavelengths in parts (b) and (c) are equal to the length of the string and two-thirds the length of the string, respectively, which agrees with the drawings of standing waves in Fig. 15.26.

Example 15.8 From waves on a string to sound waves in air

What are the frequency and wavelength of the sound waves produced in the air when the string in Example 15.7 is vibrating at its fundamental frequency? The speed of sound in air at 20°C is 344 m/s.

SOLUTION

IDENTIFY and SET UP: Our target variables are the frequency and wavelength for the *sound wave* produced by the bass viol string. The frequency of the sound wave is the same as the fundamental frequency f_1 of the standing wave, because the string forces the surrounding air to vibrate at the same frequency. The wavelength of the sound wave is $\lambda_{1(\text{sound})} = v_{\text{sound}}/f_1$.

EXECUTE: We have $f = f_1 = 20.0$ Hz, so

$$\lambda_{1(\text{sound})} = \frac{v_{\text{sound}}}{f_1} = \frac{344\ \text{m/s}}{20.0\ \text{Hz}} = 17.2\ \text{m}$$

EVALUATE: In Example 15.7, the wavelength of the fundamental on the string was $\lambda_{1(\text{string})} = 2L = 2(5.00\ \text{m}) = 10.0\ \text{m}$. Here $\lambda_{1(\text{sound})} = 17.2$ m is greater than that by the factor of $17.2/10.0 = 1.72$. This is as it should be: Because the frequencies of the sound wave and the standing wave are equal, $\lambda = v/f$ says that the wavelengths in air and on the string are in the same ratio as the corresponding wave speeds; here $v_{\text{sound}} = 344$ m/s is greater than $v_{\text{string}} = (10.0\ \text{m})(20.0\ \text{Hz}) = 200$ m/s by just the factor 1.72.

Test Your Understanding of Section 15.8 While a guitar string is vibrating, you gently touch the midpoint of the string to ensure that the string does not vibrate at that point. Which normal modes *cannot* be present on the string while you are touching it in this way? ❙

CHAPTER 15 SUMMARY

Waves and their properties: A wave is any disturbance that propagates from one region to another. A mechanical wave travels within some material called the medium. The wave speed v depends on the type of wave and the properties of the medium.

In a periodic wave, the motion of each point of the medium is periodic with frequency f and period T. The wavelength λ is the distance over which the wave pattern repeats, and the amplitude A is the maximum displacement of a particle in the medium. The product of λ and f equals the wave speed. A sinusoidal wave is a special periodic wave in which each point moves in simple harmonic motion. (See Example 15.1.)

$$v = \lambda f \qquad (15.1)$$

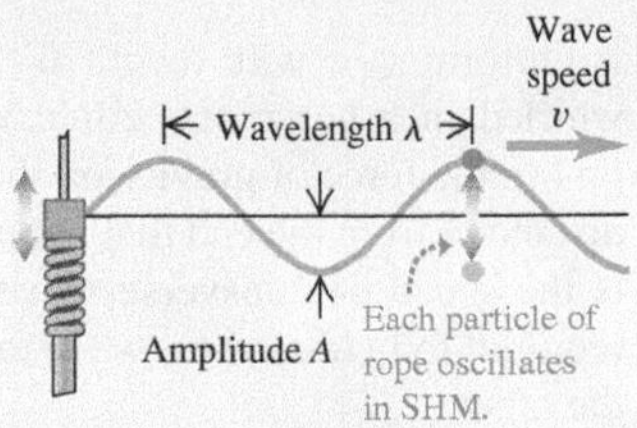

Wave functions and wave dynamics: The wave function $y(x, t)$ describes the displacements of individual particles in the medium. Equations (15.3), (15.4), and (15.7) give the wave equation for a sinusoidal wave traveling in the $+x$-direction. If the wave is moving in the $-x$-direction, the minus signs in the cosine functions are replaced by plus signs. (See Example 15.2.)

The wave function obeys a partial differential equation called the wave equation, Eq. (15.12).

The speed of transverse waves on a string depends on the tension F and mass per unit length μ. (See Example 15.3.)

$$y(x, t) = A\cos\left[\omega\left(\frac{x}{v} - t\right)\right] = A\cos 2\pi f\left(\frac{x}{v} - t\right) \qquad (15.3)$$

$$y(x, t) = A\cos 2\pi\left(\frac{x}{\lambda} - \frac{t}{T}\right) \qquad (15.4)$$

$$y(x, t) = A\cos(kx - \omega t) \qquad (15.7)$$

where $k = 2\pi/\lambda$ and $\omega = 2\pi f = vk$

$$\frac{\partial^2 y(x, t)}{\partial x^2} = \frac{1}{v^2}\frac{\partial^2 y(x, t)}{\partial t^2} \qquad (15.12)$$

$$v = \sqrt{\frac{F}{\mu}} \quad \text{(waves on a string)} \qquad (15.13)$$

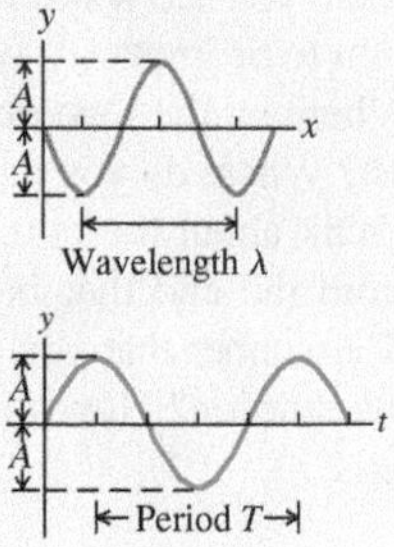

Wave power: Wave motion conveys energy from one region to another. For a sinusoidal mechanical wave, the average power P_{av} is proportional to the square of the wave amplitude and the square of the frequency. For waves that spread out in three dimensions, the wave intensity I is inversely proportional to the square of the distance from the source. (See Examples 15.4 and 15.5.)

$$P_{av} = \tfrac{1}{2}\sqrt{\mu F}\,\omega^2 A^2 \qquad (15.25)$$

(average power, sinusoidal wave)

$$\frac{I_1}{I_2} = \frac{r_2^{\,2}}{r_1^{\,2}} \qquad (15.26)$$

(inverse-square law for intensity)

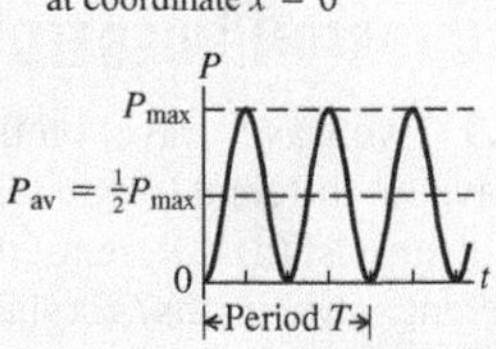

Wave superposition: A wave reflects when it reaches a boundary of its medium. At any point where two or more waves overlap, the total displacement is the sum of the displacements of the individual waves (principle of superposition).

$$y(x, t) = y_1(x, t) + y_2(x, t) \qquad (15.27)$$

(principle of superposition)

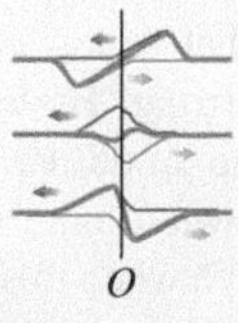

Standing waves on a string: When a sinusoidal wave is reflected from a fixed or free end of a stretched string, the incident and reflected waves combine to form a standing sinusoidal wave with nodes and antinodes. Adjacent nodes are spaced a distance $\lambda/2$ apart, as are adjacent antinodes. (See Example 15.6.)

When both ends of a string with length L are held fixed, standing waves can occur only when L is an integer multiple of $\lambda/2$. Each frequency with its associated vibration pattern is called a normal mode. (See Examples 15.7 and 15.8.)

$$y(x, t) = (A_{SW}\sin kx)\sin\omega t \qquad (15.28)$$

(standing wave on a string, fixed end at $x = 0$)

$$f_n = n\frac{v}{2L} = nf_1 \quad (n = 1, 2, 3, \ldots) \qquad (15.33)$$

$$f_1 = \frac{1}{2L}\sqrt{\frac{F}{\mu}} \qquad (15.35)$$

(string fixed at both ends)

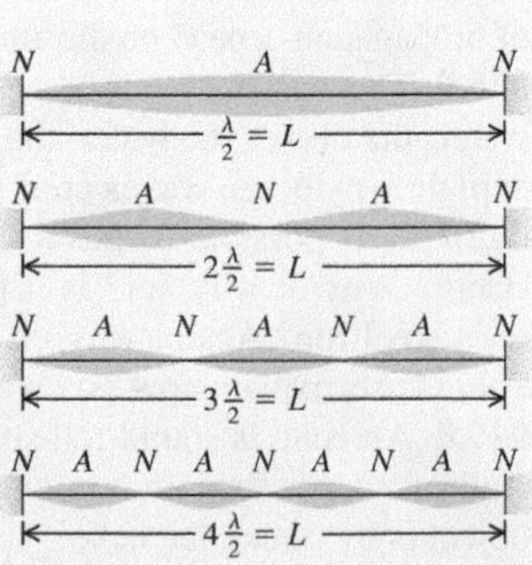

BRIDGING PROBLEM Waves on a Rotating Rope

A uniform rope with length L and mass m is held at one end and whirled in a horizontal circle with angular velocity ω. You can ignore the force of gravity on the rope. (a) At a point on the rope a distance r from the end that is held, what is the tension F? (b) What is the speed of transverse waves at this point? (c) Find the time required for a transverse wave to travel from one end of the rope to the other.

SOLUTION GUIDE

See MasteringPhysics® Study Area for a Video Tutor solution.

IDENTIFY and SET UP

1. Draw a sketch of the situation and label the distances r and L. The tension in the rope will be different at different values of r. Do you see why? Where on the rope do you expect the tension to be greatest? Where do you expect it will be least?
2. Where on the rope do you expect the wave speed to be greatest? Where do you expect it will be least?
3. Think about the portion of the rope that is farther out than r from the end that is held. What forces act on this portion? (Remember that you can ignore gravity.) What is the mass of this portion? How far is its center of mass from the rotation axis?
4. Make a list of the unknown quantities and decide which are your target variables.

EXECUTE

5. Draw a free-body diagram for the portion of the rope that is farther out than r from the end that is held.
6. Use your free-body diagram to help you determine the tension in the rope at distance r.
7. Use your result from step 6 to find the wave speed at distance r.
8. Use your result from step 7 to find the time for a wave to travel from one end to the other. (*Hint:* The wave speed is $v = dr/dt$, so the time for the wave to travel a distance dr along the rope is $dt = dr/v$. Integrate this to find the total time. See Appendix B.)

EVALUATE

9. Do your results for parts (a) and (b) agree with your expectations from steps 1 and 2? Are the units correct?
10. Check your result for part (a) by considering the net force on a small segment of the rope at distance r with length dr and mass $dm = (m/L)dr$. [*Hint:* The tension forces on this segment are $F(r)$ on one side and $F(r + dr)$ on the other side. You will get an equation for dF/dr that you can integrate to find F as a function of r.]

Problems

For instructor-assigned homework, go to www.masteringphysics.com

•, ••, •••: Problems of increasing difficulty. **CP**: Cumulative problems incorporating material from earlier chapters. **CALC**: Problems requiring calculus. **BIO**: Biosciences problems.

DISCUSSION QUESTIONS

Q15.1 Two waves travel on the same string. Is it possible for them to have (a) different frequencies; (b) different wavelengths; (c) different speeds; (d) different amplitudes; (e) the same frequency but different wavelengths? Explain your reasoning.

Q15.2 Under a tension F, it takes 2.00 s for a pulse to travel the length of a taut wire. What tension is required (in terms of F) for the pulse to take 6.00 s instead?

Q15.3 What kinds of energy are associated with waves on a stretched string? How could you detect such energy experimentally?

Q15.4 The amplitude of a wave decreases gradually as the wave travels down a long, stretched string. What happens to the energy of the wave when this happens?

Q15.5 For the wave motions discussed in this chapter, does the speed of propagation depend on the amplitude? What makes you say this?

Q15.6 The speed of ocean waves depends on the depth of the water; the deeper the water, the faster the wave travels. Use this to explain why ocean waves crest and "break" as they near the shore.

Q15.7 Is it possible to have a longitudinal wave on a stretched string? Why or why not? Is it possible to have a transverse wave on a steel rod? Again, why or why not? If your answer is yes in either case, explain how you would create such a wave.

Q15.8 An echo is sound reflected from a distant object, such as a wall or a cliff. Explain how you can determine how far away the object is by timing the echo.

Q15.9 Why do you see lightning before you hear the thunder? A familiar rule of thumb is to start counting slowly, once per second, when you see the lightning; when you hear the thunder, divide the number you have reached by 3 to obtain your distance from the lightning in kilometers (or divide by 5 to obtain your distance in miles). Why does this work, or does it?

Q15.10 For transverse waves on a string, is the wave speed the same as the speed of any part of the string? Explain the difference between these two speeds. Which one is constant?

Q15.11 Children make toy telephones by sticking each end of a long string through a hole in the bottom of a paper cup and knotting it so it will not pull out. When the spring is pulled taut, sound can be transmitted from one cup to the other. How does this work? Why is the transmitted sound louder than the sound traveling through air for the same distance?

Q15.12 The four strings on a violin have different thicknesses, but are all under approximately the same tension. Do waves travel faster on the thick strings or the thin strings? Why? How does the fundamental vibration frequency compare for the thick versus the thin strings?

Q15.13 A sinusoidal wave can be described by a cosine function, which is negative just as often as positive. So why isn't the average power delivered by this wave zero?

Q15.14 Two strings of different mass per unit length μ_1 and μ_2 are tied together and stretched with a tension F. A wave travels along the string and passes the discontinuity in μ. Which of the following wave properties will be the same on both sides of the discontinuity, and which ones will change? speed of the wave; frequency; wavelength. Explain the physical reasoning behind each of your answers.

Q15.15 A long rope with mass m is suspended from the ceiling and hangs vertically. A wave pulse is produced at the lower end of the rope, and the pulse travels up the rope. Does the speed of the wave pulse change as it moves up the rope, and if so, does it increase or decrease?

Q15.16 In a transverse wave on a string, the motion of the string is perpendicular to the length of the string. How, then, is it possible for energy to move along the length of the string?

Q15.17 Both wave intensity and gravitation obey inverse-square laws. Do they do so for the same reason? Discuss the reason for each of these inverse-square laws as well as you can.

Q15.18 Energy can be transferred along a string by wave motion. However, in a standing wave on a string, no energy can ever be transferred past a node. Why not?

Q15.19 Can a standing wave be produced on a string by superposing two waves traveling in opposite directions with the same frequency but different amplitudes? Why or why not? Can a standing wave be produced by superposing two waves traveling in opposite directions with different frequencies but the same amplitude? Why or why not?

Q15.20 If you stretch a rubber band and pluck it, you hear a (somewhat) musical tone. How does the frequency of this tone change as you stretch the rubber band further? (Try it!) Does this agree with Eq. (15.35) for a string fixed at both ends? Explain.

Q15.21 A musical interval of an *octave* corresponds to a factor of 2 in frequency. By what factor must the tension in a guitar or violin string be increased to raise its pitch one octave? To raise it two octaves? Explain your reasoning. Is there any danger in attempting these changes in pitch?

Q15.22 By touching a string lightly at its center while bowing, a violinist can produce a note exactly one octave above the note to which the string is tuned—that is, a note with exactly twice the frequency. Why is this possible?

Q15.23 As we discussed in Section 15.1, water waves are a combination of longitudinal and transverse waves. Defend the following statement: "When water waves hit a vertical wall, the wall is a node of the longitudinal displacement but an antinode of the transverse displacement."

Q15.24 Violins are short instruments, while cellos and basses are long. In terms of the frequency of the waves they produce, explain why this is so.

Q15.25 What is the purpose of the frets on a guitar? In terms of the frequency of the vibration of the strings, explain their use.

EXERCISES

Section 15.2 Periodic Waves

15.1 • The speed of sound in air at 20°C is 344 m/s. (a) What is the wavelength of a sound wave with a frequency of 784 Hz, corresponding to the note G_5 on a piano, and how many milliseconds does each vibration take? (b) What is the wavelength of a sound wave one octave higher than the note in part (a)?

15.2 • BIO **Audible Sound.** Provided the amplitude is sufficiently great, the human ear can respond to longitudinal waves over a range of frequencies from about 20.0 Hz to about 20.0 kHz. (a) If you were to mark the beginning of each complete wave pattern with a red dot for the long-wavelength sound and a blue dot for the short-wavelength sound, how far apart would the red dots be, and how far apart would the blue dots be? (b) In reality would adjacent dots in each set be far enough apart for you to easily measure their separation with a meter stick? (c) Suppose you repeated part (a) in water, where sound travels at 1480 m/s. How far apart would the dots be in each set? Could you readily measure their separation with a meter stick?

15.3 • **Tsunami!** On December 26, 2004, a great earthquake occurred off the coast of Sumatra and triggered immense waves (tsunami) that killed some 200,000 people. Satellites observing these waves from space measured 800 km from one wave crest to the next and a period between waves of 1.0 hour. What was the speed of these waves in m/s and in km/h? Does your answer help you understand why the waves caused such devastation?

15.4 • BIO **Ultrasound Imaging.** Sound having frequencies above the range of human hearing (about 20,000 Hz) is called *ultrasound.* Waves above this frequency can be used to penetrate the body and to produce images by reflecting from surfaces. In a typical ultrasound scan, the waves travel through body tissue with a speed of 1500 m/s. For a good, detailed image, the wavelength should be no more than 1.0 mm. What frequency sound is required for a good scan?

15.5 • BIO (a) **Audible wavelengths.** The range of audible frequencies is from about 20 Hz to 20,000 Hz. What is the range of the wavelengths of audible sound in air? (b) **Visible light.** The range of visible light extends from 400 nm to 700 nm. What is the range of visible frequencies of light? (c) **Brain surgery.** Surgeons can remove brain tumors by using a cavitron ultrasonic surgical aspirator, which produces sound waves of frequency 23 kHz. What is the wavelength of these waves in air? (d) **Sound in the body.** What would be the wavelength of the sound in part (c) in bodily fluids in which the speed of sound is 1480 m/s but the frequency is unchanged?

15.6 •• A fisherman notices that his boat is moving up and down periodically, owing to waves on the surface of the water. It takes 2.5 s for the boat to travel from its highest point to its lowest, a total distance of 0.62 m. The fisherman sees that the wave crests are spaced 6.0 m apart. (a) How fast are the waves traveling? (b) What is the amplitude of each wave? (c) If the total vertical distance traveled by the boat were 0.30 m but the other data remained the same, how would the answers to parts (a) and (b) be affected?

Section 15.3 Mathematical Description of a Wave

15.7 • Transverse waves on a string have wave speed 8.00 m/s, amplitude 0.0700 m, and wavelength 0.320 m. The waves travel in the $-x$-direction, and at $t = 0$ the $x = 0$ end of the string has its maximum upward displacement. (a) Find the frequency, period, and wave number of these waves. (b) Write a wave function describing the wave. (c) Find the transverse displacement of a particle at $x = 0.360$ m at time $t = 0.150$ s. (d) How much time must elapse from the instant in part (c) until the particle at $x = 0.360$ m next has maximum upward displacement?

15.8 • A certain transverse wave is described by

$$y(x, t) = (6.50 \text{ mm}) \cos 2\pi \left(\frac{x}{28.0 \text{ cm}} - \frac{t}{0.0360 \text{ s}} \right)$$

Determine the wave's (a) amplitude; (b) wavelength; (c) frequency; (d) speed of propagation; (e) direction of propagation.

15.9 • CALC Which of the following wave functions satisfies the wave equation, Eq. (15.12)? (a) $y(x, t) = A\cos(kx + \omega t)$; (b) $y(x, t) = A\sin(kx + \omega t)$; (c) $y(x, t) = A(\cos kx + \cos \omega t)$. (d) For the wave of part (b), write the equations for the transverse velocity and transverse acceleration of a particle at point x.

15.10 • A water wave traveling in a straight line on a lake is described by the equation

$$y(x, t) = (3.75 \text{ cm}) \cos(0.450 \text{ cm}^{-1}\, x + 5.40 \text{ s}^{-1}\, t)$$

where y is the displacement perpendicular to the undisturbed surface of the lake. (a) How much time does it take for one complete wave pattern to go past a fisherman in a boat at anchor, and what horizontal distance does the wave crest travel in that time? (b) What are the wave number and the number of waves per second that pass the fisherman? (c) How fast does a wave crest travel past the fisherman, and what is the maximum speed of his cork floater as the wave causes it to bob up and down?

15.11 • A sinusoidal wave is propagating along a stretched string that lies along the x-axis. The displacement of the string as a function of time is graphed in Fig. E15.11 for particles at $x = 0$ and at $x = 0.0900$ m. (a) What is the amplitude of the wave? (b) What is the period of the wave? (c) You are told that the two points $x = 0$ and $x = 0.0900$ m are within one wavelength of each other. If the wave is moving in the $+x$-direction, determine the wavelength and the wave speed. (d) If instead the wave is moving in the $-x$-direction, determine the wavelength and the wave speed. (e) Would it be possible to determine definitively the wavelength in parts (c) and (d) if you were not told that the two points were within one wavelength of each other? Why or why not?

Figure **E15.11**

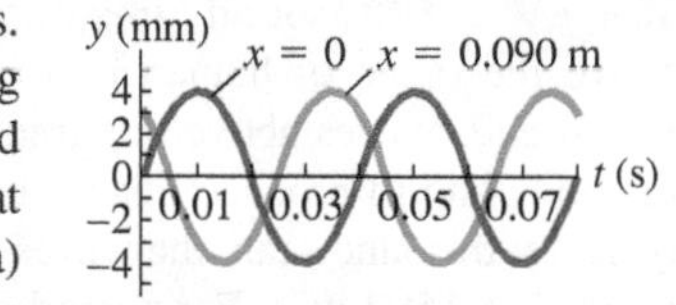

15.12 •• **CALC Speed of Propagation vs. Particle Speed.** (a) Show that Eq. (15.3) may be written as

$$y(x, t) = A \cos\left[\frac{2\pi}{\lambda}(x - vt)\right]$$

(b) Use $y(x, t)$ to find an expression for the transverse velocity v_y of a particle in the string on which the wave travels. (c) Find the maximum speed of a particle of the string. Under what circumstances is this equal to the propagation speed v? Less than v? Greater than v?

15.13 •• A transverse wave on a string has amplitude 0.300 cm, wavelength 12.0 cm, and speed 6.00 cm/s. It is represented by $y(x, t)$ as given in Exercise 15.12. (a) At time $t = 0$, compute y at 1.5-cm intervals of x (that is, at $x = 0$, $x = 1.5$ cm, $x = 3.0$ cm, and so on) from $x = 0$ to $x = 12.0$ cm. Graph the results. This is the shape of the string at time $t = 0$. (b) Repeat the calculations for the same values of x at times $t = 0.400$ s and $t = 0.800$ s. Graph the shape of the string at these instants. In what direction is the wave traveling?

15.14 • A wave on a string is described by $y(x, t) = A\cos(kx - \omega t)$. (a) Graph y, v_y, and a_y as functions of x for time $t = 0$. (b) Consider the following points on the string: (i) $x = 0$; (ii) $x = \pi/4k$; (iii) $x = \pi/2k$; (iv) $x = 3\pi/4k$; (v) $x = \pi/k$; (vi) $x = 5\pi/4k$; (vii) $x = 3\pi/2k$; (viii) $x = 7\pi/4k$. For a particle at each of these points at $t = 0$, describe in words whether the particle is moving and in what direction, and whether the particle is speeding up, slowing down, or instantaneously not accelerating.

Section 15.4 Speed of a Transverse Wave

15.15 • One end of a horizontal rope is attached to a prong of an electrically driven tuning fork that vibrates the rope transversely at 120 Hz. The other end passes over a pulley and supports a 1.50-kg mass. The linear mass density of the rope is 0.0550 kg/m. (a) What is the speed of a transverse wave on the rope? (b) What is the wavelength? (c) How would your answers to parts (a) and (b) change if the mass were increased to 3.00 kg?

15.16 • With what tension must a rope with length 2.50 m and mass 0.120 kg be stretched for transverse waves of frequency 40.0 Hz to have a wavelength of 0.750 m?

15.17 •• The upper end of a 3.80-m-long steel wire is fastened to the ceiling, and a 54.0-kg object is suspended from the lower end of the wire. You observe that it takes a transverse pulse 0.0492 s to travel from the bottom to the top of the wire. What is the mass of the wire?

15.18 •• A 1.50-m string of weight 0.0125 N is tied to the ceiling at its upper end, and the lower end supports a weight W. Neglect the very small variation in tension along the length of the string that is produced by the weight of the string. When you pluck the string slightly, the waves traveling up the string obey the equation

$$y(x, t) = (8.50 \text{ mm}) \cos(172 \text{ m}^{-1}\, x - 4830 \text{ s}^{-1}\, t)$$

Assume that the tension of the string is constant and equal to W. (a) How much time does it take a pulse to travel the full length of the string? (b) What is the weight W? (c) How many wavelengths are on the string at any instant of time? (d) What is the equation for waves traveling *down* the string?

15.19 • A thin, 75.0-cm wire has a mass of 16.5 g. One end is tied to a nail, and the other end is attached to a screw that can be adjusted to vary the tension in the wire. (a) To what tension (in newtons) must you adjust the screw so that a transverse wave of wavelength 3.33 cm makes 875 vibrations per second? (b) How fast would this wave travel?

15.20 • **Weighty Rope.** If in Example 15.3 (Section 15.4) we do *not* neglect the weight of the rope, what is the wave speed (a) at the bottom of the rope; (b) at the middle of the rope; (c) at the top of the rope?

15.21 • A simple harmonic oscillator at the point $x = 0$ generates a wave on a rope. The oscillator operates at a frequency of 40.0 Hz and with an amplitude of 3.00 cm. The rope has a linear mass density of 50.0 g/m and is stretched with a tension of 5.00 N. (a) Determine the speed of the wave. (b) Find the wavelength. (c) Write the wave function $y(x, t)$ for the wave. Assume that the oscillator has its maximum upward displacement at time $t = 0$. (d) Find the maximum transverse acceleration of points on the rope. (e) In the discussion of transverse waves in this chapter, the force of gravity was ignored. Is that a reasonable approximation for this wave? Explain.

Section 15.5 Energy in Wave Motion

15.22 •• A piano wire with mass 3.00 g and length 80.0 cm is stretched with a tension of 25.0 N. A wave with frequency 120.0 Hz and amplitude 1.6 mm travels along the wire. (a) Calculate the average power carried by the wave. (b) What happens to the average power if the wave amplitude is halved?

15.23 • A horizontal wire is stretched with a tension of 94.0 N, and the speed of transverse waves for the wire is 492 m/s. What must the amplitude of a traveling wave of frequency 69.0 Hz be in order for the average power carried by the wave to be 0.365 W?

15.24 •• A light wire is tightly stretched with tension F. Transverse traveling waves of amplitude A and wavelength λ_1 carry average power $P_{av,1} = 0.400$ W. If the wavelength of the waves is doubled, so $\lambda_2 = 2\lambda_1$, while the tension F and amplitude A are not altered, what then is the average power $P_{av,2}$ carried by the waves?

15.25 •• A jet plane at takeoff can produce sound of intensity 10.0 W/m^2 at 30.0 m away. But you prefer the tranquil sound of normal conversation, which is 1.0 $\mu W/m^2$. Assume that the plane behaves like a point source of sound. (a) What is the closest distance you should live from the airport runway to preserve your peace of mind? (b) What intensity from the jet does your friend experience if she lives twice as far from the runway as you do? (c) What power of sound does the jet produce at takeoff?

15.26 •• **Threshold of Pain.** You are investigating the report of a UFO landing in an isolated portion of New Mexico, and you encounter a strange object that is radiating sound waves uniformly in all directions. Assume that the sound comes from a point source and that you can ignore reflections. You are slowly walking toward the source. When you are 7.5 m from it, you measure its intensity to be 0.11 W/m^2. An intensity of 1.0 W/m^2 is often used as the "threshold of pain." How much closer to the source can you move before the sound intensity reaches this threshold?

15.27 • **Energy Output.** By measurement you determine that sound waves are spreading out equally in all directions from a point source and that the intensity is 0.026 W/m^2 at a distance of 4.3 m from the source. (a) What is the intensity at a distance of 3.1 m from the source? (b) How much sound energy does the source emit in one hour if its power output remains constant?

15.28 • A fellow student with a mathematical bent tells you that the wave function of a traveling wave on a thin rope is $y(x, t) = 2.30\text{ mm}\cos[(6.98\text{ rad/m})x + (742\text{ rad/s})t]$. Being more practical, you measure the rope to have a length of 1.35 m and a mass of 0.00338 kg. You are then asked to determine the following: (a) amplitude; (b) frequency; (c) wavelength; (d) wave speed; (e) direction the wave is traveling; (f) tension in the rope; (g) average power transmitted by the wave.

15.29 • At a distance of 7.00×10^{12} m from a star, the intensity of the radiation from the star is 15.4 W/m^2. Assuming that the star radiates uniformly in all directions, what is the total power output of the star?

Section 15.6 Wave Interference, Boundary Conditions, and Superposition

15.30 • **Reflection.** A wave pulse on a string has the dimensions shown in Fig. E15.30 at $t = 0$. The wave speed is 40 cm/s. (a) If point O is a fixed end, draw the total wave on the string at t = 15 ms, 20 ms, 25 ms, 30 ms, 35 ms, 40 ms, and 45 ms. (b) Repeat part (a) for the case in which point O is a free end.

Figure **E15.30**

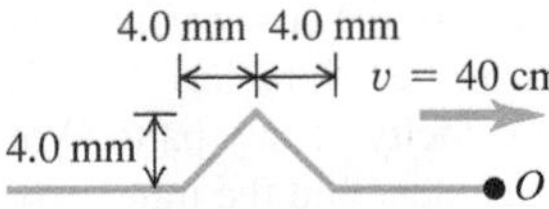

Figure **E15.31**

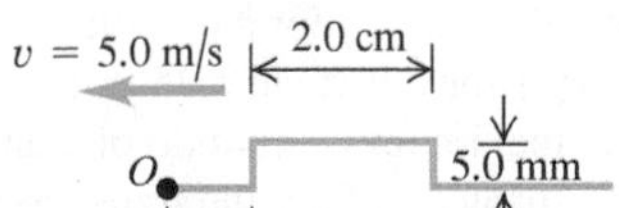

15.31 • **Reflection.** A wave pulse on a string has the dimensions shown in Fig. E15.31 at $t = 0$. The wave speed is 5.0 m/s. (a) If point O is a fixed end, draw the total wave on the string at t = 1.0 ms, 2.0 ms, 3.0 ms, 4.0 ms, 5.0 ms, 6.0 ms, and 7.0 ms. (b) Repeat part (a) for the case in which point O is a free end.

15.32 • **Interference of Triangular Pulses.** Two triangular wave pulses are traveling toward each other on a stretched string as shown in Fig. E15.32. Each pulse is identical to the other and travels at 2.00 cm/s. The leading edges of the pulses are 1.00 cm apart at $t = 0$. Sketch the shape of the string at t = 0.250 s, t = 0.500 s, t = 0.750 s, t = 1.000 s, and t = 1.250 s.

Figure **E15.32**

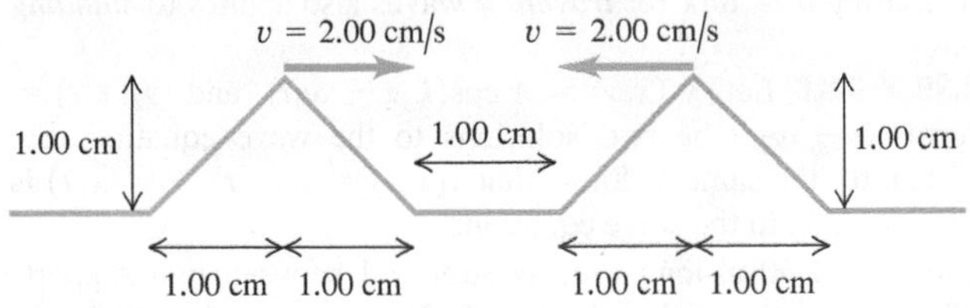

15.33 • Suppose that the left-traveling pulse in Exercise 15.32 is *below* the level of the unstretched string instead of above it. Make the same sketches that you did in that exercise.

15.34 •• Two pulses are moving in opposite directions at 1.0 cm/s on a taut string, as shown in Fig. E15.34. Each square is 1.0 cm. Sketch the shape of the string at the end of (a) 6.0 s; (b) 7.0 s; (c) 8.0 s.

Figure **E15.34**

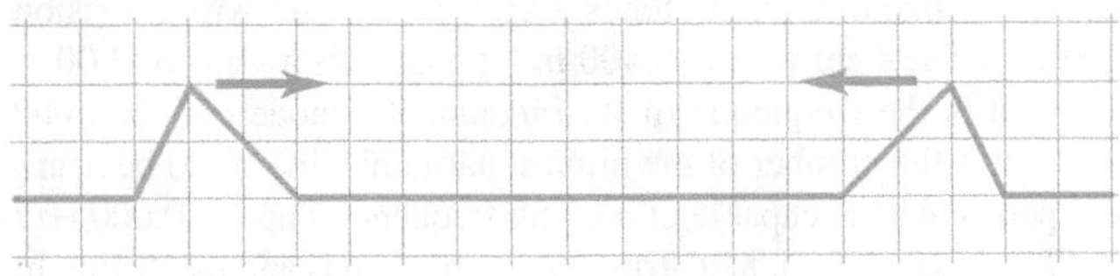

15.35 •• **Interference of Rectangular Pulses.** Figure E15.35 shows two rectangular wave pulses on a stretched string traveling toward each other. Each pulse is traveling with a speed of 1.00 mm/s and has the height and width shown in the figure. If the leading edges of the pulses are 8.00 mm apart at $t = 0$, sketch the shape of the string at t = 4.00 s, t = 6.00 s, and t = 10.0 s.

Figure **E15.35**

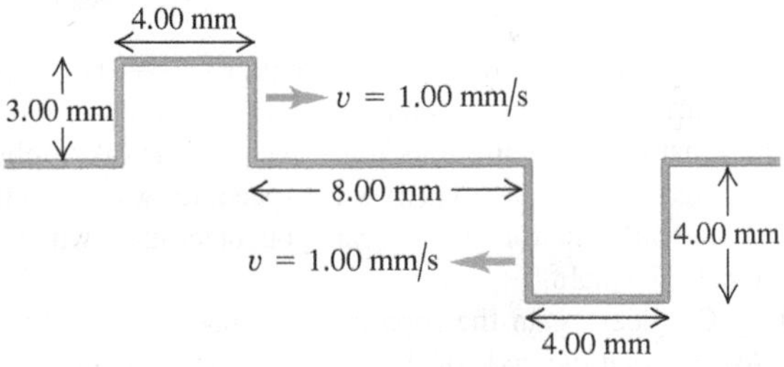

Section 15.7 Standing Waves on a String
Section 15.8 Normal Modes of a String

15.36 •• CALC Adjacent antinodes of a standing wave on a string are 15.0 cm apart. A particle at an antinode oscillates in simple harmonic motion with amplitude 0.850 cm and period 0.0750 s. The string lies along the $+x$-axis and is fixed at $x = 0$. (a) How far apart are the adjacent nodes? (b) What are the wavelength, amplitude, and speed of the two traveling waves that form this pattern? (c) Find the maximum and minimum transverse speeds of a point at an antinode. (d) What is the shortest distance along the string between a node and an antinode?

15.37 • Standing waves on a wire are described by Eq. (15.28), with A_{SW} = 2.50 mm, ω = 942 rad/s, and $k = 0.750\pi$ rad/m. The left end of the wire is at $x = 0$. At what distances from the left end are (a) the nodes of the standing wave and (b) the antinodes of the standing wave?

15.38 • CALC **Wave Equation and Standing Waves.** (a) Prove by direct substitution that $y(x, t) = (A_{SW}\sin kx)\sin\omega t$ is a solution of the wave equation, Eq. (15.12), for $v = \omega/k$. (b) Explain why the relationship $v = \omega/k$ for *traveling* waves also applies to *standing* waves.

15.39 • **CALC** Let $y_1(x, t) = A\cos(k_1x - \omega_1t)$ and $y_2(x, t) = A\cos(k_2x - \omega_2t)$ be two solutions to the wave equation, Eq. (15.12), for the same v. Show that $y(x, t) = y_1(x, t) + y_2(x, t)$ is also a solution to the wave equation.

15.40 • A 1.50-m-long rope is stretched between two supports with a tension that makes the speed of transverse waves 48.0 m/s. What are the wavelength and frequency of (a) the fundamental; (b) the second overtone; (c) the fourth harmonic?

15.41 • A wire with mass 40.0 g is stretched so that its ends are tied down at points 80.0 cm apart. The wire vibrates in its fundamental mode with frequency 60.0 Hz and with an amplitude at the antinodes of 0.300 cm. (a) What is the speed of propagation of transverse waves in the wire? (b) Compute the tension in the wire. (c) Find the maximum transverse velocity and acceleration of particles in the wire.

15.42 • A piano tuner stretches a steel piano wire with a tension of 800 N. The steel wire is 0.400 m long and has a mass of 3.00 g. (a) What is the frequency of its fundamental mode of vibration? (b) What is the number of the highest harmonic that could be heard by a person who is capable of hearing frequencies up to 10,000 Hz?

15.43 • **CALC** A thin, taut string tied at both ends and oscillating in its third harmonic has its shape described by the equation $y(x, t) = (5.60\text{ cm})\sin[(0.0340\text{ rad/cm})x]\sin[(50.0\text{ rad/s})t]$, where the origin is at the left end of the string, the x-axis is along the string, and the y-axis is perpendicular to the string. (a) Draw a sketch that shows the standing-wave pattern. (b) Find the amplitude of the two traveling waves that make up this standing wave. (c) What is the length of the string? (d) Find the wavelength, frequency, period, and speed of the traveling waves. (e) Find the maximum transverse speed of a point on the string. (f) What would be the equation $y(x, t)$ for this string if it were vibrating in its eighth harmonic?

15.44 • The wave function of a standing wave is $y(x, t) = 4.44\text{ mm}\sin[(32.5\text{ rad/m})x]\sin[(754\text{ rad/s})t]$. For the two traveling waves that make up this standing wave, find the (a) amplitude; (b) wavelength; (c) frequency; (d) wave speed; (e) wave functions. (f) From the information given, can you determine which harmonic this is? Explain.

15.45 •• Consider again the rope and traveling wave of Exercise 15.28. Assume that the ends of the rope are held fixed and that this traveling wave and the reflected wave are traveling in the opposite direction. (a) What is the wave function $y(x, t)$ for the standing wave that is produced? (b) In which harmonic is the standing wave oscillating? (c) What is the frequency of the fundamental oscillation?

15.46 •• One string of a certain musical instrument is 75.0 cm long and has a mass of 8.75 g. It is being played in a room where the speed of sound is 344 m/s. (a) To what tension must you adjust the string so that, when vibrating in its second overtone, it produces sound of wavelength 0.765 m? (Assume that the breaking stress of the wire is very large and isn't exceeded.) (b) What frequency sound does this string produce in its fundamental mode of vibration?

15.47 • The portion of the string of a certain musical instrument between the bridge and upper end of the finger board (that part of the string that is free to vibrate) is 60.0 cm long, and this length of the string has mass 2.00 g. The string sounds an A_4 note (440 Hz) when played. (a) Where must the player put a finger (what distance x from the bridge) to play a D_5 note (587 Hz)? (See Fig. E15.47.) For both the A_4 and D_5 notes, the string vibrates in its fundamental mode. (b) Without retuning, is it possible to play a G_4 note (392 Hz) on this string? Why or why not?

Figure **E15.47**

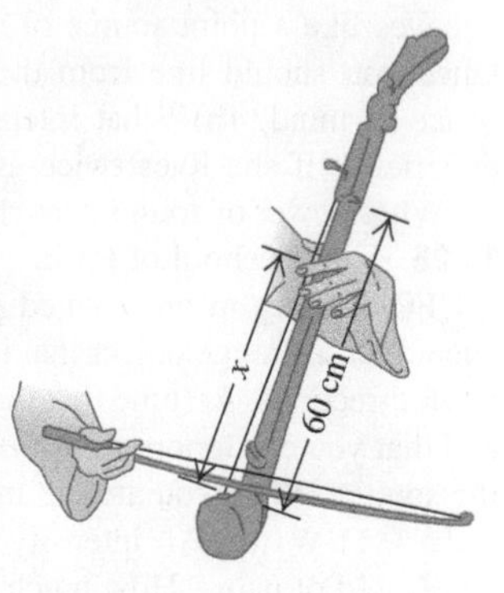

15.48 •• (a) A horizontal string tied at both ends is vibrating in its fundamental mode. The traveling waves have speed v, frequency f, amplitude A, and wavelength λ. Calculate the maximum transverse velocity and maximum transverse acceleration of points located at (i) $x = \lambda/2$, (ii) $x = \lambda/4$, and (iii) $x = \lambda/8$ from the left-hand end of the string. (b) At each of the points in part (a), what is the amplitude of the motion? (c) At each of the points in part (a), how much time does it take the string to go from its largest upward displacement to its largest downward displacement?

15.49 • **Guitar String.** One of the 63.5-cm-long strings of an ordinary guitar is tuned to produce the note B_3 (frequency 245 Hz) when vibrating in its fundamental mode. (a) Find the speed of transverse waves on this string. (b) If the tension in this string is increased by 1.0%, what will be the new fundamental frequency of the string? (c) If the speed of sound in the surrounding air is 344 m/s, find the frequency and wavelength of the sound wave produced in the air by the vibration of the B_3 string. How do these compare to the frequency and wavelength of the standing wave on the string?

15.50 • **Waves on a Stick.** A flexible stick 2.0 m long is not fixed in any way and is free to vibrate. Make clear drawings of this stick vibrating in its first three harmonics, and then use your drawings to find the wavelengths of each of these harmonics. (*Hint:* Should the ends be nodes or antinodes?)

PROBLEMS

15.51 • **CALC** A transverse sine wave with an amplitude of 2.50 mm and a wavelength of 1.80 m travels from left to right along a long, horizontal, stretched string with a speed of 36.0 m/s. Take the origin at the left end of the undisturbed string. At time $t = 0$ the left end of the string has its maximum upward displacement. (a) What are the frequency, angular frequency, and wave number of the wave? (b) What is the function $y(x, t)$ that describes the wave? (c) What is $y(t)$ for a particle at the left end of the string? (d) What is $y(t)$ for a particle 1.35 m to the right of the origin? (e) What is the maximum magnitude of transverse velocity of any particle of the string? (f) Find the transverse displacement and the transverse velocity of a particle 1.35 m to the right of the origin at time $t = 0.0625$ s.

15.52 • A transverse wave on a rope is given by

$$y(x, t) = (0.750\text{ cm})\cos\pi[(0.400\text{ cm}^{-1})x + (250\text{ s}^{-1})t]$$

(a) Find the amplitude, period, frequency, wavelength, and speed of propagation. (b) Sketch the shape of the rope at these values of t: 0, 0.0005 s, 0.0010 s. (c) Is the wave traveling in the $+x$- or $-x$-direction? (d) The mass per unit length of the rope is 0.0500 kg/m. Find the tension. (e) Find the average power of this wave.

15.53 •• Three pieces of string, each of length L, are joined together end to end, to make a combined string of length $3L$. The first piece of string has mass per unit length μ_1, the second piece has mass per unit length $\mu_2 = 4\mu_1$, and the third piece has mass per unit length $\mu_3 = \mu_1/4$. (a) If the combined string is under tension F, how much time does it take a transverse wave to travel the entire length $3L$? Give your answer in terms of L, F, and μ_1. (b) Does your answer to part (a) depend on the order in which the three pieces are joined together? Explain.

15.54 •• **CP** A 1750-N irregular beam is hanging horizontally by its ends from the ceiling by two vertical wires (A and B), each 1.25 m long and weighing 0.360 N. The center of gravity of this beam is one-third of the way along the beam from the end where wire A is attached. If you pluck both strings at the same time at the beam, what is the time delay between the arrival of the two pulses at the ceiling? Which pulse arrives first? (Neglect the effect of the weight of the wires on the tension in the wires.)

15.55 • **CALC** **Ant Joy Ride.** You place your pet ant Klyde (mass m) on top of a horizontal, stretched rope, where he holds on tightly. The rope has mass M and length L and is under tension F. You start a sinusoidal transverse wave of wavelength λ and amplitude A propagating along the rope. The motion of the rope is in a vertical plane. Klyde's mass is so small that his presence has no effect on the propagation of the wave. (a) What is Klyde's top speed as he oscillates up and down? (b) Klyde enjoys the ride and begs for more. You decide to double his top speed by changing the tension while keeping the wavelength and amplitude the same. Should the tension be increased or decreased, and by what factor?

15.56 •• **Weightless Ant.** An ant with mass m is standing peacefully on top of a horizontal, stretched rope. The rope has mass per unit length μ and is under tension F. Without warning, Cousin Throckmorton starts a sinusoidal transverse wave of wavelength λ propagating along the rope. The motion of the rope is in a vertical plane. What minimum wave amplitude will make the ant become momentarily weightless? Assume that m is so small that the presence of the ant has no effect on the propagation of the wave.

15.57 • **CP** When a transverse sinusoidal wave is present on a string, the particles of the string undergo SHM. This is the same motion as that of a mass m attached to an ideal spring of force constant k', for which the angular frequency of oscillation was found in Chapter 14 to be $\omega = \sqrt{k'/m}$. Consider a string with tension F and mass per unit length μ, along which is propagating a sinusoidal wave with amplitude A and wavelength λ. (a) Find the "force constant" $k'$of the restoring force that acts on a short segment of the string of length Δx (where$\Delta x \ll \lambda$). (b) How does the "force constant" calculated in part (b) depend on F, μ, A, and λ? Explain the physical reasons this should be so.

15.58 •• **Music.** You are designing a two-string instrument with metal strings 35.0 cm long, as shown in Fig. P15.58. Both strings are under the *same tension.* String S_1 has a mass of 8.00 g and produces the note middle C (frequency 262 Hz) in its fundamental mode. (a) What should be the tension in the string? (b) What should be the mass of string S_2 so that it will produce A-sharp (frequency 466 Hz) as its fundamental? (c) To extend the range of your instrument, you include a fret located just under the strings but not normally touching them. How far from the upper end should you put this fret so that when you press S_1 tightly against it, this string will produce C-sharp (frequency 277 Hz) in its fundamental? That is, what is x in the figure?

Figure **P15.58**

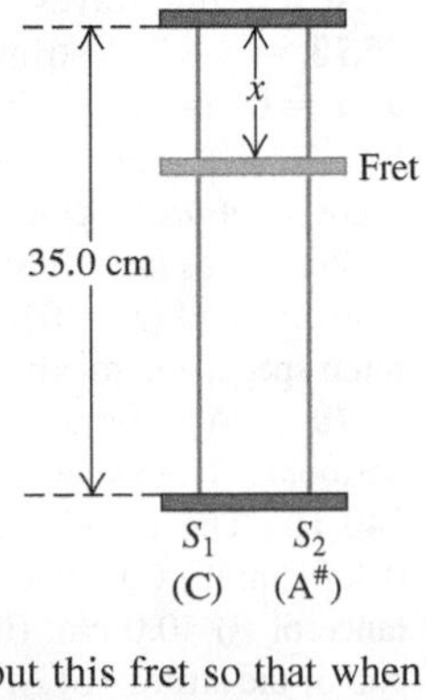

(d) If you press S_2 against the fret, what frequency of sound will it produce in its fundamental?

15.59 ••• **CP** The lower end of a uniform bar of mass 45.0 kg is attached to a wall by a frictionless hinge. The bar is held by a horizontal wire attached at its upper end so that the bar makes an angle of 30.0° with the wall. The wire has length 0.330 m and mass 0.0920 kg. What is the frequency of the fundamental standing wave for transverse waves on the wire?

15.60 ••• **CP** You are exploring a newly discovered planet. The radius of the planet is 7.20×10^7 m. You suspend a lead weight from the lower end of a light string that is 4.00 m long and has mass 0.0280 kg. You measure that it takes 0.0600 s for a transverse pulse to travel from the lower end to the upper end of the string. On earth, for the same string and lead weight, it takes 0.0390 s for a transverse pulse to travel the length of the string. The weight of the string is small enough that its effect on the tension in the string can be neglected. Assuming that the mass of the planet is distributed with spherical symmetry, what is its mass?

15.61 •• For a string stretched between two supports, two successive standing-wave frequencies are 525 Hz and 630 Hz. There are other standing-wave frequencies lower than 525 Hz and higher than 630 Hz. If the speed of transverse waves on the string is 384 m/s, what is the length of the string? Assume that the mass of the wire is small enough for its effect on the tension in the wire to be neglected.

15.62 ••• **CP** A 5.00-m, 0.732-kg wire is used to support two uniform 235-N posts of equal length (Fig. P15.62). Assume that the wire is essentially horizontal and that the speed of sound is 344 m/s. A strong wind is blowing, causing the wire to vibrate in its 5th overtone. What are the frequency and wavelength of the sound this wire produces?

Figure **P15.62**

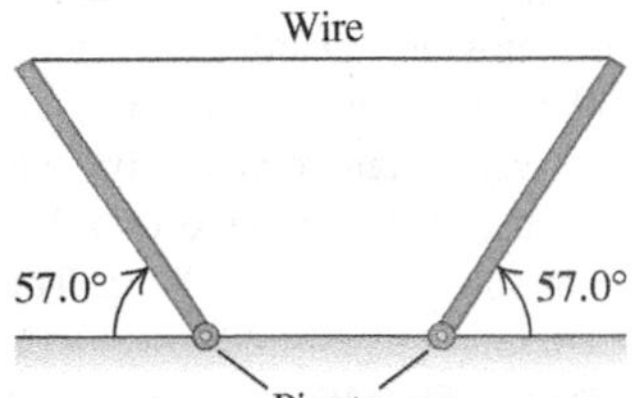

15.63 ••• **CP** A 1.80-m-long uniform bar that weighs 536 N is suspended in a horizontal position by two vertical wires that are attached to the ceiling. One wire is aluminum and the other is copper. The aluminum wire is attached to the left-hand end of the bar, and the copper wire is attached 0.40 m to the left of the right-hand end. Each wire has length 0.600 m and a circular cross section with radius 0.280 mm. What is the fundamental frequency of transverse standing waves for each wire?

15.64 •• A continuous succession of sinusoidal wave pulses are produced at one end of a very long string and travel along the length of the string. The wave has frequency 70.0 Hz, amplitude 5.00 mm, and wavelength 0.600 m. (a) How long does it take the wave to travel a distance of 8.00 m along the length of the string? (b) How long does it take a point on the string to travel a distance of 8.00 m, once the wave train has reached the point and set it into motion? (c) In parts (a) and (b), how does the time change if the amplitude is doubled?

15.65 ••• **CALC** **Waves of Arbitrary Shape.** (a) Explain why *any* wave described by a function of the form $y(x, t) = f(x - vt)$ moves in the $+x$-direction with speed v. (b) Show that $y(x, t) = f(x - vt)$ satisfies the wave equation, no matter what the functional form of f. To do this, write $y(x, t) = f(u)$, where

$u = x - vt$. Then, to take partial derivatives of $y(x, t)$, use the chain rule:

$$\frac{\partial y(x,t)}{\partial t} = \frac{df(u)}{du}\frac{\partial u}{\partial t} = \frac{df(u)}{du}(-v)$$

$$\frac{\partial y(x,t)}{\partial t} = \frac{df(u)}{du}\frac{\partial u}{\partial x} = \frac{df(u)}{du}$$

(c) A wave pulse is described by the function $y(x, t) = De^{-(Bx - Ct)^2}$, where B, C, and D are all positive constants. What is the speed of this wave?

15.66 ••• **CP** A vertical, 1.20-m length of 18-gauge (diameter of 1.024 mm) copper wire has a 100.0-N ball hanging from it. (a) What is the wavelength of the third harmonic for this wire? (b) A 500.0-N ball now *replaces* the original ball. What is the change in the wavelength of the third harmonic caused by replacing the light ball with the heavy one? (*Hint:* See Table 11.1 for Young's modulus.)

15.67 • (a) Show that Eq. (15.25) can also be written as $P_{av} = \frac{1}{2}Fk\omega A^2$, where k is the wave number of the wave. (b) If the tension F in the string is quadrupled while the amplitude A is kept the same, how must k and ω each change to keep the average power constant? [*Hint:* Recall Eq. (15.6).]

15.68 ••• **CALC** Equation (15.7) for a sinusoidal wave can be made more general by including a phase angle ϕ, where $0 \le \phi \le 2\pi$ (in radians). Then the wave function $y(x, t)$ becomes

$$y(x,t) = A\cos(kx - \omega t + \phi)$$

(a) Sketch the wave as a function of x at $t = 0$ for $\phi = 0$, $\phi = \pi/4$, $\phi = \pi/2$, $\phi = 3\pi/4$, and $\phi = 3\pi/2$. (b) Calculate the transverse velocity $v_y = \partial y/\partial t$. (c) At $t = 0$, a particle on the string at $x = 0$ has displacement $y = A/\sqrt{2}$. Is this enough information to determine the value of ϕ? In addition, if you are told that a particle at $x = 0$ is moving toward $y = 0$ at $t = 0$, what is the value of ϕ? (d) Explain in general what you must know about the wave's behavior at a given instant to determine the value of ϕ.

15.69 ••• A sinusoidal transverse wave travels on a string. The string has length 8.00 m and mass 6.00 g. The wave speed is 30.0 m/s, and the wavelength is 0.200 m. (a) If the wave is to have an average power of 50.0 W, what must be the amplitude of the wave? (b) For this same string, if the amplitude and wavelength are the same as in part (a), what is the average power for the wave if the tension is increased such that the wave speed is doubled?

15.70 ••• **CALC** **Energy in a Triangular Pulse.** A triangular wave pulse on a taut string travels in the positive x-direction with speed v. The tension in the string is F, and the linear mass density of the string is μ. At $t = 0$, the shape of the pulse is given by

$$y(x,0) = \begin{cases} 0 & \text{if } x < -L \\ h(L + x)/L & \text{for } -L < x < 0 \\ h(L - x)/L & \text{for } 0 < x < L \\ 0 & \text{for } x > L \end{cases}$$

(a) Draw the pulse at $t = 0$. (b) Determine the wave function $y(x, t)$ at all times t. (c) Find the instantaneous power in the wave. Show that the power is zero except for $-L < (x - vt) < L$ and that in this interval the power is constant. Find the value of this constant power.

15.71 ••• **CALC** **Instantaneous Power in a Wave.** (a) Graph $y(x, t)$ as given by Eq. (15.7) as a function of x for a given time t (say, $t = 0$). On the same axes, make a graph of the instantaneous power $P(x, t)$ as given by Eq. (15.23). (b) Explain the connection between the slope of the graph of $y(x, t)$ versus x and the value of $P(x, t)$. In particular, explain what is happening at points where $P = 0$, where there is no instantaneous energy transfer. (c) The quantity $P(x, t)$ always has the same sign. What does this imply about the direction of energy flow? (d) Consider a wave moving in the $-x$-direction, for which $y(x, t) = A\cos(kx + \omega t)$. Calculate $P(x, t)$ for this wave, and make a graph of $y(x, t)$ and $P(x, t)$ as functions of x for a given time t (say, $t = 0$). What differences arise from reversing the direction of the wave?

15.72 •• A vibrating string 50.0 cm long is under a tension of 1.00 N. The results from five successive stroboscopic pictures are shown in Fig. P15.72. The strobe rate is set at 5000 flashes per minute, and observations reveal that the maximum displacement occurred at flashes 1 and 5 with no other maxima in between. (a) Find the period, frequency, and wavelength for the traveling waves on this string. (b) In what normal mode (harmonic) is the string vibrating? (c) What is the speed of the traveling waves on the string? (d) How fast is point P moving when the string is in (i) position 1 and (ii) position 3? (e) What is the mass of this string? (See Section 15.3.)

Figure **P15.72**

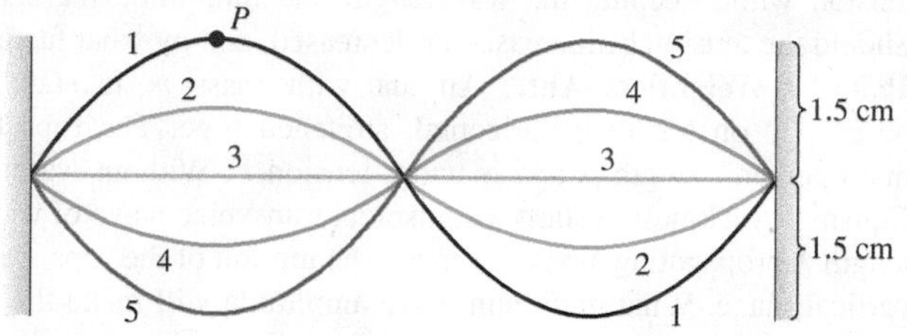

15.73 • **Clothesline Nodes.** Cousin Throckmorton is once again playing with the clothesline in Example 15.2 (Section 15.3). One end of the clothesline is attached to a vertical post. Throcky holds the other end loosely in his hand, so that the speed of waves on the clothesline is a relatively slow 0.720 m/s. He finds several frequencies at which he can oscillate his end of the clothesline so that a light clothespin 45.0 cm from the post doesn't move. What are these frequencies?

15.74 ••• **CALC** A guitar string is vibrating in its fundamental mode, with nodes at each end. The length of the segment of the string that is free to vibrate is 0.386 m. The maximum transverse acceleration of a point at the middle of the segment is $8.40 \times 10^3\ \text{m/s}^2$ and the maximum transverse velocity is 3.80 m/s. (a) What is the amplitude of this standing wave? (b) What is the wave speed for the transverse traveling waves on this string?

15.75 •• **CALC** A string that lies along the $+x$-axis has a free end at $x = 0$. (a) By using steps similar to those used to derive Eq. (15.28), show that an incident traveling wave $y_1(x, t) = A\cos(kx + \omega t)$ gives rise to a standing wave $y(x, t) = 2A\cos\omega t\cos kx$. (b) Show that the standing wave has an antinode at its free end ($x = 0$). (c) Find the maximum displacement, maximum speed, and maximum acceleration of the free end of the string.

15.76 •• A string with both ends held fixed is vibrating in its third harmonic. The waves have a speed of 192 m/s and a frequency of 240 Hz. The amplitude of the standing wave at an antinode is 0.400 cm. (a) Calculate the amplitude at points on the string a distance of (i) 40.0 cm; (ii) 20.0 cm; and (iii) 10.0 cm from the left end of the string. (b) At each point in part (a), how much time does it take the string to go from its largest upward displacement to its largest downward displacement? (c) Calculate the maximum transverse velocity and the maximum transverse acceleration of the string at each of the points in part (a).

15.77 ••• A uniform cylindrical steel wire, 55.0 cm long and 1.14 mm in diameter, is fixed at both ends. To what tension must it be adjusted so that, when vibrating in its first overtone, it produces the note D-sharp of frequency 311 Hz? Assume that it stretches an insignificant amount. (*Hint:* See Table 12.1.)

15.78 • **Holding Up Under Stress.** A string or rope will break apart if it is placed under too much tensile stress [Eq. (11.8)]. Thicker ropes can withstand more tension without breaking because the thicker the rope, the greater the cross-sectional area and the smaller the stress. One type of steel has density 7800 kg/m^3 and will break if the tensile stress exceeds 7.0×10^8 N/m^2. You want to make a guitar string from 4.0 g of this type of steel. In use, the guitar string must be able to withstand a tension of 900 N without breaking. Your job is the following: (a) Determine the maximum length and minimum radius the string can have. (b) Determine the highest possible fundamental frequency of standing waves on this string, if the entire length of the string is free to vibrate.

15.79 ••• **Combining Standing Waves.** A guitar string of length L is plucked in such a way that the total wave produced is the sum of the fundamental and the second harmonic. That is, the standing wave is given by

$$y(x,t) = y_1(x,t) + y_2(x,t)$$

where

$$y_1(x,t) = C \sin \omega_1 t \sin k_1 x$$
$$y_2(x,t) = C \sin \omega_2 t \sin k_2 x$$

with $\omega_1 = vk_1$ and $\omega_2 = vk_2$. (a) At what values of x are the nodes of y_1? (b) At what values of x are the nodes of y_2? (c) Graph the total wave at $t = 0$, $t = \frac{1}{8}f_1$, $t = \frac{1}{4}f_1$, $t = \frac{3}{8}f_1$, and $t = \frac{1}{2}f_1$. (d) Does the sum of the two standing waves y_1 and y_2 produce a standing wave? Explain.

15.80 •• **CP** When a massive aluminum sculpture is hung from a steel wire, the fundamental frequency for transverse standing waves on the wire is 250.0 Hz. The sculpture (but not the wire) is then completely submerged in water. (a) What is the new fundamental frequency? (*Hint:* See Table 12.1.) (b) Why is it a good approximation to treat the wire as being fixed at both ends?

15.81 ••• **CP** A large rock that weighs 164.0 N is suspended from the lower end of a thin wire that is 3.00 m long. The density of the rock is 3200 kg/m^3. The mass of the wire is small enough that its effect on the tension in the wire can be neglected. The upper end of the wire is held fixed. When the rock is in air, the fundamental frequency for transverse standing waves on the wire is 42.0 Hz. When the rock is totally submerged in a liquid, with the top of the rock just below the surface, the fundamental frequency for the wire is 28.0 Hz. What is the density of the liquid?

15.82 •• **Tuning an Instrument.** A musician tunes the C-string of her instrument to a fundamental frequency of 65.4 Hz. The vibrating portion of the string is 0.600 m long and has a mass of 14.4 g. (a) With what tension must the musician stretch it? (b) What percent increase in tension is needed to increase the frequency from 65.4 Hz to 73.4 Hz, corresponding to a rise in pitch from C to D?

15.83 ••• One type of steel has a density of 7.8×10^3 kg/m^3 and a breaking stress of 7.0×10^8 N/m^2. A cylindrical guitar string is to be made of 4.00 g of this steel. (a) What are the length and radius of the longest and thinnest string that can be placed under a tension of 900 N without breaking? (b) What is the highest fundamental frequency that this string could have?

CHALLENGE PROBLEMS

15.84 ••• **CP CALC** A deep-sea diver is suspended beneath the surface of Loch Ness by a 100-m-long cable that is attached to a boat on the surface (Fig. P15.84). The diver and his suit have a total mass of 120 kg and a volume of 0.0800 m^3. The cable has a diameter of 2.00 cm and a linear mass density of $\mu = 1.10$ kg/m. The diver thinks he sees something moving in the murky depths and jerks the end of the cable back and forth to send transverse waves up the cable as a signal to his companions in the boat. (a) What is the tension in the cable at its lower end, where it is attached to the diver? Do not forget to include the buoyant force that the water (density 1000 kg/m^3) exerts on him. (b) Calculate the tension in the cable a distance x above the diver. The buoyant force on the cable must be included in your calculation. (c) The speed of transverse waves on the cable is given by $v = \sqrt{F/\mu}$ (Eq. 15.13). The speed therefore varies along the cable, since the tension is not constant. (This expression neglects the damping force that the water exerts on the moving cable.) Integrate to find the time required for the first signal to reach the surface.

Figure **P15.84**

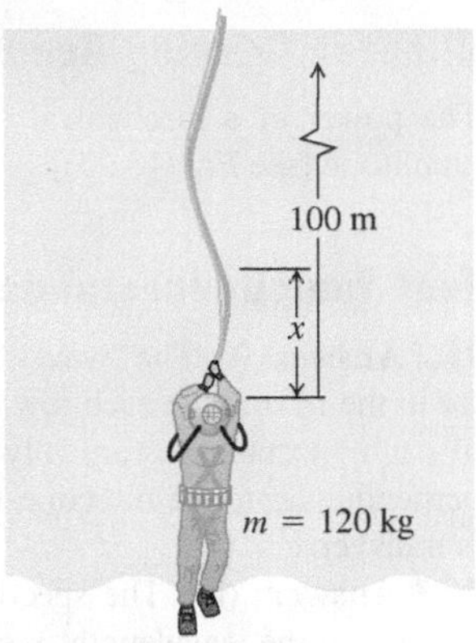

15.85 ••• **CALC** (a) Show that for a wave on a string, the kinetic energy *per unit length of string* is

$$u_k(x,t) = \tfrac{1}{2}\mu v_y{}^2(x,t) = \tfrac{1}{2}\mu\left(\frac{\partial y(x,t)}{\partial t}\right)^2$$

where μ is the mass per unit length. (b) Calculate $u_k(x,t)$ for a sinusoidal wave given by Eq. (15.7). (c) There is also elastic potential energy in the string, associated with the work required to deform and stretch the string. Consider a short segment of string at position x that has unstretched length Δx, as in Fig. 15.13. Ignoring the (small) curvature of the segment, its slope is $\partial y(x,t)/\partial x$. Assume that the displacement of the string from equilibrium is small, so that $\partial y/\partial x$ has a magnitude much less than unity. Show that the stretched length of the segment is approximately

$$\Delta x\left[1 + \tfrac{1}{2}\left(\frac{\partial y(x,t)}{\partial x}\right)^2\right]$$

(*Hint:* Use the relationship $\sqrt{1+u} \approx 1 + \frac{1}{2}u$, valid for $|u| \ll 1$.) (d) The potential energy stored in the segment equals the work done by the string tension F (which acts along the string) to stretch the segment from its unstretched length Δx to the length calculated in part (c). Calculate this work and show that the potential energy *per unit length of string* is

$$u_p(x,t) = \tfrac{1}{2}F\left(\frac{\partial y(x,t)}{\partial x}\right)^2$$

(e) Calculate $u_p(x,t)$ for a sinusoidal wave given by Eq. (15.7). (f) Show that $u_k(x,t)$, $= u_p(x,t)$, for all x and t. (g) Show $y(x,t)$, $u_k(x,t)$, and $u_p(x,t)$ as functions of x for $t = 0$ in one graph with all three functions on the same axes. Explain why u_k and u_p are maximum where y is zero, and vice versa. (h) Show that the instantaneous power in the wave, given by Eq. (15.22), is equal to the total energy per unit length multiplied by the wave speed v. Explain why this result is reasonable.

Answers

Chapter Opening Question ?

The power of a mechanical wave depends on its frequency and amplitude [see Eq. (15.25)].

Test Your Understanding Questions

15.1 Answer: (i) The "wave" travels horizontally from one spectator to the next along each row of the stadium, but the displacement of each spectator is vertically upward. Since the displacement is perpendicular to the direction in which the wave travels, the wave is transverse.

15.2 Answer: (iv) The speed of waves on a string, v, does not depend on the wavelength. We can rewrite the relationship $v = \lambda f$ as $f = v/\lambda$, which tells us that if the wavelength λ doubles, the frequency f becomes one-half as great.

15.3 Answers: (a) $\frac{2}{8}T$, (b) $\frac{4}{8}T$, (c) $\frac{5}{8}T$ Since the wave is sinusoidal, each point on the string oscillates in simple harmonic motion (SHM). Hence we can apply all of the ideas from Chapter 14 about SHM to the wave depicted in Fig. 15.8. (a) A particle in SHM has its maximum speed when it is passing through the equilibrium position ($y = 0$ in Fig. 15.8). The particle at point A is moving upward through this position at $t = \frac{2}{8}T$. (b) In vertical SHM the greatest *upward* acceleration occurs when a particle is at its maximum *downward* displacement. This occurs for the particle at point B at $t = \frac{4}{8}T$. (c) A particle in vertical SHM has a *downward* acceleration when its displacement is *upward*. The particle at C has an upward displacement and is moving downward at $t = \frac{5}{8}T$.

15.4 Answer: (ii) The relationship $v = \sqrt{F/\mu}$ [Eq. (15.13)] says that the wave speed is greatest on the string with the smallest linear mass density. This is the thinnest string, which has the smallest amount of mass m and hence the smallest linear mass density $\mu = m/L$ (all strings are the same length).

15.5 Answer: (iii), (iv), (ii), (i) Equation (15.25) says that the average power in a sinusoidal wave on a string is $P_{av} = \frac{1}{2}\sqrt{\mu F}\omega^2 A^2$. All four strings are identical, so all have the same mass, the same length, and the same linear mass density μ. The frequency f is the same for each wave, as is the angular frequency $\omega = 2\pi f$. Hence the average wave power for each string is proportional to the square root of the string tension F and the square of the amplitude A. Compared to string (i), the average power in each string is (ii) $\sqrt{4} = 2$ times greater; (iii) $4^2 = 16$ times greater; and (iv) $\sqrt{2}(2)^2 = 4\sqrt{2}$ times greater.

15.6 Answer:

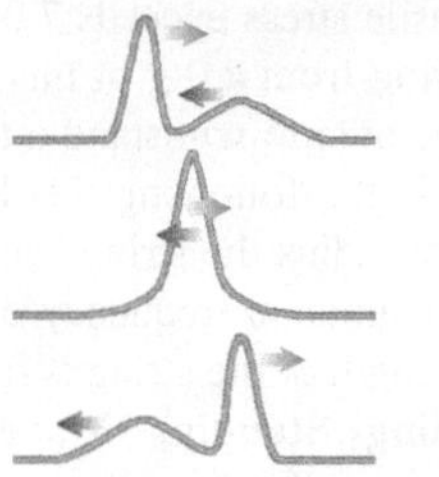

15.7 Answers: yes, yes Doubling the frequency makes the wavelength half as large. Hence the spacing between nodes (equal to $\lambda/2$) is also half as large. There are nodes at all of the previous positions, but there is also a new node between every pair of old nodes.

15.8 Answers: $n = 1, 3, 5, \ldots$ When you touch the string at its center, you are demanding that there be a node at the center. Hence only standing waves with a node at $x = L/2$ are allowed. From Figure 15.26 you can see that the normal modes $n = 1, 3, 5, \ldots$ cannot be present.

Bridging Problem

Answers: **(a)** $F(r) = \dfrac{m\omega^2}{2L}(L^2 - r^2)$

(b) $v(r) = \omega\sqrt{\dfrac{L^2 - r^2}{2}}$

(c) $\dfrac{\pi}{\omega\sqrt{2}}$

SOUND AND HEARING

16

? Most people like to listen to music, but hardly anyone likes to listen to noise. What is the physical difference between musical sound and noise?

LEARNING GOALS

By studying this chapter, you will learn:

- How to describe a sound wave in terms of either particle displacements or pressure fluctuations.
- How to calculate the speed of sound waves in different materials.
- How to calculate the intensity of a sound wave.
- What determines the particular frequencies of sound produced by an organ or a flute.
- How resonance occurs in musical instruments.
- What happens when sound waves from different sources overlap.
- How to describe what happens when two sound waves of slightly different frequencies are combined.
- Why the pitch of a siren changes as it moves past you.

Of all the mechanical waves that occur in nature, the most important in our everyday lives are longitudinal waves in a medium—usually air—called *sound* waves. The reason is that the human ear is tremendously sensitive and can detect sound waves even of very low intensity. Besides their use in spoken communication, our ears allow us to pick up a myriad of cues about our environment, from the welcome sound of a meal being prepared to the warning sound of an approaching car. The ability to hear an unseen nocturnal predator was essential to the survival of our ancestors, so it is no exaggeration to say that we humans owe our existence to our highly evolved sense of hearing.

Up to this point we have described mechanical waves primarily in terms of displacement; however, a description of sound waves in terms of *pressure* fluctuations is often more appropriate, largely because the ear is primarily sensitive to changes in pressure. We'll study the relationships among displacement, pressure fluctuation, and intensity and the connections between these quantities and human sound perception.

When a source of sound or a listener moves through the air, the listener may hear a frequency different from the one emitted by the source. This is the Doppler effect, which has important applications in medicine and technology.

16.1 Sound Waves

The most general definition of **sound** is a longitudinal wave in a medium. Our main concern in this chapter is with sound waves in air, but sound can travel through any gas, liquid, or solid. You may be all too familiar with the propagation of sound through a solid if your neighbor's stereo speakers are right next to your wall.

The simplest sound waves are sinusoidal waves, which have definite frequency, amplitude, and wavelength. The human ear is sensitive to waves in the frequency range from about 20 to 20,000 Hz, called the **audible range,** but we also use the

16.1 A sinusoidal longitudinal wave traveling to the right in a fluid. (Compare to Fig. 15.7.)

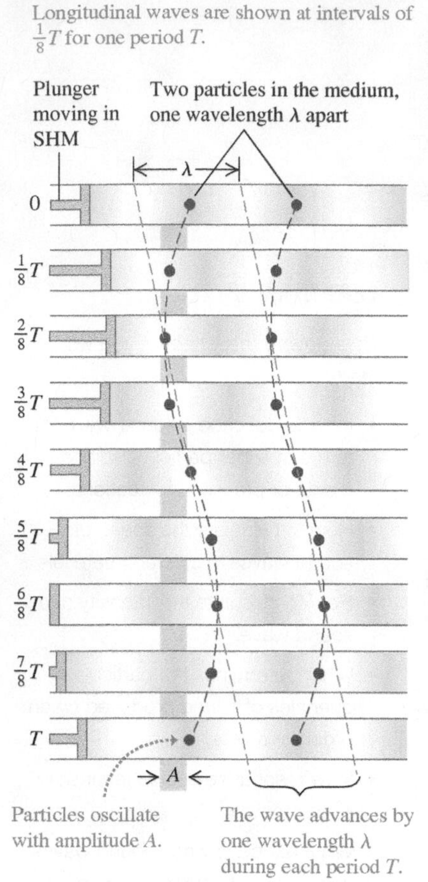

16.2 As a sound wave propagates along the x-axis, the left and right ends undergo different displacements y_1 and y_2.

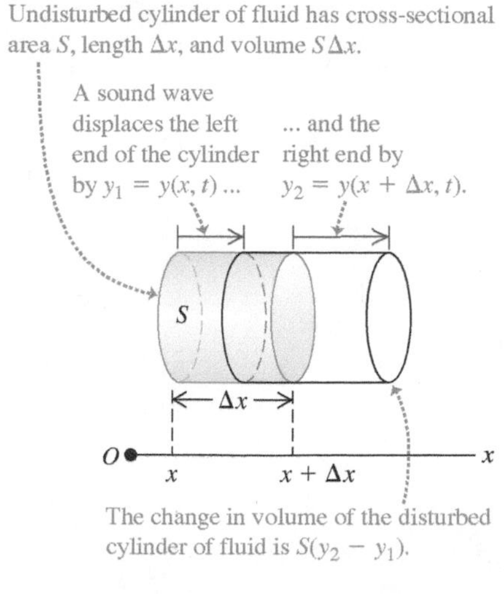

term "sound" for similar waves with frequencies above **(ultrasonic)** and below **(infrasonic)** the range of human hearing.

Sound waves usually travel out in all directions from the source of sound, with an amplitude that depends on the direction and distance from the source. We'll return to this point in the next section. For now, we concentrate on the idealized case of a sound wave that propagates in the positive x-direction only. As we discussed in Section 15.3, such a wave is described by a wave function $y(x, t)$, which gives the instantaneous displacement y of a particle in the medium at position x at time t. If the wave is sinusoidal, we can express it using Eq. (15.7):

$$y(x, t) = A\cos(kx - \omega t) \quad \text{(sound wave propagating in the } +x\text{-direction)} \qquad (16.1)$$

Remember that in a longitudinal wave the displacements are *parallel* to the direction of travel of the wave, so distances x and y are measured parallel to each other, not perpendicular as in a transverse wave. The amplitude A is the maximum displacement of a particle in the medium from its equilibrium position (Fig. 16.1). Hence A is also called the **displacement amplitude.**

Sound Waves As Pressure Fluctuations

Sound waves may also be described in terms of variations of *pressure* at various points. In a sinusoidal sound wave in air, the pressure fluctuates above and below atmospheric pressure p_a in a sinusoidal variation with the same frequency as the motions of the air particles. The human ear operates by sensing such pressure variations. A sound wave entering the ear canal exerts a fluctuating pressure on one side of the eardrum; the air on the other side of the eardrum, vented to the outside by the Eustachian tube, is at atmospheric pressure. The pressure difference on the two sides of the eardrum sets it into motion. Microphones and similar devices also usually sense pressure differences, not displacements, so it is very useful to develop a relationship between these two descriptions.

Let $p(x, t)$ be the instantaneous pressure fluctuation in a sound wave at any point x at time t. That is, $p(x, t)$ is the amount by which the pressure *differs* from normal atmospheric pressure p_a. Think of $p(x, t)$ as the *gauge pressure* defined in Section 12.2; it can be either positive or negative. The *absolute* pressure at a point is then $p_a + p(x, t)$.

To see the connection between the pressure fluctuation $p(x, t)$ and the displacement $y(x, t)$ in a sound wave propagating in the $+x$-direction, consider an imaginary cylinder of a wave medium (gas, liquid, or solid) with cross-sectional area S and axis along the direction of propagation (Fig. 16.2). When no sound wave is present, the cylinder has length Δx and volume $V = S\Delta x$, as shown by the shaded volume in Fig. 16.2. When a wave is present, at time t the end of the cylinder that is initially at x is displaced by $y_1 = y(x, t)$, and the end that is initially at $x + \Delta x$ is displaced by $y_2 = y(x + \Delta x, t)$; this is shown by the red lines. If $y_2 > y_1$, as shown in Fig. 16.2, the cylinder's volume has increased, which causes a decrease in pressure. If $y_2 < y_1$, the cylinder's volume has decreased and the pressure has increased. If $y_2 = y_1$, the cylinder is simply shifted to the left or right; there is no volume change and no pressure fluctuation. The pressure fluctuation depends on the *difference* between the displacements at neighboring points in the medium.

Quantitatively, the change in volume ΔV of the cylinder is

$$\Delta V = S(y_2 - y_1) = S[y(x + \Delta x, t) - y(x, t)]$$

In the limit as $\Delta x \to 0$, the fractional change in volume dV/V (volume change divided by original volume) is

$$\frac{dV}{V} = \lim_{\Delta x \to 0} \frac{S[y(x + \Delta x, t) - y(x, t)]}{S\Delta x} = \frac{\partial y(x, t)}{\partial x} \qquad (16.2)$$

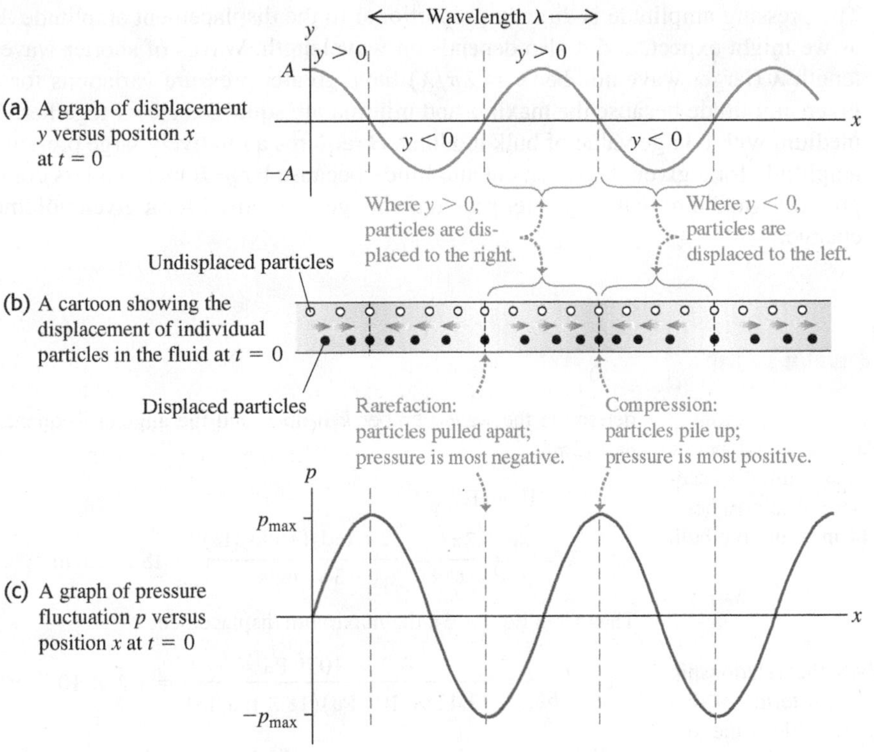

16.3 Three ways to describe a sound wave.

The fractional volume change is related to the pressure fluctuation by the bulk modulus B, which by definition [Eq. (11.13)] is $B = -p(x, t)/(dV/V)$ (see Section 11.4). Solving for $p(x, t)$, we have

$$p(x, t) = -B\frac{\partial y(x, t)}{\partial x} \tag{16.3}$$

The negative sign arises because when $\partial y(x, t)/\partial x$ is positive, the displacement is greater at $x + \Delta x$ than at x, corresponding to an increase in volume and a *decrease* in pressure.

When we evaluate $\partial y(x, t)/\partial x$ for the sinusoidal wave of Eq. (16.1), we find

$$p(x, t) = BkA\sin(kx - \omega t) \tag{16.4}$$

Figure 16.3 shows $y(x, t)$ and $p(x, t)$ for a sinusoidal sound wave at $t = 0$. It also shows how individual particles of the wave are displaced at this time. While $y(x, t)$ and $p(x, t)$ describe the same wave, these two functions are one-quarter cycle out of phase: At any time, the displacement is greatest where the pressure fluctuation is zero, and vice versa. In particular, note that the compressions (points of greatest pressure and density) and rarefactions (points of lowest pressure and density) are points of *zero* displacement.

CAUTION **Graphs of a sound wave** Keep in mind that the graphs in Fig. 16.3 show the wave at only *one* instant of time. Because the wave is propagating in the $+x$-direction, as time goes by the wave patterns in the functions $y(x, t)$ and $p(x, t)$ move to the right at the wave speed $v = \omega/k$. Hence the positions of the compressions and rarefactions also move to the right at this same speed. The particles, by contrast, simply oscillate back and forth in simple harmonic motion as shown in Fig. 16.1.

Equation (16.4) shows that the quantity BkA represents the maximum pressure fluctuation. We call this the **pressure amplitude,** denoted by p_{max}:

$$p_{max} = BkA \quad \text{(sinusoidal sound wave)} \tag{16.5}$$

The pressure amplitude is directly proportional to the displacement amplitude A, as we might expect, and it also depends on wavelength. Waves of shorter wavelength λ (larger wave number $k = 2\pi/\lambda$) have greater pressure variations for a given amplitude because the maxima and minima are squeezed closer together. A medium with a large value of bulk modulus B requires a relatively large pressure amplitude for a given displacement amplitude because large B means a less compressible medium; that is, greater pressure change is required for a given volume change.

Example 16.1 Amplitude of a sound wave in air

In a sinusoidal sound wave of moderate loudness, the maximum pressure variations are about 3.0×10^{-2} Pa above and below atmospheric pressure. Find the corresponding maximum displacement if the frequency is 1000 Hz. In air at normal atmospheric pressure and density, the speed of sound is 344 m/s and the bulk modulus is 1.42×10^5 Pa.

SOLUTION

IDENTIFY and SET UP: This problem involves the relationship between two ways of describing a sound wave: in terms of displacement and in terms of pressure. The target variable is the displacement amplitude A. We are given the pressure amplitude p_{max}, wave speed v, frequency f, and bulk modulus B. Equation (16.5) relates the target variable A to p_{max}. We use $\omega = vk$ [Eq. (15.6)] to determine the wave number k from v and the angular frequency $\omega = 2\pi f$.

EXECUTE: From Eq. (15.6),

$$k = \frac{\omega}{v} = \frac{2\pi f}{v} = \frac{(2\pi \text{ rad})(1000 \text{ Hz})}{344 \text{ m/s}} = 18.3 \text{ rad/m}$$

Then from Eq. (16.5), the maximum displacement is

$$A = \frac{p_{max}}{Bk} = \frac{3.0 \times 10^{-2} \text{ Pa}}{(1.42 \times 10^5 \text{ Pa})(18.3 \text{ rad/m})} = 1.2 \times 10^{-8} \text{ m}$$

EVALUATE: This displacement amplitude is only about $\frac{1}{100}$ the size of a human cell. The ear actually senses pressure fluctuations; it detects these minuscule displacements only indirectly.

Example 16.2 Amplitude of a sound wave in the inner ear

A sound wave that enters the human ear sets the eardrum into oscillation, which in turn causes oscillation of the *ossicles*, a chain of three tiny bones in the middle ear (Fig. 16.4). The ossicles transmit this oscillation to the fluid (mostly water) in the inner ear; there the fluid motion disturbs hair cells that send nerve impulses to the brain with information about the sound. The area of the moving part of the eardrum is about 43 mm^2, and that of the stapes (the smallest of the ossicles) where it connects to the inner ear is about 3.2 mm^2. For the sound in Example 16.1, determine (a) the pressure amplitude and (b) the displacement amplitude of the wave in the fluid of the inner ear, in which the speed of sound is 1500 m/s.

SOLUTION

IDENTIFY and SET UP: Although the sound wave here travels in liquid rather than air, the same principles and relationships among the properties of the wave apply. We can neglect the mass of the tiny ossicles (about 58 mg $= 5.8 \times 10^{-5}$ kg), so the force they exert on the inner-ear fluid is the same as that exerted on the eardrum and ossicles by the incident sound wave. (In Chapters 4 and 5 we used the same idea to say that the tension is the same at either end of a massless rope.) Hence the pressure amplitude in the inner ear, $p_{max\,(inner\ ear)}$, is greater than in the outside air, $p_{max\,(air)}$, because the same force is exerted on a smaller area (the area of the stapes versus the area of the eardrum). Given $p_{max\,(inner\ ear)}$, we find the displacement amplitude $A_{inner\ ear}$ using Eq. (16.5).

16.4 The anatomy of the human ear. The middle ear is the size of a small marble; the ossicles (incus, malleus, and stapes) are the smallest bones in the human body.

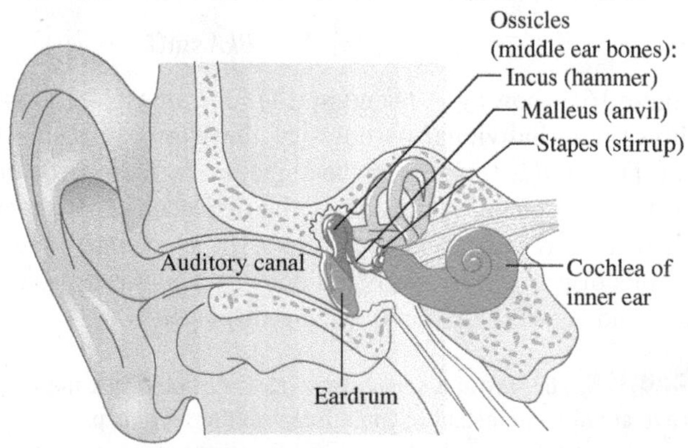

EXECUTE: (a) From the area of the eardrum and the pressure amplitude in air found in Example 16.1, the maximum force exerted by the sound wave in air on the eardrum is $F_{max} = p_{max\,(air)}S_{eardrum}$. Then

$$p_{max\,(inner\ ear)} = \frac{F_{max}}{S_{stapes}} = p_{max\,(air)}\frac{S_{eardrum}}{S_{stapes}}$$

$$= (3.0 \times 10^{-2} \text{ Pa})\frac{43 \text{ mm}^2}{3.2 \text{ mm}^2} = 0.40 \text{ Pa}$$

(b) To find the maximum displacement $A_{\text{inner ear}}$, we use $A = p_{max}/Bk$ as in Example 16.1. The inner-ear fluid is mostly water, which has a much greater bulk modulus B than air. From Table 11.2 the compressibility of water (unfortunately also called k) is $45.8 \times 10^{-11}\ \text{Pa}^{-1}$, so $B_{\text{fluid}} = 1/(45.8 \times 10^{-11}\ \text{Pa}^{-1}) = 2.18 \times 10^9$ Pa.

The wave in the inner ear has the same angular frequency ω as the wave in the air because the air, eardrum, ossicles, and inner-ear fluid all oscillate together (see Example 15.8 in Section 15.8). But because the wave speed v is greater in the inner ear than in the air (1500 m/s versus 344 m/s), the wave number $k = \omega/v$ is smaller. Using the value of ω from Example 16.1,

$$k_{\text{inner ear}} = \frac{\omega}{v_{\text{inner ear}}} = \frac{(2\pi \text{ rad})(1000 \text{ Hz})}{1500 \text{ m/s}} = 4.2 \text{ rad/m}$$

Putting everything together, we have

$$A_{\text{inner ear}} = \frac{p_{\max(\text{inner ear})}}{B_{\text{fluid}} k_{\text{inner ear}}} = \frac{0.40 \text{ Pa}}{(2.18 \times 10^9 \text{ Pa})(4.2 \text{ rad/m})}$$
$$= 4.4 \times 10^{-11} \text{ m}$$

EVALUATE: In part (a) we see that the ossicles increase the pressure amplitude by a factor of $(43\ \text{mm}^2)/(3.2\ \text{mm}^2) = 13$. This amplification helps give the human ear its great sensitivity.

The displacement amplitude in the inner ear is even smaller than in the air. But *pressure* variations within the inner-ear fluid are what set the hair cells into motion, so what matters is that the pressure amplitude is larger in the inner ear than in the air.

Perception of Sound Waves

The physical characteristics of a sound wave are directly related to the perception of that sound by a listener. For a given frequency, the greater the pressure amplitude of a sinusoidal sound wave, the greater the perceived **loudness.** The relationship between pressure amplitude and loudness is not a simple one, and it varies from one person to another. One important factor is that the ear is not equally sensitive to all frequencies in the audible range. A sound at one frequency may seem louder than one of equal pressure amplitude at a different frequency. At 1000 Hz the minimum pressure amplitude that can be perceived with normal hearing is about 3×10^{-5} Pa; to produce the same loudness at 200 Hz or 15,000 Hz requires about 3×10^{-4} Pa. Perceived loudness also depends on the health of the ear. A loss of sensitivity at the high-frequency end usually happens naturally with age but can be further aggravated by excessive noise levels.

Application Hearing Loss from Amplified Sound
Due to exposure to highly amplified music, many young popular musicians have suffered permanent ear damage and have hearing typical of persons 65 years of age. Headphones for personal music players used at high volume pose similar threats to hearing. Be careful!

The frequency of a sound wave is the primary factor in determining the **pitch** of a sound, the quality that lets us classify the sound as "high" or "low." The higher the frequency of a sound (within the audible range), the higher the pitch that a listener will perceive. Pressure amplitude also plays a role in determining pitch. When a listener compares two sinusoidal sound waves with the same frequency but different pressure amplitudes, the one with the greater pressure amplitude is usually perceived as louder but also as slightly lower in pitch.

Musical sounds have wave functions that are more complicated than a simple sine function. The pressure fluctuation in the sound wave produced by a clarinet is shown in Fig. 16.5a. The pattern is so complex because the column of air in a wind instrument like a clarinet vibrates at a fundamental frequency and at many harmonics at the same time. (In Section 15.8, we described this same behavior for a string that has been plucked, bowed, or struck. We'll examine the physics of wind instruments in Section 16.5.) The sound wave produced in the surrounding air has a similar amount of each harmonic—that is, a similar *harmonic content.* Figure 16.5b shows the harmonic content of the sound of a clarinet. The mathematical process of translating a pressure–time graph like Fig. 16.5a into a graph of harmonic content like Fig. 16.5b is called *Fourier analysis.*

Two tones produced by different instruments might have the same fundamental frequency (and thus the same pitch) but sound different because of different harmonic content. The difference in sound is called *tone color, quality,* or **timbre** and is often described in subjective terms such as reedy, golden, round, mellow, and tinny. A tone that is rich in harmonics, like the clarinet tone in Figs. 16.5a and 16.5b, usually sounds thin and "stringy" or "reedy," while a tone containing mostly a fundamental, like the alto recorder tone in Figs. 16.5c and 16.5d, is more mellow and flutelike. The same principle applies to the human voice, which is another example of a wind instrument; the vowels "a" and "e" sound different because of differences in harmonic content.

16.5 Different representations of the sound of (a), (b) a clarinet and (c), (d) an alto recorder. (Graphs adapted from R.E. Berg and D.G. Stork, *The Physics of Sound,* Prentice-Hall, 1982.)

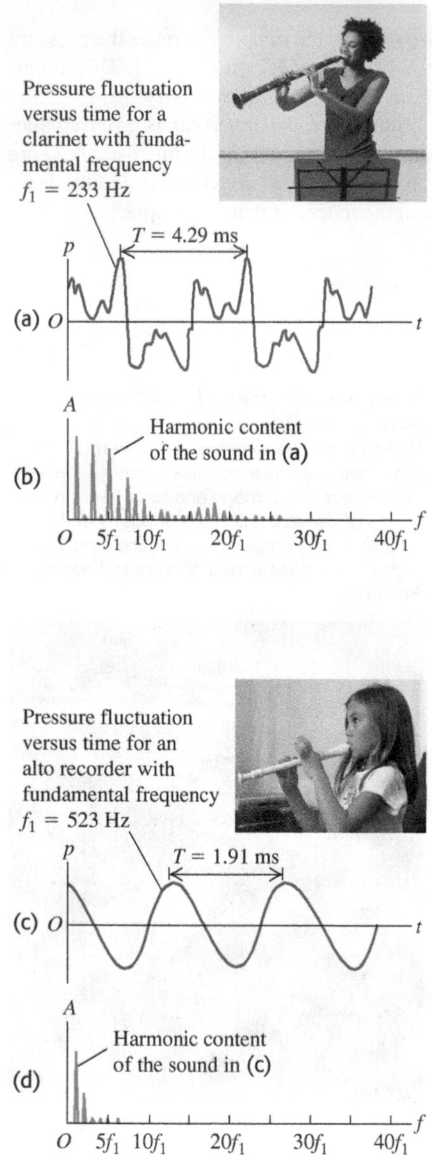

Another factor in determining tone quality is the behavior at the beginning (*attack*) and end (*decay*) of a tone. A piano tone begins with a thump and then dies away gradually. A harpsichord tone, in addition to having different harmonic content, begins much more quickly with a click, and the higher harmonics begin before the lower ones. When the key is released, the sound also dies away much more rapidly with a harpsichord than with a piano. Similar effects are present in other musical instruments. With wind and string instruments the player has considerable control over the attack and decay of the tone, and these characteristics help to define the unique characteristics of each instrument.

Unlike the tones made by musical instruments or the vowels in human speech, **noise** is a combination of *all* frequencies, not just frequencies that are integer multiples of a fundamental frequency. (An extreme case is "white noise," which contains equal amounts of all frequencies across the audible range.) Examples include the sound of the wind and the hissing sound you make in saying the consonant "s."

Test Your Understanding of Section 16.1 You use an electronic signal generator to produce a sinusoidal sound wave in air. You then increase the frequency of the wave from 100 Hz to 400 Hz while keeping the pressure amplitude constant. What effect does this have on the displacement amplitude of the sound wave? (i) It becomes four times greater; (ii) it becomes twice as great; (iii) it is unchanged; (iv) it becomes $\frac{1}{2}$ as great; (v) it becomes $\frac{1}{4}$ as great. ❙

16.2 Speed of Sound Waves

We found in Section 15.4 that the speed v of a transverse wave on a string depends on the string tension F and the linear mass density μ: $v = \sqrt{F/\mu}$. What, we may ask, is the corresponding expression for the speed of sound waves in a gas or liquid? On what properties of the medium does the speed depend?

We can make an educated guess about these questions by remembering a claim that we made in Section 15.4: For mechanical waves in general, the expression for the wave speed is of the form

$$v = \sqrt{\frac{\text{Restoring force returning the system to equilibrium}}{\text{Inertia resisting the return to equilibrium}}}$$

A sound wave in a bulk fluid causes compressions and rarefactions of the fluid, so the restoring-force term in the above expression must be related to how easy or difficult it is to compress the fluid. This is precisely what the bulk modulus B of the medium tells us. According to Newton's second law, inertia is related to mass. The "massiveness" of a bulk fluid is described by its density, or mass per unit volume, ρ. (The corresponding quantity for a string is the mass per unit length, μ.) Hence we expect that the speed of sound waves should be of the form $v = \sqrt{B/\rho}$.

To check our guess, we'll derive the speed of sound waves in a fluid in a pipe. This is a situation of some importance, since all musical wind instruments are fundamentally pipes in which a longitudinal wave (sound) propagates in a fluid (air) (Fig. 16.6). Human speech works on the same principle; sound waves propagate in your vocal tract, which is basically an air-filled pipe connected to the lungs at one end (your larynx) and to the outside air at the other end (your mouth). The steps in our derivation are completely parallel to those we used in Section 15.4 to find the speed of transverse waves, so you'll find it useful to review that section.

Speed of Sound in a Fluid

Figure 16.7 shows a fluid (either liquid or gas) with density ρ in a pipe with cross-sectional area A. In the equilibrium state, the fluid is under a uniform pressure p. In Fig. 16.7a the fluid is at rest. We take the x-axis along the length of the pipe. This is also the direction in which we make a longitudinal wave propagate, so the displacement y is also measured along the pipe, just as in Section 16.1 (see Fig. 16.2).

At time $t = 0$ we start the piston at the left end moving toward the right with constant speed v_y. This initiates a wave motion that travels to the right along the length of the pipe, in which successive sections of fluid begin to move and become compressed at successively later times.

Figure 16.7b shows the fluid at time t. All portions of fluid to the left of point P are moving to the right with speed v_y, and all portions to the right of P are still at rest. The boundary between the moving and stationary portions travels to the right with a speed equal to the speed of propagation or wave speed v. At time t the piston has moved a distance $v_y t$, and the boundary has advanced a distance vt. As with a transverse disturbance in a string, we can compute the speed of propagation from the impulse–momentum theorem.

The quantity of fluid set in motion in time t is the amount that originally occupied a section of the cylinder with length vt, cross-sectional area A, and volume vtA. The mass of this fluid is ρvtA, and its longitudinal momentum (that is, momentum along the length of the pipe) is

$$\text{Longitudinal momentum} = (\rho vtA)v_y$$

Next we compute the increase of pressure, Δp, in the moving fluid. The original volume of the moving fluid, Avt, has decreased by an amount $Av_y t$. From the definition of the bulk modulus B, Eq. (11.13) in Section 11.5,

$$B = \frac{-\text{Pressure change}}{\text{Fractional volume change}} = \frac{-\Delta p}{-Av_y t/Avt}$$

$$\Delta p = B\frac{v_y}{v}$$

The pressure in the moving fluid is $p + \Delta p$ and the force exerted on it by the piston is $(p + \Delta p)A$. The net force on the moving fluid (see Fig. 16.7b) is ΔpA, and the longitudinal impulse is

$$\text{Longitudinal impulse} = \Delta pAt = B\frac{v_y}{v}At$$

Because the fluid was at rest at time $t = 0$, the change in momentum up to time t is equal to the momentum at that time. Applying the impulse–momentum theorem (see Section 8.1), we find

$$B\frac{v_y}{v}At = \rho vtAv_y \tag{16.6}$$

When we solve this expression for v, we get

$$v = \sqrt{\frac{B}{\rho}} \quad \text{(speed of a longitudinal wave in a fluid)} \tag{16.7}$$

which agrees with our educated guess. Thus the speed of propagation of a longitudinal pulse in a fluid depends only on the bulk modulus B and the density ρ of the medium.

While we derived Eq. (16.7) for waves in a pipe, it also applies to longitudinal waves in a bulk fluid. Thus the speed of sound waves traveling in air or water is determined by this equation.

Speed of Sound in a Solid

When a longitudinal wave propagates in a *solid* rod or bar, the situation is somewhat different. The rod expands sideways slightly when it is compressed

16.6 When a wind instrument like this French horn is played, sound waves propagate through the air within the instrument's pipes. The properties of the sound that emerges from the large bell depend on the speed of these waves.

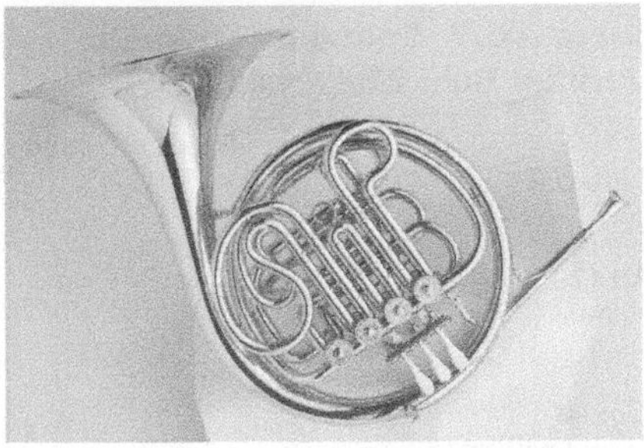

16.7 A sound wave propagating in a fluid confined to a tube. (a) Fluid in equilibrium. (b) A time t after the piston begins moving to the right at speed v_y, the fluid between the piston and point P is in motion. The speed of sound waves is v.

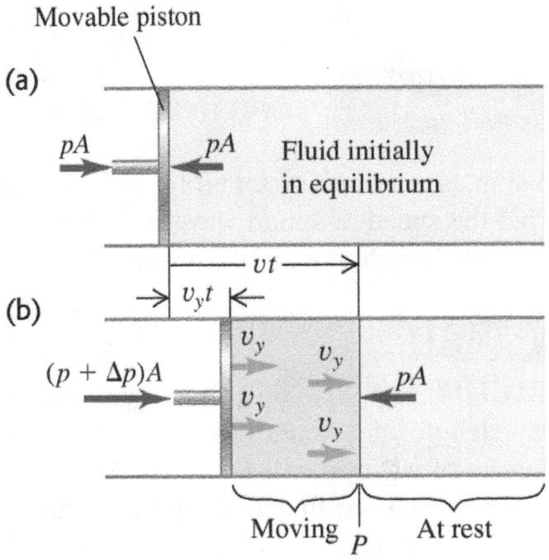

longitudinally, while a fluid in a pipe with constant cross section cannot move sideways. Using the same kind of reasoning that led us to Eq. (16.7), we can show that the speed of a longitudinal pulse in the rod is given by

$$v = \sqrt{\frac{Y}{\rho}} \quad \text{(speed of a longitudinal wave in a solid rod)} \qquad (16.8)$$

where Y is Young's modulus, defined in Section 11.4.

CAUTION **Solid rods vs. bulk solids** Equation (16.8) applies only to a rod or bar whose sides are free to bulge and shrink a little as the wave travels. It does not apply to longitudinal waves in a *bulk* solid, since in these materials, sideways motion in any element of material is prevented by the surrounding material. The speed of longitudinal waves in a bulk solid depends on the density, the bulk modulus, and the *shear* modulus; a full discussion is beyond the scope of this book.

As with the derivation for a transverse wave on a string, Eqs. (16.7) and (16.8) are valid for sinusoidal and other periodic waves, not just for the special case discussed here.

Table 16.1 lists the speed of sound in several bulk materials. Sound waves travel more slowly in lead than in aluminum or steel because lead has a lower bulk modulus and shear modulus and a higher density.

Table 16.1 Speed of Sound in Various Bulk Materials

Material	Speed of Sound (m/s)
Gases	
Air (20°C)	344
Helium (20°C)	999
Hydrogen (20°C)	1330
Liquids	
Liquid helium (4 K)	211
Mercury (20°C)	1451
Water (0°C)	1402
Water (20°C)	1482
Water (100°C)	1543
Solids	
Aluminum	6420
Lead	1960
Steel	5941

Example 16.3 Wavelength of sonar waves

A ship uses a sonar system (Fig. 16.8) to locate underwater objects. Find the speed of sound waves in water using Eq. (16.7), and find the wavelength of a 262-Hz wave.

SOLUTION

IDENTIFY and SET UP: Our target variables are the speed and wavelength of a sound wave in water. In Eq. (16.7), we use the density of water, $\rho = 1.00 \times 10^3\ \text{kg/m}^3$, and the bulk modulus of water, which we find from the compressibility (see Table 11.2). Given the speed and the frequency $f = 262$ Hz, we find the wavelength from $v = f\lambda$.

EXECUTE: In Example 16.2, we used Table 11.2 to find $B = 2.18 \times 10^9$ Pa. Then

$$v = \sqrt{\frac{B}{\rho}} = \sqrt{\frac{2.18 \times 10^9\ \text{Pa}}{1.00 \times 10^3\ \text{kg/m}^3}} = 1480\ \text{m/s}$$

and

$$\lambda = \frac{v}{f} = \frac{1480\ \text{m/s}}{262\ \text{s}^{-1}} = 5.65\ \text{m}$$

EVALUATE: The calculated value of v agrees well with the value in Table 16.1. Water is denser than air (ρ is larger) but is also much more incompressible (B is much larger), and so the speed $v = \sqrt{B/\rho}$ is greater than the 344-m/s speed of sound in air at ordinary temperatures. The relationship $\lambda = v/f$ then says that a sound wave in water must have a longer wavelength than a wave of the same frequency in air. Indeed, we found in Example 15.1 (Section 15.2) that a 262-Hz sound wave in air has a wavelength of only 1.31 m.

16.8 A sonar system uses underwater sound waves to detect and locate submerged objects.

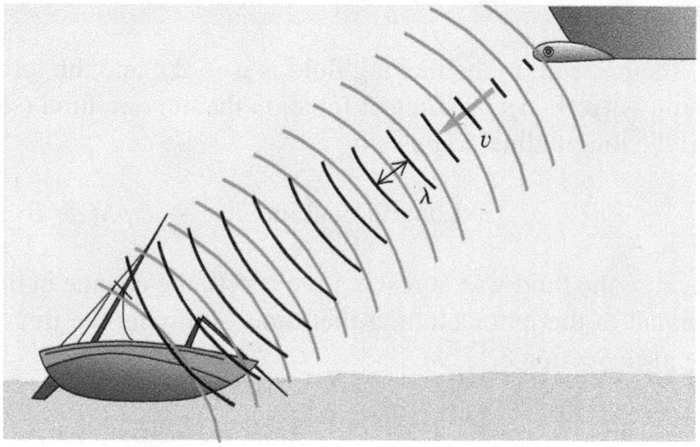

Dolphins emit high-frequency sound waves (typically 100,000 Hz) and use the echoes for guidance and for hunting. The corresponding wavelength in water is 1.48 cm. With this high-frequency "sonar" system they can sense objects that are roughly as small as the wavelength (but not much smaller). *Ultrasonic imaging* is a medical technique that uses exactly the same physical principle; sound waves of very high frequency and very short wavelength, called *ultrasound,* are scanned over the human body, and the "echoes" from interior organs are used to create an image. With ultrasound of frequency 5 MHz $= 5 \times 10^6$ Hz, the wavelength in water (the primary constituent of the body) is 0.3 mm, and features as small as this can be discerned in the image. Ultrasound is used for the study of heart-valve action, detection of tumors, and prenatal examinations (Fig. 16.9). Ultrasound is more sensitive than x rays in distinguishing various kinds of tissues and does not have the radiation hazards associated with x rays.

16.9 This three-dimensional image of a fetus in the womb was made using a sequence of ultrasound scans. Each individual scan reveals a two-dimensional "slice" through the fetus; many such slices were then combined digitally.

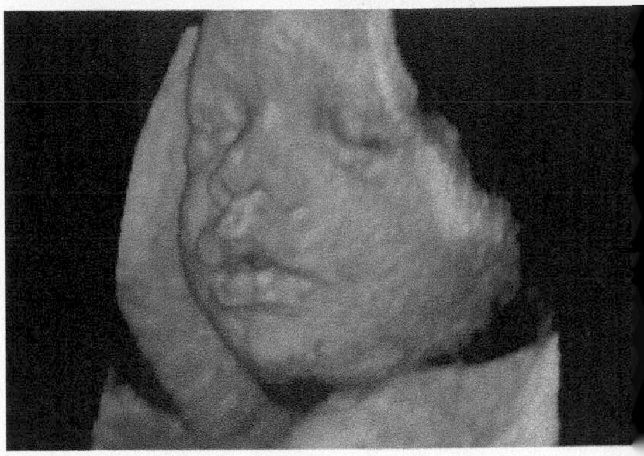

Speed of Sound in a Gas

Most of the sound waves that we encounter on a daily basis propagate in air. To use Eq. (16.7) to find the speed of sound waves in air, we must keep in mind that the bulk modulus of a gas depends on the pressure of the gas: The greater the pressure applied to a gas to compress it, the more it resists further compression and hence the greater the bulk modulus. (That's why specific values of the bulk modulus for gases are not given in Table 11.1.) The expression for the bulk modulus of a gas for use in Eq. (16.7) is

$$B = \gamma p_0 \qquad (16.9)$$

where p_0 is the equilibrium pressure of the gas. The quantity γ (the Greek letter gamma) is called the *ratio of heat capacities.* It is a dimensionless number that characterizes the thermal properties of the gas. (We'll learn more about this quantity in Chapter 19.) As an example, the ratio of heat capacities for air is $\gamma = 1.40$. At normal atmospheric pressure $p_0 = 1.013 \times 10^5$ Pa, so $B = (1.40)(1.013 \times 10^5 \text{ Pa}) = 1.42 \times 10^5$ Pa. This value is minuscule compared to the bulk modulus of a typical solid (see Table 11.1), which is approximately 10^{10} to 10^{11} Pa. This shouldn't be surprising: It's simply a statement that air is far easier to compress than steel.

The density ρ of a gas also depends on the pressure, which in turn depends on the temperature. It turns out that the ratio B/ρ for a given type of ideal gas does *not* depend on the pressure at all, only the temperature. From Eq. (16.7), this means that the speed of sound in a gas is fundamentally a function of temperature T:

$$v = \sqrt{\frac{\gamma R T}{M}} \quad \text{(speed of sound in an ideal gas)} \qquad (16.10)$$

This expression incorporates several quantities that you may recognize from your study of ideal gases in chemistry and that we will study in Chapters 17, 18, and 19. The temperature T is the *absolute* temperature in kelvins (K), equal to the Celsius temperature plus 273.15; thus 20.00°C corresponds to $T = 293.15$ K. The quantity M is the *molar mass,* or mass per mole of the substance of which the gas is composed. The *gas constant* R has the same value for all gases. The current best numerical value of R is

$$R = 8.314472(15) \text{ J/mol} \cdot \text{K}$$

which for practical calculations we can write as 8.314 J/mol · K.

For any particular gas, γ, R, and M are constants, and the wave speed is proportional to the square root of the absolute temperature. We will see in Chapter 18 that Eq. (16.10) is almost identical to the expression for the average speed of molecules in an ideal gas. This shows that sound speeds and molecular speeds are closely related.

Example 16.4 Speed of sound in air

Find the speed of sound in air at $T = 20°$C, and find the range of wavelengths in air to which the human ear (which can hear frequencies in the range of 20–20,000 Hz) is sensitive. The mean molar mass for air (a mixture of mostly nitrogen and oxygen) is $M = 28.8 \times 10^{-3}$ kg/mol and the ratio of heat capacities is $\gamma = 1.40$.

Continued

SOLUTION

IDENTIFY and SET UP: We use Eq. (16.10) to find the sound speed from γ, T, and M, and we use $v = f\lambda$ to find the wavelengths corresponding to the frequency limits. Note that in Eq. (16.10) temperature T *must* be expressed in kelvins, not Celsius degrees.

EXECUTE: At $T = 20°\text{C} = 293\ \text{K}$, we find

$$v = \sqrt{\frac{\gamma RT}{M}} = \sqrt{\frac{(1.40)(8.314\ \text{J/mol}\cdot\text{K})(293\ \text{K})}{28.8 \times 10^{-3}\ \text{kg/mol}}} = 344\ \text{m/s}$$

Using this value of v in $\lambda = v/f$, we find that at 20°C the frequency $f = 20\ \text{Hz}$ corresponds to $\lambda = 17\ \text{m}$ and $f = 20{,}000\ \text{Hz}$ to $\lambda = 1.7\ \text{cm}$.

EVALUATE: Our calculated value of v agrees with the measured sound speed at $T = 20°\text{C}$ to within 0.3%.

In this discussion we have treated a gas as a continuous medium. A gas is actually composed of molecules in random motion, separated by distances that are large in comparison with their diameters. The vibrations that constitute a wave in a gas are superposed on the random thermal motion. At atmospheric pressure, a molecule travels an average distance of about 10^{-7} m between collisions, while the displacement amplitude of a faint sound may be only 10^{-9} m. We can think of a gas with a sound wave passing through as being comparable to a swarm of bees; the swarm as a whole oscillates slightly while individual insects move about through the swarm, apparently at random.

Test Your Understanding of Section 16.2 Mercury is 13.6 times denser than water. Based on Table 16.1, at 20°C which of these liquids has the greater bulk modulus? (i) mercury; (ii) water; (iii) both are about the same; (iv) not enough information is given to decide. MP ❙

16.3 Sound Intensity

Traveling sound waves, like all other traveling waves, transfer energy from one region of space to another. We saw in Section 15.5 that a useful way to describe the energy carried by a sound wave is through the *wave intensity* I, equal to the time average rate at which energy is transported per unit area across a surface perpendicular to the direction of propagation. Let's see how to express the intensity of a sound wave in terms of the displacement amplitude A or pressure amplitude p_{max}.

Intensity and Displacement Amplitude

For simplicity, let us consider a sound wave propagating in the $+x$-direction so that we can use our expressions from Section 16.1 for the displacement $y(x, t)$ and pressure fluctuation $p(x, t)$—Eqs. (16.1) and (16.4), respectively. In Section 6.4 we saw that power equals the product of force and velocity [see Eq. (6.18)]. So the power per unit area in this sound wave equals the product of $p(x, t)$ (force per unit area) and the *particle* velocity $v_y(x, t)$. The particle velocity $v_y(x, t)$ is the velocity at time t of that portion of the wave medium at coordinate x. Using Eqs. (16.1) and (16.4), we find

$$v_y(x, t) = \frac{\partial y(x, t)}{\partial t} = \omega A \sin(kx - \omega t)$$

$$p(x, t)v_y(x, t) = [BkA \sin(kx - \omega t)][\omega A \sin(kx - \omega t)]$$
$$= B\omega k A^2 \sin^2(kx - \omega t)$$

CAUTION **Wave velocity vs. particle velocity** Remember that the velocity of the wave as a whole is *not* the same as the particle velocity. While the wave continues to move in the direction of propagation, individual particles in the wave medium merely slosh back and forth, as shown in Fig. 16.1. Furthermore, the maximum speed of a particle of the medium can be very different from the wave speed.

The intensity is, by definition, the time average value of $p(x, t)v_y(x, t)$. For any value of x the average value of the function $\sin^2(kx - \omega t)$ over one period $T = 2\pi/\omega$ is $\frac{1}{2}$, so

$$I = \tfrac{1}{2}B\omega kA^2 \tag{16.11}$$

By using the relationships $\omega = vk$ and $v^2 = B/\rho$, we can transform Eq. (16.11) into the form

$$I = \tfrac{1}{2}\sqrt{\rho B}\,\omega^2A^2 \quad \text{(intensity of a sinusoidal sound wave)} \tag{16.12}$$

This equation shows why in a stereo system, a low-frequency woofer has to vibrate with much larger amplitude than a high-frequency tweeter to produce the same sound intensity.

Intensity and Pressure Amplitude

It is usually more useful to express I in terms of the pressure amplitude p_{max}. Using Eq. (16.5) and the relationship $\omega = vk$, we find

$$I = \frac{\omega p_{max}^2}{2Bk} = \frac{v p_{max}^2}{2B} \tag{16.13}$$

By using the wave speed relationship $v^2 = B/\rho$, we can also write Eq. (16.13) in the alternative forms

$$I = \frac{p_{max}^2}{2\rho v} = \frac{p_{max}^2}{2\sqrt{\rho B}} \quad \text{(intensity of a sinusoidal sound wave)} \tag{16.14}$$

You should verify these expressions. Comparison of Eqs. (16.12) and (16.14) shows that sinusoidal sound waves of the same intensity but different frequency have different displacement amplitudes A but the *same* pressure amplitude p_{max}. This is another reason it is usually more convenient to describe a sound wave in terms of pressure fluctuations, not displacement.

The *total* average power carried across a surface by a sound wave equals the product of the intensity at the surface and the surface area, if the intensity over the surface is uniform. The average total sound power emitted by a person speaking in an ordinary conversational tone is about 10^{-5} W, while a loud shout corresponds to about 3×10^{-2} W. If all the residents of New York City were to talk at the same time, the total sound power would be about 100 W, equivalent to the electric power requirement of a medium-sized light bulb. On the other hand, the power required to fill a large auditorium or stadium with loud sound is considerable (see Example 16.7.)

If the sound source emits waves in all directions equally, the intensity decreases with increasing distance r from the source according to the inverse-square law: The intensity is proportional to $1/r^2$. We discussed this law and its consequences in Section 15.5. If the sound goes predominantly in one direction, the inverse-square law does not apply and the intensity decreases with distance more slowly than $1/r^2$ (Fig. 16.10).

16.10 By cupping your hands like this, you direct the sound waves emerging from your mouth so that they don't propagate to the sides. Hence the intensity decreases with distance more slowly than the inverse-square law would predict, and you can be heard at greater distances.

The inverse-square relationship also does not apply indoors because sound energy can reach a listener by reflection from the walls and ceiling. Indeed, part of the architect's job in designing an auditorium is to tailor these reflections so that the intensity is as nearly uniform as possible over the entire auditorium.

Problem-Solving Strategy 16.1 Sound Intensity

IDENTIFY *the relevant concepts:* The relationships between the intensity and amplitude of a sound wave are straightforward. Other quantities are involved in these relationships, however, so it's particularly important to decide which is your target variable.

SET UP *the problem* using the following steps:

1. Sort the physical quantities into categories. Wave properties include the displacement and pressure amplitudes A and p_{max} and the frequency f, which can be determined from the angular frequency ω, the wave number k, or the wavelength λ. These quantities are related through the wave speed v, which is determined by properties of the medium (B and ρ for a liquid, and γ, T, and M for a gas).
2. List the given quantities and identify the target variables. Find relationships that take you where you want to go.

EXECUTE *the solution*: Use your selected equations to solve for the target variables. Express the temperature in kelvins (Celsius temperature plus 273.15) to calculate the speed of sound in a gas.

EVALUATE *your answer:* If possible, use an alternative relationship to check your results.

Example 16.5 Intensity of a sound wave in air

Find the intensity of the sound wave in Example 16.1, with $p_{max} = 3.0 \times 10^{-2}$ Pa. Assume the temperature is 20°C so that the density of air is $\rho = 1.20\ \text{kg/m}^3$ and the speed of sound is $v = 344$ m/s.

SOLUTION

IDENTIFY and SET UP: Our target variable is the intensity I of the sound wave. We are given the pressure amplitude p_{max} of the wave as well as the density ρ and wave speed v for the medium. We can determine I from p_{max}, ρ, and v using Eq. (16.14).

EXECUTE: From Eq. (16.14),

$$I = \frac{{p_{max}}^2}{2\rho v} = \frac{(3.0 \times 10^{-2}\ \text{Pa})^2}{2(1.20\ \text{kg/m}^3)(344\ \text{m/s})}$$
$$= 1.1 \times 10^{-6}\ \text{J/(s}\cdot\text{m}^2) = 1.1 \times 10^{-6}\ \text{W/m}^2$$

EVALUATE: This seems like a very low intensity, but it is well within the range of sound intensities encountered on a daily basis. A very loud sound wave at the threshold of pain has a pressure amplitude of about 30 Pa and an intensity of about 1 W/m^2. The pressure amplitude of the faintest sound wave that can be heard is about 3×10^{-5} Pa, and the corresponding intensity is about 10^{-12} W/m^2. (Try these values of p_{max} in Eq. (16.14) to check that the corresponding intensities are as we have stated.)

Example 16.6 Same intensity, different frequencies

What are the pressure and displacement amplitudes of a 20-Hz sound wave with the same intensity as the 1000-Hz sound wave of Examples 16.1 and 16.5?

SOLUTION

IDENTIFY and SET UP: In Examples 16.1 and 16.5 we found that for a 1000-Hz sound wave with $p_{max} = 3.0 \times 10^{-2}$ Pa, $A = 1.2 \times 10^{-8}$ m and $I = 1.1 \times 10^{-6}$ W/m^2. Our target variables are p_{max} and A for a 20-Hz sound wave of the same intensity I. We can find these using Eqs. (16.14) and (16.12), respectively.

EXECUTE: We can rearrange Eqs. (16.14) and (16.12) as ${p_{max}}^2 = 2I\sqrt{\rho B}$ and $\omega^2 A^2 = 2I/\sqrt{\rho B}$, respectively. These tell us that for a given sound intensity I in a given medium (constant ρ and B), the quantities p_{max} and ωA (or, equivalently, fA) are both *constants* that don't depend on frequency. From the first result we immediately have $p_{max} = 3.0 \times 10^{-2}$ Pa for $f = 20$ Hz, the same as for $f = 1000$ Hz. If write the second result as $f_{20}A_{20} = f_{1000}A_{1000}$, we have

$$A_{20} = \left(\frac{f_{1000}}{f_{20}}\right)A_{1000}$$
$$= \left(\frac{1000\ \text{Hz}}{20\ \text{Hz}}\right)(1.2 \times 10^{-8}\ \text{m}) = 6.0 \times 10^{-7}\ \text{m} = 0.60\ \mu\text{m}$$

EVALUATE: Our result reinforces the idea that pressure amplitude is a more convenient description of a sound wave and its intensity than displacement amplitude.

Example 16.7 "Play it loud!"

For an outdoor concert we want the sound intensity to be $1\ \text{W/m}^2$ at a distance of 20 m from the speaker array. If the sound intensity is uniform in all directions, what is the required acoustic power output of the array?

SOLUTION

IDENTIFY, SET UP, and EXECUTE: This example uses the definition of sound intensity as power per unit area. The total power is the target variable; the area in question is a hemisphere centered on the speaker array. We assume that the speakers are on the ground and that none of the acoustic power is directed into the ground, so the acoustic power is uniform over a hemisphere 20 m in radius. The surface area of this hemisphere is $(\frac{1}{2})(4\pi)(20\ \text{m})^2$, or about $2500\ \text{m}^2$. The required power is the product of this area and the intensity: $(1\ \text{W/m}^2)(2500\ \text{m}^2) = 2500\ \text{W} = 2.5\ \text{kW}$.

EVALUATE: The electrical power input to the speaker would need to be considerably greater than 2.5 kW, because speaker efficiency is not very high (typically a few percent for ordinary speakers, and up to 25% for horn-type speakers).

The Decibel Scale

Because the ear is sensitive over a broad range of intensities, a *logarithmic* intensity scale is usually used. The **sound intensity level** β of a sound wave is defined by the equation

$$\beta = (10\ \text{dB}) \log \frac{I}{I_0} \quad \text{(definition of sound intensity level)} \quad (16.15)$$

In this equation, I_0 is a reference intensity, chosen to be $10^{-12}\ \text{W/m}^2$, approximately the threshold of human hearing at 1000 Hz. Recall that "log" means the logarithm to base 10. Sound intensity levels are expressed in **decibels,** abbreviated dB. A decibel is $\frac{1}{10}$ of a *bel,* a unit named for Alexander Graham Bell (the inventor of the telephone). The bel is inconveniently large for most purposes, and the decibel is the usual unit of sound intensity level.

If the intensity of a sound wave equals I_0 or $10^{-12}\ \text{W/m}^2$, its sound intensity level is 0 dB. An intensity of $1\ \text{W/m}^2$ corresponds to 120 dB. Table 16.2 gives the sound intensity levels in decibels of some familiar sounds. You can use Eq. (16.15) to check the value of sound intensity level β given for each intensity in the table.

Because the ear is not equally sensitive to all frequencies in the audible range, some sound-level meters weight the various frequencies unequally. One such scheme leads to the so-called dBA scale; this scale deemphasizes the low and very high frequencies, where the ear is less sensitive than at midrange frequencies.

Table 16.2 Sound Intensity Levels from Various Sources (Representative Values)

Source or Description of Sound	Sound Intensity Level, β (dB)	Intensity, I (W/m^2)
Military jet aircraft 30 m away	140	10^2
Threshold of pain	120	1
Riveter	95	3.2×10^{-3}
Elevated train	90	10^{-3}
Busy street traffic	70	10^{-5}
Ordinary conversation	65	3.2×10^{-6}
Quiet automobile	50	10^{-7}
Quiet radio in home	40	10^{-8}
Average whisper	20	10^{-10}
Rustle of leaves	10	10^{-11}
Threshold of hearing at 1000 Hz	0	10^{-12}

Example 16.8 Temporary—or permanent—hearing loss

A 10-min exposure to 120-dB sound will temporarily shift your threshold of hearing at 1000 Hz from 0 dB up to 28 dB. Ten years of exposure to 92-dB sound will cause a *permanent* shift to 28 dB. What sound intensities correspond to 28 dB and 92 dB?

SOLUTION

IDENTIFY and SET UP: We are given two sound intensity levels β; our target variables are the corresponding intensities. We can solve Eq. (16.15) to find the intensity I that corresponds to each value of β.

EXECUTE: We solve Eq. (16.15) for I by dividing both sides by 10 dB and using the relationship $10^{\log x} = x$:

$$I = I_0 10^{\beta/(10\ \text{dB})}$$

For $\beta = 28$ dB and $\beta = 92$ dB, the exponents are $\beta/(10\ \text{dB}) = 2.8$ and 9.2, respectively, so that

$$I_{28\ \text{dB}} = (10^{-12}\ \text{W/m}^2)10^{2.8} = 6.3 \times 10^{-10}\ \text{W/m}^2$$
$$I_{92\ \text{dB}} = (10^{-12}\ \text{W/m}^2)10^{9.2} = 1.6 \times 10^{-3}\ \text{W/m}^2$$

EVALUATE: If your answers are a factor of 10 too large, you may have entered 10×10^{-12} in your calculator instead of 1×10^{-12}. Be careful!

Example 16.9 A bird sings in a meadow

Consider an idealized bird (treated as a point source) that emits constant sound power, with intensity obeying the inverse-square law (Fig. 16.11). If you move twice the distance from the bird, by how many decibels does the sound intensity level drop?

SOLUTION

IDENTIFY and SET UP: The decibel scale is logarithmic, so the *difference* between two sound intensity levels (the target variable) corresponds to the *ratio* of the corresponding intensities, which is determined by the inverse-square law. We label the two points P_1 and P_2 (Fig. 16.11). We use Eq. (16.15), the definition of sound intensity level, at each point. We use Eq. (15.26), the inverse-square law, to relate the intensities at the two points.

EXECUTE: The difference $\beta_2 - \beta_1$ between any two sound intensity levels is related to the corresponding intensities by

$$\begin{aligned}\beta_2 - \beta_1 &= (10\ \text{dB})\left(\log\frac{I_2}{I_0} - \log\frac{I_1}{I_0}\right)\\ &= (10\ \text{dB})[(\log I_2 - \log I_0) - (\log I_1 - \log I_0)]\\ &= (10\ \text{dB})\log\frac{I_2}{I_1}\end{aligned}$$

For this inverse-square-law source, Eq. (15.26) yields $I_2/I_1 = r_1^2/r_2^2 = \frac{1}{4}$, so

$$\beta_2 - \beta_1 = (10\ \text{dB})\log\frac{I_1}{I_2} = (10\ \text{dB})\log\tfrac{1}{4} = -6.0\ \text{dB}$$

16.11 When you double your distance from a point source of sound, by how much does the sound intensity level decrease?

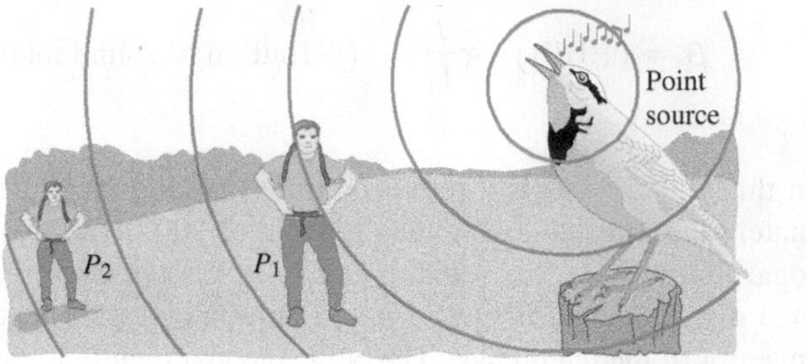

EVALUATE: Our result is negative, which tells us (correctly) that the sound intensity level is less at P_2 than at P_1. The 6-dB difference doesn't depend on the sound intensity level at P_1; *any* doubling of the distance from an inverse-square-law source reduces the sound intensity level by 6 dB.

Note that the perceived *loudness* of a sound is not directly proportional to its intensity. For example, most people interpret an increase of 8 dB to 10 dB in sound intensity level (corresponding to increasing intensity by a factor of 6 to 10) as a doubling of loudness.

Test Your Understanding of Section 16.3 You double the intensity of a sound wave in air while leaving the frequency unchanged. (The pressure, density, and temperature of the air remain unchanged as well.) What effect does this have on the displacement amplitude, pressure amplitude, bulk modulus, sound speed, and sound intensity level?

16.4 Standing Sound Waves and Normal Modes

When longitudinal (sound) waves propagate in a fluid in a pipe with finite length, the waves are reflected from the ends in the same way that transverse waves on a string are reflected at its ends. The superposition of the waves traveling in opposite directions again forms a standing wave. Just as for transverse standing waves on a string (see Section 15.7), standing sound waves (normal modes) in a pipe can

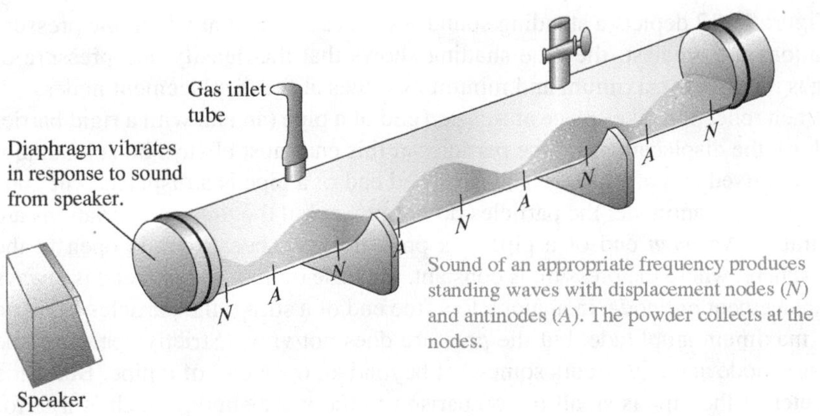

16.12 Demonstrating standing sound waves using a Kundt's tube. The blue shading represents the density of the gas at an instant when the gas pressure at the displacement nodes is a maximum or a minimum.

be used to create sound waves in the surrounding air. This is the operating principle of the human voice as well as many musical instruments, including woodwinds, brasses, and pipe organs.

Transverse waves on a string, including standing waves, are usually described only in terms of the displacement of the string. But, as we have seen, sound waves in a fluid may be described either in terms of the displacement of the fluid or in terms of the pressure variation in the fluid. To avoid confusion, we'll use the terms **displacement node** and **displacement antinode** to refer to points where particles of the fluid have zero displacement and maximum displacement, respectively.

We can demonstrate standing sound waves in a column of gas using an apparatus called a Kundt's tube (Fig. 16.12). A horizontal glass tube a meter or so long is closed at one end and has a flexible diaphragm at the other end that can transmit vibrations. A nearby loudspeaker is driven by an audio oscillator and amplifier; this produces sound waves that force the diaphragm to vibrate sinusoidally with a frequency that we can vary. The sound waves within the tube are reflected at the other, closed end of the tube. We spread a small amount of light powder uniformly along the bottom of the tube. As we vary the frequency of the sound, we pass through frequencies at which the amplitude of the standing waves becomes large enough for the powder to be swept along the tube at those points where the gas is in motion. The powder therefore collects at the displacement nodes (where the gas is not moving). Adjacent nodes are separated by a distance equal to $\lambda/2$, and we can measure this distance. Given the wavelength, we can use this experiment to determine the wave speed: We read the frequency f from the oscillator dial, and we can then calculate the speed v of the waves from the relationship $v = \lambda f$.

Figure 16.13 shows the motions of nine different particles within a gas-filled tube in which there is a standing sound wave. A particle at a displacement node (*N*) does not move, while a particle at a displacement antinode (*A*) oscillates with maximum amplitude. Note that particles on opposite sides of a displacement node vibrate in opposite phase. When these particles approach each other, the gas between them is compressed and the pressure rises; when they recede from each other, there is an expansion and the pressure drops. Hence at a displacement *node* the gas undergoes the maximum amount of compression and expansion, and the variations in pressure and density above and below the average have their maximum value. By contrast, particles on opposite sides of a displacement *antinode* vibrate *in phase;* the distance between the particles is nearly constant, and there is *no* variation in pressure or density at a displacement antinode.

We use the term **pressure node** to describe a point in a standing sound wave at which the pressure and density do not vary and the term **pressure antinode** to describe a point at which the variations in pressure and density are greatest. Using these terms, we can summarize our observations about standing sound waves as follows:

A pressure node is always a displacement antinode, and a pressure antinode is always a displacement node.

16.13 In a standing sound wave, a displacement node *N* is a pressure antinode (a point where the pressure fluctuates the most) and a displacement antinode *A* is a pressure node (a point where the pressure does not fluctuate at all).

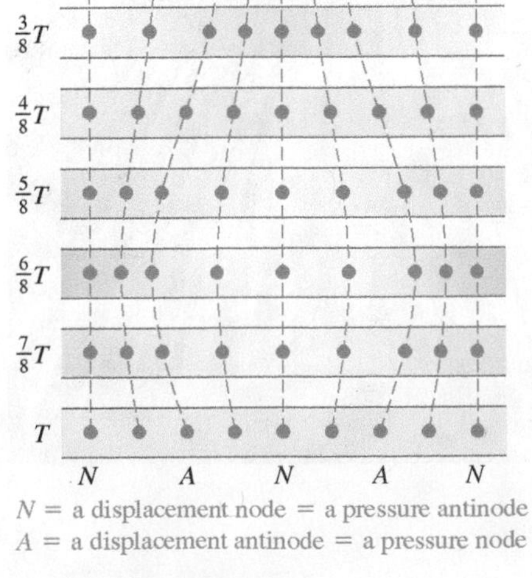

Figure 16.12 depicts a standing sound wave at an instant at which the pressure variations are greatest; the blue shading shows that the density and pressure of the gas have their maximum and minimum values at the displacement nodes.

When reflection takes place at a *closed* end of a pipe (an end with a rigid barrier or plug), the displacement of the particles at this end must always be zero, analogous to a fixed end of a string. Thus a closed end of a pipe is a displacement node and a pressure antinode; the particles do not move, but the pressure variations are maximum. An *open* end of a pipe is a pressure node because it is open to the atmosphere, where the pressure is constant. Because of this, an open end is always a displacement *antinode,* in analogy to a free end of a string; the particles oscillate with maximum amplitude, but the pressure does not vary. (Strictly speaking, the pressure node actually occurs somewhat beyond an open end of a pipe. But if the diameter of the pipe is small in comparison to the wavelength, which is true for most musical instruments, this effect can safely be neglected.) Thus longitudinal waves in a column of fluid are reflected at the closed and open ends of a pipe in the same way that transverse waves in a string are reflected at fixed and free ends, respectively.

Conceptual Example 16.10 The sound of silence

A directional loudspeaker directs a sound wave of wavelength λ at a wall (Fig. 16.14). At what distances from the wall could you stand and hear no sound at all?

SOLUTION

Your ear detects pressure variations in the air; you will therefore hear no sound if your ear is at a *pressure node,* which is a displacement antinode. The wall is at a displacement node; the distance from any node to an adjacent antinode is $\lambda/4$, and the distance from one antinode to the next is $\lambda/2$ (Fig. 16.14). Hence the displacement antinodes (pressure nodes), at which no sound will be heard, are at distances $d = \lambda/4$, $d = \lambda/4 + \lambda/2 = 3\lambda/4$, $d = 3\lambda/4 + \lambda/2 = 5\lambda/4$, . . . from the wall. If the loudspeaker is not highly directional, this effect is hard to notice because of reflections of sound waves from the floor, ceiling, and other walls.

16.14 When a sound wave is directed at a wall, it interferes with the reflected wave to create a standing wave. The *N*'s and *A*'s are *displacement* nodes and antinodes.

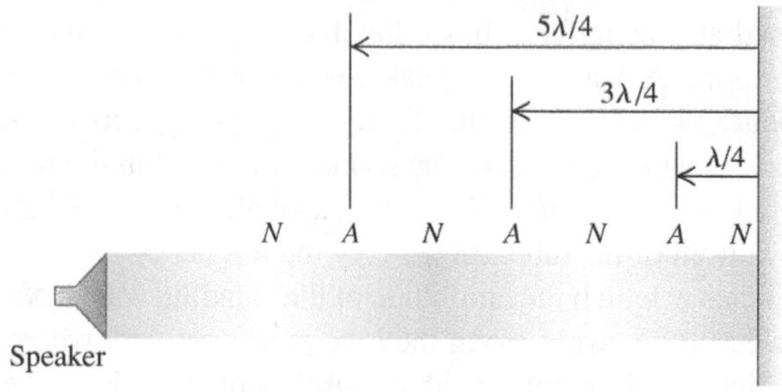

Organ Pipes and Wind Instruments

16.15 Organ pipes of different sizes produce tones with different frequencies.

The most important application of standing sound waves is the production of musical tones by wind instruments. Organ pipes are one of the simplest examples (Fig. 16.15). Air is supplied by a blower, at a gauge pressure typically of the order of 10^3 Pa (10^{-2} atm), to the bottom end of the pipe (Fig. 16.16). A stream of air emerges from the narrow opening at the edge of the horizontal surface and is directed against the top edge of the opening, which is called the *mouth* of the pipe. The column of air in the pipe is set into vibration, and there is a series of possible normal modes, just as with the stretched string. The mouth always acts as an open end; thus it is a pressure node and a displacement antinode. The other end of the pipe (at the top in Fig. 16.16) may be either open or closed.

In Fig. 16.17, both ends of the pipe are open, so both ends are pressure nodes and displacement antinodes. An organ pipe that is open at both ends is called an *open pipe.* The fundamental frequency f_1 corresponds to a standing-wave pattern with a displacement antinode at each end and a displacement node in the middle (Fig. 16.17a). The distance between adjacent antinodes is always equal to one half-wavelength, and in this case that is equal to the length L of the pipe; $\lambda/2 = L$. The corresponding frequency, obtained from the relationship $f = v/\lambda$, is

$$f_1 = \frac{v}{2L} \quad \text{(open pipe)} \tag{16.16}$$

Figures 16.17b and 16.17c show the second and third harmonics (first and second overtones); their vibration patterns have two and three displacement nodes, respectively. For these, a half-wavelength is equal to $L/2$ and $L/3$, respectively, and the frequencies are twice and three times the fundamental, respectively. That is, $f_2 = 2f_1$ and $f_3 = 3f_1$. For *every* normal mode of an open pipe the length L must be an integer number of half-wavelengths, and the possible wavelengths λ_n are given by

$$L = n\frac{\lambda_n}{2} \quad \text{or} \quad \lambda_n = \frac{2L}{n} \quad (n = 1, 2, 3, \ldots) \quad \text{(open pipe)} \tag{16.17}$$

The corresponding frequencies f_n are given by $f_n = v/\lambda_n$, so all the normal-mode frequencies for a pipe that is open at both ends are given by

$$f_n = \frac{nv}{2L} \quad (n = 1, 2, 3, \ldots) \quad \text{(open pipe)} \tag{16.18}$$

The value $n = 1$ corresponds to the fundamental frequency, $n = 2$ to the second harmonic (or first overtone), and so on. Alternatively, we can say

$$f_n = nf_1 \quad (n = 1, 2, 3, \ldots) \quad \text{(open pipe)} \tag{16.19}$$

with f_1 given by Eq. (16.16).

Figure 16.18 shows a pipe that is open at the left end but closed at the right end. This is called a *stopped pipe*. The left (open) end is a displacement antinode (pressure node), but the right (closed) end is a displacement node (pressure antinode). The distance between a node and the adjacent antinode is always one quarter-wavelength. Figure 16.18a shows the lowest-frequency mode; the length

16.16 Cross sections of an organ pipe at two instants one half-period apart. The N's and A's are *displacement* nodes and antinodes; as the blue shading shows, these are points of maximum pressure variation and zero pressure variation, respectively.

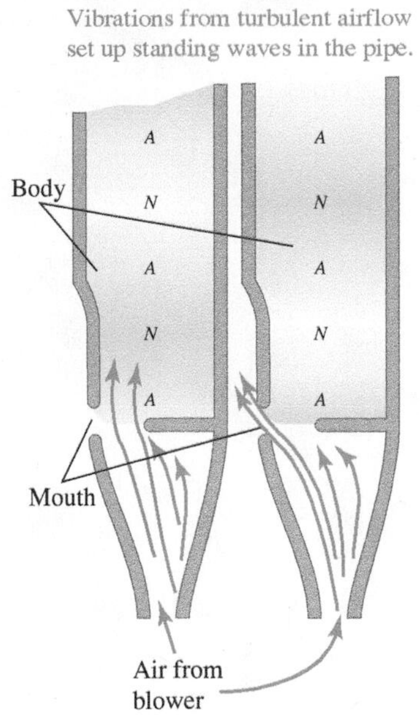

16.17 A cross section of an open pipe showing the first three normal modes. The shading indicates the pressure variations. The red curves are graphs of the displacement along the pipe axis at two instants separated in time by one half-period. The N's and A's are the *displacement* nodes and antinodes; interchange these to show the *pressure* nodes and antinodes.

(a) Fundamental: $f_1 = \frac{v}{2L}$ (b) Second harmonic: $f_2 = 2\frac{v}{2L} = 2f_1$ (c) Third harmonic: $f_3 = 3\frac{v}{2L} = 3f_1$

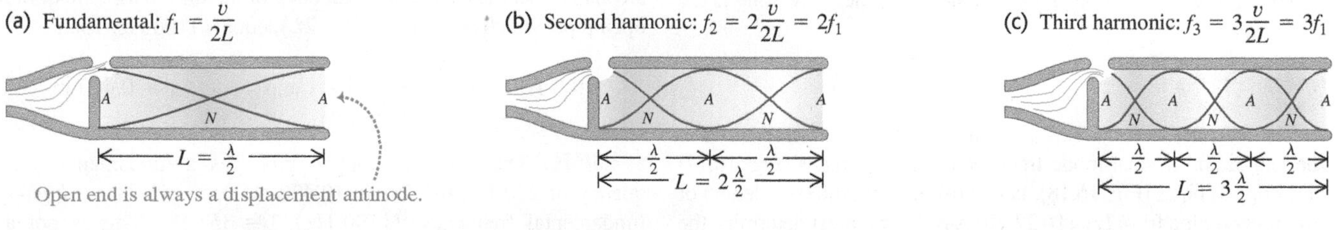

16.18 A cross section of a stopped pipe showing the first three normal modes as well as the *displacement* nodes and antinodes. Only odd harmonics are possible.

(a) Fundamental: $f_1 = \frac{v}{4L}$ (b) Third harmonic: $f_3 = 3\frac{v}{4L} = 3f_1$ (c) Fifth harmonic: $f_5 = 5\frac{v}{4L} = 5f_1$

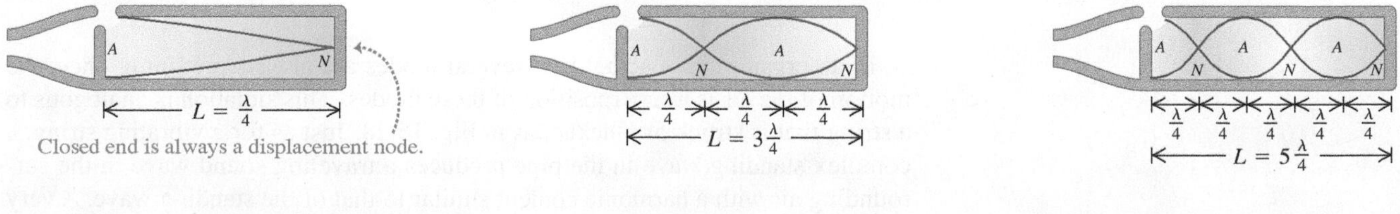

of the pipe is a quarter-wavelength ($L = \lambda_1/4$). The fundamental frequency is $f_1 = v/\lambda_1$, or

$$f_1 = \frac{v}{4L} \quad \text{(stopped pipe)} \tag{16.20}$$

This is one-half the fundamental frequency for an *open* pipe of the same length. In musical language, the *pitch* of a closed pipe is one octave lower (a factor of 2 in frequency) than that of an open pipe of the same length. Figure 16.18b shows the next mode, for which the length of the pipe is *three-quarters* of a wavelength, corresponding to a frequency $3f_1$. For Fig. 16.18c, $L = 5\lambda/4$ and the frequency is $5f_1$. The possible wavelengths are given by

$$L = n\frac{\lambda_n}{4} \quad \text{or} \quad \lambda_n = \frac{4L}{n} \quad (n = 1, 3, 5, \dots) \quad \text{(stopped pipe)} \tag{16.21}$$

The normal-mode frequencies are given by $f_n = v/\lambda_n$, or

$$f_n = \frac{nv}{4L} \quad (n = 1, 3, 5, \dots) \quad \text{(stopped pipe)} \tag{16.22}$$

or

$$f_n = nf_1 \quad (n = 1, 3, 5, \dots) \quad \text{(stopped pipe)} \tag{16.23}$$

with f_1 given by Eq. (16.20). We see that the second, fourth, and all *even* harmonics are missing. In a pipe that is closed at one end, the fundamental frequency is $f_1 = v/4L$, and only the odd harmonics in the series $(3f_1, 5f_1, \dots)$ are possible.

A final possibility is a pipe that is closed at *both* ends, with displacement nodes and pressure antinodes at both ends. This wouldn't be of much use as a musical instrument because there would be no way for the vibrations to get out of the pipe.

Example 16.11 A tale of two pipes

On a day when the speed of sound is 345 m/s, the fundamental frequency of a particular stopped organ pipe is 220 Hz. (a) How long is this pipe? (b) The second *overtone* of this pipe has the same wavelength as the third *harmonic* of an *open* pipe. How long is the open pipe?

SOLUTION

IDENTIFY and SET UP: This problem uses the relationship between the length and normal-mode frequencies of open pipes (Fig. 16.17) and stopped pipes (Fig. 16.18). In part (a), we determine the length of the stopped pipe from Eq. (16.22). In part (b), we must determine the length of an open pipe, for which Eq. (16.18) gives the frequencies.

EXECUTE: (a) For a stopped pipe $f_1 = v/4L$, so

$$L_{\text{stopped}} = \frac{v}{4f_1} = \frac{345 \text{ m/s}}{4(220 \text{ s}^{-1})} = 0.392 \text{ m}$$

(b) The frequency of the second overtone of a stopped pipe (the *third* possible frequency) is $f_5 = 5f_1 = 5(220 \text{ Hz}) = 1100 \text{ Hz}$. If the wavelengths for the two pipes are the same, the frequencies are also the same. Hence the frequency of the third harmonic of the open pipe, which is at $3f_1 = 3(v/2L)$, equals 1100 Hz. Then

$$1100 \text{ Hz} = 3\left(\frac{345 \text{ m/s}}{2L_{\text{open}}}\right) \quad \text{and} \quad L_{\text{open}} = 0.470 \text{ m}$$

EVALUATE: The 0.392-m stopped pipe has a fundamental frequency of 220 Hz; the *longer* (0.470-m) open pipe has a *higher* fundamental frequency, $(1100 \text{ Hz})/3 = 367$ Hz. This is not a contradiction, as you can see if you compare Figs. 16.17a and 16.18a.

In an organ pipe in actual use, several modes are always present at once; the motion of the air is a superposition of these modes. This situation is analogous to a string that is struck or plucked, as in Fig. 15.28. Just as for a vibrating string, a complex standing wave in the pipe produces a traveling sound wave in the surrounding air with a harmonic content similar to that of the standing wave. A very narrow pipe produces a sound wave rich in higher harmonics, which we hear as a thin and "stringy" tone; a fatter pipe produces mostly the fundamental mode, heard as a softer, more flutelike tone. The harmonic content also depends on the shape of the pipe's mouth.

We have talked about organ pipes, but this discussion is also applicable to other wind instruments. The flute and the recorder are directly analogous. The most significant difference is that those instruments have holes along the pipe. Opening and closing the holes with the fingers changes the effective length L of the air column and thus changes the pitch. Any individual organ pipe, by comparison, can play only a single note. The flute and recorder behave as *open* pipes, while the clarinet acts as a *stopped* pipe (closed at the reed end, open at the bell).

Equations (16.18) and (16.22) show that the frequencies of any wind instrument are proportional to the speed of sound v in the air column inside the instrument. As Eq. (16.10) shows, v depends on temperature; it increases when temperature increases. Thus the pitch of all wind instruments rises with increasing temperature. An organ that has some of its pipes at one temperature and others at a different temperature is bound to sound out of tune.

Test Your Understanding of Section 16.4 If you connect a hose to one end of a metal pipe and blow compressed air into it, the pipe produces a musical tone. If instead you blow compressed helium into the pipe at the same pressure and temperature, will the pipe produce (i) the same tone, (ii) a higher-pitch tone, or (iii) a lower-pitch tone? ❙

16.5 Resonance and Sound

Many mechanical systems have normal modes of oscillation. As we have seen, these include columns of air (as in an organ pipe) and stretched strings (as in a guitar; see Section 15.8). In each mode, every particle of the system oscillates with simple harmonic motion at the same frequency as the mode. Air columns and stretched strings have an infinite series of normal modes, but the basic concept is closely related to the simple harmonic oscillator, discussed in Chapter 14, which has only a single normal mode (that is, only one frequency at which it oscillates after being disturbed).

Suppose we apply a periodically varying force to a system that can oscillate. The system is then forced to oscillate with a frequency equal to the frequency of the applied force (called the *driving frequency*). This motion is called a *forced oscillation.* We talked about forced oscillations of the harmonic oscillator in Section 14.8, and we suggest that you review that discussion. In particular, we described the phenomenon of mechanical **resonance.** A simple example of resonance is pushing Cousin Throckmorton on a swing. The swing is a pendulum; it has only a single normal mode, with a frequency determined by its length. If we push the swing periodically with this frequency, we can build up the amplitude of the motion. But if we push with a very different frequency, the swing hardly moves at all.

Resonance also occurs when a periodically varying force is applied to a system with many normal modes. An example is shown in Fig. 16.19a. An open organ pipe is placed next to a loudspeaker that is driven by an amplifier and emits pure sinusoidal sound waves of frequency f, which can be varied by adjusting the amplifier. The air in the pipe is forced to vibrate with the same frequency f as the *driving force* provided by the loudspeaker. In general the amplitude of this motion is relatively small, and the air inside the pipe will not move in any of the normal-mode patterns shown in Fig. 16.17. But if the frequency f of the force is close to one of the normal-mode frequencies, the air in the pipe moves in the normal-mode pattern for that frequency, and the amplitude can become quite large. Figure 16.19b shows the amplitude of oscillation of the air

16.19 (a) The air in an open pipe is forced to oscillate at the same frequency as the sinusoidal sound waves coming from the loudspeaker. (b) The resonance curve of the open pipe graphs the amplitude of the standing sound wave in the pipe as a function of the driving frequency.

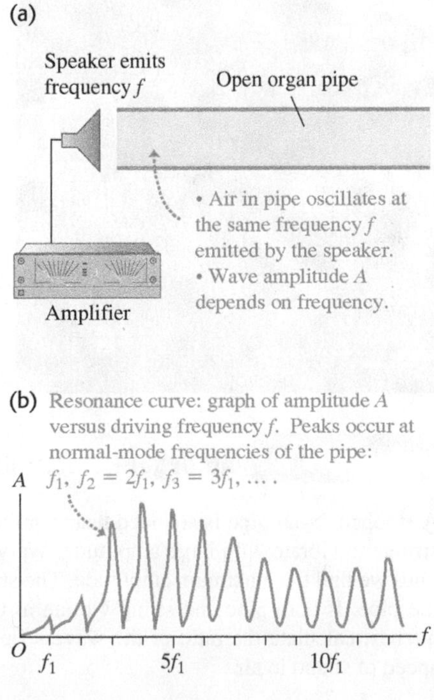

Application Resonance and the Sensitivity of the Ear
The auditory canal of the human ear (see Fig. 16.4) is an air-filled pipe open at one end and closed at the other (eardrum) end. The canal is about 2.5 cm = 0.025 m long, so it has a resonance at its fundamental frequency $f_1 = v/4L = (344 \text{ m/s})/[4(0.025 \text{ m})] = 3440$ Hz. The resonance means that a sound at this frequency produces a strong oscillation of the eardrum. That's why your ear is most sensitive to sounds near 3440 Hz.

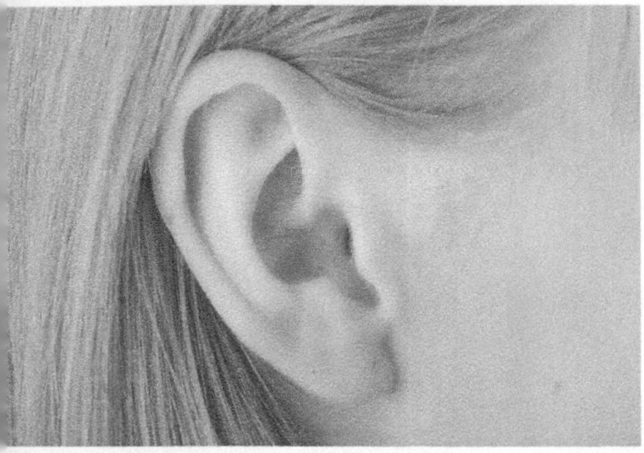

in the pipe as a function of the driving frequency f. The shape of this graph is called the **resonance curve** of the pipe; it has peaks where f equals the normal-mode frequencies of the pipe. The detailed shape of the resonance curve depends on the geometry of the pipe.

If the frequency of the force is precisely *equal* to a normal-mode frequency, the system is in resonance, and the amplitude of the forced oscillation is maximum. If there were no friction or other energy-dissipating mechanism, a driving force at a normal-mode frequency would continue to add energy to the system, and the amplitude would increase indefinitely. In such an idealized case the peaks in the resonance curve of Fig. 16.19b would be infinitely high. But in any real system there is always some dissipation of energy, or damping, as we discussed in Section 14.8; the amplitude of oscillation in resonance may be large, but it cannot be infinite.

The "sound of the ocean" you hear when you put your ear next to a large seashell is due to resonance. The noise of the outside air moving past the seashell is a mixture of sound waves of almost all audible frequencies, which forces the air inside the seashell to oscillate. The seashell behaves like an organ pipe, with a set of normal-mode frequencies; hence the inside air oscillates most strongly at those frequencies, producing the seashell's characteristic sound. To hear a similar phenomenon, uncap a full bottle of your favorite beverage and blow across the open top. The noise is provided by your breath blowing across the top, and the "organ pipe" is the column of air inside the bottle above the surface of the liquid. If you take a drink and repeat the experiment, you will hear a lower tone because the "pipe" is longer and the normal-mode frequencies are lower.

Resonance also occurs when a stretched string is forced to oscillate (see Section 15.8). Suppose that one end of a stretched string is held fixed while the other is given a transverse sinusoidal motion with small amplitude, setting up standing waves. If the frequency of the driving mechanism is *not* equal to one of the normal-mode frequencies of the string, the amplitude at the antinodes is fairly small. However, if the frequency is equal to any one of the normal-mode frequencies, the string is in resonance, and the amplitude at the antinodes is very much larger than that at the driven end. The driven end is not precisely a node, but it lies much closer to a node than to an antinode when the string is in resonance. The photographs in Fig. 15.23 were made this way, with the left end of the string fixed and the right end oscillating vertically with small amplitude; large-amplitude standing waves resulted when the frequency of oscillation of the right end was equal to the fundamental frequency or to one of the first three overtones.

It is easy to demonstrate resonance with a piano. Push down the damper pedal (the right-hand pedal) so that the dampers are lifted and the strings are free to vibrate, and then sing a steady tone into the piano. When you stop singing, the piano seems to continue to sing the same note. The sound waves from your voice excite vibrations in the strings that have natural frequencies close to the frequencies (fundamental and harmonics) present in the note you sang.

A more spectacular example is a singer breaking a wine glass with her amplified voice. A good-quality wine glass has normal-mode frequencies that you can hear by tapping it. If the singer emits a loud note with a frequency corresponding exactly to one of these normal-mode frequencies, large-amplitude oscillations can build up and break the glass (Fig. 16.20).

16.20 The frequency of the sound from this trumpet exactly matches one of the normal-mode frequencies of the goblet. The resonant vibrations of the goblet have such large amplitude that the goblet tears itself apart.

Example 16.12 An organ–guitar duet

A stopped organ pipe is sounded near a guitar, causing one of the strings to vibrate with large amplitude. We vary the string tension until we find the maximum amplitude. The string is 80% as long as the pipe. If both pipe and string vibrate at their fundamental frequency, calculate the ratio of the wave speed on the string to the speed of sound in air.

SOLUTION

IDENTIFY and SET UP: The large response of the string is an example of resonance. It occurs because the organ pipe and the guitar string have the same fundamental frequency. Letting the subscripts a and s stand for the air in the pipe and the string, respectively, the condition for resonance is $f_{1a} = f_{1s}$. Equation (16.20) gives the fundamental frequency for a stopped pipe, and Eq. (15.32) gives the fundamental frequency for a guitar string held at both ends. These expressions involve the wave speed in air (v_a) and on the string (v_s) and the lengths of the pipe and string. We are given that $L_s = 0.80L_a$; our target variable is the ratio v_s/v_a.

EXECUTE: From Eqs. (16.20) and (15.32), $f_{1a} = v_a/4L_a$ and $f_{1s} = v_s/2L_s$. These frequencies are equal, so

$$\frac{v_a}{4L_a} = \frac{v_s}{2L_s}$$

Substituting $L_s = 0.80L_a$ and rearranging, we get $v_s/v_a = 0.40$.

EVALUATE: As an example, if the speed of sound in air is 345 m/s, the wave speed on the string is $(0.40)(345\text{ m/s}) = 138\text{ m/s}$. Note that while the standing waves in the pipe and on the string have the same frequency, they have different *wavelengths* $\lambda = v/f$ because the two media have different wave speeds v. Which standing wave has the greater wavelength?

Test Your Understanding of Section 16.5 A stopped organ pipe of length L has a fundamental frequency of 220 Hz. For which of the following organ pipes will there be a resonance if a tuning fork of frequency 660 Hz is sounded next to the pipe? (There may be more than one correct answer.) (i) a stopped organ pipe of length L; (ii) a stopped organ pipe of length $2L$; (iii) an open organ pipe of length L; (iii) an open organ pipe of length $2L$.

16.6 Interference of Waves

MasteringPHYSICS
PhET: Sound
PhET: Wave Interference

Wave phenomena that occur when two or more waves overlap in the same region of space are grouped under the heading *interference.* As we have seen, standing waves are a simple example of an interference effect: Two waves traveling in opposite directions in a medium combine to produce a standing wave pattern with nodes and antinodes that do not move.

Figure 16.21 shows an example of another type of interference that involves waves that spread out in space. Two speakers, driven in phase by the same amplifier, emit identical sinusoidal sound waves with the same constant frequency. We place a microphone at point P in the figure, equidistant from the speakers. Wave crests emitted from the two speakers at the same time travel equal distances and arrive at point P at the same time; hence the waves arrive in phase, and there is constructive interference. The total wave amplitude at P is twice the amplitude from each individual wave, and we can measure this combined amplitude with the microphone.

Now let's move the microphone to point Q, where the distances from the two speakers to the microphone differ by a half-wavelength. Then the two waves arrive a half-cycle out of step, or *out of phase;* a positive crest from one speaker arrives at the same time as a negative crest from the other. Destructive interference takes place, and the amplitude measured by the microphone is much *smaller* than when only one speaker is present. If the amplitudes from the two speakers are equal, the two waves cancel each other out completely at point Q, and the total amplitude there is zero.

CAUTION Interference and traveling waves Although this situation bears some resemblance to standing waves in a pipe, the total wave in Fig. 16.21 is a *traveling* wave, not a standing wave. To see why, recall that in a standing wave there is no net flow of energy in any direction. By contrast, in Fig. 16.21 there is an overall flow of energy from the speakers into the surrounding air; this is characteristic of a traveling wave. The interference between the waves from the two speakers simply causes the energy flow to be *channeled* into certain directions (for example, toward P) and away from other directions (for example, away from Q). You can see another difference between Fig. 16.21 and a standing wave by considering a point, such as Q, where destructive interference occurs. Such a point is *both* a displacement node *and* a pressure node because there is no wave at all at this point. Compare this to a standing wave, in which a pressure node is a displacement antinode, and vice versa.

16.21 Two speakers driven by the same amplifier. Constructive interference occurs at point P, and destructive interference occurs at point Q.

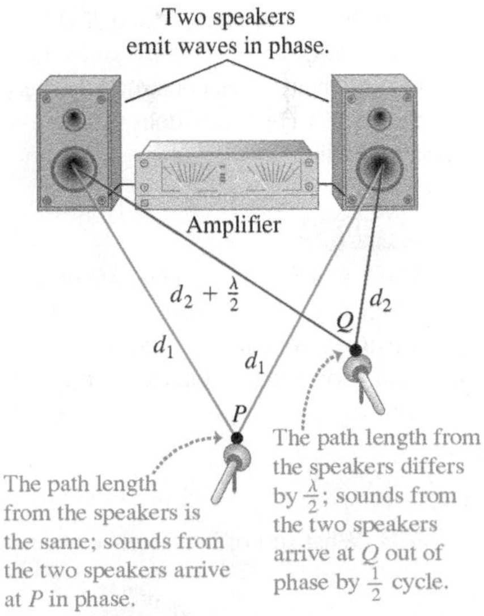

Constructive interference occurs wherever the distances traveled by the two waves differ by a whole number of wavelengths, 0, λ, 2λ, 3λ, ...; in all these cases the waves arrive at the microphone in phase (Fig. 16.22a). If the distances from the two speakers to the microphone differ by any half-integer number of wavelengths, $\lambda/2$, $3\lambda/2$, $5\lambda/2$, ..., the waves arrive at the microphone out of phase and there will be destructive interference (Fig. 16.22b). In this case, little or no sound energy flows toward the microphone directly in front of the speakers. The energy is instead directed to the sides, where constructive interference occurs.

16.22 Two speakers driven by the same amplifier, emitting waves in phase. Only the waves directed toward the microphone are shown, and they are separated for clarity. (a) Constructive interference occurs when the path difference is 0, λ, 2λ, 3λ, ... (b) Destructive interference occurs when the path difference is $\lambda/2$, $3\lambda/2$, $5\lambda/2$, ...

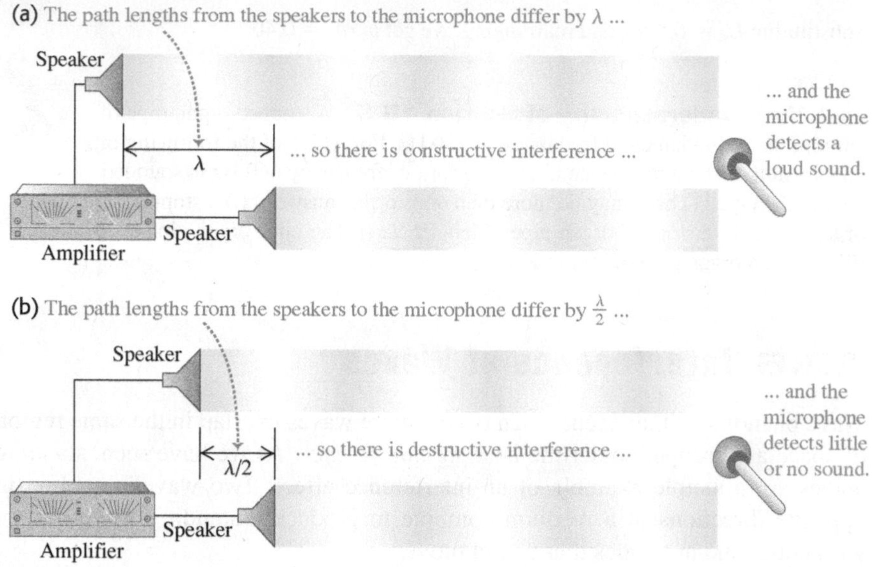

Example 16.13 Loudspeaker interference

Two small loudspeakers, A and B (Fig. 16.23), are driven by the same amplifier and emit pure sinusoidal waves in phase. (a) For what frequencies does constructive interference occur at point P? (b) For what frequencies does destructive interference occur? The speed of sound is 350 m/s.

SOLUTION

IDENTIFY and SET UP: The nature of the interference at P depends on the difference d in path lengths from point A to P and from point B to P. We calculate the path lengths using the Pythagorean theorem. Constructive interference occurs when d equals a whole number of wavelengths, while destructive interference occurs when d is a half-integer number of wavelengths. To find the corresponding frequencies, we use $v = f\lambda$.

16.23 What sort of interference occurs at P?

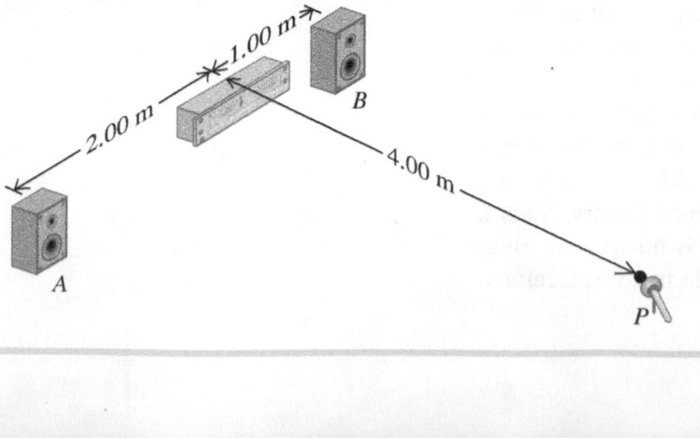

EXECUTE: The distance from A to P is $[(2.00\ \text{m})^2 + (4.00\ \text{m})^2]^{1/2} = 4.47$ m, and the distance from B to P is $[(1.00\ \text{m})^2 + (4.00\ \text{m})^2]^{1/2} = 4.12$ m. The path difference is $d = 4.47\ \text{m} - 4.12\ \text{m} = 0.35$ m.

(a) Constructive interference occurs when $d = 0, \lambda, 2\lambda, \ldots$ or $d = 0, v/f, 2v/f, \ldots = nv/f$. So the possible frequencies are

$$f_n = \frac{nv}{d} = n\frac{350\ \text{m/s}}{0.35\ \text{m}} \qquad (n = 1, 2, 3, \ldots)$$
$$= 1000\ \text{Hz},\ 2000\ \text{Hz},\ 3000\ \text{Hz}, \ldots$$

(b) Destructive interference occurs when $d = \lambda/2, 3\lambda/2, 5\lambda/2, \ldots$ or $d = v/2f, 3v/2f, 5v/2f, \ldots$. The possible frequencies are

$$f_n = \frac{nv}{2d} = n\frac{350\ \text{m/s}}{2(0.35\ \text{m})} \qquad (n = 1, 3, 5, \ldots)$$
$$= 500\ \text{Hz},\ 1500\ \text{Hz},\ 2500\ \text{Hz}, \ldots$$

EVALUATE: As we increase the frequency, the sound at point P alternates between large and small (near zero) amplitudes, with maxima and minima at the frequencies given above. This effect may not be strong in an ordinary room because of reflections from the walls, floor, and ceiling. It is stronger outdoors and best in an anechoic chamber, which has walls that absorb almost all sound and thereby eliminate reflections.

Interference effects are used to control noise from very loud sound sources such as gas-turbine power plants or jet engine test cells. The idea is to use additional sound sources that in some regions of space interfere destructively with the unwanted sound and cancel it out. Microphones in the controlled area feed signals back to the sound sources, which are continuously adjusted for optimum cancellation of noise in the controlled area.

Test Your Understanding of Section 16.6 Suppose that speaker *A* in Fig. 16.23 emits a sinusoidal sound wave of frequency 500 Hz and speaker *B* emits a sinusoidal sound wave of frequency 1000 Hz. What sort of interference will there be between these two waves? (i) constructive interference at various points, including point *P*, and destructive interference at various other points; (ii) destructive interference at various points, including point *P*, and constructive interference at various points; (iii) neither (i) nor (ii). ❙

16.7 Beats

MasteringPHYSICS
ActivPhysics 10.7: Beats and Beat Frequency

In Section 16.6 we talked about *interference* effects that occur when two different waves with the same frequency overlap in the same region of space. Now let's look at what happens when we have two waves with equal amplitude but slightly different frequencies. This occurs, for example, when two tuning forks with slightly different frequencies are sounded together, or when two organ pipes that are supposed to have exactly the same frequency are slightly "out of tune."

Consider a particular point in space where the two waves overlap. The displacements of the individual waves at this point are plotted as functions of time in Fig. 16.24a. The total length of the time axis represents 1 second, and the frequencies are 16 Hz (blue graph) and 18 Hz (red graph). Applying the principle of superposition, we add the two displacements at each instant of time to find the total displacement at that time. The result is the graph of Fig. 16.24b. At certain times the two waves are in phase; their maxima coincide and their amplitudes add. But because of their slightly different frequencies, the two waves cannot be in phase at all times. Indeed, at certain times (like $t = 0.50$ s in Fig. 16.24) the two waves are exactly *out* of phase. The two waves then cancel each other, and the total amplitude is zero.

The resultant wave in Fig. 16.24b looks like a single sinusoidal wave with a varying amplitude that goes from a maximum to zero and back. In this example the amplitude goes through two maxima and two minima in 1 second, so the frequency of this amplitude variation is 2 Hz. The amplitude variation causes variations of loudness called **beats,** and the frequency with which the loudness varies is called the **beat frequency.** In this example the beat frequency is the *difference*

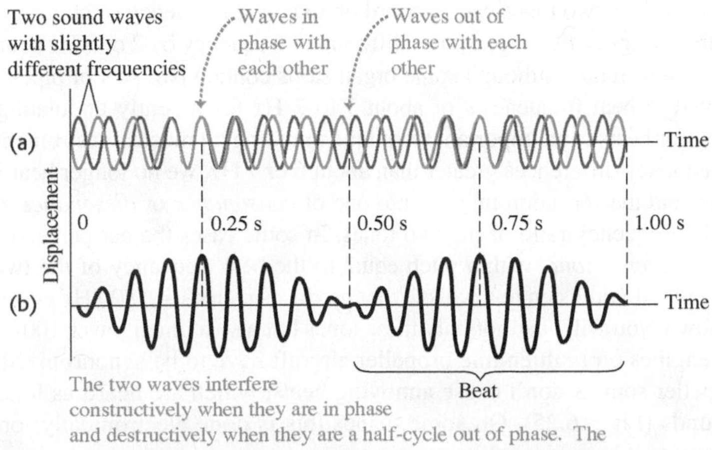

16.24 Beats are fluctuations in amplitude produced by two sound waves of slightly different frequency, here 16 Hz and 18 Hz. (a) Individual waves. (b) Resultant wave formed by superposition of the two waves. The beat frequency is 18 Hz − 16 Hz = 2 Hz.

of the two frequencies. If the beat frequency is a few hertz, we hear it as a waver or pulsation in the tone.

We can prove that the beat frequency is *always* the difference of the two frequencies f_a and f_b. Suppose f_a is larger than f_b; the corresponding periods are T_a and T_b, with $T_a < T_b$. If the two waves start out in phase at time $t = 0$, they are again in phase when the first wave has gone through exactly one more cycle than the second. This happens at a value of t equal to T_{beat}, the *period* of the beat. Let n be the number of cycles of the first wave in time T_{beat}; then the number of cycles of the second wave in the same time is $(n - 1)$, and we have the relationships

$$T_{\text{beat}} = nT_a \quad \text{and} \quad T_{\text{beat}} = (n - 1)T_b$$

Eliminating n between these two equations, we find

$$T_{\text{beat}} = \frac{T_a T_b}{T_b - T_a}$$

The reciprocal of the beat period is the beat *frequency*, $f_{\text{beat}} = 1/T_{\text{beat}}$, so

$$f_{\text{beat}} = \frac{T_b - T_a}{T_a T_b} = \frac{1}{T_a} - \frac{1}{T_b}$$

and finally

$$f_{\text{beat}} = f_a - f_b \quad \text{(beat frequency)} \tag{16.24}$$

As claimed, the beat frequency is the difference of the two frequencies. In using Eq. (16.24), remember that f_a is the higher frequency.

An alternative way to derive Eq. (16.24) is to write functions to describe the curves in Fig. 16.24a and then add them. Suppose that at a certain position the two waves are given by $y_a(t) = A\sin 2\pi f_a t$ and $y_b(t) = -A\sin 2\pi f_b t$. We use the trigonometric identity

$$\sin a - \sin b = 2\sin\tfrac{1}{2}(a - b)\cos\tfrac{1}{2}(a + b)$$

We can then express the total wave $y(t) = y_a(t) + y_b(t)$ as

$$y_a(t) + y_b(t) = \left[2A\sin\tfrac{1}{2}(2\pi)(f_a - f_b)t\right]\cos\tfrac{1}{2}(2\pi)(f_a + f_b)t$$

The amplitude factor (the quantity in brackets) varies slowly with frequency $\frac{1}{2}(f_a - f_b)$. The cosine factor varies with a frequency equal to the *average* frequency $\frac{1}{2}(f_a + f_b)$. The *square* of the amplitude factor, which is proportional to the intensity that the ear hears, goes through two maxima and two minima per cycle. So the beat frequency f_{beat} that is heard is twice the quantity $\frac{1}{2}(f_a - f_b)$, or just $f_a - f_b$, in agreement with Eq. (16.24).

Beats between two tones can be heard up to a beat frequency of about 6 or 7 Hz. Two piano strings or two organ pipes differing in frequency by 2 or 3 Hz sound wavery and "out of tune," although some organ stops contain two sets of pipes deliberately tuned to beat frequencies of about 1 to 2 Hz for a gently undulating effect. Listening for beats is an important technique in tuning all musical instruments.

At frequency differences greater than about 6 or 7 Hz, we no longer hear individual beats, and the sensation merges into one of *consonance* or *dissonance*, depending on the frequency ratio of the two tones. In some cases the ear perceives a tone called a *difference tone*, with a pitch equal to the beat frequency of the two tones. For example, if you listen to a whistle that produces sounds at 1800 Hz and 1900 Hz when blown, you will hear not only these tones but also a much lower 100-Hz tone.

The engines on multiengine propeller aircraft have to be synchronized so that the propeller sounds don't cause annoying beats, which are heard as loud throbbing sounds (Fig. 16.25). On some planes this is done electronically; on others the pilot does it by ear, just like tuning a piano.

16.25 If the two propellers on this airplane are not precisely synchronized, the pilots, passengers, and listeners on the ground will hear beats.

Test Your Understanding of Section 16.7 One tuning fork vibrates at 440 Hz, while a second tuning fork vibrates at an unknown frequency. When both tuning forks are sounded simultaneously, you hear a tone that rises and falls in intensity three times per second. What is the frequency of the second tuning fork? (i) 434 Hz; (ii) 437 Hz; (iii) 443 Hz; (iv) 446 Hz; (v) either 434 Hz or 446 Hz; (vi) either 437 Hz or 443 Hz.

16.8 The Doppler Effect

MasteringPHYSICS

ActivPhysics 10.8: Doppler Effect: Conceptual Introduction
ActivPhysics 10.9: Doppler Effect: Problems

You've probably noticed that when a car approaches you with its horn sounding, the pitch seems to drop as the car passes. This phenomenon, first described by the 19th-century Austrian scientist Christian Doppler, is called the **Doppler effect.** When a source of sound and a listener are in motion relative to each other, the frequency of the sound heard by the listener is not the same as the source frequency. A similar effect occurs for light and radio waves; we'll return to this later in this section.

To analyze the Doppler effect for sound, we'll work out a relationship between the frequency shift and the velocities of source and listener relative to the medium (usually air) through which the sound waves propagate. To keep things simple, we consider only the special case in which the velocities of both source and listener lie along the line joining them. Let v_S and v_L be the velocity components along this line for the source and the listener, respectively, relative to the medium. We choose the positive direction for both v_S and v_L to be the direction from the listener L to the source S. The speed of sound relative to the medium, v, is always considered positive.

Moving Listener and Stationary Source

Let's think first about a listener L moving with velocity v_L toward a stationary source S (Fig. 16.26). The source emits a sound wave with frequency f_S and wavelength $\lambda = v/f_S$. The figure shows four wave crests, separated by equal distances λ. The wave crests approaching the moving listener have a speed of propagation *relative to the listener* of $(v + v_L)$. So the frequency f_L with which the crests arrive at the listener's position (that is, the frequency the listener hears) is

$$f_L = \frac{v + v_L}{\lambda} = \frac{v + v_L}{v/f_S} \tag{16.25}$$

or

$$f_L = \left(\frac{v + v_L}{v}\right) f_S = \left(1 + \frac{v_L}{v}\right) f_S \quad \text{(moving listener, stationary source)} \tag{16.26}$$

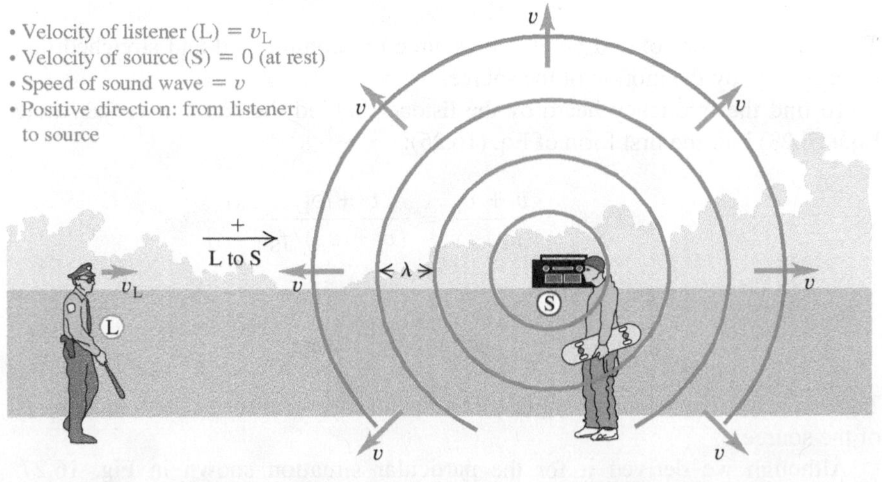

16.26 A listener moving toward a stationary source hears a frequency that is higher than the source frequency. This is because the relative speed of listener and wave is greater than the wave speed v.

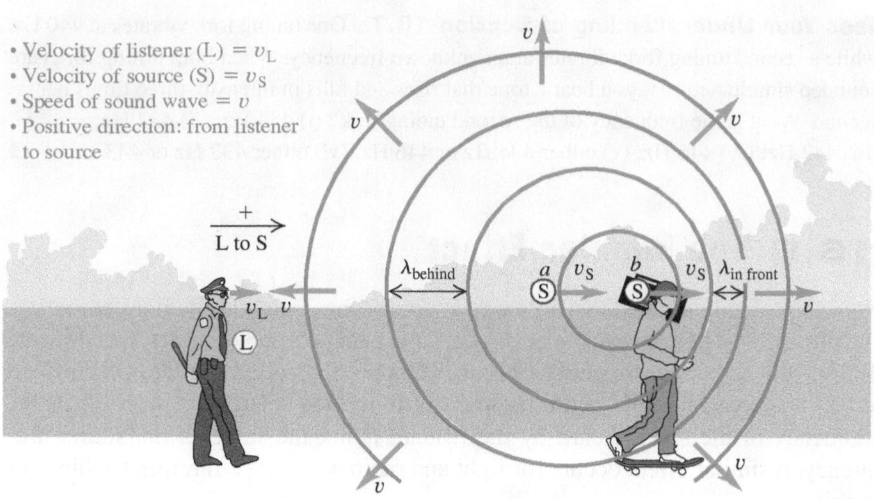

16.27 Wave crests emitted by a moving source are crowded together in front of the source (to the right of this source) and stretched out behind it (to the left of this source).

So a listener moving toward a source ($v_L > 0$), as in Fig. 16.26, hears a higher frequency (higher pitch) than does a stationary listener. A listener moving away from the source ($v_L < 0$) hears a lower frequency (lower pitch).

Moving Source and Moving Listener

Now suppose the source is also moving, with velocity v_S (Fig. 16.27). The wave speed relative to the wave medium (air) is still v; it is determined by the properties of the medium and is not changed by the motion of the source. But the wavelength is no longer equal to v/f_S. Here's why. The time for emission of one cycle of the wave is the period $T = 1/f_S$. During this time, the wave travels a distance $vT = v/f_S$ and the source moves a distance $v_S T = v_S/f_S$. The wavelength is the distance between successive wave crests, and this is determined by the *relative* displacement of source and wave. As Fig. 16.27 shows, this is different in front of and behind the source. In the region to the right of the source in Fig. 16.27 (that is, in front of the source), the wavelength is

$$\lambda_{\text{in front}} = \frac{v}{f_S} - \frac{v_S}{f_S} = \frac{v - v_S}{f_S} \quad \text{(wavelength in front of a moving source)} \tag{16.27}$$

In the region to the left of the source (that is, behind the source), it is

$$\lambda_{\text{behind}} = \frac{v + v_S}{f_S} \quad \text{(wavelength behind a moving source)} \tag{16.28}$$

The waves in front of and behind the source are compressed and stretched out, respectively, by the motion of the source.

To find the frequency heard by the listener behind the source, we substitute Eq. (16.28) into the first form of Eq. (16.25):

$$f_L = \frac{v + v_L}{\lambda_{\text{behind}}} = \frac{v + v_L}{(v + v_S)/f_S}$$

$$f_L = \frac{v + v_L}{v + v_S} f_S \quad \text{(Doppler effect, moving source and moving listener)} \tag{16.29}$$

This expresses the frequency f_L heard by the listener in terms of the frequency f_S of the source.

Although we derived it for the particular situation shown in Fig. 16.27, Eq. (16.29) includes *all* possibilities for motion of source and listener (relative to the medium) along the line joining them. If the listener happens to be at rest in the medium, v_L is zero. When both source and listener are at rest or have the same velocity relative to the medium, $v_L = v_S$ and $f_L = f_S$. Whenever the direction of the source or listener velocity is opposite to the direction from the listener toward the source (which we have defined as positive), the corresponding velocity to be used in Eq. (16.29) is negative.

As an example, the frequency heard by a listener at rest ($v_L = 0$) is $f_L = [v/(v + v_S)]f_S$. If the source is moving toward the listener (in the negative direction), then $v_S < 0$, $f_L > f_S$, and the listener hears a higher frequency than that emitted by the source. If instead the source is moving away from the listener (in the positive direction), then $v_S > 0$, $f_L < f_S$, and the listener hears a lower frequency. This explains the change in pitch that you hear from the siren of an ambulance as it passes you (Fig. 16.28).

16.28 The Doppler effect explains why the siren on a fire engine or ambulance has a high pitch ($f_L > f_S$) when it is approaching you ($v_S < 0$) and a low pitch ($f_L < f_S$) when it is moving away ($v_S > 0$).

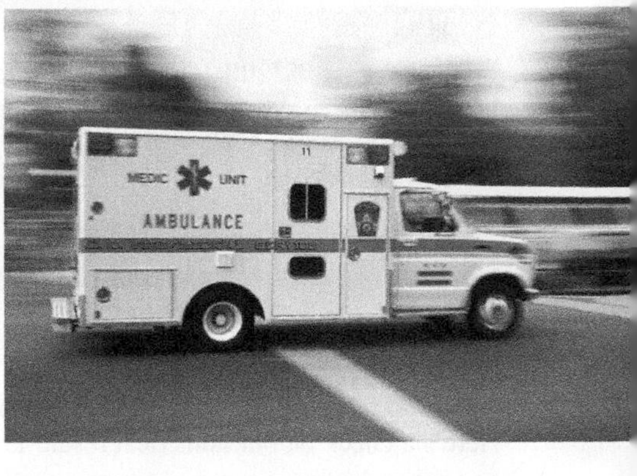

Problem-Solving Strategy 16.2 Doppler Effect

IDENTIFY *the relevant concepts:* The Doppler effect occurs whenever the source of waves, the wave detector (listener), or both are in motion.

SET UP *the problem* using the following steps:

1. Establish a coordinate system, with the positive direction from the listener toward the source. Carefully determine the signs of all relevant velocities. A velocity in the direction from the listener toward the source is positive; a velocity in the opposite direction is negative. All velocities must be measured relative to the air in which the sound travels.
2. Use consistent subscripts to identify the various quantities: S for source and L for listener.
3. Identify which unknown quantities are the target variables.

EXECUTE *the solution* as follows:

1. Use Eq. (16.29) to relate the frequencies at the source and the listener, the sound speed, and the velocities of the source and the listener according to the sign convention of step 1. If the source is moving, you can find the wavelength measured by the listener using Eq. (16.27) or (16.28).
2. When a wave is reflected from a stationary or moving surface, solve the problem in two steps. In the first, the surface is the "listener"; the frequency with which the wave crests arrive at the surface is f_L. In the second, the surface is the "source," emitting waves with this same frequency f_L. Finally, determine the frequency heard by a listener detecting this new wave.

EVALUATE *your answer:* Is the *direction* of the frequency shift reasonable? If the source and the listener are moving toward each other, $f_L > f_S$; if they are moving apart, $f_L < f_S$. If the source and the listener have no relative motion, $f_L = f_S$.

Example 16.14 Doppler effect I: Wavelengths

A police car's siren emits a sinusoidal wave with frequency $f_S = 300$ Hz. The speed of sound is 340 m/s and the air is still. (a) Find the wavelength of the waves if the siren is at rest. (b) Find the wavelengths of the waves in front of and behind the siren if it is moving at 30 m/s.

SOLUTION

IDENTIFY and SET UP: In part (a) there is no Doppler effect because neither source nor listener is moving with respect to the air; $v = \lambda f$ gives the wavelength. Figure 16.29 shows the situation in part (b): The source is in motion, so we find the wavelengths using Eqs. (16.27) and (16.28) for the Doppler effect.

EXECUTE: (a) When the source is at rest,

$$\lambda = \frac{v}{f_S} = \frac{340\ \text{m/s}}{300\ \text{Hz}} = 1.13\ \text{m}$$

16.29 Our sketch for this problem.

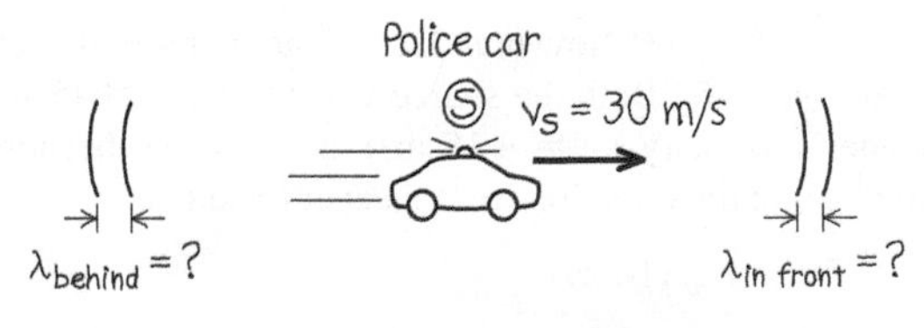

(b) From Eq. (16.27), in front of the siren

$$\lambda_{\text{in front}} = \frac{v - v_S}{f_S} = \frac{340\ \text{m/s} - 30\ \text{m/s}}{300\ \text{Hz}} = 1.03\ \text{m}$$

From Eq. (16.28), behind the siren

$$\lambda_{\text{behind}} = \frac{v + v_S}{f_S} = \frac{340\ \text{m/s} + 30\ \text{m/s}}{300\ \text{Hz}} = 1.23\ \text{m}$$

EVALUATE: The wavelength is shorter in front of the siren and longer behind it, as we expect.

Example 16.15 Doppler effect II: Frequencies

If a listener L is at rest and the siren in Example 16.14 is moving away from L at 30 m/s, what frequency does the listener hear?

SOLUTION

IDENTIFY and SET UP: Our target variable is the frequency f_L heard by a listener behind the moving source. Figure 16.30 shows the situation. We have $v_L = 0$ and $v_S = +30$ m/s (positive, since the velocity of the source is in the direction from listener to source).

EXECUTE: From Eq. (16.29),

$$f_L = \frac{v}{v + v_S} f_S = \frac{340 \text{ m/s}}{340 \text{ m/s} + 30 \text{ m/s}}(300 \text{ Hz}) = 276 \text{ Hz}$$

EVALUATE: The source and listener are moving apart, so $f_L < f_S$. Here's a check on our numerical result. From Example 16.14, the wavelength behind the source (where the listener in Fig. 16.30 is located) is 1.23 m. The wave speed relative to the stationary listener is $v = 340$ m/s even though the source is moving, so

$$f_L = \frac{v}{\lambda} = \frac{340 \text{ m/s}}{1.23 \text{ m}} = 276 \text{ Hz}$$

16.30 Our sketch for this problem.

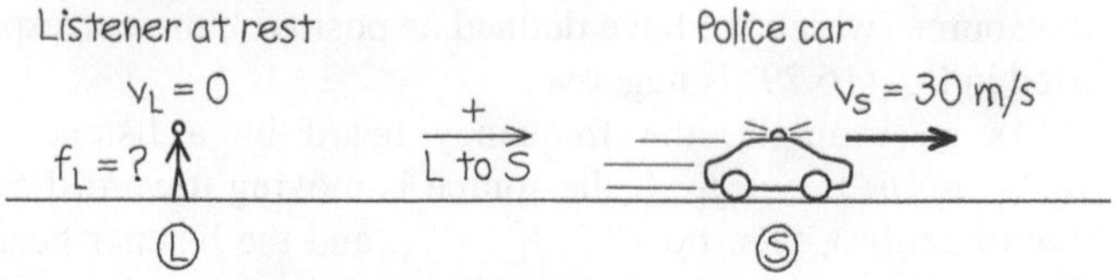

Example 16.16 Doppler effect III: A moving listener

If the siren is at rest and the listener is moving away from it at 30 m/s, what frequency does the listener hear?

SOLUTION

IDENTIFY and SET UP: Again our target variable is f_L, but now L is in motion and S is at rest. Figure 16.31 shows the situation. The velocity of the listener is $v_L = -30$ m/s (negative, since the motion is in the direction from source to listener).

EXECUTE: From Eq. (16.29),

$$f_L = \frac{v + v_L}{v} f_S = \frac{340 \text{ m/s} + (-30 \text{ m/s})}{340 \text{ m/s}}(300 \text{ Hz}) = 274 \text{ Hz}$$

16.31 Our sketch for this problem.

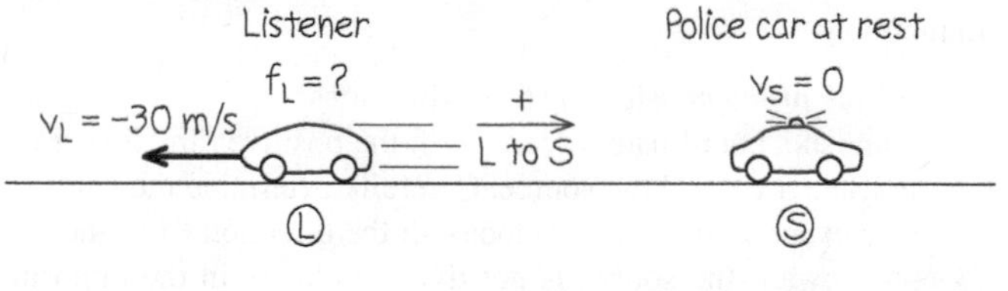

EVALUATE: Again the source and listener are moving apart, so $f_L < f_S$. Note that the *relative velocity* of source and listener is the same as in Example 16.15, but the Doppler shift is different because v_S and v_L are different.

Example 16.17 Doppler effect IV: Moving source, moving listener

The siren is moving away from the listener with a speed of 45 m/s relative to the air, and the listener is moving toward the siren with a speed of 15 m/s relative to the air. What frequency does the listener hear?

SOLUTION

IDENTIFY and SET UP: Now *both* L and S are in motion. Again our target variable is f_L. Both the source velocity $v_S = +45$ m/s and the listener's velocity $v_L = +15$ m/s are positive because both velocities are in the direction from listener to source.

EXECUTE: From Eq. (16.29),

$$f_L = \frac{v + v_L}{v + v_S} f_S = \frac{340 \text{ m/s} + 15 \text{ m/s}}{340 \text{ m/s} + 45 \text{ m/s}}(300 \text{ Hz}) = 277 \text{ Hz}$$

16.32 Our sketch for this problem.

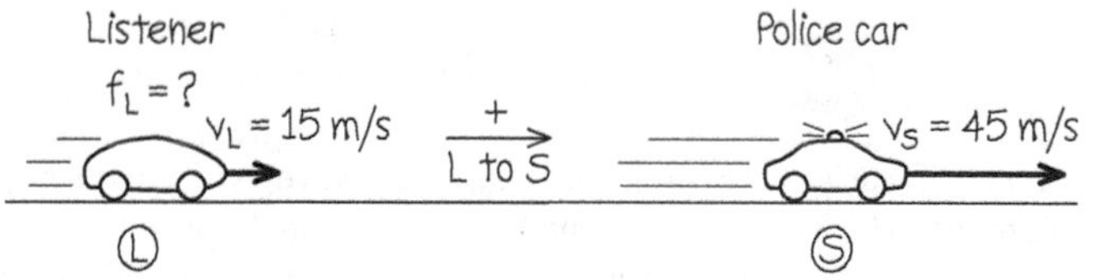

EVALUATE: As in Examples 16.15 and 16.16, the source and listener again move away from each other at 30 m/s, so again $f_L < f_S$. But f_L is different in all three cases because the Doppler effect for sound depends on how the source and listener are moving relative to the *air*, not simply on how they move relative to each other.

Example 16.18 Doppler effect V: A double Doppler shift

The police car is moving toward a warehouse at 30 m/s. What frequency does the driver hear reflected from the warehouse?

SOLUTION

IDENTIFY: In this situation there are *two* Doppler shifts (Fig. 16.33). In the first shift, the warehouse is the stationary "listener."

16.33 Two stages of the sound wave's motion from the police car to the warehouse and back to the police car.

(a) Sound travels from police car's siren (source S) to warehouse ("listener" L).

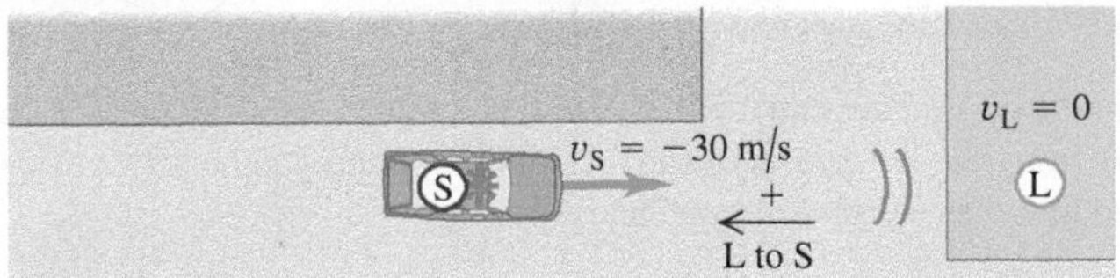

(b) Reflected sound travels from warehouse (source S) to police car (listener L).

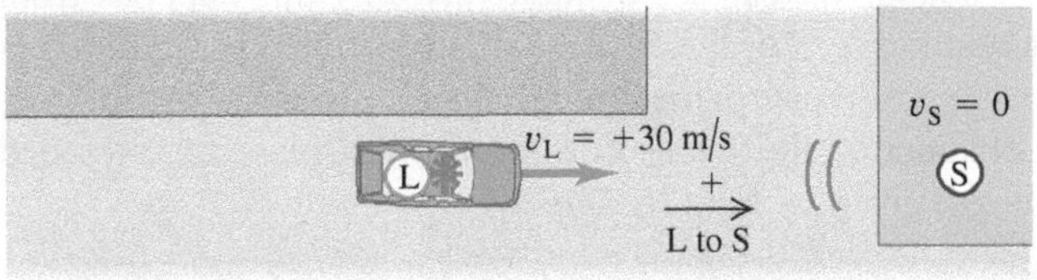

The frequency of sound reaching the warehouse, which we call f_W, is greater than 300 Hz because the source is approaching. In the second shift, the warehouse acts as a source of sound with frequency f_W, and the listener is the driver of the police car; she hears a frequency greater than f_W because she is approaching the source.

SET UP: To determine f_W, we use Eq. (16.29) with f_L replaced by f_W. For this part of the problem, $v_L = v_W = 0$ (the warehouse is at rest) and $v_S = -30$ m/s (the siren is moving in the negative direction from source to listener).

To determine the frequency heard by the driver (our target variable), we again use Eq. (16.29) but now with f_S replaced by f_W. For this second part of the problem, $v_S = 0$ because the stationary warehouse is the source and the velocity of the listener (the driver) is $v_L = +30$ m/s. (The listener's velocity is positive because it is in the direction from listener to source.)

EXECUTE: The frequency reaching the warehouse is

$$f_W = \frac{v}{v + v_S} f_S = \frac{340 \text{ m/s}}{340 \text{ m/s} + (-30 \text{ m/s})}(300 \text{ Hz}) = 329 \text{ Hz}$$

Then the frequency heard by the driver is

$$f_L = \frac{v + v_L}{v} f_W = \frac{340 \text{ m/s} + 30 \text{ m/s}}{340 \text{ m/s}}(329 \text{ Hz}) = 358 \text{ Hz}$$

EVALUATE: Because there are two Doppler shifts, the reflected sound heard by the driver has an even higher frequency than the sound heard by a stationary listener in the warehouse.

Doppler Effect for Electromagnetic Waves

In the Doppler effect for sound, the velocities v_L and v_S are always measured relative to the *air* or whatever medium we are considering. There is also a Doppler effect for *electromagnetic* waves in empty space, such as light waves or radio waves. In this case there is no medium that we can use as a reference to measure velocities, and all that matters is the *relative* velocity of source and receiver. (By contrast, the Doppler effect for sound does not depend simply on this relative velocity, as discussed in Example 16.17.)

To derive the expression for the Doppler frequency shift for light, we have to use the special theory of relativity. We will discuss this in Chapter 37, but for now we quote the result without derivation. The wave speed is the speed of light, usually denoted by c, and it is the same for both source and receiver. In the frame of reference in which the receiver is at rest, the source is moving away from the receiver with velocity v. (If the source is *approaching* the receiver, v is negative.) The source frequency is again f_S. The frequency f_R measured by the receiver R (the frequency of arrival of the waves at the receiver) is then

$$f_R = \sqrt{\frac{c - v}{c + v}}\, f_S \qquad \text{(Doppler effect for light)} \qquad (16.30)$$

When v is positive, the source is moving directly *away* from the receiver and f_R is always *less* than f_S; when v is negative, the source is moving directly *toward* the receiver and f_R is *greater* than f_S. The qualitative effect is the same as for sound, but the quantitative relationship is different.

A familiar application of the Doppler effect for radio waves is the radar device mounted on the side window of a police car to check other cars' speeds. The electromagnetic wave emitted by the device is reflected from a moving car, which acts as a moving source, and the wave reflected back to the device is Doppler-shifted in frequency. The transmitted and reflected signals are combined to produce beats, and the speed can be computed from the frequency of the beats. Similar techniques ("Doppler radar") are used to measure wind velocities in the atmosphere.

16.34 Change of velocity component along the line of sight of a satellite passing a tracking station. The frequency received at the tracking station changes from high to low as the satellite passes overhead.

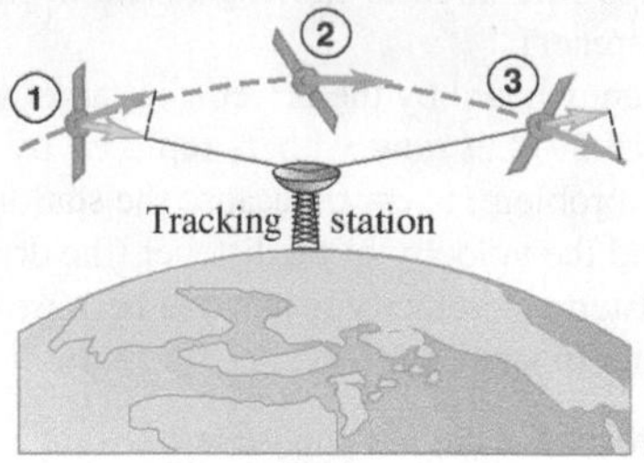

The Doppler effect is also used to track satellites and other space vehicles. In Fig. 16.34 a satellite emits a radio signal with constant frequency f_S. As the satellite orbits past, it first approaches and then moves away from the receiver; the frequency f_R of the signal received on earth changes from a value greater than f_S to a value less than f_S as the satellite passes overhead.

Test Your Understanding of Section 16.8 You are at an outdoor concert with a wind blowing at 10 m/s from the performers toward you. Is the sound you hear Doppler-shifted? If so, is it shifted to lower or higher frequencies? ❙

16.9 Shock Waves

You may have experienced "sonic booms" caused by an airplane flying overhead faster than the speed of sound. We can see qualitatively why this happens from Fig. 16.35. Let v_S denote the *speed* of the airplane relative to the air, so that it is always positive. The motion of the airplane through the air produces sound; if v_S is less than the speed of sound v, the waves in front of the airplane are crowded together with a wavelength given by Eq. (16.27):

$$\lambda_{\text{in front}} = \frac{v - v_S}{f_S}$$

As the speed v_S of the airplane approaches the speed of sound v, the wavelength approaches zero and the wave crests pile up on each other (Fig. 16.35a). The airplane must exert a large force to compress the air in front of it; by Newton's third law, the air exerts an equally large force back on the airplane. Hence there is a large increase in aerodynamic drag (air resistance) as the airplane approaches the speed of sound, a phenomenon known as the "sound barrier."

When v_S is greater in magnitude than v, the source of sound is **supersonic,** and Eqs. (16.27) and (16.29) for the Doppler effect no longer describe the sound wave in front of the source. Figure 16.35b shows a cross section of what happens. As the airplane moves, it displaces the surrounding air and produces sound. A series of wave crests is emitted from the nose of the airplane; each spreads out in a circle centered at the position of the airplane when it emitted the crest. After a time t the crest emitted from point S_1 has spread to a circle with radius vt, and the airplane has moved a greater distance $v_S t$ to position S_2. You can see that the circular crests interfere constructively at points along the blue line that makes an angle α with

16.35 Wave crests around a sound source S moving (a) slightly slower than the speed of sound v and (b) faster than the sound speed v. (c) This photograph shows a T-38 jet airplane moving at 1.1 times the speed of sound. Separate shock waves are produced by the nose, wings, and tail. The angles of these waves vary because the air speeds up and slows down as it moves around the airplane, so the relative speed v_S of the airplane and air is different for shock waves produced at different points.

(a) Sound source S (airplane) moving at nearly the speed of sound

(b) Sound source moving faster than the speed of sound

(c) Shock waves around a supersonic airplane

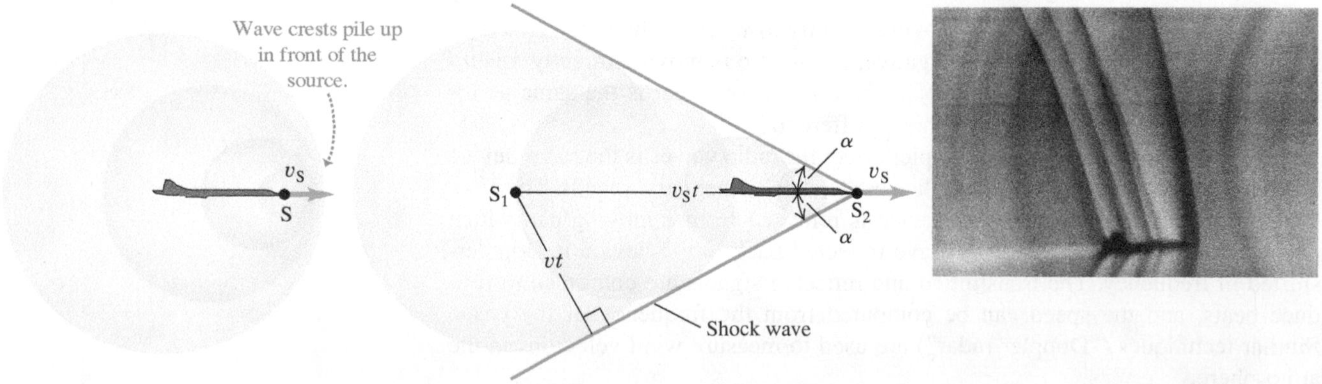

the direction of the airplane velocity, leading to a very-large-amplitude wave crest along this line. This large-amplitude crest is called a **shock wave** (Fig. 16.35c).

From the right triangle in Fig. 16.35b we can see that the angle α is given by

$$\sin\alpha = \frac{vt}{v_S t} = \frac{v}{v_S} \quad \text{(shock wave)} \tag{16.31}$$

In this relationship, v_S is the *speed* of the source (the magnitude of its velocity) relative to the air and is always positive. The ratio v_S/v is called the **Mach number.** It is greater than unity for all supersonic speeds, and $\sin\alpha$ in Eq. (16.31) is the reciprocal of the Mach number. The first person to break the sound barrier was Capt. Chuck Yeager of the U.S. Air Force, flying the Bell X-1 at Mach 1.06 on October 14, 1947 (Fig. 16.36).

16.36 The first supersonic airplane, the Bell X-1, was shaped much like a 50-caliber bullet—which was known to be able to travel faster than sound.

Shock waves are actually three-dimensional; a shock wave forms a *cone* around the direction of motion of the source. If the source (possibly a supersonic jet airplane or a rifle bullet) moves with constant velocity, the angle α is constant, and the shock-wave cone moves along with the source. It's the arrival of this shock wave that causes the sonic boom you hear after a supersonic airplane has passed by. The larger the airplane, the stronger the sonic boom; the shock wave produced at ground level by the (now retired) Concorde supersonic airliner flying at 12,000 m (40,000 ft) caused a sudden jump in air pressure of about 20 Pa. In front of the shock-wave cone, there is no sound. Inside the cone a stationary listener hears the Doppler-shifted sound of the airplane moving away.

CAUTION **Shock waves** We emphasize that a shock wave is produced *continuously* by any object that moves through the air at supersonic speed, not only at the instant that it "breaks the sound barrier." The sound waves that combine to form the shock wave, as in Fig. 16.35b, are created by the motion of the object itself, not by any sound source that the object may carry. The cracking noises of a bullet and of the tip of a circus whip are due to their supersonic motion. A supersonic jet airplane may have very loud engines, but these do not cause the shock wave. Indeed, a space shuttle makes a very loud sonic boom when coming in for a landing; its engines are out of fuel at this point, so it is a supersonic glider. ❙

Shock waves have applications outside of aviation. They are used to break up kidney stones and gallstones without invasive surgery, using a technique with the impressive name *extracorporeal shock-wave lithotripsy.* A shock wave produced outside the body is focused by a reflector or acoustic lens so that as much of it as possible converges on the stone. When the resulting stresses in the stone exceed its tensile strength, it breaks into small pieces and can be eliminated. This technique requires accurate determination of the location of the stone, which may be done using ultrasonic imaging techniques (see Fig. 16.9).

Example 16.19 Sonic boom from a supersonic airplane

An airplane is flying at Mach 1.75 at an altitude of 8000 m, where the speed of sound is 320 m/s. How long after the plane passes directly overhead will you hear the sonic boom?

SOLUTION

IDENTIFY and SET UP: The shock wave forms a cone trailing backward from the airplane, so the problem is really asking for how much time elapses from when the airplane flies overhead to when the shock wave reaches you at point L (Fig. 16.37). During the time t (our target variable) since the airplane traveling at speed v_S passed overhead, it has traveled a distance $v_S t$. Equation (16.31) gives the shock cone angle α; we use trigonometry to solve for t.

EXECUTE: From Eq. (16.31) the angle α of the shock cone is

$$\alpha = \arcsin\frac{1}{1.75} = 34.8°$$

The speed of the plane is the speed of sound multiplied by the Mach number:

$$v_S = (1.75)(320\ \text{m/s}) = 560\ \text{m/s}$$

Continued

16.37 You hear a sonic boom when the shock wave reaches you at L (*not* just when the plane breaks the sound barrier). A listener to the right of L has not yet heard the sonic boom but will shortly; a listener to the left of L has already heard the sonic boom.

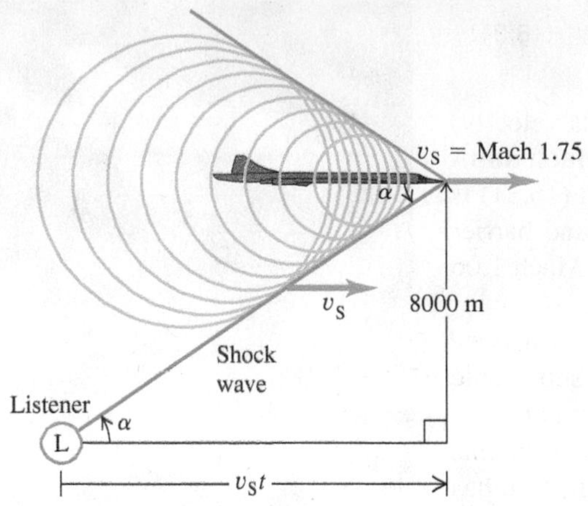

From Fig. 16.37 we have

$$\tan\alpha = \frac{8000\ \text{m}}{v_S t}$$

$$t = \frac{8000\ \text{m}}{(560\ \text{m/s})(\tan 34.8°)} = 20.5\ \text{s}$$

EVALUATE: You hear the boom 20.5 s after the airplane passes overhead, at which time it has traveled (560 m/s)(20.5 s) = 11.5 km since it passed overhead. We have assumed that the speed of sound is the same at all altitudes, so that $\alpha = \arcsin v/v_S$ is constant and the shock wave forms a perfect cone. In fact, the speed of sound decreases with increasing altitude. How would this affect the value of t?

Test Your Understanding of Section 16.9 What would you hear if you were directly behind (to the left of) the supersonic airplane in Fig. 16.37? (i) a sonic boom; (ii) the sound of the airplane, Doppler-shifted to higher frequencies; (iii) the sound of the airplane, Doppler-shifted to lower frequencies; (iv) nothing.

CHAPTER 16 SUMMARY

Sound waves: Sound consists of longitudinal waves in a medium. A sinusoidal sound wave is characterized by its frequency f and wavelength λ (or angular frequency ω and wave number k) and by its displacement amplitude A. The pressure amplitude p_{max} is directly proportional to the displacement amplitude, the wave number, and the bulk modulus B of the wave medium. (See Examples 16.1 and 16.2.)

The speed of a sound wave in a fluid depends on the bulk modulus B and density ρ. If the fluid is an ideal gas, the speed can be expressed in terms of the temperature T, molar mass M, and ratio of heat capacities γ of the gas. The speed of longitudinal waves in a solid rod depends on the density and Young's modulus Y. (See Examples 16.3 and 16.4.)

$$p_{max} = BkA \quad (16.5)$$
(sinusoidal sound wave)

$$v = \sqrt{\frac{B}{\rho}} \quad (16.7)$$
(longitudinal wave in a fluid)

$$v = \sqrt{\frac{\gamma RT}{M}} \quad (16.10)$$
(sound wave in an ideal gas)

$$v = \sqrt{\frac{Y}{\rho}} \quad (16.8)$$
(longitudinal wave in a solid rod)

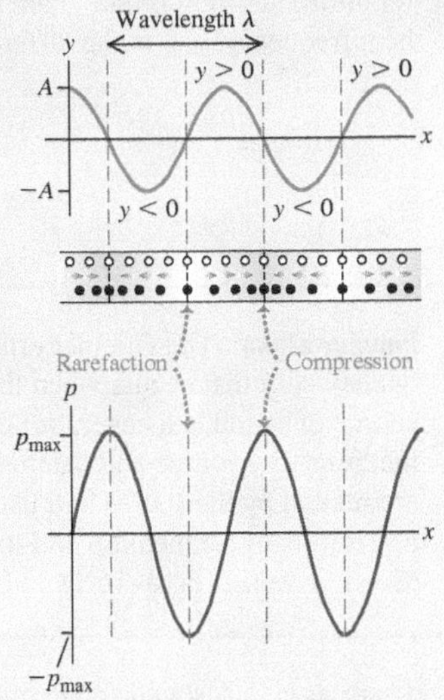

Intensity and sound intensity level: The intensity I of a sound wave is the time average rate at which energy is transported by the wave, per unit area. For a sinusoidal wave, the intensity can be expressed in terms of the displacement amplitude A or the pressure amplitude p_{max}. (See Examples 16.5–16.7.)

The sound intensity level β of a sound wave is a logarithmic measure of its intensity. It is measured relative to I_0, an arbitrary intensity defined to be $10^{-12}\ \text{W/m}^2$. Sound intensity levels are expressed in decibels (dB). (See Examples 16.8 and 16.9.)

$$I = \tfrac{1}{2}\sqrt{\rho B}\,\omega^2 A^2 = \frac{p_{max}^2}{2\rho v}$$
$$= \frac{p_{max}^2}{2\sqrt{\rho B}} \quad (16.12), (16.14)$$
(intensity of a sinusoidal sound wave)

$$\beta = (10\ \text{dB}) \log \frac{I}{I_0} \quad (16.15)$$
(definition of sound intensity level)

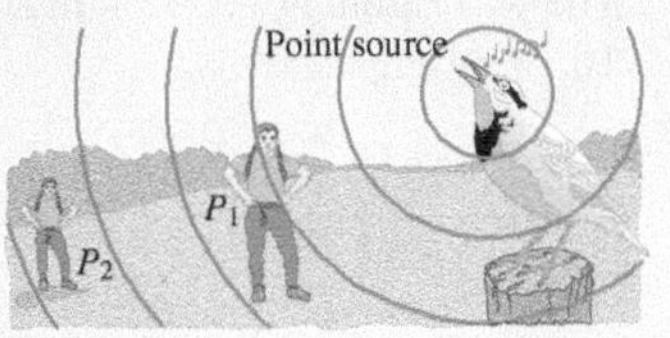

Standing sound waves: Standing sound waves can be set up in a pipe or tube. A closed end is a displacement node and a pressure antinode; an open end is a displacement antinode and a pressure node. For a pipe of length L open at both ends, the normal-mode frequencies are integer multiples of the sound speed divided by $2L$. For a stopped pipe (one that is open at only one end), the normal-mode frequencies are the odd multiples of the sound speed divided by $4L$. (See Examples 16.10 and 16.11.)

A pipe or other system with normal-mode frequencies can be driven to oscillate at any frequency. A maximum response, or resonance, occurs if the driving frequency is close to one of the normal-mode frequencies of the system. (See Example 16.12.)

$$f_n = \frac{nv}{2L} \quad (n = 1, 2, 3, \ldots) \quad (16.18)$$
(open pipe)

$$f_n = \frac{nv}{4L} \quad (n = 1, 3, 5, \ldots) \quad (16.22)$$
(stopped pipe)

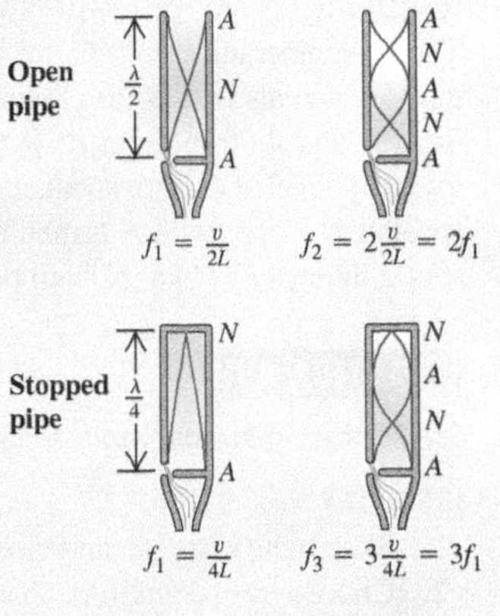

Interference: When two or more waves overlap in the same region of space, the resulting effects are called interference. The resulting amplitude can be either larger or smaller than the amplitude of each individual wave, depending on whether the waves are in phase (constructive interference) or out of phase (destructive interference). (See Example 16.13.)

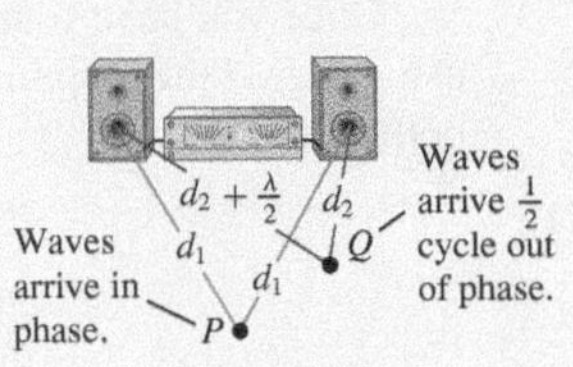

Beats: Beats are heard when two tones with slightly different frequencies f_a and f_b are sounded together. The beat frequency f_{beat} is the difference between f_a and f_b.

$$f_{beat} = f_a - f_b \quad (16.24)$$
(beat frequency)

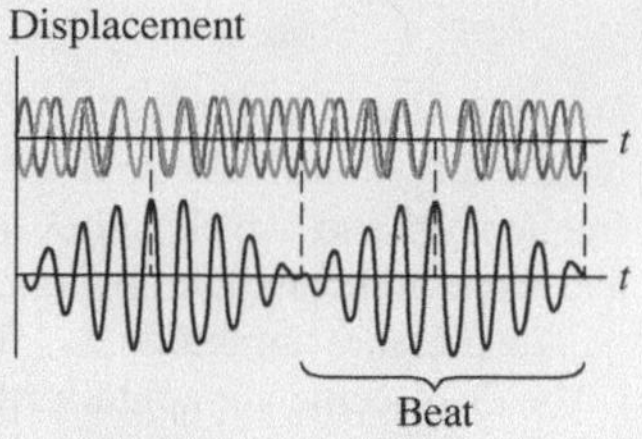

Doppler effect: The Doppler effect for sound is the frequency shift that occurs when there is motion of a source of sound, a listener, or both, relative to the medium. The source and listener frequencies f_S and f_L are related by the source and listener velocities v_S and v_L relative to the medium and to the speed of sound v. (See Examples 16.14–16.18.)

$$f_L = \frac{v + v_L}{v + v_S} f_S \quad (16.29)$$
(Doppler effect, moving source and moving listener)

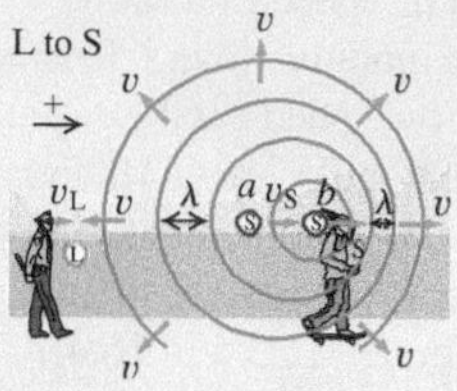

Shock waves: A sound source moving with a speed v_S greater than the speed of sound v creates a shock wave. The wave front is a cone with angle α. (See Example 16.19.)

$$\sin\alpha = \frac{v}{v_S} \quad \text{(shock wave)} \quad (16.31)$$

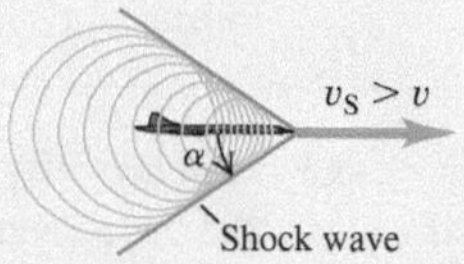

BRIDGING PROBLEM Loudspeaker Interference

Loudspeakers A and B are 7.00 m apart and vibrate in phase at 172 Hz. They radiate sound uniformly in all directions. Their acoustic power outputs are 8.00×10^{-4} W and 6.00×10^{-5} W, respectively. The air temperature is 20°C. (a) Determine the difference in phase of the two signals at a point C along the line joining A and B, 3.00 m from B and 4.00 m from A. (b) Determine the intensity and sound intensity level at C from speaker A alone (with B turned off) and from speaker B alone (with A turned off). (c) Determine the intensity and sound intensity level at C from both speakers together.

SOLUTION GUIDE

See MasteringPhysics® study area for a Video Tutor solution.

IDENTIFY and SET UP

1. Sketch the situation and label the distances between A, B, and C.
2. Choose the equations that relate power, distance from the source, intensity, pressure amplitude, and sound intensity level.
3. Decide how you will determine the phase difference in part (a). Once you have found the phase difference, how can you use it to find the amplitude of the combined wave at C due to both sources?
4. List the unknown quantities for each part of the problem and identify your target variables.

EXECUTE

5. Determine the phase difference at point C.
6. Find the intensity, sound intensity level, and pressure amplitude at C due to each speaker alone.
7. Use your results from steps 5 and 6 to find the pressure amplitude at C due to both loudspeakers together.
8. Use your result from step 7 to find the intensity and sound intensity level at C due to both loudspeakers together.

EVALUATE

9. How do your results from part (c) for intensity and sound intensity level at C compare to those from part (b)? Does this make sense?
10. What result would you have gotten in part (c) if you had (incorrectly) combined the *intensities* from A and B directly, rather than (correctly) combining the *pressure amplitudes* as you did in step 7?

Problems

For instructor-assigned homework, go to www.masteringphysics.com

•, ••, •••: Problems of increasing difficulty. **CP**: Cumulative problems incorporating material from earlier chapters. **CALC**: Problems requiring calculus. **BIO**: Biosciences problems.

DISCUSSION QUESTIONS

Q16.1 When sound travels from air into water, does the frequency of the wave change? The speed? The wavelength? Explain your reasoning.

Q16.2 The hero of a western movie listens for an oncoming train by putting his ear to the track. Why does this method give an earlier warning of the approach of a train than just listening in the usual way?

Q16.3 Would you expect the pitch (or frequency) of an organ pipe to increase or decrease with increasing temperature? Explain.

Q16.4 In most modern wind instruments the pitch is changed by using keys or valves to change the length of the vibrating air column. The bugle, however, has no valves or keys, yet it can play many notes. How might this be possible? Are there restrictions on what notes a bugle can play?

Q16.5 Symphonic musicians always "warm up" their wind instruments by blowing into them before a performance. What purpose does this serve?

Q16.6 In a popular and amusing science demonstration, a person inhales helium and then his voice becomes high and squeaky. Why does this happen? (*Warning:* Inhaling too much helium can cause unconsciousness or death.)

Q16.7 Lane dividers on highways sometimes have regularly spaced ridges or ripples. When the tires of a moving car roll along such a divider, a musical note is produced. Why? Explain how this phenomenon could be used to measure the car's speed.

Q16.8 The tone quality of an acoustic guitar is different when the strings are plucked near the bridge (the lower end of the strings) than when they are plucked near the sound hole (close to the center of the strings). Why?

Q16.9 Which has a more direct influence on the loudness of a sound wave: the *displacement* amplitude or the *pressure* amplitude? Explain your reasoning.

Q16.10 If the pressure amplitude of a sound wave is halved, by what factor does the intensity of the wave decrease? By what factor must the pressure amplitude of a sound wave be increased in order to increase the intensity by a factor of 16? Explain.

Q16.11 Does the sound intensity level β obey the inverse-square law? Why?

Q16.12 A small fraction of the energy in a sound wave is absorbed by the air through which the sound passes. How does this modify the inverse-square relationship between intensity and distance from the source? Explain your reasoning.

Q16.13 A wire under tension and vibrating in its first overtone produces sound of wavelength λ. What is the new wavelength of the sound (in terms of λ) if the tension is doubled?

Q16.14 A small metal band is slipped onto one of the tines of a tuning fork. As this band is moved closer and closer to the end of the tine, what effect does this have on the wavelength and frequency of the sound the tine produces? Why?

Q16.15 An organist in a cathedral plays a loud chord and then releases the keys. The sound persists for a few seconds and gradually dies away. Why does it persist? What happens to the sound energy when the sound dies away?

Q16.16 Two vibrating tuning forks have identical frequencies, but one is stationary and the other is mounted at the rim of a rotating platform. What does a listener hear? Explain.

Q16.17 A large church has part of the organ in the front of the church and part in the back. A person walking rapidly down the aisle while both segments are playing at once reports that the two segments sound out of tune. Why?

Q16.18 A sound source and a listener are both at rest on the earth, but a strong wind is blowing from the source toward the listener. Is there a Doppler effect? Why or why not?

Q16.19 Can you think of circumstances in which a Doppler effect would be observed for surface waves in water? For elastic waves propagating in a body of water deep below the surface? If so, describe the circumstances and explain your reasoning. If not, explain why not.

Q16.20 Stars other than our sun normally appear featureless when viewed through telescopes. Yet astronomers can readily use the light from these stars to determine that they are rotating and even measure the speed of their surface. How do you think they can do this?

Q16.21 If you wait at a railroad crossing as a train approaches and passes, you hear a Doppler shift in its sound. But if you listen closely, you hear that the change in frequency is continuous; it does not suddenly go from one high frequency to another low frequency. Instead the frequency *smoothly* (but rather quickly) changes from high to low as the train passes. Why does this smooth change occur?

Q16.22 In case 1, a source of sound approaches a stationary observer at speed v. In case 2, the observer moves toward the stationary source at the same speed v. If the source is always producing the same frequency sound, will the observer hear the same frequency in both cases, since the relative speed is the same each time? Why or why not?

Q16.23 Does an aircraft make a sonic boom only at the instant its speed exceeds Mach 1? Explain your reasoning.

Q16.24 If you are riding in a supersonic aircraft, what do you hear? Explain your reasoning. In particular, do you hear a continuous sonic boom? Why or why not?

Q16.25 A jet airplane is flying at a constant altitude at a steady speed v_S greater than the speed of sound. Describe what observers at points A, B, and C hear at the instant shown in Fig. Q16.25, when the shock wave has just reached point B. Explain your reasoning.

Figure **Q16.25**

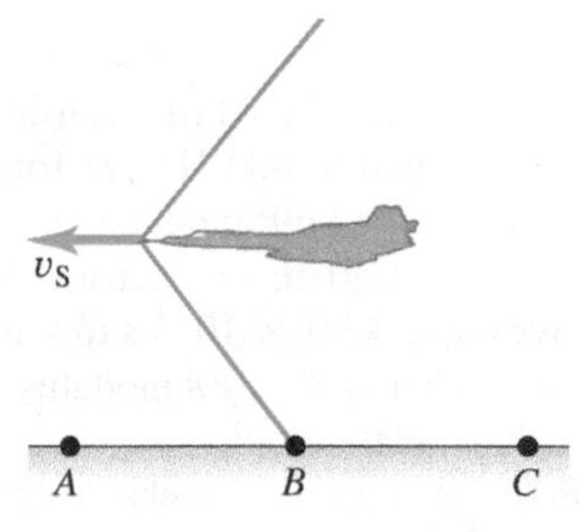

EXERCISES

Unless indicated otherwise, assume the speed of sound in air to be $v = 344$ m/s.

Section 16.1 Sound Waves

16.1 • Example 16.1 (Section 16.1) showed that for sound waves in air with frequency 1000 Hz, a displacement amplitude of

1.2×10^{-8} m produces a pressure amplitude of 3.0×10^{-2} Pa. (a) What is the wavelength of these waves? (b) For 1000-Hz waves in air, what displacement amplitude would be needed for the pressure amplitude to be at the pain threshold, which is 30 Pa? (c) For what wavelength and frequency will waves with a displacement amplitude of 1.2×10^{-8} m produce a pressure amplitude of 1.5×10^{-3} Pa?

16.2 • Example 16.1 (Section 16.1) showed that for sound waves in air with frequency 1000 Hz, a displacement amplitude of 1.2×10^{-8} m produces a pressure amplitude of 3.0×10^{-2} Pa. Water at 20°C has a bulk modulus of 2.2×10^{9} Pa, and the speed of sound in water at this temperature is 1480 m/s. For 1000-Hz sound waves in 20°C water, what displacement amplitude is produced if the pressure amplitude is 3.0×10^{-2} Pa? Explain why your answer is much less than 1.2×10^{-8} m.

16.3 • Consider a sound wave in air that has displacement amplitude 0.0200 mm. Calculate the pressure amplitude for frequencies of (a) 150 Hz; (b) 1500 Hz; (c) 15,000 Hz. In each case compare the result to the pain threshold, which is 30 Pa.

16.4 • A loud factory machine produces sound having a displacement amplitude of 1.00 μm, but the frequency of this sound can be adjusted. In order to prevent ear damage to the workers, the maximum pressure amplitude of the sound waves is limited to 10.0 Pa. Under the conditions of this factory, the bulk modulus of air is 1.42×10^{5} Pa. What is the highest-frequency sound to which this machine can be adjusted without exceeding the prescribed limit? Is this frequency audible to the workers?

16.5 • BIO **Ultrasound and Infrasound.** (a) **Whale communication.** Blue whales apparently communicate with each other using sound of frequency 17 Hz, which can be heard nearly 1000 km away in the ocean. What is the wavelength of such a sound in seawater, where the speed of sound is 1531 m/s? (b) **Dolphin clicks.** One type of sound that dolphins emit is a sharp click of wavelength 1.5 cm in the ocean. What is the frequency of such clicks? (c) **Dog whistles.** One brand of dog whistles claims a frequency of 25 kHz for its product. What is the wavelength of this sound? (d) **Bats.** While bats emit a wide variety of sounds, one type emits pulses of sound having a frequency between 39 kHz and 78 kHz. What is the range of wavelengths of this sound? (e) **Sonograms.** Ultrasound is used to view the interior of the body, much as x rays are utilized. For sharp imagery, the wavelength of the sound should be around one-fourth (or less) the size of the objects to be viewed. Approximately what frequency of sound is needed to produce a clear image of a tumor that is 1.0 mm across if the speed of sound in the tissue is 1550 m/s?

Section 16.2 Speed of Sound Waves

16.6 • (a) In a liquid with density 1300 kg/m^3, longitudinal waves with frequency 400 Hz are found to have wavelength 8.00 m. Calculate the bulk modulus of the liquid. (b) A metal bar with a length of 1.50 m has density 6400 kg/m^3. Longitudinal sound waves take 3.90×10^{-4} s to travel from one end of the bar to the other. What is Young's modulus for this metal?

16.7 • A submerged scuba diver hears the sound of a boat horn directly above her on the surface of the lake. At the same time, a friend on dry land 22.0 m from the boat also hears the horn (Fig. E16.7). The horn is 1.2 m above the surface of the water. What is the distance (labeled by "?" in Fig. E16.7) from the horn to the diver? Both air and water are at 20°C.

Figure **E16.7**

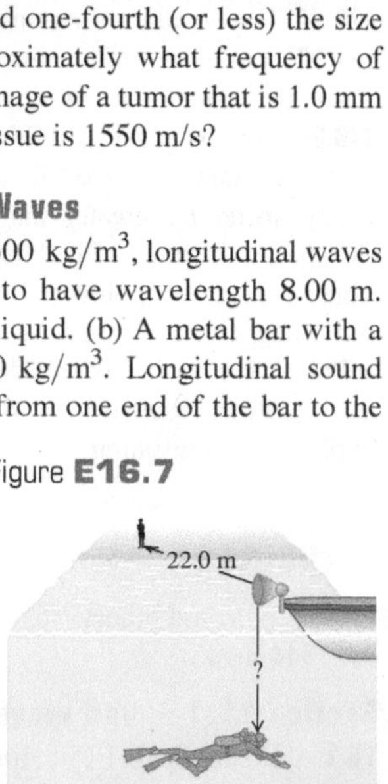

16.8 • At a temperature of 27.0°C, what is the speed of longitudinal waves in (a) hydrogen (molar mass 2.02 g/mol); (b) helium (molar mass 4.00 g/mol); (c) argon (molar mass 39.9 g/mol)? See Table 19.1 for values of γ. (d) Compare your answers for parts (a), (b), and (c) with the speed in air at the same temperature.

16.9 • An oscillator vibrating at 1250 Hz produces a sound wave that travels through an ideal gas at 325 m/s when the gas temperature is 22.0°C. For a certain experiment, you need to have the same oscillator produce sound of wavelength 28.5 cm in this gas. What should the gas temperature be to achieve this wavelength?

16.10 •• CALC (a) Show that the fractional change in the speed of sound (dv/v) due to a very small temperature change dT is given by $dv/v = \frac{1}{2}dT/T$. (*Hint:* Start with Eq. 16.10.) (b) The speed of sound in air at 20°C is found to be 344 m/s. Use the result in part (a) to find the change in the speed of sound for a 1.0°C change in air temperature.

16.11 •• An 80.0-m-long brass rod is struck at one end. A person at the other end hears two sounds as a result of two longitudinal waves, one traveling in the metal rod and the other traveling in the air. What is the time interval between the two sounds? (The speed of sound in air is 344 m/s; relevant information about brass can be found in Table 11.1 and Table 12.1.)

16.12 •• What must be the stress (F/A) in a stretched wire of a material whose Young's modulus is Y for the speed of longitudinal waves to equal 30 times the speed of transverse waves?

Section 16.3 Sound Intensity

16.13 •• BIO **Energy Delivered to the Ear.** Sound is detected when a sound wave causes the tympanic membrane (the eardrum) to vibrate. Typically, the diameter of this membrane is about 8.4 mm in humans. (a) How much energy is delivered to the eardrum each second when someone whispers (20 dB) a secret in your ear? (b) To comprehend how sensitive the ear is to very small amounts of energy, calculate how fast a typical 2.0-mg mosquito would have to fly (in mm/s) to have this amount of kinetic energy.

16.14 • Use information from Table 16.2 to answer the following questions about sound in air. At 20°C the bulk modulus for air is 1.42×10^{5} Pa and its density is 1.20 kg/m^3. At this temperature, what are the pressure amplitude (in Pa and atm) and the displacement amplitude (in m and nm) (a) for the softest sound a person can normally hear at 1000 Hz and (b) for the sound from a riveter at the same frequency? (c) How much energy per second does each wave deliver to a square 5.00 mm on a side?

16.15 •• **Longitudinal Waves in Different Fluids.** (a) A longitudinal wave propagating in a water-filled pipe has intensity 3.00×10^{-6} W/m^2 and frequency 3400 Hz. Find the amplitude A and wavelength λ of the wave. Water has density 1000 kg/m^3 and bulk modulus 2.18×10^{9} Pa. (b) If the pipe is filled with air at pressure 1.00×10^{5} Pa and density 1.20 kg/m^3, what will be the amplitude A and wavelength λ of a longitudinal wave with the same intensity and frequency as in part (a)? (c) In which fluid is the amplitude larger, water or air? What is the ratio of the two amplitudes? Why is this ratio so different from 1.00?

16.16 •• BIO **Human Hearing.** A fan at a rock concert is 30 m from the stage, and at this point the sound intensity level is 110 dB. (a) How much energy is transferred to her eardrums each second? (b) How fast would a 2.0-mg mosquito have to fly (in mm/s) to have this much kinetic energy? Compare the mosquito's speed with that found for the whisper in part (a) of Exercise 16.13.

16.17 • A sound wave in air at 20°C has a frequency of 150 Hz and a displacement amplitude of 5.00×10^{-3} mm. For this sound wave calculate the (a) pressure amplitude (in Pa); (b) intensity (in W/m^2); (c) sound intensity level (in decibels).

16.18 •• You live on a busy street, but as a music lover, you want to reduce the traffic noise. (a) If you install special sound-reflecting windows that reduce the sound intensity level (in dB) by 30 dB, by what fraction have you lowered the sound intensity (in W/m^2)? (b) If, instead, you reduce the intensity by half, what change (in dB) do you make in the sound intensity level?

16.19 • BIO For a person with normal hearing, the faintest sound that can be heard at a frequency of 400 Hz has a pressure amplitude of about 6.0×10^{-5} Pa. Calculate the (a) intensity; (b) sound intensity level; (c) displacement amplitude of this sound wave at 20°C.

16.20 •• The intensity due to a number of independent sound sources is the sum of the individual intensities. (a) When four quadruplets cry simultaneously, how many decibels greater is the sound intensity level than when a single one cries? (b) To increase the sound intensity level again by the same number of decibels as in part (a), how many more crying babies are required?

16.21 • CP A baby's mouth is 30 cm from her father's ear and 1.50 m from her mother's ear. What is the difference between the sound intensity levels heard by the father and by the mother?

16.22 •• The Sacramento City Council adopted a law to reduce the allowed sound intensity level of the much-despised leaf blowers from their current level of about 95 dB to 70 dB. With the new law, what is the ratio of the new allowed intensity to the previously allowed intensity?

16.23 •• CP At point A, 3.0 m from a small source of sound that is emitting uniformly in all directions, the sound intensity level is 53 dB. (a) What is the intensity of the sound at A? (b) How far from the source must you go so that the intensity is one-fourth of what it was at A? (c) How far must you go so that the sound intensity level is one-fourth of what it was at A? (d) Does intensity obey the inverse-square law? What about sound intensity level?

16.24 •• (a) If two sounds differ by 5.00 dB, find the ratio of the intensity of the louder sound to that of the softer one. (b) If one sound is 100 times as intense as another, by how much do they differ in sound intensity level (in decibels)? (c) If you increase the volume of your stereo so that the intensity doubles, by how much does the sound intensity level increase?

Section 16.4 Standing Sound Waves and Normal Modes

16.25 • Standing sound waves are produced in a pipe that is 1.20 m long. For the fundamental and first two overtones, determine the locations along the pipe (measured from the left end) of the displacement nodes and the pressure nodes if (a) the pipe is open at both ends and (b) the pipe is closed at the left end and open at the right end.

16.26 • The fundamental frequency of a pipe that is open at both ends is 594 Hz. (a) How long is this pipe? If one end is now closed, find (b) the wavelength and (c) the frequency of the new fundamental.

16.27 • BIO **The Human Voice.** The human vocal tract is a pipe that extends about 17 cm from the lips to the vocal folds (also called "vocal cords") near the middle of your throat. The vocal folds behave rather like the reed of a clarinet, and the vocal tract acts like a stopped pipe. Estimate the first three standing-wave frequencies of the vocal tract. Use $v = 344$ m/s. (The answers are only an estimate, since the position of lips and tongue affects the motion of air in the vocal tract.)

16.28 •• BIO **The Vocal Tract.** Many opera singers (and some pop singers) have a range of about $2\frac{1}{2}$ octaves or even greater. Suppose a soprano's range extends from A below middle C (frequency 220 Hz) up to E^b-flat above high C (frequency 1244 Hz). Although the vocal tract is quite complicated, we can model it as a resonating air column, like an organ pipe, that is open at the top and closed at the bottom. The column extends from the mouth down to the diaphragm in the chest cavity, and we can also assume that the lowest note is the fundamental. How long is this column of air if $v = 354$ m/s? Does your result seem reasonable, on the basis of observations of your own body?

16.29 •• A certain pipe produces a fundamental frequency of 262 Hz in air. (a) If the pipe is filled with helium at the same temperature, what fundamental frequency does it produce? (The molar mass of air is 28.8 g/mol, and the molar mass of helium is 4.00 g/mol.) (b) Does your answer to part (a) depend on whether the pipe is open or stopped? Why or why not?

16.30 • **Singing in the Shower.** A pipe closed at both ends can have standing waves inside of it, but you normally don't hear them because little of the sound can get out. But you *can* hear them if you are *inside* the pipe, such as someone singing in the shower. (a) Show that the wavelengths of standing waves in a pipe of length L that is closed at both ends are $\lambda_n = 2L/n$ and the frequencies are given by $f_n = nv/2L = nf_1$, where $n = 1, 2, 3, \ldots$. (b) Modeling it as a pipe, find the frequency of the fundamental and the first two overtones for a shower 2.50 m tall. Are these frequencies audible?

Section 16.5 Resonance and Sound

16.31 • You blow across the open mouth of an empty test tube and produce the fundamental standing wave of the air column inside the test tube. The speed of sound in air is 344 m/s and the test tube acts as a stopped pipe. (a) If the length of the air column in the test tube is 14.0 cm, what is the frequency of this standing wave? (b) What is the frequency of the fundamental standing wave in the air column if the test tube is half filled with water?

16.32 •• CP You have a stopped pipe of adjustable length close to a taut 85.0-cm, 7.25-g wire under a tension of 4110 N. You want to adjust the length of the pipe so that, when it produces sound at its fundamental frequency, this sound causes the wire to vibrate in its second *overtone* with very large amplitude. How long should the pipe be?

Section 16.6 Interference of Waves

16.33 • Two loudspeakers, A and B (Fig. E16.33), are driven by the same amplifier and emit sinusoidal waves in phase. Speaker B is 2.00 m to the right of speaker A. Consider point Q along the extension of the line connecting the speakers, 1.00 m to the right of speaker B. Both speakers emit sound waves that travel directly from the speaker to point Q. (a) What is the lowest frequency for which *constructive* interference occurs at point Q? (b) What is the lowest frequency for which *destructive* interference occurs at point Q?

Figure **E16.33**

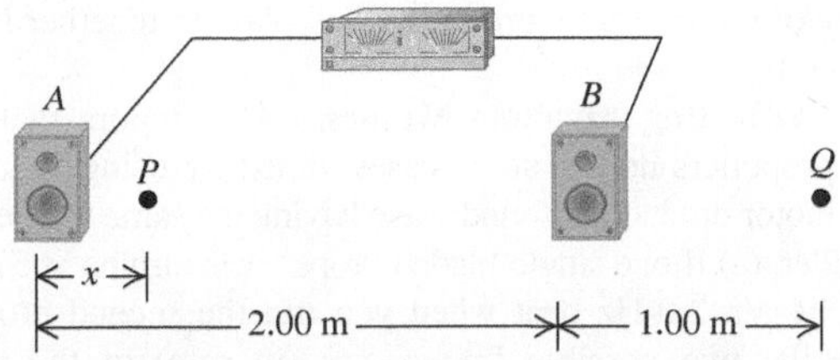

16.34 •• Two loudspeakers, A and B (see Fig. E16.33), are driven by the same amplifier and emit sinusoidal waves in phase. Speaker B is 2.00 m to the right of speaker A. The frequency of the sound waves produced by the loudspeakers is 206 Hz. Consider point P between the speakers and along the line connecting them, a distance x to the right of speaker A. Both speakers emit sound waves that travel directly from the speaker to point P. (a) For what values of x will *destructive* interference occur at point P? (b) For what values of x will *constructive* interference occur at point P? (c) Interference effects like those in parts (a) and (b) are almost never a factor in listening to home stereo equipment. Why not?

16.35 •• Two loudspeakers, A and B, are driven by the same amplifier and emit sinusoidal waves in phase. Speaker B is 12.0 m to the right of speaker A. The frequency of the waves emitted by each speaker is 688 Hz. You are standing between the speakers, along the line connecting them, and are at a point of constructive interference. How far must you walk toward speaker B to move to a point of destructive interference?

16.36 • Two loudspeakers, A and B, are driven by the same amplifier and emit sinusoidal waves in phase. The frequency of the waves emitted by each speaker is 172 Hz. You are 8.00 m from A. What is the closest you can be to B and be at a point of destructive interference?

16.37 • Two loudspeakers, A and B, are driven by the same amplifier and emit sinusoidal waves in phase. The frequency of the waves emitted by each speaker is 860 Hz. Point P is 12.0 m from A and 13.4 m from B. Is the interference at P constructive or destructive? Give the reasoning behind your answer.

16.38 •• Two small stereo speakers are driven in step by the same variable-frequency oscillator. Their sound is picked up by a microphone arranged as shown in Fig. E16.38. For what frequencies does their sound at the speakers produce (a) constructive interference and (b) destructive interference?

Figure **E16.38**

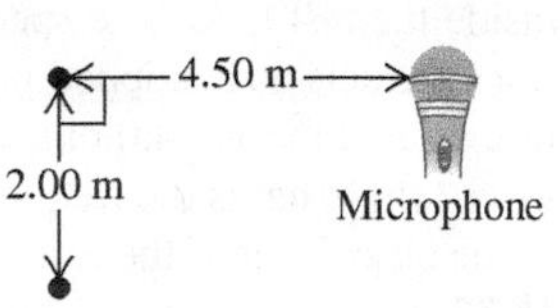

Section 16.7 Beats

16.39 •• **Tuning a Violin.** A violinist is tuning her instrument to concert A (440 Hz). She plays the note while listening to an electronically generated tone of exactly that frequency and hears a beat of frequency 3 Hz, which increases to 4 Hz when she tightens her violin string slightly. (a) What was the frequency of the note played by her violin when she heard the 3-Hz beat? (b) To get her violin perfectly tuned to concert A, should she tighten or loosen her string from what it was when she heard the 3-Hz beat?

16.40 •• Two guitarists attempt to play the same note of wavelength 6.50 cm at the same time, but one of the instruments is slightly out of tune and plays a note of wavelength 6.52 cm instead. What is the frequency of the beat these musicians hear when they play together?

16.41 •• Two organ pipes, open at one end but closed at the other, are each 1.14 m long. One is now lengthened by 2.00 cm. Find the frequency of the beat they produce when playing together in their fundamental.

16.42 •• **Adjusting Airplane Motors.** The motors that drive airplane propellers are, in some cases, tuned by using beats. The whirring motor produces a sound wave having the same frequency as the propeller. (a) If one single-bladed propeller is turning at 575 rpm and you hear a 2.0-Hz beat when you run the second propeller, what are the two possible frequencies (in rpm) of the second propeller? (b) Suppose you increase the speed of the second propeller slightly and find that the beat frequency changes to 2.1 Hz. In part (a), which of the two answers was the correct one for the frequency of the second single-bladed propeller? How do you know?

Section 16.8 The Doppler Effect

16.43 •• On the planet Arrakis a male ornithoid is flying toward his mate at 25.0 m/s while singing at a frequency of 1200 Hz. If the stationary female hears a tone of 1240 Hz, what is the speed of sound in the atmosphere of Arrakis?

16.44 •• In Example 16.18 (Section 16.8), suppose the police car is moving away from the warehouse at 20 m/s. What frequency does the driver of the police car hear reflected from the warehouse?

16.45 • Two train whistles, A and B, each have a frequency of 392 Hz. A is stationary and B is moving toward the right (away from A) at a speed of 35.0 m/s. A listener is between the two whistles and is moving toward the right with a speed of 15.0 m/s (Fig. E16.45). No wind is blowing. (a) What is the frequency from A as heard by the listener? (b) What is the frequency from B as heard by the listener? (c) What is the beat frequency detected by the listener?

Figure **E16.45**

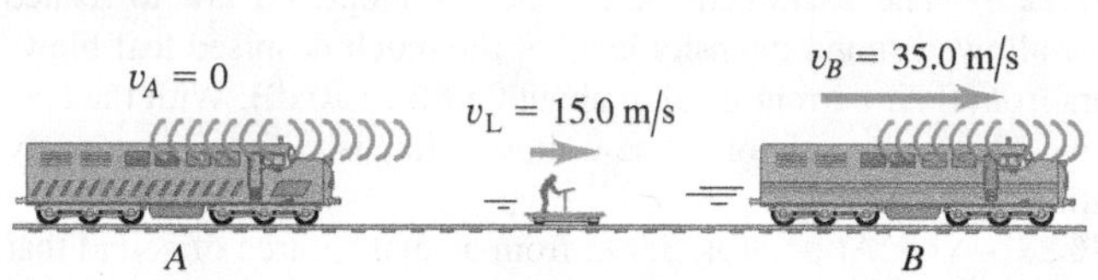

16.46 • A railroad train is traveling at 25.0 m/s in still air. The frequency of the note emitted by the locomotive whistle is 400 Hz. What is the wavelength of the sound waves (a) in front of the locomotive and (b) behind the locomotive? What is the frequency of the sound heard by a stationary listener (c) in front of the locomotive and (d) behind the locomotive?

16.47 • A swimming duck paddles the water with its feet once every 1.6 s, producing surface waves with this period. The duck is moving at constant speed in a pond where the speed of surface waves is 0.32 m/s, and the crests of the waves ahead of the duck are spaced 0.12 m apart. (a) What is the duck's speed? (b) How far apart are the crests behind the duck?

16.48 • **Moving Source vs. Moving Listener.** (a) A sound source producing 1.00-kHz waves moves toward a stationary listener at one-half the speed of sound. What frequency will the listener hear? (b) Suppose instead that the source is stationary and the listener moves toward the source at one-half the speed of sound. What frequency does the listener hear? How does your answer compare to that in part (a)? Explain on physical grounds why the two answers differ.

16.49 • A car alarm is emitting sound waves of frequency 520 Hz. You are on a motorcycle, traveling directly away from the car. How fast must you be traveling if you detect a frequency of 490 Hz?

16.50 • A railroad train is traveling at 30.0 m/s in still air. The frequency of the note emitted by the train whistle is 262 Hz. What frequency is heard by a passenger on a train moving in the opposite direction to the first at 18.0 m/s and (a) approaching the first and (b) receding from the first?

16.51 • Two swift canaries fly toward each other, each moving at 15.0 m/s relative to the ground, each warbling a note of frequency 1750 Hz. (a) What frequency note does each bird hear from the other one? (b) What wavelength will each canary measure for the note from the other one?

16.52 •• The siren of a fire engine that is driving northward at 30.0 m/s emits a sound of frequency 2000 Hz. A truck in front of this fire engine is moving northward at 20.0 m/s. (a) What is the frequency of the siren's sound that the fire engine's driver hears reflected from the back of the truck? (b) What wavelength would this driver measure for these reflected sound waves?

16.53 •• How fast (as a percentage of light speed) would a star have to be moving so that the frequency of the light we receive from it is 10.0% higher than the frequency of the light it is emitting? Would it be moving away from us or toward us? (Assume it is moving either directly away from us or directly toward us.)

16.54 • **Extrasolar Planets.** In the not-too-distant future, it should be possible to detect the presence of planets moving around other stars by measuring the Doppler shift in the infrared light they emit. If a planet is going around its star at 50.00 km/s while emitting infrared light of frequency 3.330×10^{14} Hz, what frequency light will be received from this planet when it is moving directly away from us? (*Note:* Infrared light is light having wavelengths longer than those of visible light.)

Section 16.9 Shock Waves

16.55 •• A jet plane flies overhead at Mach 1.70 and at a constant altitude of 950 m. (a) What is the angle α of the shock-wave cone? (b) How much time after the plane passes directly overhead do you hear the sonic boom? Neglect the variation of the speed of sound with altitude.

16.56 • The shock-wave cone created by the space shuttle at one instant during its reentry into the atmosphere makes an angle of 58.0° with its direction of motion. The speed of sound at this altitude is 331 m/s. (a) What is the Mach number of the shuttle at this instant, and (b) how fast (in m/s and in mi/h) is it traveling relative to the atmosphere? (c) What would be its Mach number and the angle of its shock-wave cone if it flew at the same speed but at low altitude where the speed of sound is 344 m/s?

PROBLEMS

16.57 ••• **CP** Two identical taut strings under the same tension F produce a note of the same fundamental frequency f_0. The tension in one of them is now increased by a very small amount ΔF. (a) If they are played together in their fundamental, show that the frequency of the beat produced is $f_{beat} = f_0(\Delta F/2F)$. (b) Two identical violin strings, when in tune and stretched with the same tension, have a fundamental frequency of 440.0 Hz. One of the strings is retuned by increasing its tension. When this is done, 1.5 beats per second are heard when both strings are plucked simultaneously at their centers. By what percentage was the string tension changed?

16.58 •• **CALC** (a) Defend the following statement: "In a sinusoidal sound wave, the pressure variation given by Eq. (16.4) is greatest where the displacement given by Eq. (16.1) is zero." (b) For a sinusoidal sound wave given by Eq. (16.1) with amplitude $A = 10.0\ \mu\text{m}$ and wavelength $\lambda = 0.250$ m, graph the displacement y and pressure fluctuation p as functions of x at time $t = 0$. Show at least two wavelengths of the wave on your graphs. (c) The displacement y in a *non*sinusoidal sound wave is shown in Fig. P16.58 as a function of x for $t = 0$. Draw a graph showing the pressure fluctuation p in this wave as a function of x at $t = 0$. This sound wave has the same 10.0-μm amplitude as the wave in part (b). Does it have the same pressure amplitude? Why or why not? (d) Is the statement in part (a) necessarily true if the sound wave is *not* sinusoidal? Explain your reasoning.

Figure **P16.58**

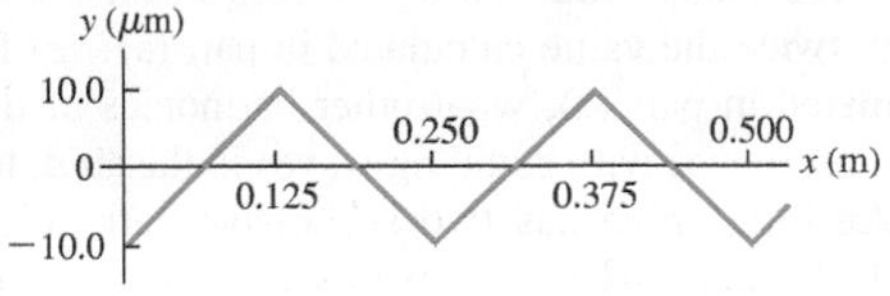

16.59 •• A soprano and a bass are singing a duet. While the soprano sings an A-sharp at 932 Hz, the bass sings an A-sharp but three octaves lower. In this concert hall, the density of air is $1.20\ \text{kg/m}^3$ and its bulk modulus is 1.42×10^5 Pa. In order for their notes to have the same sound intensity level, what must be (a) the ratio of the pressure amplitude of the bass to that of the soprano and (b) the ratio of the displacement amplitude of the bass to that of the soprano? (c) What displacement amplitude (in m and in nm) does the soprano produce to sing her A-sharp at 72.0 dB?

16.60 •• **CP** The sound from a trumpet radiates uniformly in all directions in 20°C air. At a distance of 5.00 m from the trumpet the sound intensity level is 52.0 dB. The frequency is 587 Hz. (a) What is the pressure amplitude at this distance? (b) What is the displacement amplitude? (c) At what distance is the sound intensity level 30.0 dB?

16.61 ••• **A Thermometer.** Suppose you have a tube of length L containing a gas whose temperature you want to take, but you cannot get inside the tube. One end is closed, and the other end is open but a small speaker producing sound of variable frequency is at that end. You gradually increase the frequency of the speaker until the sound from the tube first becomes very loud. With further increase of the frequency, the loudness decreases but then gets very loud again at still higher frequencies. Call f_0 the lowest frequency at which the sound is very loud. (a) Show that the absolute temperature of this gas is given by $T = 16ML^2f_0^2/\gamma R$, where M is the molar mass of the gas, γ is the ratio of its heat capacities, and R is the ideal gas constant. (b) At what frequency above f_0 will the sound from the tube next reach a maximum in loudness? (c) How could you determine the speed of sound in this tube at temperature T?

16.62 •• **CP** A uniform 165-N bar is supported horizontally by two identical wires A and B (Fig. P16.62). A small 185-N cube of lead is placed three-fourths of the way from A to B. The wires are each 75.0 cm long and have a mass of 5.50 g. If both of them are simultaneously plucked at the center, what is the frequency of the beats that they will produce when vibrating in their fundamental?

Figure **P16.62**

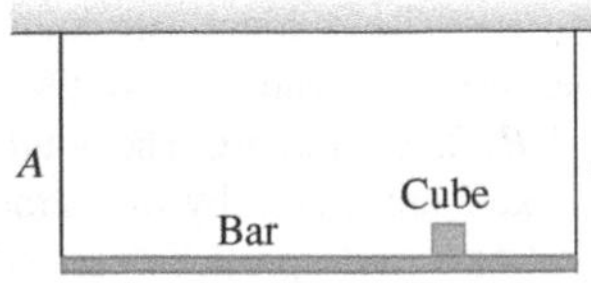

16.63 • **CP** A person is playing a small flute 10.75 cm long, open at one end and closed at the other, near a taut string having a fundamental frequency of 600.0 Hz. If the speed of sound is 344.0 m/s, for which harmonics of the flute will the string resonate? In each case, which harmonic of the string is in resonance?

16.64 ••• **CP** **A New Musical Instrument.** You have designed a new musical instrument of very simple construction. Your design consists of a metal tube with length L and diameter $L/10$. You have stretched a string of mass per unit length μ across the open end of the tube. The other end of the tube is closed. To produce the musical effect you're looking for, you want the frequency of the third-harmonic standing wave on the string to be the same as the fundamental frequency for sound waves in the air column in the tube. The speed of sound waves in this air column is v_s. (a) What must be the tension of the string to produce the desired effect? (b) What happens to the sound produced by the instrument if the tension is changed to twice the value calculated in part (a)? (c) For the tension calculated in part (a), what other harmonics of the string, if any, are in resonance with standing waves in the air column?

16.65 • An organ pipe has two successive harmonics with frequencies 1372 and 1764 Hz. (a) Is this an open or a stopped pipe? Explain. (b) What two harmonics are these? (c) What is the length of the pipe?

16.66 • **Longitudinal Standing Waves in a Solid.** Longitudinal standing waves can be produced in a solid rod by holding it at some point between the fingers of one hand and stroking it with the other hand. The rod oscillates with antinodes at both ends. (a) Why are the ends antinodes and not nodes? (b) The fundamental frequency can be obtained by stroking the rod while it is held at its center. Explain why this is the *only* place to hold the rod to obtain the fundamental. (c) Calculate the fundamental frequency of a steel rod of length 1.50 m (see Table 16.1). (d) What is the next possible standing-wave frequency of this rod? Where should the rod be held to excite a standing wave of this frequency?

16.67 •• A long tube contains air at a pressure of 1.00 atm and a temperature of 77.0°C. The tube is open at one end and closed at the other by a movable piston. A tuning fork near the open end is vibrating with a frequency of 500 Hz. Resonance is produced when the piston is at distances 18.0, 55.5, and 93.0 cm from the open end. (a) From these measurements, what is the speed of sound in air at 77.0°C? (b) From the result of part (a), what is the value of γ? (c) These data show that a displacement antinode is slightly outside of the open end of the tube. How far outside is it?

16.68 ••• The frequency of the note F_4 is 349 Hz. (a) If an organ pipe is open at one end and closed at the other, what length must it have for its fundamental mode to produce this note at 20.0°C? (b) At what air temperature will the frequency be 370 Hz, corresponding to a rise in pitch from F to F-sharp? (Ignore the change in length of the pipe due to the temperature change.)

16.69 • A standing wave with a frequency of 1100 Hz in a column of methane (CH_4) at 20.0°C produces nodes that are 0.200 m apart. What is the value of γ for methane? (The molar mass of methane is 16.0 g/mol.)

16.70 •• Two identical loudspeakers are located at points A and B, 2.00 m apart. The loudspeakers are driven by the same amplifier and produce sound waves with a frequency of 784 Hz. Take the speed of sound in air to be 344 m/s. A small microphone is moved out from point B along a line perpendicular to the line connecting A and B (line BC in Fig. P16.70). (a) At what distances from B will there be *destructive* interference? (b) At what distances from B will there be *constructive* interference? (c) If the frequency is made low enough, there will be no positions along the line BC at which destructive interference occurs. How low must the frequency be for this to be the case?

Figure **P16.70**

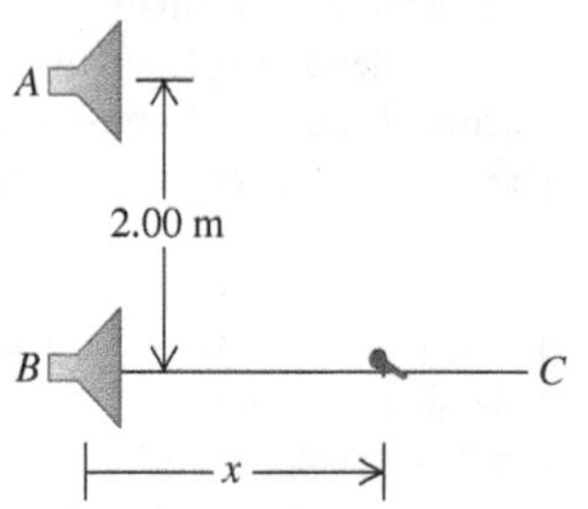

16.71 • **Wagnerian Opera.** A man marries a great Wagnerian soprano but, alas, he discovers he cannot stand Wagnerian opera. In order to save his eardrums, the unhappy man decides he must silence his larklike wife for good. His plan is to tie her to the front of his car and send car and soprano speeding toward a brick wall. This soprano is quite shrewd, however, having studied physics in her student days at the music conservatory. She realizes that this wall has a resonant frequency of 600 Hz, which means that if a continuous sound wave of this frequency hits the wall, it will fall down, and she will be saved to sing more Isoldes. The car is heading toward the wall at a high speed of 30 m/s. (a) At what frequency must the soprano sing so that the wall will crumble? (b) What frequency will the soprano hear reflected from the wall just before it crumbles?

16.72 •• A bat flies toward a wall, emitting a steady sound of frequency 1.70 kHz. This bat hears its own sound plus the sound reflected by the wall. How fast should the bat fly in order to hear a beat frequency of 10.0 Hz?

16.73 •• CP A person leaning over a 125-m-deep well accidentally drops a siren emitting sound of frequency 2500 Hz. Just before this siren hits the bottom of the well, find the frequency and wavelength of the sound the person hears (a) coming directly from the siren and (b) reflected off the bottom of the well. (c) What beat frequency does this person perceive?

16.74 ••• BIO **Ultrasound in Medicine.** A 2.00-MHz sound wave travels through a pregnant woman's abdomen and is reflected from the fetal heart wall of her unborn baby. The heart wall is moving toward the sound receiver as the heart beats. The reflected sound is then mixed with the transmitted sound, and 72 beats per second are detected. The speed of sound in body tissue is 1500 m/s. Calculate the speed of the fetal heart wall at the instant this measurement is made.

16.75 •• The sound source of a ship's sonar system operates at a frequency of 22.0 kHz. The speed of sound in water (assumed to be at a uniform 20°C) is 1482 m/s. (a) What is the wavelength of the waves emitted by the source? (b) What is the difference in frequency between the directly radiated waves and the waves reflected from a whale traveling directly toward the ship at 4.95 m/s? The ship is at rest in the water.

16.76 • CP A police siren of frequency f_{siren} is attached to a vibrating platform. The platform and siren oscillate up and down in simple harmonic motion with amplitude A_p and frequency f_p. (a) Find the maximum and minimum sound frequencies that you would hear at a position directly above the siren. (b) At what point in the motion of the platform is the maximum frequency heard? The minimum frequency? Explain.

16.77 ••• BIO Horseshoe bats (genus *Rhinolophus*) emit sounds from their nostrils and then listen to the frequency of the sound reflected from their prey to determine the prey's speed. (The "horseshoe" that gives the bat its name is a depression around the nostrils that acts like a focusing mirror, so that the bat emits sound in a narrow beam like a flashlight.) A *Rhinolophus* flying at speed v_{bat} emits sound of frequency f_{bat}; the sound it hears reflected from an insect flying toward it has a higher frequency f_{refl}. (a) Show that the speed of the insect is

$$v_{insect} = v\left[\frac{f_{refl}(v - v_{bat}) - f_{bat}(v + v_{bat})}{f_{refl}(v - v_{bat}) + f_{bat}(v + v_{bat})}\right]$$

where v is the speed of sound. (b) If $f_{bat} = 80.7$ kHz, $f_{refl} = 83.5$ kHz, and $v_{bat} = 3.9$ m/s, calculate the speed of the insect.

16.78 •• (a) Show that Eq. (16.30) can be written as

$$f_R = f_S\left(1 - \frac{v}{c}\right)^{1/2}\left(1 + \frac{v}{c}\right)^{-1/2}$$

(b) Use the binomial theorem to show that if $v \ll c$, this is approximately equal to

$$f_R = f_S\left(1 - \frac{v}{c}\right)$$

(c) A pilotless reconnaissance aircraft emits a radio signal with a frequency of 243 MHz. It is flying directly toward a test engineer on the ground. The engineer detects beats between the received signal and a local signal also of frequency 243 MHz. The beat frequency is 46.0 Hz. What is the speed of the aircraft? (Radio waves travel at the speed of light, $c = 3.00 \times 10^8$ m/s.)

16.79 •• **Supernova!** The gas cloud known as the Crab Nebula can be seen with even a small telescope. It is the remnant of a *supernova,* a cataclysmic explosion of a star. The explosion was seen on the earth on July 4, 1054 C.E. The streamers glow with the characteristic red color of heated hydrogen gas. In a laboratory on the earth, heated hydrogen produces red light with frequency 4.568×10^{14} Hz; the red light received from streamers in the Crab Nebula pointed toward the earth has frequency 4.586×10^{14} Hz. (a) Estimate the speed with which the outer edges of the Crab Nebula are expanding. Assume that the speed of the center of the nebula relative to the earth is negligible. (You may use the formulas derived in Problem 16.78. The speed of light is 3.00×10^8 m/s.) (b) Assuming that the expansion speed has been constant since the supernova explosion, estimate the diameter of the Crab Nebula. Give your answer in meters and in light-years. (c) The angular diameter of the Crab Nebula as seen from earth is about 5 arc minutes (1 arc minute $= \frac{1}{60}$ degree). Estimate the distance (in light-years) to the Crab Nebula, and estimate the year in which the supernova explosion actually took place.

16.80 •• **CP** A turntable 1.50 m in diameter rotates at 75 rpm. Two speakers, each giving off sound of wavelength 31.3 cm, are attached to the rim of the table at opposite ends of a diameter. A listener stands in front of the turntable. (a) What is the greatest beat frequency the listener will receive from this system? (b) Will the listener be able to distinguish individual beats?

16.81 •• A woman stands at rest in front of a large, smooth wall. She holds a vibrating tuning fork of frequency f_0 directly in front of her (between her and the wall). (a) The woman now runs toward the wall with speed v_W. She detects beats due to the interference between the sound waves reaching her directly from the fork and those reaching her after being reflected from the wall. How many beats per second will she detect? (*Note:* If the beat frequency is too large, the woman may have to use some instrumentation other than her ears to detect and count the beats.) (b) If the woman instead runs away from the wall, holding the tuning fork at her back so it is between her and the wall, how many beats per second will she detect?

16.82 •• On a clear day you see a jet plane flying overhead. From the apparent size of the plane, you determine that it is flying at a constant altitude h. You hear the sonic boom at time T after the plane passes directly overhead. Show that if the speed of sound v is the same at all altitudes, the speed of the plane is

$$v_S = \frac{hv}{\sqrt{h^2 - v^2T^2}}$$

(*Hint:* Trigonometric identities will be useful.)

CHALLENGE PROBLEMS

16.83 ••• **CALC** Figure P16.83 shows the pressure fluctuation p of a nonsinusoidal sound wave as a function of x for $t = 0$. The wave is traveling in the $+x$-direction. (a) Graph the pressure fluctuation p as a function of t for $x = 0$. Show at least two cycles of oscillation. (b) Graph the displacement y in this sound wave as a function of x at $t = 0$. At $x = 0$, the displacement at $t = 0$ is zero. Show at least two wavelengths of the wave. (c) Graph the displacement y as a function of t for $x = 0$. Show at least two cycles of oscillation. (d) Calculate the maximum velocity and the maximum acceleration of an element of the air through which this sound wave is traveling. (e) Describe how the cone of a loudspeaker must move as a function of time to produce the sound wave in this problem.

Figure **P16.83**

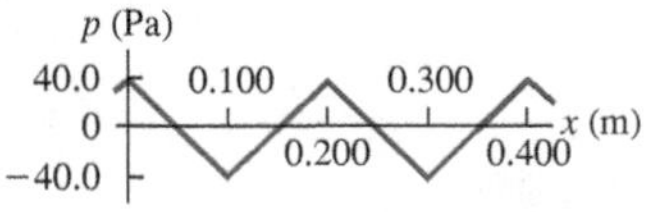

16.84 ••• **CP Longitudinal Waves on a Spring.** A long spring such as a Slinky™ is often used to demonstrate longitudinal waves. (a) Show that if a spring that obeys Hooke's law has mass m, length L, and force constant k', the speed of longitudinal waves on the spring is $v = L\sqrt{k'/m}$. (see Section 16.2). (b) Evaluate v for a spring with $m = 0.250$ kg, $L = 2.00$ m, and $k' = 1.50$ N/m.

Answers

Chapter Opening Question ?

Both musical sound and noise are made up of a combination of sinusoidal sound waves. The difference is that the frequencies of the sine waves in musical sound are all integer multiples of a fundamental frequency, while *all* frequencies are present in noise.

Test Your Understanding Questions

16.1 Answer: (v) From Eq. (16.5), the displacement amplitude is $A = p_{max}/Bk$. The pressure amplitude p_{max} and bulk modulus B remain the same, but the frequency f increases by a factor of 4. Hence the wave number $k = \omega/v = 2\pi f/v$ also increases by a factor of 4. Since A is inversely proportional to k, the displacement amplitude becomes $\frac{1}{4}$ as great. In other words, at higher frequency a smaller maximum displacement is required to produce the same maximum pressure fluctuation.

16.2 Answer: (i) From Eq. (16.7), the speed of longitudinal waves (sound) in a fluid is $v = \sqrt{B/\rho}$. We can rewrite this to give an expression for the bulk modulus B in terms of the fluid density ρ and the sound speed v: $B = \rho v^2$. At 20°C the speed of sound in mercury is slightly less than in water (1451 m/s versus 1482 m/s), but the density of mercury is greater than that of water by a large factor (13.6). Hence the bulk modulus of mercury is greater than that of water by a factor of $(13.6)(1451/1482)^2 = 13.0$.

16.3 Answer: A and p_{max} increase by a factor of $\sqrt{2}$, B and v are unchanged, β increases by 3.0 dB Equations (16.9) and (16.10) show that the bulk modulus B and sound speed v remain the same because the physical properties of the air are unchanged. From Eqs. (16.12) and (16.14), the intensity is proportional to the square of the displacement amplitude or the square of the pressure amplitude. Hence doubling the intensity means that A and p_{max} both increase by a factor of $\sqrt{2}$. Example 16.9 shows that *multiplying* the intensity by a factor of $2 (I_2/I_1 = 2)$ corresponds to *adding* to the sound intensity level by $(10\text{ dB})\log(I_2/I_1) = (10\text{ dB})\log 2 = 3.0\text{ dB}$.

16.4 Answer: (ii) Helium is less dense and has a lower molar mass than air, so sound travels faster in helium than in air. The normal-mode frequencies for a pipe are proportional to the sound speed v, so the frequency and hence the pitch increase when the air in the pipe is replaced with helium.

16.5 Answer: (i) and (iv) There will be a resonance if 660 Hz is one of the pipe's normal-mode frequencies. A stopped organ pipe has normal-mode frequencies that are odd multiples of its fundamental frequency [see Eq. (16.22) and Fig. 16.18]. Hence pipe (i), which has fundamental frequency 220 Hz, also has a normal-mode frequency of $3(220\text{ Hz}) = 660\text{ Hz}$. Pipe (ii) has twice the length of pipe (i); from Eq. (16.20), the fundamental frequency of a stopped pipe is inversely proportional to the length, so pipe (ii) has a fundamental frequency of $\left(\frac{1}{2}\right)(220\text{ Hz}) = 110\text{ Hz}$. Its other normal-mode frequencies are 330 Hz, 550 Hz, 770 Hz, . . . , so a 660-Hz tuning fork will not cause resonance. Pipe (iii) is an open pipe of the same length as pipe (i), so its fundamental frequency is twice as great as for pipe (i) [compare Eqs. (16.16) and (16.20)], or $2(220\text{ Hz}) = 440\text{ Hz}$. Its other normal-mode frequencies are integer multiples of the fundamental frequency [see Eq. (16.19)], or 880 Hz, 1320 Hz, . . . , none of which match the 660-Hz frequency of the tuning fork. Pipe (iv) is also an open pipe but with twice the length of pipe (iii) [see Eq. (16.18)], so its normal-mode frequencies are one-half those of pipe (iii): 220 Hz, 440 Hz, 660 Hz, . . . , so the third harmonic will resonate with the tuning fork.

16.6 Answer: (iii) Constructive and destructive interference between two waves can occur only if the two waves have the same frequency. In this case the frequencies are different, so there are no points where the two waves always reinforce each other (constructive interference) or always cancel each other (destructive interference).

16.7 Answer: (vi) The beat frequency is 3 Hz, so the difference between the two tuning fork frequencies is also 3 Hz. Hence the second tuning fork vibrates at a frequency of either 443 Hz or 437 Hz. You can distinguish between the two possibilities by comparing the pitches of the two tuning forks sounded one at a time: The frequency is 437 Hz if the second tuning fork has a lower pitch and 443 Hz if it has a higher pitch.

16.8 Answer: no The air (the medium for sound waves) is moving from the source toward the listener. Hence, relative to the air, both the source and the listener are moving in the direction from listener to source. So both velocities are positive and $v_S = v_L = +10\text{ m/s}$. The equality of these two velocities means that the numerator and the denominator in Eq. (16.29) are the same, so $f_L = f_S$ and there is *no* Doppler shift.

16.9 Answer: (iii) Figure 16.37 shows that there are sound waves inside the cone of the shock wave. Behind the airplane the wave crests are spread apart, just as they are behind the moving source in Fig. 16.27. Hence the waves that reach you have an increased wavelength and a lower frequency.

Bridging Problem

Answers: (a) $180° = \pi\text{ rad}$
(b) A alone: $I = 3.98 \times 10^{-6}\text{ W/m}^2$, $\beta = 66.0\text{ dB}$;
B alone: $I = 5.31 \times 10^{-7}\text{ W/m}^2$, $\beta = 57.2\text{ dB}$
(c) $I = 1.60 \times 10^{-6}\text{ W/m}^2$, $\beta = 62.1\text{ dB}$

ELECTROMAGNETIC WAVES

32

? Metal objects reflect not only visible light but also radio waves. What aspect of metals makes them so reflective?

LEARNING GOALS

By studying this chapter, you will learn:

- Why there are both electric and magnetic fields in a light wave.
- How the speed of light is related to the fundamental constants of electricity and magnetism.
- How to describe the propagation of a sinusoidal electromagnetic wave.
- What determines the amount of power carried by an electromagnetic wave.
- How to describe standing electromagnetic waves.

What is light? This question has been asked by humans for centuries, but there was no answer until electricity and magnetism were unified into *electromagnetism,* as described by Maxwell's equations. These equations show that a time-varying magnetic field acts as a source of electric field and that a time-varying electric field acts as a source of magnetic field. These $\vec{E}$ and $\vec{B}$ fields can sustain each other, forming an *electromagnetic wave* that propagates through space. Visible light emitted by the glowing filament of a light bulb is one example of an electromagnetic wave; other kinds of electromagnetic waves are produced by TV and radio stations, x-ray machines, and radioactive nuclei.

In this chapter we'll use Maxwell's equations as the theoretical basis for understanding electromagnetic waves. We'll find that these waves carry both energy and momentum. In sinusoidal electromagnetic waves, the $\vec{E}$ and $\vec{B}$ fields are sinusoidal functions of time and position, with a definite frequency and wavelength. Visible light, radio, x rays, and other types of electromagnetic waves differ only in their frequency and wavelength. Our study of optics in the following chapters will be based in part on the electromagnetic nature of light.

Unlike waves on a string or sound waves in a fluid, electromagnetic waves do not require a material medium; the light that you see coming from the stars at night has traveled without difficulty across tens or hundreds of light-years of (nearly) empty space. Nonetheless, electromagnetic waves and mechanical waves have much in common and are described in much the same language. Before reading further in this chapter, you should review the properties of mechanical waves as discussed in Chapters 15 and 16.

32.1 Maxwell's Equations and Electromagnetic Waves

In the last several chapters we studied various aspects of electric and magnetic fields. We learned that when the fields don't vary with time, such as an electric field produced by charges at rest or the magnetic field of a steady current, we can analyze the electric and magnetic fields independently without considering interactions between them. But when the fields vary with time, they are no longer independent. Faraday's law (see Section 29.2) tells us that a time-varying magnetic field acts as a source of electric field, as shown by induced emfs in inductors and transformers. Ampere's law, including the displacement current discovered by Maxwell (see Section 29.7), shows that a time-varying electric field acts as a source of magnetic field. This mutual interaction between the two fields is summarized in Maxwell's equations, presented in Section 29.7.

Thus, when *either* an electric or a magnetic field is changing with time, a field of the other kind is induced in adjacent regions of space. We are led (as Maxwell was) to consider the possibility of an electromagnetic disturbance, consisting of time-varying electric and magnetic fields, that can propagate through space from one region to another, even when there is no matter in the intervening region. Such a disturbance, if it exists, will have the properties of a *wave,* and an appropriate term is **electromagnetic wave.**

Such waves do exist; radio and television transmission, light, x rays, and many other kinds of radiation are examples of electromagnetic waves. Our goal in this chapter is to see how such waves are explained by the principles of electromagnetism that we have studied thus far and to examine the properties of these waves.

Electricity, Magnetism, and Light

As often happens in the development of science, the theoretical understanding of electromagnetic waves evolved along a considerably more devious path than the one just outlined. In the early days of electromagnetic theory (the early 19th century), two different units of electric charge were used: one for electrostatics and the other for magnetic phenomena involving currents. In the system of units used at that time, these two units of charge had different physical dimensions. Their *ratio* had units of velocity, and measurements showed that the ratio had a numerical value that was precisely equal to the speed of light, 3.00×10^8 m/s. At the time, physicists regarded this as an extraordinary coincidence and had no idea how to explain it.

32.1 James Clerk Maxwell (1831–1879) was the first person to truly understand the fundamental nature of light. He also made major contributions to thermodynamics, optics, astronomy, and color photography. Albert Einstein described Maxwell's accomplishments as "the most profound and the most fruitful that physics has experienced since the time of Newton."

In searching to understand this result, Maxwell (Fig. 32.1) proved in 1865 that an electromagnetic disturbance should propagate in free space with a speed equal to that of light and hence that light waves were likely to be electromagnetic in nature. At the same time, he discovered that the basic principles of electromagnetism can be expressed in terms of the four equations that we now call **Maxwell's equations,** which we discussed in Section 29.7. These four equations are (1) Gauss's law for electric fields; (2) Gauss's law for magnetic fields, showing the absence of magnetic monopoles; (3) Ampere's law, including displacement current; and (4) Faraday's law:

$$\oint \vec{E} \cdot d\vec{A} = \frac{Q_{\text{encl}}}{\epsilon_0} \qquad \text{(Gauss's law)} \qquad (29.18)$$

$$\oint \vec{B} \cdot d\vec{A} = 0 \qquad \text{(Gauss's law for magnetism)} \qquad (29.19)$$

$$\oint \vec{B} \cdot d\vec{l} = \mu_0 \left(i_C + \epsilon_0 \frac{d\Phi_E}{dt} \right)_{\text{encl}} \qquad \text{(Ampere's law)} \qquad (29.20)$$

$$\oint \vec{E} \cdot d\vec{l} = -\frac{d\Phi_B}{dt} \qquad \text{(Faraday's law)} \qquad (29.21)$$

These equations apply to electric and magnetic fields *in vacuum.* If a material is present, the permittivity ϵ_0 and permeability μ_0 of free space are replaced by the permittivity ϵ and permeability μ of the material. If the values of ϵ and μ are different at different points in the regions of integration, then ϵ and μ have to be transferred to the left sides of Eqs. (29.18) and (29.20), respectively, and placed inside the integrals. The ϵ in Eq. (29.20) also has to be included in the integral that gives $d\Phi_E/dt$.

According to Maxwell's equations, a point charge at rest produces a static $\vec{E}$ field but no $\vec{B}$ field; a point charge moving with a constant velocity (see Section 28.1) produces both $\vec{E}$ and $\vec{B}$ fields. Maxwell's equations can also be used to show that in order for a point charge to produce electromagnetic waves, the charge must *accelerate.* In fact, it's a general result of Maxwell's equations that *every* accelerated charge radiates electromagnetic energy (Fig. 32.2).

32.2 (Top) Every mobile phone, wireless modem, or radio transmitter emits signals in the form of electromagnetic waves that are made by accelerating charges. (Bottom) Power lines carry a strong alternating current, which means that a substantial amount of charge is accelerating back and forth and generating electromagnetic waves. These waves can produce a buzzing sound from your car radio when you drive near the lines.

Generating Electromagnetic Radiation

One way in which a point charge can be made to emit electromagnetic waves is by making it oscillate in simple harmonic motion, so that it has an acceleration at almost every instant (the exception is when the charge is passing through its equilibrium position). Figure 32.3 shows some of the electric field lines produced by such an oscillating point charge. Field lines are *not* material objects, but you may nonetheless find it helpful to think of them as behaving somewhat like strings that extend from the point charge off to infinity. Oscillating the charge up and down makes waves that propagate outward from the charge along these "strings." Note that the charge does not emit waves equally in all directions; the waves are strongest at 90° to the axis of motion of the charge, while there are *no* waves along this axis. This is just what the "string" picture would lead you to conclude. There is also a *magnetic* disturbance that spreads outward from the charge; this is not shown in Fig. 32.3. Because the electric and magnetic disturbances spread or radiate away from the source, the name **electromagnetic radiation** is used interchangeably with the phrase "electromagnetic waves."

Electromagnetic waves with macroscopic wavelengths were first produced in the laboratory in 1887 by the German physicist Heinrich Hertz. As a source of waves, he used charges oscillating in *L-C* circuits of the sort discussed in Section 30.5; he detected the resulting electromagnetic waves with other circuits tuned to the same frequency. Hertz also produced electromagnetic *standing waves* and measured the distance between adjacent nodes (one half-wavelength) to determine the wavelength. Knowing the resonant frequency of his circuits, he then found the speed of the waves from the wavelength–frequency relationship $v = \lambda f$. He established that their speed was the same as that of light; this verified Maxwell's theoretical prediction directly. The SI unit of frequency is named in honor of Hertz: One hertz (1 Hz) equals one cycle per second.

32.3 Electric field lines of a point charge oscillating in simple harmonic motion, seen at five instants during an oscillation period T. The charge's trajectory is in the plane of the drawings. At $t = 0$ the point charge is at its maximum upward displacement. The arrow shows one "kink" in the lines of $\vec{E}$ as it propagates outward from the point charge. The magnetic field (not shown) comprises circles that lie in planes perpendicular to these figures and concentric with the axis of oscillation.

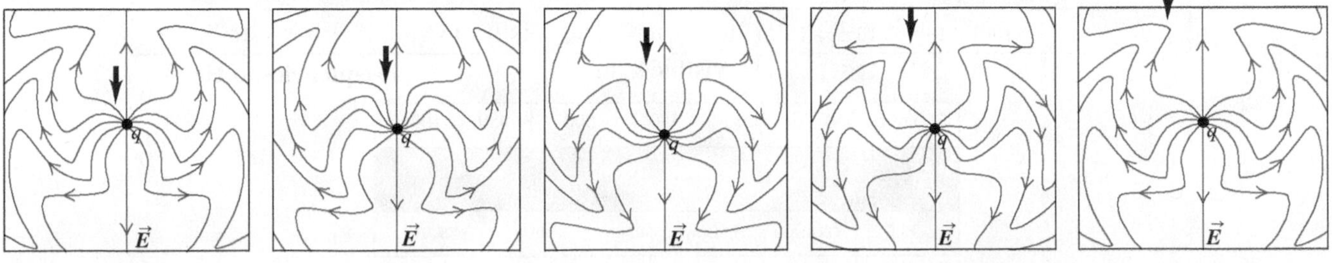

The modern value of the speed of light, which we denote by the symbol c, is 299,792,458 m/s. (Recall from Section 1.3 that this value is the basis of our standard of length: One meter is defined to be the distance that light travels in 1/299,792,458 second.) For our purposes, $c = 3.00 \times 10^8$ m/s is sufficiently accurate.

The possible use of electromagnetic waves for long-distance communication does not seem to have occurred to Hertz. It was left to Marconi and others to make radio communication a familiar household experience. In a radio *transmitter,* electric charges are made to oscillate along the length of the conducting antenna, producing oscillating field disturbances like those shown in Fig. 32.3. Since many charges oscillate together in the antenna, the disturbances are much stronger than those of a single oscillating charge and can be detected at a much greater distance. In a radio *receiver* the antenna is also a conductor; the fields of the wave emanating from a distant transmitter exert forces on free charges within the receiver antenna, producing an oscillating current that is detected and amplified by the receiver circuitry.

For the remainder of this chapter our concern will be with electromagnetic waves themselves, not with the rather complex problem of how they are produced.

The Electromagnetic Spectrum

The **electromagnetic spectrum** encompasses electromagnetic waves of all frequencies and wavelengths. Figure 32.4 shows approximate wavelength and frequency ranges for the most commonly encountered portion of the spectrum. Despite vast differences in their uses and means of production, these are all electromagnetic waves with the same propagation speed (in vacuum) $c = 299{,}792{,}458$ m/s. Electromagnetic waves may differ in frequency f and wavelength λ, but the relationship $c = \lambda f$ in vacuum holds for each.

We can detect only a very small segment of this spectrum directly through our sense of sight. We call this range **visible light.** Its wavelengths range from about 380 to 750 nm ($380 \text{ to } 750 \times 10^{-9}$ m), with corresponding frequencies from about 790 to 400 THz ($7.9 \text{ to } 4.0 \times 10^{14}$ Hz). Different parts of the visible spectrum evoke in humans the sensations of different colors. Table 32.1 gives the approximate wavelengths for colors in the visible spectrum.

Ordinary white light includes all visible wavelengths. However, by using special sources or filters, we can select a narrow band of wavelengths within a range of a few nm. Such light is approximately *monochromatic* (single-color) light. Absolutely monochromatic light with only a single wavelength is an unattainable idealization. When we use the expression "monochromatic light with λ = 550 nm" with reference to a laboratory experiment, we really mean a small band

Table 32.1 Wavelengths of Visible Light

380–450 nm	Violet
450–495 nm	Blue
495–570 nm	Green
570–590 nm	Yellow
590–620 nm	Orange
620–750 nm	Red

32.4 The electromagnetic spectrum. The frequencies and wavelengths found in nature extend over such a wide range that we have to use a logarithmic scale to show all important bands. The boundaries between bands are somewhat arbitrary.

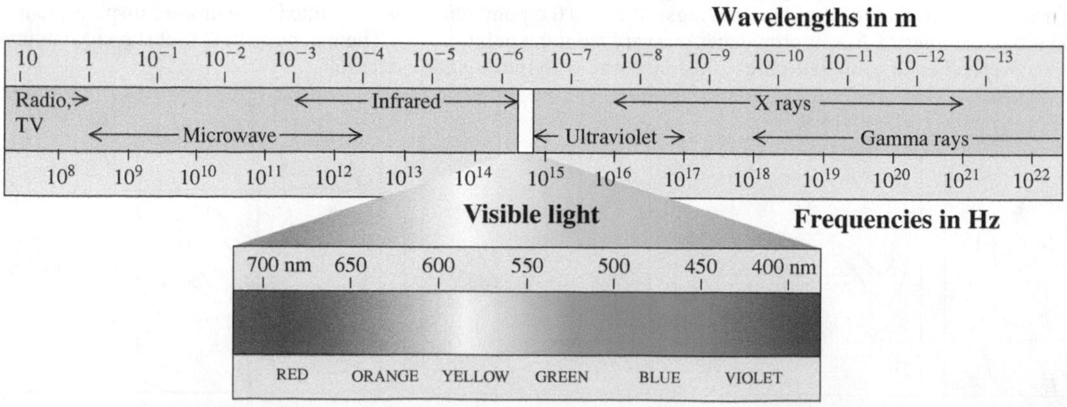

of wavelengths *around* 550 nm. Light from a *laser* is much more nearly monochromatic than is light obtainable in any other way.

Invisible forms of electromagnetic radiation are no less important than visible light. Our system of global communication, for example, depends on radio waves: AM radio uses waves with frequencies from 5.4×10^5 Hz to 1.6×10^6 Hz, while FM radio broadcasts are at frequencies from 8.8×10^7 Hz to 1.08×10^8 Hz. (Television broadcasts use frequencies that bracket the FM band.) Microwaves are also used for communication (for example, by cellular phones and wireless networks) and for weather radar (at frequencies near 3×10^9 Hz). Many cameras have a device that emits a beam of infrared radiation; by analyzing the properties of the infrared radiation reflected from the subject, the camera determines the distance to the subject and automatically adjusts the focus. X rays are able to penetrate through flesh, which makes them invaluable in dentistry and medicine. Gamma rays, the shortest-wavelength type of electromagnetic radiation, are used in medicine to destroy cancer cells.

Application Ultraviolet Vision
Many insects and birds can see ultraviolet wavelengths that humans cannot. As an example, the left-hand photo shows how black-eyed Susans (genus *Rudbeckia*) look to us. The right-hand photo (in false color), taken with an ultraviolet-sensitive camera, shows how these same flowers appear to the bees that pollinate them. Note the prominent central spot that is invisible to humans. Similarly, many birds with ultraviolet vision—including budgies, parrots, and peacocks—have ultraviolet patterns on their bodies that make them even more vivid to each other than they appear to us.

Test Your Understanding of Section 32.1 (a) Is it possible to have a purely electric wave propagate through empty space—that is, a wave made up of an electric field but no magnetic field? (b) What about a purely magnetic wave, with a magnetic field but no electric field? ❙

32.2 Plane Electromagnetic Waves and the Speed of Light

We are now ready to develop the basic ideas of electromagnetic waves and their relationship to the principles of electromagnetism. Our procedure will be to postulate a simple field configuration that has wavelike behavior. We'll assume an electric field $\vec{E}$ that has only a y-component and a magnetic field $\vec{B}$ with only a z-component, and we'll assume that both fields move together in the $+x$-direction with a speed c that is initially unknown. (As we go along, it will become clear why we choose $\vec{E}$ and $\vec{B}$ to be perpendicular to the direction of propagation as well as to each other.) Then we will test whether these fields are physically possible by asking whether they are consistent with Maxwell's equations, particularly Ampere's law and Faraday's law. We'll find that the answer is yes, provided that c has a particular value. We'll also show that the *wave equation,* which we encountered during our study of mechanical waves in Chapter 15, can be derived from Maxwell's equations.

A Simple Plane Electromagnetic Wave

Using an xyz-coordinate system (Fig. 32.5), we imagine that all space is divided into two regions by a plane perpendicular to the x-axis (parallel to the yz-plane). At every point to the left of this plane there are a uniform electric field $\vec{E}$ in the $+y$-direction and a uniform magnetic field $\vec{B}$ in the $+z$-direction, as shown. Furthermore, we suppose that the boundary plane, which we call the *wave front,* moves to the right in the $+x$-direction with a constant speed c, the value of which we'll leave undetermined for now. Thus the $\vec{E}$ and $\vec{B}$ fields travel to the right into previously field-free regions with a definite speed. This is a rudimentary electromagnetic wave. A wave such as this, in which at any instant the fields are uniform over any plane perpendicular to the direction of propagation, is called a **plane wave.** In the case shown in Fig. 32.5, the fields are zero for planes to the right of the wave front and have the same values on all planes to the left of the wave front; later we will consider more complex plane waves.

We won't concern ourselves with the problem of actually *producing* such a field configuration. Instead, we simply ask whether it is consistent with the laws of electromagnetism—that is, with Maxwell's equations. We'll consider each of these four equations in turn.

32.5 An electromagnetic wave front. The plane representing the wave front moves to the right (in the positive x-direction) with speed c.

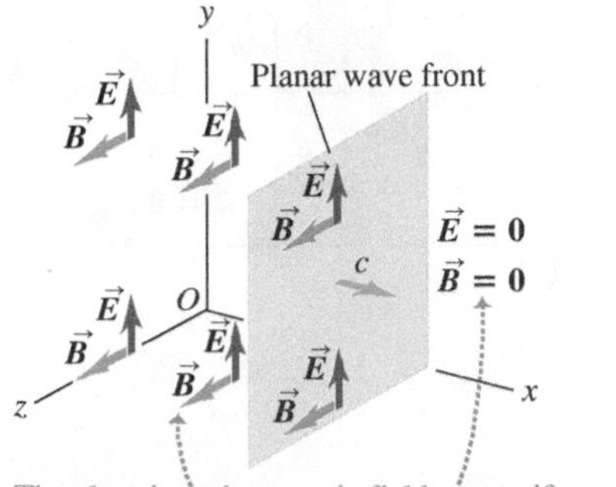

32.6 Gaussian surface for a transverse plane electromagnetic wave.

The electric field is the same on the top and bottom sides of the Gaussian surface, so the total electric flux through the surface is zero.

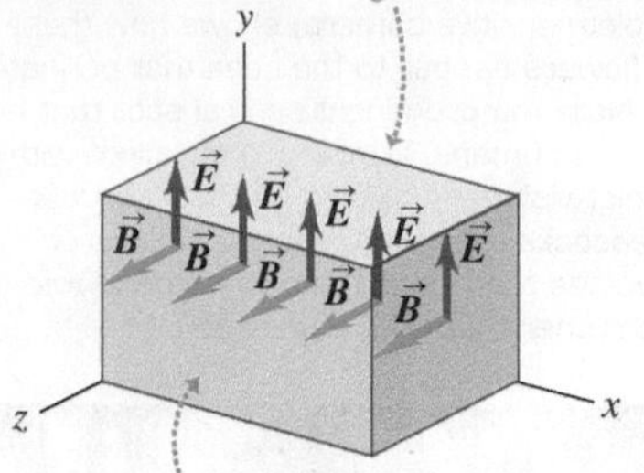

The magnetic field is the same on the left and right sides of the Gaussian surface, so the total magnetic flux through the surface is zero.

32.7 (a) Applying Faraday's law to a plane wave. (b) In a time dt, the magnetic flux through the rectangle in the xy-plane increases by an amount $d\Phi_B$. This increase equals the flux through the shaded rectangle with area $ac\,dt$; that is, $d\Phi_B = Bac\,dt$. Thus $d\Phi_B/dt = Bac$.

(a) In time dt, the wave front moves a distance $c\,dt$ in the $+x$-direction.

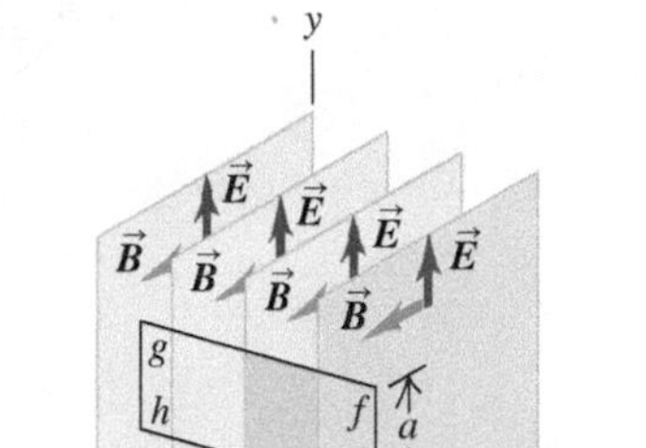

(b) Side view of situation in (a)

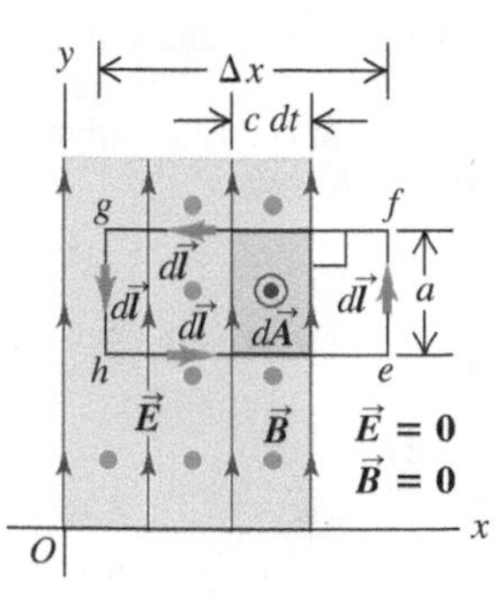

Let us first verify that our wave satisfies Maxwell's first and second equations—that is, Gauss's laws for electric and magnetic fields. To do this, we take as our Gaussian surface a rectangular box with sides parallel to the xy, xz, and yz coordinate planes (Fig. 32.6). The box encloses no electric charge. The total electric flux and magnetic flux through the box are both zero, even if part of the box is in the region where $E = B = 0$. This would *not* be the case if $\vec{E}$ or $\vec{B}$ had an x-component, parallel to the direction of propagation; if the wave front were inside the box, there would be flux through the left-hand side of the box (at $x = 0$) but not the right-hand side (at $x > 0$). Thus to satisfy Maxwell's first and second equations, the electric and magnetic fields must be perpendicular to the direction of propagation; that is, the wave must be **transverse.**

The next of Maxwell's equations to be considered is Faraday's law:

$$\oint \vec{E} \cdot d\vec{l} = -\frac{d\Phi_B}{dt} \tag{32.1}$$

To test whether our wave satisfies Faraday's law, we apply this law to a rectangle $efgh$ that is parallel to the xy-plane (Fig. 32.7a). As shown in Fig. 32.7b, a cross section in the xy-plane, this rectangle has height a and width Δx. At the time shown, the wave front has progressed partway through the rectangle, and $\vec{E}$ is zero along the side ef. In applying Faraday's law we take the vector area $d\vec{A}$ of rectangle $efgh$ to be in the $+z$-direction. With this choice the right-hand rule requires that we integrate $\vec{E} \cdot d\vec{l}$ *counterclockwise* around the rectangle. At every point on side ef, $\vec{E}$ is zero. At every point on sides fg and he, $\vec{E}$ is either zero or perpendicular to $d\vec{l}$. Only side gh contributes to the integral. On this side, $\vec{E}$ and $d\vec{l}$ are opposite, and we obtain

$$\oint \vec{E} \cdot d\vec{l} = -Ea \tag{32.2}$$

Hence, the left-hand side of Eq. (32.1) is nonzero.

To satisfy Faraday's law, Eq. (32.1), there must be a component of $\vec{B}$ in the z-direction (perpendicular to $\vec{E}$) so that there can be a nonzero magnetic flux Φ_B through the rectangle $efgh$ and a nonzero derivative $d\Phi_B/dt$. Indeed, in our wave, $\vec{B}$ has *only* a z-component. We have assumed that this component is in the *positive* z-direction; let's see whether this assumption is consistent with Faraday's law. During a time interval dt the wave front moves a distance $c\,dt$ to the right in Fig. 32.7b, sweeping out an area $ac\,dt$ of the rectangle $efgh$. During this interval the magnetic flux Φ_B through the rectangle $efgh$ increases by $d\Phi_B = B(ac\,dt)$, so the rate of change of magnetic flux is

$$\frac{d\Phi_B}{dt} = Bac \tag{32.3}$$

Now we substitute Eqs. (32.2) and (32.3) into Faraday's law, Eq. (32.1); we get

$$-Ea = -Bac$$

$$E = cB \quad \text{(electromagnetic wave in vacuum)} \tag{32.4}$$

This shows that our wave is consistent with Faraday's law only if the wave speed c and the magnitudes of the perpendicular vectors $\vec{E}$ and $\vec{B}$ are related as in Eq. (32.4). Note that if we had assumed that $\vec{B}$ was in the *negative* z-direction, there would have been an additional minus sign in Eq. (32.4); since E, c, and B are all positive magnitudes, no solution would then have been possible. Furthermore, any component of $\vec{B}$ in the y-direction (parallel to $\vec{E}$) would not contribute to the changing magnetic flux Φ_B through the rectangle $efgh$ (which is parallel to the xy-plane) and so would not be part of the wave.

Finally, we carry out a similar calculation using Ampere's law, the remaining member of Maxwell's equations. There is no conduction current ($i_C = 0$), so Ampere's law is

$$\oint \vec{B} \cdot d\vec{l} = \mu_0 \epsilon_0 \frac{d\Phi_E}{dt} \tag{32.5}$$

To check whether our wave is consistent with Ampere's law, we move our rectangle so that it lies in the xz-plane, as shown in Fig. 32.8, and we again look at the situation at a time when the wave front has traveled partway through the rectangle. We take the vector area $d\vec{A}$ in the $+y$-direction, and so the right-hand rule requires that we integrate $\vec{B} \cdot d\vec{l}$ counterclockwise around the rectangle. The $\vec{B}$ field is zero at every point along side ef, and at each point on sides fg and he it is either zero or perpendicular to $d\vec{l}$. Only side gh, where $\vec{B}$ and $d\vec{l}$ are parallel, contributes to the integral, and we find

$$\oint \vec{B} \cdot d\vec{l} = Ba \tag{32.6}$$

Hence, the left-hand side of Ampere's law, Eq. (32.5), is nonzero; the right-hand side must be nonzero as well. Thus $\vec{E}$ must have a y-component (perpendicular to $\vec{B}$) so that the electric flux Φ_E through the rectangle and the time derivative $d\Phi_E/dt$ can be nonzero. We come to the same conclusion that we inferred from Faraday's law: In an electromagnetic wave, $\vec{E}$ and $\vec{B}$ must be mutually perpendicular.

In a time interval dt the electric flux Φ_E through the rectangle increases by $d\Phi_E = E(ac\,dt)$. Since we chose $d\vec{A}$ to be in the $+y$-direction, this flux change is positive; the rate of change of electric field is

$$\frac{d\Phi_E}{dt} = Eac \tag{32.7}$$

Substituting Eqs. (32.6) and (32.7) into Ampere's law, Eq. (32.5), we find

$$Ba = \epsilon_0 \mu_0 Eac$$

$$B = \epsilon_0 \mu_0 cE \quad \text{(electromagnetic wave in vacuum)} \tag{32.8}$$

Thus our assumed wave obeys Ampere's law only if B, c, and E are related as in Eq. (32.8).

Our electromagnetic wave must obey *both* Ampere's law and Faraday's law, so Eqs. (32.4) and (32.8) must both be satisfied. This can happen only if $\epsilon_0 \mu_0 c = 1/c$, or

$$c = \frac{1}{\sqrt{\epsilon_0 \mu_0}} \quad \text{(speed of electromagnetic waves in vacuum)} \tag{32.9}$$

Inserting the numerical values of these quantities, we find

$$c = \frac{1}{\sqrt{(8.85 \times 10^{-12}\ \text{C}^2/\text{N}\cdot\text{m}^2)(4\pi \times 10^{-7}\ \text{N/A}^2)}}$$
$$= 3.00 \times 10^8\ \text{m/s}$$

Our assumed wave is consistent with all of Maxwell's equations, provided that the wave front moves with the speed given above, which you should recognize as the speed of light! Note that the *exact* value of c is defined to be 299,792,458 m/s; the modern value of ϵ_0 is defined to agree with this when used in Eq. (32.9) (see Section 21.3).

32.8 (a) Applying Ampere's law to a plane wave. (Compare to Fig. 32.7a.) (b) In a time dt, the electric flux through the rectangle in the xz-plane increases by an amount $d\Phi_E$. This increase equals the flux through the shaded rectangle with area $ac\,dt$; that is, $d\Phi_E = Eac\,dt$. Thus $d\Phi_E/dt = Eac$.

(a) In time dt, the wave front moves a distance $c\,dt$ in the $+x$-direction.

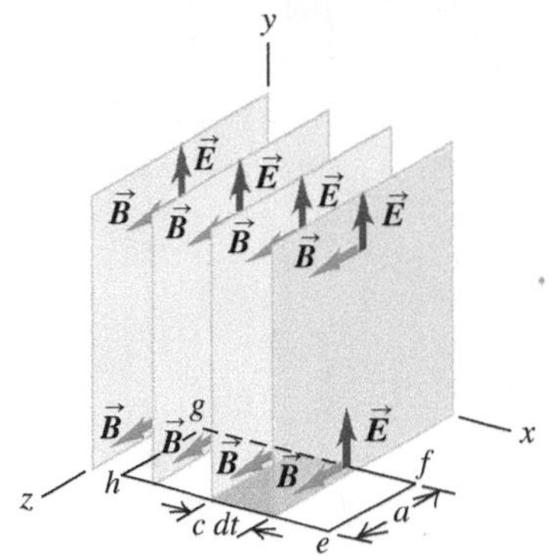

(b) Top view of situation in (a)

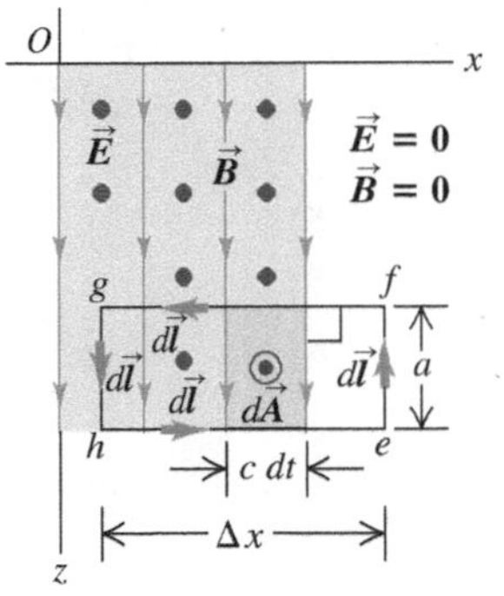

32.9 A right-hand rule for electromagnetic waves relates the directions of $\vec{E}$ and $\vec{B}$ and the direction of propagation.

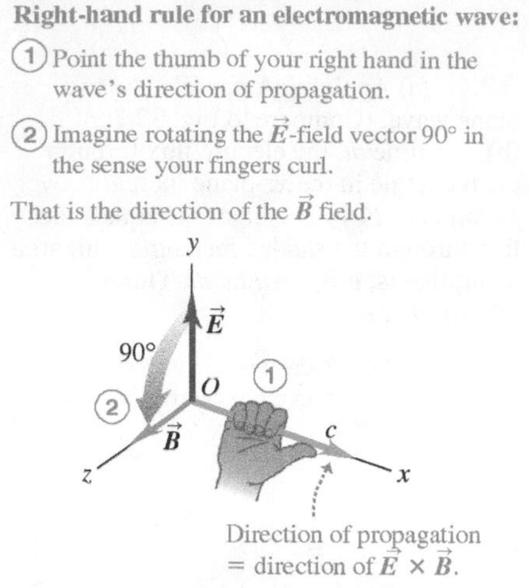

Key Properties of Electromagnetic Waves

We chose a simple wave for our study in order to avoid mathematical complications, but this special case illustrates several important features of *all* electromagnetic waves:

1. The wave is *transverse;* both $\vec{E}$ and $\vec{B}$ are perpendicular to the direction of propagation of the wave. The electric and magnetic fields are also perpendicular to each other. The direction of propagation is the direction of the vector product $\vec{E} \times \vec{B}$ (Fig. 32.9).
2. There is a definite ratio between the magnitudes of $\vec{E}$ and $\vec{B}$: $E = cB$.
3. The wave travels in vacuum with a definite and unchanging speed.
4. Unlike mechanical waves, which need the oscillating particles of a medium such as water or air to transmit a wave, electromagnetic waves require no medium.

We can generalize this discussion to a more realistic situation. Suppose we have several wave fronts in the form of parallel planes perpendicular to the x-axis, all of which are moving to the right with speed c. Suppose that the $\vec{E}$ and $\vec{B}$ fields are the same at all points within a single region between two planes, but that the fields differ from region to region. The overall wave is a plane wave, but one in which the fields vary in steps along the x-axis. Such a wave could be constructed by superposing several of the simple step waves we have just discussed (shown in Fig. 32.5). This is possible because the $\vec{E}$ and $\vec{B}$ fields obey the superposition principle in waves just as in static situations: When two waves are superposed, the total $\vec{E}$ field at each point is the vector sum of the $\vec{E}$ fields of the individual waves, and similarly for the total $\vec{B}$ field.

We can extend the above development to show that a wave with fields that vary in steps is also consistent with Ampere's and Faraday's laws, provided that the wave fronts all move with the speed c given by Eq. (32.9). In the limit that we make the individual steps infinitesimally small, we have a wave in which the $\vec{E}$ and $\vec{B}$ fields at any instant vary *continuously* along the x-axis. The entire field pattern moves to the right with speed c. In Section 32.3 we will consider waves in which $\vec{E}$ and $\vec{B}$ are *sinusoidal* functions of x and t. Because at each point the magnitudes of $\vec{E}$ and $\vec{B}$ are related by $E = cB$, the periodic variations of the two fields in any periodic traveling wave must be *in phase.*

Electromagnetic waves have the property of **polarization.** In the above discussion the choice of the y-direction for $\vec{E}$ was arbitrary. We could just as well have specified the z-axis for $\vec{E}$; then $\vec{B}$ would have been in the $-y$-direction. A wave in which $\vec{E}$ is always parallel to a certain axis is said to be **linearly polarized** along that axis. More generally, *any* wave traveling in the x-direction can be represented as a superposition of waves linearly polarized in the y- and z-directions. We will study polarization in greater detail in Chapter 33.

Derivation of the Electromagnetic Wave Equation

Here is an alternative derivation of Eq. (32.9) for the speed of electromagnetic waves. It is more mathematical than our other treatment, but it includes a derivation of the wave equation for electromagnetic waves. This part of the section can be omitted without loss of continuity in the chapter.

During our discussion of mechanical waves in Section 15.3, we showed that a function $y(x, t)$ that represents the displacement of any point in a mechanical wave traveling along the x-axis must satisfy a differential equation, Eq. (15.12):

$$\frac{\partial^2 y(x,t)}{\partial x^2} = \frac{1}{v^2}\frac{\partial^2 y(x,t)}{\partial t^2} \tag{32.10}$$

This equation is called the **wave equation,** and v is the speed of propagation of the wave.

To derive the corresponding equation for an electromagnetic wave, we again consider a plane wave. That is, we assume that at each instant, E_y and B_z are uniform over any plane perpendicular to the x-axis, the direction of propagation. But now we let E_y and B_z vary continuously as we go along the x-axis; then each is a function of x and t. We consider the values of E_y and B_z on two planes perpendicular to the x-axis, one at x and one at $x + \Delta x$.

Following the same procedure as previously, we apply Faraday's law to a rectangle lying parallel to the xy-plane, as in Fig. 32.10. This figure is similar to Fig. 32.7. Let the left end gh of the rectangle be at position x, and let the right end ef be at position $(x + \Delta x)$. At time t, the values of E_y on these two sides are $E_y(x, t)$ and $E_y(x + \Delta x, t)$, respectively. When we apply Faraday's law to this rectangle, we find that instead of $\oint \vec{E} \cdot d\vec{l} = -Ea$ as before, we have

$$\oint \vec{E} \cdot d\vec{l} = -E_y(x, t)a + E_y(x + \Delta x, t)a$$

$$= a[E_y(x + \Delta x, t) - E_y(x, t)] \tag{32.11}$$

To find the magnetic flux Φ_B through this rectangle, we assume that Δx is small enough that B_z is nearly uniform over the rectangle. In that case, $\Phi_B = B_z(x, t)A = B_z(x, t)a\,\Delta x$, and

$$\frac{d\Phi_B}{dt} = \frac{\partial B_z(x, t)}{\partial t} a\,\Delta x$$

We use partial-derivative notation because B_z is a function of both x and t. When we substitute this expression and Eq. (32.11) into Faraday's law, Eq. (32.1), we get

$$a[E_y(x + \Delta x, t) - E_y(x, t)] = -\frac{\partial B_z}{\partial t} a\,\Delta x$$

$$\frac{E_y(x + \Delta x, t) - E_y(x, t)}{\Delta x} = -\frac{\partial B_z}{\partial t}$$

Finally, imagine shrinking the rectangle down to a sliver so that Δx approaches zero. When we take the limit of this equation as $\Delta x \rightarrow 0$, we get

$$\frac{\partial E_y(x, t)}{\partial x} = -\frac{\partial B_z(x, t)}{\partial t} \tag{32.12}$$

This equation shows that if there is a time-varying component B_z of magnetic field, there must also be a component E_y of electric field that varies with x, and conversely. We put this relationship on the shelf for now; we'll return to it soon.

Next we apply Ampere's law to the rectangle shown in Fig. 32.11. The line integral $\oint \vec{B} \cdot d\vec{l}$ becomes

$$\oint \vec{B} \cdot d\vec{l} = -B_z(x + \Delta x, t)a + B_z(x, t)a \tag{32.13}$$

Again assuming that the rectangle is narrow, we approximate the electric flux Φ_E through it as $\Phi_E = E_y(x, t)A = E_y(x, t)a\,\Delta x$. The rate of change of Φ_E, which we need for Ampere's law, is then

$$\frac{d\Phi_E}{dt} = \frac{\partial E_y(x, t)}{\partial t} a\,\Delta x$$

Now we substitute this expression and Eq. (32.13) into Ampere's law, Eq. (32.5):

$$-B_z(x + \Delta x, t)a + B_z(x, t)a = \epsilon_0 \mu_0 \frac{\partial E_y(x, t)}{\partial t} a\,\Delta x$$

Again we divide both sides by $a\,\Delta x$ and take the limit as $\Delta x \rightarrow 0$. We find

$$-\frac{\partial B_z(x, t)}{\partial x} = \epsilon_0 \mu_0 \frac{\partial E_y(x, t)}{\partial t} \tag{32.14}$$

32.10 Faraday's law applied to a rectangle with height a and width Δx parallel to the xy-plane.

(a)

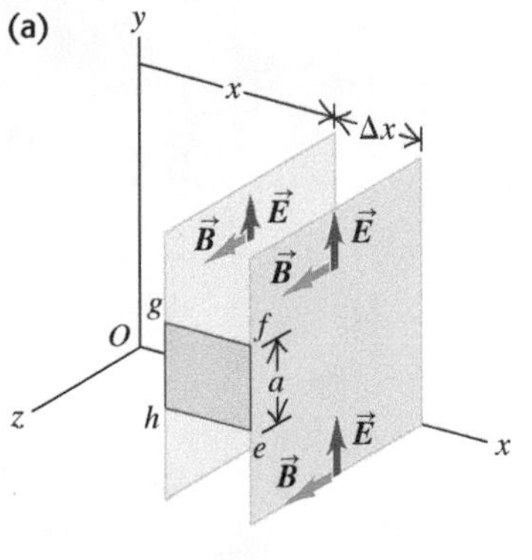

(b) Side view of the situation in (a)

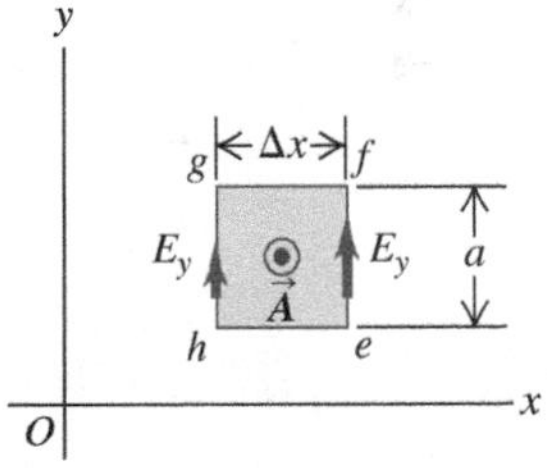

32.11 Ampere's law applied to a rectangle with height a and width Δx parallel to the xz-plane.

(a)

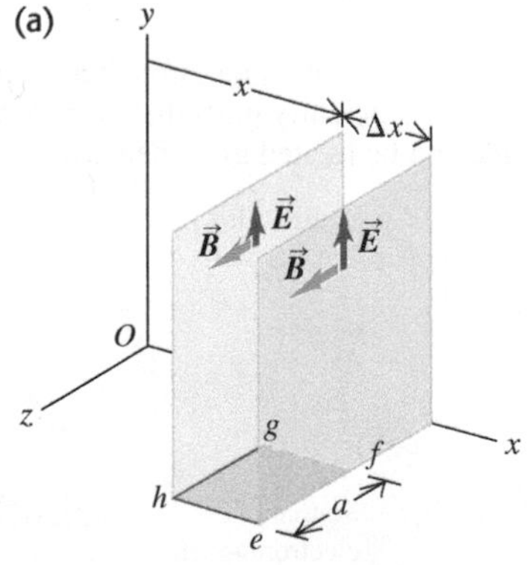

(b) Top view of the situation in (a)

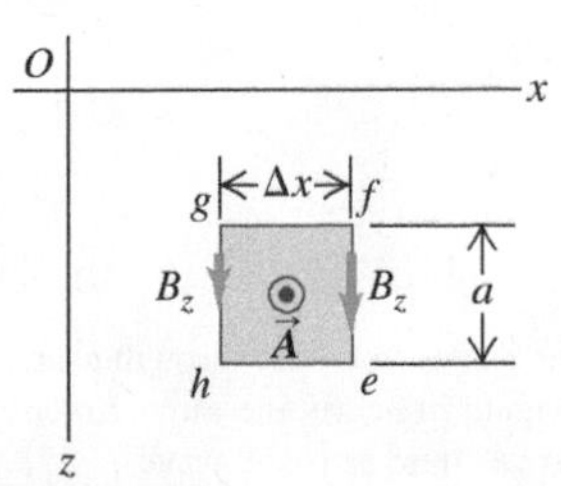

Now comes the final step. We take the partial derivatives with respect to x of both sides of Eq. (32.12), and we take the partial derivatives with respect to t of both sides of Eq. (32.14). The results are

$$-\frac{\partial^2 E_y(x,t)}{\partial x^2} = \frac{\partial^2 B_z(x,t)}{\partial x \partial t}$$

$$-\frac{\partial^2 B_z(x,t)}{\partial x \partial t} = \epsilon_0 \mu_0 \frac{\partial^2 E_y(x,t)}{\partial t^2}$$

Combining these two equations to eliminate B_z, we finally find

$$\frac{\partial^2 E_y(x,t)}{\partial x^2} = \epsilon_0 \mu_0 \frac{\partial^2 E_y(x,t)}{\partial t^2} \quad \text{(electromagnetic wave equation in vacuum)} \qquad (32.15)$$

This expression has the same form as the general wave equation, Eq. (32.10). Because the electric field E_y must satisfy this equation, it behaves as a wave with a pattern that travels through space with a definite speed. Furthermore, comparison of Eqs. (32.15) and (32.10) shows that the wave speed v is given by

$$\frac{1}{v^2} = \epsilon_0 \mu_0 \quad \text{or} \quad v = \frac{1}{\sqrt{\epsilon_0 \mu_0}}$$

This agrees with Eq. (32.9) for the speed c of electromagnetic waves.

We can show that B_z also must satisfy the same wave equation as E_y, Eq. (32.15). To prove this, we take the partial derivative of Eq. (32.12) with respect to t and the partial derivative of Eq. (32.14) with respect to x and combine the results. We leave this derivation for you to carry out.

Test Your Understanding of Section 32.2 For each of the following electromagnetic waves, state the direction of the magnetic field. (a) The wave is propagating in the positive z-direction, and $\vec{E}$ is in the positive x-direction; (b) the wave is propagating in the positive y-direction, and $\vec{E}$ is in the negative z-direction; (c) the wave is propagating in the negative x-direction, and $\vec{E}$ is in the positive z-direction. ❙

32.3 Sinusoidal Electromagnetic Waves

Sinusoidal electromagnetic waves are directly analogous to sinusoidal transverse mechanical waves on a stretched string, which we studied in Section 15.3. In a sinusoidal electromagnetic wave, $\vec{E}$ and $\vec{B}$ at any point in space are sinusoidal functions of time, and at any instant of time the *spatial* variation of the fields is also sinusoidal.

Some sinusoidal electromagnetic waves are *plane waves;* they share with the waves described in Section 32.2 the property that at any instant the fields are uniform over any plane perpendicular to the direction of propagation. The entire pattern travels in the direction of propagation with speed c. The directions of $\vec{E}$ and $\vec{B}$ are perpendicular to the direction of propagation (and to each other), so the wave is *transverse.* Electromagnetic waves produced by an oscillating point charge, shown in Fig. 32.3, are an example of sinusoidal waves that are *not* plane waves. But if we restrict our observations to a relatively small region of space at a sufficiently great distance from the source, even these waves are well approximated by plane waves (Fig. 32.12). In the same way, the curved surface of the (nearly) spherical earth appears flat to us because of our small size relative to the earth's radius. In this section we'll restrict our discussion to plane waves.

32.12 Waves passing through a small area at a sufficiently great distance from a source can be treated as plane waves.

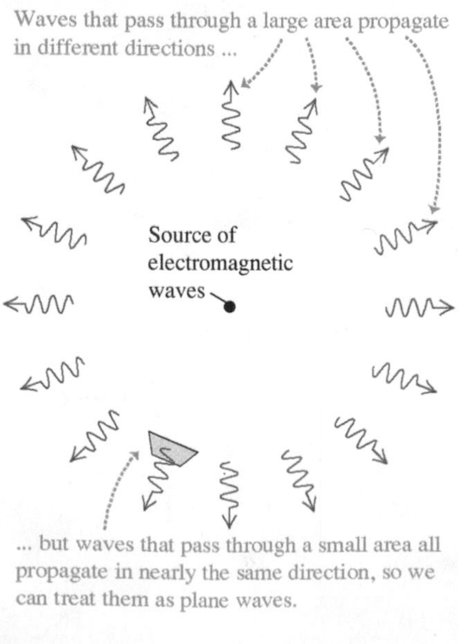

The frequency f, the wavelength λ, and the speed of propagation c of any periodic wave are related by the usual wavelength–frequency relationship $c = \lambda f$. If the frequency f is 10^8 Hz (100 MHz), typical of commercial FM radio broadcasts, the wavelength is

$$\lambda = \frac{3 \times 10^8 \text{ m/s}}{10^8 \text{ Hz}} = 3 \text{ m}$$

Figure 32.4 shows the inverse proportionality between wavelength and frequency.

Fields of a Sinusoidal Wave

Figure 32.13 shows a linearly polarized sinusoidal electromagnetic wave traveling in the $+x$-direction. The $\vec{E}$ and $\vec{B}$ vectors are shown for only a few points on the positive x-axis. Note that the electric and magnetic fields oscillate in phase: $\vec{E}$ is maximum where $\vec{B}$ is maximum and $\vec{E}$ is zero where $\vec{B}$ is zero. Note also that where $\vec{E}$ is in the $+y$-direction, $\vec{B}$ is in the $+z$-direction; where $\vec{E}$ is in the $-y$-direction, $\vec{B}$ is in the $-z$-direction. At all points the vector product $\vec{E} \times \vec{B}$ is in the direction in which the wave is propagating (the $+x$-direction). We mentioned this in Section 32.2 in the list of characteristics of electromagnetic waves.

32.13 Representation of the electric and magnetic fields as functions of x for a linearly polarized sinusoidal plane electromagnetic wave. One wavelength of the wave is shown at time $t = 0$. The fields are shown only for points along the x-axis.

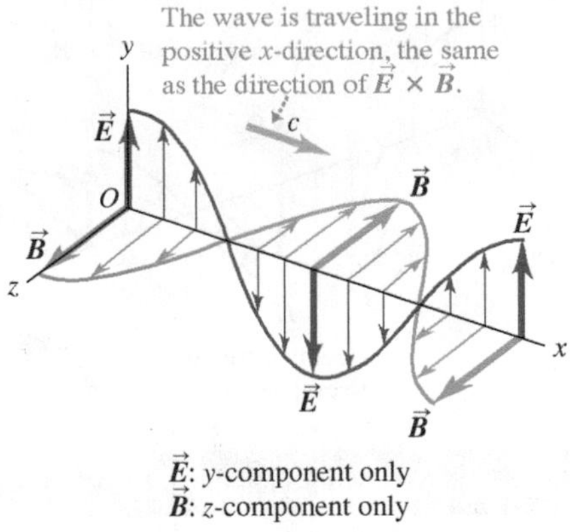

CAUTION **In a plane wave, $\vec{E}$ and $\vec{B}$ are everywhere** Figure 32.13 may give you the erroneous impression that the electric and magnetic fields exist only along the x-axis. In fact, in a sinusoidal plane wave there are electric and magnetic fields at *all* points in space. Imagine a plane perpendicular to the x-axis (that is, parallel to the yz-plane) at a particular point, at a particular time; the fields have the same values at all points in that plane. The values are different on different planes.

MasteringPHYSICS

PhET: Radio Waves & Electromagnetic Fields
ActivPhysics 10.1: Properties of Mechanical Waves

We can describe electromagnetic waves by means of *wave functions,* just as we did in Section 15.3 for waves on a string. One form of the wave function for a transverse wave traveling in the $+x$-direction along a stretched string is Eq. (15.7):

$$y(x, t) = A\cos(kx - \omega t)$$

where $y(x, t)$ is the transverse displacement from its equilibrium position at time t of a point with coordinate x on the string. The quantity A is the maximum displacement, or *amplitude,* of the wave; ω is its *angular frequency,* equal to 2π times the frequency f; and k is the *wave number,* equal to $2\pi/\lambda$, where λ is the wavelength.

Let $E_y(x, t)$ and $B_z(x, t)$ represent the instantaneous values of the y-component of $\vec{E}$ and the z-component of $\vec{B}$, respectively, in Fig. 32.13, and let E_{max} and B_{max} represent the maximum values, or *amplitudes,* of these fields. The wave functions for the wave are then

$$E_y(x, t) = E_{max}\cos(kx - \omega t) \qquad B_z(x, t) = B_{max}\cos(kx - \omega t) \tag{32.16}$$

(sinusoidal electromagnetic plane wave, propagating in $+x$-direction)

We can also write the wave functions in vector form:

$$\begin{aligned} \vec{E}(x, t) &= \hat{\jmath}E_{max}\cos(kx - \omega t) \\ \vec{B}(x, t) &= \hat{k}B_{max}\cos(kx - \omega t) \end{aligned} \tag{32.17}$$

CAUTION **The symbol k has two meanings** Note the two different k's: the unit vector $\hat{k}$ in the z-direction and the wave number k. Don't get these confused!

The sine curves in Fig. 32.13 represent instantaneous values of the electric and magnetic fields as functions of x at time $t = 0$—that is, $\vec{E}(x, t = 0)$ and $\vec{B}(x, t = 0)$. As time goes by, the wave travels to the right with speed c. Equations (32.16) and (32.17) show that at any point the sinusoidal oscillations of $\vec{E}$ and $\vec{B}$ are *in phase.* From Eq. (32.4) the amplitudes must be related by

$$E_{max} = cB_{max} \quad \text{(electromagnetic wave in vacuum)} \tag{32.18}$$

These amplitude and phase relationships are also required for $E(x, t)$ and $B(x, t)$ to satisfy Eqs. (32.12) and (32.14), which came from Faraday's law and Ampere's law, respectively. Can you verify this statement? (See Problem 32.38.)

32.14 Representation of one wavelength of a linearly polarized sinusoidal plane electromagnetic wave traveling in the negative x-direction at $t = 0$. The fields are shown only for points along the x-axis. (Compare with Fig. 32.13.)

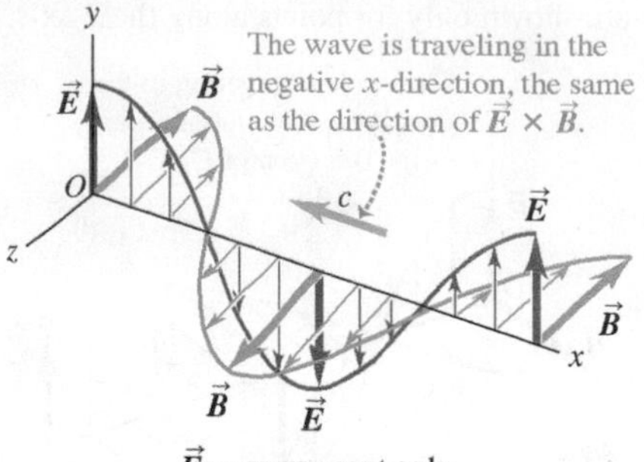

Figure 32.14 shows the electric and magnetic fields of a wave traveling in the *negative* x-direction. At points where $\vec{E}$ is in the positive y-direction, $\vec{B}$ is in the *negative* z-direction; where $\vec{E}$ is in the negative y-direction, $\vec{B}$ is in the *positive* z-direction. The wave functions for this wave are

$$E_y(x, t) = E_{max} \cos(kx + \omega t) \quad B_z(x, t) = -B_{max} \cos(kx + \omega t) \tag{32.19}$$

(sinusoidal electromagnetic plane wave, propagating in $-x$-direction)

As with the wave traveling in the $+x$-direction, at any point the sinusoidal oscillations of the $\vec{E}$ and $\vec{B}$ fields are *in phase,* and the vector product $\vec{E} \times \vec{B}$ points in the direction of propagation.

The sinusoidal waves shown in Figs. 32.13 and 32.14 are both linearly polarized in the y-direction; the $\vec{E}$ field is always parallel to the y-axis. Example 32.1 concerns a wave that is linearly polarized in the z-direction.

Problem-Solving Strategy 32.1 Electromagnetic Waves

IDENTIFY *the relevant concepts:* Many of the same ideas that apply to mechanical waves apply to electromagnetic waves. One difference is that electromagnetic waves are described by two quantities (in this case, electric field $\vec{E}$ and magnetic field $\vec{B}$), rather than by a single quantity, such as the displacement of a string.

SET UP *the problem* using the following steps:

1. Draw a diagram showing the direction of wave propagation and the directions of $\vec{E}$ and $\vec{B}$.
2. Identify the target variables.

EXECUTE *the solution* as follows:

1. Review the treatment of sinusoidal mechanical waves in Chapters 15 and 16, and particularly the four problem-solving strategies suggested there.
2. Keep in mind the basic relationships for periodic waves: $v = \lambda f$ and $\omega = vk$. For electromagnetic waves in vacuum, $v = c$. Distinguish between ordinary frequency f, usually expressed in hertz, and angular frequency $\omega = 2\pi f$, expressed in rad/s. Remember that the wave number is $k = 2\pi/\lambda$.
3. Concentrate on basic relationships, such as those between $\vec{E}$ and $\vec{B}$ (magnitude, direction, and relative phase), how the wave speed is determined, and the transverse nature of the waves.

EVALUATE *your answer:* Check that your result is reasonable. For electromagnetic waves in vacuum, the magnitude of the magnetic field in teslas is much smaller (by a factor of 3.00×10^8) than the magnitude of the electric field in volts per meter. If your answer suggests otherwise, you probably made an error using the relationship $E = cB$. (We'll see later in this section that the relationship between E and B is different for electromagnetic waves in a material medium.)

Example 32.1 Electric and magnetic fields of a laser beam

A carbon dioxide laser emits a sinusoidal electromagnetic wave that travels in vacuum in the negative x-direction. The wavelength is 10.6 μm (in the infrared; see Fig. 32.4) and the $\vec{E}$ field is parallel to the z-axis, with $E_{max} = 1.5$ MV/m. Write vector equations for $\vec{E}$ and $\vec{B}$ as functions of time and position.

SOLUTION

IDENTIFY and SET UP: Equations (32.19) describe a wave traveling in the negative x-direction with $\vec{E}$ along the y-axis—that is, a wave that is linearly polarized along the y-axis. By contrast, the wave in this example is linearly polarized along the z-axis. At points where $\vec{E}$ is in the positive z-direction, $\vec{B}$ must be in the positive y-direction for the vector product $\vec{E} \times \vec{B}$ to be in the negative x-direction (the direction of propagation). Figure 32.15 shows a wave that satisfies these requirements.

32.15 Our sketch for this problem.

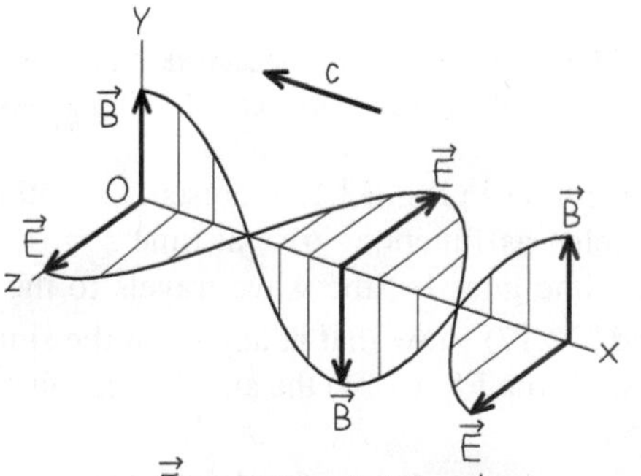

EXECUTE: A possible pair of wave functions that describe the wave shown in Fig. 32.15 are

$$\vec{E}(x, t) = \hat{k} E_{max} \cos(kx + \omega t)$$
$$\vec{B}(x, t) = \hat{j} B_{max} \cos(kx + \omega t)$$

The plus sign in the arguments of the cosine functions indicates that the wave is propagating in the negative x-direction, as it should. Faraday's law requires that $E_{max} = cB_{max}$ [Eq. (32.18)], so

$$B_{max} = \frac{E_{max}}{c} = \frac{1.5 \times 10^6 \text{ V/m}}{3.0 \times 10^8 \text{ m/s}} = 5.0 \times 10^{-3} \text{ T}$$

To check unit consistency, note that $1 \text{ V} = 1 \text{ Wb/s}$ and $1 \text{ Wb/m}^2 = 1 \text{ T}$.

We have $\lambda = 10.6 \times 10^{-6}$ m, so the wave number and angular frequency are

$$k = \frac{2\pi}{\lambda} = \frac{2\pi \text{ rad}}{10.6 \times 10^{-6} \text{ m}} = 5.93 \times 10^5 \text{ rad/m}$$

$$\omega = ck = (3.00 \times 10^8 \text{ m/s})(5.93 \times 10^5 \text{ rad/m})$$
$$= 1.78 \times 10^{14} \text{ rad/s}$$

Substituting these values into the above wave functions, we get

$$\vec{E}(x, t) = \hat{k}(1.5 \times 10^6 \text{ V/m}) \times \cos[(5.93 \times 10^5 \text{ rad/m})x + (1.78 \times 10^{14} \text{ rad/s})t]$$

$$\vec{B}(x, t) = \hat{j}(5.0 \times 10^{-3} \text{ T}) \times \cos[(5.93 \times 10^5 \text{ rad/m})x + (1.78 \times 10^{14} \text{ rad/s})t]$$

EVALUATE: As we expect, the magnitude B_{max} in teslas is much smaller than the magnitude E_{max} in volts per meter. To check the directions of $\vec{E}$ and $\vec{B}$, note that $\vec{E} \times \vec{B}$ is in the direction of $\hat{k} \times \hat{j} = -\hat{\imath}$. This is as it should be for a wave that propagates in the negative x-direction.

Our expressions for $\vec{E}(x, t)$ and $\vec{B}(x, t)$ are not the only possible solutions. We could always add a phase angle ϕ to the arguments of the cosine function, so that $kx + \omega t$ would become $kx + \omega t + \phi$. To determine the value of ϕ we would need to know $\vec{E}$ and $\vec{B}$ either as functions of x at a given time t or as functions of t at a given coordinate x. However, the statement of the problem doesn't include this information.

Electromagnetic Waves in Matter

So far, our discussion of electromagnetic waves has been restricted to waves in *vacuum*. But electromagnetic waves can also travel in *matter;* think of light traveling through air, water, or glass. In this subsection we extend our analysis to electromagnetic waves in nonconducting materials—that is, *dielectrics.*

In a dielectric the wave speed is not the same as in vacuum, and we denote it by v instead of c. Faraday's law is unaltered, but in Eq. (32.4), derived from Faraday's law, the speed c is replaced by v. In Ampere's law the displacement current is given not by $\epsilon_0\, d\Phi_E/dt$, where Φ_E is the flux of $\vec{E}$ through a surface, but by $\epsilon\, d\Phi_E/dt = K\epsilon_0\, d\Phi_E/dt$, where K is the dielectric constant and ϵ is the permittivity of the dielectric. (We introduced these quantities in Section 24.4.) Also, the constant μ_0 in Ampere's law must be replaced by $\mu = K_m\mu_0$, where K_m is the relative permeability of the dielectric and μ is its permeability (see Section 28.8). Hence Eqs. (32.4) and (32.8) are replaced by

$$E = vB \quad \text{and} \quad B = \epsilon\mu v E \tag{32.20}$$

Following the same procedure as for waves in vacuum, we find that the wave speed v is

$$v = \frac{1}{\sqrt{\epsilon\mu}} = \frac{1}{\sqrt{KK_m}}\frac{1}{\sqrt{\epsilon_0\mu_0}} = \frac{c}{\sqrt{KK_m}} \quad \text{(speed of electromagnetic waves in a dielectric)} \tag{32.21}$$

For most dielectrics the relative permeability K_m is very nearly equal to unity (except for insulating ferromagnetic materials). When $K_m \cong 1$,

$$v = \frac{1}{\sqrt{K}}\frac{1}{\sqrt{\epsilon_0\mu_0}} = \frac{c}{\sqrt{K}}$$

Because K is always greater than unity, the speed v of electromagnetic waves in a dielectric is always *less* than the speed c in vacuum by a factor of $1/\sqrt{K}$ (Fig. 32.16). The ratio of the speed c in vacuum to the speed v in a material is known in optics as the **index of refraction** n of the material. When $K_m \cong 1$,

$$\frac{c}{v} = n = \sqrt{KK_m} \cong \sqrt{K} \tag{32.22}$$

Usually, we can't use the values of K in Table 24.1 in this equation because those values are measured using *constant* electric fields. When the fields oscillate rapidly,

32.16 The dielectric constant K of water is about 1.8 for visible light, so the speed of visible light in water is slower than in vacuum by a factor of $1/\sqrt{K} = 1/\sqrt{1.8} = 0.75$.

there is usually not time for the reorientation of electric dipoles that occurs with steady fields. Values of K with rapidly varying fields are usually much *smaller* than the values in the table. For example, K for water is 80.4 for steady fields but only about 1.8 in the frequency range of visible light. Thus the dielectric "constant" K is actually a function of frequency (the *dielectric function*).

Example 32.2 Electromagnetic waves in different materials

(a) Visiting a jewelry store one evening, you hold a diamond up to the light of a sodium-vapor street lamp. The heated sodium vapor emits yellow light with a frequency of 5.09×10^{14} Hz. Find the wavelength in vacuum and the wave speed and wavelength in diamond, for which $K = 5.84$ and $K_m = 1.00$ at this frequency. (b) A 90.0-MHz radio wave (in the FM radio band) passes from vacuum into an insulating ferrite (a ferromagnetic material used in computer cables to suppress radio interference). Find the wavelength in vacuum and the wave speed and wavelength in the ferrite, for which $K = 10.0$ and $K_m = 1000$ at this frequency.

SOLUTION

IDENTIFY and SET UP: In each case we find the wavelength in vacuum using $c = \lambda f$. To use the corresponding equation $v = \lambda f$ to find the wavelength in a material medium, we find the speed v of electromagnetic waves in the medium using Eq. (32.21), which relates v to the values of dielectric constant K and relative permeability K_m for the medium.

EXECUTE: (a) The wavelength in vacuum of the sodium light is

$$\lambda_{\text{vacuum}} = \frac{c}{f} = \frac{3.00 \times 10^8 \text{ m/s}}{5.09 \times 10^{14} \text{ Hz}} = 5.89 \times 10^{-7} \text{ m} = 589 \text{ nm}$$

The wave speed and wavelength in diamond are

$$v_{\text{diamond}} = \frac{c}{\sqrt{KK_m}} = \frac{3.00 \times 10^8 \text{ m/s}}{\sqrt{(5.84)(1.00)}} = 1.24 \times 10^8 \text{ m/s}$$

$$\lambda_{\text{diamond}} = \frac{v_{\text{diamond}}}{f} = \frac{1.24 \times 10^8 \text{ m/s}}{5.09 \times 10^{14} \text{ Hz}}$$
$$= 2.44 \times 10^{-7} \text{ m} = 244 \text{ nm}$$

(b) Following the same steps as in part (a), we find

$$\lambda_{\text{vacuum}} = \frac{c}{f} = \frac{3.00 \times 10^8 \text{ m/s}}{90.0 \times 10^6 \text{ Hz}} = 3.33 \text{ m}$$

$$v_{\text{ferrite}} = \frac{c}{\sqrt{KK_m}} = \frac{3.00 \times 10^8 \text{ m/s}}{\sqrt{(10.0)(1000)}} = 3.00 \times 10^6 \text{ m/s}$$

$$\lambda_{\text{ferrite}} = \frac{v_{\text{ferrite}}}{f} = \frac{3.00 \times 10^6 \text{ m/s}}{90.0 \times 10^6 \text{ Hz}}$$
$$= 3.33 \times 10^{-2} \text{ m} = 3.33 \text{ cm}$$

EVALUATE: The speed of light in transparent materials is typically between $0.2c$ and c; our result in part (a) shows that $v_{\text{diamond}} = 0.414c$. As our results in part (b) show, the speed of electromagnetic waves in dense materials like ferrite (for which $v_{\text{ferrite}} = 0.010c$) can be *far* slower than in vacuum.

Test Your Understanding of Section 32.3 The first of Eqs. (32.17) gives the electric field for a plane wave as measured at points along the x-axis. For this plane wave, how does the electric field at points *off* the x-axis differ from the expression in Eqs. (32.17)? (i) The amplitude is different; (ii) the phase is different; (iii) both the amplitude and phase are different; (iv) none of these.

32.4 Energy and Momentum in Electromagnetic Waves

It is a familiar fact that energy is associated with electromagnetic waves; think of the energy in the sun's radiation. Microwave ovens, radio transmitters, and lasers for eye surgery all make use of the energy that these waves carry. To understand how to utilize this energy, it's helpful to derive detailed relationships for the energy in an electromagnetic wave.

We begin with the expressions derived in Sections 24.3 and 30.3 for the **energy densities** in electric and magnetic fields; we suggest you review those derivations now. Equations (24.11) and (30.10) show that in a region of empty space where $\vec{E}$ and $\vec{B}$ fields are present, the total energy density u is given by

$$u = \tfrac{1}{2}\epsilon_0 E^2 + \frac{1}{2\mu_0}B^2 \tag{32.23}$$

where ϵ_0 and μ_0 are, respectively, the permittivity and permeability of free space. For electromagnetic waves in vacuum, the magnitudes E and B are related by

$$B = \frac{E}{c} = \sqrt{\epsilon_0 \mu_0}\, E \qquad (32.24)$$

Combining Eqs. (32.23) and (32.24), we can also express the energy density u in a simple electromagnetic wave in vacuum as

$$u = \tfrac{1}{2}\epsilon_0 E^2 + \frac{1}{2\mu_0}(\sqrt{\epsilon_0 \mu_0}\, E)^2 = \epsilon_0 E^2 \qquad (32.25)$$

This shows that in vacuum, the energy density associated with the $\vec{E}$ field in our simple wave is equal to the energy density of the $\vec{B}$ field. In general, the electric-field magnitude E is a function of position and time, as for the sinusoidal wave described by Eqs. (32.16); thus the energy density u of an electromagnetic wave, given by Eq. (32.25), also depends in general on position and time.

Electromagnetic Energy Flow and the Poynting Vector

Electromagnetic waves such as those we have described are *traveling* waves that transport energy from one region to another. We can describe this energy transfer in terms of energy transferred *per unit time per unit cross-sectional area,* or *power per unit area,* for an area perpendicular to the direction of wave travel.

To see how the energy flow is related to the fields, consider a stationary plane, perpendicular to the x-axis, that coincides with the wave front at a certain time. In a time dt after this, the wave front moves a distance $dx = c\,dt$ to the right of the plane. Considering an area A on this stationary plane (Fig. 32.17), we note that the energy in the space to the right of this area must have passed through the area to reach the new location. The volume dV of the relevant region is the base area A times the length $c\,dt$, and the energy dU in this region is the energy density u times this volume:

$$dU = u\,dV = (\epsilon_0 E^2)(Ac\,dt)$$

This energy passes through the area A in time dt. The energy flow per unit time per unit area, which we will call S, is

$$S = \frac{1}{A}\frac{dU}{dt} = \epsilon_0 c E^2 \quad \text{(in vacuum)} \qquad (32.26)$$

Using Eqs. (32.4) and (32.9), we can derive the alternative forms

$$S = \frac{\epsilon_0}{\sqrt{\epsilon_0 \mu_0}} E^2 = \sqrt{\frac{\epsilon_0}{\mu_0}} E^2 = \frac{EB}{\mu_0} \quad \text{(in vacuum)} \qquad (32.27)$$

We leave the derivation of Eq. (32.27) from Eq. (32.26) as an exercise for you. The units of S are energy per unit time per unit area, or power per unit area. The SI unit of S is $1\ \text{J/s} \cdot \text{m}^2$ or $1\ \text{W/m}^2$.

We can define a *vector* quantity that describes both the magnitude and direction of the energy flow rate:

$$\vec{S} = \frac{1}{\mu_0}\vec{E} \times \vec{B} \quad \text{(Poynting vector in vacuum)} \qquad (32.28)$$

The vector $\vec{S}$ is called the **Poynting vector;** it was introduced by the British physicist John Poynting (1852–1914). Its direction is in the direction of propagation of the wave (Fig. 32.18). Since $\vec{E}$ and $\vec{B}$ are perpendicular, the magnitude of $\vec{S}$ is $S = EB/\mu_0$; from Eqs. (32.26) and (32.27) this is the energy flow per unit area and per unit time through a cross-sectional area perpendicular to the propagation direction. The total energy flow per unit time (power, P) out of any closed surface is the integral of $\vec{S}$ over the surface:

$$P = \oint \vec{S} \cdot d\vec{A}$$

32.17 A wave front at a time dt after it passes through the stationary plane with area A.

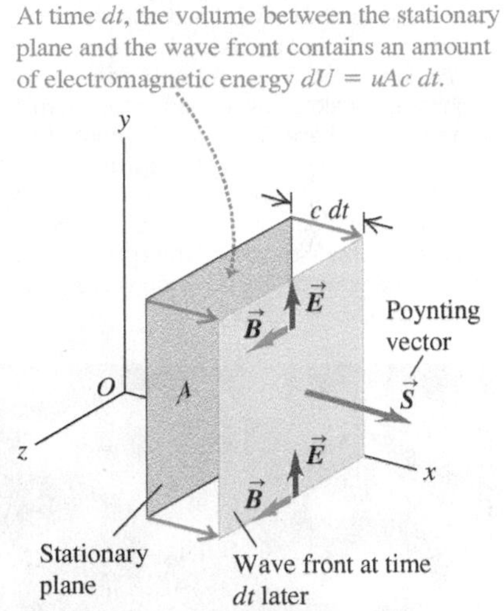

32.18 These rooftop solar panels are tilted to be face-on to the sun—that is, face-on to the Poynting vector of electromagnetic waves from the sun, so that the panels can absorb the maximum amount of wave energy.

For the sinusoidal waves studied in Section 32.3, as well as for other more complex waves, the electric and magnetic fields at any point vary with time, so the Poynting vector at any point is also a function of time. Because the frequencies of typical electromagnetic waves are very high, the time variation of the Poynting vector is so rapid that it's most appropriate to look at its *average* value. The magnitude of the average value of $\vec{S}$ at a point is called the **intensity** of the radiation at that point. The SI unit of intensity is the same as for S, 1 W/m^2 (watt per square meter).

Let's work out the intensity of the sinusoidal wave described by Eqs. (32.17). We first substitute $\vec{E}$ and $\vec{B}$ into Eq. (32.28):

$$\vec{S}(x,t) = \frac{1}{\mu_0}\vec{E}(x,t) \times \vec{B}(x,t)$$

$$= \frac{1}{\mu_0}[\hat{\jmath}E_{max}\cos(kx - \omega t)] \times [\hat{k}B_{max}\cos(kx - \omega t)]$$

The vector product of the unit vectors is $\hat{\jmath} \times \hat{k} = \hat{\imath}$ and $\cos^2(kx - \omega t)$ is never negative, so $\vec{S}(x,t)$ always points in the positive x-direction (the direction of wave propagation). The x-component of the Poynting vector is

$$S_x(x,t) = \frac{E_{max}B_{max}}{\mu_0}\cos^2(kx - \omega t) = \frac{E_{max}B_{max}}{2\mu_0}[1 + \cos 2(kx - \omega t)]$$

The time average value of $\cos 2(kx - \omega t)$ is zero because at any point, it is positive during one half-cycle and negative during the other half. So the average value of the Poynting vector over a full cycle is $\vec{S}_{av} = \hat{\imath}S_{av}$, where

$$S_{av} = \frac{E_{max}B_{max}}{2\mu_0}$$

That is, the magnitude of the average value of $\vec{S}$ for a sinusoidal wave (the intensity I of the wave) is $\frac{1}{2}$ the maximum value. By using the relationships $E_{max} = B_{max}c$ and $\epsilon_0\mu_0 = 1/c^2$, we can express the intensity in several equivalent forms:

$$I = S_{av} = \frac{E_{max}B_{max}}{2\mu_0} = \frac{E_{max}{}^2}{2\mu_0 c} = \frac{1}{2}\sqrt{\frac{\epsilon_0}{\mu_0}}E_{max}{}^2 = \frac{1}{2}\epsilon_0 c E_{max}{}^2 \quad \text{(intensity of a sinusoidal wave in vacuum)} \qquad (32.29)$$

We invite you to verify that these expressions are all equivalent.

For a wave traveling in the $-x$-direction, represented by Eqs. (32.19), the Poynting vector is in the $-x$-direction at every point, but its magnitude is the same as for a wave traveling in the $+x$-direction. Verifying these statements is left to you (see Exercise 32.24).

CAUTION **Poynting vector vs. intensity** At any point x, the magnitude of the Poynting vector varies with time. Hence, the *instantaneous* rate at which electromagnetic energy in a sinusoidal plane wave arrives at a surface is not constant. This may seem to contradict everyday experience; the light from the sun, a light bulb, or the laser in a grocery-store scanner appears steady and unvarying in strength. In fact the Poynting vector from these sources *does* vary in time, but the variation isn't noticeable because the oscillation frequency is so high (around 5×10^{14} Hz for visible light). All that you sense is the *average* rate at which energy reaches your eye, which is why we commonly use intensity (the average value of S) to describe the strength of electromagnetic radiation.

Application Laser Surgery
Lasers are used widely in medicine as ultra-precise, bloodless "scalpels." They can reach and remove tumors with minimal damage to neighboring healthy tissues, as in the brain surgery shown here. The power output of the laser is typically below 40 W, less than that of a typical light bulb. However, this power is concentrated into a spot from 0.1 to 2.0 mm in diameter, so the intensity of the light (equal to the average value of the Poynting vector) can be as high as 5×10^9 W/m^2.

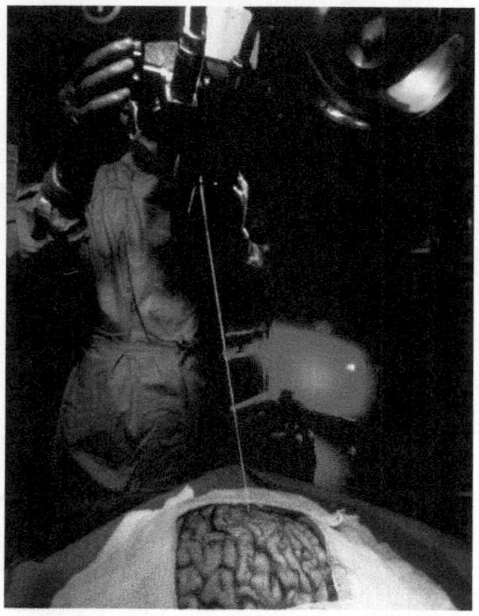

Throughout this discussion we have considered only electromagnetic waves propagating in vacuum. If the waves are traveling in a dielectric medium, however, the expressions for energy density [Eq. (32.23)], the Poynting vector [Eq. (32.28)], and the intensity of a sinusoidal wave [Eq. (32.29)] must be modified. It turns out that the required modifications are quite simple: Just replace ϵ_0 with the permittivity ϵ of the dielectric, replace μ_0 with the permeability μ of the dielectric, and replace c with the speed v of electromagnetic waves in the dielectric. Remarkably, the energy densities in the $\vec{E}$ and $\vec{B}$ fields are equal even in a dielectric.

Example 32.3 Energy in a nonsinusoidal wave

For the nonsinusoidal wave described in Section 32.2, suppose that $E = 100\ \text{V/m} = 100\ \text{N/C}$. Find the value of B, the energy density u, and the rate of energy flow per unit area S.

SOLUTION

IDENTIFY and SET UP: In this wave $\vec{E}$ and $\vec{B}$ are uniform behind the wave front (and zero ahead of it). Hence the target variables B, u, and S must also be uniform behind the wave front. Given the magnitude E, we use Eq. (32.4) to find B, Eq. (32.25) to find u, and Eq. (32.27) to find S. (We cannot use Eq. (32.29), which applies to sinusoidal waves only.)

EXECUTE: From Eq. (32.4),

$$B = \frac{E}{c} = \frac{100\ \text{V/m}}{3.00 \times 10^8\ \text{m/s}} = 3.33 \times 10^{-7}\ \text{T}$$

From Eq. (32.25),

$$u = \epsilon_0 E^2 = (8.85 \times 10^{-12}\ \text{C}^2/\text{N}\cdot\text{m}^2)(100\ \text{N/C})^2$$
$$= 8.85 \times 10^{-8}\ \text{N/m}^2 = 8.85 \times 10^{-8}\ \text{J/m}^3$$

The magnitude of the Poynting vector is

$$S = \frac{EB}{\mu_0} = \frac{(100\ \text{V/m})(3.33 \times 10^{-7}\ \text{T})}{4\pi \times 10^{-7}\ \text{T}\cdot\text{m/A}}$$
$$= 26.5\ \text{V}\cdot\text{A/m}^2 = 26.5\ \text{W/m}^2$$

EVALUATE: We can check our result for S by using Eq. (32.26):

$$S = \epsilon_0 c E^2 = (8.85 \times 10^{-12}\ \text{C}^2/\text{N}\cdot\text{m}^2)(3.00 \times 10^8\ \text{m/s})$$
$$\times (100\ \text{N/C})^2 = 26.5\ \text{W/m}^2$$

Since $\vec{E}$ and $\vec{B}$ have the same values at all points behind the wave front, u and S likewise have the same value everywhere behind the wave front. In front of the wave front, $\vec{E} = \mathbf{0}$ and $\vec{B} = \mathbf{0}$, and so $u = 0$ and $S = 0$; where there are no fields, there is no field energy.

Example 32.4 Energy in a sinusoidal wave

A radio station on the earth's surface emits a sinusoidal wave with average total power 50 kW (Fig. 32.19). Assuming that the transmitter radiates equally in all directions above the ground (which is unlikely in real situations), find the electric-field and magnetic-field amplitudes E_{max} and B_{max} detected by a satellite 100 km from the antenna.

SOLUTION

IDENTIFY and SET UP: We are given the transmitter's average total power P. The intensity I is just the average power per unit area, so to find I at 100 km from the transmitter we divide P by the surface area of the hemisphere shown in Fig. 32.19. For a sinusoidal wave, I is also equal to the magnitude of the average value S_{av} of the Poynting vector, so we can use Eqs. (32.29) to find E_{max}; Eq. (32.4) then yields B_{max}.

32.19 A radio station radiates waves into the hemisphere shown.

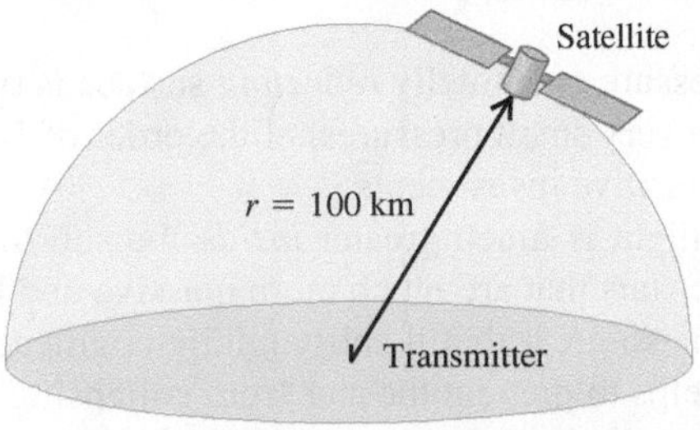

EXECUTE: The surface area of a hemisphere of radius $r = 100\ \text{km} = 1.00 \times 10^5\ \text{m}$ is

$$A = 2\pi R^2 = 2\pi(1.00 \times 10^5\ \text{m})^2 = 6.28 \times 10^{10}\ \text{m}^2$$

All the radiated power passes through this surface, so the average power per unit area (that is, the intensity) is

$$I = \frac{P}{A} = \frac{P}{2\pi R^2} = \frac{5.00 \times 10^4\ \text{W}}{6.28 \times 10^{10}\ \text{m}^2} = 7.96 \times 10^{-7}\ \text{W/m}^2$$

From Eqs. (32.29), $I = S_{av} = E_{max}{}^2/2\mu_0 c$, so

$$E_{max} = \sqrt{2\mu_0 c S_{av}}$$
$$= \sqrt{2(4\pi \times 10^{-7}\ \text{T}\cdot\text{m/A})(3.00 \times 10^8\ \text{m/s})(7.96 \times 10^{-7}\ \text{W/m}^2)}$$
$$= 2.45 \times 10^{-2}\ \text{V/m}$$

Then from Eq. (32.4),

$$B_{max} = \frac{E_{max}}{c} = 8.17 \times 10^{-11}\ \text{T}$$

EVALUATE: Note that E_{max} is comparable to fields commonly seen in the laboratory, but B_{max} is extremely small in comparison to $\vec{B}$ fields we saw in previous chapters. For this reason, most detectors of electromagnetic radiation respond to the effect of the electric field, not the magnetic field. Loop radio antennas are an exception (see the Bridging Problem at the end of this chapter).

Electromagnetic Momentum Flow and Radiation Pressure

By using the observation that energy is required to establish electric and magnetic fields, we have shown that electromagnetic waves transport energy. It can also be shown that electromagnetic waves carry *momentum* p, with a corresponding momentum density (momentum dp per volume dV) of magnitude

$$\frac{dp}{dV} = \frac{EB}{\mu_0 c^2} = \frac{S}{c^2} \qquad (32.30)$$

This momentum is a property of the field; it is not associated with the mass of a moving particle in the usual sense.

There is also a corresponding momentum flow rate. The volume dV occupied by an electromagnetic wave (speed c) that passes through an area A in time dt is $dV = Ac\,dt$. When we substitute this into Eq. (32.30) and rearrange, we find that the momentum flow rate per unit area is

$$\frac{1}{A}\frac{dp}{dt} = \frac{S}{c} = \frac{EB}{\mu_0 c} \quad \text{(flow rate of electromagnetic momentum)} \qquad (32.31)$$

This is the momentum transferred per unit surface area per unit time. We obtain the *average* rate of momentum transfer per unit area by replacing S in Eq. (32.31) by $S_{av} = I$.

This momentum is responsible for **radiation pressure.** When an electromagnetic wave is completely absorbed by a surface, the wave's momentum is also transferred to the surface. For simplicity we'll consider a surface perpendicular to the propagation direction. Using the ideas developed in Section 8.1, we see that the rate dp/dt at which momentum is transferred to the absorbing surface equals the *force* on the surface. The average force per unit area due to the wave, or *radiation pressure* p_{rad}, is the average value of dp/dt divided by the absorbing area A. (We use the subscript "rad" to distinguish pressure from momentum, for which the symbol p is also used.) From Eq. (32.31) the radiation pressure is

$$p_{rad} = \frac{S_{av}}{c} = \frac{I}{c} \quad \text{(radiation pressure, wave totally absorbed)} \qquad (32.32)$$

If the wave is totally reflected, the momentum change is twice as great, and the pressure is

$$p_{rad} = \frac{2S_{av}}{c} = \frac{2I}{c} \quad \text{(radiation pressure, wave totally reflected)} \qquad (32.33)$$

For example, the value of I (or S_{av}) for direct sunlight, before it passes through the earth's atmosphere, is approximately 1.4 kW/m^2. From Eq. (32.32) the corresponding average pressure on a completely absorbing surface is

$$p_{rad} = \frac{I}{c} = \frac{1.4 \times 10^3\ \text{W/m}^2}{3.0 \times 10^8\ \text{m/s}} = 4.7 \times 10^{-6}\ \text{Pa}$$

From Eq. (32.33) the average pressure on a totally *reflecting* surface is twice this: $2I/c$ or 9.4×10^{-6} Pa. These are very small pressures, of the order of 10^{-10} atm, but they can be measured with sensitive instruments.

The radiation pressure of sunlight is much greater *inside* the sun than at the earth (see Problem 32.45). Inside stars that are much more massive and luminous than the sun, radiation pressure is so great that it substantially augments the gas pressure within the star and so helps to prevent the star from collapsing under its own gravity. In some cases the radiation pressure of stars can have dramatic effects on the material surrounding them (Fig. 32.20).

32.20 At the center of this interstellar gas cloud is a group of intensely luminous stars that exert tremendous radiation pressure on their surroundings. Aided by a "wind" of particles emanating from the stars, over the past million years the radiation pressure has carved out a bubble within the cloud 70 light-years across.

Example 32.5 Power and pressure from sunlight

An earth-orbiting satellite has solar energy–collecting panels with a total area of 4.0 m^2 (Fig. 32.21). If the sun's radiation is perpendicular to the panels and is completely absorbed, find the average solar power absorbed and the average radiation-pressure force.

SOLUTION

IDENTIFY and SET UP: This problem uses the relationships among intensity, power, radiation pressure, and force. In the above discussion we calculated the intensity I (power per unit area) of sunlight as well as the radiation pressure p_{rad} (force per unit area) of sunlight on an absorbing surface. (We calculated these values for points above the atmosphere, which is where the satellite orbits.) Multiplying each value by the area of the solar panels gives the average power absorbed and the net radiation force on the panels.

32.21 Solar panels on a satellite.

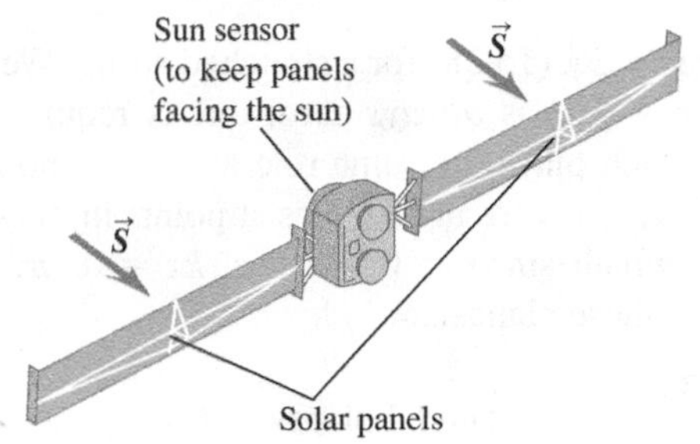

EXECUTE: The intensity I (power per unit area) is $1.4 \times 10^3\ \text{W/m}^2$. Although the light from the sun is not a simple sinusoidal wave, we can still use the relationship that the average power P is the intensity I times the area A:

$$P = IA = (1.4 \times 10^3\ \text{W/m}^2)(4.0\ \text{m}^2) = 5.6 \times 10^3\ \text{W} = 5.6\ \text{kW}$$

The radiation pressure of sunlight on an absorbing surface is $p_{rad} = 4.7 \times 10^{-6}\ \text{Pa} = 4.7 \times 10^{-6}\ \text{N/m}^2$. The total force F is the pressure p_{rad} times the area A:

$$F = p_{rad}A = (4.7 \times 10^{-6}\ \text{N/m}^2)(4.0\ \text{m}^2) = 1.9 \times 10^{-5}\ \text{N}$$

EVALUATE: The absorbed power is quite substantial. Part of it can be used to power the equipment aboard the satellite; the rest goes into heating the panels, either directly or due to inefficiencies in the photocells contained in the panels.

The total radiation force is comparable to the weight (on earth) of a single grain of salt. Over time, however, this small force can have a noticeable effect on the orbit of a satellite like that in Fig. 32.21, and so radiation pressure must be taken into account.

Test Your Understanding of Section 32.4 Figure 32.13 shows one wavelength of a sinusoidal electromagnetic wave at time $t = 0$. For which of the following four values of x is (a) the energy density a maximum; (b) the energy density a minimum; (c) the magnitude of the instantaneous (not average) Poynting vector a maximum; (d) the magnitude of the instantaneous (not average) Poynting vector a minimum? (i) $x = 0$; (ii) $x = \lambda/4$; (iii) $x = \lambda/2$; (iv) $x = 3\lambda/4$.

32.5 Standing Electromagnetic Waves

Electromagnetic waves can be *reflected;* the surface of a conductor (like a polished sheet of metal) or of a dielectric (such as a sheet of glass) can serve as a reflector. The superposition principle holds for electromagnetic waves just as for electric and magnetic fields. The superposition of an incident wave and a reflected wave forms a **standing wave.** The situation is analogous to standing waves on a stretched string, discussed in Section 15.7; you should review that discussion.

Suppose a sheet of a perfect conductor (zero resistivity) is placed in the yz-plane of Fig. 32.22 and a linearly polarized electromagnetic wave, traveling in the negative x-direction, strikes it. As we discussed in Section 23.4, $\vec{E}$ cannot have a component parallel to the surface of a perfect conductor. Therefore in the present situation, $\vec{E}$ must be zero everywhere in the yz-plane. The electric field of the *incident* electromagnetic wave is *not* zero at all times in the yz-plane. But this incident wave induces oscillating currents on the surface of the conductor, and these currents give rise to an additional electric field. The *net* electric field, which is the vector sum of this field and the incident $\vec{E}$, *is* zero everywhere inside and on the surface of the conductor.

The currents induced on the surface of the conductor also produce a *reflected* wave that travels out from the plane in the $+x$-direction. Suppose the incident wave is described by the wave functions of Eqs. (32.19) (a sinusoidal wave traveling in the $-x$-direction) and the reflected wave by the negative of Eqs. (32.16) (a sinusoidal wave traveling in the $+x$-direction). We take the *negative* of the

32.22 Representation of the electric and magnetic fields of a linearly polarized electromagnetic standing wave when $\omega t = 3\pi/4$ rad. In any plane perpendicular to the x-axis, E is maximum (an antinode) where B is zero (a node), and vice versa. As time elapses, the pattern does *not* move along the x-axis; instead, at every point the $\vec{E}$ and $\vec{B}$ vectors simply oscillate.

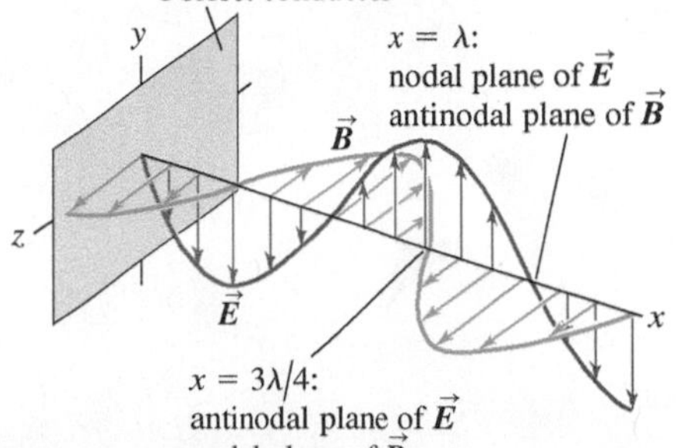

MasteringPHYSICS
PhET: Microwaves

wave given by Eqs. (32.16) so that the incident and reflected electric fields cancel at $x = 0$ (the plane of the conductor, where the total electric field must be zero). The superposition principle states that the total $\vec{E}$ field at any point is the vector sum of the $\vec{E}$ fields of the incident and reflected waves, and similarly for the $\vec{B}$ field. Therefore the wave functions for the superposition of the two waves are

$$E_y(x, t) = E_{max}[\cos(kx + \omega t) - \cos(kx - \omega t)]$$

$$B_z(x, t) = B_{max}[-\cos(kx + \omega t) - \cos(kx - \omega t)]$$

We can expand and simplify these expressions, using the identities

$$\cos(A \pm B) = \cos A \cos B \mp \sin A \sin B$$

The results are

$$E_y(x, t) = -2E_{max} \sin kx \sin \omega t \tag{32.34}$$

$$B_z(x, t) = -2B_{max} \cos kx \cos \omega t \tag{32.35}$$

Equation (32.34) is analogous to Eq. (15.28) for a stretched string. We see that at $x = 0$ the electric field $E_y(x = 0, t)$ is *always* zero; this is required by the nature of the ideal conductor, which plays the same role as a fixed point at the end of a string. Furthermore, $E_y(x, t)$ is zero at *all* times at points in those planes perpendicular to the x-axis for which $\sin kx = 0$—that is, $kx = 0, \pi, 2\pi, \ldots$. Since $k = 2\pi/\lambda$, the positions of these planes are

$$x = 0, \frac{\lambda}{2}, \lambda, \frac{3\lambda}{2}, \ldots \quad \text{(nodal planes of } \vec{E}\text{)} \tag{32.36}$$

These planes are called the **nodal planes** of the $\vec{E}$ field; they are the equivalent of the nodes, or nodal points, of a standing wave on a string. Midway between any two adjacent nodal planes is a plane on which $\sin kx = \pm 1$; on each such plane, the magnitude of $E(x, t)$ equals the maximum possible value of $2E_{max}$ twice per oscillation cycle. These are the **antinodal planes** of $\vec{E}$, corresponding to the antinodes of waves on a string.

The total magnetic field is zero at all times at points in planes on which $\cos kx = 0$. This occurs where

$$x = \frac{\lambda}{4}, \frac{3\lambda}{4}, \frac{5\lambda}{4}, \ldots \quad \text{(nodal planes of } \vec{B}\text{)} \tag{32.37}$$

These are the nodal planes of the $\vec{B}$ field; there is an antinodal plane of $\vec{B}$ midway between any two adjacent nodal planes.

Figure 32.22 shows a standing-wave pattern at one instant of time. The magnetic field is *not* zero at the conducting surface ($x = 0$). The surface currents that must be present to make $\vec{E}$ exactly zero at the surface cause magnetic fields at the surface. The nodal planes of each field are separated by one half-wavelength. The nodal planes of one field are midway between those of the other; hence the nodes of $\vec{E}$ coincide with the antinodes of $\vec{B}$, and conversely. Compare this situation to the distinction between pressure nodes and displacement nodes in Section 16.4.

The total electric field is a *sine* function of t, and the total magnetic field is a *cosine* function of t. The sinusoidal variations of the two fields are therefore 90° out of phase at each point. At times when $\sin \omega t = 0$, the electric field is zero *everywhere,* and the magnetic field is maximum. When $\cos \omega t = 0$, the magnetic field is zero everywhere, and the electric field is maximum. This is in contrast to a wave traveling in one direction, as described by Eqs. (32.16) or (32.19) separately, in which the sinusoidal variations of $\vec{E}$ and $\vec{B}$ at any particular point are *in phase.* You can show that Eqs. (32.34) and (32.35) satisfy the wave equation, Eq. (32.15). You can also show that they satisfy Eqs. (32.12) and (32.14), the equivalents of Faraday's and Ampere's laws (see Exercise 32.36).

Standing Waves in a Cavity

Let's now insert a second conducting plane, parallel to the first and a distance L from it, along the $+x$-axis. The cavity between the two planes is analogous to a stretched string held at the points $x = 0$ and $x = L$. Both conducting planes must be nodal planes for $\vec{E}$; a standing wave can exist only when the second plane is placed at one of the positions where $E(x, t) = 0$, so L must be an integer multiple of $\lambda/2$. The wavelengths that satisfy this condition are

$$\lambda_n = \frac{2L}{n} \quad (n = 1, 2, 3, \ldots) \tag{32.38}$$

The corresponding frequencies are

$$f_n = \frac{c}{\lambda_n} = n\frac{c}{2L} \quad (n = 1, 2, 3, \ldots) \tag{32.39}$$

Thus there is a set of *normal modes,* each with a characteristic frequency, wave shape, and node pattern (Fig. 32.23). By measuring the node positions, we can measure the wavelength. If the frequency is known, the wave speed can be determined. This technique was first used by Hertz in the 1880s in his pioneering investigations of electromagnetic waves.

Conducting surfaces are not the only reflectors of electromagnetic waves. Reflections also occur at an interface between two insulating materials with different dielectric or magnetic properties. The mechanical analog is a junction of two strings with equal tension but different linear mass density. In general, a wave incident on such a boundary surface is partly transmitted into the second material and partly reflected back into the first. For example, light is transmitted through a glass window, but its surfaces also reflect light.

32.23 A typical microwave oven sets up a standing electromagnetic wave with $\lambda = 12.2$ cm, a wavelength that is strongly absorbed by the water in food. Because the wave has nodes spaced $\lambda/2 = 6.1$ cm apart, the food must be rotated while cooking. Otherwise, the portion that lies at a node—where the electric-field amplitude is zero—will remain cold.

Example 32.6 Intensity in a standing wave

Calculate the intensity of the standing wave represented by Eqs. (32.34) and (32.35).

SOLUTION

IDENTIFY and SET UP: The intensity I of the wave is the time-averaged value S_{av} of the magnitude of the Poynting vector $\vec{S}$. To find S_{av}, we first use Eq. (32.28) to find the instantaneous value of $\vec{S}$ and then average it over a whole number of cycles of the wave.

EXECUTE: Using the wave functions of Eqs. (32.34) and (32.35) in Eq. (32.28) for the Poynting vector $\vec{S}$, we find

$$\begin{aligned}\vec{S}(x, t) &= \frac{1}{\mu_0}\vec{E}(x, t) \times \vec{B}(x, t) \\ &= \frac{1}{\mu_0}[-2\hat{j}E_{max}\sin kx \cos \omega t] \times [-2\hat{k}B_{max}\cos kx \sin \omega t] \\ &= \hat{\imath}\frac{E_{max}B_{max}}{\mu_0}(2\sin kx \cos kx)(2\sin \omega t \cos \omega t) \\ &= \hat{\imath}S_x(x, t)\end{aligned}$$

Using the identity $\sin 2A = 2\sin A\cos A$, we can rewrite $S_x(x, t)$ as

$$S_x(x, t) = \frac{E_{max}B_{max}\sin 2kx \sin 2\omega t}{\mu_0}$$

The average value of a sine function over any whole number of cycles is zero. Thus *the time average of $\vec{S}$ at any point is zero;* $I = S_{av} = 0$.

EVALUATE: This result is what we should expect. The standing wave is a superposition of two waves with the same frequency and amplitude, traveling in opposite directions. All the energy transferred by one wave is cancelled by an equal amount transferred in the opposite direction by the other wave. When we use electromagnetic waves to transmit power, it is important to avoid reflections that give rise to standing waves.

Example 32.7 Standing waves in a cavity

Electromagnetic standing waves are set up in a cavity with two parallel, highly conducting walls 1.50 cm apart. (a) Calculate the longest wavelength λ and lowest frequency f of these standing waves. (b) For a standing wave of this wavelength, where in the cavity does $\vec{E}$ have maximum magnitude? Where is $\vec{E}$ zero? Where does $\vec{B}$ have maximum magnitude? Where is $\vec{B}$ zero?

Continued

SOLUTION

IDENTIFY and SET UP: Only certain normal modes are possible for electromagnetic waves in a cavity, just as only certain normal modes are possible for standing waves on a string. The longest possible wavelength and lowest possible frequency correspond to the $n = 1$ mode in Eqs. (32.38) and (32.39); we use these to find λ and f. Equations (32.36) and (32.37) then give the locations of the nodal planes of $\vec{E}$ and $\vec{B}$. The antinodal planes of each field are midway between adjacent nodal planes.

EXECUTE: (a) From Eqs. (32.38) and (32.39), the $n = 1$ wavelength and frequency are

$$\lambda_1 = 2L = 2(1.50\ \text{cm}) = 3.00\ \text{cm}$$

$$f_1 = \frac{c}{2L} = \frac{3.00 \times 10^8\ \text{m/s}}{2(1.50 \times 10^{-2}\ \text{m})} = 1.00 \times 10^{10}\ \text{Hz} = 10\ \text{GHz}$$

(b) With $n = 1$ there is a single half-wavelength between the walls. The electric field has nodal planes ($\vec{E} = \mathbf{0}$) at the walls and an antinodal plane (where $\vec{E}$ has its maximum magnitude) midway between them. The magnetic field has *antinodal* planes at the walls and a nodal plane midway between them.

EVALUATE: One application of such standing waves is to produce an oscillating $\vec{E}$ field of definite frequency, which is used to probe the behavior of a small sample of material placed in the cavity. To subject the sample to the strongest possible field, it should be placed near the center of the cavity, at the antinode of $\vec{E}$.

Test Your Understanding of Section 32.5 In the standing wave described in Example 32.7, is there any point in the cavity where the energy density is zero at all times? If so, where? If not, why not? ▎

CHAPTER 32 SUMMARY

Maxwell's equations and electromagnetic waves: Maxwell's equations predict the existence of electromagnetic waves that propagate in vacuum at the speed of light c. The electromagnetic spectrum covers frequencies from at least 1 to 10^{24} Hz and a correspondingly broad range of wavelengths. Visible light, with wavelengths from 380 to 750 nm, is only a very small part of this spectrum. In a plane wave, $\vec{E}$ and $\vec{B}$ are uniform over any plane perpendicular to the propagation direction. Faraday's law and Ampere's law both give relationships between the magnitudes of $\vec{E}$ and $\vec{B}$; requiring both of these relationships to be satisfied gives an expression for c in terms of ϵ_0 and μ_0. Electromagnetic waves are transverse; the $\vec{E}$ and $\vec{B}$ fields are perpendicular to the direction of propagation and to each other. The direction of propagation is the direction of $\vec{E} \times \vec{B}$.

$$E = cB \tag{32.4}$$

$$B = \epsilon_0 \mu_0 c E \tag{32.8}$$

$$c = \frac{1}{\sqrt{\epsilon_0 \mu_0}} \tag{32.9}$$

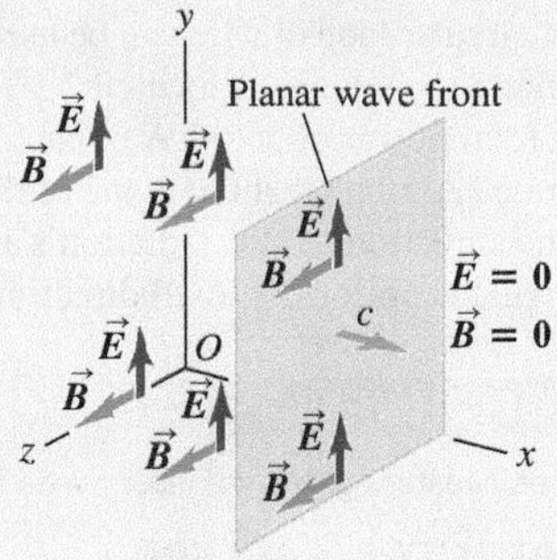

Sinusoidal electromagnetic waves: Equations (32.17) and (32.18) describe a sinusoidal plane electromagnetic wave traveling in vacuum in the $+x$-direction. If the wave is propagating in the $-x$-direction, replace $kx - \omega t$ by $kx + \omega t$. (See Example 32.1.)

$$\vec{E}(x,t) = \hat{\jmath} E_{max} \cos(kx - \omega t)$$
$$\vec{B}(x,t) = \hat{k} B_{max} \cos(kx - \omega t) \tag{32.17}$$

$$E_{max} = cB_{max} \tag{32.18}$$

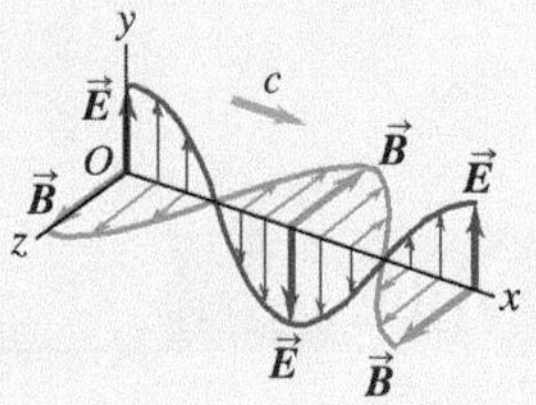

Electromagnetic waves in matter: When an electromagnetic wave travels through a dielectric, the wave speed v is less than the speed of light in vacuum c. (See Example 32.2.)

$$v = \frac{1}{\sqrt{\epsilon\mu}} = \frac{1}{\sqrt{KK_m}}\frac{1}{\sqrt{\epsilon_0\mu_0}} = \frac{c}{\sqrt{KK_m}} \tag{32.21}$$

Energy and momentum in electromagnetic waves: The energy flow rate (power per unit area) in an electromagnetic wave in vacuum is given by the Poynting vector $\vec{S}$. The magnitude of the time-averaged value of the Poynting vector is called the intensity I of the wave. Electromagnetic waves also carry momentum. When an electromagnetic wave strikes a surface, it exerts a radiation pressure p_{rad}. If the surface is perpendicular to the wave propagation direction and is totally absorbing, $p_{rad} = I/c$; if the surface is a perfect reflector, $p_{rad} = 2I/c$. (See Examples 32.3–32.5.)

$$\vec{S} = \frac{1}{\mu_0}\vec{E} \times \vec{B} \tag{32.28}$$

$$I = S_{av} = \frac{E_{max}B_{max}}{2\mu_0} = \frac{E_{max}{}^2}{2\mu_0 c} = \frac{1}{2}\sqrt{\frac{\epsilon_0}{\mu_0}}E_{max}{}^2 = \frac{1}{2}\epsilon_0 c E_{max}{}^2 \tag{32.29}$$

$$\frac{1}{A}\frac{dp}{dt} = \frac{S}{c} = \frac{EB}{\mu_0 c} \tag{32.31}$$

(flow rate of electromagnetic momentum)

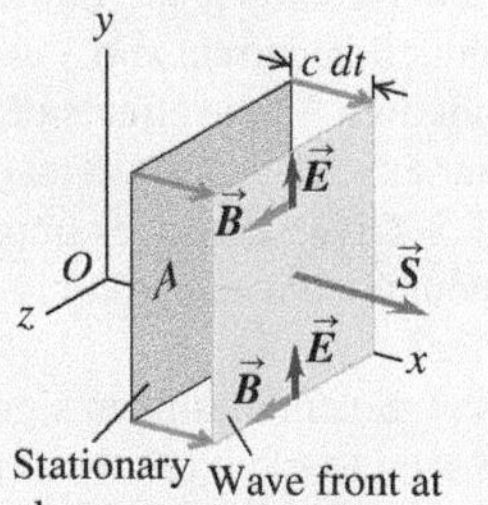

Standing electromagnetic waves: If a perfect reflecting surface is placed at $x = 0$, the incident and reflected waves form a standing wave. Nodal planes for $\vec{E}$ occur at $kx = 0, \pi, 2\pi, \ldots$, and nodal planes for $\vec{B}$ at $kx = \pi/2, 3\pi/2, 5\pi/2, \ldots$. At each point, the sinusoidal variations of $\vec{E}$ and $\vec{B}$ with time are 90° out of phase. (See Examples 32.6 and 32.7.)

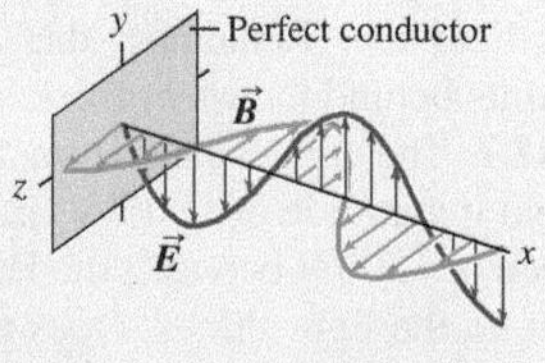

BRIDGING PROBLEM Detecting Electromagnetic Waves

A circular loop of wire can be used as a radio antenna. If an 18.0-cm-diameter antenna is located 2.50 km from a 95.0-MHz source with a total power of 55.0 kW, what is the maximum emf induced in the loop? Assume that the plane of the antenna loop is perpendicular to the direction of the radiation's magnetic field and that the source radiates uniformly in all directions.

SOLUTION GUIDE

See MasteringPhysics® study area for a Video Tutor solution.

IDENTIFY and SET UP:

1. The electromagnetic wave has an oscillating magnetic field. This causes a magnetic flux through the loop antenna that varies sinusoidally with time. By Faraday's law, this produces an emf equal in magnitude to the rate of change of the flux. The target variable is the magnitude of this emf.
2. Select the equations that you will need to find (i) the intensity of the wave at the position of the loop, a distance $r = 2.50$ km from the source of power $P = 55.0$ kW; (ii) the amplitude of the sinusoidally varying magnetic field at that position; (iii) the magnetic flux through the loop as a function of time; and (iv) the emf produced by the flux.

EXECUTE

3. Find the wave intensity at the position of the loop.
4. Use your result from step 3 to write expressions for the time-dependent magnetic field at this position and the time-dependent magnetic flux through the loop.
5. Use the results of step 4 to find the time-dependent induced emf in the loop. The amplitude of this emf is your target variable.

EVALUATE

6. Is the induced emf large enough to detect? (If it is, a receiver connected to this antenna will be able to pick up signals from the source.)

Problems

For instructor-assigned homework, go to www.masteringphysics.com

•, ••, •••: Problems of increasing difficulty. **CP**: Cumulative problems incorporating material from earlier chapters. **CALC**: Problems requiring calculus. **BIO**: Biosciences problems.

DISCUSSION QUESTIONS

Q32.1 By measuring the electric and magnetic fields at a point in space where there is an electromagnetic wave, can you determine the direction from which the wave came? Explain.

Q32.2 According to Ampere's law, is it possible to have both a conduction current and a displacement current at the same time? Is it possible for the effects of the two kinds of current to cancel each other exactly so that *no* magnetic field is produced? Explain.

Q32.3 Give several examples of electromagnetic waves that are encountered in everyday life. How are they all alike? How do they differ?

Q32.4 Sometimes neon signs located near a powerful radio station are seen to glow faintly at night, even though they are not turned on. What is happening?

Q32.5 Is polarization a property of all electromagnetic waves, or is it unique to visible light? Can sound waves be polarized? What fundamental distinction in wave properties is involved? Explain.

Q32.6 Suppose that a positive point charge q is initially at rest on the x-axis, in the path of the electromagnetic plane wave described in Section 32.2. Will the charge move after the wave front reaches it? If not, why not? If the charge does move, describe its motion qualitatively. (Remember that $\vec{E}$ and $\vec{B}$ have the same value at all points behind the wave front.)

Q32.7 The light beam from a searchlight may have an electric-field magnitude of 1000 V/m, corresponding to a potential difference of 1500 V between the head and feet of a 1.5-m-tall person on whom the light shines. Does this cause the person to feel a strong electric shock? Why or why not?

Q32.8 For a certain sinusoidal wave of intensity I, the amplitude of the magnetic field is B. What would be the amplitude (in terms of B) in a similar wave of twice the intensity?

Q32.9 The magnetic-field amplitude of the electromagnetic wave from the laser described in Example 32.1 (Section 32.3) is about 100 times greater than the earth's magnetic field. If you illuminate a compass with the light from this laser, would you expect the compass to deflect? Why or why not?

Q32.10 Most automobiles have vertical antennas for receiving radio broadcasts. Explain what this tells you about the direction of polarization of $\vec{E}$ in the radio waves used in broadcasting.

Q32.11 If a light beam carries momentum, should a person holding a flashlight feel a recoil analogous to the recoil of a rifle when it is fired? Why is this recoil not actually observed?

Q32.12 A light source radiates a sinusoidal electromagnetic wave uniformly in all directions. This wave exerts an average pressure p on a perfectly reflecting surface a distance R away from it. What average pressure (in terms of p) would this wave exert on a perfectly absorbing surface that was twice as far from the source?

Q32.13 Does an electromagnetic *standing* wave have energy? Does it have momentum? Are your answers to these questions the same as for a *traveling* wave? Why or why not?

Q32.14 When driving on the upper level of the Bay Bridge, westbound from Oakland to San Francisco, you can easily pick up a number of radio stations on your car radio. But when driving eastbound on the lower level of the bridge, which has steel girders on either side to support the upper level, the radio reception is much worse. Why is there a difference?

EXERCISES

Section 32.2 Plane Electromagnetic Waves and the Speed of Light

32.1 • (a) How much time does it take light to travel from the moon to the earth, a distance of 384,000 km? (b) Light from the star Sirius takes 8.61 years to reach the earth. What is the distance from earth to Sirius in kilometers?

32.2 • Consider each of the electric- and magnetic-field orientations given next. In each case, what is the direction of propagation of the wave? (a) $\vec{E}$ in the $+x$-direction, $\vec{B}$ in the $+y$-direction; (b) $\vec{E}$ in the $-y$-direction, $\vec{B}$ in the $+x$-direction; (c) $\vec{E}$ in the $+z$-direction, $\vec{B}$ in the $-x$-direction; (d) $\vec{E}$ in the $+y$-direction, $\vec{B}$ in the $-z$-direction.

32.3 • A sinusoidal electromagnetic wave is propagating in vacuum in the $+z$-direction. If at a particular instant and at a certain point in space the electric field is in the $+x$-direction and has magnitude 4.00 V/m, what are the magnitude and direction of the magnetic field of the wave at this same point in space and instant in time?

32.4 • Consider each of the following electric- and magnetic-field orientations. In each case, what is the direction of propagation of the wave? (a) $\vec{E} = E\hat{\imath}$, $\vec{B} = -B\hat{\jmath}$; (b) $\vec{E} = E\hat{\jmath}$, $\vec{B} = B\hat{\imath}$; (c) $\vec{E} = -E\hat{k}$, $\vec{B} = -B\hat{\imath}$; (d) $\vec{E} = E\hat{\imath}$, $\vec{B} = -B\hat{k}$.

Section 32.3 Sinusoidal Electromagnetic Waves

32.5 • BIO **Medical X rays.** Medical x rays are taken with electromagnetic waves having a wavelength of around 0.10 nm. What are the frequency, period, and wave number of such waves?

32.6 • BIO **Ultraviolet Radiation.** There are two categories of ultraviolet light. Ultraviolet A (UVA) has a wavelength ranging from 320 nm to 400 nm. It is not harmful to the skin and is necessary for the production of vitamin D. UVB, with a wavelength between 280 nm and 320 nm, is much more dangerous because it causes skin cancer. (a) Find the frequency ranges of UVA and UVB. (b) What are the ranges of the wave numbers for UVA and UVB?

32.7 • A sinusoidal electromagnetic wave having a magnetic field of amplitude 1.25 μT and a wavelength of 432 nm is traveling in the $+x$-direction through empty space. (a) What is the frequency of this wave? (b) What is the amplitude of the associated electric field? (c) Write the equations for the electric and magnetic fields as functions of x and t in the form of Eqs. (32.17).

32.8 • An electromagnetic wave of wavelength 435 nm is traveling in vacuum in the $-z$-direction. The electric field has amplitude 2.70×10^{-3} V/m and is parallel to the x-axis. What are (a) the frequency and (b) the magnetic-field amplitude? (c) Write the vector equations for $\vec{E}(z, t)$ and $\vec{B}(z, t)$.

32.9 • Consider electromagnetic waves propagating in air. (a) Determine the frequency of a wave with a wavelength of (i) 5.0 km, (ii) 5.0 μm, (iii) 5.0 nm. (b) What is the wavelength (in meters and nanometers) of (i) gamma rays of frequency 6.50×10^{21} Hz and (ii) an AM station radio wave of frequency 590 kHz?

32.10 • The electric field of a sinusoidal electromagnetic wave obeys the equation $E = (375\ \text{V/m})\cos[(1.99 \times 10^{7}\ \text{rad/m})x + (5.97 \times 10^{15}\ \text{rad/s})t]$. (a) What are the amplitudes of the electric and magnetic fields of this wave? (b) What are the frequency, wavelength, and period of the wave? Is this light visible to humans? (c) What is the speed of the wave?

32.11 • An electromagnetic wave has an electric field given by $\vec{E}(y, t) = (3.10 \times 10^{5}\ \text{V/m})\hat{k}\cos[ky - (12.65 \times 10^{12}\ \text{rad/s})t]$. (a) In which direction is the wave traveling? (b) What is the wavelength of the wave? (c) Write the vector equation for $\vec{B}(y, t)$.

32.12 • An electromagnetic wave has a magnetic field given by $\vec{B}(x, t) = -(8.25 \times 10^{-9}\ \text{T})\hat{\jmath}\cos[(1.38 \times 10^{4}\ \text{rad/m})x + \omega t]$. (a) In which direction is the wave traveling? (b) What is the frequency f of the wave? (c) Write the vector equation for $\vec{E}(x, t)$.

32.13 • Radio station WCCO in Minneapolis broadcasts at a frequency of 830 kHz. At a point some distance from the transmitter, the magnetic-field amplitude of the electromagnetic wave from WCCO is 4.82×10^{-11} T. Calculate (a) the wavelength; (b) the wave number; (c) the angular frequency; (d) the electric-field amplitude.

32.14 • An electromagnetic wave with frequency 65.0 Hz travels in an insulating magnetic material that has dielectric constant 3.64 and relative permeability 5.18 at this frequency. The electric field has amplitude 7.20×10^{-3} V/m. (a) What is the speed of propagation of the wave? (b) What is the wavelength of the wave? (c) What is the amplitude of the magnetic field?

32.15 • An electromagnetic wave with frequency 5.70×10^{14} Hz propagates with a speed of 2.17×10^{8} m/s in a certain piece of glass. Find (a) the wavelength of the wave in the glass; (b) the wavelength of a wave of the same frequency propagating in air; (c) the index of refraction n of the glass for an electromagnetic wave with this frequency; (d) the dielectric constant for glass at this frequency, assuming that the relative permeability is unity.

Section 32.4 Energy and Momentum in Electromagnetic Waves

32.16 • BIO **High-Energy Cancer Treatment.** Scientists are working on a new technique to kill cancer cells by zapping them with ultrahigh-energy (in the range of 10^{12} W) pulses of light that last for an extremely short time (a few nanoseconds). These short pulses scramble the interior of a cell without causing it to explode, as long pulses would do. We can model a typical such cell as a disk 5.0 μm in diameter, with the pulse lasting for 4.0 ns with an average power of 2.0×10^{12} W. We shall assume that the energy is spread uniformly over the faces of 100 cells for each pulse. (a) How much energy is given to the cell during this pulse? (b) What is the intensity (in W/m^2) delivered to the cell? (c) What are the maximum values of the electric and magnetic fields in the pulse?

32.17 •• **Fields from a Light Bulb.** We can reasonably model a 75-W incandescent light bulb as a sphere 6.0 cm in diameter. Typically, only about 5% of the energy goes to visible light; the rest goes largely to nonvisible infrared radiation. (a) What is the visible-light intensity (in W/m^2) at the surface of the bulb? (b) What are the amplitudes of the electric and magnetic fields at this surface, for a sinusoidal wave with this intensity?

32.18 •• A sinusoidal electromagnetic wave from a radio station passes perpendicularly through an open window that has area 0.500 m^2. At the window, the electric field of the wave has rms value 0.0200 V/m. How much energy does this wave carry through the window during a 30.0-s commercial?

32.19 •• **Testing a Space Radio Transmitter.** You are a NASA mission specialist on your first flight aboard the space shuttle. Thanks to your extensive training in physics, you have been assigned to evaluate the performance of a new radio transmitter on board the International Space Station (ISS). Perched on the shuttle's movable arm, you aim a sensitive detector at the ISS, which is 2.5 km away. You find that the electric-field amplitude of the radio waves coming from the ISS transmitter is 0.090 V/m and that the frequency of the waves is 244 MHz. Find the following: (a) the intensity of the radio wave at your location; (b) the magnetic-field amplitude of the wave at your location; (c) the total power output of the ISS radio transmitter. (d) What assumptions, if any, did you make in your calculations?

32.20 • The intensity of a cylindrical laser beam is 0.800 W/m^2. The cross-sectional area of the beam is 3.0×10^{-4} m^2 and the intensity is uniform across the cross section of the beam. (a) What is the average power output of the laser? (b) What is the rms value of the electric field in the beam?

32.21 • A space probe 2.0×10^{10} m from a star measures the total intensity of electromagnetic radiation from the star to be 5.0×10^3 W/m^2. If the star radiates uniformly in all directions, what is its total average power output?

32.22 • A sinusoidal electromagnetic wave emitted by a cellular phone has a wavelength of 35.4 cm and an electric-field amplitude of 5.40×10^{-2} V/m at a distance of 250 m from the phone. Calculate (a) the frequency of the wave; (b) the magnetic-field amplitude; (c) the intensity of the wave.

32.23 • A monochromatic light source with power output 60.0 W radiates light of wavelength 700 nm uniformly in all directions. Calculate E_{max} and B_{max} for the 700-nm light at a distance of 5.00 m from the source.

32.24 • For the electromagnetic wave represented by Eqs. (32.19), show that the Poynting vector (a) is in the same direction as the propagation of the wave and (b) has average magnitude given by Eqs. (32.29).

32.25 •• An intense light source radiates uniformly in all directions. At a distance of 5.0 m from the source, the radiation pressure on a perfectly absorbing surface is 9.0×10^{-6} Pa. What is the total average power output of the source?

32.26 • **Television Broadcasting.** Public television station KQED in San Francisco broadcasts a sinusoidal radio signal at a power of 316 kW. Assume that the wave spreads out uniformly into a hemisphere above the ground. At a home 5.00 km away from the antenna, (a) what average pressure does this wave exert on a totally reflecting surface, (b) what are the amplitudes of the electric and magnetic fields of the wave, and (c) what is the average density of the energy this wave carries? (d) For the energy density in part (c), what percentage is due to the electric field and what percentage is due to the magnetic field?

32.27 •• BIO **Laser Safety.** If the eye receives an average intensity greater than 1.0×10^2 W/m^2, damage to the retina can occur. This quantity is called the *damage threshold* of the retina. (a) What is the largest average power (in mW) that a laser beam 1.5 mm in diameter can have and still be considered safe to view head-on? (b) What are the maximum values of the electric and magnetic fields for the beam in part (a)? (c) How much energy would the beam in part (a) deliver per second to the retina? (d) Express the damage threshold in W/cm^2.

32.28 • In the 25-ft Space Simulator facility at NASA's Jet Propulsion Laboratory, a bank of overhead arc lamps can produce light of intensity 2500 W/m^2 at the floor of the facility. (This simulates the intensity of sunlight near the planet Venus.) Find the average radiation pressure (in pascals and in atmospheres) on (a) a totally absorbing section of the floor and (b) a totally reflecting section of the floor. (c) Find the average momentum density (momentum per unit volume) in the light at the floor.

32.29 • **Laboratory Lasers.** He–Ne lasers are often used in physics demonstrations. They produce light of wavelength 633 nm and a power of 0.500 mW spread over a cylindrical beam 1.00 mm in diameter (although these quantities can vary). (a) What is the intensity of this laser beam? (b) What are the maximum values of the electric and magnetic fields? (c) What is the average energy density in the laser beam?

32.30 •• **Solar Sail 1.** During 2004, Japanese scientists successfully tested two solar sails. One had a somewhat complicated shape that we shall model as a disk 9.0 m in diameter and 7.5 μm thick. The intensity of solar energy at that location was about 1400 W/m^2. (a) What force did the sun's light exert on this sail, assuming that it struck perpendicular to the sail and that the sail was perfectly reflecting? (b) If the sail was made of magnesium, of density 1.74 g/cm^3, what acceleration would the sun's radiation give to the sail? (c) Does the acceleration seem large enough to be feasible for space flight? In what ways could the sail be modified to increase its acceleration?

Section 32.5 Standing Electromagnetic Waves

32.31 • **Microwave Oven.** The microwaves in a certain microwave oven have a wavelength of 12.2 cm. (a) How wide must this oven be so that it will contain five antinodal planes of the electric field along its width in the standing-wave pattern? (b) What is the frequency of these microwaves? (c) Suppose a manufacturing error occurred and the oven was made 5.0 cm longer than specified in part (a). In this case, what would have to be the frequency of the microwaves for there still to be five antinodal planes of the electric field along the width of the oven?

32.32 • An electromagnetic standing wave in air of frequency 750 MHz is set up between two conducting planes 80.0 cm apart. At which positions between the planes could a point charge be placed at rest so that it would *remain* at rest? Explain.

32.33 • A standing electromagnetic wave in a certain material has frequency 2.20×10^{10} Hz. The nodal planes of $\vec{B}$ are 3.55 mm apart. Find (a) the wavelength of the wave in this material; (b) the distance between adjacent nodal planes of the $\vec{E}$ field; (c) the speed of propagation of the wave.

32.34 • An electromagnetic standing wave in air has frequency 75.0 MHz. (a) What is the distance between nodal planes of the $\vec{E}$ field? (b) What is the distance between a nodal plane of $\vec{E}$ and the closest nodal plane of $\vec{B}$?

32.35 • An electromagnetic standing wave in a certain material has frequency 1.20×10^{10} Hz and speed of propagation 2.10×10^8 m/s. (a) What is the distance between a nodal plane of $\vec{B}$ and the closest antinodal plane of $\vec{B}$? (b) What is the distance between an antinodal plane of $\vec{E}$ and the closest antinodal plane of $\vec{B}$? (c) What is the distance between a nodal plane of $\vec{E}$ and the closest nodal plane of $\vec{B}$?

32.36 • CALC Show that the electric and magnetic fields for standing waves given by Eqs. (32.34) and (32.35) (a) satisfy the wave equation, Eq. (32.15), and (b) satisfy Eqs. (32.12) and (32.14).

PROBLEMS

32.37 •• BIO **Laser Surgery.** Very short pulses of high-intensity laser beams are used to repair detached portions of the retina of the eye. The brief pulses of energy absorbed by the retina weld the detached portions back into place. In one such procedure, a laser beam has a wavelength of 810 nm and delivers 250 mW of power spread over a circular spot 510 μm in diameter. The vitreous humor (the transparent fluid that fills most of the eye) has an index of refraction of 1.34. (a) If the laser pulses are each 1.50 ms long, how much energy is delivered to the retina with each pulse? (b) What average pressure does the pulse of the laser beam exert on the retina as it is fully absorbed by the circular spot? (c) What are the wavelength and frequency of the laser light inside the vitreous humor of the eye? (d) What are the maximum values of the electric and magnetic fields in the laser beam?

32.38 •• CALC Consider a sinusoidal electromagnetic wave with fields $\vec{E} = E_{max}\hat{\jmath}\cos(kx - \omega t)$ and $\vec{B} = B_{max}\hat{k}\cos(kx - \omega t + \phi)$, with $-\pi \le \phi \le \pi$. Show that if $\vec{E}$ and $\vec{B}$ are to satisfy Eqs. (32.12) and (32.14), then $E_{max} = cB_{max}$ and $\phi = 0$. (The result $\phi = 0$ means the $\vec{E}$ and $\vec{B}$ fields oscillate in phase.)

32.39 •• You want to support a sheet of fireproof paper horizontally, using only a vertical upward beam of light spread uniformly over the sheet. There is no other light on this paper. The sheet measures 22.0 cm by 28.0 cm and has a mass of 1.50 g. (a) If the paper is black and hence absorbs all the light that hits it, what must be the intensity of the light beam? (b) For the light in part (a), what are the amplitudes of its electric and magnetic fields? (c) If the paper is white and hence reflects all the light that hits it, what intensity of light beam is needed to support it? (d) To see if it is physically reasonable to expect to support a sheet of paper this way, calculate the intensity in a typical 0.500-mW laser beam that is 1.00 mm in diameter, and compare this value with your answer in part (a).

32.40 •• For a sinusoidal electromagnetic wave in vacuum, such as that described by Eq. (32.16), show that the *average* energy density in the electric field is the same as that in the magnetic field.

32.41 • A satellite 575 km above the earth's surface transmits sinusoidal electromagnetic waves of frequency 92.4 MHz uniformly in all directions, with a power of 25.0 kW. (a) What is the intensity of these waves as they reach a receiver at the surface of the earth directly below the satellite? (b) What are the amplitudes of the electric and magnetic fields at the receiver? (c) If the receiver has a totally absorbing panel measuring 15.0 cm by 40.0 cm oriented with its plane perpendicular to the direction the waves travel, what average force do these waves exert on the panel? Is this force large enough to cause significant effects?

32.42 • A plane sinusoidal electromagnetic wave in air has a wavelength of 3.84 cm and an $\vec{E}$-field amplitude of 1.35 V/m. (a) What is the frequency? (b) What is the $\vec{B}$-field amplitude? (c) What is the intensity? (d) What average force does this radiation exert on a totally absorbing surface with area $0.240\ m^2$ perpendicular to the direction of propagation?

32.43 • A small helium–neon laser emits red visible light with a power of 4.60 mW in a beam that has a diameter of 2.50 mm. (a) What are the amplitudes of the electric and magnetic fields of the light? (b) What are the average energy densities associated with the electric field and with the magnetic field? (c) What is the total energy contained in a 1.00-m length of the beam?

32.44 •• The electric-field component of a sinusoidal electromagnetic wave traveling through a plastic cylinder is given by the equation $E = (5.35\ \text{V/m})\cos[(1.39 \times 10^7\ \text{rad/m})x - (3.02 \times 10^{15}\ \text{rad/s})t]$. (a) Find the frequency, wavelength, and speed of this wave in the plastic. (b) What is the index of refraction of the plastic? (c) Assuming that the amplitude of the electric field does not change, write a comparable equation for the electric field if the light is traveling in air instead of in plastic.

32.45 • The sun emits energy in the form of electromagnetic waves at a rate of 3.9×10^{26} W. This energy is produced by nuclear reactions deep in the sun's interior. (a) Find the intensity of electromagnetic radiation and the radiation pressure on an absorbing object at the surface of the sun (radius $r = R = 6.96 \times 10^5$ km) and at $r = R/2$, in the sun's interior. Ignore any scattering of the waves as they move radially outward from the center of the sun. Compare to the values given in Section 32.4 for sunlight just before it enters the earth's atmosphere. (b) The gas pressure at the sun's surface is about 1.0×10^4 Pa; at $r = R/2$, the gas pressure is calculated from solar models to be about 4.7×10^{13} Pa. Comparing with your results in part (a), would you expect that radiation pressure is an important factor in determining the structure of the sun? Why or why not?

32.46 •• A source of sinusoidal electromagnetic waves radiates uniformly in all directions. At 10.0 m from this source, the amplitude of the electric field is measured to be 1.50 N/C. What is the electric-field amplitude at a distance of 20.0 cm from the source?

32.47 •• **CP** Two square reflectors, each 1.50 cm on a side and of mass 4.00 g, are located at opposite ends of a thin, extremely light, 1.00-m rod that can rotate without friction and in vacuum about an axle perpendicular to it through its center (Fig. P32.47). These reflectors are small enough to be treated as point masses in moment-of-inertia calculations. Both reflectors are illuminated on one face by a sinusoidal light wave having an electric field of amplitude 1.25 N/C that falls uniformly on both surfaces and always strikes them perpendicular to the plane of their surfaces. One reflector is covered with a perfectly absorbing coating, and the other is covered with a perfectly reflecting coating. What is the angular acceleration of this device?

Figure **P32.47**

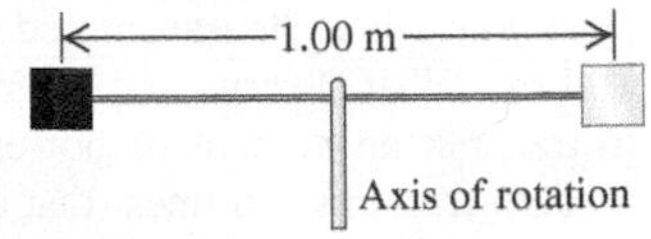

32.48 •• **CP** A circular loop of wire has radius 7.50 cm. A sinusoidal electromagnetic plane wave traveling in air passes through the loop, with the direction of the magnetic field of the wave perpendicular to the plane of the loop. The intensity of the wave at the location of the loop is $0.0195\ W/m^2$, and the wavelength of the wave is 6.90 m. What is the maximum emf induced in the loop?

32.49 • **CALC** **CP** A cylindrical conductor with a circular cross section has a radius a and a resistivity ρ and carries a constant current I. (a) What are the magnitude and direction of the electric-field vector $\vec{E}$ at a point just inside the wire at a distance a from the axis? (b) What are the magnitude and direction of the magnetic-field vector $\vec{B}$ at the same point? (c) What are the magnitude and direction of the Poynting vector $\vec{S}$ at the same point? (The direction of $\vec{S}$ is the direction in which electromagnetic energy flows into or out of the conductor.) (d) Use the result in part (c) to find the rate of flow of energy into the volume occupied by a length l of the conductor. (*Hint:* Integrate $\vec{S}$ over the surface of this volume.) Compare your result to the rate of generation of thermal energy in the same volume. Discuss why the energy dissipated in a current-carrying conductor, due to its resistance, can be thought of as entering through the cylindrical sides of the conductor.

32.50 • In a certain experiment, a radio transmitter emits sinusoidal electromagnetic waves of frequency 110.0 MHz in opposite directions inside a narrow cavity with reflectors at both ends, causing a standing-wave pattern to occur. (a) How far apart are the nodal planes of the magnetic field? (b) If the standing-wave pattern is determined to be in its eighth harmonic, how long is the cavity?

32.51 •• **CP** **Flashlight to the Rescue.** You are the sole crew member of the interplanetary spaceship *T:1339 Vorga,* which makes regular cargo runs between the earth and the mining colonies in the asteroid belt. You are working outside the ship one day while at a distance of 2.0 AU from the sun. [1 AU (astronomical unit) is the average distance from the earth to the sun, 149,600,000 km.] Unfortunately, you lose contact with the ship's hull and begin to drift away into space. You use your spacesuit's rockets to try to push yourself back toward the ship, but they run out of fuel and stop working before you can return to the ship. You find yourself in an awkward position, floating 16.0 m from the spaceship with zero velocity relative to it. Fortunately, you are carrying a 200-W flashlight. You turn on the flashlight and use its beam as a "light rocket" to push yourself back toward the ship. (a) If you, your spacesuit, and the flashlight have a combined mass of 150 kg, how long will it take you to get back to the ship? (b) Is there another way you could use the flashlight to accomplish the same job of returning you to the ship?

32.52 • The 19th-century inventor Nikola Tesla proposed to transmit electric power via sinusoidal electromagnetic waves. Suppose power is to be transmitted in a beam of cross-sectional area 100 m^2. What electric- and magnetic-field amplitudes are required to transmit an amount of power comparable to that handled by modern transmission lines (that carry voltages and currents of the order of 500 kV and 1000 A)?

32.53 •• **CP Global Positioning System (GPS).** The GPS network consists of 24 satellites, each of which makes two orbits around the earth per day. Each satellite transmits a 50.0-W (or even less) sinusoidal electromagnetic signal at two frequencies, one of which is 1575.42 MHz. Assume that a satellite transmits half of its power at each frequency and that the waves travel uniformly in a downward hemisphere. (a) What average intensity does a GPS receiver on the ground, directly below the satellite, receive? (*Hint:* First use Newton's laws to find the altitude of the satellite.) (b) What are the amplitudes of the electric and magnetic fields at the GPS receiver in part (a), and how long does it take the signal to reach the receiver? (c) If the receiver is a square panel 1.50 cm on a side that absorbs all of the beam, what average pressure does the signal exert on it? (d) What wavelength must the receiver be tuned to?

32.54 •• **CP Solar Sail 2.** NASA is giving serious consideration to the concept of *solar sailing*. A solar sailcraft uses a large, low-mass sail and the energy and momentum of sunlight for propulsion. (a) Should the sail be absorbing or reflective? Why? (b) The total power output of the sun is 3.9×10^{26} W. How large a sail is necessary to propel a 10,000-kg spacecraft against the gravitational force of the sun? Express your result in square kilometers. (c) Explain why your answer to part (b) is independent of the distance from the sun.

32.55 •• **CP** Interplanetary space contains many small particles referred to as *interplanetary dust.* Radiation pressure from the sun sets a lower limit on the size of such dust particles. To see the origin of this limit, consider a spherical dust particle of radius R and mass density ρ. (a) Write an expression for the gravitational force exerted on this particle by the sun (mass M) when the particle is a distance r from the sun. (b) Let L represent the luminosity of the sun, equal to the rate at which it emits energy in electromagnetic radiation. Find the force exerted on the (totally absorbing) particle due to solar radiation pressure, remembering that the intensity of the sun's radiation also depends on the distance r. The relevant area is the cross-sectional area of the particle, *not* the total surface area of the particle. As part of your answer, explain why this is so. (c) The mass density of a typical interplanetary dust particle is about 3000 kg/m^3. Find the particle radius R such that the gravitational and radiation forces acting on the particle are equal in magnitude. The luminosity of the sun is 3.9×10^{26} W. Does your answer depend on the distance of the particle from the sun? Why or why not? (d) Explain why dust particles with a radius less than that found in part (c) are unlikely to be found in the solar system. [*Hint:* Construct the ratio of the two force expressions found in parts (a) and (b).]

CHALLENGE PROBLEMS

32.56 ••• **CALC** Electromagnetic waves propagate much differently in *conductors* than they do in dielectrics or in vacuum. If the resistivity of the conductor is sufficiently low (that is, if it is a sufficiently good conductor), the oscillating electric field of the wave gives rise to an oscillating conduction current that is much larger than the displacement current. In this case, the wave equation for an electric field $\vec{E}(x,t) = E_y(x,t)\hat{j}$ propagating in the $+x$-direction within a conductor is

$$\frac{\partial^2 E_y(x,t)}{\partial x^2} = \frac{\mu}{\rho}\frac{\partial E_y(x,t)}{\partial t}$$

where μ is the permeability of the conductor and ρ is its resistivity. (a) A solution to this wave equation is

$$E_y(x,t) = E_{max}e^{-k_C x}\cos(k_C x - \omega t)$$

where $k_C = \sqrt{\omega\mu/2\rho}$. Verify this by substituting $E_y(x,t)$ into the above wave equation. (b) The exponential term shows that the electric field decreases in amplitude as it propagates. Explain why this happens. (*Hint:* The field does work to move charges within the conductor. The current of these moving charges causes i^2R heating within the conductor, raising its temperature. Where does the energy to do this come from?) (c) Show that the electric-field amplitude decreases by a factor of $1/e$ in a distance $1/k_C = \sqrt{2\rho/\omega\mu}$, and calculate this distance for a radio wave with frequency f = 1.0 MHz in copper (resistivity $1.72 \times 10^{-8}\ \Omega \cdot m$; permeability $\mu = \mu_0$). Since this distance is so short, electromagnetic waves of this frequency can hardly propagate at all into copper. Instead, they are reflected at the surface of the metal. This is why radio waves cannot penetrate through copper or other metals, and why radio reception is poor inside a metal structure.

32.57 ••• **CP** Electromagnetic radiation is emitted by accelerating charges. The rate at which energy is emitted from an accelerating charge that has charge q and acceleration a is given by

$$\frac{dE}{dt} = \frac{q^2a^2}{6\pi\epsilon_0 c^3}$$

where c is the speed of light. (a) Verify that this equation is dimensionally correct. (b) If a proton with a kinetic energy of 6.0 MeV is traveling in a particle accelerator in a circular orbit of radius 0.750 m, what fraction of its energy does it radiate per second? (c) Consider an electron orbiting with the same speed and radius. What fraction of its energy does it radiate per second?

32.58 ••• **CP The Classical Hydrogen Atom.** The electron in a hydrogen atom can be considered to be in a circular orbit with a radius of 0.0529 nm and a kinetic energy of 13.6 eV. If the electron behaved classically, how much energy would it radiate per second (see Challenge Problem 32.57)? What does this tell you about the use of classical physics in describing the atom?

Answers

Chapter Opening Question ?

Metals are reflective because they are good conductors of electricity. When an electromagnetic wave strikes a conductor, the electric field of the wave sets up currents on the conductor surface that generate a reflected wave. For a perfect conductor, this reflected wave is just as intense as the incident wave. Tarnished metals are less shiny because their surface is oxidized and less conductive; polishing the metal removes the oxide and exposes the conducting metal.

Test Your Understanding Questions

32.1 Answers: (a) no, (b) no A purely electric wave would have a varying electric field. Such a field necessarily generates a magnetic field through Ampere's law, Eq. (29.20), so a purely electric wave is impossible. In the same way, a purely magnetic wave is impossible: The varying magnetic field in such a wave would automatically give rise to an electric field through Faraday's law, Eq. (29.21).
32.2 Answers: (a) positive y-direction, (b) negative x-direction, (c) positive y-direction You can verify these answers by using the right-hand rule to show that $\vec{E} \times \vec{B}$ in each case is in the direction of propagation, or by using the rule shown in Fig. 32.9.
32.3 Answer: (iv) In an ideal electromagnetic plane wave, at any instant the fields are the same anywhere in a plane perpendicular to the direction of propagation. The plane wave described by Eqs. (32.17) is propagating in the x-direction, so the fields depend on the coordinate x and time t but do *not* depend on the coordinates y and z.
32.4 Answers: (a) (i) and (iii), (b) (ii) and (iv), (c) (i) and (iii), (d) (ii) and (iv) Both the energy density u and the Poynting vector magnitude S are maximum where the $\vec{E}$ and $\vec{B}$ fields have their maximum magnitudes. (The directions of the fields doesn't matter.) From Fig. 32.13, this occurs at $x = 0$ and $x = \lambda/2$. Both u and S have a minimum value of zero; that occurs where $\vec{E}$ and $\vec{B}$ are both zero. From Fig. 32.13, this occurs at $x = \lambda/4$ and $x = 3\lambda/4$.
32.5 Answer: no There are places where $\vec{E} = \mathbf{0}$ at all times (at the walls) and the electric energy density $\frac{1}{2}\epsilon_0 E^2$ is always zero. There are also places where $\vec{B} = \mathbf{0}$ at all times (on the plane midway between the walls) and the magnetic energy density $B^2/2\mu_0$ is always zero. However, there are *no* locations where both $\vec{E}$ and $\vec{B}$ are always zero. Hence the energy density at any point in the standing wave is always nonzero.

Bridging Problem

Answer: 0.0368 V

33 THE NATURE AND PROPAGATION OF LIGHT

? These drafting tools are made of clear plastic, but a rainbow of colors appears when they are placed between two special filters called polarizers. How does this cause the colors?

LEARNING GOALS

By studying this chapter, you will learn:

- What light rays are, and how they are related to wave fronts.
- The laws that govern the reflection and refraction of light.
- The circumstances under which light is totally reflected at an interface.
- How to make polarized light out of ordinary light.
- How Huygens's principle helps us analyze reflection and refraction.

Blue lakes, ochre deserts, green forests, and multicolored rainbows can be enjoyed by anyone who has eyes with which to see them. But by studying the branch of physics called **optics,** which deals with the behavior of light and other electromagnetic waves, we can reach a deeper appreciation of the visible world. A knowledge of the properties of light allows us to understand the blue color of the sky and the design of optical devices such as telescopes, microscopes, cameras, eyeglasses, and the human eye. The same basic principles of optics also lie at the heart of modern developments such as the laser, optical fibers, holograms, optical computers, and new techniques in medical imaging.

The importance of optics to physics, and to science and engineering in general, is so great that we will devote the next four chapters to its study. In this chapter we begin with a study of the laws of reflection and refraction and the concepts of dispersion, polarization, and scattering of light. Along the way we compare the various possible descriptions of light in terms of particles, rays, or waves, and we introduce Huygens's principle, an important link that connects the ray and wave viewpoints. In Chapter 34 we'll use the ray description of light to understand how mirrors and lenses work, and we'll see how mirrors and lenses are used in optical instruments such as cameras, microscopes, and telescopes. We'll explore the wave characteristics of light further in Chapters 35 and 36.

33.1 The Nature of Light

Until the time of Isaac Newton (1642–1727), most scientists thought that light consisted of streams of particles (called *corpuscles*) emitted by light sources. Galileo and others tried (unsuccessfully) to measure the speed of light. Around 1665, evidence of *wave* properties of light began to be discovered. By the early 19th century, evidence that light is a wave had grown very persuasive.

In 1873, James Clerk Maxwell predicted the existence of electromagnetic waves and calculated their speed of propagation, as we learned in Chapter 32. This development, along with the experimental work of Heinrich Hertz starting in 1887, showed conclusively that light is indeed an electromagnetic wave.

The Two Personalities of Light

The wave picture of light is not the whole story, however. Several effects associated with emission and absorption of light reveal a particle aspect, in that the energy carried by light waves is packaged in discrete bundles called *photons* or *quanta.* These apparently contradictory wave and particle properties have been reconciled since 1930 with the development of quantum electrodynamics, a comprehensive theory that includes *both* wave and particle properties. The *propagation* of light is best described by a wave model, but understanding emission and absorption requires a particle approach.

The fundamental sources of all electromagnetic radiation are electric charges in accelerated motion. All bodies emit electromagnetic radiation as a result of thermal motion of their molecules; this radiation, called *thermal radiation,* is a mixture of different wavelengths. At sufficiently high temperatures, all matter emits enough visible light to be self-luminous; a very hot body appears "red-hot" (Fig. 33.1) or "white-hot." Thus hot matter in any form is a light source. Familiar examples are a candle flame, hot coals in a campfire, the coils in an electric room heater, and an incandescent lamp filament (which usually operates at a temperature of about 3000°C).

33.1 An electric heating element emits primarily infrared radiation. But if its temperature is high enough, it also emits a discernible amount of visible light.

Light is also produced during electrical discharges through ionized gases. The bluish light of mercury-arc lamps, the orange-yellow of sodium-vapor lamps, and the various colors of "neon" signs are familiar. A variation of the mercury-arc lamp is the *fluorescent* lamp (see Fig. 30.7). This light source uses a material called a *phosphor* to convert the ultraviolet radiation from a mercury arc into visible light. This conversion makes fluorescent lamps more efficient than incandescent lamps in transforming electrical energy into light.

In most light sources, light is emitted independently by different atoms within the source; in a *laser,* by contrast, atoms are induced to emit light in a cooperative, coherent fashion. The result is a very narrow beam of radiation that can be enormously intense and that is much more nearly *monochromatic,* or single-frequency, than light from any other source. Lasers are used by physicians for microsurgery, in a DVD or Blu-ray player to scan the information recorded on a video disc, in industry to cut through steel and to fuse high-melting-point materials, and in many other applications (Fig. 33.2).

33.2 Ophthalmic surgeons use lasers for repairing detached retinas and for cauterizing blood vessels in retinopathy. Pulses of blue-green light from an argon laser are ideal for this purpose, since they pass harmlessly through the transparent part of the eye but are absorbed by red pigments in the retina.

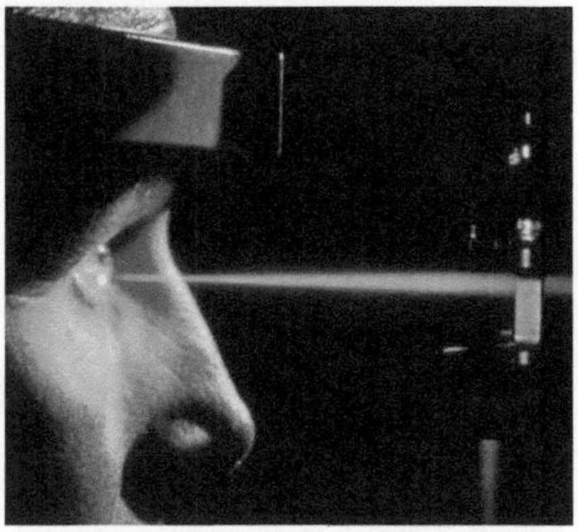

No matter what its source, electromagnetic radiation travels in vacuum at the same speed. As we saw in Sections 1.3 and 32.1, the speed of light in vacuum is defined to be

$$c = 2.99792458 \times 10^8 \text{ m/s}$$

or 3.00×10^8 m/s to three significant figures. The duration of one second is defined by the cesium clock (see Section 1.3), so one meter is defined to be the distance that light travels in 1/299,792,458 s.

Waves, Wave Fronts, and Rays

We often use the concept of a **wave front** to describe wave propagation. We introduced this concept in Section 32.2 to describe the leading edge of a wave. More generally, we define a wave front as *the locus of all adjacent points at which the phase of vibration of a physical quantity associated with the wave is the same.* That is, at any instant, all points on a wave front are at the same part of the cycle of their variation.

When we drop a pebble into a calm pool, the expanding circles formed by the wave crests, as well as the circles formed by the wave troughs between

33.3 Spherical wave fronts of sound spread out uniformly in all directions from a point source in a motionless medium, such as still air, that has the same properties in all regions and in all directions. Electromagnetic waves in vacuum also spread out as shown here.

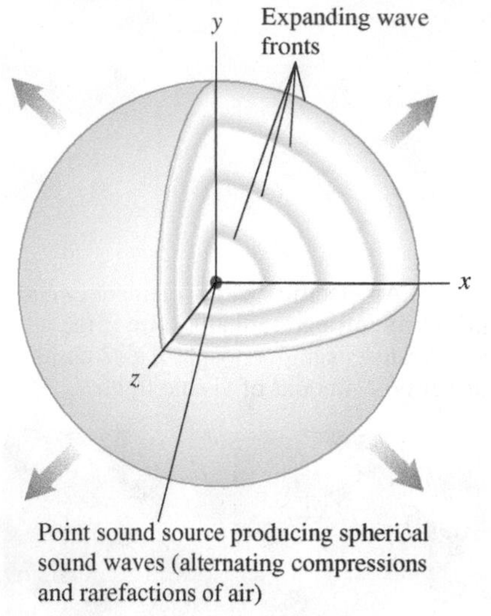

33.4 Wave fronts (blue) and rays (purple).

(a)

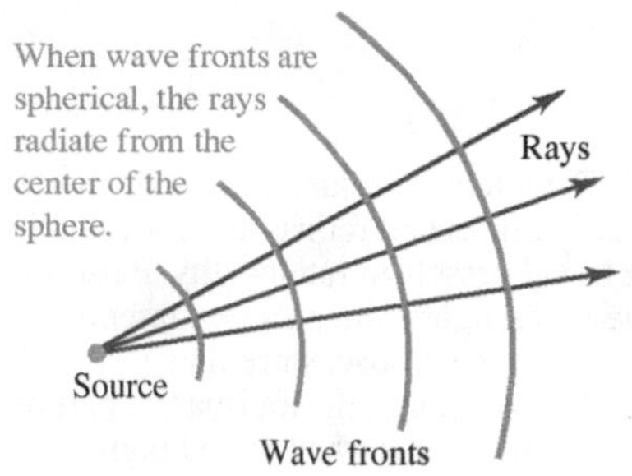

(b)

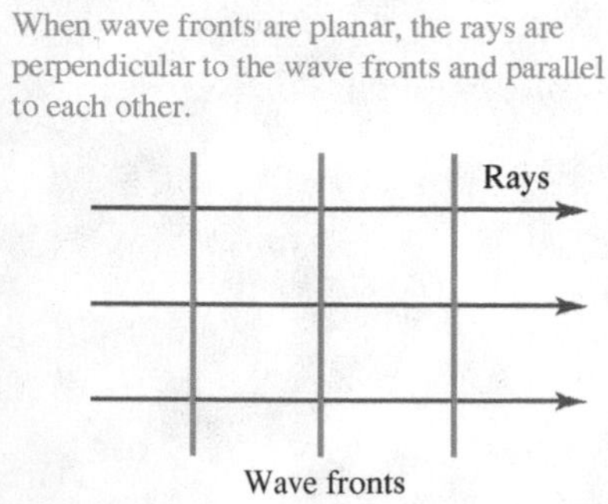

them, are wave fronts. Similarly, when sound waves spread out in still air from a pointlike source, or when electromagnetic radiation spreads out from a pointlike emitter, any spherical surface that is concentric with the source is a wave front, as shown in Fig. 33.3. In diagrams of wave motion we usually draw only parts of a few wave fronts, often choosing consecutive wave fronts that have the same phase and thus are one wavelength apart, such as crests of water waves. Similarly, a diagram for sound waves might show only the "pressure crests," the surfaces over which the pressure is maximum, and a diagram for electromagnetic waves might show only the "crests" on which the electric or magnetic field is maximum.

We will often use diagrams that show the shapes of the wave fronts or their cross sections in some reference plane. For example, when electromagnetic waves are radiated by a small light source, we can represent the wave fronts as spherical surfaces concentric with the source or, as in Fig. 33.4a, by the circular intersections of these surfaces with the plane of the diagram. Far away from the source, where the radii of the spheres have become very large, a section of a spherical surface can be considered as a plane, and we have a *plane* wave like those discussed in Sections 32.2 and 32.3 (Fig, 33.4b).

To describe the directions in which light propagates, it's often convenient to represent a light wave by **rays** rather than by wave fronts. Rays were used to describe light long before its wave nature was firmly established. In a particle theory of light, rays are the paths of the particles. From the wave viewpoint *a ray is an imaginary line along the direction of travel of the wave.* In Fig. 33.4a the rays are the radii of the spherical wave fronts, and in Fig. 33.4b they are straight lines perpendicular to the wave fronts. When waves travel in a homogeneous isotropic material (a material with the same properties in all regions and in all directions), the rays are always straight lines normal to the wave fronts. At a boundary surface between two materials, such as the surface of a glass plate in air, the wave speed and the direction of a ray may change, but the ray segments in the air and in the glass are straight lines.

The next several chapters will give you many opportunities to see the interplay of the ray, wave, and particle descriptions of light. The branch of optics for which the ray description is adequate is called **geometric optics;** the branch dealing specifically with wave behavior is called **physical optics.** This chapter and the following one are concerned mostly with geometric optics. In Chapters 35 and 36 we will study wave phenomena and physical optics.

Test Your Understanding of Section 33.1 Some crystals are *not* isotropic: Light travels through the crystal at a higher speed in some directions than in others. In a crystal in which light travels at the same speed in the x- and z-directions but at a faster speed in the y-direction, what would be the shape of the wave fronts produced by a light source at the origin? (i) spherical, like those shown in Fig. 33.3; (ii) ellipsoidal, flattened along the y-axis; (iii) ellipsoidal, stretched out along the y-axis. ❙

33.2 Reflection and Refraction

In this section we'll use the *ray* model of light to explore two of the most important aspects of light propagation: **reflection** and **refraction.** When a light wave strikes a smooth interface separating two transparent materials (such as air and glass or water and glass), the wave is in general partly *reflected* and partly *refracted* (transmitted) into the second material, as shown in Fig. 33.5a. For example, when you look into a restaurant window from the street, you see a reflection of the street scene, but a person inside the restaurant can look out through the window at the same scene as light reaches him by refraction.

MasteringPHYSICS
ActivPhysics 15.1: Reflection and Refraction
ActivPhysics 15.3: Refraction Applications

33.5 (a) A plane wave is in part reflected and in part refracted at the boundary between two media (in this case, air and glass). The light that reaches the inside of the coffee shop is refracted twice, once entering the glass and once exiting the glass. (b), (c) How light behaves at the interface between the air outside the coffee shop (material a) and the glass (material b). For the case shown here, material b has a larger index of refraction than material $a (n_b > n_a)$ and the angle θ_b is smaller than θ_a.

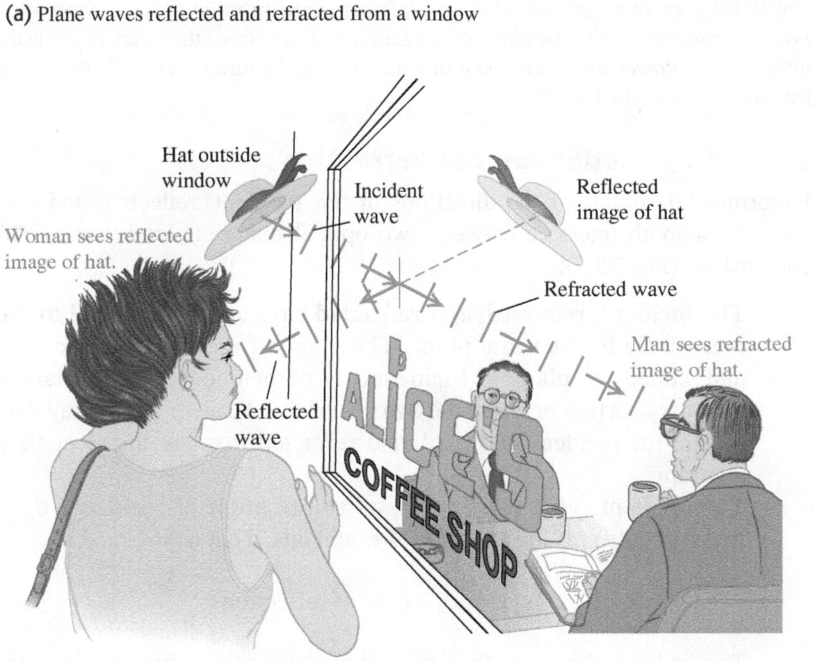

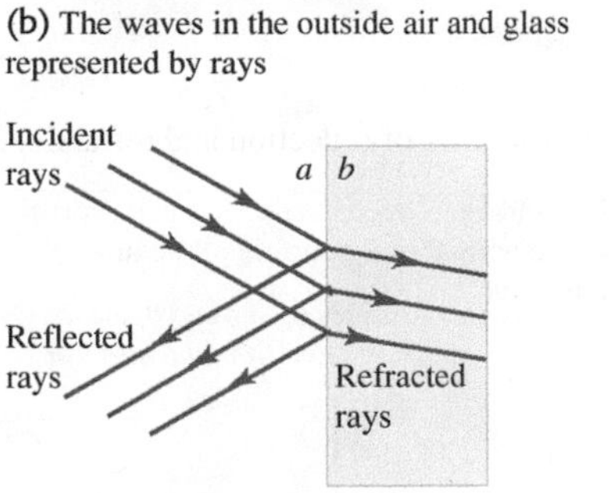

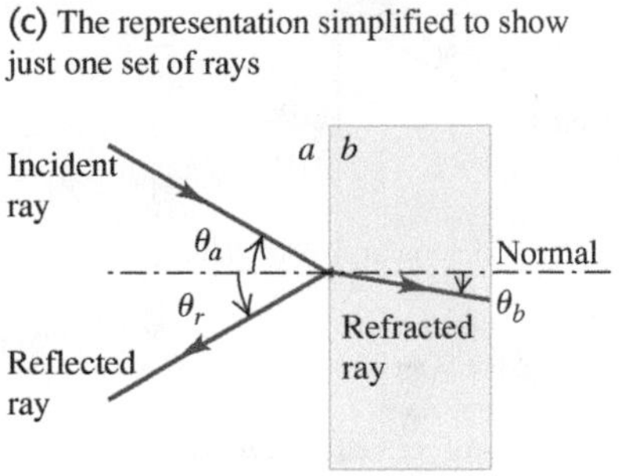

The segments of plane waves shown in Fig. 33.5a can be represented by bundles of rays forming *beams* of light (Fig. 33.5b). For simplicity we often draw only one ray in each beam (Fig. 33.5c). Representing these waves in terms of rays is the basis of geometric optics. We begin our study with the behavior of an individual ray.

We describe the directions of the incident, reflected, and refracted (transmitted) rays at a smooth interface between two optical materials in terms of the angles they make with the *normal* (perpendicular) to the surface at the point of incidence, as shown in Fig. 33.5c. If the interface is rough, both the transmitted light and the reflected light are scattered in various directions, and there is no single angle of transmission or reflection. Reflection at a definite angle from a very smooth surface is called **specular reflection** (from the Latin word for "mirror"); scattered reflection from a rough surface is called **diffuse reflection.** This distinction is shown in Fig. 33.6. Both kinds of reflection can occur with either transparent materials or *opaque* materials that do not transmit light. The vast majority of objects in your environment (including plants, other people, and this book) are visible to you because they reflect light in a diffuse manner from their surfaces. Our primary concern, however, will be with specular reflection from a very smooth surface such as highly polished glass or metal. Unless stated otherwise, when referring to "reflection" we will always mean *specular* reflection.

The **index of refraction** of an optical material (also called the **refractive index**), denoted by n, plays a central role in geometric optics. It is the ratio of the speed of light c in vacuum to the speed v in the material:

$$n = \frac{c}{v} \quad \text{(index of refraction)} \tag{33.1}$$

Light always travels *more slowly* in a material than in vacuum, so the value of n in anything other than vacuum is always greater than unity. For vacuum, $n = 1$.

33.6 Two types of reflection.

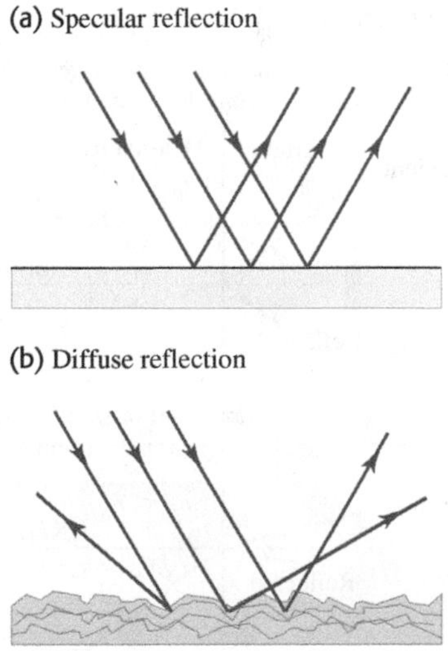

Since n is a ratio of two speeds, it is a pure number without units. (The relationship of the value of n to the electric and magnetic properties of a material is described in Section 32.3.)

CAUTION **Wave speed and index of refraction** Keep in mind that the wave speed v is *inversely* proportional to the index of refraction n. The greater the index of refraction in a material, the *slower* the wave speed in that material. Failure to remember this point can lead to serious confusion!

33.7 The laws of reflection and refraction.

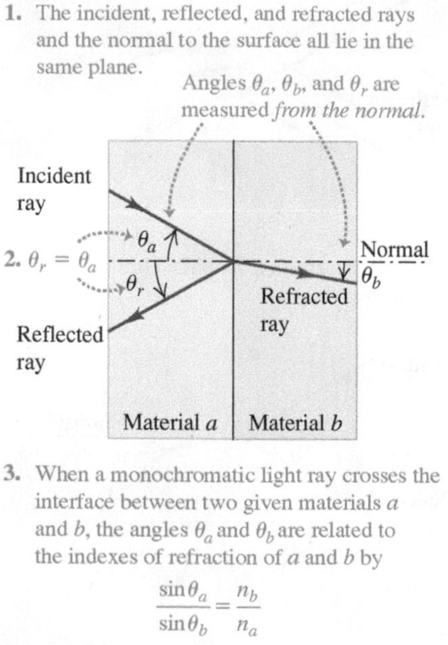

33.8 Refraction and reflection in three cases. (a) Material b has a larger index of refraction than material a. (b) Material b has a smaller index of refraction than material a. (c) The incident light ray is normal to the interface between the materials.

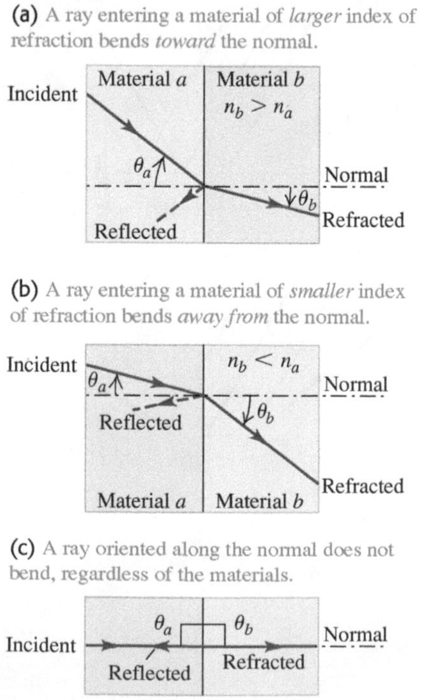

The Laws of Reflection and Refraction

Experimental studies of the directions of the incident, reflected, and refracted rays at a smooth interface between two optical materials lead to the following conclusions (Fig. 33.7):

1. **The incident, reflected, and refracted rays and the normal to the surface all lie in the same plane.** The plane of the three rays and the normal, called the **plane of incidence,** is perpendicular to the plane of the boundary surface between the two materials. We always draw ray diagrams so that the incident, reflected, and refracted rays are in the plane of the diagram.
2. **The angle of reflection θ_r is equal to the angle of incidence θ_a for all wavelengths and for any pair of materials.** That is, in Fig. 33.5c,

$$\theta_r = \theta_a \quad \text{(law of reflection)} \tag{33.2}$$

   This relationship, together with the observation that the incident and reflected rays and the normal all lie in the same plane, is called the **law of reflection.**

3. For monochromatic light and for a given pair of materials, a and b, on opposite sides of the interface, **the ratio of the sines of the angles θ_a and θ_b, where both angles are measured from the normal to the surface, is equal to the inverse ratio of the two indexes of refraction:**

$$\frac{\sin\theta_a}{\sin\theta_b} = \frac{n_b}{n_a} \tag{33.3}$$

   or

$$n_a \sin\theta_a = n_b \sin\theta_b \quad \text{(law of refraction)} \tag{33.4}$$

   This experimental result, together with the observation that the incident and refracted rays and the normal all lie in the same plane, is called the **law of refraction** or **Snell's law,** after the Dutch scientist Willebrord Snell (1591–1626). There is some doubt that Snell actually discovered it. The discovery that $n = c/v$ came much later.

While these results were first observed experimentally, they can be derived theoretically from a wave description of light. We do this in Section 33.7.

Equations (33.3) and (33.4) show that when a ray passes from one material (a) into another material (b) having a larger index of refraction ($n_b > n_a$) and hence a slower wave speed, the angle θ_b with the normal is *smaller* in the second material than the angle θ_a in the first; hence the ray is bent *toward* the normal (Fig. 33.8a). When the second material has a *smaller* index of refraction than the first material ($n_b < n_a$) and hence a faster wave speed, the ray is bent *away from* the normal (Fig. 33.8b).

No matter what the materials on either side of the interface, in the case of *normal* incidence the transmitted ray is not bent at all (Fig. 33.8c). In this case

33.9 (a) This ruler is actually straight, but it appears to bend at the surface of the water. (b) Light rays from any submerged object bend away from the normal when they emerge into the air. As seen by an observer above the surface of the water, the object appears to be much closer to the surface than it actually is.

(a) A straight ruler half-immersed in water (b) Why the ruler appears bent

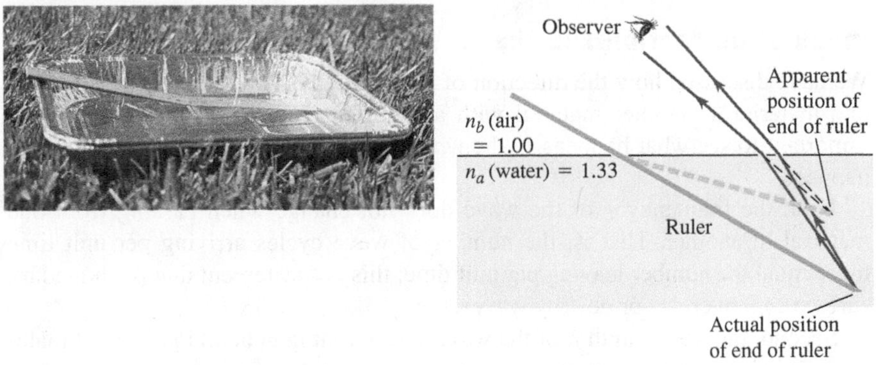

$\theta_a = 0$ and $\sin\theta_a = 0$, so from Eq. (33.4) θ_b is also equal to zero, so the transmitted ray is also normal to the interface. Equation (33.2) shows that θ_r, too, is equal to zero, so the reflected ray travels back along the same path as the incident ray.

The law of refraction explains why a partially submerged ruler or drinking straw appears bent; light rays coming from below the surface change in direction at the air–water interface, so the rays appear to be coming from a position above their actual point of origin (Fig. 33.9). A similar effect explains the appearance of the setting sun (Fig. 33.10).

An important special case is refraction that occurs at an interface between vacuum, for which the index of refraction is unity by definition, and a material. When a ray passes from vacuum into a material (*b*), so that $n_a = 1$ and $n_b > 1$, the ray is always bent *toward* the normal. When a ray passes from a material into vacuum, so that $n_a > 1$ and $n_b = 1$, the ray is always bent *away from* the normal.

The laws of reflection and refraction apply regardless of which side of the interface the incident ray comes from. If a ray of light approaches the interface in Fig. 33.8a or 33.8b from the right rather than from the left, there are again reflected and refracted rays; these two rays, the incident ray, and the normal to the surface again lie in the same plane. Furthermore, the path of a refracted ray is *reversible;* it follows the same path when going from *b* to *a* as when going from *a* to *b*. [You can verify this using Eq. (33.4).] Since reflected and incident rays make the same angle with the normal, the path of a reflected ray is also reversible. That's why when you see someone's eyes in a mirror, they can also see you.

The *intensities* of the reflected and refracted rays depend on the angle of incidence, the two indexes of refraction, and the polarization (that is, the direction of the electric-field vector) of the incident ray. The fraction reflected is smallest at normal incidence ($\theta_a = 0°$), where it is about 4% for an air–glass interface. This fraction increases with increasing angle of incidence to 100% at grazing incidence, when $\theta_a = 90°$.

It's possible to use Maxwell's equations to predict the amplitude, intensity, phase, and polarization states of the reflected and refracted waves. Such an analysis is beyond our scope, however.

The index of refraction depends not only on the substance but also on the wavelength of the light. The dependence on wavelength is called *dispersion;* we will consider it in Section 33.4. Indexes of refraction for several solids and liquids are given in Table 33.1 for a particular wavelength of yellow light.

33.10 (a) The index of refraction of air is slightly greater than 1, so light rays from the setting sun bend downward when they enter our atmosphere. (The effect is exaggerated in this figure.) (b) Stronger refraction occurs for light coming from the lower limb of the sun (the part that appears closest to the horizon), which passes through denser air in the lower atmosphere. As a result, the setting sun appears flattened vertically. (See Problem 33.55.)

(a)

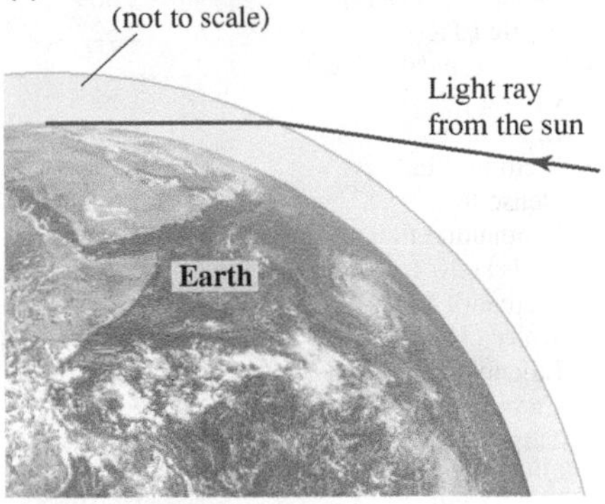

(b)

Application Transparency and Index of Refraction

An eel in its larval stage is nearly as transparent as the seawater in which it swims. The larva in this photo is nonetheless easy to see because its index of refraction is higher than that of seawater, so that some of the light striking it is reflected instead of transmitted. The larva appears particularly shiny around its edges because the light reaching the camera from those points struck the larva at near-grazing incidence ($\theta_a = 90°$), resulting in almost 100% reflection.

Table 33.1 Index of Refraction for Yellow Sodium Light, $\lambda_0 = 589$ nm

Substance	Index of Refraction, n
Solids	
Ice (H_2O)	1.309
Fluorite (CaF_2)	1.434
Polystyrene	1.49
Rock salt (NaCl)	1.544
Quartz (SiO_2)	1.544
Zircon ($ZrO_2 \cdot SiO_2$)	1.923
Diamond (C)	2.417
Fabulite ($SrTiO_3$)	2.409
Rutile (TiO_2)	2.62
Glasses (typical values)	
Crown	1.52
Light flint	1.58
Medium flint	1.62
Dense flint	1.66
Lanthanum flint	1.80
Liquids at 20°C	
Methanol (CH_3OH)	1.329
Water (H_2O)	1.333
Ethanol (C_2H_5OH)	1.36
Carbon tetrachloride (CCl_4)	1.460
Turpentine	1.472
Glycerine	1.473
Benzene	1.501
Carbon disulfide (CS_2)	1.628

The index of refraction of air at standard temperature and pressure is about 1.0003, and we will usually take it to be exactly unity. The index of refraction of a gas increases as its density increases. Most glasses used in optical instruments have indexes of refraction between about 1.5 and 2.0. A few substances have larger indexes; one example is diamond, with 2.417.

Index of Refraction and the Wave Aspects of Light

We have discussed how the direction of a light ray changes when it passes from one material to another material with a different index of refraction. It's also important to see what happens to the *wave* characteristics of the light when this happens.

First, the frequency f of the wave does not change when passing from one material to another. That is, the number of wave cycles arriving per unit time must equal the number leaving per unit time; this is a statement that the boundary surface cannot create or destroy waves.

Second, the wavelength λ of the wave *is* different in general in different materials. This is because in any material, $v = \lambda f$; since f is the same in any material as in vacuum and v is always less than the wave speed c in vacuum, λ is also correspondingly reduced. Thus the wavelength λ of light in a material is *less than* the wavelength λ_0 of the same light in vacuum. From the above discussion, $f = c/\lambda_0 = v/\lambda$. Combining this with Eq. (33.1), $n = c/v$, we find

$$\lambda = \frac{\lambda_0}{n} \quad \text{(wavelength of light in a material)} \qquad (33.5)$$

When a wave passes from one material into a second material with larger index of refraction, so that $n_b > n_a$, the wave speed decreases. The wavelength $\lambda_b = \lambda_0/n_b$ in the second material is then shorter than the wavelength $\lambda_a = \lambda_0/n_a$ in the first material. If instead the second material has a smaller index of refraction than the first material, so that $n_b < n_a$, then the wave speed increases. Then the wavelength λ_b in the second material is longer than the wavelength λ_a in the first material. This makes intuitive sense; the waves get "squeezed" (the wavelength gets shorter) if the wave speed decreases and get "stretched" (the wavelength gets longer) if the wave speed increases.

Problem-Solving Strategy 33.1 Reflection and Refraction

MP

IDENTIFY *the relevant concepts:* Use geometric optics, discussed in this section, whenever light (or electromagnetic radiation of *any* frequency and wavelength) encounters a boundary between materials. In general, part of the light is reflected back into the first material and part is refracted into the second material.

SET UP *the problem* using the following steps:

1. In problems involving rays and angles, start by drawing a large, neat diagram. Label all known angles and indexes of refraction.
2. Identify the target variables.

EXECUTE *the solution* as follows:

1. Apply the laws of reflection, Eq. (33.2), and refraction, Eq. (33.4). Measure angles of incidence, reflection, and refraction with respect to the *normal* to the surface, *never* from the surface itself.
2. Apply geometry or trigonometry in working out angular relationships. Remember that the sum of the acute angles of a right triangle is 90° (they are *complementary*) and the sum of the interior angles in any triangle is 180°.
3. The frequency of the electromagnetic radiation does not change when it moves from one material to another; the wavelength changes in accordance with Eq. (33.5), $\lambda = \lambda_0/n$.

EVALUATE *your answer:* In problems that involve refraction, check that your results are consistent with Snell's law ($n_a \sin\theta_a = n_b \sin\theta_b$). If the second material has a higher index of refraction than the first, the angle of refraction must be *smaller* than the angle of incidence: The refracted ray bends toward the normal. If the first material has the higher index of refraction, the refracted angle must be larger than the incident angle: The refracted ray bends away from the normal.

Example 33.1 Reflection and refraction

In Fig. 33.11, material a is water and material b is glass with index of refraction 1.52. The incident ray makes an angle of 60.0° with the normal; find the directions of the reflected and refracted rays.

SOLUTION

IDENTIFY and SET UP: This is a problem in geometric optics. We are given the angle of incidence $\theta_a = 60.0°$ and the indexes of refraction $n_a = 1.33$ and $n_b = 1.52$. We must find the angles of reflection and refraction θ_r and θ_b; to do this we use Eqs. (33.2) and (33.4), respectively. Figure 33.11 shows the rays and angles; n_b is slightly greater than n_a, so by Snell's law [Eq. (33.4)] θ_b is slightly smaller than θ_a, as the figure shows.

33.11 Reflection and refraction of light passing from water to glass.

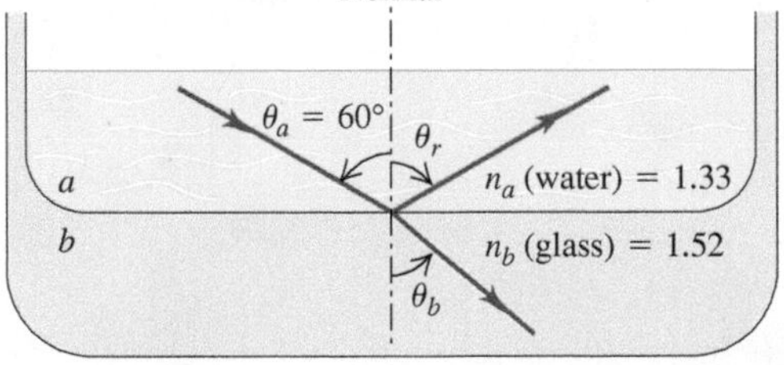

EXECUTE: According to Eq. (33.2), the angle the reflected ray makes with the normal is the same as that of the incident ray, so $\theta_r = \theta_a = 60.0°$.

To find the direction of the refracted ray we use Snell's law, Eq. (33.4):

$$n_a \sin\theta_a = n_b \sin\theta_b$$

$$\sin\theta_b = \frac{n_a}{n_b}\sin\theta_a = \frac{1.33}{1.52}\sin 60.0° = 0.758$$

$$\theta_b = \arcsin(0.758) = 49.3°$$

EVALUATE: The second material has a larger refractive index than the first, as in Fig. 33.8a. Hence the refracted ray is bent toward the normal and $\theta_b < \theta_a$.

Example 33.2 Index of refraction in the eye

The wavelength of the red light from a helium-neon laser is 633 nm in air but 474 nm in the aqueous humor inside your eyeball. Calculate the index of refraction of the aqueous humor and the speed and frequency of the light in it.

SOLUTION

IDENTIFY and SET UP: The key ideas here are (i) the definition of index of refraction n in terms of the wave speed v in a medium and the speed c in vacuum, and (ii) the relationship between wavelength λ_0 in vacuum and wavelength λ in a medium of index n. We use Eq. (33.1), $n = c/v$; Eq. (33.5), $\lambda = \lambda_0/n$; and $v = \lambda f$.

EXECUTE: The index of refraction of air is very close to unity, so we assume that the wavelength λ_0 in vacuum is the same as that in air, 633 nm. Then from Eq. (33.5),

$$\lambda = \frac{\lambda_0}{n} \qquad n = \frac{\lambda_0}{\lambda} = \frac{633\text{ nm}}{474\text{ nm}} = 1.34$$

This is about the same index of refraction as for water. Then, using $n = c/v$ and $v = \lambda f$, we find

$$v = \frac{c}{n} = \frac{3.00 \times 10^8\text{ m/s}}{1.34} = 2.25 \times 10^8\text{ m/s}$$

$$f = \frac{v}{\lambda} = \frac{2.25 \times 10^8\text{ m/s}}{474 \times 10^{-9}\text{ m}} = 4.74 \times 10^{14}\text{ Hz}$$

EVALUATE: Note that while the speed and wavelength have different values in air and in the aqueous humor, the *frequency* in air, f_0, is the same as the frequency f in the aqueous humor:

$$f_0 = \frac{c}{\lambda_0} = \frac{3.00 \times 10^8\text{ m/s}}{633 \times 10^{-9}\text{ m}} = 4.74 \times 10^{14}\text{ Hz}$$

When a light wave passes from one material into another, the wave speed and wavelength both change but the wave frequency is unchanged.

Example 33.3 A twice-reflected ray

Two mirrors are perpendicular to each other. A ray traveling in a plane perpendicular to both mirrors is reflected from one mirror, then the other, as shown in Fig. 33.12. What is the ray's final direction relative to its original direction?

SOLUTION

IDENTIFY and SET UP: This problem involves the law of reflection, which we must apply twice (once for each mirror).

EXECUTE: For mirror 1 the angle of incidence is θ_1, and this equals the angle of reflection. The sum of interior angles in the triangle shown in the figure is 180°, so we see that the angles of incidence and reflection for mirror 2 are both $90° - \theta_1$. The total change in direction of the ray after both reflections is therefore $2(90° - \theta_1) + 2\theta_1 = 180°$. That is, the ray's final direction is opposite to its original direction.

Continued

33.12 A ray moving in the xy-plane. The first reflection changes the sign of the y-component of its velocity, and the second reflection changes the sign of the x-component. For a different ray with a z-component of velocity, a third mirror (perpendicular to the two shown) could be used to change the sign of that component.

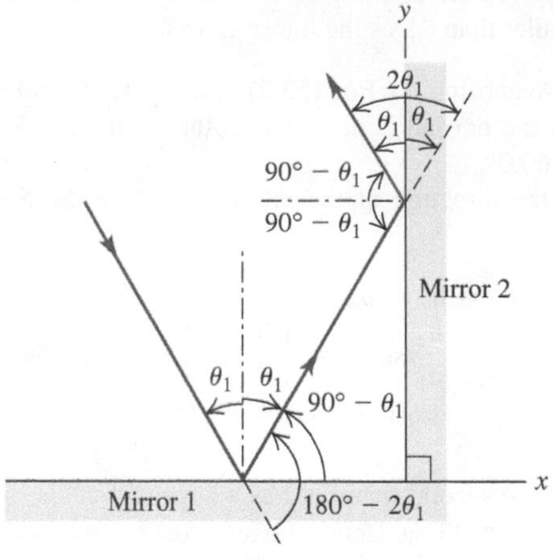

EVALUATE: An alternative viewpoint is that reflection reverses the sign of the component of light velocity perpendicular to the surface but leaves the other components unchanged. We invite you to verify this in detail. You should also be able to use this result to show that when a ray of light is successively reflected by three mirrors forming a corner of a cube (a "corner reflector"), its final direction is again opposite to its original direction. This principle is widely used in tail-light lenses and bicycle reflectors to improve their night-time visibility. Apollo astronauts placed arrays of corner reflectors on the moon. By use of laser beams reflected from these arrays, the earth–moon distance has been measured to within 0.15 m.

Test Your Understanding of Section 33.2 You are standing on the shore of a lake. You spot a tasty fish swimming some distance below the lake surface. (a) If you want to spear the fish, should you aim the spear (i) above, (ii) below, or (iii) directly at the apparent position of the fish? (b) If instead you use a high-power laser to simultaneously kill and cook the fish, should you aim the laser (i) above, (ii) below, or (iii) directly at the apparent position of the fish? ❙

MasteringPHYSICS

ActivPhysics 15.2: Total Internal Reflection

33.3 Total Internal Reflection

We have described how light is partially reflected and partially transmitted at an interface between two materials with different indexes of refraction. Under certain circumstances, however, *all* of the light can be reflected back from the interface, with none of it being transmitted, even though the second material is transparent. Figure 33.13a shows how this can occur. Several rays are shown radiating from a point source in material a with index of refraction n_a. The rays

33.13 (a) Total internal reflection. The angle of incidence for which the angle of refraction is 90° is called the critical angle: This is the case for ray 3. The reflected portions of rays 1, 2, and 3 are omitted for clarity. (b) Rays of laser light enter the water in the fishbowl from above; they are reflected at the bottom by mirrors tilted at slightly different angles. One ray undergoes total internal reflection at the air–water interface.

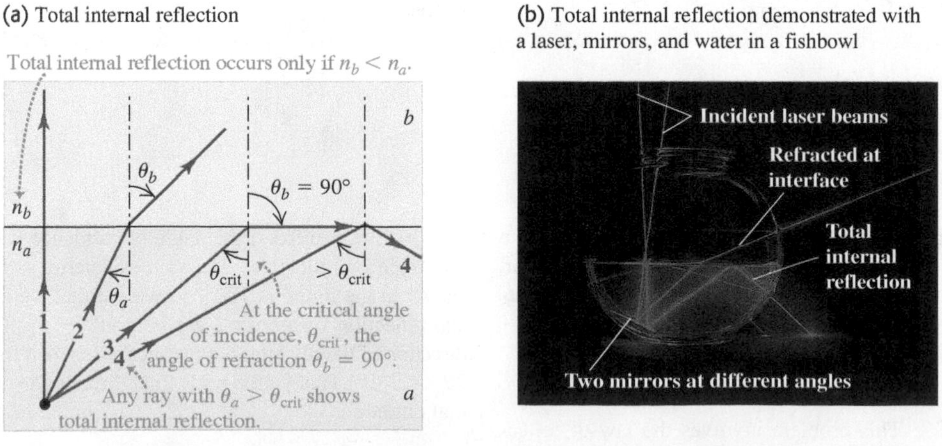

strike the surface of a second material b with index n_b, where $n_a > n_b$. (Materials a and b could be water and air, respectively.) From Snell's law of refraction,

$$\sin\theta_b = \frac{n_a}{n_b}\sin\theta_a$$

Because n_a/n_b is greater than unity, $\sin\theta_b$ is larger than $\sin\theta_a$; the ray is bent *away from* the normal. Thus there must be some value of θ_a *less than* 90° for which $\sin\theta_b = 1$ and $\theta_b = 90°$. This is shown by ray 3 in the diagram, which emerges just grazing the surface at an angle of refraction of 90°. Compare Fig. 33.13a to the photograph of light rays in Fig. 33.13b.

The angle of incidence for which the refracted ray emerges tangent to the surface is called the **critical angle,** denoted by θ_{crit}. (A more detailed analysis using Maxwell's equations shows that as the incident angle approaches the critical angle, the transmitted intensity approaches zero.) If the angle of incidence is *larger* than the critical angle, the sine of the angle of refraction, as computed by Snell's law, would have to be greater than unity, which is impossible. Beyond the critical angle, the ray *cannot* pass into the upper material; it is trapped in the lower material and is completely reflected at the boundary surface. This situation, called **total internal reflection,** occurs only when a ray in material a is incident on a second material b whose index of refraction is *smaller* than that of material a (that is, $n_b < n_a$).

We can find the critical angle for two given materials a and b by setting $\theta_b = 90°(\sin\theta_b = 1)$ in Snell's law. We then have

$$\sin\theta_{crit} = \frac{n_b}{n_a} \quad \text{(critical angle for total internal reflection)} \quad (33.6)$$

Total internal reflection will occur if the angle of incidence θ_a is larger than or equal to θ_{crit}.

33.14 (a) Total internal reflection in a Porro prism. (b) A combination of two Porro prisms in binoculars.

(a) Total internal reflection in a Porro prism

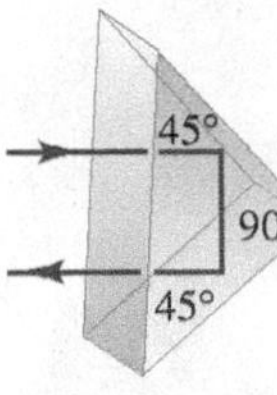

If the incident beam is oriented as shown, total internal reflection occurs on the 45° faces (because, for a glass–air interface, $\theta_{crit} = 41.1$).

(b) Binoculars use Porro prisms to reflect the light to each eyepiece.

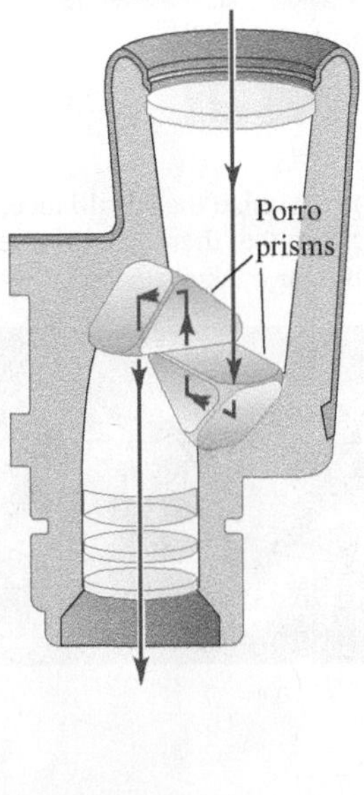

Applications of Total Internal Reflection

Total internal reflection finds numerous uses in optical technology. As an example, consider glass with index of refraction $n = 1.52$. If light propagating within this glass encounters a glass–air interface, the critical angle is

$$\sin\theta_{crit} = \frac{1}{1.52} = 0.658 \qquad \theta_{crit} = 41.1°$$

The light will be *totally reflected* if it strikes the glass–air surface at an angle of 41.1° or larger. Because the critical angle is slightly smaller than 45°, it is possible to use a prism with angles of 45°–45°–90° as a totally reflecting surface. As reflectors, totally reflecting prisms have some advantages over metallic surfaces such as ordinary coated-glass mirrors. While no metallic surface reflects 100% of the light incident on it, light can be *totally* reflected by a prism. These reflecting properties of a prism are permanent and unaffected by tarnishing.

A 45°– 45°– 90° prism, used as in Fig. 33.14a, is called a *Porro* prism. Light enters and leaves at right angles to the hypotenuse and is totally reflected at each of the shorter faces. The total change of direction of the rays is 180°. Binoculars often use combinations of two Porro prisms, as in Fig. 33.14b.

When a beam of light enters at one end of a transparent rod (Fig. 33.15), the light can be totally reflected internally if the index of refraction of the rod is greater than that of the surrounding material. The light is "trapped" within the rod even if the rod is curved, provided that the curvature is not too great. Such a

33.15 A transparent rod with refractive index greater than that of the surrounding material.

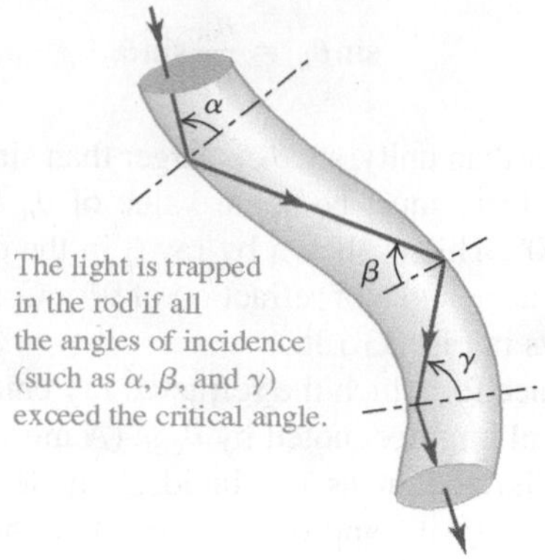

33.16 This colored x-ray image of a patient's abdomen shows an endoscope winding through the colon.

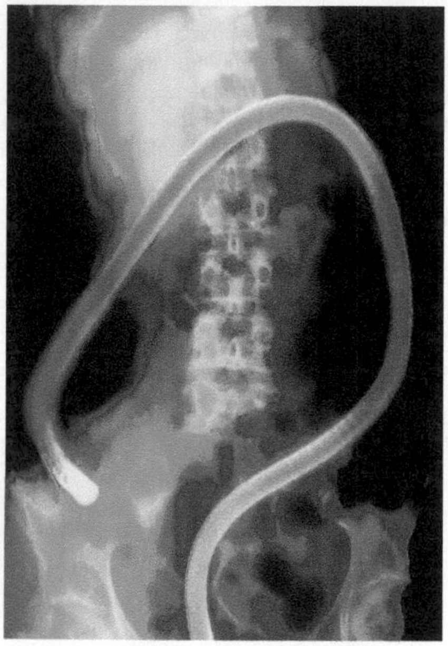

rod is sometimes called a *light pipe.* A bundle of fine glass or plastic fibers behaves in the same way and has the advantage of being flexible. A bundle may consist of thousands of individual fibers, each of the order of 0.002 to 0.01 mm in diameter. If the fibers are assembled in the bundle so that the relative positions of the ends are the same (or mirror images) at both ends, the bundle can transmit an image.

Fiber-optic devices have found a wide range of medical applications in instruments called *endoscopes,* which can be inserted directly into the bronchial tubes, the bladder, the colon, and other organs for direct visual examination (Fig. 33.16). A bundle of fibers can even be enclosed in a hypodermic needle for studying tissues and blood vessels far beneath the skin.

Fiber optics also have applications in communication systems, in which they are used to transmit a modulated laser beam. The rate at which information can be transmitted by a wave (light, radio, or whatever) is proportional to the frequency. To see qualitatively why this is so, consider modulating (modifying) the wave by chopping off some of the wave crests. Suppose each crest represents a binary digit, with a chopped-off crest representing a zero and an unmodified crest representing a one. The number of binary digits we can transmit per unit time is thus proportional to the frequency of the wave. Infrared and visible-light waves have much higher frequency than do radio waves, so a modulated laser beam can transmit an enormous amount of information through a single fiber-optic cable.

Another advantage of optical fibers is that they can be made thinner than conventional copper wire, so more fibers can be bundled together in a cable of a given diameter. Hence more distinct signals (for instance, different phone lines) can be sent over the same cable. Because fiber-optic cables are electrical insulators, they are immune to electrical interference from lightning and other sources, and they don't allow unwanted currents between source and receiver. For these and other reasons, fiber-optic cables play an important role in long-distance telephone, television, and Internet communication.

33.17 To maximize their brilliance, diamonds are cut so that there is total internal reflection on their back surfaces.

Total internal reflection also plays an important role in the design of jewelry. The brilliance of diamond is due in large measure to its very high index of refraction ($n = 2.417$) and correspondingly small critical angle. Light entering a cut diamond is totally internally reflected from facets on its back surface, and then emerges from its front surface (Fig. 33.17). "Imitation diamond" gems, such as cubic zirconia, are made from less expensive crystalline materials with comparable indexes of refraction.

Conceptual Example 33.4 **A leaky periscope**

A submarine periscope uses two totally reflecting 45°–45°–90° prisms with total internal reflection on the sides adjacent to the 45° angles. Explain why the periscope will no longer work if it springs a leak and the bottom prism is covered with water.

SOLUTION

The critical angle for water ($n_b = 1.33$) on glass ($n_a = 1.52$) is

$$\theta_{crit} = \arcsin\frac{1.33}{1.52} = 61.0°$$

The 45° angle of incidence for a totally reflecting prism is *smaller* than this new 61° critical angle, so total internal reflection does not occur at the glass–water interface. Most of the light is transmitted into the water, and very little is reflected back into the prism.

Test Your Understanding of Section 33.3 In which of the following situations is there total internal reflection? (i) Light propagating in water ($n = 1.33$) strikes a water–air interface at an incident angle of 70°; (ii) light propagating in glass ($n = 1.52$) strikes a glass–water interface at an incident angle of 70°; (iii) light propagating in water strikes a water–glass interface at an incident angle of 70°.

33.4 Dispersion

Ordinary white light is a superposition of waves with wavelengths extending throughout the visible spectrum. The speed of light *in vacuum* is the same for all wavelengths, but the speed in a material substance is different for different wavelengths. Therefore the index of refraction of a material depends on wavelength. The dependence of wave speed and index of refraction on wavelength is called **dispersion.**

Figure 33.18 shows the variation of index of refraction n with wavelength for some common optical materials. Note that the horizontal axis of this figure is the wavelength of the light *in vacuum,* λ_0; the wavelength in the material is given by Eq. (33.5), $\lambda = \lambda_0/n$. In most materials the value of n *decreases* with increasing wavelength and decreasing frequency, and thus n *increases* with decreasing wavelength and increasing frequency. In such a material, light of longer wavelength has greater speed than light of shorter wavelength.

Figure 33.19 shows a ray of white light incident on a prism. The deviation (change of direction) produced by the prism increases with increasing index of refraction and frequency and decreasing wavelength. Violet light is deviated most, and red is deviated least; other colors are in intermediate positions. When it comes out of the prism, the light is spread out into a fan-shaped beam, as shown. The light is said to be *dispersed* into a spectrum. The amount of dispersion depends on the *difference* between the refractive indexes for violet light and for red light. From Fig. 33.18 we can see that for a substance such as fluorite, the difference between the indexes for red and violet is small, and the dispersion will also be small. A better choice of material for a prism whose purpose is to produce a spectrum would be silicate flint glass, for which there is a larger difference in the value of n between red and violet.

33.18 Variation of index of refraction n with wavelength for different transparent materials. The horizontal axis shows the wavelength λ_0 of the light *in vacuum;* the wavelength in the material is equal to $\lambda = \lambda_0/n$.

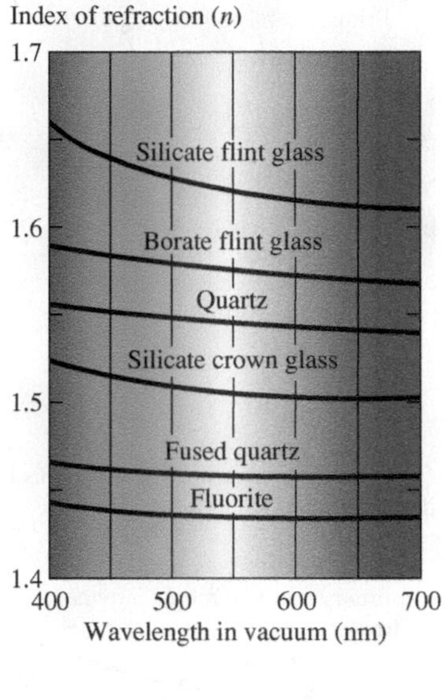

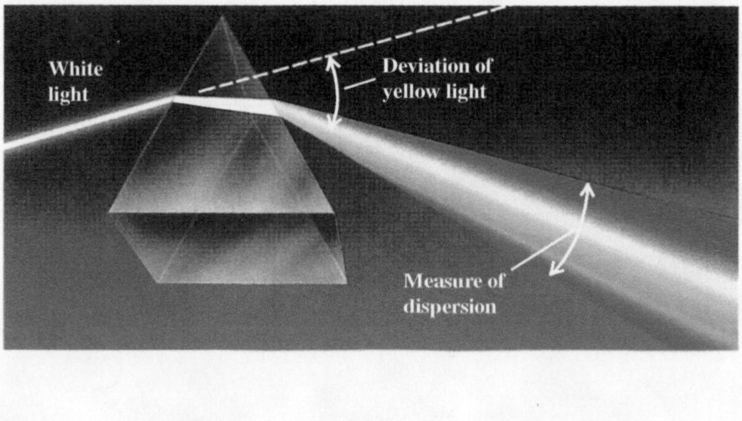

33.19 Dispersion of light by a prism. The band of colors is called a spectrum.

As we mentioned in Section 33.3, the brilliance of diamond is due in part to its unusually large refractive index; another important factor is its large dispersion, which causes white light entering a diamond to emerge as a multicolored spectrum. Crystals of rutile and of strontium titanate, which can be produced synthetically, have about eight times the dispersion of diamond.

Rainbows

When you experience the beauty of a rainbow, as in Fig. 33.20a, you are seeing the combined effects of dispersion, refraction, and reflection. Sunlight comes from behind you, enters a water droplet, is (partially) reflected from the back surface of the droplet, and is refracted again upon exiting the droplet (Fig. 33.20b). A light ray that enters the middle of the raindrop is reflected straight back. All other rays

33.20 How rainbows form.

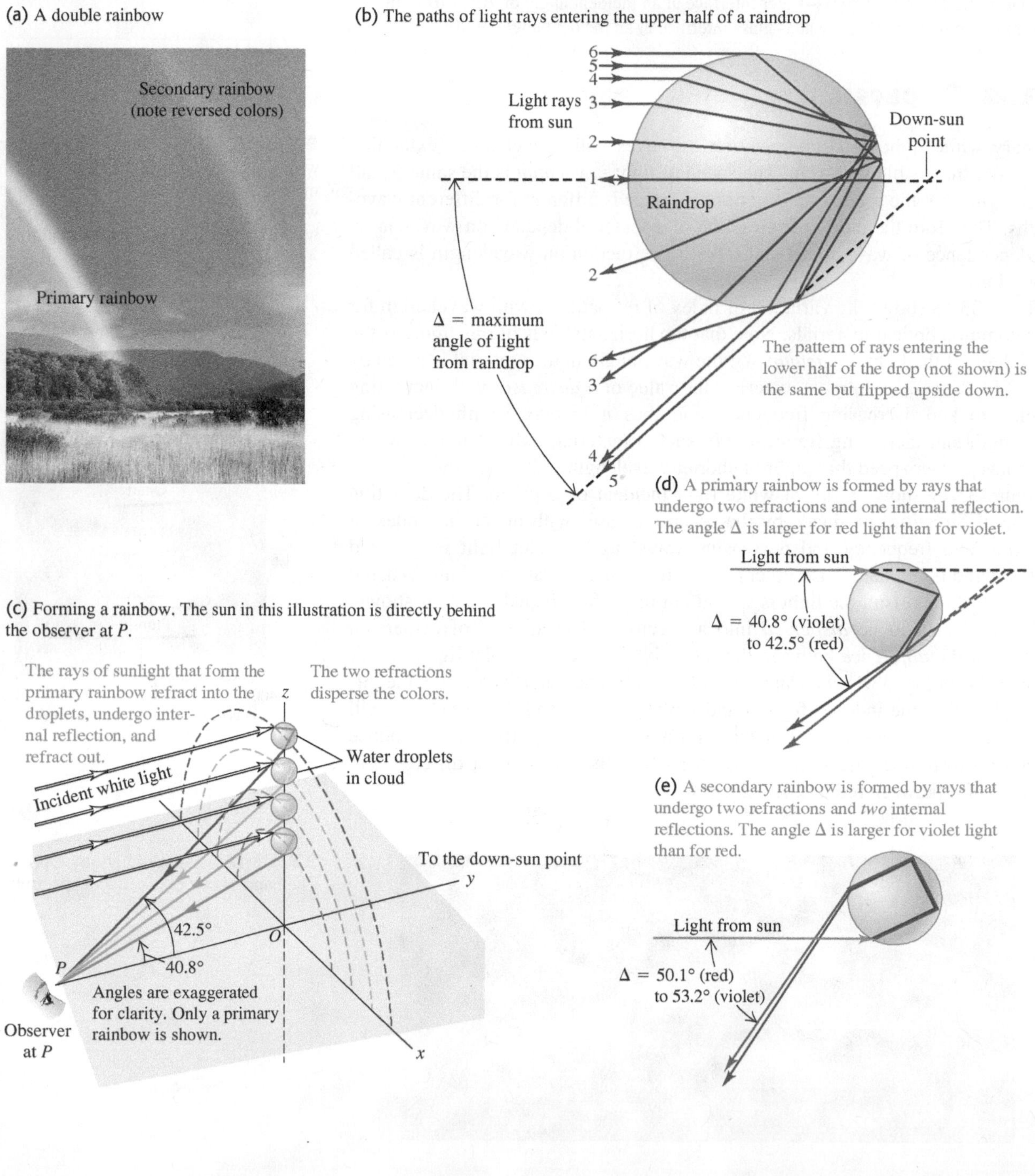

exit the raindrop within an angle Δ of that middle ray, with many rays "piling up" at the angle Δ. What you see is a disk of light of angular radius Δ centered on the down-sun point (the point in the sky opposite the sun); due to the "piling up" of light rays, the disk is brightest around its rim, which we see as a rainbow (Fig. 33.20c). Because no light reaches your eye from angles larger than Δ, the sky looks dark outside the rainbow (see Fig. 33.20a). The value of the angle Δ depends on the index of refraction of the water that makes up the raindrops, which in turn depends on the wavelength (Fig. 33.20d). The bright disk of red light is slightly larger than that for orange light, which in turn is slightly larger than that for yellow light, and so on. As a result, you see the rainbow as a band of colors.

In many cases you can see a second, larger rainbow. It is the result of dispersion, refraction, and *two* reflections from the back surface of the droplet (Fig. 33.20e). Each time a light ray hits the back surface, part of the light is refracted out of the drop (not shown in Fig. 33.20); after two such hits, relatively little light is left inside the drop, which is why the secondary rainbow is noticeably fainter than the primary rainbow. Just as a mirror held up to a book reverses the printed letters, so the second reflection reverses the sequence of colors in the secondary rainbow. You can see this effect in Fig. 33.20a.

33.5 Polarization

MasteringPHYSICS

ActivPhysics 16.9: Physical Optics: Polarization

Polarization is a characteristic of all transverse waves. This chapter is about light, but to introduce some basic polarization concepts, let's go back to the transverse waves on a string that we studied in Chapter 15. For a string that in equilibrium lies along the x-axis, the displacements may be along the y-direction, as in Fig. 33.21a. In this case the string always lies in the xy-plane. But the displacements might instead be along the z-axis, as in Fig. 33.21b; then the string always lies in the xz-plane.

When a wave has only y-displacements, we say that it is **linearly polarized** in the y-direction; a wave with only z-displacements is linearly polarized in the z-direction. For mechanical waves we can build a **polarizing filter,** or **polarizer,** that permits only waves with a certain polarization direction to pass. In Fig. 33.21c the string can slide vertically in the slot without friction, but no horizontal motion is possible. This filter passes waves that are polarized in the y-direction but blocks those that are polarized in the z-direction.

This same language can be applied to electromagnetic waves, which also have polarization. As we learned in Chapter 32, an electromagnetic wave is a *transverse* wave; the fluctuating electric and magnetic fields are perpendicular to each other and to the direction of propagation. We always define the direction of polarization of an electromagnetic wave to be the direction of the *electric*-field vector $\vec{E}$, not the magnetic field, because many common electromagnetic-wave detectors respond to the electric forces on electrons in materials, not the magnetic forces. Thus the electromagnetic wave described by Eq. (32.17),

$$\vec{E}(x,t) = \hat{j}E_{max}\cos(kx - \omega t)$$
$$\vec{B}(x,t) = \hat{k}B_{max}\cos(kx - \omega t)$$

33.21 (a), (b) Polarized waves on a string. (c) Making a polarized wave on a string from an unpolarized one using a polarizing filter.

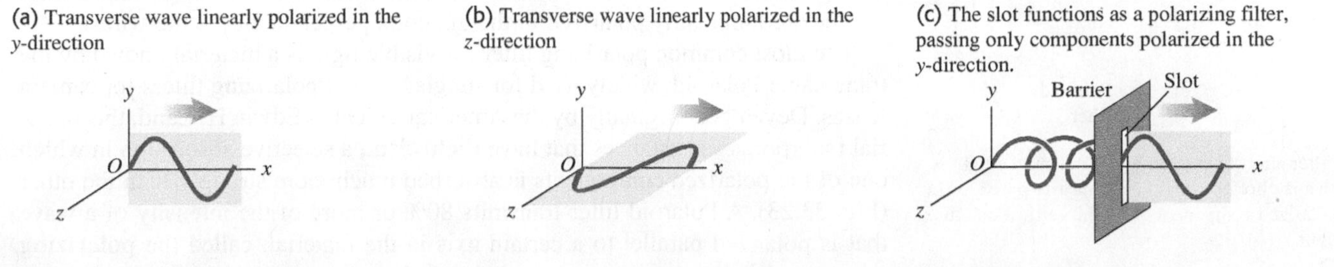

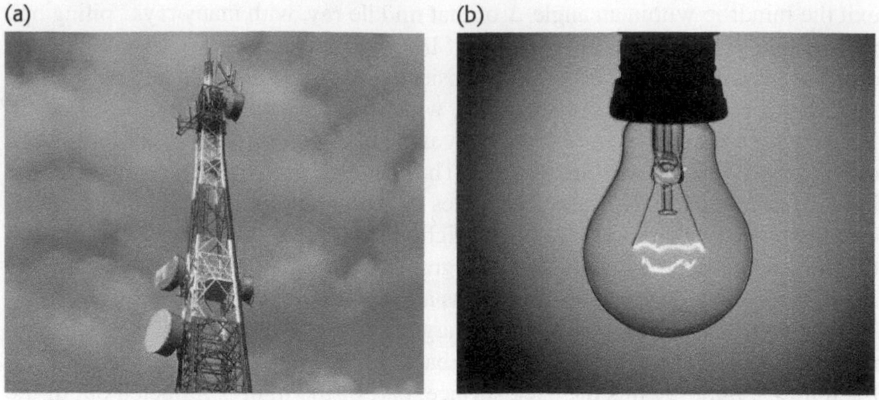

33.22 (a) Electrons in the red and white broadcast antenna oscillate vertically, producing vertically polarized electromagnetic waves that propagate away from the antenna in the horizontal direction. (The small gray antennas are for relaying cellular phone signals.) (b) No matter how this light bulb is oriented, the random motion of electrons in the filament produces unpolarized light waves.

is said to be polarized in the y-direction because the electric field has only a y-component.

CAUTION **The meaning of "polarization"** It's unfortunate that the same word "polarization" that is used to describe the direction of $\vec{E}$ in an electromagnetic wave is also used to describe the shifting of electric charge within a body, such as in response to a nearby charged body; we described this latter kind of polarization in Section 21,2 (see Fig. 21.7). You should remember that while these two concepts have the same name, they do not describe the same phenomenon. ❙

Polarizing Filters

Waves emitted by a radio transmitter are usually linearly polarized. The vertical antennas that are used for radio broadcasting emit waves that, in a horizontal plane around the antenna, are polarized in the vertical direction (parallel to the antenna) (Fig. 33.22a).

The situation is different for visible light. Light from incandescent light bulbs and fluorescent light fixtures is *not* polarized (Fig. 33.22b). The "antennas" that radiate light waves are the molecules that make up the sources. The waves emitted by any one molecule may be linearly polarized, like those from a radio antenna. But any actual light source contains a tremendous number of molecules with random orientations, so the emitted light is a random mixture of waves linearly polarized in all possible transverse directions. Such light is called **unpolarized light** or **natural light.** To create polarized light from unpolarized natural light requires a filter that is analogous to the slot for mechanical waves in Fig. 33.21c.

33.23 A Polaroid filter is illuminated by unpolarized natural light (shown by $\vec{E}$ vectors that point in all directions perpendicular to the direction of propagation). The transmitted light is linearly polarized along the polarizing axis (shown by $\vec{E}$ vectors along the polarization direction only).

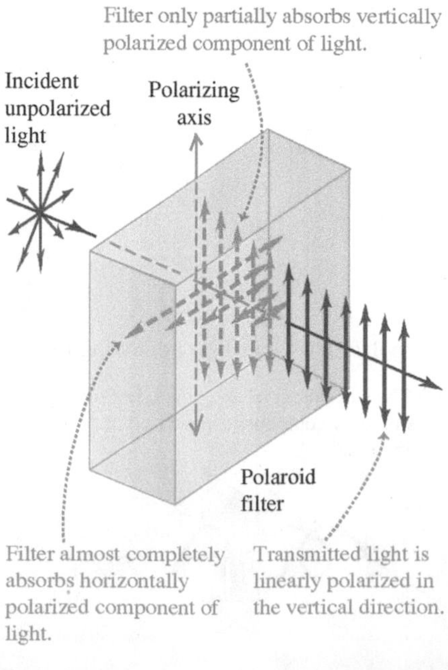

Polarizing filters for electromagnetic waves have different details of construction, depending on the wavelength. For microwaves with a wavelength of a few centimeters, a good polarizer is an array of closely spaced, parallel conducting wires that are insulated from each other. (Think of a barbecue grill with the outer metal ring replaced by an insulating one.) Electrons are free to move along the length of the conducting wires and will do so in response to a wave whose $\vec{E}$ field is parallel to the wires. The resulting currents in the wires dissipate energy by I^2R heating; the dissipated energy comes from the wave, so whatever wave passes through the grid is greatly reduced in amplitude. Waves with $\vec{E}$ oriented perpendicular to the wires pass through almost unaffected, since electrons cannot move through the air between the wires. Hence a wave that passes through such a filter will be predominantly polarized in the direction perpendicular to the wires.

The most common polarizing filter for visible light is a material known by the trade name Polaroid, widely used for sunglasses and polarizing filters for camera lenses. Developed originally by the American scientist Edwin H. Land, this material incorporates substances that have **dichroism,** a selective absorption in which one of the polarized components is absorbed much more strongly than the other (Fig. 33.23). A Polaroid filter transmits 80% or more of the intensity of a wave that is polarized parallel to a certain axis in the material, called the **polarizing**

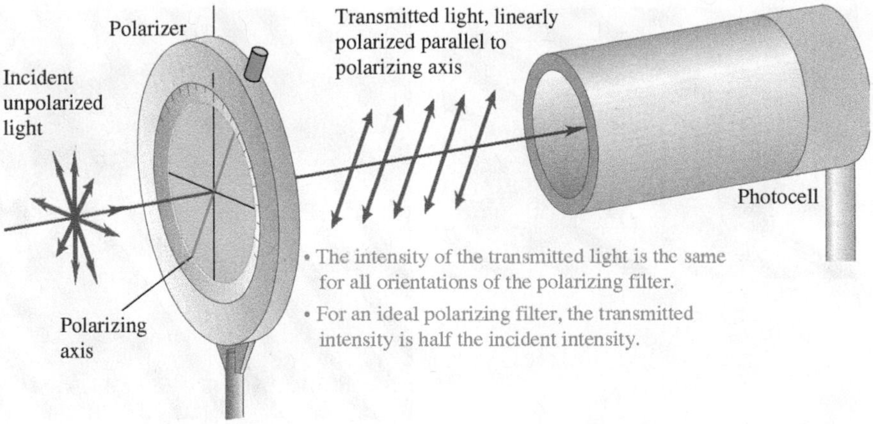

33.24 Unpolarized natural light is incident on the polarizing filter. The photocell measures the intensity of the transmitted linearly polarized light.

axis, but only 1% or less for waves that are polarized perpendicular to this axis. In one type of Polaroid filter, long-chain molecules within the filter are oriented with their axis perpendicular to the polarizing axis; these molecules preferentially absorb light that is polarized along their length, much like the conducting wires in a polarizing filter for microwaves.

Using Polarizing Filters

An *ideal* polarizing filter (polarizer) passes 100% of the incident light that is polarized parallel to the filter's polarizing axis but completely blocks all light that is polarized perpendicular to this axis. Such a device is an unattainable idealization, but the concept is useful in clarifying the basic ideas. In the following discussion we will assume that all polarizing filters are ideal. In Fig. 33.24 unpolarized light is incident on a flat polarizing filter. The $\vec{E}$ vector of the incident wave can be represented in terms of components parallel and perpendicular to the polarizer axis (shown in blue); only the component of $\vec{E}$ parallel to the polarizing axis is transmitted. Hence the light emerging from the polarizer is linearly polarized parallel to the polarizing axis.

When unpolarized light is incident on an ideal polarizer as in Fig. 33.24, the intensity of the transmitted light is *exactly half* that of the incident unpolarized light, no matter how the polarizing axis is oriented. Here's why: We can resolve the $\vec{E}$ field of the incident wave into a component parallel to the polarizing axis and a component perpendicular to it. Because the incident light is a random mixture of all states of polarization, these two components are, on average, equal. The ideal polarizer transmits only the component that is parallel to the polarizing axis, so half the incident intensity is transmitted.

What happens when the linearly polarized light emerging from a polarizer passes through a second polarizer, or *analyzer*, as in Fig. 33.25? Suppose the polarizing axis of the analyzer makes an angle ϕ with the polarizing axis of the

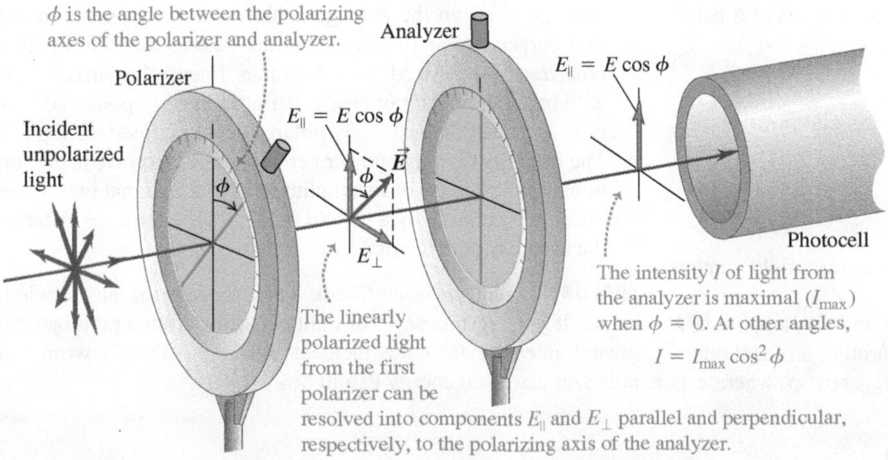

33.25 An ideal analyzer transmits only the electric field component parallel to its transmission direction (that is, its polarizing axis).

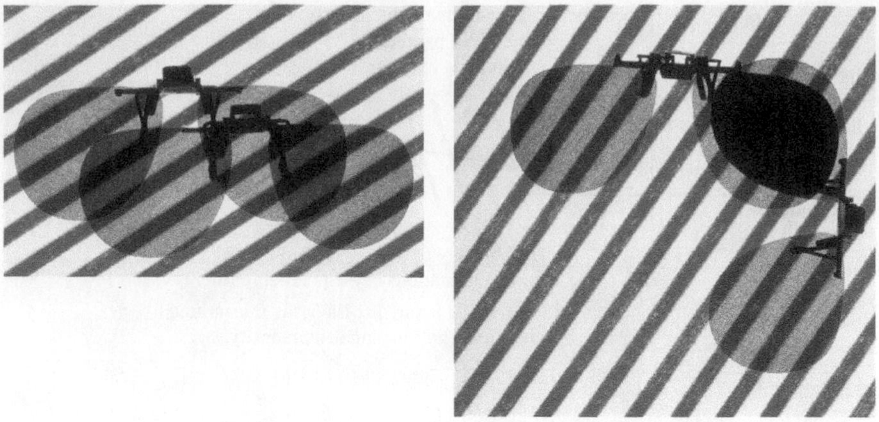

33.26 These photos show the view through Polaroid sunglasses whose polarizing axes are (left) aligned ($\phi = 0$) and (right) perpendicular ($\phi = 90°$). The transmitted intensity is greatest when the axes are aligned; it is zero when the axes are perpendicular.

first polarizer. We can resolve the linearly polarized light that is transmitted by the first polarizer into two components, as shown in Fig. 33.25, one parallel and the other perpendicular to the axis of the analyzer. Only the parallel component, with amplitude $E \cos \phi$, is transmitted by the analyzer. The transmitted intensity is greatest when $\phi = 0$, and it is zero when the polarizer and analyzer are *crossed* so that $\phi = 90°$ (Fig. 33.26). To determine the direction of polarization of the light transmitted by the first polarizer, rotate the analyzer until the photocell in Fig. 33.25 measures zero intensity; the polarization axis of the first polarizer is then perpendicular to that of the analyzer.

To find the transmitted intensity at intermediate values of the angle ϕ, we recall from our energy discussion in Section 32.4 that the intensity of an electromagnetic wave is proportional to the *square* of the amplitude of the wave [see Eq. (32.29)]. The ratio of transmitted to incident *amplitude* is $\cos \phi$, so the ratio of transmitted to incident *intensity* is $\cos^2 \phi$. Thus the intensity of the light transmitted through the analyzer is

$$I = I_{max} \cos^2 \phi \quad \text{(Malus's law, polarized light passing through an analyzer)} \tag{33.7}$$

where I_{max} is the maximum intensity of light transmitted (at $\phi = 0$) and I is the amount transmitted at angle ϕ. This relationship, discovered experimentally by Etienne Louis Malus in 1809, is called **Malus's law.** Malus's law applies *only* if the incident light passing through the analyzer is already linearly polarized.

Problem-Solving Strategy 33.2 Linear Polarization

MP

IDENTIFY *the relevant concepts:* In all electromagnetic waves, including light waves, the direction of polarization is the direction of the $\vec{E}$ field and is perpendicular to the propagation direction. Problems about polarizers are therefore about the components of $\vec{E}$ parallel and perpendicular to the polarizing axis.

SET UP *the problem* using the following steps:

1. Start by drawing a large, neat diagram. Label all known angles, including the angles of all polarizing axes.
2. Identify the target variables.

EXECUTE *the solution* as follows:

1. Remember that a polarizer lets pass only electric-field components parallel to its polarizing axis.
2. If the incident light is linearly polarized and has amplitude E and intensity I_{max}, the light that passes through an ideal polarizer has amplitude $E \cos \phi$ and intensity $I_{max} \cos^2 \phi$, where ϕ is the angle between the incident polarization direction and the filter's polarizing axis.
3. Unpolarized light is a random mixture of all possible polarization states, so on the average it has equal components in any two perpendicular directions. When passed through an ideal polarizer, unpolarized light becomes linearly polarized light with half the incident intensity. Partially linearly polarized light is a superposition of linearly polarized and unpolarized light.
4. The intensity (average power per unit area) of a wave is proportional to the *square* of its amplitude. If you find that two waves differ in amplitude by a certain factor, their intensities differ by the square of that factor.

EVALUATE *your answer:* Check your answer for any obvious errors. If your results say that light emerging from a polarizer has greater intensity than the incident light, something's wrong: A polarizer can't add energy to a light wave.

Example 33.5 Two polarizers in combination

In Fig. 33.25 the incident unpolarized light has intensity I_0. Find the intensities transmitted by the first and second polarizers if the angle between the axes of the two filters is 30°.

SOLUTION

IDENTIFY and SET UP: This problem involves a polarizer (a polarizing filter on which unpolarized light shines, producing polarized light) and an analyzer (a second polarizing filter on which the polarized light shines). We are given the intensity I_0 of the incident light and the angle $\phi = 30°$ between the axes of the polarizers. We use Malus's law, Eq. (33.7), to solve for the intensities of the light emerging from each polarizer.

EXECUTE: The incident light is unpolarized, so the intensity of the linearly polarized light transmitted by the first polarizer is $I_0/2$. From Eq. (33.7) with $\phi = 30°$, the second polarizer reduces the intensity by a further factor of $\cos^2 30° = \frac{3}{4}$. Thus the intensity transmitted by the second polarizer is

$$\left(\frac{I_0}{2}\right)\left(\frac{3}{4}\right) = \frac{3}{8}I_0$$

EVALUATE: Note that the intensity decreases after each passage through a polarizer. The only situation in which the transmitted intensity does *not* decrease is if the polarizer is ideal (so it absorbs none of the light that passes through it) and if the incident light is linearly polarized along the polarizing axis, so $\phi = 0$.

33.27 When light is incident on a reflecting surface at the polarizing angle, the reflected light is linearly polarized.

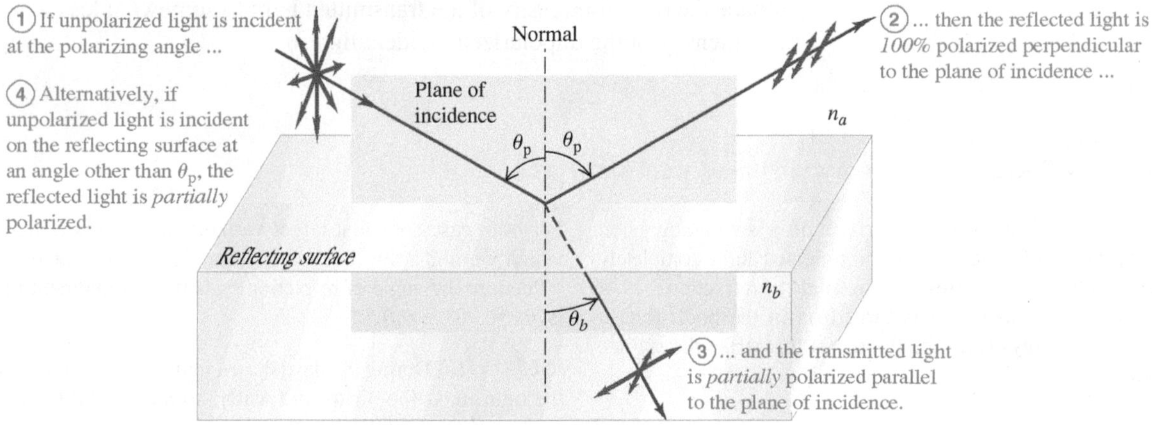

Polarization by Reflection

Unpolarized light can be polarized, either partially or totally, by *reflection.* In Fig. 33.27, unpolarized natural light is incident on a reflecting surface between two transparent optical materials. For most angles of incidence, waves for which the electric-field vector $\vec{E}$ is perpendicular to the plane of incidence (that is, parallel to the reflecting surface) are reflected more strongly than those for which $\vec{E}$ lies in this plane. In this case the reflected light is *partially polarized* in the direction perpendicular to the plane of incidence.

But at one particular angle of incidence, called the **polarizing angle** θ_p, the light for which $\vec{E}$ lies in the plane of incidence is *not reflected at all* but is completely refracted. At this same angle of incidence the light for which $\vec{E}$ is perpendicular to the plane of incidence is partially reflected and partially refracted. The *reflected* light is therefore *completely* polarized perpendicular to the plane of incidence, as shown in Fig. 33.27. The *refracted* (transmitted) light is *partially* polarized parallel to this plane; the refracted light is a mixture of the component parallel to the plane of incidence, all of which is refracted, and the remainder of the perpendicular component.

In 1812 the British scientist Sir David Brewster discovered that when the angle of incidence is equal to the polarizing angle θ_p, the reflected ray and the refracted ray are perpendicular to each other (Fig. 33.28). In this case the angle of refraction θ_b equals $90° - \theta_p$. From the law of refraction,

$$n_a \sin\theta_p = n_b \sin\theta_b$$

33.28 The significance of the polarizing angle. The open circles represent a component of $\vec{E}$ that is perpendicular to the plane of the figure (the plane of incidence) and parallel to the surface between the two materials.

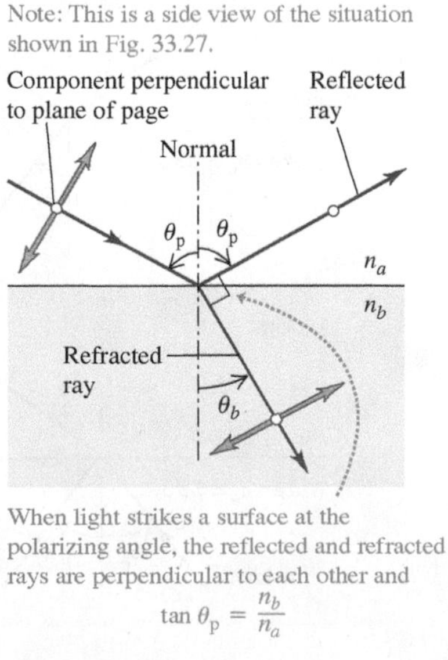

so we find

$$n_a \sin\theta_p = n_b \sin(90° - \theta_p) = n_b \cos\theta_p$$

$$\tan\theta_p = \frac{n_b}{n_a} \quad \text{(Brewster's law for the polarizing angle)} \qquad (33.8)$$

This relationship is known as **Brewster's law.** Although discovered experimentally, it can also be *derived* from a wave model using Maxwell's equations.

Polarization by reflection is the reason polarizing filters are widely used in sunglasses (Fig. 33.26). When sunlight is reflected from a horizontal surface, the plane of incidence is vertical, and the reflected light contains a preponderance of light that is polarized in the horizontal direction. When the reflection occurs at a smooth asphalt road surface or the surface of a lake, it causes unwanted glare. Vision can be improved by eliminating this glare. The manufacturer makes the polarizing axis of the lens material vertical, so very little of the horizontally polarized light reflected from the road is transmitted to the eyes. The glasses also reduce the overall intensity of the transmitted light to somewhat less than 50% of the intensity of the unpolarized incident light.

Example 33.6 Reflection from a swimming pool's surface

Sunlight reflects off the smooth surface of a swimming pool. (a) For what angle of reflection is the reflected light completely polarized? (b) What is the corresponding angle of refraction? (c) At night, an underwater floodlight is turned on in the pool. Repeat parts (a) and (b) for rays from the floodlight that strike the surface from below.

SOLUTION

IDENTIFY and SET UP: This problem involves polarization by reflection at an air–water interface in parts (a) and (b) and at a water–air interface in part (c). Figure 33.29 shows our sketches.

33.29 Our sketches for this problem.

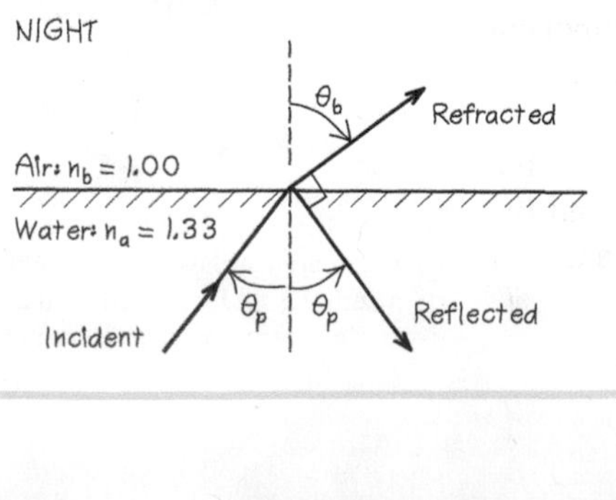

For both cases our first target variable is the polarizing angle θ_p, which we find using Brewster's law, Eq. (33.8). For this angle of reflection, the angle of refraction θ_b is the complement of θ_p (that is, $\theta_b = 90° - \theta_p$).

EXECUTE: (a) During the day (shown in the upper part of Fig. 33.29) the light moves in air toward water, so $n_a = 1.00$ (air) and $n_b = 1.33$ (water). From Eq. (33.8),

$$\theta_p = \arctan\frac{n_b}{n_a} = \arctan\frac{1.33}{1.00} = 53.1°$$

(b) The incident light is at the polarizing angle, so the reflected and refracted rays are perpendicular; hence

$$\theta_b = 90° - \theta_p = 90° - 53.1° = 36.9°$$

(c) At night (shown in the lower part of Fig. 33.29) the light moves in water toward air, so now $n_a = 1.33$ and $n_b = 1.00$. Again using Eq. (33.8), we have

$$\theta_p = \arctan\frac{1.00}{1.33} = 36.9°$$

$$\theta_b = 90° - 36.9° = 53.1°$$

EVALUATE: We check our answer in part (b) by using Snell's law, $n_a \sin\theta_a = n_b \sin\theta_b$, to solve for θ_b:

$$\sin\theta_b = \frac{n_a \sin\theta_p}{n_b} = \frac{1.00 \sin 53.1°}{1.33} = 0.600$$

$$\theta_b = \arcsin(0.600) = 36.9°$$

Note that the two polarizing angles found in parts (a) and (c) add to 90°. This is *not* an accident; can you see why?

Circular and Elliptical Polarization

Light and other electromagnetic radiation can also have *circular* or *elliptical* polarization. To introduce these concepts, let's return once more to mechanical waves on a stretched string. In Fig. 33.21, suppose the two linearly polarized waves in parts (a) and (b) are in phase and have equal amplitude. When they are superposed, each point in the string has simultaneous y- and z-displacements of equal magnitude. A little thought shows that the resultant wave lies in a plane oriented at 45° to the y- and z-axes (i.e., in a plane making a 45° angle with the xy- and xz-planes). The amplitude of the resultant wave is larger by a factor of $\sqrt{2}$ than that of either component wave, and the resultant wave is linearly polarized.

But now suppose the two equal-amplitude waves differ in phase by a quarter-cycle. Then the resultant motion of each point corresponds to a superposition of two simple harmonic motions at right angles, with a quarter-cycle phase difference. The y-displacement at a point is greatest at times when the z-displacement is zero, and vice versa. The motion of the string as a whole then no longer takes place in a single plane. It can be shown that each point on the rope moves in a *circle* in a plane parallel to the yz-plane. Successive points on the rope have successive phase differences, and the overall motion of the string has the appearance of a rotating helix. This is shown to the left of the polarizing filter in Fig. 33.21c. This particular superposition of two linearly polarized waves is called **circular polarization.**

Figure 33.30 shows the analogous situation for an electromagnetic wave. Two sinusoidal waves of equal amplitude, polarized in the y- and z-directions and with a quarter-cycle phase difference, are superposed. The result is a wave in which the $\vec{E}$ vector at each point has a constant magnitude but *rotates* around the direction of propagation. The wave in Fig. 33.30 is propagating toward you and the $\vec{E}$ vector appears to be rotating clockwise, so it is called a *right circularly polarized* electromagnetic wave. If instead the $\vec{E}$ vector of a wave coming toward you appears to be rotating counterclockwise, it is called a *left circularly polarized* electromagnetic wave.

If the phase difference between the two component waves is something other than a quarter-cycle, or if the two component waves have different amplitudes, then each point on the string traces out not a circle but an *ellipse.* The resulting wave is said to be **elliptically polarized.**

For electromagnetic waves with radio frequencies, circular or elliptical polarization can be produced by using two antennas at right angles, fed from the same

33.30 Circular polarization of an electromagnetic wave moving toward you parallel to the x-axis. The y-component of $\vec{E}$ lags the z-component by a quarter-cycle. This phase difference results in right circular polarization.

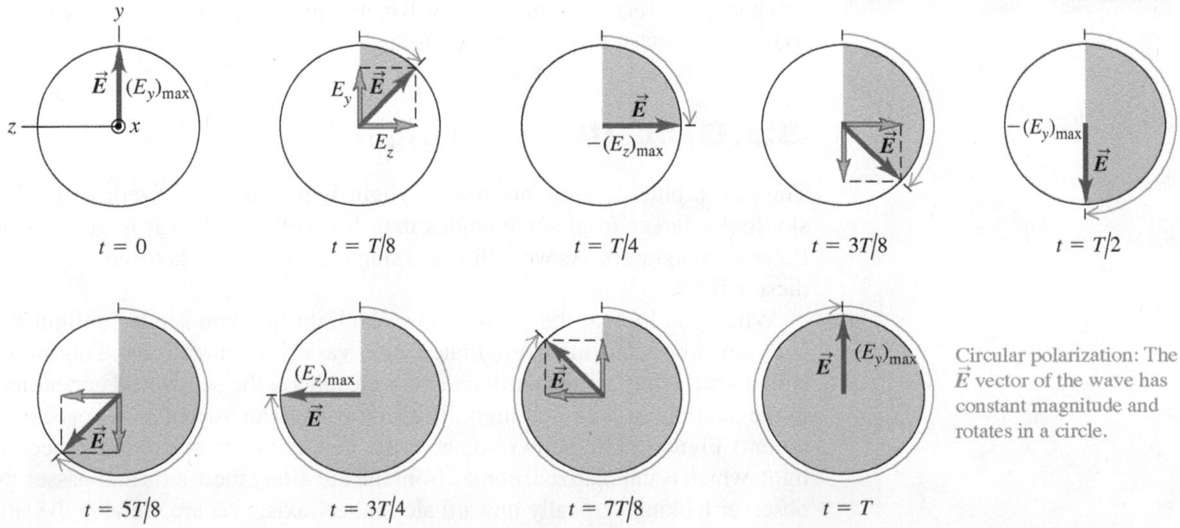

Circular polarization: The $\vec{E}$ vector of the wave has constant magnitude and rotates in a circle.

transmitter but with a phase-shifting network that introduces the appropriate phase difference. For light, the phase shift can be introduced by use of a material that exhibits *birefringence*—that is, has different indexes of refraction for different directions of polarization. A common example is calcite ($CaCO_3$). When a calcite crystal is oriented appropriately in a beam of unpolarized light, its refractive index (for a wavelength in vacuum of 589 nm) is 1.658 for one direction of polarization and 1.486 for the perpendicular direction. When two waves with equal amplitude and with perpendicular directions of polarization enter such a material, they travel with different speeds. If they are in phase when they enter the material, then in general they are no longer in phase when they emerge. If the crystal is just thick enough to introduce a quarter-cycle phase difference, then the crystal converts linearly polarized light to circularly polarized light. Such a crystal is called a *quarter-wave plate.* Such a plate also converts circularly polarized light to linearly polarized light. Can you prove this?

Photoelasticity

33.31 This plastic model of an artificial hip joint was photographed between two polarizing filters (a polarizer and an analyzer) with perpendicular polarizing axes. The colored interference pattern reveals the direction and magnitude of stresses in the model. Engineers use these results to help design the metal artificial hip joint used in medicine.

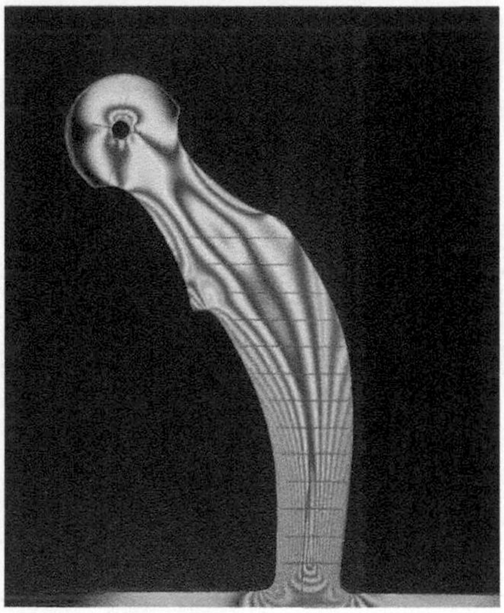

Some optical materials that are not normally birefringent become so when they are subjected to mechanical stress. This is the basis of the science of *photoelasticity.* Stresses in girders, boiler plates, gear teeth, and cathedral pillars can be analyzed by constructing a transparent model of the object, usually of a plastic material, subjecting it to stress, and examining it between a polarizer and an analyzer in the crossed position. Very complicated stress distributions can be studied by these optical methods.

Figure 33.31 is a photograph of a photoelastic model under stress. The polarized light that enters the model can be thought of as having a component along each of the two directions of the birefringent plastic. Since these two components travel through the plastic at different speeds, the light that emerges from the other side of the model can have a different overall direction of polarization. Hence some of this transmitted light will be able to pass through the analyzer even though its polarization axis is at a 90° angle to the polarizer's axis, and the stressed areas in the plastic will appear as bright spots. The amount of birefringence is different for different wavelengths and hence different colors of light; the color that appears at each location in Fig. 33.31 is that for which the transmitted light is most nearly polarized along the analyzer's polarization axis.

Test Your Understanding of Section 33.5 You are taking a photograph of a sunlit high-rise office building. In order to minimize the reflections from the building's windows, you place a polarizing filter on the camera lens. How should you orient the filter? (i) with the polarizing axis vertical; (ii) with the polarizing axis horizontal; (iii) either orientation will minimize the reflections just as well; (iv) neither orientation will have any effect.

33.6 Scattering of Light

The sky is blue. Sunsets are red. Skylight is partially polarized; that's why the sky looks darker from some angles than from others when it is viewed through Polaroid sunglasses. As we will see, a single phenomenon is responsible for all of these effects.

When you look at the daytime sky, the light that you see is sunlight that has been absorbed and then re-radiated in a variety of directions. This process is called **scattering.** (If the earth had no atmosphere, the sky would appear as black in the daytime as it does at night, just as it does to an astronaut in space or on the moon.) Figure 33.32 shows some of the details of the scattering process. Sunlight, which is unpolarized, comes from the left along the x-axis and passes over an observer looking vertically upward along the y-axis. (We are viewing the situation

33.32 When the sunbathing observer on the left looks up, he sees blue, polarized sunlight that has been scattered by air molecules. The observer on the right sees reddened, unpolarized light when he looks at the sun.

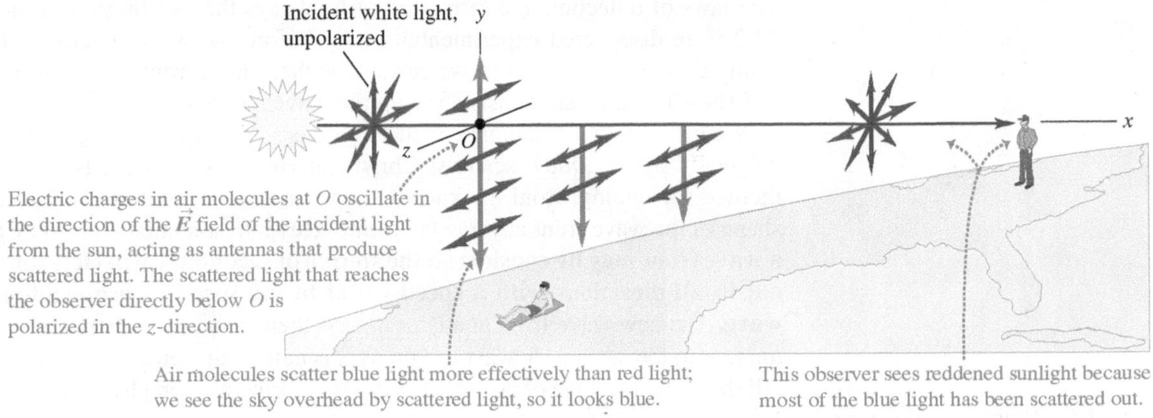

from the side.) Consider the molecules of the earth's atmosphere located at point O. The electric field in the beam of sunlight sets the electric charges in these molecules into vibration. Since light is a transverse wave, the direction of the electric field in any component of the sunlight lies in the yz-plane, and the motion of the charges takes place in this plane. There is no field, and hence no motion of charges, in the direction of the x-axis.

An incident light wave sets the electric charges in the molecules at point O vibrating along the line of $\vec{E}$. We can resolve this vibration into two components, one along the y-axis and the other along the z-axis. Each component in the incident light produces the equivalent of two molecular "antennas," oscillating with the same frequency as the incident light and lying along the y- and z-axes.

We mentioned in Chapter 32 that an oscillating charge, like those in an antenna, does not radiate in the direction of its oscillation. (See Fig. 32.3 in Section 32.1.) Thus the "antenna" along the y-axis does not send any light to the observer directly below it, although it does emit light in other directions. Therefore the only light reaching this observer comes from the other molecular "antenna," corresponding to the oscillation of charge along the z-axis. This light is linearly polarized, with its electric field along the z-axis (parallel to the "antenna"). The red vectors on the y-axis below point O in Fig. 33.32 show the direction of polarization of the light reaching the observer.

As the original beam of sunlight passes though the atmosphere, its intensity decreases as its energy goes into the scattered light. Detailed analysis of the scattering process shows that the intensity of the light scattered from air molecules increases in proportion to the fourth power of the frequency (inversely to the fourth power of the wavelength). Thus the intensity ratio for the two ends of the visible spectrum is $(750\text{ nm}/380\text{ nm})^4 = 15$. Roughly speaking, scattered light contains 15 times as much blue light as red, and that's why the sky is blue.

Clouds contain a high concentration of water droplets or ice crystals, which also scatter light. Because of this high concentration, light passing through the cloud has many more opportunities for scattering than does light passing through a clear sky. Thus light of *all* wavelengths is eventually scattered out of the cloud, so the cloud looks white (Fig. 33.33). Milk looks white for the same reason; the scattering is due to fat globules in the milk.

Near sunset, when sunlight has to travel a long distance through the earth's atmosphere, a substantial fraction of the blue light is removed by scattering. White light minus blue light looks yellow or red. This explains the yellow or red hue that we so often see from the setting sun (and that is seen by the observer at the far right of Fig. 33.32).

Application Bee Vision and Polarized Light from the Sky

The eyes of a bee can detect the polarization of light. Bees use this to help them navigate between the hive and food sources. As Fig. 33.32 shows, a bee sees unpolarized light if it looks directly toward the sun and sees completely polarized light if it looks 90° away from the sun. These polarizations are unaffected by the presence of clouds, so a bee can navigate relative to the sun even on an overcast day.

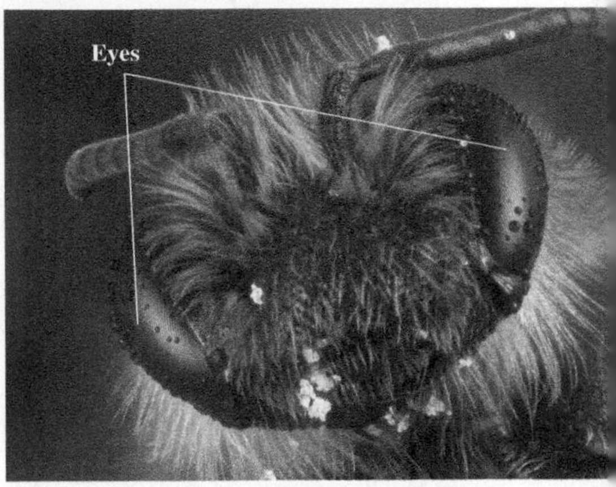

33.33 Clouds are white because they efficiently scatter sunlight of all wavelengths.

33.7 Huygens's Principle

The laws of reflection and refraction of light rays that we introduced in Section 33.2 were discovered experimentally long before the wave nature of light was firmly established. However, we can *derive* these laws from wave considerations and show that they are consistent with the wave nature of light.

We begin with a principle called **Huygens's principle.** This principle, stated originally by the Dutch scientist Christiaan Huygens in 1678, is a geometrical method for finding, from the known shape of a wave front at some instant, the shape of the wave front at some later time. Huygens assumed that **every point of a wave front may be considered the source of secondary wavelets that spread out in all directions with a speed equal to the speed of propagation of the wave.** The new wave front at a later time is then found by constructing a surface *tangent* to the secondary wavelets or, as it is called, the *envelope* of the wavelets. All the results that we obtain from Huygens's principle can also be obtained from Maxwell's equations. Thus it is not an independent principle, but it is often very convenient for calculations with wave phenomena.

33.34 Applying Huygens's principle to wave front AA' to construct a new wave front BB'.

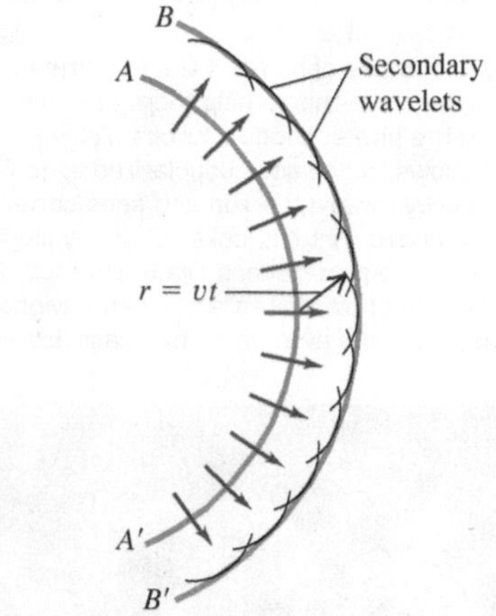

Huygens's principle is shown in Fig. 33.34. The original wave front AA' is traveling outward from a source, as indicated by the arrows. We want to find the shape of the wave front after a time interval t. We assume that v, the speed of propagation of the wave, is the same at all points. Then in time t the wave front travels a distance vt. We construct several circles (traces of spherical wavelets) with radius $r = vt$, centered at points along AA'. The trace of the envelope of these wavelets, which is the new wave front, is the curve BB'.

Reflection and Huygens's Principle

To derive the law of reflection from Huygens's principle, we consider a plane wave approaching a plane reflecting surface. In Fig. 33.35a the lines AA', OB', and NC' represent successive positions of a wave front approaching the surface MM'. Point A on the wave front AA' has just arrived at the reflecting surface. We can use Huygens's principle to find the position of the wave front after a time interval t. With points on AA' as centers, we draw several secondary wavelets with radius vt. The wavelets that originate near the upper end of AA' spread out unhindered, and their envelope gives the portion OB' of the new wave front. If the reflecting surface were not there, the wavelets originating near the lower end of AA' would similarly reach the positions shown by the broken circular arcs. Instead, these wavelets strike the reflecting surface.

33.35 Using Huygens's principle to derive the law of reflection.

(a) Successive positions of a plane wave AA' as it is reflected from a plane surface

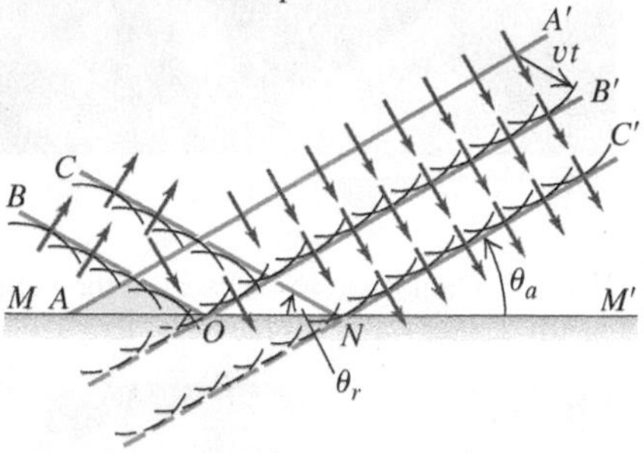

(b) Magnified portion of (a)

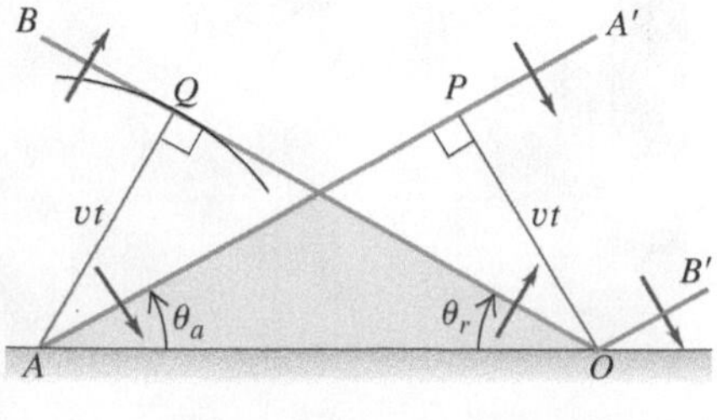

The effect of the reflecting surface is to *change the direction* of travel of those wavelets that strike it, so the part of a wavelet that would have penetrated the surface actually lies to the left of it, as shown by the full lines. The first such wavelet is centered at point A; the envelope of all such reflected wavelets is the portion OB of the wave front. The trace of the entire wave front at this instant is the bent line BOB'. A similar construction gives the line CNC' for the wave front after another interval t.

From plane geometry the angle θ_a between the incident *wave front* and the *surface* is the same as that between the incident *ray* and the *normal* to the surface and is therefore the angle of incidence. Similarly, θ_r is the angle of reflection. To find the relationship between these angles, we consider Fig. 33.35b. From O we draw $OP = vt$, perpendicular to AA'. Now OB, by construction, is tangent to a circle of radius vt with center at A. If we draw AQ from A to the point of tangency, the triangles APO and OQA are congruent because they are right triangles with the side AO in common and with $AQ = OP = vt$. The angle θ_a therefore equals the angle θ_r, and we have the law of reflection.

Refraction and Huygens's Principle

We can derive the law of *refraction* by a similar procedure. In Fig. 33.36a we consider a wave front, represented by line AA', for which point A has just arrived at the boundary surface SS' between two transparent materials a and b, with indexes of refraction n_a and n_b and wave speeds v_a and v_b. (The *reflected* waves are not shown in the figure; they proceed as in Fig. 33.35.) We can apply Huygens's principle to find the position of the refracted wave fronts after a time t.

With points on AA' as centers, we draw several secondary wavelets. Those originating near the upper end of AA' travel with speed v_a and, after a time interval t, are spherical surfaces of radius $v_a t$. The wavelet originating at point A, however, is traveling in the second material b with speed v_b and at time t is a spherical surface of radius $v_b t$. The envelope of the wavelets from the original wave front is the plane whose trace is the bent line BOB'. A similar construction leads to the trace CPC' after a second interval t.

The angles θ_a and θ_b between the surface and the incident and refracted wave fronts are the angle of incidence and the angle of refraction, respectively. To find the relationship between these angles, refer to Fig. 33.36b. We draw $OQ = v_a t$, perpendicular to AQ, and we draw $AB = v_b t$, perpendicular to BO. From the right triangle AOQ,

$$\sin\theta_a = \frac{v_a t}{AO}$$

and from the right triangle AOB,

$$\sin\theta_b = \frac{v_b t}{AO}$$

Combining these, we find

$$\frac{\sin\theta_a}{\sin\theta_b} = \frac{v_a}{v_b} \qquad (33.9)$$

We have defined the index of refraction n of a material as the ratio of the speed of light c in vacuum to its speed v in the material: $n_a = c/v_a$ and $n_b = c/v_b$. Thus

$$\frac{n_b}{n_a} = \frac{c/v_b}{c/v_a} = \frac{v_a}{v_b}$$

and we can rewrite Eq. (33.9) as

$$\frac{\sin\theta_a}{\sin\theta_b} = \frac{n_b}{n_a} \quad \text{or}$$

$$n_a \sin\theta_a = n_b \sin\theta_b$$

which we recognize as Snell's law, Eq. (33.4). So we have derived Snell's law from a wave theory. Alternatively, we may choose to regard Snell's law as an experimental result that defines the index of refraction of a material; in that case this analysis helps to confirm the relationship $v = c/n$ for the speed of light in a material.

Mirages offer an interesting example of Huygens's principle in action. When the surface of pavement or desert sand is heated intensely by the sun, a hot, less dense, smaller-n layer of air forms near the surface. The speed of light is slightly greater in the hotter air near the ground, the Huygens wavelets have slightly larger radii, the wave fronts tilt slightly, and rays that were headed toward the surface with a large angle of incidence (near 90°) can be bent up as shown in Fig. 33.37. Light farther from the ground is bent less and travels nearly in a straight line. The observer sees the object in its natural position, with an inverted image below it, as though seen in a horizontal reflecting surface. The mind of a thirsty traveler can interpret the apparent reflecting surface as a sheet of water.

33.36 Using Huygens's principle to derive the law of refraction. The case $v_b < v_a$ ($n_b > n_a$) is shown.

(a) Successive positions of a plane wave AA' as it is refracted by a plane surface

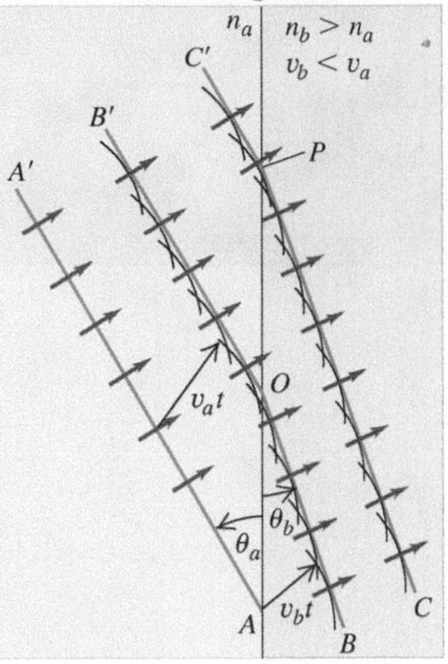

(b) Magnified portion of (a)

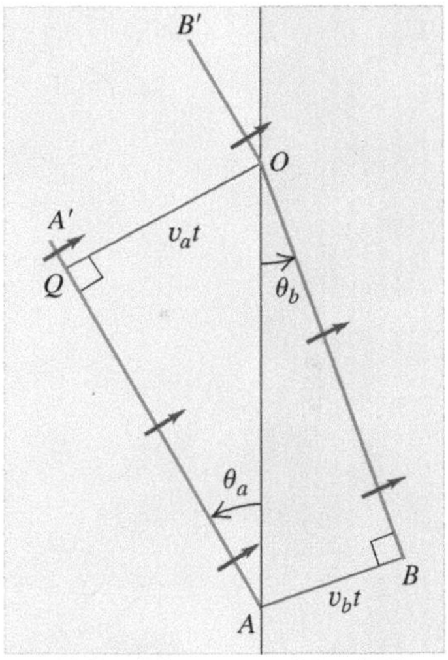

33.37 How mirages are formed.

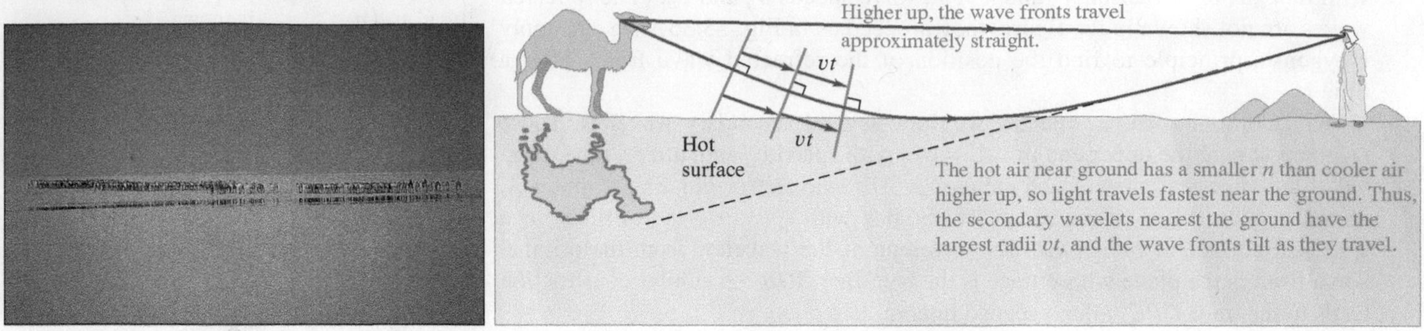

It is important to keep in mind that Maxwell's equations are the fundamental relationships for electromagnetic wave propagation. But Huygens's principle provides a convenient way to visualize this propagation.

Test Your Understanding of Section 33.7 Sound travels faster in warm air than in cold air. Imagine a weather front that runs north-south, with warm air to the west of the front and cold air to the east. A sound wave traveling in a northeast direction in the warm air encounters this front. How will the direction of this sound wave change when it passes into the cold air? (i) The wave direction will deflect toward the north; (ii) the wave direction will deflect toward the east; (iii) the wave direction will be unchanged. ❙

CHAPTER 33 SUMMARY

Light and its properties: Light is an electromagnetic wave. When emitted or absorbed, it also shows particle properties. It is emitted by accelerated electric charges.

A wave front is a surface of constant phase; wave fronts move with a speed equal to the propagation speed of the wave. A ray is a line along the direction of propagation, perpendicular to the wave fronts.

When light is transmitted from one material to another, the frequency of the light is unchanged, but the wavelength and wave speed can change. The index of refraction n of a material is the ratio of the speed of light in vacuum c to the speed v in the material. If λ_0 is the wavelength in vacuum, the same wave has a shorter wavelength λ in a medium with index of refraction n. (See Example 33.2.)

$$n = \frac{c}{v} \tag{33.1}$$

$$\lambda = \frac{\lambda_0}{n} \tag{33.5}$$

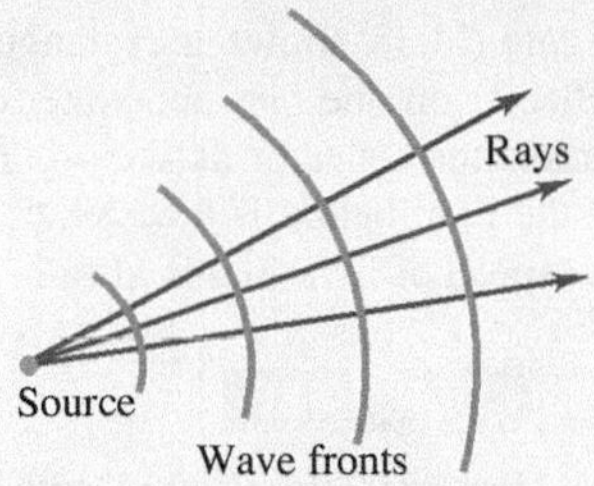

Reflection and refraction: At a smooth interface between two optical materials, the incident, reflected, and refracted rays and the normal to the interface all lie in a single plane called the plane of incidence. The law of reflection states that the angles of incidence and reflection are equal. The law of refraction relates the angles of incidence and refraction to the indexes of refraction of the materials. (See Examples 33.1 and 33.3.)

$$\theta_r = \theta_a \tag{33.2}$$
(law of reflection)

$$n_a \sin\theta_a = n_b \sin\theta_b \tag{33.4}$$
(law of refraction)

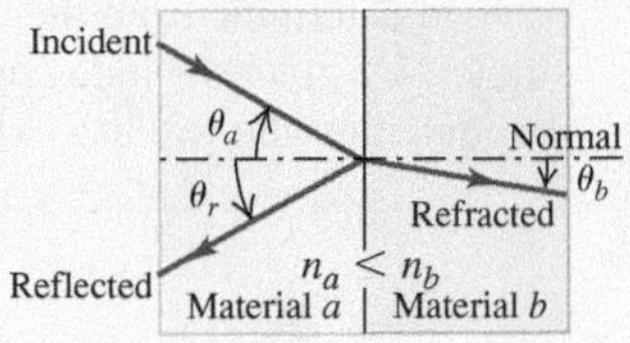

Total internal reflection: When a ray travels in a material of greater index of refraction n_a toward a material of smaller index n_b, total internal reflection occurs at the interface when the angle of incidence exceeds a critical angle θ_{crit}. (See Example 33.4.)

$$\sin\theta_{crit} = \frac{n_b}{n_a} \tag{33.6}$$

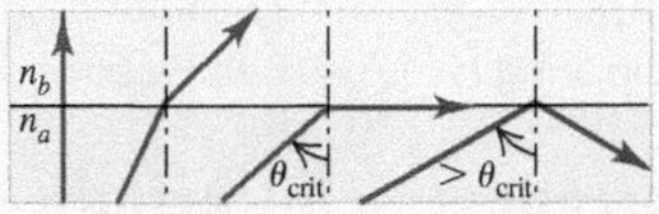

Polarization of light: The direction of polarization of a linearly polarized electromagnetic wave is the direction of the $\vec{E}$ field. A polarizing filter passes waves that are linearly polarized along its polarizing axis and blocks waves polarized perpendicularly to that axis. When polarized light of intensity I_{max} is incident on a polarizing filter used as an analyzer, the intensity I of the light transmitted through the analyzer depends on the angle ϕ between the polarization direction of the incident light and the polarizing axis of the analyzer. (See Example 33.5.)

$$I = I_{max}\cos^2\phi \tag{33.7}$$
(Malus's law)

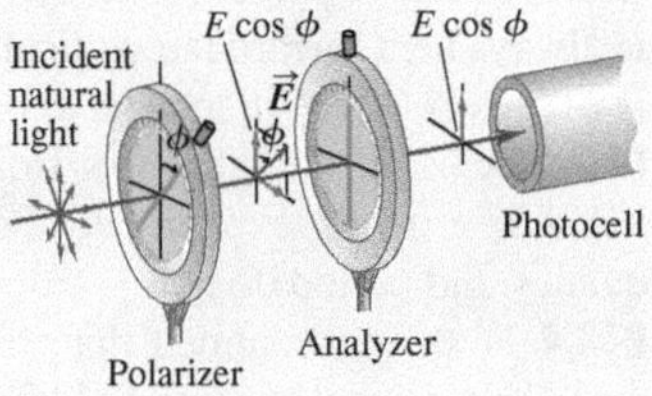

Polarization by reflection: When unpolarized light strikes an interface between two materials, Brewster's law states that the reflected light is completely polarized perpendicular to the plane of incidence (parallel to the interface) if the angle of incidence equals the polarizing angle θ_p. (See Example 33.6.)

$$\tan\theta_p = \frac{n_b}{n_a} \tag{33.8}$$
(Brewster's law)

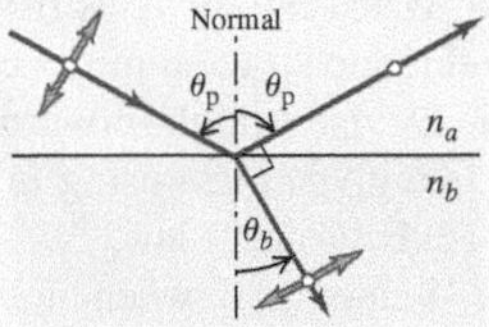

Huygens's principle: Huygens's principle states that if the position of a wave front at one instant is known, then the position of the front at a later time can be constructed by imagining the front as a source of secondary wavelets. Huygens's principle can be used to derive the laws of reflection and refraction.

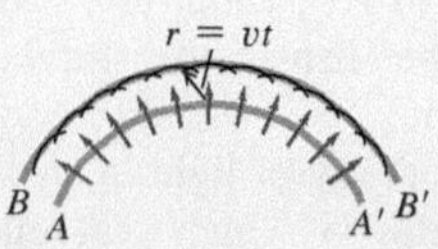

BRIDGING PROBLEM Reflection and Refraction

Figure 33.38 shows a rectangular glass block that has a metal reflector on one face and water on an adjoining face. A light beam strikes the reflector as shown. You gradually increase the angle θ of the light beam. If $\theta \geq 59.2°$, no light enters the water. What is the speed of light in this glass?

33.38

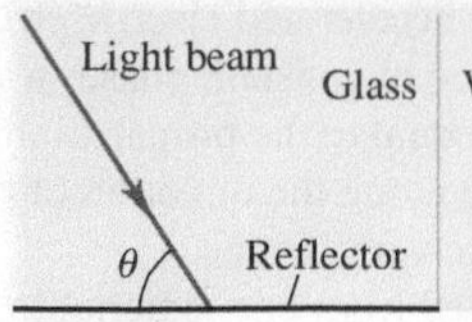

SOLUTION GUIDE

See MasteringPhysics® study area for a Video Tutor solution.

IDENTIFY and SET UP

1. Specular reflection occurs where the light ray in the glass strikes the reflector. If no light is to enter the water, we require that there be reflection only and no refraction where this ray strikes the glass–water interface—that is, there must be total internal reflection.
2. The target variable is the speed of light v in the glass, which you can determine from the index of refraction n of the glass. (Table 33.1 gives the index of refraction of water.) Write down the equations you will use to find n and v.

EXECUTE

3. Use the figure to find the angle of incidence of the ray at the glass–water interface.
4. Use the result of step 3 to find n.
5. Use the result of step 4 to find v.

EVALUATE

6. How does the speed of light in the glass compare to the speed in water? Does this make sense?

Problems

For instructor-assigned homework, go to www.masteringphysics.com

•, ••, •••: Problems of increasing difficulty. **CP**: Cumulative problems incorporating material from earlier chapters. **CALC**: Problems requiring calculus. **BIO**: Biosciences problems.

DISCUSSION QUESTIONS

Q33.1 Light requires about 8 minutes to travel from the sun to the earth. Is it delayed appreciably by the earth's atmosphere? Explain.

Q33.2 Sunlight or starlight passing through the earth's atmosphere is always bent toward the vertical. Why? Does this mean that a star is not really where it appears to be? Explain.

Q33.3 A beam of light goes from one material into another. On *physical* grounds, explain *why* the wavelength changes but the frequency and period do not.

Q33.4 A student claimed that, because of atmospheric refraction (see Discussion Question Q33.2), the sun can be seen after it has set and that the day is therefore longer than it would be if the earth had no atmosphere. First, what does she mean by saying that the sun can be seen after it has set? Second, comment on the validity of her conclusion.

Q33.5 When hot air rises from a radiator or heating duct, objects behind it appear to shimmer or waver. What causes this?

Q33.6 Devise straightforward experiments to measure the speed of light in a given glass using (a) Snell's law; (b) total internal reflection; (c) Brewster's law.

Q33.7 Sometimes when looking at a window, you see two reflected images slightly displaced from each other. What causes this?

Q33.8 If you look up from underneath toward the surface of the water in your aquarium, you may see an upside-down reflection of your pet fish in the surface of the water. Explain how this can happen.

Q33.9 A ray of light in air strikes a glass surface. Is there a range of angles for which total reflection occurs? Explain.

Q33.10 When light is incident on an interface between two materials, the angle of the refracted ray depends on the wavelength, but the angle of the reflected ray does not. Why should this be?

Q33.11 A salesperson at a bargain counter claims that a certain pair of sunglasses has Polaroid filters; you suspect that the glasses are just tinted plastic. How could you find out for sure?

Q33.12 Does it make sense to talk about the polarization of a *longitudinal* wave, such as a sound wave? Why or why not?

Q33.13 How can you determine the direction of the polarizing axis of a single polarizer?

Q33.14 It has been proposed that automobile windshields and headlights should have polarizing filters to reduce the glare of oncoming lights during night driving. Would this work? How should the polarizing axes be arranged? What advantages would this scheme have? What disadvantages?

Q33.15 When a sheet of plastic food wrap is placed between two crossed polarizers, no light is transmitted. When the sheet is stretched in one direction, some light passes through the crossed polarizers. What is happening?

Q33.16 If you sit on the beach and look at the ocean through Polaroid sunglasses, the glasses help to reduce the glare from sunlight reflecting off the water. But if you lie on your side on the beach, there is little reduction in the glare. Explain why there is a difference.

Q33.17 When unpolarized light is incident on two crossed polarizers, no light is transmitted. A student asserted that if a third polarizer is inserted between the other two, some transmission will occur. Does this make sense? How can adding a third filter *increase* transmission?

Q33.18 For the old "rabbit-ear" style TV antennas, it's possible to alter the quality of reception considerably simply by changing the orientation of the antenna. Why?

Q33.19 In Fig. 33.32, since the light that is scattered out of the incident beam is polarized, why is the transmitted beam not also partially polarized?

Q33.20 You are sunbathing in the late afternoon when the sun is relatively low in the western sky. You are lying flat on your back, looking straight up through Polaroid sunglasses. To minimize the amount of sky light reaching your eyes, how should you lie: with your feet pointing north, east, south, west, or in some other direction? Explain your reasoning.

Q33.21 Light scattered from blue sky is strongly polarized because of the nature of the scattering process described in Section 33.6. But light scattered from white clouds is usually *not* polarized. Why not?

Q33.22 Atmospheric haze is due to water droplets or smoke particles ("smog"). Such haze reduces visibility by scattering light, so that the light from distant objects becomes randomized and images become indistinct. Explain why visibility through haze can be improved by wearing red-tinted sunglasses, which filter out blue light.

Q33.23 The explanation given in Section 33.6 for the color of the setting sun should apply equally well to the *rising* sun, since sunlight travels the same distance through the atmosphere to reach your eyes at either sunrise or sunset. Typically, however, sunsets are redder than sunrises. Why? (*Hint:* Particles of all kinds in the atmosphere contribute to scattering.)

Q33.24 Huygens's principle also applies to sound waves. During the day, the temperature of the atmosphere decreases with increasing altitude above the ground. But at night, when the ground cools, there is a layer of air just above the surface in which the temperature *increases* with altitude. Use this to explain why sound waves from distant sources can be heard more clearly at night than in the daytime. (*Hint:* The speed of sound increases with increasing temperature. Use the ideas displayed in Fig. 33.37 for light.)

Q33.25 Can water waves be reflected and refracted? Give examples. Does Huygens's principle apply to water waves? Explain.

EXERCISES

Section 33.2 Reflection and Refraction

33.1 • Two plane mirrors intersect at right angles. A laser beam strikes the first of them at a point 11.5 cm from their point of intersection, as shown in Fig. E33.1 For what angle of incidence at the first mirror will this ray strike the midpoint of the second mirror (which is 28.0 cm long) after reflecting from the first mirror?

Figure **E33.1**

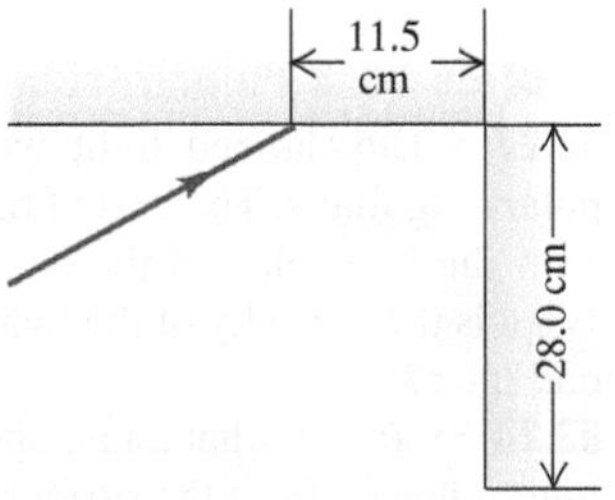

33.2 • BIO **Light Inside the Eye.** The vitreous humor, a transparent, gelatinous fluid that fills most of the eyeball, has an index of refraction of 1.34. Visible light ranges in wavelength from 380 nm (violet) to 750 nm (red), as measured in air. This light travels through the vitreous humor and strikes the rods and cones at the surface of the retina. What are the ranges of (a) the wavelength, (b) the frequency, and (c) the speed of the light just as it approaches the retina within the vitreous humor?

33.3 • A beam of light has a wavelength of 650 nm in vacuum. (a) What is the speed of this light in a liquid whose index of refraction at this wavelength is 1.47? (b) What is the wavelength of these waves in the liquid?

33.4 • Light with a frequency of 5.80×10^{14} Hz travels in a block of glass that has an index of refraction of 1.52. What is the wavelength of the light (a) in vacuum and (b) in the glass?

33.5 • A light beam travels at 1.94×10^8 m/s in quartz. The wavelength of the light in quartz is 355 nm. (a) What is the index of refraction of quartz at this wavelength? (b) If this same light travels through air, what is its wavelength there?

33.6 •• Light of a certain frequency has a wavelength of 438 nm in water. What is the wavelength of this light in benzene?

33.7 •• A parallel beam of light in air makes an angle of 47.5° with the surface of a glass plate having a refractive index of 1.66. (a) What is the angle between the reflected part of the beam and the surface of the glass? (b) What is the angle between the refracted beam and the surface of the glass?

33.8 •• A laser beam shines along the surface of a block of transparent material (see Fig. E33.8.). Half of the beam goes straight to a detector, while the other half travels through the block and then hits the detector. The time delay between the arrival of the two light beams at the detector is 6.25 ns. What is the index of refraction of this material?

Figure **E33.8**

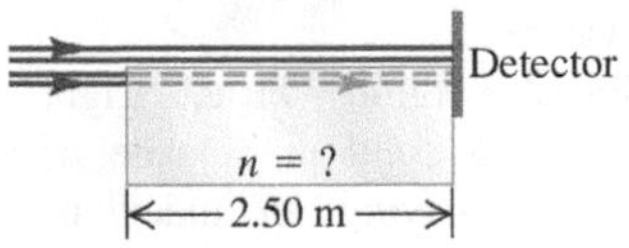

33.9 • Light traveling in air is incident on the surface of a block of plastic at an angle of 62.7° to the normal and is bent so that it makes a 48.1° angle with the normal in the plastic. Find the speed of light in the plastic.

33.10 • (a) A tank containing methanol has walls 2.50 cm thick made of glass of refractive index 1.550. Light from the outside air strikes the glass at a 41.3° angle with the normal to the glass. Find the angle the light makes with the normal in the methanol. (b) The tank is emptied and refilled with an unknown liquid. If light incident at the same angle as in part (a) enters the liquid in the tank at an angle of 20.2° from the normal, what is the refractive index of the unknown liquid?

33.11 •• As shown in Fig. E33.11, a layer of water covers a slab of material X in a beaker. A ray of light traveling upward follows the path indicated. Using the information on the figure, find (a) the index of refraction of material X and (b) the angle the light makes with the normal in the *air*.

Figure **E33.11**

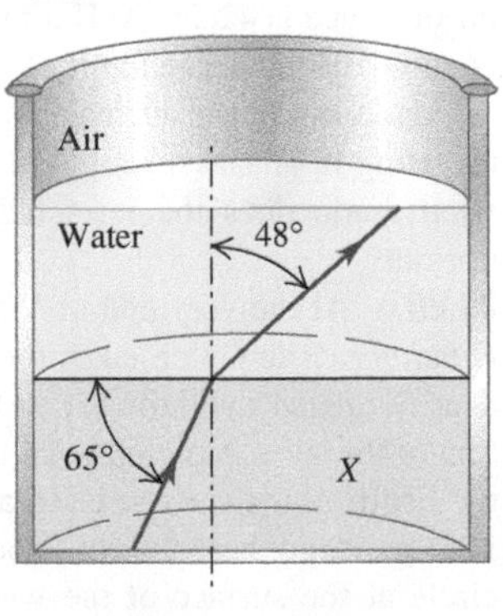

33.12 •• A horizontal, parallel-sided plate of glass having a refractive index of 1.52 is in contact with the surface of water in a tank. A ray coming from above in air makes an angle of incidence of 35.0° with the normal to the top surface of the glass. (a) What angle does the ray refracted into the water make with the normal to the surface? (b) What is the dependence of this angle on the refractive index of the glass?

33.13 •• In a material having an index of refraction n, a light ray has frequency f, wavelength λ, and speed v. What are the frequency, wavelength, and speed of this light (a) in vacuum and

(b) in a material having refractive index n'? In each case, express your answers in terms of *only* f, λ, v, n, and n'.

33.14 • A ray of light traveling in water is incident on an interface with a flat piece of glass. The wavelength of the light in the water is 726 nm and its wavelength in the glass is 544 nm. If the ray in water makes an angle of 42.0° with respect to the normal to the interface, what angle does the refracted ray in the glass make with respect to the normal?

33.15 • A ray of light is incident on a plane surface separating two sheets of glass with refractive indexes 1.70 and 1.58. The angle of incidence is 62.0°, and the ray originates in the glass with $n = 1.70$. Compute the angle of refraction.

Section 33.3 Total Internal Reflection

33.16 • A flat piece of glass covers the top of a vertical cylinder that is completely filled with water. If a ray of light traveling in the glass is incident on the interface with the water at an angle of $\theta_a = 36.2°$, the ray refracted into the water makes an angle of 49.8° with the normal to the interface. What is the smallest value of the incident angle θ_a for which none of the ray refracts into the water?

33.17 • **Light Pipe.** Light enters a solid pipe made of plastic having an index of refraction of 1.60. The light travels parallel to the upper part of the pipe (Fig. E33.17). You want to cut the face AB so that all the light will reflect back into the pipe after it first strikes that face. (a) What is the largest that θ can be if the pipe is in air? (b) If the pipe is immersed in water of refractive index 1.33, what is the largest that θ can be?

Figure **E33.17**

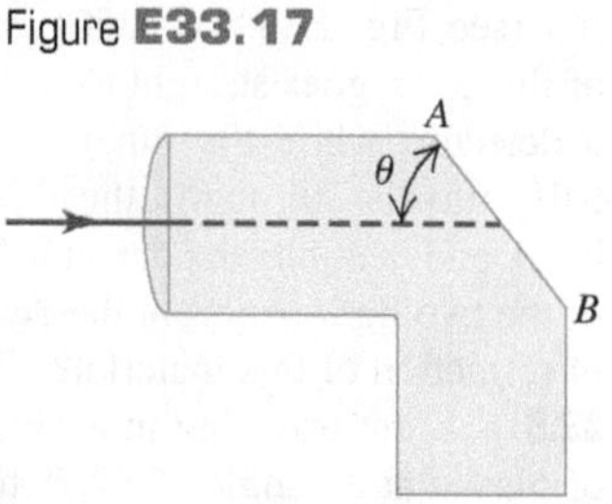

33.18 • A beam of light is traveling inside a solid glass cube having index of refraction 1.53. It strikes the surface of the cube from the inside. (a) If the cube is in air, at what minimum angle with the normal inside the glass will this light *not* enter the air at this surface? (b) What would be the minimum angle in part (a) if the cube were immersed in water?

33.19 •• The critical angle for total internal reflection at a liquid–air interface is 42.5°. (a) If a ray of light traveling in the liquid has an angle of incidence at the interface of 35.0°, what angle does the refracted ray in the air make with the normal? (b) If a ray of light traveling in air has an angle of incidence at the interface of 35.0°, what angle does the refracted ray in the liquid make with the normal?

33.20 • At the very end of Wagner's series of operas *Ring of the Nibelung,* Brünnhilde takes the golden ring from the finger of the dead Siegfried and throws it into the Rhine, where it sinks to the bottom of the river. Assuming that the ring is small enough compared to the depth of the river to be treated as a point and that the Rhine is 10.0 m deep where the ring goes in, what is the area of the largest circle at the surface of the water over which light from the ring could escape from the water?

33.21 • A ray of light is traveling in a glass cube that is totally immersed in water. You find that if the ray is incident on the glass–water interface at an angle to the normal larger than 48.7°, no light is refracted into the water. What is the refractive index of the glass?

33.22 • Light is incident along the normal on face AB of a glass prism of refractive index 1.52, as shown in Fig. E33.22. Find the largest value the angle α can have without any light refracted out of the prism at face AC if (a) the prism is immersed in air and (b) the prism is immersed in water.

Figure **E33.22**

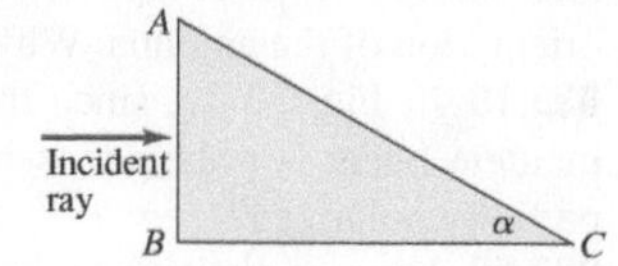

33.23 • A piece of glass with a flat surface is at the bottom of a tank of water. If a ray of light traveling in the glass is incident on the interface with the water at an angle with respect to the normal that is greater than 62.0°, no light is refracted into the water. For smaller angles of incidence, part of the ray is refracted into the water. If the light has wavelength 408 nm in the glass, what is the wavelength of the light in the water?

33.24 •• We define the index of refraction of a material for sound waves to be the ratio of the speed of sound in air to the speed of sound in the material. Snell's law then applies to the refraction of sound waves. The speed of a sound wave is 344 m/s in air and 1320 m/s in water. (a) Which medium has the higher index of refraction for sound? (b) What is the critical angle for a sound wave incident on the surface between air and water? (c) For total internal reflection to occur, must the sound wave be traveling in the air or in the water? (d) Use your results to explain why it is possible to hear people on the opposite shore of a river or small lake extremely clearly.

Section 33.4 Dispersion

33.25 •• A narrow beam of white light strikes one face of a slab of silicate flint glass. The light is traveling parallel to the two adjoining faces, as shown in Fig. E33.25. For the transmitted light inside the glass, through what angle $\Delta\theta$ is the portion of the visible spectrum between 400 nm and 700 nm dispersed? (Consult the graph in Fig. 33.18.)

Figure **E33.25**

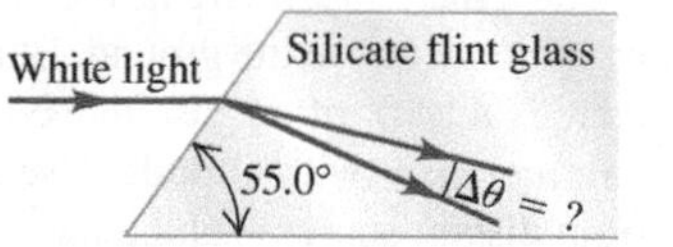

33.26 • A beam of light strikes a sheet of glass at an angle of 57.0° with the normal in air. You observe that red light makes an angle of 38.1° with the normal in the glass, while violet light makes a 36.7° angle. (a) What are the indexes of refraction of this glass for these colors of light? (b) What are the speeds of red and violet light in the glass?

Section 33.5 Polarization

33.27 • Unpolarized light with intensity I_0 is incident on two polarizing filters. The axis of the first filter makes an angle of 60.0° with the vertical, and the axis of the second filter is horizontal. What is the intensity of the light after it has passed through the second filter?

33.28 •• (a) At what angle above the horizontal is the sun if sunlight reflected from the surface of a calm lake is completely polarized? (b) What is the plane of the electric-field vector in the reflected light?

33.29 •• A beam of unpolarized light of intensity I_0 passes through a series of ideal polarizing filters with their polarizing directions turned to various angles as shown in Fig. E33.29. (a) What is the light intensity (in terms of I_0) at points A, B, and C? (b) If we remove the middle filter, what will be the light intensity at point C?

Figure **E33.29**

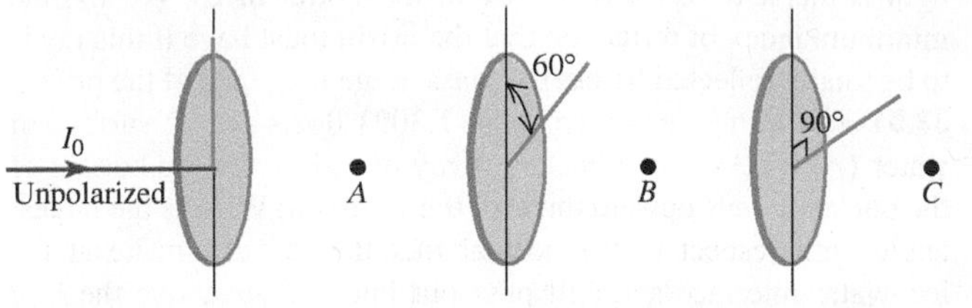

33.30 • Light traveling in water strikes a glass plate at an angle of incidence of 53.0°; part of the beam is reflected and part is refracted. If the reflected and refracted portions make an angle of 90.0° with each other, what is the index of refraction of the glass?

33.31 • A parallel beam of unpolarized light in air is incident at an angle of 54.5° (with respect to the normal) on a plane glass surface. The reflected beam is completely linearly polarized. (a) What is the refractive index of the glass? (b) What is the angle of refraction of the transmitted beam?

33.32 •• Light of original intensity I_0 passes through two ideal polarizing filters having their polarizing axes oriented as shown in Fig. E33.32. You want to adjust the angle ϕ so that the intensity at point P is equal to $I_0/10$. (a) If the original light is unpolarized, what should ϕ be? (b) If the original light is linearly polarized in the same direction as the polarizing axis of the first polarizer the light reaches, what should ϕ be?

Figure **E33.32**

33.33 •• A beam of polarized light passes through a polarizing filter. When the angle between the polarizing axis of the filter and the direction of polarization of the light is θ, the intensity of the emerging beam is I. If you now want the intensity to be $I/2$, what should be the angle (in terms of θ) between the polarizing angle of the filter and the original direction of polarization of the light?

33.34 • The refractive index of a certain glass is 1.66. For what incident angle is light reflected from the surface of this glass completely polarized if the glass is immersed in (a) air and (b) water?

33.35 •• Unpolarized light of intensity 20.0 W/cm^2 is incident on two polarizing filters. The axis of the first filter is at an angle of 25.0° counterclockwise from the vertical (viewed in the direction the light is traveling), and the axis of the second filter is at 62.0° counterclockwise from the vertical. What is the intensity of the light after it has passed through the second polarizer?

33.36 ••• Three polarizing filters are stacked, with the polarizing axis of the second and third filters at 23.0° and 62.0°, respectively, to that of the first. If unpolarized light is incident on the stack, the light has intensity 75.0 W/cm^2 after it passes through the stack. If the incident intensity is kept constant, what is the intensity of the light after it has passed through the stack if the second polarizer is removed?

33.37 • **Three Polarizing Filters.** Three polarizing filters are stacked with the polarizing axes of the second and third at 45.0° and 90.0°, respectively, with that of the first. (a) If unpolarized light of intensity I_0 is incident on the stack, find the intensity and state of polarization of light emerging from each filter. (b) If the second filter is removed, what is the intensity of the light emerging from each remaining filter?

Section 33.6 Scattering of Light

33.38 • A beam of white light passes through a uniform thickness of air. If the intensity of the scattered light in the middle of the green part of the visible spectrum is I, find the intensity (in terms of I) of scattered light in the middle of (a) the red part of the spectrum and (b) the violet part of the spectrum. Consult Table 32.1.

PROBLEMS

33.39 •• **The Corner Reflector.** An inside corner of a cube is lined with mirrors to make a corner reflector (see Example 33.3 in Section 33.2). A ray of light is reflected successively from each of three mutually perpendicular mirrors; show that its final direction is always exactly opposite to its initial direction.

33.40 • A light beam is directed parallel to the axis of a hollow cylindrical tube. When the tube contains only air, it takes the light 8.72 ns to travel the length of the tube, but when the tube is filled with a transparent jelly, it takes the light 2.04 ns longer to travel its length. What is the refractive index of this jelly?

33.41 •• BIO **Heart Sonogram.** Physicians use high-frequency ($f = 1-5$ MHz) sound waves, called ultrasound, to image internal organs. The speed of these ultrasound waves is 1480 m/s in muscle and 344 m/s in air. We define the index of refraction of a material for sound waves to be the ratio of the speed of sound in air to the speed of sound in the material. Snell's law then applies to the refraction of sound waves. (a) At what angle from the normal does an ultrasound beam enter the heart if it leaves the lungs at an angle of 9.73° from the normal to the heart wall? (Assume that the speed of sound in the lungs is 344 m/s.) (b) What is the critical angle for sound waves in air incident on muscle?

33.42 ••• In a physics lab, light with wavelength 490 nm travels in air from a laser to a photocell in 17.0 ns. When a slab of glass 0.840 m thick is placed in the light beam, with the beam incident along the normal to the parallel faces of the slab, it takes the light 21.2 ns to travel from the laser to the photocell. What is the wavelength of the light in the glass?

33.43 •• A ray of light is incident in air on a block of a transparent solid whose index of refraction is n. If $n = 1.38$, what is the *largest* angle of incidence θ_a for which total internal reflection will occur at the vertical face (point A shown in Fig. P33.43)?

Figure **P33.43**

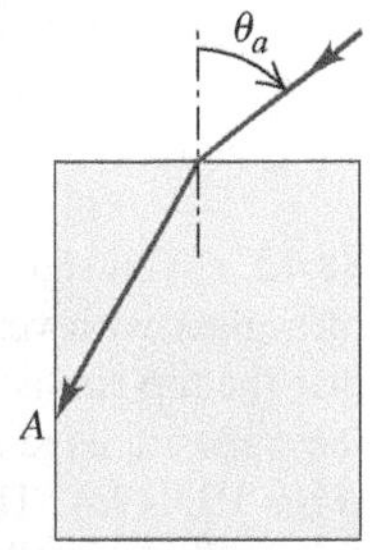

33.44 • A light ray in air strikes the right-angle prism shown in Fig. P33.44. The prism angle at B is 30.0°. This ray consists of two different wavelengths. When it emerges at face AB, it has been split into two different rays that diverge from each other by 8.50°. Find the index of refraction of the prism for each of the two wavelengths.

Figure **P33.44**

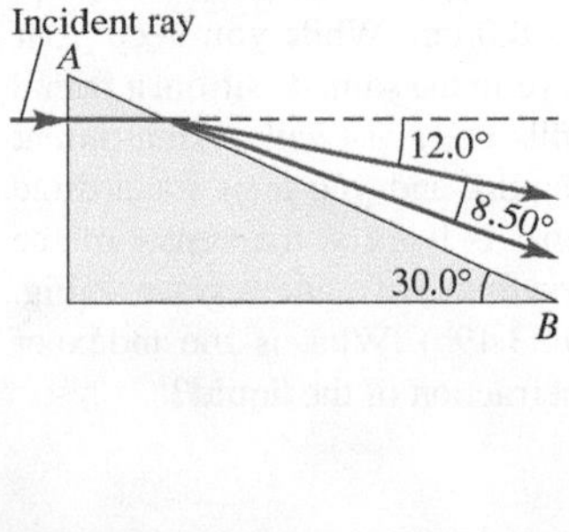

33.45 •• A ray of light traveling *in* a block of glass ($n = 1.52$) is incident on the top surface at an angle of 57.2° with respect to the normal in the glass. If a layer of oil is placed on the top surface of the glass, the ray is totally reflected. What is the maximum possible index of refraction of the oil?

33.46 ••• A glass plate 2.50 mm thick, with an index of refraction of 1.40, is placed between a point source of light with wavelength 540 nm (in vacuum) and a screen. The distance from source to screen is 1.80 cm. How many wavelengths are there between the source and the screen?

33.47 •• Old photographic plates were made of glass with a light-sensitive emulsion on the front surface. This emulsion was somewhat transparent. When a bright point source is focused on the front of the plate, the developed photograph will show a halo around the image of the spot. If the glass plate is 3.10 mm thick and the halos have an inner radius of 5.34 mm, what is the index of refraction of the glass? (*Hint:* Light from the spot on the front surface is scattered in all directions by the emulsion. Some of it is then totally reflected at the back surface of the plate and returns to the front surface.)

33.48 • After a long day of driving you take a late-night swim in a motel swimming pool. When you go to your room, you realize that you have lost your room key in the pool. You borrow a powerful flashlight and walk around the pool, shining the light into it. The light shines on the key, which is lying on the bottom of the pool, when the flashlight is held 1.2 m above the water surface and is directed at the surface a horizontal distance of 1.5 m from the edge (Fig. P33.48). If the water here is 4.0 m deep, how far is the key from the edge of the pool?

Figure **P33.48**

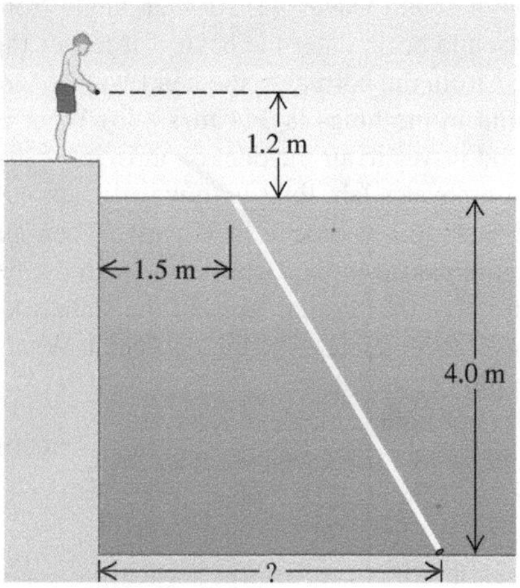

33.49 • You sight along the rim of a glass with vertical sides so that the top rim is lined up with the opposite edge of the bottom (Fig. P33.49a). The glass is a thin-walled, hollow cylinder 16.0 cm high. The diameter of the top and bottom of the glass is 8.0 cm. While you keep your eye in the same position, a friend fills the glass with a transparent liquid, and you then see a dime that is lying at the center of the bottom of the glass (Fig. P33.49b). What is the index of refraction of the liquid?

Figure **P33.49**

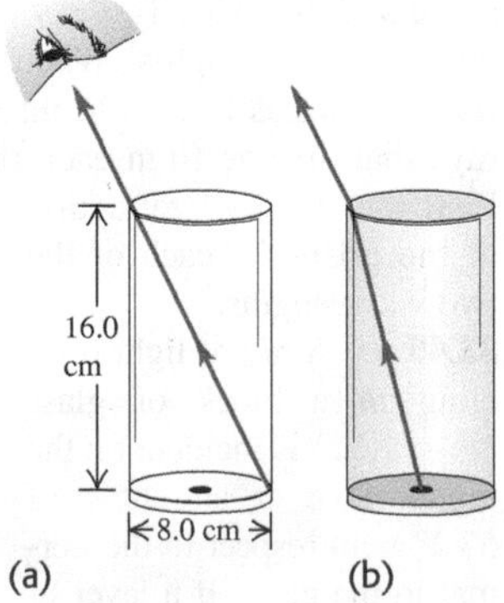

33.50 •• A 45°–45°–90° prism is immersed in water. A ray of light is incident normally on one of its shorter faces. What is the minimum index of refraction that the prism must have if this ray is to be totally reflected within the glass at the long face of the prism?

33.51 • A thin layer of ice ($n = 1.309$) floats on the surface of water ($n = 1.333$) in a bucket. A ray of light from the bottom of the bucket travels upward through the water. (a) What is the largest angle with respect to the normal that the ray can make at the ice–water interface and still pass out into the air above the ice? (b) What is this angle after the ice melts?

33.52 •• Light is incident normally on the short face of a 30°–60°–90° prism (Fig. P33.52). A drop of liquid is placed on the hypotenuse of the prism. If the index of refraction of the prism is 1.62, find the maximum index that the liquid may have if the light is to be totally reflected.

Figure **P33.52**

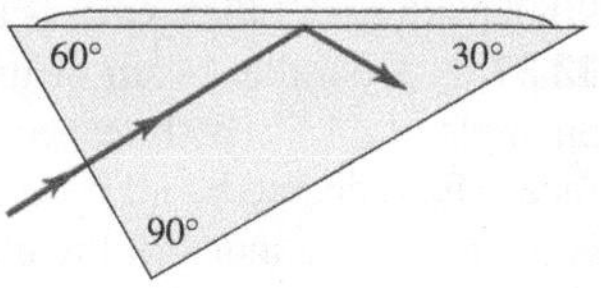

33.53 •• The prism shown in Fig. P33.53 has a refractive index of 1.66, and the angles A are 25.0°. Two light rays m and n are parallel as they enter the prism. What is the angle between them after they emerge?

Figure **P33.53**

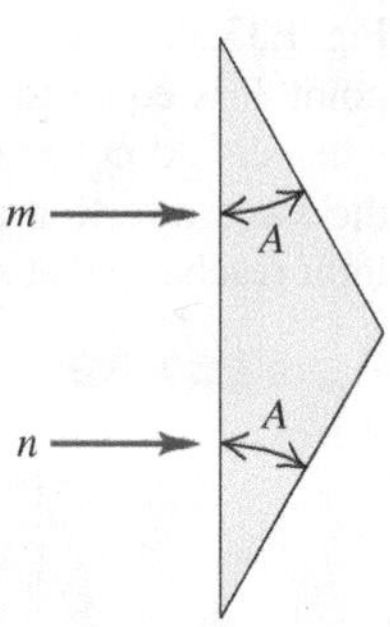

33.54 •• A horizontal cylindrical tank 2.20 m in diameter is half full of water. The space above the water is filled with a pressurized gas of unknown refractive index. A small laser can move along the curved bottom of the water and aims a light beam toward the center of the water surface (Fig. P33.54). You observe that when the laser has moved a distance $S = 1.09$ m or more (measured along the curved surface) from the lowest point in the water, no light enters the gas. (a) What is the index of refraction of the gas? (b) What minimum time does it take the light beam to travel from the laser to the rim of the tank when (i) $S > 1.09$ m and (ii) $S < 1.09$ m?

Figure **P33.54**

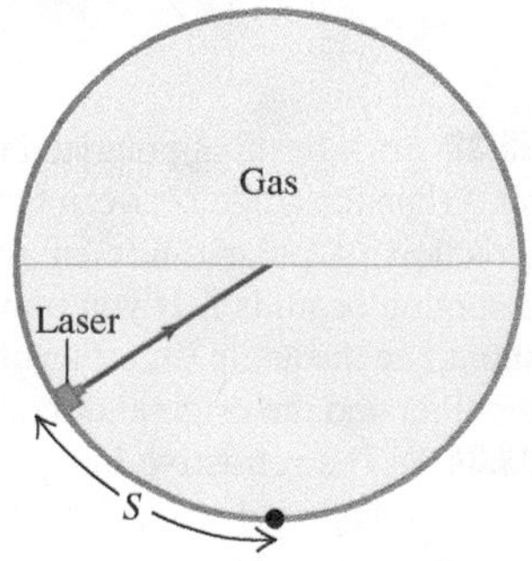

33.55 •• When the sun is either rising or setting and appears to be just on the horizon, it is in fact *below* the horizon. The explanation for this seeming paradox is that light from the sun bends slightly when entering the earth's atmosphere, as shown in Fig. P33.55. Since our perception is based on the idea that light travels in straight lines, we perceive the light to be coming from an apparent position that is an angle δ above the sun's true position. (a) Make the simplifying assumptions that the atmosphere has uniform density, and hence uniform index of refraction n, and extends to a height h above the earth's surface, at which point it abruptly stops. Show that the angle δ is given by

$$\delta = \arcsin\left(\frac{nR}{R+h}\right) - \arcsin\left(\frac{R}{R+h}\right)$$

where $R = 6378$ km is the radius of the earth. (b) Calculate δ using $n = 1.0003$ and $h = 20$ km. How does this compare to the angular radius of the sun, which is about one quarter of a degree?

(In actuality a light ray from the sun bends gradually, not abruptly, since the density and refractive index of the atmosphere change gradually with altitude.)

Figure **P33.55**

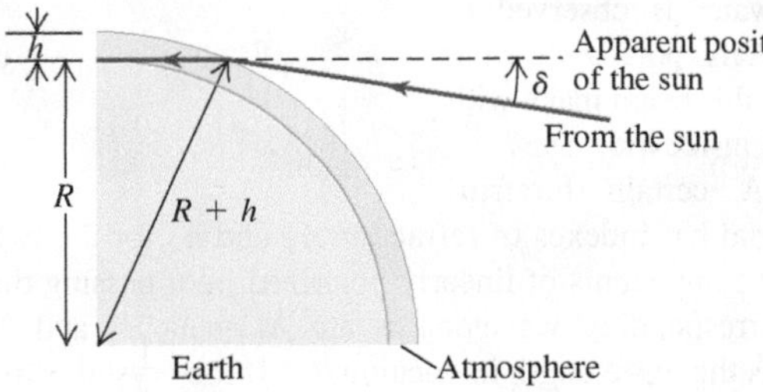

33.56 •• **CALC** **Fermat's Principle of Least Time.** A ray of light traveling with speed c leaves point 1 shown in Fig. P33.56 and is reflected to point 2. The ray strikes the reflecting surface a horizontal distance x from point 1. (a) Show that the time t required for the light to travel from 1 to 2 is

$$t = \frac{\sqrt{y_1^2 + x^2} + \sqrt{y_2^2 + (l - x)^2}}{c}$$

(b) Take the derivative of t with respect to x. Set the derivative equal to zero to show that this time reaches its *minimum* value when $\theta_1 = \theta_2$, which is the law of reflection and corresponds to the actual path taken by the light. This is an example of Fermat's *principle of least time,* which states that among all possible paths between two points, the one actually taken by a ray of light is that for which the time of travel is a *minimum.* (In fact, there are some cases in which the time is a maximum rather than a minimum.)

Figure **P33.56**

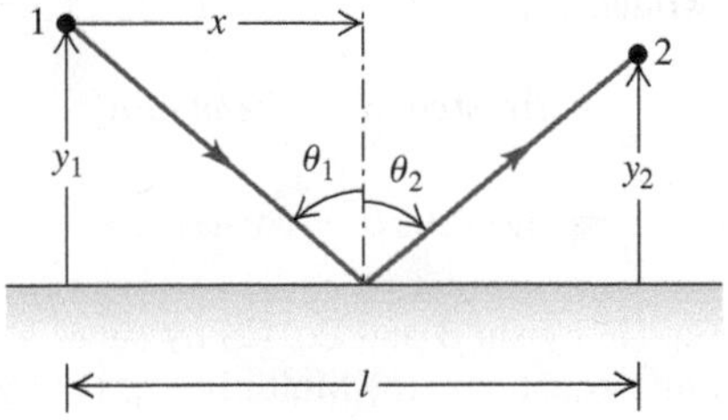

33.57 •• **CALC** A ray of light goes from point A in a medium in which the speed of light is v_1 to point B in a medium in which the speed is v_2 (Fig. P33.57). The ray strikes the interface a horizontal distance x to the right of point A. (a) Show that the time required for the light to go from A to B is

Figure **P33.57**

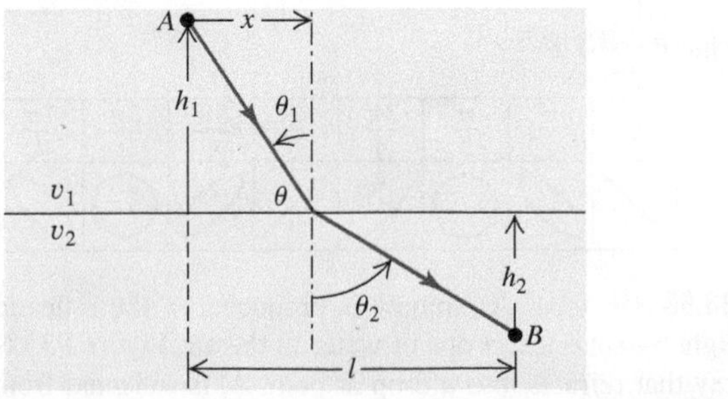

$$t = \frac{\sqrt{h_1^2 + x^2}}{v_1} + \frac{\sqrt{h_2^2 + (l - x)^2}}{v_2}$$

(b) Take the derivative of t with respect to x. Set this derivative equal to zero to show that this time reaches its *minimum* value when $n_1 \sin\theta_1 = n_2 \sin\theta_2$. This is Snell's law and corresponds to the actual path taken by the light. This is another example of Fermat's principle of least time (see Problem 33.56).

33.58 •• Light is incident in air at an angle θ_a (Fig. P33.58) on the upper surface of a transparent plate, the surfaces of the plate being plane and parallel to each other. (a) Prove that $\theta_a = \theta_a'$. (b) Show that this is true for any number of different parallel plates. (c) Prove that the lateral displacement d of the emergent beam is given by the relationship

$$d = t\frac{\sin(\theta_a - \theta_b')}{\cos\theta_b'}$$

where t is the thickness of the plate. (d) A ray of light is incident at an angle of 66.0° on one surface of a glass plate 2.40 cm thick with an index of refraction of 1.80. The medium on either side of the plate is air. Find the lateral displacement between the incident and emergent rays.

Figure **P33.58**

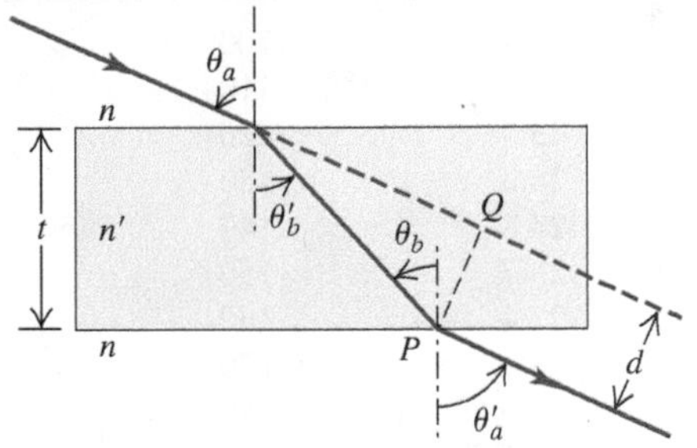

33.59 •• **Angle of Deviation.** The incident angle θ_a shown in Fig. P33.59 is chosen so that the light passes symmetrically through the prism, which has refractive index n and apex angle A. (a) Show that the angle of deviation δ (the angle between the initial and final directions of the ray) is given by

$$\sin\frac{A + \delta}{2} = n\sin\frac{A}{2}$$

(When the light passes through symmetrically, as shown, the angle of deviation is a minimum.) (b) Use the result of part (a) to find the angle of deviation for a ray of light passing symmetrically through a prism having three equal angles ($A = 60.0°$) and $n = 1.52$. (c) A certain glass has a refractive index of 1.61 for red light (700 nm) and 1.66 for violet light (400 nm). If both colors pass through symmetrically, as described in part (a), and if $A = 60.0°$, find the difference between the angles of deviation for the two colors.

Figure **P33.59**

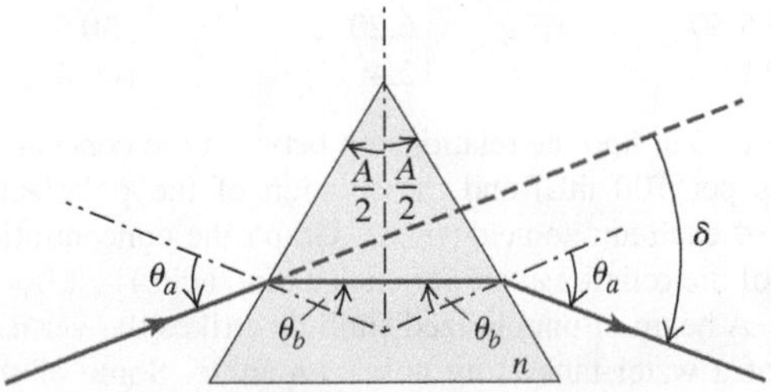

33.60 • A thin beam of white light is directed at a flat sheet of silicate flint glass at an angle of 20.0° to the surface of the sheet. Due to dispersion in the glass, the beam is spread out in a spectrum as shown in Fig. P33.60. The refractive index of silicate flint glass versus wavelength is graphed in Fig. 33.18. (a) The rays a and b shown in Fig. P33.60 correspond to the extreme wavelengths shown in Fig. 33.18. Which corresponds to red and which to violet? Explain your reasoning. (b) For what thickness d of the glass sheet will the spectrum be 1.0 mm wide, as shown (see Problem 33.58)?

Figure **P33.60**

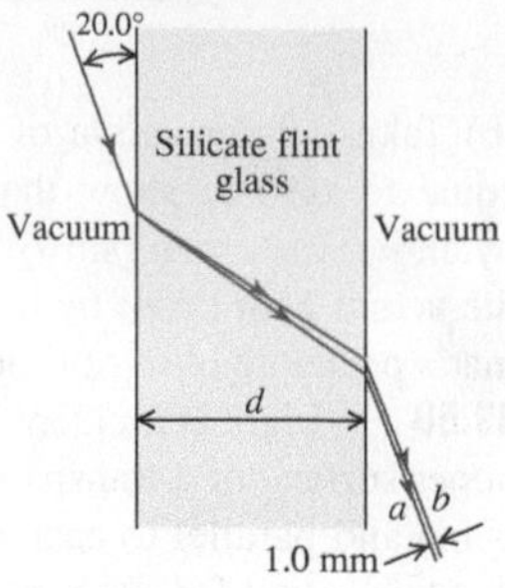

33.61 • A beam of light traveling horizontally is made of an unpolarized component with intensity I_0 and a polarized component with intensity I_p. The plane of polarization of the polarized component is oriented at an angle of θ with respect to the vertical. The data in the table give the intensity measured through a polarizer with an orientation of ϕ with respect to the vertical. (a) What is the orientation of the polarized component? (That is, what is the angle θ?) (b) What are the values of I_0 and I_p?

ϕ(°)	I_{total} (W/m²)	ϕ(°)	I_{total} (W/m²)
0	18.4	100	8.6
10	21.4	110	6.3
20	23.7	120	5.2
30	24.8	130	5.2
40	24.8	140	6.3
50	23.7	150	8.6
60	21.4	160	11.6
70	18.4	170	15.0
80	15.0	180	18.4
90	11.6		

33.62 •• BIO **Optical Activity of Biological Molecules.** Many biologically important molecules are optically active. When linearly polarized light traverses a solution of compounds containing these molecules, its plane of polarization is rotated. Some compounds rotate the polarization clockwise; others rotate the polarization counterclockwise. The amount of rotation depends on the amount of material in the path of the light. The following data give the amount of rotation through two amino acids over a path length of 100 cm:

Rotation (°)		
l-leucine	*d*-glutamic acid	Concentration (g/100 mL)
−0.11	0.124	1.0
−0.22	0.248	2.0
−0.55	0.620	5.0
−1.10	1.24	10.0
−2.20	2.48	20.0
−5.50	6.20	50.0
−11.0	12.4	100.0

From these data, find the relationship between the concentration C (in grams per 100 mL) and the rotation of the polarization (in degrees) of each amino acid. (*Hint:* Graph the concentration as a function of the rotation angle for each amino acid.)

33.63 •• A beam of unpolarized sunlight strikes the vertical plastic wall of a water tank at an unknown angle. Some of the light reflects from the wall and enters the water (Fig. P33.63). The refractive index of the plastic wall is 1.61. If the light that has been reflected from the wall into the water is observed to be completely polarized, what angle does this beam make with the normal inside the water?

Figure **P33.63**

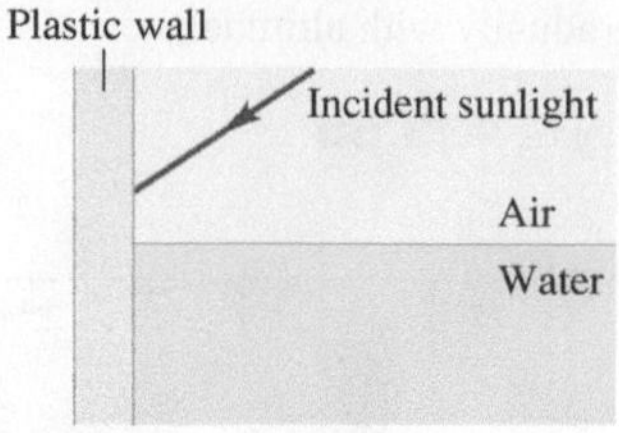

33.64 •• A certain birefringent material has indexes of refraction n_1 and n_2 for the two perpendicular components of linearly polarized light passing through it. The corresponding wavelengths are $\lambda_1 = \lambda_0/n_1$ and λ_0/n_2, where λ_0 is the wavelength in vacuum. (a) If the crystal is to function as a quarter-wave plate, the number of wavelengths of each component within the material must differ by $\frac{1}{4}$. Show that the minimum thickness for a quarter-wave plate is

$$d = \frac{\lambda_0}{4(n_1 - n_2)}$$

(b) Find the minimum thickness of a quarter-wave plate made of siderite ($FeO \cdot CO_2$) if the indexes of refraction are $n_1 = 1.875$ and $n_2 = 1.635$ and the wavelength in vacuum is $\lambda_0 = 589$ nm.

CHALLENGE PROBLEMS

33.65 ••• Consider two vibrations of equal amplitude and frequency but differing in phase, one along the x-axis,

$$x = a \sin(\omega t - \alpha)$$

and the other along the y-axis,

$$y = a \sin(\omega t - \beta)$$

These can be written as follows:

$$\frac{x}{a} = \sin \omega t \cos \alpha - \cos \omega t \sin \alpha \qquad (1)$$

$$\frac{y}{a} = \sin \omega t \cos \beta - \cos \omega t \sin \beta \qquad (2)$$

(a) Multiply Eq. (1) by $\sin \beta$ and Eq. (2) by $\sin \alpha$, and then subtract the resulting equations. (b) Multiply Eq. (1) by $\cos \beta$ and Eq. (2) by $\cos \alpha$, and then subtract the resulting equations. (c) Square and add the results of parts (a) and (b). (d) Derive the equation $x^2 + y^2 - 2xy\cos\delta = a^2\sin^2\delta$, where $\delta = \alpha - \beta$. (e) Use the above result to justify each of the diagrams in Fig. P33.65. In the figure, the angle given is the phase difference between two simple harmonic motions of the same frequency and amplitude, one horizontal (along the x-axis) and the other vertical (along the y-axis). The figure thus shows the resultant motion from the superposition of the two perpendicular harmonic motions.

Figure **P33.65**

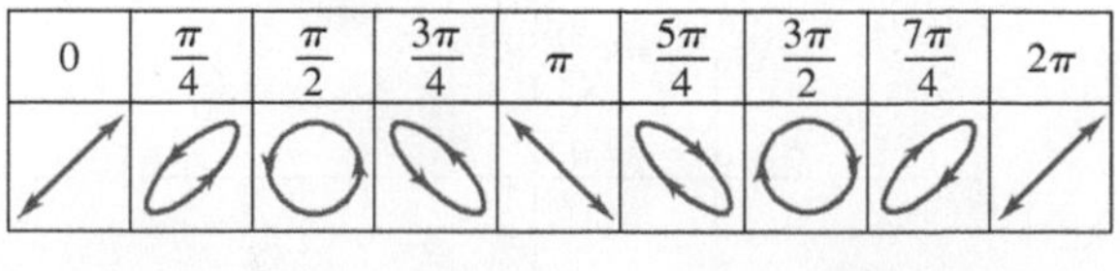

33.66 ••• CALC A rainbow is produced by the reflection of sunlight by spherical drops of water in the air. Figure P33.66 shows a ray that refracts into a drop at point A, is reflected from the back surface of the drop at point B, and refracts back into the air at point C. The angles of incidence and refraction, θ_a and θ_b, are shown at points A and C, and the angles of incidence and reflection, θ_a and θ_r, are shown at point B. (a) Show that $\theta_a{}^B = \theta_b{}^A$, $\theta_a{}^C = \theta_b{}^A$, and $\theta_b{}^C = \theta_a{}^A$. (b) Show that the angle in radians between the ray before it enters the drop at A and after it exits at C (the total angular deflection of the ray) is $\Delta = 2\theta_a{}^A - 4\theta_b{}^A + \pi$. (*Hint:* Find the angular deflections that occur at A, B, and C, and add them to get Δ.) (c) Use Snell's law to write Δ in terms of $\theta_a{}^A$ and n, the refractive index of the water in the drop. (d) A rainbow will form when the angular deflection Δ is *stationary* in the incident angle $\theta_a{}^A$—that is, when $d\Delta/d\theta_a{}^A = 0$. If this condition is satisfied, all the rays with incident angles close to $\theta_a{}^A$ will be sent back in the same direction, producing a bright zone in the sky. Let θ_1 be the value of $\theta_a{}^A$ for which this occurs. Show that $\cos^2\theta_1 = \frac{1}{3}(n^2 - 1)$. (*Hint:* You may find the derivative formula $d(\arcsin u(x))/dx = (1 - u^2)^{-1/2}(du/dx)$ helpful.) (e) The index of refraction in water is 1.342 for violet light and 1.330 for red light. Use the results of parts (c) and (d) to find θ_1 and Δ for violet and red light. Do your results agree with the angles shown in Fig. 33.20d? When you view the rainbow, which color, red or violet, is higher above the horizon?

Figure **P33.66**

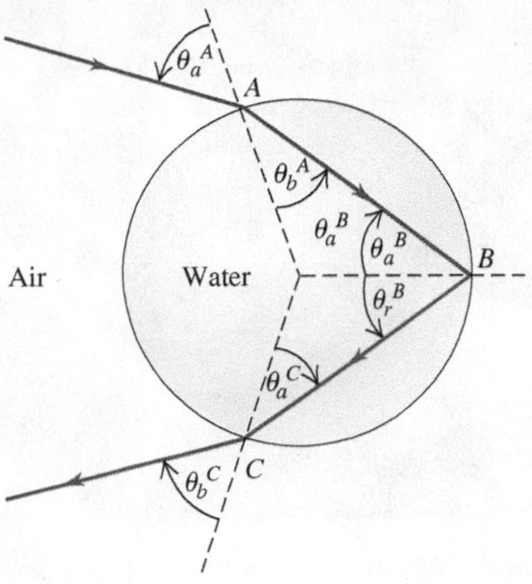

33.67 ••• **CALC** A *secondary rainbow* is formed when the incident light undergoes two internal reflections in a spherical drop of water as shown in Fig. 33.20e. (See Challenge Problem 33.66.) (a) In terms of the incident angle θ_a^A and the refractive index n of the drop, what is the angular deflection Δ of the ray? That is, what is the angle between the ray before it enters the drop and after it exits? (b) What is the incident angle θ_2 for which the derivative of Δ with respect to the incident angle θ_a^A is zero? (c) The indexes of refraction for red and violet light in water are given in part (e) of Challenge Problem 33.66. Use the results of parts (a) and (b) to find θ_2 and Δ for violet and red light. Do your results agree with the angles shown in Fig. 33.20e? When you view a secondary rainbow, is red or violet higher above the horizon? Explain.

Answers

Chapter Opening Question ?

This is the same effect as shown in Fig. 33.31. The drafting tools are placed between two polarizing filters whose polarizing axes are perpendicular. In places where the clear plastic is under stress, the plastic becomes birefringent; that is, light travels through it at a speed that depends on its polarization. The result is that the light that emerges from the plastic has a different polarization than the light that enters. A spot on the plastic appears bright if the emerging light has the same polarization as the second polarizing filter. The amount of birefringence depends on the wavelength of the light as well as the amount of stress on the plastic, so different colors are seen at different locations on the plastic.

Test Your Understanding Questions

33.1 Answer: (iii) The waves go farther in the y-direction in a given amount of time than in the other directions, so the wave fronts are elongated in the y-direction.

33.2 Answers: (a) (ii), (b) (iii) As shown in the figure, light rays coming from the fish bend away from the normal when they pass from the water ($n = 1.33$) into the air ($n = 1.00$). As a result, the fish appears to be higher in the water than it actually is. Hence you should aim a spear *below* the apparent position of the fish. If you use a laser beam, you should aim *at* the apparent position of the fish: The beam of laser light takes the same path from you to the fish as ordinary light takes from the fish to you (though in the opposite direction).

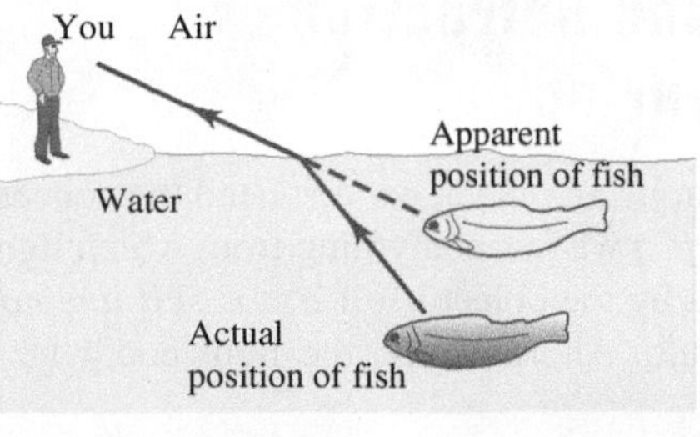

33.3 Answers: (i), (ii) Total internal reflection can occur only if two conditions are met: n_b must be less than n_a, and the critical angle θ_{crit} (where $\sin\theta_{crit} = n_b/n_a$) must be smaller than the angle of incidence θ_a. In the first two cases both conditions are met: The critical angles are (i) $\theta_{crit} = \sin^{-1}(1/1.33) = 48.8°$ and (ii) $\theta_{crit} = \sin^{-1}(1.33/1.52) = 61.0°$, both of which are smaller than $\theta_a = 70°$. In the third case $n_b = 1.52$ is greater than $n_a = 1.33$, so total internal reflection cannot occur for any incident angle.

33.5 Answer: (ii) The sunlight reflected from the windows of the high-rise building is partially polarized in the vertical direction, since each window lies in a vertical plane. The Polaroid filter in front of the lens is oriented with its polarizing axis perpendicular to the dominant direction of polarization of the reflected light.

33.7 Answer: (ii) Huygens's principle applies to waves of all kinds, including sound waves. Hence this situation is exactly like that shown in Fig. 33.36, with material a representing the warm air, material b representing the cold air in which the waves travel more slowly, and the interface between the materials representing the weather front. North is toward the top of the figure and east is toward the right, so Fig. 33.36 shows that the rays (which indicate the direction of propagation) deflect toward the east.

Bridging Problem

Answer: 1.93×10^8 m/s

34 GEOMETRIC OPTICS

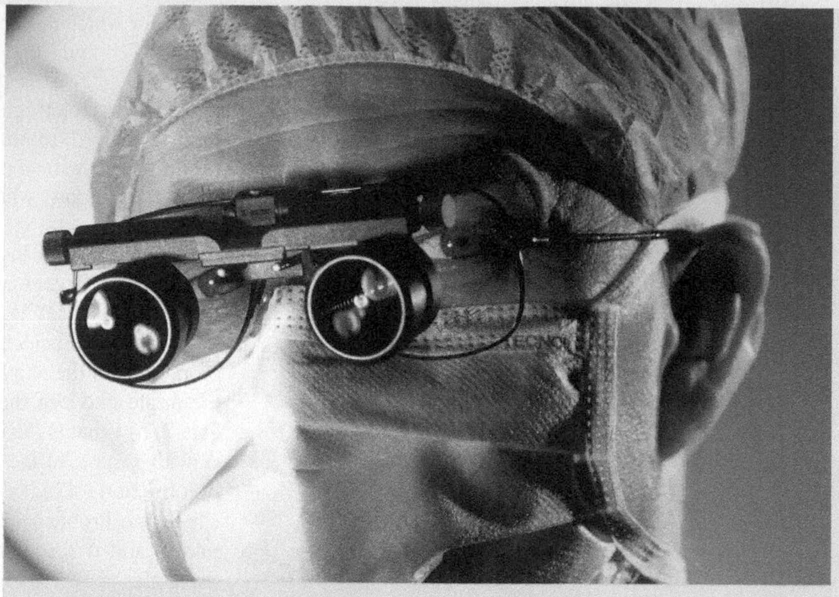

? How do magnifying lenses work? At what distance from the object being examined do they provide the sharpest view?

LEARNING GOALS

By studying this chapter, you will learn:

- How a plane mirror forms an image.
- Why concave and convex mirrors form different kinds of image.
- How images can be formed by a curved interface between two transparent materials.
- What aspects of a lens determine the type of image that it produces.
- What determines the field of view of a camera lens.
- What causes various defects in human vision, and how they can be corrected.
- The principle of the simple magnifier.
- How microscopes and telescopes work.

Your reflection in the bathroom mirror, the view of the moon through a telescope, the patterns seen in a kaleidoscope—all of these are examples of *images.* In each case the object that you're looking at appears to be in a different place than its actual position: Your reflection is on the other side of the mirror, the moon appears to be much closer when seen through a telescope, and objects seen in a kaleidoscope seem to be in many places at the same time. In each case, light rays that come from a point on an object are deflected by reflection or refraction (or a combination of the two), so they converge toward or appear to diverge from a point called an *image point.* Our goal in this chapter is to see how this is done and to explore the different kinds of images that can be made with simple optical devices.

To understand images and image formation, all we need are the ray model of light, the laws of reflection and refraction, and some simple geometry and trigonometry. The key role played by geometry in our analysis is the reason for the name *geometric optics* that is given to the study of how light rays form images. We'll begin our analysis with one of the simplest image-forming optical devices, a plane mirror. We'll go on to study how images are formed by curved mirrors, by refracting surfaces, and by thin lenses. Our results will lay the foundation for understanding many familiar optical instruments, including camera lenses, magnifiers, the human eye, microscopes, and telescopes.

MasteringPHYSICS

ActivPhysics 15.4: Geometric Optics: Plane Mirrors

34.1 Reflection and Refraction at a Plane Surface

Before discussing what is meant by an image, we first need the concept of **object** as it is used in optics. By an *object* we mean anything from which light rays radiate. This light could be emitted by the object itself if it is *self-luminous,* like the glowing filament of a light bulb. Alternatively, the light could be emitted by another source (such as a lamp or the sun) and then reflected from the object; an example is the light you see coming from the pages of this book. Figure 34.1 shows light rays radiating in all directions from an object at a point *P*. For an observer to see this object directly, there must be no obstruction between the object and the observer's eyes. Note that light rays from the object reach the observer's left and right eyes at different angles; these differences are processed by the observer's brain to infer the *distance* from the observer to the object.

The object in Fig. 34.1 is a **point object** that has no physical extent. Real objects with length, width, and height are called **extended objects.** To start with, we'll consider only an idealized point object, since we can always think of an extended object as being made up of a very large number of point objects.

Suppose some of the rays from the object strike a smooth, plane reflecting surface (Fig. 34.2). This could be the surface of a material with a different index of refraction, which reflects part of the incident light, or a polished metal surface that reflects almost 100% of the light that strikes it. We will always draw the reflecting surface as a black line with a shaded area behind it, as in Fig. 34.2. Bathroom mirrors have a thin sheet of glass that lies in front of and protects the reflecting surface; we'll ignore the effects of this thin sheet.

According to the law of reflection, all rays striking the surface are reflected at an angle from the normal equal to the angle of incidence. Since the surface is plane, the normal is in the same direction at all points on the surface, and we have *specular* reflection. After the rays are reflected, their directions are the same as though they had come from point P'. We call point P an *object point* and point P' the corresponding *image point,* and we say that the reflecting surface forms an **image** of point P. An observer who can see only the rays reflected from the surface, and who doesn't know that he's seeing a reflection, *thinks* that the rays originate from the image point P'. The image point is therefore a convenient way to describe the directions of the various reflected rays, just as the object point P describes the directions of the rays arriving at the surface *before* reflection.

If the surface in Fig. 34.2 were *not* smooth, the reflection would be *diffuse,* and rays reflected from different parts of the surface would go in uncorrelated directions (see Fig. 33.6b). In this case there would not be a definite image point P' from which all reflected rays seem to emanate. You can't see your reflection in the surface of a tarnished piece of metal because its surface is rough; polishing the metal smoothes the surface so that specular reflection occurs and a reflected image becomes visible.

An image is also formed by a plane *refracting* surface, as shown in Fig. 34.3. Rays coming from point P are refracted at the interface between two optical materials. When the angles of incidence are small, the final directions of the rays after refraction are the same as though they had come from point P', as shown, and again we call P' an *image point.* In Section 33.2 we described how this effect makes underwater objects appear closer to the surface than they really are (see Fig. 33.9).

In both Figs. 34.2 and 34.3 the rays do not actually pass through the image point P'. Indeed, if the mirror in Fig. 34.2 is opaque, there is no light at all on its right side. If the outgoing rays don't actually pass through the image point, we call the image a **virtual image.** Later we will see cases in which the outgoing rays really *do* pass through an image point, and we will call the resulting image a **real image.** The images that are formed on a projection screen, on the photographic film in a camera, and on the retina of your eye are real images.

Image Formation by a Plane Mirror

Let's concentrate for now on images produced by *reflection;* we'll return to refraction later in the chapter. To find the precise location of the virtual image P' that a plane mirror forms of an object at P, we use the construction shown in Fig. 34.4. The figure shows two rays diverging from an object point P at a

34.1 Light rays radiate from a point object P in all directions.

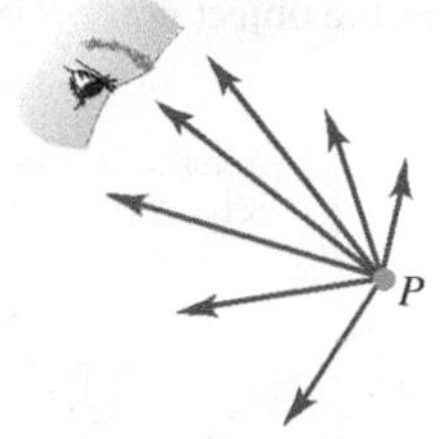

34.2 Light rays from the object at point P are reflected from a plane mirror. The reflected rays entering the eye look as though they had come from image point P'.

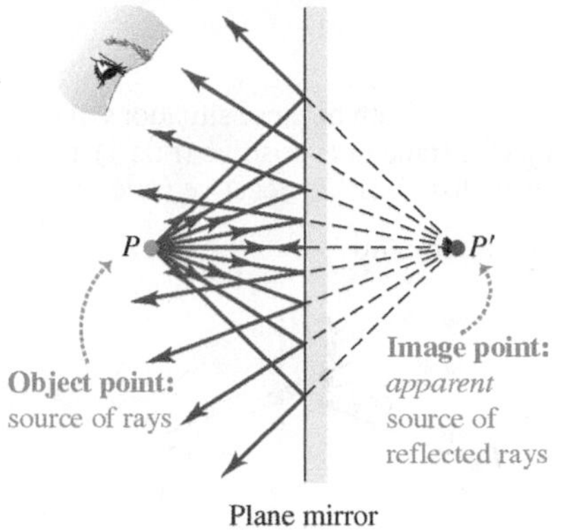

34.3 Light rays from the object at point P are refracted at the plane interface. The refracted rays entering the eye look as though they had come from image point P'.

When $n_a > n_b$, P' is closer to the surface than P; for $n_a < n_b$, the reverse is true.

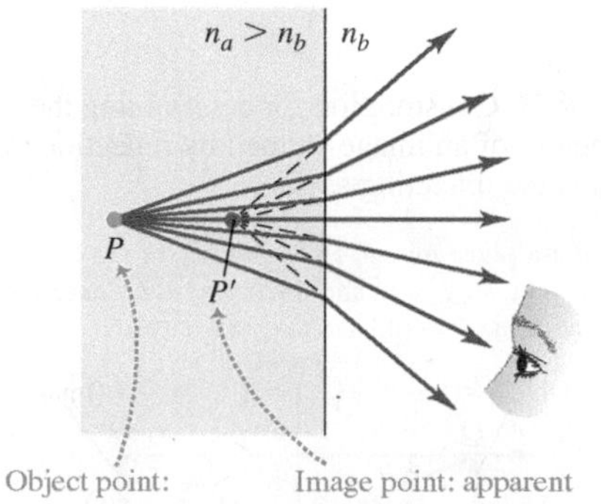

34.4 Construction for determining the location of the image formed by a plane mirror. The image point P' is as far behind the mirror as the object point P is in front of it.

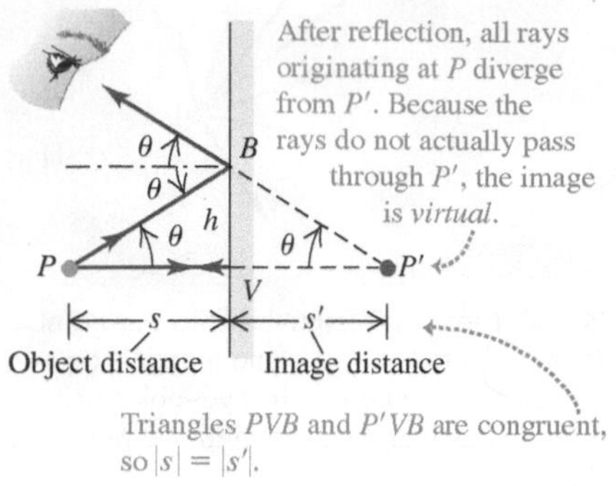

34.5 For both of these situations, the object distance s is positive (rule 1) and the image distance s' is negative (rule 2).

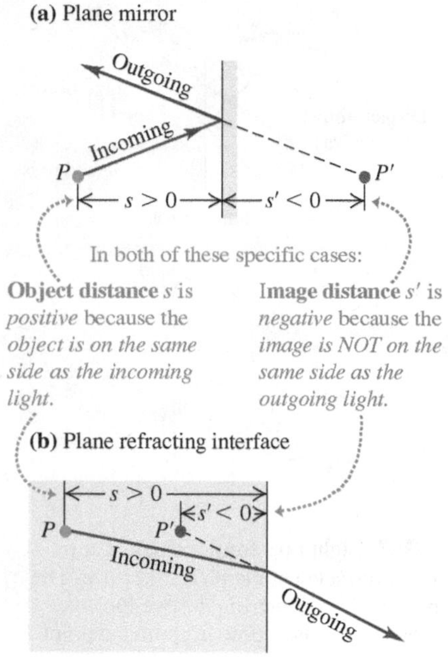

34.6 Construction for determining the height of an image formed by reflection at a plane reflecting surface.

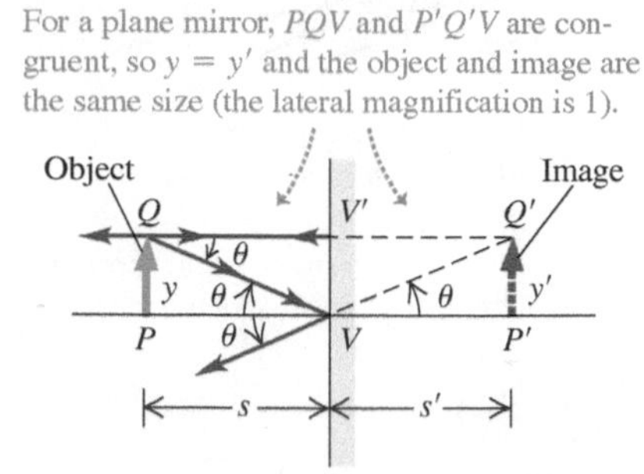

distance s to the left of a plane mirror. We call s the **object distance.** The ray PV is incident normally on the mirror (that is, it is perpendicular to the mirror surface), and it returns along its original path.

The ray PB makes an angle θ with PV. It strikes the mirror at an angle of incidence θ and is reflected at an equal angle with the normal. When we extend the two reflected rays backward, they intersect at point P', at a distance s' behind the mirror. We call s' the **image distance.** The line between P and P' is perpendicular to the mirror. The two triangles PVB and $P'VB$ are congruent, so P and P' are at equal distances from the mirror, and s and s' have equal magnitudes. The image point P' is located exactly opposite the object point P as far *behind* the mirror as the object point is from the front of the mirror.

We can repeat the construction of Fig. 34.4 for each ray diverging from P. The directions of *all* the outgoing reflected rays are the same as though they had originated at point P', confirming that P' is the *image* of P. No matter where the observer is located, she will always see the image at the point P'.

Sign Rules

Before we go further, let's introduce some general sign rules. These may seem unnecessarily complicated for the simple case of an image formed by a plane mirror, but we want to state the rules in a form that will be applicable to *all* the situations we will encounter later. These will include image formation by a plane or spherical reflecting or refracting surface, or by a pair of refracting surfaces forming a lens. Here are the rules:

1. **Sign rule for the object distance:** When the object is on the same side of the reflecting or refracting surface as the incoming light, the object distance s is positive; otherwise, it is negative.
2. **Sign rule for the image distance:** When the image is on the same side of the reflecting or refracting surface as the outgoing light, the image distance s' is positive; otherwise, it is negative.
3. **Sign rule for the radius of curvature of a spherical surface:** When the center of curvature C is on the same side as the outgoing light, the radius of curvature is positive; otherwise, it is negative.

Figure 34.5 illustrates rules 1 and 2 for two different situations. For a mirror the incoming and outgoing sides are always the same; for example, in Figs. 34.2, 34.4, and 34.5a they are both on the left side. For the refracting surfaces in Figs. 34.3 and 34.5b the incoming and outgoing sides are on the left and right sides, respectively, of the interface between the two materials. (Note that other textbooks may use different rules.)

In Figs. 34.4 and 34.5a the object distance s is *positive* because the object point P is on the incoming side (the left side) of the reflecting surface. The image distance s' is *negative* because the image point P' is *not* on the outgoing side (the left side) of the surface. The object and image distances s and s' are related simply by

$$s = -s' \qquad \text{(plane mirror)} \tag{34.1}$$

For a plane reflecting or refracting surface, the radius of curvature is infinite and not a particularly interesting or useful quantity; in these cases we really don't need sign rule 3. But this rule will be of great importance when we study image formation by *curved* reflecting and refracting surfaces later in the chapter.

Image of an Extended Object: Plane Mirror

Next we consider an *extended* object with finite size. For simplicity we often consider an object that has only one dimension, like a slender arrow, oriented parallel to the reflecting surface; an example is the arrow PQ in Fig. 34.6. The distance from the head to the tail of an arrow oriented in this way is called its *height;* in Fig. 34.6 the height is y. The image formed by such an extended object is an extended image; to each point on the object, there corresponds a point on the image. Two of the rays from Q are shown; *all* the rays from Q appear to diverge from its image point Q' after reflection. The image of the arrow is the line $P'Q'$, with height y'. Other points of the object PQ have image points between P' and Q'. The triangles PQV and $P'Q'V$ are congruent, so the object PQ and image $P'Q'$ have the same size and orientation, and $y = y'$.

The ratio of image height to object height, y'/y, in *any* image-forming situation is called the **lateral magnification** m; that is,

$$m = \frac{y'}{y} \quad \text{(lateral magnification)} \qquad (34.2)$$

Thus for a plane mirror the lateral magnification m is unity. When you look at yourself in a plane mirror, your image is the same size as the real you.

In Fig. 34.6 the image arrow points in the *same* direction as the object arrow; we say that the image is **erect.** In this case, y and y' have the same sign, and the lateral magnification m is positive. The image formed by a plane mirror is always erect, so y and y' have both the same magnitude and the same sign; from Eq. (34.2) the lateral magnification of a plane mirror is always $m = +1$. Later we will encounter situations in which the image is **inverted;** that is, the image arrow points in the direction *opposite* to that of the object arrow. For an inverted image, y and y' have *opposite* signs, and the lateral magnification m is *negative.*

The object in Fig. 34.6 has only one dimension. Figure 34.7 shows a *three-dimensional* object and its three-dimensional virtual image formed by a plane mirror. The object and image are related in the same way as a left hand and a right hand.

CAUTION **Reflections in a plane mirror** At this point, you may be asking, "Why does a plane mirror reverse images left and right but not top and bottom?" This question is quite misleading! As Fig. 34.7 shows, the up-down image $P'Q'$ and the left-right image $P'S'$ are parallel to their objects and are not reversed at all. Only the front-back image $P'R'$ is reversed relative to PR. Hence it's most correct to say that a plane mirror reverses *back to front.* To verify this object-image relationship, point your thumbs along PR and $P'R'$, your forefingers along PQ and $P'Q'$, and your middle fingers along PS and $P'S'$. When an object and its image are related in this way, the image is said to be **reversed;** this means that *only* the front-back dimension is reversed.

The reversed image of a three-dimensional object formed by a plane mirror is the same *size* as the object in all its dimensions. When the transverse dimensions of object and image are in the same direction, the image is erect. Thus a plane mirror always forms an erect but reversed image. Figure 34.8 illustrates this point.

An important property of all images formed by reflecting or refracting surfaces is that an *image* formed by one surface or optical device can serve as the *object* for a second surface or device. Figure 34.9 shows a simple example. Mirror 1 forms an image P_1' of the object point P, and mirror 2 forms another image P_2', each in the way we have just discussed. But in addition, the image P_1' formed by mirror 1 serves an object for mirror 2, which then forms an image of this object at point P_3' as shown. Similarly, mirror 1 uses the image P_2' formed by mirror 2 as an object and forms an image of it. We leave it to you to show that this image point is also at P_3'. The idea that an image formed by one device can act as the object for a second device is of great importance in geometric optics. We will use it later in this chapter to locate the image formed by two successive curved-surface refractions in a lens. This idea will help us to understand image formation by combinations of lenses, as in a microscope or a refracting telescope.

34.7 The image formed by a plane mirror is virtual, erect, and reversed. It is the same size as the object.

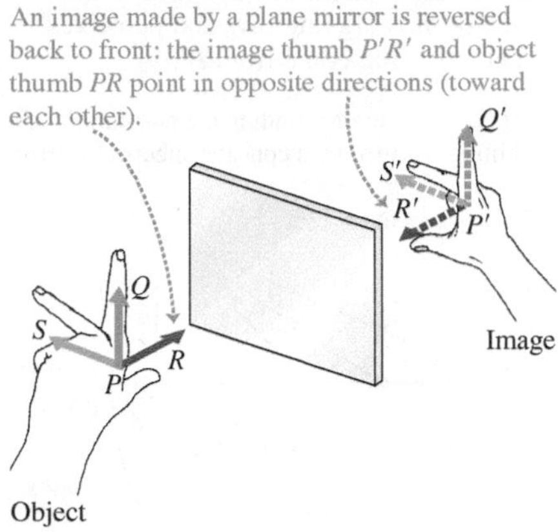

34.8 The image formed by a plane mirror is reversed; the image of a right hand is a left hand, and so on. (The hand is resting on a horizontal mirror.) Are images of the letters H and A reversed?

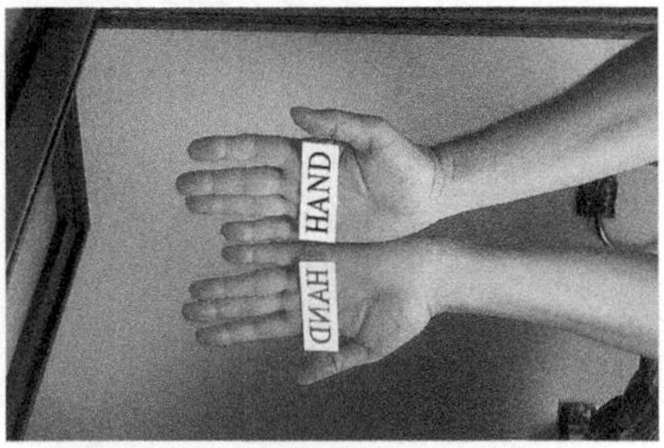

34.9 Images P_1' and P_2' are formed by a single reflection of each ray from the object at P. Image P_3', located by treating either of the other images as an object, is formed by a double reflection of each ray.

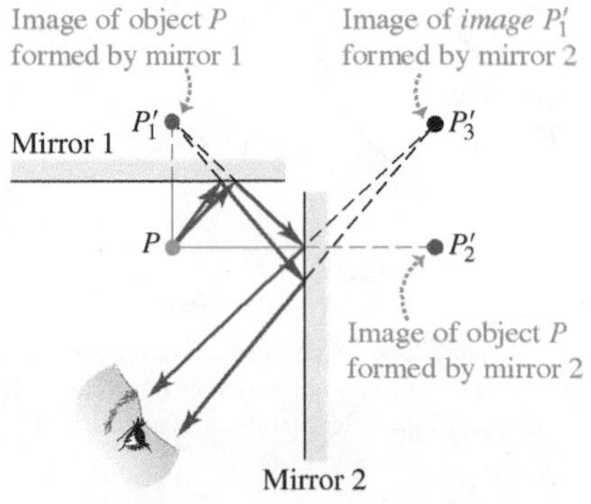

Test Your Understanding of Section 34.1 If you walk directly toward a plane mirror at a speed v, at what speed does your image approach you? (i) slower than v; (ii) v; (iii) faster than v but slower than $2v$; (iv) $2v$; (v) faster than $2v$.

34.2 Reflection at a Spherical Surface

A plane mirror produces an image that is the same size as the object. But there are many applications for mirrors in which the image and object must be of different sizes. A magnifying mirror used when applying makeup gives an image that is *larger* than the object, and surveillance mirrors (used in stores to help spot shoplifters) give an image that is *smaller* than the object. There are also applications of mirrors in which a *real* image is desired, so light rays do indeed pass through the image point P'. A plane mirror by itself cannot perform any of these tasks. Instead, *curved* mirrors are used.

34.10 (a) A concave spherical mirror forms a real image of a point object P on the mirror's optic axis. (b) The eye sees some of the outgoing rays and perceives them as having come from P'.

(a) Construction for finding the position P' of an image formed by a concave spherical mirror

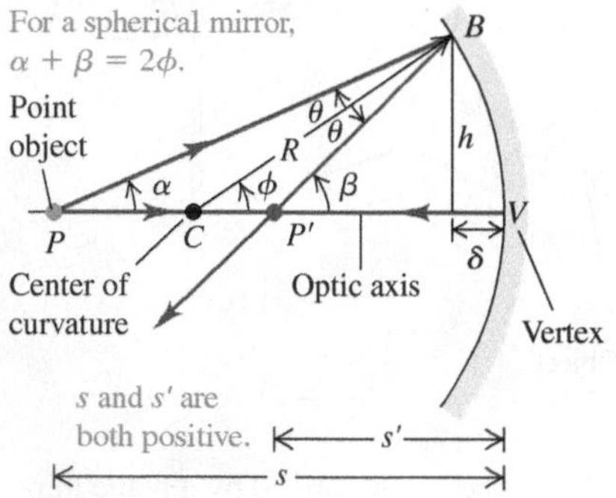

(b) The paraxial approximation, which holds for rays with small α

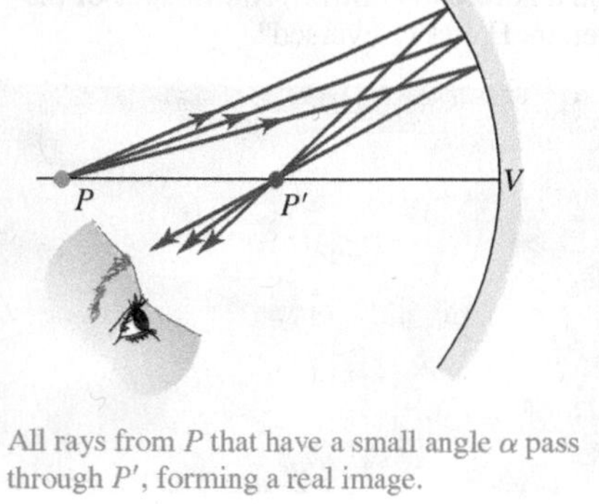

Image of a Point Object: Spherical Mirror

We'll consider the special (and easily analyzed) case of image formation by a *spherical* mirror. Figure 34.10a shows a spherical mirror with radius of curvature R, with its concave side facing the incident light. The **center of curvature** of the surface (the center of the sphere of which the surface is a part) is at C, and the **vertex** of the mirror (the center of the mirror surface) is at V. The line CV is called the **optic axis.** Point P is an object point that lies on the optic axis; for the moment, we assume that the distance from P to V is greater than R.

Ray PV, passing through C, strikes the mirror normally and is reflected back on itself. Ray PB, at an angle α with the axis, strikes the mirror at B, where the angles of incidence and reflection are θ. The reflected ray intersects the axis at point P'. We will show shortly that *all* rays from P intersect the axis at the *same* point P', as in Fig. 34.10b, provided that the angle α is small. Point P' is therefore the *image* of object point P. Unlike the reflected rays in Fig. 34.1, the reflected rays in Fig. 34.10b actually do intersect at point P', then diverge from P' *as if* they had originated at this point. Thus P' is a *real* image.

To see the usefulness of having a real image, suppose that the mirror is in a darkened room in which the only source of light is a self-luminous object at P. If you place a small piece of photographic film at P', all the rays of light coming from point P that reflect off the mirror will strike the same point P' on the film; when developed, the film will show a single bright spot, representing a sharply focused image of the object at point P. This principle is at the heart of most astronomical telescopes, which use large concave mirrors to make photographs of celestial objects. With a *plane* mirror like that in Fig. 34.2, placing a piece of film at the image point P' would be a waste of time; the light rays never actually pass through the image point, and the image can't be recorded on film. Real images are *essential* for photography.

34.11 The sign rule for the radius of a spherical mirror.

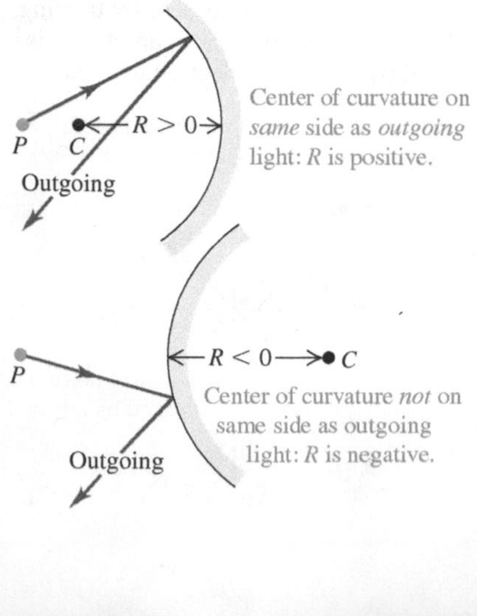

Let's now find the location of the real image point P' in Fig. 34.10a and prove the assertion that all rays from P intersect at P' (provided that their angle with the optic axis is small). The object distance, measured from the vertex V, is s; the image distance, also measured from V, is s'. The signs of s, s', and the radius of curvature R are determined by the sign rules given in Section 34.1. The object point P is on the same side as the incident light, so according to sign rule 1, s is positive. The image point P' is on the same side as the reflected light, so according to sign rule 2, the image distance s' is also positive. The center of curvature C is on the same side as the reflected light, so according to sign rule 3, R, too, is positive; R is always positive when reflection occurs at the *concave* side of a surface (Fig. 34.11).

We now use the following theorem from plane geometry: An exterior angle of a triangle equals the sum of the two opposite interior angles. Applying this theorem to triangles PBC and $P'BC$ in Fig. 34.10a, we have

$$\phi = \alpha + \theta \qquad \beta = \phi + \theta$$

Eliminating θ between these equations gives

$$\alpha + \beta = 2\phi \tag{34.3}$$

We may now compute the image distance s'. Let h represent the height of point B above the optic axis, and let δ represent the short distance from V to the foot of this vertical line. We now write expressions for the tangents of α, β, and ϕ, remembering that s, s', and R are all positive quantities:

$$\tan\alpha = \frac{h}{s-\delta} \qquad \tan\beta = \frac{h}{s'-\delta} \qquad \tan\phi = \frac{h}{R-\delta}$$

These trigonometric equations cannot be solved as simply as the corresponding algebraic equations for a plane mirror. However, *if the angle* α *is small,* the angles β and ϕ are also small. The tangent of an angle that is much less than one radian is nearly equal to the angle itself (measured in radians), so we can replace $\tan\alpha$ by α, and so on, in the equations above. Also, if α is small, we can neglect the distance δ compared with s', s, and R. So for small angles we have the following approximate relationships:

$$\alpha = \frac{h}{s} \qquad \beta = \frac{h}{s'} \qquad \phi = \frac{h}{R}$$

Substituting these into Eq. (34.3) and dividing by h, we obtain a general relationship among s, s', and R:

$$\frac{1}{s} + \frac{1}{s'} = \frac{2}{R} \quad \text{(object–image relationship, spherical mirror)} \tag{34.4}$$

This equation does not contain the angle α. Hence *all* rays from P that make sufficiently small angles with the axis intersect at P' after they are reflected; this verifies our earlier assertion. Such rays, nearly parallel to the axis and close to it, are called **paraxial rays.** (The term **paraxial approximation** is often used for the approximations we have just described.) Since all such reflected light rays converge on the image point, a concave mirror is also called a *converging mirror.*

Be sure you understand that Eq. (34.4), as well as many similar relationships that we will derive later in this chapter and the next, is only *approximately* correct. It results from a calculation containing approximations, and it is valid only for paraxial rays. If we increase the angle α that a ray makes with the optic axis, the point P' where the ray intersects the optic axis moves somewhat closer to the vertex than for a paraxial ray. As a result, a spherical mirror, unlike a plane mirror, does not form a precise point image of a point object; the image is "smeared out." This property of a spherical mirror is called **spherical aberration.** When the primary mirror of the Hubble Space Telescope (Fig. 34.12a) was manufactured, tiny errors were made in its shape that led to an unacceptable amount of spherical aberration (Fig. 34.12b). The performance of the telescope improved dramatically after the installation of corrective optics (Fig. 34.12c).

If the radius of curvature becomes infinite ($R = \infty$), the mirror becomes *plane,* and Eq. (34.4) reduces to Eq. (34.1) for a plane reflecting surface.

Focal Point and Focal Length

When the object point P is very far from the spherical mirror ($s = \infty$), the incoming rays are parallel. (The star shown in Fig. 34.12c is an example of such a distant object.) From Eq. (34.4) the image distance s' in this case is given by

$$\frac{1}{\infty} + \frac{1}{s'} = \frac{2}{R} \qquad s' = \frac{R}{2}$$

34.12 (a), (b) Soon after the Hubble Space Telescope (HST) was placed in orbit in 1990, it was discovered that the concave primary mirror (also called the *objective mirror*) was too shallow by about $\frac{1}{50}$ the width of a human hair, leading to spherical aberration of the star's image. (c) After corrective optics were installed in 1993, the effects of spherical aberration were almost completely eliminated.

(a) The 2.4-m-diameter primary mirror of the Hubble Space Telescope

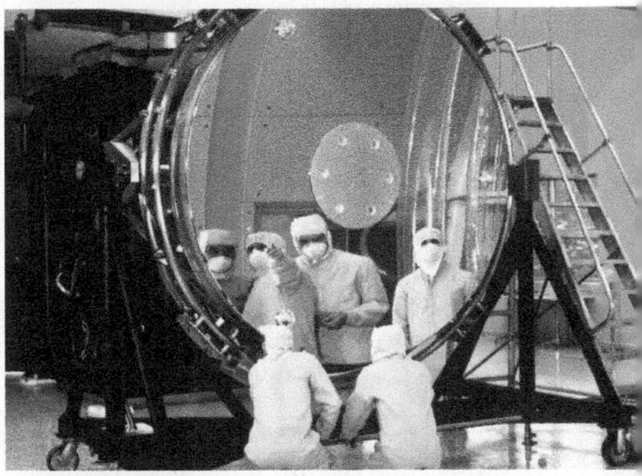

(b) A star seen with the original mirror

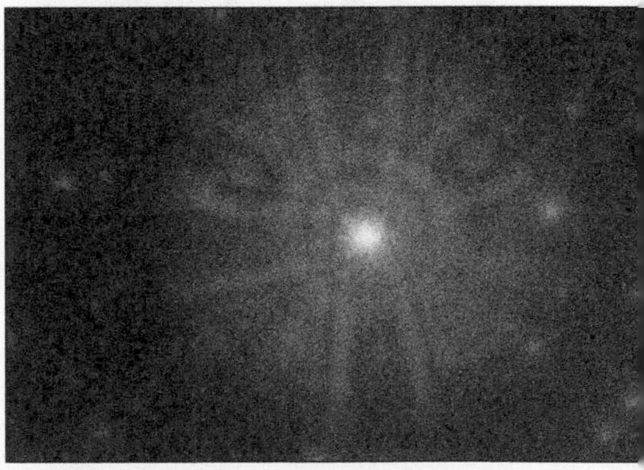

(c) The same star with corrective optics

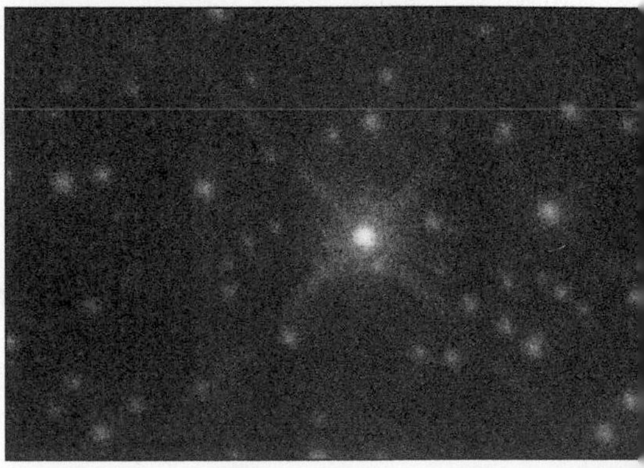

34.13 The focal point and focal length of a concave mirror.

(a) All parallel rays incident on a spherical mirror reflect through the focal point.

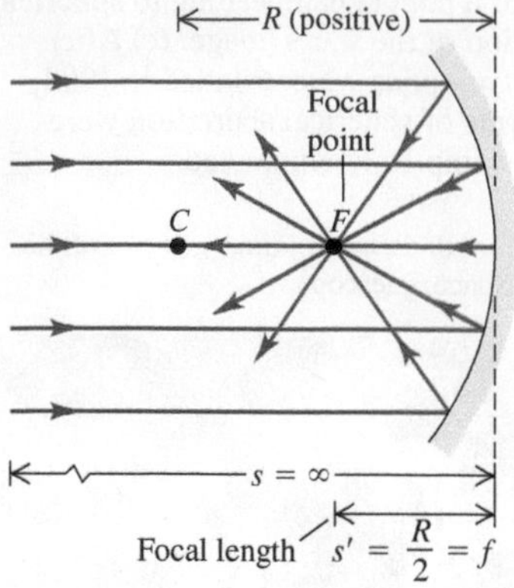

(b) Rays diverging from the focal point reflect to form parallel outgoing rays.

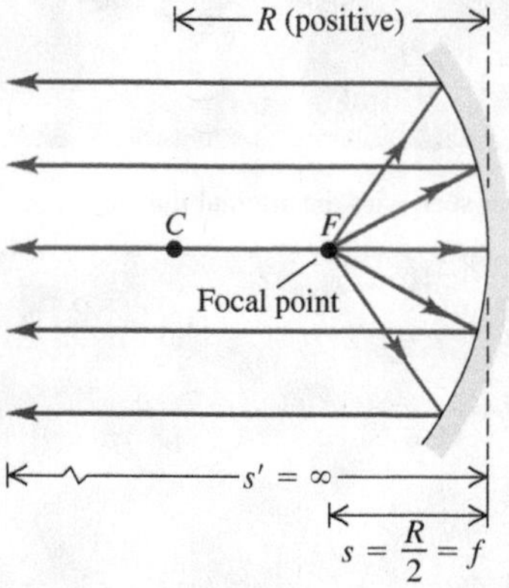

The situation is shown in Fig. 34.13a. The beam of incident parallel rays converges, after reflection from the mirror, to a point F at a distance $R/2$ from the vertex of the mirror. The point F at which the incident parallel rays converge is called the **focal point;** we say that these rays are brought to a focus. The distance from the vertex to the focal point, denoted by f, is called the **focal length.** We see that f is related to the radius of curvature R by

$$f = \frac{R}{2} \quad \text{(focal length of a spherical mirror)} \tag{34.5}$$

The opposite situation is shown in Fig. 34.13b. Now the *object* is placed at the focal point F, so the object distance is $s = f = R/2$. The image distance s' is again given by Eq. (34.4):

$$\frac{2}{R} + \frac{1}{s'} = \frac{2}{R} \qquad \frac{1}{s'} = 0 \qquad s' = \infty$$

With the object at the focal point, the reflected rays in Fig. 34.13b are parallel to the optic axis; they meet only at a point infinitely far from the mirror, so the image is at infinity.

Thus the focal point F of a spherical mirror has the properties that (1) any incoming ray parallel to the optic axis is reflected through the focal point and (2) any incoming ray that passes through the focal point is reflected parallel to the optic axis. For spherical mirrors these statements are true only for paraxial rays. For parabolic mirrors these statements are *exactly* true; this is why parabolic mirrors are preferred for astronomical telescopes. Spherical or parabolic mirrors are used in flashlights and headlights to form the light from the bulb into a parallel beam. Some solar-power plants use an array of plane mirrors to simulate an approximately spherical concave mirror; light from the sun is collected by the mirrors and directed to the focal point, where a steam boiler is placed. (The concepts of focal point and focal length also apply to lenses, as we'll see in Section 34.4.)

We will usually express the relationship between object and image distances for a mirror, Eq. (34.4), in terms of the focal length f:

$$\frac{1}{s} + \frac{1}{s'} = \frac{1}{f} \quad \text{(object–image relationship, spherical mirror)} \tag{34.6}$$

Image of an Extended Object: Spherical Mirror

Now suppose we have an object with *finite* size, represented by the arrow PQ in Fig. 34.14, perpendicular to the optic axis CV. The image of P formed by paraxial rays is at P'. The object distance for point Q is very nearly equal to that for point P, so the image $P'Q'$ is nearly straight and perpendicular to the axis. Note that the object and image arrows have different sizes, y and y', respectively, and that they have opposite orientation. In Eq. (34.2) we defined the *lateral magnification* m as the ratio of image size y' to object size y:

$$m = \frac{y'}{y}$$

34.14 Construction for determining the position, orientation, and height of an image formed by a concave spherical mirror.

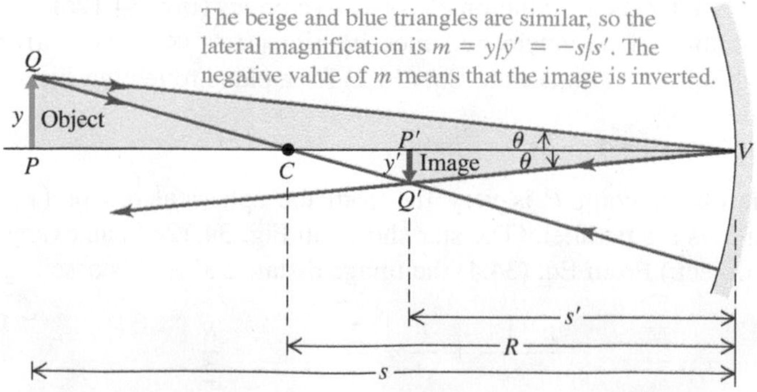

Because triangles PVQ and $P'VQ'$ in Fig. 34.14 are *similar,* we also have the relationship $y/s = -y'/s'$. The negative sign is needed because object and image are on opposite sides of the optic axis; if y is positive, y' is negative. Therefore

$$m = \frac{y'}{y} = -\frac{s'}{s} \quad \text{(lateral magnification, spherical mirror)} \qquad (34.7)$$

If m is positive, the image is erect in comparison to the object; if m is negative, the image is *inverted* relative to the object, as in Fig. 34.14. For a *plane* mirror, $s = -s'$, so $y' = y$ and $m = +1$; since m is positive, the image is erect, and since $|m| = 1$, the image is the same size as the object.

MasteringPHYSICS

ActivPhysics 15.5: Spherical Mirrors: Ray Diagrams
ActivPhysics 15.6: Spherical Mirrors: The Mirror Equation
ActivPhysics 15.7: Spherical Mirrors: Linear Magnification
ActivPhysics 15.8: Spherical Mirrors: Problems

CAUTION **Lateral magnification can be less than 1** Although the ratio of image size to object size is called the *lateral magnification,* the image formed by a mirror or lens may be larger than, smaller than, or the same size as the object. If it is smaller, then the lateral magnification is less than unity in absolute value: $|m| < 1$. The image formed by an astronomical telescope mirror or a camera lens is usually *much* smaller than the object. For example, the image of the bright star shown in Fig. 34.12c is just a few millimeters across, while the star itself is hundreds of thousands of kilometers in diameter.

In our discussion of concave mirrors we have so far considered only objects that lie *outside* or at the focal point, so that the object distance s is greater than or equal to the (positive) focal length f. In this case the image point is on the same side of the mirror as the outgoing rays, and the image is real and inverted. If an object is placed *inside* the focal point of a concave mirror, so that $s < f$, the resulting image is *virtual* (that is, the image point is on the opposite side of the mirror from the object), *erect,* and *larger* than the object. Mirrors used when applying makeup (referred to at the beginning of this section) are concave mirrors; in use, the distance from the face to the mirror is less than the focal length, and an enlarged, erect image is seen. You can prove these statements about concave mirrors by applying Eqs. (34.6) and (34.7) (see Exercise 34.11). We'll also be able to verify these results later in this section, after we've learned some graphical methods for relating the positions and sizes of the object and the image.

Example 34.1 Image formation by a concave mirror I

A concave mirror forms an image, on a wall 3.00 m in front of the mirror, of a headlamp filament 10.0 cm in front of the mirror. (a) What are the radius of curvature and focal length of the mirror? (b) What is the lateral magnification? What is the image height if the object height is 5.00 mm?

SOLUTION

IDENTIFY and SET UP: Figure 34.15 shows our sketch. Our target variables are the radius of curvature R, focal length f, lateral magnification m, and image height y'. We are given the distances from the mirror to the object (s) and from the mirror to the image (s'). We solve Eq. (34.4) for R, and then use Eq. (34.5) to find f. Equation (34.7) yields both m and y'.

34.15 Our sketch for this problem.

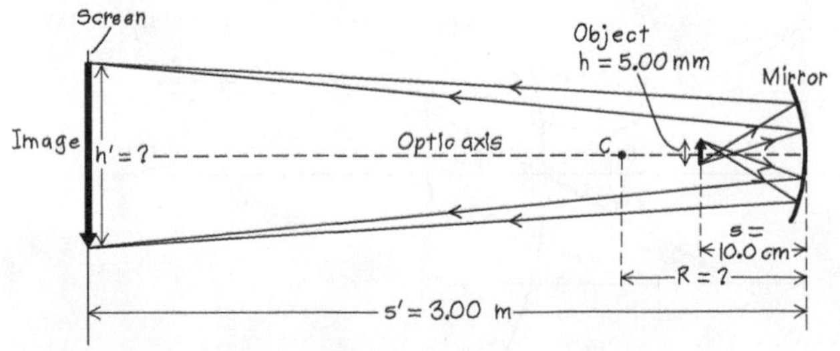

EXECUTE: (a) Both the object and the image are on the concave (reflective) side of the mirror, so both s and s' are positive; we have $s = 10.0$ cm and $s' = 300$ cm. We solve Eq. (34.4) for R:

$$\frac{1}{10.0\text{ cm}} + \frac{1}{300\text{ cm}} = \frac{2}{R}$$

$$R = 2\left(\frac{1}{10.0\text{ cm}} + \frac{1}{300\text{ cm}}\right)^{-1} = 19.4\text{ cm}$$

The focal length of the mirror is $f = R/2 = 9.7$ cm.

(b) From Eq. (34.7) the lateral magnification is

$$m = -\frac{s'}{s} = -\frac{300\text{ cm}}{10.0\text{ cm}} = -30.0$$

Because m is negative, the image is inverted. The height of the image is 30.0 times the height of the object, or $(30.0)(5.00\text{ mm}) = 150$ mm.

Continued

EVALUATE: Our sketch indicates that the image is inverted; our calculations agree. Note that the object (at $s = 10.0$ cm) is just outside the focal point ($f = 9.7$ cm). This is very similar to what is done in automobile headlights. With the filament close to the focal point, the concave mirror produces a beam of nearly parallel rays.

Conceptual Example 34.2 Image formation by a concave mirror II

In Example 34.1, suppose that the lower half of the mirror's reflecting surface is covered with nonreflective soot. What effect will this have on the image of the filament?

SOLUTION

It would be natural to guess that the image would now show only half of the filament. But in fact the image will still show the *entire* filament. You can see why by examining Fig. 34.10b. Light rays coming from any object point P are reflected from *all* parts of the mirror and converge on the corresponding image point P'. If part of the mirror surface is made nonreflective (or is removed altogether), rays from the remaining reflective surface still form an image of every part of the object.

Reducing the reflecting area reduces the light energy reaching the image point, however: The image becomes *dimmer*. If the area is reduced by one-half, the image will be one-half as bright. Conversely, *increasing* the reflective area makes the image brighter. To make reasonably bright images of faint stars, astronomical telescopes use mirrors that are up to several meters in diameter (see Fig. 34.12a).

Convex Mirrors

In Fig. 34.16a the *convex* side of a spherical mirror faces the incident light. The center of curvature is on the side opposite to the outgoing rays; according to sign rule 3 in Section 34.1, R is negative (see Fig. 34.11). Ray PB is reflected, with the angles of incidence and reflection both equal to θ. The reflected ray, projected backward, intersects the axis at P'. As with a concave mirror, *all* rays from P that are reflected by the mirror diverge from the same point P', provided that the angle α is small. Therefore P' is the image of P. The object distance s is positive, the image distance s' is negative, and the radius of curvature R is *negative* for a *convex* mirror.

Figure 34.16b shows two rays diverging from the head of the arrow PQ and the virtual image $P'Q'$ of this arrow. The same procedure that we used for a concave mirror can be used to show that for a convex mirror,

$$\frac{1}{s} + \frac{1}{s'} = \frac{2}{R}$$

and the lateral magnification is

$$m = \frac{y'}{y} = -\frac{s'}{s}$$

34.16 Image formation by a convex mirror.

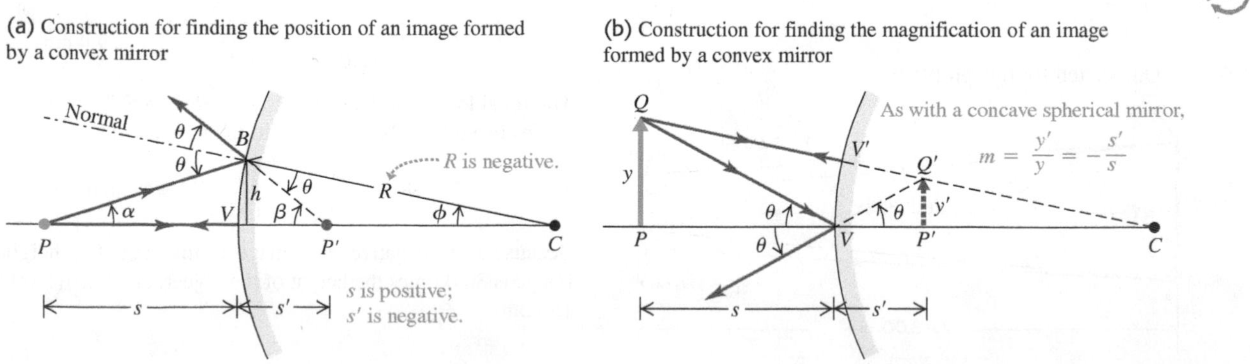

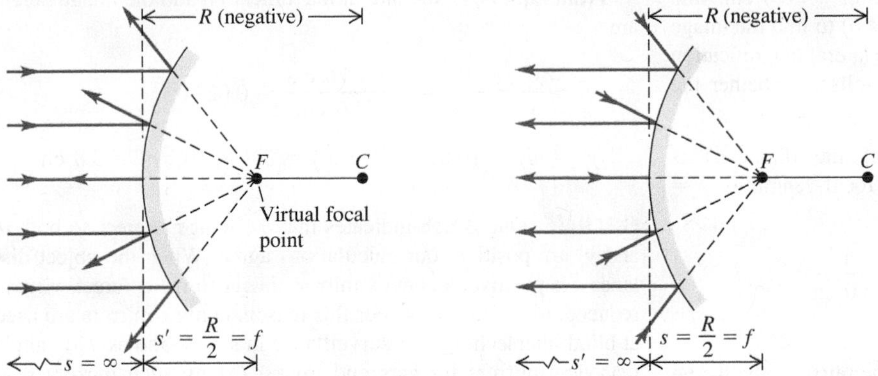

34.17 The focal point and focal length of a convex mirror.

These expressions are exactly the same as Eqs. (34.4) and (34.7) for a concave mirror. Thus when we use our sign rules consistently, Eqs. (34.4) and (34.7) are valid for both concave and convex mirrors.

When R is negative (convex mirror), incoming rays that are parallel to the optic axis are not reflected through the focal point F. Instead, they diverge as though they had come from the point F at a distance f *behind* the mirror, as shown in Fig. 34.17a. In this case, f is the focal length, and F is called a *virtual focal point.* The corresponding image distance s' is negative, so both f and R are negative, and Eq. (34.5), $f = R/2$, holds for convex as well as concave mirrors. In Fig. 34.17b the incoming rays are converging as though they would meet at the virtual focal point F, and they are reflected parallel to the optic axis.

In summary, Eqs. (34.4) through (34.7), the basic relationships for image formation by a spherical mirror, are valid for both concave and convex mirrors, provided that we use the sign rules consistently.

Example 34.3 Santa's image problem

Santa checks himself for soot, using his reflection in a silvered Christmas tree ornament 0.750 m away (Fig. 34.18a). The diameter of the ornament is 7.20 cm. Standard reference texts state that he is a "right jolly old elf," so we estimate his height to be 1.6 m. Where and how tall is the image of Santa formed by the ornament? Is it erect or inverted?

SOLUTION

IDENTIFY and SET UP: Figure 34.18b shows the situation. Santa is the object, and the surface of the ornament closest to him acts as a convex mirror. The relationships among object distance, image distance, focal length, and magnification are the same as for

34.18 (a) The ornament forms a virtual, reduced, erect image of Santa. (b) Our sketch of two of the rays forming the image.

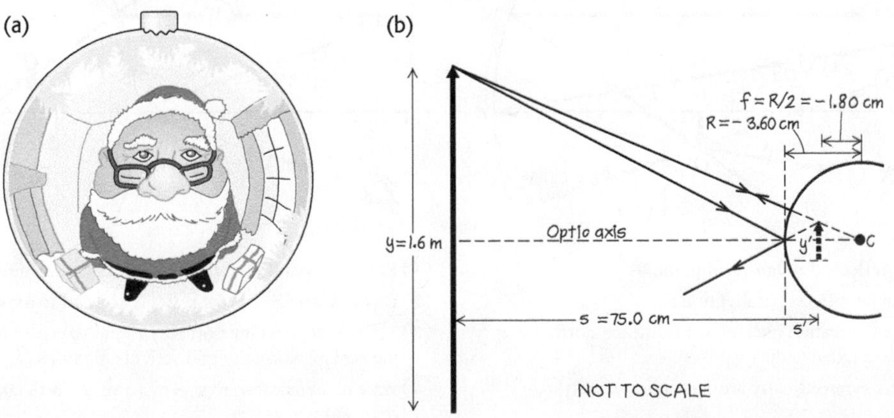

Continued

concave mirrors, provided we use the sign rules consistently. The radius of curvature and the focal length of a convex mirror are *negative*. The object distance is $s = 0.750\ \text{m} = 75.0\ \text{cm}$, and Santa's height is $y = 1.6\ \text{m}$. We solve Eq. (34.6) to find the image distance s', and then use Eq. (34.7) to find the lateral magnification m and the image height y'. The sign of m tells us whether the image is erect or inverted.

EXECUTE: The radius of the mirror (half the diameter) is $R = -(7.20\ \text{cm})/2 = -3.60\ \text{cm}$, and the focal length is $f = R/2 = -1.80\ \text{cm}$. From Eq. (34.6),

$$\frac{1}{s'} = \frac{1}{f} - \frac{1}{s} = \frac{1}{-1.80\ \text{cm}} - \frac{1}{75.0\ \text{cm}}$$

$$s' = -1.76\ \text{cm}$$

Because s' is negative, the image is behind the mirror—that is, on the side opposite to the outgoing light (Fig. 34.18b)—and it is virtual. The image is about halfway between the front surface of the ornament and its center.

From Eq. (34.7), the lateral magnification and the image height are

$$m = \frac{y'}{y} = -\frac{s'}{s} = -\frac{-1.76\ \text{cm}}{75.0\ \text{cm}} = 0.0234$$

$$y' = my = (0.0234)(1.6\ \text{m}) = 3.8 \times 10^{-2}\ \text{m} = 3.8\ \text{cm}$$

EVALUATE: Our sketch indicates that the image is erect so both m and y' are positive; our calculations agree. When the object distance s is positive, a convex mirror *always* forms an erect, virtual, reduced, reversed image. For this reason, convex mirrors are used at blind intersections, for surveillance in stores, and as wide-angle rear-view mirrors for cars and trucks. (Many such mirrors read "Objects in mirror are closer than they appear.")

Graphical Methods for Mirrors

In Examples 34.1 and 34.3, we used Eqs. (34.6) and (34.7) to find the position and size of the image formed by a mirror. We can also determine the properties of the image by a simple *graphical* method. This method consists of finding the point of intersection of a few particular rays that diverge from a point of the object (such as point Q in Fig. 34.19) and are reflected by the mirror. Then (neglecting aberrations) *all* rays from this object point that strike the mirror will intersect at the same point. For this construction we always choose an object point that is *not* on the optic axis. Four rays that we can usually draw easily are shown in Fig. 34.19. These are called **principal rays.**

1. *A ray parallel to the axis,* after reflection, passes through the focal point F of a concave mirror or appears to come from the (virtual) focal point of a convex mirror.
2. *A ray through (or proceeding toward) the focal point F* is reflected parallel to the axis.
3. *A ray along the radius* through or away from the center of curvature C intersects the surface normally and is reflected back along its original path.
4. *A ray to the vertex V* is reflected forming equal angles with the optic axis.

34.19 The graphical method of locating an image formed by a spherical mirror. The colors of the rays are for identification only; they do not refer to specific colors of light.

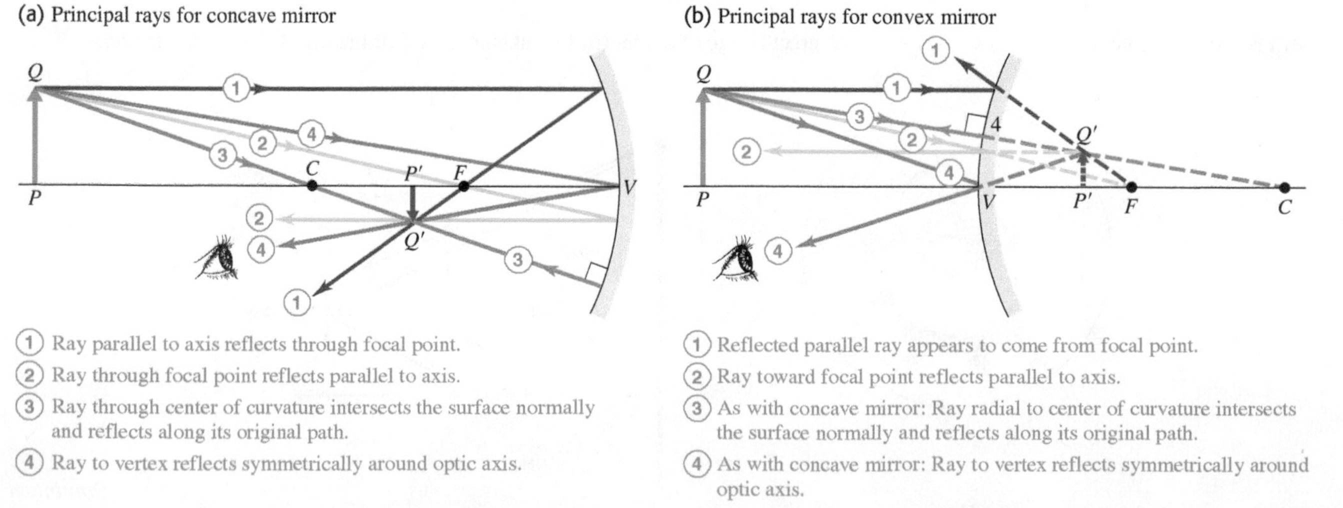

Once we have found the position of the image point by means of the intersection of any two of these principal rays (1, 2, 3, 4), we can draw the path of any other ray from the object point to the same image point.

CAUTION **Principal rays are not the only rays** Although we've emphasized the principal rays, in fact *any* ray from the object that strikes the mirror will pass through the image point (for a real image) or appear to originate from the image point (for a virtual image). Usually, you only need to draw the principal rays, because these are all you need to locate the image.

Problem-Solving Strategy 34.1 Image Formation by Mirrors

IDENTIFY *the relevant concepts:* Problems involving image formation by mirrors can be solved in two ways: using principal-ray diagrams and using equations. A successful problem solution uses *both* approaches.

SET UP *the problem:* Identify the target variables. One of them is likely to be the focal length, the object distance, or the image distance, with the other two quantities given.

EXECUTE *the solution* as follows:

1. Draw a large, clear principal-ray diagram if you have enough information.
2. Orient your diagram so that incoming rays go from left to right. Draw only the principal rays; color-code them as in Fig. 34.19. If possible, use graph paper or quadrille-ruled paper. Use a ruler and measure distances carefully! A freehand sketch will *not* give good results.
3. If your principal rays don't converge at a real image point, you may have to extend them straight backward to locate a virtual image point, as in Fig. 34.19b. We recommend drawing the extensions with broken lines.
4. Measure the resulting diagram to obtain the magnitudes of the target variables.
5. Solve for the target variables using Eq. (34.6), $1/s + 1/s' = 1/f$, and the lateral magnification equation, Eq. (34.7), as appropriate. Apply the sign rules given in Section 34.1 to object and image distances, radii of curvature, and object and image heights.
6. Use the sign rules to interpret the results that you deduced from your ray diagram and calculations. Note that the *same* sign rules (given in Section 34.1) work for all four cases in this chapter: reflection and refraction from plane and spherical surfaces.

EVALUATE *your answer:* Check that the results of your calculations agree with your ray-diagram results for image position, image size, and whether the image is real or virtual.

Example 34.4 Concave mirror with various object distances

A concave mirror has a radius of curvature with absolute value 20 cm. Find graphically the image of an object in the form of an arrow perpendicular to the axis of the mirror at object distances of (a) 30 cm, (b) 20 cm, (c) 10 cm, and (d) 5 cm. Check the construction by *computing* the size and lateral magnification of each image.

SOLUTION

IDENTIFY and SET UP: We must use graphical methods *and* calculations to analyze the image made by a mirror. The mirror is concave, so its radius of curvature is $R = +20$ cm and its focal length is $f = R/2 = +10$ cm. Our target variables are the image distances s' and lateral magnifications m corresponding to four cases with successively smaller object distances s. In each case we solve Eq. (34.6) for s' and use $m = -s'/s$ to find m.

EXECUTE: Figure 34.20 shows the principal-ray diagrams for the four cases. Study each of these diagrams carefully and confirm that each numbered ray is drawn in accordance with the rules given earlier (under "Graphical Methods for Mirrors"). Several points are worth noting. First, in case (b) the object and image distances are equal. Ray 3 cannot be drawn in this case because a ray from Q through the center of curvature C does not strike the mirror. In case (c), ray 2 cannot be drawn because a ray from Q through F does not strike the mirror. In this case the outgoing rays are parallel, corresponding to an infinite image distance. In case (d), the outgoing rays diverge; they have been extended backward to the *virtual image point* Q', from which they appear to diverge. Case (d) illustrates the general observation that an object placed inside the focal point of a concave mirror produces a virtual image.

Measurements of the figures, with appropriate scaling, give the following approximate image distances: (a) 15 cm; (b) 20 cm; (c) ∞ or $-\infty$ (because the outgoing rays are parallel and do not converge at any finite distance); (d) -10 cm. To *compute* these distances, we solve Eq. (34.6) for s' and insert $f = 10$ cm:

$$\text{(a)}\ \frac{1}{30\text{ cm}} + \frac{1}{s'} = \frac{1}{10\text{ cm}} \qquad s' = 15\text{ cm}$$

$$\text{(b)}\ \frac{1}{20\text{ cm}} + \frac{1}{s'} = \frac{1}{10\text{ cm}} \qquad s' = 20\text{ cm}$$

$$\text{(c)}\ \frac{1}{10\text{ cm}} + \frac{1}{s'} = \frac{1}{10\text{ cm}} \qquad s' = \infty\ (\text{or } -\infty)$$

$$\text{(d)}\ \frac{1}{5\text{ cm}} + \frac{1}{s'} = \frac{1}{10\text{ cm}} \qquad s' = -10\text{ cm}$$

The signs of s' tell us that the image is real in cases (a) and (b) and virtual in case (d).

Continued

The lateral magnifications measured from the figures are approximately (a) $-\frac{1}{2}$; (b) -1; (c) ∞ or $-\infty$; (d) $+2$. From Eq. (34.7),

$$\text{(a) } m = -\frac{15\text{ cm}}{30\text{ cm}} = -\frac{1}{2}$$

$$\text{(b) } m = -\frac{20\text{ cm}}{20\text{ cm}} = -1$$

$$\text{(c) } m = -\frac{\infty\text{ cm}}{10\text{ cm}} = -\infty \text{ (or } +\infty\text{)}$$

$$\text{(d) } m = -\frac{-10\text{ cm}}{5\text{ cm}} = +2$$

The signs of m tell us that the image is inverted in cases (a) and (b) and erect in case (d).

EVALUATE: Notice the trend of the results in the four cases. When the object is far from the mirror, as in Fig. 34.20a, the image is smaller than the object, inverted, and real. As the object distance s decreases, the image moves farther from the mirror and gets larger (Fig. 34.20b). When the object is at the focal point, the image is at infinity (Fig. 34.20c). When the object is inside the focal point, the image becomes larger than the object, erect, and virtual (Fig. 34.20d). You can confirm these conclusions by looking at objects reflected in the concave bowl of a shiny metal spoon.

34.20 Using principal-ray diagrams to locate the image $P'Q'$ made by a concave mirror.

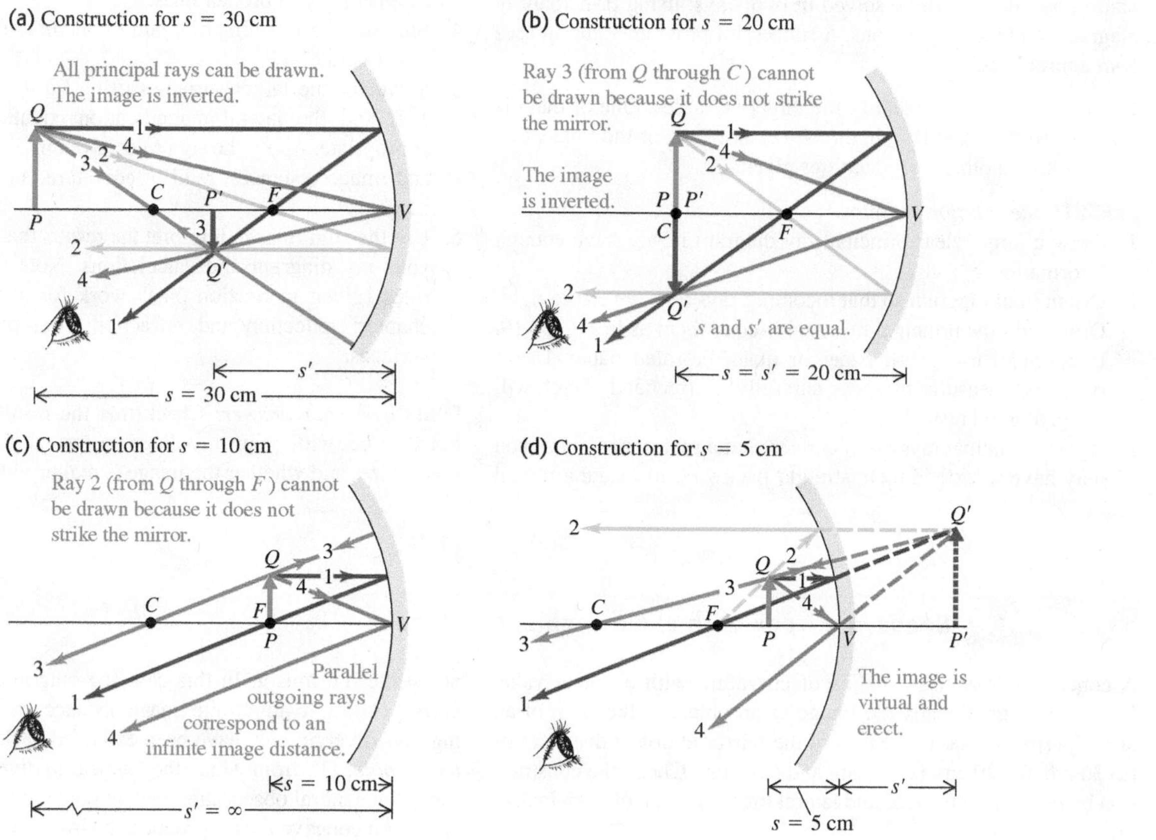

Test Your Understanding of Section 34.2 A cosmetics mirror is designed so that your reflection appears right-side up and enlarged. (a) Is the mirror concave or convex? (b) To see an enlarged image, what should be the distance from the mirror (of focal length f) to your face? (i) $|f|$; (ii) less than $|f|$; (iii) greater than $|f|$. ❙

34.3 Refraction at a Spherical Surface

As we mentioned in Section 34.1, images can be formed by refraction as well as by reflection. To begin with, let's consider refraction at a spherical surface—that is, at a spherical interface between two optical materials with different indexes of refraction. This analysis is directly applicable to some real optical systems, such as the human eye. It also provides a stepping-stone for the analysis of lenses, which usually have *two* spherical (or nearly spherical) surfaces.

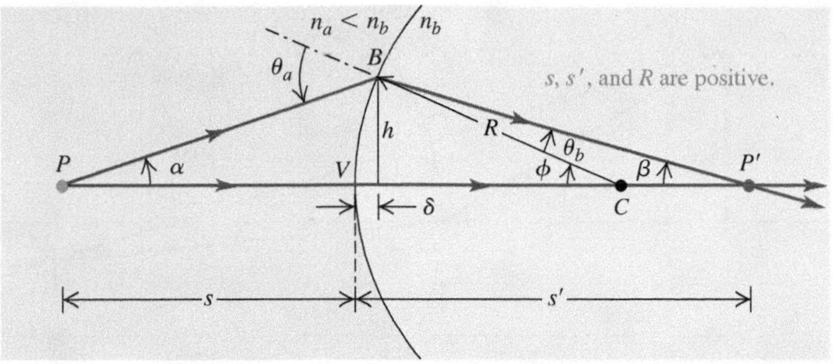

34.21 Construction for finding the position of the image point P' of a point object P formed by refraction at a spherical surface. The materials to the left and right of the interface have refractive indexes n_a and n_b, respectively. In the case shown here, $n_a < n_b$.

Image of a Point Object: Spherical Refracting Surface

In Fig. 34.21 a spherical surface with radius R forms an interface between two materials with different indexes of refraction n_a and n_b. The surface forms an image P' of an object point P; we want to find how the object and image distances (s and s') are related. We will use the same sign rules that we used for spherical mirrors. The center of curvature C is on the outgoing side of the surface, so R is positive. Ray PV strikes the vertex V and is perpendicular to the surface (that is, to the plane that is tangent to the surface at the point of incidence V). It passes into the second material without deviation. Ray PB, making an angle α with the axis, is incident at an angle θ_a with the normal and is refracted at an angle θ_b. These rays intersect at P', a distance s' to the right of the vertex. The figure is drawn for the case $n_a < n_b$. The object and image distances are both positive.

We are going to prove that if the angle α is small, *all* rays from P intersect at the same point P', so P' is the *real image* of P. We use much the same approach as we did for spherical mirrors in Section 34.2. We again use the theorem that an exterior angle of a triangle equals the sum of the two opposite interior angles; applying this to the triangles PBC and $P'BC$ gives

$$\theta_a = \alpha + \phi \qquad \phi = \beta + \theta_b \tag{34.8}$$

From the law of refraction,

$$n_a \sin\theta_a = n_b \sin\theta_b$$

Also, the tangents of α, β, and ϕ are

$$\tan\alpha = \frac{h}{s + \delta} \qquad \tan\beta = \frac{h}{s' - \delta} \qquad \tan\phi = \frac{h}{R - \delta} \tag{34.9}$$

For paraxial rays, θ_a and θ_b are both small in comparison to a radian, and we may approximate both the sine and tangent of either of these angles by the angle itself (measured in radians). The law of refraction then gives

$$n_a\theta_a = n_b\theta_b$$

Combining this with the first of Eqs. (34.8), we obtain

$$\theta_b = \frac{n_a}{n_b}(\alpha + \phi)$$

When we substitute this into the second of Eqs. (34.8), we get

$$n_a\alpha + n_b\beta = (n_b - n_a)\phi \tag{34.10}$$

Now we use the approximations $\tan\alpha = \alpha$, and so on, in Eqs. (34.9) and also neglect the small distance δ; those equations then become

$$\alpha = \frac{h}{s} \qquad \beta = \frac{h}{s'} \qquad \phi = \frac{h}{R}$$

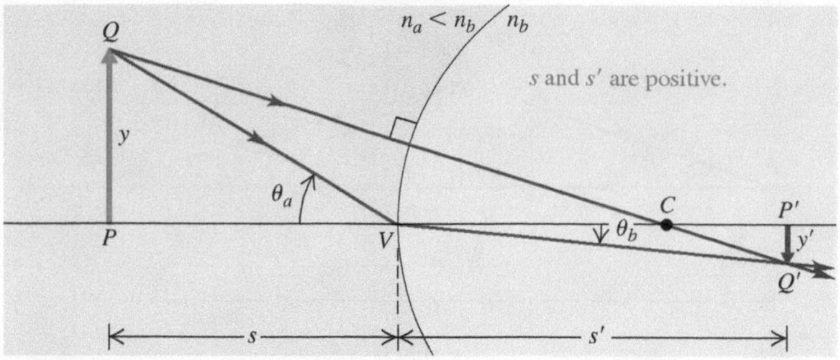

34.22 Construction for determining the height of an image formed by refraction at a spherical surface. In the case shown here, $n_a < n_b$.

Finally, we substitute these into Eq. (34.10) and divide out the common factor h. We obtain

$$\frac{n_a}{s} + \frac{n_b}{s'} = \frac{n_b - n_a}{R} \qquad \text{(object–image relationship, spherical refracting surface)} \tag{34.11}$$

This equation does not contain the angle α, so the image distance is the same for *all* paraxial rays emanating from P; this proves our assertion that P' is the image of P.

To obtain the lateral magnification m for this situation, we use the construction in Fig. 34.22. We draw two rays from point Q, one through the center of curvature C and the other incident at the vertex V. From the triangles PQV and $P'Q'V$,

$$\tan\theta_a = \frac{y}{s} \qquad \tan\theta_b = \frac{-y'}{s'}$$

and from the law of refraction,

$$n_a \sin\theta_a = n_b \sin\theta_b$$

For small angles,

$$\tan\theta_a = \sin\theta_a \qquad \tan\theta_b = \sin\theta_b$$

so finally

$$\frac{n_a y}{s} = -\frac{n_b y'}{s'} \qquad \text{or}$$

$$m = \frac{y'}{y} = -\frac{n_a s'}{n_b s} \qquad \text{(lateral magnification, spherical refracting surface)} \tag{34.12}$$

Equations (34.11) and (34.12) can be applied to both convex and concave refracting surfaces, provided that you use the sign rules consistently. It doesn't matter whether n_b is greater or less than n_a. To verify these statements, you should construct diagrams like Figs. 34.21 and 34.22 for the following three cases: (i) $R > 0$ and $n_a > n_b$, (ii) $R < 0$ and $n_a < n_b$, and (iii) $R < 0$ and $n_a > n_b$. Then in each case, use your diagram to again derive Eqs. (34.11) and (34.12).

Here's a final note on the sign rule for the radius of curvature R of a surface. For the convex reflecting surface in Fig. 34.16, we considered R negative, but the convex *refracting* surface in Fig. 34.21 has a *positive* value of R. This may seem inconsistent, but it isn't. The rule is that R is positive if the center of curvature C is on the outgoing side of the surface and negative if C is on the other side. For the convex reflecting surface in Fig. 34.16, R is negative because point C is to the right of the surface but outgoing rays are to the left. For the convex refracting surface in Fig. 34.21, R is positive because both C and the outgoing rays are to the right of the surface.

Refraction at a curved surface is one reason gardeners avoid watering plants at midday. As sunlight enters a water drop resting on a leaf (Fig. 34.23), the light rays are refracted toward each other as in Figs. 34.21 and 34.22. The sunlight that strikes the leaf is therefore more concentrated and able to cause damage.

An important special case of a spherical refracting surface is a *plane* surface between two optical materials. This corresponds to setting $R = \infty$ in Eq. (34.11). In this case,

$$\frac{n_a}{s} + \frac{n_b}{s'} = 0 \quad \text{(plane refracting surface)} \tag{34.13}$$

To find the lateral magnification m for this case, we combine this equation with the general relationship, Eq. (34.12), obtaining the simple result

$$m = 1$$

That is, the image formed by a *plane* refracting surface always has the same lateral size as the object, and it is always erect.

An example of image formation by a plane refracting surface is the appearance of a partly submerged drinking straw or canoe paddle. When viewed from some angles, the object appears to have a sharp bend at the water surface because the submerged part appears to be only about three-quarters of its actual distance below the surface. (We commented on the appearance of a submerged object in Section 33.2; see Fig. 33.9.)

34.23 Light rays refract as they pass through the curved surfaces of these water droplets.

Example 34.5 Image formation by refraction I

A cylindrical glass rod (Fig. 34.24) has index of refraction 1.52. It is surrounded by air. One end is ground to a hemispherical surface with radius $R = 2.00$ cm. A small object is placed on the axis of the rod, 8.00 cm to the left of the vertex. Find (a) the image distance and (b) the lateral magnification.

SOLUTION

IDENTIFY and SET UP: This problem uses the ideas of refraction at a curved surface. Our target variables are the image distance s' and the lateral magnification m. Here material a is air ($n_a = 1.00$) and material b is the glass of which the rod is made ($n_b = 1.52$). We are given $s = 8.00$ cm. The center of curvature of the spherical surface is on the outgoing side of the surface, so the radius is positive: $R = +2.00$ cm. We solve Eq. (34.11) for s', and we use Eq. (34.12) to find m.

34.24 The glass rod in air forms a real image.

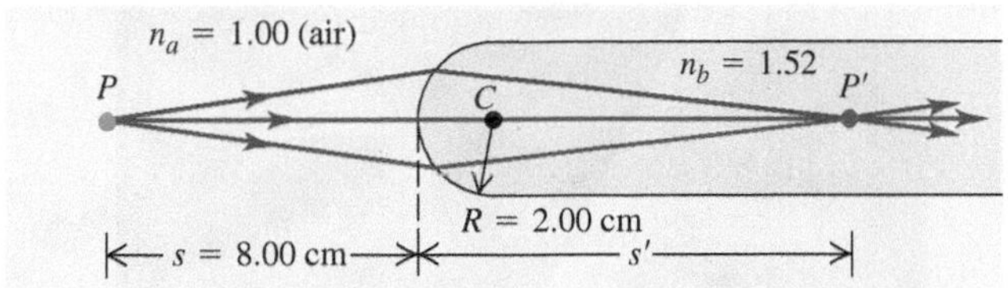

EXECUTE: (a) From Eq. (34.11),

$$\frac{1.00}{8.00 \text{ cm}} + \frac{1.52}{s'} = \frac{1.52 - 1.00}{+2.00 \text{ cm}}$$

$$s' = +11.3 \text{ cm}$$

(b) From Eq. (34.12),

$$m = -\frac{n_a s'}{n_b s} = -\frac{(1.00)(11.3 \text{ cm})}{(1.52)(8.00 \text{ cm})} = -0.929$$

EVALUATE: Because the image distance s' is positive, the image is formed 11.3 cm to the *right* of the vertex (on the outgoing side), as Fig. 34.24 shows. The value of m tells us that the image is somewhat smaller than the object and that it is inverted. If the object is an arrow 1.000 mm high, pointing upward, the image is an arrow 0.929 mm high, pointing downward.

Example 34.6 Image formation by refraction II

The glass rod of Example 34.5 is immersed in water, which has index of refraction $n = 1.33$ (Fig. 34.25). The object distance is again 8.00 cm. Find the image distance and lateral magnification.

SOLUTION

IDENTIFY and SET UP: The situation is the same as in Example 34.5 except that now $n_a = 1.33$. We again use Eqs. (34.11) and (34.12) to determine s' and m, respectively.

EXECUTE: Our solution of Eq. (34.11) in Example 34.5 yields

$$\frac{1.33}{8.00 \text{ cm}} + \frac{1.52}{s'} = \frac{1.52 - 1.33}{+2.00 \text{ cm}}$$

$$s' = -21.3 \text{ cm}$$

Continued

34.25 When immersed in water, the glass rod forms a virtual image.

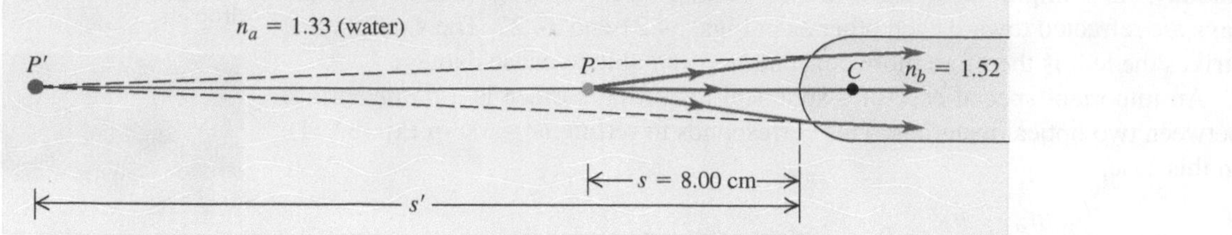

The lateral magnification in this case is

$$m = -\frac{(1.33)(-21.3 \text{ cm})}{(1.52)(8.00 \text{ cm})} = +2.33$$

EVALUATE: The negative value of s' means that the refracted rays do not converge, but appear to diverge from a point 21.3 cm to the *left* of the vertex. We saw a similar case in the reflection of light from a convex mirror; in both cases we call the result a *virtual image*. The vertical image is erect (because m is positive) and 2.33 times as large as the object.

Example 34.7 Apparent depth of a swimming pool

If you look straight down into a swimming pool where it is 2.00 m deep, how deep does it appear to be?

SOLUTION

IDENTIFY and SET UP: Figure 34.26 shows the situation. The surface of the water acts as a plane refracting surface. To determine the pool's apparent depth, we imagine an arrow PQ painted on the bottom. The pool's refracting surface forms a virtual image $P'Q'$ of this arrow. We solve Eq. (34.13) to find the image depth s'; that's the pool's apparent depth.

EXECUTE: The object distance is the actual depth of the pool, $s = 2.00$ m. Material a is water ($n_a = 1.33$) and material b is air ($n_b = 1.00$). From Eq. (34.13),

$$\frac{n_a}{s} + \frac{n_b}{s'} = \frac{1.33}{2.00 \text{ m}} + \frac{1.00}{s'} = 0$$

$$s' = -1.50 \text{ m}$$

The image distance is negative. By the sign rules in Section 34.1, this means that the image is virtual and on the incoming side of the refracting surface—that is, on the same side as the object, namely underwater. The pool's apparent depth is 1.50 m, or just 75% of its true depth.

EVALUATE: Recall that the lateral magnification for a plane refracting surface is $m = 1$. Hence the image $P'Q'$ of the arrow has the same *horizontal length* as the actual arrow PQ (Fig. 34.27). Only its depth is different from that of PQ.

34.26 Arrow $P'Q'$ is the virtual image of the underwater arrow PQ. The angles of the ray with the vertical are exaggerated for clarity.

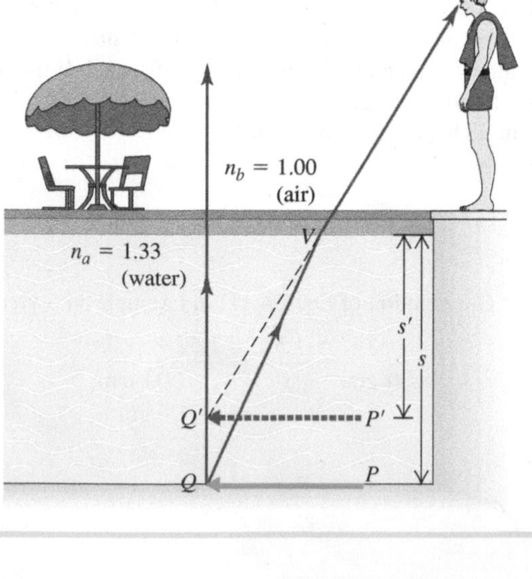

34.27 The submerged portion of this straw appears to be at a shallower depth (closer to the surface) than it actually is.

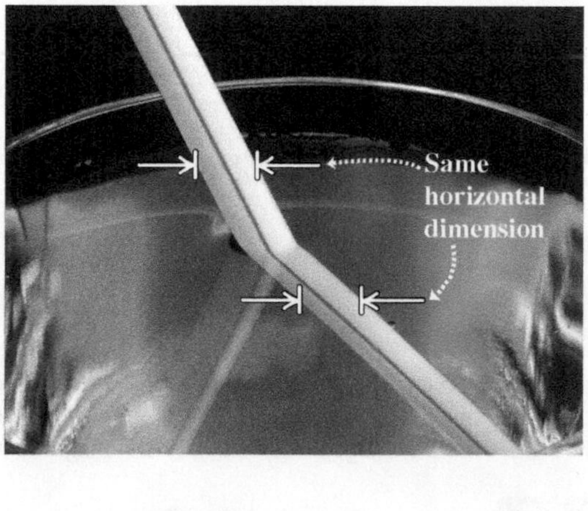

Test Your Understanding of Section 34.3 The water droplets in Fig. 34.23 have radius of curvature R and index of refraction $n = 1.33$. Can they form an image of the sun on the leaf?

34.4 Thin Lenses

The most familiar and widely used optical device (after the plane mirror) is the *lens.* A lens is an optical system with two refracting surfaces. The simplest lens has two *spherical* surfaces close enough together that we can neglect the distance between them (the thickness of the lens); we call this a **thin lens.** If you wear eyeglasses or contact lenses while reading, you are viewing these words through a pair of thin lenses. We can analyze thin lenses in detail using the results of Section 34.3 for refraction by a single spherical surface. However, we postpone this analysis until later in the section so that we can first discuss the properties of thin lenses.

Properties of a Lens

A lens of the shape shown in Fig. 34.28 has the property that when a beam of rays parallel to the axis passes through the lens, the rays converge to a point F_2 (Fig. 34.28a) and form a real image at that point. Such a lens is called a **converging lens.** Similarly, rays passing through point F_1 emerge from the lens as a beam of parallel rays (Fig. 34.28b). The points F_1 and F_2 are called the first and second *focal points,* and the distance f (measured from the center of the lens) is called the *focal length.* Note the similarities between the two focal points of a converging lens and the single focal point of a concave mirror (see Fig. 34.13). As for a concave mirror, the focal length of a converging lens is defined to be a *positive* quantity, and such a lens is also called a *positive lens.*

The central horizontal line in Fig. 34.28 is called the *optic axis,* as with spherical mirrors. The centers of curvature of the two spherical surfaces lie on and define the optic axis. The two focal lengths in Fig. 34.28, both labeled f, *are always equal* for a thin lens, even when the two sides have different curvatures. We will derive this somewhat surprising result later in the section, when we derive the relationship of f to the index of refraction of the lens and the radii of curvature of its surfaces.

34.28 F_1 and F_2 are the first and second focal points of a converging thin lens. The numerical value of f is positive.

(a)

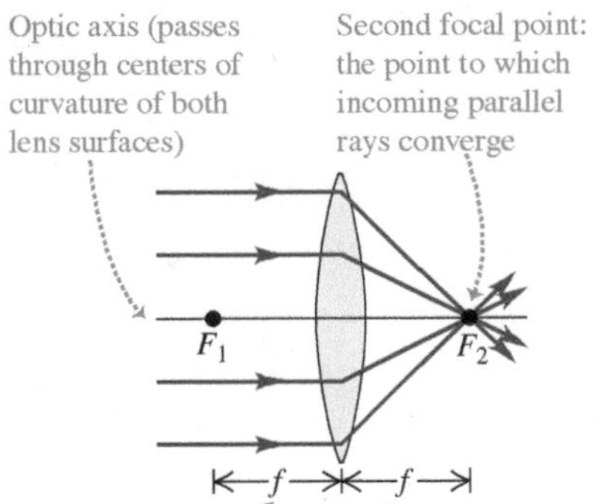

(b)

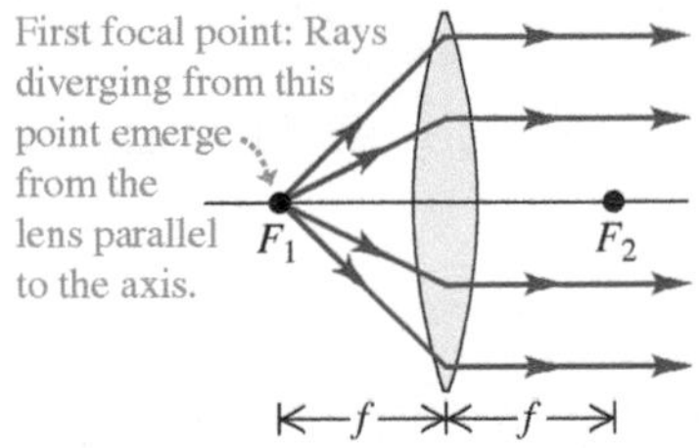

Image of an Extended Object: Converging Lens

Like a concave mirror, a converging lens can form an image of an extended object. Figure 34.29 shows how to find the position and lateral magnification of an image made by a thin converging lens. Using the same notation and sign rules as before, we let s and s' be the object and image distances, respectively, and let y and y' be the object and image heights. Ray QA, parallel to the optic axis before refraction, passes through the second focal point F_2 after refraction. Ray QOQ' passes undeflected straight through the center of the lens because at the center the two surfaces are parallel and (we have assumed) very close together. There is refraction where the ray enters and leaves the material but no net change in direction.

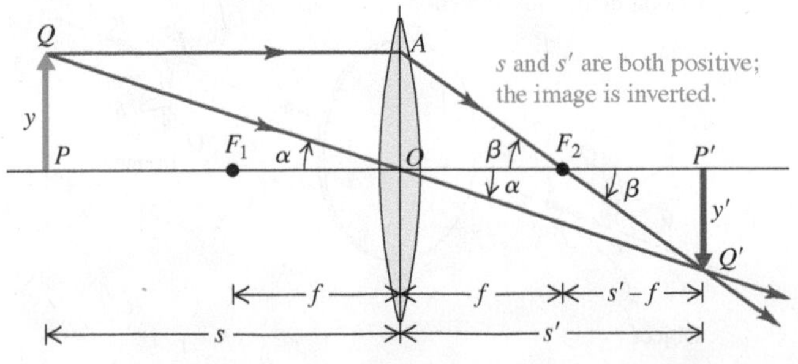

34.29 Construction used to find image position for a thin lens. To emphasize that the lens is assumed to be very thin, the ray QAQ' is shown as bent at the midplane of the lens rather than at the two surfaces and ray QOQ' is shown as a straight line.

The two angles labeled α in Fig. 34.29 are equal. Therefore the two right triangles PQO and $P'Q'O$ are *similar,* and ratios of corresponding sides are equal. Thus

$$\frac{y}{s} = -\frac{y'}{s'} \quad \text{or} \quad \frac{y'}{y} = -\frac{s'}{s} \tag{34.14}$$

(The reason for the negative sign is that the image is below the optic axis and y' is negative.) Also, the two angles labeled β are equal, and the two right triangles OAF_2 and $P'Q'F_2$ are similar, so

$$\frac{y}{f} = -\frac{y'}{s' - f} \quad \text{or}$$

$$\frac{y'}{y} = -\frac{s' - f}{f} \tag{34.15}$$

We now equate Eqs. (34.14) and (34.15), divide by s', and rearrange to obtain

$$\frac{1}{s} + \frac{1}{s'} = \frac{1}{f} \quad \text{(object–image relationship, thin lens)} \tag{34.16}$$

This analysis also gives the lateral magnification $m = y'/y$ for the lens; from Eq. (34.14),

$$m = -\frac{s'}{s} \quad \text{(lateral magnification, thin lens)} \tag{34.17}$$

The negative sign tells us that when s and s' are both positive, as in Fig. 34.29, the image is *inverted,* and y and y' have opposite signs.

Equations (34.16) and (34.17) are the basic equations for thin lenses. They are *exactly* the same as the corresponding equations for spherical mirrors, Eqs. (34.6) and (34.7). As we will see, the same sign rules that we used for spherical mirrors are also applicable to lenses. In particular, consider a lens with a positive focal length (a converging lens). When an object is outside the first focal point F_1 of this lens (that is, when $s > f$), the image distance s' is positive (that is, the image is on the same side as the outgoing rays); this image is real and inverted, as in Fig. 34.29. An object placed inside the first focal point of a converging lens, so that $s < f$, produces an image with a negative value of s'; this image is located on the same side of the lens as the object and is virtual, erect, and larger than the object. You can verify these statements algebraically using Eqs. (34.16) and (34.17); we'll also verify them in the next section, using graphical methods analogous to those introduced for mirrors in Section 34.2.

Figure 34.30 shows how a lens forms a three-dimensional image of a three-dimensional object. Point R is nearer the lens than point P. From Eq. (34.16), image point R' is farther from the lens than is image point P', and the image $P'R'$

34.30 The image $S'P'Q'R'$ of a three-dimensional object $SPQR$ is not reversed by a lens.

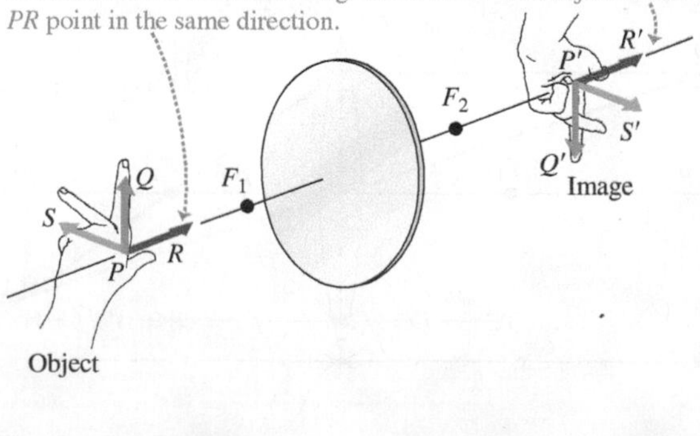

points in the same direction as the object PR. Arrows $P'S'$ and $P'Q'$ are reversed relative to PS and PQ.

Let's compare Fig. 34.30 with Fig. 34.7, which shows the image formed by a plane *mirror.* We note that the image formed by the lens is inverted, but it is *not* reversed front to back along the optic axis. That is, if the object is a left hand, its image is also a left hand. You can verify this by pointing your left thumb along PR, your left forefinger along PQ, and your left middle finger along PS. Then rotate your hand 180°, using your thumb as an axis; this brings the fingers into coincidence with $P'Q'$ and $P'S'$. In other words, an *inverted* image is equivalent to an image that has been rotated by 180° about the lens axis.

Diverging Lenses

So far we have been discussing *converging* lenses. Figure 34.31 shows a **diverging lens;** the beam of parallel rays incident on this lens *diverges* after refraction. The focal length of a diverging lens is a negative quantity, and the lens is also called a *negative lens.* The focal points of a negative lens are reversed, relative to those of a positive lens. The second focal point, F_2, of a negative lens is the point from which rays that are originally parallel to the axis *appear to diverge* after refraction, as in Fig. 34.31a. Incident rays converging toward the first focal point F_1, as in Fig. 34.31b, emerge from the lens parallel to its axis. Comparing with Section 34.2, you can see that a diverging lens has the same relationship to a converging lens as a convex mirror has to a concave mirror.

Equations (34.16) and (34.17) apply to *both* positive and negative lenses. Figure 34.32 shows various types of lenses, both converging and diverging. Here's an important observation: *Any lens that is thicker at its center than at its edges is a converging lens with positive f; and any lens that is thicker at its edges than at its center is a diverging lens with negative f* (provided that the lens has a greater index of refraction than the surrounding material). We can prove this using the *lensmaker's equation,* which it is our next task to derive.

34.31 F_2 and F_1 are the second and first focal points of a diverging thin lens, respectively. The numerical value of f is negative.

(a)

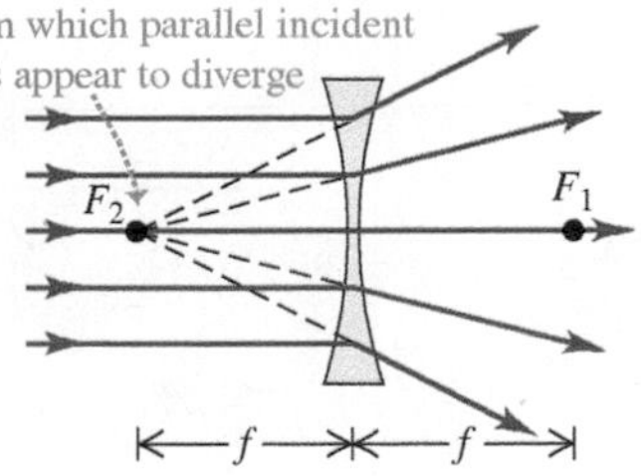

(b)

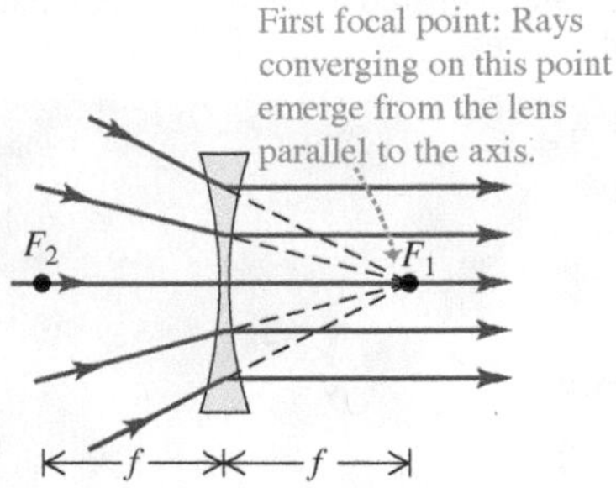

34.32 Various types of lenses.

(a) **Converging lenses**

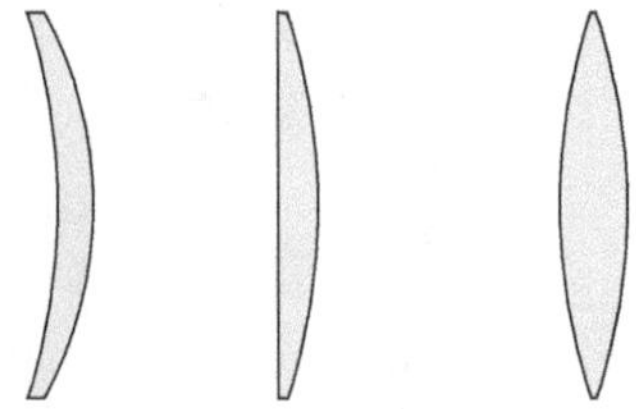

(b) **Diverging lenses**

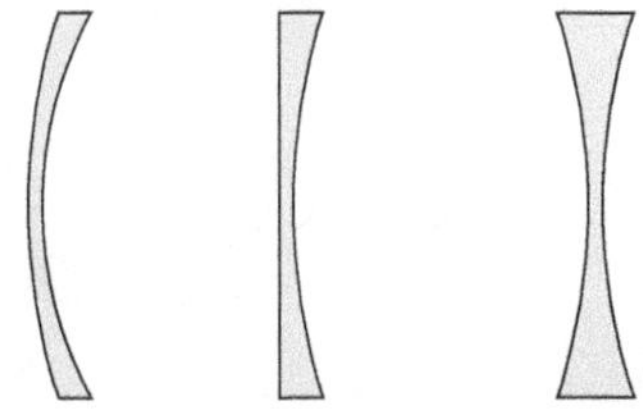

The Lensmaker's Equation

We'll now derive Eq. (34.16) in more detail and at the same time derive the *lensmaker's equation,* which is a relationship among the focal length f, the index of refraction n of the lens, and the radii of curvature R_1 and R_2 of the lens surfaces. We use the principle that an image formed by one reflecting or refracting surface can serve as the object for a second reflecting or refracting surface.

We begin with the somewhat more general problem of two spherical interfaces separating three materials with indexes of refraction n_a, n_b, and n_c, as shown in Fig. 34.33. The object and image distances for the first surface are s_1 and s'_1, and those for the second surface are s_2 and s'_2. We assume that the lens is thin, so that the distance t between the two surfaces is small in comparison with the object and image distances and can therefore be neglected. This is usually the case with eyeglass lenses (Fig. 34.34). Then s_2 and s'_1 have the same magnitude but opposite sign. For example, if the first image is on the outgoing side of the first surface, s'_1 is positive. But when viewed as an object for the second surface, the first image is *not* on the incoming side of that surface. So we can say that $s_2 = -s'_1$.

We need to use the single-surface equation, Eq. (34.11), twice, once for each surface. The two resulting equations are

$$\frac{n_a}{s_1} + \frac{n_b}{s'_1} = \frac{n_b - n_a}{R_1}$$

$$\frac{n_b}{s_2} + \frac{n_c}{s'_2} = \frac{n_c - n_b}{R_2}$$

Ordinarily, the first and third materials are air or vacuum, so we set $n_a = n_c = 1$. The second index n_b is that of the lens, which we can call simply n. Substituting these values and the relationship $s_2 = -s'_1$, we get

34.33 The image formed by the first surface of a lens serves as the object for the second surface. The distances s'_1 and s_2 are taken to be equal; this is a good approximation if the lens thickness t is small.

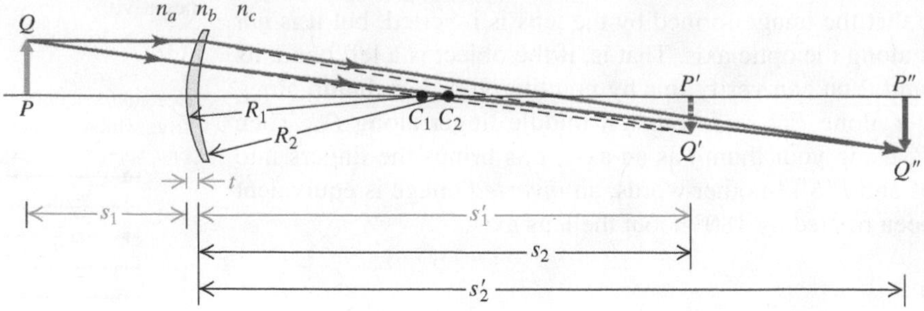

34.34 These eyeglass lenses satisfy the thin-lens approximation: Their thickness is small compared to the object and image distances.

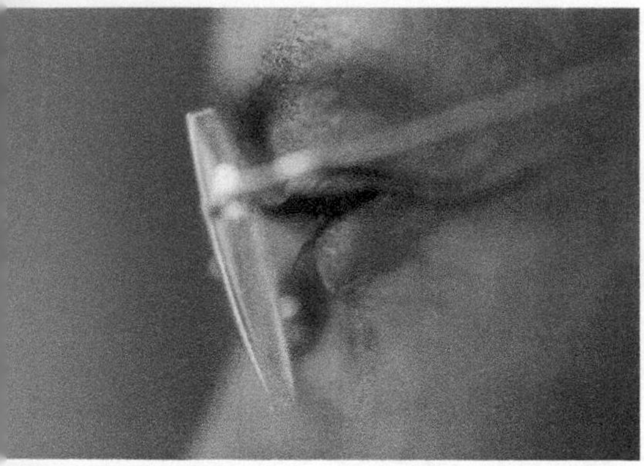

$$\frac{1}{s_1} + \frac{n}{s'_1} = \frac{n-1}{R_1}$$

$$-\frac{n}{s'_1} + \frac{1}{s'_2} = \frac{1-n}{R_2}$$

To get a relationship between the initial object position s_1 and the final image position s'_2, we add these two equations. This eliminates the term n/s'_1, and we obtain

$$\frac{1}{s_1} + \frac{1}{s'_2} = (n-1)\left(\frac{1}{R_1} - \frac{1}{R_2}\right)$$

Finally, thinking of the lens as a single unit, we call the object distance simply s instead of s_1, and we call the final image distance s' instead of s'_2. Making these substitutions, we have

$$\frac{1}{s} + \frac{1}{s'} = (n-1)\left(\frac{1}{R_1} - \frac{1}{R_2}\right) \quad (34.18)$$

Now we compare this with the other thin-lens equation, Eq. (34.16). We see that the object and image distances s and s' appear in exactly the same places in both equations and that the focal length f is given by

$$\frac{1}{f} = (n-1)\left(\frac{1}{R_1} - \frac{1}{R_2}\right) \quad \text{(lensmaker's equation for a thin lens)} \quad (34.19)$$

This is the **lensmaker's equation.** In the process of rederiving the relationship among object distance, image distance, and focal length for a thin lens, we have also derived an expression for the focal length f of a lens in terms of its index of refraction n and the radii of curvature R_1 and R_2 of its surfaces. This can be used to show that all the lenses in Fig. 34.32a are converging lenses with positive focal lengths and that all the lenses in Fig. 34.32b are diverging lenses with negative focal lengths.

We use all our sign rules from Section 34.1 with Eqs. (34.18) and (34.19). For example, in Fig. 34.35, s, s', and R_1 are positive, but R_2 is negative.

It is not hard to generalize Eq. (34.19) to the situation in which the lens is immersed in a material with an index of refraction greater than unity. We invite you to work out the lensmaker's equation for this more general situation.

We stress that the paraxial approximation is indeed an approximation! Rays that are at sufficiently large angles to the optic axis of a spherical lens will not be brought to the same focus as paraxial rays; this is the same problem of spherical aberration that plagues spherical *mirrors* (see Section 34.2). To avoid this and other limitations of thin spherical lenses, lenses of more complicated shape are used in precision optical instruments.

34.35 A converging thin lens with a positive focal length f.

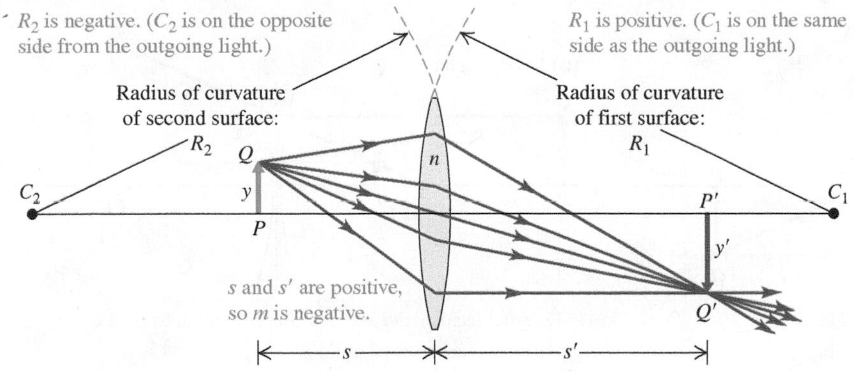

Example 34.8 Determining the focal length of a lens

(a) Suppose the absolute values of the radii of curvature of the lens surfaces in Fig. 34.35 are both equal to 10 cm and the index of refraction of the glass is $n = 1.52$. What is the focal length f of the lens? (b) Suppose the lens in Fig. 34.31 also has $n = 1.52$ and the absolute values of the radii of curvature of its lens surfaces are also both equal to 10 cm. What is the focal length of this lens?

SOLUTION

IDENTIFY and SET UP: We are asked to find the focal length f of (a) a lens that is convex on both sides (Fig. 34.35) and (b) a lens that is concave on both sides (Fig. 34.31). In both cases we solve the lensmaker's equation, Eq. (34.19), to determine f. We apply the sign rules given in Section 34.1 to the radii of curvature R_1 and R_2 to take account of whether the surfaces are convex or concave.

EXECUTE: (a) The lens in Fig. 34.35 is *double convex:* The center of curvature of the first surface (C_1) is on the outgoing side of the lens, so R_1 is positive, and the center of curvature of the second surface (C_2) is on the *incoming* side, so R_2 is negative. Hence $R_1 = +10$ cm and $R_2 = -10$ cm. Then from Eq. (34.19),

$$\frac{1}{f} = (1.52 - 1)\left(\frac{1}{+10\text{ cm}} - \frac{1}{-10\text{ cm}}\right)$$

$$f = 9.6\text{ cm}$$

(b) The lens in Fig. 34.31 is *double concave:* The center of curvature of the first surface is on the *incoming* side, so R_1 is negative, and the center of curvature of the second surface is on the outgoing side, so R_2 is positive. Hence in this case $R_1 = -10$ cm and $R_2 = +10$ cm. Again using Eq. (34.19),

$$\frac{1}{f} = (1.52 - 1)\left(\frac{1}{-10\text{ cm}} - \frac{1}{+10\text{ cm}}\right)$$

$$f = -9.6\text{ cm}$$

EVALUATE: In part (a) the focal length is *positive,* so this is a converging lens; this makes sense, since the lens is thicker at its center than at its edges. In part (b) the focal length is *negative,* so this is a diverging lens; this also makes sense, since the lens is thicker at its edges than at its center.

Graphical Methods for Lenses

We can determine the position and size of an image formed by a thin lens by using a graphical method very similar to the one we used in Section 34.2 for spherical mirrors. Again we draw a few special rays called *principal rays* that diverge from a point of the object that is *not* on the optic axis. The intersection of these rays, after they pass through the lens, determines the position and size of the image. In using this graphical method, we will consider the entire deviation of a ray as occurring at the midplane of the lens, as shown in Fig. 34.36. This is consistent with the assumption that the distance between the lens surfaces is negligible.

The three principal rays whose paths are usually easy to trace for lenses are shown in Fig. 34.36:

1. *A ray parallel to the axis* emerges from the lens in a direction that passes through the second focal point F_2 of a converging lens, or appears to come from the second focal point of a diverging lens.
2. *A ray through the center of the lens* is not appreciably deviated; at the center of the lens the two surfaces are parallel, so this ray emerges at essentially the same angle at which it enters and along essentially the same line.
3. *A ray through (or proceeding toward) the first focal point F_1* emerges parallel to the axis.

34.36 The graphical method of locating an image formed by a thin lens. The colors of the rays are for identification only; they do not refer to specific colors of light. (Compare Fig. 34.19 for spherical mirrors.)

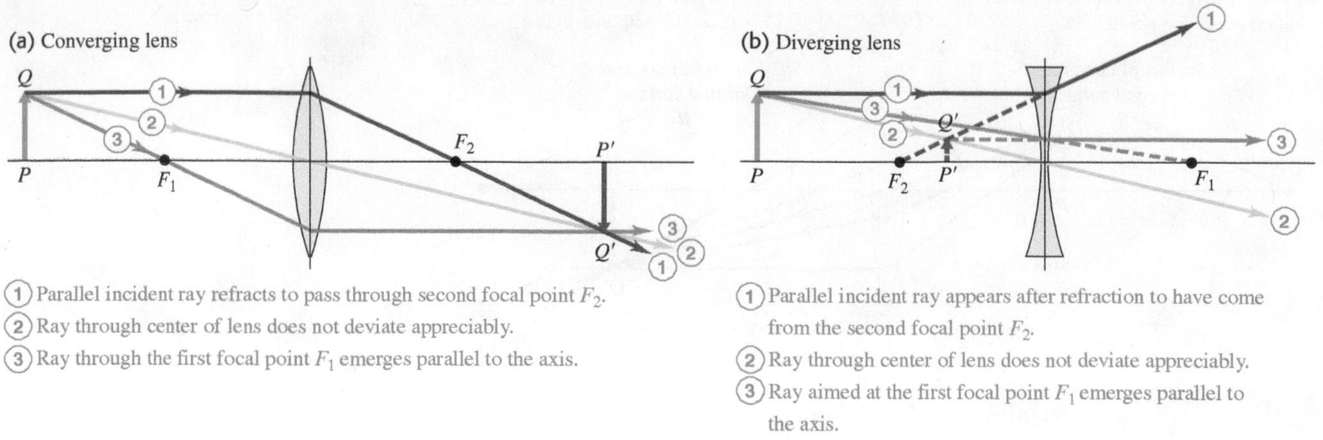

When the image is real, the position of the image point is determined by the intersection of any two rays 1, 2, and 3 (Fig. 34.36a). When the image is virtual, we extend the diverging outgoing rays backward to their intersection point to find the image point (Fig. 34.36b).

CAUTION **Principal rays are not the only rays** Keep in mind that *any* ray from the object that strikes the lens will pass through the image point (for a real image) or appear to originate from the image point (for a virtual image). (We made a similar comment about image formation by mirrors in Section 34.2.) We've emphasized the principal rays because they're the only ones you need to draw to locate the image.

Figure 34.37 shows principal-ray diagrams for a converging lens for several object distances. We suggest you study each of these diagrams very carefully, comparing each numbered ray with the above description.

34.37 Formation of images by a thin converging lens for various object distances. The principal rays are numbered. (Compare Fig. 34.20 for a concave spherical mirror.)

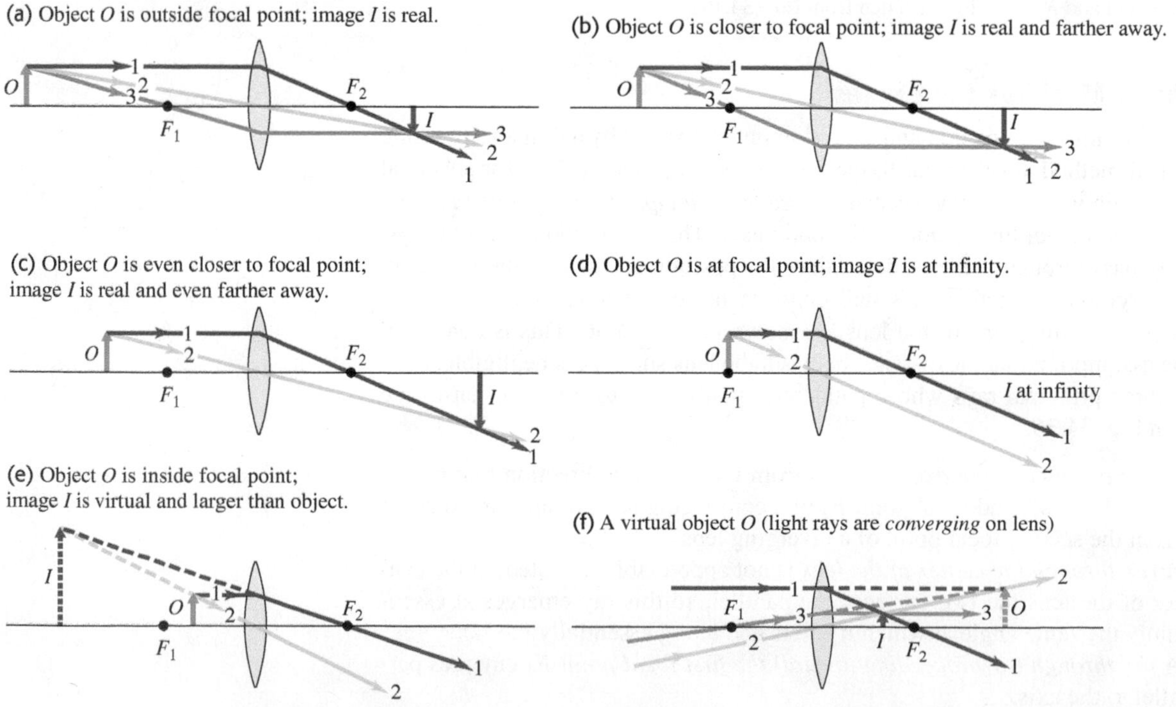

Parts (a), (b), and (c) of Fig. 34.37 help explain what happens in focusing a camera. For a photograph to be in sharp focus, the film must be at the position of the real image made by the camera's lens. The image distance increases as the object is brought closer, so the film is moved farther behind the lens (i.e., the lens is moved farther in front of the film). In Fig. 34.37d the object is at the focal point; ray 3 can't be drawn because it doesn't pass through the lens. In Fig. 34.37e the object distance is less than the focal length. The outgoing rays are divergent, and the image is *virtual;* its position is located by extending the outgoing rays backward, so the image distance s' is negative. Note also that the image is erect and larger than the object. (We'll see the usefulness of this in Section 34.6.) Figure 34.37f corresponds to a *virtual object.* The incoming rays do not diverge from a real object, but are *converging* as though they would meet at the tip of the virtual object O on the right side; the object distance s is negative in this case. The image is real and is located between the lens and the second focal point. This situation can arise if the rays that strike the lens in Fig. 34.37f emerge from another converging lens (not shown) to the left of the figure.

Problem-Solving Strategy 34.2 Image Formation by Thin Lenses

MP

IDENTIFY *the relevant concepts:* Review Problem-Solving Strategy 34.1 (Section 34.2) for mirrors, which is equally applicable here. As for mirrors, you should solve problems involving image formation by lenses using *both* principal-ray diagrams and equations.

SET UP *the problem:* Identify the target variables.

EXECUTE *the solution* as follows:

1. Draw a large principal-ray diagram if you have enough information, using graph paper or quadrille-ruled paper. Orient your diagram so that incoming rays go from left to right. Draw the rays with a ruler, and measure distances carefully.
2. Draw the principal rays so they change direction at the midplane of the lens, as in Fig. 34.36. For a lens there are only three principal rays (compared to four for a mirror). Draw all three whenever possible; the intersection of any two rays determines the image location, but the third ray should pass through the same point.
3. If the outgoing principal rays diverge, extend them backward to find the virtual image point on the *incoming* side of the lens, as in Fig. 34.27e.
4. Solve Eqs. (34.16) and (34.17), as appropriate, for the target variables. Make sure that you carefully use the sign rules given in Section 34.1.
5. The *image* from a first lens or mirror may serve as the *object* for a second lens or mirror. In finding the object and image distances for this intermediate image, be sure you include the distance between the two elements (lenses and/or mirrors) correctly.

EVALUATE *your answer:* Your calculated results must be consistent with your ray-diagram results. Check that they give the same image position and image size, and that they agree on whether the image is real or virtual.

Example 34.9 Image position and magnification with a converging lens

Use ray diagrams to find the image position and magnification for an object at each of the following distances from a converging lens with a focal length of 20 cm: (a) 50 cm; (b) 20 cm; (c) 15 cm; (d) −40 cm. Check your results by calculating the image position and lateral magnification using Eqs. (34.16) and (34.17), respectively.

SOLUTION

IDENTIFY and SET UP: We are given the focal length $f = 20\text{ cm}$ and four object distances s. Our target variables are the corresponding image distances s' and lateral magnifications m. We solve Eq. (34.16) for s', and find m from Eq. (34.17), $m = -s'/s$.

EXECUTE: Figures 34.37a, d, e, and f, respectively, show the appropriate principal-ray diagrams. You should be able to reproduce these without referring to the figures. Measuring these diagrams yields the approximate results: $s' = 35\text{ cm}$, $-\infty$, -40 cm, and 15 cm, and $m = -\frac{2}{3}$, $+\infty$, $+3$, and $+\frac{1}{3}$, respectively.

Calculating the image distances from Eq. (34.16), we find

$$\text{(a)}\ \frac{1}{50\text{ cm}} + \frac{1}{s'} = \frac{1}{20\text{ cm}} \qquad s' = 33.3\text{ cm}$$

$$\text{(b)}\ \frac{1}{20\text{ cm}} + \frac{1}{s'} = \frac{1}{20\text{ cm}} \qquad s' = \pm\infty$$

$$\text{(c)}\ \frac{1}{15\text{ cm}} + \frac{1}{s'} = \frac{1}{20\text{ cm}} \qquad s' = -60\text{ cm}$$

$$\text{(d)}\ \frac{1}{-40\text{ cm}} + \frac{1}{s'} = \frac{1}{20\text{ cm}} \qquad s' = 13.3\text{ cm}$$

The graphical results are fairly close to these except for part (c); the accuracy of the diagram in Fig. 34.37e is limited because the rays extended backward have nearly the same direction.

From Eq. (34.17),

$$\text{(a)}\ m = -\frac{33.3\text{ cm}}{50\text{ cm}} = -\tfrac{2}{3} \qquad \text{(b)}\ m = -\frac{\pm\infty\text{ cm}}{20\text{ cm}} = \pm\infty$$

$$\text{(c)}\ m = -\frac{-60\text{ cm}}{15\text{ cm}} = +4 \qquad \text{(d)}\ m = -\frac{13.3\text{ cm}}{-40\text{ cm}} = +\tfrac{1}{3}$$

Continued

EVALUATE: Note that the image distance s' is positive in parts (a) and (d) but negative in part (c). This makes sense: The image is real in parts (a) and (d) but virtual in part (c). The light rays that emerge from the lens in part (b) are parallel and never converge, so the image can be regarded as being at either $+\infty$ or $-\infty$.

The values of magnification m tell us that the image is inverted in part (a) and erect in parts (c) and (d), in agreement with the principal-ray diagrams. The infinite value of magnification in part (b) is another way of saying that the image is formed infinitely far away.

Example 34.10 Image formation by a diverging lens

A beam of parallel rays spreads out after passing through a thin diverging lens, as if the rays all came from a point 20.0 cm from the center of the lens. You want to use this lens to form an erect, virtual image that is $\frac{1}{3}$ the height of the object. (a) Where should the object be placed? Where will the image be? (b) Draw a principal-ray diagram.

SOLUTION

IDENTIFY and SET UP: The result with parallel rays shows that the focal length is $f = -20$ cm. We want the lateral magnification to be $m = +\frac{1}{3}$ (positive because the image is to be erect). Our target variables are the object distance s and the image distance s'. In part (a), we solve the magnification equation, Eq. (34.17), for s' in terms of s; we then use the object–image relationship, Eq. (34.16), to find s and s' individually.

EXECUTE: (a) From Eq. (34.17), $m = +\frac{1}{3} = -s'/s$, so $s' = -s/3$. We insert this result into Eq. (34.16) and solve for the object distance s:

$$\frac{1}{s} + \frac{1}{-s/3} = \frac{1}{s} - \frac{3}{s} = -\frac{2}{s} = \frac{1}{f}$$

$$s = -2f = -2(-20.0\text{ cm}) = 40.0\text{ cm}$$

The object should be 40.0 cm from the lens. The image distance will be

$$s' = -\frac{s}{3} = -\frac{40.0\text{ cm}}{3} = -13.3\text{ cm}$$

The image distance is negative, so the object and image are on the same side of the lens.

(b) Figure 34.38 is a principal-ray diagram for this problem, with the rays numbered as in Fig. 34.36b.

EVALUATE: You should be able to draw a principal-ray diagram like Fig. 34.38 without referring to the figure. From your diagram, you can confirm our results in part (a) for the object and image distances. You can also check our results for s and s' by substituting them back into Eq. (34.16).

34.38 Principal-ray diagram for an image formed by a thin diverging lens.

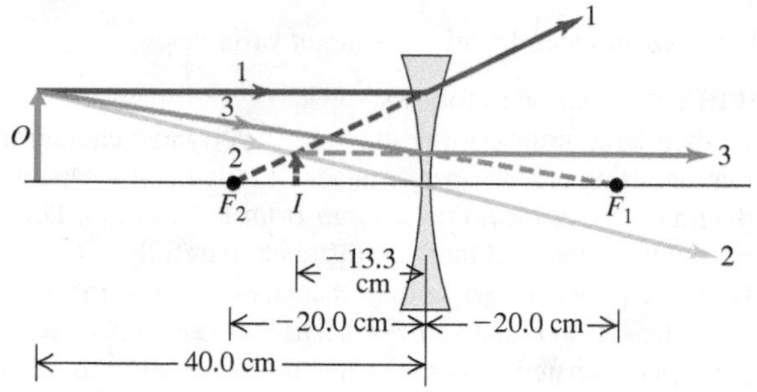

Example 34.11 An image of an image

Converging lenses A and B, of focal lengths 8.0 cm and 6.0 cm, respectively, are placed 36.0 cm apart. Both lenses have the same optic axis. An object 8.0 cm high is placed 12.0 cm to the left of lens A. Find the position, size, and orientation of the image produced by the lenses in combination. (Such combinations are used in telescopes and microscopes, to be discussed in Section 34.7.)

SOLUTION

IDENTIFY and SET UP: Figure 34.39 shows the situation. The object O lies outside the first focal point F_1 of lens A, which therefore produces a real image I. The light rays that strike lens B diverge from this real image just as if I was a material object; image I therefore acts as an *object* for lens B. Our goal is to determine the properties of the image I' made by lens B. We use both ray-diagram and computational methods to do this.

EXECUTE: In Fig. 34.39 we have drawn principal rays 1, 2, and 3 from the head of the object arrow O to find the position of the image I made by lens A, and principal rays 1′, 2′, and 3′ from the head of I to find the position of the image I' made by lens B (even though rays 2′ and 3′ don't actually exist in this case). The image is inverted *twice,* once by each lens, so the second image I' has the same orientation as the original object.

34.39 Principal-ray diagram for a combination of two converging lenses. The first lens (A) makes a real image of the object. This real image acts as an object for the second lens (B).

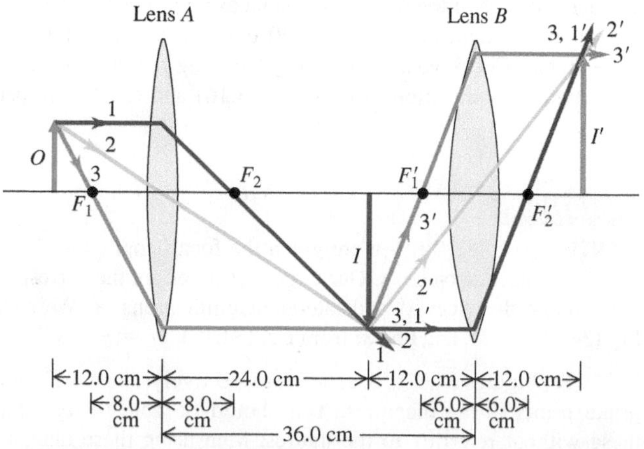

We first find the position and size of the first image I. Applying Eq. (34.16), $1/s + 1/s' = 1/f$, to lens A gives

$$\frac{1}{12.0\text{ cm}} + \frac{1}{s'_{I,A}} = \frac{1}{8.0\text{ cm}} \qquad s'_{I,A} = +24.0\text{ cm}$$

Image I is 24.0 cm to the right of lens A. The lateral magnification is $m_A = -(24.0\text{ cm})/(12.0\text{ cm}) = -2.00$, so image I is inverted and twice as tall as object O.

Image I is $36.0\text{ cm} - 24.0\text{ cm} = 12.0\text{ cm}$ to the left of lens B, so the object distance for lens B is $+12.0$ cm. Applying Eq. (34.16) to lens B then gives

$$\frac{1}{12.0\text{ cm}} + \frac{1}{s'_{I',B}} = \frac{1}{6.0\text{ cm}} \qquad s'_{I',B} = +12.0\text{ cm}$$

The final image I' is 12.0 cm to the right of lens B. The magnification produced by lens B is $m_B = -(12.0\text{ cm})/(12.0\text{ cm}) = -1.00$.

EVALUATE: The value of m_B means that the final image I' is just as large as the first image I but has the opposite orientation. The *overall* magnification is $m_A m_B = (-2.00)(-1.00) = +2.00$. Hence the final image I' is $(2.00)(8.0\text{ cm}) = 16$ cm tall and has the same orientation as the original object O, just as Fig. 34.39 shows.

Test Your Understanding of Section 34.4 A diverging lens and an object are positioned as shown in the figure at right. Which of the rays A, B, C, and D could emanate from point Q at the top of the object? ❙

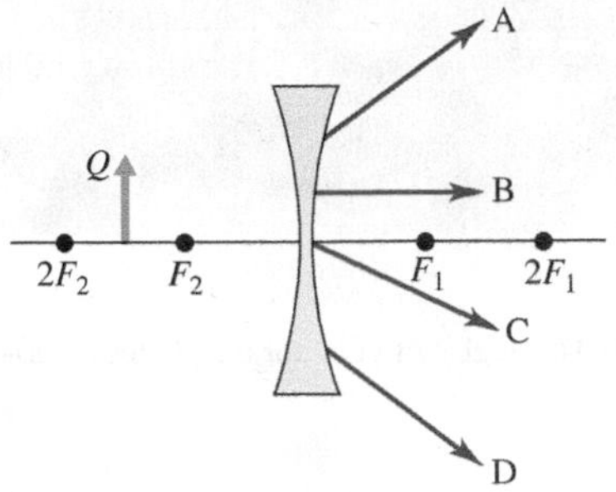

34.5 Cameras

The concept of *image,* which is so central to understanding simple mirror and lens systems, plays an equally important role in the analysis of optical instruments (also called *optical devices*). Among the most common optical devices are cameras, which make an image of an object and record it either electronically or on film.

The basic elements of a **camera** are a light-tight box ("camera" is a Latin word meaning "a room or enclosure"), a converging lens, a shutter to open the lens for a prescribed length of time, and a light-sensitive recording medium (Fig. 34.40). In a digital camera this is an electronic detector called a charge-coupled device (CCD) array; in an older camera, this is photographic film. The lens forms an inverted real image on the recording medium of the object being photographed. High-quality camera lenses have several elements, permitting partial correction of various *aberrations,* including the dependence of index of refraction on wavelength and the limitations imposed by the paraxial approximation.

When the camera is in proper *focus,* the position of the recording medium coincides with the position of the real image formed by the lens. The resulting photograph will then be as sharp as possible. With a converging lens, the image distance increases as the object distance decreases (see Figs. 34.41a, 34.41b, and 34.41c, and the discussion in Section 34.4). Hence in "focusing" the camera, we move the lens closer to the film for a distant object and farther from the film for a nearby object.

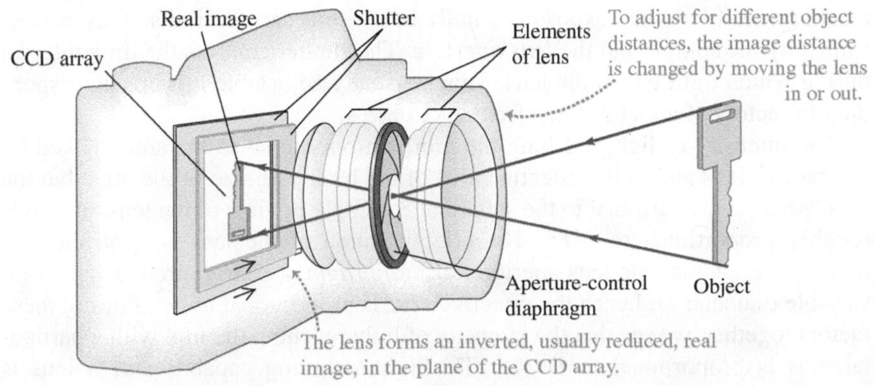

34.40 Key elements of a digital camera.

34.41 (a), (b), (c) Three photographs taken with the same camera from the same position in the Boston Public Garden using lenses with focal lengths $f = 28$ mm, 105 mm, and 300 mm. Increasing the focal length increases the image size proportionately. (d) The larger the value of f, the smaller the angle of view. The angles shown here are for a camera with image area 24 mm × 36 mm (corresponding to 35-mm film) and refer to the angle of view along the diagonal dimension of the film.

(a) $f = 28$ mm

(b) $f = 105$ mm

(c) $f = 300$ mm

(d) The angles of view for the photos in (a)–(c)

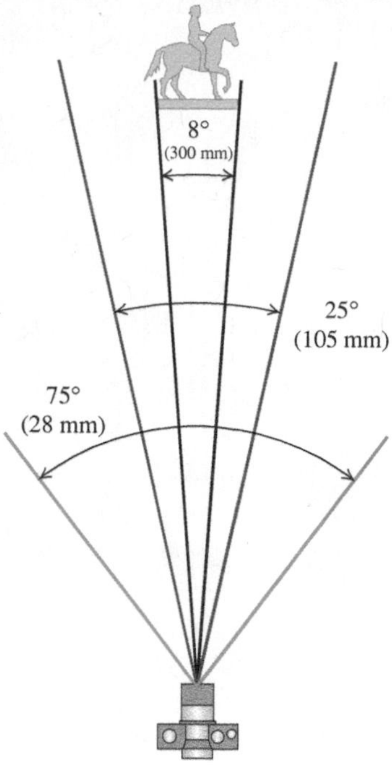

Camera Lenses: Focal Length

The choice of the focal length f for a camera lens depends on the film size and the desired angle of view. Figure 34.41 shows three photographs taken on 35-mm film with the same camera at the same position, but with lenses of different focal lengths. A lens of long focal length, called a *telephoto* lens, gives a small angle of view and a large image of a distant object (such as the statue in Fig. 34.41c); a lens of short focal length gives a small image and a wide angle of view (as in Fig. 34.41a) and is called a *wide-angle* lens. To understand this behavior, recall that the focal length is the distance from the lens to the image when the object is infinitely far away. In general, for *any* object distance, using a lens of longer focal length gives a greater image distance. This also increases the height of the image; as was discussed in Section 34.4, the ratio of the image height y' to the object height y (the *lateral magnification*) is equal in absolute value to the ratio of image distance s' to the object distance s [Eq. (34.17)]:

$$m = \frac{y'}{y} = -\frac{s'}{s}$$

With a lens of short focal length, the ratio s'/s is small, and a distant object gives only a small image. When a lens with a long focal length is used, the image of this same object may entirely cover the area of the film. Hence the longer the focal length, the narrower the angle of view (Fig. 34.41d).

Camera Lenses: f-Number

For the film to record the image properly, the total light energy per unit area reaching the film (the "exposure") must fall within certain limits. This is controlled by the *shutter* and the *lens aperture.* The shutter controls the time interval during which light enters the lens. This is usually adjustable in steps corresponding to factors of about 2, often from 1 s to $\frac{1}{1000}$ s.

The intensity of light reaching the film is proportional to the area viewed by the camera lens and to the effective area of the lens. The size of the area that the lens "sees" is proportional to the square of the angle of view of the lens, and so is roughly proportional to $1/f^2$. The effective area of the lens is controlled by means of an adjustable lens aperture, or *diaphragm,* a nearly circular hole with variable diameter D; hence the effective area is proportional to D^2. Putting these factors together, we see that the intensity of light reaching the film with a particular lens is proportional to D^2/f^2. The light-gathering capability of a lens is commonly expressed by photographers in terms of the ratio f/D, called the ***f*-number** of the lens:

$$f\text{-number} = \frac{\text{Focal length}}{\text{Aperture diameter}} = \frac{f}{D} \qquad (34.20)$$

For example, a lens with a focal length $f = 50$ mm and an aperture diameter $D = 25$ mm is said to have an f-number of 2, or "an aperture of $f/2$." The light intensity reaching the film is *inversely* proportional to the square of the f-number.

For a lens with a variable-diameter aperture, increasing the diameter by a factor of $\sqrt{2}$ changes the f-number by $1/\sqrt{2}$ and increases the intensity at the film by a factor of 2. Adjustable apertures usually have scales labeled with successive numbers (often called *f-stops)* related by factors of $\sqrt{2}$, such as

$$f/2 \quad f/2.8 \quad f/4 \quad f/5.6 \quad f/8 \quad f/11 \quad f/16$$

and so on. The larger numbers represent smaller apertures and exposures, and each step corresponds to a factor of 2 in intensity (Fig. 34.42). The actual *exposure* (total amount of light reaching the film) is proportional to both the aperture area and the time of exposure. Thus $f/4$ and $\frac{1}{500}$ s, $f/5.6$ and $\frac{1}{250}$ s, and $f/8$ and $\frac{1}{125}$ s all correspond to the same exposure.

Zoom Lenses and Projectors

Many photographers use a *zoom lens,* which is not a single lens but a complex collection of several lens elements that give a continuously variable focal length, often over a range as great as 10 to 1. Figures 34.43a and 34.43b show a simple system with variable focal length, and Fig. 34.43c shows a typical zoom lens for a single-lens reflex camera. Zoom lenses give a range of image sizes of a given object. It is an enormously complex problem in optical design to keep the image in focus and maintain a constant f-number while the focal length changes. When you vary the focal length of a typical zoom lens, two groups of elements move within the lens and a diaphragm opens and closes.

A *projector* for viewing slides, digital images, or motion pictures operates very much like a camera in reverse. In a movie projector, a lamp shines on the film, which acts as an object for the projection lens. The lens forms a real, enlarged, inverted image of the film on the projection screen. Because the image is inverted, the film goes through the projector upside down so that the image on the screen appears right-side up.

Application Inverting an Inverted Image
A camera lens makes an inverted image on the camera's light-sensitive electronic detector. The internal software of the camera then inverts the image again so it appears the right way around on the camera's display. A similar thing happens with your vision: The image formed on the retina of your eye is inverted, but your brain's "software" erects the image so you see the world right-side up.

34.42 A camera lens with an adjustable diaphragm.

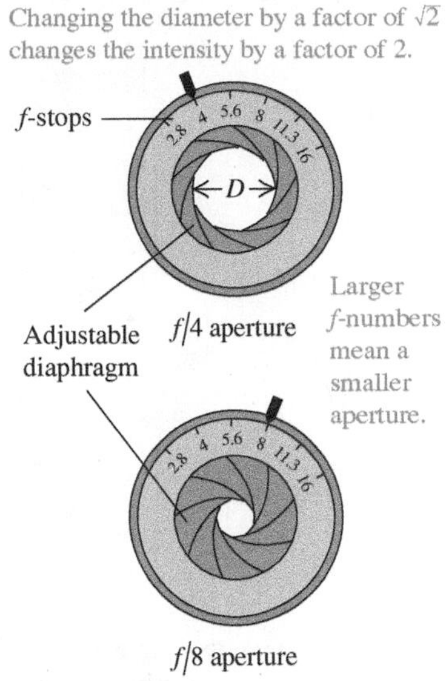

34.43 A simple zoom lens uses a converging lens and a diverging lens in tandem. (a) When the two lenses are close together, the combination behaves like a single lens of long focal length. (b) If the two lenses are moved farther apart, the combination behaves like a short-focal-length lens. (c) A typical zoom lens for a single-lens reflex camera, containing twelve elements arranged in four groups.

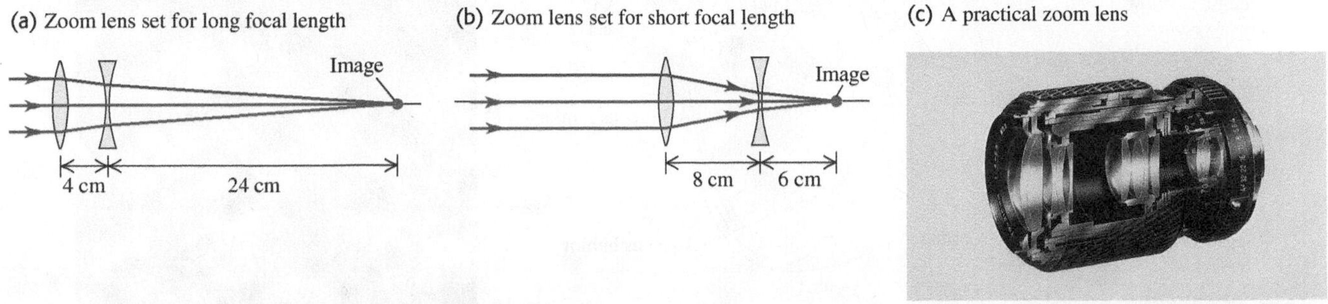

Example 34.12 Photographic exposures

A common telephoto lens for a 35-mm camera has a focal length of 200 mm; its f-stops range from $f/2.8$ to $f/22$. (a) What is the corresponding range of aperture diameters? (b) What is the corresponding range of image intensities on the film?

SOLUTION

IDENTIFY and SET UP: Part (a) of this problem uses the relationship among lens focal length f, aperture diameter D, and f-number. Part (b) uses the relationship between intensity and aperture diameter. We use Eq. (34.20) to relate D (the target variable) to the f-number and the focal length $f = 200$ mm. The intensity of the light reaching the film is proportional to D^2/f^2; since f is the same in each case, we conclude that the intensity in this case is proportional to D^2, the square of the aperture diameter.

EXECUTE: (a) From Eq. (34.20), the diameter ranges from

$$D = \frac{f}{f\text{-number}} = \frac{200\text{ mm}}{2.8} = 71\text{ mm}$$

to

$$D = \frac{200\text{ mm}}{22} = 9.1\text{ mm}$$

(b) Because the intensity is proportional to D^2, the ratio of the intensity at $f/2.8$ to the intensity at $f/22$ is

$$\left(\frac{71\text{ mm}}{9.1\text{ mm}}\right)^2 = \left(\frac{22}{2.8}\right)^2 = 62 \qquad (\text{about } 2^6)$$

EVALUATE: If the correct exposure time at $f/2.8$ is $\frac{1}{1000}$ s, then the exposure at $f/22$ is $(62)\left(\frac{1}{1000}\text{ s}\right) = \frac{1}{16}$ s to compensate for the lower intensity. In general, the smaller the aperture and the larger the f-number, the longer the required exposure. Nevertheless, many photographers prefer to use small apertures so that only the central part of the lens is used to make the image. This minimizes aberrations that occur near the edges of the lens and gives the sharpest possible image.

Test Your Understanding of Section 34.5 When used with 35-mm film (image area 24 mm × 36 mm), a lens with $f = 50$ mm gives a 45° angle of view and is called a "normal lens." When used with a CCD array that measures 5 mm × 5 mm, this same lens is (i) a wide-angle lens; (ii) a normal lens; (iii) a telephoto lens. ❙

MasteringPHYSICS

PhET: Color Vision

34.6 The Eye

The optical behavior of the eye is similar to that of a camera. The essential parts of the human eye, considered as an optical system, are shown in Fig. 34.44a. The eye is nearly spherical and about 2.5 cm in diameter. The front portion is somewhat more sharply curved and is covered by a tough, transparent membrane called the *cornea.* The region behind the cornea contains a liquid called the *aqueous humor.* Next comes the *crystalline lens,* a capsule containing a fibrous jelly, hard at the center and progressively softer at the outer portions. The crystalline lens is

34.44 (a) The eye. (b) There are two types of light-sensitive cells on the retina. The rods are more sensitive to light than the cones, but only the cones are sensitive to differences in color. A typical human eye contains about 1.3×10^8 rods and about 7×10^6 cones.

(a) Diagram of the eye

(b) Scanning electron micrograph showing retinal rods and cones in different colors

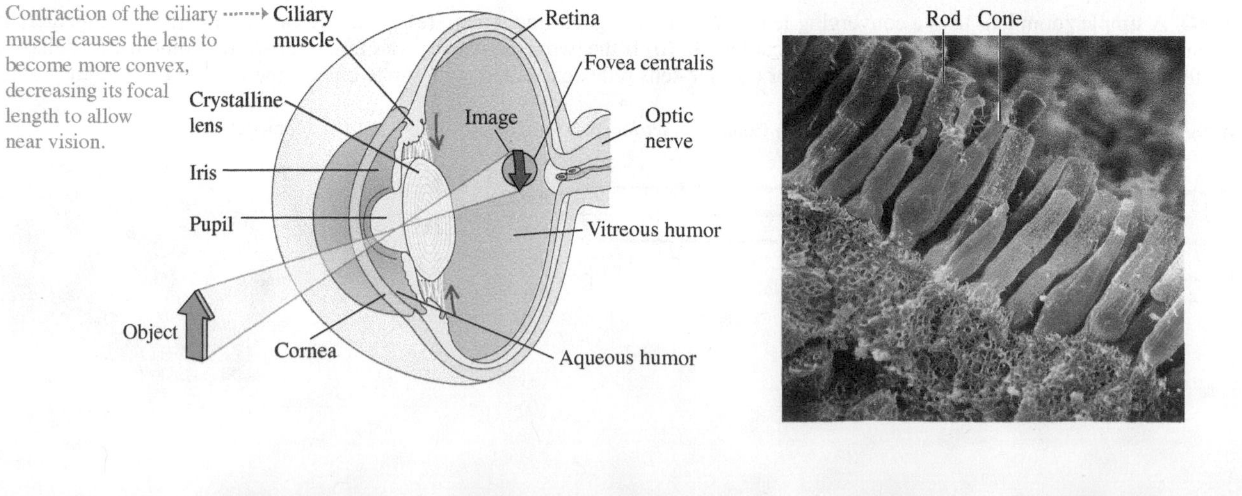

held in place by ligaments that attach it to the ciliary muscle, which encircles it. Behind the lens, the eye is filled with a thin watery jelly called the *vitreous humor.* The indexes of refraction of both the aqueous humor and the vitreous humor are about 1.336, nearly equal to that of water. The crystalline lens, while not homogeneous, has an average index of 1.437. This is not very different from the indexes of the aqueous and vitreous humors. As a result, most of the refraction of light entering the eye occurs at the outer surface of the cornea.

Refraction at the cornea and the surfaces of the lens produces a *real image* of the object being viewed. This image is formed on the light-sensitive *retina,* lining the rear inner surface of the eye. The retina plays the same role as the film in a camera. The *rods* and *cones* in the retina act like an array of miniature photocells (Fig. 34.44b); they sense the image and transmit it via the *optic nerve* to the brain. Vision is most acute in a small central region called the *fovea centralis,* about 0.25 mm in diameter.

In front of the lens is the *iris.* It contains an aperture with variable diameter called the *pupil,* which opens and closes to adapt to changing light intensity. The receptors of the retina also have intensity adaptation mechanisms.

For an object to be seen sharply, the image must be formed exactly at the location of the retina. The eye adjusts to different object distances s by changing the focal length f of its lens; the lens-to-retina distance, corresponding to s', does not change. (Contrast this with focusing a camera, in which the focal length is fixed and the lens-to-film distance is changed.) For the normal eye, an object at infinity is sharply focused when the ciliary muscle is relaxed. To permit sharp imaging on the retina of closer objects, the tension in the ciliary muscle surrounding the lens increases, the ciliary muscle contracts, the lens bulges, and the radii of curvature of its surfaces decrease; this decreases the focal length. This process is called *accommodation.*

The extremes of the range over which distinct vision is possible are known as the *far point* and the *near point* of the eye. The far point of a normal eye is at infinity. The position of the near point depends on the amount by which the ciliary muscle can increase the curvature of the crystalline lens. The range of accommodation gradually diminishes with age because the crystalline lens grows throughout a person's life (it is about 50% larger at age 60 than at age 20) and the ciliary muscles are less able to distort a larger lens. For this reason, the near point gradually recedes as one grows older. This recession of the near point is called *presbyopia.* Table 34.1 shows the approximate position of the near point for an average person at various ages. For example, an average person 50 years of age cannot focus on an object that is closer than about 40 cm.

Table 34.1 Receding of Near Point with Age

Age (years)	Near Point (cm)
10	7
20	10
30	14
40	22
50	40
60	200

34.45 Refractive errors for (a) a normal eye, (b) a myopic (nearsighted) eye, and (c) a hyperopic (farsighted) eye viewing a very distant object. The dashed blue curve indicates the required position of the retina.

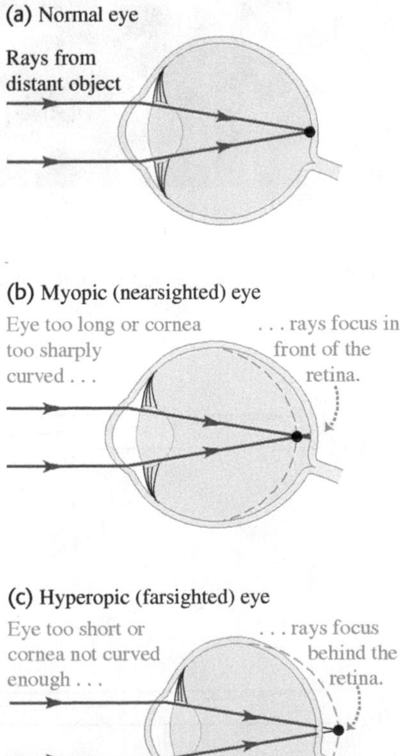

Defects of Vision

Several common defects of vision result from incorrect distance relationships in the eye. A normal eye forms an image on the retina of an object at infinity when the eye is relaxed (Fig. 34.45a). In the *myopic* (nearsighted) eye, the eyeball is too long from front to back in comparison with the radius of curvature of the cornea (or the cornea is too sharply curved), and rays from an object at infinity are focused in front of the retina (Fig. 34.45b). The most distant object for which an image can be formed on the retina is then nearer than infinity. In the *hyperopic* (farsighted) eye, the eyeball is too short or the cornea is not curved enough, and the image of an infinitely distant object is behind the retina (Fig. 34.45c). The myopic eye produces *too much* convergence in a parallel bundle of rays for an image to be formed on the retina; the hyperopic eye, *not enough* convergence.

All of these defects can be corrected by the use of corrective lenses (eyeglasses or contact lenses). The near point of either a presbyopic or a hyperopic eye is *farther* from the eye than normal. To see clearly an object at normal reading distance (often assumed to be 25 cm), we need a lens that forms a virtual image of the object at or beyond the near point. This can be accomplished by a

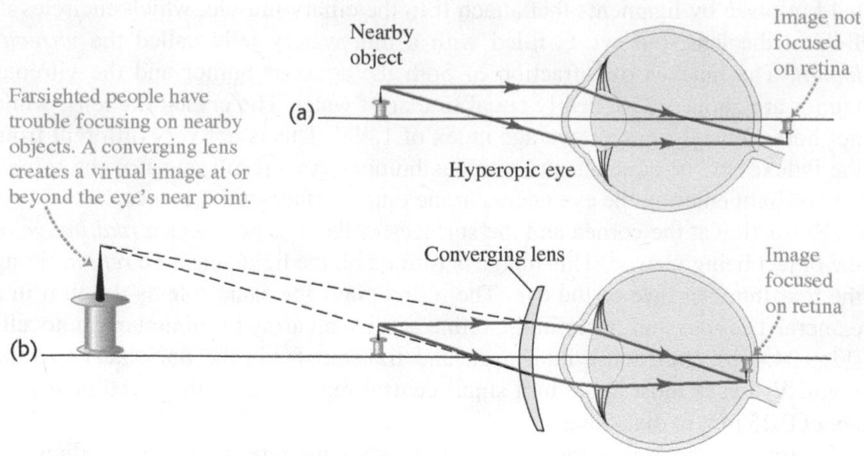

34.46 (a) An uncorrected hyperopic (farsighted) eye. (b) A positive (converging) lens gives the extra convergence needed for a hyperopic eye to focus the image on the retina.

Application Focusing in the Animal Kingdom
The crystalline lens and ciliary muscle found in humans and other mammals are among a number of focusing mechanisms used by animals. Birds can change the shape not only of their lens but also of the corneal surface. In aquatic animals the corneal surface is not very useful for focusing because its refractive index is close to that of water. Thus, focusing is accomplished entirely by the lens, which is nearly spherical. Fish focus by using a muscle to move the lens either inward or outward. Whales and dolphins achieve the same effect by filling or emptying a fluid chamber behind the lens to move the lens in or out.

converging (positive) lens, as shown in Fig. 34.46. In effect the lens moves the object farther away from the eye to a point where a sharp retinal image can be formed. Similarly, correcting the myopic eye involves using a diverging (negative) lens to move the image closer to the eye than the actual object, as shown in Fig. 34.47.

Astigmatism is a different type of defect in which the surface of the cornea is not spherical but rather more sharply curved in one plane than in another. As a result, horizontal lines may be imaged in a different plane from vertical lines (Fig. 34.48a). Astigmatism may make it impossible, for example, to focus clearly on both the horizontal and vertical bars of a window at the same time.

Astigmatism can be corrected by use of a lens with a *cylindrical* surface. For example, suppose the curvature of the cornea in a horizontal plane is correct to focus rays from infinity on the retina but the curvature in the vertical plane is too great to form a sharp retinal image. When a cylindrical lens with its axis horizontal is placed before the eye, the rays in a horizontal plane are unaffected, but the additional divergence of the rays in a vertical plane causes these to be sharply imaged on the retina (Fig. 34.48b).

Lenses for vision correction are usually described in terms of the **power,** defined as the reciprocal of the focal length expressed in meters. The unit of power is the **diopter.** Thus a lens with $f = 0.50$ m has a power of 2.0 diopters, $f = -0.25$ m corresponds to -4.0 diopters, and so on. The numbers on a prescription for glasses

34.47 (a) An uncorrected myopic (nearsighted) eye. (b) A negative (diverging) lens spreads the rays farther apart to compensate for the excessive convergence of the myopic eye.

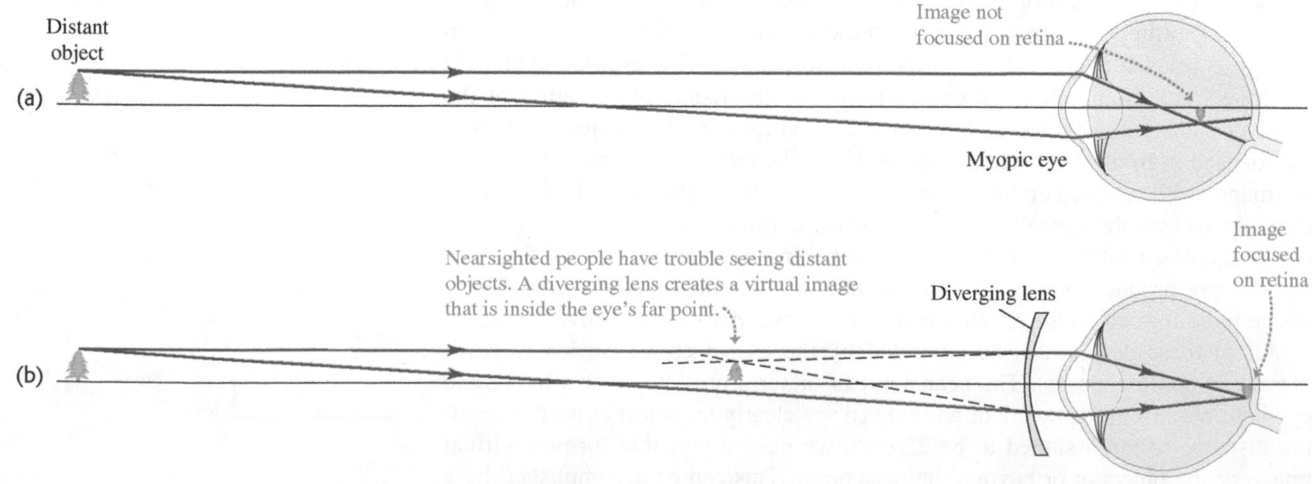

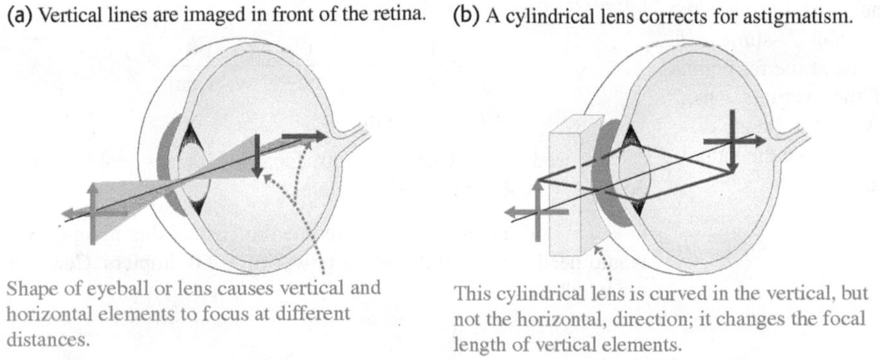

34.48 One type of astigmatism and how it is corrected.

are usually powers expressed in diopters. When the correction involves both astigmatism and myopia or hyperopia, there are three numbers: one for the spherical power, one for the cylindrical power, and an angle to describe the orientation of the cylinder axis.

Example 34.13 Correcting for farsightedness

The near point of a certain hyperopic eye is 100 cm in front of the eye. Find the focal length and power of the contact lens that will permit the wearer to see clearly an object that is 25 cm in front of the eye.

SOLUTION

IDENTIFY and SET UP: Figure 34.49 shows the situation. We want the lens to form a virtual image of the object at the near point of the eye, 100 cm from it. The contact lens (which we treat as having negligible thickness) is at the surface of the cornea, so the object distance is $s = 25$ cm. The virtual image is on the incoming side of the contact lens, so the image distance is $s' = -100$ cm. We use Eq. (34.16) to determine the required focal length f of the contact lens; the corresponding power is $1/f$.

EXECUTE: From Eq. (34.16),

$$\frac{1}{f} = \frac{1}{s} + \frac{1}{s'} = \frac{1}{+25\text{ cm}} + \frac{1}{-100\text{ cm}}$$

$$f = +33\text{ cm}$$

34.49 Using a contact lens to correct for farsightedness. For clarity, the eye and contact lens are shown much larger than the scale of the figure; the 2.5-cm diameter of the eye is actually much smaller than the focal length f of the contact lens.

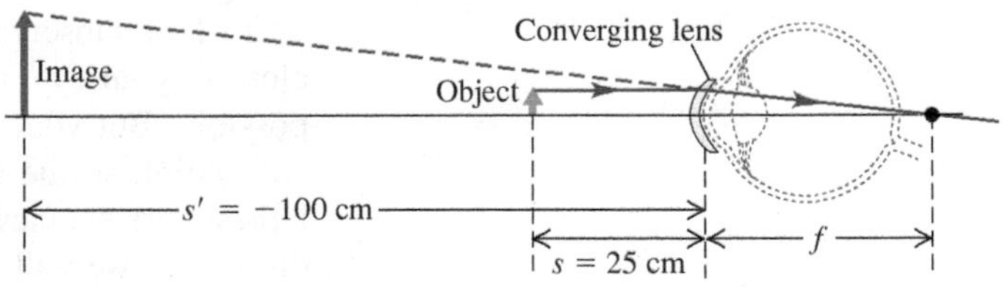

We need a converging lens with focal length $f = 33$ cm and power $1/(0.33\text{ m}) = +3.0$ diopters.

EVALUATE: In this example we used a contact lens to correct hyperopia. Had we used eyeglasses, we would have had to account for the separation between the eye and the eyeglass lens, and a somewhat different power would have been required (see Example 34.14).

Example 34.14 Correcting for nearsightedness

The far point of a certain myopic eye is 50 cm in front of the eye. Find the focal length and power of the eyeglass lens that will permit the wearer to see clearly an object at infinity. Assume that the lens is worn 2 cm in front of the eye.

SOLUTION

IDENTIFY and SET UP: Figure 34.50 shows the situation. The far point of a myopic eye is nearer than infinity. To see clearly objects

34.50 Using an eyeglass lens to correct for nearsightedness. For clarity, the eye and eyeglass lens are shown much larger than the scale of the figure.

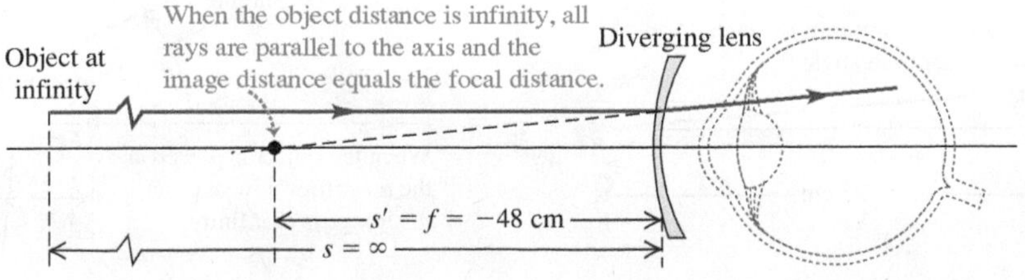

Continued

beyond the far point, we need a lens that forms a virtual image of such objects no farther from the eye than the far point. Assume that the virtual image of the object at infinity is formed at the far point, 50 cm in front of the eye (48 cm in front of the eyeglass lens). Then when the object distance is $s = \infty$, we want the image distance to be $s' = -48$ cm. As in Example 34.13, we use the values of s and s' to calculate the required focal length.

EXECUTE: From Eq. (34.16),

$$\frac{1}{f} = \frac{1}{s} + \frac{1}{s'} = \frac{1}{\infty} + \frac{1}{-48\text{ cm}}$$

$$f = -48\text{ cm}$$

We need a *diverging* lens with focal length $f = -48$ cm and power $1/(-0.48\text{ m}) = -2.1$ diopters.

EVALUATE: If a *contact* lens were used to correct this myopia, we would need $f = -50$ cm and a power of -2.0 diopters. Can you see why?

Test Your Understanding of Section 34.6 A certain eyeglass lens is thin at its center, even thinner at its top and bottom edges, and relatively thick at its left and right edges. What defects of vision is this lens intended to correct? (i) hyperopia for objects oriented both vertically and horizontally; (ii) myopia for objects oriented both vertically and horizontally; (iii) hyperopia for objects oriented vertically and myopia for objects oriented horizontally; (iv) hyperopia for objects oriented horizontally and myopia for objects oriented vertically.

34.7 The Magnifier

The apparent size of an object is determined by the size of its image on the retina. If the eye is unaided, this size depends on the *angle* θ subtended by the object at the eye, called its **angular size** (Fig. 34.51a).

To look closely at a small object, such as an insect or a crystal, you bring it close to your eye, making the subtended angle and the retinal image as large as possible. But your eye cannot focus sharply on objects that are closer than the near point, so the angular size of an object is greatest (that is, it subtends the largest possible viewing angle) when it is placed at the near point. In the following discussion we will assume an average viewer for whom the near point is 25 cm from the eye.

A converging lens can be used to form a virtual image that is larger and farther from the eye than the object itself, as shown in Fig. 34.51b. Then the object can be moved closer to the eye, and the angular size of the image may be substantially larger than the angular size of the object at 25 cm without the lens. A lens used in this way is called a **magnifier,** otherwise known as a *magnifying glass* or a *simple magnifier.* The virtual image is most comfortable to view when it is placed at infinity, so that the ciliary muscle of the eye is relaxed; this means that the object is placed at the focal point F_1 of the magnifier. In the following discussion we assume that this is done.

34.51 (a) The angular size θ is largest when the object is at the near point. (b) The magnifier gives a virtual image at infinity. This virtual image appears to the eye to be a real object subtending a larger angle θ' at the eye.

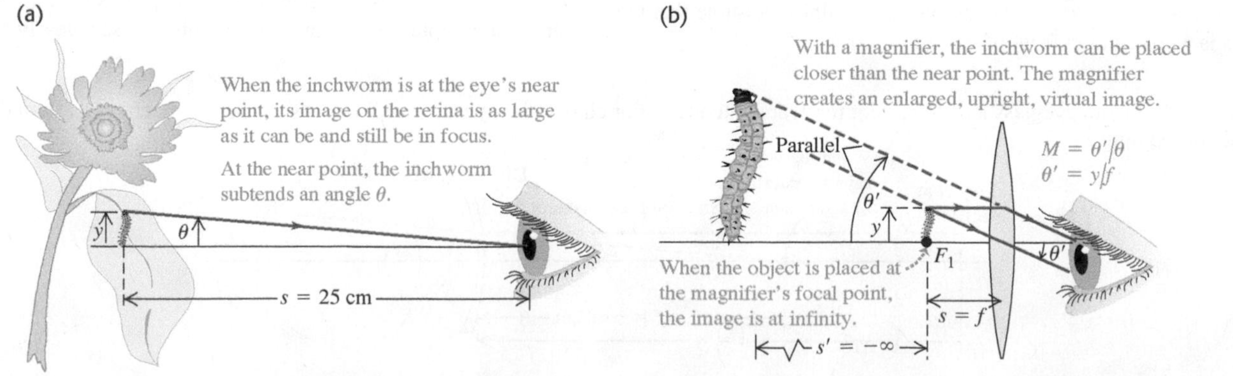

In Fig. 34.51a the object is at the near point, where it subtends an angle θ at the eye. In Fig. 34.51b a magnifier in front of the eye forms an image at infinity, and the angle subtended at the magnifier is θ'. The usefulness of the magnifier is given by the ratio of the angle θ' (with the magnifier) to the angle θ (without the magnifier). This ratio is called the **angular magnification** M:

$$M = \frac{\theta'}{\theta} \quad \text{(angular magnification)} \qquad (34.21)$$

CAUTION **Angular magnification vs. lateral magnification** Don't confuse the *angular* magnification M with the *lateral* magnification m. Angular magnification is the ratio of the *angular* size of an image to the angular size of the corresponding object; lateral magnification refers to the ratio of the *height* of an image to the height of the corresponding object. For the situation shown in Fig. 34.51b, the angular magnification is about 3×, since the inchworm subtends an angle about three times larger than that in Fig. 34.51a; hence the inchworm will look about three times larger to the eye. The *lateral* magnification $m = -s'/s$ in Fig. 34.51b is *infinite* because the virtual image is at infinity, but that doesn't mean that the inchworm looks infinitely large through the magnifier! (That's why we didn't attempt to draw an infinitely large inchworm in Fig. 34.51b.) When dealing with a magnifier, M is useful but m is not. ❙

To find the value of M, we first assume that the angles are small enough that each angle (in radians) is equal to its sine and its tangent. Using Fig. 34.451a and drawing the ray in Fig. 34.51b that passes undeviated through the center of the lens, we find that θ and θ' (in radians) are

$$\theta = \frac{y}{25\text{ cm}} \qquad \theta' = \frac{y}{f}$$

Combining these expressions with Eq. (34.21), we find

$$M = \frac{\theta'}{\theta} = \frac{y/f}{y/25\text{ cm}} = \frac{25\text{ cm}}{f} \quad \begin{array}{l}\text{(angular magnification}\\ \text{for a simple magnifier)}\end{array} \qquad (34.22)$$

It may seem that we can make the angular magnification as large as we like by decreasing the focal length f. In fact, the aberrations of a simple double-convex lens set a limit to M of about 3× to 4×. If these aberrations are corrected, the angular magnification may be made as great as 20×. When greater magnification than this is needed, we usually use a compound microscope, discussed in the next section.

Test Your Understanding of Section 34.7 You are examining a gem using a magnifier. If you change to a different magnifier with twice the focal length of the first one, (i) you will have to hold the object at twice the distance and the angular magnification will be twice as great; (ii) you will have to hold the object at twice the distance and the angular magnification will be $\frac{1}{2}$ as great; (iii) you will have to hold the object at $\frac{1}{2}$ the distance and the angular magnification will be twice as great; (iv) you will have to hold the object at $\frac{1}{2}$ the distance and the angular magnification will be $\frac{1}{2}$ as great. ❙

34.8 Microscopes and Telescopes

MasteringPHYSICS

ActivPhysics 15.12: Two-Lens Optical Systems

Cameras, eyeglasses, and magnifiers use a single lens to form an image. Two important optical devices that use *two* lenses are the microscope and the telescope. In each device a primary lens, or *objective,* forms a real image, and a second lens, or *eyepiece,* is used as a magnifier to make an enlarged, virtual image.

Microscopes

When we need greater magnification than we can get with a simple magnifier, the instrument that we usually use is the **microscope,** sometimes called a *compound*

34.52 (a) Elements of a microscope. (b) The object O is placed just outside the first focal point of the objective (the distance s_1 has been exaggerated for clarity). (c) This microscope image shows single-celled organisms about 2×10^{-4} m (0.2 mm) across. Typical light microscopes can resolve features as small as 2×10^{-7} m, comparable to the wavelength of light.

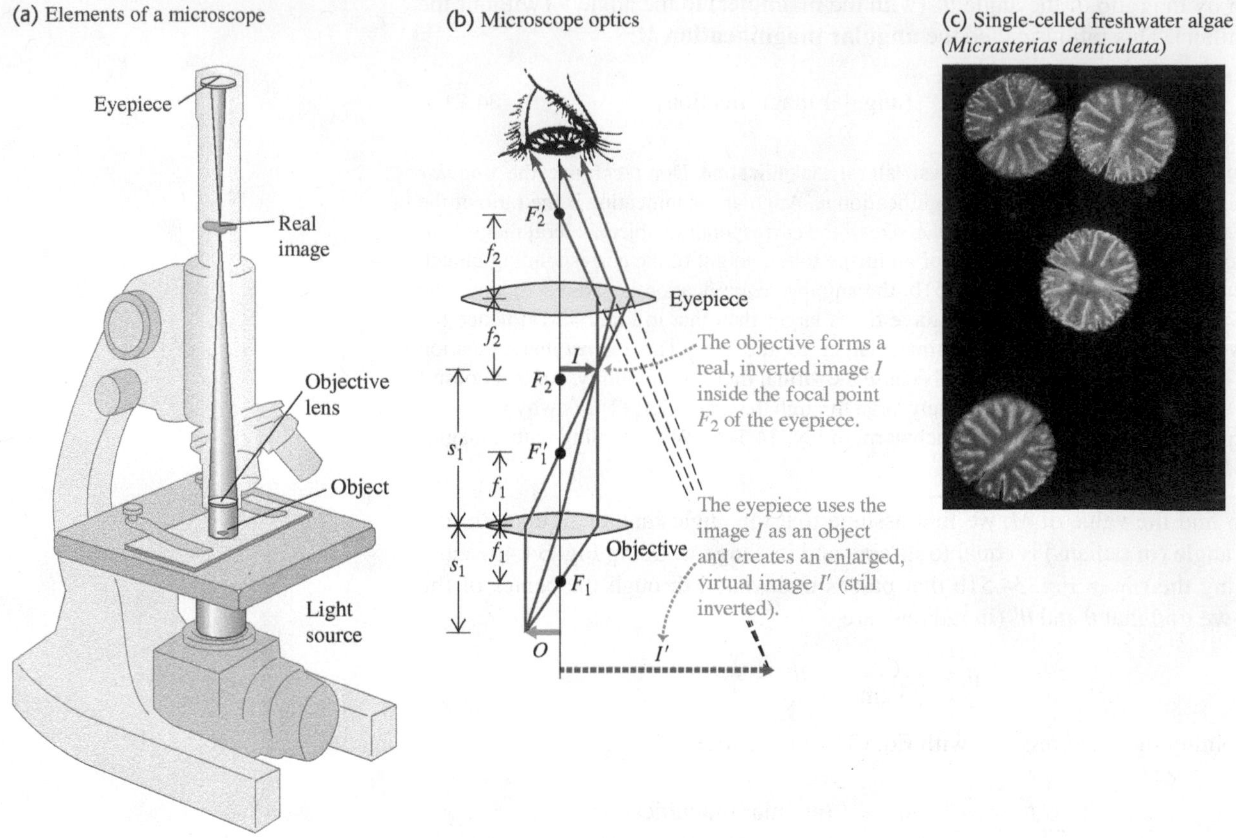

microscope. The essential elements of a microscope are shown in Fig. 34.52a. To analyze this system, we use the principle that an image formed by one optical element such as a lens or mirror can serve as the object for a second element. We used this principle in Section 34.4 when we derived the thin-lens equation by repeated application of the single-surface refraction equation; we used this principle again in Example 34.11 (Section 34.4), in which the image formed by a lens was used as the object of a second lens.

The object O to be viewed is placed just beyond the first focal point F_1 of the **objective,** a converging lens that forms a real and enlarged image I (Fig. 34.52b). In a properly designed instrument this image lies just inside the first focal point F_1' of a second converging lens called the **eyepiece** or *ocular.* (The reason the image should lie just *inside* F_1' is left for you to discover; see Problem 34.108.) The eyepiece acts as a simple magnifier, as discussed in Section 34.7, and forms a final virtual image I' of I. The position of I' may be anywhere between the near and far points of the eye. Both the objective and the eyepiece of an actual microscope are highly corrected compound lenses with several optical elements, but for simplicity we show them here as simple thin lenses.

As for a simple magnifier, what matters when viewing through a microscope is the *angular* magnification M. The overall angular magnification of the compound microscope is the product of two factors. The first factor is the *lateral* magnification m_1 of the objective, which determines the linear size of the real image I; the second factor is the *angular* magnification M_2 of the eyepiece, which relates the angular size of the virtual image seen through the eyepiece to the angular size that the real image I would have if you viewed it *without* the eyepiece. The first of these factors is given by

$$m_1 = -\frac{s'_1}{s_1} \qquad (34.23)$$

where s_1 and s'_1 are the object and image distances, respectively, for the objective lens. Ordinarily, the object is very close to the focal point, and the resulting image distance s'_1 is very great in comparison to the focal length f_1 of the objective lens. Thus s_1 is approximately equal to f_1, and we can write $m_1 = -s'_1/f_1$.

The real image I is close to the focal point F'_1 of the eyepiece, so to find the eyepiece angular magnification, we can use Eq. (34.22): $M_2 = (25\text{ cm})/f_2$, where f_2 is the focal length of the eyepiece (considered as a simple lens). The overall angular magnification M of the compound microscope (apart from a negative sign, which is customarily ignored) is the product of the two magnifications:

$$M = m_1 M_2 = \frac{(25\text{ cm})s'_1}{f_1 f_2} \quad \text{(angular magnification for a microscope)} \qquad (34.24)$$

where s'_1, f_1, and f_2 are measured in centimeters. The final image is inverted with respect to the object. Microscope manufacturers usually specify the values of m_1 and M_2 for microscope components rather than the focal lengths of the objective and eyepiece.

Equation (34.24) shows that the angular magnification of a microscope can be increased by using an objective of shorter focal length f_1, thereby increasing m_1 and the size of the real image I. Most optical microscopes have a rotating "turret" with three or more objectives of different focal lengths so that the same object can be viewed at different magnifications. The eyepiece should also have a short focal length f_2 to help to maximize the value of M.

To take a photograph using a microscope (called a *photomicrograph* or *micrograph*), the eyepiece is removed and a camera placed so that the real image I falls on the camera's CCD array or film. Figure 34.52c shows such a photograph. In this case what matters is the *lateral* magnification of the microscope as given by Eq. (34.23).

Telescopes

The optical system of a **telescope** is similar to that of a compound microscope. In both instruments the image formed by an objective is viewed through an eyepiece. The key difference is that the telescope is used to view large objects at large distances and the microscope is used to view small objects close at hand. Another difference is that many telescopes use a curved mirror, not a lens, as an objective.

Figure 34.53 shows an *astronomical telescope.* Because this telescope uses a lens as an objective, it is called a *refracting telescope* or *refractor.* The objective lens forms a real, reduced image I of the object. This image is the object for the eyepiece lens, which forms an enlarged, virtual image of I. Objects that are viewed with a telescope are usually so far away from the instrument that the first image I is formed very nearly at the second focal point of the objective lens. If the final image I' formed by the eyepiece is at infinity (for most comfortable viewing by a normal eye), the first image must also be at the first focal point of the eyepiece. The distance between objective and eyepiece, which is the length of the telescope, is therefore the *sum* of the focal lengths of objective and eyepiece, $f_1 + f_2$.

The angular magnification M of a telescope is defined as the ratio of the angle subtended at the eye by the final image I' to the angle subtended at the (unaided) eye by the object. We can express this ratio in terms of the focal lengths of objective and eyepiece. In Fig. 34.53 the ray passing through F_1, the first focal point of the objective, and through F'_2, the second focal point of the eyepiece, is shown in red. The object (not shown) subtends an angle θ at the objective and would subtend essentially the same angle at the unaided eye. Also, since the observer's eye is placed just to the right of the focal point F'_2, the angle subtended at the eye by the final image is very nearly equal to the angle θ'. Because bd is parallel to the

34.53 Optical system of an astronomical refracting telescope.

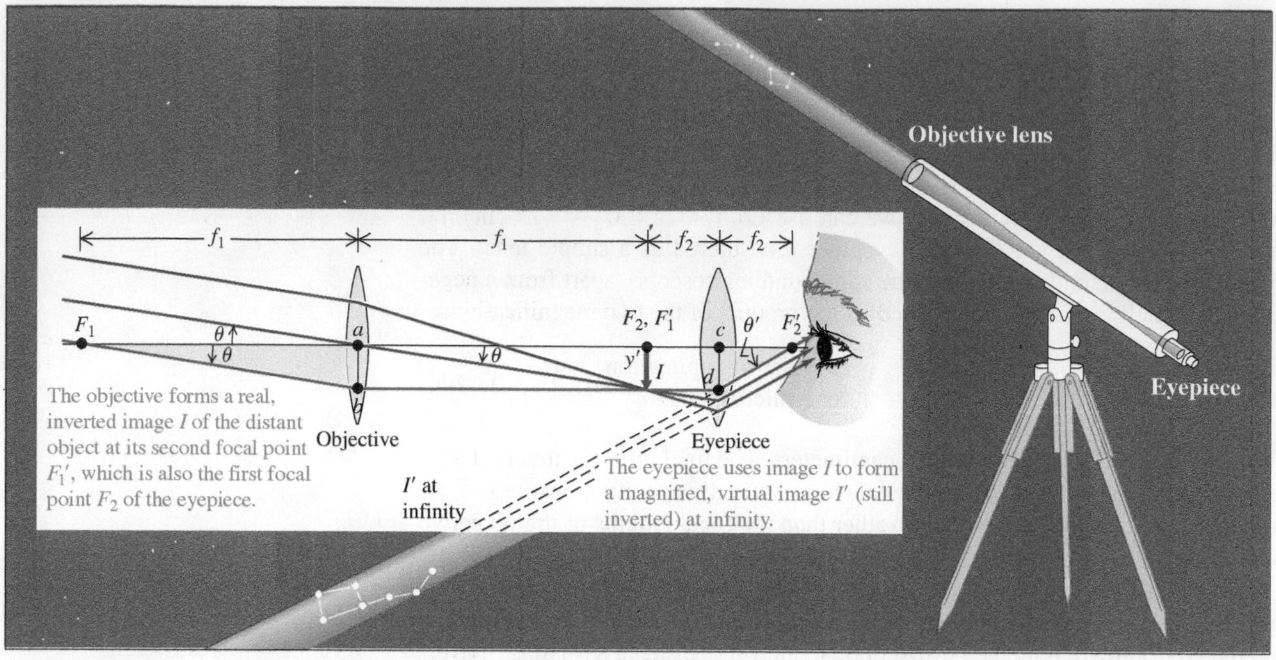

optic axis, the distances ab and cd are equal to each other and also to the height y' of the real image I. Because the angles θ and θ' are small, they may be approximated by their tangents. From the right triangles F_1ab and $F_2'cd$,

$$\theta = \frac{-y'}{f_1} \qquad \theta' = \frac{y'}{f_2}$$

and the angular magnification M is

$$M = \frac{\theta'}{\theta} = -\frac{y'/f_2}{y'/f_1} = -\frac{f_1}{f_2} \quad \text{(angular magnification for a telescope)} \tag{34.25}$$

The angular magnification M of a telescope is equal to the ratio of the focal length of the objective to that of the eyepiece. The negative sign shows that the final image is inverted. Equation (34.25) shows that to achieve good angular magnification, a *telescope* should have a *long* objective focal length f_1. By contrast, Eq. (34.24) shows that a *microscope* should have a *short* objective focal length. However, a telescope objective with a long focal length should also have a large diameter D so that the f-number f_1/D will not be too large; as described in Section 34.5, a large f-number means a dim, low-intensity image. Telescopes typically do not have interchangeable objectives; instead, the magnification is varied by using different eyepieces with different focal lengths f_2. Just as for a microscope, smaller values of f_2 give larger angular magnifications.

An inverted image is no particular disadvantage for astronomical observations. When we use a telescope or binoculars—essentially a pair of telescopes mounted side by side—to view objects on the earth, though, we want the image to be right-side up. In prism binoculars, this is accomplished by reflecting the light several times along the path from the objective to the eyepiece. The combined effect of the reflections is to flip the image both horizontally and vertically. Binoculars are usually described by two numbers separated by a multiplication sign, such as 7×50. The first number is the angular magnification M, and the second is the diameter of the objective lenses (in millimeters). The diameter helps to determine the light-gathering capacity of the objective lenses and thus the brightness of the image.

In the *reflecting telescope* (Fig. 34.54a) the objective lens is replaced by a concave mirror. In large telescopes this scheme has many advantages. Mirrors are

34.54 (a), (b), (c) Three designs for reflecting telescopes. (d) This photo shows the interior of the Gemini North telescope, which uses the design shown in (c). The objective mirror is 8 meters in diameter.

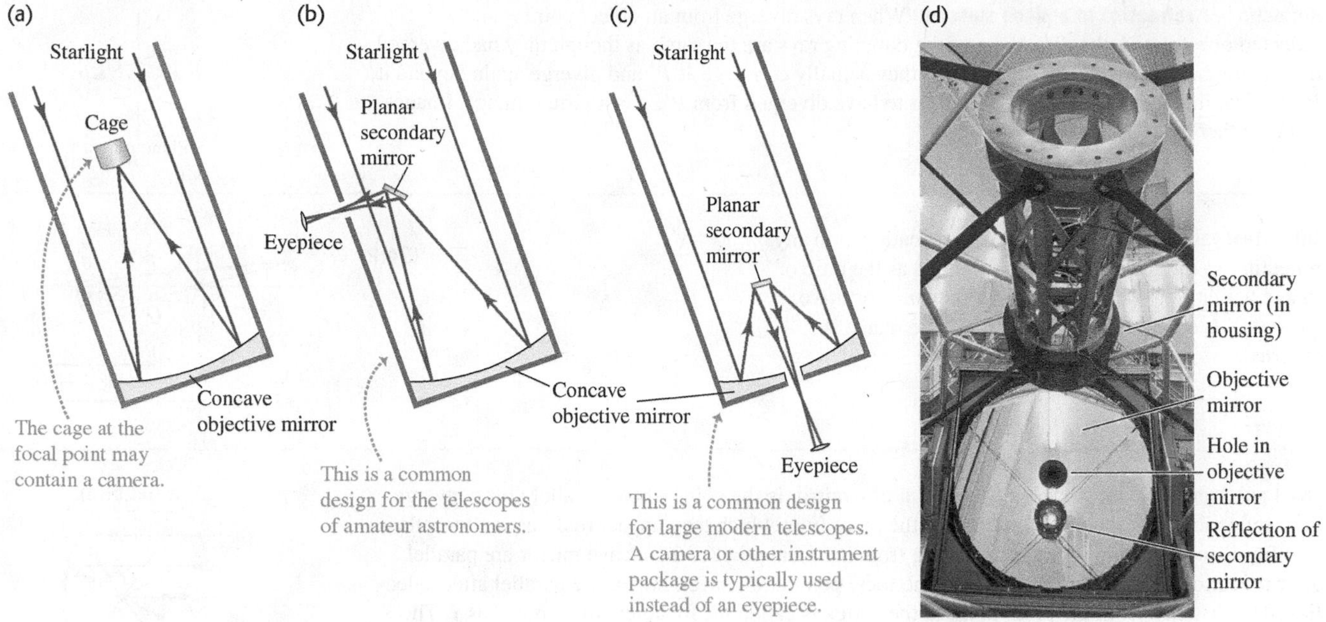

inherently free of chromatic aberrations (dependence of focal length on wavelength), and spherical aberrations (associated with the paraxial approximation) are easier to correct than with a lens. The reflecting surface is sometimes parabolic rather than spherical. The material of the mirror need not be transparent, and it can be made more rigid than a lens, which has to be supported only at its edges.

The largest reflecting telescopes in the world, the Keck telescopes atop Mauna Kea in Hawaii, each have an objective mirror of overall diameter 10 m made up of 36 separate hexagonal reflecting elements.

One challenge in designing reflecting telescopes is that the image is formed in front of the objective mirror, in a region traversed by incoming rays. Isaac Newton devised one solution to this problem. A flat secondary mirror oriented at 45° to the optic axis causes the image to be formed in a hole on the side of the telescope, where it can be magnified with an eyepiece (Fig. 34.54b). Another solution uses a secondary mirror that causes the focused light to pass through a hole in the objective mirror (Fig. 34.54c). Large research telescopes, as well as many amateur telescopes, use this design (Fig. 34.54d).

Like a microscope, when a telescope is used for photography the eyepiece is removed and a CCD array or photographic film is placed at the position of the real image formed by the objective. (Some long-focal-length "lenses" for photography are actually reflecting telescopes used in this way.) Most telescopes used for astronomical research are never used with an eyepiece.

Test Your Understanding of Section 34.8 Which gives a lateral magnification of greater absolute value: (i) the objective lens in a microscope (Fig. 34.52); (ii) the objective lens in a refracting telescope (Fig. 34.53); or (iii) not enough information is given to decide? ❙

CHAPTER 34 SUMMARY

Reflection or refraction at a plane surface: When rays diverge from an object point P and are reflected or refracted, the directions of the outgoing rays are the same as though they had diverged from a point P' called the image point. If they actually converge at P' and diverge again beyond it, P' is a real image of P; if they only appear to have diverged from P', it is a virtual image. Images can be either erect or inverted.

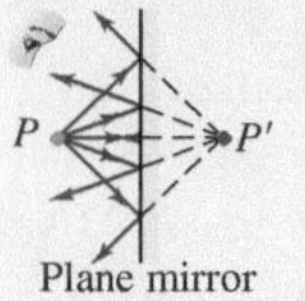

Lateral magnification: The lateral magnification m in any reflecting or refracting situation is defined as the ratio of image height y' to object height y. When m is positive, the image is erect; when m is negative, the image is inverted.

$$m = \frac{y'}{y} \qquad (34.2)$$

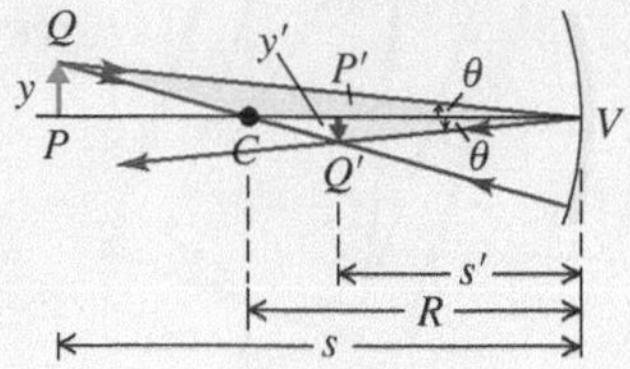

Focal point and focal length: The focal point of a mirror is the point where parallel rays converge after reflection from a concave mirror, or the point from which they appear to diverge after reflection from a convex mirror. Rays diverging from the focal point of a concave mirror are parallel after reflection; rays converging toward the focal point of a convex mirror are parallel after reflection. The distance from the focal point to the vertex is called the focal length, denoted as f. The focal points of a lens are defined similarly.

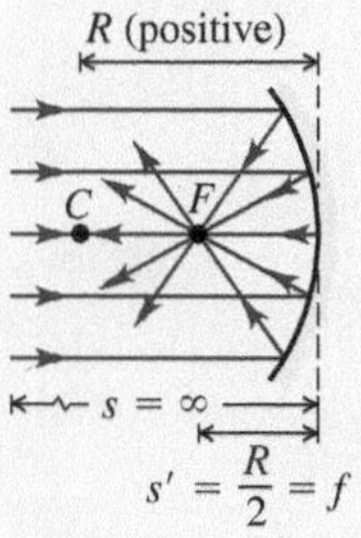

Relating object and image distances: The formulas for object distance s and image distance s' for plane and spherical mirrors and single refracting surfaces are summarized in the table. The equation for a plane surface can be obtained from the corresponding equation for a spherical surface by setting $R = \infty$. (See Examples 34.1–34.7.)

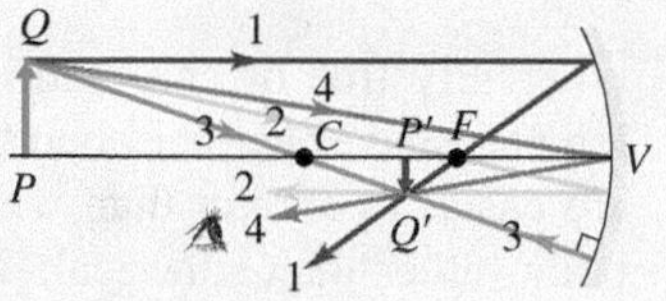

	Plane Mirror	Spherical Mirror	Plane Refracting Surface	Spherical Refracting Surface
Object and image distances	$\frac{1}{s} + \frac{1}{s'} = 0$	$\frac{1}{s} + \frac{1}{s'} = \frac{2}{R} = \frac{1}{f}$	$\frac{n_a}{s} + \frac{n_b}{s'} = 0$	$\frac{n_a}{s} + \frac{n_b}{s'} = \frac{n_b - n_a}{R}$
Lateral magnification	$m = -\frac{s'}{s} = 1$	$m = -\frac{s'}{s}$	$m = -\frac{n_a s'}{n_b s} = 1$	$m = -\frac{n_a s'}{n_b s}$

Object–image relationships derived in this chapter are valid only for rays close to and nearly parallel to the optic axis; these are called paraxial rays. Nonparaxial rays do not converge precisely to an image point. This effect is called spherical aberration.

Thin lenses: The object–image relationship, given by Eq. (34.16), is the same for a thin lens as for a spherical mirror. Equation (34.19), the lensmaker's equation, relates the focal length of a lens to its index of refraction and the radii of curvature of its surfaces. (See Examples 34.8–34.11.)

$$\frac{1}{s} + \frac{1}{s'} = \frac{1}{f} \qquad (34.16)$$

$$\frac{1}{f} = (n - 1)\left(\frac{1}{R_1} - \frac{1}{R_2}\right) \qquad (34.19)$$

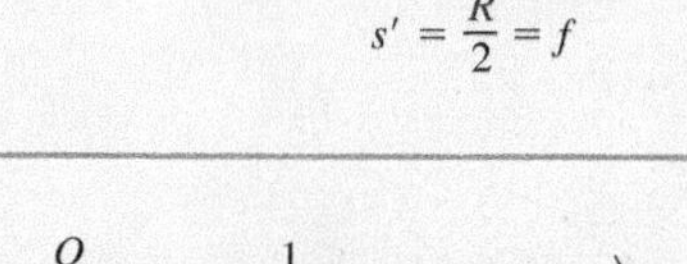

Sign rules: The following sign rules are used with all plane and spherical reflecting and refracting surfaces.

- $s > 0$ when the object is on the incoming side of the surface (a real object); $s < 0$ otherwise.
- $s' > 0$ when the image is on the outgoing side of the surface (a real image); $s' < 0$ otherwise.
- $R > 0$ when the center of curvature is on the outgoing side of the surface; $R < 0$ otherwise.
- $m > 0$ when the image is erect; $m < 0$ when inverted.

Cameras: A camera forms a real, inverted, reduced image of the object being photographed on a light-sensitive surface. The amount of light striking this surface is controlled by the shutter speed and the aperture. The intensity of this light is inversely proportional to the square of the f-number of the lens. (See Example 34.12.)

$$f\text{-number} = \frac{\text{Focal length}}{\text{Aperture diameter}} = \frac{f}{D} \quad (34.20)$$

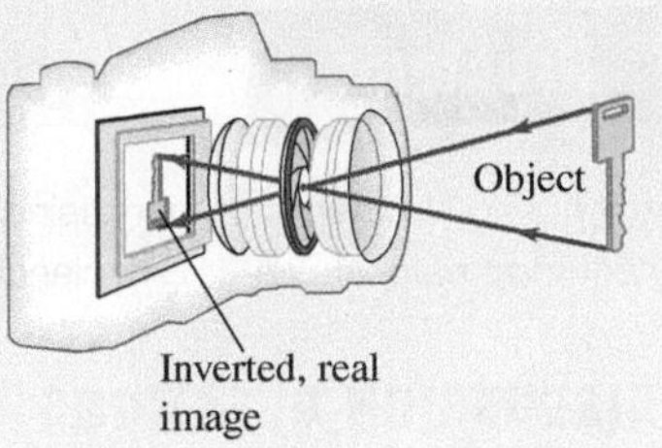

The eye: In the eye, refraction at the surface of the cornea forms a real image on the retina. Adjustment for various object distances is made by squeezing the lens, thereby making it bulge and decreasing its focal length. A nearsighted eye is too long for its lens; a farsighted eye is too short. The power of a corrective lens, in diopters, is the reciprocal of the focal length in meters. (See Examples 34.13 and 34.14.)

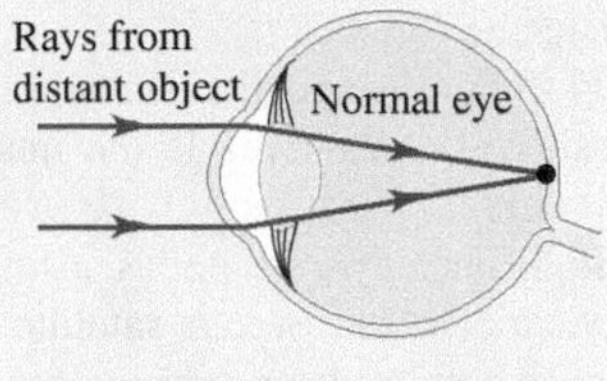

The simple magnifier: The simple magnifier creates a virtual image whose angular size θ' is larger than the angular size θ of the object itself at a distance of 25 cm, the nominal closest distance for comfortable viewing. The angular magnification M of a simple magnifier is the ratio of the angular size of the virtual image to that of the object at this distance.

$$M = \frac{\theta'}{\theta} = \frac{25\text{ cm}}{f} \quad (34.22)$$

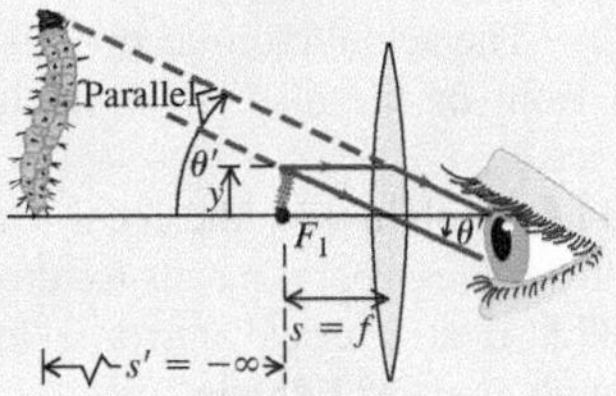

Microscopes and telescopes: In a compound microscope, the objective lens forms a first image in the barrel of the instrument, and the eyepiece forms a final virtual image, often at infinity, of the first image. The telescope operates on the same principle, but the object is far away. In a reflecting telescope, the objective lens is replaced by a concave mirror, which eliminates chromatic aberrations.

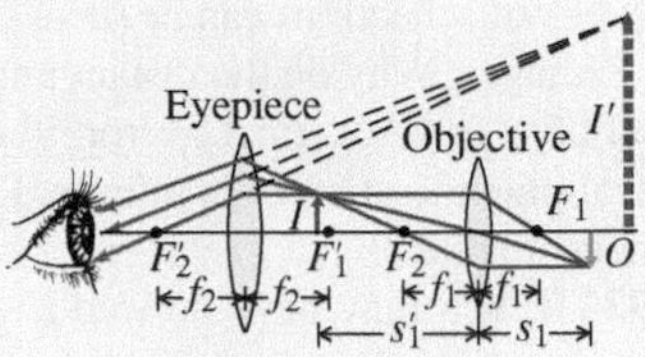

BRIDGING PROBLEM Image Formation by a Wine Goblet

A thick-walled wine goblet can be considered to be a hollow glass sphere with an outer radius of 4.00 cm and an inner radius of 3.40 cm. The index of refraction of the goblet glass is 1.50. (a) A beam of parallel light rays enters the side of the empty goblet along a horizontal radius. Where, if anywhere, will an image be formed? (b) The goblet is filled with white wine ($n = 1.37$). Where is the image formed?

SOLUTION GUIDE

See MasteringPhysics® study area for a Video Tutor solution. MP

IDENTIFY and SET UP

1. The goblet is *not* a thin lens, so you cannot use the thin-lens formula. Instead, you must think of the inner and outer surfaces of the goblet walls as spherical refracting surfaces. The image formed by one surface serves as the object for the next surface.
2. Choose the appropriate equation that relates the image and object distances for a spherical refracting surface.

EXECUTE

3. For the empty goblet, each refracting surface has glass on one side and air on the other. Find the position of the image formed by the first surface, the outer wall of the goblet. Use this as the object for the second surface (the inner wall of the same side of the goblet) and find the position of the second image. (*Hint:* Be sure to account for the thickness of the goblet wall.)
4. Continue the process of step 3. Consider the refractions at the inner and outer surfaces of the glass on the opposite side of the goblet, and find the position of the final image. (*Hint:* Be sure to account for the distance between the two sides of the goblet.)
5. Repeat steps 3 and 4 for the case in which the goblet is filled with wine.

EVALUATE

6. Are the images real or virtual? How can you tell?

Problems

For instructor-assigned homework, go to www.masteringphysics.com

•, ••, •••: Problems of increasing difficulty. **CP**: Cumulative problems incorporating material from earlier chapters. **CALC**: Problems requiring calculus. **BIO**: Biosciences problems.

DISCUSSION QUESTIONS

Q34.1 A spherical mirror is cut in half horizontally. Will an image be formed by the bottom half of the mirror? If so, where will the image be formed?

Q34.2 For the situation shown in Fig. 34.3, is the image distance s' positive or negative? Is the image real or virtual? Explain your answers.

Q34.3 The laws of optics also apply to electromagnetic waves invisible to the eye. A satellite TV dish is used to detect radio waves coming from orbiting satellites. Why is a curved reflecting surface (a "dish") used? The dish is always concave, never convex; why? The actual radio receiver is placed on an arm and suspended in front of the dish. How far in front of the dish should it be placed?

Q34.4 Explain why the focal length of a *plane* mirror is infinite, and explain what it means for the focal point to be at infinity.

Q34.5 If a spherical mirror is immersed in water, does its focal length change? Explain.

Q34.6 For what range of object positions does a concave spherical mirror form a real image? What about a convex spherical mirror?

Q34.7 When a room has mirrors on two opposite walls, an infinite series of reflections can be seen. Discuss this phenomenon in terms of images. Why do the distant images appear fainter?

Q34.8 For a spherical mirror, if $s = f$, then $s' = \infty$, and the lateral magnification m is infinite. Does this make sense? If so, what does it mean?

Q34.9 You may have noticed a small convex mirror next to your bank's ATM. Why is this mirror convex, as opposed to flat or concave? What considerations determine its radius of curvature?

Q34.10 A student claims that she can start a fire on a sunny day using just the sun's rays and a concave mirror. How is this done? Is the concept of image relevant? Can she do the same thing with a convex mirror? Explain.

Q34.11 A person looks at his reflection in the concave side of a shiny spoon. Is it right side up or inverted? Does it matter how far his face is from the spoon? What if he looks in the convex side? (Try this yourself!)

Q34.12 In Example 34.4 (Section 34.2), there appears to be an ambiguity for the case $s = 10$ cm as to whether s' is $+\infty$ or $-\infty$ and whether the image is erect or inverted. How is this resolved? Or is it?

Q34.13 Suppose that in the situation of Example 34.7 of Section 34.3 (see Fig. 34.26) a vertical arrow 2.00 m tall is painted on the side of the pool beneath the water line. According to the calculations in the example, this arrow would appear to the person shown in Fig. 34.26 to be 1.50 m long. But the discussion following Eq. (34.13) states that the magnification for a plane refracting surface is $m = 1$, which suggests that the arrow would appear to the person to be 2.00 m long. How can you resolve this apparent contradiction?

Q34.14 The bottom of the passenger-side mirror on your car notes, "Objects in mirror are closer than they appear." Is this true? Why?

Q34.15 How could you very quickly make an approximate measurement of the focal length of a converging lens? Could the same method be applied if you wished to use a diverging lens? Explain.

Q34.16 The focal length of a simple lens depends on the color (wavelength) of light passing through it. Why? Is it possible for a lens to have a positive focal length for some colors and negative for others? Explain.

Q34.17 When a converging lens is immersed in water, does its focal length increase or decrease in comparison with the value in air? Explain.

Q34.18 A spherical air bubble in water can function as a lens. Is it a converging or diverging lens? How is its focal length related to its radius?

Q34.19 Can an image formed by one reflecting or refracting surface serve as an object for a second reflection or refraction? Does it matter whether the first image is real or virtual? Explain.

Q34.20 If a piece of photographic film is placed at the location of a real image, the film will record the image. Can this be done with a virtual image? How might one record a virtual image?

Q34.21 According to the discussion in Section 34.2, light rays are reversible. Are the formulas in the table in this chapter's Summary still valid if object and image are interchanged? What does reversibility imply with respect to the *forms* of the various formulas?

Q34.22 You've entered a survival contest that will include building a crude telescope. You are given a large box of lenses. Which two lenses do you pick? How do you quickly identify them?

Q34.23 **BIO** You can't see clearly underwater with the naked eye, but you *can* if you wear a face mask or goggles (with air between your eyes and the mask or goggles). Why is there a difference? Could you instead wear eyeglasses (with water between your eyes and the eyeglasses) in order to see underwater? If so, should the lenses be converging or diverging? Explain.

Q34.24 You take a lens and mask it so that light can pass through only the bottom half of the lens. How does the image formed by the masked lens compare to the image formed before masking?

EXERCISES

Section 34.1 Reflection and Refraction at a Plane Surface

34.1 • A candle 4.85 cm tall is 39.2 cm to the left of a plane mirror. Where is the image formed by the mirror, and what is the height of this image?

34.2 • The image of a tree just covers the length of a plane mirror 4.00 cm tall when the mirror is held 35.0 cm from the eye. The tree is 28.0 m from the mirror. What is its height?

34.3 • A pencil that is 9.0 cm long is held perpendicular to the surface of a plane mirror with the tip of the pencil lead 12.0 cm from the mirror surface and the end of the eraser 21.0 cm from the mirror surface. What is the length of the image of the pencil that is formed by the mirror? Which end of the image is closer to the mirror surface: the tip of the lead or the end of the eraser?

Section 34.2 Reflection at a Spherical Surface

34.4 • A concave mirror has a radius of curvature of 34.0 cm. (a) What is its focal length? (b) If the mirror is immersed in water (refractive index 1.33), what is its focal length?

34.5 • An object 0.600 cm tall is placed 16.5 cm to the left of the vertex of a concave spherical mirror having a radius of curvature of 22.0 cm. (a) Draw a principal-ray diagram showing the formation of the image. (b) Determine the position, size, orientation, and nature (real or virtual) of the image.

34.6 • Repeat Exercise 34.5 for the case in which the mirror is convex.

34.7 •• The diameter of Mars is 6794 km, and its minimum distance from the earth is 5.58×10^7 km. When Mars is at this distance, find the diameter of the image of Mars formed by a spherical, concave telescope mirror with a focal length of 1.75 m.

34.8 •• An object is 24.0 cm from the center of a silvered spherical glass Christmas tree ornament 6.00 cm in diameter. What are the position and magnification of its image?

34.9 • A coin is placed next to the convex side of a thin spherical glass shell having a radius of curvature of 18.0 cm. Reflection from the surface of the shell forms an image of the 1.5-cm-tall coin that is 6.00 cm behind the glass shell. Where is the coin located? Determine the size, orientation, and nature (real or virtual) of the image.

34.10 • You hold a spherical salad bowl 90 cm in front of your face with the bottom of the bowl facing you. The salad bowl is made of polished metal with a 35-cm radius of curvature. (a) Where is the image of your 2.0-cm-tall nose located? (b) What are the image's size, orientation, and nature (real or virtual)?

34.11 • (a) Show that Eq. (34.6) can be written as $s' = sf/(s - f)$ and hence the lateral magnification given by Eq. (34.7) can be expressed as $m = f/(f - s)$. (b) A concave spherical mirror has focal length $f = +14.0$ cm. What is the nonzero distance of the object from the mirror vertex if the image has the same height as the object? In this case, is the image erect or inverted? (c) A convex spherical mirror has $f = -8.00$ cm. What is the nonzero distance of the object from the mirror vertex if the height of the image is one-half the height of the object?

34.12 • The thin glass shell shown in Fig. E34.12 has a spherical shape with a radius of curvature of 12.0 cm, and both of its surfaces can act as mirrors. A seed 3.30 mm high is placed 15.0 cm from the center of the mirror along the optic axis, as shown in the figure. (a) Calculate the location and height of the image of this seed. (b) Suppose now that the shell is reversed. Find the location and height of the seed's image.

Figure **E34.12**

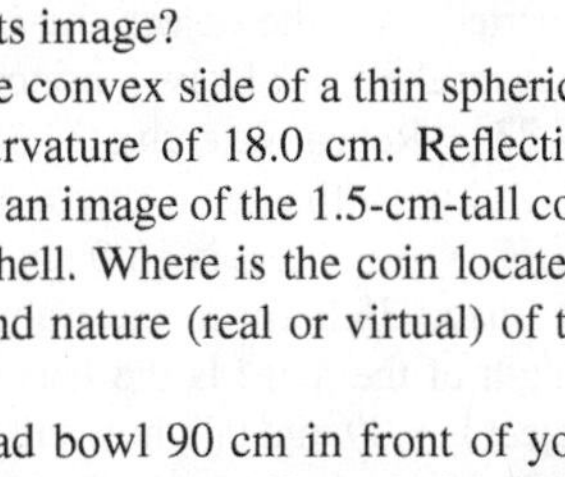

34.13 • **Dental Mirror.** A dentist uses a curved mirror to view teeth on the upper side of the mouth. Suppose she wants an erect image with a magnification of 2.00 when the mirror is 1.25 cm from a tooth. (Treat this problem as though the object and image lie along a straight line.) (a) What kind of mirror (concave or convex) is needed? Use a ray diagram to decide, without performing any calculations. (b) What must be the focal length and radius of curvature of this mirror? (c) Draw a principal-ray diagram to check your answer in part (b).

34.14 • A spherical, concave shaving mirror has a radius of curvature of 32.0 cm. (a) What is the magnification of a person's face when it is 12.0 cm to the left of the vertex of the mirror? (b) Where is the image? Is the image real or virtual? (c) Draw a principal-ray diagram showing the formation of the image.

Section 34.3 Refraction at a Spherical Surface

34.15 • A speck of dirt is embedded 3.50 cm below the surface of a sheet of ice ($n = 1.309$). What is its apparent depth when viewed at normal incidence?

34.16 •• A tank whose bottom is a mirror is filled with water to a depth of 20.0 cm. A small fish floats motionless 7.0 cm under the surface of the water. (a) What is the apparent depth of the fish when viewed at normal incidence? (b) What is the apparent depth of the image of the fish when viewed at normal incidence?

34.17 • A person swimming 0.80 m below the surface of the water in a swimming pool looks at the diving board that is directly overhead and sees the image of the board that is formed by refraction at the surface of the water. This image is a height of 5.20 m above the swimmer. What is the actual height of the diving board above the surface of the water?

34.18 • A person is lying on a diving board 3.00 m above the surface of the water in a swimming pool. The person looks at a penny that is on the bottom of the pool directly below her. The penny appears to the person to be a distance of 8.00 m from her. What is the depth of the water at this point?

34.19 •• **A Spherical Fish Bowl.** A small tropical fish is at the center of a water-filled, spherical fish bowl 28.0 cm in diameter. (a) Find the apparent position and magnification of the fish to an observer outside the bowl. The effect of the thin walls of the bowl may be ignored. (b) A friend advised the owner of the bowl to keep it out of direct sunlight to avoid blinding the fish, which might swim into the focal point of the parallel rays from the sun. Is the focal point actually within the bowl?

34.20 • The left end of a long glass rod 6.00 cm in diameter has a convex hemispherical surface 3.00 cm in radius. The refractive index of the glass is 1.60. Determine the position of the image if an object is placed in air on the axis of the rod at the following distances to the left of the vertex of the curved end: (a) infinitely far, (b) 12.0 cm; (c) 2.00 cm.

34.21 •• The glass rod of Exercise 34.20 is immersed in oil ($n = 1.45$). An object placed to the left of the rod on the rod's axis is to be imaged 1.20 m inside the rod. How far from the left end of the rod must the object be located to form the image?

34.22 •• The left end of a long glass rod 8.00 cm in diameter, with an index of refraction of 1.60, is ground and polished to a convex hemispherical surface with a radius of 4.00 cm. An object in the form of an arrow 1.50 mm tall, at right angles to the axis of the rod, is located on the axis 24.0 cm to the left of the vertex of the convex surface. Find the position and height of the image of the arrow formed by paraxial rays incident on the convex surface. Is the image erect or inverted?

34.23 •• Repeat Exercise 34.22 for the case in which the end of the rod is ground to a *concave* hemispherical surface with radius 4.00 cm.

34.24 •• The glass rod of Exercise 34.23 is immersed in a liquid. An object 14.0 cm from the vertex of the left end of the rod and on its axis is imaged at a point 9.00 cm from the vertex inside the liquid. What is the index of refraction of the liquid?

Section 34.4 Thin Lenses

34.25 • An insect 3.75 mm tall is placed 22.5 cm to the left of a thin planoconvex lens. The left surface of this lens is flat, the right surface has a radius of curvature of magnitude 13.0 cm, and the index of refraction of the lens material is 1.70. (a) Calculate the location and size of the image this lens forms of the insect. Is it real or virtual? Erect or inverted? (b) Repeat part (a) if the lens is reversed.

34.26 • A lens forms an image of an object. The object is 16.0 cm from the lens. The image is 12.0 cm from the lens on the same side as the object. (a) What is the focal length of the lens? Is the lens converging or diverging? (b) If the object is 8.50 mm tall, how tall is the image? Is it erect or inverted? (c) Draw a principal-ray diagram.

34.27 • A converging meniscus lens (see Fig. 34.32a) with a refractive index of 1.52 has spherical surfaces whose radii are 7.00 cm and 4.00 cm. What is the position of the image if an object is placed 24.0 cm to the left of the lens? What is the magnification?

34.28 • A converging lens with a focal length of 90.0 cm forms an image of a 3.20-cm-tall real object that is to the left of the lens. The image is 4.50 cm tall and inverted. Where are the object and image located in relation to the lens? Is the image real or virtual?

34.29 •• A converging lens forms an image of an 8.00-mm-tall real object. The image is 12.0 cm to the left of the lens, 3.40 cm tall, and erect. What is the focal length of the lens? Where is the object located?

34.30 • A photographic slide is to the left of a lens. The lens projects an image of the slide onto a wall 6.00 m to the right of the slide. The image is 80.0 times the size of the slide. (a) How far is the slide from the lens? (b) Is the image erect or inverted? (c) What is the focal length of the lens? (d) Is the lens converging or diverging?

34.31 •• A double-convex thin lens has surfaces with equal radii of curvature of magnitude 2.50 cm. Looking through this lens, you observe that it forms an image of a very distant tree at a distance of 1.87 cm from the lens. What is the index of refraction of the lens?

34.32 • BIO **The Lens of the Eye.** The crystalline lens of the human eye is a double-convex lens made of material having an index of refraction of 1.44 (although this varies). Its focal length in air is about 8.0 mm, which also varies. We shall assume that the radii of curvature of its two surfaces have the same magnitude. (a) Find the radii of curvature of this lens. (b) If an object 16 cm tall is placed 30.0 cm from the eye lens, where would the lens focus it and how tall would the image be? Is this image real or virtual? Is it erect or inverted? (*Note:* The results obtained here are not strictly accurate because the lens is embedded in fluids having refractive indexes different from that of air.)

34.33 • BIO **The Cornea As a Simple Lens.** The cornea behaves as a thin lens of focal length approximately 1.8 cm, although this varies a bit. The material of which it is made has an index of refraction of 1.38, and its front surface is convex, with a radius of curvature of 5.0 mm. (a) If this focal length is in air, what is the radius of curvature of the back side of the cornea? (b) The closest distance at which a typical person can focus on an object (called the near point) is about 25 cm, although this varies considerably with age. Where would the cornea focus the image of an 8.0-mm-tall object at the near point? (c) What is the height of the image in part (b)? Is this image real or virtual? Is it erect or inverted? (*Note:* The results obtained here are not strictly accurate because, on one side, the cornea has a fluid with a refractive index different from that of air.)

34.34 • A converging lens with a focal length of 7.00 cm forms an image of a 4.00-mm-tall real object that is to the left of the lens. The image is 1.30 cm tall and erect. Where are the object and image located? Is the image real or virtual?

34.35 • For each thin lens shown in Fig. E34.35, calculate the location of the image of an object that is 18.0 cm to the left of the lens. The lens material has a refractive index of 1.50, and the radii of curvature shown are only the magnitudes.

Figure **E34.35**

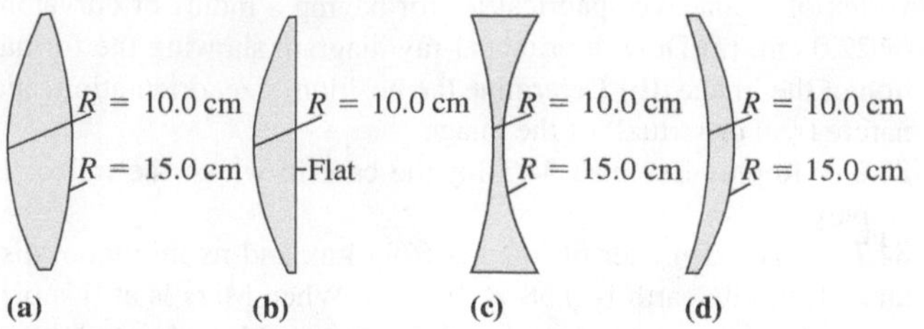

34.36 • A converging lens with a focal length of 12.0 cm forms a virtual image 8.00 mm tall, 17.0 cm to the right of the lens. Determine the position and size of the object. Is the image erect or inverted? Are the object and image on the same side or opposite sides of the lens? Draw a principal-ray diagram for this situation.

34.37 • Repeat Exercise 34.36 for the case in which the lens is diverging, with a focal length of −48.0 cm.

34.38 • An object is 16.0 cm to the left of a lens. The lens forms an image 36.0 cm to the right of the lens. (a) What is the focal length of the lens? Is the lens converging or diverging? (b) If the object is 8.00 mm tall, how tall is the image? Is it erect or inverted? (c) Draw a principal-ray diagram.

34.39 •• **Combination of Lenses I.** A 1.20-cm-tall object is 50.0 cm to the left of a converging lens of focal length 40.0 cm. A second converging lens, this one having a focal length of 60.0 cm, is located 300.0 cm to the right of the first lens along the same optic axis. (a) Find the location and height of the image (call it I_1) formed by the lens with a focal length of 40.0 cm. (b) I_1 is now the object for the second lens. Find the location and height of the image produced by the second lens. This is the final image produced by the combination of lenses.

34.40 •• **Combination of Lenses II.** Repeat Problem 34.39 using the same lenses except for the following changes: (a) The second lens is a *diverging* lens having a focal length of magnitude 60.0 cm. (b) The first lens is a *diverging* lens having a focal length of magnitude 40.0 cm. (c) Both lenses are diverging lenses having focal lengths of the same *magnitudes* as in Problem 34.39.

34.41 •• **Combination of Lenses III.** Two thin lenses with a focal length of magnitude 12.0 cm, the first diverging and the second converging, are located 9.00 cm apart. An object 2.50 mm tall is placed 20.0 cm to the left of the first (diverging) lens. (a) How far from this first lens is the final image formed? (b) Is the final image real or virtual? (c) What is the height of the final image? Is it erect or inverted? (*Hint:* See the preceding two problems.)

Section 34.5 Cameras

34.42 • You wish to project the image of a slide on a screen 9.00 m from the lens of a slide projector. (a) If the slide is placed 15.0 cm from the lens, what focal length lens is required? (b) If the dimensions of the picture on a 35-mm color slide are 24 mm × 36 mm, what is the minimum size of the projector screen required to accommodate the image?

34.43 •• A camera lens has a focal length of 200 mm. How far from the lens should the subject for the photo be if the lens is 20.4 cm from the film?

34.44 • When a camera is focused, the lens is moved away from or toward the film. If you take a picture of your friend, who is standing 3.90 m from the lens, using a camera with a lens with a 85-mm focal length, how far from the film is the lens? Will the whole image of your friend, who is 175 cm tall, fit on film that is 24 × 36 mm?

34.45 • Figure 34.41 shows photographs of the same scene taken with the same camera with lenses of different focal length. If the object is 200 m from the lens, what is the magnitude of the lateral magnification for a lens of focal length (a) 28 mm; (b) 105 mm; (c) 300 mm?

34.46 • A photographer takes a photograph of a Boeing 747 airliner (length 70.7 m) when it is flying directly overhead at an altitude of 9.50 km. The lens has a focal length of 5.00 m. How long is the image of the airliner on the film?

34.47 • **Choosing a Camera Lens.** The picture size on ordinary 35-mm camera film is 24 mm × 36 mm. Focal lengths of lenses available for 35-mm cameras typically include 28, 35, 50 (the "normal" lens), 85, 100, 135, 200, and 300 mm, among others. Which of these lenses should be used to photograph the following objects, assuming that the object is to fill most of the picture area? (a) a building 240 m tall and 160 m wide at a distance of 600 m, and (b) a mobile home 9.6 m in length at a distance of 40.0 m.

34.48 • **Zoom Lens.** Consider the simple model of the zoom lens shown in Fig. 34.43a. The converging lens has focal length $f_1 = 12$ cm, and the diverging lens has focal length $f_2 = -12$ cm. The lenses are separated by 4 cm as shown in Fig. 34.43a. (a) For a distant object, where is the image of the converging lens? (b) The image of the converging lens serves as the object for the diverging lens. What is the object distance for the diverging lens? (c) Where is the final image? Compare your answer to Fig. 34.43a. (d) Repeat parts (a), (b), and (c) for the situation shown in Fig. 34.43b, in which the lenses are separated by 8 cm.

34.49 •• A camera lens has a focal length of 180.0 mm and an aperture diameter of 16.36 mm. (a) What is the f-number of the lens? (b) If the correct exposure of a certain scene is $\frac{1}{30}$ s at $f/11$, what is the correct exposure at $f/2.8$?

34.50 •• Recall that the intensity of light reaching film in a camera is proportional to the effective area of the lens. Camera A has a lens with an aperture diameter of 8.00 mm. It photographs an object using the correct exposure time of $\frac{1}{30}$ s. What exposure time should be used with camera B in photographing the same object with the same film if this camera has a lens with an aperture diameter of 23.1 mm?

34.51 • **Photography.** A 35-mm camera has a standard lens with focal length 50 mm and can focus on objects between 45 cm and infinity. (a) Is the lens for such a camera a concave or a convex lens? (b) The camera is focused by rotating the lens, which moves it on the camera body and changes its distance from the film. In what range of distances between the lens and the film plane must the lens move to focus properly over the 45 cm to infinity range?

Section 34.6 The Eye

34.52 •• BIO **Curvature of the Cornea.** In a simplified model of the human eye, the aqueous and vitreous humors and the lens all have a refractive index of 1.40, and all the refraction occurs at the cornea, whose vertex is 2.60 cm from the retina. What should be the radius of curvature of the cornea such that the image of an object 40.0 cm from the cornea's vertex is focused on the retina?

34.53 •• BIO (a) Where is the near point of an eye for which a contact lens with a power of +2.75 diopters is prescribed? (b) Where is the far point of an eye for which a contact lens with a power of −1.30 diopters is prescribed for distant vision?

34.54 • BIO **Contact Lenses.** Contact lenses are placed right on the eyeball, so the distance from the eye to an object (or image) is the same as the distance from the lens to that object (or image). A certain person can see distant objects well, but his near point is 45.0 cm from his eyes instead of the usual 25.0 cm. (a) Is this person nearsighted or farsighted? (b) What type of lens (converging or diverging) is needed to correct his vision? (c) If the correcting lenses will be contact lenses, what focal length lens is needed and what is its power in diopters?

34.55 •• BIO **Ordinary Glasses.** Ordinary glasses are worn in front of the eye and usually 2.0 cm in front of the eyeball. Suppose that the person in Problem 34.54 prefers ordinary glasses to contact lenses. What focal length lenses are needed to correct his vision, and what is their power in diopters?

34.56 • BIO A person can see clearly up close but cannot focus on objects beyond 75.0 cm. She opts for contact lenses to correct her vision. (a) Is she nearsighted or farsighted? (b) What type of lens (converging or diverging) is needed to correct her vision? (c) What focal length contact lens is needed, and what is its power in diopters?

34.57 •• BIO If the person in Problem 34.56 chooses ordinary glasses over contact lenses, what power lens (in diopters) does she need to correct her vision if the lenses are 2.0 cm in front of the eye?

Section 34.7 The Magnifier

34.58 •• A thin lens with a focal length of 6.00 cm is used as a simple magnifier. (a) What angular magnification is obtainable with the lens if the object is at the focal point? (b) When an object is examined through the lens, how close can it be brought to the lens? Assume that the image viewed by the eye is at the near point, 25.0 cm from the eye, and that the lens is very close to the eye.

34.59 • The focal length of a simple magnifier is 8.00 cm. Assume the magnifier is a thin lens placed very close to the eye. (a) How far in front of the magnifier should an object be placed if the image is formed at the observer's near point, 25.0 cm in front of her eye? (b) If the object is 1.00 mm high, what is the height of its image formed by the magnifier?

34.60 • You want to view an insect 2.00 mm in length through a magnifier. If the insect is to be at the focal point of the magnifier, what focal length will give the image of the insect an angular size of 0.025 radian?

Section 34.8 Microscopes and Telescopes

34.61 • A certain microscope is provided with objectives that have focal lengths of 16 mm, 4 mm, and 1.9 mm and with eyepieces that have angular magnifications of 5× and 10×. Each objective forms an image 120 mm beyond its second focal point. Determine (a) the largest overall angular magnification obtainable and (b) the smallest overall angular magnification obtainable.

34.62 •• **Resolution of a Microscope.** The image formed by a microscope objective with a focal length of 5.00 mm is 160 mm from its second focal point. The eyepiece has a focal length of 26.0 mm. (a) What is the angular magnification of the microscope? (b) The unaided eye can distinguish two points at its near point as separate if they are about 0.10 mm apart. What is the minimum separation between two points that can be observed (or resolved) through this microscope?

34.63 •• The focal length of the eyepiece of a certain microscope is 18.0 mm. The focal length of the objective is 8.00 mm. The distance between objective and eyepiece is 19.7 cm. The final image formed by the eyepiece is at infinity. Treat all lenses as thin. (a) What is the distance from the objective to the object being viewed? (b) What is the magnitude of the linear magnification produced by the objective? (c) What is the overall angular magnification of the microscope?

34.64 •• The eyepiece of a refracting telescope (see Fig. 34.53) has a focal length of 9.00 cm. The distance between objective and eyepiece is 1.80 m, and the final image is at infinity. What is the angular magnification of the telescope?

34.65 •• A telescope is constructed from two lenses with focal lengths of 95.0 cm and 15.0 cm, the 95.0-cm lens being used as the objective. Both the object being viewed and the final image are at infinity. (a) Find the angular magnification for the telescope. (b) Find the height of the image formed by the objective of a building 60.0 m tall, 3.00 km away. (c) What is the angular size of the final image as viewed by an eye very close to the eyepiece?

34.66 •• Saturn is viewed through the Lick Observatory refracting telescope (objective focal length 18 m). If the diameter of the image of Saturn produced by the objective is 1.7 mm, what angle does Saturn subtend from when viewed from earth?

34.67 •• A reflecting telescope (Fig. E34.67) is to be made by using a spherical mirror with a radius of curvature of 1.30 m and an eyepiece with a focal length of 1.10 cm. The final image is at infinity. (a) What should the distance between the eyepiece and the mirror vertex be if the object is taken to be at infinity? (b) What will the angular magnification be?

Figure **E34.67**

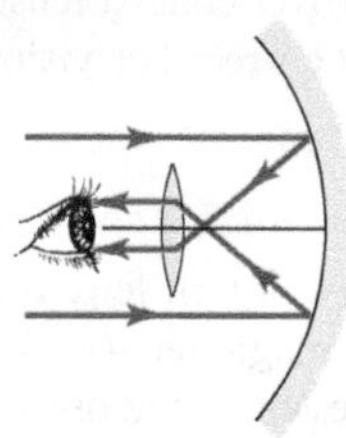

PROBLEMS

34.68 • Where must you place an object in front of a concave mirror with radius R so that the image is erect and $2\frac{1}{2}$ times the size of the object? Where is the image?

34.69 • If you run away from a plane mirror at 3.60 m/s, at what speed does your image move away from you?

34.70 • An object is placed between two plane mirrors arranged at right angles to each other at a distance d_1 from the surface of one mirror and a distance d_2 from the other. (a) How many images are formed? Show the location of the images in a diagram. (b) Draw the paths of rays from the object to the eye of an observer.

34.71 •• What is the size of the smallest vertical plane mirror in which a woman of height h can see her full-length image?

34.72 • A light bulb is 3.00 m from a wall. You are to use a concave mirror to project an image of the bulb on the wall, with the image 2.25 times the size of the object. How far should the mirror be from the wall? What should its radius of curvature be?

34.73 •• A concave mirror is to form an image of the filament of a headlight lamp on a screen 8.00 m from the mirror. The filament is 6.00 mm tall, and the image is to be 24.0 cm tall. (a) How far in front of the vertex of the mirror should the filament be placed? (b) What should be the radius of curvature of the mirror?

34.74 •• **Rear-View Mirror.** A mirror on the passenger side of your car is convex and has a radius of curvature with magnitude 18.0 cm. (a) Another car is behind your car, 9.00 m from the mirror, and this car is viewed in the mirror by your passenger. If this car is 1.5 m tall, what is the height of the image? (b) The mirror has a warning attached that objects viewed in it are closer than they appear. Why is this so?

34.75 • Suppose the lamp filament shown in Example 34.1 (Section 34.2) is moved to a position 8.0 cm in front of the mirror. (a) Where is the image located now? Is it real or virtual? (b) What is the height of the image? Is it erect or inverted? (c) In Example 34.1, the filament is 10.0 cm in front of the mirror, and an image of the filament is formed on a wall 3.00 m from the mirror. If the filament is 8.0 cm from the mirror, can a wall be placed so that an image is formed on it? If so, where should the wall be placed? If not, why not?

34.76 •• A layer of benzene ($n = 1.50$) 4.20 cm deep floats on water ($n = 1.33$) that is 6.50 cm deep. What is the apparent distance from the upper benzene surface to the bottom of the water layer when it is viewed at normal incidence?

34.77 •• **CP CALC** You are in your car driving on a highway at 25 m/s when you glance in the passenger-side mirror (a convex mirror with radius of curvature 150 cm) and notice a truck approaching. If the image of the truck is approaching the vertex of the mirror at a speed of 1.9 m/s when the truck is 2.0 m from the mirror, what is the speed of the truck relative to the highway?

34.78 •• Figure P34.78 shows a small plant near a thin lens. The ray shown is one of the principal rays for the lens. Each square is 2.0 cm along the horizontal direction, but the vertical direction is not to the same scale. Use information from the diagram for the following: (a) Using only the ray shown, decide what type of lens (converging or diverging) this is. (b) What is the focal length of the lens? (c) Locate the image by drawing the other two principal rays. (d) Calculate where the image should be, and compare this result with the graphical solution in part (c).

Figure **P34.78**

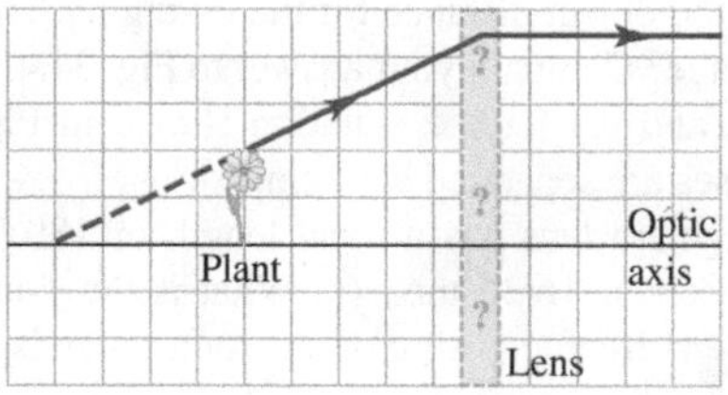

34.79 •• **Pinhole Camera.** A pinhole camera is just a rectangular box with a tiny hole in one face. The film is on the face opposite this hole, and that is where the image is formed. The camera forms an image *without* a lens. (a) Make a clear ray diagram to show how a pinhole camera can form an image on the film without using a lens. (*Hint:* Put an object outside the hole, and then draw rays passing through the hole to the opposite side of the box.) (b) A certain pinhole camera is a box that is 25 cm square and 20.0 cm deep, with the hole in the middle of one of the 25 cm × 25 cm faces. If this camera is used to photograph a fierce chicken that is 18 cm high and 1.5 m in front of the camera, how large is the image of this bird on the film? What is the magnification of this camera?

34.80 ••• A microscope is focused on the upper surface of a glass plate. A second plate is then placed over the first. To focus on the bottom surface of the second plate, the microscope must be raised 0.780 mm. To focus on the upper surface, it must be raised another 2.50 mm. Find the index of refraction of the second plate.

34.81 •• What should be the index of refraction of a transparent sphere in order for paraxial rays from an infinitely distant object to be brought to a focus at the vertex of the surface opposite the point of incidence?

34.82 •• **A Glass Rod.** Both ends of a glass rod with index of refraction 1.60 are ground and polished to convex hemispherical surfaces. The radius of curvature at the left end is 6.00 cm, and the radius of curvature at the right end is 12.0 cm. The length of the rod between vertices is 40.0 cm. The object for the surface at the left end is an arrow that lies 23.0 cm to the left of the vertex of this surface. The arrow is 1.50 mm tall and at right angles to the axis. (a) What constitutes the object for the surface at the right end of the rod? (b) What is the object distance for this surface? (c) Is the object for this surface real or virtual? (d) What is the position of the final image? (e) Is the final image real or virtual? Is it erect or inverted with respect to the original object? (f) What is the height of the final image?

34.83 •• The rod in Problem 34.82 is shortened to a distance of 25.0 cm between its vertices; the curvatures of its ends remain the same. As in Problem 34.82, the object for the surface at the left end is an arrow that lies 23.0 cm to the left of the vertex of this surface. The arrow is 1.50 mm tall and at right angles to the axis. (a) What is the object distance for the surface at the right end of the rod? (b) Is the object for this surface real or virtual? (c) What is the position of the final image? (d) Is the final image real or virtual? Is it erect or inverted with respect to the original object? (e) What is the height of the final image?

34.84 • Figure P34.84 shows an object and its image formed by a thin lens. (a) What is the focal length of the lens, and what type of lens (converging or diverging) is it? (b) What is the height of the image? Is it real or virtual?

Figure **P34.84**

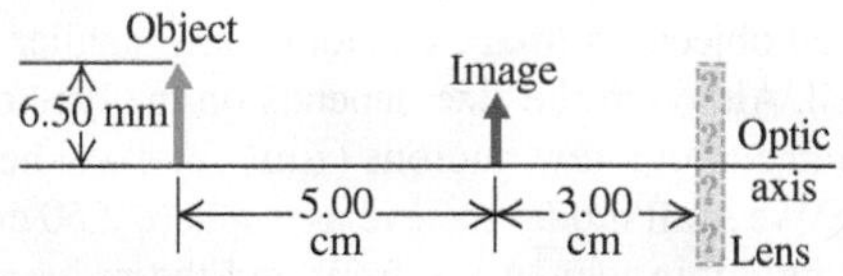

34.85 • Figure P34.85 shows an object and its image formed by a thin lens. (a) What is the focal length of the lens, and what type of lens (converging or diverging) is it? (b) What is the height of the image? Is it real or virtual?

Figure **P34.85**

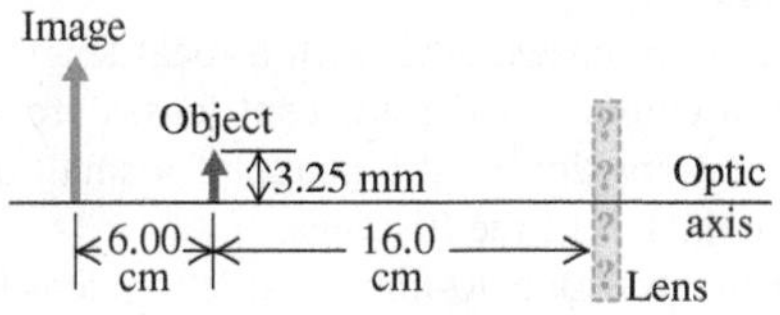

34.86 ••• A transparent rod 30.0 cm long is cut flat at one end and rounded to a hemispherical surface of radius 10.0 cm at the other end. A small object is embedded within the rod along its axis and halfway between its ends, 15.0 cm from the flat end and 15.0 cm from the vertex of the curved end. When viewed from the flat end of the rod, the apparent depth of the object is 9.50 cm from the flat end. What is its apparent depth when viewed from the curved end?

34.87 • BIO **Focus of the Eye.** The cornea of the eye has a radius of curvature of approximately 0.50 cm, and the aqueous humor behind it has an index of refraction of 1.35. The thickness of the cornea itself is small enough that we shall neglect it. The depth of a typical human eye is around 25 mm. (a) What would have to be the radius of curvature of the cornea so that it alone would focus the image of a distant mountain on the retina, which is at the back of the eye opposite the cornea? (b) If the cornea focused the mountain correctly on the retina as described in part (a), would it also focus the text from a computer screen on the retina if that screen were 25 cm in front of the eye? If not, where would it focus that text: in front of or behind the retina? (c) Given that the cornea has a radius of curvature of about 5.0 mm, where does it actually focus the mountain? Is this in front of or behind the retina? Does this help you see why the eye needs help from a lens to complete the task of focusing?

34.88 ••• A transparent rod 50.0 cm long and with a refractive index of 1.60 is cut flat at the right end and rounded to a hemispherical surface with a 15.0-cm radius at the left end. An object is placed on the axis of the rod 12.0 cm to the left of the vertex of the hemispherical end. (a) What is the position of the final image? (b) What is its magnification?

34.89 ••• A glass rod with a refractive index of 1.55 is ground and polished at both ends to hemispherical surfaces with radii of 6.00 cm. When an object is placed on the axis of the rod, 25.0 cm to the left of the left-hand end, the final image is formed 65.0 cm to the right of the right-hand end. What is the length of the rod measured between the vertices of the two hemispherical surfaces?

34.90 • The radii of curvature of the surfaces of a thin converging meniscus lens are $R_1 = +12.0$ cm and $R_2 = +28.0$ cm. The index of refraction is 1.60. (a) Compute the position and size of the image of an object in the form of an arrow 5.00 mm tall, perpendicular to the lens axis, 45.0 cm to the left of the lens. (b) A second converging lens with the same focal length is placed 3.15 m to the right of the first. Find the position and size of the final image. Is the final image erect or inverted with respect to the original object? (c) Repeat part (b) except with the second lens 45.0 cm to the right of the first.

34.91 • An object to the left of a lens is imaged by the lens on a screen 30.0 cm to the right of the lens. When the lens is moved 4.00 cm to the right, the screen must be moved 4.00 cm to the left to refocus the image. Determine the focal length of the lens.

34.92 • An object is placed 18.0 cm from a screen. (a) At what two points between object and screen may a converging lens with a 3.00-cm focal length be placed to obtain an image on the screen? (b) What is the magnification of the image for each position of the lens?

34.93 •• A convex mirror and a concave mirror are placed on the same optic axis, separated by a distance $L = 0.600$ m. The radius of curvature of each mirror has a magnitude of 0.360 m. A light source is located a distance x from the concave mirror, as shown in Fig. P34.93. (a) What distance x will result in the rays from the source returning to the source after reflecting first from the convex mirror and then from the concave mirror? (b) Repeat part (a), but now let the rays reflect first from the concave mirror and then from the convex one.

Figure **P34.93**

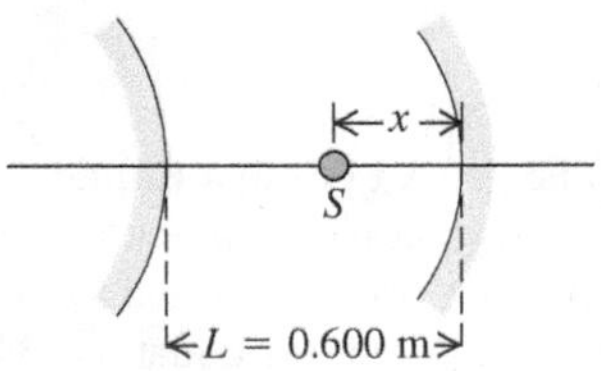

34.94 •• As shown in Fig. P34.94 the candle is at the center of curvature of the concave mirror, whose focal length is 10.0 cm. The converging lens has a focal length of 32.0 cm and is 85.0 cm to the right of the candle. The candle is viewed looking through the lens from the right. The lens forms two images of the candle. The first is formed by light passing directly through the lens. The second image is formed from the light that goes from the candle to the mirror, is reflected, and then passes through the lens. (a) For each of these two images, draw a principal-ray diagram that locates the image. (b) For each image, answer the following questions: (i) Where is the image? (ii) Is the image real or virtual? (iii) Is the image erect or inverted with respect to the original object?

Figure **P34.94**

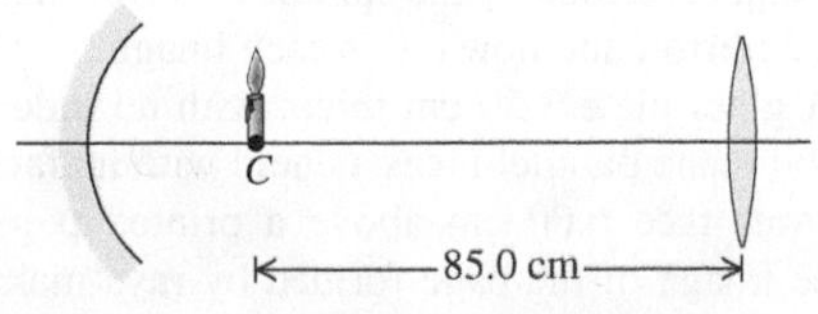

34.95 ••• One end of a long glass rod is ground to a convex hemispherical shape. This glass has an index of refraction of 1.55. When a small leaf is placed 20.0 cm in front of the center of the hemisphere along the optic axis, an image is formed inside the glass 9.12 cm from the spherical surface. Where would the image be formed if the glass were now immersed in water (refractive index 1.33) but nothing else were changed?

34.96 •• **Two Lenses in Contact.** (a) Prove that when two thin lenses with focal lengths f_1 and f_2 are placed *in contact*, the focal length f of the combination is given by the relationship

$$\frac{1}{f} = \frac{1}{f_1} + \frac{1}{f_2}$$

(b) A converging meniscus lens (see Fig. 34.32a) has an index of refraction of 1.55 and radii of curvature for its surfaces of magnitudes 4.50 cm and 9.00 cm. The concave surface is placed upward and filled with carbon tetrachloride (CCl_4), which has $n = 1.46$. What is the focal length of the CCl_4–glass combination?

34.97 ••• Rays from a lens are converging toward a point image P located to the right of the lens. What thickness t of glass with index of refraction 1.60 must be interposed between the lens and P for the image to be formed at P', located 0.30 cm to the right of P? The locations of the piece of glass and of points P and P' are shown in Fig. P34.97.

Figure **P34.97**

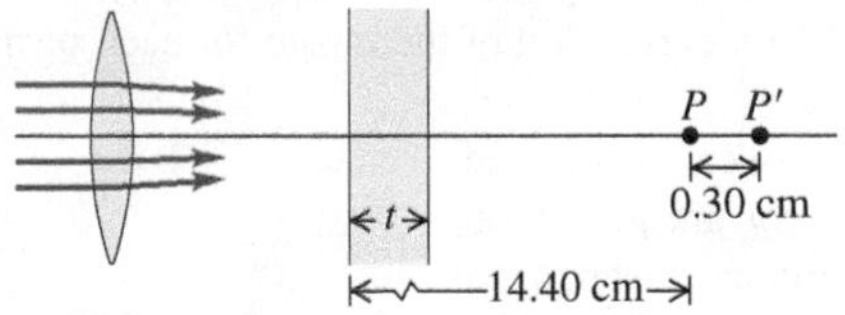

34.98 •• **A Lens in a Liquid.** A lens obeys Snell's law, bending light rays at each surface an amount determined by the index of refraction of the lens and the index of the medium in which the lens is located. (a) Equation (34.19) assumes that the lens is surrounded by air. Consider instead a thin lens immersed in a liquid with refractive index n_{liq}. Prove that the focal length f' is then given by Eq. (34.19) with n replaced by n/n_{liq}. (b) A thin lens with index n has focal length f in vacuum. Use the result of part (a) to show that when this lens is immersed in a liquid of index n_{liq}, it will have a new focal length given by

$$f' = \left[\frac{n_{liq}(n-1)}{n - n_{liq}}\right] f$$

34.99 ••• When an object is placed at the proper distance to the left of a converging lens, the image is focused on a screen 30.0 cm to the right of the lens. A diverging lens is now placed 15.0 cm to the right of the converging lens, and it is found that the screen must be moved 19.2 cm farther to the right to obtain a sharp image. What is the focal length of the diverging lens?

34.100 ••• A convex spherical mirror with a focal length of magnitude 24.0 cm is placed 20.0 cm to the left of a plane mirror. An object 0.250 cm tall is placed midway between the surface of the plane mirror and the vertex of the spherical mirror. The spherical mirror forms multiple images of the object. Where are the two images of the object formed by the spherical mirror that are closest to the spherical mirror, and how tall is each image?

34.101 ••• A glass plate 3.50 cm thick, with an index of refraction of 1.55 and plane parallel faces, is held with its faces horizontal and its lower face 6.00 cm above a printed page. Find the position of the image of the page formed by rays making a small angle with the normal to the plate.

34.102 •• A symmetric, double-convex, thin lens made of glass with index of refraction 1.52 has a focal length in air of 40.0 cm. The lens is sealed into an opening in the left-hand end of a tank filled with water. At the right-hand end of the tank, opposite the lens, is a plane mirror 90.0 cm from the lens. The index of refraction of the water is $\frac{4}{3}$. (a) Find the position of the image formed by the lens–water–mirror system of a small object outside the tank on the lens axis and 70.0 cm to the left of the lens. (b) Is the image real or virtual? (c) Is it erect or inverted? (d) If the object has a height of 4.00 mm, what is the height of the image?

34.103 • You have a camera with a 35.0-mm-focal-length lens and 36.0-mm-wide film. You wish to take a picture of a 12.0-m-long sailboat but find that the image of the boat fills only $\frac{1}{4}$ of the width of the film. (a) How far are you from the boat? (b) How much closer must the boat be to you for its image to fill the width of the film?

34.104 •• BIO **What Is the Smallest Thing We Can See?** The smallest object we can resolve with our eye is limited by the size of the light receptor cells in the retina. In order for us to distinguish any detail in an object, its image cannot be any smaller than a single retinal cell. Although the size depends on the type of cell (rod or cone), a diameter of a few microns (μm) is typical near the center of the eye. We shall model the eye as a sphere 2.50 cm in diameter with a single thin lens at the front and the retina at the rear, with light receptor cells 5.0 μm in diameter. (a) What is the smallest object you can resolve at a near point of 25 cm? (b) What angle is subtended by this object at the eye? Express your answer in units of minutes ($1° = 60$ min), and compare it with the typical experimental value of about 1.0 min. (*Note:* There are other limitations, such as the bending of light as it passes through the pupil, but we shall ignore them here.)

34.105 • Three thin lenses, each with a focal length of 40.0 cm, are aligned on a common axis; adjacent lenses are separated by 52.0 cm. Find the position of the image of a small object on the axis, 80.0 cm to the left of the first lens.

34.106 •• A camera with a 90-mm-focal-length lens is focused on an object 1.30 m from the lens. To refocus on an object 6.50 m from the lens, by how much must the distance between the lens and the film be changed? To refocus on the more distant object, is the lens moved toward or away from the film?

34.107 •• The derivation of the expression for angular magnification, Eq. (34.22), assumed a near point of 25 cm. In fact, the near point changes with age as shown in Table 34.1. In order to achieve an angular magnification of 2.0×, what focal length should be used by a person of (a) age 10; (b) age 30; (c) age 60? (d) If the lens that gives $M = 2.0$ for a 10-year-old is used by a 60-year-old, what angular magnification will the older viewer obtain? (e) Does your answer in part (d) mean that older viewers are able to see more highly magnified images than younger viewers? Explain.

34.108 •• **Angular Magnification.** In deriving Eq. (34.22) for the angular magnification of a magnifier, we assumed that the object is placed at the focal point of the magnifier so that the virtual image is formed at infinity. Suppose instead that the object is placed so that the virtual image appears at an average viewer's near point of 25 cm, the closest point at which the viewer can bring an object into focus. (a) Where should the object be placed to achieve this? Give your answer in terms of the magnifier focal length f. (b) What angle θ' will an object of height y subtend at the position found in part (a)? (c) Find the angular magnification M with the object at the position found in part (a). The angle θ is the same as in Fig. 34.51a, since it refers to viewing the object *without* the magnifier. (d) For a convex lens with $f = +10.0$ cm, what is the value of M with the object at the position found in part (a)? How many times greater is M in this case than in the case where the image is formed at infinity? (e) In the description of a compound microscope in Section 34.8, it is stated that in a properly designed instrument, the real image formed by the objective lies *just inside* the first focal point F_1' of the eyepiece. What advantages are gained by having the image formed by the objective be just inside F_1', as opposed to precisely at F_1'? What happens if the image formed by the objective is *just outside* F_1'?

34.109 •• BIO In one form of cataract surgery the person's natural lens, which has become cloudy, is replaced by an artificial lens. The refracting properties of the replacement lens can be chosen so that the person's eye focuses on distant objects. But there is no accommodation, and glasses or contact lenses are needed for close vision. What is the power, in diopters, of the corrective contact lenses that will enable a person who has had such surgery to focus on the page of a book at a distance of 24 cm?

34.110 •• BIO **A Nearsighted Eye.** A certain very nearsighted person cannot focus on anything farther than 36.0 cm from the eye. Consider the simplified model of the eye described in Exercise 34.52. If the radius of curvature of the cornea is 0.75 cm when the eye is focusing on an object 36.0 cm from the cornea vertex and the indexes of refraction are as described in Exercise 34.52, what is the distance from the cornea vertex to the retina? What does this tell you about the shape of the nearsighted eye?

34.111 •• BIO A person with a near point of 85 cm, but excellent distant vision, normally wears corrective glasses. But he loses them while traveling. Fortunately, he has his old pair as a spare. (a) If the lenses of the old pair have a power of +2.25 diopters, what is his near point (measured from his eye) when he is wearing the old glasses if they rest 2.0 cm in front of his eye? (b) What would his near point be if his old glasses were contact lenses instead?

34.112 •• **The Galilean Telescope.** Figure P34.112 is a diagram of a *Galilean telescope,* or *opera glass,* with both the object and its final image at infinity. The image I serves as a virtual object for the eyepiece. The final image is virtual and erect. (a) Prove that the angular magnification is $M = -f_1/f_2$. (b) A Galilean telescope is to be constructed with the same objective lens as in Exercise 34.65. What focal length should the eyepiece have if this telescope is to have the same magnitude of angular magnification as the one in Exercise 34.65? (c) Compare the lengths of the telescopes.

Figure **P34.112**

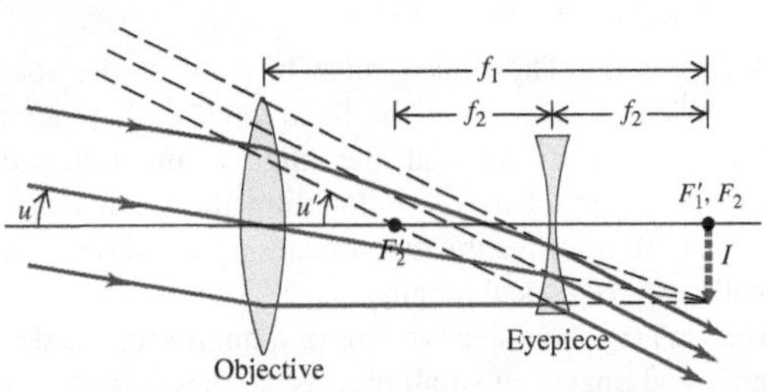

34.113 ••• **Focal Length of a Zoom Lens.** Figure P34.113 shows a simple version of a zoom lens. The converging lens has focal length f_1, and the diverging lens has focal length $f_2 = -|f_2|$. The two lenses are separated by a variable distance d that is always less than f_1. Also, the magnitude of the focal length of the diverging lens satisfies the inequality $|f_2| > (f_1 - d)$. To determine the effective focal length of the combination lens, consider a bundle of parallel rays of radius r_0 entering the converging lens. (a) Show that the radius of the ray bundle decreases to $r_0' = r_0(f_1 - d)/f_1$ at the point that it enters the diverging lens. (b) Show that the final image I' is formed a distance $s_2' = |f_2|(f_1 - d)/(|f_2| - f_1 + d)$ to the right of the diverging lens. (c) If the rays that emerge from the diverging lens and reach the final image point are extended backward to the left of the diverging lens, they will eventually expand to the original radius r_0 at some point Q. The distance from the final image I' to the point Q is the *effective focal length* f of the lens combination; if the combination were replaced by a single lens of focal length f placed at Q, parallel rays would still be brought to a focus at I'. Show that the effective focal length is given by $f = f_1|f_2|/(|f_2| - f_1 + d)$. (d) If $f_1 = 12.0$ cm, $f_2 = -18.0$ cm, and the separation d is adjustable between 0 and 4.0 cm, find the maximum and minimum focal lengths of the combination. What value of d gives $f = 30.0$ cm?

Figure **P34.113**

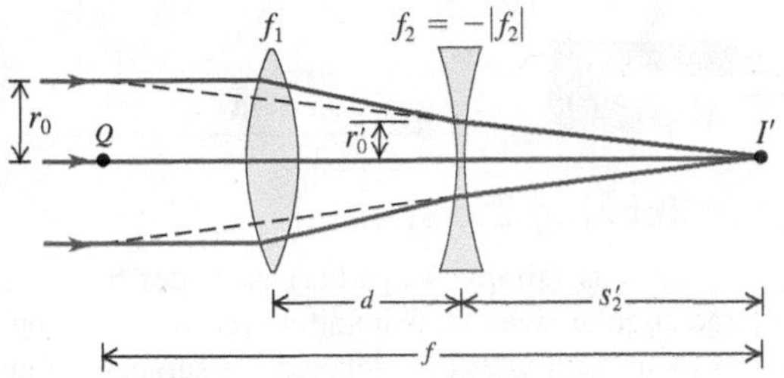

34.114 • A certain reflecting telescope, constructed as shown in Fig. E34.67, has a spherical mirror with a radius of curvature of 96.0 cm and an eyepiece with a focal length of 1.20 cm. If the angular magnification has a magnitude of 36 and the object is at infinity, find the position of the eyepiece and the position and nature (real or virtual) of the final image. (*Note:* $|M|$ is *not* equal to $|f_1|/|f_2|$, so the image formed by the eyepiece is *not* at infinity.)

34.115 • A microscope with an objective of focal length 8.00 mm and an eyepiece of focal length 7.50 cm is used to project an image on a screen 2.00 m from the eyepiece. Let the image distance of the objective be 18.0 cm. (a) What is the lateral magnification of the image? (b) What is the distance between the objective and the eyepiece?

CHALLENGE PROBLEMS

34.116 ••• *Spherical aberration* is a blurring of the image formed by a spherical mirror. It occurs because parallel rays striking the mirror far from the optic axis are focused at a different point than are rays near the axis. This problem is usually minimized by using only the center of a spherical mirror. (a) Show that for a spherical concave mirror, the focus moves toward the mirror as the parallel rays move toward the outer edge of the mirror. (*Hint:* Derive an analytic expression for the distance from the vertex to the focus of the ray for a particular parallel ray. This expression should be in terms of (i) the radius of curvature R of the mirror and (ii) the angle θ between the incident ray and a line connecting the center of curvature of the mirror with the point where the ray strikes the mirror.) (b) What value of θ produces a 2% change in the location of the focus, compared to the location for θ very close to zero?

34.117 ••• CALC (a) For a lens with focal length f, find the smallest distance possible between the object and its real image. (b) Graph the distance between the object and the real image as a function of the distance of the object from the lens. Does your graph agree with the result you found in part (a)?

34.118 ••• **An Object at an Angle.** A 16.0-cm-long pencil is placed at a 45.0° angle, with its center 15.0 cm above the optic axis and 45.0 cm from a lens with a 20.0-cm focal length as shown in Fig. P34.118. (Note that the figure is not drawn to scale.) Assume that the diameter of the lens is large enough for the paraxial approximation to be valid. (a) Where is the image of the pencil? (Give the location of the images of the points A, B, and C on the object, which are located at the eraser, point, and center of the pencil, respectively.) (b) What is the length of the image (that is, the distance between the images of points A and B)? (c) Show the orientation of the image in a sketch.

Figure **P34.118**

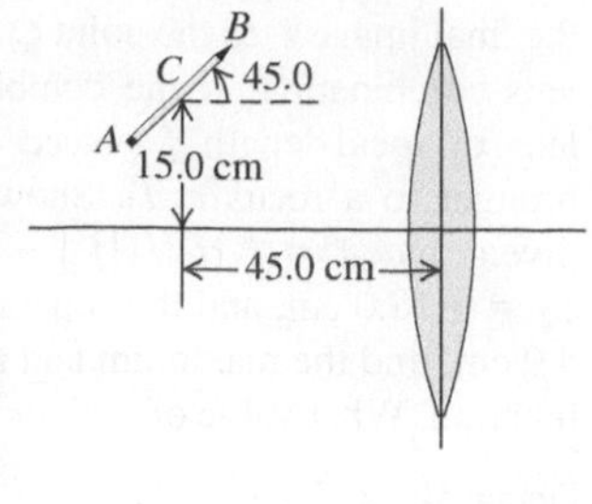

34.119 ••• BIO People with normal vision cannot focus their eyes underwater if they aren't wearing a face mask or goggles and there is water in contact with their eyes (see Discussion Question Q34.23). (a) Why not? (b) With the simplified model of the eye described in Exercise 34.52, what corrective lens (specified by focal length as measured in air) would be needed to enable a person underwater to focus an infinitely distant object? (Be careful—the focal length of a lens underwater is *not* the same as in air! See Problem 34.98. Assume that the corrective lens has a refractive index of 1.62 and that the lens is used in eyeglasses, not goggles, so there is water on both sides of the lens. Assume that the eyeglasses are 2.00 cm in front of the eye.)

Answers

Chapter Opening Question ?

A magnifying lens (simple magnifier) produces a virtual image with a large angular size that is infinitely far away, so you can see it in sharp focus with your eyes relaxed. (A surgeon doing microsurgery would not appreciate having to strain his eyes while working.) The object should be at the focal point of the lens, so the object and lens are separated by one focal length.

Test Your Understanding Questions

34.1 Answer: (iv) When you are a distance s from the mirror, your image is a distance s on the other side of the mirror and the distance from you to your image is $2s$. As you move toward the mirror, the distance $2s$ changes at twice the rate of the distance s, so your image moves toward you at speed $2v$.

34.2 Answers: (a) concave, (b) (ii) A convex mirror always produces an erect image, but that image is smaller than the object (see Fig. 34.16b). Hence a concave mirror must be used. The image will be erect and enlarged only if the distance from the object (your face) to the mirror is less than the focal length of the mirror, as in Fig. 34.20d.

34.3 Answer: no The sun is very far away, so the object distance is essentially infinite: $s = \infty$ and $1/s = 0$. Material a is air ($n_a = 1.00$) and material b is water ($n_b = 1.33$), so the image position s' is given by

$$\frac{n_a}{s} + \frac{n_b}{s'} = \frac{n_b - n_a}{R} \quad \text{or} \quad 0 + \frac{1.33}{s'} = \frac{1.33 - 1.00}{R}$$

$$s' = \frac{1.33}{0.33}R = 4.0R$$

The image would be formed 4.0 drop radii from the front surface of the drop. But since each drop is only a part of a complete sphere, the distance from the front to the back of the drop is less than $2R$. Thus the rays of sunlight never reach the image point, and the drops do not form an image of the sun on the leaf. While the rays are not focused to a point, they are nonetheless concentrated and can cause damage to the leaf.

34.4 Answers: A and C When rays A and D are extended backward, they pass through focal point F_2; thus, before they passed through the lens, they were parallel to the optic axis. The figures show that ray A emanated from point Q, but ray D did not. Ray B is parallel to the optic axis, so before it passed through the lens, it was directed toward focal point F_1. Hence it cannot have come from point Q. Ray C passes through the center of the lens and hence is not deflected by its passage; tracing the ray backward shows that it emanates from point Q.

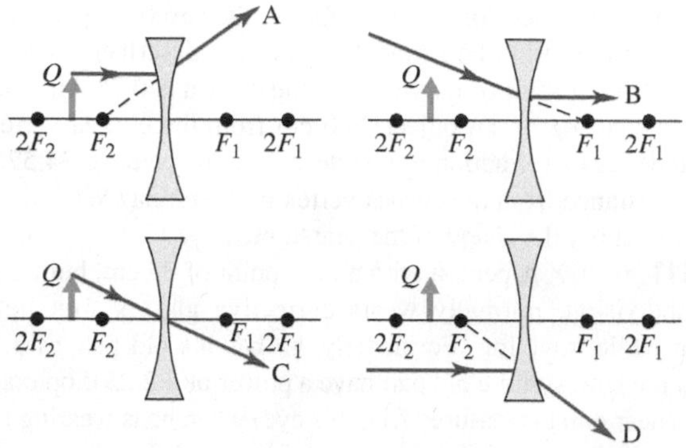

34.5 Answer: (iii) The smaller image area of the CCD array means that the angle of view is decreased for a given focal length. Individual objects make images of the same size in either case; when a smaller light-sensitive area is used, fewer images fit into the area and the field of view is narrower.

34.6 Answer: (iii) This lens is designed to correct for a type of astigmatism. Along the vertical axis, the lens is configured as a converging lens; along the horizontal axis, the lens is configured as a diverging lens. Hence the eye is hyperopic (see Fig. 34.46) for objects that are oriented vertically but myopic for objects that are oriented horizontally (see Fig. 34.47). Without correction, the eye focuses vertical objects behind the retina but horizontal objects in front of the retina.

34.7 Answer: (ii) The object must be held at the focal point, which is twice as far away if the focal length f is twice as great. Equation (24.22) shows that the angular magnification M is inversely proportional to f, so doubling the focal length makes M $\frac{1}{2}$ as great. To improve the magnification, you should use a magnifier with a *shorter* focal length.

34.8 Answer: (i) The objective lens of a microscope is designed to make enlarged images of small objects, so the absolute value of its lateral magnification m is greater than 1. By contrast, the objective lens of a refracting telescope is designed to make *reduced* images. For example, the moon is thousands of kilometers in diameter, but its image may fit on a CCD array a few centimeters across. Thus $|m|$ is much less than 1 for a refracting telescope. (In both cases m is negative because the objective makes an inverted image, which is why the question asks about the absolute value of m.)

Bridging Problem

Answers: (a) 29.9 cm to the left of the goblet
(b) 3.73 cm to the right of the goblet

35

INTERFERENCE

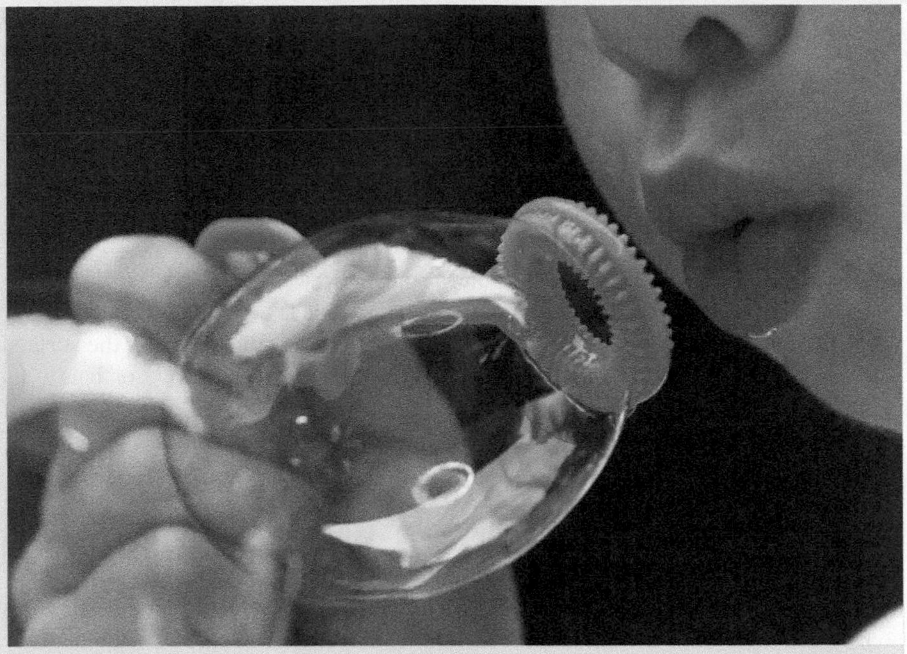

? Soapy water is colorless, but when blown into bubbles it shows vibrant colors. How does the thickness of the bubble walls determine the particular colors that appear?

LEARNING GOALS

By studying this chapter, you will learn:

- What happens when two waves combine, or interfere, in space.
- How to understand the interference pattern formed by the interference of two coherent light waves.
- How to calculate the intensity at various points in an interference pattern.
- How interference occurs when light reflects from the two surfaces of a thin film.
- How interference makes it possible to measure extremely small distances.

An ugly black oil spot on the pavement can become a thing of beauty after a rain, when the oil reflects a rainbow of colors. Multicolored reflections can also be seen from the surfaces of soap bubbles and DVDs. How is it possible for colorless objects to produce these remarkable colors?

In our discussion of lenses, mirrors, and optical instruments we used the model of *geometric optics,* in which we represent light as *rays,* straight lines that are bent at a reflecting or refracting surface. But many aspects of the behavior of light *can't* be understood on the basis of rays. We have already learned that light is fundamentally a *wave,* and in some situations we have to consider its wave properties explicitly. If two or more light waves of the same frequency overlap at a point, the total effect depends on the *phases* of the waves as well as their amplitudes. The resulting patterns of light are a result of the *wave* nature of light and cannot be understood on the basis of rays. Optical effects that depend on the wave nature of light are grouped under the heading **physical optics.**

In this chapter we'll look at *interference* phenomena that occur when two waves combine. The colors seen in oil films and soap bubbles are a result of interference between light reflected from the front and back surfaces of a thin film of oil or soap solution. Effects that occur when *many* sources of waves are present are called *diffraction* phenomena; we'll study these in Chapter 36. In that chapter we'll see that diffraction effects occur whenever a wave passes through an aperture or around an obstacle. They are important in practical applications of physical optics such as diffraction gratings, x-ray diffraction, and holography.

While our primary concern is with light, interference and diffraction can occur with waves of *any* kind. As we go along, we'll point out applications to other types of waves such as sound and water waves.

35.1 Interference and Coherent Sources

As we discussed in Chapter 15, the term **interference** refers to any situation in which two or more waves overlap in space. When this occurs, the total wave at any point at any instant of time is governed by the **principle of superposition,** which we introduced in Section 15.6 in the context of waves on a string. This principle also applies to electromagnetic waves and is the most important principle in all of physical optics. The principle of superposition states:

When two or more waves overlap, the resultant displacement at any point and at any instant is found by adding the instantaneous displacements that would be produced at the point by the individual waves if each were present alone.

(In some special situations, such as electromagnetic waves propagating in a crystal, this principle may not apply. A discussion of these is beyond our scope.)

We use the term "displacement" in a general sense. With waves on the surface of a liquid, we mean the actual displacement of the surface above or below its normal level. With sound waves, the term refers to the excess or deficiency of pressure. For electromagnetic waves, we usually mean a specific component of electric or magnetic field.

Interference in Two or Three Dimensions

We have already discussed one important case of interference, in which two identical waves propagating in opposite directions combine to produce a *standing wave.* We saw this in Chapters 15 and 16 for transverse waves on a string and for longitudinal waves in a fluid filling a pipe; we described the same phenomenon for electromagnetic waves in Section 32.5. In all of these cases the waves propagated along only a single axis: along a string, along the length of a fluid-filled pipe, or along the propagation direction of an electromagnetic plane wave. But light waves can (and do) travel in *two* or *three* dimensions, as can any kind of wave that propagates in a two- or three-dimensional medium. In this section we'll see what happens when we combine waves that spread out in two or three dimensions from a pair of identical wave sources.

35.1 A "snapshot" of sinusoidal waves of frequency f and wavelength λ spreading out from source S_1 in all directions.

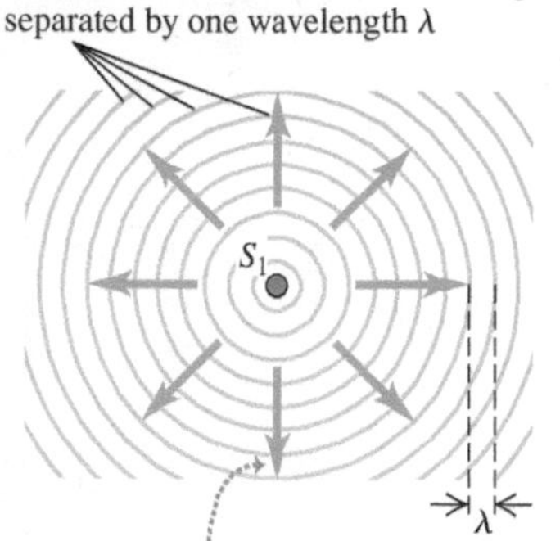

Interference effects are most easily seen when we combine *sinusoidal* waves with a single frequency f and wavelength λ. Figure 35.1 shows a "snapshot" of a *single* source S_1 of sinusoidal waves and some of the wave fronts produced by this source. The figure shows only the wave fronts corresponding to wave *crests,* so the spacing between successive wave fronts is one wavelength. The material surrounding S_1 is uniform, so the wave speed is the same in all directions, and there is no refraction (and hence no bending of the wave fronts). If the waves are two-dimensional, like waves on the surface of a liquid, the circles in Fig. 35.1 represent circular wave fronts; if the waves propagate in three dimensions, the circles represent spherical wave fronts spreading away from S_1.

In optics, sinusoidal waves are characteristic of **monochromatic light** (light of a single color). While it's fairly easy to make water waves or sound waves of a single frequency, common sources of light *do not* emit monochromatic (single-frequency) light. For example, incandescent light bulbs and flames emit a continuous distribution of wavelengths. By far the most nearly monochromatic source that is available at present is the *laser.* An example is the helium–neon laser, which emits red light at 632.8 nm with a wavelength range of the order of ± 0.000001 nm, or about one part in 10^9. As we analyze interference and diffraction effects in this chapter and the next, we will assume that we are working with monochromatic waves (unless we explicitly state otherwise).

Constructive and Destructive Interference

Two identical sources of monochromatic waves, S_1 and S_2, are shown in Fig. 35.2a. The two sources produce waves of the same amplitude and the same wavelength λ.

In addition, the two sources are permanently *in phase;* they vibrate in unison. They might be two loudspeakers driven by the same amplifier, two radio antennas powered by the same transmitter, or two small slits in an opaque screen, illuminated by the same monochromatic light source. We will see that if there were not a constant phase relationship between the two sources, the phenomena we are about to discuss would not occur. Two monochromatic sources of the same frequency and with a constant phase relationship (not necessarily in phase) are said to be **coherent.** We also use the term *coherent waves* (or, for light waves, *coherent light*) to refer to the waves emitted by two such sources.

If the waves emitted by the two coherent sources are *transverse,* like electromagnetic waves, then we will also assume that the wave disturbances produced by both sources have the same *polarization* (that is, they lie along the same line). For example, the sources S_1 and S_2 in Fig. 35.2a could be two radio antennas in the form of long rods oriented parallel to the z-axis (perpendicular to the plane of the figure); at any point in the xy-plane the waves produced by both antennas have $\vec{E}$ fields with only a z-component. Then we need only a single scalar function to describe each wave; this makes the analysis much easier.

We position the two sources of equal amplitude, equal wavelength, and (if the waves are transverse) the same polarization along the y-axis in Fig. 35.2a, equidistant from the origin. Consider a point a on the x-axis. From symmetry the two distances from S_1 to a and from S_2 to a are *equal;* waves from the two sources thus require equal times to travel to a. Hence waves that leave S_1 and S_2 in phase arrive at a in phase. The two waves add, and the total amplitude at a is *twice* the amplitude of each individual wave. This is true for *any* point on the x-axis.

Similarly, the distance from S_2 to point b is exactly two wavelengths *greater* than the distance from S_1 to b. A wave crest from S_1 arrives at b exactly two cycles earlier than a crest emitted at the same time from S_2, and again the two waves arrive in phase. As at point a, the total amplitude is the sum of the amplitudes of the waves from S_1 and S_2.

In general, when waves from two or more sources arrive at a point *in phase,* they reinforce each other: The amplitude of the resultant wave is the *sum* of the amplitudes of the individual waves. This is called **constructive interference** (Fig. 35.2b). Let the distance from S_1 to any point P be r_1, and let the distance from S_2 to P be r_2. For constructive interference to occur at P, the path difference $r_2 - r_1$ for the two sources must be an integral multiple of the wavelength λ:

$$r_2 - r_1 = m\lambda \qquad (m = 0, \pm 1, \pm 2, \pm 3, \ldots) \qquad \text{(constructive interference, sources in phase)} \tag{35.1}$$

In Fig. 35.2a, points a and b satisfy Eq. (35.1) with $m = 0$ and $m = +2$, respectively.

Something different occurs at point c in Fig. 35.2a. At this point, the path difference $r_2 - r_1 = -2.50\lambda$, which is a *half-integral* number of wavelengths. Waves from the two sources arrive at point c exactly a half-cycle out of phase. A crest of one wave arrives at the same time as a crest in the opposite direction (a "trough") of the other wave (Fig. 35.2c). The resultant amplitude is the *difference* between the two individual amplitudes. If the individual amplitudes are equal, then the total amplitude is *zero*! This cancellation or partial cancellation of the individual waves is called **destructive interference.** The condition for destructive interference in the situation shown in Fig. 35.2a is

$$r_2 - r_1 = \left(m + \tfrac{1}{2}\right)\lambda \quad (m = 0, \pm 1, \pm 2, \pm 3, \ldots) \quad \text{(destructive interference, sources in phase)} \tag{35.2}$$

The path difference at point c in Fig. 35.2a satisfies Eq. (35.2) with $m = -3$.

35.2 (a) A "snapshot" of sinusoidal waves spreading out from two coherent sources S_1 and S_2. Constructive interference occurs at point a (equidistant from the two sources) and (b) at point b. (c) Destructive interference occurs at point c.

(a) Two coherent wave sources separated by a distance 4λ

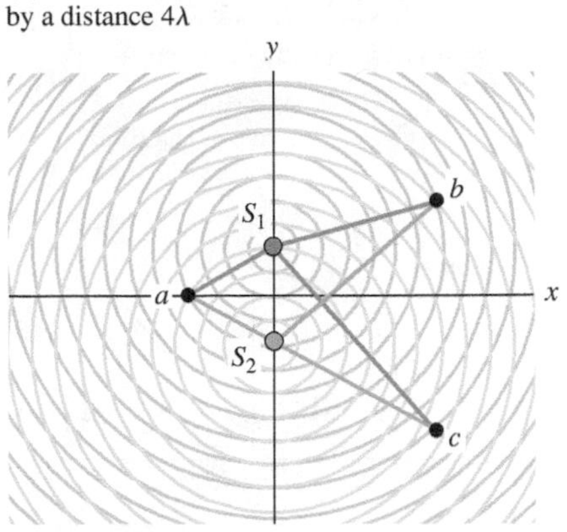

(b) Conditions for constructive interference: Waves interfere constructively if their path lengths differ by an integral number of wavelengths: $r_2 - r_1 = m\lambda$.

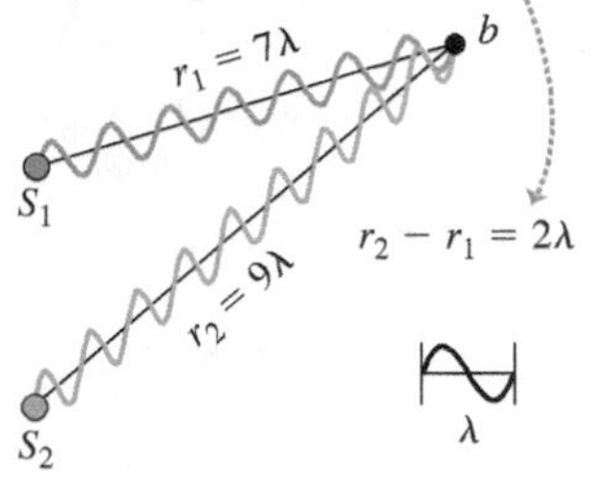

(c) Conditions for destructive interference: Waves interfere destructively if their path lengths differ by a half-integral number of wavelengths: $r_2 - r_1 = (m + \frac{1}{2})\lambda$.

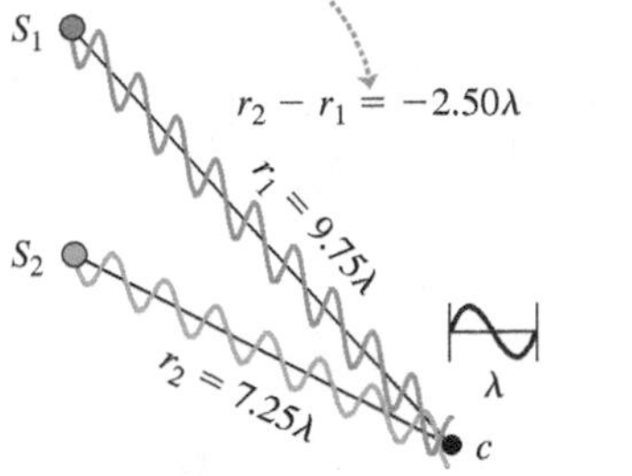

35.3 The same as Fig. 35.2a, but with red antinodal curves (curves of maximum amplitude) superimposed. All points on each curve satisfy Eq. (35.1) with the value of m shown. The nodal curves (not shown) lie between each adjacent pair of antinodal curves.

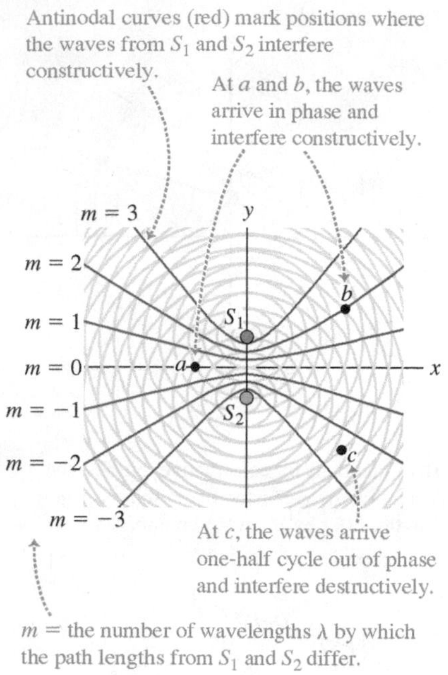

Figure 35.3 shows the same situation as in Fig. 35.2a, but with red curves that show all positions where *constructive* interference occurs. On each curve, the path difference $r_2 - r_1$ is equal to an integer m times the wavelength, as in Eq. (35.1). These curves are called **antinodal curves.** They are directly analogous to *antinodes* in the standing-wave patterns described in Chapters 15 and 16 and Section 32.5. In a standing wave formed by interference between waves propagating in opposite directions, the antinodes are points at which the amplitude is maximum; likewise, the wave amplitude in the situation of Fig. 35.3 is maximum along the antinodal curves. Not shown in Fig. 35.3 are the **nodal curves,** which are the curves that show where *destructive* interference occurs in accordance with Eq. (35.2); these are analogous to the *nodes* in a standing-wave pattern. A nodal curve lies between each two adjacent antinodal curves in Fig. 35.3; one such curve, corresponding to $r_2 - r_1 = -2.50\lambda$, passes through point c.

In some cases, such as two loudspeakers or two radio-transmitter antennas, the interference pattern is three-dimensional. Think of rotating the color curves of Fig. 35.3 around the y-axis; then maximum constructive interference occurs at all points on the resulting surfaces of revolution.

CAUTION **Interference patterns are not standing waves** The interference patterns in Figs. 35.2a and 35.3 are *not* standing waves, though they have some similarities to the standing-wave patterns described in Chapters 15 and 16 and Section 32.5. In a standing wave, the interference is between two waves propagating in opposite directions; there is *no* net energy flow in either direction (the energy in the wave is left "standing"). In the situations shown in Figs. 35.2a and 35.3, there is likewise a stationary pattern of antinodal and nodal curves, but there is a net flow of energy *outward* from the two sources. All that interference does is to "channel" the energy flow so that it is greatest along the antinodal curves and least along the nodal curves. ❙

For Eqs. (35.1) and (35.2) to hold, the two sources must have the same wavelength and must *always* be in phase. These conditions are rather easy to satisfy for sound waves. But with *light* waves there is no practical way to achieve a constant phase relationship (coherence) with two independent sources. This is because of the way light is emitted. In ordinary light sources, atoms gain excess energy by thermal agitation or by impact with accelerated electrons. Such an "excited" atom begins to radiate energy and continues until it has lost all the energy it can, typically in a time of the order of 10^{-8} s. The many atoms in a source ordinarily radiate in an unsynchronized and random phase relationship, and the light that is emitted from *two* such sources has no definite phase relationship.

However, the light from a single source can be split so that parts of it emerge from two or more regions of space, forming two or more *secondary sources.* Then any random phase change in the source affects these secondary sources equally and does not change their *relative* phase.

The distinguishing feature of light from a *laser* is that the emission of light from many atoms is synchronized in frequency and phase. As a result, the random phase changes mentioned above occur much less frequently. Definite phase relationships are preserved over correspondingly much greater lengths in the beam, and laser light is much more coherent than ordinary light.

Test Your Understanding of Section 35.1 Consider a point in Fig. 35.3 on the positive y-axis above S_1. Does this point lie on (i) an antinodal curve; (ii) a nodal curve; or (iii) neither? (*Hint:* The distance between S_1 and S_2 is 4λ.) MP ❙

35.2 Two-Source Interference of Light

The interference pattern produced by two coherent sources of *water* waves of the same wavelength can be readily seen in a ripple tank with a shallow layer of water (Fig. 35.4). This pattern is not directly visible when the interference is between *light* waves, since light traveling in a uniform medium cannot be seen. (A shaft of afternoon sunlight in a room is made visible by scattering from airborne dust particles.)

One of the earliest quantitative experiments to reveal the interference of light from two sources was performed in 1800 by the English scientist Thomas Young. We will refer back to this experiment several times in this and later chapters, so it's important to understand it in detail. Young's apparatus is shown in perspective in Fig. 35.5a. A light source (not shown) emits monochromatic light; however, this light is not suitable for use in an interference experiment because emissions from different parts of an ordinary source are not synchronized. To remedy this, the light is directed at a screen with a narrow slit S_0, 1 μm or so wide. The light emerging from the slit originated from only a small region of the light source; thus slit S_0 behaves more nearly like the idealized source shown in Fig. 35.1. (In modern versions of the experiment, a laser is used as a source of coherent light, and the slit S_0 isn't needed.) The light from slit S_0 falls on a screen with two other narrow slits S_1 and S_2, each 1 μm or so wide and a few tens or hundreds of micrometers apart. Cylindrical wave fronts spread out from slit S_0 and reach slits S_1 and S_2 *in phase* because they travel equal distances from S_0. The waves *emerging* from slits S_1 and S_2 are therefore also always in phase, so S_1 and S_2 are *coherent* sources. The interference of waves from S_1 and S_2 produces a pattern in space like that to the right of the sources in Figs. 35.2a and 35.3.

To visualize the interference pattern, a screen is placed so that the light from S_1 and S_2 falls on it (Fig. 35.5b). The screen will be most brightly illuminated at points P, where the light waves from the slits interfere constructively, and will be darkest at points where the interference is destructive.

To simplify the analysis of Young's experiment, we assume that the distance R from the slits to the screen is so large in comparison to the distance d between the slits that the lines from S_1 and S_2 to P are very nearly parallel, as in Fig. 35.5c. This is usually the case for experiments with light; the slit separation is typically a few millimeters, while the screen may be a meter or more away. The difference in path length is then given by

35.4 The concepts of constructive interference and destructive interference apply to these water waves as well as to light waves and sound waves.

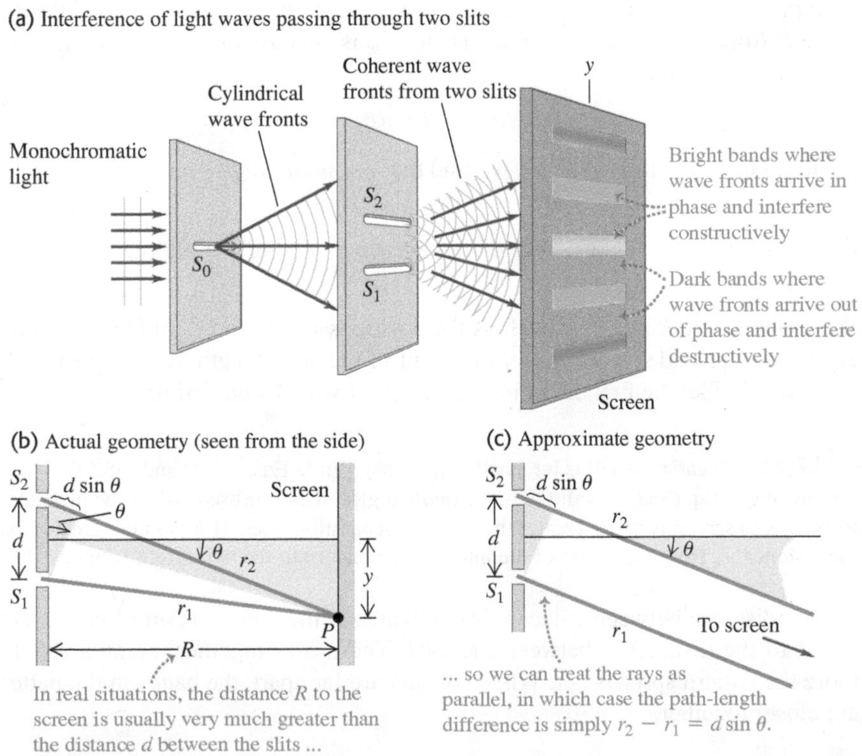

35.5 (a) Young's experiment to show interference of light passing through two slits. A pattern of bright and dark areas appears on the screen (see Fig. 35.6). (b) Geometrical analysis of Young's experiment. For the case shown, $r_2 > r_1$ and both y and θ are positive. If point P is on the other side of the screen's center, $r_2 < r_1$ and both y and θ are negative. (c) Approximate geometry when the distance R to the screen is much greater than the distance d between the slits.

MasteringPHYSICS

PhET: Wave Interference
ActivPhysics 16.1: Two-Source Interference: Introduction
ActivPhysics 16.2: Two-Source Interference: Qualitative Questions
ActivPhysics 16.3: Two-Source Interference: Problems

$$r_2 - r_1 = d\sin\theta \qquad (35.3)$$

where θ is the angle between a line from slits to screen (shown in blue in Fig. 35.5c) and the normal to the plane of the slits (shown as a thin black line).

Constructive and Destructive Two-Slit Interference

We found in Section 35.1 that constructive interference (reinforcement) occurs at points where the path difference is an integral number of wavelengths, $m\lambda$, where $m = 0, \pm1, \pm2, \pm3, \ldots$. So the bright regions on the screen in Fig. 35.5a occur at angles θ for which

$$d\sin\theta = m\lambda \quad (m = 0, \pm1, \pm2, \ldots) \quad \text{(constructive interference, two slits)} \qquad (35.4)$$

Similarly, destructive interference (cancellation) occurs, forming dark regions on the screen, at points for which the path difference is a half-integral number of wavelengths, $\left(m + \frac{1}{2}\right)\lambda$:

$$d\sin\theta = \left(m + \tfrac{1}{2}\right)\lambda \quad (m = 0, \pm1, \pm2, \ldots) \quad \text{(destructive interference, two slits)} \qquad (35.5)$$

Thus the pattern on the screen of Figs. 35.5a and 35.5b is a succession of bright and dark bands, or **interference fringes,** parallel to the slits S_1 and S_2. A photograph of such a pattern is shown in Fig. 35.6. The center of the pattern is a bright band corresponding to $m = 0$ in Eq. (35.4); this point on the screen is equidistant from the two slits.

35.6 Photograph of interference fringes produced on a screen in Young's double-slit experiment.

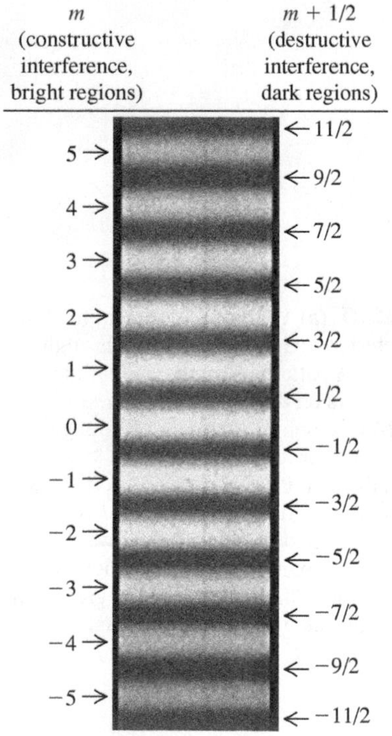

We can derive an expression for the positions of the centers of the bright bands on the screen. In Fig. 35.5b, y is measured from the center of the pattern, corresponding to the distance from the center of Fig. 35.6. Let y_m be the distance from the center of the pattern ($\theta = 0$) to the center of the mth bright band. Let θ_m be the corresponding value of θ; then

$$y_m = R\tan\theta_m$$

In experiments such as this, the distances y_m are often much smaller than the distance R from the slits to the screen. Hence θ_m is very small, $\tan\theta_m$ is very nearly equal to $\sin\theta_m$, and

$$y_m = R\sin\theta_m$$

Combining this with Eq. (35.4), we find that *for small angles only,*

$$y_m = R\frac{m\lambda}{d} \quad \text{(constructive interference in Young's experiment)} \qquad (35.6)$$

We can measure R and d, as well as the positions y_m of the bright fringes, so this experiment provides a direct measurement of the wavelength λ. Young's experiment was in fact the first direct measurement of wavelengths of light.

CAUTION **Equation (35.6) is for small angles only** While Eqs. (35.4) and (35.5) are valid for any angle, Eq. (35.6) is valid only for *small* angles. It can be used *only* if the distance R from slits to screen is much greater than the slit separation d and if R is much greater than the distance y_m from the center of the interference pattern to the mth bright fringe.

The distance between adjacent bright bands in the pattern is *inversely* proportional to the distance d between the slits. The closer together the slits are, the more the pattern spreads out. When the slits are far apart, the bands in the pattern are closer together.

While we have described the experiment that Young performed with visible light, the results given in Eqs. (35.4) and (35.5) are valid for *any* type of wavc, provided that the resultant wave from two coherent sources is detected at a point that is far away in comparison to the separation d.

Example 35.1 Two-slit interference

Figure 35.7 shows a two-slit interference experiment in which the slits are 0.200 mm apart and the screen is 1.00 m from the slits. The $m = 3$ bright fringe in the figure is 9.49 mm from the central fringe. Find the wavelength of the light.

35.7 Using a two-slit interference experiment to measure the wavelength of light.

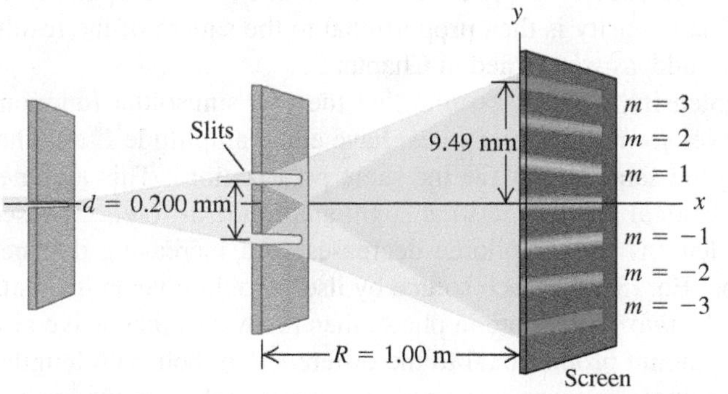

SOLUTION

IDENTIFY and SET UP: Our target variable in this two-slit interference problem is the wavelength λ. We are given the slit separation $d = 0.200$ mm, the distance from slits to screen $R = 1.00$ m, and the distance $y_3 = 9.49$ mm on the screen from the center of the interference pattern to the $m = 3$ bright fringe. We may use Eq. (35.6) to find λ, since the value of R is so much greater than the values of d or y_3.

EXECUTE: We solve Eq. (35.6) for λ for the case $m = 3$:

$$\lambda = \frac{y_m d}{mR} = \frac{(9.49 \times 10^{-3}\ \text{m})(0.200 \times 10^{-3}\ \text{m})}{(3)(1.00\ \text{m})}$$
$$= 633 \times 10^{-9}\ \text{m} = 633\ \text{nm}$$

EVALUATE: This bright fringe could also correspond to $m = -3$. Can you show that this gives the same result for λ?

Example 35.2 Broadcast pattern of a radio station

It is often desirable to radiate most of the energy from a radio transmitter in particular directions rather than uniformly in all directions. Pairs or rows of antennas are often used to produce the desired radiation pattern. As an example, consider two identical vertical antennas 400 m apart, operating at 1500 kHz $= 1.5 \times 10^6$ Hz (near the top end of the AM broadcast band) and oscillating in phase. At distances much greater than 400 m, in what directions is the intensity from the two antennas greatest?

SOLUTION

IDENTIFY and SET UP: The antennas, shown in Fig. 35.8, correspond to sources S_1 and S_2 in Fig. 35.5. Hence we can apply the ideas of two-slit interference to this problem. Since the resultant wave is detected at distances much greater than $d = 400$ m, we may use Eq. (35.4) to give the directions of the intensity maxima, the values of θ for which the path difference is zero or a whole number of wavelengths.

35.8 Two radio antennas broadcasting in phase. The purple arrows indicate the directions of maximum intensity. The waves that are emitted toward the lower half of the figure are not shown.

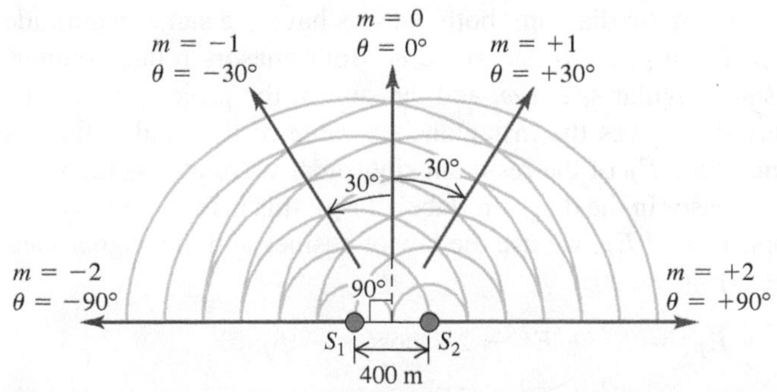

EXECUTE: The wavelength is $\lambda = c/f = 200$ m. From Eq. (35.4) with $m = 0, \pm 1$, and ± 2, the intensity maxima are given by

$$\sin\theta = \frac{m\lambda}{d} = \frac{m(200\ \text{m})}{400\ \text{m}} = \frac{m}{2} \qquad \theta = 0, \pm 30°, \pm 90°$$

In this example, values of m greater than 2 or less than -2 give values of $\sin\theta$ greater than 1 or less than -1, which is impossible. There is *no* direction for which the path difference is three or more wavelengths, so values of m of ± 3 or beyond have no meaning in this example.

EVALUATE: We can check our result by calculating the angles for *minimum* intensity, using Eq. (35.5). There should be one intensity minimum between each pair of intensity maxima, just as in Fig. 35.6. From Eq. (35.5), with $m = -2, -1, 0$, and 1,

$$\sin\theta = \frac{(m + \frac{1}{2})\lambda}{d} = \frac{m + \frac{1}{2}}{2} \qquad \theta = \pm 14.5°, \pm 48.6°$$

These angles fall between the angles for intensity maxima, as they should. The angles are not small, so the angles for the minima are *not* exactly halfway between the angles for the maxima.

Test Your Understanding of Section 35.2 You shine a tunable laser (whose wavelength can be adjusted by turning a knob) on a pair of closely spaced slits. The light emerging from the two slits produces an interference pattern on a screen like that shown in Fig. 35.6. If you adjust the wavelength so that the laser light changes from red to blue, how will the spacing between bright fringes change? (i) The spacing increases; (ii) the spacing decreases; (iii) the spacing is unchanged; (iv) not enough information is given to decide.

35.3 Intensity in Interference Patterns

In Section 35.2 we found the positions of maximum and minimum intensity in a two-source interference pattern. Let's now see how to find the intensity at *any* point in the pattern. To do this, we have to combine the two sinusoidally varying fields (from the two sources) at a point P in the radiation pattern, taking proper account of the phase difference of the two waves at point P, which results from the path difference. The intensity is then proportional to the square of the resultant electric-field amplitude, as we learned in Chapter 32.

To calculate the intensity, we will assume that the two sinusoidal functions (corresponding to waves from the two sources) have equal amplitude E and that the $\vec{E}$ fields lie along the same line (have the same polarization). This assumes that the sources are identical and neglects the slight amplitude difference caused by the unequal path lengths (the amplitude decreases with increasing distance from the source). From Eq. (32.29), each source by itself would give an intensity $\frac{1}{2}\epsilon_0 cE^2$ at point P. If the two sources are in phase, then the waves that arrive at P differ in phase by an amount proportional to the difference in their path lengths, $(r_2 - r_1)$. If the phase angle between these arriving waves is ϕ, then we can use the following expressions for the two electric fields superposed at P:

$$E_1(t) = E\cos(\omega t + \phi)$$
$$E_2(t) = E\cos\omega t$$

The superposition of the two fields at P is a sinusoidal function with some amplitude E_P that depends on E and the phase difference ϕ. First we'll work on finding the amplitude E_P if E and ϕ are known. Then we'll find the intensity I of the resultant wave, which is proportional to E_P^2. Finally, we'll relate the phase difference ϕ to the path difference, which is determined by the geometry of the situation.

Amplitude in Two-Source Interference

To add the two sinusoidal functions with a phase difference, we use the same *phasor* representation that we used for simple harmonic motion (see Section 14.2) and for voltages and currents in ac circuits (see Section 31.1). We suggest that you review these sections now. Each sinusoidal function is represented by a rotating vector (phasor) whose projection on the horizontal axis at any instant represents the instantaneous value of the sinusoidal function.

35.9 Phasor diagram for the superposition at a point P of two waves of equal amplitude E with a phase difference ϕ.

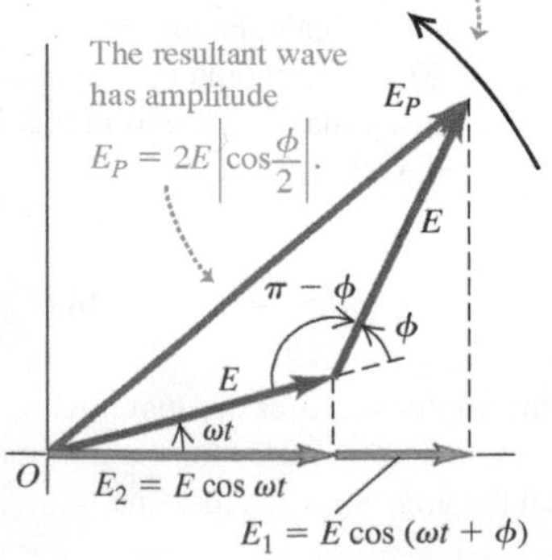

In Fig. 35.9, E_1 is the horizontal component of the phasor representing the wave from source S_1, and E_2 is the horizontal component of the phasor for the wave from S_2. As shown in the diagram, both phasors have the same magnitude E, but E_1 is *ahead* of E_2 in phase by an angle ϕ. Both phasors rotate counterclockwise with constant angular speed ω, and the sum of the projections on the horizontal axis at any time gives the instantaneous value of the total E field at point P. Thus the amplitude E_P of the resultant sinusoidal wave at P is the magnitude of the dark red phasor in the diagram (labeled E_P); this is the *vector sum* of the other two phasors. To find E_P, we use the law of cosines and the trigonometric identity $\cos(\pi - \phi) = -\cos\phi$:

$$E_P^2 = E^2 + E^2 - 2E^2\cos(\pi - \phi)$$
$$= E^2 + E^2 + 2E^2\cos\phi$$

Then, using the identity $1 + \cos\phi = 2\cos^2(\phi/2)$, we obtain

$$E_P{}^2 = 2E^2(1 + \cos\phi) = 4E^2\cos^2\left(\frac{\phi}{2}\right)$$

$$E_P = 2E\left|\cos\frac{\phi}{2}\right| \quad \text{(amplitude in two-source interference)} \tag{35.7}$$

You can also obtain this result without using phasors (see Problem 35.50).

When the two waves are in phase, $\phi = 0$ and $E_P = 2E$. When they are exactly a half-cycle out of phase, $\phi = \pi\ \text{rad} = 180°$, $\cos(\phi/2) = \cos(\pi/2) = 0$, and $E_P = 0$. Thus the superposition of two sinusoidal waves with the same frequency and amplitude but with a phase difference yields a sinusoidal wave with the same frequency and an amplitude between zero and twice the individual amplitudes, depending on the phase difference.

Intensity in Two-Source Interference

To obtain the intensity I at point P, we recall from Section 32.4 that I is equal to the average magnitude of the Poynting vector, S_{av}. For a sinusoidal wave with electric-field amplitude E_P, this is given by Eq. (32.29) with E_{max} replaced by E_P. Thus we can express the intensity in several equivalent forms:

$$I = S_{av} = \frac{E_P{}^2}{2\mu_0 c} = \frac{1}{2}\sqrt{\frac{\epsilon_0}{\mu_0}}E_P{}^2 = \frac{1}{2}\epsilon_0 c E_P{}^2 \tag{35.8}$$

The essential content of these expressions is that I is proportional to $E_P{}^2$. When we substitute Eq. (35.7) into the last expression in Eq. (35.8), we get

$$I = \frac{1}{2}\epsilon_0 c E_P{}^2 = 2\epsilon_0 c E^2 \cos^2\frac{\phi}{2} \tag{35.9}$$

In particular, the *maximum* intensity I_0, which occurs at points where the phase difference is zero ($\phi = 0$), is

$$I_0 = 2\epsilon_0 c E^2$$

Note that the maximum intensity I_0 is *four times* (not twice) as great as the intensity $\frac{1}{2}\epsilon_0 c E^2$ from each individual source.

Substituting the expression for I_0 into Eq. (35.9), we can express the intensity I at any point very simply in terms of the maximum intensity I_0:

$$I = I_0\cos^2\frac{\phi}{2} \quad \text{(intensity in two-source interference)} \tag{35.10}$$

For some phase angles ϕ the intensity is I_0, four times as great as for an individual wave source, but for other phase angles the intensity is zero. If we average Eq. (35.10) over all possible phase differences, the result is $I_0/2 = \epsilon_0 c E^2$ (the average of $\cos^2(\phi/2)$ is $\frac{1}{2}$). This is just twice the intensity from each individual source, as we should expect. The total energy output from the two sources isn't changed by the interference effects, but the energy is redistributed (as we mentioned in Section 35.1).

Phase Difference and Path Difference

Our next task is to find the phase difference ϕ between the two fields at any point P. We know that ϕ is proportional to the difference in path length from the two sources to point P. When the path difference is one wavelength, the phase difference is one cycle, and $\phi = 2\pi\ \text{rad} = 360°$. When the path difference is

$\lambda/2$, $\phi = \pi$ rad $= 180°$, and so on. That is, the ratio of the phase difference ϕ to 2π is equal to the ratio of the path difference $r_2 - r_1$ to λ:

$$\frac{\phi}{2\pi} = \frac{r_2 - r_1}{\lambda}$$

Thus a path difference $(r_2 - r_1)$ causes a phase difference given by

$$\phi = \frac{2\pi}{\lambda}(r_2 - r_1) = k(r_2 - r_1) \quad \text{(phase difference related to path difference)} \tag{35.11}$$

where $k = 2\pi/\lambda$ is the *wave number* introduced in Section 15.3.

If the material in the space between the sources and P is anything other than vacuum, we must use the wavelength *in the material* in Eq. (35.11). If the material has index of refraction n, then

$$\lambda = \frac{\lambda_0}{n} \quad \text{and} \quad k = nk_0 \tag{35.12}$$

where λ_0 and k_0 are the wavelength and the wave number, respectively, in vacuum.

Finally, if the point P is far away from the sources in comparison to their separation d, the path difference is given by Eq. (35.3):

$$r_2 - r_1 = d\sin\theta$$

Combining this with Eq. (35.11), we find

$$\phi = k(r_2 - r_1) = kd\sin\theta = \frac{2\pi d}{\lambda}\sin\theta \tag{35.13}$$

When we substitute this into Eq. (35.10), we find

$$I = I_0\cos^2\left(\tfrac{1}{2}kd\sin\theta\right) = I_0\cos^2\left(\frac{\pi d}{\lambda}\sin\theta\right) \quad \text{(intensity far from two sources)} \tag{35.14}$$

The directions of *maximum* intensity occur when the cosine has the values ± 1—that is, when

$$\frac{\pi d}{\lambda}\sin\theta = m\pi \qquad (m = 0, \pm 1, \pm 2, \dots)$$

or

$$d\sin\theta = m\lambda$$

in agreement with Eq. (35.4). You can also derive Eq. (35.5) for the zero-intensity directions from Eq. (35.14).

As we noted in Section 35.2, in experiments with light we visualize the interference pattern due to two slits by using a screen placed at a distance R from the slits. We can describe positions on the screen with the coordinate y; the positions of the bright fringes are given by Eq. (35.6), where ordinarily $y \ll R$. In that case, $\sin\theta$ is approximately equal to y/R, and we obtain the following expressions for the intensity at *any* point on the screen as a function of y:

$$I = I_0\cos^2\left(\frac{kdy}{2R}\right) = I_0\cos^2\left(\frac{\pi dy}{\lambda R}\right) \quad \text{(intensity in two-slit interference)} \tag{35.15}$$

Figure 35.10 shows a graph of Eq. (35.15); we can compare this with the photographically recorded pattern of Fig. 35.6. The peaks in Fig. 35.10 all have the same intensity, while those in Fig. 35.6 fade off as we go away from the center. We'll explore the reasons for this variation in peak intensity in Chapter 36.

35.10 Intensity distribution in the interference pattern from two identical slits.

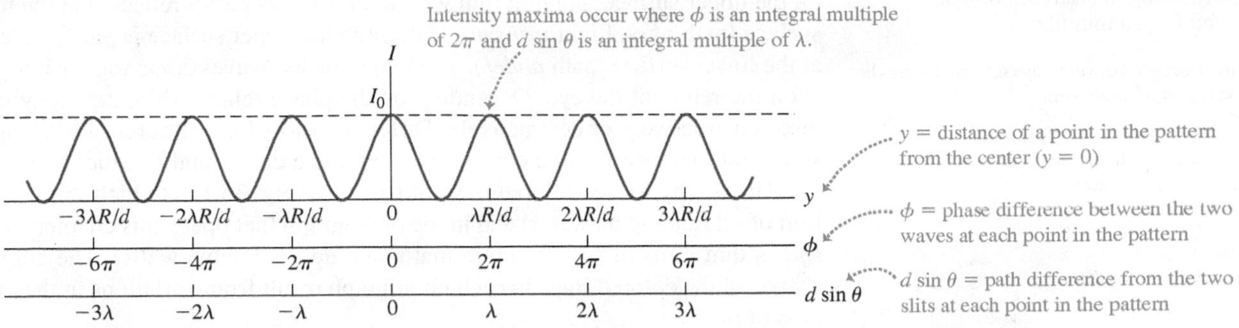

Example 35.3 A directional transmitting antenna array

Suppose the two identical radio antennas of Fig. 35.8 are moved to be only 10.0 m apart and the broadcast frequency is increased to $f = 60.0$ MHz. At a distance of 700 m from the point midway between the antennas and in the direction $\theta = 0$ (see Fig. 35.8), the intensity is $I_0 = 0.020\ \text{W/m}^2$. At this same distance, find (a) the intensity in the direction $\theta = 4.0°$; (b) the direction near $\theta = 0$ for which the intensity is $I_0/2$; and (c) the directions in which the intensity is zero.

SOLUTION

IDENTIFY and SET UP: This problem involves the intensity distribution as a function of angle. Because the 700-m distance from the antennas to the point at which the intensity is measured is much greater than the distance $d = 10.0$ m between the antennas, the amplitudes of the waves from the two antennas are very nearly equal. Hence we can use Eq. (35.14) to relate intensity I and angle θ.

EXECUTE: The wavelength is $\lambda = c/f = 5.00$ m. The spacing $d = 10.0$ m between the antennas is just twice the wavelength (as was the case in Example 35.2), so $d/\lambda = 2.00$ and Eq. (35.14) becomes

$$I = I_0 \cos^2\left(\frac{\pi d}{\lambda}\sin\theta\right) = I_0 \cos^2[(2.00\pi\ \text{rad})\sin\theta]$$

(a) When $\theta = 4.0°$,

$$I = I_0 \cos^2[(2.00\pi\ \text{rad})\sin 4.0°] = 0.82 I_0$$
$$= (0.82)(0.020\ \text{W/m}^2) = 0.016\ \text{W/m}^2$$

(b) The intensity I equals $I_0/2$ when the cosine in Eq. (35.14) has the value $\pm 1/\sqrt{2}$. The smallest angles at which this occurs correspond to $2.00\pi \sin\theta = \pm\pi/4$ rad, so that $\sin\theta = \pm(1/8.00) = \pm 0.125$ and $\theta = \pm 7.2°$.

(c) The intensity is zero when $\cos[(2.00\pi\ \text{rad})\sin\theta] = 0$. This occurs for $2.00\pi \sin\theta = \pm\pi/2, \pm 3\pi/2, \pm 5\pi/2, \ldots$, or $\sin\theta = \pm 0.250, \pm 0.750, \pm 1.25, \ldots$. Values of $\sin\theta$ greater than 1 have no meaning, so the answers are

$$\theta = \pm 14.5°, \pm 48.6°$$

EVALUATE: The condition in part (b) that $I = I_0/2$, so that $(2.00\pi\ \text{rad})\sin\theta = \pm\pi/4$ rad, is also satisfied when $\sin\theta = \pm 0.375, \pm 0.625$, or ± 0.875 so that $\theta = \pm 22.0°, \pm 38.7°$, or $\pm 61.0°$. (Can you verify this?) It would be incorrect to include these angles in the solution, however, because the problem asked for the angle *near* $\theta = 0$ at which $I = I_0/2$. These additional values of θ aren't the ones we're looking for.

Test Your Understanding of Section 35.3 A two-slit interference experiment uses coherent light of wavelength 5.00×10^{-7} m. Rank the following points in the interference pattern according to the intensity at each point, from highest to lowest. (i) a point that is closer to one slit than the other by 4.00×10^{-7} m; (ii) a point where the light waves received from the two slits are out of phase by 4.00 rad; (iii) a point that is closer to one slit than the other by 7.50×10^{-7} m; (iv) a point where the light waves received by the two slits are out of phase by 2.00 rad. |

35.4 Interference in Thin Films

You often see bright bands of color when light reflects from a thin layer of oil floating on water or from a soap bubble (see the photograph that opens this chapter). These are the results of interference. Light waves are reflected from the front and back surfaces of such thin films, and constructive interference between the two reflected waves (with different path lengths) occurs in different

35.11 (a) A diagram and (b) a photograph showing interference of light reflected from a thin film.

(a) Interference between rays reflected from the two surfaces of a thin film

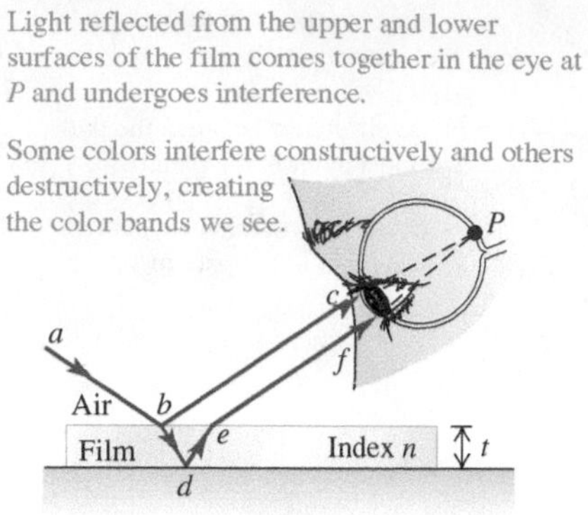

(b) The rainbow fringes of an oil slick on water

places for different wavelengths. Figure 35.11a shows the situation. Light shining on the upper surface of a thin film with thickness t is partly reflected at the upper surface (path *abc*). Light *transmitted* through the upper surface is partly reflected at the lower surface (path *abdef*). The two reflected waves come together at point P on the retina of the eye. Depending on the phase relationship, they may interfere constructively or destructively. Different colors have different wavelengths, so the interference may be constructive for some colors and destructive for others. That's why we see colored rings or fringes in Fig. 35.11b (which shows a thin film of oil floating on water) and in the photograph that opens this chapter (which shows thin films of soap solution that make up the bubble walls). The complex shapes of the colored rings in each photograph result from variations in the thickness of the film.

Thin-Film Interference and Phase Shifts During Reflection

Let's look at a simplified situation in which *monochromatic* light reflects from two nearly parallel surfaces at nearly normal incidence. Figure 35.12 shows two plates of glass separated by a thin wedge, or film, of air. We want to consider interference between the two light waves reflected from the surfaces adjacent to the air wedge, as shown. (Reflections also occur at the top surface of the upper plate and the bottom surface of the lower plate; to keep our discussion simple, we won't include these.) The situation is the same as in Fig. 35.11a except that the film (wedge) thickness is not uniform. The path difference between the two waves is just twice the thickness t of the air wedge at each point. At points where $2t$ is an integer number of wavelengths, we expect to see constructive interference and a bright area; where it is a half-integer number of wavelengths, we expect to see destructive interference and a dark area. Along the line where the plates are in contact, there is practically *no* path difference, and we expect a bright area.

When we carry out the experiment, the bright and dark fringes appear, but they are interchanged! Along the line where the plates are in contact, we find a *dark* fringe, not a bright one. This suggests that one or the other of the reflected waves has undergone a half-cycle phase shift during its reflection. In that case the two waves that are reflected at the line of contact are a half-cycle out of phase even though they have the same path length.

35.12 Interference between light waves reflected from the two sides of an air wedge separating two glass plates. The angles and the thickness of the air wedge have been exaggerated for clarity; in the text we assume that the light strikes the upper plate at normal incidence and that the distances h and t are much less than l.

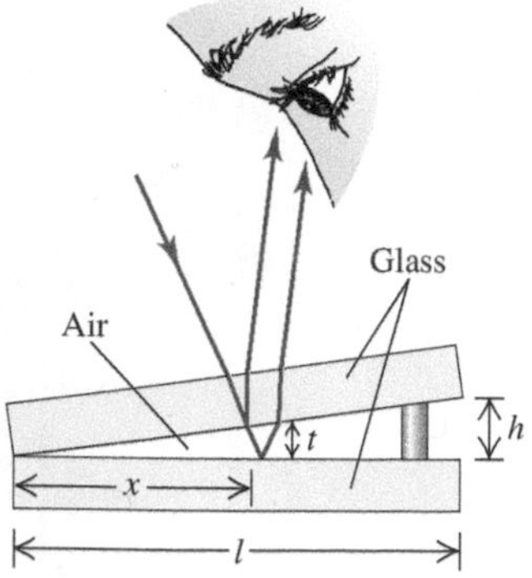

In fact, this phase shift can be predicted from Maxwell's equations and the electromagnetic nature of light. The details of the derivation are beyond our scope, but here is the result. Suppose a light wave with electric-field amplitude E_i is traveling in an optical material with index of refraction n_a. It strikes, at normal incidence, an interface with another optical material with index n_b. The amplitude E_r of the wave reflected from the interface is proportional to the amplitude E_i of the incident wave and is given by

$$E_r = \frac{n_a - n_b}{n_a + n_b} E_i \quad \text{(normal incidence)} \tag{35.16}$$

This result shows that the incident and reflected amplitudes have the same sign when n_a is larger than n_b and opposite sign when n_b is larger than n_a. We can distinguish three cases, as shown in Fig. 35.13:

Figure 35.13a: When $n_a > n_b$, light travels more slowly in the first material than in the second. In this case, E_r and E_i have the same sign, and the phase shift of the reflected wave relative to the incident wave is zero. This is analogous to reflection of a transverse mechanical wave on a heavy rope at a point where it is tied to a lighter rope or a ring that can move vertically without friction.

Figure 35.13b: When $n_a = n_b$, the amplitude E_r of the reflected wave is zero. The incident light wave can't "see" the interface, and there is *no* reflected wave.

35.13 Upper figures: electromagnetic waves striking an interface between optical materials at normal incidence (shown as a small angle for clarity). Lower figures: mechanical wave pulses on ropes.

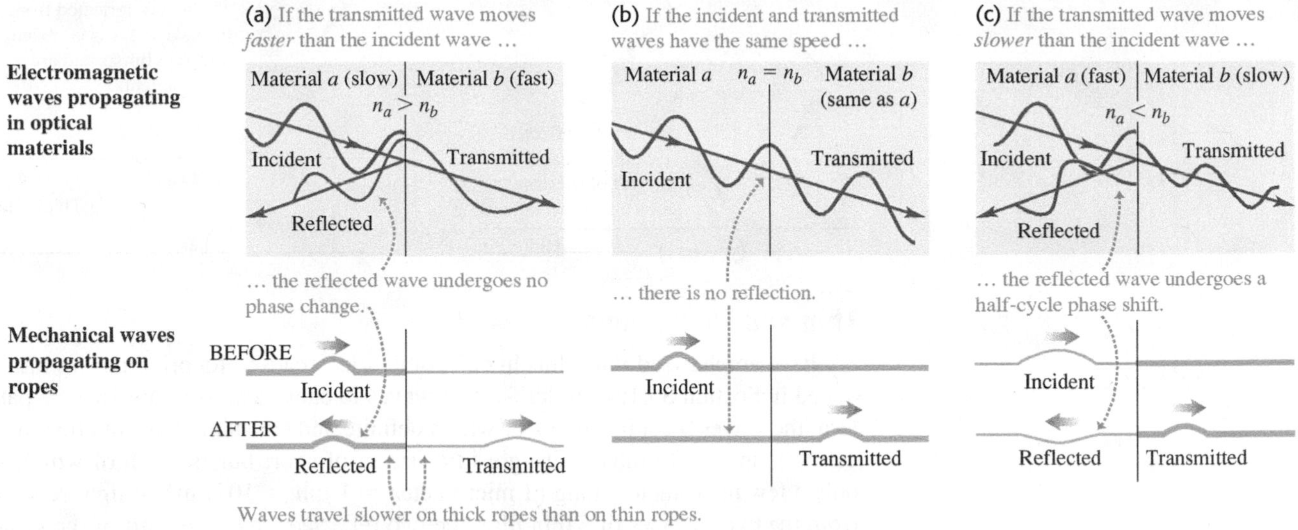

Figure 35.13c: When $n_a < n_b$, light travels more slowly in the second material than in the first. In this case, E_r and E_i have opposite signs, and the phase shift of the reflected wave relative to the incident wave is π rad (180° or a half-cycle). This is analogous to reflection (with inversion) of a transverse mechanical wave on a light rope at a point where it is tied to a heavier rope or a rigid support.

Let's compare with the situation of Fig. 35.12. For the wave reflected from the upper surface of the air wedge, n_a (glass) is greater than n_b, so this wave has zero phase shift. For the wave reflected from the lower surface, n_a (air) is less than n_b (glass), so this wave has a half-cycle phase shift. Waves that are reflected from the line of contact have no path difference to give additional phase shifts, and they interfere destructively; this is what we observe. You can use the above principle to show that for normal incidence, the wave reflected at point *b* in Fig. 35.11a is shifted by a half-cycle, while the wave reflected at *d* is not (if there is air below the film).

We can summarize this discussion mathematically. If the film has thickness *t*, the light is at normal incidence and has wavelength λ in the film; if neither or both of the reflected waves from the two surfaces have a half-cycle reflection phase shift, the conditions for constructive and destructive interference are

$$2t = m\lambda \quad (m = 0, 1, 2, \dots) \quad \text{(constructive reflection from thin film, no relative phase shift)} \tag{35.17a}$$

$$2t = \left(m + \tfrac{1}{2}\right)\lambda \quad (m = 0, 1, 2, \dots) \quad \text{(destructive reflection from thin film, no relative phase shift)} \tag{35.17b}$$

If *one* of the two waves has a half-cycle reflection phase shift, the conditions for constructive and destructive interference are reversed:

$$2t = \left(m + \tfrac{1}{2}\right)\lambda \quad (m = 0, 1, 2, \dots) \quad \text{(constructive reflection from thin film, half-cycle relative phase shift)} \tag{35.18a}$$

$$2t = m\lambda \quad (m = 0, 1, 2, \dots) \quad \text{(destructive reflection from thin film, half-cycle relative phase shift)} \tag{35.18b}$$

35.14 (a) Light reflecting from a thin film produces a steady interference pattern, but (b) light reflecting from a thick film does not.

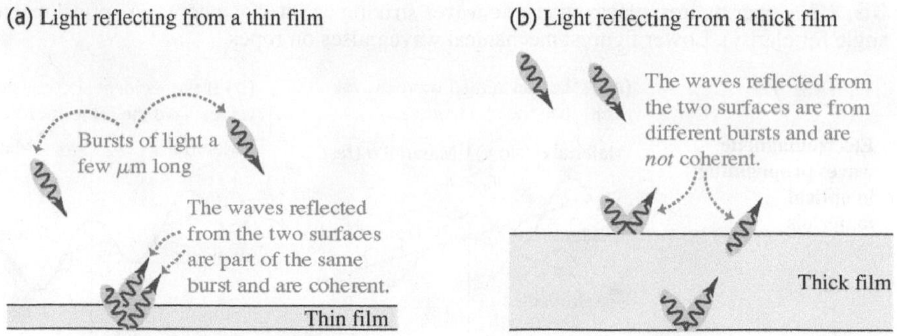

Thin and Thick Films

We have emphasized *thin* films in our discussion because of a principle we introduced in Section 35.1: In order for two waves to cause a steady interference pattern, the waves must be *coherent,* with a definite and constant phase relationship. The sun and light bulbs emit light in a stream of short bursts, each of which is only a few micrometers long $(1 \text{ micrometer} = 1\ \mu m = 10^{-6}\text{ m})$. If light reflects from the two surfaces of a thin film, the two reflected waves are part of the same burst (Fig. 35.14a). Hence these waves are coherent and interference occurs as we have described. If the film is too thick, however, the two reflected waves will belong to different bursts (Fig. 35.14b). There is no definite phase relationship between different light bursts, so the two waves are incoherent and there is no fixed interference pattern. That's why you see interference colors in light reflected from an oil slick a few micrometers thick (see Fig. 35.11b), but you do *not* see such colors in the light reflected from a pane of window glass with a thickness of a few millimeters (a thousand times greater).

Problem-Solving Strategy 35.1 Interference in Thin Films

MP

IDENTIFY *the relevant concepts:* Problems with thin films involve interference of two waves, one reflected from the film's front surface and one reflected from the back surface. Typically you will be asked to relate the wavelength, the film thickness, and the index of refraction of the film.

SET UP *the problem* using the following steps:

1. Make a drawing showing the geometry of the film. Identify the materials that adjoin the film; their properties determine whether one or both of the reflected waves have a half-cycle phase shift.
2. Identify the target variable.

EXECUTE *the solution* as follows:

1. Apply the rule for phase changes to each reflected wave: There is a half-cycle phase shift when $n_b > n_a$ and none when $n_b < n_a$.
2. If *neither* reflected wave undergoes a phase shift, or if *both* do, use Eqs. (35.17). If only one reflected wave undergoes a phase shift, use Eqs. (35.18).
3. Solve the resulting equation for the target variable. Use the wavelength $\lambda = \lambda_0/n$ of light *in the film* in your calculations, where n is the index of refraction of the film. (For air, $n = 1.000$ to four-figure precision.)
4. If you are asked about the wave that is transmitted through the film, remember that minimum intensity in the reflected wave corresponds to maximum *transmitted* intensity, and vice versa.

EVALUATE *your answer:* Interpret your results by examining what would happen if the wavelength were changed or if the film had a different thickness.

Example 35.4 Thin-film interference I

Suppose the two glass plates in Fig. 35.12 are two microscope slides 10.0 cm long. At one end they are in contact; at the other end they are separated by a piece of paper 0.0200 mm thick. What is the spacing of the interference fringes seen by reflection? Is the fringe at the line of contact bright or dark? Assume monochromatic light with a wavelength in air of $\lambda = \lambda_0 = 500$ nm.

SOLUTION

IDENTIFY and SET UP: Figure 35.15 depicts the situation. We'll consider only interference between the light reflected from the upper and lower surfaces of the air wedge between the microscope slides. [The top slide has a relatively great thickness, about 1 mm,

35.15 Our sketch for this problem.

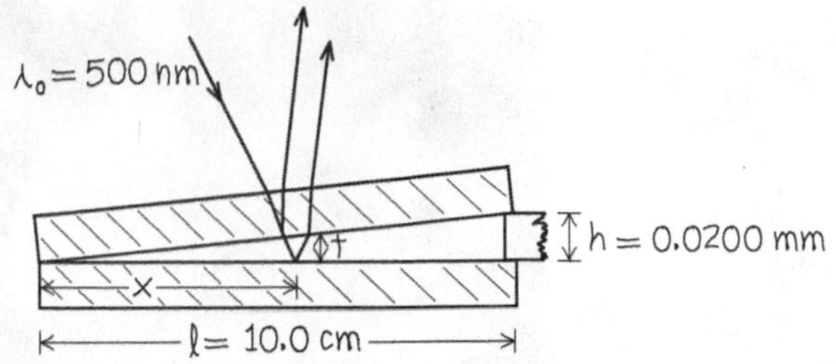

so we can ignore interference between the light reflected from its upper and lower surfaces (see Fig. 35.14b).] Light travels more slowly in the glass of the slides than it does in air. Hence the wave reflected from the upper surface of the air wedge has no phase shift (see Fig. 35.13a), while the wave reflected from the lower surface has a half-cycle phase shift (see Fig. 35.13c).

EXECUTE: Since only one of the reflected waves undergoes a phase shift, the condition for *destructive* interference (a dark fringe) is Eq. (35.18b):

$$2t = m\lambda_0 \qquad (m = 0, 1, 2, \ldots)$$

From similar triangles in Fig. 35.15 the thickness t of the air wedge at each point is proportional to the distance x from the line of contact:

$$\frac{t}{x} = \frac{h}{l}$$

Combining this with Eq. (35.18b), we find

$$\frac{2xh}{l} = m\lambda_0$$

$$x = m\frac{l\lambda_0}{2h} = m\frac{(0.100 \text{ m})(500 \times 10^{-9} \text{ m})}{(2)(0.0200 \times 10^{-3} \text{ m})} = m(1.25 \text{ mm})$$

Successive dark fringes, corresponding to $m = 1, 2, 3, \ldots$, are spaced 1.25 mm apart. Substituting $m = 0$ into this equation gives $x = 0$, which is where the two slides touch (at the left-hand side of Fig. 35.15). Hence there is a dark fringe at the line of contact.

EVALUATE: Our result shows that the fringe spacing is proportional to the wavelength of the light used; the fringes would be farther apart with red light (larger λ_0) than with blue light (smaller λ_0). If we use white light, the reflected light at any point is a mixture of wavelengths for which constructive interference occurs; the wavelengths that interfere destructively are weak or absent in the reflected light. (This same effect explains the colors seen when an oil film on water is illuminated by white light, as in Fig. 35.11b).

Example 35.5 Thin-film interference II

Suppose the glass plates of Example 35.4 have $n = 1.52$ and the space between plates contains water ($n = 1.33$) instead of air. What happens now?

SOLUTION

IDENTIFY and SET UP: The index of refraction of the water wedge is still less than that of the glass on either side of it, so the phase shifts are the same as in Example 35.4. Once again we use Eq. (35.18b) to find the positions of the dark fringes; the only difference is that the wavelength λ in this equation is now the wavelength in water instead of in air.

EXECUTE: In the film of water ($n = 1.33$), the wavelength is $\lambda = \lambda_0/n = (500 \text{ nm})/(1.33) = 376$ nm. When we replace λ_0 by λ in the expression from Example 35.4 for the position x of the mth dark fringe, we find that the fringe spacing is reduced by the same factor of 1.33 and is equal to 0.940 mm. There is still a dark fringe at the line of contact.

EVALUATE: Can you see that to obtain the same fringe spacing as in Example 35.4, the dimension h in Fig. 35.15 would have to be reduced to $(0.0200 \text{ mm})/1.33 = 0.0150$ mm? This shows that what matters in thin-film interference is the *ratio* t/λ between film thickness and wavelength. [You can see this by considering Eqs. (35.17) and (35.18).]

Example 35.6 Thin-film interference III

Suppose the upper of the two plates of Example 35.4 is a plastic with $n = 1.40$, the wedge is filled with a silicone grease with $n = 1.50$, and the bottom plate is a dense flint glass with $n = 1.60$. What happens now?

SOLUTION

IDENTIFY and SET UP: The geometry is again the same as shown in Fig. 35.15, but now half-cycle phase shifts occur at *both* surfaces of the grease wedge (see Fig. 35.13c). Hence there is no *relative* phase shift and we must use Eq. (35.17b) to find the positions of the dark fringes.

EXECUTE: The value of λ to use in Eq. (35.17b) is the wavelength in the silicone grease, $\lambda = \lambda_0/n = (500 \text{ nm})/1.50 = 333$ nm. You can readily show that the fringe spacing is 0.833 mm. Note that the two reflected waves from the line of contact are in phase (they both undergo the same phase shift), so the line of contact is at a *bright* fringe.

EVALUATE: What would happen if you carefully removed the upper microscope slide so that the grease wedge retained its shape? There would still be half-cycle phase changes at the upper and lower surfaces of the wedge, so the pattern of fringes would be the same as with the upper slide present.

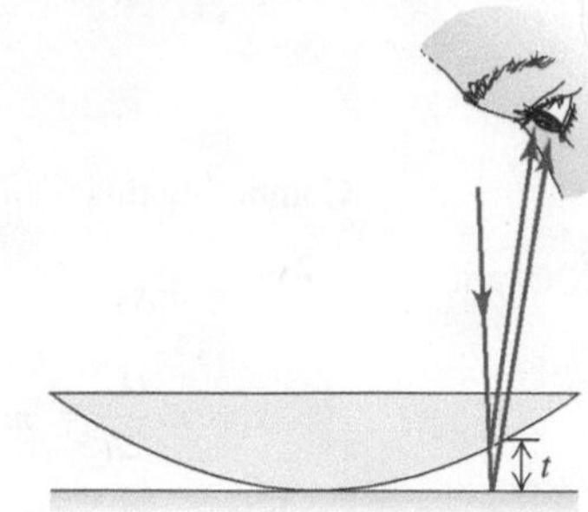

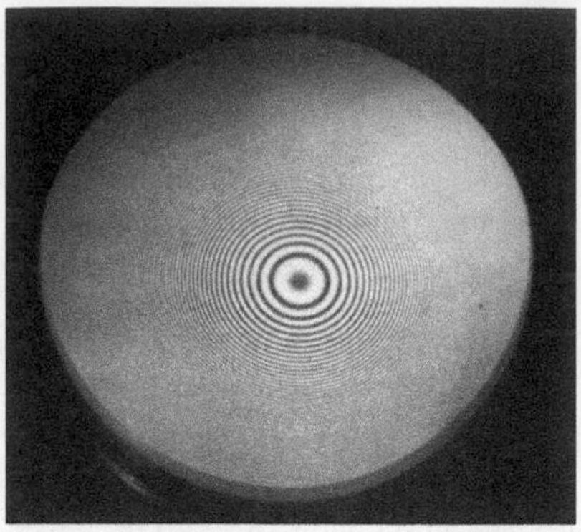

35.16 (a) Air film between a convex lens and a plane surface. The thickness of the film t increases from zero as we move out from the center, giving (b) a series of alternating dark and bright rings for monochromatic light.

Newton's Rings

Figure 35.16a shows the convex surface of a lens in contact with a plane glass plate. A thin film of air is formed between the two surfaces. When you view the setup with monochromatic light, you see circular interference fringes (Fig. 35.16b). These were studied by Newton and are called **Newton's rings.**

We can use interference fringes to compare the surfaces of two optical parts by placing the two in contact and observing the interference fringes. Figure 35.17 is a photograph made during the grinding of a telescope objective lens. The lower, larger-diameter, thicker disk is the correctly shaped master, and the smaller, upper disk is the lens under test. The "contour lines" are Newton's interference fringes; each one indicates an additional distance between the specimen and the master of one half-wavelength. At 10 lines from the center spot the distance between the two surfaces is five wavelengths, or about 0.003 mm. This isn't very good; high-quality lenses are routinely ground with a precision of less than one wavelength. The surface of the primary mirror of the Hubble Space Telescope was ground to a precision of better than $\frac{1}{50}$ wavelength. Unfortunately, it was ground to incorrect specifications, creating one of the most precise errors in the history of optical technology (see Section 34.2).

35.17 The surface of a telescope objective lens under inspection during manufacture.

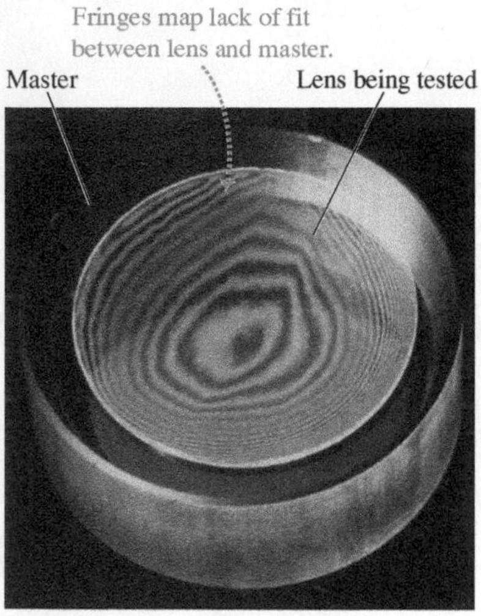

Nonreflective and Reflective Coatings

Nonreflective coatings for lens surfaces make use of thin-film interference. A thin layer or film of hard transparent material with an index of refraction smaller than that of the glass is deposited on the lens surface, as in Fig. 35.18. Light is reflected from both surfaces of the layer. In both reflections the light is reflected from a medium of greater index than that in which it is traveling, so the same phase change occurs in both reflections. If the film thickness is a quarter (one-fourth) of the wavelength *in the film* (assuming normal incidence), the total path difference is a half-wavelength. Light reflected from the first surface is then a half-cycle out of phase with light reflected from the second, and there is destructive interference.

The thickness of the nonreflective coating can be a quarter-wavelength for only one particular wavelength. This is usually chosen in the central yellow-green portion of the spectrum ($\lambda = 550$ nm), where the eye is most sensitive. Then there is somewhat more reflection at both longer (red) and shorter (blue) wavelengths, and the reflected light has a purple hue. The overall reflection from a lens or prism surface can be reduced in this way from 4–5% to less than 1%. This also increases the net amount of light that is *transmitted* through the lens, since light that is not reflected will be transmitted. The same principle is used to minimize reflection from silicon photovoltaic solar cells ($n = 3.5$) by use of a thin surface layer of silicon monoxide (SiO, $n = 1.45$); this helps to increase the amount of light that actually reaches the solar cells.

35.18 A nonreflective coating has an index of refraction intermediate between those of glass and air.

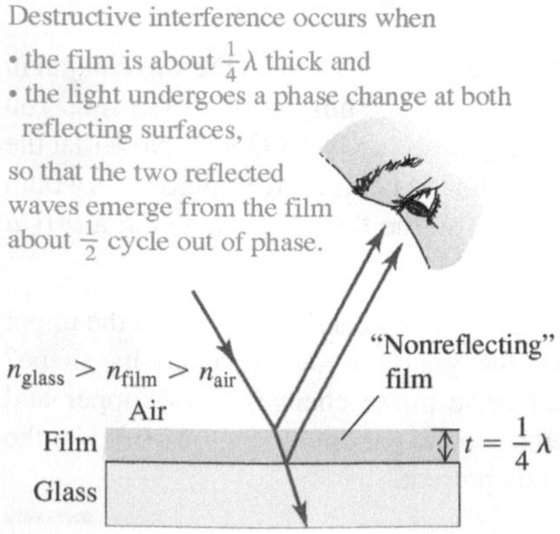

If a quarter-wavelength thickness of a material with an index of refraction *greater* than that of glass is deposited on glass, then the reflectivity is *increased,* and the deposited material is called a **reflective coating.** In this case there is a half-cycle phase shift at the air–film interface but none at the film–glass interface, and reflections from the two sides of the film interfere constructively. For example, a coating with refractive index 2.5 causes 38% of the incident energy to be reflected, compared with 4% or so with no coating. By use of multiple-layer coatings, it is possible to achieve nearly 100% transmission or reflection for particular wavelengths. Some practical applications of these coatings are for color separation in television cameras and for infrared "heat reflectors" in motion-picture projectors, solar cells, and astronauts' visors.

Example 35.7 A nonreflective coating

A common lens coating material is magnesium fluoride (MgF_2), with $n = 1.38$. What thickness should a nonreflective coating have for 550-nm light if it is applied to glass with $n = 1.52$?

SOLUTION

IDENTIFY and SET UP: This coating is of the sort shown in Fig. 35.18. The thickness must be one-quarter of the wavelength of this light *in the coating*.

EXECUTE: The wavelength in air is $\lambda_0 = 550$ nm, so its wavelength in the MgF_2 coating is $\lambda = \lambda_0/n = (550\text{ nm})/1.38 = 400$ nm. The coating thickness should be one-quarter of this, or $\lambda/4 = 100$ nm.

EVALUATE: This is a very thin film, no more than a few hundred molecules thick. Note that this coating is *reflective* for light whose wavelength is *twice* the coating thickness; light of that wavelength reflected from the coating's lower surface travels one wavelength farther than light reflected from the upper surface, so the two waves are in phase and interfere constructively. This occurs for light with a wavelength in MgF_2 of 200 nm and a wavelength in air of $(200\text{ nm})(1.38) = 276$ nm. This is an ultraviolet wavelength (see Section 32.1), so designers of optical lenses with nonreflective coatings need not worry about such enhanced reflection.

Test Your Understanding of Section 35.4 A thin layer of benzene ($n = 1.501$) ties on top of a sheet of fluorite ($n = 1.434$). It is illuminated from above with light whose wavelength in benzene is 400 nm. Which of the following possible thicknesses of the benzene layer will maximize the brightness of the reflected light? (i) 100 nm; (ii) 200 nm; (iii) 300 nm; (iv) 400 nm.

Application Interference and Butterfly Wings

Many of the most brilliant colors in the animal world are created by *interference* rather than by pigments. These photos show the butterfly *Morpho rhetenor* and the microscopic scales that cover the upper surfaces of its wings. The scales have a profusion of tiny ridges (middle photo); these carry regularly spaced flanges (bottom photo) that function as reflectors. These are spaced so that the reflections interfere constructively for blue light. The multilayered structure reflects 70% of the blue light that strikes it, giving the wings a mirror-like brilliance. (The undersides of the wings do not have these structures and are a dull brown.)

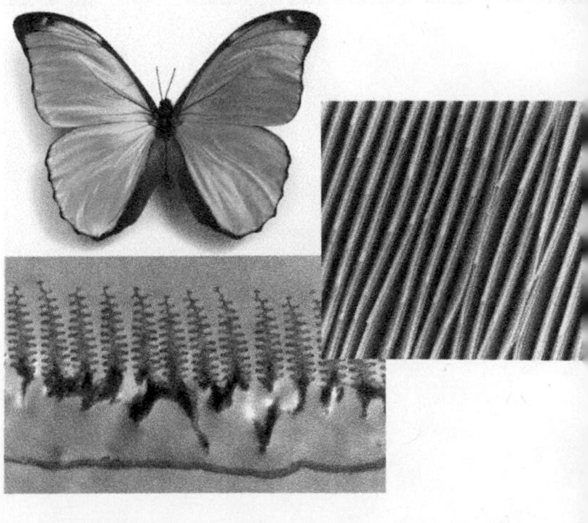

35.5 The Michelson Interferometer

An important experimental device that uses interference is the **Michelson interferometer.** Michelson interferometers are used to make precise measurements of wavelengths and of very small distances, such as the minute changes in thickness of an axon when a nerve impulse propagates along its length. Like the Young two-slit experiment, a Michelson interferometer takes monochromatic light from a single source and divides it into two waves that follow different paths. In Young's experiment, this is done by sending part of the light through one slit and part through another; in a Michelson interferometer a device called a *beam splitter* is used. Interference occurs in both experiments when the two light waves are recombined.

How a Michelson Interferometer Works

Figure 35.19 shows the principal components of a Michelson interferometer. A ray of light from a monochromatic source *A* strikes the beam splitter *C*, which is a glass plate with a thin coating of silver on its right side. Part of the light (ray 1) passes through the silvered surface and the compensator plate *D* and is reflected from mirror M_1. It then returns through *D* and is reflected from the silvered surface of *C* to the observer. The remainder of the light (ray 2) is reflected from the silvered surface at point *P* to the mirror M_2 and back through *C* to the observer's eye.

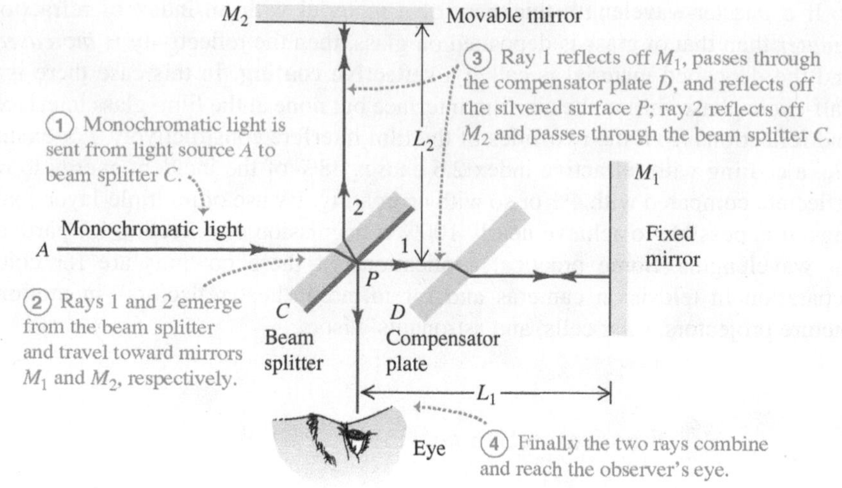

35.19 A schematic Michelson interferometer. The observer sees an interference pattern that results from the difference in path lengths for rays 1 and 2.

Application Imaging Cells with a Michelson Interferometer
This false-color image of a human colon cancer cell was made using a microscope that was mated to a Michelson interferometer. The cell is in one arm of the interferometer, and light passing through the cell undergoes a phase shift that depends on the cell thickness and the organelles within the cell. The fringe pattern can then be used to construct a three-dimensional view of the cell. Scientists have used this technique to observe how different types of cells behave when prodded by microscopic probes. Cancer cells turn out to be "softer" than normal cells, a distinction that may make cancer stem cells easier to identify.

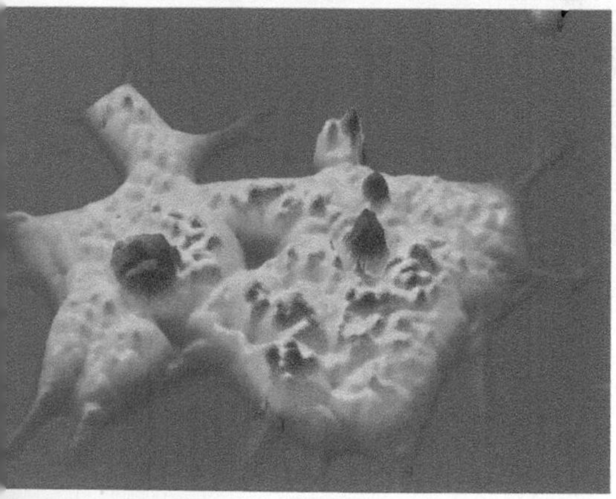

The purpose of the compensator plate D is to ensure that rays 1 and 2 pass through the same thickness of glass; plate D is cut from the same piece of glass as plate C, so their thicknesses are identical to within a fraction of a wavelength.

The whole apparatus in Fig. 35.19 is mounted on a very rigid frame, and the position of mirror M_2 can be adjusted with a fine, very accurate micrometer screw. If the distances L_1 and L_2 are exactly equal and the mirrors M_1 and M_2 are exactly at right angles, the virtual image of M_1 formed by reflection at the silvered surface of plate C coincides with mirror M_2. If L_1 and L_2 are *not* exactly equal, the image of M_1 is displaced slightly from M_2; and if the mirrors are not exactly perpendicular, the image of M_1 makes a slight angle with M_2. Then the mirror M_2 and the virtual image of M_1 play the same roles as the two surfaces of a wedge-shaped thin film (see Section 35.4), and light reflected from these surfaces forms the same sort of interference fringes.

Suppose the angle between mirror M_2 and the virtual image of M_1 is just large enough that five or six vertical fringes are present in the field of view. If we now move the mirror M_2 slowly either backward or forward a distance $\lambda/2$, the difference in path length between rays 1 and 2 changes by λ, and each fringe moves to the left or right a distance equal to the fringe spacing. If we observe the fringe positions through a telescope with a crosshair eyepiece and m fringes cross the crosshairs when we move the mirror a distance y, then

$$y = m\frac{\lambda}{2} \quad \text{or} \quad \lambda = \frac{2y}{m} \tag{35.19}$$

If m is several thousand, the distance y is large enough that it can be measured with good accuracy, and we can obtain an accurate value for the wavelength λ. Alternatively, if the wavelength is known, a distance y can be measured by simply counting fringes when M_2 is moved by this distance. In this way, distances that are comparable to a wavelength of light can be measured with relative ease.

The Michelson-Morley Experiment

The original application of the Michelson interferometer was to the historic **Michelson-Morley experiment.** Before the electromagnetic theory of light became established, most physicists thought that the propagation of light waves occurred in a medium called the **ether,** which was believed to permeate all space. In 1887 the American scientists Albert Michelson and Edward Morley used the Michelson interferometer in an attempt to detect the motion of the earth through the ether. Suppose the interferometer in Fig. 35.19 is moving from left to right relative to the ether. According to the ether theory, this would lead to changes in the speed of light in the portions of the path shown as horizontal lines in the figure. There would be fringe shifts relative to the positions that the fringes would have if the instrument were at rest in the ether. Then when the entire instrument was rotated 90°, the other portions of the paths would be similarly affected, giving a fringe shift in the opposite direction.

Michelson and Morley expected that the motion of the earth through the ether would cause a shift of about four-tenths of a fringe when the instrument was rotated. The shift that was actually observed was less than a hundredth of a fringe and, within the limits of experimental uncertainty, appeared to be exactly zero. Despite its orbital motion around the sun, the earth appeared to be *at rest* relative to the ether. This negative result baffled physicists until 1905, when Albert Einstein developed the special theory of relativity (which we will study in detail in Chapter 37). Einstein postulated that the speed of a light wave in vacuum has the same magnitude c relative to *all* inertial reference frames, no matter what their velocity may be relative to each other. The presumed ether then plays no role, and the concept of an ether has been abandoned.

Test Your Understanding of Section 35.5 You are observing the pattern of fringes in a Michelson interferometer like that shown in Fig. 35.19. If you change the index of refraction (but not the thickness) of the compensator plate, will the pattern change? ❙

CHAPTER 35 SUMMARY

Interference and coherent sources: Monochromatic light is light with a single frequency. Coherence is a definite, unchanging phase relationship between two waves. The overlap of waves from two coherent sources of monochromatic light forms an interference pattern. The principle of superposition states that the total wave disturbance at any point is the sum of the disturbances from the separate waves.

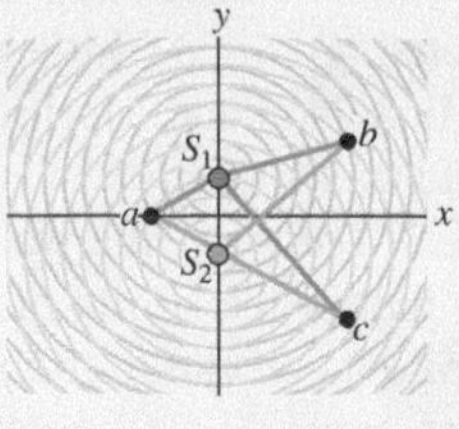

Two-source interference of light: When two sources are in phase, constructive interference occurs where the difference in path length from the two sources is zero or an integer number of wavelengths; destructive interference occurs where the path difference is a half-integer number of wavelengths. If two sources separated by a distance d are both very far from a point P, and the line from the sources to P makes an angle θ with the line perpendicular to the line of the sources, then the condition for constructive interference at P is Eq. (35.4). The condition for destructive interference is Eq. (35.5). When θ is very small, the position y_m of the mth bright fringe on a screen located a distance R from the sources is given by Eq. (35.6). (See Examples 35.1 and 35.2.)

$$d\sin\theta = m\lambda \quad (m = 0, \pm1, \pm2, \ldots)$$
(constructive interference) (35.4)

$$d\sin\theta = \left(m + \tfrac{1}{2}\right)\lambda$$
$(m = 0, \pm1, \pm2, \ldots)$ (35.5)
(destructive interference)

$$y_m = R\frac{m\lambda}{d}$$ (35.6)
(bright fringes)

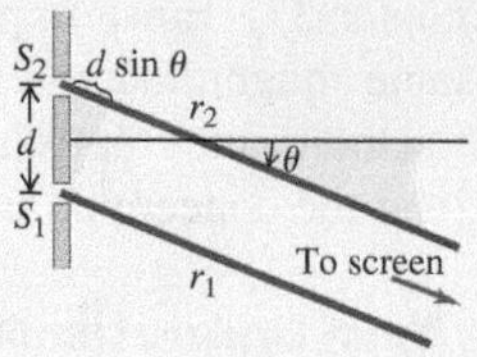

Intensity in interference patterns: When two sinusoidal waves with equal amplitude E and phase difference ϕ are superimposed, the resultant amplitude E_P and intensity I are given by Eqs. (35.7) and (35.10), respectively. If the two sources emit in phase, the phase difference ϕ at a point P (located a distance r_1 from source 1 and a distance r_2 from source 2) is directly proportional to the difference in path length $r_2 - r_1$. (See Example 35.3.)

$$E_P = 2E\left|\cos\frac{\phi}{2}\right|$$ (35.7)

$$I = I_0\cos^2\frac{\phi}{2}$$ (35.10)

$$\phi = \frac{2\pi}{\lambda}(r_2 - r_1) = k(r_2 - r_1)$$ (35.11)

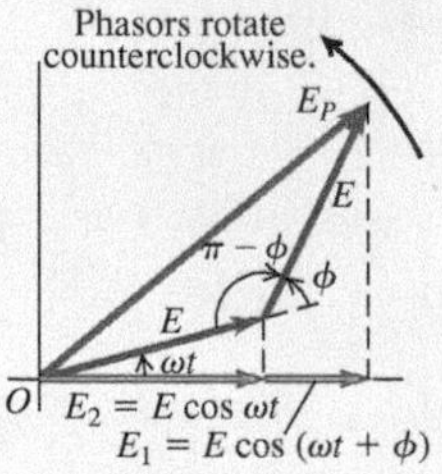

Interference in thin films: When light is reflected from both sides of a thin film of thickness t and no phase shift occurs at either surface, constructive interference between the reflected waves occurs when $2t$ is equal to an integral number of wavelengths. If a half-cycle phase shift occurs at one surface, this is the condition for destructive interference. A half-cycle phase shift occurs during reflection whenever the index of refraction in the second material is greater than that in the first. (See Examples 35.4–35.7.)

$$2t = m\lambda \quad (m = 0, 1, 2, \ldots)$$
(constructive reflection from thin film, no relative phase shift) (35.17a)

$$2t = \left(m + \tfrac{1}{2}\right)\lambda \quad (m = 0, 1, 2, \ldots)$$
(destructive reflection from thin film, no relative phase shift) (35.17b)

$$2t = \left(m + \tfrac{1}{2}\right)\lambda \quad (m = 0, 1, 2, \ldots)$$
(constructive reflection from thin film, half-cycle relative phase shift) (35.18a)

$$2t = m\lambda \quad (m = 0, 1, 2, \ldots)$$
(destructive reflection from thin film, half-cycle relative phase shift) (35.18b)

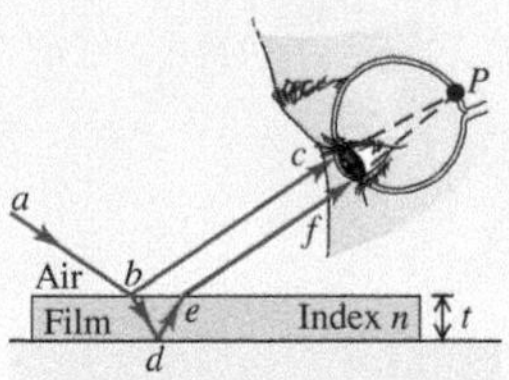

Michelson interferometer: The Michelson interferometer uses a monochromatic light source and can be used for high-precision measurements of wavelengths. Its original purpose was to detect motion of the earth relative to a hypothetical ether, the supposed medium for electromagnetic waves. The ether has never been detected, and the concept has been abandoned; the speed of light is the same relative to all observers. This is part of the foundation of the special theory of relativity.

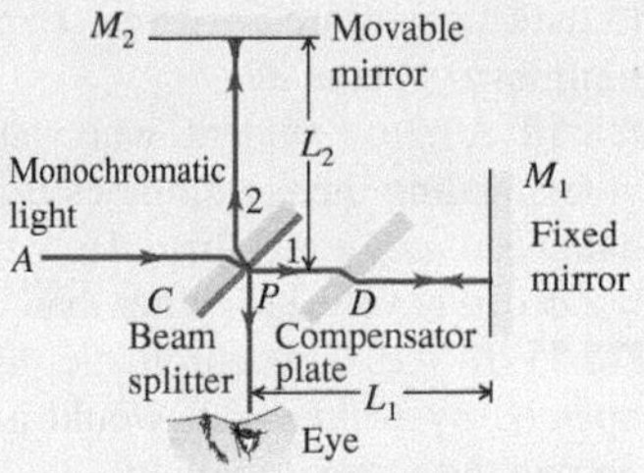

BRIDGING PROBLEM Modifying a Two-Slit Experiment

An oil tanker spills a large amount of oil ($n = 1.45$) into the sea ($n = 1.33$). (a) If you look down onto the oil spill from overhead, what predominant wavelength of light do you see at a point where the oil is 380 nm thick? What color is the light? (*Hint:* See Table 32.1.) (b) In the water under the slick, what visible wavelength (as measured in air) is predominant in the transmitted light at the same place in the slick as in part (a)?

SOLUTION GUIDE

See MasteringPhysics® study area for a Video Tutor solution.

IDENTIFY and SET UP

1. The oil layer acts as a thin film, so we must consider interference between light that reflects from the top and bottom surfaces of the oil. If a wavelength is prominent in the *transmitted* light, there is destructive interference for that wavelength in the *reflected* light.
2. Choose the appropriate interference equations that relate the thickness of the oil film and the wavelength of light. Take account of the indexes of refraction of the air, oil, and water.

EXECUTE

3. For part (a), find the wavelengths for which there is constructive interference as seen from above the oil film. Which of these are in the visible spectrum?
4. For part (b), find the visible wavelength for which there is destructive interference as seen from above the film. (This will ensure that there is substantial transmitted light at the wavelength.)

EVALUATE

5. If a diver below the water's surface shines a light up at the bottom of the oil film, at what wavelengths would there be constructive interference in the light that reflects back downward?

Problems

For instructor-assigned homework, go to www.masteringphysics.com

•, ••, •••: Problems of increasing difficulty. **CP**: Cumulative problems incorporating material from earlier chapters. **CALC**: Problems requiring calculus. **BIO**: Biosciences problems.

DISCUSSION QUESTIONS

Q35.1 A two-slit interference experiment is set up, and the fringes are displayed on a screen. Then the whole apparatus is immersed in the nearest swimming pool. How does the fringe pattern change?

Q35.2 Could an experiment similar to Young's two-slit experiment be performed with sound? How might this be carried out? Does it matter that sound waves are longitudinal and electromagnetic waves are transverse? Explain.

Q35.3 Monochromatic coherent light passing through two thin slits is viewed on a distant screen. Are the bright fringes equally spaced on the screen? If so, why? If not, which ones are closest to being equally spaced?

Q35.4 In a two-slit interference pattern on a distant screen, are the bright fringes midway between the dark fringes? Is this ever a good approximation?

Q35.5 Would the headlights of a distant car form a two-source interference pattern? If so, how might it be observed? If not, why not?

Q35.6 The two sources S_1 and S_2 shown in Fig. 35.3 emit waves of the same wavelength λ and are in phase with each other. Suppose S_1 is a weaker source, so that the waves emitted by S_1 have half the amplitude of the waves emitted by S_2. How would this affect the positions of the antinodal lines and nodal lines? Would there be total reinforcement at points on the antinodal curves? Would there be total cancellation at points on the nodal curves? Explain your answers.

Q35.7 Could the Young two-slit interference experiment be performed with gamma rays? If not, why not? If so, discuss differences in the experimental design compared to the experiment with visible light.

Q35.8 Coherent red light illuminates two narrow slits that are 25 cm apart. Will a two-slit interference pattern be observed when the light from the slits falls on a screen? Explain.

Q35.9 Coherent light with wavelength λ falls on two narrow slits separated by a distance d. If d is less than some minimum value, no dark fringes are observed. Explain. In terms of λ, what is this minimum value of d?

Q35.10 A fellow student, who values memorizing equations above understanding them, combines Eqs. (35.4) and (35.13) to "prove" that ϕ can *only* equal $2\pi m$. How would you explain to this student that ϕ can have values other than $2\pi m$?

Q35.11 If the monochromatic light shown in Fig. 35.5a were replaced by white light, would a two-slit interference pattern be seen on the screen? Explain.

Q35.12 In using the superposition principle to calculate intensities in interference patterns, could you add the intensities of the waves instead of their amplitudes? Explain.

Q35.13 A glass windowpane with a thin film of water on it reflects less than when it is perfectly dry. Why?

Q35.14 A *very* thin soap film ($n = 1.33$), whose thickness is much less than a wavelength of visible light, looks black; it appears to reflect no light at all. Why? By contrast, an equally thin layer of soapy water ($n = 1.33$) on glass ($n = 1.50$) appears quite shiny. Why is there a difference?

Q35.15 Interference can occur in thin films. Why is it important that the films be *thin*? Why don't you get these effects with a relatively *thick* film? Where should you put the dividing line between "thin" and "thick"? Explain your reasoning.

Q35.16 If we shine white light on an air wedge like that shown in Fig. 35.12, the colors that are weak in the light *reflected* from any point along the wedge are strong in the light *transmitted* through the wedge. Explain why this should be so.

Q35.17 Monochromatic light is directed at normal incidence on a thin film. There is destructive interference for the reflected light, so the intensity of the reflected light is very low. What happened to the energy of the incident light?

Q35.18 When a thin oil film spreads out on a puddle of water, the thinnest part of the film looks dark in the resulting interference pattern. What does this tell you about the relative magnitudes of the refractive indexes of oil and water?

EXERCISES

Section 35.1 Interference and Coherent Sources

35.1 • Two small stereo speakers A and B that are 1.40 m apart are sending out sound of wavelength 34 cm in all directions and all in phase. A person at point P starts out equidistant from both speakers and walks so that he is always 1.50 m from speaker B (Fig. E35.1). For what values of x will the sound this person hears be (a) maximally reinforced, (b) cancelled? Limit your solution to the cases where $x \leq 1.50$ m.

Figure E35.1

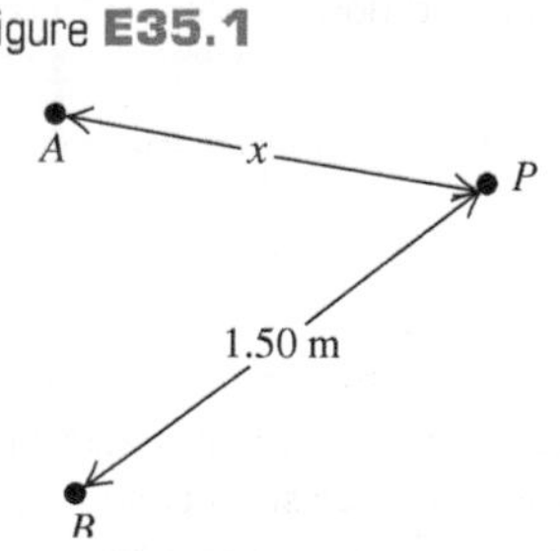

35.2 •• Two speakers that are 15.0 m apart produce in-phase sound waves of frequency 250.0 Hz in a room where the speed of sound is 340.0 m/s. A woman starts out at the midpoint between the two speakers. The room's walls and ceiling are covered with absorbers to eliminate reflections, and she listens with only one ear for best precision. (a) What does she hear: constructive or destructive interference? Why? (b) She now walks slowly toward one of the speakers. How far from the center must she walk before she first hears the sound reach a minimum intensity? (c) How far from the center must she walk before she first hears the sound maximally enhanced?

35.3 •• Two identical audio speakers connected to the same amplifier produce in-phase sound waves with a single frequency that can be varied between 300 and 600 Hz. The speed of sound is 340 m/s. You find that where you are standing, you hear minimum-intensity sound. (a) Explain why you hear minimum-intensity sound. (b) If one of the speakers is moved 39.8 cm toward you, the sound you hear has maximum intensity. What is the frequency of the sound? (c) How much closer to you from the position in part (b) must the speaker be moved to the next position where you hear maximum intensity?

35.4 • **Radio Interference.** Two radio antennas A and B radiate in phase. Antenna B is 120 m to the right of antenna A. Consider point Q along the extension of the line connecting the antennas, a horizontal distance of 40 m to the right of antenna B. The frequency, and hence the wavelength, of the emitted waves can be varied. (a) What is the longest wavelength for which there will be destructive interference at point Q? (b) What is the longest wavelength for which there will be constructive interference at point Q?

35.5 •• A radio transmitting station operating at a frequency of 120 MHz has two identical antennas that radiate in phase. Antenna B is 9.00 m to the right of antenna A. Consider point P between the antennas and along the line connecting them, a horizontal distance x to the right of antenna A. For what values of x will constructive interference occur at point P?

35.6 • Two light sources can be adjusted to emit monochromatic light of any visible wavelength. The two sources are coherent, 2.04 μm apart, and in line with an observer, so that one source is 2.04 μm farther from the observer than the other. (a) For what visible wavelengths (380 to 750 nm) will the observer see the brightest light, owing to constructive interference? (b) How would your answers to part (a) be affected if the two sources were not in line with the observer, but were still arranged so that one source is 2.04 μm farther away from the observer than the other? (c) For what visible wavelengths will there be *destructive* interference at the location of the observer?

35.7 • Two speakers, emitting identical sound waves of wavelength 2.0 m in phase with each other, and an observer are located as shown in Fig. E35.7. (a) At the observer's location, what is the path difference for waves from the two speakers? (b) Will the sound waves interfere constructively or destructively at the observer's location—or something in between constructive and destructive? (c) Suppose the observer now increases her distance from the closest speaker to 17.0 m, staying directly in front of the same speaker as initially. Answer the questions of parts (a) and (b) for this new situation.

Figure E35.7

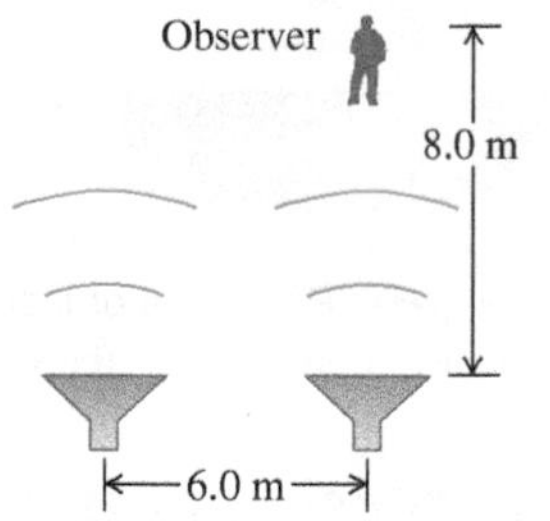

35.8 •• Figure 35.3 shows the wave pattern produced by two identical, coherent sources emitting waves with wavelength λ and separated by a distance $d = 4\lambda$. (a) Explain why the positive y-axis above S_1 constitutes an antinodal curve with $m = +4$ and why the negative y-axis below S_2 constitutes an antinodal curve with $m = -4$. (b) Draw the wave pattern produced when the separation between the sources is reduced to 3λ. In your drawing, sketch all antinodal curves—that is, the curves on which $r_2 - r_1 = m\lambda$. Label each curve by its value of m. (c) In general, what determines the maximum (most positive) and minimum (most negative) values of the integer m that labels the antinodal lines? (d) Suppose the separation between the sources is increased to $7\frac{1}{2}\lambda$. How many antinodal curves will there be? To what values of m do they correspond? Explain your reasoning. (You should not have to make a drawing to answer these questions.)

Section 35.2 Two-Source Interference of Light

35.9 • Young's experiment is performed with light from excited helium atoms ($\lambda = 502$ nm). Fringes are measured carefully on a screen 1.20 m away from the double slit, and the center of the 20th fringe (not counting the central bright fringe) is found to be 10.6 mm from the center of the central bright fringe. What is the separation of the two slits?

35.10 •• Coherent light with wavelength 450 nm falls on a double slit. On a screen 1.80 m away, the distance between dark fringes is 4.20 mm. What is the separation of the slits?

35.11 •• Two slits spaced 0.450 mm apart are placed 75.0 cm from a screen. What is the distance between the second and third dark lines of the interference pattern on the screen when the slits are illuminated with coherent light with a wavelength of 500 nm?

35.12 •• If the entire apparatus of Exercise 35.11 (slits, screen, and space in between) is immersed in water, what then is the distance between the second and third dark lines?

35.13 •• Two thin parallel slits that are 0.0116 mm apart are illuminated by a laser beam of wavelength 585 nm. (a) On a very large distant screen, what is the *total* number of bright fringes (those indicating complete constructive interference), including the central fringe and those on both sides of it? Solve this problem without calculating all the angles! (*Hint:* What is the largest that $\sin\theta$ can be? What does this tell you is the largest value of m?) (b) At what angle, relative to the original direction of the beam, will the fringe that is most distant from the central bright fringe occur?

35.14 • Coherent light with wavelength 400 nm passes through two very narrow slits that are separated by 0.200 mm, and the interference pattern is observed on a screen 4.00 m from the slits. (a) What is the width (in mm) of the central interference maximum? (b) What is the width of the first-order bright fringe?

35.15 •• Two very narrow slits are spaced 1.80 μm apart and are placed 35.0 cm from a screen. What is the distance between the first and second dark lines of the interference pattern when the slits are illuminated with coherent light with $\lambda = 550$ nm? (*Hint:* The angle θ in Eq. (35.5) is *not* small.)

35.16 •• Coherent light that contains two wavelengths, 660 nm (red) and 470 nm (blue), passes through two narrow slits separated by 0.300 mm, and the interference pattern is observed on a screen 5.00 m from the slits. What is the distance on the screen between the first-order bright fringes for the two wavelengths?

35.17 •• Coherent light with wavelength 600 nm passes through two very narrow slits and the interference pattern is observed on a screen 3.00 m from the slits. The first-order bright fringe is at 4.84 mm from the center of the central bright fringe. For what wavelength of light will the first-order dark fringe be observed at this same point on the screen?

35.18 •• Coherent light of frequency 6.32×10^{14} Hz passes through two thin slits and falls on a screen 85.0 cm away. You observe that the third bright fringe occurs at ± 3.11 cm on either side of the central bright fringe. (a) How far apart are the two slits? (b) At what distance from the central bright fringe will the third dark fringe occur?

Section 35.3 Intensity in Interference Patterns

35.19 •• In a two-slit interference pattern, the intensity at the peak of the central maximum is I_0. (a) At a point in the pattern where the phase difference between the waves from the two slits is 60.0°, what is the intensity? (b) What is the path difference for 480-nm light from the two slits at a point where the phase angle is 60.0°?

35.20 • Coherent sources A and B emit electromagnetic waves with wavelength 2.00 cm. Point P is 4.86 m from A and 5.24 m from B. What is the phase difference at P between these two waves?

35.21 • Coherent light with wavelength 500 nm passes through narrow slits separated by 0.340 mm. At a distance from the slits large compared to their separation, what is the phase difference (in radians) in the light from the two slits at an angle of 23.0° from the centerline?

35.22 • Two slits spaced 0.260 mm apart are placed 0.700 m from a screen and illuminated by coherent light with a wavelength of 660 nm. The intensity at the center of the central maximum ($\theta = 0°$) is I_0. (a) What is the distance on the screen from the center of the central maximum to the first minimum? (b) What is the distance on the screen from the center of the central maximum to the point where the intensity has fallen to $I_0/2$?

35.23 •• Points A and B are 56.0 m apart along an east-west line. At each of these points, a radio transmitter is emitting a 12.5-MHz signal horizontally. These transmitters are in phase with each other and emit their beams uniformly in a horizontal plane. A receiver is taken 0.500 km north of the AB line and initially placed at point C, directly opposite the midpoint of AB. The receiver can be moved only along an east-west direction but, due to its limited sensitivity, it must always remain within a range so that the intensity of the signal it receives from the transmitter is no less than $\frac{1}{4}$ of its maximum value. How far from point C (along an east-west line) can the receiver be moved and always be able to pick up the signal?

35.24 • Consider two antennas separated by 9.00 m that radiate in phase at 120 MHz, as described in Exercise 35.5. A receiver placed 150 m from both antennas measures an intensity I_0. The receiver is moved so that it is 1.8 m closer to one antenna than to the other. (a) What is the phase difference ϕ between the two radio waves produced by this path difference? (b) In terms of I_0, what is the intensity measured by the receiver at its new position?

Section 35.4 Interference in Thin Films

35.25 • What is the thinnest film of a coating with $n = 1.42$ on glass ($n = 1.52$) for which destructive interference of the red component (650 nm) of an incident white light beam in air can take place by reflection?

35.26 •• **Nonglare Glass.** When viewing a piece of art that is behind glass, one often is affected by the light that is reflected off the front of the glass (called *glare*), which can make it difficult to see the art clearly. One solution is to coat the outer surface of the glass with a film to cancel part of the glare. (a) If the glass has a refractive index of 1.62 and you use TiO_2, which has an index of refraction of 2.62, as the coating, what is the minimum film thickness that will cancel light of wavelength 505 nm? (b) If this coating is too thin to stand up to wear, what other thickness would also work? Find only the three thinnest ones.

35.27 •• Two rectangular pieces of plane glass are laid one upon the other on a table. A thin strip of paper is placed between them at one edge so that a very thin wedge of air is formed. The plates are illuminated at normal incidence by 546-nm light from a mercury-vapor lamp. Interference fringes are formed, with 15.0 fringes per centimeter. Find the angle of the wedge.

35.28 •• A plate of glass 9.00 cm long is placed in contact with a second plate and is held at a small angle with it by a metal strip

0.0800 mm thick placed under one end. The space between the plates is filled with air. The glass is illuminated from above with light having a wavelength in air of 656 nm. How many interference fringes are observed per centimeter in the reflected light?

35.29 •• A uniform film of TiO_2, 1036 nm thick and having index of refraction 2.62, is spread uniformly over the surface of crown glass of refractive index 1.52. Light of wavelength 520.0 nm falls at normal incidence onto the film from air. You want to increase the thickness of this film so that the reflected light cancels. (a) What is the *minimum* thickness of TiO_2 that you must *add* so the reflected light cancels as desired? (b) After you make the adjustment in part (a), what is the path difference between the light reflected off the top of the film and the light that cancels it after traveling through the film? Express your answer in (i) nanometers and (ii) wavelengths of the light in the TiO_2 film.

35.30 • A plastic film with index of refraction 1.85 is put on the surface of a car window to increase the reflectivity and thus to keep the interior of the car cooler. The window glass has index of refraction 1.52. (a) What minimum thickness is required if light with wavelength 550 nm in air reflected from the two sides of the film is to interfere constructively? (b) It is found to be difficult to manufacture and install coatings as thin as calculated in part (a). What is the next greatest thickness for which there will also be constructive interference?

35.31 • The walls of a soap bubble have about the same index of refraction as that of plain water, $n = 1.33$. There is air both inside and outside the bubble. (a) What wavelength (in air) of visible light is most strongly reflected from a point on a soap bubble where its wall is 290 nm thick? To what color does this correspond (see Fig. 32.4 and Table 32.1)? (b) Repeat part (a) for a wall thickness of 340 nm.

35.32 •• Light with wavelength 648 nm in air is incident perpendicularly from air on a film 8.76 μm thick and with refractive index 1.35. Part of the light is reflected from the first surface of the film, and part enters the film and is reflected back at the second surface, where the film is again in contact with air. (a) How many waves are contained along the path of this second part of the light in its round trip through the film? (b) What is the phase difference between these two parts of the light as they leave the film?

35.33 •• **Compact Disc Player.** A compact disc (CD) is read from the bottom by a semiconductor laser with wavelength 790 nm passing through a plastic substrate of refractive index 1.8. When the beam encounters a pit, part of the beam is reflected from the pit and part from the flat region between the pits, so these two beams interfere with each other (Fig. E35.33). What must the minimum pit depth be so that the part of the beam reflected from a pit cancels the part of the beam reflected from the flat region? (It is this cancellation that allows the player to recognize the beginning and end of a pit.)

Figure **E35.33**

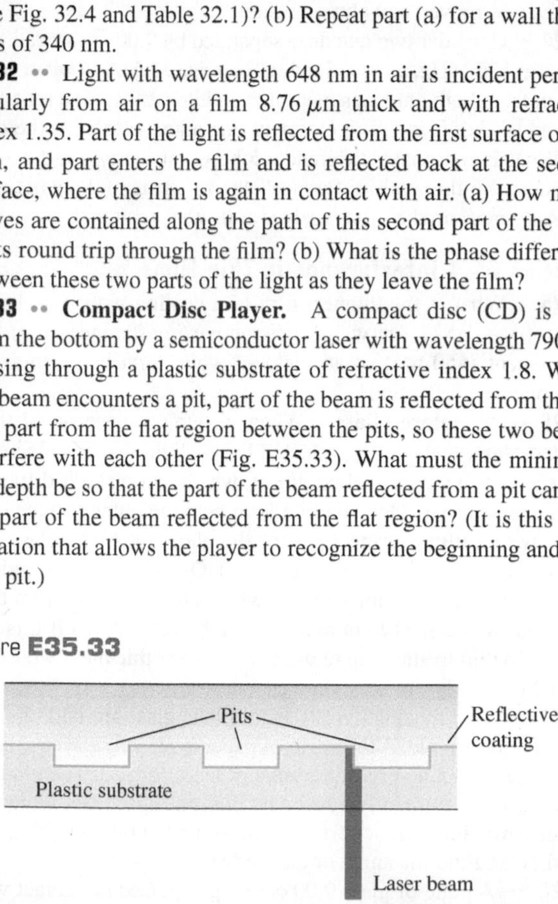

35.34 • What is the thinnest soap film (excluding the case of zero thickness) that appears black when illuminated with light with wavelength 480 nm? The index of refraction of the film is 1.33, and there is air on both sides of the film.

Section 35.5 The Michelson Interferometer

35.35 • How far must the mirror M_2 (see Fig. 35.19) of the Michelson interferometer be moved so that 1800 fringes of He-Ne laser light ($\lambda = 633$ nm) move across a line in the field of view?

35.36 • Jan first uses a Michelson interferometer with the 606-nm light from a krypton-86 lamp. He displaces the movable mirror away from him, counting 818 fringes moving across a line in his field of view. Then Linda replaces the krypton lamp with filtered 502-nm light from a helium lamp and displaces the movable mirror toward her. She also counts 818 fringes, but they move across the line in her field of view opposite to the direction they moved for Jan. Assume that both Jan and Linda counted to 818 correctly. (a) What distance did each person move the mirror? (b) What is the resultant displacement of the mirror?

PROBLEMS

35.37 ••• The radius of curvature of the convex surface of a planoconvex lens is 68.4 cm. The lens is placed convex side down on a perfectly flat glass plate that is illuminated from above with red light having a wavelength of 580 nm. Find the diameter of the second bright ring in the interference pattern.

35.38 •• Newton's rings can be seen when a planoconvex lens is placed on a flat glass surface. For a particular lens with an index of refraction of $n = 1.50$ and a glass plate with an index of $n = 1.80$, the diameter of the third bright ring is 0.720 mm. If water ($n = 1.33$) now fills the space between the lens and the plate, what is the new diameter of this ring?

35.39 • BIO **Coating Eyeglass Lenses.** Eyeglass lenses can be coated on the *inner* surfaces to reduce the reflection of stray light to the eye. If the lenses are medium flint glass of refractive index 1.62 and the coating is fluorite of refractive index 1.432, (a) what minimum thickness of film is needed on the lenses to cancel light of wavelength 550 nm reflected toward the eye at normal incidence? (b) Will any other wavelengths of visible light be cancelled or enhanced in the reflected light?

35.40 •• BIO **Sensitive Eyes.** After an eye examination, you put some eyedrops on your sensitive eyes. The cornea (the front part of the eye) has an index of refraction of 1.38, while the eyedrops have a refractive index of 1.45. After you put in the drops, your friends notice that your eyes look red, because red light of wavelength 600 nm has been reinforced in the reflected light. (a) What is the minimum thickness of the film of eyedrops on your cornea? (b) Will any other wavelengths of visible light be reinforced in the reflected light? Will any be cancelled? (c) Suppose you had contact lenses, so that the eyedrops went on them instead of on your corneas. If the refractive index of the lens material is 1.50 and the layer of eyedrops has the same thickness as in part (a), what wavelengths of visible light will be reinforced? What wavelengths will be cancelled?

35.41 •• Two flat plates of glass with parallel faces are on a table, one plate on the other. Each plate is 11.0 cm long and has a refractive index of 1.55. A very thin sheet of metal foil is inserted under the end of the upper plate to raise it slightly at that end, in a manner similar to that discussed in Example 35.4. When you view the glass plates from above with reflected white light, you observe that, at 1.15 mm from the line where the sheets are in contact, the violet light of wavelength 400.0 nm is enhanced in this reflected light, but no visible light is enhanced closer to the line of contact.

(a) How far from the line of contact will green light (of wavelength 550 nm) and orange light (of wavelength 600.0 nm) first be enhanced? (b) How far from the line of contact will the violet, green, and orange light again be enhanced in the reflected light? (c) How thick is the metal foil holding the ends of the plates apart?

35.42 •• In a setup similar to that of Problem 35.41, the glass has an index of refraction of 1.53, the plates are each 8.00 cm long, and the metal foil is 0.015 mm thick. The space between the plates is filled with a jelly whose refractive index is not known precisely, but is known to be greater than that of the glass. When you illuminate these plates from above with light of wavelength 525 nm, you observe a series of equally spaced dark fringes in the reflected light. You measure the spacing of these fringes and find that there are 10 of them every 6.33 mm. What is the index of refraction of the jelly?

35.43 ••• Suppose you illuminate two thin slits by monochromatic coherent light in air and find that they produce their first interference *minima* at $\pm 35.20°$ on either side of the central bright spot. You then immerse these slits in a transparent liquid and illuminate them with the same light. Now you find that the first minima occur at $\pm 19.46°$ instead. What is the index of refraction of this liquid?

35.44 •• **CP CALC** A very thin sheet of brass contains two thin parallel slits. When a laser beam shines on these slits at normal incidence and room temperature (20.0°C), the first interference dark fringes occur at $\pm 32.5°$ from the original direction of the laser beam when viewed from some distance. If this sheet is now slowly heated up to 135°C, by how many degrees do these dark fringes change position? Do they move closer together or get farther apart? See Table 17.1 for pertinent information, and ignore any effects that might occur due to change in the thickness of the slits. (*Hint:* Since thermal expansion normally produces very small changes in length, you can use differentials to find the change in the angle.)

35.45 •• Two speakers, 2.50 m apart, are driven by the same audio oscillator so that each one produces a sound consisting of *two* distinct frequencies, 0.900 kHz and 1.20 kHz. The speed of sound in the room is 344 m/s. Find all the angles relative to the usual centerline in front of (and far from) the speakers at which *both* frequencies interfere constructively.

35.46 •• Two radio antennas radiating in phase are located at points A and B, 200 m apart (Fig. P35.46). The radio waves have a frequency of 5.80 MHz. A radio receiver is moved out from point B along a line perpendicular to the line connecting A and B (line BC shown in Fig. P35.46). At what distances from B will there be *destructive* interference? (*Note:* The distance of the receiver from the sources is not large in comparison to the separation of the sources, so Eq. (35.5) does not apply.)

Figure **P35.46**

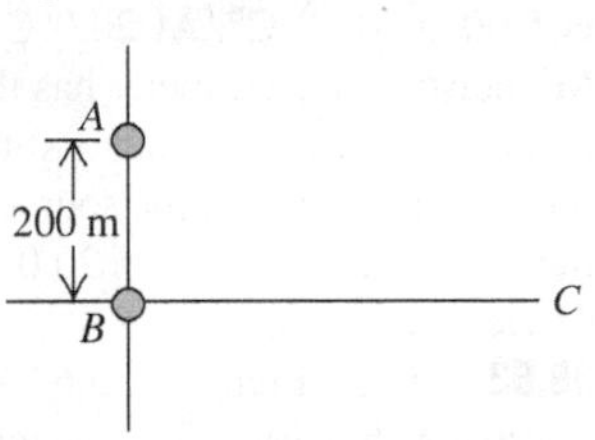

35.47 •• One round face of a 3.25-m, solid, cylindrical plastic pipe is covered with a thin black coating that completely blocks light. The opposite face is covered with a fluorescent coating that glows when it is struck by light. Two straight, thin, parallel scratches, 0.225 mm apart, are made in the center of the black face. When laser light of wavelength 632.8 nm shines through the slits perpendicular to the black face, you find that the central bright fringe on the opposite face is 5.82 mm wide, measured between the dark fringes that border it on either side. What is the index of refraction of the plastic?

35.48 • A uniform thin film of material of refractive index 1.40 coats a glass plate of refractive index 1.55. This film has the proper thickness to cancel normally incident light of wavelength 525 nm that strikes the film surface from air, but it is somewhat greater than the minimum thickness to achieve this cancellation. As time goes by, the film wears away at a steady rate of 4.20 nm per year. What is the minimum number of years before the reflected light of this wavelength is now enhanced instead of cancelled?

35.49 •• Two speakers A and B are 3.50 m apart, and each one is emitting a frequency of 444 Hz. However, because of signal delays in the cables, speaker A is one-fourth of a period *ahead* of speaker B. For points far from the speakers, find all the angles relative to the centerline (Fig. P35.49) at which the sound from these speakers cancels. Include angles on *both* sides of the centerline. The speed of sound is 340 m/s.

Figure **P35.49**

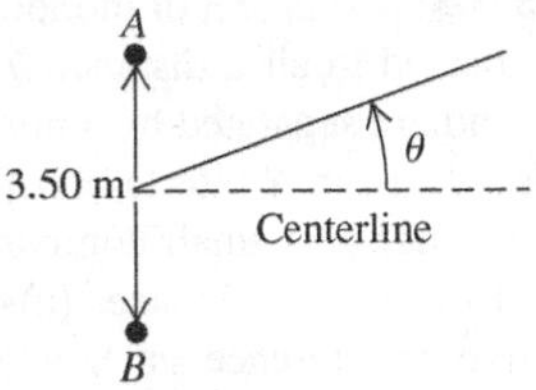

35.50 ••• **CP** The electric fields received at point P from two identical, coherent wave sources are $E_1(t) = E\cos(\omega t + \phi)$ and $E_2(t) = E\cos\omega t$. (a) Use the trigonometric identities in Appendix B to show that the resultant wave is $E_P(t) = 2E\cos(\phi/2)\cos(\omega t + \phi/2)$. (b) Show that the amplitude of this resultant wave is given by Eq. (35.7). (c) Use the result of part (a) to show that at an interference maximum, the amplitude of the resultant wave is in phase with the original waves $E_1(t)$ and $E_2(t)$. (d) Use the result of part (a) to show that near an interference minimum, the resultant wave is approximately $\frac{1}{4}$ cycle out of phase with either of the original waves. (e) Show that the *instantaneous* Poynting vector at point P has magnitude $S = 4\epsilon_0 cE^2\cos^2(\phi/2)\cos^2(\omega t + \phi/2)$ and that the *time-averaged* Poynting vector is given by Eq. (35.9).

35.51 •• **CP** A thin uniform film of refractive index 1.750 is placed on a sheet of glass of refractive index 1.50. At room temperature (20.0°C), this film is just thick enough for light with wavelength 582.4 nm reflected off the top of the film to be cancelled by light reflected from the top of the glass. After the glass is placed in an oven and slowly heated to 170°C, you find that the film cancels reflected light with wavelength 588.5 nm. What is the coefficient of linear expansion of the film? (Ignore any changes in the refractive index of the film due to the temperature change.)

35.52 ••• **GPS Transmission.** The GPS (Global Positioning System) satellites are approximately 5.18 m across and transmit two low-power signals, one of which is at 1575.42 MHz (in the UHF band). In a series of laboratory tests on the satellite, you put two 1575.42-MHz UHF transmitters at opposite ends of the satellite. These broadcast in phase uniformly in all directions. You measure the intensity at points on a circle that is several hundred meters in radius and centered on the satellite. You measure angles on this circle relative to a point that lies along the centerline of the satellite (that is, the perpendicular bisector of a line that extends from one transmitter to the other). At this point on the circle, the measured intensity is 2.00 W/m^2. (a) At how many other angles in the range $0° < \theta < 90°$ is the intensity also 2.00 W/m^2? (b) Find the four smallest angles in the range $0° < \theta < 90°$ for which the intensity is 2.00 W/m^2. (c) What is the intensity at a point on the circle at an angle of 4.65° from the centerline?

35.53 •• Consider a two-slit interference pattern, for which the intensity distribution is given by Eq. (35.14). Let θ_m be the angular position of the mth bright fringe, where the intensity is I_0. Assume that θ_m is small, so that $\sin\theta_m \cong \theta_m$. Let θ_m^+ and θ_m^- be the two angles on either side of θ_m for which $I = \frac{1}{2}I_0$. The quantity $\Delta\theta_m = |\theta_m^+ - \theta_m^-|$ is the half-width of the mth fringe. Calculate $\Delta\theta_m$. How does $\Delta\theta_m$ depend on m?

35.54 •• White light reflects at normal incidence from the top and bottom surfaces of a glass plate ($n = 1.52$). There is air above and below the plate. Constructive interference is observed for light whose wavelength in air is 477.0 nm. What is the thickness of the plate if the next longer wavelength for which there is constructive interference is 540.6 nm?

35.55 ••• A source S of monochromatic light and a detector D are both located in air a distance h above a horizontal plane sheet of glass and are separated by a horizontal distance x. Waves reaching D directly from S interfere with waves that reflect off the glass. The distance x is small compared to h so that the reflection is at close to normal incidence. (a) Show that the condition for constructive interference is $\sqrt{x^2 + 4h^2} - x = \left(m + \frac{1}{2}\right)\lambda$, and the condition for destructive interference is $\sqrt{x^2 + 4h^2} - x = m\lambda$. (*Hint:* Take into account the phase change on reflection.) (b) Let $h = 24$ cm and $x = 14$ cm. What is the longest wavelength for which there will be constructive interference?

35.56 •• BIO **Reflective Coatings and Herring.** Herring and related fish have a brilliant silvery appearance that camouflages them while they are swimming in a sunlit ocean. The silveriness is due to *platelets* attached to the surfaces of these fish. Each platelet is made up of several alternating layers of crystalline guanine ($n = 1.80$) and of cytoplasm ($n = 1.333$, the same as water), with a guanine layer on the outside in contact with the surrounding water (Fig. P35.56). In one typical platelet, the guanine layers are 74 nm thick and the cytoplasm layers are 100 nm thick. (a) For light striking the platelet surface at normal incidence, for which vacuum wavelengths of visible light will all of the reflections R_1, R_2, R_3, R_4, and R_5, shown in Fig. P35.56, be approximately in phase? If white light is shone on this platelet, what color will be most strongly reflected (see Fig. 32.4)? The surface of a herring has very many platelets side by side with layers of different thickness, so that *all* visible wavelengths are reflected. (b) Explain why such a "stack" of layers is more reflective than a single layer of guanine with cytoplasm underneath. (A stack of five guanine layers separated by cytoplasm layers reflects more than 80% of incident light at the wavelength for which it is "tuned.") (c) The color that is most strongly reflected from a platelet depends on the angle at which it is viewed. Explain why this should be so. (You can see these changes in color by examining a herring from different angles. Most of the platelets on these fish are oriented in the same way, so that they are vertical when the fish is swimming.)

Figure **P35.56**

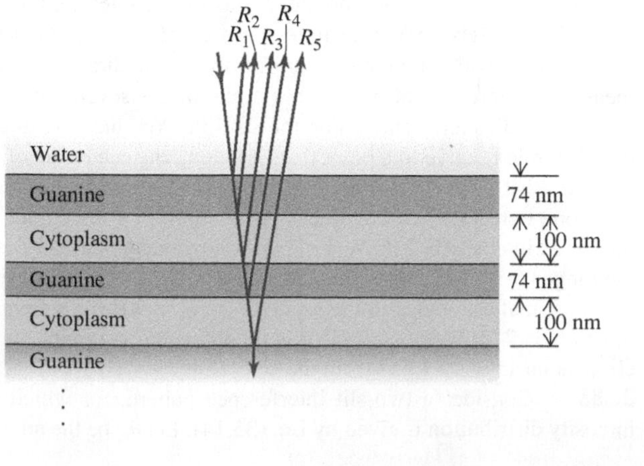

35.57 • Two thin parallel slits are made in an opaque sheet of film. When a monochromatic beam of light is shone through them at normal incidence, the first bright fringes in the transmitted light occur in air at ±18.0° with the original direction of the light beam on a distant screen when the apparatus is in air. When the apparatus is immersed in a liquid, the same bright fringes now occur at ±12.6°. Find the index of refraction of the liquid.

35.58 •• Red light with wavelength 700 nm is passed through a two-slit apparatus. At the same time, monochromatic visible light with another wavelength passes through the same apparatus. As a result, most of the pattern that appears on the screen is a mixture of two colors; however, the center of the third bright fringe ($m = 3$) of the red light appears pure red, with none of the other color. What are the possible wavelengths of the second type of visible light? Do you need to know the slit spacing to answer this question? Why or why not?

35.59 ••• In a Young's two-slit experiment a piece of glass with an index of refraction n and a thickness L is placed in front of the upper slit. (a) Describe qualitatively what happens to the interference pattern. (b) Derive an expression for the intensity I of the light at points on a screen as a function of n, L, and θ. Here θ is the usual angle measured from the center of the two slits. That is, determine the equation analogous to Eq. (35.14) but that also involves L and n for the glass plate. (c) From your result in part (b) derive an expression for the values of θ that locate the maxima in the interference pattern [that is, derive an equation analogous to Eq. (35.4)].

35.60 •• After a laser beam passes through two thin parallel slits, the first completely dark fringes occur at ±19.0° with the original direction of the beam, as viewed on a screen far from the slits. (a) What is the ratio of the distance between the slits to the wavelength of the light illuminating the slits? (b) What is the smallest angle, relative to the original direction of the laser beam, at which the intensity of the light is $\frac{1}{10}$ the maximum intensity on the screen?

CHALLENGE PROBLEMS

35.61 ••• CP The index of refraction of a glass rod is 1.48 at $T = 20.0$°C and varies linearly with temperature, with a coefficient of 2.50×10^{-5}/C°. The coefficient of linear expansion of the glass is 5.00×10^{-6}/C°. At 20.0°C the length of the rod is 3.00 cm. A Michelson interferometer has this glass rod in one arm, and the rod is being heated so that its temperature increases at a rate of 5.00 C°/min. The light source has wavelength $\lambda = 589$ nm, and the rod initially is at $T = 20.0$°C. How many fringes cross the field of view each minute?

35.62 ••• CP Figure P35.62 shows an interferometer known as *Fresnel's biprism.* The magnitude of the prism angle A is

Figure **P35.62**

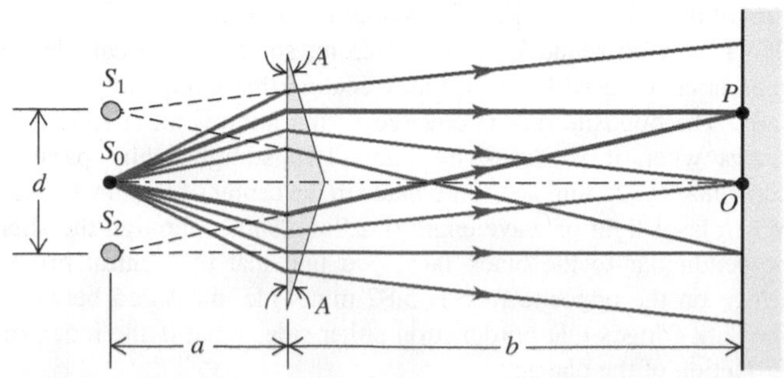

extremely small. (a) If S_0 is a very narrow source slit, show that the separation of the two virtual coherent sources S_1 and S_2 is given by $d = 2aA(n - 1)$, where n is the index of refraction of the material of the prism. (b) Calculate the spacing of the fringes of green light with wavelength 500 nm on a screen 2.00 m from the biprism. Take $a = 0.200$ m, $A = 3.50$ mrad, and $n = 1.50$.

Answers

Chapter Opening Question ?

The colors appear due to constructive interference between light waves reflected from the outer and inner surfaces of the soap bubble. The thickness of the bubble walls at each point determines the wavelength of light for which the most constructive interference occurs and hence the color that appears the brightest at that point (see Example 35.4 in Section 35.4).

Test Your Understanding Questions

35.1 Answer: (i) At any point P on the positive y-axis above S_1, the distance r_2 from S_2 to P is greater than the distance r_1 from S_1 to P by 4λ. This corresponds to $m = 4$ in Eq. (35.1), the equation for constructive interference. Hence all such points make up an antinodal curve.

35.2 Answer: (ii) Blue light has a shorter wavelength than red light (see Section 32.1). Equation (35.6) tells us that the distance y_m from the center of the pattern to the mth bright fringe is proportional to the wavelength λ. Hence all of the fringes will move toward the center of the pattern as the wavelength decreases, and the spacing between fringes will decrease.

35.3 Answer: (i), (iv), (ii), (iii) In cases (i) and (iii) we are given the wavelength λ and path difference $d\sin\theta$. Hence we use Eq. (35.14), $I = I_0\cos^2[(\pi d\sin\theta)/\lambda]$. In parts (ii) and (iii) we are given the phase difference ϕ and we use Eq. (35.10), $I = I_0\cos^2(\phi/2)$. We find:
(i) $I = I_0\cos^2[\pi(4.00 \times 10^{-7}\text{ m})/(5.00 \times 10^{-7}\text{ m})] = I_0\cos^2(0.800\pi\text{ rad}) = 0.655I_0$;
(ii) $I = I_0\cos^2[(4.00\text{ rad})/2] = I_0\cos^2(2.00\text{ rad}) = 0.173I_0$;
(iii) $I = I_0\cos^2[\pi(7.50 \times 10^{-7}\text{ m})/(5.00 \times 10^{-7}\text{ m})] = I_0\cos^2(1.50\pi\text{ rad}) = 0$;
(iv) $I = I_0\cos^2[(2.00\text{ rad})/2] = I_0\cos^2(1.00\text{ rad}) = 0.292I_0$.

35.4 Answers: (i) and (iii) Benzene has a larger index of refraction than air, so light that reflects off the upper surface of the benzene undergoes a half-cycle phase shift. Fluorite has a *smaller* index of refraction than benzene, so light that reflects off the benzene–fluorite interface does not undergo a phase shift. Hence the equation for constructive reflection is Eq. (35.18a), $2t = \left(m + \frac{1}{2}\right)\lambda$, which we can rewrite as $t = \left(m + \frac{1}{2}\right)\lambda/2 = \left(m + \frac{1}{2}\right)(400\text{ mm})/2 = 100\text{ nm}, 300\text{ nm}, 500\text{ nm}, \ldots$.

35.5 Answer: yes Changing the index of refraction changes the wavelength of the light inside the compensator plate, and so changes the number of wavelengths within the thickness of the plate. Hence this has the same effect as changing the distance L_1 from the beam splitter to mirror M_1, which would change the interference pattern.

Bridging Problem

Answers: (a) 441 nm **(b)** 551 nm

36 DIFFRACTION

? The laser used to read a DVD has a wavelength of 650 nm, while the laser used to read a Blu-ray disc has a shorter 405-nm wavelength. How does this make it possible for a Blu-ray disc to hold more information than a DVD?

LEARNING GOALS

By studying this chapter, you will learn:

- What happens when coherent light shines on an object with an edge or aperture.
- How to understand the diffraction pattern formed when coherent light passes through a narrow slit.
- How to calculate the intensity at various points in a single-slit diffraction pattern.
- What happens when coherent light shines on an array of narrow, closely spaced slits.
- How scientists use diffraction gratings for precise measurements of wavelength.
- How x-ray diffraction reveals the arrangement of atoms in a crystal.
- How diffraction sets limits on the smallest details that can be seen with a telescope.

Everyone is used to the idea that sound bends around corners. If sound didn't behave this way, you couldn't hear a police siren that's out of sight around a corner or the speech of a person whose back is turned to you. What may surprise you (and certainly surprised many scientists of the early 19th century) is that *light* can bend around corners as well. When light from a point source falls on a straightedge and casts a shadow, the edge of the shadow is never perfectly sharp. Some light appears in the area that we expect to be in the shadow, and we find alternating bright and dark fringes in the illuminated area. In general, light emerging from apertures doesn't behave precisely according to the predictions of the straight-line ray model of geometric optics.

The reason for these effects is that light, like sound, has wave characteristics. In Chapter 35 we studied the interference patterns that can arise when two light waves are combined. In this chapter we'll investigate interference effects due to combining *many* light waves. Such effects are referred to as *diffraction.* We'll find that the behavior of waves after they pass through an aperture is an example of diffraction; each infinitesimal part of the aperture acts as a source of waves, and the resulting pattern of light and dark is a result of interference among the waves emanating from these sources.

Light emerging from arrays of apertures also forms patterns whose character depends on the color of the light and the size and spacing of the apertures. Examples of this effect include the colors of iridescent butterflies and the "rainbow" you see reflected from the surface of a compact disc. We'll explore similar effects with x rays that are used to study the atomic structure of solids and liquids. Finally, we'll look at the physics of a *hologram,* a special kind of interference pattern recorded on photographic film and reproduced. When properly illuminated, it forms a three-dimensional image of the original object.

36.1 Fresnel and Fraunhofer Diffraction

36.1 A point source of light illuminates a straightedge.

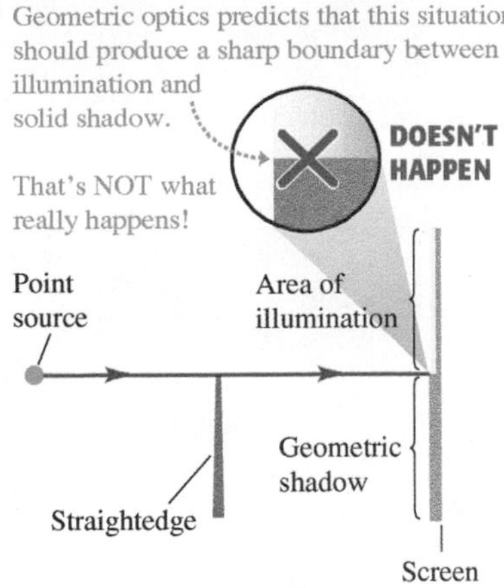

According to geometric optics, when an opaque object is placed between a point light source and a screen, as in Fig. 36.1, the shadow of the object forms a perfectly sharp line. No light at all strikes the screen at points within the shadow, and the area outside the shadow is illuminated nearly uniformly. But as we saw in Chapter 35, the *wave* nature of light causes effects that can't be understood with geometric optics. An important class of such effects occurs when light strikes a barrier that has an aperture or an edge. The interference patterns formed in such a situation are grouped under the heading **diffraction.**

Figure 36.2 shows an example of diffraction. The photograph in Fig. 36.2a was made by placing a razor blade halfway between a pinhole, illuminated by monochromatic light, and a photographic film. The film recorded the shadow cast by the blade. Figure 36.2b is an enlargement of a region near the shadow of the right edge of the blade. The position of the *geometric* shadow line is indicated by arrows. The area outside the geometric shadow is bordered by alternating bright and dark bands. There is some light in the shadow region, although this is not very visible in the photograph. The first bright band in Fig. 36.2b, just to the right of the geometric shadow, is considerably brighter than in the region of uniform illumination to the extreme right. This simple experiment gives us some idea of the richness and complexity of what might seem to be a simple idea, the casting of a shadow by an opaque object.

We don't often observe diffraction patterns such as Fig. 36.2 in everyday life because most ordinary light sources are neither monochromatic nor point sources. If we use a white frosted light bulb instead of a point source to illuminate the razor blade in Fig. 36.2, each wavelength of the light from every point of the bulb forms its own diffraction pattern, but the patterns overlap so much that we can't see any individual pattern.

Diffraction and Huygens's Principle

We can analyze diffraction patterns using Huygens's principle (see Section 33.7). This principle states that we can consider every point of a wave front as a source of secondary wavelets. These spread out in all directions with a speed equal to the speed of propagation of the wave. The position of the wave front at any later time is the *envelope* of the secondary wavelets at that time. To find the resultant displacement at any point, we combine all the individual displacements produced by these secondary waves, using the superposition principle and taking into account their amplitudes and relative phases.

36.2 An example of diffraction.

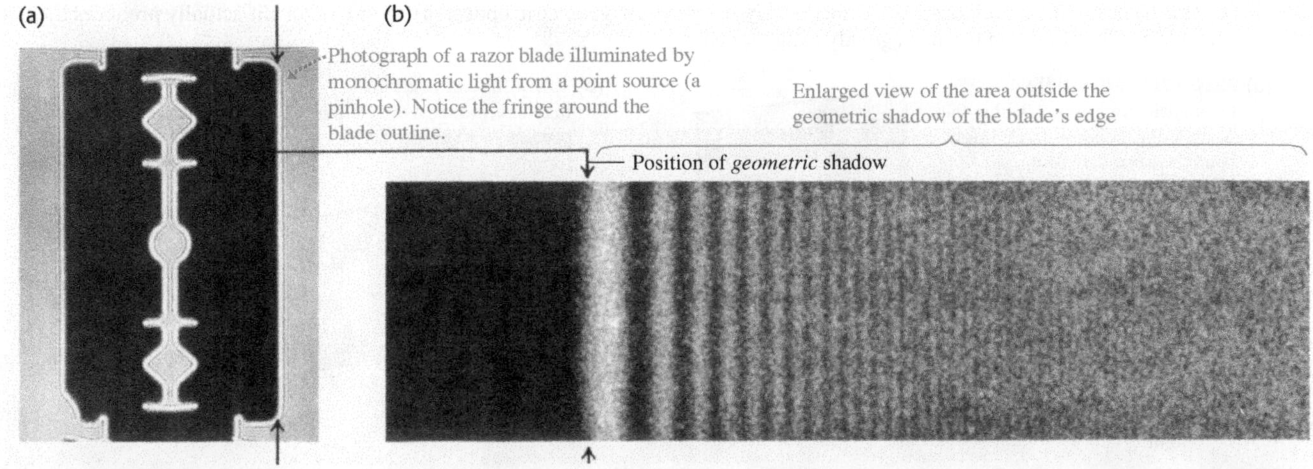

In Fig. 36.1, both the point source and the screen are relatively close to the obstacle forming the diffraction pattern. This situation is described as *near-field diffraction* or **Fresnel diffraction,** pronounced "Freh-nell" (after the French scientist Augustin Jean Fresnel, 1788–1827). By contrast, we use the term **Fraunhofer diffraction** (after the German physicist Joseph von Fraunhofer, 1787–1826) for situations in which the source, obstacle, and screen are far enough apart that we can consider all lines from the source to the obstacle to be parallel, and can likewise consider all lines from the obstacle to a given point on the screen to be parallel. We will restrict the following discussion to Fraunhofer diffraction, which is usually simpler to analyze in detail than Fresnel diffraction.

Diffraction is sometimes described as "the bending of light around an obstacle." But the process that causes diffraction is present in the propagation of *every* wave. When part of the wave is cut off by some obstacle, we observe diffraction effects that result from interference of the remaining parts of the wave fronts. Optical instruments typically use only a limited portion of a wave; for example, a telescope uses only the part of a wave that is admitted by its objective lens or mirror. Thus diffraction plays a role in nearly all optical phenomena.

Finally, we emphasize that there is no fundamental distinction between *interference* and *diffraction.* In Chapter 35 we used the term *interference* for effects involving waves from a small number of sources, usually two. *Diffraction* usually involves a *continuous* distribution of Huygens's wavelets across the area of an aperture, or a very large number of sources or apertures. But both interference and diffraction are consequences of superposition and Huygens's principle.

Test Your Understanding of Section 36.1 Can *sound* waves undergo diffraction around an edge?

Mastering**PHYSICS**

PhET: Wave Interference
ActivPhysics 16.6: Single-Slit Diffraction

36.2 Diffraction from a Single Slit

In this section we'll discuss the diffraction pattern formed by plane-wave (parallel-ray) monochromatic light when it emerges from a long, narrow slit, as shown in Fig. 36.3. We call the narrow dimension the *width,* even though in this figure it is a vertical dimension.

According to geometric optics, the transmitted beam should have the same cross section as the slit, as in Fig. 36.3a. What is *actually* observed is the pattern shown in Fig. 36.3b. The beam spreads out vertically after passing through the slit. The diffraction pattern consists of a central bright band, which may be much broader than the width of the slit, bordered by alternating dark and bright bands with rapidly decreasing intensity. About 85% of the power in the

36.3 (a) The "shadow" of a horizontal slit as incorrectly predicted by geometric optics. (b) A horizontal slit actually produces a diffraction pattern. The slit width has been greatly exaggerated.

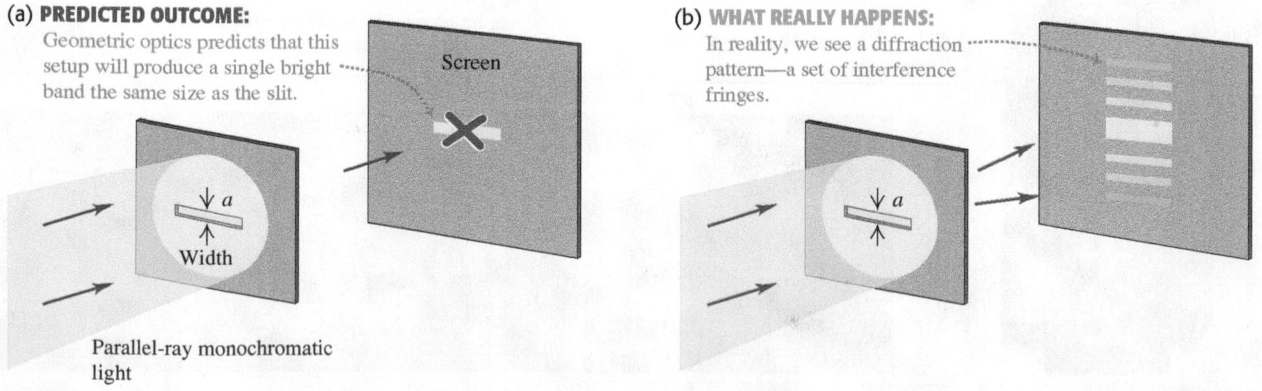

36.4 Diffraction by a single rectangular slit. The long sides of the slit are perpendicular to the figure.

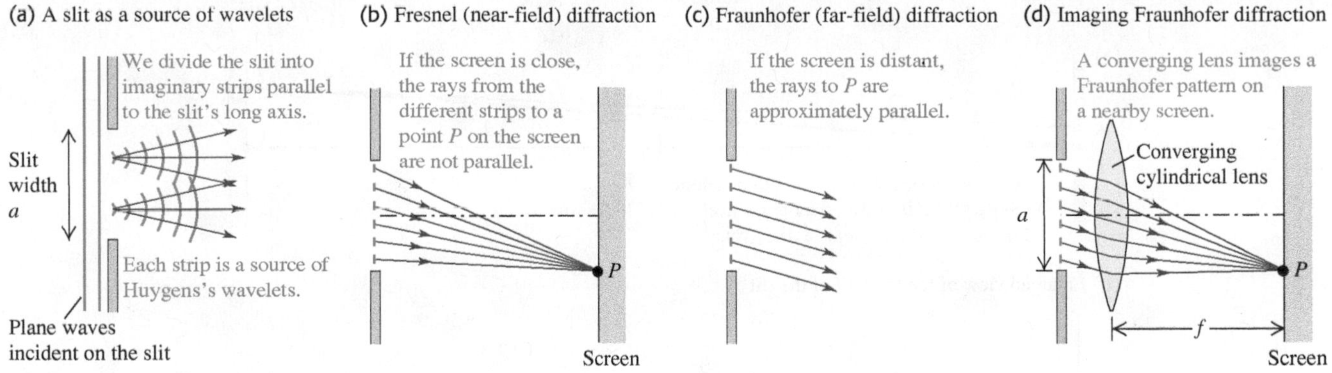

transmitted beam is in the central bright band, whose width is *inversely* proportional to the width of the slit. In general, the smaller the width of the slit, the broader the entire diffraction pattern. (The *horizontal* spreading of the beam in Fig. 36.3b is negligible because the horizontal dimension of the slit is relatively large.) You can observe a similar diffraction pattern by looking at a point source, such as a distant street light, through a narrow slit formed between your two thumbs held in front of your eye; the retina of your eye corresponds to the screen.

Single-Slit Diffraction: Locating the Dark Fringes

Figure 36.4 shows a side view of the same setup; the long sides of the slit are perpendicular to the figure, and plane waves are incident on the slit from the left. According to Huygens's principle, each element of area of the slit opening can be considered as a source of secondary waves. In particular, imagine dividing the slit into several narrow strips of equal width, parallel to the long edges and perpendicular to the page. Figure 36.4a shows two such strips. Cylindrical secondary wavelets, shown in cross section, spread out from each strip.

In Fig. 36.4b a screen is placed to the right of the slit. We can calculate the resultant intensity at a point P on the screen by adding the contributions from the individual wavelets, taking proper account of their various phases and amplitudes. It's easiest to do this calculation if we assume that the screen is far enough away that all the rays from various parts of the slit to a particular point P on the screen are parallel, as in Fig. 36.4c. An equivalent situation is Fig. 36.4d, in which the rays to the lens are parallel and the lens forms a reduced image of the same pattern that would be formed on an infinitely distant screen without the lens. We might expect that the various light paths through the lens would introduce additional phase shifts, but in fact it can be shown that all the paths have *equal* phase shifts, so this is not a problem.

The situation of Fig. 36.4b is Fresnel diffraction; those in Figs. 36.4c and 36.4d, where the outgoing rays are considered parallel, are Fraunhofer diffraction. We can derive quite simply the most important characteristics of the Fraunhofer diffraction pattern from a single slit. First consider two narrow strips, one just below the top edge of the drawing of the slit and one at its center, shown in end view in Fig. 36.5. The difference in path length to point P is $(a/2)\sin\theta$, where a is the slit width and θ is the angle between the perpendicular to the slit and a line from the center of the slit to P. Suppose this path difference happens to be equal to $\lambda/2$; then light from these two strips arrives at point P with a half-cycle phase difference, and cancellation occurs.

Similarly, light from two strips immediately *below* the two in the figure also arrives at P a half-cycle out of phase. In fact, the light from *every* strip in the top half of the slit cancels out the light from a corresponding strip in the bottom half.

36.5 Side view of a horizontal slit. When the distance x to the screen is much greater than the slit width a, the rays from a distance $a/2$ apart may be considered parallel.

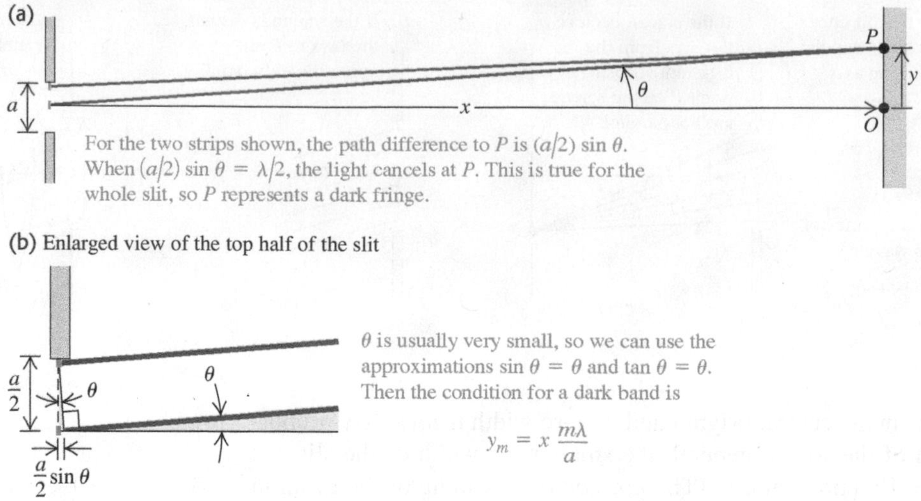

Hence the combined light from the entire slit completely cancels at P, giving a dark fringe in the interference pattern. A dark fringe occurs whenever

$$\frac{a}{2}\sin\theta = \pm\frac{\lambda}{2} \quad \text{or} \quad \sin\theta = \pm\frac{\lambda}{a} \tag{36.1}$$

The plus-or-minus ($\pm$) sign in Eq. (36.1) says that there are symmetric dark fringes above and below point O in Fig. 36.5a. The upper fringe ($\theta > 0$) occurs at a point P where light from the bottom half of the slit travels $\lambda/2$ farther to P than does light from the top half; the lower fringe ($\theta < 0$) occurs where light from the *top* half travels $\lambda/2$ farther than light from the *bottom* half.

We may also divide the screen into quarters, sixths, and so on, and use the above argument to show that a dark fringe occurs whenever $\sin\theta = \pm 2\lambda/a$, $\pm 3\lambda/a$, and so on. Thus the condition for a *dark* fringe is

$$\sin\theta = \frac{m\lambda}{a} \quad (m = \pm1, \pm2, \pm3, \dots) \quad \text{(dark fringes in single-slit diffraction)} \tag{36.2}$$

For example, if the slit width is equal to ten wavelengths ($a = 10\lambda$), dark fringes occur at $\sin\theta = \pm\frac{1}{10}, \pm\frac{2}{10}, \pm\frac{3}{10}, \dots$. Between the dark fringes are bright fringes. We also note that $\sin\theta = 0$ corresponds to a *bright* band; in this case, light from the entire slit arrives at P in phase. Thus it would be wrong to put $m = 0$ in Eq. (36.2). The central bright fringe is wider than the other bright fringes, as Fig. 36.3b shows. In the small-angle approximation that we will use below, it is exactly *twice* as wide.

With light, the wavelength λ is of the order of $500 \text{ nm} = 5 \times 10^{-7}$ m. This is often much smaller than the slit width a; a typical slit width is $10^{-2} \text{ cm} = 10^{-4}$ m. Therefore the values of θ in Eq. (36.2) are often so small that the approximation $\sin\theta \approx \theta$ (where θ is in radians) is a very good one. In that case we can rewrite this equation as

$$\theta = \frac{m\lambda}{a} \quad (m = \pm1, \pm2, \pm3, \dots) \quad \text{(for small angles } \theta\text{)}$$

where θ is in *radians.* Also, if the distance from slit to screen is x, as in Fig. 36.5a, and the vertical distance of the mth dark band from the center of the pattern is y_m, then $\tan\theta = y_m/x$. For small θ we may also approximate $\tan\theta$ by θ (in radians), and we then find

$$y_m = x\frac{m\lambda}{a} \quad (\text{for } y_m \ll x) \qquad (36.3)$$

Figure 36.6 is a photograph of a single-slit diffraction pattern with the $m = \pm 1$, ± 2, and ± 3 minima labeled.

36.6 Photograph of the Fraunhofer diffraction pattern of a single horizontal slit.

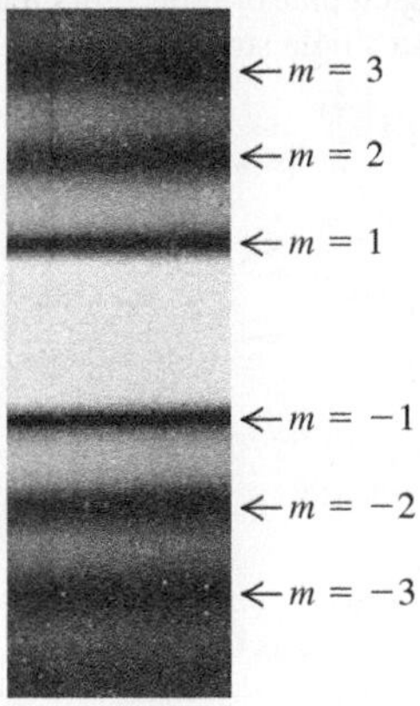

CAUTION **Single-slit diffraction vs. two-slit interference** Equation (36.3) has the same form as the equation for the two-slit pattern, Eq. (35.6), except that in Eq. (36.3) we use x rather than R for the distance to the screen. But Eq. (36.3) gives the positions of the *dark* fringes in a *single-slit* pattern rather than the *bright* fringes in a *double-slit* pattern. Also, $m = 0$ in Eq. (36.2) is *not* a dark fringe. Be careful!

Example 36.1 **Single-slit diffraction**

You pass 633-nm laser light through a narrow slit and observe the diffraction pattern on a screen 6.0 m away. The distance on the screen between the centers of the first minima on either side of the central bright fringe is 32 mm (Fig. 36.7). How wide is the slit?

SOLUTION

IDENTIFY and SET UP: This problem involves the relationship between the positions of dark fringes in a single-slit diffraction pattern and the slit width a (our target variable). The distances between fringes on the screen are much smaller than the slit-to-screen distance, so the angle θ shown in Fig. 36.5a is very small and we can use Eq. (36.3) to solve for a.

36.7 A single-slit diffraction experiment.

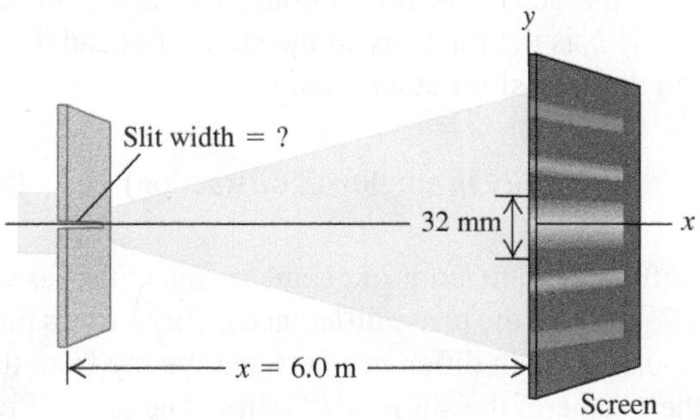

EXECUTE: The first minimum corresponds to $m = 1$ in Eq. (36.3). The distance y_1 from the central maximum to the first minimum on either side is half the distance between the two first minima, so $y_1 = (32\text{ mm})/2 = 16$ mm. Solving Eq. (36.3) for a, we find

$$a = \frac{x\lambda}{y_1} = \frac{(6.0\text{ m})(633 \times 10^{-9}\text{ m})}{16 \times 10^{-3}\text{ m}} = 2.4 \times 10^{-4}\text{ m} = 0.24\text{ mm}$$

EVALUATE: The angle θ is small only if the wavelength is small compared to the slit width. Since $\lambda = 633\text{ nm} = 6.33 \times 10^{-7}$ m and we have found $a = 0.24\text{ mm} = 2.4 \times 10^{-4}$ m, our result is consistent with this: The wavelength is $(6.33 \times 10^{-7}\text{ m})/(2.4 \times 10^{-4}\text{ m}) = 0.0026$ as large as the slit width. Can you show that the distance between the *second* minima on either side is $2(32\text{ mm}) = 64$ mm, and so on?

Test Your Understanding of Section 36.2 Rank the following single-slit diffraction experiments in order of the size of the angle from the center of the diffraction pattern to the first dark fringe, from largest to smallest: (i) wavelength 400 nm, slit width 0.20 mm; (ii) wavelength 600 nm, slit width 0.20 mm; (iii) wavelength 400 nm, slit width 0.30 mm; (iv) wavelength 600 nm, slit width 0.30 mm.

36.3 Intensity in the Single-Slit Pattern

We can derive an expression for the intensity distribution for the single-slit diffraction pattern by the same phasor-addition method that we used in Section 35.3 to obtain Eqs. (35.10) and (35.14) for the two-slit interference pattern. We again imagine a plane wave front at the slit subdivided into a large number of strips. We superpose the contributions of the Huygens wavelets from all the strips at a point P on a distant screen at an angle θ from the normal to the slit plane (Fig. 36.8a). To do this, we use a phasor to represent the sinusoidally varying $\vec{E}$ field from

36.8 Using phasor diagrams to find the amplitude of the $\vec{E}$ field in single-slit diffraction. Each phasor represents the $\vec{E}$ field from a single strip within the slit.

(a)

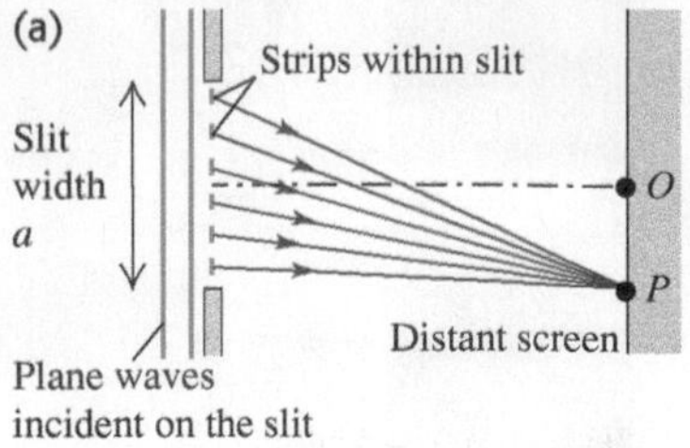

(b) At the center of the diffraction pattern (point O), the phasors from all strips within the slit are in phase.

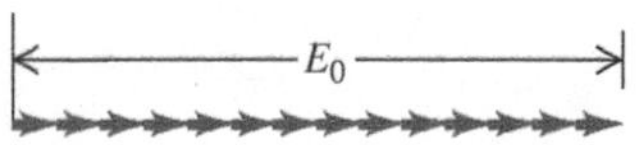

(c) Phasor diagram at a point slightly off the center of the pattern; β = total phase difference between the first and last phasors.

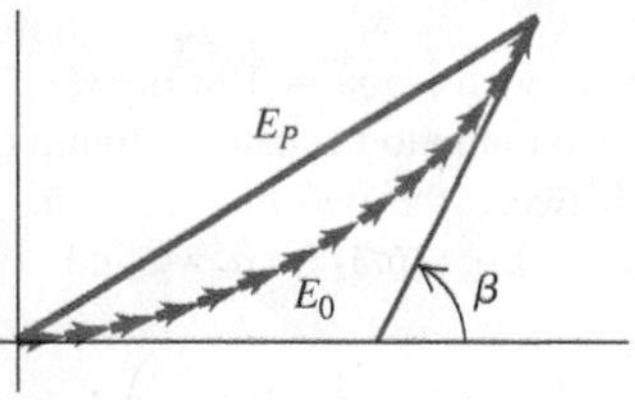

(d) As in (c), but in the limit that the slit is subdivided into infinitely many strips

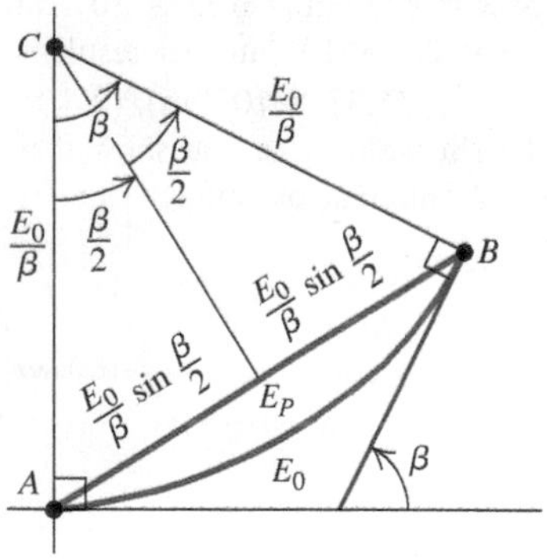

each individual strip. The magnitude of the vector sum of the phasors at each point P is the amplitude E_P of the total $\vec{E}$ field at that point. The intensity at P is proportional to $E_P{}^2$.

At the point O shown in Fig. 36.8a, corresponding to the center of the pattern where $\theta = 0$, there are negligible path differences for $x \gg a$; the phasors are all essentially *in phase* (that is, have the same direction). In Fig. 36.8b we draw the phasors at time $t = 0$ and denote the resultant amplitude at O by E_0. In this illustration we have divided the slit into 14 strips.

Now consider wavelets arriving from different strips at point P in Fig. 36.8a, at an angle θ from point O. Because of the differences in path length, there are now phase differences between wavelets coming from adjacent strips; the corresponding phasor diagram is shown in Fig. 36.8c. The vector sum of the phasors is now part of the perimeter of a many-sided polygon, and E_P, the amplitude of the resultant electric field at P, is the *chord.* The angle β is the total phase difference between the wave from the top strip of Fig. 36.8a and the wave from the bottom strip; that is, β is the phase of the wave received at P from the top strip with respect to the wave received at P from the bottom strip.

We may imagine dividing the slit into narrower and narrower strips. In the limit that there is an infinite number of infinitesimally narrow strips, the curved trail of phasors becomes an *arc of a circle* (Fig. 36.8d), with arc length equal to the length E_0 in Fig. 36.8b. The center C of this arc is found by constructing perpendiculars at A and B. From the relationship among arc length, radius, and angle, the radius of the arc is E_0/β; the amplitude E_P of the resultant electric field at P is equal to the chord AB, which is $2(E_0/\beta)\sin(\beta/2)$. (Note that β *must* be in radians!) We then have

$$E_P = E_0\frac{\sin(\beta/2)}{\beta/2} \qquad \text{(amplitude in single-slit diffraction)} \qquad (36.4)$$

The intensity at each point on the screen is proportional to the square of the amplitude given by Eq. (36.4). If I_0 is the intensity in the straight-ahead direction where $\theta = 0$ and $\beta = 0$, then the intensity I at any point is

$$I = I_0\left[\frac{\sin(\beta/2)}{\beta/2}\right]^2 \qquad \text{(intensity in single-slit diffraction)} \qquad (36.5)$$

We can express the phase difference β in terms of geometric quantities, as we did for the two-slit pattern. From Eq. (35.11) the phase difference is $2\pi/\lambda$ times the path difference. Figure 36.5 shows that the path difference between the ray from the top of the slit and the ray from the middle of the slit is $(a/2)\sin\theta$. The path difference between the rays from the top of the slit and the bottom of the slit is twice this, so

$$\beta = \frac{2\pi}{\lambda}a\sin\theta \qquad (36.6)$$

and Eq. (36.5) becomes

$$I = I_0\left\{\frac{\sin[\pi a(\sin\theta)/\lambda]}{\pi a(\sin\theta)/\lambda}\right\}^2 \qquad \text{(intensity in single-slit diffraction)} \qquad (36.7)$$

This equation expresses the intensity directly in terms of the angle θ. In many calculations it is easier first to calculate the phase angle β, using Eq. (36.6), and then to use Eq. (36.5).

Equation (36.7) is plotted in Fig. 36.9a. Note that the central intensity peak is much larger than any of the others. This means that most of the power in the wave remains within an angle θ from the perpendicular to the slit, where $\sin\theta = \lambda/a$ (the first diffraction minimum). You can see this easily in Fig. 36.9b, which is a photograph of water waves undergoing single-slit diffraction. Note also that the peak intensities in Fig. 36.9a decrease rapidly as we go away from the center of the pattern. (Compare Fig. 36.6, which shows a single-slit diffraction pattern for light.)

The dark fringes in the pattern are the places where $I = 0$. These occur at points for which the numerator of Eq. (36.5) is zero so that β is a multiple of 2π. From Eq. (36.6) this corresponds to

$$\frac{a\sin\theta}{\lambda} = m \qquad (m = \pm1, \pm2, \dots)$$

$$\sin\theta = \frac{m\lambda}{a} \qquad (m = \pm1, \pm2, \dots) \tag{36.8}$$

This agrees with our previous result, Eq. (36.2). Note again that $\beta = 0$ (corresponding to $\theta = 0$) is *not* a minimum. Equation (36.5) is indeterminate at $\beta = 0$, but we can evaluate the limit as $\beta \rightarrow 0$ using L'Hôpital's rule. We find that at $\beta = 0$, $I = I_0$, as we should expect.

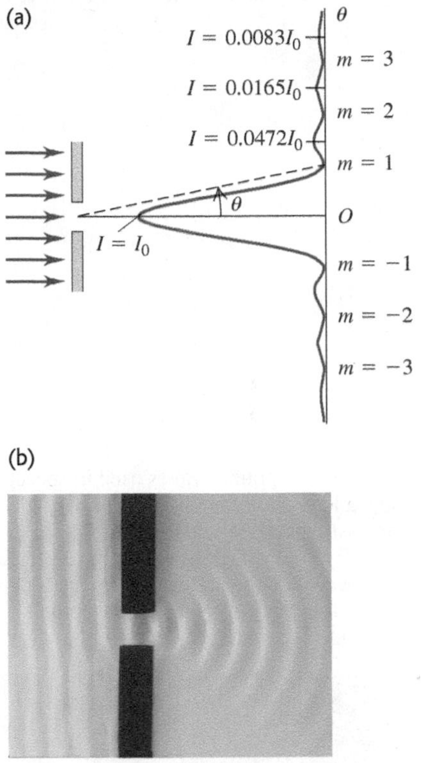

36.9 (a) Intensity versus angle in single-slit diffraction. The values of m label intensity minima given by Eq. (36.8). Most of the wave power goes into the central intensity peak (between the $m = 1$ and $m = -1$ intensity minima). (b) These water waves passing through a small aperture behave exactly like light waves in single-slit diffraction. Only the diffracted waves within the central intensity peak are visible; the waves at larger angles are too faint to see.

Intensity Maxima in the Single-Slit Pattern

We can also use Eq. (36.5) to calculate the positions of the peaks, or *intensity maxima,* and the intensities at these peaks. This is not quite as simple as it may appear. We might expect the peaks to occur where the sine function reaches the value ±1—namely, where $\beta = \pm\pi, \pm3\pi, \pm5\pi$, or in general,

$$\beta \approx \pm(2m + 1)\pi \qquad (m = 0, 1, 2, \dots) \tag{36.9}$$

This is *approximately* correct, but because of the factor $(\beta/2)^2$ in the denominator of Eq. (36.5), the maxima don't occur precisely at these points. When we take the derivative of Eq. (36.5) with respect to β and set it equal to zero to try to find the maxima and minima, we get a transcendental equation that has to be solved numerically. In fact there is *no* maximum near $\beta = \pm\pi$. The first maxima on either side of the central maximum, near $\beta = \pm3\pi$, actually occur at $\pm2.860\pi$. The second side maxima, near $\beta = \pm5\pi$, are actually at $\pm4.918\pi$, and so on. The error in Eq. (36.9) vanishes in the limit of large m—that is, for intensity maxima far from the center of the pattern.

To find the intensities at the side maxima, we substitute these values of β back into Eq. (36.5). Using the approximate expression in Eq. (36.9), we get

$$I_m \approx \frac{I_0}{\left(m + \frac{1}{2}\right)^2\pi^2} \tag{36.10}$$

where I_m is the intensity of the mth side maximum and I_0 is the intensity of the central maximum. Equation (36.10) gives the series of intensities

$$0.0450I_0 \qquad 0.0162I_0 \qquad 0.0083I_0$$

and so on. As we have pointed out, this equation is only approximately correct. The actual intensities of the side maxima turn out to be

$$0.0472I_0 \qquad 0.0165I_0 \qquad 0.0083I_0 \qquad \dots$$

Note that the intensities of the side maxima decrease very rapidly, as Fig. 36.9a also shows. Even the first side maxima have less than 5% of the intensity of the central maximum.

Width of the Single-Slit Pattern

For small angles the angular spread of the diffraction pattern is inversely proportional to the slit width a or, more precisely, to the ratio of a to the wavelength λ. Figure 36.10 shows graphs of intensity I as a function of the angle θ for three values of the ratio a/λ.

36.10 The single-slit diffraction pattern depends on the ratio of the slit width a to the wavelength λ.

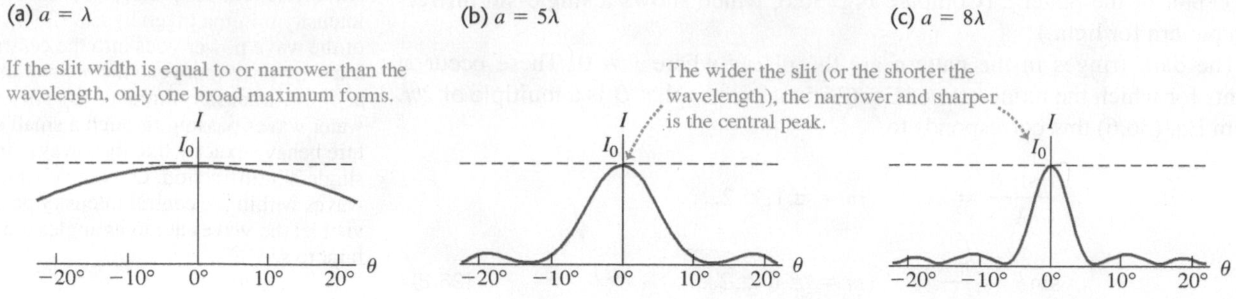

With light waves, the wavelength λ is often much smaller than the slit width a, and the values of θ in Eqs. (36.6) and (36.7) are so small that the approximation $\sin\theta = \theta$ is very good. With this approximation the position θ_1 of the first minimum beside the central maximum, corresponding to $\beta/2 = \pi$, is, from Eq. (36.7),

$$\theta_1 = \frac{\lambda}{a} \qquad (36.11)$$

This characterizes the width (angular spread) of the central maximum, and we see that it is *inversely* proportional to the slit width a. When the small-angle approximation is valid, the central maximum is exactly twice as wide as each side maximum. When a is of the order of a centimeter or more, θ_1 is so small that we can consider practically all the light to be concentrated at the geometrical focus. But when a is less than λ, the central maximum spreads over 180°, and the fringe pattern is not seen at all.

It's important to keep in mind that diffraction occurs for *all* kinds of waves, not just light. Sound waves undergo diffraction when they pass through a slit or aperture such as an ordinary doorway. The sound waves used in speech have wavelengths of about a meter or greater, and a typical doorway is less than 1 m wide; in this situation, a is less than λ, and the central intensity maximum extends over 180°. This is why the sounds coming through an open doorway can easily be heard by an eavesdropper hiding out of sight around the corner. In the same way, sound waves can bend around the head of an instructor who faces the blackboard while lecturing (Fig. 36.11). By contrast, there is essentially no diffraction of visible light through a doorway because the width a is very much greater than the wavelength λ (of order 5×10^{-7} m). You can *hear* around corners because typical sound waves have relatively long wavelengths; you cannot *see* around corners because the wavelength of visible light is very short.

36.11 The sound waves used in speech have a long wavelength (about 1 m) and can easily bend around this instructor's head. By contrast, light waves have very short wavelengths and undergo very little diffraction. Hence you can't *see* around his head!

Example 36.2 Single-slit diffraction: Intensity I

(a) The intensity at the center of a single-slit diffraction pattern is I_0. What is the intensity at a point in the pattern where there is a 66-radian phase difference between wavelets from the two edges of the slit? (b) If this point is 7.0° away from the central maximum, how many wavelengths wide is the slit?

SOLUTION

IDENTIFY and SET UP: In our analysis of Fig. 36.8 we used the symbol β for the phase difference between wavelets from the two edges of the slit. In part (a) we use Eq. (36.5) to find the intensity I at the point in the pattern where $\beta = 66$ rad. In part (b) we need to find the slit width a as a multiple of the wavelength λ so our target variable is a/λ. We are given the angular position θ of the point where $\beta = 66$ rad, so we can use Eq. (36.6) to solve for a/λ.

EXECUTE: (a) We have $\beta/2 = 33$ rad, so from Eq. (36.5),

$$I = I_0\left[\frac{\sin(33\text{ rad})}{33\text{ rad}}\right]^2 = (9.2 \times 10^{-4})I_0$$

(b) From Eq. (36.6),

$$\frac{a}{\lambda} = \frac{\beta}{2\pi\sin\theta} = \frac{66\text{ rad}}{(2\pi\text{ rad})\sin 7.0°} = 86$$

For example, for 550-nm light the slit width is $a = (86)(550\text{ nm}) = 4.7 \times 10^{-5}\text{ m} = 0.047$ mm, or roughly $\frac{1}{20}$ mm.

EVALUATE: To what point in the diffraction pattern does this value of β correspond? To find out, note that $\beta = 66$ rad is approximately equal to 21π. This is an odd multiple of π, corresponding to the form $(2m + 1)\pi$ found in Eq. (36.9) for the intensity *maxima*. Hence $\beta = 66$ rad corresponds to a point near the tenth ($m = 10$) maximum. This is well beyond the range shown in Fig. 36.9a, which shows only maxima out to $m = \pm 3$.

Example 36.3 Single-slit diffraction: Intensity II

In the experiment described in Example 36.1 (Section 36.2), the intensity at the center of the pattern is I_0. What is the intensity at a point on the screen 3.0 mm from the center of the pattern?

SOLUTION

IDENTIFY and SET UP: This is similar to Example 36.2, except that we are not given the value of the phase difference β at the point in question. We use geometry to determine the angle θ for our point and then use Eq. (36.7) to find the intensity I (the target variable).

EXECUTE: Referring to Fig. 36.5a, we have $y = 3.0$ mm and $x = 6.0$ m, so $\tan\theta = y/x = (3.0 \times 10^{-3}\text{ m})/(6.0\text{ m}) = 5.0 \times 10^{-4}$. This is so small that the values of $\tan\theta$, $\sin\theta$, and θ (in radians) are all nearly the same. Then, using Eq. (36.7),

$$\frac{\pi a \sin\theta}{\lambda} = \frac{\pi(2.4 \times 10^{-4}\text{ m})(5.0 \times 10^{-4})}{6.33 \times 10^{-7}\text{ m}} = 0.60$$

$$I = I_0\left(\frac{\sin 0.60}{0.60}\right)^2 = 0.89 I_0$$

EVALUATE: Figure 36.9a shows that an intensity this high can occur only within the central intensity maximum. This checks out; from Example 36.1, the first intensity minimum ($m = 1$ in Fig. 36.9a) is $(32\text{ mm})/2 = 16$ mm from the center of the pattern, so the point in question here at $y = 3$ mm does, indeed, lie within the central maximum.

Test Your Understanding of Section 36.3 Coherent electromagnetic radiation is sent through a slit of width 0.0100 mm. For which of the following wavelengths will there be *no* points in the diffraction pattern where the intensity is zero? (i) blue light of wavelength 500 nm; (ii) infrared light of wavelength 10.6 μm; (iii) microwaves of wavelength 1.00 mm; (iv) ultraviolet light of wavelength 50.0 nm. ❙

36.4 Multiple Slits

In Sections 35.2 and 35.3 we analyzed interference from two point sources or from two very narrow slits; in this analysis we ignored effects due to the finite (that is, nonzero) slit width. In Sections 36.2 and 36.3 we considered the diffraction effects that occur when light passes through a single slit of finite width. Additional interesting effects occur when we have two slits with finite width or when there are several very narrow slits.

Two Slits of Finite Width

Let's take another look at the two-slit pattern in the more realistic case in which the slits have finite width. If the slits are narrow in comparison to the wavelength, we can assume that light from each slit spreads out uniformly in all directions to the right of the slit. We used this assumption in Section 35.3 to calculate the interference pattern described by Eq. (35.10) or (35.15), consisting of a series of equally spaced, equally intense maxima. However, when the slits have finite width, the peaks in the two-slit interference pattern are modulated by the single-slit diffraction pattern characteristic of the width of each slit.

Figure 36.12a shows the intensity in a single-slit diffraction pattern with slit width a. The *diffraction minima* are labeled by the integer $m_d = \pm 1, \pm 2, \ldots$ ("d" for "diffraction"). Figure 36.12b shows the pattern formed by two very narrow slits with distance d between slits, where d is four times as great as the single-slit width a in Fig. 36.12a; that is, $d = 4a$. The *interference maxima* are labeled by the integer $m_i = 0, \pm 1, \pm 2, \ldots$ ("i" for "interference"). We note that the spacing between adjacent minima in the single-slit pattern is four times as great as in the two-slit pattern. Now suppose we widen each of the narrow slits to the same width a as that of the single slit in Fig. 36.12a. Figure 36.12c shows the pattern

36.12 Finding the intensity pattern for two slits of finite width.

(a) Single-slit diffraction pattern for a slit width a

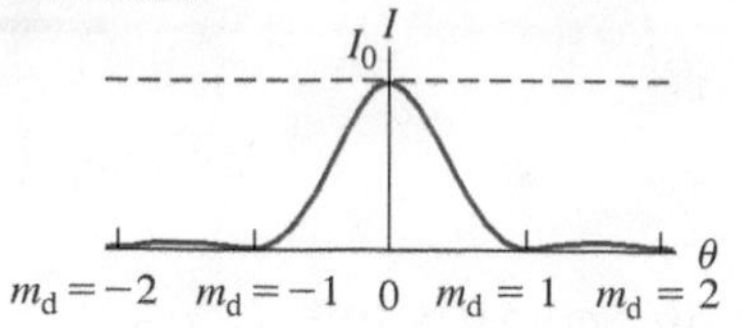

(b) Two-slit interference pattern for narrow slits whose separation d is four times the width of the slit in (a)

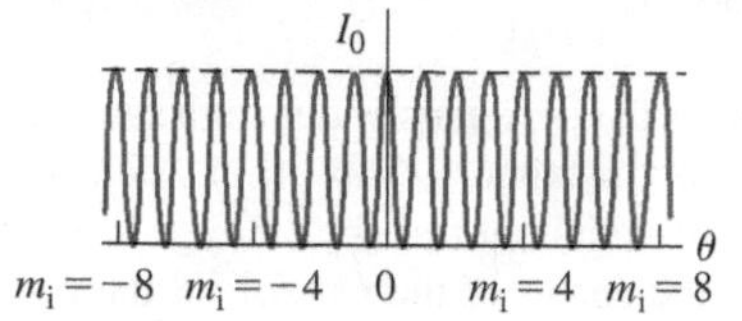

(c) Calculated intensity pattern for two slits of width a and separation $d = 4a$, including both interference and diffraction effects

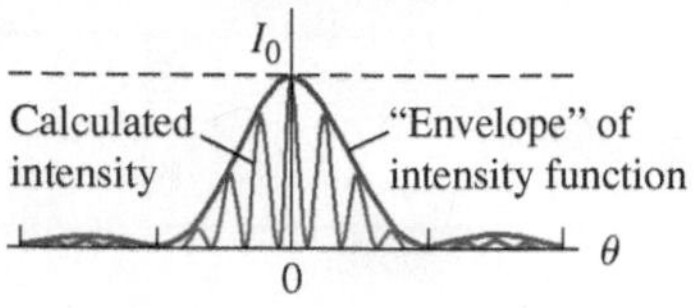

(d) Actual photograph of the pattern calculated in (c)

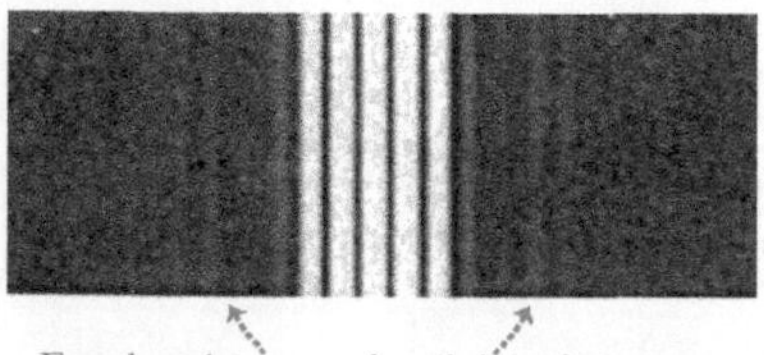

For $d = 4a$, every fourth interference maximum at the sides ($m_i = \pm 4, \pm 8, \ldots$) is missing.

from two slits with width a, separated by a distance (between centers) $d = 4a$. The effect of the finite width of the slits is to superimpose the two patterns—that is, to multiply the two intensities at each point. The two-slit peaks are in the same positions as before, but their intensities are modulated by the single-slit pattern, which acts as an "envelope" for the intensity function. The expression for the intensity shown in Fig. 36.12c is proportional to the product of the two-slit and single-slit expressions, Eqs. (35.10) and (36.5):

$$I = I_0 \cos^2\frac{\phi}{2}\left[\frac{\sin(\beta/2)}{\beta/2}\right]^2 \quad \text{(two slits of finite width)} \qquad (36.12)$$

where, as before,

$$\phi = \frac{2\pi d}{\lambda}\sin\theta \qquad \beta = \frac{2\pi a}{\lambda}\sin\theta$$

Note that in Fig. 36.12c, every fourth interference maximum at the sides is *missing* because these interference maxima ($m_i = \pm 4, \pm 8, \ldots$) coincide with diffraction minima ($m_d = \pm 1, \pm 2, \ldots$). This can also be seen in Fig. 36.12d, which is a photograph of an actual pattern with $d = 4a$. You should be able to convince yourself that there will be "missing" maxima whenever d is an integer multiple of a.

Figures 36.12c and 36.12d show that as you move away from the central bright maximum of the two-slit pattern, the intensity of the maxima decreases. This is a result of the single-slit modulating pattern shown in Fig. 36.12a; mathematically, the decrease in intensity arises from the factor $(\beta/2)^2$ in the denominator of Eq. (36.12). This decrease in intensity can also be seen in Fig. 35.6 (Section 35.2). The narrower the slits, the broader the single-slit pattern (as in Fig. 36.10) and the slower the decrease in intensity from one interference maximum to the next.

Shall we call the pattern in Fig. 36.12d *interference* or *diffraction*? It's really both, since it results from the superposition of waves coming from various parts of the two apertures.

Several Slits

Next let's consider patterns produced by *several* very narrow slits. As we will see, systems of narrow slits are of tremendous practical importance in *spectroscopy*, the determination of the particular wavelengths of light coming from a source. Assume that each slit is narrow in comparison to the wavelength, so its diffraction pattern spreads out nearly uniformly. Figure 36.13 shows an array of eight narrow slits, with distance d between adjacent slits. Constructive interference occurs for rays at angle θ to the normal that arrive at point P with a path difference between adjacent slits equal to an integer number of wavelengths:

$$d\sin\theta = m\lambda \qquad (m = 0, \pm 1, \pm 2, \ldots)$$

36.13 Multiple-slit diffraction. Here a lens is used to give a Fraunhofer pattern on a nearby screen, as in Fig. 36.4d.

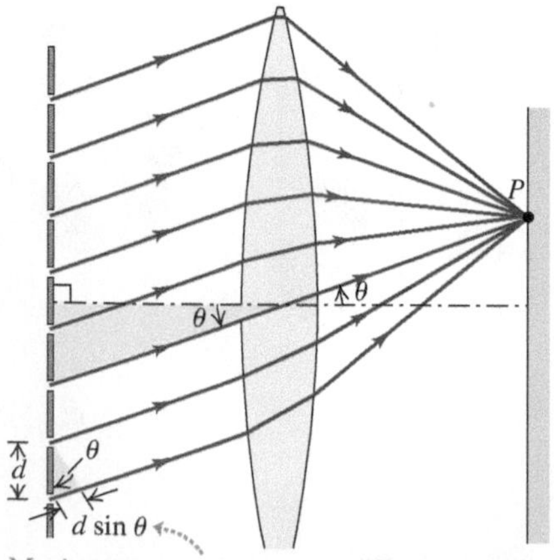

Maxima occur where the path difference for adjacent slits is a whole number of wavelengths: $d \sin\theta = m\lambda$.

This means that reinforcement occurs when the phase difference ϕ at P for light from adjacent slits is an integer multiple of 2π. That is, the maxima in the pattern occur at the *same* positions as for *two* slits with the same spacing. To this extent the pattern resembles the two-slit pattern.

But what happens *between* the maxima? In the two-slit pattern, there is exactly one intensity minimum located midway between each pair of maxima, corresponding to angles for which the phase difference between waves from the two sources is π, 3π, 5π, and so on. In the eight-slit pattern these are also minima because the light from adjacent slits cancels out in pairs, corresponding to the phasor diagram in Fig. 36.14a. But these are not the only minima in the eight-slit pattern. For example, when the phase difference ϕ from adjacent sources is $\pi/4$, the phasor diagram is as shown in Fig. 36.14b; the total (resultant) phasor is zero, and the intensity is zero. When $\phi = \pi/2$, we get the phasor diagram of Fig. 36.14c, and again both the total phasor and the intensity are zero. More

36.14 Phasor diagrams for light passing through eight narrow slits. Intensity maxima occur when the phase difference $\phi = 0, 2\pi, 4\pi, \ldots$. Between the maxima at $\phi = 0$ and $\phi = 2\pi$ are seven minima, corresponding to $\phi = \pi/4, \pi/2, 3\pi/4, \pi, 5\pi/4, 3\pi/2$, and $7\pi/4$. Can you draw phasor diagrams for the other minima?

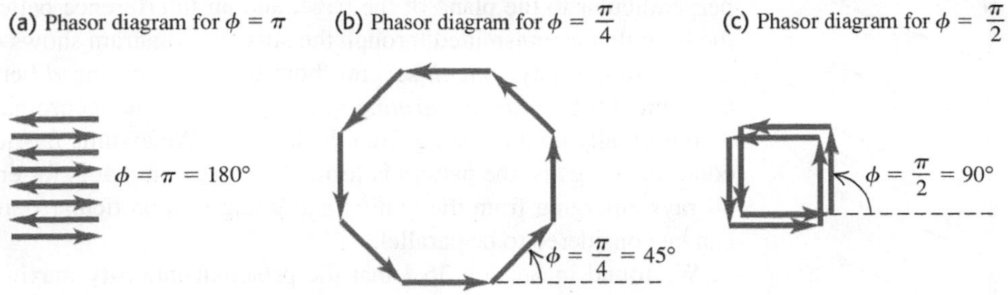

generally, the intensity with eight slits is zero whenever ϕ is an integer multiple of $\pi/4$, *except* when ϕ is a multiple of 2π. Thus there are seven minima for every maximum.

Figure 36.15b shows the result of a detailed calculation of the eight-slit pattern. The large maxima, called *principal maxima,* are in the same positions as for the two-slit pattern of Fig. 36.15a but are much narrower. If the phase difference ϕ between adjacent slits is slightly different from a multiple of 2π, the waves from slits 1 and 2 will be only a little out of phase; however, the phase difference between slits 1 and 3 will be greater, that between slits 1 and 4 will be greater still, and so on. This leads to a partial cancellation for angles that are only slightly different from the angle for a maximum, giving the narrow maxima in Fig. 36.15b. The maxima are even narrower with 16 slits (Fig. 36.15c).

You should show that when there are N slits, there are $(N - 1)$ minima between each pair of principal maxima and a minimum occurs whenever ϕ is an integral multiple of $2\pi/N$ (except when ϕ is an integral multiple of 2π, which gives a principal maximum). There are small *secondary* intensity maxima between the minima; these become smaller in comparison to the principal maxima as N increases. The greater the value of N, the narrower the principal maxima become. From an energy standpoint the total power in the entire pattern is proportional to N. The height of each principal maximum is proportional to N^2, so from energy conservation the width of each principal maximum must be proportional to $1/N$. As we will see in the next section, the narrowness of the principal maxima in a multiple-slit pattern is of great practical importance.

Test Your Understanding of Section 36.4 Suppose two slits, each of width a, are separated by a distance $d = 2.5a$. Are there any missing maxima in the interference pattern produced by these slits? If so, which are missing? If not, why not?

36.5 The Diffraction Grating

We have just seen that increasing the number of slits in an interference experiment (while keeping the spacing of adjacent slits constant) gives interference patterns in which the maxima are in the same positions, but progressively narrower, than with two slits. Because these maxima are so narrow, their angular position, and hence the wavelength, can be measured to very high precision. As we will see, this effect has many important applications.

An array of a large number of parallel slits, all with the same width a and spaced equal distances d between centers, is called a **diffraction grating.** The first one was constructed by Fraunhofer using fine wires. Gratings can be made by using a diamond point to scratch many equally spaced grooves on a glass or metal surface,

36.15 Interference patterns for N equally spaced, very narrow slits. (a) Two slits. (b) Eight slits. (c) Sixteen slits. The vertical scales are different for each graph; I_0 is the maximum intensity for a single slit, and the maximum intensity for N slits is $N^2 I_0$. The width of each peak is proportional to $1/N$.

(a) $N = 2$: two slits produce one minimum between adjacent maxima.

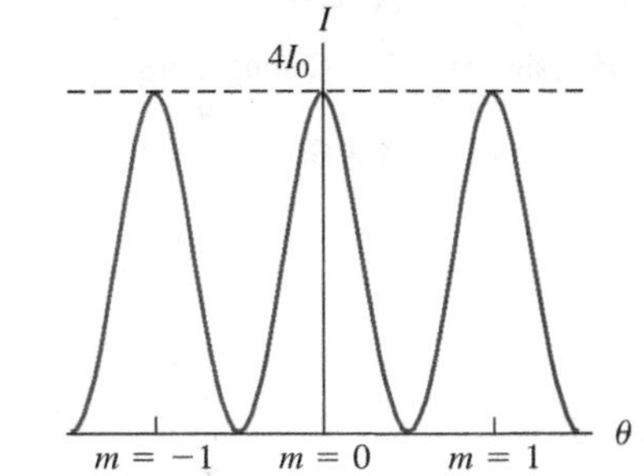

(b) $N = 8$: eight slits produce taller, narrower maxima in the same locations, separated by seven minima.

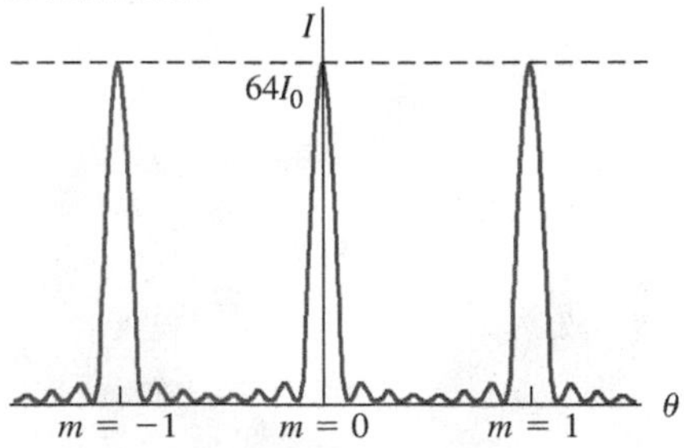

(c) $N = 16$: with 16 slits, the maxima are even taller and narrower, with more intervening minima.

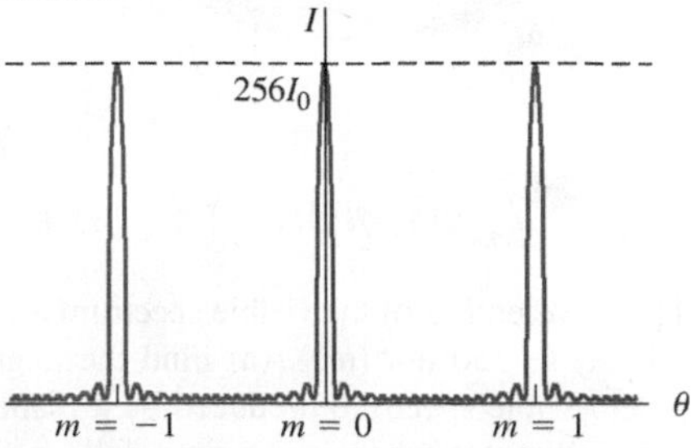

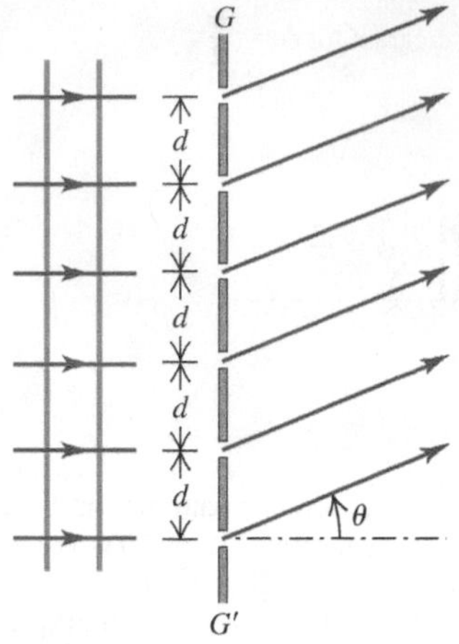

36.16 A portion of a transmission diffraction grating. The separation between the centers of adjacent slits is d.

or by photographic reduction of a pattern of black and white stripes on paper. For a grating, what we have been calling *slits* are often called *rulings* or *lines.*

In Fig. 36.16, GG' is a cross section of a *transmission grating;* the slits are perpendicular to the plane of the page, and an interference pattern is formed by the light that is transmitted through the slits. The diagram shows only six slits; an actual grating may contain several thousand. The spacing d between centers of adjacent slits is called the *grating spacing.* A plane monochromatic wave is incident normally on the grating from the left side. We assume far-field (Fraunhofer) conditions; that is, the pattern is formed on a screen that is far enough away that all rays emerging from the grating and going to a particular point on the screen can be considered to be parallel.

We found in Section 36.4 that the principal intensity maxima with multiple slits occur in the same directions as for the two-slit pattern. These are the directions for which the path difference for adjacent slits is an integer number of wavelengths. So the positions of the maxima are once again given by

$$d\sin\theta = m\lambda \qquad (m = 0, \pm1, \pm2, \pm3, \dots) \qquad \text{(intensity maxima, multiple slits)} \tag{36.13}$$

The intensity patterns for two, eight, and 16 slits displayed in Fig. 36.15 show the progressive increase in sharpness of the maxima as the number of slits increases.

MasteringPHYSICS

ActivPhysics 16.4: The Grating: Introduction and Questions
ActivPhysics 16.5: The Grating: Problems

When a grating containing hundreds or thousands of slits is illuminated by a beam of parallel rays of monochromatic light, the pattern is a series of very sharp lines at angles determined by Eq. (36.13). The $m = \pm1$ lines are called the *first-order lines,* the $m = \pm2$ lines the *second-order lines,* and so on. If the grating is illuminated by white light with a continuous distribution of wavelengths, each value of m corresponds to a continuous spectrum in the pattern. The angle for each wavelength is determined by Eq. (36.13); for a given value of m, long wavelengths (the red end of the spectrum) lie at larger angles (that is, are deviated more from the straight-ahead direction) than do the shorter wavelengths at the violet end of the spectrum.

As Eq. (36.13) shows, the sines of the deviation angles of the maxima are proportional to the ratio λ/d. For substantial deviation to occur, the grating spacing d should be of the same order of magnitude as the wavelength λ. Gratings for use with visible light (λ from 400 to 700 nm) usually have about 1000 slits per millimeter; the value of d is the *reciprocal* of the number of slits per unit length, so d is of the order of $\frac{1}{1000}$ mm = 1000 nm.

36.17 Microscopic pits on the surface of this DVD act as a reflection grating, splitting white light into its component colors.

In a *reflection grating,* the array of equally spaced slits shown in Fig. 36.16 is replaced by an array of equally spaced ridges or grooves on a reflective screen. The reflected light has maximum intensity at angles where the phase difference between light waves reflected from adjacent ridges or grooves is an integral multiple of 2π. If light of wavelength λ is incident normally on a reflection grating with a spacing d between adjacent ridges or grooves, the *reflected* angles at which intensity maxima occur are given by Eq. (36.13).

The rainbow-colored reflections from the surface of a DVD are a reflection-grating effect (Fig. 36.17). The "grooves" are tiny pits 0.12 μm deep in the surface of the disc, with a uniform radial spacing of 0.74 μm = 740 nm. Information is coded on the DVD by varying the *length* of the pits. The reflection-grating aspect of the disc is merely an aesthetic side benefit.

Example 36.4 Width of a grating spectrum

The wavelengths of the visible spectrum are approximately 380 nm (violet) to 750 nm (red). (a) Find the angular limits of the first-order visible spectrum produced by a plane grating with 600 slits per millimeter when white light falls normally on the grating. (b) Do the first-order and second-order spectra overlap? What about the second-order and third-order spectra? Do your answers depend on the grating spacing?

SOLUTION

IDENTIFY and SET UP: We must find the angles spanned by the visible spectrum in the first-, second-, and third-order spectra. These correspond to $m = 1, 2,$ and 3 in Eq. (36.13).

EXECUTE: (a) The grating spacing is

$$d = \frac{1}{600 \text{ slits/mm}} = 1.67 \times 10^{-6} \text{ m}$$

We solve Eq. (36.13) for θ:

$$\theta = \arcsin\frac{m\lambda}{d}$$

Then for $m = 1$, the angular deviations θ_{v1} and θ_{r1} for violet and red light, respectively, are

$$\theta_{v1} = \arcsin\left(\frac{380 \times 10^{-9}\text{ m}}{1.67 \times 10^{-6}\text{ m}}\right) = 13.2°$$

$$\theta_{r1} = \arcsin\left(\frac{750 \times 10^{-9}\text{ m}}{1.67 \times 10^{-6}\text{ m}}\right) = 26.7°$$

That is, the first-order visible spectrum appears with deflection angles from $\theta_{v1} = 13.2°$ (violet) to $\theta_{r1} = 26.7°$ (red).

(b) With $m = 2$ and $m = 3$, our equation $\theta = \arcsin(m\lambda/d)$ for 380-mm violet light yields

$$\theta_{v2} = \arcsin\left(\frac{2(380 \times 10^{-9}\text{ m})}{1.67 \times 10^{-6}\text{ m}}\right) = 27.1°$$

$$\theta_{v3} = \arcsin\left(\frac{3(380 \times 10^{-9}\text{ m})}{1.67 \times 10^{-6}\text{ m}}\right) = 43.0°$$

For 750-nm red light, this same equation gives

$$\theta_{r2} = \arcsin\left(\frac{2(750 \times 10^{-9}\text{ m})}{1.67 \times 10^{-6}\text{ m}}\right) = 63.9°$$

$$\theta_{r3} = \arcsin\left(\frac{3(750 \times 10^{-9}\text{ m})}{1.67 \times 10^{-6}\text{ m}}\right) = \arcsin(1.35) = \text{undefined}$$

Hence the second-order spectrum extends from 27.1° to 63.9° and the third-order spectrum extends from 43.0° to 90° (the largest possible value of θ). The undefined value of θ_{r3} means that the third-order spectrum reaches $\theta = 90° = \arcsin(1)$ at a wavelength shorter than 750 nm; you should be able to show that this happens for $\lambda = 557$ nm. Hence the first-order spectrum (from 13.2° to 26.7°) does not overlap with the second-order spectrum, but the second- and third-order spectra do overlap. You can convince yourself that this is true for any value of the grating spacing d.

EVALUATE: The fundamental reason the first-order and second-order visible spectra don't overlap is that the human eye is sensitive to only a narrow range of wavelengths. Can you show that if the eye could detect wavelengths from 380 nm to 900 nm (in the near-infrared range), the first and second orders *would* overlap?

Grating Spectrographs

Diffraction gratings are widely used to measure the spectrum of light emitted by a source, a process called *spectroscopy* or *spectrometry*. Light incident on a grating of known spacing is dispersed into a spectrum. The angles of deviation of the maxima are then measured, and Eq. (36.13) is used to compute the wavelength. With a grating that has many slits, very sharp maxima are produced, and the angle of deviation (and hence the wavelength) can be measured very precisely.

An important application of this technique is to astronomy. As light generated within the sun passes through the sun's atmosphere, certain wavelengths are selectively absorbed. The result is that the spectrum of sunlight produced by a diffraction grating has dark *absorption lines* (Fig. 36.18). Experiments in the laboratory show that different types of atoms and ions absorb light of different wavelengths. By comparing these laboratory results with the wavelengths of absorption lines in the spectrum of sunlight, astronomers can deduce the chemical composition of the sun's atmosphere. The same technique is used to make chemical assays of galaxies that are millions of light-years away.

Figure 36.19 shows one design for a *grating spectrograph* used in astronomy. A transmission grating is used in the figure; in other setups, a reflection grating is used. In older designs a prism was used rather than a grating, and a spectrum was formed by dispersion (see Section 33.4) rather than diffraction. However, there is no simple relationship between wavelength and angle of deviation for a prism, prisms absorb some of the light that passes through them, and they are less effective for many nonvisible wavelengths that are important in astronomy. For these and other reasons, gratings are preferred in precision applications.

36.18 (a) A visible-light photograph of the sun. (b) Sunlight is dispersed into a spectrum by a diffraction grating. Specific wavelengths are absorbed as sunlight passes through the sun's atmosphere, leaving dark lines in the spectrum.

(a) (b)

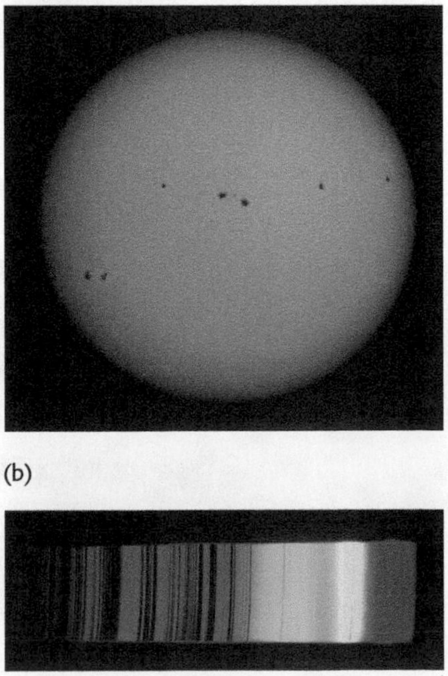

Resolution of a Grating Spectrograph

In spectroscopy it is often important to distinguish slightly differing wavelengths. The minimum wavelength difference $\Delta\lambda$ that can be distinguished by a spectrograph is described by the **chromatic resolving power** R, defined as

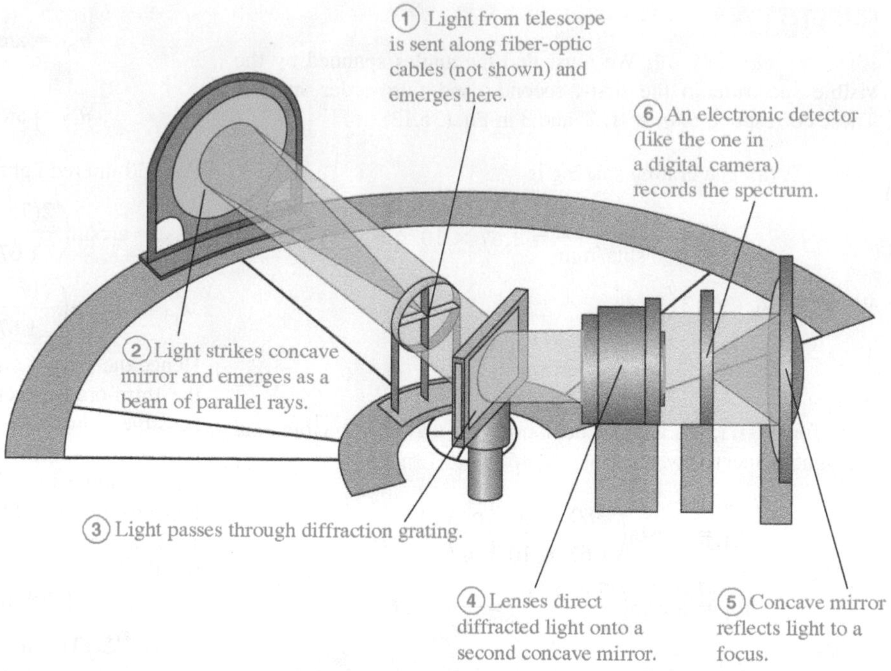

36.19 A schematic diagram of a diffraction-grating spectrograph for use in astronomy. Note that the light does not strike the grating normal to its surface, so the intensity maxima are given by a somewhat different expression than Eq. (36.13). (See Problem 36.64.)

$$R = \frac{\lambda}{\Delta\lambda} \quad \text{(chromatic resolving power)} \tag{36.14}$$

As an example, when sodium atoms are heated, they emit strongly at the yellow wavelengths 589.00 nm and 589.59 nm. A spectrograph that can barely distinguish these two lines in the spectrum (called the *sodium doublet*) has a chromatic resolving power $R = (589.00\text{ nm})/(0.59\text{ nm}) = 1000$. (You can see these wavelengths when boiling water on a gas range. If the water boils over onto the flame, dissolved sodium from table salt emits a burst of yellow light.)

We can derive an expression for the resolving power of a diffraction grating used in a spectrograph. Two different wavelengths give diffraction maxima at slightly different angles. As a reasonable (though arbitrary) criterion, let's assume that we can distinguish them as two separate peaks if the maximum of one coincides with the first minimum of the other.

From our discussion in Section 36.4 the mth-order maximum occurs when the phase difference ϕ for adjacent slits is $\phi = 2\pi m$. The first minimum beside that maximum occurs when $\phi = 2\pi m + 2\pi/N$, where N is the number of slits. The phase difference is also given by $\phi = (2\pi d \sin\theta)/\lambda$, so the angular interval $d\theta$ corresponding to a small increment $d\phi$ in the phase shift can be obtained from the differential of this equation:

$$d\phi = \frac{2\pi d \cos\theta \, d\theta}{\lambda}$$

When $d\phi = 2\pi/N$, this corresponds to the angular interval $d\theta$ between a maximum and the first adjacent minimum. Thus $d\theta$ is given by

$$\frac{2\pi}{N} = \frac{2\pi d \cos\theta \, d\theta}{\lambda} \quad \text{or} \quad d\cos\theta \, d\theta = \frac{\lambda}{N}$$

CAUTION **Watch out for different uses of the symbol d** Don't confuse the spacing d with the differential "d" in the angular interval $d\theta$ or in the phase shift increment $d\phi$!

Now we need to find the angular spacing $d\theta$ between maxima for two slightly different wavelengths. We have $d\sin\theta = m\lambda$, so the differential of this equation gives

$$d\cos\theta \, d\theta = m \, d\lambda$$

Application Detecting DNA with Diffraction

Diffraction gratings are used in a common piece of laboratory equipment known as a spectrophotometer. Light shining across a diffraction grating is dispersed into its component wavelengths. A slit is used to block all but a very narrow range of wavelengths, producing a beam of almost perfectly monochromatic light. The instrument then measures how much of that light is absorbed by a solution of biological molecules. For example, the sample tube shown here contains a solution of DNA, which is transparent to visible light but which strongly absorbs ultraviolet light with a wavelength of exactly 260 nm. Therefore, by illuminating the sample with 260-nm light and measuring the amount absorbed, we can determine the concentration of DNA in the solution.

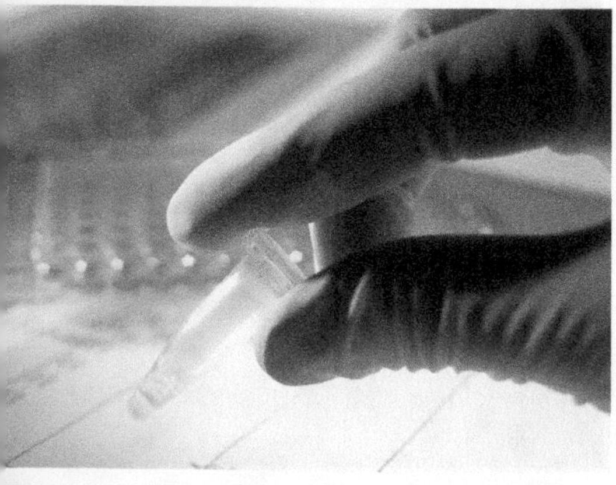

According to our criterion, the limit or resolution is reached when these two angular spacings are equal. Equating the two expressions for the quantity $(d\cos\theta\, d\theta)$, we find

$$\frac{\lambda}{N} = m\,d\lambda \quad \text{and} \quad \frac{\lambda}{d\lambda} = Nm$$

If $\Delta\lambda$ is small, we can replace $d\lambda$ by $\Delta\lambda$, and the resolving power R is given by

$$R = \frac{\lambda}{\Delta\lambda} = Nm \tag{36.15}$$

The greater the number of slits N, the better the resolution; also, the higher the order m of the diffraction-pattern maximum that we use, the better the resolution.

Test Your Understanding of Section 36.5 What minimum number of slits would be required in a grating to resolve the sodium doublet in the fourth order? (i) 250; (ii) 400; (iii) 1000; (iv) 4000.

36.6 X-Ray Diffraction

X rays were discovered by Wilhelm Röntgen (1845–1923) in 1895, and early experiments suggested that they were electromagnetic waves with wavelengths of the order of 10^{-10} m. At about the same time, the idea began to emerge that in a crystalline solid the atoms are arranged in a regular repeating pattern, with spacing between adjacent atoms also of the order of 10^{-10} m. Putting these two ideas together, Max von Laue (1879–1960) proposed in 1912 that a crystal might serve as a kind of three-dimensional diffraction grating for x rays. That is, a beam of x rays might be scattered (that is, absorbed and re-emitted) by the individual atoms in a crystal, and the scattered waves might interfere just like waves from a diffraction grating.

The first **x-ray diffraction** experiments were performed in 1912 by Friederich, Knipping, and von Laue, using the experimental setup shown in Fig. 36.20a. The scattered x rays *did* form an interference pattern, which they recorded on photographic film. Figure 36.20b is a photograph of such a pattern. These experiments verified that x rays *are* waves, or at least have wavelike properties, and also that the atoms in a crystal *are* arranged in a regular pattern (Fig. 36.21). Since that time, x-ray diffraction has proved to be an invaluable research tool, both for measuring x-ray wavelengths and for studying the structure of crystals and complex molecules.

36.20 (a) An x-ray diffraction experiment. (b) Diffraction pattern (or *Laue pattern*) formed by directing a beam of x rays at a thin section of quartz crystal.

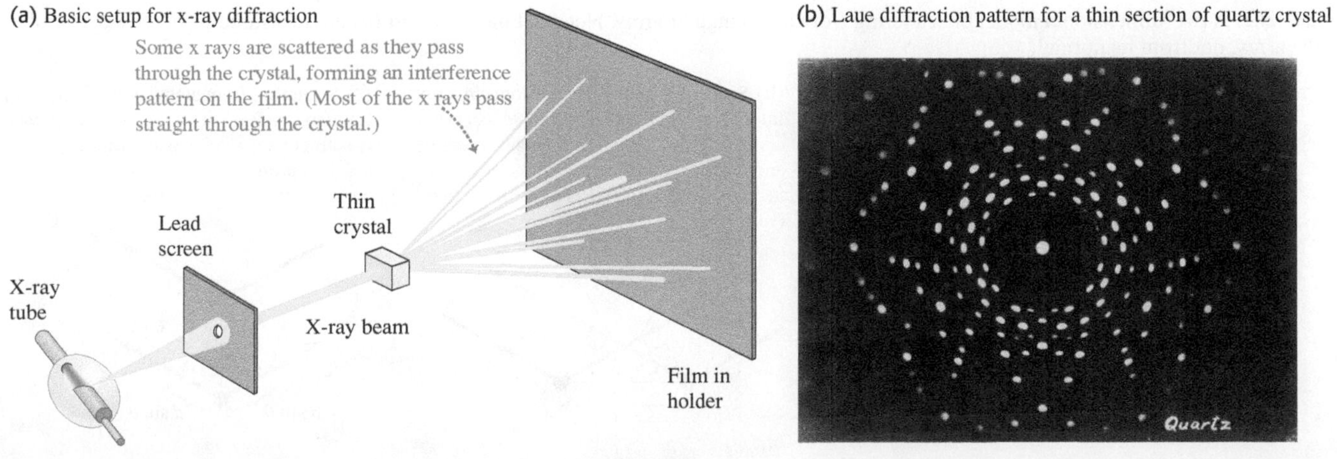

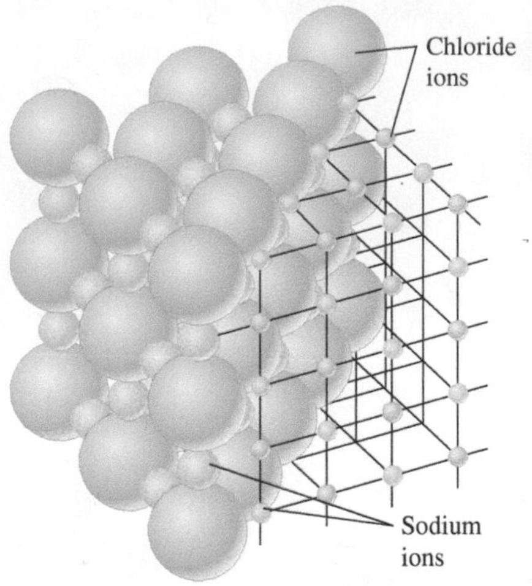

36.21 Model of the arrangement of ions in a crystal of NaCl (table salt). The spacing of adjacent atoms is 0.282 nm. (The electron clouds of the atoms actually overlap slightly.)

A Simple Model of X-Ray Diffraction

To better understand x-ray diffraction, we consider first a two-dimensional scattering situation, as shown in Fig. 36.22a, in which a plane wave is incident on a rectangular array of scattering centers. The situation might be a ripple tank with an array of small posts, 3-cm microwaves striking an array of small conducting spheres, or x rays incident on an array of atoms. In the case of electromagnetic waves, the wave induces an oscillating electric dipole moment in each scatterer. These dipoles act like little antennas, emitting scattered waves. The resulting interference pattern is the superposition of all these scattered waves. The situation is different from that with a diffraction grating, in which the waves from all the slits are emitted *in phase* (for a plane wave at normal incidence). Here the scattered waves are *not* all in phase because their distances from the *source* are different. To compute the interference pattern, we have to consider the *total* path differences for the scattered waves, including the distances from source to scatterer and from scatterer to observer.

As Fig. 36.22b shows, the path length from source to observer is the same for all the scatterers in a single row if the two angles θ_a and θ_r are equal. Scattered radiation from *adjacent* rows is *also* in phase if the path difference for adjacent rows is an integer number of wavelengths. Figure 36.22c shows that this path difference is $2d\sin\theta$, where θ is the common value of θ_a and θ_r. Therefore the conditions for radiation from the *entire array* to reach the observer in phase are (1) the angle of incidence must equal the angle of scattering and (2) the path difference for adjacent rows must equal $m\lambda$, where m is an integer. We can express the second condition as

$$2d\sin\theta = m\lambda \quad (m = 1, 2, 3, \ldots) \qquad \text{(Bragg condition for constructive interference from an array)} \qquad (36.16)$$

CAUTION **Scattering from an array** In Eq. (36.16) the angle θ is measured with respect to the *surface* of the crystal, rather than with respect to the *normal* to the plane of an array of slits or a grating. Also, note that the path difference in Eq. (36.16) is $2d\sin\theta$, not $d\sin\theta$ as in Eq. (36.13) for a diffraction grating.

In directions for which Eq. (36.16) is satisfied, we see a strong maximum in the interference pattern. We can describe this interference in terms of *reflections* of the wave from the horizontal rows of scatterers in Fig. 36.22a. Strong reflection (constructive interference) occurs at angles such that the incident and scattered angles are equal and Eq. (36.16) is satisfied. Since $\sin\theta$ can never be greater than 1, Eq. (36.16) says that to have constructive interference the quantity $m\lambda$

36.22 A two-dimensional model of scattering from a rectangular array. Note that the angles in **(b)** are measured from the *surface* of the array, not from its normal.

(a) Scattering of waves from a rectangular array

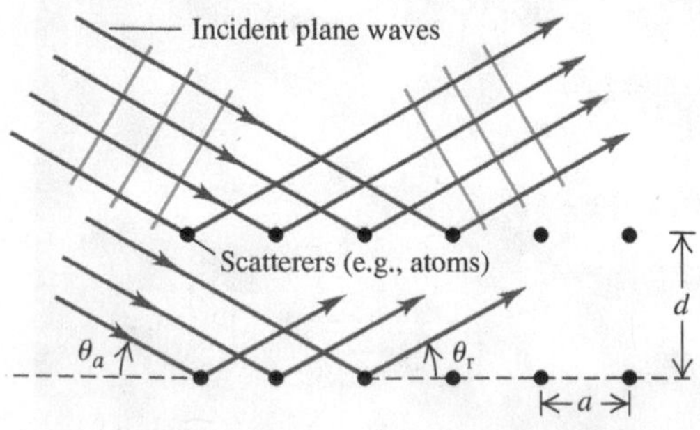

(b) Scattering from adjacent atoms in a row
Interference from adjacent atoms in a row is constructive when the path lengths $a\cos\theta_a$ and $a\cos\theta_r$ are equal, so that the angle of incidence θ_a equals the angle of reflection (scattering) θ_r.

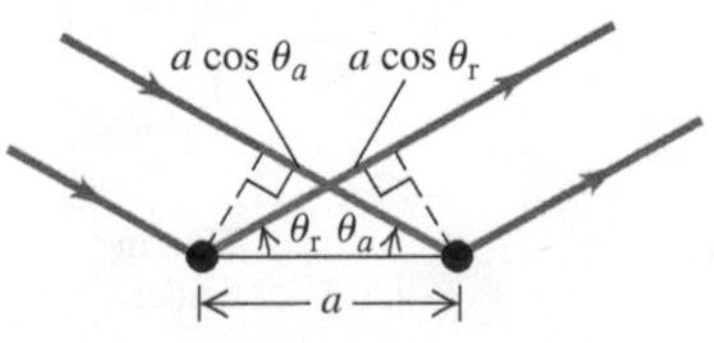

(c) Scattering from atoms in adjacent rows
Interference from atoms in adjacent rows is constructive when the path difference $2d\sin\theta$ is an integral number of wavelengths, as in Eq. (36.16).

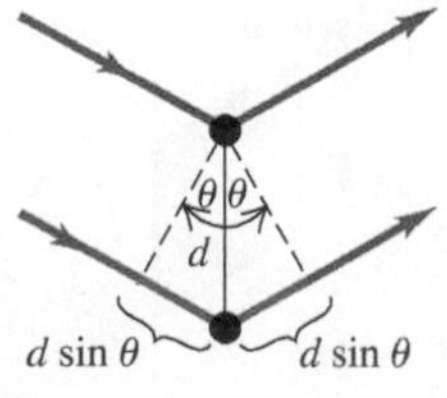

36.23 A cubic crystal and two different families of crystal planes. There are also three sets of planes parallel to the cube faces, with spacing a.

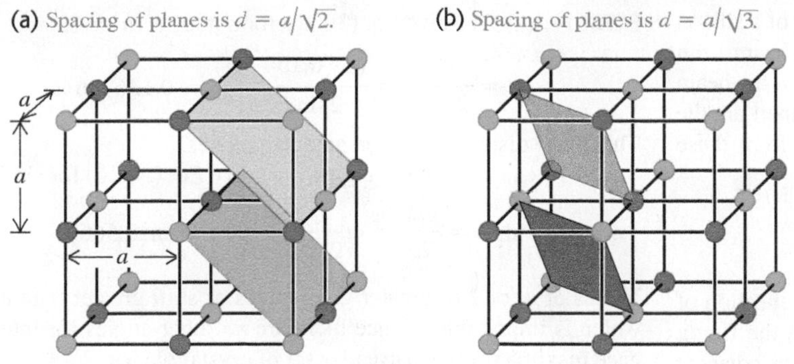

must be less than $2d$ and so λ must be less than $2d/m$. For example, the value of d in an NaCl crystal (see Fig. 36.21) is only 0.282 nm. Hence to have the mth-order maximum present in the diffraction pattern, λ must be less than $2(0.282\text{ nm})/m$; that is, $\lambda < 0.564$ nm for $m = 1$, $\lambda < 0.282$ nm for $m = 2$, $\lambda < 0.188$ nm for $m = 3$, and so on. These are all x-ray wavelengths (see Fig. 32.4), which is why x rays are used for studying crystal structure.

We can extend this discussion to a three-dimensional array by considering *planes* of scatterers instead of *rows.* Figure 36.23 shows two different sets of parallel planes that pass through all the scatterers. Waves from all the scatterers in a given plane interfere constructively if the angles of incidence and scattering are equal. There is also constructive interference between planes when Eq. (36.16) is satisfied, where d is now the distance between adjacent planes. Because there are many different sets of parallel planes, there are also many values of d and many sets of angles that give constructive interference for the whole crystal lattice. This phenomenon is called **Bragg reflection,** and Eq. (36.16) is called the **Bragg condition,** in honor of Sir William Bragg and his son Laurence Bragg, two pioneers in x-ray analysis.

CAUTION **Bragg *reflection* is really Bragg *interference*** While we are using the term *reflection,* remember that we are dealing with an *interference* effect. In fact, the reflections from various planes are closely analogous to interference effects in thin films (see Section 35.4).

As Fig. 36.20b shows, in x-ray diffraction there is nearly complete cancellation in all but certain very specific directions in which constructive interference occurs and forms bright spots. Such a pattern is usually called an x-ray *diffraction* pattern, although *interference* pattern might be more appropriate.

We can determine the wavelength of x rays by examining the diffraction pattern for a crystal of known structure and known spacing between atoms, just as we determined wavelengths of visible light by measuring patterns from slits or gratings. (The spacing between atoms in simple crystals of known structure, such as sodium chloride, can be found from the density of the crystal and Avogadro's number.) Then, once we know the x-ray wavelength, we can use x-ray diffraction to explore the structure and determine the spacing between atoms in crystals with unknown structure.

X-ray diffraction is by far the most important experimental tool in the investigation of crystal structure of solids. X-ray diffraction also plays an important role in studies of the structures of liquids and of organic molecules. It has been one of the chief experimental techniques in working out the double-helix structure of DNA (Fig. 36.24) and subsequent advances in molecular genetics.

36.24 The British scientist Rosalind Franklin made this groundbreaking x-ray diffraction image of DNA in 1953. The dark bands arranged in a cross provided the first evidence of the helical structure of the DNA molecule.

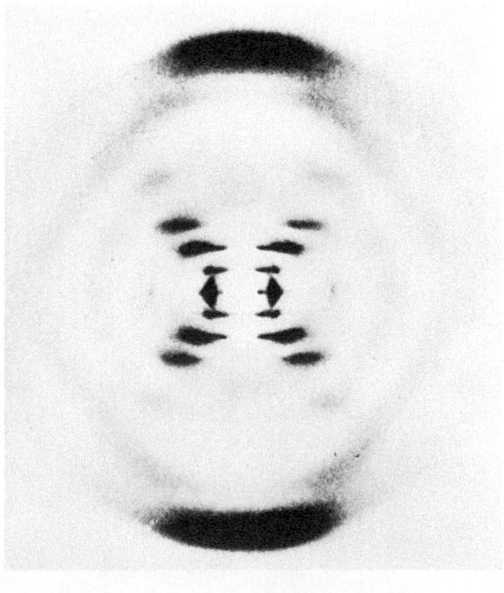

Example 36.5 X-ray diffraction

You direct a beam of 0.154-nm x rays at certain planes of a silicon crystal. As you increase the angle of incidence of the beam from zero, the first strong interference maximum occurs when the beam makes an angle of 34.5° with the planes. (a) How far apart are the planes? (b) Will you find other interference maxima from these planes at greater angles of incidence?

SOLUTION

IDENTIFY and SET UP: This problem involves Bragg reflection of x rays from the planes of a crystal. In part (a) we use the Bragg condition, Eq. (36.16), to find the distance d between adjacent planes from the known wavelength $\lambda = 0.154$ nm and angle of incidence $\theta = 34.5°$ for the $m = 1$ interference maximum. Given the value of d, we use the Bragg condition again in part (b) to find the values of θ for interference maxima corresponding to other values of m.

EXECUTE: (a) We solve Eq. (36.16) for d and set $m = 1$:

$$d = \frac{m\lambda}{2\sin\theta} = \frac{(1)(0.154\text{ nm})}{2\sin 34.5°} = 0.136\text{ nm}$$

This is the distance between adjacent planes.

(b) To calculate other angles, we solve Eq. (36.16) for $\sin\theta$:

$$\sin\theta = \frac{m\lambda}{2d} = m\frac{0.154\text{ nm}}{2(0.136\text{ nm})} = m(0.566)$$

Values of m of 2 or greater give values of $\sin\theta$ greater than unity, which is impossible. Hence there are *no* other angles for interference maxima for this particular set of crystal planes.

EVALUATE: Our result in part (b) shows that there *would* be a second interference maximum if the quantity $2\lambda/2d = \lambda/d$ were less than 1. This would be the case if the wavelength of the x rays were less than $d = 0.136$ nm. How short would the wavelength need to be to have *three* interference maxima?

Test Your Understanding of Section 36.6 You are doing an x-ray diffraction experiment with a crystal in which the atomic planes are 0.200 nm apart. You are using x rays of wavelength 0.100 nm. Will the fifth-order maximum be present in the diffraction pattern?

MasteringPHYSICS

ActivPhysics 16.7: Circular Hole Diffraction
ActivPhysics 16.8: Resolving Power

36.7 Circular Apertures and Resolving Power

We have studied in detail the diffraction patterns formed by long, thin slits or arrays of slits. But an aperture of *any* shape forms a diffraction pattern. The diffraction pattern formed by a *circular* aperture is of special interest because of its role in limiting how well an optical instrument can resolve fine details. In principle, we could compute the intensity at any point P in the diffraction pattern by dividing the area of the aperture into small elements, finding the resulting wave amplitude and phase at P, and then integrating over the aperture area to find the resultant amplitude and intensity at P. In practice, the integration cannot be carried out in terms of elementary functions. We will simply *describe* the pattern and quote a few relevant numbers.

The diffraction pattern formed by a circular aperture consists of a central bright spot surrounded by a series of bright and dark rings, as Fig. 36.25 shows.

36.25 Diffraction pattern formed by a circular aperture of diameter D. The pattern consists of a central bright spot and alternating dark and bright rings. The angular radius θ_1 of the first dark ring is shown. (This diagram is not drawn to scale.)

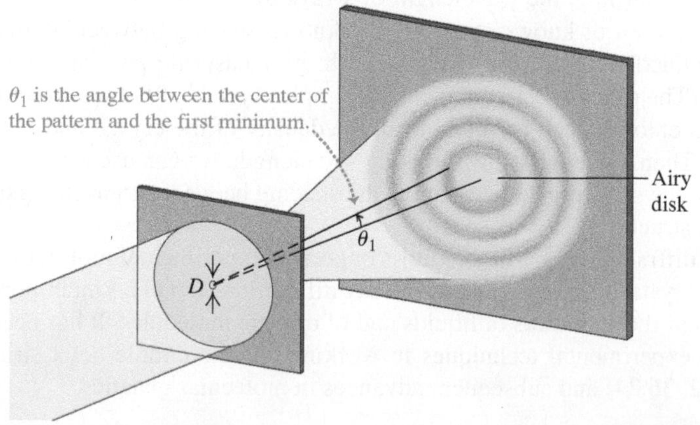

We can describe the pattern in terms of the angle θ, representing the angular radius of each ring. If the aperture diameter is D and the wavelength is λ, the angular radius θ_1 of the first *dark* ring is given by

$$\sin\theta_1 = 1.22\frac{\lambda}{D} \qquad \text{(diffraction by a circular aperture)} \qquad (36.17)$$

The angular radii of the next two dark rings are given by

$$\sin\theta_2 = 2.23\frac{\lambda}{D} \qquad \sin\theta_3 = 3.24\frac{\lambda}{D} \qquad (36.18)$$

Between these are bright rings with angular radii given by

$$\sin\theta = 1.63\frac{\lambda}{D}, \qquad 2.68\frac{\lambda}{D}, \qquad 3.70\frac{\lambda}{D} \qquad (36.19)$$

and so on. The central bright spot is called the **Airy disk,** in honor of Sir George Airy (1801–1892), Astronomer Royal of England, who first derived the expression for the intensity in the pattern. The angular radius of the Airy disk is that of the first dark ring, given by Eq. (36.17).

The intensities in the bright rings drop off very quickly with increasing angle. When D is much larger than the wavelength λ, the usual case for optical instruments, the peak intensity in the first ring is only 1.7% of the value at the center of the Airy disk, and the peak intensity of the second ring is only 0.4%. Most (85%) of the light energy falls within the Airy disk. Figure 36.26 shows a diffraction pattern from a circular aperture.

36.26 Photograph of the diffraction pattern formed by a circular aperture.

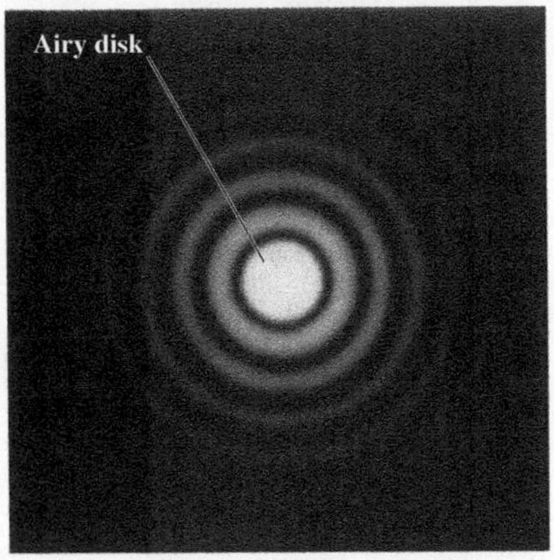

Diffraction and Image Formation

Diffraction has far-reaching implications for image formation by lenses and mirrors. In our study of optical instruments in Chapter 34 we assumed that a lens with focal length f focuses a parallel beam (plane wave) to a *point* at a distance f from the lens. This assumption ignored diffraction effects. We now see that what we get is not a point but the diffraction pattern just described. If we have two point objects, their images are not two points but two diffraction patterns. When the objects are close together, their diffraction patterns overlap; if they are close enough, their patterns overlap almost completely and cannot be distinguished. The effect is shown in Fig. 36.27, which presents the patterns for four very small "point" sources of light. In Fig. 36.27a the image of the left-hand source is well separated from the others, but the images of the middle and right-hand sources have merged. In Fig. 36.27b, with a larger aperture diameter and hence smaller Airy disks, the middle and right-hand images are better resolved. In Fig. 36.27c, with a still larger aperture, they are well resolved.

A widely used criterion for resolution of two point objects, proposed by the English physicist Lord Rayleigh (1842–1919) and called **Rayleigh's criterion,** is that the objects are just barely resolved (that is, distinguishable) if the center of one diffraction pattern coincides with the first minimum of the other. In that case the angular separation of the image centers is given by Eq. (36.17). The angular separation of the *objects* is the same as that of the *images* made by a telescope, microscope, or other optical device. So two point objects are barely resolved, according to Rayleigh's criterion, when their angular separation is given by Eq. (36.17).

The minimum separation of two objects that can just be resolved by an optical instrument is called the **limit of resolution** of the instrument. The smaller the limit of resolution, the greater the *resolution,* or **resolving power,** of the instrument. Diffraction sets the ultimate limits on resolution of lenses. *Geometric* optics may make it seem that we can make images as large as we like. Eventually, though, we always reach a point at which the image becomes larger but does not

36.27 Diffraction patterns of four very small ("point") sources of light. The photographs were made with a circular aperture in front of the lens. (a) The aperture is so small that the patterns of sources 3 and 4 overlap and are barely resolved by Rayleigh's criterion. Increasing the size of the aperture decreases the size of the diffraction patterns, as shown in (b) and (c).

(a) Small aperture

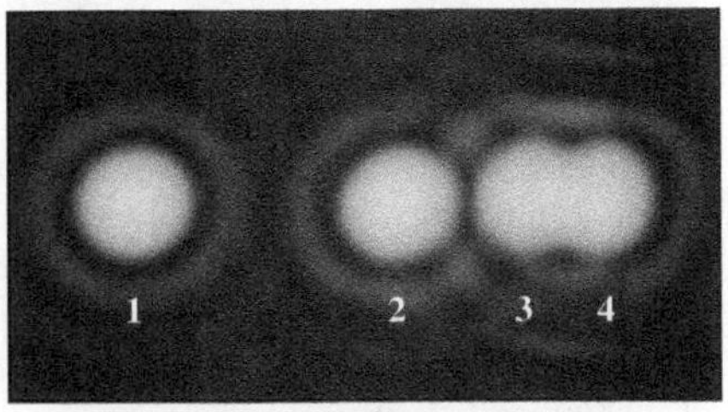

(b) Medium aperture

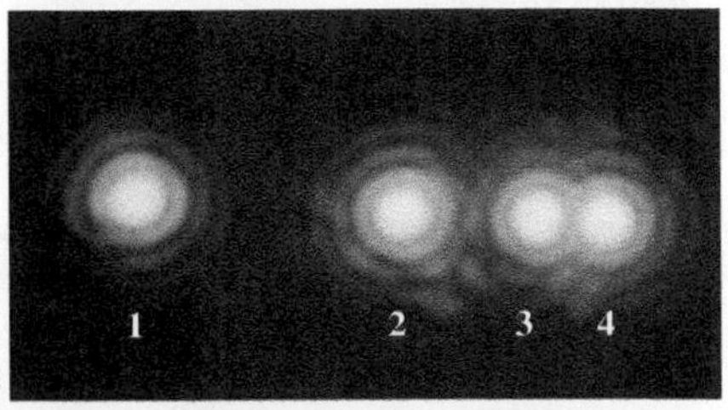

(c) Large aperture

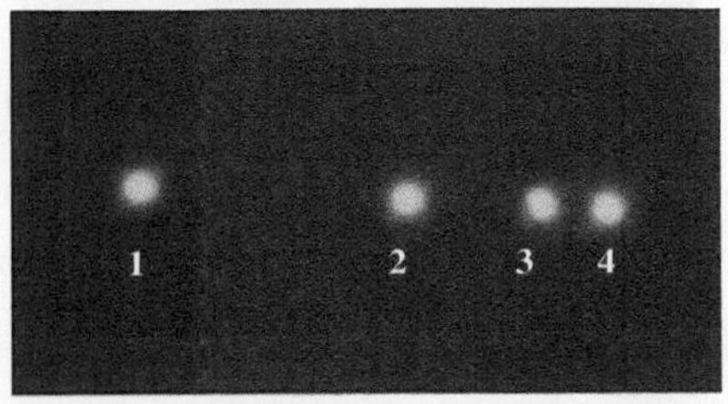

gain in detail. The images in Fig. 36.27 would not become sharper with further enlargement.

Application Bigger Telescope, Better Resolution

One reason for building very large telescopes is to increase the aperture diameter and thus minimize diffraction effects. The effective diameter of a telescope can be increased by using arrays of smaller telescopes. The Very Large Array (VLA) in New Mexico is a collection of 27 radio telescopes, each 25 m in diameter, that can be spread out in a Y-shaped arrangement 36 km across. Hence the effective aperture diameter is 36 km, giving the VLA a limit of resolution of 5×10^{-8} rad at a radio wavelength of 1.5 cm. If your eye had this angular resolution, you could read the "20/20" line on an eye chart more than 30 km away!

CAUTION **Resolving power vs. chromatic resolving power** Be careful not to confuse the resolving power of an optical instrument with the *chromatic* resolving power of a grating (described in Section 36.5). Resolving power refers to the ability to distinguish the images of objects that appear close to each other, when looking either through an optical instrument or at a photograph made with the instrument. Chromatic resolving power describes how well different wavelengths can be distinguished in a spectrum formed by a diffraction grating. ❙

Rayleigh's criterion combined with Eq. (36.17) shows that resolution (resolving power) improves with larger diameter; it also improves with shorter wavelengths. Ultraviolet microscopes have higher resolution than visible-light microscopes. In electron microscopes the resolution is limited by the wavelengths associated with the electrons, which have wavelike aspects (to be discussed further in Chapter 39). These wavelengths can be made 100,000 times smaller than wavelengths of visible light, with a corresponding gain in resolution. Resolving power also explains the difference in storage capacity between DVDs (introduced in 1995) and Blu-ray discs (introduced in 2003). Information is stored in both of these in a series of tiny pits. In order not to lose information in the scanning process, the scanning optics must be able to resolve two adjacent pits so that they do not seem to blend into a single pit (see sources 3 and 4 in Fig. 36.27). The blue scanning laser used in a Blu-ray player has a shorter wavelength (405 nm) and hence better resolving power than the 650-nm red laser in a DVD player. Hence pits can be spaced closer together in a Blu-ray disc than in a DVD, and more information can be stored on a disc of the same size (50 gigabytes on a Blu-ray disc versus 4.7 gigabytes on a DVD).

Example 36.6 Resolving power of a camera lens

A camera lens with focal length $f = 50$ mm and maximum aperture $f/2$ forms an image of an object 9.0 m away. (a) If the resolution is limited by diffraction, what is the minimum distance between two points on the object that are barely resolved? What is the corresponding distance between image points? (b) How does the situation change if the lens is "stopped down" to $f/16$? Use $\lambda = 500$ nm in both cases.

SOLUTION

IDENTIFY and SET UP: This example uses the ideas about resolving power, image formation by a lens (Section 34.4), and f-number (Section 34.5). From Eq. (34.20), the f-number of a lens is its focal length f divided by the aperture diameter D. We use this equation to determine D and then use Eq. (36.17) (the Rayleigh criterion) to find the angular separation θ between two barely resolved points on the object. We then use the geometry of image formation by a lens to determine the distance y between those points and the distance y' between the corresponding image points.

EXECUTE: (a) The aperture diameter is $D = f/(f\text{-number}) = (50\text{ mm})/2 = 25\text{ mm} = 25 \times 10^{-3}$ m. From Eq. (36.17) the angular separation θ of two object points that are barely resolved is

$$\theta \approx \sin\theta = 1.22\frac{\lambda}{D} = 1.22\frac{500 \times 10^{-9}\text{ m}}{25 \times 10^{-3}\text{ m}} = 2.4 \times 10^{-5}\text{ rad}$$

We know from our thin-lens analysis in Section 34.4 that, apart from sign, $y/s = y'/s'$ [see Eq. (34.14)]. Thus the angular separations of the object points and the corresponding image points are both equal to θ. Because the object distance s is much greater than the focal length $f = 50$ mm, the image distance s' is approximately equal to f. Thus

$$\frac{y}{9.0\text{ m}} = 2.4 \times 10^{-5} \qquad y = 2.2 \times 10^{-4}\text{ m} = 0.22\text{ mm}$$

$$\frac{y'}{50\text{ mm}} = 2.4 \times 10^{-5} \qquad y' = 1.2 \times 10^{-3}\text{ mm}$$

$$= 0.0012\text{ mm} \approx \tfrac{1}{800}\text{ mm}$$

(b) The aperture diameter is now $(50\text{ mm})/16$, or one-eighth as large as before. The angular separation between barely resolved points is eight times as great, and the values of y and y' are also eight times as great as before:

$$y = 1.8\text{ mm} \qquad y' = 0.0096\text{ mm} = \tfrac{1}{100}\text{ mm}$$

Only the best camera lenses can approach this resolving power.

EVALUATE: Many photographers use the smallest possible aperture for maximum sharpness, since lens aberrations cause light rays that are far from the optic axis to converge to a different image point than do rays near the axis. But as this example shows, diffraction effects become more significant at small apertures. One cause of fuzzy images has to be balanced against another.

Test Your Understanding of Section 36.7 You have been asked to compare four different proposals for telescopes to be placed in orbit, above the blurring effects of the earth's atmosphere. Rank the proposed telescopes in order of their ability to resolve small details, from best to worst. (i) a radio telescope 100 m in diameter observing at a wavelength of 21 cm; (ii) an optical telescope 2.0 m in diameter observing at a wavelength of 500 nm; (iii) an ultraviolet telescope 1.0 m in diameter observing at a wavelength of 100 nm; (iv) an infrared telescope 2.0 m in diameter observing at a wavelength of 10 μm. ❙

36.8 Holography

Holography is a technique for recording and reproducing an image of an object through the use of interference effects. Unlike the two-dimensional images recorded by an ordinary photograph or television system, a holographic image is truly three-dimensional. Such an image can be viewed from different directions to reveal different sides and from various distances to reveal changing perspective. If you had never seen a hologram, you wouldn't believe it was possible!

Figure 36.28a shows the basic procedure for making a hologram. We illuminate the object to be holographed with monochromatic light, and we place a photographic film so that it is struck by scattered light from the object and also by direct light from the source. In practice, the light source must be a laser, for reasons we will discuss later. Interference between the direct and scattered light leads to the formation and recording of a complex interference pattern on the film.

To form the images, we simply project light through the developed film (Fig. 36.28b). Two images are formed: a virtual image on the side of the film nearer the source and a real image on the opposite side.

Holography and Interference Patterns

A complete analysis of holography is beyond our scope, but we can gain some insight into the process by looking at how a single point is holographed and imaged. Consider the interference pattern that is formed on a sheet of photographic negative film by the superposition of an incident plane wave and a

36.28 (a) A hologram is the record on film of the interference pattern formed with light from the coherent source and light scattered from the object. (b) Images are formed when light is projected through the hologram. The observer sees the virtual image formed behind the hologram.

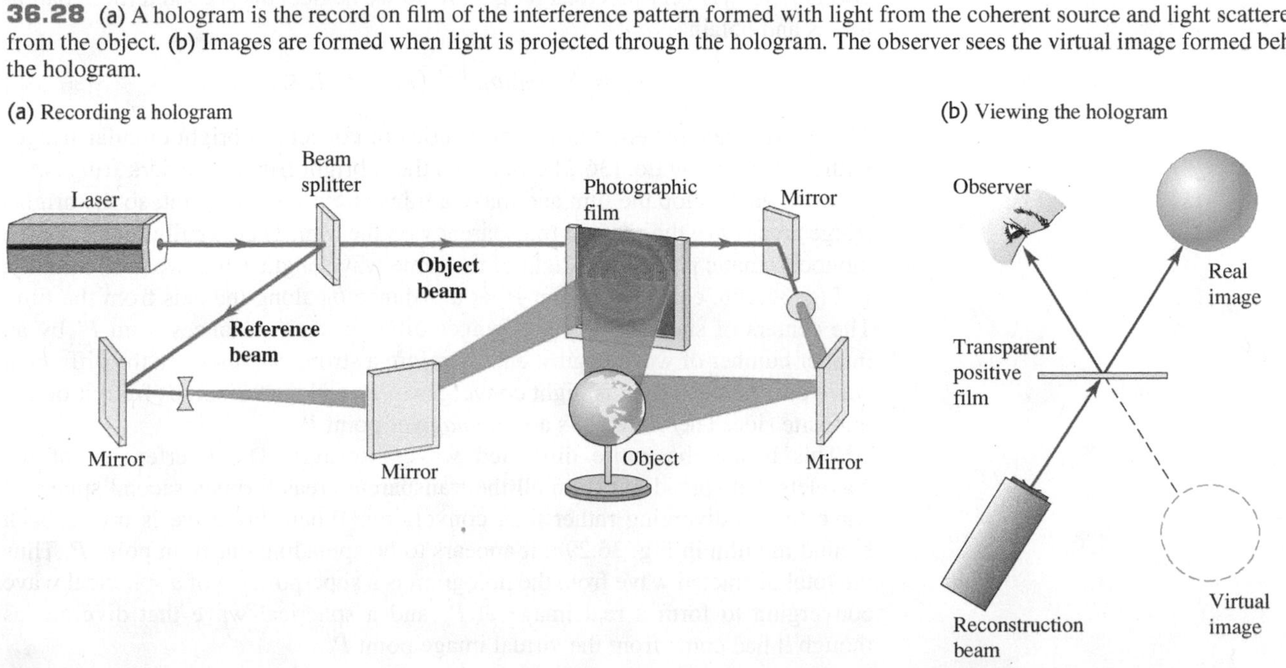

36.29 (a) Constructive interference of the plane and spherical waves occurs in the plane of the film at every point Q for which the distance b_m from P is greater than the distance b_0 from P to O by an integral number of wavelengths $m\lambda$. For the point Q shown, $m = 2$. (b) When a plane wave strikes a transparent positive print of the developed film, the diffracted wave consists of a wave converging to P' and then diverging again and a diverging wave that appears to originate at P. These waves form the real and virtual images, respectively.

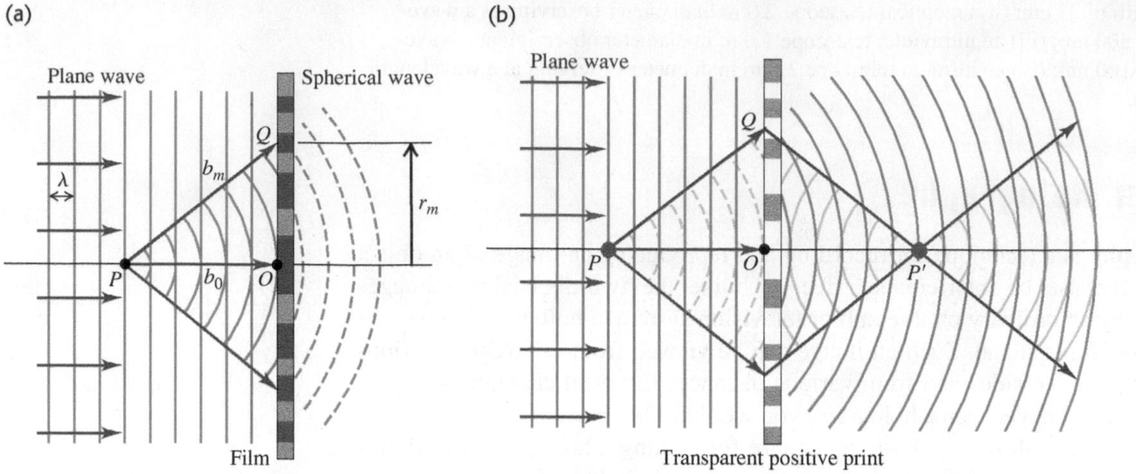

spherical wave, as shown in Fig. 36.29a. The spherical wave originates at a point source P at a distance b_0 from the film; P may in fact be a small object that scatters part of the incident plane wave. We assume that the two waves are monochromatic and coherent and that the phase relationship is such that constructive interference occurs at point O on the diagram. Then constructive interference will *also* occur at any point Q on the film that is farther from P than O is by an integer number of wavelengths. That is, if $b_m - b_0 = m\lambda$, where m is an integer, then constructive interference occurs. The points where this condition is satisfied form circles on the film centered at O, with radii r_m given by

$$b_m - b_0 = \sqrt{b_0^2 + r_m^2} - b_0 = m\lambda \qquad (m = 1, 2, 3, \ldots) \quad (36.20)$$

Solving this for r_m^2, we find

$$r_m^2 = \lambda(2mb_0 + m^2\lambda)$$

Ordinarily, b_0 is very much larger than λ, so we neglect the second term in parentheses and obtain

$$r_m = \sqrt{2m\lambda b_0} \qquad (m = 1, 2, 3, \ldots) \quad (36.21)$$

The interference pattern consists of a series of concentric bright circular fringes with radii given by Eq. (36.21). Between these bright fringes are dark fringes.

Now we develop the film and make a transparent positive print, so the bright-fringe areas have the greatest transparency on the film. Then we illuminate it with monochromatic plane-wave light of the same wavelength λ that we used initially. In Fig. 36.29b, consider a point P' at a distance b_0 along the axis from the film. The centers of successive bright fringes differ in their distances from P' by an integer number of wavelengths, and therefore a strong *maximum* in the diffracted wave occurs at P'. That is, light converges to P' and then diverges from it on the opposite side. Therefore P' is a *real image* of point P.

This is not the entire diffracted wave, however. The interference of the wavelets that spread out from all the transparent areas forms a second spherical wave that is diverging rather than converging. When this wave is traced back behind the film in Fig. 36.29b, it appears to be spreading out from point P. Thus the total diffracted wave from the hologram is a superposition of a spherical wave converging to form a real image at P' and a spherical wave that diverges as though it had come from the virtual image point P.

Because of the principle of superposition for waves, what is true for the imaging of a single point is also true for the imaging of any number of points. The film records the superposed interference pattern from the various points, and when light is projected through the film, the various image points are reproduced simultaneously. Thus the images of an extended object can be recorded and reproduced just as for a single point object. Figure 36.30 shows photographs of a holographic image from two different angles, showing the changing perspective in this three-dimensional image.

In making a hologram, we have to overcome two practical problems. First, the light used must be *coherent* over distances that are large in comparison to the dimensions of the object and its distance from the film. Ordinary light sources *do not* satisfy this requirement, for reasons that we discussed in Section 35.1. Therefore laser light is essential for making a hologram. (Ordinary white light can be used for *viewing* certain types of hologram, such as those used on credit cards.) Second, extreme mechanical stability is needed. If any relative motion of source, object, or film occurs during exposure, even by as much as a quarter of a wavelength, the interference pattern on the film is blurred enough to prevent satisfactory image formation. These obstacles are not insurmountable, however, and holography has become important in research, entertainment, and a wide variety of technological applications.

36.30 Two views of the same hologram seen from different angles.

CHAPTER 36 SUMMARY

Fresnel and Fraunhofer diffraction: Diffraction occurs when light passes through an aperture or around an edge. When the source and the observer are so far away from the obstructing surface that the outgoing rays can be considered parallel, it is called Fraunhofer diffraction. When the source or the observer is relatively close to the obstructing surface, it is Fresnel diffraction.

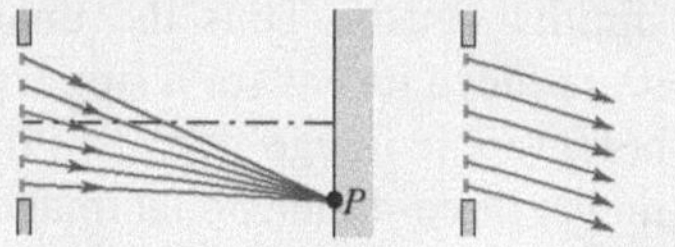

Single-slit diffraction: Monochromatic light sent through a narrow slit of width a produces a diffraction pattern on a distant screen. Equation (36.2) gives the condition for destructive interference (a dark fringe) at a point P in the pattern at angle θ. Equation (36.7) gives the intensity in the pattern as a function of θ. (See Examples 36.1–36.3.)

$$\sin\theta = \frac{m\lambda}{a} \quad (m = \pm1, \pm2, \dots) \tag{36.2}$$

$$I = I_0\left\{\frac{\sin[\pi a(\sin\theta)/\lambda]}{\pi a(\sin\theta)/\lambda}\right\}^2 \tag{36.7}$$

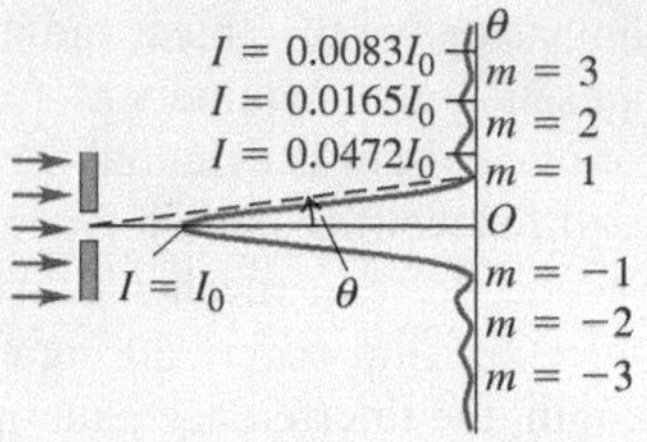

Diffraction gratings: A diffraction grating consists of a large number of thin parallel slits, spaced a distance d apart. The condition for maximum intensity in the interference pattern is the same as for the two-source pattern, but the maxima for the grating are very sharp and narrow. (See Example 36.4.)

$$d\sin\theta = m\lambda$$
$$(m = 0, \pm1, \pm2, \pm3, \dots) \tag{36.13}$$

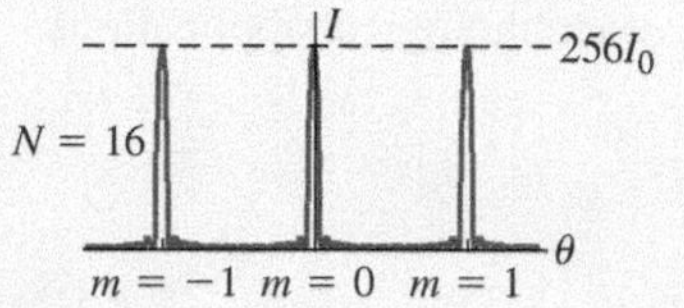

X-ray diffraction: A crystal serves as a three-dimensional diffraction grating for x rays with wavelengths of the same order of magnitude as the spacing between atoms in the crystal. For a set of crystal planes spaced a distance d apart, constructive interference occurs when the angles of incidence and scattering (measured from the crystal planes) are equal and when the Bragg condition [Eq. (36.16)] is satisfied. (See Example 36.5.)

$$2d\sin\theta = m\lambda \quad (m = 1, 2, 3, \dots) \tag{36.16}$$

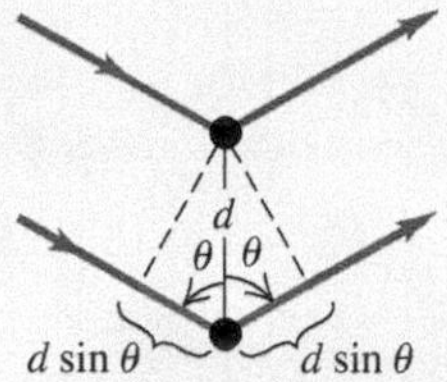

Circular apertures and resolving power: The diffraction pattern from a circular aperture of diameter D consists of a central bright spot, called the Airy disk, and a series of concentric dark and bright rings. Equation (36.17) gives the angular radius θ_1 of the first dark ring, equal to the angular size of the Airy disk. Diffraction sets the ultimate limit on resolution (image sharpness) of optical instruments. According to Rayleigh's criterion, two point objects are just barely resolved when their angular separation θ is given by Eq. (36.17). (See Example 36.6.)

$$\sin\theta_1 = 1.22\frac{\lambda}{D} \tag{36.17}$$

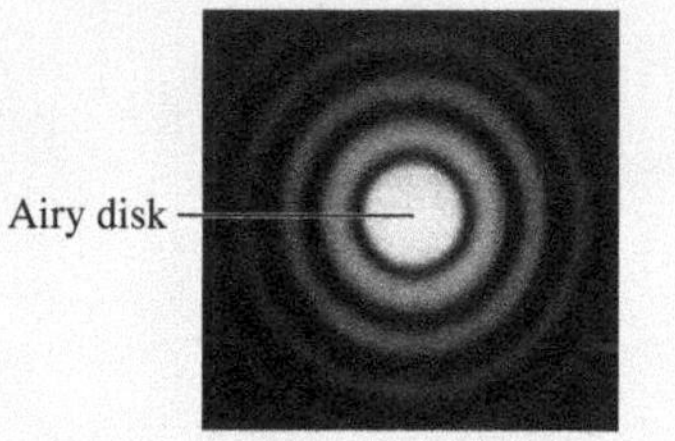

BRIDGING PROBLEM Observing the Expanding Universe

An astronomer who is studying the light from a galaxy has identified the spectrum of hydrogen but finds that the wavelengths are somewhat shifted from those found in the laboratory. In the lab, the H_α line in the hydrogen spectrum has a wavelength of 656.3 nm. The astronomer is using a transmission diffraction grating having 5758 lines/cm in the first order and finds that the first bright fringe for the H_α line occurs at $\pm 23.41°$ from the central spot. How fast is the galaxy moving? Express your answer in m/s and as a percentage of the speed of light. Is the galaxy moving toward us or away from us?

SOLUTION GUIDE

See MasteringPhysics® study area for a Video Tutor solution.

IDENTIFY and SET UP

1. You can use the information about the grating to find the wavelength of the H_α line in the galaxy's spectrum.
2. In Section 16.8 we learned about the Doppler effect for electromagnetic radiation: The frequency that we receive from a moving source, such as the galaxy, is different from the frequency that is emitted. Equation (16.30) relates the emitted frequency, the received frequency, and the velocity of the source (the target variable). The equation $c = f\lambda$ relates the frequency f and wavelength λ through the speed of light c.

EXECUTE

3. Find the wavelength of the H_α spectral line in the received light.
4. Rewrite Eq. (16.30) as a formula for the velocity v of the galaxy in terms of the received wavelength and the wavelength emitted by the source.
5. Solve for v. Express it in m/s and as a percentage of c, and decide whether the galaxy is moving toward us or moving away.

EVALUATE

6. Is your answer consistent with the relative sizes of the received wavelength and the emitted wavelength?

Problems

For instructor-assigned homework, go to www.masteringphysics.com

•, ••, •••: Problems of increasing difficulty. **CP**: Cumulative problems incorporating material from earlier chapters. **CALC**: Problems requiring calculus. **BIO**: Biosciences problems.

DISCUSSION QUESTIONS

Q36.1 Why can we readily observe diffraction effects for sound waves and water waves, but not for light? Is this because light travels so much faster than these other waves? Explain.

Q36.2 What is the difference between Fresnel and Fraunhofer diffraction? Are they different *physical* processes? Explain.

Q36.3 You use a lens of diameter D and light of wavelength λ and frequency f to form an image of two closely spaced and distant objects. Which of the following will increase the resolving power? (a) Use a lens with a smaller diameter; (b) use light of higher frequency; (c) use light of longer wavelength. In each case justify your answer.

Q36.4 Light of wavelength λ and frequency f passes through a single slit of width a. The diffraction pattern is observed on a screen a distance x from the slit. Which of the following will *decrease* the width of the central maximum? (a) Decrease the slit width; (b) decrease the frequency f of the light; (c) decrease the wavelength λ of the light; (d) decrease the distance x of the screen from the slit. In each case justify your answer.

Q36.5 In a diffraction experiment with waves of wavelength λ, there will be *no* intensity minima (that is, no dark fringes) if the slit width is small enough. What is the maximum slit width for which this occurs? Explain your answer.

Q36.6 The predominant sound waves used in human speech have wavelengths in the range from 1.0 to 3.0 meters. Using the ideas of diffraction, explain how it is possible to hear a person's voice even when he is facing away from you.

Q36.7 In single-slit diffraction, what is $\sin(\beta/2)$ when $\theta = 0$? In view of your answer, why is the single-slit intensity *not* equal to zero at the center?

Q36.8 A rainbow ordinarily shows a range of colors (see Section 33.4). But if the water droplets that form the rainbow are small enough, the rainbow will appear white. Explain why, using diffraction ideas. How small do you think the raindrops would have to be for this to occur?

Q36.9 Some loudspeaker horns for outdoor concerts (at which the entire audience is seated on the ground) are wider vertically than horizontally. Use diffraction ideas to explain why this is more efficient at spreading the sound uniformly over the audience than either a square speaker horn or a horn that is wider horizontally than vertically. Would this still be the case if the audience were seated at different elevations, as in an amphitheater? Why or why not?

Q36.10 Figure 31.12 (Section 31.2) shows a loudspeaker system. Low-frequency sounds are produced by the *woofer,* which is a speaker with large diameter; the *tweeter,* a speaker with smaller diameter, produces high-frequency sounds. Use diffraction ideas to explain why the tweeter is more effective for distributing high-frequency sounds uniformly over a room than is the woofer.

Q36.11 Information is stored on an audio compact disc, CD-ROM, or DVD disc in a series of pits on the disc. These pits are scanned by a laser beam. An important limitation on the amount of information that can be stored on such a disc is the width of the laser beam. Explain why this should be, and explain how using a shorter-wavelength laser allows more information to be stored on a disc of the same size.

Q36.12 With which color of light can the Hubble Space Telescope see finer detail in a distant astronomical object: red, blue, or ultraviolet? Explain your answer.

Q36.13 At the end of Section 36.4, the following statements were made about an array of N slits. Explain, using phasor diagrams, why each statement is true. (a) A minimum occurs whenever ϕ is an integral multiple of $2\pi/N$, except when ϕ is an integral multiple of 2π (which gives a principal maximum). (b) There are $(N - 1)$ minima between each pair of principal maxima.

Q36.14 Could x-ray diffraction effects with crystals be observed by using visible light instead of x rays? Why or why not?

Q36.15 Why is a diffraction grating better than a two-slit setup for measuring wavelengths of light?

Q36.16 One sometimes sees rows of evenly spaced radio antenna towers. A student remarked that these act like diffraction gratings. What did she mean? Why would one want them to act like a diffraction grating?

Q36.17 If a hologram is made using 600-nm light and then viewed with 500-nm light, how will the images look compared to those observed when viewed with 600-nm light? Explain.

Q36.18 A hologram is made using 600-nm light and then viewed by using white light from an incandescent bulb. What will be seen? Explain.

Q36.19 Ordinary photographic film reverses black and white, in the sense that the most brightly illuminated areas become blackest upon development (hence the term *negative*). Suppose a hologram negative is viewed directly, without making a positive transparency. How will the resulting images differ from those obtained with the positive? Explain.

EXERCISES

Section 36.2 Diffraction from a Single Slit

36.1 •• Monochromatic light from a distant source is incident on a slit 0.750 mm wide. On a screen 2.00 m away, the distance from the central maximum of the diffraction pattern to the first minimum is measured to be 1.35 mm. Calculate the wavelength of the light.

36.2 • Parallel rays of green mercury light with a wavelength of 546 nm pass through a slit covering a lens with a focal length of 60.0 cm. In the focal plane of the lens the distance from the central maximum to the first minimum is 10.2 mm. What is the width of the slit?

36.3 •• Light of wavelength 585 nm falls on a slit 0.0666 mm wide. (a) On a very large and distant screen, how many *totally* dark fringes (indicating complete cancellation) will there be, including both sides of the central bright spot? Solve this problem *without* calculating all the angles! (*Hint:* What is the largest that $\sin\theta$ can be? What does this tell you is the largest that m can be?) (b) At what angle will the dark fringe that is most distant from the central bright fringe occur?

36.4 • Light of wavelength 633 nm from a distant source is incident on a slit 0.750 mm wide, and the resulting diffraction pattern is observed on a screen 3.50 m away. What is the distance between the two dark fringes on either side of the central bright fringe?

36.5 •• Diffraction occurs for all types of waves, including sound waves. High-frequency sound from a distant source with wavelength 9.00 cm passes through a slit 12.0 cm wide. A microphone is placed 8.00 m directly in front of the center of the slit, corresponding to point O in Fig. 36.5a. The microphone is then moved in a direction perpendicular to the line from the center of the slit to point O. At what distances from O will the intensity detected by the microphone be zero?

36.6 • CP **Tsunami!** On December 26, 2004, a violent earthquake of magnitude 9.1 occurred off the coast of Sumatra. This quake triggered a huge tsunami (similar to a tidal wave) that killed more than 150,000 people. Scientists observing the wave on the open ocean measured the time between crests to be 1.0 h and the speed of the wave to be 800 km/h. Computer models of the evolution of this enormous wave showed that it bent around the continents and spread to all the oceans of the earth. When the wave reached the gaps between continents, it diffracted between them as through a slit. (a) What was the wavelength of this tsunami? (b) The distance between the southern tip of Africa and northern Antarctica is about 4500 km, while the distance between the southern end of Australia and Antarctica is about 3700 km. As an approximation, we can model this wave's behavior by using Fraunhofer diffraction. Find the smallest angle away from the central maximum for which the waves would cancel after going through each of these continental gaps.

36.7 •• CP A series of parallel linear water wave fronts are traveling directly toward the shore at 15.0 cm/s on an otherwise placid lake. A long concrete barrier that runs parallel to the shore at a distance of 3.20 m away has a hole in it. You count the wave crests and observe that 75.0 of them pass by each minute, and you also observe that no waves reach the shore at ± 61.3 cm from the point directly opposite the hole, but waves do reach the shore everywhere within this distance. (a) How wide is the hole in the barrier? (b) At what other angles do you find no waves hitting the shore?

36.8 • Monochromatic electromagnetic radiation with wavelength λ from a distant source passes through a slit. The diffraction pattern is observed on a screen 2.50 m from the slit. If the width of the central maximum is 6.00 mm, what is the slit width a if the wavelength is (a) 500 nm (visible light); (b) 50.0 μm (infrared radiation); (c) 0.500 nm (x rays)?

36.9 •• **Doorway Diffraction.** Sound of frequency 1250 Hz leaves a room through a 1.00-m-wide doorway (see Exercise 36.5). At which angles relative to the centerline perpendicular to the doorway will someone outside the room hear no sound? Use 344 m/s for the speed of sound in air and assume that the source and listener are both far enough from the doorway for Fraunhofer diffraction to apply. You can ignore effects of reflections.

36.10 • CP Light waves, for which the electric field is given by $E_y(x, t) = E_{max}\sin[(1.20 \times 10^7\ \text{m}^{-1})x - \omega t]$, pass through a slit and produce the first dark bands at $\pm 28.6°$ from the center of the diffraction pattern. (a) What is the frequency of this light? (b) How wide is the slit? (c) At which angles will other dark bands occur?

36.11 •• Parallel rays of light with wavelength 620 nm pass through a slit covering a lens with a focal length of 40.0 cm. The diffraction pattern is observed in the focal plane of the lens, and the distance from the center of the central maximum to the first minimum is 36.5 cm. What is the width of the slit? (*Note:* The angle that locates the first minimum is *not* small.)

36.12 •• Red light of wavelength 633 nm from a helium–neon laser passes through a slit 0.350 mm wide. The diffraction pattern is observed on a screen 3.00 m away. Define the width of a bright fringe as the distance between the minima on either side. (a) What is the width of the central bright fringe? (b) What is the width of the first bright fringe on either side of the central one?

Section 36.3 Intensity in the Single-Slit Pattern

36.13 •• Monochromatic light of wavelength 580 nm passes through a single slit and the diffraction pattern is observed on a screen. Both the source and screen are far enough from the slit for Fraunhofer diffraction to apply. (a) If the first diffraction minima are at $\pm 90.0°$, so the central maximum completely fills the screen, what is the width of the slit? (b) For the width of the slit as calculated in part (a), what is the ratio of the intensity at $\theta = 45.0°$ to the intensity at $\theta = 0$?

36.14 •• Monochromatic light of wavelength $\lambda = 620$ nm from a distant source passes through a slit 0.450 mm wide. The diffraction pattern is observed on a screen 3.00 m from the slit. In terms of the intensity I_0 at the peak of the central maximum, what is the intensity of the light at the screen the following distances from the center of the central maximum: (a) 1.00 mm; (b) 3.00 mm; (c) 5.00 mm?

36.15 •• A slit 0.240 mm wide is illuminated by parallel light rays of wavelength 540 nm. The diffraction pattern is observed on a screen that is 3.00 m from the slit. The intensity at the center of the central maximum ($\theta = 0°$) is $6.00 \times 10^{-6}\ \text{W/m}^2$. (a) What is the distance on the screen from the center of the central maximum to the first minimum? (b) What is the intensity at a point on the screen midway between the center of the central maximum and the first minimum?

36.16 • Monochromatic light of wavelength 486 nm from a distant source passes through a slit that is 0.0290 mm wide. In the resulting diffraction pattern, the intensity at the center of the central maximum ($\theta = 0°$) is $4.00 \times 10^{-5}\ \text{W/m}^2$. What is the intensity at a point on the screen that corresponds to $\theta = 1.20°$.

36.17 •• A single-slit diffraction pattern is formed by monochromatic electromagnetic radiation from a distant source passing through a slit 0.105 mm wide. At the point in the pattern 3.25° from the center of the central maximum, the total phase difference between wavelets from the top and bottom of the slit is 56.0 rad. (a) What is the wavelength of the radiation? (b) What is the intensity at this point, if the intensity at the center of the central maximum is I_0?

36.18 • Consider a single-slit diffraction experiment in which the amplitude of the wave at point O in Fig. 36.5a is E_0. For each of the following cases, draw a phasor diagram like that in Fig. 36.8c and determine *graphically* the amplitude of the wave at the point in question. (*Hint:* Use Eq. (36.6) to determine the value of β for each case.) Compute the intensity and compare to Eq. (36.5). (a) $\sin\theta = \lambda/2a$; (b) $\sin\theta = \lambda/a$; (c) $\sin\theta = 3\lambda/2a$.

36.19 •• Public Radio station KXPR-FM in Sacramento broadcasts at 88.9 MHz. The radio waves pass between two tall skyscrapers that are 15.0 m apart along their closest walls. (a) At what horizontal angles, relative to the original direction of the waves, will a distant antenna not receive any signal from this station? (b) If the maximum intensity is $3.50\ \text{W/m}^2$ at the antenna, what is the intensity at $\pm 5.00°$ from the center of the central maximum at the distant antenna?

Section 36.4 Multiple Slits

36.20 •• **Diffraction and Interference Combined.** Consider the interference pattern produced by two parallel slits of width a and separation d, in which $d = 3a$. The slits are illuminated by normally incident light of wavelength λ. (a) First we ignore diffraction effects due to the slit width. At what angles θ from the central maximum will the next four maxima in the two-slit interference pattern occur? Your answer will be in terms of d and λ. (b) Now we include the effects of diffraction. If the intensity at $\theta = 0$ is I_0, what is the intensity at each of the angles in part (a)? (c) Which double-slit interference maxima are missing in the pattern? (d) Compare your results to those illustrated in Fig. 36.12c. In what ways is your result different?

36.21 • **Number of Fringes in a Diffraction Maximum.** In Fig. 36.12c the central diffraction maximum contains exactly seven interference fringes, and in this case $d/a = 4$. (a) What must the ratio d/a be if the central maximum contains exactly five fringes? (b) In the case considered in part (a), how many fringes are contained within the first diffraction maximum on one side of the central maximum?

36.22 • An interference pattern is produced by eight parallel and equally spaced, narrow slits. There is an interference minimum when the phase difference ϕ between light from adjacent slits is $\pi/4$. The phasor diagram is given in Fig. 36.14b. For which pairs of slits is there totally destructive interference?

36.23 •• An interference pattern is produced by light of wavelength 580 nm from a distant source incident on two identical parallel slits separated by a distance (between centers) of 0.530 mm. (a) If the slits are very narrow, what would be the angular positions of the first-order and second-order, two-slit, interference maxima? (b) Let the slits have width 0.320 mm. In terms of the intensity I_0 at the center of the central maximum, what is the intensity at each of the angular positions in part (a)?

36.24 • Parallel rays of monochromatic light with wavelength 568 nm illuminate two identical slits and produce an interference pattern on a screen that is 75.0 cm from the slits. The centers of the slits are 0.640 mm apart and the width of each slit is 0.434 mm. If the intensity at the center of the central maximum is $5.00 \times 10^{-4}\ \text{W/m}^2$, what is the intensity at a point on the screen that is 0.900 mm from the center of the central maximum?

36.25 •• An interference pattern is produced by four parallel and equally spaced, narrow slits. By drawing appropriate phasor diagrams, show that there is an interference minimum when the phase difference ϕ from adjacent slits is (a) $\pi/2$; (b) π; (c) $3\pi/2$. In each case, for which pairs of slits is there totally destructive interference?

36.26 •• A diffraction experiment involving two thin parallel slits yields the pattern of closely spaced bright and dark fringes shown in Fig. E36.26. Only the central portion of the pattern is shown in the figure. The bright spots are equally spaced at 1.53 mm center to center (except for the missing spots) on a screen 2.50 m from the slits. The light source was a He-Ne laser producing a wavelength of 632.8 nm. (a) How far apart are the two slits? (b) How wide is each one?

Figure E36.26

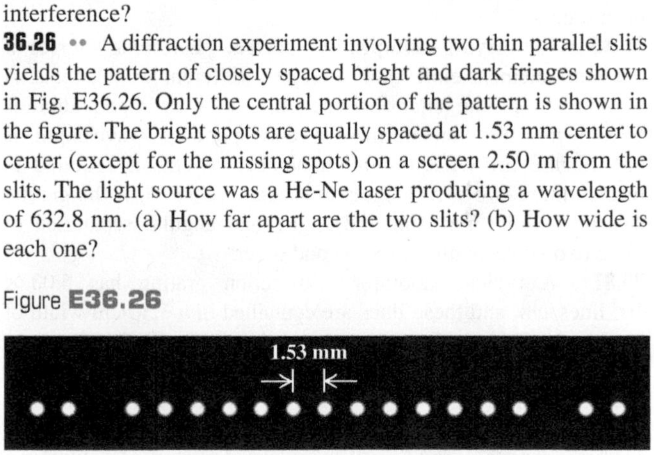

36.27 •• Laser light of wavelength 500.0 nm illuminates two identical slits, producing an interference pattern on a screen 90.0 cm from the slits. The bright bands are 1.00 cm apart, and the third bright bands on either side of the central maximum are missing in the pattern. Find the width and the separation of the two slits.

Section 36.5 The Diffraction Grating

36.28 •• Monochromatic light is at normal incidence on a plane transmission grating. The first-order maximum in the interference pattern is at an angle of 8.94°. What is the angular position of the fourth-order maximum?

36.29 • If a diffraction grating produces its third-order bright band at an angle of 78.4° for light of wavelength 681 nm, find (a) the number of slits per centimeter for the grating and (b) the angular location of the first-order and second-order bright bands. (c) Will there be a fourth-order bright band? Explain.

36.30 • If a diffraction grating produces a third-order bright spot for red light (of wavelength 700 nm) at 65.0° from the central maximum, at what angle will the second-order bright spot be for violet light (of wavelength 400 nm)?

36.31 • Visible light passes through a diffraction grating that has 900 slits/cm, and the interference pattern is observed on a screen that is 2.50 m from the grating. (a) Is the angular position of the first-order spectrum small enough for $\sin\theta \approx \theta$ to be a good approximation? (b) In the first-order spectrum, the maxima for two different wavelengths are separated on the screen by 3.00 mm. What is the difference in these wavelengths?

36.32 • The wavelength range of the visible spectrum is approximately 380–750 nm. White light falls at normal incidence on a diffraction grating that has 350 slits/mm. Find the angular width of the visible spectrum in (a) the first order and (b) the third order. (*Note:* An advantage of working in higher orders is the greater angular spread and better resolution. A disadvantage is the overlapping of different orders, as shown in Example 36.4.)

36.33 • When laser light of wavelength 632.8 nm passes through a diffraction grating, the first bright spots occur at $\pm 17.8°$ from the central maximum. (a) What is the line density (in lines/cm) of this grating? (b) How many additional bright spots are there beyond the first bright spots, and at what angles do they occur?

36.34 • (a) What is the wavelength of light that is deviated in the first order through an angle of 13.5° by a transmission grating having 5000 slits/cm? (b) What is the second-order deviation of this wavelength? Assume normal incidence.

36.35 • Plane monochromatic waves with wavelength 520 nm are incident normally on a plane transmission grating having 350 slits/mm. Find the angles of deviation in the first, second, and third orders.

36.36 • **Identifying Isotopes by Spectra.** Different isotopes of the same element emit light at slightly different wavelengths. A wavelength in the emission spectrum of a hydrogen atom is 656.45 nm; for deuterium, the corresponding wavelength is 656.27 nm. (a) What minimum number of slits is required to resolve these two wavelengths in second order? (b) If the grating has 500.00 slits/mm, find the angles and angular separation of these two wavelengths in the second order.

36.37 • A typical laboratory diffraction grating has 5.00×10^3 lines/cm, and these lines are contained in a 3.50-cm width of grating. (a) What is the chromatic resolving power of such a grating in the first order? (b) Could this grating resolve the lines of the sodium doublet (see Section 36.5) in the first order? (c) While doing spectral analysis of a star, you are using this grating in the *second* order to resolve spectral lines that are very close to the 587.8002-nm spectral line of iron. (i) For wavelengths longer than the iron line, what is the shortest wavelength you could distinguish from the iron line? (ii) For wavelengths shorter than the iron line, what is the longest wavelength you could distinguish from the iron line? (iii) What is the range of wavelengths you could *not* distinguish from the iron line?

36.38 • The light from an iron arc includes many different wavelengths. Two of these are at $\lambda = 587.9782$ nm and $\lambda = 587.8002$ nm. You wish to resolve these spectral lines in first order using a grating 1.20 cm in length. What minimum number of slits per centimeter must the grating have?

Section 36.6 X-Ray Diffraction

36.39 • X rays of wavelength 0.0850 nm are scattered from the atoms of a crystal. The second-order maximum in the Bragg reflection occurs when the angle θ in Fig. 36.22 is 21.5°. What is the spacing between adjacent atomic planes in the crystal?

36.40 • If the planes of a crystal are 3.50 Å (1 Å = 10^{-10} m = 1 Ångstrom unit) apart, (a) what wavelength of electromagnetic waves is needed so that the first strong interference maximum in the Bragg reflection occurs when the waves strike the planes at an angle of 15.0°, and in what part of the electromagnetic spectrum do these waves lie? (See Fig. 32.4.) (b) At what other angles will strong interference maxima occur?

36.41 • Monochromatic x rays are incident on a crystal for which the spacing of the atomic planes is 0.440 nm. The first-order maximum in the Bragg reflection occurs when the incident and reflected x rays make an angle of 39.4° with the crystal planes. What is the wavelength of the x rays?

Section 36.7 Circular Apertures and Resolving Power

36.42 • BIO If you can read the bottom row of your doctor's eye chart, your eye has a resolving power of 1 arcminute, equal to $\frac{1}{60}$ degree. If this resolving power is diffraction limited, to what effective diameter of your eye's optical system does this correspond? Use Rayleigh's criterion and assume $\lambda = 550$ nm.

36.43 • Two satellites at an altitude of 1200 km are separated by 28 km. If they broadcast 3.6-cm microwaves, what minimum receiving-dish diameter is needed to resolve (by Rayleigh's criterion) the two transmissions?

36.44 •• The VLBA (Very Long Baseline Array) uses a number of individual radio telescopes to make one unit having an equivalent diameter of about 8000 km. When this radio telescope is focusing radio waves of wavelength 2.0 cm, what would have to be the diameter of the mirror of a visible-light telescope focusing light of wavelength 550 nm so that the visible-light telescope has the same resolution as the radio telescope?

36.45 •• Monochromatic light with wavelength 620 nm passes through a circular aperture with diameter 7.4 μm. The resulting diffraction pattern is observed on a screen that is 4.5 m from the aperture. What is the diameter of the Airy disk on the screen?

36.46 • **Photography.** A wildlife photographer uses a moderate telephoto lens of focal length 135 mm and maximum aperture $f/4.00$ to photograph a bear that is 11.5 m away. Assume the wavelength is 550 nm. (a) What is the width of the smallest feature on the bear that this lens can resolve if it is opened to its maximum aperture? (b) If, to gain depth of field, the photographer stops the lens down to $f/22.0$, what would be the width of the smallest resolvable feature on the bear?

36.47 • **Observing Jupiter.** You are asked to design a space telescope for earth orbit. When Jupiter is 5.93×10^8 km away (its closest approach to the earth), the telescope is to resolve, by Rayleigh's criterion, features on Jupiter that are 250 km apart. What minimum-diameter mirror is required? Assume a wavelength of 500 nm.

36.48 • A converging lens 7.20 cm in diameter has a focal length of 300 mm. If the resolution is diffraction limited, how far away can an object be if points on it 4.00 mm apart are to be resolved (according to Rayleigh's criterion)? Use $\lambda = 550$ nm.

36.49 •• **Hubble Versus Arecibo.** The Hubble Space Telescope has an aperture of 2.4 m and focuses visible light (380–750 nm). The Arecibo radio telescope in Puerto Rico is 305 m (1000 ft) in diameter (it is built in a mountain valley) and focuses radio waves of wavelength 75 cm. (a) Under optimal viewing conditions, what is the smallest crater that each of these telescopes could resolve on our moon? (b) If the Hubble Space Telescope were to be converted to surveillance use, what is the highest orbit above the surface of the earth it could have and still be able to resolve the license plate (not the letters, just the plate) of a car on the ground? Assume optimal viewing conditions, so that the resolution is diffraction limited.

36.50 • **Searching for Starspots.** The Hale Telescope on Palomar Mountain in California has a mirror 200 in. (5.08 m) in diameter and it focuses visible light. Given that a large sunspot is about 10,000 mi in diameter, what is the most distant star on which this telescope could resolve a sunspot to see whether other stars have them? (Assume optimal viewing conditions, so that the resolution is diffraction limited.) Are there any stars this close to us, besides our sun?

PROBLEMS

36.51 •• BIO **Thickness of Human Hair.** Although we have discussed single-slit diffraction only for a slit, a similar result holds when light bends around a straight, thin object, such as a strand of hair. In that case, a is the width of the strand. From actual laboratory measurements on a human hair, it was found that when a beam of light of wavelength 632.8 nm was shone on a single strand of hair, and the diffracted light was viewed on a screen 1.25 m away, the first dark fringes on either side of the central bright spot were 5.22 cm apart. How thick was this strand of hair?

36.52 •• Suppose the entire apparatus (slit, screen, and space in between) in Exercise 36.4 is immersed in water ($n = 1.333$). Then what is the distance between the two dark fringes?

36.53 ••• Laser light of wavelength 632.8 nm falls normally on a slit that is 0.0250 mm wide. The transmitted light is viewed on a distant screen where the intensity at the center of the central bright fringe is 8.50 W/m^2. (a) Find the maximum number of totally dark fringes on the screen, assuming the screen is large enough to show them all. (b) At what angle does the dark fringe that is most distant from the center occur? (c) What is the maximum intensity of the bright fringe that occurs immediately before the dark fringe in part (b)? Approximate the angle at which this fringe occurs by assuming it is midway between the angles to the dark fringes on either side of it.

36.54 •• CP A loudspeaker having a diaphragm that vibrates at 1250 Hz is traveling at 80.0 m/s directly toward a pair of holes in a very large wall in a region for which the speed of sound is 344 m/s. You observe that the sound coming through the openings first cancels at $\pm 11.4°$ with respect to the original direction of the speaker when observed far from the wall. (a) How far apart are the two openings? (b) At what angles would the sound first cancel if the source stopped moving?

36.55 • **Measuring Refractive Index.** A thin slit illuminated by light of frequency f produces its first dark band at $\pm 38.2°$ in air. When the entire apparatus (slit, screen, and space in between) is immersed in an unknown transparent liquid, the slit's first dark bands occur instead at $\pm 21.6°$. Find the refractive index of the liquid.

36.56 • **Grating Design.** Your boss asks you to design a diffraction grating that will disperse the first-order visible spectrum through an angular range of 21.0° (see Example 36.4 in Section 36.5). (a) What must the number of slits per centimeter be for this grating? (b) At what angles will the first-order visible spectrum begin and end?

36.57 •• A slit 0.360 mm wide is illuminated by parallel rays of light that have a wavelength of 540 nm. The diffraction pattern is observed on a screen that is 1.20 m from the slit. The intensity at the center of the central maximum ($\theta = 0°$) is I_0. (a) What is the distance on the screen from the center of the central maximum to the first minimum? (b) What is the distance on the screen from the center of the central maximum to the point where the intensity has fallen to $I_0/2$?

36.58 ••• CALC The intensity of light in the Fraunhofer diffraction pattern of a single slit is

$$I = I_0\left(\frac{\sin\gamma}{\gamma}\right)^2$$

where

$$\gamma = \frac{\pi a \sin\theta}{\lambda}$$

(a) Show that the equation for the values of γ at which I is a maximum is $\tan\gamma = \gamma$. (b) Determine the three smallest positive values of γ that are solutions of this equation. (*Hint:* You can use a trial-and-error procedure. Guess a value of γ and adjust your guess to bring $\tan\gamma$ closer to γ. A graphical solution of the equation is very helpful in locating the solutions approximately, to get good initial guesses.)

36.59 •• **Angular Width of a Principal Maximum.** Consider N evenly spaced, narrow slits. Use the small-angle approximation $\sin\theta = \theta$ (for θ in radians) to prove the following: For an intensity maximum that occurs at an angle θ, the intensity minima immediately adjacent to this maximum are at angles $\theta + \lambda/Nd$ and $\theta - \lambda/Nd$, so that the angular width of the principal maximum is $2\lambda/Nd$. This is proportional to $1/N$, as we concluded in Section 36.4 on the basis of energy conservation.

36.60 •• CP CALC In a large vacuum chamber, monochromatic laser light passes through a narrow slit in a thin aluminum plate and forms a diffraction pattern on a screen that is 0.620 m from the slit. When the aluminum plate has a temperature of 20.0°C, the width of the central maximum in the diffraction pattern is 2.75 mm. What is the change in the width of the central maximum when the temperature of the plate is raised to 520.0°C? Does the width of the central diffraction maximum increase or decrease when the temperature is increased?

36.61 • **Phasor Diagram for Eight Slits.** An interference pattern is produced by eight equally spaced, narrow slits. Figure 36.14 shows phasor diagrams for the cases in which the phase difference ϕ between light from adjacent slits is $\phi = \pi$, $\phi = \pi/4$, and $\phi = \pi/2$. Each of these cases gives an intensity minimum. The caption for Fig. 36.14 also claims that minima occur for $\phi = 3\pi/4$, $\phi = 5\pi/4$, $\phi = 3\pi/2$, and $\phi = 7\pi/4$. (a) Draw the phasor diagram for each of these four cases, and explain why each diagram proves that there is in fact a minimum. (*Note:* You may find it helpful to use a different colored pencil for each slit!) (b) For each of the four cases $\phi = 3\pi/4$, $\phi = 5\pi/4$, $\phi = 3\pi/2$, and $\phi = 7\pi/4$, for which pairs of slits is there totally destructive interference?

36.62 •• CP In a laboratory, light from a particular spectrum line of helium passes through a diffraction grating and the second-order maximum is at 18.9° from the center of the central bright fringe. The same grating is then used for light from a distant galaxy that is moving away from the earth with a speed of 2.65×10^7 m/s. For the light from the galaxy, what is the angular location of the second-order maximum for the same spectral line as was observed in the lab? (See Section 16.8.)

36.63 • What is the longest wavelength that can be observed in the third order for a transmission grating having 9200 slits/cm? Assume normal incidence.

36.64 •• (a) Figure 36.16 shows plane waves of light incident *normally* on a diffraction grating. If instead the light strikes the grating at an angle of incidence θ' (measured from the normal), show that the condition for an intensity maximum is *not* Eq. (36.13), but rather

$$d(\sin\theta + \sin\theta') = m\lambda \quad (m = 0, \pm 1, \pm 2, \pm 3, \ldots)$$

(b) For the grating described in Example 36.4 (Section 36.5), with 600 slits/mm, find the angles of the maxima corresponding to $m = 0$, 1, and -1 with red light ($\lambda = 650$ nm) for the cases $\theta' = 0$ (normal incidence) and $\theta' = 20.0°$.

36.65 • A diffraction grating has 650 slits/mm. What is the highest order that contains the entire visible spectrum? (The wavelength range of the visible spectrum is approximately 380–750 nm.)

36.66 •• *Quasars,* an abbreviation for *quasi-stellar radio sources,* are distant objects that look like stars through a telescope but that emit far more electromagnetic radiation than an entire normal galaxy of stars. An example is the bright object below and to the left of center in Fig. P36.66; the other elongated objects in this image are normal galaxies. The leading model for the structure of a quasar is a galaxy with a supermassive black hole at its center. In this model, the radiation is emitted by interstellar gas and dust within the galaxy as this material falls toward the black hole. The radiation is thought to emanate from a region just a few light-years in diameter. (The diffuse glow surrounding the bright quasar shown in Fig. P36.66 is thought to be this quasar's host galaxy.) To investigate this model of quasars and to study other exotic astronomical objects, the Russian Space Agency plans to place a radio telescope in an orbit that extends to 77,000 km from the earth. When the signals from this telescope are combined with signals from the ground-based telescopes of the VLBA, the resolution will be that of a single radio telescope 77,000 km in diameter. What is the size of the smallest detail that this arrangement could resolve in quasar 3C 405, which is 7.2×10^8 light-years from earth, using radio waves at a frequency of 1665 MHz? (*Hint:* Use Rayleigh's criterion.) Give your answer in light-years and in kilometers.

Figure **P36.66**

36.67 ••• **Phased-Array Radar.** In one common type of radar installation, a rotating antenna sweeps a radio beam around the sky. But in a *phased-array* radar system, the antennas remain stationary and the beam is swept electronically. To see how this is done, consider an array of N antennas that are arranged along the horizontal x-axis at $x = 0, \pm d, \pm 2d, \ldots, \pm(N-1)d/2$. (The number N is odd.) Each antenna emits radiation uniformly in all directions in the horizontal xy-plane. The antennas all emit radiation coherently, with the same amplitude E_0 and the same wavelength λ. The relative phase δ of the emission from adjacent antennas can be varied, however. If the antenna at $x = 0$ emits a signal that is given by $E_0 \cos \omega t$, as measured at a point next to the antenna, the antenna at $x = d$ emits a signal given by $E_0 \cos(\omega t + \delta)$, as measured at a point next to that antenna. The corresponding quantity for the antenna at $x = -d$ is $E_0 \cos(\omega t - \delta)$; for the antennas at $x = \pm 2d$, it is $E_0 \cos(\omega t \pm 2\delta)$; and so on. (a) If $\delta = 0$, the interference pattern at a distance from the antennas is large compared to d and has a principal maximum at $\theta = 0$ (that is, in the $+y$-direction, perpendicular to the line of the antennas). Show that if $d < \lambda$, this is the *only* principal interference maximum in the angular range $-90° < \theta < 90°$. Hence this principal maximum describes a beam emitted in the direction $\theta = 0$. As described in Section 36.4, if N is large, the beam will have a large intensity and be quite narrow. (b) If $\delta \neq 0$, show that the principal intensity maximum described in part (a) is located at

$$\theta = \arcsin\left(\frac{\delta\lambda}{2\pi d}\right)$$

where δ is measured in radians. Thus, by varying δ from positive to negative values and back again, which can easily be done electronically, the beam can be made to sweep back and forth around $\theta = 0$. (c) A weather radar unit to be installed on an airplane emits radio waves at 8800 MHz. The unit uses 15 antennas in an array 28.0 cm long (from the antenna at one end of the array to the antenna at the other end). What must the maximum and minimum values of δ be (that is, the most positive and most negative values) if the radar beam is to sweep 45° to the left or right of the airplane's direction of flight? Give your answer in radians.

36.68 •• **Underwater Photography.** An underwater camera has a lens of focal length 35.0 mm and a maximum aperture of $f/2.80$. The film it uses has an emulsion that is sensitive to light of frequency 6.00×10^{14} Hz. If the photographer takes a picture of an object 2.75 m in front of the camera with the lens wide open, what is the width of the smallest resolvable detail on the subject if the object is (a) a fish underwater with the camera in the water and (b) a person on the beach with the camera out of the water?

36.69 •• An astronaut in the space shuttle can just resolve two point sources on earth that are 65.0 m apart. Assume that the resolution is diffraction limited and use Rayleigh's criterion. What is the astronaut's altitude above the earth? Treat his eye as a circular aperture with a diameter of 4.00 mm (the diameter of his pupil), and take the wavelength of the light to be 550 nm. Ignore the effect of fluid in the eye.

36.70 •• BIO **Resolution of the Eye.** The maximum resolution of the eye depends on the diameter of the opening of the pupil (a diffraction effect) and the size of the retinal cells. The size of the retinal cells (about 5.0 μm in diameter) limits the size of an object at the near point (25 cm) of the eye to a height of about 50 μm. (To get a reasonable estimate without having to go through complicated calculations, we shall ignore the effect of the fluid in the eye.) (a) Given that the diameter of the human pupil is about 2.0 mm, does the Rayleigh criterion allow us to resolve a 50-μm-tall object at 25 cm from the eye with light of wavelength 550 nm? (b) According to the Rayleigh criterion, what is the shortest object we could resolve at the 25-cm near point with light of wavelength 550 nm? (c) What angle would the object in part (b) subtend at the eye? Express your answer in minutes (60 min = 1°), and compare it with the experimental value of about 1 min. (d) Which effect is more important in limiting the resolution of our eyes: diffraction or the size of the retinal cells?

36.71 •• A glass sheet is covered by a very thin opaque coating. In the middle of this sheet there is a thin scratch 0.00125 mm thick. The sheet is totally immersed beneath the surface of a liquid. Parallel rays of monochromatic coherent light with wavelength 612 nm in air strike the sheet perpendicular to its surface and pass through the scratch. A screen is placed in the liquid a distance of 30.0 cm away from the sheet and parallel to it. You observe that the first dark fringes on either side of the central bright fringe on the screen are 22.4 cm apart. What is the refractive index of the liquid?

36.72 •• **Observing Planets Beyond Our Solar System.** NASA is considering a project called *Planet Imager* that would give astronomers the ability to see details on planets orbiting other stars. Using the same principle as the Very Large Array (see Section 36.7), *Planet Imager* will use an array of infrared telescopes spread over thousands of kilometers of space. (Visible light would give even better resolution. Unfortunately, at visible wavelengths, stars are so bright that a planet would be lost in the glare. This is less of a problem at infrared wavelengths.) (a) If *Planet Imager* has an effective diameter of 6000 km and observes infrared radiation at a wavelength of 10 μm, what is the greatest distance at which it would be able to observe details as small as 250 km across (about the size of the greater Los Angeles area) on a planet? Give your answer in light-years (see Appendix E). (*Hint:* Use Rayleigh's criterion.) (b) For comparison, consider the resolution of a single infrared telescope in space that has a diameter of 1.0 m and that observes 10-μm radiation. What is the size of the smallest details that such a telescope could resolve at the distance of the nearest star to the sun, Proxima Centauri, which is 4.22 light-years distant? How does this compare to the diameter of the earth (1.27×10^4 km)? To the average distance from the earth to the sun (1.50×10^8 km)? Would a single telescope of this kind be able to detect the presence of a planet like the earth, in an orbit the size of the earth's orbit, around *any* other star? Explain. (c) Suppose *Planet Imager* is used to observe a planet orbiting the star 70 Virginis, which is 59 light-years from our solar system. A planet (though not an earthlike one) has in fact been detected orbiting this star, not by imaging it directly but by observing the slight "wobble" of the star as both it and the planet orbit their common center of mass. What is the size of the smallest details that *Planet Imager* could hope to resolve on the planet of 70 Virginis? How does this compare to the diameter of the planet, assumed to be comparable to that of Jupiter (1.38×10^5 km)? (Although the planet of 70 Virginis is thought to be at least 6.6 times more massive than Jupiter, its radius is probably not too different from that of Jupiter. The reason is that such large planets are thought to be composed primarily of gases, not rocky material, and hence can be greatly compressed by the mutual gravitational attraction of different parts of the planet.)

CHALLENGE PROBLEMS

36.73 ••• CALC It is possible to calculate the intensity in the single-slit Fraunhofer diffraction pattern *without* using the phasor method of Section 36.3. Let y' represent the position of a point within the slit of width a in Fig. 36.5a, with $y' = 0$ at the center of the slit so that the slit extends from $y' = -a/2$ to $y' = a/2$. We imagine dividing the slit up into infinitesimal strips of width dy', each of which acts as a source of secondary wavelets. (a) The amplitude of the total wave at the point O on the distant screen in Fig. 36.5a is E_0. Explain why the amplitude of the wavelet from each infinitesimal strip within the slit is $E_0(dy'/a)$, so that the electric field of the wavelet a distance x from the infinitesimal strip is $dE = E_0(dy'/a)\sin(kx - \omega t)$. (b) Explain why the wavelet from each strip as detected at point P in Fig. 36.5a can be expressed as

$$dE = E_0\frac{dy'}{a}\sin[k(D - y'\sin\theta) - \omega t]$$

where D is the distance from the center of the slit to point P and $k = 2\pi/\lambda$. (c) By integrating the contributions dE from all parts of the slit, show that the total wave detected at point P is

$$E = E_0\sin(kD - \omega t)\frac{\sin[ka(\sin\theta)/2]}{ka(\sin\theta)/2}$$
$$= E_0\sin(kD - \omega t)\frac{\sin[\pi a(\sin\theta)/\lambda]}{\pi a(\sin\theta)/\lambda}$$

(The trigonometric identities in Appendix B will be useful.) Show that at $\theta = 0$, corresponding to point O in Fig. 36.5a, the wave is $E = E_0\sin(kD - \omega t)$ and has amplitude E_0, as stated in part (a). (d) Use the result of part (c) to show that if the intensity at point O is I_0, then the intensity at a point P is given by Eq. (36.7).

36.74 ••• **Intensity Pattern of N Slits.** (a) Consider an arrangement of N slits with a distance d between adjacent slits. The slits emit coherently and in phase at wavelength λ. Show that at a time t, the electric field at a distant point P is

$$E_P(t) = E_0\cos(kR - \omega t) + E_0\cos(kR - \omega t + \phi) + E_0\cos(kR - \omega t + 2\phi) + \cdots + E_0\cos(kR - \omega t + (N-1)\phi)$$

where E_0 is the amplitude at P of the electric field due to an individual slit, $\phi = (2\pi d\sin\theta)/\lambda$, θ is the angle of the rays reaching P (as measured from the perpendicular bisector of the slit arrangement), and R is the distance from P to the most distant slit. In this problem, assume that R is much larger than d. (b) To carry out the sum in part (a), it is convenient to use the complex-number relationship

$$e^{iz} = \cos z + i\sin z$$

where $i = \sqrt{-1}$. In this expression, $\cos z$ is the *real part* of the complex number e^{iz}, and $\sin z$ is its *imaginary part.* Show that the electric field $E_P(t)$ is equal to the real part of the complex quantity

$$\sum_{n=0}^{N-1} E_0 e^{i(kR - \omega t + n\phi)}$$

(c) Using the properties of the exponential function that $e^A e^B = e^{(A+B)}$ and $(e^A)^n = e^{nA}$, show that the sum in part (b) can be written as

$$E_0\left(\frac{e^{iN\phi} - 1}{e^{i\phi} - 1}\right)e^{i(kR-\omega t)}$$
$$= E_0\left(\frac{e^{iN\phi/2} - e^{-iN\phi/2}}{e^{i\phi/2} - e^{-i\phi/2}}\right)e^{i[kR-\omega t+(N-1)\phi/2]}$$

Then, using the relationship $e^{iz} = \cos z + i\sin z$, show that the (real) electric field at point P is

$$E_P(t) = \left[E_0\frac{\sin(N\phi/2)}{\sin(\phi/2)}\right]\cos[kR - \omega t + (N-1)\phi/2]$$

The quantity in the first square brackets in this expression is the amplitude of the electric field at P. (d) Use the result for the electric-field amplitude in part (c) to show that the intensity at an angle θ is

$$I = I_0\left[\frac{\sin(N\phi/2)}{\sin(\phi/2)}\right]^2$$

where I_0 is the maximum intensity for an individual slit. (e) Check the result in part (d) for the case $N = 2$. It will help to recall that $\sin 2A = 2\sin A\cos A$. Explain why your result differs from Eq. (35.10), the expression for the intensity in two-source interference, by a factor of 4. (*Hint:* Is I_0 defined in the same way in both expressions?)

36.75 ••• CALC Intensity Pattern of N Slits, Continued. Part (d) of Challenge Problem 36.74 gives an expression for the intensity in the interference pattern of N identical slits. Use this result to verify the following statements. (a) The maximum intensity in the pattern is N^2I_0. (b) The principal maximum at the center of the pattern extends from $\phi = -2\pi/N$ to $\phi = 2\pi/N$, so its width is inversely proportional to $1/N$. (c) A minimum occurs whenever ϕ is an integral multiple of $2\pi/N$, except when ϕ is an integral multiple of 2π (which gives a principal maximum). (d) There are $(N - 1)$ minima between each pair of principal maxima. (e) Halfway between two principal maxima, the intensity can be no greater than I_0; that is, it can be no greater than $1/N^2$ times the intensity at a principal maximum.

Answers

Chapter Opening Question ?

The shorter wavelength of a Blu-ray scanning laser gives it superior resolving power, so information can be more tightly packed onto a Blu-ray disc than a DVD. See Section 36.7 for details.

Test Your Understanding Questions

36.1 Answer: yes When you hear the voice of someone standing around a corner, you are hearing sound waves that underwent diffraction. If there were no diffraction of sound, you could hear sounds only from objects that were in plain view.

36.2 Answer: (ii), (i) and (iv) (tie), (iii) The angle θ of the first dark fringe is given by Eq. (36.2) with $m = 1$, or $\sin\theta = \lambda/a$. The larger the value of the ratio λ/a, the larger the value of $\sin\theta$ and hence the value of θ. The ratio λ/a in each case is (i) $(400\text{ nm})/(0.20\text{ mm}) = (4.0 \times 10^{-7}\text{ m})/(2.0 \times 10^{-4}\text{ m}) = 2.0 \times 10^{-3}$; (ii) $(600\text{ nm})/(0.20\text{ mm}) = (6.0 \times 10^{-7}\text{ m})/(2.0 \times 10^{-4}\text{ m}) = 3.0 \times 10^{-3}$; (iii) $(400\text{ nm})/(0.30\text{ mm}) = (4.0 \times 10^{-7}\text{ m})/(3.0 \times 10^{-4}\text{ m}) = 1.3 \times 10^{-3}$; (iv) $(600\text{ nm})/(0.30\text{ mm}) = (6.0 \times 10^{-7}\text{ m})/(3.0 \times 10^{-4}\text{ m}) = 2.0 \times 10^{-3}$.

36.3 Answers: (ii) and (iii) If the slit width a is less than the wavelength λ, there are no points in the diffraction pattern at which the intensity is zero (see Fig. 36.10a). The slit width is $0.0100\text{ mm} = 1.00 \times 10^{-5}\text{ m}$, so this condition is satisfied for (ii) $(\lambda = 10.6\ \mu\text{m} = 1.06 \times 10^{-5}\text{ m})$ and (iii) $(\lambda = 1.00\text{ mm} = 1.00 \times 10^{-3}\text{ m})$ but not for (i) $(\lambda = 500\text{ nm} = 5.00 \times 10^{-7}\text{ m})$ or (iv) $(\lambda = 50.0\text{ nm} = 5.00 \times 10^{-8}\text{ m})$.

36.4 Answers: yes; $m_i = \pm 5, \pm 10, \ldots$ A "missing maximum" satisfies both $d\sin\theta = m_i\lambda$ (the condition for an interference maximum) and $a\sin\theta = m_d\lambda$ (the condition for a diffraction minimum). Substituting $d = 2.5a$, we can combine these two conditions into the relationship $m_i = 2.5m_d$. This is satisfied for $m_i = \pm 5$ and $m_d = \pm 2$ (the fifth interference maximum is missing because it coincides with the second diffraction minimum), $m_i = \pm 10$ and $m_d = \pm 4$ (the tenth interference maximum is missing because it coincides with the fourth diffraction minimum), and so on.

36.5 Answer: (i) As described in the text, the resolving power needed is $R = Nm = 1000$. In the first order $(m = 1)$ we need $N = 1000$ slits, but in the fourth order $(m = 4)$ we need only $N = R/m = 1000/4 = 250$ slits. (These numbers are only approximate because of the arbitrary nature of our criterion for resolution and because real gratings always have slight imperfections in the shapes and spacings of the slits.)

36.6 Answer: no The angular position of the mth maximum is given by Eq. (36.16), $2d\sin\theta = m\lambda$. With $d = 0.200\text{ nm}$, $\lambda = 0.100\text{ nm}$, and $m = 5$, this gives $\sin\theta = m\lambda/2d = (5)(0.100\text{ nm})/(2)(0.200\text{ nm}) = 1.25$. Since the sine function can never be greater than 1, this means that there is no solution to this equation and the $m = 5$ maximum does not appear.

36.7 Answer: (iii), (ii), (iv), (i) Rayleigh's criterion combined with Eq. (36.17) shows that the smaller the value of the ratio λ/D, the better the resolving power of a telescope of diameter D. For the four telescopes, this ratio is equal to (i) $(21\text{ cm})/(100\text{ m}) = (0.21\text{ m})/(100\text{ m}) = 2.1 \times 10^{-3}$; (ii) $(500\text{ nm})/(2.0\text{ m}) = (5.0 \times 10^{-7}\text{ m})/(2.0\text{ m}) = 2.5 \times 10^{-7}$; (iii) $(100\text{ nm})/(1.0\text{ m}) = (1.0 \times 10^{-7}\text{ m})/(1.0\text{ m}) = 1.0 \times 10^{-7}$; (iv) $(10\ \mu\text{m})/(2.0\text{ m}) = (1.0 \times 10^{-5}\text{ m})/(2.0\text{ m}) = 5.0 \times 10^{-6}$.

Bridging Problem

Answers: 1.501×10^7 m/s or 5.00% of c; away from us

APPENDIX A

THE INTERNATIONAL SYSTEM OF UNITS

The Système International d'Unités, abbreviated SI, is the system developed by the General Conference on Weights and Measures and adopted by nearly all the industrial nations of the world. The following material is adapted from the National Institute of Standards and Technology (**http://physics.nist.gov/cuu).**

Quantity	Name of unit	Symbol	
	SI base units		
length	meter	m	
mass	kilogram	kg	
time	second	s	
electric current	ampere	A	
thermodynamic temperature	kelvin	K	
amount of substance	mole	mol	
luminous intensity	candela	cd	
	SI derived units		**Equivalent units**
area	square meter	m^2	
volume	cubic meter	m^3	
frequency	hertz	Hz	s^{-1}
mass density (density)	kilogram per cubic meter	kg/m^3	
speed, velocity	meter per second	m/s	
angular velocity	radian per second	rad/s	
acceleration	meter per second squared	m/s^2	
angular acceleration	radian per second squared	rad/s^2	
force	newton	N	$kg \cdot m/s^2$
pressure (mechanical stress)	pascal	Pa	N/m^2
kinematic viscosity	square meter per second	m^2/s	
dynamic viscosity	newton-second per square meter	$N \cdot s/m^2$	
work, energy, quantity of heat	joule	J	$N \cdot m$
power	watt	W	J/s
quantity of electricity	coulomb	C	$A \cdot s$
potential difference, electromotive force	volt	V	J/C, W/A
electric field strength	volt per meter	V/m	N/C
electric resistance	ohm	Ω	V/A
capacitance	farad	F	$A \cdot s/V$
magnetic flux	weber	Wb	$V \cdot s$
inductance	henry	H	$V \cdot s/A$
magnetic flux density	tesla	T	Wb/m^2
magnetic field strength	ampere per meter	A/m	
magnetomotive force	ampere	A	
luminous flux	lumen	lm	$cd \cdot sr$
luminance	candela per square meter	cd/m^2	
illuminance	lux	lx	lm/m^2
wave number	1 per meter	m^{-1}	
entropy	joule per kelvin	J/K	
specific heat capacity	joule per kilogram-kelvin	$J/kg \cdot K$	
thermal conductivity	watt per meter-kelvin	$W/m \cdot K$	

Quantity	Name of unit	Symbol	Equivalent units
radiant intensity	watt per steradian	W/sr	
activity (of a radioactive source)	becquerel	Bq	s^{-1}
radiation dose	gray	Gy	J/kg
radiation dose equivalent	sievert	Sv	J/kg
	SI supplementary units		
plane angle	radian	rad	
solid angle	steradian	sr	

Definitions of SI Units

meter (m) The *meter* is the length equal to the distance traveled by light, in vacuum, in a time of 1/299,792,458 second.

kilogram (kg) The *kilogram* is the unit of mass; it is equal to the mass of the international prototype of the kilogram. (The international prototype of the kilogram is a particular cylinder of platinum-iridium alloy that is preserved in a vault at Sévres, France, by the International Bureau of Weights and Measures.)

second (s) The *second* is the duration of 9,192,631,770 periods of the radiation corresponding to the transition between the two hyperfine levels of the ground state of the cesium-133 atom.

ampere (A) The *ampere* is that constant current that, if maintained in two straight parallel conductors of infinite length, of negligible circular cross section, and placed 1 meter apart in vacuum, would produce between these conductors a force equal to 2×10^{-7} newton per meter of length.

kelvin (K) The *kelvin*, unit of thermodynamic temperature, is the fraction 1/273.16 of the thermodynamic temperature of the triple point of water.

ohm (Ω) The *ohm* is the electric resistance between two points of a conductor when a constant difference of potential of 1 volt, applied between these two points, produces in this conductor a current of 1 ampere, this conductor not being the source of any electromotive force.

coulomb (C) The *coulomb* is the quantity of electricity transported in 1 second by a current of 1 ampere.

candela (cd) The *candela* is the luminous intensity, in a given direction, of a source that emits monochromatic radiation of frequency 540×10^{12} hertz and that has a radiant intensity in that direction of 1/683 watt per steradian.

mole (mol) The *mole* is the amount of substance of a system that contains as many elementary entities as there are carbon atoms in 0.012 kg of carbon 12. The elementary entities must be specified and may be atoms, molecules, ions, electrons, other particles, or specified groups of such particles.

newton (N) The *newton* is that force that gives to a mass of 1 kilogram an acceleration of 1 meter per second per second.

joule (J) The *joule* is the work done when the point of application of a constant force of 1 newton is displaced a distance of 1 meter in the direction of the force.

watt (W) The *watt* is the power that gives rise to the production of energy at the rate of 1 joule per second.

volt (V) The *volt* is the difference of electric potential between two points of a conducting wire carrying a constant current of 1 ampere, when the power dissipated between these points is equal to 1 watt.

weber (Wb) The *weber* is the magnetic flux that, linking a circuit of one turn, produces in it an electromotive force of 1 volt as it is reduced to zero at a uniform rate in 1 second.

lumen (lm) The *lumen* is the luminous flux emitted in a solid angle of 1 steradian by a uniform point source having an intensity of 1 candela.

farad (F) The *farad* is the capacitance of a capacitor between the plates of which there appears a difference of potential of 1 volt when it is charged by a quantity of electricity equal to 1 coulomb.

henry (H) The *henry* is the inductance of a closed circuit in which an electromotive force of 1 volt is produced when the electric current in the circuit varies uniformly at a rate of 1 ampere per second.

radian (rad) The *radian* is the plane angle between two radii of a circle that cut off on the circumference an arc equal in length to the radius.

steradian (sr) The *steradian* is the solid angle that, having its vertex in the center of a sphere, cuts off an area of the surface of the sphere equal to that of a square with sides of length equal to the radius of the sphere.

SI Prefixes To form the names of multiples and submultiples of SI units, apply the prefixes listed in Appendix F.

APPENDIX B

USEFUL MATHEMATICAL RELATIONS

Algebra

$$a^{-x} = \frac{1}{a^x} \qquad a^{(x+y)} = a^x a^y \qquad a^{(x-y)} = \frac{a^x}{a^y}$$

Logarithms: If $\log a = x$, then $a = 10^x$. $\log a + \log b = \log(ab)$ $\log a - \log b = \log(a/b)$ $\log(a^n) = n\log a$

If $\ln a = x$, then $a = e^x$. $\ln a + \ln b = \ln(ab)$ $\ln a - \ln b = \ln(a/b)$ $\ln(a^n) = n\ln a$

Quadratic formula: If $ax^2 + bx + c = 0$, $x = \dfrac{-b \pm \sqrt{b^2 - 4ac}}{2a}$.

Binomial Theorem

$$(a+b)^n = a^n + na^{n-1}b + \frac{n(n-1)a^{n-2}b^2}{2!} + \frac{n(n-1)(n-2)a^{n-3}b^3}{3!} + \cdots$$

Trigonometry

In the right triangle ABC, $x^2 + y^2 = r^2$.

Definitions of the trigonometric functions:

$\sin\alpha = y/r \qquad \cos\alpha = x/r \qquad \tan\alpha = y/x$

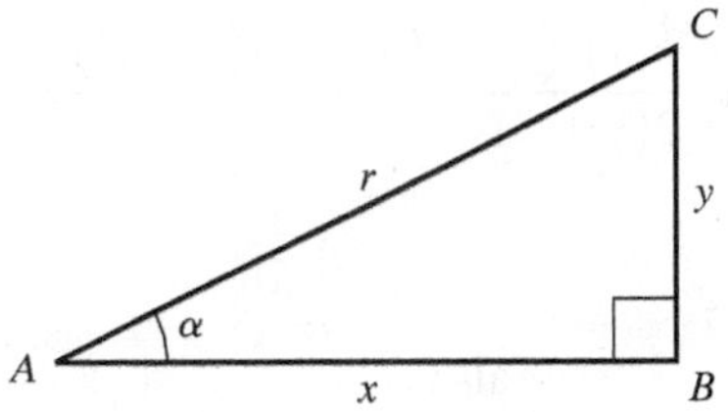

Identities:

$$\sin^2\alpha + \cos^2\alpha = 1 \qquad \tan\alpha = \frac{\sin\alpha}{\cos\alpha}$$

$$\sin 2\alpha = 2\sin\alpha\cos\alpha \qquad \cos 2\alpha = \cos^2\alpha - \sin^2\alpha = 2\cos^2\alpha - 1 = 1 - 2\sin^2\alpha$$

$$\sin\tfrac{1}{2}\alpha = \sqrt{\frac{1-\cos\alpha}{2}} \qquad \cos\tfrac{1}{2}\alpha = \sqrt{\frac{1+\cos\alpha}{2}}$$

$$\sin(-\alpha) = -\sin\alpha \qquad \sin(\alpha \pm \beta) = \sin\alpha\cos\beta \pm \cos\alpha\sin\beta$$

$$\cos(-\alpha) = \cos\alpha \qquad \cos(\alpha \pm \beta) = \cos\alpha\cos\beta \mp \sin\alpha\sin\beta$$

$$\sin(\alpha \pm \pi/2) = \pm\cos\alpha \qquad \sin\alpha + \sin\beta = 2\sin\tfrac{1}{2}(\alpha+\beta)\cos\tfrac{1}{2}(\alpha-\beta)$$

$$\cos(\alpha \pm \pi/2) = \mp\sin\alpha \qquad \cos\alpha + \cos\beta = 2\cos\tfrac{1}{2}(\alpha+\beta)\cos\tfrac{1}{2}(\alpha-\beta)$$

For *any* triangle $A'B'C'$ (not necessarily a right triangle) with sides a, b, and c and angles α, β, and γ:

Law of sines: $\dfrac{\sin\alpha}{a} = \dfrac{\sin\beta}{b} = \dfrac{\sin\gamma}{c}$

Law of cosines: $c^2 = a^2 + b^2 - 2ab\cos\gamma$

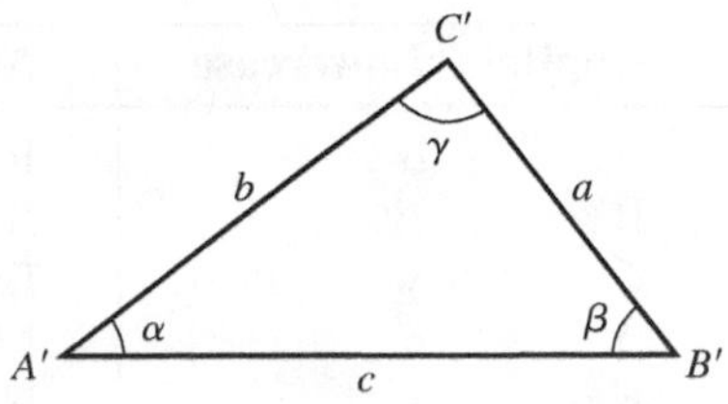

Geometry

Circumference of circle of radius r: $C = 2\pi r$

Area of circle of radius r: $A = \pi r^2$

Volume of sphere of radius r: $V = 4\pi r^3/3$

Surface area of sphere of radius r: $A = 4\pi r^2$

Volume of cylinder of radius r and height h: $V = \pi r^2 h$

Calculus

Derivatives:

$$\frac{d}{dx}x^n = nx^{n-1} \qquad \frac{d}{dx}\ln ax = \frac{1}{x} \qquad \frac{d}{dx}e^{ax} = ae^{ax}$$

$$\frac{d}{dx}\sin ax = a\cos ax \qquad \frac{d}{dx}\cos ax = -a\sin ax$$

Integrals:

$$\int x^n\,dx = \frac{x^{n+1}}{n+1} \quad (n \neq -1) \qquad \int \frac{dx}{x} = \ln x \qquad \int e^{ax}\,dx = \frac{1}{a}e^{ax}$$

$$\int \sin ax\,dx = -\frac{1}{a}\cos ax \qquad \int \cos ax\,dx = \frac{1}{a}\sin ax \qquad \int \frac{dx}{\sqrt{a^2 - x^2}} = \arcsin\frac{x}{a}$$

$$\int \frac{dx}{\sqrt{x^2 + a^2}} = \ln\left(x + \sqrt{x^2 + a^2}\right) \qquad \int \frac{dx}{x^2 + a^2} = \frac{1}{a}\arctan\frac{x}{a} \qquad \int \frac{dx}{(x^2 + a^2)^{3/2}} = \frac{1}{a^2}\frac{x}{\sqrt{x^2 + a^2}}$$

$$\int \frac{x\,dx}{(x^2 + a^2)^{3/2}} = -\frac{1}{\sqrt{x^2 + a^2}}$$

Power series (convergent for range of x shown):

$$(1 + x)^n = 1 + nx + \frac{n(n-1)x^2}{2!} + \frac{n(n-1)(n-2)}{3!}x^3 + \cdots \quad (|x| < 1)$$

$$\sin x = x - \frac{x^3}{3!} + \frac{x^5}{5!} - \frac{x^7}{7!} + \cdots \quad (\text{all } x)$$

$$\cos x = 1 - \frac{x^2}{2!} + \frac{x^4}{4!} - \frac{x^6}{6!} + \cdots \quad (\text{all } x)$$

$$\tan x = x + \frac{x^3}{3} + \frac{2x^2}{15} + \frac{17x^7}{315} + \cdots \quad (|x| < \pi/2)$$

$$e^x = 1 + x + \frac{x^2}{2!} + \frac{x^3}{3!} + \cdots \quad (\text{all } x)$$

$$\ln(1 + x) = x - \frac{x^2}{2} + \frac{x^3}{3} - \frac{x^4}{4} + \cdots \quad (|x| < 1)$$

APPENDIX C

THE GREEK ALPHABET

Name	Capital	Lowercase	Name	Capital	Lowercase	Name	Capital	Lowercase
Alpha	A	α	Iota	I	ι	Rho	P	ρ
Beta	B	β	Kappa	K	κ	Sigma	Σ	σ
Gamma	Γ	γ	Lambda	Λ	λ	Tau	T	τ
Delta	Δ	δ	Mu	M	μ	Upsilon	Υ	υ
Epsilon	E	ϵ	Nu	N	ν	Phi	Φ	ϕ
Zeta	Z	ζ	Xi	Ξ	ξ	Chi	X	χ
Eta	H	η	Omicron	O	o	Psi	Ψ	ψ
Theta	Θ	θ	Pi	Π	π	Omega	Ω	ω

APPENDIX D

PERIODIC TABLE OF THE ELEMENTS

Group / Period	1	2	3	4	5	6	7	8	9	10	11	12	13	14	15	16	17	18
1	1 **H** 1.008																	2 **He** 4.003
2	3 **Li** 6.941	4 **Be** 9.012											5 **B** 10.811	6 **C** 12.011	7 **N** 14.007	8 **O** 15.999	9 **F** 18.998	10 **Ne** 20.180
3	11 **Na** 22.990	12 **Mg** 24.305											13 **Al** 26.982	14 **Si** 28.086	15 **P** 30.974	16 **S** 32.065	17 **Cl** 35.453	18 **Ar** 39.948
4	19 **K** 39.098	20 **Ca** 40.078	21 **Sc** 44.956	22 **Ti** 47.867	23 **V** 50.942	24 **Cr** 51.996	25 **Mn** 54.938	26 **Fe** 55.845	27 **Co** 58.933	28 **Ni** 58.693	29 **Cu** 63.546	30 **Zn** 65.409	31 **Ga** 69.723	32 **Ge** 72.64	33 **As** 74.922	34 **Se** 78.96	35 **Br** 79.904	36 **Kr** 83.798
5	37 **Rb** 85.468	38 **Sr** 87.62	39 **Y** 88.906	40 **Zr** 91.224	41 **Nb** 92.906	42 **Mo** 95.94	43 **Tc** (98)	44 **Ru** 101.07	45 **Rh** 102.906	46 **Pd** 106.42	47 **Ag** 107.868	48 **Cd** 112.411	49 **In** 114.818	50 **Sn** 118.710	51 **Sb** 121.760	52 **Te** 127.60	53 **I** 126.904	54 **Xe** 131.293
6	55 **Cs** 132.905	56 **Ba** 137.327	71 **Lu** 174.967	72 **Hf** 178.49	73 **Ta** 180.948	74 **W** 183.84	75 **Re** 186.207	76 **Os** 190.23	77 **Ir** 192.217	78 **Pt** 195.078	79 **Au** 196.967	80 **Hg** 200.59	81 **Tl** 204.383	82 **Pb** 207.2	83 **Bi** 208.980	84 **Po** (209)	85 **At** (210)	86 **Rn** (222)
7	87 **Fr** (223)	88 **Ra** (226)	103 **Lr** (262)	104 **Rf** (261)	105 **Db** (262)	106 **Sg** (266)	107 **Bh** (264)	108 **Hs** (269)	109 **Mt** (268)	110 **Ds** (271)	111 **Rg** (272)	112 **Uub** (285)	113 **Uut** (284)	114 **Uuq** (289)	115 **Uup** (288)	116 **Uuh** (292)	117 **Uus** (294)	118 **Uuo**

Lanthanoids	57 **La** 138.905	58 **Ce** 140.116	59 **Pr** 140.908	60 **Nd** 144.24	61 **Pm** (145)	62 **Sm** 150.36	63 **Eu** 151.964	64 **Gd** 157.25	65 **Tb** 158.925	66 **Dy** 162.500	67 **Ho** 164.930	68 **Er** 167.259	69 **Tm** 168.934	70 **Yb** 173.04
Actinoids	89 **Ac** (227)	90 **Th** (232)	91 **Pa** (231)	92 **U** (238)	93 **Np** (237)	94 **Pu** (244)	95 **Am** (243)	96 **Cm** (247)	97 **Bk** (247)	98 **Cf** (251)	99 **Es** (252)	100 **Fm** (257)	101 **Md** (258)	102 **No** (259)

For each element the average atomic mass of the mixture of isotopes occurring in nature is shown. For elements having no stable isotope, the approximate atomic mass of the longest-lived isotope is shown in parentheses. For elements that have been predicted but not yet confirmed, no atomic mass is given. All atomic masses are expressed in atomic mass units ($1\ u = 1.660538782(83) \times 10^{-27}$ kg), equivalent to grams per mole (g/mol).

APPENDIX E

UNIT CONVERSION FACTORS

Length
1 m = 100 cm = 1000 mm = 10^6 μm = 10^9 nm
1 km = 1000 m = 0.6214 mi
1 m = 3.281 ft = 39.37 in.
1 cm = 0.3937 in.
1 in. = 2.540 cm
1 ft = 30.48 cm
1 yd = 91.44 cm
1 mi = 5280 ft = 1.609 km
1 Å = 10^{-10} m = 10^{-8} cm = 10^{-1} nm
1 nautical mile = 6080 ft
1 light year = 9.461×10^{15} m

Area
1 cm^2 = 0.155 $in.^2$
1 m^2 = 10^4 cm^2 = 10.76 ft^2
1 $in.^2$ = 6.452 cm^2
1 ft^2 = 144 $in.^2$ = 0.0929 m^2

Volume
1 liter = 1000 cm^3 = 10^{-3} m^3 = 0.03531 ft^3 = 61.02 $in.^3$
1 ft^3 = 0.02832 m^3 = 28.32 liters = 7.477 gallons
1 gallon = 3.788 liters

Time
1 min = 60 s
1 h = 3600 s
1 d = 86,400 s
1 y = 365.24 d = 3.156×10^7 s

Angle
1 rad = 57.30° = 180°/π
1° = 0.01745 rad = π/180 rad
1 revolution = 360° = 2π rad
1 rev/min (rpm) = 0.1047 rad/s

Speed
1 m/s = 3.281 ft/s
1 ft/s = 0.3048 m/s
1 mi/min = 60 mi/h = 88 ft/s
1 km/h = 0.2778 m/s = 0.6214 mi/h
1 mi/h = 1.466 ft/s = 0.4470 m/s = 1.609 km/h
1 furlong/fortnight = 1.662×10^{-4} m/s

Acceleration
1 m/s^2 = 100 cm/s^2 = 3.281 ft/s^2
1 cm/s^2 = 0.01 m/s^2 = 0.03281 ft/s^2
1 ft/s^2 = 0.3048 m/s^2 = 30.48 cm/s^2
1 mi/h · s = 1.467 ft/s^2

Mass
1 kg = 10^3 g = 0.0685 slug
1 g = 6.85×10^{-5} slug
1 slug = 14.59 kg
1 u = 1.661×10^{-27} kg
1 kg has a weight of 2.205 lb when g = 9.80 m/s^2

Force
1 N = 10^5 dyn = 0.2248 lb
1 lb = 4.448 N = 4.448×10^5 dyn

Pressure
1 Pa = 1 N/m^2 = 1.450×10^{-4} $lb/in.^2$ = 0.209 lb/ft^2
1 bar = 10^5 Pa
1 $lb/in.^2$ = 6895 Pa
1 lb/ft^2 = 47.88 Pa
1 atm = 1.013×10^5 Pa = 1.013 bar
= 14.7 $lb/in.^2$ = 2117 lb/ft^2
1 mm Hg = 1 torr = 133.3 Pa

Energy
1 J = 10^7 ergs = 0.239 cal
1 cal = 4.186 J (based on 15° calorie)
1 ft · lb = 1.356 J
1 Btu = 1055 J = 252 cal = 778 ft · lb
1 eV = 1.602×10^{-19} J
1 kWh = 3.600×10^6 J

Mass–Energy Equivalence
1 kg ↔ 8.988×10^{16} J
1 u ↔ 931.5 MeV
1 eV ↔ 1.074×10^{-9} u

Power
1 W = 1 J/s
1 hp = 746 W = 550 ft · lb/s
1 Btu/h = 0.293 W

APPENDIX F

NUMERICAL CONSTANTS

Fundamental Physical Constants*

Name	Symbol	Value
Speed of light in vacuum	c	2.99792458×10^8 m/s
Magnitude of charge of electron	e	$1.602176487(40) \times 10^{-19}$ C
Gravitational constant	G	$6.67428(67) \times 10^{-11}\ \mathrm{N \cdot m^2/kg^2}$
Planck's constant	h	$6.62606896(33) \times 10^{-34}\ \mathrm{J \cdot s}$
Boltzmann constant	k	$1.3806504(24) \times 10^{-23}$ J/K
Avogadro's number	N_A	$6.02214179(30) \times 10^{23}$ molecules/mol
Gas constant	R	$8.314472(15)\ \mathrm{J/mol \cdot K}$
Mass of electron	m_e	$9.10938215(45) \times 10^{-31}$ kg
Mass of proton	m_p	$1.672621637(83) \times 10^{-27}$ kg
Mass of neutron	m_n	$1.674927211(84) \times 10^{-27}$ kg
Permeability of free space	μ_0	$4\pi \times 10^{-7}\ \mathrm{Wb/A \cdot m}$
Permittivity of free space	$\epsilon_0 = 1/\mu_0 c^2$	$8.854187817\ldots \times 10^{-12}\ \mathrm{C^2/N \cdot m^2}$
	$1/4\pi\epsilon_0$	$8.987551787\ldots \times 10^9\ \mathrm{N \cdot m^2/C^2}$

Other Useful Constants*

Mechanical equivalent of heat		4.186 J/cal (15° calorie)
Standard atmospheric pressure	1 atm	1.01325×10^5 Pa
Absolute zero	0 K	−273.15°C
Electron volt	1 eV	$1.602176487(40) \times 10^{-19}$ J
Atomic mass unit	1 u	$1.660538782(83) \times 10^{-27}$ kg
Electron rest energy	$m_e c^2$	0.510998910(13) MeV
Volume of ideal gas (0°C and 1 atm)		22.413996(39) liter/mol
Acceleration due to gravity (standard)	g	$9.80665\ \mathrm{m/s^2}$

*Source: National Institute of Standards and Technology (**http://physics.nist.gov/cuu**). Numbers in parentheses show the uncertainty in the final digits of the main number; for example, the number 1.6454(21) means 1.6454 ± 0.0021. Values shown without uncertainties are exact.

Astronomical Data[†]

Body	Mass (kg)	Radius (m)	Orbit radius (m)	Orbit period
Sun	1.99×10^{30}	6.96×10^{8}	—	—
Moon	7.35×10^{22}	1.74×10^{6}	3.84×10^{8}	27.3 d
Mercury	3.30×10^{23}	2.44×10^{6}	5.79×10^{10}	88.0 d
Venus	4.87×10^{24}	6.05×10^{6}	1.08×10^{11}	224.7 d
Earth	5.97×10^{24}	6.38×10^{6}	1.50×10^{11}	365.3 d
Mars	6.42×10^{23}	3.40×10^{6}	2.28×10^{11}	687.0 d
Jupiter	1.90×10^{27}	6.91×10^{7}	7.78×10^{11}	11.86 y
Saturn	5.68×10^{26}	6.03×10^{7}	1.43×10^{12}	29.45 y
Uranus	8.68×10^{25}	2.56×10^{7}	2.87×10^{12}	84.02 y
Neptune	1.02×10^{26}	2.48×10^{7}	4.50×10^{12}	164.8 y
Pluto[‡]	1.31×10^{22}	1.15×10^{6}	5.91×10^{12}	247.9 y

[†]Source: NASA Jet Propulsion Laboratory Solar System Dynamics Group **(http://ssd.jpl.nasa.gov)**, and P. Kenneth Seidelmann, ed., ***Explanatory Supplement to the Astronomical Almanac*** (University Science Books, Mill Valley, CA, 1992), pp. 704–706. For each body, "radius" is its radius at its equator and "orbit radius" is its average distance from the sun or (for the moon) from the earth.

[‡]In August 2006, the International Astronomical Union reclassified Pluto and other small objects that orbit the sun as "dwarf planets."

Prefixes for Powers of 10

Power of ten	Prefix	Abbreviation	Pronunciation
10^{-24}	yocto-	y	*yoc*-toe
10^{-21}	zepto-	z	*zep*-toe
10^{-18}	atto-	a	*at*-toe
10^{-15}	femto-	f	*fem*-toe
10^{-12}	pico-	p	*pee*-koe
10^{-9}	nano-	n	*nan*-oe
10^{-6}	micro-	μ	*my*-crow
10^{-3}	milli-	m	*mil*-i
10^{-2}	centi-	c	*cen*-ti
10^{3}	kilo-	k	*kil*-oe
10^{6}	mega-	M	*meg*-a
10^{9}	giga-	G	*jig*-a or *gig*-a
10^{12}	tera-	T	*ter*-a
10^{15}	peta-	P	*pet*-a
10^{18}	exa-	E	*ex*-a
10^{21}	zetta-	Z	*zet*-a
10^{24}	yotta-	Y	*yot*-a

Examples:

1 femtometer $= 1\ \text{fm} = 10^{-15}\ \text{m}$

1 picosecond $= 1\ \text{ps} = 10^{-12}\ \text{s}$

1 nanocoulomb $= 1\ \text{nC} = 10^{-9}\ \text{C}$

1 microkelvin $= 1\ \mu\text{K} = 10^{-6}\ \text{K}$

1 millivolt $= 1\ \text{mV} = 10^{-3}\ \text{V}$

1 kilopascal $= 1\ \text{kPa} = 10^{3}\ \text{Pa}$

1 megawatt $= 1\ \text{MW} = 10^{6}\ \text{W}$

1 gigahertz $= 1\ \text{GHz} = 10^{9}\ \text{Hz}$

ANSWERS TO ODD-NUMBERED PROBLEMS

Chapter 12

12.1 41.8 N, no
12.3 7020 kg/m^3, yes
12.5 1.6
12.7 61.6 N
12.9 a) 1.86×10^6 Pa b) 184 m
12.11 0.581 m
12.13 a) 1.90×10^4 Pa
b) causes additional force on the walls of the blood vessels
12.15 2.8 m
12.17 6.0×10^4 Pa
12.19 2.27×10^5 N
12.21 a) 636 Pa b) (i) 1170 Pa (ii) 1170 Pa
12.23 10.9
12.25 0.107 m
12.27 6.43×10^{-4} m^3, 2.78×10^3 kg/m^3
12.29 a) $\rho < \rho_{\text{fluid}}$
c) above: $1 - \dfrac{\rho}{\rho_{\text{fluid}}}$, submerged: $\dfrac{\rho}{\rho_{\text{fluid}}}$
d) 32%
12.31 a) 116 Pa b) 921 Pa c) 0.822 kg, 822 kg/m^3
12.33 1910 kg/m^3
12.35 9.6 m/s
12.37 a) 17.0 m/s b) 0.317 m
12.39 0.956 m
12.41 28.4 m/s
12.43 1.47×10^5 Pa
12.45 2.03×10^4 Pa
12.47 2.25×10^5 Pa
12.49 $1.19D$
12.51 a) $(p_0 - p)\pi \dfrac{D^2}{4}$ b) 776 N
12.53 a) 5.9×10^5 N b) 1.8×10^5 N
12.55 c) independent of surface area
12.57 0.964 cm, rises
12.59 a) 1470 Pa b) 13.9 cm
12.61 9.8×10^6 kg, yes
12.63 a) 0.30 b) 0.70
12.65 3.50×10^{-4} m^3, 3.95 kg
12.67 a) 8.27×10^3 m^3 b) 83.8 kN
12.69 2.05 m
12.71 a) $H/2$ b) H
12.73 0.116 kg
12.75 33.4 N
12.77 b) 12.2 N c) 11.8 N
12.79 b) 2.52×10^{-4} m^3, 0.124
12.81 5.57×10^{-4} m
12.83 a) $1 - \dfrac{\rho_B}{\rho_L}$ b) $\left(\dfrac{\rho_L - \rho_B}{\rho_L - \rho_w}\right)L$ c) 4.60 cm
12.85 a) al/g b) $\omega^2 l^2/2g$
12.89 a) $2\sqrt{h(H-h)}$ b) h
12.91 a) 0.200 m^3/s b) 6.97×10^4 Pa
12.93 $3h_1$
12.95 a) $r = \dfrac{r_0\sqrt{v_0}}{(v_0^2 + 2gy)^{1/4}}$ b) 1.10 m
12.97 a) 80.4 N

Chapter 14

14.1 a) 2.15 ms, 2930 rad/s
b) 2.00×10^4 Hz, 1.26×10^5 rad/s
c) 4.3×10^{14} Hz $\leq f \leq 7.5 \times 10^{14}$ Hz;
1.3×10^{-15} s $\leq T \leq 2.3 \times 10^{-15}$ s
d) 2.0×10^{-7} s, 3.1×10^7 rad/s

14.3 5530 rad/s, 1.14 ms

14.5 0.0500 s

14.7 a) 0.167 s b) 37.7 rad/s c) 0.0844 kg

14.9 a) 0.150 s b) 0.0750 s

14.11 a) 0.98 m b) $\pi/2$ rad
c) $x = (-0.98 \text{ m}) \sin[(12.2 \text{ rad/s})t]$

14.13 a) -2.71 m/s²
b) $x = (1.46 \text{ cm}) \cos[(15.7 \text{ rad/s})t + 0.715 \text{ rad}]$,
$v_x = (-22.9 \text{ cm/s}) \sin[(15.7 \text{ rad/s})t + 0.715 \text{ rad}]$,
$a_x = (-359 \text{ cm/s}^2) \cos[(15.7 \text{ rad/s})t + 0.715 \text{ rad}]$

14.15 120 kg

14.17 a) 0.253 kg b) 1.21 cm
c) 3.03 N

14.19 a) 1.51 s b) 26.0 N/m
c) 30.8 cm/s d) 1.92 N
e) -0.0125 m, 30.4 cm/s, 0.216 m/s²
f) 0.324 N

14.21 a) $x = (0.0030 \text{ m}) \cos[(2760 \text{ rad/s})t]$
b) 8.3 m/s, 2.3×10^4 m/s²
c) $da_x/dt = (6.3 \times 10^7 \text{ m/s}^3) \times \sin[(2760 \text{ rad/s})t]$, 6.3×10^7 m/s³

14.23 127 m/s²

14.25 a) 1.48 m/s b) 2.96×10^{-5} J

14.27 a) 1.20 m/s b) 1.11 m/s
c) 36 m/s² d) 13.5 m/s² e) 0.36 J

14.29 $3M$, $^3/_4$

14.31 0.240 m

14.33 $A/\sqrt{2}$

14.35 a) 0.0778 m b) 1.28 Hz c) 0.624 m/s

14.37 a) 4.06 cm b) 1.21 m/s c) 29.8 rad/s

14.39 b) 23.9 cm, 1.45 Hz

14.41 a) 2.7×10^{-8} kg · m²
b) 4.3×10^{-6} N · m/rad

14.43 0.0512 kg · m²

14.45 a) 0.25 s b) 0.25 s

14.47 0.407 swings per second

14.49 10.7 m/s²

14.51 a) 2.84 s b) 2.89 s
c) 2.89 s, -2%

14.53 0.129 kg · m²

14.55 A: $2\pi\sqrt{\frac{L}{g}}$, B: $\frac{2\sqrt{2}}{3}\left(2\pi\sqrt{\frac{L}{g}}\right)$, pendulum A

14.57 A: $2\pi\sqrt{\frac{L}{g}}$, B: $\sqrt{\frac{11}{10}}\left(2\pi\sqrt{\frac{L}{g}}\right)$, pendulum B

14.59 a) 0.393 Hz b) 1.73 kg/s

14.61 a) A b) $-Ab/2m$
c) $A\left(\frac{b^2}{2m^2} - \frac{k}{m}\right)$; negative if $b < \sqrt{2km}$, zero if $b = \sqrt{2km}$, positive if $b > \sqrt{2km}$

14.63 a) kg/s
c) (i) $5.0\frac{F_{max}}{k}$ (ii) $2.5\frac{F_{max}}{k}$

14.65 0.353 m

14.67 a) 1.11×10^4 m/s² b) 5.00×10^3 N
c) 23.6 m/s, 125 J d) 37.5 kW
e) 1.21×10^4 N, 36.7 m/s, 302 J, 141 kW

14.69 a) none of them change
b) $^1/_4$ as great c) $^1/_2$ as great
d) $1/\sqrt{5}$ as great
e) potential energy is the same, kinetic energy is 1/5 as great

14.71 a) 24.4 cm b) 0.221 s c) 1.19 m/s

14.73 a) 0.373 Hz, 0.426 m, 2.68 s b) 1.34 s

14.75 2.00 m

14.77 a) 0.107 m b) 2.42 s

14.79 $(0.921)\left(\frac{1}{2\pi}\sqrt{\frac{g}{L}}\right)$

14.81 a) 1.49 s b) -2.12×10^{-4} s per s, shorter
c) 0.795 s

14.83 a) 0.150 m/s b) 0.112 m/s² downward
c) 0.700 s d) 4.38 m

14.85 a) 2.6 m/s b) 0.21 m c) 0.49 s

14.87 9.08×10^{24} kg

14.89 1.17 s

14.91 0.505 s

14.93 c) -7.57×10^{-19} J e) 8.39×10^{12} Hz

14.95 0.705 Hz, 14.5°

14.97 $2\pi\sqrt{\frac{M}{3k}}$

14.99 $\frac{1}{4\pi}\sqrt{\frac{6g}{\sqrt{2}L}}$

14.101 a) $k_1 + k_2$ b) $k_1 + k_2$
c) $\frac{k_1 k_2}{k_1 + k_2}$ d) $\sqrt{2}$

14.103 a) $Mv^2/6$ c) $\omega = \sqrt{\frac{3k}{M}}$, $M' = M/3$

Chapter 15

15.1 a) 0.439 m, 1.28 ms
b) 0.219 m

15.3 220 m/s = 800 km/h

15.5 a) 1.7 cm to 17 m
b) 4.3×10^{14} Hz to 7.5×10^{14} Hz
c) 1.5 cm d) 6.4 cm

15.7 a) 25.0 Hz, 0.0400 s, 19.6 rad/m
b) $y(x, t) = (0.0700 \text{ m}) \cos[(19.6 \text{ m}^{-1})x + (157 \text{ rad/s})t]$ c) 4.95 cm
d) 0.0050 s

15.9 a) yes b) yes c) no
d) $v_y = \omega A \cos(kx + \omega t)$,
$a_y = -\omega^2 A \sin(kx + \omega t)$

15.11 a) 4 mm b) 0.040 s c) 0.14 m, 3.5 m/s
d) 0.24 m, 6.0 m/s e) no

15.13 b) $+x$-direction

15.15 a) 16.3 m/s b) 0.136 m
c) both increase by a factor of $\sqrt{2}$

15.17 0.337 kg

15.19 a) 18.6 N b) 29.1 m/s

15.21 a) 10.0 m/s b) 0.250 m
c) $y(x, t) = (3.00 \text{ cm}) \cos[\pi(8.00 \text{ rad/m})x - (80.0\pi \text{ rad/s})t]$ d) 1890 m/s² e) yes

15.23 4.51 mm

15.25 a) 95 km b) 0.25 μW/m²
c) 110 kW

15.27 a) 0.050 W/m² b) 22 kJ

15.29 9.48×10^{27} W

15.37 a) $(1.33 \text{ m})n$, $n = 0, 1, 2, \ldots$
b) $(1.33 \text{ m})(n + {}^1/_2)$, $n = 0, 1, 2, \ldots$

15.41 a) 96.0 m/s b) 461 N
c) 1.13 m/s, 426 m/s²

15.43 b) 2.80 cm c) 277 cm
d) 185 cm, 7.96 Hz, 0.126 s, 1470 cm/s
e) 280 cm/s
f) $y(x, t) = (5.60 \text{ cm}) \times \sin[(0.0906 \text{ rad/cm})x] \sin[(133 \text{ rad/s})t]$

15.45 a) $y(x, t) = (4.60 \text{ mm}) \times \sin[(6.98 \text{ rad/m})x] \sin[(742 \text{ rad/s})t]$
b) 3rd harmonic c) 39.4 Hz

15.47 a) 45.0 cm b) no

15.49 a) 311 m/s b) 246 Hz
c) 245 Hz, 1.40 m

15.51 a) 20.0 Hz, 126 rad/s, 3.49 rad/m
b) $y(x, t) = (2.50 \times 10^{-3} \text{ m}) \times \cos[(3.49 \text{ rad/m})x - (126 \text{ rad/s})t]$
c) $y(0, t) = (2.50 \times 10^{-3} \text{ m}) \times \cos[(126 \text{ rad/s})t]$
d) $y(1.35 \text{ m}, t) = (2.50 \times 10^{-3} \text{ m}) \times \cos[(126 \text{ rad/s})t - 3\pi/2 \text{ rad}]$
e) 0.315 m/s
f) -2.50×10^{-3} m, 0

15.53 a) $\frac{7L}{2}\sqrt{\frac{\mu_1}{F}}$ b) no

15.55 a) $\frac{2\pi A}{\lambda}\sqrt{\frac{FL}{M}}$ b) increase F by a factor of 4

15.57 a) $\frac{4\pi^2 F \Delta x}{\lambda^2}$

15.59 32.4 Hz

15.61 1.83 m

15.63 330 Hz (copper), 447 Hz (aluminum)

15.65 c) C/B

15.67 b) ω must be decreased by a factor of $1/\sqrt{2}$, k must be decreased by a factor of $1/\sqrt{8}$

15.69 a) 7.07 cm b) 0.400 kW

15.71 d) $P(x, t) = -Fk\omega A^2 \sin^2(kx + \omega t)$

15.73 $(0.800 \text{ Hz})n$, $n = 1, 2, 3, \ldots$

15.75 c) $2A$, $2A\omega$, $2A\omega^2$

15.77 233 N

15.79 a) 0, L b) 0, $L/2$, L d) no

15.81 1780 kg/m³

15.83 a) $r = 0.640$ mm, $L = 0.40$ m
b) 380 Hz

15.85 b) $u_k = \frac{1}{2}\mu\omega^2 A^2 \sin^2(kx - \omega t)$
e) $u_p = \frac{1}{2}Fk^2 A^2 \sin^2(kx - \omega t)$

Chapter 16

16.1 a) 0.344 m b) 1.2×10^{-5} m
c) 6.9 m, 50 Hz
16.3 a) 7.78 Pa b) 77.8 Pa c) 778 Pa
16.5 a) 90 m b) 102 kHz c) 1.4 cm
d) 4.4 mm to 8.8 mm e) 6.2 MHz
16.7 90.8 m
16.9 81.4°C
16.11 0.208 s
16.13 a) 5.5×10^{-15} J b) 0.074 mm/s
16.15 a) 9.44×10^{-11} m, 0.434 m
b) 5.66×10^{-9} m, 0.100 m
16.17 a) 1.95 Pa b) 4.58×10^{-3} W/m^2
c) 96.6 dB
16.19 a) 4.4×10^{-12} W/m^2 b) 6.4 dB
c) 5.8×10^{-11} m
16.21 14.0 dB
16.23 a) 2.0×10^{-7} W/m^2 b) 6.0 m c) 290 m
16.25 a) *fundamental:* displacement node at 0.60 m, pressure nodes at 0 and 1.20 m; *first overtone:* displacement nodes at 0.30 m and 0.90 m, pressure nodes at 0, 0.60 m, 1.20 m; *second overtone:* displacement nodes at 0.20 m, 0.60 m, 1.00 m, pressure nodes at 0, 0.40 m, 0.80 m, 1.20 m
b) *fundamental:* displacement node at 0, pressure node at 1.20 m; *first overtone:* displacement nodes at 0 and 0.80 m, pressure nodes at 0.40 m and 1.20 m; *second overtone:* displacement nodes at 0, 0.48 m, 0.96 m, pressure nodes at 0.24 m, 0.72 m, 1.20 m
16.27 506 Hz, 1517 Hz, 2529 Hz
16.29 a) 767 Hz b) no
16.31 a) 614 Hz b) 1230 Hz
16.33 a) 172 Hz b) 86 Hz
16.35 0.125 m
16.37 destructive
16.39 a) 433 Hz b) loosen
16.41 1.3 Hz
16.43 780 m/s
16.45 a) 375 Hz b) 371 Hz c) 4 Hz
16.47 a) 0.25 m/s b) 0.91 m
16.49 19.8 m/s
16.51 a) 1910 Hz b) 0.188 m
16.53 0.0950*c*, toward us
16.55 a) 36.0° b) 2.23 s
16.57 b) 0.68%
16.59 a) 1.00 b) 8.00
c) 4.73×10^{-8} m = 47.3 nm
16.61 b) $3f_0$
16.63 flute harmonic 3*N* resonates with string harmonic 4*N*, *N* = 1, 3, 5, . . .
16.65 a) stopped b) 7th and 9th c) 0.439 m
16.67 a) 375 m/s b) 1.39 c) 0.8 cm
16.69 1.27
16.71 a) 548 Hz b) 652 Hz
16.73 a) 2186 Hz, 0.157 m b) 2920 Hz, 0.118 m
c) 734 Hz
16.75 a) 0.0674 m b) 147 Hz
16.77 b) 2.0 m/s
16.79 a) 1.2×10^6 m/s
b) 3.6×10^{16} m = 3.8 ly
c) 5200 ly, about 4100 BCE
16.81 a) $f_0\left(\frac{2v_w}{v - v_w}\right)$ b) $f_0\left(\frac{2v_w}{v + v_w}\right)$
16.83 d) 9.69 cm/s, 667 m/s^2

Chapter 32

32.1 a) 1.28 s b) 8.15×10^{13} km
32.3 13.3 nT, $+y$-direction
32.5 3.0×10^{18} Hz, 3.3×10^{-19} s, 6.3×10^{10} rad/m
32.7 a) 6.94×10^{14} Hz b) 375 V/m c) $E(x, t) = (375\ \text{V/m}) \cos[(1.45 \times 10^7\ \text{rad/m})x - (4.36 \times 10^{15}\ \text{rad/s})t]$, $B(x, t) = (1.25\ \mu\text{T}) \cos[(1.45 \times 10^7\ \text{rad/m})x - (4.36 \times 10^{15}\ \text{rad/s})t]$
32.9 a) (i) 60 kHz (ii) 6.0×10^{13} Hz (iii) 6.0×10^{16} Hz b) (i) 4.62×10^{-14} m = 4.62×10^{-5} nm (ii) 508 m = 5.08×10^{11} nm
32.11 a) $+y$-direction b) 0.149 mm c) $\vec{B} = (1.03\ \text{mT})\hat{\imath} \cos[(4.22 \times 10^4\ \text{rad/m})y - (1.265 \times 10^{13}\ \text{rad/s})t]$
32.13 a) 361 m b) 0.0174 rad/m c) 5.22×10^6 rad/s d) 0.0144 V/m
32.15 a) 0.381 μm b) 0.526 μm c) 1.38 d) 1.90
32.17 a) 330 W/m² b) 500 V/m, 1.7 μT
32.19 a) 11 μW/m² b) 0.30 nT c) 840 W
32.21 2.5×10^{25} W
32.23 12.0 V/m, 40.0 nT
32.25 850 kW
32.27 a) 0.18 mW b) 274 V/m, 0.913 μT c) 0.18 mJ/s d) 0.010 W/cm²
32.29 a) 637 W/m² b) 693 V/m, 2.31 μT c) 2.12 μJ/m³
32.31 a) 30.5 cm b) 2.46 GHz c) 2.11 GHz
32.33 a) 7.10 mm b) 3.55 mm c) 1.56×10^8 m/s
32.35 a) 4.38 mm b) 4.38 mm c) 4.38 mm
32.37 a) 0.375 mJ b) 4.08 mPa c) 604 nm, 3.70×10^{14} Hz d) 30.3 kV/m, 101 μT
32.39 a) 71.6 MW/m² b) 232 kV/m, 774 μT c) 35.8 MW/m² d) 637 W/m²
32.41 a) 0.00602 W/m² b) 2.13 V/m, 7.10 nT c) 1.20 pN, no
32.43 a) 840 V/m, 2.80 μT b) 1.56 μJ/m³ for each c) 15.3 pJ
32.45 a) at $r = R$: 64 MW/m², 0.21 Pa; at $r = R/2$: 260 MW/m², 0.85 Pa b) no
32.47 3.89×10^{-13} rad/s²
32.49 a) $\rho I/\pi a^2$, in the direction of the current b) $\mu_0 I/2\pi a$, counterclockwise if the current is out of the page c) $\dfrac{\rho I^2}{2\pi^2 a^3}$, radially inward d) $\dfrac{\rho l I^2}{\pi a^2} = I^2 R$
32.51 a) 23.6 h b) throw it
32.53 a) 9.75×10^{-15} W/m² b) 2.71 μV/m, 9.03×10^{-15} T, 67.3 ms c) 3.25×10^{-23} Pa d) 0.190 m
32.55 a) $\dfrac{4\rho G\pi M R^3}{3r^2}$ b) $\dfrac{LR^2}{4cr^2}$ c) 0.19 μm, no
32.57 b) 1.39×10^{-11} c) 2.54×10^{-8}

Chapter 33

33.1 39.4°
33.3 a) 2.04×10^8 m/s b) 442 nm
33.5 a) 1.55 b) 550 nm
33.7 a) 47.5° b) 66.0°
33.9 2.51×10^8 m/s
33.11 a) 2.34 b) 82°
33.13 a) f, $n\lambda$, nv b) f, $(n/n')\lambda$, $(n/n')v$
33.15 71.8°
33.17 a) 51.3° b) 33.6°
33.19 a) 58.1° b) 22.8°
33.21 1.77
33.23 462 nm
33.25 0.6°
33.27 $0.375I_0$
33.29 a) $I_0/2$, $0.125I_0$, $0.0938I_0$ b) 0
33.31 a) 1.40 b) 35.5°
33.33 $\arccos\left(\dfrac{\cos\theta}{\sqrt{2}}\right)$ 2 linearly
33.35 6.38 W/m²
33.37 a) $I_0/2$, $0.250I_0$, $0.125I_0$, linearly polarized along the axis of each filter b) $I_0/$ polarized along the axis of the filter; 0
33.41 a) 46.7° b) 13.4°
33.43 72.1°
33.45 1.28
33.47 1.53
33.49 1.84
33.51 a) 48.6° b) 48.6°
33.53 39.1° 10.1 W m²
33.55 0.23°, about the same
33.59 b) 38.9° c) 5.0°
33.61 a) 35° b) I_p = 19.9 W/m², I_0 = /
33.63 23.3°
33.67 a) $\Delta = 2\theta_a^A - 6 \arcsin\left(\dfrac{\sin\theta_a^A}{n}\right) + 2\pi$ b) $\cos^2\theta_2 = \dfrac{n^2 - 1}{8}$ c) violet: $\theta_2 = 71.55°$, $\Delta = 233.2°$; red: $\theta_2 = 71.94°$, $\Delta = 230.1°$

Chapter 34

34.1 39.2 cm to the right of the mirror, 4.85 cm
34.3 9.0 cm, tip of the lead
34.5 b) 33.0 cm to the left of the vertex, 1.20 cm, inverted, real
34.7 0.213 mm
34.9 18.0 cm from the vertex, 0.50 cm, erect, virtual
34.11 b) 28.0 cm, inverted c) 8.00 cm
34.13 a) concave b) 2.50 cm, 5.00 cm
34.15 2.67 cm
34.17 3.30 m
34.19 a) at the center of the bowl, 1.33 b) no
34.21 39.5 cm
34.23 8.35 cm to the left of the vertex, 0.326 mm, erect
34.25 a) 107 cm to the right of the lens, 17.8 mm, real, inverted b) same as part (a)
34.27 a) 71.2 cm to the right of the lens b) −2.97
34.29 3.69 cm, 2.82 cm to the left of the lens
34.31 1.67
34.33 a) 18.6 mm b) 19 mm from the cornea c) 0.61 mm, real, inverted
34.35 a) 36.0 cm to the right of the lens b) 180 cm to the left of the lens c) 7.20 cm to the left of the lens d) 13.8 cm to the left of the lens
34.37 26.3 cm from the lens, 12.4 mm, erect, same side
34.39 a) 200 cm to the right of the first lens, 4.80 cm b) 150 cm to the right of the second lens, 7.20 cm
34.41 a) 53.0 cm b) real c) 2.50 mm, inverted
34.43 10.2 m
34.45 a) 1.4×10^{-4} b) 5.3×10^{-4} c) 1.5×10^{-3}
34.47 a) 85 mm b) 135 mm
34.49 a) $f/11$ b) 1/480 s = 2.1 ms
34.51 a) convex b) 50 mm to 56 mm
34.53 a) 80.0 cm b) 76.9 cm
34.55 49.4 cm, 2.02 diopters
34.57 −1.37 diopters
34.59 a) 6.06 cm b) 4.12 mm
34.61 a) 640 b) 43
34.63 a) 8.37 mm b) 21.4 c) −297
34.65 a) −6.33 b) 1.90 cm c) 0.127 rad
34.67 a) 0.661 m b) 59.1
34.69 7.20 m/s
34.71 $h/2$
34.73 a) 20.0 cm b) 39.0 cm
34.75 a) 46 cm from the mirror, on the opposite side of the mirror, virtual b) 29 mm, erect c) no
34.77 51 m/s
34.79 b) 2.4 cm, −0.133
34.81 2.00
34.83 a) −3.3 cm b) virtual c) 1.9 cm to the right of the vertex at the right-hand end of the rod d) real, inverted, 1.06 mm
34.85 a) 58.7 cm, converging b) 4.48 mm, virtual
34.87 a) 6.48 mm b) no, behind the retina c) 19.3 mm from the cornea, in front of the retina
34.89 50.3 cm
34.91 10.6 cm
34.93 a) 0.24 m b) 0.24 m
34.95 72.1 cm to the right of the surface vertex
34.97 0.80 cm
34.99 −26.7 cm
34.101 1.24 cm above the page
34.103 a) 46.7 m b) 35.0 m
34.105 134 cm to the left of the object
34.107 a) 3.5 cm b) 7.0 cm c) 100 cm d) 57 e) no
34.109 4.17 diopters
34.111 a) 30.9 cm b) 29.2 cm
34.113 d) 36.0 cm, 21.6 cm, d = 1.2 cm
34.115 a) 552 b) 25.8 cm
34.117 a) $4f$
34.119 b) 1.35 cm

Chapter 35

35.1 a) 14 cm, 48 cm, 82 cm, 116 cm, 150 cm
b) 31 cm, 65 cm, 99 cm, 133 cm
35.3 b) 427 Hz b) 0.796 m
35.5 0.75 m, 2.00 m, 3.25 m, 4.50 m, 5.75 m, 7.00 m, 8.25 m
35.7 a) 2.0 m b) constructively
c) 1.0 m, destructively
35.9 1.14 mm
35.11 0.83 mm
35.13 a) 39 b) $\pm 73.3°$
35.15 12.6 cm
35.17 1200 nm
35.19 a) $0.750 I_0$ b) 80 nm
35.21 1670 rad
35.23 71.4 m
35.25 114 nm
35.27 0.0234°
35.29 a) 55.6 nm b) (i) 2180 nm (ii) 11.0 wavelengths
35.31 a) 514 nm, green b) 603 nm, orange
35.33 0.11 μm
35.35 0.570 mm
35.37 1.54 mm
35.39 a) 96.0 nm b) no, no
35.41 a) 1.58 mm (green), 1.72 mm (orange)
b) 3.45 mm (violet), 4.74 mm (green), 5.16 mm (orange) c) 9.57 μm
35.43 1.730
35.45 0°, 27.3°, 66.5°
35.47 1.57
35.49 above centerline: 3.14°, 15.9°, 29.5°, 45.4°, 68.6°; below centerline: 9.45°, 22.5°, 37.0°, 55.2°
35.51 6.8×10^{-5} $(C°)^{-1}$
35.53 $\lambda/2d$, independent of m
35.55 b) 0.72 m
35.57 1.42
35.59 b) $I = I_0 \cos^2\left\{\dfrac{\pi[d\sin\theta + L(n-1)]}{\lambda_0}\right\}$
c) $\sin\theta = \dfrac{m\lambda_0 - L(n-1)}{d}$
35.61 14.0

Chapter 36

36.1 506 nm
36.3 a) 226 b) $\pm 83.0°$
36.5 9.07 m
36.7 a) 63.8 cm
b) $\pm 22.1°$, $\pm 34.3°$, $\pm 48.8°$, $\pm 70.1°$
36.9 $\pm 16.0°$, $\pm 33.4°$, $\pm 55.6°$
36.11 0.920 μm
36.13 a) 580 nm b) 0.128
36.15 a) 6.75 mm b) 2.43 $\mu W/m^2$
36.17 a) 668 nm b) $9.36 \times 10^{-5} I_0$
36.19 a) $\pm 13.0°$, $\pm 26.7°$, $\pm 42.4°$, $\pm 64.1°$
b) 2.08 W/m^2
36.21 a) 3 b) 2
36.23 a) 0.0627°, 0.125° b) $0.249 I_0$, 0.0256
36.25 a) 1 & 3, 2 & 4 b) 1 & 2, 3 & 4
c) 1 & 3, 2 & 4
36.27 15.0 μm (width), 45.0 μm (separation)
36.29 a) 4790 slits/cm b) 19.1°, 40.8° c) no
36.31 a) yes b) 13.3 nm
36.33 a) 4830 lines/cm b) $\pm 37.7°$, $\pm 66.5°$
36.35 10.5°, 21.3°, 33.1°
36.37 a) 17,500 b) yes
c) (i) 587.8170 nm (ii) 587.7834 nm
(iii) 587.7834 nm $< \lambda <$ 587.8170 nm
36.39 0.232 nm
36.41 0.559 nm
36.43 1.88 m
36.45 92 cm
36.47 1.45 m
36.49 a) 77 m (Hubble), 1100 km (Arecibo)
b) 1500 km
36.51 30.2 μm
36.53 a) 78 b) $\pm 80.8°$ c) 555 $\mu W/m^2$
36.55 1.68
36.57 a) 1.80 mm b) 0.796 mm
36.61 b) for $3\pi/2$: any two slits separated by one other slit; for the other cases: any two slits separated by three other slits
36.63 360 nm
36.65 second
36.67 c) ± 2.61 rad
36.69 387 km
36.71 1.40

PHOTO CREDITS

About the Author Hugh D. Young; Roger Freedman

Chapter 1 Opener: Ralph Wetmore/Getty Images; 1.1a: Shutterstock; 1.1b: CERN/European Organization for Nuclear Research; 1.4: National Institute of Standards and Technology (NIST); 1.5a: R. Williams (STScI), the HDF-S Team, and NASA; 1.5b: SOHO (ESA & NASA); 1.5c: Courtesy of NASA/JPL/Caltech; 1.5d: Photodisc Green/Getty Images; 1.5e: PhotoDisc/Getty Images; 1.5f: Purdue University. Veeco Instruments, Inc.; 1.5g: SPL/Photo Researchers, Inc.; 1.6: Pearson Education; 1.7: Liaison/Getty Images; App. 1.1: Scott Bauer - USDA Agricultural Research Service

Chapter 2 Opener: Terje Rakke/Getty Images; 2.4: Bob Thomas/iStockphoto; 2.5: Shutterstock; App.2.1: NASA; 2.22: Richard Megna/Fundamental Photographs; 2.26: Corbis; 2.27: iStockphoto

Chapter 3 Opener: Feng Li/Getty Images; App. 3.1: Luca Lozzi/Getty Images; 3.8: PhotoAlto/Getty Images; 3.16: Richard Megna/Fundamental Photographs; 3.19a: Richard Megna/Fundamental Photographs; 3.19b: Fotolia; App. 3.2: David Wall/Alamy; 3.31: Hart Matthews/Reuters

Chapter 4 Opener: Brian Cleary/Getty Images; App. 4.1: Fotolia; 4.12: Wayne Eastep/Getty Images; 4.17: Shutterstock; App.4.2: Stan Kujawa/Alamy; 4.20: Shutterstock; 4.29: Shutterstock; 4.30a: John McDonough/Time Inc. Magazines/Sports Illustrated; 4.30b: John McDonough/Getty Images; 4.30c: Mark M. Lawrence/Corbis

Chapter 5 Opener: U.S. Air Force photo by Tech. Sgt. Jeremy Lock/Released; 5.11: NASA; 5.16: Dave Sandford/Getty Images; App. 5.1: Radim Spitzer/iStockphoto; App. 5.2: David Scharf /Photo Researchers, Inc.; 5.26b: Joggie Botma/iStockphoto; 5.35: AOPA/Aircraft Owners and Pilots Association; 5.38a: NASA; 5.38b: Helen Hansma, University of California, Santa Barbara; 5.38c: Nicholas Roemmelt/iStockphoto; 5.38d: David Malin, Anglo-Australian Observatory

Chapter 6 Opener: Flickr RM/Getty Images; 6.1: Allison Michael Orenstein/Getty Images; App. 6.1: Steve Gschmeissner/Photo Researchers, Inc.; 6.13: Bojan Fatur/iStockphoto; App. 6.2: Steve Gschmeissner/Photo Researchers, Inc.; 6.26: Hulton Archive/Getty Images; 6.27a: Keystone/Getty Images; 6.27b: Adrian Pingstone; 6.28: Shutterstock

Chapter 7 Opener: Geoff de Feu/Getty Images; 7.1: Shutterstock; App. 7.1: Yuji Sakai/Getty Images; 7.3: Robert F. Bukaty/AP; 7.5: Joggie Botma/iStockphoto; 7.12: Jupiterimages/Brand X/Corbis; App. 7.2: iStockphoto; 7.15: William Loy/iStockphoto; 7.21: Bill Grove/iStockphoto; App. 7.3: Matt Naylor/iStockphoto; App. 7.4: Peter Menzel/Photo Researchers, Inc.

Chapter 8 Opener: Flickr RM/Getty Images; 8.2: David Woods/Corbis; App. 8.1: Shutterstock; 8.4: Jim Cummins/Getty Images; 8.6: Andrew Davidhazy; 8.16: Hulton Archive/Getty Images; 8.21: David Leah/Getty Images; 8.29: Richard Megna/Fundamental Photographs; 8.31b: Shutterstock; App. 8.2: Dr. James B. Wood; 8.33: NASA

Chapter 9 Opener: Todd Klassy; 9.3: Mike Powell/Getty Images; App. 9.1: Hybrid Medical Animation/Photo Researchers, Inc.; App. 9.2a: Shutterstock; App. 9.2b: Jakob Leitner/iStockphoto; 9.18: David J. Phillip/AP; 9.21: NASA/Johnson Space Center; P9.98: NASA

Chapter 10 Opener: Ilia Shalamaev/Photolibrary; 10.7: Corbis; App. 10.1 (right): Shutterstock; App. 10.1 (left): David Lentink/SPL/Photo Researchers, Inc.; 10.14: James Warren/iStockphoto; 10.17: Loic Bernard/iStockphoto; 10.22: Images Source/Getty Images; 10.28: Gerard Lacz/Natural History Photographic Agency

Chapter 11 Opener: iStockphoto; 11.3: Jeremy Woodhouse/Getty Images; 11.12a: Shutterstock; 11.12b: Jonathan Blair/Corbis; 11.12c: Photodisc Green/Getty Images; App. 11.2: Dante Fenolio/Photo Researchers, Inc.

Chapter 12 Opener: Digital Vision/AGE Fotostock; App. 12.1: Sean Locke/iStockphoto; 12.6: Cenco Physics; 12.9: Shutterstock; 12.14: Fotolia; 12.19: Pearson Education; 12.20: Cordelia Molloy/Photo Researchers, Inc.; 12.27: Shutterstock; App. 12.2: Sean Locke/iStockphoto; 12.29a: Photodisc Green/Getty Images; 12.29b: Colin Barker/Getty Images; 12.30f: The Harold E. Edgerton 1992 Trust, Palm Press, Inc.

Chapter 13 Opener: NASA/JPL/Space Science Institute; 13.3: NASA/JPL/Caltech; 13.6: NASA; App. 13.1: NASA; 13.7: George Hall/Corbis; 13.13: NASA and Hubble Space Telescope (STSc1); 13.16: NASA; 13.17: NASA; App. 13.2: NASA; 13.20b: NASA; 13.26: NASA; 13.27: NASA; 13.28: Prof. Andrea Ghez/UCLA - W. M. Keck Telescopes

Chapter 14 Opener: Tim McCaig/iStockphoto; App. 14.1: Nigel Cattlin/Photo Researchers, Inc.; 14.7: American Diagnostic Corporation; 14.21: Frank Herholdt/Getty Images; 14.25: Christopher Griffin/Alamy; App. 14.2: Shutterstock

Chapter 15 Opener: REUTERS/Nicky Loh; App. 15.1: MARCO POLO COLLECTION/Alamy; 15.2: REUTERS/Charles Platiau; 15.5: David Parker/Photo Researchers, Inc.; 15.12: iStockphoto; App. 15.2: iStockphoto; 15.18: Reproduced from *PSSC Physics*, 2nd ed. (1965), D.C. Heath & Company with Educational Development Center, Inc., Newton Massachusets; 15.23: Richard Megna/Fundamental Photographs; 15.25: iStockphoto; 15.27: National Optical Astronomy Observatories

Chapter 16 Opener: iStockphoto; App. 16.1: Steve Thorne/Getty Images; 16.5a: Lisa Pines/Getty Images; 16.5c: David Young-Wolff/PhotoEdit Inc.; 16.6: Dorling Kindersley; 16.9: Kretztechnik/Photo Researchers, Inc.; 16.10: Eastcott-Momatiuk/The Image Works; 16.15: Dorothy Y Riess/The Image Works; App. 16.2: iStockphoto; 16.20: Martin Bough/Fundamental Photographs; 16.25: Shutterstock; 16.28: Mark Reinstein/The Image Works; 16.35c: NASA/Langley Research Center; 16.36: NASA/Robert A. Hoover, Dryden Flight Research Center

Chapter 17 Opener: Shutterstock; 17.4: Exergen Corporation; App.17.1: Shutterstock; 17.5: Sargent-Welch/VWR International, Courtesy of Cenco Physics; 17.11: NASA/Jim Ross, Dryden Flight Research Center; 17.13: Eric Schrader - Pearson Science; 17.16: Roger Freedman; 17.18: Paul Seheult/Corbis; 17.19: Adam Hart-Davis/Photo Researchers, Inc.; 17.20: Richard Megna/Fundamental Photographs; 17.22: Shutterstock; App. 17.2a: iStockphoto; App. 17.2b: Paul Nicklen/National Geographic Creative/Getty Image; 17.27: Hugh D. Young; 17.28: Dr. Arthur Tucker/Photo Researchers, Inc.

Chapter 18 Opener: iStockphoto; 18.2: John Powell/The Image Works; 18.10: ThermoMicroscopes/Park Scientific Instruments; 18.13: Stone/Getty Images; 18.14: ARCTIC IMAGES/Alamy; 18.16: David Grossman/The Image Works; App. 18.2: Ray Coleman/Photo Researchers, Inc.; 18.25: PhotoDisc/Getty Images; E18.25: David Malin, Royal Observatory, Edinburgh and Anglo-Australian Telescope Board; P18.91: David Malin, Royal Observatory, Edinburgh and Anglo-Australian Telescope Board

Chapter 19 Opener: Richard A. Cooke III/Getty Images; 19.1: John P. Surey; 19.2a: PhotoDisc/StockTrek/Getty Images; 19.2b: iStockphoto; App. 19.1: iStockphoto; 19.10: Shutterstock; 19.14: Tom Branch/Photo Researchers, Inc.; 19.15: Shutterstock; P19.57: Photolibrary

Chapter 20 Opener: G. Brad Lewis/Getty Images; 20.2: Shutterstock; App. 20.1: Shutterstock; 20.12: Bill Bachman/Photo Researchers, Inc.; 20.16: U.S. Air Force photo by Staff Sgt. Robert Zoellner; 20.17: Erich Schrempp/Photo Researchers, Inc.; App. 20.2: iStockphoto; 20.20: Eric Schrader - Pearson Science

Chapter 21 Opener: iStockphoto; 21.5: Journal-Courier/The Image Works; 21.8a: Richard Megna/Fundamental Photographs; 21.29a: Reproduced from *PSSC Physics*, 2nd ed. (1965), D.C. Heath & Company with Education Development Center, Inc., Newton, Massachusetts; 21.30b: Tony Craddock/Photo Researchers, Inc.; App. 21.1 iStockphoto; App. 21.2: Albert Kok; P21.94: David Parker/Photo Researchers, Inc.

Chapter 22 Opener: U.S. Department of Energy; 22.10: AKG London Ltd.; 22.27b: Peter Terren/Tesladownunder.com; 22.28b: Russ Kinne/Comstock; App. 22.1a: Mark Webster/Photolibrary; App. 22.2: Dr. David Furness, Keele University/SPL/Photo Researchers, Inc.

Chapter 23 Opener: Ted Kurihara/Getty Images; 23.9: NASA/JPL/Caltech; 23.11: Lester V. Berman/Corbis; 23.17: Hulton Archive/Keystone/Getty Images; 23.22: iStockphoto; App. 23.1: iStockphoto; App. 23.2: 3D4Medical.com/Getty Images

Chapter 24 Opener: Shutterstock; 24.3: Shutterstock; 24.4: Andrew Lambert/Photo Researchers, Inc.; 24.7: Eric Schrader - Pearson Science; 24.11: Sandia National Laboratories; App. 24.1: iStockphoto; App. 24.2: H Heller, M Schaefer, & K Schulten, "Molecular dynamics simulation of a bilayer of 200 lipids in the gel and in the liquid-crystal phases," J. Phys. Chem. 97:8343-60, 1993.

Chapter 25 Opener: iStockphoto; 25.4: Eric Schrader - Pearson Science; 25.5: PhotoDisc/Getty Images; 25.8: iStockphoto; 25.12: iStockphoto; App. 25.1: Dr. David Furness, Keele University/Photo Researchers, Inc.; App. 25.2: Andrew J. Martinez/Photo Researchers, Inc.; 25.15 Richard Megna/Fundamental Photographs

Chapter 26 Opener: Maximilian Stock/Photo Researchers, Inc.; 26.2 Photos.com; 26.5: John P. Surey; 26.13: John P. Surey; App. 26.1: Dorling Kindersley Media Library; 26.18: Richard Megna/Fundamental Photographs; App. 26.2: Mehau Kulyk/Photo Researchers, Inc.; 26.25a: Banana Stock/Alamy; 26.25b: Wikipedia

Chapter 27 Opener: Simon Fraser/Photo Researchers, Inc.; 27.2b: Bill Aron/PhotoEdit Inc.; 27.14: Richard Megna/Fundamental Photographs; 27.17b: Sargent-Welch/VWR International; 27.20b: Shutterstock; 27.21: Lawrence Berkeley National Laboratory; 27.40: Jeremy Burgess/Photo Researchers, Inc.; App. 27.1: Robert Smith/Photolibrary; App. 27.2: iStockphoto

Chapter 28 Opener: CERN/European Organization for Nuclear Research; 28.8: Definitive Stock; 28.11: Jeremy Walker/Photo Researchers, Inc.; App. 28.1: iStockphoto; Test Your Understanding, page 941: Mark Antman/The Image Works; App. 28.2: Scarberry, K. E., Dickerson, E. B., Zhang, Z. J., Benigno, B. B. & McDonald, J. F., "Selective removal of ovarian cancer cells from human ascites fluid using magnetic nanoparticles." Nanomedicine: Nanotechnology, Biology and Medicine. 6, 399-408 (2010)

Chapter 29 Opener: iStockphoto; App. 29.1: Simon Fraser/University of Durham/Photo Researchers, Inc.; 29.9: Maximilian Stock Ltd./Photo Researchers, Inc.; 29.18a: Photodisc Red/Getty Images; 29.18b: Toyota Motor Sales USA; 29.18c: CIRRUS Design Corporation; App. 29.2: NASA/JPL/Caltech; 29.25: Ken Gatherum, Boeing Computer Services

Chapter 30 Opener: EschCollection/Getty Images; 30.2: Shutterstock; App. 30.1: Ron Chapple/Getty Images; 30.7: Photodisc/Getty Images; App. 30.2: SOHO/NASA; 30.10: John Walsh/Photo Researchers, Inc.

Chapter 31 Opener: John P. Surey & Caroline J. Robillard; 31.5: Rubberball/Getty Images; 31.14: Lawrence Migdale/Photo Researchers, Inc.; App. 31.1: Mauro Fermariello/Photo Researchers, Inc.; App. 31.2: iStockphoto; 31.22: Shutterstock; 31.23: Roger A. Freedman

Chapter 32 Opener: Shutterstock; 32.1: Bettmann/Corbis; 32.2a: iStockphoto; 32.2b: Malcolm Fife/Getty Images; App. 32.1: Ted Kinsman/Photo Researchers, Inc.; 32.16: The Image Bank/Getty Images; 32.18: iStockphoto; App. 32.2: Alexander Tsiaras/Photo Researchers, Inc.; 32.20: NASA/JPL-Caltech/E.Churchwell (University of Wisconsin-Madison); 32.23: iStockphoto

Chapter 33 Opener: Peter Aprahamian/Photo Researchers, Inc.; 33.1: iStockphoto; 33.2: National Institutes of Health/Photo Researchers, Inc.; 33.9: Roger A. Freedman; 33.10a: NASA/John F. Kennedy Space Center; 33.10b: iStockphoto; App. 33.1: Peter Herring/imagequestmarine.com; 33.13b: Susan Schwartzenberg, The Exploratorium; 33.16: VEM / Photo Researchers, Inc.; 33.17: iStockphoto; 33.20a: Randy O'Rourke/Corbis; 33.22a: Dougal Walters/Getty Images; 33.22b: Pixtal/AGE Fotostock; 33.26: Diane Hirsch/Fundamental Photographs; 33.31: Peter Aprahamian/Sharples Stress Engineers/Photo Researchers, Inc.; App. 33.2: iStockphoto; 33.33: Roger Freedman; 33.37a: K. Nomachi/Photo Researchers, Inc.

Chapter 34 Opener: Tek Image/Photo Researchers, Inc.; 34.8: Marshall Henrichs; 34.12a: NASA; 34.12b-c: NASA Headquarters; 34.23: iStockphoto; 34.27: Richard Megna/Fundamental Photographs; 34.34: PhotoDisc/Getty Images; 34.41a-c: Marshall Henrichs; App. 34.1: Shutterstock; 34.43c: THK Photo Products, Inc.; 34.44b: Omikron/Photo Researchers, Inc.; App. 34.2: Shutterstock; 34.52c: Jan Hinsch/Photo Researchers, Inc.; 34.54d: National Optical Astronomy Observatories

Chapter 35 Opener: iStockphoto; 35.4: Roger Freedman; 35.6: Pearson Education; 35.11b: Shutterstock; 35.16b: Bausch & Lomb Incorporated; 35.17: Bausch & Lomb Incorporated; App. 35.1, top: iStockphoto; App. 35.1, right and bottom: Peter Vukusic; App. 35.2: J. Reed and J.K.Gimzewski, UCLA California Nanosystems Institute, 2007

Chapter 36 Opener: Eric Schrader - Pearson Science; 36.2a-b: Pearson Education; 36.6: Pearson Education; 36.9b: Richard Megna/Fundamental Photographs; 36.11: Dane Hornsleth; 36.12d: Pearson Education; 36.17: iStockphoto; 36.18a: NSO/AURA/NSF; 36.18b: Physics Dept., Imperial College/Photo Researchers, Inc.; App.36.1: Tek Image/Photo Researchers, Inc.; 36.20b: Estate of Bertram Eugene Warren; 36.24: Science Photo Library/Photo Researchers, Inc.; 36.26: Pearson Education; 36.27a-c: Pearson Education; App. 36.2: National Radio Astronomy Observatory/Associated Universities, Inc./National Science Foundation; 36.30: Paul Silverman/Fundamental Photographs; P36.66: NASA

Chapter 37 Opener: Brookhaven National Laboratory/Corbis; 37.4: Shutterstock; 37.7: NASA/John F. Kennedy Space Center; App. 37.1: iStockphoto; 37.11: Jack Fields/Photo Researchers, Inc.; 37.18: Adam Hart-Davis/Photo Researchers, Inc.; 37.19: NASA and The Hubble Heritage Team (STScI/AURA); App. 37.2: Imaginechina/AP Images; 37.25: Thinkstock/Getty Images

Chapter 38 Opener: Kim Steele/Photolibrary; 38.2a: U.S. Air Force photo/Master Sgt. Lance Cheung; 38.2b: Bill Corwin; App. 38.1: Linda Bartlett/National Cancer Institute; 38.9: Thinkstock/Getty Images; App. 38.2: iStockphoto; 38.14a: Ernest Orlando, Lawrence Berkeley National Laboratory; 38.16: From Huggins, *Physics 1*, ©1968 by W.A. Benjamin, Inc. Pearson Addison Wesley

Chapter 39 Opener: Lee D. Simon/Photo Researchers, Inc.; 39.1: AIP Meggers Gallery of Nobel Laureates; 39.4: Reproduced from *PSSC Physics*, 2nd ed. (1965), D.C. Heath & Company with Educational Development Center, Inc., Newton Massachusetts; 39.6: Scimat/Photo Researchers, Inc.; 39.8: Ted Kinsman/Photo Researchers, Inc.; App. 39.1: NASA; 39.9: N.A.Sharp, NOAO/NSO/Kitt Peak FTS/AURA/NSF; 39.10: American Institute of Physics/Emilio Segré Visual Archives; 39.15: Roger Viollet/Getty Images; 39.19b: Andrew Lambert/Photo Researchers, Inc.; App. 39.2: Louise Murray/Photo Researchers, Inc.; 39.31: Royal Swedish Academy of Sciences; 39.34: From Huggins, *Physics 1*, ©1968 by W.A. Benjamin, Inc. Pearson Addison Wesley; 39.36: NASA

Chapter 40 Opener: Dr. Dmitry Talapin, University of Hamburg; 40.1: JGI/Agefotostock; 40.2: UPI/Corbis; 40.4: Churchill Archives Centre, Born Papers, BORN Acc 1498 Box 12; 40.17: Almaden Research Center/Research Division; 40.21: Hewlett-Packard Lab/Photo Researchers, Inc.; App. 40.1: SPL/Photo Researchers, Inc.

Chapter 41 Opener Left: SPL/Photo Researchers, Inc.; Opener Right: Shutterstock; 41.7: NASA; 41.11 a-b: National Optical Astronomy Observatories; 41.19: National Radio Astronomy Observatory/Associated Universities, Inc./National Science Foundation; 41.20: American Institute of Physics/Emilio Segré Visual Archives; 41.22: iStockphoto; App.41.1: SPL/Photo Researchers, Inc.; App. 41.2a: Thinkstock/Getty Images; App. 41.2b: SPL/Photo Researchers, Inc.

Chapter 42 Opener: NASA; App. 42.1: Alfred Pasieka/Photo Researchers, Inc.; 42.9: Roger A. Freedman; 42.17: Stanford University, AIP Emilio Segré Visual Archives; App. 42.2: Andy Crump/Photo Researchers, Inc.; 42.36: PhotoDisc/Getty Images; P42.44: NASA

Chapter 43 Opener: Juraj Liptak/Deutsche Presse-Agentur/Newscom; 43.1b: Science Photo Library/Photo Researchers, Inc.; App.43.1: Steve Gschmeissner & Carol Upton/Photo Researchers, Inc.; 43.6: Lloyd Cluff/Corbis; 43.10: Dept. of Nuclear Medicine, Charing Cross Hospital/Photo Researchers, Inc.; App.43.2: Argonne National Laboratory; 43.17: David Malin, Royal Observatory Edinburgh & Anglo-Australian Observatory; 43.18: LLNL/Photo Researchers, Inc.; Summary: Dept. of Nuclear Medicine, Charing Cross Hospital/Photo Researchers, Inc.

Chapter 44 Opener: NASA/JPL-Caltech/ESA/CXC/STScI; 44.1: Lawrence Berkeley National Laboratory; 44.3: Ernest Orlando, Lawrence Berkeley National Laboratory; App.44.1: Susan Landau; 44.7 a-b: CERN/European Organization for Nuclear Research; 44.8: CERN/European Organization for Nuclear Research; 44.9: Mark R. Lowenstine; 44.14: Institute for Cosmic Ray Research, University of Tokyo; 44.15 a-b: NASA; 44.19: NASA/CXC/INAF/S. Andreon et al; App.44.2: Shutterstock; 44.21: N.A. Sharp, REU program/NOAO/AURA/NSF; 44.22: NASA/WMAP/Science Team; Summary (particle collisions): Brookhaven National Laboratory; Summary (nebula): N.A. Sharp, REU program/NOAO/AURA/NSF

INDEX

For users of the three-volume edition: pages 1–686 are in Volume 1; pages 687–1260 are in Volume 2; and pages 1223–1522 are in Volume 3. Pages 1261–1522 are not in the Standard Edition.

Note: Page numbers followed by f indicate figures; those followed by t indicate tables.

A

D

E

F

S

T